Getting Started is as EASY as 1, 2, 3 . . . 4!

1. Sign Up

Instructors register with myBusinessCourse.com

2. Setup Your Course

Add your class details and additional materials.

3. Invite Your Students

Students register using your unique course code.

4. Manage Your Course

Study, test, and grade assignments. It's simple!

Provide Instruction and Practice 24/7

◆ Assign homework from your Cambridge Business Publishers textbook and have myBusinessCourse grade it for you automatically.

◆ With our eLectures, your students can revisit accounting topics as often as they like or until they master the topic.

◆ Guided Examples show students how to solve select problems.

◆ Make homework due before class to ensure students enter your classroom prepared.

◆ Additional practice and exam preparation materials are available to help students achieve better grades and content mastery.

STUDENT SELF-STUDY OPTION

Not all instructors choose to incorporate **myBusinessCourse** into their course. In such cases, students can access the Self-Study option for MBC. The Self-Study option provides most of the learning tools available in the Instructor-Led courses, including:

◆ eLectures
◆ Guided Examples
◆ Practice Quizzes

The Self-Study option does not include homework assignments from the textbook. Only the Instructor-Led option includes homework assignments.

Want to learn more about myBusinessCourse?

Contact your sales representative or visit **www.mybusinesscourse.com**.

STUDENTS: Find your access code on the myBusinessCourse insert on the following pages. If you have a used copy of this textbook, you can purchase access online at **www.mybusinesscourse.com**.

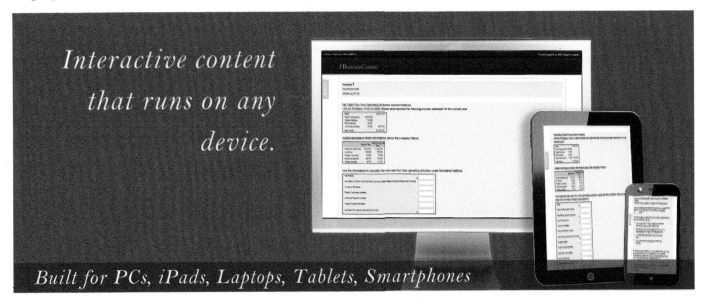

Advanced Accounting

Third Edition

SUSAN S. HAMLEN
University at Buffalo, The State University of New York

RONALD J. HUEFNER
University at Buffalo, The State University of New York

JAMES A. LARGAY III
Lehigh University

Cambridge
BUSINESS PUBLISHERS

Cambridge Business Publishers
ADVANCED ACCOUNTING, Third Edition, by Susan S. Hamlen, Ronald J. Huefner, and James A. Largay III.

STUDENT EDITION ISBN: 978-1-61853-151-3

**Bookstores & Faculty: to order this book, call 800-619-6473 or email
customerservice@cambridgepub.com.**

Students: to order this book, please visit the book's Website and order directly online.

Printed in the United States of America.
10 9 8 7 6 5 4 3 2

PREFACE

W elcome to *Advanced Accounting*. We wrote this book with two major objectives in mind. First, we seek to reflect the changing topical emphases and content in the advanced accounting course; coverage is completely updated for new developments concerning applicable reporting issues and requirements, including the newest FASB and GASB pronouncements and proposals. We extensively discuss International Financial Reporting Standards where appropriate throughout the book. Second, we write from the perspective of enhancing teachability; many of the topics in this course are complex and require careful explanation. We highlight the major issues in each topic and provide the student with the background and logical structure needed to analyze these issues, rather than merely explaining current practice. This view equips students to analyze and assess future reporting developments.

This book is the product of extensive market research including focus groups, market surveys, class tests, manuscript reviews, and interviews with faculty from across the country. We are grateful to the students and faculty who provided us with useful feedback during the preparation of this book.

TARGET AUDIENCE

Advanced Accounting is intended for use, at either the undergraduate or graduate level, in the course commonly known as advanced accounting. It is also designed to be used in courses focusing on mergers and acquisitions that are often part of the MBA curriculum or that are offered as a nondegree, professional development program.

HOW THIS BOOK EFFECTIVELY TEACHES ADVANCED ACCOUNTING TOPICS

Conceptual Focus

Conceptual explanations focus on the logic underlying reporting standards rather than merely explaining procedures. We develop each topic by explaining the underlying business activity, the reporting goals, and how standards and procedures achieve these goals. Each topic is clearly developed in terms students can understand. We use illustrations from actual practice to enhance understanding and familiarize students with the information presented in real financial statements. Accounting standards are increasingly **principles based**, requiring substantial **judgment** in their application. And standards change every year. Conceptual understanding prepares students to evaluate and effectively apply future standards throughout their professional careers.

Logical Flow of Topical Coverage

The organization of chapters reflects the logical flow of topics:

- **Mergers and acquisitions** material is covered in Chapters 1–6.
- **Foreign currency translation, foreign currency transactions and hedging,** and **other financial derivatives** (futures, options, and swaps) are in Chapters 7–9.
- Reporting standards for **state and local government and NFP organizations** are in Chapters 10–13.
- **Partnerships, bankruptcy and reorganization,** and the **SEC** are covered in Chapters 14–16.

Relevant Real Company Illustrations

Each chapter begins with a description of a familiar **focus company**, and how its activities and reporting practices relate to that chapter's topics. For example, in Chapter 2, **IBM**'s extensive acquisitions illustrate accounting for mergers and acquisitions. Noncontrolling interests are common in the resort industry, and in Chapter 5 **Las Vegas Sands Corporation** illustrates reporting for noncontrolling interests in subsidiaries. In Chapter 9, **Kellogg's** hedging practices illustrate hedge accounting for futures, options and swaps. In Chapter 13, **Beta Alpha Psi**'s financial statements illustrate NFP reporting standards. Throughout each chapter, examples from actual practice highlight major topics, using either the focus company or other companies in the same industry.

Following is a list of focus companies by chapter.

Chapter 1	Coca-Cola	**Chapter 9**	Kellogg's
Chapter 2	IBM	**Chapter 10**	Mecklenburg County, NC
Chapter 3	General Motors	**Chapter 11**	Alameda County, CA
Chapter 4	Time Warner	**Chapter 12**	St. Louis, MO
Chapter 5	Las Vegas Sands Corporation	**Chapter 13**	Beta Alpha Psi
Chapter 6	Nike	**Chapter 14**	Suburban Propane Partners
Chapter 7	Wal-Mart	**Chapter 15**	Quiznos
Chapter 8	McDonald's	**Chapter 16**	Securities and Exchange Commission

Emphasis on Current Issues and Trends

Business Applications

Taken from current news and actual financial statements, Business Application boxes illustrate reporting practices, current issues, and controversies. The following is an example from Chapter 3.

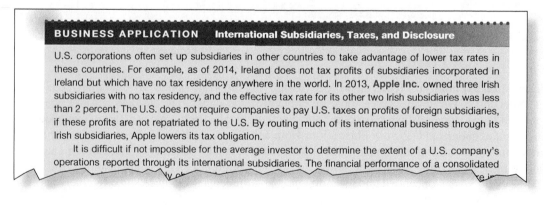

BUSINESS APPLICATION International Subsidiaries, Taxes, and Disclosure

U.S. corporations often set up subsidiaries in other countries to take advantage of lower tax rates in these countries. For example, as of 2014, Ireland does not tax profits of subsidiaries incorporated in Ireland but which have no tax residency anywhere in the world. In 2013, **Apple Inc.** owned three Irish subsidiaries with no tax residency, and the effective tax rate for its other two Irish subsidiaries was less than 2 percent. The U.S. does not require companies to pay U.S. taxes on profits of foreign subsidiaries, if these profits are not repatriated to the U.S. By routing much of its international business through its Irish subsidiaries, Apple lowers its tax obligation.

It is difficult if not impossible for the average investor to determine the extent of a U.S. company's operations reported through its international subsidiaries. The financial performance of a consolidated

Reporting Perspectives

Reporting Perspectives comment on topics such as the strengths and weaknesses in reporting standards, motivations for changes in standards, ethical issues, implications for information quality, and proposals for new standards. The following is an example from Chapter 4.

● ●

Reporting Perspective

The FASB added the qualitative assessment option (Step 0) to make impairment testing less onerous. Prior to 2012, all companies were required to compare the fair value of each indefinite life intangible and reporting unit to its book value. Companies complained that estimating the fair value of each intangible asset and reporting unit was costly and time consuming, and unnecessary when fair value was obviously higher than book value.

Critics claim that this option weakens the impairment test, by giving managers additional earnings management opportunities. The subjective nature of the qualitative assessment increases the ability to delay recognition of impairment losses. Management can also choose to perform the quantitative test in good years, but take the qualitative option in bad years, thus increasing the likelihood of impairment recognition when earnings are high and avoiding it when earnings are low.

IFRS

Extensive discussion and illustration of international financial reporting standards and proposals appear in each of the business combinations, foreign currency translation and transactions, and futures, options and swaps chapters. The following is an excerpt from Chapter 5.

INTERNATIONAL FINANCIAL REPORTING STANDARDS FOR NONCONTROLLING INTERESTS

IFRS 3(R) presents IFRS for valuing and reporting noncontrolling interests in consolidated financial statements. Although IFRS agrees with U.S. GAAP that the noncontrolling interest should be reported at acquisition-date fair value, *IFRS 3(R)* actually allows the acquirer to choose between **two different valuation methods**:

LO4 Explain IFRS for noncontrolling interests.

1. Value the noncontrolling interest at **full fair value** at the acquisition date, as in U.S. GAAP.
2. Value the noncontrolling interest at its share of the **fair value of the subsidiary's identifiable net assets** at the acquisition date.

Using valuation method #2, the noncontrolling interest is not allocated any goodwill: only the controlling interest's share of goodwill is recognized. Therefore the IFRS alternative reports goodwill

Clear and Logical Development of Business Combinations Topics

Reporting issues related to business combinations cover a variety of topics. Consolidation procedures are difficult to comprehend and can be confusing to students. We emphasize the **measurement aspects** of combinations—reporting assets and liabilities acquired, determining acquisition cost, valuing noncontrolling interests, and eliminating intercompany accounts.

To make consolidation procedures more comprehensible, eliminations subsequent to acquisition (covered in Chapters 4–6) presume that the parent uses the **complete (full) equity method**. Exclusive use of the complete (full) equity method allows students to focus on the goals of consolidation and the key issues in consolidation procedures. Once students develop a solid understanding of the consolidation process, changes in procedures required when the parent uses the **cost method** can be introduced. The appendix to Chapter 4 explains the eliminating entries necessary to adjust the parent's accounts to the complete equity method before proceeding with consolidation. The appendix also compares complete equity method eliminations to cost method eliminations.

Additional Pedagogy

To reinforce concepts presented in each chapter and ensure student comprehension, we include two or more **In-Chapter Review Problems** that require students to recall and apply the accounting techniques and concepts described in the chapter. The solutions to the review problems are included after each chapter's assignments. The following example is from Chapter 2.

REVIEW 1   •   Reporting Assets Acquired and Liabilities Assumed

IBM acquires SoftCloud Technologies in an acquisition reported as a merger, for $1.2 billion in cash. At the acquisition date, the reported assets and liabilities of SoftCloud have fair values as follows:

(in millions)	**Fair value**
Cash and receivables...	$ 400
Inventories	800
Property, plant and equipment......................................	3,500
Accounts payable..	300
Long-term debt	3,850

In addition, the following items are not currently reported on SoftCloud's balance sheet:

(in millions)	**Fair value**
Favorable lease agreements	$150
Skilled workforce	15
Favorable press reviews on products	5

Required: Prepare the entry IBM makes to record its acquisition of SoftCloud.

Solutions are located after the chapter assignments.

Learning Objectives identify the primary learning outcomes for each chapter. An end-of-chapter **Review of Key Concepts** summarizes the key topics of each chapter.

Extensive Class-Tested End-of-Chapter Material

Outstanding assignment material is an essential component of a successful textbook. End-of-chapter **questions, exercises and problems** cover all major topics and have a range of difficulty levels, allowing students ample opportunity to practice their understanding of the chapter. Some problems require students to use real company data in applying their knowledge. Assignment material is class-tested, with an emphasis on relevance and accuracy.

Certain **business combination problems continue from chapter to chapter**. For example, P3.2 covers consolidation at the date of acquisition, and P4.8 covers consolidation of the same two companies in subsequent years. P4.2 covers subsequent year consolidation of a wholly owned subsidiary, and P5.7 addresses subsequent year consolidation of the same subsidiary, when the subsidiary has outside ownership. In P2.5, an acquisition is reported as a merger, and in P3.11 the same acquisition is reported as a stock investment and consolidation. P3.4, P4.4, P5.2, P5.4 and P5.5 use the same acquisition data to illustrate consolidation of a bargain purchase at the date of acquisition, subsequent years, and with a noncontrolling interest. Each of these problems can also be assigned separately. In working through these problems, students gain a clearer understanding of accounting for business combinations.

FEATURES NEW TO THIS EDITION

- In the consolidation chapters, we use **color** pedagogically to identify eliminating entries, both in journal form and in the consolidation working papers, making it easier for students to navigate the complexities of consolidation procedures.

- All consolidation chapters emphasize consolidation of the **statement of income and comprehensive income**. Because in practice companies use a variety of formats to present consolidated operating results, the working paper consolidates the **trial balances** of the parent and subsidiary, which students then package into financial statements in whatever format desired. This approach increases students' flexibility and understanding of basic concepts.

- Discussion of consolidation policy more clearly emphasizes the goal of consolidating **controlled entities**, and includes updates on development stage entities, kick-out rights, and partnerships as illustrations of this concept.

- A new section on **valuation of acquired intangibles** discusses and illustrates the cost, market and income approaches, with emphasis on appropriate judgments and related audit risks.

- We added new material on common reporting issues related to acquisitions, including valuation of acquired **deferred taxes**, classification of **contingent consideration** as acquisition cost versus future compensation, acquisition of entities previously reported as **significant influence investments**, and fair value measurement issues for **impairment testing**.

- In the governmental chapters, all illustrations are updated for current standards and practice in the areas of **fund balance classifications**, recognition of **deferred inflows and outflows**, and reporting for **defined benefit pensions**. We added new material on accounting for **debt refundings**, a common activity in state and local governments.

- We emphasize the **commonality of reporting issues** for different types of entities—businesses, NFPs, governments, and even partnerships. Examples include consolidation policy, acquisition reporting, and hedge accounting.

- Chapter 16, covering **SEC** financial reporting and governance issues, is completely updated for current activities in the areas of **regulation, enforcement, and monitoring**.

- All **illustrations**, **current practices**, and **reporting perspectives** are completely updated.

- There are **over 150 new exercises and problems**, and a **net increase of about 80** exercises and problems, and various levels of difficulty.

- In response to requests from adopters, more assignments have been added to myBusinessCourse for the 3rd edition, including the multiple choice questions at the end of each chapter.

The Website for this text provides updates for changes in standards occurring subsequent to the publication date.

ONLINE INSTRUCTION AND HOMEWORK MANAGEMENT SYSTEM

myBusinessCourse: Is a web-based learning and assessment program intended to complement your textbook and faculty instruction. This easy-to-use program grades homework automatically (Instructor-Led course only) and provides students with access to narrated demonstrations and eLecture videos. Assignments with the ✓ in the margin are available in the Instructor-Led version of myBusinessCourse. Access is free with new copies of this textbook (look for a page containing the access code near the front of the book). If you buy a used copy of the book, you can purchase access at www.mybusinesscourse.com.

SUPPLEMENT PACKAGE

For Instructors

myBusinessCourse: Is a web-based learning and assessment program intended to complement your textbook and classroom instruction. This easy-to-use program grades homework automatically (Instructor-Led course only) and provides students with access to narrated demonstrations and eLecture videos. Assignments with the ✓ in the margin are available in the Instructor-Led version of myBusinessCourse. Visit www.mybusinesscourse.com to sign up or to learn more about this program's features and benefits. In addition, detailed diagnostic tools assess class and individual performance. myBusinessCourse is ideal for online courses, blended courses, and traditional face-to-face courses for which you want to offer students more resources to succeed.

Instructor CD-ROM: This convenient supplement provides the text's ancillary materials on a portable CD-ROM. All the faculty supplements that accompany the textbook are available, including PowerPoint, Solutions Manual, Test Bank, Excel Templates, and Computerized Test Bank.

Solutions Manual: Created by the textbook authors, the *Solutions Manual* contains complete solutions to all the assignments in the textbook.

Test Bank: Written by the textbook authors, the test bank includes multiple-choice questions and problems.

 Excel Templates: Excel spreadsheets for select assignments are provided on the book's Website. These spreadsheets will save time in data entry and allow students to dedicate additional time to learning the material. The Excel spreadsheets are identified by the Excel icon.

PowerPoint: Edited by the textbook authors, the PowerPoint slides outline key elements of each chapter.

Computerized Test Bank: This computerized version of the test bank enables an instructor to add and edit questions; create up to 99 versions of each test; attach graphic files to questions; import and export ASCII files; and select questions based on type or learning objective. It provides password protection for saved tests and question databases and is able to run on a network.

Website: All instructor materials are accessible via the book's Website (password protected). **www.cambridgepub.com**

For Students

BusinessCourse: Is a web-based learning and assessment program intended to complement your textbook and faculty instruction. This easy-to-use program grades homework automatically (Instructor-Led course only) and provides students with access to narrated demonstrations and eLecture videos. Access is free with new copies of this textbook (look for page containing the access code towards the front of the book). If you buy a used copy of the book, you can purchase access at **www.mybusinesscourse.com**.

 Excel Templates: Excel spreadsheets for select assignments are provided on the book's Website. These spreadsheets will save time in data entry and allow students to dedicate additional time to learning the material. The Excel spreadsheets are identified by the Excel icon.

Website: Practice quizzes, Excel templates, and other useful links are available to students free of charge on the book's Website.

ACKNOWLEDGEMENTS

Many individuals helped us develop this textbook. We gratefully acknowledge their assistance, and list their names and affiliations below.

Mark Anderson, *University of Texas—Dallas*
Mark Barfield, *Baylor University*
Mark Bauman, *University Northern Iowa*
Frank Beil, *University of Minnesota—Twin Cities*
John Bildersee, *New York University*
Andy Borchers, *Lipscomb University*
Gary Braun, *University of Texas—El Paso*
Kimberly Brickler-Ulrich, *Lindenwood University*
Richard Brown, *Concordia University Wisconsin*
Gene Bryson, *University of Alabama—Huntsville*
Kerry Calnan, *Nichols College*
Tina Carpenter, *University of Georgia*
Charles Carslaw, *University of Nevada, Reno*
Lynn Clements, *Florida Southern College*

Jacklyn Collins, *University of Miami*
Laurie Corradino, *Colorado State University-Pueblo*
Chris Cowles, *Central Connecticut State University*
Jean Crawford, *Alabama State University*
Donald Danner, *Aurora University*
Patricia Davis, *Keystone College*
Michael Davis, *University of Alaska*
Dennis Debrecht, *Carroll University*
Hemang Desai, *Southern Methodist University*
John Dexter, *Northwood University*
David Diehl, *Aurora University*
Cynthia Dittmer, *St. Ambrose University*
Reed Easton, *Seton Hall University*
Jack Elfrink, *Western Illinois University*

Michael Ettredge, *University of Kansas*

Mary Fischer, *University of Texas at Tyler*

Linda Flaming, *Monmouth University*

Sheila Foster, *The Citadel*

Carl Gabrini, *College of Coastal Georgia*

George Gardner, *Bemidji State University*

Earl Godfrey, *Gardner-Webb University*

Angela Gore, *George Washington University*

Ronald Guidry, *Illinois State University*

Michael Gurevitz, *Montgomery College*

Ling Harris, *University of South Carolina*

Judith Harris, *NOVA Southeastern University*

Anthony Herron, *University of Oklahoma*

Arlene Hibschweiler, *University at Buffalo*

Kenneth Hiltebeitel, *Villanova University*

Joan Hollister, *SUNY at New Paltz*

Yongtao Hong, *North Dakota State University*

Peter Hosker, *Southern New Hampshire University*

Huichi Huang, *Oregon State University*

Jodi Hunter, *Lake Superior State University*

Teresa Iannaconi, *KPMG LLP*

Marianne L. James, *CSU—Los Angeles*

Patricia Johnson, *Canisius College*

Bill Joyce, *Bemidji State University*

Roger Kerkenbush, *Loras College*

Ed Ketz, *Penn State University*

Myungsun Kim, *University at Buffalo*

Gordon Klein, *University of California—Los Angeles*

Lisa Koonce, *University of Texas—Austin*

Stanley Kratchman, *Texas A&M University*

Sudha Krishnan, *CSU—Long Beach*

Steve LaFever, *Wichita State University*

Robert Larson, *University of Dayton*

Mike Luehlfing, *Louisiana Tech University*

Cathy Margolin, *Brandman University*

Maureen Mascha, *Purdue University Calumet*

Dawn Massey, *Fairfield University*

Betsy Matz, *University of Pittsburgh—Bradford*

Katie Maxwell, *University of Arizona*

Reed McKnight, *University of New Mexico*

Allison McLeod, *University of North Texas*

Greg Merrill, *St. Mary's College*

Scott Miller, *Edinboro University*

Ramin Mirsaidi, *University of Washington—Tacoma*

Maria Mitchell, *Thomas More College*

Adam Myers, *Texas A&M University*

Hugo Nurnberg, *CUNY—Baruch*

Bruce Oliver, *Rochester Institute of Technology*

Gary Olsen, *Carroll University*

Michael Owens, *University of Tennessee—Chattanooga*

Tina Quinn, *Arkansas State University*

Sara Reiter, *Binghamton University*

Susan Riffe, *Southern Methodist University*

Jane Romal, *College at Brockport*

John Rossi, *Moravian College*

Kenneth Shaw, *University of Missouri*

Margaret Shelton, *University of St. Thomas*

Andreas Simon, *Pepperdine University*

Richard Simpson, *University of Massachusetts*

Sheldon Smith, *Utah Valley University*

Ira Stolzenberg, *Molloy College*

William Stout, *University of Louisville*

Gina Sturgill, *Bluefield State College*

John Surdick, *Xavier University*

Margaret Tanner, *University of Arkansas—Fort Smith*

Diane Tanner, *University of North Florida*

Randy Thomas, *Upper Iowa University*

Carmelita Troy, *Andrews University*

Kenton B. Walker, *University of Wyoming*

David Wallin, *Ohio State University*

Larry Walther, *Utah State University*

Jamie Wang, *University of Wisconsin—Parkside*

Donna Whitten, *Purdue University North Central*

Latasha Williams, *Keiser University*

Debbie Williams, *West Virginia State University*

Jan Williams, *University of Baltimore*

Sung Wook Yoon, *CSU—Northridge*

Suzanne Wright, *Penn State University*

Jia Wu, *University of Massachusetts—Dartmouth*

Stephen Zeff, *Rice University*

Ling Zhou, *Tulane University*

We express our appreciation for the support of the School of Management, University at Buffalo, and the Department of Accounting, Lehigh University. A special acknowledgement goes to Angela Gore for her very valuable assistance in updating the state and local government chapters. Her help is much appreciated. We also thank Mark Bauman for his contributions to myBusinessCourse. In addition, we are extremely grateful to George Werthman, Lorraine Gleeson, Beth Nodus, Jill Sternard, Jocelyn Mousel, Debbie McQuade, Terry McQuade, and the entire team at Cambridge Business Publishers for their encouragement, enthusiasm, and guidance. Comments are invited and encouraged from all instructors, students, and readers.

Susan S. Hamlen (hamlen@buffalo.edu)

Ronald J. Huefner (rhuefner@buffalo.edu)

James A. Largay III (jal3@lehigh.edu)

Brief Contents

Contents

Chapter 3

Consolidated Financial Statements: Date of Acquisition   78

Chapter 4

Consolidated Financial Statements Subsequent to Acquisition   118

Chapter 5

Consolidated Financial Statements: Outside Interests   176

Chapter 6

Consolidated Financial Statements: Intercompany Transactions   228

Chapter 7

Consolidating Foreign Currency Financial Statements   272

Chapter 11

State and Local Governments:
Other Transactions   468

Chapter 12

State and Local Governments:
External Financial Reporting   518

1 Intercorporate Investments: An Overview

LEARNING OBJECTIVES

LO1 Describe the reporting for trading, available-for-sale, and held-to-maturity intercorporate investments. (p. 5)

LO2 Explain the reporting for equity method intercorporate investments. (p. 9)

LO3 Describe the reporting for controlling interests in other companies. (p. 15)

LO4 Discuss International Financial Reporting Standards (IFRS) for intercorporate investments. (p. 17)

THE COCA-COLA COMPANY
www.coca-cola.com

The Coca-Cola Company is the world's largest beverage company. In addition to Coca-Cola, its brands include Sprite, Dasani, and Minute Maid. Coca-Cola produces beverage syrup in concentrated form, and sells it to bottlers. The bottlers mix the syrup with water and other ingredients, and bottle or can the finished beverages for delivery to retailers, restaurants, and food distributors.

Coca-Cola's investments in its bottlers and other companies take a variety of forms. At the end of 2013, Coca-Cola owned several legally separate bottling companies, including Coca-Cola Refreshments Canada and BCI Coca-Cola Bottling Company of Los Angeles. These companies are **subsidiaries** of Coca-Cola Company. Coca-Cola has a **significant interest** in some of its bottlers through equity ownership. It is involved in several **joint ventures**, where Coca-Cola shares decision-making authority with another company, and has certain financial relationships with other companies, called **variable interests**, which must be disclosed in its financial statements. Coca-Cola also holds **marketable debt and equity investments** in other companies, categorized as trading, available-for-sale, or held-to-maturity. These accounts appear as current and noncurrent assets on Coca-Cola's balance sheet.

Coca-Cola's financial statements illustrate the variety of intercorporate investments held by companies. Each investment type involves a different set of reporting requirements. This chapter presents an overview of reporting for the major types of investments in other companies. *Source*: The Coca-Cola Company 2013 annual report.

CHAPTER ORGANIZATION

Introduction	Marketable debt and equity investments	Investments with significant influence	Controlling investments	International Financial Reporting Standards
• Motivations for intercorporate investments • Types of investments	• Trading investments • Available-for-sale investments • Held-to-maturity investments	• Equity method investments • Joint ventures	• Mergers, consolidations, and asset acquisitions • Stock acquisitions • Variable interest entities	• Marketable debt and equity investments • Investments with significant influence • Joint ventures • Controlling investments

INTRODUCTION

Companies invest in other companies for many reasons, using a variety of financing arrangements, operating relationships and legal structures. Intercorporate investments are pervasive business activities, affect financial performance in profound ways, and have detailed and complex reporting requirements. How firms value investments and report gains and losses depends on the purpose of the investment and whether the investor has significant influence or control over the investee.

Motivations for Intercorporate Investments

Intercorporate investments achieve a variety of business purposes.

- A company purchases debt or equity securities of another company as a temporary investment of excess cash or as part of a longer-term risk-adjusted portfolio, expecting to receive dividends and capital gains.
- A company makes strategic investments to develop relationships with suppliers or customers or to gain access to new product or geographic markets.
- A company obtains a controlling interest in another company to facilitate activity along its supply chain.

The balance sheet and footnotes to **The Coca-Cola Company**'s December 31, 2013, annual report illustrate some of the most common types of intercorporate investments.

The Coca-Cola Company, Balance Sheet, Investments Lines Only		
December 31 *(in millions)*	2013	2012
Trading securities	$ 372	$ 266
Available-for-sale securities	4,842	4,593
Equity method investments	10,393	9,216

Coca-Cola holds trading and available-for-sale investments in the securities of other companies to generate investment income and capital gains. These investments are reported in various asset lines on Coca-Cola's balance sheet, including "marketable securities," "other investments, principally bottling companies," and "other assets."

Coca-Cola uses the **equity method** to account for investments in which it has significant influence. In 2013, Coca-Cola had a 29 percent ownership interest in Coca-Cola Amatil, one of the largest bottlers in the Asia-Pacific region, a 28 percent interest in the bottler Coca-Cola FEMSA, operating in Latin America, and a 23 percent interest in Coca-Cola Hellenic, operating in 28 European countries. Coca-Cola holds these investments for strategic reasons and exerts significant influence over the operations of these companies. Coca-Cola shares decision making authority in joint ventures with other companies. For example, Beverage Partners Worldwide is a 50/50 joint venture between Coca-Cola and Nestlé S.A., distributing Nestea products primarily in Europe and Canada. These investments are also reported using the equity method.

In recent years, beverage companies have changed strategy with respect to their bottlers, in some cases concluding that full ownership rather than significant influence results in more flexible, efficient and timely manufacture and delivery of products. For many years Coca-Cola held between 30 and 35 percent ownership in Coca-Cola Enterprises (CCE), a major bottler. In 2010 it acquired full ownership of CCE's North American production, sales, and distribution operations. On the other hand, in 2013 Coca-Cola sold 51 percent of its investment in Coca-Cola Bottlers Philippines, Inc. to Coca-Cola FEMSA. Coca-Cola has controlling ownership of more than 50 companies.

Coca-Cola has financial relationships with other companies. In some cases these relationships give Coca-Cola the power to direct these companies' activities and expose Coca-Cola to their benefits and losses, even though it does not have any ownership interests. The individual assets and liabilities of all these companies are included with Coca-Cola's assets and liabilities on its balance sheet, through a process known as **consolidation**. There is no separate investment line for these companies.

Types of Investments

For reporting purposes, intercorporate investments are divided into the following categories:

- *Trading* debt or equity securities are held on a short-term basis to generate profits through realized gains. Investors typically buy and sell these securities frequently.

- *Held-to-maturity* investments are *debt* securities intended to be held to maturity. Companies hold these investments for the interest and principal payments.

- *Available-for-sale* investments are debt or equity securities held for income or gains in value that are not classified as trading or held-to-maturity.

- *Equity method* investments are stock investments that provide the investor with a significant influence over the investee. This category includes *joint ventures*, where the investor shares joint control of an entity.

- Debt or equity securities can be held as *hedges* of the investor's financial risk. For example, a U.S. company with payables denominated in euros may neutralize the risk of a weakening U.S. dollar by investing in euro-denominated debt securities, which gain in value to offset the loss on the payables if the U.S. dollar weakens.

- A company can acquire some or all of the assets and liabilities of another business to expand into new markets, develop new products or services, or for other strategic purposes. These transactions are *mergers*, *consolidations*, or *asset acquisitions* depending on the acquisition structure.

- A company can gain a *controlling interest* in another legally separate company, either through ownership of all or the majority of its voting stock—termed a *stock acquisition*—or through a legal agreement that gives the investor the right to the majority of the investee's risks and rewards. These acquired companies are called *subsidiaries*. Entities controlled through a legal agreement rather than equity ownership are also known as *variable interest entities*.

FASB ASC Topic 825 allows companies to elect fair value reporting (the "fair value option") for eligible noncontrolling intercorporate investments. These include trading, held-to-maturity, available-for-sale, or equity method investments. Investments for which the fair value option is chosen are reported at fair value and value changes appear in income. The discussion that follows assumes the investor does *not* elect the fair value option. Controlling equity investments, in the form of mergers, consolidations, asset acquisitions and stock acquisitions, are not eligible for the fair value option.

MARKETABLE DEBT AND EQUITY INVESTMENTS

Many businesses invest in the debt and equity securities of other companies to generate investment income and capital gains. Examples of debt securities include commercial paper, corporate bonds, and redeemable preferred stock. Equity investments typically take the form of shares of a company's common or preferred stock, but often involve put or call options on the shares, allowing the investor to sell or buy shares at a fixed price. Such investors have no significant influence over the investee, either because the investments are debt securities, or the equity investment is a small fraction of total ownership. *ASC Topic 320* describes reporting requirements for these securities.

LO1 Describe the reporting for trading, available-for-sale, and held-to-maturity intercorporate investments.

The FASB is currently considering major changes in reporting requirements for investments covered by *ASC Topic 320*. As this edition goes to press, no Accounting Standards Update has been issued. The discussion below reflects GAAP in effect in 2014.

ASC Topic 320 divides investments with readily determinable market values into three categories: trading, available-for-sale, and held-to-maturity investments. When market value is not determinable, investments are reported at cost. Because intermediate accounting courses detail the reporting for these investments, we provide only a brief discussion.

Trading Investments

Trading investments can be in the form of debt or equity securities. These investments appear on the balance sheet as current assets reported at fair value, with gains and losses reported on the income statement as market prices change. Investment income, in the form of interest or dividends, is reported in income as earned. An illustration is based on the information in Exhibit 1.1.

EXHIBIT 1.1 Securities Portfolio

Security	Date Acquired	Cost	Dec. 31, 2015 Fair Value	Date Sold	Selling Price
A.........	10/15/15	$100,000	$125,000	1/15/16	$120,000
B.........	10/15/15	500,000	485,000	1/15/16	496,000
C.........	10/15/15	200,000	N/A	12/5/15	214,000

When these securities are classified as trading securities, the journal entries related to these securities are as follows:

2015			
Oct. 15	Investment in trading securities................................	800,000	
	Cash		800,000
	To record investment in trading securities costing a total of $800,000 in cash.		
2015			
Dec. 5	Cash..	214,000	
	Investment in trading securities...........................		200,000
	Gain on trading securities (income)........................		14,000
	To record sale of trading security C.		
2015			
Dec. 31	Investment in trading securities..............................	10,000	
	Gain on trading securities (income)........................		10,000
	To record unrealized value change in securities A and B; unrealized gain of $25,000 on security A and unrealized loss of $15,000 on security B.		
2016			
Jan. 15	Cash..	616,000	
	Investment in trading securities...........................		610,000
	Gain on trading securities (income)........................		6,000
	To record sale of trading securities A and B; cash received = $120,000 + $496,000, credit to Investment = $125,000 + $485,000.		

All unrealized and realized gains and losses on trading securities are reported on the income statement.

Available-for-Sale Investments

Investments in available-for-sale (AFS) securities are debt or equity securities reported at fair value as current or noncurrent assets on the balance sheet. As market prices change, unrealized gains and losses on AFS securities are reported in other comprehensive income (OCI), which is closed to accumulated other comprehensive income (AOCI) in the equity section of the balance sheet. When AFS securities are sold, the related unrealized gain or loss is recategorized from AOCI to the income statement. As a result, the entire gain or loss appears in income when the securities are sold. Interest or dividend income is reported in income as earned.

Assume that the securities in Exhibit 1.1 are classified as AFS securities. Journal entries are as follows:

2015			
Oct. 15	Investment in AFS securities	800,000	
	Cash		800,000
	To record investment in AFS securities A, B and C.		
2015			
Dec. 5	Cash.	214,000	
	Investment in AFS securities		200,000
	Gain on AFS securities (income)		14,000
	To record the sale of AFS security C. When AFS securities are purchased and sold in the same reporting period, gains and losses can be reported directly in income without going through OCI.		
2015			
Dec. 31	Investment in AFS securities	10,000	
	Gain on AFS securities (OCI).		10,000
	To record unrealized value changes for AFS securities A and B in OCI; OCI is closed to AOCI on the balance sheet.		
2016			
Jan. 15	Cash.	616,000	
	Reclassification of gain on AFS securities (OCI)	10,000	
	Investment in AFS securities		610,000
	Gain on AFS securities (income)		16,000
	To record sale of AFS securities A and B.		

Note that the effect of the January 15, 2016, entry is to *reduce* 2016 OCI by $10,000. To put this in perspective, look at Coca-Cola's 2013 Statement of Comprehensive Income.

The Coca-Cola Company and Subsidiaries Consolidated Statements of Comprehensive Income			
Year Ended December 31, (In millions)	**2013**	**2012**	**2011**
Consolidated Net Income	**$8,626**	**$9,086**	**$8,646**
Other comprehensive income:			
Net foreign currency translation adjustment	(1,187)	(182)	(692)
Net gain (loss) on derivatives	151	99	145
Net unrealized gain (loss) on available-for-sale securities	(80)	178	(7)
Net change in pension and other benefit liabilities.	1,066	(668)	(763)
Total Comprehensive Income.	8,576	8,513	7,329
Less: Comprehensive income (loss) attributable to noncontrolling interests. . .	39	105	10
Total Comprehensive Income Attributable to Shareowners of **the Coca-Cola Company**	**$8,537**	**$8,408**	**$7,319**

Each type of other comprehensive income appears as one line. Coca-Cola's 2013 net unrealized loss on available-for-sale securities of $80 million consists of two parts: (1) unrealized gains and losses on AFS securities held by Coca-Cola at December 31, 2013, and (2) reclassifications from other comprehensive income for AFS securities sold during 2013. In our example, the 2015 Statement of Comprehensive Income reports an unrealized *gain* of $10,000 for AFS securities held at year-end. The 2016 Statement of Comprehensive Income reports the reclassification of the unrealized gain to income when the securities are sold, as a *reduction* in other comprehensive income.

Beginning in 2013, U.S. companies are required to separately report reclassifications of AOCI, by type, either on the Statement of Comprehensive Income or in the footnotes. For example, if Coca-Cola's $80 million loss on AFS securities consists of $20 million in unrealized gains on securities held at year-end, and $100 million in reclassifications of previously recognized unrealized gains on securities sold in 2013, Coca-Cola is required to report each amount separately.

The principal difference in reporting for trading and available-for-sale investments is the timing of gain and loss recognition on the income statement. For trading securities, gains and losses affect net income *as prices change*. For AFS securities, gains and losses affect net income *when they are sold*. Note that in the previous illustration, the gain reported in 2016 income is the difference between the selling price and the original cost of the investment ($16,000 = $616,000 − $600,000).

Impairment Testing for AFS Securities   Although available-for-sale debt and equity securities are already carried at fair value on the balance sheet, *ASC Section 320-10-35* requires impairment testing for these securities. Impairment losses differ from other declines in value because they are reported on the income statement, not in other comprehensive income. There are two steps to the impairment test.

1. Determine whether the investment is impaired. Impairment occurs if the security's fair value is below its *cost*.

2. Decide whether the impairment is "**other than temporary**." If the investor intends to sell the security soon after the balance sheet date, the impairment is clearly other than temporary. If not, the investor must assess whether, during the time it intends to hold the security, it will recover the security's cost.

Suppose the $15,000 decline in value of AFS security B at December 31, 2015, is determined to be other than temporary. The entry to adjust securities A and B to fair value is:

2015			
Dec. 31	Investment in AFS securities	10,000	
	Impairment loss on security B (income)	15,000	
	Gain on security A (OCI)		25,000
	To record unrealized gain on security A and impairment loss on security B.		

For future impairment testing, security B's "cost" is $485,000. Any subsequent increases in fair value are not reported. Note that the amount of the impairment loss reported on the income statement is the decline in value below *cost*, not carrying value. If unrealized gains or losses have previously been recorded, and the security incurs an other-than-temporary impairment loss, any amounts recorded in AOCI are reclassified to income. Suppose an AFS investment, carried at $200,000, was originally acquired for $160,000. Therefore unrealized gains of $40,000 have previously been reported in OCI. Its fair value is currently $90,000. The $70,000 loss (= $160,000 − $90,000) is determined to be other-than-temporary. The entry to record the impairment loss is:

Reclassification of gain on AFS securities (OCI)	40,000	
Impairment loss on AFS securities (income)	70,000	
Investment in AFS securities		110,000
To record impairment loss on AFS securities.		

Held-to-Maturity Investments

Investments in held-to-maturity (HTM) securities can only be debt securities, since equity securities have no maturity date. They appear on the balance sheet as noncurrent assets until the year of maturity, and are reported at amortized cost. No gains or losses are reported unless the securities are not held to maturity as intended, and this only occurs under limited circumstances, such as financial distress on the part of the issuer. When debt securities are purchased above or below face value, the premium or discount is amortized over time as interest income is reported.

Assume investment of $965,349 in a $1,000,000 face value corporate bond on January 1, 2015, a price producing a 6 percent yield to maturity. The bond pays 5 percent interest annually on December 31, matures on December 31, 2018, and is classified as an HTM security. We use the effective interest method to amortize the discount. Journal entries to maturity are as follows:

2015				
Jan. 1	Investment in HTM securities...............................		965,349	
	Cash			965,349
	To record investment in HTM securities.			
2015				
Dec. 31	Cash...		50,000	
	Investment in HTM securities................................		7,921	
	Interest income			57,921
	To record interest income for 2015; $50,000 = 5% × $1,000,000;			
	$57,921 = 6% × $965,349.			
2016				
Dec. 31	Cash...		50,000	
	Investment in HTM securities................................		8,396	
	Interest income			58,396
	To record interest income for 2016; $58,396 = 6% × $973,270			
	(= $965,349 + $7,921).			
2017				
Dec. 31	Cash...		50,000	
	Investment in HTM securities................................		8,900	
	Interest income			58,900
	To record interest income for 2017; $58,900 = 6% × $981,666			
	(= $973,270 + $8,396).			
2018				
Dec. 31	Cash...		50,000	
	Investment in HTM securities................................		9,434	
	Interest income			59,434
	To record interest income for 2018; $59,434 = 6% × $990,566			
	(= $981,666 + $8,900).			
Dec. 31	Cash...		1,000,000	
	Investment in HTM securities			1,000,000
	To record receipt of the face value of the matured bond.			

Impairment Testing for HTM Investments   Although companies normally report HTM securities at amortized cost, *ASC Section 320-10-35* requires that they be evaluated for impairment. If the fair value of the security declines below amortized cost, and the decline is judged to be "**other than temporary**," we write the security down to fair value and report the impairment loss on the income statement. Any subsequent increases in fair value are not reported. The Codification offers the following guidance in measuring other-than-temporary impairment:

> If the present value of cash flows expected to be collected is less than the amortized cost basis of the security, the entire amortized cost basis of the security will not be recovered (that is, a credit loss exists), and an other-than-temporary impairment shall be considered to have occurred. *(ASC para. 320-10-35-33C)*

The original yield on the investment is the discount rate used in determining present value. In the illustration above, assume that a significant decrease in the bond issuer's profitability, and analysts' severe downgrade of company prospects, reduced the December 31, 2016, fair value of the corporate bond to $200,000 when the amortized cost of the bond is $981,666. If the decline in fair value is attributed to other-than-temporary impairment, the investor reports the impairment loss in income, as follows:

2016			
Dec. 31	Impairment loss on HTM securities (income)......................	781,666	
	Investment in HTM securities		781,666
	To record other-than-temporary impairment of HTM securities;		
	$781,666 = $200,000 − $981,666.		

Proposed Reporting Changes for Financial Instruments

Since the 2008 credit crisis, the FASB has been working on a project to update reporting requirements for investments in debt and equity financial instruments that are currently classified as trading, AFS, and HTM. As of 2014, no new standards are effective. However, in 2013 the FASB issued a proposed Accounting Standards Update focusing on classification and measurement of financial instruments.

For debt instruments involving contractual payments of principal and interest, the proposal retains the three current measurement classifications of fair value through income, fair value through OCI, and amortized cost. The fair values of debt instruments reported at amortized cost would be reported parenthetically on the face of the balance sheet. A company determines an investment's classification based on investment objectives. Equity investments are reported at fair value through income, or at cost if fair value is not readily determinable.

A 2012 proposed ASU focuses on reporting for impairment of debt instruments. A company would recognize an allowance for expected credit losses, measured as management's estimate of the investment's lifetime uncollectible contractual cash flows. The 2013 proposed ASU addresses impairment testing of equity investments reported at cost. The investment is considered impaired if it is more likely than not that its fair value is less than its book value.

The proposals, if adopted, would significantly change the reporting for financial instruments. Reporting classification would depend on investment strategy rather than legal form. A company would no longer be able to report equity investments at fair value through OCI. A more straightforward likelihood assessment replaces the "other-than-temporary" criterion for impairment recognition. Note that these changes are only proposals as of 2014. Consult the FASB web site for current updates.

REVIEW 1 • Trading, AFS, and HTM Investments

Assume **The Coca-Cola Company** makes the following intercorporate investments on January 2, 2016:

Security	Type	Cost
A.........	Trading	$ 300,000
B.........	AFS	1,000,000
C.........	HTM	486,384

Security C is a 3-year $500,000 face value corporate bond paying 4% interest annually on December 31 and yielding 5% to maturity. Coca-Cola sells Security A for $265,000 on June 15, 2016, and acquires Security D on October 15, 2016, for $250,000. Security D is classified as a trading security.

December 31, 2016, fair values are as follows:

Security	Type	Fair Value
B.........	AFS	$920,000
C.........	HTM	495,000
D.........	Trading	260,000

Cash dividends of $12,000 are received on the investments in Securities B and D on December 1, 2016. Interest of $20,000 is received on Security C on December 31, 2016.

Required: Prepare all entries related to the above investments for 2016.

Solutions are located after the chapter assignments.

INVESTMENTS WITH SIGNIFICANT INFLUENCE

LO2 Explain the reporting for equity method intercorporate investments.

Unless a company elects the *ASC Section 825-10-25* fair value option, *ASC Topic 323* requires that the **equity method** be used to account for equity investments that allow the investor to exercise *significant influence* over the operating and financial decisions of the investee. **Significant influence** is assumed to be present if the investor owns between 20 and 50 percent of the investee's voting stock. However, this is only a guideline to aid in assessing significant influence. The Codification offers indicators of the investor's ability to exert significant influence, including:

- representation on the investee's board of directors
- involvement in the development of investee operating and financial policies
- significant transactions between investor and investee

The *key issue* is whether the investor *in fact* exerts significant influence over the investee's operations. Significant influence may exist with less than 20 percent ownership of the investee's voting shares, or there may be circumstances where a large minority ownership does not indicate significant influence. *ASC para. 323-10-15-10* provides guidance on this point. For example, if the investor has given up significant shareholder rights, has tried but failed to gain representation on the investee's board, or if other owners not influenced by the investor control the investee's operations, the equity method is not appropriate even if the investor holds 20 to 50 percent of the voting stock.

Accounting Using the Equity Method

When the investor can influence the investee's operating and financial decisions and the amount and timing of dividends the investee pays, performance of the investment is not accurately measured by dividend payout. Instead, investment performance should parallel the investee's performance. The equity method achieves this goal with the following procedures:

- Increase (decrease) the investment account by the investor's share of the investee's income (loss).
- The investor reports its share of the investee's income (loss) in income.
- Reduce the investment account for dividends from the investee.

The investor's investment balance therefore changes in proportion to the changes in the investee's retained earnings.

Suppose that on January 2, 2016, The Coca-Cola Company acquires 300,000, or 30 percent, of the voting shares of Rocky Mountain Bottlers for $40 per share, a total of $12 million in cash. Coca-Cola has a significant influence over Rocky Mountain, and therefore the equity method is appropriate. Rocky Mountain reports net income of $2 million for the year ended December 31, 2016. It declares a cash dividend of $0.50 per share on November 1, 2016, and pays the dividend on December 2, 2016. Coca-Cola records the following entries for 2016 relative to its equity method investment in Rocky Mountain:

2016			
Jan. 2	Investment in Rocky Mountain Bottlers.............................	12,000,000	
	Cash		12,000,000
	To record the investment.		
2016			
Nov. 1	Dividends receivable	150,000	
	Investment in Rocky Mountain Bottlers......................		150,000
	To record the declared dividend; $150,000 = $0.50 × 300,000.		
2016			
Dec. 2	Cash..	150,000	
	Dividends receivable		150,000
	To record receipt of the declared dividend.		
2016			
Dec. 31	Investment in Rocky Mountain Bottlers...........................	600,000	
	Equity in net income of Rocky Mountain Bottlers (income)........		600,000
	To accrue the earnings of the investee; $600,000 = 30% × $2,000,000.		

The December 31, 2016, investment balance, reported on Coca-Cola's balance sheet in noncurrent assets, is $12,450,000 (= $12,000,000 − $150,000 + $600,000). Equity in net income of Rocky Mountain Bottlers of $600,000 appears as a component of Coca-Cola's income for 2016.

Equity in Net Income Calculation

The discussion above computed equity in net income as the investor's share of the investee's reported net income, based on the assumption that the investee's reported net income accurately measures the performance of the investment. When investment cost differs from the investee's book value, or the investor and investee transact business with each other, the investor must make adjustments to the investee's reported income.

At the date of acquisition, investment cost usually exceeds the book value of the investee, calculated as its reported assets less liabilities. The investee reports its noncurrent assets such as plant and equipment at cost less accumulated depreciation, not current fair value. Internally developed intangible assets, such as favorable contractual agreements, customer base, technology and reputation do not appear as assets on the investee's balance sheet. For these reasons an investee's shares usually sell at a price in excess of book value.

Companies take large noncontrolling interests in other entities for strategic reasons that facilitate business activities between the companies. Common transactions involve intercompany sales of raw materials or finished goods inventories. For example, Coca-Cola sells syrup to its 29-percent-owned bottler, Coca-Cola Amatil. When related entities sell merchandise to each other, the profit on these transactions is not considered to be earned until the merchandise is sold to an unrelated outside party.

Amortization of Investment Cost in Excess of Book Value Acquired

To accurately measure investment performance, we must consider any investment cost in excess of investee book value, also known as *basis differences*. The investee's reported income reflects appropriate write-offs of its reported assets, in the form of depreciation, amortization, and impairment losses. If investment cost reflects additional assets not recorded on the investee's books, equity in net income should in turn reflect write-offs of these additional assets. In the previous discussion, we calculated Coca-Cola's share of Rocky Mountain Bottlers' income as a proportion of Rocky Mountain's reported net income. If Coca-Cola's investment cost at the date of investment differs from Rocky Mountain's underlying book value, we must make adjustments to accurately measure investment performance.

Suppose that on January 2, 2016, Rocky Mountain's book value is $30 million. Coca-Cola therefore paid $3 million (= $12 million − 30% × $30 million) more for its 30 percent investment than its share of Rocky Mountain's reported book value. Analysis of Rocky Mountain's assets and liabilities reveals that its plant and equipment is reported at $1 million less than its fair value. It also has unreported technology valued at $5 million. We can explain the $3 million excess over acquired book value as follows:

Price paid.		$12,000,000
Share of Rocky Mountain's net assets acquired:		
Book value (30% × $30,000,000).	$9,000,000	
Revaluation of plant and equipment (30% × $1,000,000)	300,000	
Unreported technology (30% × $5,000,000)	1,500,000	10,800,000
Goodwill.		$ 1,200,000

Of the total $3 million excess cost, $1,800,000 (= $300,000 + $1,500,000) is explained by specific asset undervaluations. The remaining unexplained cost is attributed to goodwill, representing the additional cost not explained by underreported or unreported identifiable assets.

Rocky Mountain does not report depreciation or amortization of the additional assets embedded in Coca-Cola's investment cost, because these assets do not appear on Rocky Mountain's books. Coca-Cola therefore adjusts its equity in the net income of Rocky Mountain for basis difference write-offs. Equity in net income is adjusted for write-offs of *identifiable assets*, but any adjustment for goodwill impairment is *prohibited*.

Continuing Coca-Cola's investment in 30 percent of Rocky Mountain Bottlers' voting stock, assume that the revalued plant and equipment has a remaining life of 10 years as of January 2, 2016, straight-line, and the previously unreported technology is a limited life intangible asset with a five-year life. Coca-Cola's 2016 equity in the net income of Rocky Mountain Bottlers is reduced by $30,000 in depreciation on the plant and equipment revaluation (= $300,000/10) and by amortization of previously unreported technology of $300,000 (= $1,500,000/5). In practice, however, the investor often attributes the excess cost entirely to goodwill. This shortcut avoids any income adjustments for revaluation write-offs.

Unconfirmed Inventory Profits

An investor may sell inventory to its investee, termed **downstream** sales, or an investee may sell merchandise to the investor, termed **upstream** sales. Both companies record the sales on their own books as if they are selling to outside customers. If both companies sell the merchandise at a markup over cost, they will report a gross margin on these intercompany sales as part of their income. However, if the merchandise is not yet sold to an unrelated outside party at year-end, this gross margin is not yet earned and must be removed when calculating equity in the net income of the investee.

Suppose that during 2016 Rocky Mountain Bottlers sells merchandise to Coca-Cola (upstream) at an average markup of 20 percent on cost. Coca-Cola still holds $210,000 of this inventory at year-end. During 2016 Coca-Cola sells merchandise to Rocky Mountain (downstream) at an average markup of 25 percent on cost. Rocky Mountain holds $100,000 of this inventory at year-end. The total unconfirmed profit on the ending inventories is as follows:

Unconfirmed gross profit on $210,000 upstream sales:
$$\$210,000 - \$210,000/1.20 = \$35,000$$

Unconfirmed gross profit on $100,000 downstream sales:
$$\$100,000 - \$100,000/1.25 = \$20,000$$

Coca-Cola's 2016 equity in the net income of Rocky Mountain Bottlers is reduced by $10,500 (= 30% × $35,000) and $6,000 (= 30% × $20,000). When the beginning inventories are sold to outside customers, the profit is confirmed and equity in net income is increased by $10,500 and $6,000.

To summarize, Coca-Cola's equity in the 2016 net income of Rocky Mountain is calculated as follows:

Coca-Cola's share of Rocky Mountain's reported net income (30% × $2,000,000)	$600,000
Revaluation write-offs:	
Plant and equipment	(30,000)
Previously unreported technology	(300,000)
Unconfirmed inventory profits:	
Upstream sales	(10,500)
Downstream sales	(6,000)
Equity in net income of Rocky Mountain	$253,500

Coca-Cola's end-of-year entry to recognize its share of Rocky Mountain's income is:

2016			
Dec. 31	Investment in Rocky Mountain Bottlers	253,500	
	Equity in net income of Rocky Mountain Bottlers		253,500
	To accrue Coca-Cola's share of the earnings of the investee.		

The investment balance at year-end is $12,103,500 (= $12,000,000 − $150,000 + $253,500).

Other Comprehensive Income and the Equity Method

Using the equity method, the investor reports its share of the investee's performance each year on its own books. A company's performance is measured by its income, which accumulates in retained earnings, but other elements of performance are reflected in other comprehensive income, which appears in its statement of comprehensive income and accumulates in AOCI. To fully report the investee's performance, the investor adjusts its investment and other comprehensive income for its share of the investee's yearly OCI.

Assume that in 2016 Rocky Mountain reported $200,000 in unrealized gains on AFS securities, its only OCI item. In addition to the entries above, Coca-Cola makes the following entry to reflect these gains:

2016			
Dec. 31	Investment in Rocky Mountain Bottlers	60,000	
	Unrealized gains on AFS investments (OCI)		60,000
	To report 30% share of Rocky Mountain's unrealized gains on AFS securities.		

Impairment Testing

ASC para. 323-10-35-32 requires impairment testing of equity method investments. If the fair value of the investment declines below its carrying value, and the decline is judged to be other than temporary, the investment is written down and the loss appears on the investor's income statement. Any subsequent increases in fair value are not reported.

• •

Reporting Perspective

Typically the cost of equity method investments exceeds the underlying book value of the investee, because the investee has assets valued by the market but not reported on its balance sheet. When using the equity method, the investor identifies the specific assets that are undervalued or not reported on the investee's books. The investor then reports equity in the net income of the investee as its share of the investee's reported net income, adjusted for write-offs of those undervalued or unreported assets with limited lives. However, equity in net income is *not* adjusted for goodwill impairment.

Why is goodwill impairment not included when computing equity in net income? One logical explanation is that the impairment test for the investment as a whole reflects impairment losses in the investee's goodwill. If the investment is subject to other-than-temporary impairment, expectations concerning the investee's future performance have significantly declined. A financially distressed investee's goodwill is therefore impaired.

In practice, investors typically attribute to goodwill the entire difference between book value and investment cost. Therefore they rarely adjust equity in net income for write-offs of basis adjustments, since goodwill is not amortized and the FASB prohibits adjustments for goodwill impairment. For example, Coca-Cola's 2013 annual report states that at December 31, 2013, its investment in equity method investees exceeded its proportionate share of investee book value by $2,202 million, but the difference is not amortized.

• •

BUSINESS APPLICATION   Impairment Testing

In 2011, **The Coca-Cola Company** recorded $17 million in losses on its AFS securities, and a $41 million loss on one of its equity method investments. In 2012 and 2013, Coca-Cola held AFS investments whose cost exceeded fair value. However, it recorded no impairment losses on these securities, since management determined that the decline in value was not other than temporary. Note 1 to the 2013 financial statements describes Coca-Cola's impairment testing.

> Each reporting period we review all of our investments in equity and debt securities, except for those classified as trading, to determine whether a significant event or change in circumstances has occurred that may have an adverse effect on the fair value of each investment. When such events or changes occur, we evaluate the fair value compared to our cost basis in the investment. . . . The fair values of most of our investments in publicly traded companies are often readily available based on quoted market prices. For investments in nonpublicly traded companies, management's assessment of fair value is based on valuation methodologies including discounted cash flows, estimate of sales proceeds and appraisals, as appropriate.
>
> In the event the fair value of an investment declines below our cost basis, management determines if the decline in fair value is other than temporary. . . . Management's assessment as to the nature of a decline in fair value is based on, among other things, the length of time and the extent to which the market value has been less than our cost basis, the financial condition and near-term prospects of the issuer, and our intent and ability to retain the investment for a period of time sufficient to allow for any anticipated recovery in market value.

Coca-Cola uses a variety of methods to measure the fair value of its investments, and forecasts the future financial condition of the investee and the investment holding period to determine if declines in value are other than temporary. *Source*: The Coca-Cola Company 2013 annual report.

Joint Ventures

A **joint venture** is an entity formed by a group of individuals or firms that contribute resources and jointly share in managing and controlling the venture. Joint ventures are traditionally established to carry out a single business transaction or activity, often over a limited period of time. Frequently, the owners of a joint venture are themselves large firms, either partnerships or corporations. Participants form joint ventures for activities when it is mutually desirable to combine expertise, special technology, capital, or access to certain markets. Examples include research projects or development of new products, in which two areas of technology must be joined, and large-scale construction projects, in which the capital and facilities of two or more contractors are needed. Although joint ventures are frequently short-lived, they can last several years and their initial projects may lead to ongoing business activities.

We discussed Coca-Cola's joint venture with Nestlé earlier in this chapter. This joint venture expands Coca-Cola's markets internationally. U.S. companies follow the guidelines of *ASC Topic 323*: joint ventures give the investor significant influence and require use of the equity method.

• •

Reporting Perspective

If two companies form a joint venture with equal interests, U.S. GAAP allows both companies to report the venture using the equity method. As a result, the separate assets and liabilities of the joint venture do not appear on *any* balance sheet. Each investor reports its interest as a one-line equity investment in the asset section of its balance sheet. Similarly, the separate revenues and expenses of the joint venture do not appear on *any* income statement. Each investor reports its equity in the joint venture's net income on one line in its income statement.

• •

Coca-Cola and Nestlé each have 50 percent ownership in Beverage Partners Worldwide (BPW). Suppose Coca-Cola instead had 60 percent ownership, and Nestlé 40 percent, and that Coca-Cola now controls BPW. Nestlé would continue to account for its investment using the equity method, assuming it retained significant influence over BPW. Coca-Cola, on the other hand, would consolidate BPW on its financial statements. Consolidation involves combining the separate assets, liabilities, revenues and expenses of BPW with Coca-Cola's own accounts on its financial statements. The next section introduces reporting for controlling equity investments.

REVIEW 2 ● Reporting for Equity Method Investments

On January 5, 2017, Fizzy Cola Corporation, headquartered in Minneapolis, MN, acquires 25 percent of the voting stock of Armadillo Bottlers, located in Austin, TX, to support expansion in southwestern U.S. markets. Fizzy Cola pays $15 million in cash for the stock. Armadillo's book value is $20 million at the acquisition date, and its assets and liabilities are fairly stated except for unreported customer-related intangible assets valued at $10 million, with average expected lives of five years. In 2017, Armadillo reports net income of $3 million.

Armadillo sells canned and bottled beverages to Fizzy Cola at a markup of 30 percent on cost. Fizzy Cola sells syrup to Armadillo at a markup of 20 percent on cost. At December 31, 2017, Fizzy Cola's inventory includes $325,000 in merchandise acquired from Armadillo. Armadillo's inventory includes $480,000 in merchandise purchased from Fizzy Cola. Armadillo declares and pays total cash dividends of $500,000 on December 1, 2017. Fizzy Cola accounts for its investment in Armadillo using the equity method.

Required: Prepare Fizzy Cola's entries to record the above information for 2017.

Solutions are located after the chapter assignments.

CONTROLLING INVESTMENTS

Investments in other companies may give the investor control over the operating and financial decisions of the investee. The investment structures may take different forms, as follows:

- **Merger**, **consolidation**, or **asset acquisition**, where the investor directly acquires the assets and liabilities of the investee. Mergers occur when the investor acquires the investee and becomes the remaining legal entity. In a consolidation, a new entity is formed to acquire both the investor and investee. In asset acquisitions, the investor acquires a subset of the investee's assets.

- **Stock acquisition**, where the investor acquires a controlling interest in the voting stock of the investee.

- **Variable interest entity**, where the investor may not hold the investee's stock, but legal agreements give it the power to direct the investee's activities, the obligation to absorb its losses and the right to receive its benefits. The investee's actual equity holders do not have the usual rights and responsibilities pertaining to equity ownership.

Investors should be able to evaluate a company's complete financial performance by looking at its financial statements. If the company controls the resources of another company, investors should see the results of decisions affecting these resources in the controlling company's financial statements. Therefore, regardless of the investment structure used to obtain control, reporting policies are generally the same—the assets, liabilities, revenues and expenses of the controlled investee are combined with those of the investor for presentation in its financial statements.

Mergers, Consolidations, and Asset Acquisitions

When the investor acquires the assets and liabilities of the investee, it records these assets and liabilities directly on its books at fair value. Consider again Coca-Cola's acquisition of Rocky Mountain Bottlers, but assume Coca-Cola acquires *all* of Rocky Mountain's assets and liabilities in a merger. Information on this acquisition is in Exhibit 1.2 below.

EXHIBIT 1.2   Coca-Cola's Acquisition of Rocky Mountain Bottlers

Coca-Cola pays $40,000,000 in cash to acquire the assets and liabilities of Rocky Mountain Bottlers on January 2, 2016. Fair values of Rocky Mountain's reported assets and liabilities on that date are as follows:

Rocky Mountain Bottlers	Fair value
Current assets	$20,000,000
Plant and equipment	61,000,000
Current liabilities	15,000,000
Long-term liabilities	35,000,000

Coca-Cola identified and valued Rocky Mountain's previously unreported intangible assets as follows:

Technology	$ 5,000,000

The acquisition price is analyzed as follows:

Price paid		$40,000,000
Fair value of identifiable net assets acquired:		
Current assets	$20,000,000	
Plant and equipment	61,000,000	
Technology	5,000,000	
Current liabilities	(15,000,000)	
Long-term debt	(35,000,000)	36,000,000
Goodwill		$ 4,000,000

Coca-Cola makes the following January 2 entry on its books:

Current assets	20,000,000	
Plant and equipment	61,000,000	
Technology	5,000,000	
Goodwill	4,000,000	
Current liabilities		15,000,000
Long-term debt		35,000,000
Cash		40,000,000

To record the acquisition of Rocky Mountain Bottlers for $40,000,000 in cash.

Coca-Cola records Rocky Mountain's assets and liabilities directly on its books, at date-of-acquisition market values. Rocky Mountain ceases to exist as a separate entity, and Coca-Cola reports Rocky Mountain's subsequent activities directly in its own financial records.

Stock Acquisitions

When an investor obtains control over another company by investing in its *voting stock*, the investor is known as the **parent**, the acquired company is the **subsidiary**, and the two companies remain as separate legal entities, recording transactions on their own books. At the end of each reporting period, the accountant **consolidates** the separate financial records of the parent and subsidiary for presentation in the annual report.

Suppose Coca-Cola acquires and holds all of the *voting stock* of Rocky Mountain Bottlers, paying the former stockholders of Rocky Mountain $40,000,000 cash. Coca-Cola makes the following entry on its own books:

Investment in Rocky Mountain Bottlers	40,000,000	
Cash		40,000,000

To record acquisition of all Rocky Mountain's stock for $40,000,000 cash.

Rocky Mountain Bottlers continues to exist as a separate entity, and reports its financial activities on its own books. At the end of each reporting period, a *consolidation working paper* is used to combine the financial results of Coca-Cola and Rocky Mountain, as if Coca-Cola had reported Rocky Mountain's acquired assets and liabilities, and subsequent activities, directly on its books. Chapters 3 through 6 discuss this process.

Variable Interest Entities

Variable interest entities (VIEs) are similar to stock acquisitions, in that the investee is a separate legal entity controlled by another company. However, control occurs through legal relationships rather than stock ownership. Two reporting questions arise: (1) Is the entity a variable interest entity, and (2) must the investor consolidate the entity with its own financial statements? Chapter 3 provides detailed answers to these questions. The following discussion is a brief introduction.

According to *ASC para. 810-10-15-14*, if the entity must obtain guarantees from other parties in order to obtain financing, or if the equity holders do not have the usual rights and responsibilities pertaining to equity ownership, such as voting rights and the right to residual returns, the entity is a VIE. A common example is a leasing arrangement where a company creates a separate legal entity to purchase long-term assets, funded by loans guaranteed by the company. That entity leases the assets to the company, and uses the lease payments to pay interest and principal on the debt. The entity has a small outside equity ownership, but rights to dividends or returns in liquidation may be contractually guaranteed or limited, leaving the equity owners with rights similar to debtholders. The question is whether the entity can finance its activities without additional support, such as guaranteed loans or future funding commitments, from affiliated entities. If not, the entity is a VIE.

ASC para. 810-10-25-38A requires the entity that has the power to direct the VIE's activities, absorbs the majority of the VIE's expected losses and/or receives a majority of the VIE's residual gains, to consolidate the VIE. Consolidation procedures parallel those for stock investments.

INTERNATIONAL FINANCIAL REPORTING STANDARDS FOR INTERCORPORATE INVESTMENTS

LO4 Discuss International Financial Reporting Standards (IFRS) for intercorporate investments.

International Financial Reporting Standards (IFRS) for intercorporate investments are found in the following pronouncements:

- *IAS 28*, Investments in Associates
- *IAS 39*, Financial Instruments: Recognition and Measurement
- *IFRS 3(R)*, Business Combinations
- *IFRS 9*, Financial Instruments
- *IFRS 10*, Consolidated Financial Statements
- *IFRS 11*, Joint Arrangements

In light of the 2008 credit crisis, both the FASB and the IASB recently proposed significant changes in reporting for investments in debt and equity securities that do not involve significant or controlling interests. The IASB's financial instruments project has three phases: classification and measurement, impairment, and hedge accounting. The classification and measurement phase was completed in 2009, with the issuance of *IFRS 9*. The guidance in the other two phases will be added to *IFRS 9* as they are completed. Although *IFRS 9* will eventually replace *IAS 39*, its effective date has been delayed since the impairment and hedge accounting phases are not yet complete. As of 2014, the standard becomes effective in 2018. The discussion below includes current *IAS 39* guidance as well as *IFRS 9* requirements.

The IASB also changed the requirements for joint ventures (*IFRS 11*) and for deciding when to consolidate an equity investment (*IFRS 10*). Both of these standards became effective in 2013, and the discussion below reflects their requirements.

Marketable Debt and Equity Investments

IFRS for marketable investments in debt and equity securities, found in *IAS 39*, generally parallel current U.S. GAAP. Investments are classified as trading, available-for-sale, and held-to-maturity. Trading and available-for-sale securities are reported at fair value, with unrealized gains and losses on trading securities reported in income, and unrealized gains and losses on available-for-sale securities reported in equity until the securities are sold. Held-to-maturity debt securities are carried at amortized cost.

Following both U.S. GAAP and IFRS, securities classified as available-for-sale are reported at fair value through OCI. Unrealized gains and losses are reported in OCI and reclassified to income when the securities are sold. U.S. companies must report OCI items by type, and disclose actual reclassifications separately by type. Unlike U.S. GAAP, IFRS requires that OCI items be classified according to whether or not they can be reclassified to income or if they remain in AOCI indefinitely.

IFRS for impairment losses focuses on specific objective evidence of the decline in fair value, citing observance of particular *"loss events,"* such as a decline in credit rating or if the investee misses scheduled debt payments. U.S. GAAP requires loss recognition when the decline is *"other than temporary,"* which may involve more judgment. Unlike U.S. GAAP, IFRS allows impairment losses on held-to-maturity debt investments to be *reversed*, thereby increasing income, if a subsequent event reduces the previously recognized impairment loss. The maximum impairment reversal is the amount that increases book value to amortized cost without impairment. Like U.S. GAAP, IFRS does not allow reversal of impairment losses on equity investments.

IFRS 9 changes the measurement and classification of financial assets that do not give the investor significant influence or control over the investee. The default for all investments in marketable debt and equity financial instruments is to report these investments at fair value, with all value changes reported in income (FV-NI). Changes in the value of equity investments not held for trading may be reported in other comprehensive income (FV-OCI). The gains and losses reported in OCI are not reclassified to income when realized. Debt instruments held for principal and interest payments, with no intent to sell, may be reported at amortized cost.

A 2013 IASB *Exposure Draft* addresses recognition of credit losses on investments in financial instruments. Current *IAS 39* guidance looks to "loss events" to identify when impairment losses should be reported. No losses are reported until a loss event occurs. The proposal requires continuing recognition of expected credit losses, measured as the present value of expected payment defaults. The proposal therefore should lead to more timely recognition of impairment losses. However, loss recognition differs depending on if the financial instrument has "significantly deteriorated" or not. The loss is based on lifetime losses only if there is significant deterioration of credit quality. If not, the loss is based on expected credit losses over the next twelve months. The FASB proposal looks at lifetime expected losses for all investments. The FASB proposal would likely require earlier recognition of credit losses. As of 2014, no convergence between U.S. GAAP and IFRS has been achieved on this topic.

Investments with Significant Influence

IFRS for investments providing the investor with a significant influence over the investee are found in *IAS 28*. The investee in this case is defined as an **associate**. Circumstances that indicate significant influence, can take one of the following forms *(para 7)*:

- representation on the board of directors or equivalent governing body of the investee;
- participation in the policy-making process;
- material transactions between the investor and the investee;
- interchange of managerial personnel; or
- provision of essential technical information.

IFRS requires the equity method for significant influence investments, using procedures very similar to U.S. GAAP. *IAS 36* and *IAS 39* provide guidance for impairment recognition. *IAS 39* states that impairment testing is performed if one or more significant events occur that indicate the investment has become impaired. The quantitative impairment test, found in *IAS 36*, compares the investment's book value to its recoverable amount, which is the *higher of its market value or value-in-use*. **Value-in-use** is the present value of the investment's future expected cash flows while held by the investor. Current U.S. GAAP requires impairment recognition only when the decline in value is *other than temporary*. This difference in criteria is likely to result in differences in impairment loss recognition between IFRS and U.S. GAAP.

Joint Ventures

IFRS 11 defines *joint arrangements* as investments in which contractual agreements require the investors to unanimously consent to decisions concerning the investee. For example, if decisions regarding the activities of an entity are made by majority vote, and two parties each have a 50 percent interest in the entity, it is a joint arrangement. Joint arrangements may be *joint operations* or *joint ventures*, with joint operations giving the investors rights to the entity's individual assets and obligations for its liabilities, and joint ventures giving the investors rights to the entity's net assets. Most joint arrangements are joint ventures, involving rights to the entity's returns and amounts received on disposal. Similar to U.S. GAAP, *IFRS 11* requires that joint ventures be reported using the equity method.

Controlling Investments

IFRS 3(R), "Business Combinations," describes IFRS for assets and liabilities acquired in mergers, consolidations, and asset acquisitions, and consolidation of controlling stock investments. These standards are similar to U.S. GAAP.

IFRS for determining *when* an entity should be consolidated are in *IFRS 10*, "Consolidated Financial Statements." This standard applies to any entities with which the reporting entity has a relationship, whether it involves ownership of stock or some sort of contractual relationship. *IFRS 10* requires consolidation of an entity when it *controls* the entity. Control occurs when the investor has all of the following *(IFRS 10, para 7)*:

- power over the investee—the investor has existing rights that give it the ability to direct the activities that significantly affect the investee's returns
- exposure, or rights, to variable returns from its involvement with the investee
- the ability to use its power over the investee to affect the amount of the investor's returns.

The IFRS consolidation standard requires qualitative analysis of the reporting entity's relationship with another entity. Although U.S. GAAP is also based on the concept of control, U.S. GAAP is more likely to focus on the "bright line" of majority equity ownership. There is also a separate set of conditions for consolidation of entities controlled through legal relationships. As a result, IFRS and U.S. GAAP can disagree on whether a particular entity should be consolidated.

BUSINESS APPLICATION   Orange S.A.

Orange S.A. (formerly France Telecom) is an international telecommunications company with headquarters in France. Its 2013 annual report lists the following major interests in associates and joint ventures:

Entity	Co-shareholder(s)	% interest	Country of operation
EE	Deutsche Telekom (50%)	50%	UK
Médi Telecom	Groupe Caisse de Dépôt et de Gestion (30%), Groupe FinanceCom (30%)	40%	Morocco
Korek Telecom	Agility (24%), CS Ltd (56%)	20%	Iraq

Orange reports investments in associates on its balance sheet as a noncurrent asset, totaling €6,525 million at December 31, 2013. Orange reported impairment losses of €186 million in 2013, mostly related to Médi Telecom. Once a loss event is identified, book value is compared to value-in-use, measured as the present value of future expected cash flows generated by the associate. Orange's strategic business planning process is used to generate expected future cash flows. Orange discloses the key assumptions used in this calculation:

Basis of recoverable amount	Value-in-use
Source used	Internal plan
Methodology	Discounted cash flow
Growth rate to perpetuity	1.0%
Post-tax discount rate	7.8%
Pre-tax discount rate	9.0%

In 2012, Orange used a post-tax discount rate of 8.0% and a pre-tax discount rate of 9.7% to measure its associates' value-in-use. Small changes in discount rates can have significant effects on present value. As Orange's auditor, how would you evaluate the appropriateness of the discount rates used to measure impairment? *Source*: Orange 2013 annual report.

REVIEW OF KEY CONCEPTS

Describe the reporting for trading, available-for-sale, and held-to-maturity intercorporate investments. (p. 5)   **LO 1**
Investments in securities held for income and value increases are classified as **trading, available-for-sale**, and **held-to-maturity**. Trading and available-for-sale investments in debt and equity securities appear on the balance sheet at fair value. Unrealized gains and losses on trading securities are reported in income. Unrealized gains and losses on AFS debt and equity securities are reported in other comprehensive income, and are reclassified to income when the securities are sold. Held-to-maturity debt securities are reported at amortized cost. AFS and HTM securities are regularly tested for impairment. The FASB is currently deliberating significant changes in standards for financial instruments.

Explain the reporting for equity method intercorporate investments. (p. 9) The **equity method** is used to   **LO 2**
report equity investments that enable the investor to significantly influence the investee's operating and financial decisions. The investor's equity in the investee's net income or loss appears on the investor's income statement, increasing or decreasing the investment balance, and dividends received reduce the balance. Equity in the investee's net income is the investor's share of the investee's reported income, net of amortization of the excess of investment cost over the investee's book value and unconfirmed profits on intercompany transactions. Other-than-temporary

impairment losses are reported in income. Some companies pool resources and create a business enterprise to complete a particular project or expand into new markets. This enterprise is a **joint venture** if control is shared by the participating companies. Investors use the equity method to report joint ventures.

LO 3 **Describe the reporting for controlling interests in other companies. (p. 15)** Controlling investments in other companies take the form of **mergers, consolidations, asset acquisitions, stock investments**, and **variable interest entities**. The acquisition structures of mergers, consolidations and asset acquisitions differ, but they all involve investors acquiring the assets and liabilities of another company. The investor reports each acquired asset and liability at fair value. With controlling stock investments and variable interest entities controlled through legal financial agreements, the investor and investee remain legal entities with separate books, and the investor accounts for its investment as a noncurrent asset on its own books. **Consolidation procedures** bring the financial statements of the investor and investee together at the end of each reporting period for external reporting purposes.

LO 4 **Discuss International Financial Reporting Standards (IFRS) for intercorporate investments. (p. 17)** **International Financial Reporting Standards** (IFRS) for intercorporate investments currently parallel U.S. GAAP on many dimensions. Criteria for impairment loss recognition differ, and in some cases IFRS allows reversal of impairment losses. The decision to use the equity method of reporting focuses on whether the investor has significant influence. The decision to consolidate the investee under IFRS depends on whether the investor controls the investee. *IFRS 9*, effective in 2018, significantly changes financial instrument classification, valuation, and impairment recognition.

Assignments with the ✅ in the margin are available in BusinessCourse.
See the Preface of the book for details.

MULTIPLE CHOICE QUESTIONS •••••••••••••••••••••••••••••••••••••

Use the following information to answer questions 1–4:

On January 1, 2016, a company's balance sheet reports its investments in financial instruments as follows:

Assets	
Investment in trading securities	$160,000
Investment in AFS securities	100,000
Investment in HTM securities	207,544
Equity	
Accumulated other comprehensive income:	
Unrealized gains (losses) on AFS securities	$ 4,000

Additional information:

   a. The HTM securities are $200,000 face value debt securities purchased on January 1, 2014, at a yield of 4%. The securities have a 4-year total life and pay interest annually on December 31, at a coupon rate of 6%.
   b. The trading securities on hand on January 1 were sold in 2016 for $180,000.
   c. More trading securities were purchased for $100,000. They are still on hand at December 31, 2016, and have a fair value of $125,000.
   d. AFS securities, originally purchased for $26,000 with a carrying value of $25,000 as of January 1, 2016, were sold for $29,000.
   e. AFS securities on hand at December 31, 2016, have a fair value of $81,000.

✅ **LO 1**   **1.** The total gain on trading securities reported on the 2016 income statement is

   a. $20,000
   b. $25,000
   c. $45,000
   d. $60,000

✅ **LO 1**   **2.** The gain on AFS securities reported on the 2016 income statement is

   a. $ 3,000
   b. $ 4,000
   c. $ 9,000
   d. $10,000

3. Investment in HTM securities reported on the December 31, 2016 balance sheet is   **LO 1** ✓

    a. $203,846
    b. $204,938
    c. $207,544
    d. $207,997

4. What is the amount of the net gain related to AFS securities reported on the 2016 Statement of Comprehen-   **LO 1** ✓
sive Income?

    a. $1,000
    b. $5,000
    c. $6,000
    d. $7,000

5. ABC Company uses the equity method to account for its 40% interest in the voting stock of XYZ Company.   **LO 2** ✓
ABC paid $5,000,000 for the investment at the beginning of the current year, and XYZ's total book value at
the time was $6,000,000. The discrepancy between acquisition cost and share of book value acquired was
attributed to goodwill. XYZ reported income of $600,000 and paid dividends of $200,000 during the year.
ABC will report its investment in XYZ on its end-of-year balance sheet at what amount?

    a. $4,920,000
    b. $5,240,000
    c. $5,000,000
    d. $5,160,000

6. Under current standards, when is an impairment loss reported on a significant influence investment in the   **LO 2, 4** ✓
stock of another company, following U.S. GAAP and IFRS?

	U.S. GAAP	IFRS
a.	Book value > higher of market value or value-in-use	Other than temporary impairment
b.	Other than temporary impairment	Book value > higher of market value or value-in-use
c.	If a "loss event" occurs	Not reported
d.	Other than temporary impairment	If a "loss event" occurs

7. Fizzy Cola acquired 35% of the voting stock of National Bottlers on January 1, 2017, at a cost of $50,000,000,   **LO 2** ✓
an amount equal to 35% of National's book value. Fizzy reports its investment using the equity method. In
2017, National reported net income of $7,000,000 and declared and paid dividends of $2,000,000. National
sells product to Fizzy at a markup of 25% on cost. Fizzy had $6,000,000 of product purchased from National
in its ending inventory, measured at cost to Fizzy. What is Fizzy's Investment in National balance reported
on its December 31, 2017 balance sheet?

    a. $50,000,000
    b. $51,330,000
    c. $52,030,000
    d. $51,750,000

8. Fizzy Cola acquires Juicee Ltd. for $25,000,000 in cash, and accounts for its investment as a merger. Juicee's   **LO 3** ✓
balance sheet at the date of acquisition is as follows:

Current assets	$ 100,000	Liabilities	$3,000,000
Property, net	4,000,000	Equity	1,100,000
Total	$4,100,000	Total	$4,100,000

The fair value of Juicee's current assets is $75,000 less than book value. The fair value of its property is
$1,500,000 less than book value. The book value of its liabilities approximates fair value. There are no un-
reported assets or liabilities. How much goodwill does Fizzy report for this acquisition?

    a. $19,475,000
    b. $22,325,000
    c. $22,475,000
    d. $25,475,000

✔ LO 4   9. Under *IFRS 9*, companies that invest in equity securities will be able to generally choose from which of the following options for reporting their investment?

    a.   FV-NI only
    b.   FV-NI or FV-OCI
    c.   Amortized cost or FV-NI
    d.   Amortized cost or FV-OCI

✔ LO 4   10. Following both U.S. GAAP and IFRS, when should a company use the equity method to report an intercorporate investment?

    a.   The company significantly influences the decisions of the investee.
    b.   The investee is the company's major supplier.
    c.   The company owns 20–50% of the investee's voting stock.
    d.   The company is holding the investment in its long-term portfolio.

EXERCISES ••

LO 1   E1.1

THE COCA-COLA COMPANY [KO]

Investment in Trading Securities   The **Coca-Cola Company**'s December 31, 2013, balance sheet reports investments in trading securities at $372 million, with net unrealized gains of $12 million.

Required

    a.   How much did Coca-Cola pay for the trading securities reported on its 2013 balance sheet?
    b.   Where are unrealized gains and losses on trading securities reported in Coca-Cola's financial statements?
    c.   Assume the trading securities on hand at the end of 2013 were acquired during 2013. Prepare the summary journal entries made by Coca-Cola to record events related to these trading securities.
    d.   Assume the securities are sold for $370 million in 2014. Prepare the journal entry to record the sale.

✔ LO 1   E1.2   **Investment in Trading and AFS Securities**   In 2016, a company purchases securities at a cost of $450,000. Their year-end value is $475,000. In 2017, these securities are sold for $460,000 and new securities are purchased for $610,000. At the end of 2017, the securities have not yet been sold, and have a value of $580,000.

Required

Prepare the journal entries to record the above information for 2016 and 2017, assuming that:

    a.   The securities are categorized as trading securities.
    b.   The securities are categorized as AFS securities, and the securities on hand at the end of 2017 are considered (1) not impaired, or (2) impaired.

LO 1   E1.3   **Held-to-Maturity Investments**   On January 1, 2016, a company pays $5,222,591 for a 5-year corporate bond with a face value of $5 million. The bond pays interest at 5 percent on December 31 of each year, and the principal is due on December 31, 2020. The investment yields a 4 percent compound annual return to maturity. The company classifies the bond as a held-to-maturity investment.

Required

Prepare the journal entries to record the investment on January 1, 2016, receipt of the interest payments on December 31 of each year 2016 through 2020, and receipt of the bond principal on December 31, 2020, using the effective interest method.

✔ LO 1   E1.4   **Investment in Trading, AFS and HTM Securities**   Zyggy Corporation has the following investment activity during 2015, 2016, and 2017:

    •   Purchased trading investment of $200,000 in the stock of Allen Corporation on February 3, 2015. The investment was sold on June 18, 2015, for $210,000.
    •   Purchased trading investment of $400,000 in the stock of Becker Corporation on October 29, 2015. The investment had a December 31, 2015, fair value of $380,000 and was sold on March 1, 2016, for $405,000.

- Purchased AFS investment of $600,000 in the stock of Corey Corporation on November 1, 2015. Its fair value on December 31, 2015 and 2016 was $640,000 and $510,000, respectively. The 2016 decline in value was determined to be other than temporary. The investment was sold on February 15, 2017, for $500,000.
- Purchased AFS investment of $500,000 in the stock of Donata Corporation on April 4, 2017. Its fair value on December 31, 2017, was $535,000.
- Purchased HTM investment on January 2, 2016, of $194,449 in Eiffel Corporation's $200,000 face value, 3 percent bond, yielding 4 percent to maturity, interest paid annually on December 31. On December 31, 2017, the fair value of the bond is $150,000, and the decline is determined to be other than temporary.

Required

For each of the above investments, prepare the journal entries and determine the accounts and balances reported on Zyggy's December 31, 2015, 2016, and 2017 balance sheets and its 2015, 2016, and 2017 income statements and statements of comprehensive income.

E1.5 **Equity Method Investment with Intercompany Sales**   The Coca-Cola Company owns 28 per-   **LO 2** ✓ cent of the voting stock of **Coca-Cola FEMSA**, acquired at book value. Assume that Coca-Cola FEMSA reports income of $5 million for 2016. Coca-Cola FEMSA regularly sells canned beverages to Coca-Cola at a markup of 35 percent on cost. During 2016 Coca-Cola FEMSA's sales to Coca-Cola totaled $25 million. Coca-Cola's January 1, 2016, inventories include $1,350,000 purchased from Coca-Cola FEMSA. Coca-Cola's December 31, 2016, inventories include $1,215,000 purchased from Coca-Cola FEMSA.

Required

Prepare the 2016 journal entry on Coca-Cola's books to recognize its income from Coca-Cola FEMSA under the equity method.

E1.6 **Equity Method Investment with Cost in Excess of Book Value**   Revco Corporation purchases   **LO 2** 40 percent of the voting stock of Ronco Pharmaceuticals on January 1, 2016, for $15 million in cash. Ronco's book value at the date of acquisition is $6 million. Investigation reveals that Ronco's reported patents (10-year life) are undervalued by $1 million and it has unreported technology (5-year life) valued at $2 million. Ronco pays dividends of $250,000 and reports net income of $900,000 for 2016.

Required

Prepare the journal entries on Revco's books to report the above information assuming Revco accounts for its investment in Ronco using the equity method. At what amount does Revco report the investment in Ronco on its December 31, 2016, balance sheet?

E1.7 **Equity Method and Other Comprehensive Income**   Mitchell Corporation pays $6 million to   **LO 2** acquire a 25 percent interest in Turner Corporation's stock on January 1, 2017, and reports the investment using the equity method. Any basis difference is attributed to goodwill. During 2017, Turner reports net income of $900,000, which includes $25,000 in realized and unrealized gains on trading securities and $40,000 in realized gains on sales of AFS securities. Turner also reports $30,000 in unrealized losses on AFS securities and pays dividends of $240,000 in 2017.

Required

Prepare Mitchell's journal entries to record the above events for 2017.

E1.8 **Equity Method Investment Cost Computation**   Traynor Corporation reports its 40 percent in-   **LO 2** vestment in Victor Company on its December 31, 2017 balance sheet at $14,608,000. Traynor acquired its interest in Victor on January 2, 2015 and uses the equity method to account for the investment. Victor's assets and liabilities were fairly stated on January 2, 2015 except for unreported technology (5-year life) of $4 million. Victor reported net income of $1.2 million, $1.5 million, and $1.4 million, and paid dividends of $200,000, $250,000, and $230,000 in 2015, 2016, and 2017, respectively.

Required

How much did Traynor Corporation pay for its investment in Victor Company on January 2, 2015?

E1.9 **Joint Venture**   On January 2, 2017, Adena Corporation and Dillon Company form a joint venture to   **LO 2** develop a new product. Each contributes $2.5 million and has a 50 percent interest in the venture. At December 31, 2017, the joint venture's balance sheet is as follows (*in millions*):

Cash.	$ 1.8	Debt	$ 8.4
Equipment	12.2	Equity	5.6
Total	$14.0	Total	$14.0

The joint venture reported net income of $600,000 during 2017. Each investor uses the equity method to report its interest in the joint venture.

Required

Show how the joint venture is reported on each investor's financial statements for 2017. Where are the joint venture's individual assets and liabilities reported by the venturers?

✓ LO 2 E1.10 Equity Method Investment with Basis Differences Several Years Later Saxton Corporation purchased 25 percent of Taylor Company's voting stock on January 1, 2013, for $3 million in cash. At the date of acquisition, Taylor reported its total assets at $60 million and its total liabilities at $56 million. Investigation revealed that Taylor's plant and equipment (15-year life) was overvalued by $1.8 million and it had an unreported customer database (2-year life) valued at $500,000. Taylor declares and pays $100,000 in dividends and reports net income of $250,000 in 2016.

Required

Prepare the necessary journal entries on Saxton's books to report the above information for 2016 assuming Saxton uses the equity method to report its investment.

✓ LO 3 E1.11 Merger and Stock Investment (see related E1.10) Saxton Corporation purchases all of Taylor Company's assets and liabilities on January 1, 2013, for $12 million in cash. At the date of acquisition, Taylor's reported assets consist of current assets of $10 million and plant and equipment of $50 million. It reports current liabilities of $16 million and long-term debt of $40 million. Investigation reveals that Taylor's plant and equipment is overvalued by $1.8 million and it has an unreported customer database valued at $500,000.

Required

a. Prepare the necessary journal entry on Saxton's books to record its acquisition of Taylor on January 1, 2013.
b. Assume that Saxton purchases all of Taylor's voting stock on January 1, 2013, for $12 million in cash. Prepare the necessary journal entry on Saxton's books to record the acquisition.

✓ LO 3 E1.12 Merger Organic Juices, Inc. acquires Healthy Snax Corporation for $100 million in cash, in a merger. Healthy Snax's balance sheet at the date of acquisition is as follows *(in millions)*:

Current assets	$10	Current liabilities.	$12
Plant and equipment	65	Long-term debt	36
Intangible assets	5	Capital stock	18
		Retained earnings	24
		Treasury stock	(10)
Total assets	$80	Total liabilities and equity.	$80

A consulting firm values Healthy Snax's plant and equipment at $20 million and its reported intangibles at $15 million. Due to declining interest rates, long-term debt has a fair value of $38 million. There are no unreported identifiable intangibles, and all other assets and liabilities are reported at amounts approximating fair value.

Required

Prepare the journal entry Organic Juices makes to record its acquisition of Healthy Snax.

LO 1 E1.13 Investment in AFS Securities The following information appears on Anderson Corporation's balance sheet at December 31, 2017, with comparative information for December 31, 2016:

	2017	2016
Noncurrent assets:		
AFS securities....................................	$460,000	$500,000
Equity:		
Accumulated other comprehensive income (AOCI)		
Unrealized gains (losses) on AFS securities	(50,000)	(60,000)

Anderson's 2017 income statement reports the following:

Losses on sale of AFS securities	20,000

Anderson's 2017 statement of comprehensive income reports the following information:

Unrealized gains on AFS securities	15,000
Reclassification of unrealized gains on AFS securities	(5,000)

Anderson did not make any new investments in AFS securities in 2017.

Required
a. Calculate the original cost of the AFS securities held on December 31, 2017.
b. Calculate the cash Anderson received on the sale of AFS securities in 2017.

E1.14 **Impairment of AFS and HTM Investments, U.S. GAAP and IFRS** Assume **The Coca-Cola** **LO 1, 4**
Company reports the following investments at December 31, 2016, prior to any required end-of-year
valuation adjustments:

Investment in equity securities......................................	$1,500,000
Investment in debt securities	600,000

Coca-Cola classifies its investment in equity securities as AFS, and its investment in debt securities as
HTM. The December 31, 2016, fair value of the equity securities is $1,000,000, and the fair value of the
debt securities is $400,000. The equity securities were originally purchased for $1,600,000.

Required
a. Record any required journal entries to reflect fair values at year-end, assuming the investments are
    (1) not impaired, and (2) impaired, following U.S. GAAP.
b. If Coca-Cola follows IFRS, are there any differences in how the value changes are recorded? Are
    there differences in the decision to treat an investment as impaired? Explain.
c. It is now December 31, 2017. Coca-Cola still holds both investments. The fair value of the equity
    securities is $1,400,000 and the fair value of the debt securities is $640,000. On an amortized cost
    basis, the debt securities balance would be $590,000 if no impairment loss had been recorded. Re-
    cord any required journal entries at year-end, following (1) U.S. GAAP, and (2) IFRS, assuming the
    securities were impaired in 2016.

E1.15 **Consequences of Investment Reporting Choices** Assume **The Coca-Cola Company** acquires **LO 2, 3**
all of the stock of Bubbly Bottler on January 1, 2016, at a cost of $950 million in cash. Bubbly's balance
sheet on that date is as follows (in millions):

Tangible assets	$1,000	Liabilities.................	$ 900
		Equity	100
Total assets	$1,000	Total liabilities and equity....	$1,000

Bubbly's tangible assets and liabilities are reported at amounts approximating fair value, and the excess paid over book value is attributed entirely to goodwill.

Required

a. Assume that Coca-Cola reports its investment in Bubbly as a significant influence investment, because although it owns all of Bubbly's stock, the decision-making structure at Bubbly does not allow Coca-Cola to control Bubbly. How does Coca-Cola record the investment at January 1, 2016?

b. Now assume that Coca-Cola controls Bubbly and reports the acquisition as a merger. How does Coca-Cola record the investment at January 1, 2016?

c. Assume Coca-Cola's balance sheet just prior to the acquisition consists of $80,000 million in assets and $20,000 million in liabilities. Calculate Coca-Cola's leverage, measured as total liabilities divided by total assets, if Coca-Cola reports its investment in Bubbly as a significant influence investment and as a merger.

d. Which reporting choice allows Coca-Cola to appear more financially viable? As Coca-Cola's auditor, how do you evaluate Coca-Cola's reporting choice?

PROBLEMS ••

LO 1 P1.1 Investments in Trading and AFS Securities A company has the following investment activity during 2016 and 2017:

Security	Type	Date of Acquisition	Cost	Fair value at 12/31/16	Date of Sale	Selling Price	Fair value at 12/31/17
A..........	Trading	3/5/16	$350,000	N/A	6/3/16	$325,000	N/A
B..........	Trading	7/14/16	225,000	$252,000	1/15/17	235,000	N/A
C..........	Trading	9/1/17	400,000	N/A	N/A	N/A	$410,000
D..........	AFS	8/2/16	175,000	190,000	4/2/17	213,000	N/A
E..........	AFS	11/20/16	300,000	250,000	N/A	N/A	215,000
F..........	AFS	4/6/17	710,000	N/A	N/A	N/A	690,000

Security E is impaired in 2017, but is not impaired in 2016. Security F is not impaired in 2017.

Required

a. Prepare the journal entries to record the above information for 2016 and 2017, assuming the company's reporting year ends December 31.

b. Show how this information is presented in the company's balance sheet, income statement, and statement of comprehensive income for 2016 and 2017.

LO 1 P1.2 Held-to-Maturity Intercorporate Debt Investments On January 2, 2016, a U.S. company invests in the following corporate debt securities, classified as held-to-maturity per *ASC Topic 320*:

1. 5-year $1,000,000 face value corporate bond paying 6 percent interest annually on December 31. The bond is priced to yield 5 percent to maturity.
2. 4-year $500,000 face value corporate bond paying 4 percent interest annually on December 31. The bond is priced to yield 5 percent to maturity.

Required

a. Calculate the cost of each investment.

b. Calculate interest income for 2016 and 2017.

c. At what value are these investments reported on the company's December 31, 2018, balance sheet?

d. On December 31, 2019, the company determines that an impairment loss should be reported on the $1,000,000 bond. What factors indicate impairment loss? If the bond is estimated to have a value of $500,000 on December 31, 2019, what is the amount of the impairment loss, and where will it be reported on the 2019 financial statements?

LO 1 P1.3 Held-to-Maturity Intercorporate Debt Investment, Impairment Losses **Monster Beverage Corporation** is a public U.S. company that produces and distributes "alternative" energy drinks. Its 2013 balance sheet includes $396 million in held-to-maturity bonds. Monster reports its HTM securities as follows:

MONSTER BEVERAGE CORPORATION
[MNST]

> Held-to-maturity securities are recorded at amortized cost which approximates fair market value. The Company evaluates whether the decline in fair value of its investments is other-than-temporary at each quarter-end. This evaluation consists of a review by management, and includes market pricing information and maturity dates for the securities held, market and economic trends in the industry and information on the issuer's financial condition and, if applicable, information on the guarantors' financial condition. Factors considered in determining whether a loss is temporary include the length of time and extent to which the investment's fair value has been less than its cost basis, the financial condition and near-term prospects of the issuer and guarantors, including any specific events which may influence the operations of the issuer and our intent and ability to retain the investment for a reasonable period of time sufficient to allow for any anticipated recovery of fair value. (*Note 1 to Monster Beverage Corporation 2013 financial statements*)

Assume that the HTM bonds on Monster's 2013 balance sheet have a 2-year remaining life, were acquired at par, and pay interest each December 31 at 4 percent. Monster determines that due to an other-than-temporary decline in the issuer's liquidity, no additional interest payments are expected, but $325 million of principal is recoverable at maturity.

Required

a. Calculate Monster's impairment loss for 2013. Round to the nearest million.
b. Assume that on December 31, 2014, the issuer's financial health has improved and the bonds' fair value is now $396 million. How does Monster report this information?
c. If Monster receives all contractual principal and interest payments, what is the actual yield on the bond investment for 2014 and 2015?

P1.4   **Equity Method Investment Several Years After Acquisition**   On January 2, 2014, Best Beverages acquired 45 percent of the stock of Better Bottlers for $30 million in cash. Best Beverages accounts for its investment using the equity method. At the time of acquisition, Better Bottlers' balance sheet was as follows *(in millions)*:

Better Bottlers Balance Sheet, January 2, 2014	
Assets	
Current assets	$ 20
Property and equipment, net	415
Patents and trademarks	150
Total assets	$585
Liabilities and equity	
Current liabilities	$ 42
Long-term debt	518
Total liabilities	560
Capital stock	12
Retained earnings	13
Total equity	25
Total liabilities and equity	$585

Valuation of Better Bottlers' assets and liabilities revealed that its reported patents and trademarks (10-year life) had a fair value of $160 million and it had unrecognized brand names (15-year life) worth $9 million. Better Bottlers' December 31, 2017, retained earnings balance is $25 million. For 2017, it reported net income of $2.5 million and paid $650,000 in dividends.

Required

a. Prepare the 2017 entries to report the above information on Best Beverages' books.
b. Calculate the Investment in Better Bottlers balance, reported on Best Beverages' December 31, 2017, balance sheet.

LO 2   P1.5   Equity Method Investment Several Years After Acquisition   Rance Corporation paid $10 million in cash to acquire 30 percent of the voting stock of Seaway Company on January 2, 2015. Rance uses the equity method to report its investment. Seaway's book value at date of acquisition was $25 million. Analysis of Seaway's assets and liabilities reveals that Seaway's property and equipment (10-year life) was overvalued by $4 million, and its reported intangibles (2-year life) were undervalued by $6 million.

During the years 2015 and 2016, Seaway reported total income of $14 million, paid dividends of $5 million, and reported net unrealized gains on AFS securities of $1 million. During 2017, Seaway reported income of $4 million, paid dividends of $1.5 million, and reported net unrealized losses on AFS securities of $800,000.

Rance sells merchandise to Seaway at a markup of 20 percent on cost. Seaway sells merchandise to Rance at a markup of 25 percent on cost. Below are the inventories on hand at each balance sheet date, related to these sales.

December 31	2015	2016	2017
Ending inventory held by Rance Corporation	$750,000	$925,000	$625,000
Ending inventory held by Seaway Company	480,000	420,000	696,000

Required

a.   Calculate Rance's equity in net income of Seaway for 2017.
b.   Prepare Rance's journal entries to report its investment in Seaway for 2017.
c.   Calculate the investment balance, reported on Rance Corporation's balance sheet at December 31, 2017.

LO 2   P1.6   Equity Method Investment with Basis Differences   Bristol Corporation acquired 40 percent of the voting stock of Manchester Corporation on January 2, 2016, for $3.2 million in cash. Manchester's balance sheet and estimated fair values of its assets and liabilities on January 2, 2016, are as follows:

MANCHESTER CORPORATION
Balance Sheet
January 2, 2016

(in thousands)	Book Value	Fair Value
Assets		
Cash and receivables..................................	$ 400	$ 400
Inventory (FIFO)	1,200	800
Investments	300	300
Land..	800	2,000
Property and equipment..............................	4,200	1,500
Less: Accumulated depreciation	(1,300)	
Total assets	$5,600	
Liabilities and Equity		
Current liabilities...................................	$ 900	$ 900
Long-term liabilities	3,000	3,000
Common stock, $2.00 par	500	
Additional paid-in capital	1,000	
Retained earnings	800	
Accumulated other comprehensive income..............	(600)	
Total liabilities and equity............................	$5,600	

In addition to its reported assets, Manchester has unreported franchise agreements (5-year life) valued at $1 million. Its property and equipment has a 20-year average remaining life. Manchester reported income of $1.8 million for 2016.

Required

a.   How many shares of Manchester stock did Bristol acquire?
b.   Compute Bristol's equity in Manchester's net income for 2016.

P1.7   Equity Method Investment, Intercompany Sales   Harcker Corporation acquires 40 percent of   **LO 2**
Jackson Corporation's voting stock on January 3, 2017, for $40 million in cash. Jackson's net assets were
fairly reported at $100 million at the date of acquisition. During 2017, Harcker sells $130 million in merchandise to Jackson at a markup of 30 percent on cost. Jackson still holds $26 million of this merchan-
dise in its ending inventory. Also during 2017, Jackson sells $54 million in merchandise to Harcker at a
markup of 20 percent on cost. Harcker still holds $12 million of this merchandise in its ending inventory.
Jackson reports 2017 net income of $10 million.

Required

a. Calculate Harcker's equity in Jackson's net income for 2017.
b. Assume Harcker reports total 2017 sales revenue and cost of sales of $310 million and $262 million,
    respectively, while Jackson reports total 2017 sales revenue and cost of sales of $254 million and
    $235 million, respectively. Compute each company's gross margin on sales as reported following
    U.S. GAAP. Now compute gross margin on sales again, excluding intercompany sales. Comment on
    the results.

P1.8   Equity Investments, Various Reporting Methods   On January 2, 2016, Parker Corporation in-   **LO 2, 3**
vests in the stock of Quarry Corporation. Quarry's book value is $4 million and its assets and liabilities
are reported at amounts approximating fair value. Quarry reports income of $3 million in 2016. Parker's
December 31, 2016, balance sheet and 2016 income statement, ignoring its investment in Quarry's stock,
follow.

PARKER CORPORATION
Balance Sheet *(in thousands)*
December 31, 2016

Current assets	$ 40,000	Current liabilities.	$ 20,000
Property, net.	450,000	Long-term liabilities	200,000
Identifiable intangibles	5,000	Capital stock	90,000
		Retained earnings	185,000
Total assets	$495,000	Total liabilities and equity.	$495,000

PARKER CORPORATION
Income Statement *(in thousands)*
Year ended December 31, 2016

Sales revenue.	$900,000
Cost of sales.	(750,000)
Operating expenses.	(140,000)
Net income.	$ 10,000

Quarry Corporation's financial statements for 2016 are as follows:

QUARRY CORPORATION
Balance Sheet *(in thousands)*
December 31, 2016

Current assets	$ 5,000	Current liabilities.	$ 2,000
Property, net.	85,000	Long-term liabilities	81,000
		Capital stock, $1 par	1,000
		Retained earnings	6,000
Total assets	$90,000	Total liabilities and equity.	$90,000

QUARRY CORPORATION
Income Statement (in thousands)
Year ended December 31, 2016

Sales revenue.	$60,000
Cost of sales.	(20,000)
Operating expenses	(37,000)
Net income.	$ 3,000

Required

Prepare Parker's December 31, 2016, balance sheet and 2016 income statement under each of the following circumstances:

a. Parker's investment consists of 100,000 shares costing $15/share, and Parker classifies it as an AFS investment. The shares have a market value of $12/share on December 31, 2016.

b. Parker's investment consists of 400,000 shares costing $15/share, and Parker accounts for it using the equity method.

c. Parker acquires all of Quarry's shares for $15 million in cash, retires the shares and merges with Quarry. Goodwill is unimpaired in 2016.

LO 2 **P1.9** **Joint Venture** On January 3, 2016, Allen Corporation and Barkely Corporation invested $5 million each in cash to form Albar Enterprises, a joint venture that develops new products benefitting both corporations. Each corporation holds an equal ownership interest in Albar Enterprises. Albar Enterprises' balance sheet on December 31, 2016, follows *(in millions)*:

Cash.	$ 2.5	Current payables	$ 26.9
Merchandise.	12.0	Long-term debt	150.0
Equipment	120.0	Capital stock	10.0
Patents.	50.0	Retained earnings	(2.4)
Total.	$184.5	Total.	$184.5

The joint venture distributed $0.2 million in cash to each of its investors at the end of 2016.

December 31, 2016, balance sheets for each corporation are below. Each shows its investment in Albar Enterprises at original cost less the cash distribution.

Balance Sheet (in millions)	Allen Corp.	Barkely Corp.
Current assets	$ 1.2	$ 0.6
Plant and equipment, net.	150.0	65.0
Investment in Albar Enterprises	4.8	4.8
Intangibles	200.0	3.5
Total assets	$356.0	$73.9
Current liabilities.	$ 14.0	$ 0.2
Noncurrent liabilities.	265.0	55.0
Capital stock	10.0	1.0
Retained earnings	67.0	17.7
Total liabilities and equity.	$356.0	$73.9

Both corporations use the equity method to report their investment in Albar Enterprises. Barkely estimates that the fair value of its investment in Albar declined to $0.5 million as of December 31, 2016, and that the decline is other-than-temporary. Allen does not report a decline in the value of its investment.

Required

a. Prepare the adjusting entry or entries Allen and Barkely make at the end of 2016.

b. Present the December 31, 2016, balance sheets of each corporation, after appropriate adjustments for their joint venture investment.

c. Is it appropriate for Barkely to report an impairment loss on its investment in the joint venture, while Allen does not? Explain.

P1.10 **Balance Sheet After Business Acquisition**   Wilson Corporation acquires Greatbatch Company   **LO 3** ✓
for $50 million cash in a merger. The balance sheets of both companies at the date of acquisition are as
follows:

Balance Sheet *(in millions)*	Wilson	Greatbatch
Current assets	$ 60	$ 5
Property and equipment.	500	90
Intangibles	20	3
Total assets	$580	$98
Current liabilities.	$ 25	$ 2
Long-term debt	400	65
Capital stock	50	12
Retained earnings	120	15
Accumulated other comprehensive income.	(15)	4
Total liabilities and equity.	$580	$98

Greatbatch's property and equipment is overvalued by $30 million, its reported intangibles are underval-
ued by $20 million, and it has unreported intangibles, in the form of customer databases and marketing
agreements, valued at $7 million.

Required

Prepare Wilson's balance sheet immediately following the merger.

P1.11 **Merger**   Nestlé is a Swiss multinational food and beverage company. Its financial statement balances   **LO 3, 4**
are reported in Swiss francs (CHF). In late 2012 Nestlé acquired **Wyeth Nutrition**, an infant nutrition
business focusing on emerging markets. The total purchase price consisted of CHF 11,078 million in cash   **NESTLÉ**
and CHF 190 million in consideration payable in future years. The acquisition date fair values of Wyeth's   [NESN]
acquired identifiable assets and liabilities were as follows *(in millions of CHF)*:

Property, plant and equipment.	CHF 1,144
Brands and intellectual property rights	4,510
Inventories and other assets	1,092
Assets held for sale	357
Financial debt.	(6)
Employee benefits, deferred taxes and provisions	(118)
Other liabilities	(371)

Required

Assuming Nestlé records this acquisition as a merger, prepare the journal entry it made in 2012 to record
its acquisition of Wyeth Nutrition.

P1.12 **Trading and AFS Investments, Impairment**   On its January 1, 2016, balance sheet, Ericsson Cor-   **LO 1** ✓
poration reports the following balances related to its investments:

Trading investments.	$ 56,000
AFS investments	160,000
Accumulated other comprehensive gains (losses) (unrealized losses on AFS investments). . .	(30,000)

During 2016, Ericsson sold for $43,000 trading securities carried at $40,000 on its beginning balance
sheet. It sold the remaining trading securities held at the beginning of the year for $20,000. It purchased
trading securities costing $60,000; their fair value at the end of 2016 was $52,000. Ericsson sold for
$52,000 AFS securities carried at $50,000, with unrealized gains of $1,000 included in the beginning
AOCI balance. It did not purchase any new AFS securities. At the end of 2016, AFS securities with a
book value of $85,000 have a fair value of $88,000. It is determined that AFS securities with a book
value of $25,000 and unrealized losses of $5,000 have a fair value of $10,000; this decline in value is
determined to be other-than-temporary.

Required

Prepare journal entries to record the events of 2016, and determine the balances related to trading and AFS securities reported on Ericsson's 2016 income statement and December 31, 2016, balance sheet.

LO 1   **P1.13**   **Investment in AFS Securities**   The Coca-Cola Company's 2013 annual report discloses the following information regarding its investments in AFS securities:

THE COCA-COLA COMPANY [KO]

- 2013 net loss on AFS securities, from the 2013 statement of comprehensive income: $80 million
- Investment in AFS securities balances at December 31, 2013 and 2012, from the balance sheet: $4,842 million and $4,593 million, respectively
- Proceeds from 2013 sales or maturities of AFS securities: $4,212 million
- Gains and losses from 2013 sales or maturities of AFS securities, from the 2013 income statement: gross gains $12 million, gross losses $24 million

Required

Based on the above information, reconstruct Coca-Cola's 2013 journal entries, as follows:
a. Assume 2013 reclassifications to income for disposal of AFS securities increased 2013 OCI by $20 million. Prepare the summary entry to record the sale of the securities.
b. Prepare the adjusting entry to record unrealized gains or losses on AFS securities on hand at year-end.
c. Prepare the entry to record new investments in AFS securities in 2013.

LO 2, 3   **P1.14**   **Change from Significant Interest to Control**   In 2013, **The Coca-Cola Company** acquired the remaining outstanding shares of **Fresh Trading Ltd.** Coca-Cola had previously reported its investment using the equity method. Assume the following information:

THE COCA-COLA COMPANY [KO]

- Coca-Cola paid $350 million in cash for Fresh Trading's remaining shares, and reports the acquisition as a merger.
- Coca-Cola's equity method investment in Fresh Trading was carried at $4 million and had a fair value of $10 million when the transaction took place.
- At the date of the transaction, the fair values of Fresh Trading's identifiable assets were $250 million, and the fair values of its liabilities were $100 million.

Required

a. Explain why Coca-Cola carried its equity method investment at an amount that was considerably below fair value.
b. Prepare Coca-Cola's journal entry or entries to record its acquisition of the remaining shares of Fresh Trading Ltd., assuming Coca-Cola reports the acquisition as a merger.

LO 2, 3, 4   **P1.15**   **Merger with Associate**   In 2013, **AB InBev** completed its acquisition of **Grupo Modelo**. AB InBev had previously held a significant interest in Grupo Modelo. Although AB InBev is headquartered in Belgium, its financial statements are reported in U.S. dollars. The footnotes to AB InBev's 2013 annual report reveal the following information on this acquisition:

AB INBEV [ABI]

- Consideration paid: Cash, $20,103 million; fair value of previously held equity interest, $12,946 million.
- AB InBev revalued the previously held equity interest to fair value at the date of acquisition, and recycled $199 million in gains from AOCI to income, resulting in a net non-recurring non-cash gain of $6,410 million.
- The fair values of Grupo Modelo's identifiable assets and liabilities at the date of acquisition were as follows:

Noncurrent assets	$9,779 million
Current assets	8,231
Noncurrent liabilities	1,975
Current liabilities	2,578

Required

a. Calculate the amount of goodwill AB InBev reported for this acquisition.
b. Why did AB InBev recycle $199 million in gains from AOCI to income?
c. Prepare the summary journal entries AB InBev made to record the acquisition as a merger.
d. At what amount did AB InBev report its investment in Grupo Modelo just prior to the acquisition?

REVIEW SOLUTIONS

Review 1 Solution

2016			
Jan. 2	Investment in trading securities	300,000	
	Investment in AFS securities	1,000,000	
	Investment in HTM securities.	486,384	
	Cash		1,786,384
2016			
June 15	Cash.	265,000	
	Loss on trading securities (income)	35,000	
	Investment in trading securities.		300,000
2016			
Oct. 15	Investment in trading securities	250,000	
	Cash		250,000
2016			
Dec. 1	Cash.	12,000	
	Dividend income		12,000
2016			
Dec. 31	Investment in trading securities	10,000	
	Loss on AFS securities (OCI)	80,000	
	Gain on trading securities (income).		10,000
	Investment in AFS securities		80,000
Dec. 31	Cash.	20,000	
	Investment in HTM securities.	4,319	
	Interest income		24,319

$20,000 = 4\% \times \$500,000; \$24,319 = 5\% \times \$486,384.$

Review 2 Solution

2017			
Jan. 5	Investment in Armadillo Bottlers	15,000,000	
	Cash		15,000,000
	To record investment in Armadillo.		
2017			
Dec. 1	Cash.	125,000	
	Investment in Armadillo Bottlers		125,000
	To record dividends received; $125,000 = 25\% \times \$500,000.		
2017			
Dec. 31	Investment in Armadillo Bottlers	211,250	
	Equity in net income of Armadillo Bottlers (income)		211,250
	To record equity in Armadillo's net income for 2017.		

Equity in net income for 2017 is calculated as follows:

Fizzy Cola's share of Armadillo's reported net income (25% × $3 million).	$750,000
Amortization of previously unreported intangibles (25% × $10 million/5).	(500,000)
Unconfirmed profit on downstream sales (25% × ($480,000 − ($480,000/1.2)))	(20,000)
Unconfirmed profit on upstream sales (25% × ($325,000 − ($325,000/1.3)))	(18,750)
Equity in net income.	$211,250

2 Mergers and Acquisitions

LEARNING OBJECTIVES

LO1 Measure and account for the various assets and liabilities acquired in mergers and acquisitions. (p. 40)

LO2 Measure and report the various types of consideration paid. (p. 48)

LO3 Account for changes in the values of acquired assets and liabilities, and contingent consideration. (p. 51)

LO4 Account for bargain purchases. (p. 53)

LO5 Explain the reporting requirements and issues related to in-process research and development, preacquisition contingencies and deferred tax liabilities. (p. 55)

IBM CORPORATION
www.ibm.com

International Business Machines Corporation (IBM) is a world leader in systems, software, and technology services. Its business is organized in five segments: Global Technology Services, Global Business Services, Systems and Technology, Software, and Global Financing. IBM uses acquisitions of other companies to increase revenues in expanding markets. According to its 2013 annual report, IBM has spent $17 billion on more than 30 acquisitions to increase its capabilities in Big Data and analytics. It has spent $7 billion on 15 acquisitions to become a leader in enterprise cloud services. Other acquisitions have expanded IBM's mobile initiatives and data security services.

IBM made ten acquisitions costing $3,219 million in 2013, of which $1,977 million was spent to acquire cloud computing infrastructure provider SoftLayer. The Global Technology Services and Software segments shared responsibility for this acquisition. The Software segment acquired eight companies, and the Systems and Technology segment made one acquisition. All of these investments were cash acquisitions of privately held companies. The table below summarizes IBM's acquisition activity for the last few years. Clearly IBM uses acquisitions to achieve its strategic goals.

	2013	2012	2011	2010	2009	2008
Number of acquisitions	10	11	5	17	6	15
Aggregate purchase price *(in millions)* . . .	$3,219	$3,964	$1,849	$6,538	$1,471	$6,796

How does IBM report its acquisitions? Does it include all the assets and liabilities of these acquired companies on its balance sheet? If so, how are they valued? How are costs incurred in connection with acquisitions reported?

Most large companies use acquisitions to expand or refocus their business activities. This chapter explains that the reporting for acquisitions is controversial and has evolved significantly over the years. Because acquisitions often have a major impact on company financial performance, this subject deserves careful scrutiny. *Source:* IBM Corporation annual reports, 2013 and 2010.

CHAPTER ORGANIZATION

Introduction	U.S. GAAP for mergers and consolidations	IFRS for mergers and consolidations
• Motivations for combinations • Types of combinations • Overview of reporting for combinations • Standards of reporting for business combinations	• Valuation of net assets acquired • Valuation of consideration paid • Post-acquisition changes in estimated values of net assets acquired or consideration paid • Bargain purchases • Special issues: research and development, preacquisition contingencies and deferred tax liabilities	• *IFRS 3(R)*, Business Combinations • *IAS 38*, Intangible Assets

INTRODUCTION

A **business combination**—also referred to as a *merger*, *acquisition*, or *takeover*—occurs when one company obtains control over another company. Chapter 1 introduced the general reporting requirements for controlling interests in other companies. This chapter provides a detailed analysis of these requirements for acquisition of the assets and liabilities of another company.

Motivations for Mergers and Acquisitions

To survive and prosper, business firms need reliable and cost-effective sources of supply; efficient and high quality production, distribution, and administrative capabilities; and sufficient customers. Firms also seek to grow larger and diversify into new products or markets. How are these goals to be accomplished? One strategy is to deal with other companies as suppliers, subcontractors, and customers and to grow internally by adding new facilities and capabilities. Another is the acquisition of other established firms. Combining with another company enables a firm to instantly control a source of supply, acquire additional production or distribution facilities, achieve customer relationships, expand into new geographic markets, or diversify into new lines of business. The acquiring firm seeks a business combination when the firm's management believes that it can accomplish its objectives more efficiently and at lower cost than it could via internal growth or market transactions with other firms.

Growth is a major objective of most corporate enterprises and takes many forms. Growth in sales is needed to increase the firm's share of the market and to solidify the firm's position. Growth in earnings and earnings per share is essential for the firm's securities to become more attractive in the capital markets. Growth in diversification is pursued to reduce or spread business risk, insulate earnings from downturns in business, and decrease the cost of capital. Although firms can achieve growth in these areas internally as well as externally, they may prefer combination with existing firms to expansion from within, for some of the following reasons:

- A going concern has its own experienced personnel, and network of suppliers, customers, and creditors. Combination with such a firm eliminates the need to start from scratch. Although managerial and other changes may be necessary, the inescapable fact is that growth from within, whether for reasons of market share or diversification, usually requires duplication of many of the efforts already made by an existing firm. The cost of duplicating these efforts could exceed the cost of acquiring the firm outright.

- Combination with an existing firm often leads to lower levels of actual or potential competition. When two competing firms combine, competition is reduced. Similarly, if a new firm enters an industry by acquiring an existing firm, the number of competing firms remains unchanged. But entry into an industry by forming a new firm increases the number of competitors, thereby making it more difficult for the entering firm to succeed.

- The combination can lead to increased sales overall, if the combined firms have complementary products or services. For example, an organization providing tax services may acquire a large CPA firm specializing in business valuation or enterprise risk services. The combined organization offers a variety of financial services to clients. To the extent that the enterprise risk clients are persuaded to switch from outside tax services to those of the combined firm, sales increase.

Mergers and acquisitions (M&A) are pervasive, and are also a global phenomenon. The table below lists some of the largest acquisitions in recent years, measured in U.S. dollars.

EXHIBIT 2.1   Top M&A Deals Worldwide, 2000–2014

Year	Acquirer	Target	Price (USD billions)
2000	America Online	Time Warner	$165
2014	Verizon Communications	Verizon Wireless (45%)	130
2007	RFS Holdings	ABN-AMRO Holding	99
2000	Glaxo Wellcome Plc	SmithKline Beecham Plc	76
2004	Royal Dutch Petroleum Co.	Shell Transport & Trading Co.	75
2006	AT&T Inc.	BellSouth Corporation	73
2001	Comcast Corp.	AT&T Broadband & Internet Svcs	72
2009	Pfizer Inc.	Wyeth	67
2004	Sanofi-Synthelabo SA	Aventis SA	60
2002	Pfizer Inc.	Pharmacia Corp.	60
2008	InBev NV	Anheuser-Busch Cos. Inc.	60
2004	JP Morgan Chase	Bank One	59
2014	AT&T	DirecTV	49
2014	Time Warner Cable	Comcast	45

Source: Thomson Reuters

AT&T's 2014 acquisition of **DirecTV** illustrates some of the common motivations for acquisitions. In justifying the acquisition to FCC regulators, chief executives of both firms outlined these benefits to customers:

- Expansion of bundled pay-TV and internet options
- New and faster broadband connections
- Increased competition with large cable competitors such as Comcast, reducing prices
- Greater efficiencies in providing services
- More network upgrades financed by cost savings

Types of Combinations

Four types of business combinations can be identified from legal and organizational perspectives:

1. A **merger** results when one company is absorbed into another company in exchange for cash, debt or stock. The acquiring company may purchase the assets and liabilities of the acquired

company directly, or it may acquire and then retire the stock of the acquired company. In either case, the acquired company ceases to exist as a legal entity. Only the surviving firm remains as a legal entity.

2. A **consolidation** takes place when a new corporation is organized to absorb the activities of two or more existing corporations. The shares of the existing companies are retired, and only the new corporation continues to exist as a legal entity.

3. An **asset acquisition** occurs when one firm acquires a subset of the assets (and possibly liabilities) of another firm. The selling firm may continue to survive as a legal entity, or it may liquidate entirely. The acquirer typically targets key assets for acquisition, or buys the acquiree's assets but does not assume its liabilities. Often the assets acquired are in the form of a division or product line.

4. A **stock acquisition** occurs when the acquiring firm obtains all or most of the voting shares of another firm. Each firm continues as a *separate legal entity*, and the investment in the acquired firm is treated as an intercorporate investment on the books of the acquiring firm.

Mergers, consolidations and asset acquisitions involve different acquisition procedures, but the reporting process for all three types of acquisitions is the same. *All assets acquired and all liabilities assumed are recorded directly on the books of the acquiring company.* The absorbed firms cease to exist as legal entities, but their operations may continue as divisions of the combined company.

In a business combination that is a *stock acquisition*, a *parent/subsidiary relationship* is created between the acquiring and acquired companies. The acquired company remains as a separate legal entity and is treated as an intercorporate investment by the acquiring firm. Consequently, the acquiring firm *does not record the assets and liabilities of the acquired firm on its books*. Rather, the acquiring firm records the shares of stock acquired in an **Investment in Subsidiary** account. This account gives a one-line summation of the acquiring company's interest in the underlying assets and liabilities of the acquired company. A stock acquisition does not affect the books of the acquired company; there is merely a change in ownership of its already-issued stock.

We shall see in subsequent chapters that the parent/subsidiary relationship resulting from a controlling stock investment requires the preparation of consolidated financial statements. In a consolidated balance sheet, the underlying asset and liability accounts of the subsidiary replace the Investment in Subsidiary account on the acquiring company's books. Therefore the consolidated balance sheet is the same as if the acquiring company had reported the acquired company's assets and liabilities directly on its own books, as in a merger, consolidation, or asset acquisition.

Overview of Reporting for Combinations

From a reporting perspective, all acquisitions involve combining the assets and liabilities of the acquired company with those of the acquiring company. The assets and liabilities acquired are reported at their *fair value* at the date of acquisition. Consider the following simple example.

EXHIBIT 2.2   Combination Illustration

Suppose IBM pays $10,000,000 in cash to acquire DataFile Inc. on July 1, 2015. Fair values of DataFile's assets and liabilities are as follows:

Account	Fair value
Current assets	$ 5,000,000
Equipment	45,000,000
Patents and copyrights	10,000,000
Current liabilities	15,000,000
Long-term debt	35,000,000

If IBM absorbs the assets and liabilities of DataFile through a *merger*, IBM makes the following entry on its books:

Current assets	5,000,000	
Equipment	45,000,000	
Patents and copyrights	10,000,000	
Current liabilities		15,000,000
Long-term debt		35,000,000
Cash		10,000,000
To record the acquisition of DataFile for $10,000,000 in cash.		

IBM records DataFile's assets and liabilities directly on its books. DataFile ceases to exist as a separate entity, and IBM reports DataFile's subsequent activities directly in its own financial records. The *acquiring* company does not revalue its own assets and liabilities to fair value. Only the *acquired* assets and liabilities are reported at fair value at the date of acquisition. IBM reports acquisition of DataFile's assets and liabilities the same way it reports any other acquisition of property. When a company buys equipment, it reports the equipment at the price paid, which presumably is its fair value. The company probably owns other equipment, and reports it at historical cost less accumulated depreciation. The company does not revalue this equipment to current fair value when it purchases additional equipment.

Even if a new corporation absorbs both companies, as in a consolidation, one of the companies is identified as the acquirer. The new corporation's balance sheet reports the acquirer's assets and liabilities at their book values shown in the acquirer's financial records. However, the new corporation's balance sheet reports the acquired company's assets and liabilities at fair value at the date of acquisition.

Now assume IBM acquires all of the *voting stock* of DataFile Inc., paying the former stockholders of DataFile $10,000,000 in cash. This is a *stock acquisition*, and IBM makes the following entry:

Investment in DataFile Inc..	10,000,000	
Cash		10,000,000
To record acquisition of all of DataFile's stock for $10,000,000 in cash.		

In this case, DataFile continues to exist as a separate entity, and reports its financial activities on its own books. Because IBM will likely include the activities of DataFile in its financial statements, a *consolidation working paper* is used to combine the financial results of IBM and DataFile, just as if IBM had reported DataFile's acquired assets and liabilities, and subsequent activities, directly on its books.

Note, however, that whether the acquisition is initially reported as a merger or consolidation, or as a stock acquisition, the combined results are *exactly the same*. The only difference is that in a stock acquisition, a consolidation working paper combines the accounts of the two companies. In a merger, consolidation, or asset acquisition, the acquirer reports the acquired assets and liabilities directly on its books, automatically combining the assets and liabilities of two companies.

Typically the price paid by the acquiring company exceeds the total fair value of the specific net assets acquired. A company's value includes its reputation and competitive strengths, which GAAP does not recognize as specific assets. The excess amount paid is attributed to goodwill, an intangible asset. For example, in Exhibit 2.2, suppose the fair value of the patents and copyrights is only $2,000,000. Then the acquisition cost is $8,000,000 greater than the fair values of the net assets acquired, as calculated below.

Acquisition cost		$10,000,000
Fair value of identifiable net assets acquired:		
Current assets	$ 5,000,000	
Equipment..	45,000,000	
Patents and copyrights...	2,000,000	
Current liabilities..	(15,000,000)	
Long-term debt..	(35,000,000)	2,000,000
Goodwill...		$ 8,000,000

If this acquisition is a merger, IBM makes the following entry to record the acquisition:

Current assets	5,000,000	
Equipment	45,000,000	
Patents and copyrights	2,000,000	
Goodwill	8,000,000	
Current liabilities		15,000,000
Long-term debt		35,000,000
Cash		10,000,000
To record the acquisition of DataFile Inc. for $10,000,000 in cash.		

Many reporting issues arise during the acquisition of a business. How are fair values of acquired assets and liabilities measured? Should we include assets and liabilities not currently reported on the acquired company's balance sheet, such as research and development (R&D) or other specific intangibles? What does the purchase price include? Should we include consulting fees or fees for registering any stock issued by the acquiring company? What happens when the purchase price is less than the sum of the fair values of the net assets acquired? If the acquirer does not purchase all of the acquired company's stock, how do the financial reports reflect this outside or "noncontrolling" interest?

Standards of Reporting for Business Combinations

ASC Topic 805 contains current standards for reporting business combinations. Standards for valuing acquired intangible assets, including goodwill, are in *ASC Topic 350. ASC Topic 810* describes consolidation procedures for stock acquisitions. The major valuation requirements found in *ASC Topic 805* are converged with IFRS.

Definition of Business Combination   The requirements of *ASC Topics 805* and *810* apply only to *business combinations*. A **business combination** occurs when *control is obtained* over one or more *businesses*. Control may be obtained by direct acquisition of the assets and liabilities of the acquired company—merger, consolidation, or asset acquisition—or by obtaining a controlling interest in the voting shares of the acquired company—stock acquisition. To determine whether a business combination has occurred, we need a definition of **control**, and we need to identify the attributes that constitute a *business*.

This chapter focuses on mergers, consolidations, and asset acquisitions: the acquired company or division ceases to exist and the acquiring company absorbs its financial records. It is therefore obvious that the acquiring company obtains control of the acquired company. When the acquisition is structured as a *stock acquisition*, the question of control becomes more relevant. Discussion of the concept of control and related reporting issues appears in Chapter 3. The ASC glossary provides this definition of a **business**:

> An integrated set of activities and assets that is capable of being conducted and managed for the purpose of providing a return in the form of dividends, lower costs, or other economic benefits directly to investors or other owners, members, or participants.

Certain transactions do *not* constitute a business combination. Formation of a **joint venture** by two or more existing companies is not a business combination. **Establishing a new business** as a separate subsidiary is not a business combination. In both of these cases, a new business is formed without an acquisition transaction. **Combining two or more companies already under common control**—such as two or more existing subsidiaries, or merging an existing subsidiary into the parent company—similarly does not constitute a business combination because there is no change in control. *ASC Topic 805* does not prescribe the accounting for these transactions. However, acquiring a division or product line of another company *is* a business combination, even though the division or product line is not a separate legal entity.

The remainder of this chapter discusses and illustrates the requirements of *ASC Topic 805*, focusing on the initial recording of acquisitions *reported as mergers, consolidations, or asset acquisitions,* where the acquired assets and liabilities are recorded directly on the acquirer's books.

VALUATION OF ASSETS ACQUIRED AND LIABILITIES ASSUMED

LO1 Measure and account for the various assets and liabilities acquired in mergers and acquisitions.

The **acquisition method** is used to report all business combinations. This method calls for careful identification and valuation of the *fair value of the assets acquired and liabilities assumed* at the *acquisition date*.

Acquisition Date

FASB ASC para. 805-10-25-7 defines the **acquisition date** as the *date the acquiring company obtains control of the acquired company*, usually the date when the consideration is paid to the former owners of the acquired company. When control was attained at an earlier date, based on agreement with the former owners of the acquired company, the earlier date is used.

When the parties agree on an official acquisition date prior to completing all aspects of the transaction, the acquisition date typically is the beginning of an accounting period for the acquiring entity. This accounting convenience avoids including the acquired entity at some interim date during the reporting year. Subject to provisions needed to protect the interests of the equity holders of the two entities, effective control over the acquired entity must occur on or before this chosen date.

Identifying the Acquiring Company

As discussed earlier in the chapter, only the assets and liabilities of the *acquired company* are revalued to fair value at the acquisition date. It is therefore imperative that the acquiring and acquired companies be identified. When no equity interests are exchanged, determining the acquiring company is easy. The acquiring entity is the one distributing cash or other assets, and/or incurring liabilities. Business combinations that involve an equity exchange can be more difficult to resolve. The following characteristics typically describe the **acquiring company**:

- It is the entity that **issues the equity interests**.
- It is the **larger entity**, as measured by assets, revenues, or earnings.
- Its owners have the **larger voting interest** in the combined company.
- An individual or organized group of its prior owners constitute a **large minority ($\leq 50\%$) interest** in the combined entity, and there are no other significant concentrations of voting interests.
- It constitutes or selects a **majority of the governing body**—the Board of Directors—of the combined entity.
- Its senior management **dominates the senior management** of the combined entity.
- Its stockholders **did not receive a premium** over market value in the exchange, whereas stockholders of the acquired entity did receive a premium.

When these indicators do not all point in the same direction, the accountant must assess all the facts and circumstances to identify the acquiring company. Should a *new entity* be formed to serve as the combined entity—as in a consolidation—one of the prior entities must still be designated as the acquiring company, following the guidelines above.

Combinations involving *more than two entities* make identification of the acquiring company even more difficult. In such cases, additional characteristics used to identify the acquiring company include:

- It is the entity which initiated the combination.
- It is the largest entity.

Once we identify the acquiring company and the acquisition date, we measure the assets acquired and liabilities assumed at fair value. If the acquisition cost is *greater than* the fair value of the identifiable net assets acquired, **goodwill** is reported. If the acquisition cost is *less than* the fair value of identifiable net assets acquired, the acquisition is a **bargain purchase** and a *gain* is reported.

BUSINESS APPLICATION   Reverse Acquisitions

Usually the company issuing the equity interests is the acquirer. But in a **reverse acquisition**, the equity issuer does not control the combined entity. The *former* shareholders receiving the issued stock *own the majority* of the shares in the combined company, or the management of the *other company* dominates the senior management of the combined company. Reverse acquisitions are particularly popular as a technique for taking a private company public without the cost and regulatory requirements involved with an initial public offering (IPO). A private company acquires a publicly traded company, but the public company controls the combined entity. The publicly traded company is usually a shell, with very few products or transactions, which then absorbs the private company's products, operations, and management.

Private Chinese companies have used reverse acquisitions to trade on U.S. markets without being subject to the SEC's usual rigorous regulatory and auditing standards. Between 2007 and 2010, approximately 200 Chinese companies began trading on U.S. capital markets. Three quarters of these companies gained access to U.S. markets through reverse acquisitions. In 2010, the PCAOB issued an alert to investors, warning that financial information provided by these companies may not be reliable. Increased SEC scrutiny has reduced the incidence of these reverse acquisitions in recent years.

Measurement of Previously Reported Assets and Liabilities

The acquired company's balance sheet reports its assets and liabilities according to GAAP. Most of the reported values will likely *not* reflect fair value at the date of acquisition. Cash is obviously reported at fair value, and current liabilities probably reflect the amount needed to satisfy creditors. Most short-term investments are also reported at current fair values. However, even current assets such as receivables and inventories may not be reported at fair value. For example, LIFO inventories typically reflect very old historical costs, unless the entire inventory has been recently replaced. Long-term assets, such as buildings, equipment, and reported intangibles, are reported at historical cost less accumulated depreciation or amortization.

The fair value of acquired assets is based on the acquirer's planned use of those assets. Tangible operating property held by the acquired company changes in value if the acquirer intends to dispose of it or change its planned usage.

The methods of estimating fair value vary from item to item. *FASB ASC Topic 820*, Fair Value Measurements and Disclosures, provides a detailed definition and framework for determining fair value for a variety of asset types. **Fair value** may be estimated by use of quoted market prices, appraisals, estimated selling prices, estimated replacement costs, and the present value of future cash flows discounted at an appropriate interest rate. Exhibit 2.3 presents common means of determining fair values of assets and liabilities.

EXHIBIT 2.3 Estimation of Fair Values	
Asset or Liability	**Fair Value Estimated by**
Accounts receivable.	Discounted expected cash inflows
Marketable securities	Quoted market prices
Inventories: Raw materials	Current replacement cost
Inventories: Work in process	Estimated selling price, less costs to complete and sell, less reasonable profit
Inventories: Finished goods	Estimated selling price, less costs to sell, less reasonable profit
Property, plant and equipment to be used	Current replacement cost
Property, plant and equipment to be sold	Estimated selling price less costs to sell
Other tangible noncurrent assets.	Appraised value
Most liabilities.	Discounted expected cash outflows

The acquired company may have identifiable intangibles, such as trademarks and patents, reported on its balance sheet. The acquiring company reports these intangibles at fair value, usually estimated by discounted expected cash inflows.

The acquired company may also have goodwill on its books, created when it made acquisitions in the past, and deferred tax assets or liabilities. The acquired company's reported goodwill and deferred tax items are assumed to have a zero fair value for the purposes of recording the acquisition. These items are replaced with the goodwill and deferred taxes resulting from the acquisition.

Identification and Measurement of Previously Unreported Intangibles

Tangible assets acquired and most liabilities assumed should be fairly easy to identify. Virtually all of these appear on the books of the acquired company. Intangible assets, however, present special problems. The existence of significant *unrecorded* intangible assets may be both a major reason why the business combination occurred and a major factor in the total acquisition cost. Such intangibles include brand names, market share, customer base, good locations, technology, skilled workforce, and the like. Although most of these intangibles developed internally during the life of the acquired company, very few are recorded as assets on the acquired company's books under GAAP.

ASC Topic 805 specifies the requirements for reporting previously unrecognized acquired intangibles. Two criteria are employed to identify intangibles requiring separate recognition:

- The intangible asset arises from *contractual or other legal rights*, or
- The intangible is *separable*, that is, it can be separated or divided from the acquired entity and sold, rented, licensed, or otherwise transferred.

Meeting *either* criterion is sufficient to require separate recognition of an intangible. A firm must report an intangible asset arising from **contractual or other legal rights** *even if it is not separable. ASC para. 805-20-55-2* provides three examples:

- An operating lease with terms that are favorable to terms that could be obtained in the current market, even though the lease terms prohibit transfer of the lease to an outside party
- A license to operate a nuclear power plant, even though it cannot be sold or transferred to an outside party
- A patent licensed to others for a percentage of future revenues; even though the patent and the license cannot be separately sold, each is separately reported.

The **separability criterion** applies when the intangible could be separated from the acquired company and transferred through sale, licensing, leasing, or other means. Evidence of separability comes from similar observable market transactions; it does not matter whether the acquired company actually intends to sell the intangible asset or such market transactions occur regularly. However, when contractual terms prevent the company from selling the intangible asset, it does not meet the separability criterion.

Examples of Identifiable Intangible Assets   The Codification offers many examples of reportable intangibles, grouped into broad categories as follows:

- **Contract-based intangible assets**, such as lease agreements, franchise agreements, licensing agreements, construction permits, employment contracts, broadcast rights, and mineral rights.
- **Marketing-related intangible assets**, such as brand names, trademarks, internet domain names, newspaper mastheads and non-competition agreements.
- **Customer-related intangible assets**, such as customer lists, order backlogs, and customer contracts.
- **Technology-based intangible assets**, such as patent rights, computer software, databases, and trade secrets.
- **Artistic-related intangible assets**, such as television programs, motion pictures, videos, recordings, books, photographs, and advertising jingles.

Most of these intangibles meet the criteria for separate reporting based on the *existence of contractual or legal rights*. This category of intangibles is wide-ranging, as many business features and activities involve contractual agreements. Far fewer examples of intangibles meeting the *separability* criterion exist; they include customer lists, noncontractual customer relationships, databases, and unpatented technology.

Unreported Intangibles   Many intangibles do not meet the contractual or separability criteria and are not reported as assets acquired. Whether or not they meet the accounting definition of acquired intangible assets, the acquiring company views these intangibles as valuable, because they contribute to future cash flows. The consideration paid will reflect the value of these intangibles, and therefore will likely exceed the fair value of the identifiable net assets acquired. The difference is reported as **goodwill**.

ASC paras. 805-20-55-6 and 7 provide examples of intangibles that are included in goodwill.

- An **assembled workforce**, the group of employees already in place and able to run the business, including management, sales, technical and other personnel
- **Potential contracts** being negotiated with prospective customers

Other examples include favorable locations and business reputation.

Valuation of Intangibles   Although the Codification does not provide specific guidance for valuing acquired intangible assets, the general measurement guidelines of ASC Topic 820 apply. ASC paras. 820-10-35-37 through 57 define the **fair value hierarchy**, in order of priority:

- **Level 1**: Quoted prices in an active market for identical assets
- **Level 2**: Quoted market prices for similar assets, adjusted for the attributes of the assets in question
- **Level 3**: Valuation based on unobservable estimated attributes

In all cases, the asset is valued in the context of its highest and best use. If the company obtains the most value from the asset by selling it, market values are used. If the asset's value is maximized through its use within the company, market values of products it produces or the estimated present value of expected future cash inflows may be used.

The Codification identifies three approaches to valuation:

- **Market:** Quoted market prices of identical or similar assets
- **Income:** Valuation models used to calculate the present value of future cash flows or earnings
- **Cost**: Estimation of replacement cost of the services provided by the asset

The **cost approach** values the intangible asset at either replacement cost or reproduction cost. Replacement cost is the current cost to develop an intangible asset that performs the same function as the acquired intangible asset. Reproduction cost is the current cost to recreate an exact duplicate of the acquired intangible asset. The choice of approach depends on the availability of data. Costs include direct costs such as materials and labor, indirect costs paid to outside consultants, an estimated profit to the developer and opportunity costs, or income lost because the developer could not take on other projects. If the acquired intangible asset is not new, the estimated amount of obsolescence must be subtracted to obtain the asset's value at the acquisition date.

Intangible asset cost = Direct costs + Indirect costs + Developer profit + Opportunity costs

Intangible asset value = Cost − Estimated obsolescence

The cost approach is particularly applicable to supporting intangible assets that do not directly generate income and do not have observable market values. Examples may include product formulas, operating manuals, and business process documentation.

The **market approach** values the intangible asset at transaction values derived from the arm's-length sale of similar assets in active markets. This level 1 approach is generally preferred because it involves less judgment and relies on the market's assessment of value.

Intangible asset value = Market price in an active market − Selling costs

The majority of acquired intangible assets are unique, and markets are thin. Therefore the market approach is rarely used to value acquired intangible assets. Examples of intangibles with active markets may include trademarks, favorable leases, and licenses.

By far the most common valuation method for acquired intangible assets is the level 3 **income approach**. The asset's value is the present value of future estimated income, or cost savings, derived from its use. "Income" can be defined as net income before or after tax, net operating income, operating cash flow, or whatever measure is deemed appropriate to measure the asset's benefit. For example, a royalty contract's value is derived from estimated future royalty receipts. The estimates are typically based on the company's strategic plan, and represent expected future benefits from use of the intangible asset. Projected benefits are often adjusted for a capital cost, reflecting the use of existing assets to produce revenues, and incremental capital investments related to the intangible asset.

However defined, the estimated future income numbers must be discounted to present value, using an appropriate risk-adjusted discount rate. Because these assets are not expected to have infinite lives, the present value of intangible assets is most commonly calculated by estimating expected cash flows over several years, and discounting each cash flow to the present.

Intangible asset value = Present value of expected future benefits from use of the asset

To illustrate the income approach, return to IBM's acquisition of DataFile Inc. on July 1, 2015. One of DataFile's previously unreported identifiable intangible assets is contractual customer relationships. Management estimates related to the value of these customer relationships are as follows:

- Projected revenue for fiscal 2016 is $15,000,000.
- Projected annual revenue growth rate is 4%.
- Cost of sales and operating expenses are 90% of revenue.
- The effective income tax rate is 35%.
- Average remaining useful life of the contractual customer relationships is 3 years.
- The appropriate risk-adjusted discount rate is 20%.

Additional management estimates, by year, are:

Fiscal year	2016	2017	2018
Projected additional capital expenditures	$100,000	$110,000	$115,000
Depreciation expense included in operating expenses	600,000	600,000	610,000
Capital charge on the use of contributory assets	50,000	60,000	70,000

Management estimates the value of contractual customer relationships as the present value of operating cash flow, net of taxes, capital charges and additional capital expenditures. For convenience, cash flows are assumed to occur at year-end. The valuation analysis appears below.

Fiscal year	2016	2017	2018
Projected revenue	$15,000,000	$15,600,000	$16,224,000
Less cost of sales and operating expenses	(13,500,000)	(14,040,000)	(14,601,600)
Projected operating income	1,500,000	1,560,000	1,622,400
Less income tax expense	(525,000)	(546,000)	(567,840)
After-tax operating income	975,000	1,014,000	1,054,560
Plus depreciation expense	600,000	600,000	610,000
Less capital expenditures	(100,000)	(110,000)	(115,000)
Less contributory assets capital charge	(50,000)	(60,000)	(70,000)
Net cash flow	$ 1,425,000	$ 1,444,000	$ 1,479,560

Present value of net cash flow = $1,425,000/1.2 + $1,444,000/(1.2)^2 + $1,479,560/(1.2)^3 = $3,046,505, or approximately $3 million.

Note that these valuation estimates rely heavily on management's estimates of cash flows, as well as the choice of risk-adjusted discount rate. In the above illustration, if management chooses a discount rate of 10%, the value of the customer relationships jumps to $3.6 million. The income approach is appropriate when estimating the value of income-producing intangible assets. Examples include customer relationships, brand names, developed technology, and licenses.

Oracle Corporation's fiscal 2013 10-K report provides some insight into the methods it uses to value acquired intangible assets.

> Examples of critical estimates in valuing certain of the intangible assets we have acquired include but are not limited to:
>
> - Future expected cash flows from software license sales, cloud software subscriptions contracts, hardware systems product sales, support agreements, consulting contracts, other customer contracts, acquired developed technologies and patents;
>
> - Expected costs to develop the in-process research and development into commercially viable products and estimated cash flows from the projects when completed;
>
> - The acquired company's brand and competitive position, as well as assumptions about the period of time the acquired brand will continue to be used in the combined company's product portfolio; and
>
> - Discount rates.

From the above discussion, it appears that Oracle primarily uses the income (level 3) approach to value acquired intangible assets at the present value of future expected cash flows.

Illustration of Reporting Assets Acquired and Liabilities Assumed

To illustrate the reporting for assets acquired and liabilities assumed, we use the merger information in Exhibit 2.4.

EXHIBIT 2.4 Combination Illustration with Identifiable Intangibles

IBM pays $25,000,000 in cash to acquire DataFile Inc. on July 1, 2015. Fair values of DataFile's reported assets and liabilities follow:

Account	Fair value
Current assets	$ 2,000,000
Plant and equipment	60,000,000
Patents and copyrights	5,000,000
Current liabilities	10,000,000
Long-term debt	40,000,000

In addition, IBM identified and valued DataFile's previously unreported intangible assets as follows:

Brand names	$ 1,000,000
Favorable lease agreements	600,000
Assembled workforce	5,000,000
In-process contracts with potential customers	2,000,000
Contractual customer relationships	3,000,000

Other than the assembled workforce and in-process contracts, all of the previously unreported intangibles meet the contractual or separability criteria for reporting as identifiable intangibles. IBM records the acquisition as follows:

Current assets	2,000,000	
Plant and equipment	60,000,000	
Patents and copyrights	5,000,000	
Brand names	1,000,000	
Favorable lease agreements	600,000	
Contractual customer relationships	3,000,000	
Goodwill	3,400,000	
Current liabilities		10,000,000
Long-term debt		40,000,000
Cash		25,000,000
To record the acquisition of DataFile for $25,000,000 in cash.		

Goodwill in this acquisition is the difference between the acquisition price and the fair value of the identifiable net assets acquired, and is calculated as follows:

Acquisition cost		$25,000,000
Fair value of identifiable net assets acquired:		
Current assets	$ 2,000,000	
Plant and equipment.	60,000,000	
Patents and copyrights.	5,000,000	
Brand names	1,000,000	
Favorable lease agreements.	600,000	
Contractual customer relationships	3,000,000	
Current liabilities.	(10,000,000)	
Long-term debt.	(40,000,000)	21,600,000
Goodwill		$ 3,400,000

BUSINESS APPLICATION   Goodwill

The composition of goodwill is often discussed in financial statement footnotes. Below are some recent examples:

IBM   (*2013 annual report, describing goodwill recognition on all acquisitions*):

> The primary drivers that generate goodwill are the value of synergies between the acquired entities and the company and the acquired assembled workforce, neither of which qualifies as an identifiable intangible asset.

Walt Disney   (*2013 annual report, describing Lucasfilm Ltd. LLC acquisition*):

> The goodwill reflects the value to Disney from leveraging Lucasfilm intellectual property across our distribution channels, taking advantage of Disney's established global reach.

Ingram Micro Inc.   (*2013 annual report, describing acquisition of Shipwire, an e-commerce fulfillment services provider*):

> The goodwill recognized in connection with the acquisition is primarily attributable to the assembled workforce and our expectation of extending Shipwire's brand and the reach of its networked platform, while enhancing our existing portfolio of products and services. This acquisition will expand our solutions offerings into the large and growing e-commerce fulfillment market.

Sprint Corporation   (*2013 annual report, describing acquisition of Clearwire, a wireless provider*):

> Goodwill includes expected synergies from combining the businesses, such as cost synergies from reduced network-related expenses through the elimination of redundant assets and enhanced spectrum positions, which are expected to provide greater network coverage.

Reporting Perspective

Reporting standards for business combinations emphasize recognition of identifiable intangibles, to accurately reflect the types of assets acquired and to properly report write-offs of these assets over time. However, although companies identify and measure some previously unreported identifiable intangible assets acquired in a business combination, a large proportion of acquisition cost is typically allocated to goodwill. **IBM**'s yearly acquisitions, shown below, illustrate this phenomenon. The specific identifiable intangible assets IBM reports include completed technology, client relationships, in-process R&D, patents and trademarks.

IBM Acquisitions, 2009–2013 *(in millions)*	2009	2010	2011	2012	2013
Tangible net assets	$ 237	$ 204	$ (2)	$ 38	$ 51
Identifiable intangible assets	231	1,580	560	1,032	922
Goodwill	1,003	4,754	1,291	2,894	2,246
Total acquisition cost	$1,471	$6,538	$1,849	$3,964	$3,219
Identifiable intangible assets as a percent of acquisition cost	16%	24%	30%	26%	29%
Goodwill as a percent of acquisition cost	68%	73%	70%	73%	70%

The choice between recognition of identifiable intangibles versus goodwill has an impact on future income, particularly if the identifiable intangibles have finite lives and must be amortized. In contrast, goodwill is not amortized, although it is subject to impairment testing.

REVIEW 1 • Reporting Assets Acquired and Liabilities Assumed

IBM acquires SoftCloud Technologies in an acquisition reported as a merger, for $1.2 billion in cash. At the acquisition date, the reported assets and liabilities of SoftCloud have fair values as follows:

(in millions)	Fair value
Cash and receivables	$ 400
Inventories	800
Property, plant and equipment	3,500
Accounts payable	300
Long-term debt	3,850

In addition, the following items are not currently reported on SoftCloud's balance sheet:

(in millions)	Fair value
Favorable lease agreements	$150
Skilled workforce	15
Favorable press reviews on products	5

Required: Prepare the entry IBM makes to record its acquisition of SoftCloud.

Solutions are located after the chapter assignments.

MEASUREMENT OF ACQUISITION COST

LO2 Measure and report the various types of consideration paid.

The Codification requires that the acquisition cost, or consideration transferred, in a business combination be measured at *fair value at the acquisition date*. **Acquisition cost** includes the following items:

- Assets, such as cash, transferred by the acquirer to the former owners of the acquiree
- Liabilities incurred by the acquirer and owed to the former owners of the acquiree
- Stock issued by the acquirer to the former owners of the acquiree

ASC Topic 805 requires that the *stock issued to the former owners of the acquiree be valued as of the date that the acquirer achieves control*. Using the acquisition date value adds uncertainty to the acquisition cost, as the market value of the stock issued is unknown until control changes hands. **Walt Disney**'s 2009 acquisition of **Marvel Entertainment, Inc.** is an example. Under terms of the agreement, announced at the end of August, 2009, Disney paid Marvel shareholders $30 per share in cash plus 0.745 Disney shares for each Marvel share owned. The total acquisition cost of $4 billion was based on Disney's August 28, 2009, closing price of $26.84 per share. The acquisition was completed on December 31, 2009, when Disney's stock price was $32.25 per share, adding over $300 million to the acquisition cost.

Contingent Consideration

Acquisition cost may also include **contingent consideration**, where the acquirer agrees to make additional payments to the former owners of the acquiree if certain events occur or conditions are met. These arrangements are commonly used when the buyer and seller do not agree on the value of the acquiree. The additional payments, known as **earnouts**, are usually dependent on some measure of the future performance of the acquiree. For example, the acquirer may agree to pay the former owners of the acquiree an additional payment three years after the acquisition, equal to two times the amount by which the acquiree's revenue in the third year exceeds $3 billion. The earnout not only closes the expectations gap between the buyer and seller, but transfers some of the acquiree's future performance risk to the seller.

When **Oracle** acquired **Pillar Data** in 2011, the entire acquisition price was an earnout. Oracle agreed to pay Pillar investors a cash amount in early 2015 equal to three times Pillar's revenues from the sale of specific products in 2014, less the losses from the sale of specific products over the entire earnout period. If losses exceeded revenues, the acquisition price is zero. Earnout performance metrics may take many forms, but the most common are gross revenue or an operating earnings measure such as earnings before interest, taxes, depreciation and amortization (EBITDA). Nonfinancial milestones such as bringing a particular product to market or obtaining a key patent are also prevalent.

The Codification requires that contingent consideration be reported *at the date of acquisition* as part of acquisition cost. Three major reporting questions must be addressed: (1) Is the payment agreement classified as a liability or as equity? (2) Are any of the payments compensation for future services? (3) What is the value of the agreement? Answers to these questions not only affect reporting at the acquisition date, but also affect subsequent reporting of changes in the value of the agreement, with varying effects on the acquirer's income.

Classification as Liability or Equity Acquirers use *ASC Subtopic 480-10* to determine whether the contingency arrangement is classified as a liability or equity. Agreements that require the buyer to transfer cash or other assets to the seller are liabilities. Agreements requiring the buyer to transfer additional shares to the seller may be either liabilities or equity. If the buyer agrees to transfer shares of stock to the seller to meet a fixed monetary obligation, the agreement is a liability. For example, assume the buyer issues 100,000 shares of its stock to the seller. The market value of the stock at the date of acquisition is $5 million. If the market value of the stock declines in the next two years, the buyer agrees to issue additional shares to restore the total value of the stock to $5 million. The $5 million is a fixed monetary obligation, and the agreement is recorded as a liability. Classification of contingent consideration as equity generally requires that the number of shares to be transferred be indeterminate and not based on a fixed value that is known at the date of acquisition. This type of arrangement as part of a business acquisition is rare, and therefore in this text we assume all contingent consideration is classified as a liability.

Contingent Consideration or Compensation for Future Services   If former owners of the acquired company become employees of the combined entity, contingent payments to these former owners may be compensation for their future services rather than a cost of the acquisition. *ASC Topic 805* requires that if the contingent payments are terminated when the former owner is no longer employed, the payments are compensation. Otherwise, each arrangement must be analyzed to determine whether some or all of the contingent payments are compensation for future services rather than additional acquisition cost. Contingent payments classified as compensatory are not reported at the date of acquisition, but are recognized over time as *compensation expense* as the payments are earned by the employee.

Reporting and Measuring Contingent Consideration   *ASC Topic 805* requires that contingent consideration be reported as a component of acquisition cost, *at the date of acquisition*. Because the exact payment amount is unknown at that time, the acquirer must make a good-faith estimate of the *present value of the expected payment*, considering both its *probability* and its *timing*.

To illustrate the valuation of an earnout classified as contingent consideration, assume that on January 1, 2016, **Oracle** acquires Eloquant, Inc., a cloud-based revenue management software provider. In addition to cash and stock paid to the former shareholders of Eloquant at the date of acquisition, Oracle agrees to pay, two years after the date of acquisition, one dollar in cash for every dollar in EBITDA above $40 million that Eloquant reports over the next two years. In valuing an actual earnout, the acquirer may have a range of predictions of future EBITDA. For purposes of this illustration, assume Oracle expects only three possible outcomes over the next two years:

EBITDA	Probability
$25,000,000	0.20
45,000,000	0.60
75,000,000	0.20

The expected payment is calculated as follows:

$$(\$45,000,000 - \$40,000,000) \times 60\% = \$\ 3,000,000$$
$$(\$75,000,000 - \$40,000,000) \times 20\% = \underline{\ 7,000,000}$$
$$\$10,000,000$$

If the appropriate risk-adjusted discount rate is 15 percent, the present value of the expected payment is:

$$\$10,000,000/(1 + 0.15)^2 = \$7,561,437$$

The earnout of $7,561,437 increases the acquisition price, and is reported by Oracle as a liability.

Employee Compensation

Typically the acquiring company makes payments to the employees of the acquired company. These can be in the form of cash, or equity payments such as stock options and restricted stock awards. When control changes, outstanding equity awards to the acquired company's employees must be converted to awards in the acquiring company's shares and reported by the acquiring company when appropriate.

As discussed above, it is important to distinguish between payments for *services already performed* and payments for *services to be provided* after the acquisition. Severance payments and vested stock options are part of acquisition cost, since they relate to prior services. The fair value of stock options issued to replace options denominated in the acquiree's stock is part of acquisition cost if the options relate to prior services, but if they are compensation for future services, they are recognized as prepaid expenses and expensed as services are performed. Typically when the stock options are *vested* as of the date of acquisition, they relate to services performed prior to the acquisition.

Acquisition-Related Costs

Costs related to acquisitions include more than just payments to the former owners of the acquired company. Acquirers generally employ outside consultants, lawyers, accountants, and advisory services to support their acquisition activities. For example, in 2013 **Sprint Corporation** reported $19 million in costs related to its acquisition of **Clearwire**, and $129 million related to its acquisition of **SoftBank**.

These **out-of-pocket costs** to outside consultants, lawyers, accountants, and others are not included in acquisition cost. Although these costs are a necessary part of an acquisition, they do not increase the value of the acquired business. Therefore companies expense these acquisition-related costs as incurred. Similarly, costs of internally provided services, such as salaries for employees in the acquisitions department of the acquiring company, are expensed as incurred.

Registration costs for securities issued in an acquisition are treated the same as for any issue of securities—they reduce the net value of the equity accounts affected. For example, if an acquirer issues no-par stock with a fair value of $50,000,000, and registration costs are $2,000,000, the capital stock account is credited for $48,000,000. Stock registration fees do not affect the total acquisition cost—cash paid for the fees *adds* to the acquisition cost, but the fees are *netted out* of the total fair value of stock issued. In our example, consideration paid is $50,000,000, reported as $48,000,000 in capital stock and $2,000,000 in cash. If registration costs are instead $1,000,000, consideration paid is still $50,000,000, reported as $49,000,000 in capital stock and $1,000,000 in cash.

Companies often incur additional **acquisition-related restructuring costs**, including shutting down departments, reassigning or eliminating jobs, and changing suppliers or production practices in connection with business combinations. Unless represented by acquisition-date liabilities, these costs are expensed as incurred, and do not affect acquisition cost.

Illustration of Reporting Consideration Given in an Acquisition

Return to the July 1, 2015, business combination described in Exhibit 2.4. Instead of simply paying $25,000,000 in cash to the former owners of DataFile, IBM structures the deal as follows:

Cash paid to former owners of DataFile.	$ 3,000,000
Fair value of stock issued to former owners of DataFile: 1,000,000 shares, par value $0.50	20,000,000
Cash paid for registration fees on stock issued.	600,000
Cash paid for outside merger advisory services	1,200,000
Expected present value of earnout agreement	2,300,000

Acquisition cost is $25,300,000, consisting of $3,000,000 in cash paid to the former owners of Data-File, $20,000,000 fair value of stock issued, and the $2,300,000 earnout. The registration fees are netted against additional paid-in capital and advisory services are expensed; neither affects acquisition cost. Using the asset and liability data on page 45, IBM records the acquisition as follows:

Current assets	2,000,000	
Plant and equipment	60,000,000	
Patents and copyrights	5,000,000	
Brand names	1,000,000	
Favorable lease agreements	600,000	
Contractual customer relationships	3,000,000	
Goodwill	3,700,000	
Merger expenses (income).	1,200,000	
Current liabilities		10,000,000
Long-term debt		40,000,000
Earnout liability		2,300,000
Common stock, $0.50 par.		500,000
Additional paid-in capital.		18,900,000
Cash		4,800,000
To record the acquisition of DataFile Inc.		

We can separately calculate goodwill as follows:

Acquisition cost		
Cash to former owners of DataFile..............................	$ 3,000,000	
Fair value of stock issued......................................	20,000,000	
Fair value of earnout..	2,300,000	
Total acquisition cost...		$25,300,000
Fair value of identifiable net assets acquired		
Current assets	$ 2,000,000	
Plant and equipment..	60,000,000	
Patents and copyrights..	5,000,000	
Brand names	1,000,000	
Favorable lease agreements...................................	600,000	
Contractual customer relationships	3,000,000	
Current liabilities..	(10,000,000)	
Long-term debt..	(40,000,000)	(21,600,000)
Goodwill..		$ 3,700,000

SUBSEQUENT CHANGES IN ASSET, LIABILITY, OR CONTINGENT CONSIDERATION VALUES

LO3 Account for changes in the values of acquired assets and liabilities, and contingent consideration.

The prior discussion indicates, perhaps surprisingly, that most of the numbers reported in an acquisition are estimates. Assets and liabilities acquired are reported at fair value as of the date of acquisition, based on the information known at the time. Reporting contingent consideration at the date of acquisition requires estimates of expected future performance. Subsequent reporting for changes in these estimates depends on whether new information obtained is a clarification of circumstances that existed at the *date of acquisition*, or reflects events and circumstances that occur *after the acquisition*. Value changes resulting from clarification of facts existing as of the *date of acquisition* are treated as *corrections to the initial acquisition entry*. Value changes caused by events occurring *after the acquisition* are reported *following normal GAAP for these events*.

Measurement Period

ASC Section 805-10-25 defines the **measurement period** as the period during which value changes can be reported as corrections to the initial acquisition entry. During this period, the acquirer may obtain additional facts pertaining to the acquisition-date fair values of assets acquired and liabilities assumed and the consideration paid, and use this information to adjust these values.

Although the Codification does not specify exactly when the measurement period is over, it does state that *the measurement period ends when no more information can be obtained concerning estimated values as of the acquisition date*. Information obtained soon after the acquisition occurs is more likely to relate to values as of the acquisition date, so *ASC para. 805-10-25-14* puts a limit on the measurement period at **one year from the acquisition date**. However, note carefully that the choice between reporting value changes as corrections of the acquisition entry or following normal GAAP depends on whether the changes *correct values as of the acquisition date*, or are value changes caused by *subsequent events*. Accountants *cannot* assume that all value changes within the first year are corrections of the original acquisition entry.

Reporting Subsequent Changes in Asset and Liability Values

Return again to the example in Exhibit 2.4 on page 45. Three months after the acquisition, new information reveals that equipment not belonging to DataFile was mistakenly included in the original valuation, and the actual fair value of the acquired equipment was $40,000,000 at the date of acquisition, not $60,000,000. In that case, IBM corrects the original acquisition entry:

Goodwill	20,000,000	
Plant and equipment		20,000,000
To correct the value of equipment acquired.		

For an acquisition reporting goodwill, increases in the value of acquired assets during the measurement period *reduce* reported goodwill. Increases in the value of liabilities assumed *increase* reported goodwill.

But if DataFile's equipment actually was worth $60,000,000 at date of acquisition and subsequently loses value because of a fire at the storage warehouse and is now worth $40,000,000, the following entry records the asset impairment:

Loss on equipment (income)	20,000,000	
Plant and equipment		20,000,000
To report impairment of equipment.		

Changes in value caused by events subsequent to the acquisition are reported using appropriate GAAP for the value change, and do not adjust the original acquisition entry. If DataFile's equipment *increased* in value from $60,000,000 to $100,000,000 due to events subsequent to the acquisition, this value change would not be reported, because normal GAAP prohibits the reporting of unrealized gains on equipment.

Reporting Subsequent Changes in Contingent Consideration Value

The values reported at date of acquisition for earnouts are estimates, based on the best judgment of management. These estimates will undoubtedly change based on events that occur after the date of acquisition. Additionally, the present values of the estimates will change with the passage of time.

As discussed above, it is important to distinguish changes in estimated value that result from *clarification of facts that existed at the date of acquisition* from changes that result from *events that occur subsequent to the acquisition*. Changes in the value of contingent consideration resulting from clarification of facts as of the acquisition date are reported as measurement period adjustments, while changes in value due to events occurring after the acquisition date are treated as follows:

- If the contingent consideration is reported as equity, no value changes are reported. Final settlement is reported in equity.

- If the contingent consideration is reported as a liability, as in an earnout agreement, all changes in value are reported in income at each reporting date until the contingency is resolved.

The acquisition facts on page 50 show that IBM reports an earnout agreement at $2,300,000. Four months after the acquisition, new information is uncovered concerning expected performance as of the date of acquisition, and the expected earnout value increases by $400,000. IBM reports the change in earnout value as a correction to the original acquisition entry, as follows:

Goodwill	400,000	
Earnout liability		400,000
To record the change in value of the earnout during the measurement period.		

If instead the change in estimated earnout value is due to an improvement in business conditions after the acquisition, the entry is as follows:

Loss on earnout (income).	400,000	
Earnout liability		400,000
To record the change in value of the earnout due to subsequent events.		

In 2011 **Oracle** originally valued its earnout agreement with the former shareholders of **Pillar Data** at $346 million, and included this amount in its noncurrent liabilities. In 2012, the earnout increased in value to $387 million due to the passage of time. In 2013, Oracle reduced its estimate of 2014 revenues related to the agreement, and concluded that the earnout had a fair value of zero. Because changes in the value of the agreement were due to subsequent events, the earnout liability increase of $41 million in 2012 and the decline of $387 million in 2013 reduced Oracle's net income in 2012 and increased it in 2013.

REVIEW 2 • Reporting Assets and Liabilities Acquired, Consideration Paid, and Subsequent Events

Refer to the information on IBM's acquisition of SoftCloud, in review problem #1 above. Instead of paying $1.2 billion in cash, IBM incurs the following costs to acquire SoftCloud *(in millions)*:

	Fair value
Cash paid to former owners of SoftCloud	$ 600
Fair value of stock issued (15,000,000 shares, $1 par, $100 fair value per share)	1,500
Earnout agreement.	400
Cash paid for acquisition-related advisory services	200
Cash paid for registration fees for shares issued.	100

Required:
1. Prepare the entry IBM makes to record the acquisition.
2. Now assume that one month after the acquisition, new information reveals that the fair value of the property, plant and equipment acquired was $4 billion at the date of acquisition, not $3.5 billion. Six months after the acquisition, changes in the customer base since the acquisition reduce the expected present value of the earnout to $300 million. Prepare the entries necessary to report both value changes.

Solutions are located after the chapter assignments.

BARGAIN PURCHASES

Because *ASC Topic 805* focuses on the fair values of assets and liabilities acquired, rather than allocating the cost of the acquisition to the acquired company's net assets, there likely will be differences between the value of net assets acquired and the acquisition cost. We have already discussed and illustrated many cases where acquisition cost *exceeds* the fair value of identifiable net assets acquired, resulting in reporting the asset *goodwill*. However, in some cases the acquisition cost is *less than* the fair value of identifiable net assets acquired. These acquisitions are called **bargain purchases**.

LO4 Account for bargain purchases.

An acquiring company may pay less than the fair value of identifiable net assets acquired if the acquisition is a "forced sale," where the seller is attempting to avoid bankruptcy or other serious financial losses and there is no time to shop around for a better price. One example occurred in 2009 when **Republic Airlines** acquired **Frontier Airlines**. Frontier was in bankruptcy, illiquidity in the credit market limited the competitive bidding process, and Frontier was expected to generate future losses. As a result, Republic paid a price that was determined to be lower than the fair value of Frontier's net assets.

In 2013, **Avnet, Inc.**, a U.S. electronics components distributor, acquired the stock of **Internix, Inc.**, a Japanese circuit and semiconductor supplier. Avnet's acquisition cost was lower than the estimated fair value of Internix's identifiable net assets. At the time of the acquisition, Internix's markets were fragmented and highly competitive, and the Japanese economy was increasingly volatile. The stockholders of Internix likely viewed the acquisition as the most profitable way to liquidate their investment, while Avnet viewed the future business value of Internix's identifiable net assets in a more favorable light.

In these cases, the acquisition price does not reflect the fair values of assets acquired and liabilities assumed. Because the Codification emphasizes accurate reporting of asset and liability values, rather than adjusting their values downward, a **gain** on the bargain purchase is reported in income. In its acquisition of Frontier, Republic recorded a bargain gain of $203.7 million in 2009. Avnet reported a $33 million bargain gain from its acquisition of Internix, as part of its 2013 income.

Before labeling an acquisition as a bargain purchase, the acquirer must carefully evaluate the assets acquired and liabilities assumed, and the consideration paid. An acquisition that looks like a bargain purchase may actually be the result of overvaluing acquired assets or undervaluing assumed liabilities. Identification and valuation of previously unreported assets and liabilities deserve particular scrutiny. The value of consideration paid may be understated as well.

Suppose that, after careful evaluation, the acquisition is still a bargain purchase. The assets acquired and liabilities assumed are reported at fair value, the consideration is reported at fair value, and a *gain on acquisition is reported in income*.

To illustrate, return to the acquisition facts in Exhibit 2.4 on page 45. If we now assume that IBM paid $20,000,000 in cash to the former owners of DataFile, we make this entry to record the bargain purchase:

Current assets	2,000,000	
Plant and equipment	60,000,000	
Patents and copyrights	5,000,000	
Brand names	1,000,000	
Favorable lease agreements	600,000	
Contractual customer relationships	3,000,000	
Current liabilities		10,000,000
Long-term debt		40,000,000
Cash		20,000,000
Gain on bargain purchase (income)		1,600,000
To record the acquisition of DataFile Inc. for $20,000,000 in cash.		

We can calculate the gain separately as follows:

Acquisition cost		$20,000,000
Fair value of identifiable net assets acquired:		
Current assets	$ 2,000,000	
Plant and equipment	60,000,000	
Patents and copyrights	5,000,000	
Brand names	1,000,000	
Favorable lease agreements	600,000	
Contractual customer relationships	3,000,000	
Current liabilities	(10,000,000)	
Long-term debt	(40,000,000)	21,600,000
Gain on bargain purchase		$ 1,600,000

Reporting Perspective

The requirement that a gain be reported on bargain purchases appears to open the door to earnings manipulation. Acquirers may intentionally over-report bargains to present a better financial picture to investors. However, the FASB made two arguments against this position. First, in business valuation, analysts generally ignore one-time or unusual gains. Second, in order to inflate a bargain gain, the fair values of identifiable net assets would have to be overstated. This would reduce future earnings as the inflated values are depreciated, amortized, or incur impairment losses. The FASB also addressed an apparent inconsistency in reporting—if gains on bargain purchases are reported, why aren't losses on overpayments also reported? Overpayment is instead reported as goodwill. The FASB believes overpayment is not likely to be intentional, and is difficult to quantify. Overpayment is instead addressed through recognition of subsequent impairment losses on goodwill and net assets acquired.

SPECIAL ISSUES: RESEARCH AND DEVELOPMENT, PREACQUISITION CONTINGENCIES, AND DEFERRED TAX LIABILITIES

Estimating the fair values of acquired assets and liabilities requires considerable judgment. This section highlights the particularly contentious reporting issues involved in reporting an acquired company's research and development, preacquisition contingencies, and deferred tax liabilities related to the acquisition.

LO5 Explain the reporting requirements and issues related to in-process research and development, preacquisition contingencies, and deferred tax liabilities.

In-Process Research and Development

Especially in high-tech companies, ongoing research and development projects are of significant value to future performance. U.S. GAAP requires that costs of *internally* generated research and development be expensed as incurred. Prior to 2009, if such costs were part of a business combination, they were expensed at date of acquisition, unless the project had reached technological feasibility or the assets involved had alternative uses. This treatment mirrored the reporting for internally generated R&D.

The Codification now requires that in-process research and development acquired in a business combination be reported as an *asset*, at fair value, regardless of whether the R&D has an alternative future use. The requirement that in-process R&D acquired in a business combination be reported on the balance sheet is another example of the Codification's focus on accurate measurement of assets acquired and liabilities assumed. Although such projects may have a low probability of success, and estimated fair value is likely to be subject to more measurement error than other assets, the FASB believes that omitting these items from the balance sheet can mislead investors. In addition, capitalization of in-process research and development costs with no alternative future use is in agreement with international reporting standards. We discuss these standards at the end of the chapter.

Reporting Perspective

Standards effective in 2009 changed the reporting of business combinations in fundamental ways:

- Out-of-pocket fees for outside consultants, lawyers, accountants, and others were previously included in acquisition cost, increasing goodwill. Treating these costs as expenses may direct additional attention to the size of these outlays, as they now impact income immediately.

- In-process R&D was previously expensed, and is now capitalized as an indefinite-lived asset, requiring impairment testing subsequent to acquisition.

- Contingent consideration was previously reported as incurred. More timely recognition at the acquisition date requires estimation of expected future cash outflows and selection of the appropriate discount rate.

The new requirements are designed to improve information on acquisitions, but they require valuation skills and considerable judgment, which can markedly affect reported assets, liabilities, and income.

Preacquisition Contingencies

An acquired company can have business situations that will result in a gain or loss if and when future events occur. A common example is an unsettled lawsuit. When the acquired company is the plaintiff in the lawsuit, a **contingent asset** may exist. When the acquired company is the defendant, a **contingent liability** can arise. Intermediate accounting courses examine these situations in the context of *ASC Topic 450*.

ASC section 805-20-25 distinguishes between (1) known assets and liabilities with "determined" or "determinable" fair values and (2) other contingencies. We summarize the guidance as follows.

- The Codification uses a warranty liability to illustrate category (1) contingencies. Warranty obligations can be estimated, usually based on past experience, and are contractually specified. The fair value of acquired contingencies is recognized at the date of acquisition when this value can be determined during the **measurement period**, not to exceed one year after acquisition.

- Recognition of category (2) contingencies, such as an unsettled lawsuit, occurs when the following two criteria are satisfied during the measurement period:

    a. It is probable that a contingent asset or liability existed on the acquisition date, and

    b. The value of the asset or liability can be reasonably estimated.

These requirements generally bring the recognition and measurement issues in preacquisition contingencies under the umbrella of *ASC Topic 450*.

Companies must develop a systematic and logical method to identify and account for subsequent changes in the value of contingencies. A rational approach is to report these changes in the same way as changes in other estimated values related to the combination. Changes occurring within the measurement period are corrections in the original acquisition entry. Otherwise, the changes are reported in income. As emphasized throughout this chapter, the focus on complete reporting of assets acquired and liabilities assumed, even when this requires a significant amount of judgment, extends to the required treatment of preacquisition contingencies.

BUSINESS APPLICATION   Oracle's Measurement of Contingent Liabilities Assumed

In its fiscal 2013 10-K report, **Oracle Corporation** describes its process for valuing contingent liabilities assumed in an acquisition:

> We estimate the fair values of cloud software subscriptions, software license updates and product support and hardware systems support obligations assumed. The estimated fair values of these performance obligations are determined utilizing a cost build-up approach. The cost build-up approach determines fair value by estimating the costs related to fulfilling the obligations plus a normal profit margin. The estimated costs to fulfill the obligations are based on the historical direct costs related to providing the services including the correction of any errors in the products acquired. The sum of these costs and operating profit approximates, in theory, the amount that we would be required to pay a third party to assume the performance obligations.

Thus once Oracle has determined that these obligations must be reported at the date of acquisition, it uses a *cost approach* to value contingent obligations assumed in an acquisition.

Acquired Deferred Tax Liabilities

Acquirers often include deferred tax liabilities as one of the liabilities assumed. For example, in its 2013 acquisition of Mandiant Corporation, **FireEye, Inc.** reports over $90 million in deferred tax liabilities in its list of date-of-acquisition fair values of identifiable net assets acquired. This section discusses the most common reason behind this practice.

For all business acquisitions involving a change in control, the acquiring company reports the assets acquired and liabilities assumed at their fair value at the date of acquisition, and bases subsequent reporting on these fair values. For example, a trademark reported on an acquired company's books at $1,000,000 may have an acquisition-date fair value of $4,000,000. If the trademark has an estimated remaining life of five years, the acquiring company reports amortization expense of $800,000 per year (= $4,000,000/5) on its books. Tax deductions for these write-offs may differ from the book amounts reported by the acquiring company.

For tax purposes, the acquirer's basis in acquired assets depends on whether the acquisition is *taxable* or *nontaxable*. If the acquisition is taxable, the acquiree pays taxes on its gain on acquisition. This gain is the difference between the acquisition price and the tax basis of net assets sold, typically the acquiree's cost, net of accumulated depreciation or amortization taken for tax purposes. In a taxable acquisition, the acquirer's tax basis in the net assets acquired is fair value, so valuation is the same for both book and tax purposes, and no deferred tax issues arise. In a nontaxable acquisition, the acquiree does not pay taxes on its gain. Therefore the tax basis of the acquired net assets remains at the acquired company's tax basis. The acquirer still reports net assets acquired at fair value on its books. Therefore the book values of net assets acquired differ from their tax bases. In the example above, assume that the trademark's tax basis is $1,000,000, to be written off on a straight-line basis. The yearly write-off allowed for tax purposes is only $200,000 (= $1,000,000/5) rather than the $800,000 reported on the acquirer's books. The acquiring company reports a **deferred tax liability** for the additional taxes it will pay in excess of the tax expense it reports on its books, as these intangible assets are written off. If the appropriate tax rate is 30 percent, the deferred tax liability is $900,000 (= [$4,000,000 − $1,000,000] × 30%). This liability declines by $180,000 (= [$800,000 − $200,000] × 30%) each year for the next five years.

The deferred tax liability recognized by the acquirer at the date of acquisition pertains to differences between the fair value and tax basis of acquired tangible and identifiable intangible assets. Note that if the acquiree's tax basis in an acquired asset is greater than the fair value reported by the acquirer, the acquirer recognizes a deferred tax *asset*. In either case, recognition of deferred taxes changes the amount of goodwill reported on acquisition, since the deferred tax asset or liability increases or decreases the fair value of identifiable net assets acquired. In the trademark illustration, goodwill is $900,000 higher because the deferred tax liability reduces the fair value of identifiable net assets by that amount.

INTERNATIONAL FINANCIAL REPORTING STANDARDS FOR BUSINESS COMBINATIONS

IFRS for reporting mergers, consolidations, and asset acquisitions are found in the following pronouncements:

- *IFRS 3(R),* Business Combinations
- *IAS 38*, Intangible Assets

IFRS 3(R) covers the same reporting issues as *FASB ASC Topic 805*, and has similar requirements to U.S. GAAP for the issues studied in this chapter. The acquiring company reports the identifiable net assets of the acquired company at fair value at date of acquisition, including any previously unreported identifiable intangible assets. Goodwill arises if the acquired company's fair value exceeds the fair value of its identifiable net assets. Indicators of the acquiring company include size, contribution of management expertise, composition of the management team, and identity of the issuer of new stock. Acquisition-related costs are reported as expenses. Contingent consideration is reported at expected present value. The definition of the measurement period, used to guide the reporting for subsequent changes in estimated reported values at the acquisition date, mirrors the definition in U.S. GAAP.

IAS 38 criteria for capitalization of identifiable intangibles follow the contractual or separability conditions, found in U.S. GAAP. Although internally-generated *research* is expensed under IFRS, in-process research acquired in a business combination is capitalized, regardless of whether it has an alternative future use. The FASB's decision to capitalize R&D with no alternative future use was influenced by the need to converge with international standards. IFRS for *internally* generated *development* costs allow capitalization of these costs under certain circumstances; U.S. standards require expensing of all internally generated development costs except for specific items such as certain software development costs. Therefore, companies reporting under IFRS have more experience with the issues related to capitalization of R&D.

BUSINESS APPLICATION   SAP AG's Acquisitions

SAP AG is a global leader in enterprise application software. The company is headquartered in Germany, its financial information is measured in euros, and it follows IFRS. Its stock is listed on the Frankfurt and New York stock exchanges.

Similar to U.S. companies, goodwill continues to be a large percentage of acquisition cost for companies using IFRS. In 2013, SAP AG acquired six companies for a total cost of €1,136 million, of which €840 million was attributed to goodwill. Its largest acquisition was **hybris AG**, a Swiss provider of commerce technology. The €1,032 million acquisition cost was attributed to the following hybris AG assets and liabilities (in millions):

Current assets	€ 58
Property, plant and equipment	7
Identifiable intangible assets:	
Acquired technology	167
Customer relationships	144
Trade name	10
Other intangible assets	10
Software and database licenses	1
Goodwill	780
Liabilities	(145)
Total consideration paid	€1,032

Although identifiable intangibles are a significant part of net assets acquired, goodwill comprises the majority of acquisition cost.

REVIEW OF KEY CONCEPTS

LO 1 **Measure and account for the various assets and liabilities acquired in mergers and acquisitions. (p. 40)** *FASB ASC Topic 805* provides the reporting requirements for assets and liabilities acquired, and consideration paid in a business combination. One company must be identified as the **acquirer**; it reports the acquired assets and liabilities at **fair value at date of acquisition**. Complete reporting of assets acquired and liabilities assumed involves revaluing the assets and liabilities reported on the acquired company's balance sheet, and identifying and valuing previously unreported assets and liabilities. A major issue involves previously unreported **identifiable intangibles**. These intangibles are reported if they meet **contractual** or **separability** criteria, and are typically valued using the income approach.

LO 2 **Measure and report the various types of consideration paid. (p. 48)** **Acquisition cost** is measured as the fair value of assets transferred, liabilities incurred by the acquirer, and stock issued to the former owners of the acquired company. **Contingent consideration** is recorded at estimated expected present value. **Acquisition-related costs** for consulting, legal, and other advisory services are expensed as incurred.

LO 3 **Account for changes in the values of acquired assets and liabilities, and contingent consideration. (p. 51)** **Subsequent changes** in the values of assets and liabilities acquired and consideration paid are reported as adjustments to the original acquisition entry if the new information behind the changes pertains to their acquisition date values and the changes occur within the **measurement period**. Value changes that arise from events subsequent to the acquisition date are reported following normal GAAP for these events.

LO 4 **Account for bargain purchases. (p. 53)** The acquisition cost is usually greater than the fair value of identifiable net assets acquired, and is reported as **goodwill**. In some cases, especially in forced sales, the acquisition cost is less than the fair value of net assets acquired. These situations are called **bargain purchases**. If, after careful review of estimated values, an acquisition is identified as a bargain purchase, a **gain** is recognized in income.

LO 5 **Explain the reporting requirements and issues related to in-process research and development, preacquisition contingencies, and deferred tax liabilities. (p. 55)** In identifying and measuring acquired assets and liabilities, **in-process research and development projects** and **preacquisition contingencies** are particularly difficult to evaluate. In-process research and development is reported as an acquired asset, even if the R&D has no alternative use. An acquired contingent asset or liability is reported if, during the measurement period, its fair value is either determinable and it is probable that it exists. **Deferred tax liabilities** arise when the acquirer reports tangible and identifiable intangible assets acquired at fair value, but their tax basis remains at the acquiree's book value.

Assignments with the ✅ in the margin are available in B̄usinessCourse.
See the Preface of the book for details.

MULTIPLE CHOICE QUESTIONS ·····································

Use the following information to answer questions 1–7 below. All amounts are in thousands.

PR Company pays $10,000 in cash and issues no-par stock with a fair value of $40,000 to acquire all of SX Corporation's net assets. SX's balance sheet at the date of acquisition is as follows:

	SX Corporation	
	Book value	Fair value
Current assets	$ 2,000	$ 4,200
Property, plant & equipment, net	10,000	6,000
Identifiable intangible assets	4,000	14,000
Total assets	$16,000	
Current liabilities.	$ 1,600	$ 2,000
Long-term debt	12,000	11,600
Capital stock	5,000	
Retained earnings	8,000	
Accumulated other comprehensive income.	(1,000)	
Treasury stock	(9,600)	
Total liabilities & equity.	$16,000	

PR's consultants find these items that are not reported on SX's balance sheet:

	Fair value
Potential contracts with new customers	$8,000
Advanced production technology	4,000
Future cost savings	2,000
Customer lists	1,000

Outside consultants are paid $200 in cash, and registration fees to issue PR's new stock are $400. All questions below relate to the entry or entries PR makes to record the acquisition on its books.

1. PR recognizes previously unrecorded intangibles of   LO 1 ✅

    a. $ 1,000
    b. $ 5,000
    c. $13,000
    d. $15,000

2. PR credits capital stock in the amount of   LO 2 ✅

    a. $40,000
    b. $50,000
    c. $39,600
    d. $39,200

3. PR records expenses of   LO 2 ✅

    a. $ 0
    b. $200
    c. $400
    d. $600

✓ LO 3 **4.** Three months after the acquisition, a fire damages SX's equipment, reducing its fair value from $6,000 to $4,000. How does PR report this event?

    a. Loss of $2,000, reported on the income statement
    b. $2,000 increase in goodwill
    c. $2,000 decrease in goodwill
    d. Not reported

✓ LO 3 **5.** Three months after the acquisition, PR receives information revealing that the identifiable intangible assets reported on SX's books at the date of acquisition were really worth $12,000 instead of $14,000. How does PR report this information?

    a. Loss of $2,000, reported on the income statement
    b. $2,000 decrease in goodwill
    c. $2,000 increase in goodwill
    d. Not reported

✓ LO 1 **6.** Now assume the acquisition cost to PR is $60,000 (not the right answer). Other facts are the same as originally reported. Goodwill reported on this acquisition is

    a. $35,600
    b. $35,800
    c. $44,400
    d. $49,400

✓ LO 4 **7.** Now assume PR paid $8,000 in cash for SX's net assets. There are no consultant fees, and no shares are issued. Assume that SX's previously unrecorded intangible assets, capitalizable per GAAP, have a fair value of $500. PR records a bargain gain of

    a. $ 0
    b. $3,100
    c. $3,600
    d. $4,100

✓ LO 1 **8.** Which one of the following is *most* likely to be reported as part of goodwill?

    a. Brand names
    b. Broadcast rights
    c. Non-competition agreements
    d. Favorable location

✓ LO 5 **9.** What is the current standard for reporting acquired in-process R&D?

    a. Not reported; becomes part of goodwill
    b. Capitalized as an asset only if it is more likely than not that the outcome will be a viable project
    c. Capitalized as an asset only if it has a future alternative use
    d. Capitalized as an asset regardless of its probability of success or possible future use

✓ LO 5 **10.** Which of the following items related to an acquired company is *most* likely to be recorded by the acquirer?

    a. Warranty liability
    b. Pending lawsuit, where the acquired company is the defendant
    c. Pending lawsuit, where the acquired company is the plaintiff
    d. Fines that might be assessed by environmental agencies

EXERCISES ••

✓ LO 1, 2 **E2.1** **Recording a Merger and a Stock Acquisition** The Poonamalie Company paid $4,000,000 in cash to the shareholders of the Slys Company for all of Slys' outstanding shares. Attorneys' fees related to the combination were $175,000, paid in cash. A comparison of the book and fair values of Slys' assets and liabilities follows:

	Book Value	Fair Value
Cash and receivables.	$ 120,000	$ 120,000
Equity method investments	175,000	200,000
Inventory.	610,000	400,000
Plant assets.	1,600,000	1,000,000
Current liabilities.	(340,000)	(340,000)
Long-term debt	(1,090,000)	(1,100,000)
Net assets	$1,075,000	$ 280,000

Required

a. Prepare the journal entry made by Poonamalie to record the business combination as a merger.
b. Prepare the journal entry made by Poonamalie to record the business combination as a stock acquisition.

E2.2   Post-Combination Balance Sheet: Merger and Stock Acquisition   Presented below are the **LO 1** balance sheets of Allen Corporation and Benson Corporation, *immediately prior* to a business combination. The fair values of Benson's reported net assets equal their book values, and previously unreported identifiable intangible assets have a fair value of $200,000.

	Allen Corp.	Benson Corp.
Cash.	$1,000,000	$ 50,000
Other current assets.	600,000	150,000
Property, plant and equipment.	1,200,000	400,000
Total assets	$2,800,000	$600,000
Current liabilities.	$ 300,000	$100,000
Long-term liabilities	600,000	250,000
Common stock.	200,000	100,000
Additional paid-in capital	900,000	50,000
Retained earnings	800,000	100,000
Total liabilities and equity.	$2,800,000	$600,000

Required

a. Prepare the acquisition entry and the balance sheet of Allen Corporation after each of the following business combinations:
   (1) Allen acquires Benson for $800,000 cash in a transaction recorded as a merger.
   (2) Allen acquires Benson for $800,000 cash in a transaction recorded as a stock acquisition.
b. Why are Allen's total assets in part *a*(2), the stock acquisition, different from the total assets in part *a*(1)?

E2.3   Recording an Acquisition   In fiscal 2010, **Dell Inc.** acquired **Perot Systems** for $3,878 million in **LO 1, 2** cash. Perot's net assets acquired had the following fair values at the acquisition date:

DELL INC.
[DELL]

(in millions)	Fair Value
Cash and cash equivalents	$ 266
Accounts receivable, net	410
Other assets.	58
Property, plant, and equipment	323
Identifiable intangible assets	1,174
Deferred tax liability, net.	(424)
Other liabilities	(256)
Total identifiable net assets	1,551
Goodwill	2,327
Total purchase price.	$3,878

Identifiable intangible assets are:

(in millions)	Fair Value
Customer relationships	$1,081
Technology	44
Non-compete agreements	39
Tradenames	10
Total amortizable intangible assets	$1,174

Dell incurred $116 million in cash payments for bankers' fees, consulting fees, and restructuring costs.

Required

Prepare Dell's journal entry to record its acquisition of Perot Systems, as a merger.

LO 4, 5   E2.4   Bargain Purchase   Sontag Corporation's net assets have fair values as described below.

	Fair Value
Current assets	$ 250,000
Land	800,000
Buildings and equipment	1,000,000
Loans payable	(300,000)

The Pratt Company pays $3,000,000 for Sontag Corporation, and records the acquisition as a merger. Pratt Company determines that identifiable intangibles valued at $1,500,000, not previously reported on Sontag's books, also are recognized as acquired assets.

Required

a.   Prepare a schedule to calculate the gain on acquisition.
b.   Prepare Pratt's journal entry to record the merger.
c.   Now assume Pratt determines that Sontag Corporation has unreported contingent liabilities, reportable at the date of acquisition following GAAP, with a fair value of $75,000. Recalculate the gain on acquisition.

⊘ LO 1, 4   E2.5   Goodwill and Bargain Purchase   Panda Corporation paid $1,000,000 in cash for all of Sim Corporation's assets and liabilities in a merger. The following table shows three possible cases for the merger:

	Fair Value		
Account	Case 1	Case 2	Case 3
Current assets	$300,000	$ 400,000	$ 50,000
Plant assets	600,000	800,000	1,430,000
Identifiable intangible assets	700,000	300,000	200,000
Liabilities	(800,000)	(500,000)	(300,000)
Fair value of identifiable net assets	$800,000	$1,000,000	$1,380,000

Required

In each of the above cases, prepare the journal entry Panda makes to record the acquisition.

⊘ LO 3   E2.6   Changes in Acquisition Values   In 2016, Plummer Corporation acquired the net assets of Singer Company. The purchase price was $85 million. Plummer's annual reports for 2016 and 2017 provide the following information (*in millions*):

	2016	Changes	2017
Net assets acquired:			
Cash and receivables.	$ 10	$ —	$ 10
Inventories	70	(5)	65
Plant and equipment, net.	120	(30)	90
Identifiable intangible assets	35	6	41
Goodwill	500	34	534
Current liabilities.	(50)	—	(50)
Long-term liabilities	(600)	(10)	(610)
Acquisition cost.	$ 85	$ (5)	$ 80

The change in acquisition cost is a reduction in the fair value of an earnings contingency.

Required

a.   Did the changes in value between 2016 and 2017 occur within the measurement period? Explain.

b.   Prepare the entry Plummer made in 2017 to adjust the 2016 acquisition values.

E2.7   Acquisition Cost   Potluck Corp. acquired all of the net assets of Sauers Corp. on June 30, 2016, in an acquisition reported as a merger. The fair values of Sauers Corp.'s identifiable net assets at the date of acquisition are as follows: **LO 1, 2**

Tangible assets.	$25,000,000
Intangible assets.	90,000,000
Liabilities.	55,000,000

Potluck pays $100 million in cash and issues 1,500,000 shares of stock to the former owners of Sauers. Potluck's stock has a par value of $1/share. The market price of the shares at the date of acquisition, $40/share, is used to value the shares issued. Registration fees for the stock are $750,000, and legal and consulting fees connected with the acquisition are $900,000, both paid in cash.

Required

Record the acquisition on June 30, 2016.

E2.8   Identifiable Intangibles   Brightcove, Inc. acquires Ciber, Inc. for $50 million in cash and accounts for the acquisition as a merger. Ciber's balance sheet at the date of acquisition is as follows (*in thousands*):   **LO 1**

	Book Value	Fair Value
Current assets	$ 400	$ 300
Plant and equipment	12,000	4,000
Licenses and trademarks.	5,000	7,000
Total assets.	$17,400	
Current liabilities.	$ 800	800
Long-term liabilities	10,000	11,000
Capital stock	8,000	
Retained earnings	(1,400)	
Total liabilities and equity	$17,400	

Brightcove hires a consultant to identify and value any previously unreported intangible assets attributable to Ciber at the date of acquisition. The consultant identifies the following intangibles:

(in thousands)	Fair Value
Customer contracts	$ 1,000
Assembled workforce.	20,000
Brand names	5,000
Leases at rents below current market	400
Developed technology	1,500
In-process research and development	300
Future cost savings from elimination of duplicate assets	800
Additional expected revenues from bundling products.	600

Required

a.   Identify which of the above intangible assets meet the criteria for recognition as identifiable intangibles per *ASC Topic 805*.

b.   Calculate the goodwill to be reported for this acquisition.

c.   Prepare the journal entry Brightcove makes to record the acquisition.

⊘ LO 1, 5   E2.9   Preacquisition Contingency   On January 3, 2015, Prance Corporation purchased all of the business operations of Step Corporation for $10 million cash. The acquisition is recorded as a merger. Step's identifiable assets and liabilities are listed below at their fair values:

Current assets	$ 850,000
Plant and equipment	3,000,000
Estimated liability: defective product lawsuits	(400,000)
Other liabilities	(4,000,000)

The $400,000 estimated liability represented Step's best estimate of likely losses due to lawsuits pending as of January 3, 2015. Later in 2015, as favorable information regarding the January 3, 2015, status of defective products became available, the estimated liability was reduced to $300,000. Then, in late 2016, after observing large judgments awarded by courts in similar lawsuits against competitors, management revised the estimated liability upward to $500,000.

Required

Prepare the entries made by Prance to record the original acquisition entry and the subsequent value changes in 2015 and 2016.

LO 2   E2.10   Contingent Consideration   As part of its acquisition of Broadvision Inc., Aircastle Corporation enters into the following agreements:

1.   After four years, Aircastle will pay the former shareholders of Broadvision an amount equal to 25% of the amount by which Broadvision's total EBITDA over the four years exceeds $100 million. This payment will be made in cash. Aircastle has the following expectations regarding Broadvision's total EBITDA over the next four years:

EBITDA	Probability
$ 60 million	20%
90 million	10%
120 million	55%
150 million	15%

2.   Several of Broadvision's former shareholders have valuable expertise and will remain as employees with Aircastle. After the first year following the acquisition, Aircastle will pay these shareholders $5 million as incentive compensation. Of this amount, $1 million is an incentive to persuade the shareholders to agree to the merger, and $4 million relates to services to be provided after the acquisition.

Required

a. Compute the amount of contingent consideration Aircastle reports as a liability at the date of acquisition. Assume that the appropriate risk-adjusted discount rate for agreement 1. is 20%, and for agreement 2. it is 5%. Round your answer to the nearest million.

b. Assume Aircastle reported $20 million in goodwill on its acquisition of Broadvision. Assume the fair value of the earnout in agreement 1. declines by $0.5 million during the first year following the acquisition. Prepare the journal entry made by Aircastle to record the value change, assuming

  (1) The value change reflects conditions as of the date of acquisition, that Aircastle discovered subsequent to the acquisition.

  (2) The value change reflects changes in market conditions occurring subsequent to the acquisition.

E2.11 In-Process R&D, Other Previously Unreported Intangibles, Goodwill   Thorn Company acquires Underbrush Company for 2,000,000 shares of $0.50 par common stock with a market price of $15/share. Underbrush has the following assets and liabilities reported on its balance sheet at the date of acquisition: **LO 1, 5**

	Book Value	Fair Value
Current assets	$ 400,000	$500,000
Plant assets	1,200,000	700,000
Liabilities	500,000	450,000

Following are previously unreported assets identified as belonging to Underbrush:

	Fair Value
Contracts under negotiation with potential customers	$ 5,000,000
In-process research & development	2,500,000
Patent rights	3,000,000
Skilled workforce	10,000,000

Required

Prepare the journal entry to record the acquisition on Thorn's books, as a merger.

E2.12 Valuation of Earnings Contingency   As part of the acquisition agreement, Parma Corporation agrees to pay the former shareholders of Stow Company $2 in cash for every dollar of gross revenues above $30,000,000 reported by Stow at the end of the first year following acquisition. Parma projects the following outcomes for the year: **LO 2**

Gross revenues	Probability
$25,000,000	0.05
35,000,000	0.30
40,000,000	0.20
45,000,000	0.25
50,000,000	0.20

Required

Using a 15 percent discount rate, what is the appropriate value to be reported as an earnings contingency liability on Parma's books at the date of acquisition?

E2.13 Recording Asset Acquisition   In 2013, **Flowers Foods, Inc.** acquired certain assets of **Hostess Brands, Inc.**, including the Wonder and Butternut bread brands and related assets. Flowers incurred $16 million in out-of-pocket acquisition costs for this acquisition, paid in cash. These costs were reported in selling, distribution and administrative expenses. The following table summarizes information found in Flowers' 2013 10-K filing, concerning consideration paid and assets acquired (*in thousands*).   **LO 1**   **FLOWERS FOODS INC.** [FLO]

Property, plant and equipment...	$160,673
Trademarks	189,000
Financial assets	1,650
Total identifiable assets acquired.......................................	351,323
Gain on legal settlement..	(1,400)
Goodwill..	5,419
Acquisition cost, paid in cash	$355,342

Flowers had filed a trademark infringement suit against Hostess prior to the acquisition. This suit was settled for $1.4 million and reported as a gain on legal settlement. As of the 2013 balance sheet date, Flowers had not yet received payment on this settlement.

Required

a.   Flowers acquired only a subset of Hostess' assets, and none of its liabilities. Since Flowers did not acquire the company as a whole, do the requirements of *ASC 805* still apply? Cite appropriate Codification.

b.   How did Flowers report the lawsuit settlement?

b.   Prepare Flowers' summary entry to record its acquisition of Hostess' bread brands and related assets.

✔ **LO 3**   **E2.14   Changes in Acquisition Values**   On January 1, 2016, Asure Corporation acquires the net assets of BlueBox Inc. and records the acquisition as a merger. Asure's acquisition entry looks like this (*amounts in thousands*):

Current assets	6,000	
Plant and equipment	20,000	
Identifiable intangibles	40,000	
Goodwill..	350,000	
Notes payable		50,000
Cash		350,000
Earnings contingency liability		16,000

Brand names and customer lists comprise the identifiable intangibles.

Required

For each of the following independent situations, prepare Asure's journal entry, if any, to record the information (*amounts are in thousands*).

a.   On March 1, 2016, Asure receives information that the appraiser of BlueBox's plant and equipment was not qualified. A new appraiser values BlueBox's plant and equipment at $15,000 as of the date of acquisition.

b.   On January 17, 2017, Asure learns that inventory mistakenly valued at $500 at the date of acquisition was really worth $200 at that time.

c.   On June 15, 2016, BlueBox's equipment, acquired by Asure, was damaged in a fire. The amount of damage is $2,000.

d.   On September 22, 2016, Asure determines that because of an increase in demand for BlueBox's products since the date of acquisition, the brand names recorded at the date of acquisition have increased in value by $1,500. In addition, the earnout agreement's fair value has increased by $1,000.

LO 1   **E2.15   Valuing Identifiable Intangibles**   Airmedia Corporation acquires Bridgeline Inc. for cash and stock on January 1, 2015. One of Bridgeline's previously unreported identifiable intangible assets is developed technology, which Airmedia can use to produce unique media services demanded by customers, thereby increasing revenues. Management estimates related to the incremental effect of the developed technology on future cash flows are as follows:

- Projected revenue for 2015 is $25,000,000.
- Projected annual revenue growth rate is 25%.
- Cost of sales and operating expenses are 85% of revenue.
- The effective income tax rate is 30%.
- Average remaining useful life of the developed technology is 5 years.
- The appropriate risk-adjusted discount rate is 20%.

Additional management estimates, by year, are:

Year	2015	2016	2017	2018	2019
Projected additional capital expenditures	$1,000,000	$700,000	$200,000	$500,000	$400,000
Depreciation expense included in operating expenses	800,000	825,000	900,000	850,000	900,000
Capital charge on the use of contributory assets.	200,000	220,000	230,000	250,000	250,000

Airmedia uses the income approach to value the acquired developed technology, at the present value of operating cash flow, net of taxes, capital charges and additional capital expenditures. For convenience, cash flows are assumed to occur at year-end.

Required

Calculate the fair value of the acquired developed technology. Round your answer to the nearest million dollars.

PROBLEMS ••

P2.1 **Acquisition Entries, Various Types of Combinations, Acquisition Costs**   Plastic Corporation   **LO 1, 2, 4** ⊘
is contemplating a business combination with Steel Corporation at December 31, 2015. Steel's condensed balance sheet on that date appears below *(in millions):*

Assets	Book Value	Fair Value
Cash and receivables.	$ 35,000	$35,000
Inventory.	35,000	45,000
Equity method investments	18,000	20,000
Land	8,000	11,000
Buildings and equipment	7,000	14,000
Patents.	5,000	10,000
Total assets	$108,000	

Liabilities and Stockholders' Equity		
Liabilities.	$ 22,000	$ 22,000
Common stock.	50,000	—
Retained earnings	36,000	—
Total liabilities and equity.	$108,000	

Required

Prepare the journal entry to record the business combination of Plastic and Steel for each of the following acquisition costs and combination methods.

a. Plastic merges with Steel by acquiring all of Steel's stock for $125,000 cash, in a merger. Other direct cash acquisition costs are $25,000.

b. Plastic merges with Steel by acquiring all of Steel's stock for $100,000 cash, in a merger. Other direct cash acquisition costs are $10,000.

c. Plastic acquires all of Steel's stock for $135,000 cash, in a stock acquisition. Other direct cash acquisition costs are $15,000.

P2.2 **Identification of Acquirer and Balance Sheet Valuation**   Presented below are the book values   **LO 1**
and fair values of the assets and liabilities of Axtel, Inc. and Barcel, Inc. on October 4, 2016, immediately prior to a business combination.

	Axtel, Inc.		Barcel, Inc.	
	Book Value	**Fair Value**	**Book Value**	**Fair Value**
Current assets	$ 40,000	$100,000	$ 50,000	$ 25,000
Property, plant and equipment........	200,000	400,000	150,000	175,000
Total assets	$240,000		$200,000	
Current liabilities...................	$ 70,000	$ 70,000	$ 30,000	$ 30,000
Common stock....................	80,000		60,000	
Retained earnings	90,000		110,000	
Total liabilities and equity...........	$240,000		$200,000	

Previously unreported identifiable intangibles, capitalized per GAAP, are:

Axtel, Inc. $25,000
Barcel, Inc.   20,000

Required

a. Prepare the balance sheet of the acquiring firm following each of the following business combinations:
    (1) Axtel borrows $250,000 on a long-term basis and buys full ownership of Barcel for $250,000 cash. The transaction is recorded as a merger.
    (2) Barcel borrows $505,000 on a long-term basis, and buys full ownership of Axtel for $505,000 cash. The transaction is recorded as a merger.

b. Comment on how the fair value data for Axtel and Barcel were used in each of the above transactions. Why are total assets reported on the two balance sheets different, even though each transaction results in the union of the same two companies?

LO 1, 2   P2.3

FIREEYE, INC.
[FEYE]

Recording Acquisitions   In December 2013, **FireEye, Inc.** acquired all of the outstanding shares of privately held **Mandiant Corporation**, a provider of computer security products, for $106,538,000 in cash and 16,921,000 shares of FireEye common stock with a fair value of $704,414,000 and a par value of $0.0001/share. In addition, Mandiant's existing vested stock option and restricted stock awards were converted to awards denominated in FireEye stock, in the amount of 6,680,000 shares with a fair value of $86,703,000. These awards have the same terms as when they were issued by Mandiant. FireEye estimates that unvested equity awards relating to post combination services have a current fair value of $122,600,000. Out-of-pocket acquisition-related costs were $8,500,000. The following table summarizes the date-of-acquisition fair values of the identifiable net assets acquired.

Net tangible assets.	$ 9,629,000
Identifiable intangible assets:	
Developed technology	54,600,000
In-process research and development.	1,400,000
Content intangibles.	128,500,000
Customer relationships.	66,000,000
Contract backlog	12,600,000
Trade names.	12,400,000
Deferred tax liability	(90,105,000)
Identifiable net assets acquired	$195,024,000

FireEye describes the identifiable intangible assets acquired as follows:

Content intangibles represent threat intelligence, which is continually gathered from ongoing monitoring of endpoints and by incident response and remediation teams. The intangible assets attributable to customer relationships relate to Mandiant's ability to sell existing, in-process and future versions of its products and services to its existing customers. Developed technology intangibles includes a combination of patented and unpatented technology, trade secrets, and computer software and process that represent the foundation for planned new products and services.

FireEye plans to amortize the developed technology over 4–6 years, the content intangibles over 10 years, customer relationships over 8 years, contract backlog over 1–3 years, and trade names over 4 years. In-process research and development has an indefinite life.

Required

a. Calculate the total acquisition cost reported by FireEye. If any costs described above are omitted, explain your reasoning.
b. Based on the information provided, did FireEye follow *ASC Topic 805* standards for capitalizing identifiable intangible assets? If you are FireEye's auditor, what are your major concerns?
c. How much goodwill was recognized for this acquisition?
d. Prepare the journal entry FireEye would make if it recorded the combination as a merger. Round all numbers to the nearest thousand.

P2.4 Valuation of Identifiable Intangible Assets *All amounts are in € millions.* Invensus Corporation, **LO 1** headquartered in Germany, acquired Clearline Systems on January 1, 2016. Total acquisition cost was €60,000. Clearline's book value at the date of acquisition was €5,000. Clearline's reported assets and liabilities are on its books at amounts approximating fair value, but Invensus determined that Clearline had previously unreported in-process R&D and developed technology.

Valuation of previously unreported identifiable intangible assets is based on the three-year strategic plan plus estimated terminal value. Below is information on projected cash flows for the in-process R&D and the developed technology as of January 1, 2016. All cash flows are assumed to take place at the end of the year for purposes of valuation.

In-process R&D	
Year	**Net cash inflow**
2016	€400
2017	450
2018	350

Developed technology	
Year	**Net cash inflow**
2016	€1,500
2017	2,000
2018	2,100

All cash flows after 2018 are assumed to grow at a rate of 5% each year, indefinitely, based on the 2018 forecast (e.g., if the 2018 cash flow forecast is €100, cash flow for 2019 is €105, for 2020 is €110.25, etc.). Invensus uses a risk-adjusted discount rate of 20% to value in-process R&D, and a rate of 15% to value the developed technology. Round all answers to the nearest € million.

Required

a. Compute the fair values of Clearline's in-process R&D and developed technology.
b. Compute the amount of goodwill recognized for this acquisition.

P2.5 Identifiable Intangibles and Goodwill Prince Corporation acquires Squire Service Corporation **LO 1, 2** ✓ for one million shares of Prince stock, valued at $35 per share. Squire is merged into Prince, although it continues to do business under the Squire Service name. Professional fees connected with the acquisition are $1,200,000 and costs of registering and issuing the new shares are $600,000, both paid in cash. Squire performs vehicle maintenance services for owners of auto, truck and bus fleets. Squire's balance sheet at acquisition is as follows:

Cash	$ 300,000	Current liabilities	$ 3,100,000
Accounts receivable	2,700,000	Long-term liabilities	8,600,000
Parts inventory	5,200,000	Stockholders' equity	14,100,000
Equipment	17,600,000		
Total assets	$25,800,000	Total liabilities and equity	$25,800,000

In reviewing Squire's assets and liabilities, you determine the following:

1. On a discounted present value basis, the accounts receivable have a fair value of $2,600,000, and the long-term liabilities have a fair value of $8,000,000.
2. The current replacement cost of the parts inventory is $6,000,000.
3. The current replacement cost of the equipment is $19,500,000.
4. Squire occupies its service facilities under an operating lease with ten years remaining. The rent is below current market levels, giving the lease an estimated fair value of $1,250,000.
5. Squire has long-term service contracts with several large fleet owners. These contracts have been profitable; the present value of expected profits over the remaining term of the contracts is estimated at $2,000,000.
6. Squire has a skilled and experienced work force. You estimate that the cost to hire and train replacements would be $750,000.
7. Squire's trade name is well-known among fleet owners and is estimated to have a fair value of $200,000.

Required
a. Calculate the amount of goodwill that Prince records for the acquisition.
b. Prepare Prince's journal entry or entries to record the merger with Squire.

LO 1   P2.6   Goodwill   Lisa Corporation made an offer to acquire the assets and assume the liabilities of Toga Corporation. Toga's balance sheet as of December 31, 2016, appears below. Toga has no unrecorded identifiable intangible assets, liabilities or contingent liabilities. The market values of Toga's current liabilities approximate their book values. Lisa Corporation offered Toga Corporation's Board of Directors $1 billion in cash for 100 percent ownership interest.

TOGA CORPORATION
Balance Sheet
December 31, 2016
(in thousands)

Assets	
Accounts receivable.	$ 40,000
Inventories	90,000
Long-term marketable debt securities	95,000
Property, plant and equipment.	275,000
Total assets	$500,000
Liabilities and Shareholders' Equity	
Current liabilities.	$ 70,000
Capital stock	230,000
Accumulated other comprehensive income.	10,000
Retained earnings	190,000
Total liabilities and shareholders' equity	$500,000

The fair values of Toga's assets as of December 31, 2016, are estimated to be as follows:

(in thousands)	Fair Value
Accounts receivable.	$ 30,000
Inventories	50,000
Equity method investments	120,000
Property, plant and equipment.	200,000
Total fair market value	$400,000

Required
a. Identify five business factors or conditions that generally give rise to goodwill.
b. Determine the amount of goodwill that would be recorded on the books of Lisa Corporation if the $1 billion cash offer is accepted by Toga Corporation.
c. Explain why the goodwill determined in part *b* was not included on Toga Corporation's balance sheet.

P2.7 **Bargain Purchase and Preacquisition Contingency**   On January 2, 2017, Fisher Corporation   **LO 1, 3, 4, 5**
acquired all of the voting common stock of Grant Corporation for its own stock worth $10,000,000, in a
merger. Grant's condensed balance sheet on January 2, 2017, appears below:

Assets	Book Value	Fair Value
Cash and receivables....................................	$ 6,400,000	$6,400,000
Inventory..	3,800,000	5,800,000
Plant assets	4,000,000	6,500,000
Other assets...	3,000,000	3,000,000
Total assets	$17,200,000	

Liabilities and Stockholders' Equity	Book Value	Fair Value
Current liabilities......................................	$ 5,000,000	$5,000,000
Long-term debt	1,800,000	1,800,000
Capital stock	2,000,000	
Retained earnings	8,400,000	
Total liabilities and equity............................	$17,200,000	

Note: On December 31, 2016, a lawsuit alleging defective products and claiming damages of $1,000,000
was filed against Grant. The estimated liability and related loss, believed to be $800,000, have not yet been
accrued. The lawsuit meets the criteria for recognition as a contingent liability.

Required

a. Prepare the journal entry made by Fisher to record the acquisition of Grant. There are no unrecorded
identifiable intangibles.
b. During 2017, new facts are discovered that reset the value of the lawsuit at the date of acquisition to
$300,000. Prepare the journal entry to record the change in the value of the lawsuit.
c. Assume that at the end of 2018, based on events occurring after the acquisition date, the lawsuit was
settled out of court for $400,000 in cash. Prepare the journal entry to record this event.

P2.8 **Post-Combination Balance Sheet, Goodwill**   Softdata, Inc. acquires all the net assets of Datalink   **LO 1, 2**
Corporation, recording the combination as a merger. The balance sheets of Softdata and Datalink *immediately prior* to the acquisition, along with fair value information for Datalink's reported assets and
liabilities, are as follows:

(in millions)	Softdata Book Value	Datalink Book Value	Fair Value
Current assets	$1,000	$ 20	$ 5
Property, plant and equipment....................	5,000	800	400
Patents and trademarks...........................	500	100	1,000
Total assets	$6,500	$920	
Current liabilities..................................	$ 200	$ 15	$ 15
Long-term liabilities	5,400	970	990
Common stock, $1 par............................	10	2	
Additional paid-in capital	650	48	
Retained earnings	270	(110)	
Accumulated other comprehensive income..........	(25)	10	
Treasury stock	(5)	(15)	
Total liabilities and equity........................	$6,500	$920	

Datalink also has the following previously unreported intangible assets that meet U.S. GAAP requirements for asset recognition:

(in millions)	Fair Value
Brand names	$150
Software	200

Softdata issues 5 million shares of stock with a fair value of $500 million, and pays cash of $900 million to the former owners of Datalink. Stock registration fees are $5 million and legal and consulting fees are $3 million, all paid in cash.

Required

Record the acquisition entry and prepare Softdata's balance sheet immediately after it acquires Datalink.

LO 1, 2, 3

SPRINT CORP.
[S]

P2.9   **Merger Entry, Valuation Adjustments**   On August 12, 2005, **Sprint Corporation** acquired all of **Nextel Communications**, forming **Sprint Nextel Corporation**. Total consideration paid for the merger was as follows *(in millions)*:

Cash payment to Nextel shareholders	$ 969
Stock issued to Nextel shareholders	35,645
Conversion of Nextel stock-based awards to Sprint Nextel awards	1,124
Total	$37,738

Direct acquisition costs for financial advisory, legal and other services were $78 million. The 1,414 million shares issued had a par value of $2/share. The value of the stock-based awards (employee stock options) was calculated following the requirements of *ASC Topic 718*. Estimated fair values of Nextel's identifiable net assets as of September 30, 2005, are listed below, as well as purchase price adjustments made in the fourth quarter of 2005.

	Preliminary Purchase Price Allocation		
(in millions)	As of 9/30/2005	Adjustments	As of 12/31/2005
Current assets	$ 5,501	$ 4	$ 5,505
Property, plant and equipment.	8,454	(80)	8,374
Spectrum licenses and other indefinite life intangibles	14,640	—	14,640
Customer relationships and other definite life intangibles	10,448	—	10,448
Investments	2,680	(2)	2,678
Other assets	111	—	111
Current liabilities.	(2,902)	(18)	(2,920)
Long-term debt	(8,984)	—	(8,984)
Other long-term liabilities	(8,199)	105	(8,094)
Deferred compensation included in shareholders' equity	518	(33)	485
Totals	$22,267		$22,243

Required

a. Calculate the amount of goodwill reported on this acquisition, as of September 30, 2005.
b. If Sprint recorded this acquisition as a merger, what entry did it make, using September 30, 2005, fair values? Assume direct acquisition costs were paid in cash.
c. Prepare the entry Sprint made to record the fair value changes during the fourth quarter of 2005 as purchase price adjustments occurring during the measurement period.

✔ LO 1, 2, 4, 5

P2.10   **Earnings Contingency, In-Process R&D, Bargain Purchase**   On January 2, 2015, Fiser, Inc. acquired Vixen Pharmaceuticals for $1.25 billion cash, in a merger. Vixen had two promising products for treating common infections under review by the U.S. Food and Drug Administration. The balance sheets of Fiser and Vixen reflect data *immediately prior* to the acquisition. Fair value information appears for Vixen's reported assets and liabilities.

(in thousands)	Fiser, Inc. Book Value	Vixen Pharmaceuticals Book Value	Fair Value
Current assets	$ 5,000,000	$ 200,000	$ 200,000
Property, plant and equipment	60,000,000	10,000,000	5,000,000
Patents	10,000,000	500,000	3,000,000
Total assets	$75,000,000	$10,700,000	$8,200,000
Liabilities	$35,000,000	$ 7,850,000	$7,850,000
Capital stock	25,000,000	5,000,000	
Retained earnings	15,000,000	(2,150,000)	
Total liabilities and equity	$75,000,000	$10,700,000	

$1 billion of the purchase price was allocated to previously unreported in-process research and development attributed to Vixen's products under development. The purchase price was low due to Vixen's poor performance in previous years—Vixen reported a retained earnings deficit of $2.15 billion as of the date of acquisition. To close the deal, Fiser agreed to pay the former owners of Vixen $2 for every dollar of total revenue above $50 million reported on sales of Vixen's products over the next two years. This payment, if made at all, would occur at December 31, 2016. Fiser expects that there is only a 10 percent chance the payment will be made, as follows:

Total expected revenue on Vixen's products, 2015–2016	Probability
Below $50 million	0.90
$60 million	0.08
$80 million	0.02

Required

a. Calculate the present value of the earnout agreement, using a 15 percent discount rate.
b. This acquisition is a bargain purchase. Calculate the gain on acquisition reported by Fiser.
c. Prepare the entry Fiser made to record the acquisition.
d. Prepare Fiser's post-combination balance sheet.

P2.11 Bargain Gain, Contingent Consideration, and Changes in Estimates On December 31, 2009, **Manitex International, Inc.** acquired **Load King Trailers**, manufacturer of custom trailers and hauling systems, from **Genie Industries**. The acquisition cost was as follows *(in thousands)*:

LO 1, 2, 3, 4

MANITEX
INTERNATIONAL,
INC.
[MNTX]

	Fair Value
Cash	$ 100
130,890 shares of Manitex International, Inc. stock	250
Interest-bearing promissory note	2,580
Contingent consideration	30
Total purchase consideration	$2,960

Manitex also incurred $54 in legal fees related to the Load King acquisition. Manitex common stock has no par value. The promissory note is the present value of amounts owed to Genie over the period 2009–2016. The contingent consideration is described as follows:

> The agreement has a contingent consideration provision which provides for a onetime payment of $750 if net revenues are equal to or greater than $30,000 in any of the next three years, i.e., 2010, 2011 or 2012. Given the disparity between the revenue threshold and the Company's projected financial results, it was determined that a Monte Carlo simulation analysis was appropriate to determine the fair value of contingent consideration. It was determined that the probability weighted average earnout payment is $30. Based thereon, we determined the fair value of the contingent consideration to be $30.

The fair value of net assets acquired is as follows *(in thousands)*:

Inventory.	$1,841
Machinery and equipment	1,716
Land and buildings.	2,610
Accounts receivable.	464
Prepaid expenses.	5
Trade names and trademarks	420
Unpatented technology	670
Accounts payable.	(144)
Accrued expenses	(150)
Deferred tax liability	(1,557)
Fair value of net assets acquired	$5,875

Required

a. Prepare the entry made by Manitex to record its acquisition of Load King, as a merger.
b. Assume that within the measurement period, new information indicates that the date-of-acquisition fair values of some items have changed to *(in thousands)*:

Inventory.	$1,000
Machinery and equipment	800
Land and buildings.	1,200
Contingent consideration.	35

Prepare the entry to adjust the asset and contingent consideration values.

c. Now assume the fair value changes in *b.* occur outside the measurement period. Prepare the entry to adjust the asset and contingent consideration values, assuming all value changes are reported in income per normal GAAP.

LO 1, 2, 4   P2.12   Recording Acquisitions, Bargain Gain and Goodwill   In fiscal 2013, **Avnet, Inc.** acquired several companies. The following table summarizes the date-of-acquisition fair values of the net assets acquired *(in thousands)*.

AVNET, INC.
[AVT]

Cash.	$ 29,276
Accounts receivable, net	226,743
Inventory.	91,791
Other current assets.	33,689
Property, plant and equipment.	25,311
Customer relationships	35,248
Other assets.	12,044
Total identifiable assets acquired.	454,102
Current liabilities.	(157,986)
Long-term debt	(112,007)
Total liabilities assumed	(269,993)
Net identifiable assets acquired	184,109
Goodwill.	157,521
Bargain gain	(32,679)
Acquisition cost	$308,951

Avnet incurred $116,382 thousand in out-of-pocket costs related to these acquisitions.

Required

a. Avnet's disclosure of its acquisitions shows that it recorded both goodwill and a bargain gain on acquisitions. Explain how this can happen.
b. Assume Avnet paid all acquisition costs in cash. Prepare Avnet's summary entry to record its 2013 acquisitions.

LO 1, 2   P2.13   Conversion of Equity Method Investment to Merger   In October, 2010, **The Coca-Cola Company** owned 33 percent of the North American business of Coca-Cola Enterprises (CCE). That year,

THE COCA-COLA COMPANY
[KO]

Coca-Cola acquired the other 67 percent of CCE's North American business. Acquisition cost of full owner-ship of CCE's North American business was the 33 percent interest previously held, plus cash consideration and replacement share-based compensation awarded to certain employees of CCE. Note 2 of Coca-Cola's annual report states that it remeasured its investment to its $5,373 million fair value at the date of acquisi-tion, recognizing a gain of $4,978 million as other income on the 2010 consolidated income statement. Coca-Cola paid CCE's owners $1,321 million in cash and $235 million in share-based payment awards to CCE employees. The share-based payments of $154 million associated with services performed prior to the acquisition were included in the acquisition cost. The remaining $81 million will be expensed over future periods.

The fair value of net assets acquired is as follows (*in millions*):

Current assets	$2,690
Property, plant and equipment, net	5,385
Bottlers' franchise rights	6,393
Liabilities	(15,366)
Net identifiable assets assumed	(898)
Goodwill	7,746
Acquisition cost	$6,848

Required

a. Why did Coca-Cola remeasure its 33 percent interest in CCE's North American business to fair value at the date of acquisition? How did Coca-Cola account for its investment previously?

b. Total share-based payment awards connected with the acquisition were valued at $235 million. Why were $154 million of the share-based payment awards included in acquisition cost?

c. The schedule above indicates that acquisition cost was $6,848 million. What were the components of acquisition cost?

d. Assume the acquisition was a merger, and the net assets of CCE's North American business were recorded directly on Coca-Cola's books. Prepare the entry or entries Coca-Cola made on its own books to record the acquisition of CCE's North American net assets.

P2.14 Valuation Issues and Goodwill Remeasurement In mid-2013, Salesforce.com, Inc., a global leader in CRM (customer relationship management) services, acquired all of the outstanding stock of Ex-actTarget, a global provider of digital marketing technology. Acquisition cost consisted of the following (*in thousands*):

LO 1, 2, 3, 5

SALESFORCE. COM, INC. [CRM]

Cash	$2,567,098
Fair value of equity awards assumed	17,428
Total	$2,584,526

Salesforce.com assumed outstanding stock options and restricted stock related to ExactTarget's employ-ees, with an estimated fair value of $102.2 million, by converting the awards into Salesforce.com stock using a share conversion ratio of 0.84. Of this amount, $17.428 million was included in acquisition cost. The equity awards assumed represents conversion of ExactTarget's outstanding stock options to equity awards in Salesforce.com stock.

The following schedule lists the fair values of ExactTarget's identifiable net assets (*in thousands*):

	Fair Value
Current assets	$175,224
Customer contracts	205,033
Property and equipment	69,161
Identifiable intangibles	706,064
Current liabilities	(65,636)
Deferred revenue	(46,615)
Customer liability	(144,792)
Deferred tax liability	(162,566)
Identifiable net assets	$735,873

Identifiable intangibles, all amortizable, consist of the following (*in thousands*):

Developed technologies.	$307,200
Customer relationships	362,200
Trade name and trademark	29,400
Other acquired intangibles.	7,264
Total intangible assets	$706,064

The deferred tax liability is primarily the result of the difference between book and tax basis of identifiable intangible assets. Salesforce.com's fiscal year ends January 31.

Required

a. How do you think Salesforce.com determined the fair value of equity awards assumed?
b. How did Salesforce.com determine which portion of the $102.2 million in equity awards assumed was included in acquisition cost? What is the difference in reporting for the two portions of assumed equity awards?
c. Explain the nature of the deferred tax liability that is included in liabilities assumed.
d. Salesforce.com made other acquisitions in fiscal 2014, but its acquisition of ExactTarget was by far the largest. In its annual report footnotes, Salesforce.com disclosed that "finalization of acquisition date fair values" resulted in a $5,019,000 reduction in goodwill in fiscal 2014. Speculate on the reasons why goodwill was *reduced* in fiscal 2014.

LO 1, 2 **P2.15** **Valuation of Goodwill and Consideration Paid**   In 2013, the online travel company **priceline.com, Inc.** acquired **KAYAK Corporation**, a travel meta-search website. Amounts paid related to the acquisition were as follows (*dollars in thousands*):

PRICELINE.COM INC.
[PCLN]

Cash paid to the former shareholders of KAYAK.	$ 521,443
Fair value of 1,522,000 shares of $0.008 par common stock issued to	
former shareholders of KAYAK.	1,282,334
Fair value of assumed vested KAYAK stock options, related to pre-combination service . . .	264,423
Fair value of unvested KAYAK stock options, related to post-combination service	57,400
Stock issuance costs.	1,200
Professional consulting fees	8,500

The fair values of identifiable assets acquired and liabilities assumed are listed below.

Current assets	$322,000
Trade names.	496,000
Supply and distribution agreements	302,000
Technology.	73,000
Other long-term assets	11,700
Deferred tax liabilities.	(326,000)
Other liabilities	(42,800)

Required

a. Calculate the acquisition cost for KAYAK. Calculate the amount of acquisition expense reported on priceline.com's income statement in 2013.
b. Calculate priceline.com's net credit to additional paid-in capital for this acquisition. Round amounts to the nearest thousand, if necessary.
c. Calculate the amount of goodwill recognized for this acquisition.

REVIEW SOLUTIONS

Review 1 Solution (in millions)

Cash and receivables	400	
Inventories	800	
Property, plant and equipment	3,500	
Favorable lease agreements	150	
Goodwill	500	
Accounts payable		300
Long-term debt		3,850
Cash		1,200
To record acquisition of SoftCloud.		

Review 2 Solution (in millions)

1)	Cash and receivables	400	
	Inventories	800	
	Property, plant and equipment	3,500	
	Favorable lease agreements	150	
	Goodwill	1,800	
	Merger expenses (income)	200	
	Accounts payable		300
	Long-term debt		3,850
	Earnout liability		400
	Cash		900
	Common stock, $1 par		15
	Additional paid-in capital		1,385
	To record acquisition of SoftCloud.		
2)	Property, plant and equipment	500	
	Goodwill		500
	To record change in value of property, plant and equipment during measurement period.		
	Earnout liability	100	
	Gain on earnout (income)		100
	To record subsequent change in value of earnout.		

3 Consolidated Financial Statements: Date of Acquisition

LEARNING OBJECTIVES

LO1 Explain the purpose and motivation behind consolidation. (p. 80)

LO2 Apply the concept of control to equity investments. (p. 82)

LO3 Apply the concept of control to non-equity investments. (p. 83)

LO4 Prepare consolidated balance sheets at the date of acquisition. (p. 88)

LO5 Explain IFRS for consolidations. (p. 97)

GENERAL MOTORS COMPANY
www.gm.com

General Motors Company (GM) is a worldwide producer and marketer of cars, trucks, and automotive parts. It also provides automotive financing services through its finance subsidiary, GM Financial. In 2013, GM made vehicles sold in North America under the following brands: Buick, Cadillac, Chevrolet and GMC, and had the largest North American market share in retail vehicle sales, with Ford and Toyota in second and third place, respectively. GM also operates in Europe, Latin America, Africa, the Middle East, and Asia Pacific, with additional brands not as familiar to U.S. customers, including Opel, Vauxhall, and Holden.

GM presents its financial results in the form of consolidated financial statements that include the financial records of entities legally separate from GM. GM's 2013 annual report describes its consolidation policy as follows:

The consolidated financial statements include our accounts and those of our subsidiaries that we control due to ownership of a majority voting interest and our consolidated variable interest entities (VIEs) of which we are the primary beneficiary. We continually evaluate our involvement with VIEs to determine whether we have variable interests and are the primary beneficiary of the VIE. When these criteria are met, we are required to consolidate the VIE.

GM owns 31 percent of GM Egypt and 50 percent of Shanghai General Motors Co., Ltd. (SGM). It includes GM Egypt's accounts in its consolidated financial statements, but it uses the equity method to account for its investment in SGM.

How did GM decide which entities to include in its 2013 consolidated financial statements? The basis of presentation in an annual report can have major effects on the overall financial performance of a company, as reflected in its consolidated financial statements. Consolidation policy has been the subject of serious debate among accounting regulators over the years, and is continually evolving. This chapter discusses the issues involved and explains current practice.

Once management identifies which entities to be included, how are the financial records of these entities incorporated into the consolidated financial statements? Accountants must accurately combine the financial records of the various entities. This chapter introduces you to the procedures involved. *Source:* General Motors Company annual report, 2013.

CHAPTER ORGANIZATION

Criteria for consolidation	Consolidation procedures	IFRS for consolidation
• Concept of control • Motivations for off-balance-sheet financing • Application to equity investments • Application to non-equity investments	• Preliminary issues: differences in currency, GAAP, year-end • Steps in consolidation • Consolidation at the date of acquisition: three illustrations • Special issues: depreciable assets and previously reported goodwill	• *IFRS 10* requirements • Comparison with U.S. GAAP

INTRODUCTION

This chapter concentrates on business combinations structured as **stock acquisitions**, where the acquirer obtains a controlling interest in another company by *purchasing and retaining its outstanding voting shares*. The acquirer is known as the **parent**, the acquired company is the **subsidiary**, and the two companies remain as separate legal entities, recording transactions on their own books. When appropriate, the accountant **consolidates** the separate financial records of the parent and subsidiary for presentation in the annual report.

Most business combinations are stock acquisitions. Stock ownership allows the acquirer to obtain control while holding less than 100 percent of the company, thereby reducing the investment needed. Because the two companies remain as separate legal entities, the subsidiary's creditors generally can only look to the assets of the subsidiary for satisfaction of debts. The parent and its subsidiaries also can retain separate names, which may be useful for marketing purposes. For example, Adam Opel AG is a German subsidiary of General Motors, but its cars bear the Opel name.

In other situations, one company can control another separate legal entity *without* equity ownership. Such entities are commonly known as **special purpose entities**, or **variable interest entities**. Whether these entities should be consolidated in the financial statements of the "controlling" company has been and continues to be a contentious issue, and contributed to some of the accounting scandals of the early twenty-first century. This chapter also covers reporting requirements for these relationships.

The subject of reporting for controlled investments in separate legal entities should be approached one step at a time. The parent and the subsidiary each have their own separate set of books. It is the accountant's job to consolidate these ever-changing financial records at each point in time when financial statements are to be published. Because this can be a complex process, this chapter covers consolidation *immediately following an acquisition*. This decision is made for pedagogical reasons only; in the business world, consolidation occurs at the *end of the reporting period*, not at the time of a merger or acquisition.

Consolidation at date of business combination allows us to focus on problems of consolidating the balance sheet only; because no time has elapsed since the acquisition, we can ignore for now the income statement and the statement of cash flows. We can also disregard for the moment the possibility of transactions between the parent and subsidiary. And for simplicity we limit our discussion in this chapter to 100-percent, or **wholly-owned**, subsidiaries.

Subsequent chapters focus on other topics related to consolidation. Chapter 4 discusses consolidation at any point in time *subsequent to acquisition*, which requires preparation of a consolidated income statement and a consolidated statement of cash flows in addition to the consolidated balance sheet. Chapter 5 examines situations where a company controls another company, but holds *less than 100 percent* of its voting stock. Chapter 6 covers additional consolidation procedures that are necessary when the combined companies do business with each other, in the form of *intercompany transactions*.

Before we discuss consolidation procedures, we must identify the circumstances under which consolidation takes place. In other words, *when* is it appropriate to combine the results of two or more separate legal entities for presentation in financial statements?

CRITERIA FOR CONSOLIDATION

LO1 Explain the purpose and motivation behind consolidation.

As discussed in Chapter 2, the requirements of *FASB ASC Topics 805* and *810* apply only to **business combinations**. A business combination occurs when *control is obtained* over one or more businesses. The definition of a *business* was discussed in Chapter 2. Here we discuss the concept of *control*, and the related reporting issues.

Underlying the concept of consolidation is the idea that aggregated information is more relevant to investors when one company has control over another company. *ASC Topic 810* addresses this issue as follows:

> The purpose of consolidated financial statements is to present, primarily for the benefit of the owners and creditors of the parent, the results of operations and the financial position of a parent and all its subsidiaries as if the consolidated group were a single economic entity. There is a presumption that consolidated financial statements are more meaningful than separate financial statements, and that they are usually necessary for a fair presentation when one of the entities in the consolidated group directly or indirectly has a controlling financial interest in the other entities. (*ASC para. 810-10-10-1*)

Investors should be able to evaluate the complete financial performance of a company by looking at its financial statements. If the company controls the resources of another entity, investors should see the results of decisions affecting these resources in the controlled company's financial statements. Consolidated financial statements, which combine the controlled entity's accounts, line by line, with those of the controlling company, more accurately reflect that company's overall performance.

But how is "control" defined, and how does one determine whether control exists in a particular business relationship? In many cases, control is directly observable through ownership of the entity's voting shares. But for entities created for special purposes, such as joint development projects, investment funds, and financing units, control may occur by contract, debt guarantees, or board membership.

Motivations for Off-Balance-Sheet Entities

The decision to consolidate another entity directly affects the financial statements of the consolidating company, since the other entity's assets, liabilities, revenues and expenses are combined with those of the consolidating company. Therefore consolidation can significantly affect reported financial health. Companies are motivated to avoid consolidating another entity if consolidation negatively impacts their financial statements.

A simple example illustrates how a company's balance sheet is affected by the consolidation decision. Assume Manufacturing Company acquires all of the stock of Finance Corporation. Just prior to the acquisition, their separate balance sheets are as follows:

	Manufacturing Co.	Finance Corp.
Total assets	$220,000,000	$110,000,000
Total liabilities	$115,000,000	$100,000,000
Stockholders' equity	105,000,000	10,000,000
Total liabilities and equity	$220,000,000	$110,000,000

Assume Finance Corporation's assets and liabilities are reported at fair value. Manufacturing Company pays $10,000,000 in cash to Finance Corporation's shareholders for Finance Corporation's assets and liabilities, and then consolidates the assets and liabilities of Finance Corporation with its own assets and liabilities. The resulting consolidated balance sheet is:

Consolidated Balance Sheet, Manufacturing Company and Subsidiary	
Total assets	$320,000,000
Total liabilities	$215,000,000
Stockholders' equity	105,000,000
Total liabilities and equity	$320,000,000

If Manufacturing Company instead treats the transaction as an investment, accounted for by the equity method, it makes the following entry on its own books:

Investment in Finance Corporation	10,000,000	
Cash		10,000,000
To record the acquisition of Finance Corporation.		

Finance Corporation's assets and liabilities are not included with those of Manufacturing Company. Manufacturing Company's balance sheet is:

Manufacturing Company with Equity Investment	
Other assets	$210,000,000
Investment in Finance Corporation	10,000,000
Total assets	$220,000,000
Total liabilities	$115,000,000
Stockholders' equity	105,000,000
Total liabilities and equity	$220,000,000

Notice the impact on leverage ratios:

	Manufacturing Co. prior to investment	Finance Corp. prior to investment	Manufacturing Co. plus equity method investment	Manufacturing Co. plus consolidated subsidiary
Total liabilities/Total assets	0.52	0.91	0.52	0.67
Total liabilities/Total equity	1.10	10.00	1.10	2.05

Finance Corporation is much more highly leveraged—has proportionally more liabilities—than Manufacturing Company. Use of the equity method to report the investment has virtually no impact on Manufacturing Company's leverage ratios. However, when Finance Corporation is consolidated with Manufacturing Company, its liabilities are included in the consolidated entity's financial results, significantly increasing both ratios. If investors and analysts use these ratios to evaluate the risk of a company, consolidating Finance Corporation could reduce the market valuation of Manufacturing Company.

Standards for Consolidation

Over the years companies have structured affiliated entities to avoid consolidation, leading to potentially misleading financial statements. Due to the variety and complexity of financial relationships between entities, the FASB has been challenged to develop effective standards that require companies to consolidate the entities they actually control. A company can avoid consolidating a controlled entity under "bright line" standards. For example, if a standard requires consolidation when a company owns the majority of the entity's voting shares, the company can acquire slightly less than a majority of the shares. If the standard requires the company to be exposed to more than 50 percent of the other entity's risks and rewards, the company can structure its financial relationship with the entity to indicate exactly 50 percent exposure. In both cases, control may in fact exist, but the standard does not require consolidation.

U.S. GAAP criteria for consolidation are found in *ASC Topic 810*. There are currently two sets of standards used to determine whether control exists, depending on if the company owns the entity's voting shares, or if it has another type of financial relationship with the entity. Both sets of standards attempt to determine if the company controls the entity, that is, it has the power to direct the entity's major decisions and is exposed to the entity's risks and rewards.

Control and Consolidation of Equity Investments

LO2 Apply the concept of control to equity investments.

Historically, the concept of control has been applied in the context of equity investments. *ASC Topic 810* defines a "controlling financial interest" as follows:

> The usual condition for a controlling financial interest is ownership of a majority voting interest, and, therefore, as a general rule ownership by one entity, directly or indirectly, of more than fifty percent of the outstanding voting shares of another entity is a condition pointing toward consolidation. (*ASC para. 810-10-15-8*)

This approach is commonly known as the **voting interest model**. There are circumstances where majority ownership of voting shares does *not* lead to control of the entity. Current exceptions are found in *ASC para. 810-10-15-10*:

> Consolidate majority-owned subsidiaries unless the majority owner does not control the subsidiary. For example:
> - The subsidiary is in legal reorganization.
> - The subsidiary is in bankruptcy.
> - Governmentally imposed restrictions, controls, or uncertainties cast significant doubt on the parent's ability to control the subsidiary.
> - Approval or veto rights granted to the noncontrolling shareholders significantly limit the majority owner's ability to control the subsidiary.

In practice, exceptions to consolidation of a majority-owned entity are rare. A proposed FASB Accounting Standards Update, expected to become a standard in 2015, addresses the issue of a noncontrolling interest's ability to limit the majority owner's ability to control the entity, and further restricts this exception. Currently if the noncontrolling interest is required to approve *any* significant decision affecting the entity, the majority owner can claim that they don't have control over the entity. The proposal requires the noncontrolling interest to approve *all* significant decisions, not just one. Therefore it will be even more difficult for a majority shareholder to avoid consolidation.

Note that the current standards *do not prohibit* consolidation of entities where the equity investment is 50 percent or less, and a controlling interest exists. Majority ownership is merely a guideline. In U.S. practice, principles tend to evolve into rules, and today most consolidated subsidiaries are majority owned by their parent. Exceptions include GM Egypt, which General Motors consolidates even though it owns only 31 percent of its stock. Voting and other rights give GM the power to control GM Egypt's financial performance.

BUSINESS APPLICATION   2006 Deconsolidation of GMAC

General Motors Acceptance Corporation (GMAC) was founded in 1919 as a wholly-owned finance subsidiary of GM Corporation, providing GM dealers and customers with financing for their car and truck purchases. Since then, it has expanded into banking, insurance, mortgages, and other commercial and retail financing. In 2010, it changed its name to Ally Financial. Today, Ally Financial is an independent entity and GM's automotive finance unit is GM Financial, a subsidiary wholly owned by GM.

On November 30, 2006, GM sold a 51 percent controlling interest in GMAC for $7.4 billion to FIM Holdings, a group of private investors that included Cerberus Capital Management, L.P., and Citigroup, Inc. GM retained a 49 percent interest in GMAC. Although GMAC's financial records had been consolidated with those of GM, after November 30, 2006, GM no longer consolidated GMAC, instead using the equity method to account for its investment. Rather than combining GMAC's assets, liabilities, revenues and expenses with those of GM in its financial statements, GM reported its investment in GMAC as one line in the assets section of its balance sheet, and reported its share of GMAC's earnings as one line in its income statement.

This scenario applies the guidelines of *FASB ASC Topic 810*, which require that majority-owned subsidiaries be consolidated in the financial statements of the parent. Since GM's ownership declined from 100 percent to 49 percent, it no longer was required to consolidate GMAC. One might wonder, however, how the change in ownership interest was decided, and whether the requirements of U.S. GAAP had any bearing on the choice. One might also wonder whether by changing its equity ownership to 49 percent, GM actually relinquished control over GMAC at the time. *Source:* General Motors Corporation annual report, 2008.

Control and Consolidation of Non-Equity Investments

Control over another company may be obtained without paying *any* consideration, or acquiring *any* of the company's stock. A company may form and control a separate entity, known as a **special purpose entity**, with little or no equity investment.

LO3 Apply the concept of control to non-equity investments.

Motivations for Special Purpose Entities   Special purpose entities (SPEs) are legal structures formed for specific business activities. They frequently have no separate management or employees, are staffed by existing companies' personnel, typically obtain most of their financing from debt, and have a small outside equity interest that obtains a secure return with little or no risk. Common examples include:

- **Securitization:** A financial services company sets up an SPE to buy customer or loan receivables from its clients. The arrangement allows the clients to obtain immediate cash for their receivables, typically at a lower cost than factoring. The SPE issues debt securities backed (or collateralized) by the receivables, uses the money to buy the receivables, then uses the collection proceeds from the receivables to pay the interest and principal on the debt securities. A diagram of the securitization structure clarifies the relationships.

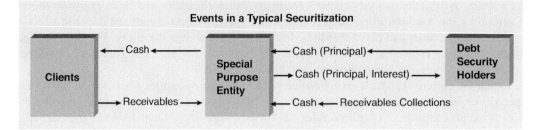

Large financial services entities such as **JP Morgan Chase** and **Citigroup** have used SPEs to securitize billions of dollars of mortgages.

• **Leasing:** A company creates an SPE to purchase long-term assets. Funding for the purchases is obtained primarily through loans. The SPE then leases the assets to the company, and uses the lease payments to pay the interest and principal on the debt. The terms of the lease usually allow the lessee to report the lease as an operating lease.

• **Joint ventures:** An SPE is formed by two or more companies for specialized projects, often requiring large amounts of specialized skill and financing. The SPE structure legally separates the project's risk from that of the sponsors, therefore allowing financing to be obtained at a lower cost. If the companies have licensing agreements requiring them to share new technology with competitors, technology developed by the SPE is legally sheltered from these agreements.

Although many SPEs have legitimate business purposes, they provide the opportunity to hide debt and losses from investors. Because the companies creating the SPEs typically do not have significant equity ownership, the consolidation requirements of *ASC paras. 810-10-15-8* and *10* do not apply.

Applying the concept of control to SPEs is particularly challenging. Equity holders control most entities by holding voting shares. With SPEs, the equity investors provide little of the funding, and do not absorb the majority of the risks and rewards of the entity. Losses absorbed by the equity holders are usually limited, and they also often have limited voting power. SPE debt may be guaranteed by parties that do not have equity ownership. Therefore non-equity holders control the SPE.

In the past, FASB standards for consolidating SPEs used simplistic "bright line" guidelines. For example, in 2001, consolidation could be avoided if the SPE's outside equity interest was at least 3 percent of its total assets. Companies, notably **Enron**, structured their SPEs to meet this standard and avoid consolidation. The collapse of Enron in 2001 highlighted the limitation of these "bright line" consolidation standards. Enron sponsored numerous legally separate "shadow entities," with limited purpose activities, that were not included in its consolidated financial statements. By not consolidating these entities, Enron understated its debt and overstated its income on "profitable" transactions with the SPEs. In one type of sham transaction, Enron issued its own stock to a nonconsolidated SPE that used the stock as collateral for a bank loan, paying Enron with the loan proceeds. When one views these transactions together, it is obvious that Enron increased its debt. However, because Enron did not consolidate the SPE, it reported the transaction as a stock issuance.

Consolidation Requirements   A company often has a financial relationship with one or more special purpose entities that are legally separate and in which the company has little or no equity ownership. Following current U.S. GAAP, the company must evaluate each of these financial relationships to determine if consolidation is appropriate. The evaluation process consists of two steps, commonly known as the **variable interest model**:

(1) Determine if the entity's equity investors are likely not the controlling interest. These entities are termed **variable interest entities** (VIEs). If the entity is not a VIE, the voting interest model, discussed above, applies.

(2) If the entity is a VIE, determine if the company controls the VIE. The controlling company is termed the VIE's **primary beneficiary**. The primary beneficiary consolidates the VIE.

What is a Variable Interest Entity?   *ASC Topic 810* defines a variable interest entity (VIE) as one having the following characteristics (*paraphrased from ASC para. 810-10-15-14*):

- The total equity investment at risk does not allow the entity to finance its activities without additional subordinated financial support provided by other parties.
- The equity investment at risk lacks any one of the following characteristics of a controlling financial interest: (1) the power through voting rights or similar rights to make decisions about an entity's activities that most significantly impact the entity's economic performance, (2) the obligation to absorb the expected losses of the entity, or (3) the right to receive the expected residual returns of the entity.
- The equity investors as a group also are considered to lack characteristics of a controlling financial interest if the voting rights of some investors are not proportional to their obligations to absorb the expected losses of the entity, their rights to receive the expected residual returns of the entity, or both, and substantially all of the entity's activities, such as providing financing or buying assets, either involve or are conducted on behalf of an investor that has disproportionately few voting rights.

In practice, determination of the sufficiency of the entity's equity is particularly challenging. Regardless of the level of equity investment, here is the key question:

> Is the entity able to finance its activities without additional support, such as guaranteed loans or future funding commitments, from affiliated entities?

There are two qualitative ways commonly used to establish the sufficiency of an entity's equity:

- Provide evidence that the entity is in fact able to obtain financing on its own.
- Show that the entity has a level of equity comparable with entities who can obtain financing without outside support.

If qualitative analysis is not conclusive, a quantitative evaluation may be used to determine if the equity investment is sufficient to absorb future expected losses.

A simple example illustrates quantitative analysis of equity sufficiency. Suppose an SPE is formed with $15,000 in equity and $133,000 in debt, for a total investment of $148,000. All cash flows are expected to occur at the end of one year. Exhibit 3.1 shows expected cash flows and expected residual losses and gains, using a 5 percent discount rate and the computational technique provided in *ASC para. 810-10-55-53*.

EXHIBIT 3.1 Calculation of Expected Losses and Residual Gains

(a) Expected Cash Flows	(b) Present Value (@5%)	(c) Probability	(d) = (b) × (c) Expected Present Value	(e) Investment Fair Value	(f) = (b) − (e) Residual Returns	(g) = (f) × (c) Expected Gains	Expected Losses
$189,000	$180,000	0.75	$135,000	$148,000	$ 32,000	$24,000	
63,000	60,000	0.15	9,000	148,000	(88,000)		$(13,200)
42,000	40,000	0.10	4,000	148,000	(108,000)		(10,800)
			$148,000			$24,000	$(24,000)

The $15,000 equity investment is less than expected losses of $24,000 and cannot absorb these losses. This quantitative analysis indicates that the entity's equity investment is not sufficient to absorb the entity's risks. Therefore, the entity is likely to be classified as a VIE.

An Accounting Standards Update to *ASC Topic 810*, effective in 2016, specifically addresses the sufficiency of equity for **development stage entities** (DSEs), defined as entities currently in the process of establishing a new business. Development stage entities are commonly used to develop new products in the software and pharmaceutical industries. Under previous guidance, DSEs were considered to have sufficient equity if they had enough cash to finance the research and development phase of their business. The new guidance requires the DSE to have enough equity to support operations over its entire life. As a result, it is likely that more DSEs will be identified as variable interest entities.

Who must consolidate a variable interest entity?   The reporting entity with a *controlling* interest in a variable interest entity is the VIE's **primary beneficiary** and must consolidate the VIE. A reporting entity has a controlling interest if it possesses both of these attributes (*paraphrased from ASC para. 810-10-25-38A*):

- The power to direct the activities of the VIE that most significantly affect its economic performance, and
- The obligation to absorb the losses or the right to receive the benefits of the VIE that are potentially significant to the VIE.

Determining whether an entity is a VIE's primary beneficiary requires an understanding of the VIE's purpose and design, who makes the day-to-day operating and capital decisions, which decisions significantly affect performance, and how performance affects the VIE's shareholders, creditors, and providers of subordinated support.

The process used to determine whether a company should consolidate an affiliated entity can be summarized in the following diagram:

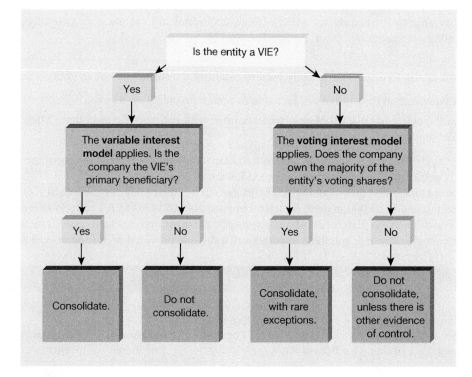

The FASB continues to work to improve standards relating to the major issues behind the consolidation decision. It is currently evaluating specific rights of investors, for example, the ability to remove ("kick out") a decision maker and the existence of liquidation rights, whether a decision maker's fee is considered a variable interest, and whether a limited partnership is a VIE. The goal is to require consolidation of all entities within a company's control. However, in practice financial relationships between entities are complex, and new structures appear regularly. Development of effective standards covering all relationships between a company and its affiliated entity is therefore very difficult.

Consolidation procedures for variable interest entities parallel those for controlling equity investments: the fair values of the VIE's assets and liabilities are consolidated with those of the primary beneficiary. If the primary beneficiary and the VIE are already under common control, however, the assets and liabilities of the VIE remain at book value. Because the primary beneficiary generally owns none of the VIE's equity, the difference between VIE assets and liabilities is reported as "noncontrolling interest" in the equity section of the primary beneficiary's consolidated balance sheet.

BUSINESS APPLICATION   GM's Variable Interest Entities

Footnote 12 of **General Motors**' 2013 annual report discusses its consolidated VIEs. Most are related to GM's financing unit, GM Financial.

> GM Financial uses special purpose entities (SPEs) that are considered VIEs to issue variable funding notes to third party bank-sponsored warehouse facilities or asset-backed securities to investors in securitization transactions. The debt issued by these VIEs is backed by the cash flows related to finance receivables and leasing related assets transferred by GM Financial to the VIEs (Securitized Assets). GM Financial holds variable interests in the VIEs that could potentially be significant to the VIEs. GM Financial determined that it is the primary beneficiary of the SPEs because (1) the servicing responsibilities for the Securitized Assets give it the power to direct the activities that most significantly impact the performance of the VIEs and (2) the variable interests in the VIEs give it the obligation to absorb losses and the right to receive residual returns that could potentially be significant.

GM Financial transfers receivables and lease-related assets to these VIEs. The VIEs issue debt, and use the cash collected from their transferred assets to pay the debt principal and interest. GM Financial consolidates these VIEs because it controls them.

Why do you think GM Financial creates these separate entities, rather than issuing debt directly? A clue comes from additional disclosure in Footnote 12.

> Investors in the notes issued by the VIEs do not have recourse to GM Financial or its other assets, with the exception of customary representation and warranty repurchase provisions and indemnities that GM Financial provides as the servicer. GM Financial is not required and does not currently intend to provide additional financial support to these SPEs. While these subsidiaries are included in our consolidated financial statements, these subsidiaries are separate legal entities and their assets are legally owned by them and are not available to GM Financial's creditors.

By creating separate VIEs to issue and repay debt, GM Financial limits its legal liability for the debt.
Source: General Motors Company 2013 annual report.

REVIEW 1 • Identifying Consolidated Entities

Assume that **General Motors** has the following relationships with other entities:

Entity	VIE	Relationship
A	No	Owns 45% of the voting stock
B	No	Owns 60% of the voting stock
C	No	Owns 60% of the nonvoting preferred stock
D	No	Owns 100% of the voting stock
E	Yes	Shares decision-making power, voting rights and board representation equally with another entity.
F	Yes	Has a small equity investment, but most funding is provided by GM-guaranteed debt. GM dictates the entity's strategies and manages its day-to-day activities.
G	Yes	Owns the entity's bonds (most of its financing) and receives fixed payments therefrom. An outside equity holder makes all operating and governance decisions.

Required: Which of the above entities are likely to be consolidated in GM's financial statements?

Solutions are located after the chapter assignments.

CONSOLIDATION AT DATE OF ACQUISITION

LO4 Prepare consolidated balance sheets at the date of acquisition.

Once it is decided that separate legal entities should present consolidated financial statements, the challenge is to implement consolidation procedures. When the business combination takes the form of a merger or consolidation, as in Chapter 2, the acquired company ceases to exist and the acquiring company records the assets and liabilities acquired on its books. However, when the two companies remain as separate legal entities they retain their separate financial records. The acquiring company reports its investment as one line on its balance sheet, and does not report the individual assets and liabilities acquired. The acquired company makes *no entry at all*—the ownership of its outstanding shares has changed hands, but the cash, other assets paid, or stock issued by the acquiring company goes to the acquired company's *shareholders*, not to the acquired company itself. The only effect on the financial records of the acquired company is that any dividends paid will now go to the parent, rather than to the previous shareholders.

Consolidation of Financial Statements: Preliminary Issues

Some important issues must be resolved before considering procedures used to consolidate the financial statements of the separate companies.

Different Currencies   Suppose a U.S. parent consolidates a subsidiary whose records are maintained in another currency, such as the euro. This issue is common in our increasingly global economy. The accountant first converts the financial records of the subsidiary into U.S. dollars before consolidation. The conversion process addresses the effects of changes in the foreign currency exchange rate over time, and how and where to report these effects, a topic covered in Chapter 7.

Different Accounting Principles   Suppose the financial records of the parent and the subsidiary follow different accounting standards. This often happens when the subsidiary is domiciled in another country. Although global standards are rapidly converging, many countries still require subsidiaries to follow country-specific accounting methods.

In many cases, the foreign subsidiary of a U.S. parent maintains its records using U.S. GAAP. If it does not, one must make adjustments during the consolidation process to convert the subsidiary's records to U.S. GAAP. For a variation on this theme, note that **HSBC Bank USA** is a subsidiary of **HSBC Holdings PLC**, a UK company headquartered in London. HSBC Holdings uses IFRS to present its financial information. Although it is a U.S. operation, when consolidated with its parent, HSBC Bank USA's financial information is reported following IFRS.

BUSINESS APPLICATION   **GM's Non-U.S. Subsidiaries**

General Motors consolidates hundreds of subsidiaries in its 2013 financial statements. Many of these subsidiaries are located in other countries, including:

- Adam Opel GmbH (Rüsselsheim, Germany)
- GM Holden Ltd. (Port Melbourne, Victoria, Australia)
- GM Korea (Bupyeong-gu, Incheon, South Korea)
- General Motors do Brasil (São Caetano do Sul, Brazil)

The financial records of these subsidiaries must be consolidated with those of General Motors itself to fairly present GM's financial statements. Consolidation procedures require adjusting the local numbers to U.S. GAAP and converting the financial records of these organizations to U.S. dollars.   *Source:* General Motors 10-K Filing, 2013.

Different Accounting Years   When the parent and subsidiary have different accounting year-ends, the subsidiary will typically adjust its year-end to conform with that of the parent. However, *ASC para. 810-10-45-12* allows consolidation of financial records with differing year-ends of up to three months.

When the fiscal year-ends of the parent and subsidiary differ, the consolidated financial statements should disclose material subsequent events that occurred. For example, if the parent's year-end is December 31, but the subsidiary's year-end is October 31, footnote disclosures should explain any material events affecting the subsidiary between October 31 and December 31.

Objectives of Consolidation

Consolidated statements stress *substance* over *form*. The fact that corporations remain as separate legal entities does not detract from the fact that they are under common control. Thus, these legally-separate affiliates constitute a single reporting entity.

The overriding objective in the preparation of consolidated statements is to report the affairs of a group of affiliated corporations *as a single economic entity*. Consolidation procedures are designed to *remove the effects of reported transactions and relationships between components of the reporting entity*. In this way, the financial statements for the consolidated entity are guided by the same accounting principles that guide any financial statement—namely, that information (revenues, expenses, gains, assets, liabilities, and so on) *reflects transactions with outside parties*. Just as a company's financial statements do not report transfers between different departments within the company, or obligations between segments of the company, consolidated financial statements do not report transactions or relationships between the parent and its subsidiaries.

Recall the procedures described in Chapter 2 to record an acquisition structured as a merger or consolidation. The acquired assets and liabilities are identified, valued at fair value, recorded directly on the books of the acquirer, and the acquired company ceases to exist as a separate entity. When the acquired company remains as a separate legal entity, and continues to maintain its separate financial records, we must combine the records of the separate entities to create consolidated financial statements. At the date of acquisition, the final product after consolidation shows consolidated financial statements *as if the acquiring company had treated the acquisition as a merger*. The consolidation process takes the assets and liabilities of the acquired company, revalues them to fair value, combines them with the assets and liabilities of the parent, and removes any intercompany transactions or account balances. This process must be performed *each time* financial statements are prepared.

Consolidation Working Paper

In this section we explain procedures used to consolidate the separate balance sheets of the parent and the subsidiary at the date of acquisition. As you work through this section, keep in mind that the goal of the consolidation process is to develop consolidated financial statements that are identical to how the parent's financial statements would appear if the parent reported the subsidiary's acquired assets and liabilities directly on its own books, as in Chapter 2.

Three acquisitions are used to illustrate the consolidation process. In the first acquisition, only assets and liabilities reported on the subsidiary's books are required to be revalued. In the second acquisition, revaluations include previously unreported intangibles and goodwill. In the third acquisition, the fair value of the subsidiary's identifiable net assets exceeds acquisition cost—a bargain purchase.

Consolidation Illustration: Revaluation of Previously Reported Net Assets   Assume that **General Motors** pays $35,000,000 in cash for all of the stock of Automagic Parts, Inc., on January 1, 2016. Exhibit 3.2 shows the balance sheets of the two companies just prior to the acquisition and the fair values of Automagic's assets and liabilities. Note that the actual balance sheet account balances are presented in trial balance format, where the debits minus the credits equal zero.

EXHIBIT 3.2   Balance Sheets of GM and Automagic, January 1, 2016, Immediately Prior to Acquisition

	General Motors	Automagic Parts	
	Book value Dr (Cr)	Book value Dr (Cr)	Fair value Dr (Cr)
Current assets	$100,000,000	$ 2,000,000	$ 1,800,000
Plant and equipment, net.	400,000,000	50,000,000	80,000,000
Patents and copyrights	10,000,000	1,000,000	3,200,000
Current liabilities.	(120,000,000)	(10,000,000)	(10,000,000)
Long-term debt	(300,000,000)	(38,000,000)	(40,000,000)
Common stock, $1 par.	(10,000,000)	(500,000)	
Additional paid-in capital	(60,000,000)	(2,000,000)	
Retained earnings	(20,000,000)	(2,500,000)	
Total	$ 0	$ 0	

Because this is a stock acquisition, GM makes the following entry on its own books:

Investment in Automagic Parts	35,000,000	
Cash		35,000,000
To record investment in the stock of Automagic Parts.		

Automagic's balance sheet remains *exactly the same as before*, showing its assets and liabilities at book value, and including its stockholders' equity. Consolidation of the two balance sheets requires preparation of financial statements for a new reporting entity—the parent and subsidiary together. No financial records (books) exist for this consolidated entity; we have only separate books for the parent and subsidiary. To create financial records for the new reporting entity, we prepare a **consolidation working paper**. This working paper has the following elements:

- Accounts of the parent company, taken from the parent's books
- Accounts of the subsidiary company, taken from the subsidiary's books
- Eliminating entries necessary to consolidate the accounts of the parent and subsidiary

Exhibit 3.3 displays the general working paper format used to consolidate the balance sheets of GM and Automagic. GM's books now reflect the acquisition entry above. The goal is to show the consolidated balance sheet as if GM had reported the assets and liabilities of Automagic directly on its own books, valued at fair value, and Automagic had ceased to exist. Given that we are starting with the separate balance sheets of the two companies, the following adjustments must be made to those numbers:

- Eliminate the investment account on GM's books.
- Eliminate the stockholders' equity accounts on Automagic's books.
- Revalue Automagic's assets and liabilities from book value to fair value.

The following working paper **eliminating entries** achieve these goals:

(E) Eliminate Automagic's Stockholders' Equity accounts against the investment account.

(R) Eliminate the remainder of the investment account, representing the difference between acquisition cost and Automagic's book value, and Revalue Automagic's assets and liabilities from book value to fair value at the acquisition date.

GM pays $35,000,000 for Automagic, but Automagic's net assets are reported on its own books at $5,000,000 (= $500,000 + $2,000,000 + $2,500,000). Therefore GM pays $30,000,000 more than Automagic's book value. The following schedule is helpful in completing the eliminating entries.

Acquisition cost		$35,000,000
Book value of Automagic..		(5,000,000)
Cost in excess of Automagic's book value		30,000,000
Differences between fair value and book value:		
Current assets	$ (200,000)	
Plant and equipment, net..	30,000,000	
Patents and copyrights..	2,200,000	
Long-term debt..	(2,000,000)	(30,000,000)
Goodwill		$ 0

GM pays $30,000,000 more than book value because the fair values of Automagic's current assets, plant and equipment, patents and copyrights and long-term debt differ from their book values. No goodwill arises in this illustration, because the differences between book and fair value for previously recorded assets and liabilities completely explain the $30,000,000 difference between the GM's cost and Automagic's book value.

The eliminating entries necessary to make these adjustments appear below, in journal entry form. Remember that the eliminations are labeled (E) and (R) to help you remember the purpose of each entry:

(E) **E**quity—eliminate the subsidiary's acquisition date equity balances.

(R) **R**evalue—recognize acquisition date fair value revaluations.

(E)	Common stock, $1 par.	500,000	
	Additional paid-in capital	2,000,000	
	Retained earnings	2,500,000	
	Investment in Automagic Parts		5,000,000
	To eliminate Automagic's equity accounts against the		
	book value portion of the investment account.		

(R)	Plant and equipment, net.	30,000,000	
	Patents and copyrights	2,200,000	
	Current assets		200,000
	Long-term debt		2,000,000
	Investment in Automagic Parts		30,000,000
	To eliminate the excess paid over book value from the investment		
	account and revalue Automagic's assets and liabilities to fair value.		

The eliminating entries are shown in the "Eliminations" columns of the working paper, and the consolidated balance sheet appears in the last column. *The elimination debits always equal the elimination credits*. Eliminations made on the working paper are *not* reported in the actual accounts of GM or Automagic. They appear *only on the working paper*.

EXHIBIT 3.3   Consolidation Working Paper for GM and Automagic, January 1, 2016

	Accounts Taken From Books		Eliminations		Consolidated Balances
	GM Dr (Cr)	Automagic Dr (Cr)	Dr	Cr	Dr (Cr)
Current assets	$ 65,000,000	$ 2,000,000		$ 200,000 (R)	$ 66,800,000
Plant and equipment, net.	400,000,000	50,000,000	(R)$30,000,000		480,000,000
Patents and copyrights	10,000,000	1,000,000	(R) 2,200,000		13,200,000
Investment in Automagic	35,000,000			5,000,000 (E)	—
				30,000,000 (R)	
Current liabilities.	(120,000,000)	(10,000,000)			(130,000,000)
Long-term debt	(300,000,000)	(38,000,000)		2,000,000 (R)	(340,000,000)
Common stock, $1 par.	(10,000,000)	(500,000)	(E) 500,000		(10,000,000)
Additional paid-in capital	(60,000,000)	(2,000,000)	(E) 2,000,000		(60,000,000)
Retained earnings	(20,000,000)	(2,500,000)	(E) 2,500,000		(20,000,000)
Total	$ 0	$ 0	$37,200,000	$37,200,000	$ 0

Consolidation Illustration: Goodwill and Previously Unreported Intangibles   Unlike the illustration above, acquisition cost typically exceeds the fair values of identifiable net assets acquired, and new assets and/or liabilities not previously reported on the acquired company's balance sheet are recognized in consolidation. To illustrate these concepts, in Exhibit 3.4 we reproduce data for the acquisition of DataFile by IBM on July 1, 2015, described in Chapter 2, Exhibit 2.4.

EXHIBIT 3.4   Consolidation Illustration with Identifiable Intangibles and Goodwill

IBM Corporation acquires all of the voting stock of DataFile Inc. on July 1, 2015, for $25,000,000 in cash. Fair values of DataFile's reported assets and liabilities are as follows:

Account	Fair value
Current assets	$ 2,000,000
Plant and equipment, net	60,000,000
Patents and copyrights	5,000,000
Current liabilities	10,000,000
Long-term debt	40,000,000

In addition, IBM identified and valued DataFile's previously unreported intangible assets as follows:

Brand names	$ 1,000,000
Favorable lease agreements	600,000
Assembled workforce	5,000,000
In-process contracts with potential customers	2,000,000
Contractual customer relationships	3,000,000

To consolidate the balance sheets of IBM and DataFile, we need their separate account balances. The balance sheet accounts of IBM and DataFile *immediately prior to* the acquisition are shown in Exhibit 3.5.

EXHIBIT 3.5   Balance Sheets of IBM and DataFile, July 1, 2015, Immediately Prior to Acquisition

	IBM Dr (Cr)	DataFile Dr (Cr)
Current assets	$ 40,000,000	$ 2,300,000
Plant and equipment, net	150,000,000	50,000,000
Patents and copyrights	3,000,000	1,000,000
Current liabilities	(15,000,000)	(10,000,000)
Long-term debt	(100,000,000)	(38,000,000)
Common stock, $0.50 par	(2,000,000)	(500,000)
Additional paid-in capital	(59,000,000)	(1,700,000)
Retained earnings	(16,000,000)	(2,800,000)
Accumulated other comprehensive income	(1,000,000)	(300,000)
Total	$ 0	$ 0

IBM records the stock acquisition as follows on its own books:

Investment in DataFile	25,000,000	
Cash		25,000,000
To record the purchase of all of DataFile's stock.		

The consolidation working paper for this acquisition appears in Exhibit 3.6. IBM's balance sheet reflects the above acquisition entry.

Although IBM pays $25,000,000 for DataFile, DataFile's net assets are reported on its own books at $5,300,000. Therefore IBM pays $19,700,000 more than DataFile's book value, explained as follows:

Acquisition cost		$25,000,000
Book value of DataFile		(5,300,000)
Cost in excess of DataFile's book value		19,700,000
Differences between fair value and book value:		
Current assets	$ (300,000)	
Plant and equipment, net	10,000,000	
Patents and copyrights.	4,000,000	
Brand names	1,000,000	
Favorable lease agreements.	600,000	
Contractual customer relationships	3,000,000	
Long-term debt.	(2,000,000)	(16,300,000)
Goodwill.		$ 3,400,000

Recall from Chapter 2 that the assembled workforce and in-process contracts listed in Exhibit 3.4 do not meet *ASC Topic 805*'s criteria for separate capitalization, and are therefore included in goodwill. The schedule above calculates the difference between the acquisition cost and the book value of Data-File—the sum of DataFile's equity accounts—and identifies why the acquisition price differs from DataFile's book value. The schedule tells the following story:

- IBM paid $19,700,000 more than the book value of DataFile's net assets.

- A comparison of book value to fair value for each of DataFile's identifiable assets and liabilities reveals that the fair value of DataFile's identifiable net assets exceeds book value by a total of $16,300,000.

- Since IBM's cost is $3,400,000 higher than the fair value of DataFile's identifiable net assets, this amount is reported as goodwill.

Working paper eliminations accomplish the tasks necessary to combine the two balance sheets:

(E) Eliminate Investment in DataFile, shown on IBM's books, against DataFile's stockholders' equity accounts.

(R) Revalue DataFile's assets and liabilities from book value to fair value. In this case, in addition to revaluing assets and liabilities currently on DataFile's balance sheet, new identifiable intangible assets and goodwill are created. These assets are reported at zero on DataFile's books.

The eliminating entries necessary to make these adjustments appear below, in journal entry form.

(E)	Common stock, $0.50 par	500,000	
	Additional paid-in capital	1,700,000	
	Retained earnings	2,800,000	
	Accumulated other comprehensive income.	300,000	
	Investment in DataFile.		5,300,000
	To eliminate DataFile's equity accounts against the book value portion of		
	the investment account.		

(R)	Plant and equipment, net.	10,000,000	
	Patents and copyrights	4,000,000	
	Brand names	1,000,000	
	Favorable lease agreements	600,000	
	Contractual customer relationships	3,000,000	
	Goodwill.	3,400,000	
	Current assets.		300,000
	Long-term debt		2,000,000
	Investment in DataFile.		19,700,000
	To eliminate the excess paid over book value from the investment account		
	and revalue DataFile's assets and liabilities to fair value.		

The eliminating entries are shown in the "Eliminations" columns of the working paper, Exhibit 3.6.

EXHIBIT 3.6   Consolidation Working Paper, July 1, 2015

	IBM Dr (Cr)	DataFile Dr (Cr)	Eliminations Dr	Eliminations Cr	Consolidated Balances Dr (Cr)
Current assets	$ 15,000,000	$ 2,300,000		$ 300,000 (R)	$ 17,000,000
Plant and equipment, net.	150,000,000	50,000,000	(R)$10,000,000		210,000,000
Patents and copyrights	3,000,000	1,000,000	(R) 4,000,000		8,000,000
Investment in DataFile	25,000,000	—		5,300,000 (E)	—
				19,700,000 (R)	
Brand names	—	—	(R) 1,000,000		1,000,000
Favorable lease agreements	—	—	(R) 600,000		600,000
Contractual customer relationships	—	—	(R) 3,000,000		3,000,000
Goodwill	—	—	(R) 3,400,000		3,400,000
Current liabilities.	(15,000,000)	(10,000,000)			(25,000,000)
Long-term debt	(100,000,000)	(38,000,000)		2,000,000 (R)	(140,000,000)
Common stock, $0.50 par	(2,000,000)	(500,000)	(E) 500,000		(2,000,000)
Additional paid-in capital	(59,000,000)	(1,700,000)	(E) 1,700,000		(59,000,000)
Retained earnings	(16,000,000)	(2,800,000)	(E) 2,800,000		(16,000,000)
Accumulated other comprehensive income.	(1,000,000)	(300,000)	(E) 300,000		(1,000,000)
Total	$ 0	$ 0	$27,300,000	$27,300,000	$ 0

The balances in the last column of Exhibit 3.6 display the consolidated balance sheet accounts at the date of acquisition. If IBM had reported the acquisition as a **merger**, the entry that IBM made on its own books is repeated from Chapter 2 below:

Current assets	2,000,000	
Plant and equipment, net.	60,000,000	
Patents and copyrights	5,000,000	
Brand names	1,000,000	
Favorable lease agreements	600,000	
Contractual customer relationships	3,000,000	
Goodwill	3,400,000	
Current liabilities		10,000,000
Long-term debt		40,000,000
Cash		25,000,000

To record the acquisition of DataFile Inc. as a merger.

If we combine this entry with IBM's balance sheet accounts immediately prior to the acquisition, shown in Exhibit 3.5, we see that IBM's balance sheet is *identical to* the consolidated balance sheet shown in the last column of the working paper in Exhibit 3.6.

Consolidation Illustration: Bargain Purchase

In a bargain purchase, the fair values of the identifiable net assets of the acquired company, including previously unrecorded intangibles, sum to more than the acquisition price. The parent reports the difference on its own books as a gain on acquisition, and reports no goodwill in consolidation. Repeat the illustration for IBM and DataFile, discussed above, but assume IBM pays only $20,000,000 in cash for all of the stock of DataFile. IBM makes the following entry to record the acquisition:

Investment in DataFile	21,600,000	
Cash		20,000,000
Gain on acquisition		1,600,000

To record the purchase of all of DataFile's stock; $21,600,000 = $5,300,000 book value + $16,300,000 revaluation of identifiable net assets.

The consolidation working paper is shown in Exhibit 3.7. Because we are consolidating *balance sheet accounts*, the $1,600,000 gain on acquisition enters IBM's retained earnings directly; $17,600,000 = $16,000,000 + $1,600,000.

EXHIBIT 3.7 Consolidation Working Paper, July 1, 2015, Bargain Purchase

| | Accounts Taken From Books | | Eliminations | | Consolidated Balances |
	IBM Dr (Cr)	DataFile Dr (Cr)	Dr	Cr	Dr (Cr)
Current assets	$ 20,000,000	$ 2,300,000		$ 300,000 (R)	$ 22,000,000
Plant and equipment, net	150,000,000	50,000,000	(R)$10,000,000		210,000,000
Patents and copyrights	3,000,000	1,000,000	(R) 4,000,000		8,000,000
Investment in DataFile	21,600,000	—		5,300,000 (E)	—
				16,300,000 (R)	
Brand names	—	—	(R) 1,000,000		1,000,000
Favorable lease agreements	—	—	(R) 600,000		600,000
Contractual customer relationships	—	—	(R) 3,000,000		3,000,000
Current liabilities	(15,000,000)	(10,000,000)			(25,000,000)
Long-term debt	(100,000,000)	(38,000,000)		2,000,000 (R)	(140,000,000)
Common stock, $0.50 par	(2,000,000)	(500,000)	(E) 500,000		(2,000,000)
Additional paid-in capital	(59,000,000)	(1,700,000)	(E) 1,700,000		(59,000,000)
Retained earnings	(17,600,000)	(2,800,000)	(E) 2,800,000		(17,600,000)
Accumulated other comprehensive income.	(1,000,000)	(300,000)	(E) 300,000		(1,000,000)
Total	$ 0	$ 0	$23,900,000	$23,900,000	$ 0

BUSINESS APPLICATION   International Subsidiaries, Taxes, and Disclosure

U.S. corporations often set up subsidiaries in other countries to take advantage of lower tax rates in these countries. For example, as of 2014, Ireland does not tax profits of subsidiaries incorporated in Ireland but which have no tax residency anywhere in the world. In 2013, **Apple Inc.** owned three Irish subsidiaries with no tax residency, and the effective tax rate for its other two Irish subsidiaries was less than 2 percent. The U.S. does not require companies to pay U.S. taxes on profits of foreign subsidiaries, if these profits are not repatriated to the U.S. By routing much of its international business through its Irish subsidiaries, Apple lowers its tax obligation.

It is difficult if not impossible for the average investor to determine the extent of a U.S. company's operations reported through its international subsidiaries. The financial performance of a consolidated subsidiary is not separately observable in an annual report, because the subsidiary's accounts are included with those of the parent. The SEC requires a listed company to disclose the names of its consolidated subsidiaries. However, names of subsidiaries may be omitted if, in the aggregate, they are not "significant." According to a May 2013 *Wall Street Journal* article, some companies have become less forthcoming about disclosing the names of their international subsidiaries. For example, in 2010 **Oracle Corporation** named over 400 subsidiaries. In 2012, the list included only eight subsidiaries. **Google Inc.** named more than 100 subsidiaries in 2009, but only two in 2012. One might wonder if the reduction in disclosure of offshore subsidiaries operating in low-tax countries is related to the public's increasing criticism of this practice.   *Source:* Jessica Holzer, "From Google to FedEx: The Incredible Vanishing Subsidiary," *Wall Street Journal*, May 22, 2013.

Special Issues: Depreciable Assets and Previously Reported Goodwill   In the previous illustrations, depreciable assets are shown net of accumulated depreciation. The books of the parent and subsidiary usually show depreciable assets in two accounts: original cost and accumulated depreciation. Also, if the subsidiary has previously acquired another company, it may report goodwill on its separate balance sheet. How do these items affect consolidation procedures?

When a company buys a **depreciable asset** from another company, the acquiring company reports the asset at fair value, which is the acquiring company's original cost. For example, assume Powerdown Inc., a manufacturer of auto parts, has equipment on its books at an original cost of $100,000 and accumulated depreciation of $40,000. It sells the equipment to General Motors for $50,000. General Motors reports the equipment at original cost of $50,000, and begins depreciating the equipment at the date it is acquired. The original cost and accumulated depreciation reported on Powerdown's books are irrelevant to General Motors. Similarly, when General Motors acquires Powerdown, Inc., it reports acquired equipment at fair value, which is original cost to the consolidated entity. The original cost and accumulated depreciation amounts reported on Powerdown's separate books are not reported on the consolidated balance sheet.

When consolidating a **subsidiary reporting goodwill** on its separate books, the previously reported goodwill is assigned a fair value of zero. The consolidation process assigns fair values to the subsidiary's identifiable assets and liabilities. The difference between acquisition cost and the fair value of net identifiable assets acquired is reported as goodwill on the consolidated balance sheet. Goodwill arising from a previous combination between the subsidiary and another company is *not* an identifiable asset and is not separately reported. For example, assume General Motors acquires Powerdown, Inc. for $40 million, and includes Powerdown on its consolidated balance sheet. Powerdown's separate balance sheet, in trial balance format, is as follows:

Powerdown, Inc., Balance Sheet	Book Value Dr (Cr)	Fair Value Dr (Cr)
Various identifiable assets	$50,000,000	$80,000,000
Goodwill	10,000,000	9,000,000
Liabilities	(55,000,000)	(55,000,000)
Stockholders' equity	(5,000,000)	
Total	$ 0	

The calculation of goodwill on the acquisition is as follows:

Acquisition cost		$40,000,000
Book value of Powerdown		(5,000,000)
Cost in excess of book value		35,000,000
Differences between fair value and book value:		
Various identifiable assets	$30,000,000	
Previously recorded goodwill	(10,000,000)	20,000,000
Goodwill		$15,000,000

The eliminating entries at the date of acquisition appear below, in journal entry form.

(E)	Stockholders' equity	5,000,000	
	Investment in Powerdown		5,000,000
	To eliminate Powerdown's equity accounts against the book value portion of the investment account.		

(R)	Various identifiable assets	30,000,000	
	Goodwill (new)	15,000,000	
	Goodwill (old)		10,000,000
	Investment in Powerdown		35,000,000
	To eliminate the excess paid over book value from the investment account and revalue Powerdown's net assets to fair value.		

REVIEW 2 • Consolidation with Identifiable Intangibles

Look at review problem #1 in Chapter 2, where **IBM** acquires SoftCloud Technologies for $1.2 billion in cash. Assume IBM acquires all of SoftCloud's stock in a stock investment. Information on book values for both companies and fair values of SoftCloud's assets and liabilities is below.

Balance Sheets of IBM and SoftCloud, Immediately *After* the Acquisition

(in millions)	IBM Book value Dr (Cr)	SoftCloud Book value Dr (Cr)	SoftCloud Fair value Dr (Cr)
Cash and receivables.	$ 800	$ 400	$ 400
Inventories	6,000	850	800
Property, plant and equipment, net	25,000	2,900	3,500
Investment in SoftCloud.	1,200	—	—
Accounts payable.	(7,000)	(300)	(300)
Long-term debt	(22,000)	(3,500)	(3,850)
Common stock, par value	(100)	(10)	
Additional paid-in capital	(2,500)	(200)	
Retained earnings	(1,300)	(260)	
Treasury stock	—	50	
Accumulated other comprehensive income.	(100)	70	
Total	$ 0	$ 0	

In addition, the following items are not currently reported on SoftCloud's balance sheet:

(in millions)	Fair value
Favorable lease agreements	$150
Skilled work force.	15
Favorable press reviews on products	5

Required: Prepare the consolidation working paper necessary to consolidate IBM and SoftCloud at the date of acquisition.

Solutions are located after the chapter assignments.

INTERNATIONAL FINANCIAL REPORTING STANDARDS FOR CONSOLIDATIONS

LO5 Explain IFRS for consolidations.

IFRS procedures to report acquisition cost and value and combine the assets and liabilities of the acquired company with that of the acquirer appear in *IFRS 3(R)*, Business Combinations, and are similar to U.S. GAAP. IFRS for determining *when* an entity should be consolidated is governed by *IFRS 10*, Consolidated Financial Statements. *IFRS 12*, Disclosures of Involvement with Other Entities, specifies required disclosures of interests in other entities, such as subsidiaries and unconsolidated structured entities.

The Concept of Control

Like U.S. GAAP, IFRS strives to require consolidation of all controlled entities. Unlike U.S. GAAP, IFRS has only one set of criteria for deciding when control exists. Recall that U.S. GAAP has two sets of standards, one for investments in voting stock and another for non-equity relationships with other entities.

IFRS 10's focus is on a principles-based definition of control, applicable to all organizations regardless of financial or governance structure. The investor must possess all three of the following elements to conclude that it controls and therefore must consolidate the investee:

- power over the investee;
- exposure or rights to the investee's variable returns;
- ability to use power over the investee to influence the amount of returns to the investor.

"Power" is defined as the ability to direct the activities that significantly affect the investee's returns, and may be the result of equity voting rights, rights to appoint or remove key personnel, the ability to dominate nomination of members to the investee's governing body, or other contractual relationships. Decision-making power may exist with less than a majority ownership of voting rights. For example, an investor may hold a large minority of the voting rights, with the remaining rights spread among many small investors. Alternatively, a minority investor may have the potential to obtain majority ownership at any time, through convertible debt securities or call options.

"Exposure or rights to variable returns" includes economic exposure to both positive and negative returns. Examples include changes in the value of the investment, dividends or interest, service or management fees, and tax benefits. "Ability to use power to affect returns" requires that the controlling investor not only have the power to influence the investee's activities and exposure to the investee's returns, but also can use its power to affect those returns. An investor who directs the investee's major activities is likely to be the controlling investor, even though the investor has a small equity ownership.

IFRS 10 is viewed as an improvement over previous IFRS because it provides a consistent standard for consolidation of all types of entities that is based on the principle of control rather than using legalistic "bright lines" that can be circumvented. Control is based on the ability to direct significant activities of the investee, rather than just contractual exposure to the investee's risks and rewards. Assessment is qualitative, not quantitative, and involves considerable judgment. *IFRS 10* also offers specific guidance for determining whether control exists with less-than-majority equity ownership.

IFRS and U.S. GAAP Compared

IFRS brings consolidation standards for variable interest entities closer to U.S. GAAP, as both standards use the same concepts of decision-making power and exposure to returns to determine whether an investor consolidates an entity—in U.S. GAAP, identification of the primary beneficiary. However, while IFRS applies these concepts to all entities, U.S. GAAP requires evaluation of each entity to determine if it meets the requirements of a variable interest entity—an entity whose equity interests are limited

---

BUSINESS APPLICATION Consolidation Policy Under IFRS

The financial statements and footnote disclosures of IFRS companies are often more detailed than those of U.S. companies. For example, many IFRS companies routinely list the names and ownership interests of their consolidated companies. An example is **Orange SA**, the major telecommunications provider in France. In its 2013 financial statements, Orange SA lists its fully consolidated companies. Orange SA owns 50 percent or less of many of these subsidiaries. Examples include:

- Côte d'Ivoire Telecom, Ivory Coast, 45.9% owned
- Orange Bissau, Guinea, 38.10% owned
- Sonatel and Subsidiaries, Senegal, 42.33% owned
- Orange Guinee, Guinea, 37.83% owned
- Orange Mali, 29.65% owned

Orange SA's footnote disclosures explain some of the reasons for consolidation. Sonatel is consolidated because "Orange SA controls Sonatel and its subsidiaries . . . under the terms of the shareholders' agreement . . . " Orange SA owns 90% of FCR Côte d'Ivoire, which owns 51% of Côte d'Ivoire Telecom. Therefore Orange SA owns 45.9% (= 90% × 51%) of Côte d'Ivoire Telecom, as reported above.   *Source:* Orange SA annual report, 2013.

or insufficient. If the entity is a VIE, one searches for the primary beneficiary, applying the concepts of power and the obligation to absorb returns significant to the VIE.

For investments involving ownership of equity voting rights, in theory U.S. GAAP follows the concept of control, but in practice typically only majority-owned equity investments are consolidated. *IFRS 10* specifically identifies situations where control exists, and consolidation occurs, with less-than-majority ownership.

As discussed earlier in this chapter, rather than adopting the IFRS's principles-based approach, the FASB continues to struggle to develop rules covering specific details of the relationship between a company and its affiliated entity. Examples include partnerships, development stage entities, and investment funds. Generally the IFRS consolidation model is intended to apply to all entities, although *IFRS 10* does exempt certain investment companies from consolidating their subsidiaries if strict conditions are met. The FASB has retained the two separate consolidation models, and convergence with IFRS is unlikely.

REVIEW OF KEY CONCEPTS ••••••••••••••••••••••••••••••••••••••

Explain the purpose and motivation behind consolidation. (p. 80) When a business combination takes place as a stock acquisition, the acquired company remains as a separate legal entity. A **parent/subsidiary** relationship is established between these affiliated corporations. For reporting purposes, **consolidated statements** are prepared so that the financial affairs of two or more affiliated corporations will be reported as if they are a single unified economic entity. Consolidation is appropriate when **control over the subsidiary** exists. Consolidation causes attributes of the subsidiary to affect the financial statements of the parent. Companies are motivated to avoid consolidating **highly leveraged** subsidiaries.   **LO 1**

Apply the concept of control to equity investments. (p. 82) For equity investments, current practice defines control as **majority ownership of voting shares**. All majority-owned subsidiaries are consolidated, unless control does not reside with the majority stockholder.   **LO 2**

Apply the concept of control to non-equity investments. (p. 83) A company may have a relationship with a **variable interest entity** and own little or none of its equity. Even without equity ownership in this entity, if the company is the **primary beneficiary** of that entity, it must consolidate it.   **LO 3**

Prepare consolidated balance sheets at the date of acquisition. (p. 88) Preparation of consolidated financial statements brings together the affiliated companies' separate statements for reporting purposes. The books of the individual affiliates are not affected by the consolidation process. **Eliminating entries** that remove the various intercompany financial relationships are made on a **consolidation working paper** designed to facilitate the consolidation process. Eliminations remove the acquirer's investment account and the acquiree's equity accounts, and revalue the acquiree's assets and liabilities to fair value. Consolidated statements incorporating wholly-owned subsidiaries **are the same as if the subsidiaries had been merged** and their assets and liabilities recorded by the acquiring company as explained in Chapter 2. In parent/subsidiary relationships, combining the asset and liability balances and revaluing the subsidiary's assets and liabilities occurs on the working paper instead of on the books.   **LO 4**

Explain IFRS for consolidations. (p. 97) Under IFRS, consolidation of any entities relies on the concept of **control**. IFRS is more principles oriented, focusing on control over decision making rather than legalistically applying majority ownership or other "bright line" rules. As a result, companies following IFRS consolidate some affiliates in which they have less than majority ownership, when they have control over these entities. The decision to consolidate a special purpose entity is also based on the existence of control, while under U.S. GAAP an entity must first qualify as a VIE and then the primary beneficiary consolidates the VIE.   **LO 5**

Assignments with the ⊘ in the margin are available in ᵐʸBusinessCourse.
See the Preface of the book for details.

MULTIPLE CHOICE QUESTIONS ••••••••••••••••••••••••••••••••

1. Companies that invest in other companies often prefer using the equity method instead of consolidating their investments, because consolidating would   **LO 1** ⊘

    a. reduce their stockholders' equity.
    b. reduce their reported net income and earnings per share.
    c. reduce their assets.
    d. increase their leverage (debt to assets ratio).

✅ LO 3   **2.**   A U.S. company consolidates a VIE with which it has a contractual relationship, but no equity investment. If the company and the entity were not previously under common control, at the date the company identifies the entity as a VIE that meets the requirements for consolidation, the U.S. company's consolidated balance sheet will report a noncontrolling interest valued at

   a.   the VIE's book value.
   b.   the VIE's fair value.
   c.   zero.
   d.   the fair value of the VIE's assets.

✅ LO 3   **3.**   A U.S. company performs a quantitative analysis of the sufficiency of a newly-formed special purpose entity's equity to absorb expected losses. The SPE was formed with $11,250 in equity and $99,750 in debt, for a total fair value of $111,000. Assume the SPE's expected net cash inflows all occur at the end of one year. Expected cash flows and probabilities are:

Expected net cash flow	Probability
$156,000	0.65
46,800	0.20
31,200	0.15

The U.S. company uses a risk-adjusted discount rate of 4 percent to determine the present value of cash flows. The SPE's expected losses are

   a. $12,150
   b. $13,200
   c. $18,150
   d. $25,350

✅ LO 4   **4.**   The consolidation working paper at the date of acquisition takes the book value balances of a parent and subsidiary and

   a.   eliminates the parent's equity accounts and revalues the parent's assets and liabilities to fair value.
   b.   eliminates the subsidiary's equity accounts and revalues the subsidiary's assets and liabilities to fair value.
   c.   eliminates the parent's equity accounts and revalues the subsidiary's assets and liabilities to fair value.
   d.   eliminates the subsidiary's equity accounts and revalues the parent's assets and liabilities to fair value.

Use the following information to answer questions 5–8 below. All amounts are in thousands.

PR Company pays $10,000 in cash and issues stock with a fair value of $40,000 to acquire all of SX Corporation's stock. SX will be a subsidiary of PR. Balance sheet accounts *just prior to the acquisition* are as follows, in trial balance format:

	PR Company	SX Corporation	
	Book value Dr (Cr)	Book value Dr (Cr)	Fair value Dr (Cr)
Current assets	$ 14,000	$ 2,000	$ 4,200
Property, plant & equipment, net	110,000	10,000	6,000
Identifiable intangible assets	800	4,000	14,000
Current liabilities	(13,000)	(1,600)	(2,000)
Long-term debt	(60,000)	(12,000)	(11,600)
Capital stock	(44,400)	(5,000)	
Retained earnings	(8,000)	(8,000)	
Accumulated other comprehensive income	(200)	1,000	
Treasury stock	800	9,600	
Total	$ 0	$ 0	

PR's consultants find these items that are not reported on SX's balance sheet:

	Fair value
Potential contracts with new customers	$6,000
Advanced production technology	4,000
Future cost savings	2,000
Customer lists	1,000

Outside consultants are paid $200 in cash, and registration fees to issue PR's new stock are $400.

5. Total acquisition cost reported by PR (the debit to Investment on PR's books) is   **LO 4** ✓

   a. $50,000
   b. $50,200
   c. $50,400
   d. $50,600

6. On the consolidation working paper at the date of acquisition, elimination (E) credits the investment account   **LO 4** ✓
   by

   a. $ 2,400
   b. $ 3,400
   c. $ 5,000
   d. $13,000

7. On the consolidation working paper at the date of acquisition, elimination (R) debits identifiable intangible   **LO 4** ✓
   assets by

   a. $10,000
   b. $13,000
   c. $15,000
   d. $23,000

8. On the consolidated balance sheet at the date of acquisition, elimination (R)   **LO 4** ✓

   a. credits long-term debt by $400.
   b. debits long-term debt by $11,600.
   c. credits long-term debt by $11,600.
   d. debits long-term debt by $400.

9. ABC Corporation has a financial relationship with XYZ Company, but does not have an equity interest in   **LO 3, 5** ✓
   XYZ. Should ABC consolidate XYZ? Which statement below is *true* concerning U.S. GAAP and IFRS on
   this question?

   a. IFRS requires XYZ to be identified as a VIE, and then requires consolidation if ABC controls XYZ.
   b. There is no significant difference in the standards; both require consolidation if XYZ is a VIE and ABC
      controls XYZ.
   c. There is no significant difference in the standards; both require consolidation if ABC controls XYZ.
   d. U.S. standards require XYZ to be identified as a VIE, and then require consolidation if ABC controls
      XYZ.

10. PX Company owns 40% of the equity of SC Corporation. Which statement is *true* concerning the choice of   **LO 5** ✓
    whether PX should consolidate SC, following IFRS?

    a. PX should always consolidate SC.
    b. PX should never consolidate SC.
    c. PX should consolidate SC if the other 60% of SC's stock is held by thousands of shareholders with less
       than 1% ownership each.
    d. PX should consolidate SC if the other 60% of SC's stock is held by thousands of shareholders with less
       than 1% ownership each, decisions are made based on majority vote, and on average 85% of votes are
       cast at SC shareholders' meetings.

EXERCISES •••

LO 4   E3.1   Eliminating Entries, Acquisition at Book Value   Polaris Company acquires all of the stock of SSC, Inc. for $35 million in cash. At the date of acquisition, SSC's current assets had a book value of $25 million, its noncurrent assets had a book value of $100 million, and its liabilities had a book value of $90 million. It is determined that the book values of SSC's net assets approximate fair value at the date of acquisition. SSC's stockholders' equity consists of capital stock of $22 million, retained earnings of $15 million (credit balance), and treasury stock of $2 million.

Required

Prepare the eliminating entry or entries necessary to consolidate the balance sheet accounts of Polaris and SSC at the date of acquisition.

LO 4   E3.2   Eliminating Entries, Revaluation of Reported Net Assets   Petrel Corporation acquires all of the stock of Samson Company for $20 million in cash. Samson's balance sheet accounts at the date of acquisition are listed below. Date-of-acquisition fair values for Samson's assets and liabilities are also displayed. Samson does not have any previously unrecorded identifiable intangible assets.

(in thousands)	Book Value Dr (Cr)	Fair Value Dr (Cr)
Cash.	$ 2,000	$ 2,000
Accounts receivable.	5,000	4,900
Inventories	30,000	20,000
Land, buildings and equipment, net.	320,000	150,000
Trademarks	10,000	60,000
Current liabilities.	(45,000)	(45,000)
Noncurrent liabilities.	(250,000)	(260,000)
Common stock, $2 par.	(1,000)	
Additional paid-in capital	(80,000)	
Retained earnings	5,500	
Accumulated other comprehensive income.	(500)	
Treasury stock	4,000	
Total	$ 0	

Required

a.   Prepare a schedule calculating the goodwill to be recognized for this acquisition.
b.   Prepare the eliminating entries to consolidate the balance sheets of Petrel and Samson at the date of acquisition.

LO 4   E3.3   Eliminating Entries, Bargain Gain   Phelps, Inc. acquires all of the stock of Skelton Company for $8 million in cash. At the date of acquisition, Skelton's current assets had a book value of $5 million and a fair value of $3 million, its noncurrent assets had a book value of $45 million and a fair value of $20 million, and its liabilities had a book value of $30 million, which approximated fair value. Skelton also has previously unreported identifiable intangibles, valued at $17 million, that meet *ASC Topic 805*'s criteria for recognition. Skelton's stockholders' equity consists of capital stock of $25 million and a retained loss of $5 million (debit balance).

Required

a.   Calculate the gain on acquisition and prepare Phelps' journal entry to record the acquisition on its own books.
b.   Prepare the eliminating entries necessary to consolidate the balance sheet accounts of Phelps and Skelton at the date of acquisition.

LO 4   E3.4   Eliminating Entries with Previously Unreported Intangibles   ProLock acquired all of the stock of Senyo for $10,000,000. At the date of acquisition, Senyo's $6,000,000 of reported net assets were fairly stated, except land was undervalued by $500,000 and unrecorded in-process R&D was valued at $1,000,000.

Required

Prepare the working paper eliminating entries needed to consolidate ProLock and Senyo at the date of acquisition.

E3.5 **Acquisition and Eliminating Entries, Acquisition Expenses** Pinnacle Corporation acquired all **LO 4** ✓ of Stengl Corporation's common stock by issuing 250,000 shares of $1 par common stock with a current market value of $10,000,000. Related accountants' and attorneys' fees were $300,000, paid in cash. The total book value of Stengl's stockholders' equity consists of capital stock of $200,000 and retained earnings of $1,800,000. Book values and fair values of Stengl's assets and liabilities are given below:

	Book Value Dr (Cr)	Fair Value Dr (Cr)
Cash and receivables...	$ 800,000	$ 800,000
Inventories	1,100,000	900,000
Plant assets, net..	1,600,000	1,000,000
Current liabilities...	(1,000,000)	(1,000,000)
Long-term debt	(500,000)	(475,000)
Totals	$2,000,000	$1,225,000

In addition, Stengl has previously unrecorded identifiable intangible assets with a fair value of $500,000 that meet *FASB ASC Topic 805* criteria for recognition.

Required

a. Prepare the entry Pinnacle makes to record the acquisition on its own books.
b. Prepare the working paper eliminating entries to consolidate the balance sheets of Pinnacle Corporation and Stengl Corporation at the date of acquisition.

E3.6 **Acquisition and Eliminating Entries, Bargain Purchase** Publix Company acquired all of Sher- **LO 4** man Company's common stock for $2,750 million cash; fees paid to an outside firm to estimate the earning power of Sherman and the fair values of its properties amounted to $40 million. Book value of Sherman's net assets was $2,500 million. Book values of Sherman's identifiable assets and liabilities approximated their fair values except as noted below:

(in millions)	Book Value	Fair Value
Inventories	$1,500	$1,600
Land..	100	200
Other plant assets, net..	800	1,050
Long-term debt	400	370

Required

a. Record Publix's acquisition entry.
b. Prepare the working paper eliminating entries necessary to prepare a consolidated balance sheet at the date of acquisition.

E3.7 **Interpreting Eliminating Entries** The following two consolidation eliminating entries were **LO 4** made immediately following Plains' acquisition of a 100 percent ownership interest in Seaboard for $88,000,000 cash:

(E)	Stockholders' equity—Seaboard..	?	
	Investment in Seaboard		48,000,000
(R)	Goodwill..	?	
	Noncurrent assets..		2,000,000
	Investment in Seaboard		?

Required

Compute the following amounts:

a. Book value of Seaboard at the date of acquisition.
b. Excess paid over the book value of net assets acquired.
c. Goodwill.

LO 4   E3.8

Acquisition Entry and Consolidation Working Paper   Phoenix, Inc. acquired all of the outstanding common stock of Spark Corporation for $400 million cash plus 25 million shares of Phoenix's $10 par value common stock having a market value of $90 per share. Registration fees were $5 million and merger-related consultant and legal fees were $8 million, paid in cash. *Immediately prior* to the acquisition, the trial balances of the two companies were as follows:

	Dr (Cr)	
(in millions)	**Phoenix**	**Spark**
Current assets	$1,000	$200
Plant and equipment, net	3,500	700
Current liabilities	(500)	(150)
Long-term liabilities	(2,000)	(300)
Common stock	(300)	(100)
Additional paid-in capital	(600)	(50)
Retained earnings	(1,100)	(300)
Totals	$ 0	$ 0

A review of the fair values of Spark's assets indicates that current assets are overvalued by $10 million, plant and equipment is undervalued by $200 million, and previously unreported brand names and trademarks have a fair value of $300 million.

Required

a. Prepare the entry Phoenix makes to record the acquisition of Spark.
b. Prepare a working paper to consolidate the balance sheets of Phoenix and Spark at the date of acquisition.

LO 4   E3.9   **Consolidation Working Paper, Simple Example**   Below are the condensed balance sheets of Princecraft and Sylvan Companies just prior to Princecraft's acquisition of all of the voting shares of Sylvan for $40 million in cash. The book values of Sylvan Company's net assets approximate fair value.

Balance Sheets	Princecraft Company	Sylvan Company
Cash	$ 60,000,000	$ 2,000,000
Other current assets	20,000,000	8,000,000
Property and equipment, net	70,000,000	15,000,000
Total assets	$150,000,000	$25,000,000
Total liabilities	$ 30,000,000	$ 8,000,000
Common stock	15,000,000	5,000,000
Additional paid-in capital	45,000,000	10,000,000
Retained earnings	60,000,000	2,000,000
Total liabilities and equity	$150,000,000	$25,000,000

Required

a. Prepare the journal entry Princecraft makes to record the acquisition on its own books.
b. Prepare the consolidation working paper at the date of acquisition.
c. Prepare the consolidated balance sheet at the date of acquisition, in good form.

E3.10 **Consolidation with Revaluations of Recorded Net Assets** Panoz Corporation issues 1 million **LO 4**
shares of stock, valued at $50 per share, to acquire all of the stock of Shelby, Inc. Panoz accounts for the
acquisition as a stock acquisition. Balance sheet information at the date of acquisition is as follows *(in
millions)*:

	Panoz Corporation	Shelby, Inc.	
	Book Value Dr (Cr)	Book Value Dr (Cr)	Fair Value Dr (Cr)
Cash and receivables.	$ 10	$ 5	$ 6
Inventory.	40	10	7
Property and equipment, net	350	100	90
Investment in Shelby	50	—	—
Current liabilities.	(60)	(20)	(20)
Long-term liabilities	(200)	(80)	(78)
Capital stock	(120)	(10)	
Retained earnings	(100)	(6)	
Accumulated other comprehensive income.	10	(1)	
Treasury stock	20	2	
Total	$ 0	$ 0	

Shelby has no previously unrecorded identifiable intangible assets.

Required
a. Calculate the amount of goodwill recognized for this acquisition.
b. Prepare the consolidation working paper at the date of acquisition.
c. Present the consolidated balance sheet, in good form, at the date of acquisition.

E3.11 **Consolidation with Previously Unrecorded Intangibles and Goodwill (see related E2.8)** **LO 4** ✔
Brightcove, Inc. acquires all of the stock of Ciber, Inc. for $50 million in cash and accounts for the
acquisition as a stock acquisition. Balance sheet information at the date of acquisition is as follows *(in
thousands)*:

	Brightcove, Inc.	Ciber, Inc.	
	Book Value Dr (Cr)	Book Value Dr (Cr)	Fair Value Dr (Cr)
Current assets	$ 70,000	$ 400	$ 300
Plant and equipment, net	200,000	12,000	4,000
Licenses and trademarks.	—	5,000	7,000
Investment in Ciber	50,000		—
Current liabilities.	(80,000)	(800)	(800)
Long-term liabilities	(150,000)	(10,000)	(11,000)
Capital stock	(35,000)	(8,000)	
Retained earnings	(55,000)	1,400	
Total	$ 0	$ 0	

Brightcove hires a consultant to identify and value any previously unreported intangible assets attributable to Ciber at the date of acquisition. The consultant identifies the following intangibles:

	Fair Value *(in thousands)*
Customer contracts	$ 1,000
Assembled workforce.	20,000
Brand names	5,000
Leases at rents below current market	400
Developed technology	1,500
In-process research and development	300
Future cost savings from elimination of duplicate assets	800
Additional expected revenues from bundling products	600

Required

a. Prepare a schedule of the excess of acquisition cost over Ciber's book value and its allocation to Ciber's identifiable net assets and goodwill.

b. Prepare a working paper to consolidate the balance sheet accounts of Brightcove and Ciber at the date of acquisition.

c. Prepare the consolidated balance sheet at the date of acquisition, in good form.

LO 4 E3.12 Reconstructing Eliminating Entries and Book Value Cove Corporation owns all of Bay Corporation's common stock, acquired for $65 million in cash. Immediately prior to the acquisition, Cove reported current assets of $75 million, noncurrent assets of $25 million, and liabilities of $15 million. The date-of-acquisition consolidated balance sheet reports consolidated total assets of $111 million, including goodwill of $37 million related to the acquisition of Bay. The book values of Bay's identifiable assets and liabilities approximated their fair values, except for previously unreported identifiable intangibles with a fair value of $16 million.

Required

a. Calculate the fair value of Bay's identifiable total assets at the date of acquisition.

b. Calculate the fair value of Bay's liabilities at the date of acquisition.

c. Calculate the book value of Bay's net assets at the date of acquisition.

d. Prepare the working paper eliminating entries to consolidate Cove and Bay at the date of acquisition.

LO 3 E3.13 Identifying and Analyzing Variable Interest Entities Corporations A and B are formed to purchase property and lease it to end users C and D.

Required

In each of these independent cases, indicate whether A and B are variable interest entities per U.S. GAAP, and, if so, whether C or D is the primary beneficiary that should consolidate it. If A or B are not variable interest entities and should be consolidated with C or D, explain why.

a. C owns 30 percent of A's equity and other investors own 70 percent. Ninety-two percent of A's assets are funded by bank loans that C guarantees. A's board of directors makes all significant operating and capital decisions. C selects six of the ten board members.

b. B reports total assets of $100 million and stockholders' equity of $2 million; D is the sole owner of B's stock.

c. Outside investor E owns all the stock behind A's stockholders' equity, which amounts to 15 percent of A's total assets. C contracts with E to compensate E for any of A's losses and to cap its residual gains at 10 percent of A's average equity in any one year. Excess residual gains will be distributed to C, who also makes the day-to-day decisions that affect A's economic performance.

d. B purchases property and leases 75 percent of it to C and 25 percent to D. Both C and D guarantee specific residual values for the property they leased and neither have any interest in the stockholders' equity amounting to 10 percent of B's total assets. The property that C leases is fairly generic and has an active aftermarket whereas the property leased by D is dedicated to D's special needs and has no alternative uses. D covers 60 percent of B's funding needs with an unsecured loan. Banks provide remaining funding that is secured by the leased property. B's operating decisions are made at the board level, and D controls the majority of the board.

LO 3 E3.14 Identification of Variable Interest Entity and Primary Beneficiary Softek Corporation forms a separate legal entity, Startek, to develop new technology. The entity is funded by $4,000,000 in outside equity and $26,000,000 in debt. Softek guarantees Startek's debt. The entity is expected to generate the following cash flows at the end of one year:

Cash Flow	Probability
$11,000,000	0.40
33,000,000	0.20
55,000,000	0.40

A discount rate of 10 percent is appropriate.

Required

a. Assume qualitative analysis of Startek's VIE status is inconclusive. Quantitatively analyze whether Startek is a variable interest entity.
b. Assume Startek is a variable interest entity. Identify the factors that determine whether Softek is the primary beneficiary that must consolidate Startek.

E3.15 Consolidation Policy: U.S. GAAP and IFRS   Marshall Corporation has 10,000,000 shares of Class   **LO 2, 5**
A common stock and 100,000,000 shares of Class B common stock outstanding. The Class A common stock has 60 percent of the voting rights and the Class B stock has the other 40 percent. All shares have equal dividend rights. Randolph Corporation owns 80 percent of the Class A shares and 40 percent of the Class B shares.

Required

a. Following U.S. GAAP, should Randolph consolidate Marshall? Explain.
b. Following IFRS, should Randolph consolidate Marshall? Explain.
c. Repeat parts a and b assuming Randolph owns no Class B shares and a single investor owns them all.
d. Repeat parts a and b assuming Randolph owns 70 percent of the Class A shares and ownership of all other shares is widely dispersed.

PROBLEMS ••

P3.1   Eliminating Entries, Goodwill   Pendragon Corporation acquired all of the stock of Sherwood, Inc.   **LO 4** ✓
for $400 million in cash. Sherwood's stockholders' equity accounts at the date of acquisition were as follows:

(in millions)	
Common stock, par	$ 5
Additional paid-in capital	15
Retained earnings (deficit)	(40)
Accumulated other comprehensive loss	(2)
Treasury stock	(3)
Total stockholders' equity (deficit)	$(25)

The following previously unreported assets of Sherwood were reported in the acquisition *(in millions)*:

Customer lists	$ 65
Brand names	100

Assume Sherwood's fixed assets are overstated by $35 million, its liabilities are understated by $1 million, and its other assets and liabilities are fairly reported.

Required

a. Calculate the goodwill for this acquisition.
b. Present the working paper eliminating entries necessary to consolidate the balance sheets of Pendragon and Sherwood at the date of acquisition.

✓ LO 4   P3.2   Consolidation Working Paper, Identifiable Intangibles, Goodwill   International Technology Inc. (ITI) acquires all of the voting stock of Global Outsourcing Corporation (GOC) on June 30, 2015. Amounts paid are as follows *(in millions)*:

Cash consideration to the former shareholders of GOC	$50
2,000,000 shares of new $1 par common stock issued	60
Registration fees on new stock issued, paid in cash.	3
Outside legal and advisory services, paid in cash	5
Fair value of earnings contingency.	2

The earnings contingency provides for a potential payout to the former shareholders of GOC at the end of the third year following acquisition. The balance sheets of both companies *immediately prior to* the acquisition are as follows. Fair values of GOC's assets and liabilities at the date of acquisition are also provided.

	ITI	GOC	
Balance Sheets (in millions)	**Book Value**	**Book Value**	**Fair Value**
Current assets	$ 200	$ 10	$ 15
Property, plant and equipment, net	500	130	70
Intangible assets	1,300	20	30
Total assets	$2,000	$160	
Current liabilities.	$ 150	$ 20	$ 20
Long-term liabilities	1,200	100	103
Common stock, par	20	4	
Additional paid-in capital	550	60	
Retained earnings	100	(25)	
Accumulated other comprehensive income.	(15)	3	
Treasury stock	(5)	(2)	
Total liabilities and equity.	$2,000	$160	

The intangible assets reported above consist of patents and trademarks. GOC also has the following previously unreported intangible assets that meet *FASB ASC Topic 805* requirements for asset recognition:

	Fair Value
Advanced technology.	$ 5
Customer lists	25

Required

a.   Prepare the journal entry or entries ITI makes to record the acquisition on its own books.
b.   Prepare a working paper to consolidate the balance sheets of ITI and GOC at June 30, 2015.

LO 4   P3.3   Stock Acquisition and Consolidation Working Paper Eliminating Entries   **Pfizer Inc.** ac-
PFIZER INC.   quired all of the stock of **Pharmacia** for 1,817 million shares of its $0.05 par value stock on April 16,
[PFE]   2003. The fair value of the stock issued was $30.75/share. Merger-related cash costs were $101 million. Pharmacia's stockholders' equity accounts at the date of acquisition totaled $7,236 million, and the fair values of its assets and liabilities differed from reported book values as follows:

(in millions)	**Fair Value Less Book Value**
Inventory.	$ 2,939
Long-term investments	40
Property, plant and equipment.	(317)
In-process research and development	5,052
Developed technology rights	37,066
Long-term debt (undervalued)	1,841
Other assets	(15,606)

Round all answers to the nearest million.

Required

a. Prepare the journal entry Pfizer made to record the acquisition on its own books, following current U.S. GAAP.
b. Calculate the goodwill purchased in this acquisition.
c. Prepare the consolidation working paper eliminating entries needed to consolidate the balance sheets of Pfizer and Pharmacia on April 16, 2003.

P3.4   Consolidated Balance Sheet Working Paper, Bargain Purchase   On January 1, 2016, Paxon   **LO 4**
Corporation acquired all of the outstanding common stock of Saxon Company for $1.8 billion cash. The balance sheets of Paxon and Saxon, *immediately prior* to the combination, are shown below:

Balance Sheets *(in millions)*		Paxon	Saxon
Assets			
Cash and receivables..		$2,860	$ 720
Inventory.......................................		1,700	900
Long-term investments		—	300
Land..		650	175
Buildings and equipment	$3,400		
Less accumulated depreciation....................	(1,000)	2,400	600 (net)
Total assets		$7,610	$2,695
Liabilities and Stockholders' Equity			
Current liabilities.......................................		$1,500	$1,000
Long-term debt		2,000	400
Common stock, par value		500	100
Additional paid-in capital...........................		1,200	350
Retained earnings		2,410	845
Total liabilities and equity........................		$7,610	$2,695

Several of Saxon's assets and liabilities had fair values that were different from their book values. Estimates of the fair values of these items follow:

(in millions)	Estimated Fair Value
Inventory..	$1,000
Long-term investments	250
Land..	420
Buildings and equipment, net	900
Long-term debt	290

Required

a. Calculate the gain on acquisition in this bargain purchase.
b. Prepare a working paper to consolidate the balance sheets of Paxon and Saxon at January 1, 2016.
c. Present the consolidated balance sheet, in good form, at the date of acquisition.

P3.5   Consolidated Balance Sheet Working Paper, Previously Reported Goodwill   Progres-   **LO 4**
sive Corporation acquired all of the outstanding stock of Static Company on June 30, 2016, by issuing 200,000 shares of its $1 par value common stock valued at $75 per share. Direct cash costs associated with the acquisition were $60,000, and the cost of registering and issuing the stock was $400,000. Condensed balance sheet data for the two companies *immediately prior* to the combination are given below.

Balance Sheets *(in thousands)*	Progressive	Static	
	Book Value	Book Value	Fair Value
Cash and receivables.	$ 8,000	$2,000	$1,800
Inventory.	7,000	2,400	2,000
Equity method investments	—	600	3,000
Plant assets, net.	10,000	3,600	1,500
Copyrights	1,000	200	3,000
Goodwill.	—	500	2,500
Total assets	$26,000	$9,300	
Current liabilities.	$ 6,000	$2,000	$2,000
Noncurrent liabilities.	4,000	3,300	3,200
Common stock, par	100	100	
Additional paid-in capital	900	400	
Retained earnings	15,000	3,500	
Total liabilities and equity.	$26,000	$9,300	

Required

a. Prepare the entry Progressive made to record the acquisition on its own books.
b. Prepare a schedule calculating the reported goodwill for this acquisition.
c. Prepare a working paper to consolidate the balance sheets of Progressive and Static at June 30, 2016.
d. Prepare the consolidated balance sheet at June 30, 2016, in good form.

LO 1, 2, 4 **P3.6** **Consolidated Balances, Different Acquirers** Microtech Corporation and Webnet Solutions, Inc. have identical balance sheets, as follows *(in millions)*:

Assets	
Current assets	$10
Property, plant and equipment, net	50
Patents	5
Total assets	$65
Liabilities and Stockholders' Equity	
Current liabilities.	$ 4
Long-term debt	20
Common stock, par value	2
Additional paid-in capital	25
Retained earnings	14
Total liabilities and equity.	$65

Microtech's property, plant and equipment has a fair value of $70 million, and its patents have a fair value of $15 million. Microtech also has developed technology with a fair value of $100 million and client relationships worth $29 million. Both intangibles satisfy the Codification's criteria for capitalization. Webnet Solution's assets and liabilities are all fairly stated and it has no previously unrecorded intangibles. Assume that the two companies have the same stock price.

Microtech and Webnet Solutions are planning a business combination. One company will issue $200 million in stock, with a par value of $1 million, for the stock of the other company. They are not sure who will issue the stock, and therefore who will be the acquirer in this transaction.

Required

a. Prepare a consolidated balance sheet working paper, assuming Microtech is the acquiring company and issues $200 million in stock for all of the stock of Webnet Solutions.
b. Prepare a consolidated balance sheet working paper, assuming Webnet Solutions is the acquiring company, and issues $200 million in stock for all of the stock of Microtech.
c. What are the similarities and differences in the consolidated balances in parts *a* and *b*? Why are the balances different? Do you think management has a preference for one set of consolidated balances over the other?

P3.7   **Tangible and Intangible Asset Revaluations**   During the period 2011–2013, **Yahoo! Inc.** made several acquisitions. Following is a summary of information from the footnotes to Yahoo's 2013 10-K report on the largest of these acquisitions. All numbers are in thousands.

LO 4

YAHOO! INC.
[YHOO]

	interclick, inc.	Tumblr, Inc.
Consideration paid.	$258,501	$990,211
Previously unrecorded intangible assets acquired:		
Customer contracts and related relationships	42,700	182,400
Developed technology	35,600	23,700
Trade name, trademark, and domain name	600	56,500
Goodwill	171,641	751,765
Company book value (assumed)	10,000	50,000

Assume that each acquiree's preacquisition balance sheet reports only tangible assets and liabilities.

Required

a.   For each acquisition, calculate the fair value of tangible net assets acquired.
b.   In the Tumblr acquisition, the fair value of tangible net assets is negative, yet book value is positive. Why do you think the fair value of Tumblr's tangible net assets is negative?
c.   Assume Yahoo records each acquisition as a stock acquisition and then uses a working paper to consolidate each subsidiary's accounts for its annual report. Prepare the eliminating entries required to consolidate each subsidiary at its acquisition date.

P3.8   **Eliminating Entries, Subsidiary's Separate Balance Sheet**   Proha Company acquired all of Sonara Company's voting stock for $40 million cash. The book value of Sonara's net assets on that date was $8 million. The book values of Sonara's individual assets and liabilities approximated fair value, except for inventory, which was undervalued by $2 million, plant assets, which were overvalued by $4 million, and unreported identifiable intangibles valued at $6 million. Given below are condensed balance sheets for Proha Company before and after consolidation of Sonara Company. Inventory is included in current assets.

LO 4

	Proha Company Prior to Consolidation	Consolidated
Assets		
Current assets	$ 5,000,000	$ 8,000,000
Plant assets, net.	25,000,000	45,000,000
Investment in Sonara	40,000,000	—
Identifiable intangible assets	—	6,000,000
Goodwill	—	28,000,000
Total assets	$70,000,000	$87,000,000
Liabilities and Stockholders' Equity		
Liabilities.	$39,000,000	$56,000,000
Stockholders' equity	31,000,000	31,000,000
Total liabilities and equity.	$70,000,000	$87,000,000

Required

a.   Determine the working paper entries that were made in consolidation.
b.   Prepare Sonara Company's separate condensed balance sheet at the date of acquisition.

P3.9   **Stock Acquisition, Previous Equity Interest and Goodwill, Merger-Related Costs, Deferred Taxes**   In 2013, **AB InBev** acquired the remainder of the stock of **Grupo Modelo** that it did not previously own. AB InBev had previously reported its investment in Grupo Modelo using the equity method. All numbers below are in millions. Acquisition cost information is as follows:

LO 4, 5

AB INBEV
[ABI]

Cash consideration paid to Grupo Modelo shareholders, at $9.15/share.	$20,103
Fair value of previously held equity investment	13,905
Merger-related transactions costs, paid in cash	100

The following table summarizes the date-of-acquisition fair and book values of Grupo Modelo's identifiable net assets acquired, as reported in the footnotes to AB InBev's 2013 financial statements (credit balances are in parentheses):

	Book Value	Fair Value
Property, plant and equipment.	$4,609	$ 4,708
Goodwill.	796	—
Intangible assets	458	4,912
Investment in associates	79	75
Investment securities	19	19
Current assets	4,922	9,255
Noncurrent liabilities:		
Employee benefits	(256)	(256)
Trade and other payables.	(78)	(587)
Deferred tax liabilities.	(418)	(1,132)
Current liabilities.	(928)	(2,578)
Net identified assets and liabilities.	$9,203	$14,416

Required

a. AB InBev reported this acquisition as a stock acquisition. Prepare the journal entry it made on its own books to record the acquisition of Grupo Modelo.

b. Grupo Modelo reported goodwill on its books at $796 million, which is adjusted to a fair value of zero. Explain why this revaluation occurs.

c. Grupo Modelo's deferred tax liabilities had a fair value that was significantly higher than book value. Explain how the acquisition caused an increase in deferred tax liabilities.

d. Calculate the goodwill recognized for this acquisition.

e. Prepare eliminating entries (E) and (R) to consolidate Grupo Modelo at the date of acquisition.

LO 3   P3.10   Consolidation of Variable Interest Entities   GM Financial, **General Motors Company**'s financing segment, has special purpose entities that are consolidated in GM's financial statements. GM Financial transfers receivables and lease-related assets to these SPEs, the SPEs issue notes, and use the cash collected from their transferred assets to pay principal and interest on the notes. Creditors of the SPEs have no recourse to the assets of GM Financial or General Motors. GM Financial has no obligation to provide additional financing to these SPEs.

GENERAL MOTORS CO. [GM]

At December 31, 2013, the assets and liabilities related to GM Financial's consolidated SPEs are as follows *(dollars in millions)*:

Restricted cash	$ 1,523
Securitized assets	23,584
Notes payable	(19,448)

Required

a. Describe the process GM used in deciding to consolidate GM Financial's SPEs. What conditions must exist to lead to the conclusion that the SPEs should be consolidated? Why do you think GM decided that these SPEs should be consolidated?

b. How does consolidation affect GM's December 31, 2013, balance sheet accounts?

⊘ LO 4   P3.11   Identifiable Intangibles and Goodwill (see related P2.5)   Prince Corporation, a wholesale vehicle distributor, acquires all of the stock of Squire Service Corporation for one million shares of Prince stock, valued at $35 per share. Squire becomes a subsidiary of Prince. Professional fees connected with the acquisition are $1,200,000 and costs of registering and issuing the new shares are $600,000, both paid in cash.

Squire performs vehicle maintenance services for owners of auto, truck and bus fleets. The balance sheets of Prince and Squire *immediately prior* to the acquisition are shown next.

Balance Sheets	Prince	Squire
Cash...	$ 2,800,000	$ 300,000
Accounts receivable......................................	6,000,000	2,700,000
Parts inventory...	—	5,200,000
Vehicle inventory	15,000,000	—
Equipment, net...	40,000,000	17,600,000
Total assets	$63,800,000	$25,800,000
Current liabilities...	$ 5,000,000	$ 3,100,000
Long-term liabilities	25,000,000	8,600,000
Stockholders' equity	33,800,000	14,100,000
Total liabilities and equity...............................	$63,800,000	$25,800,000

In reviewing Squire's assets and liabilities, you determine the following:

1. On a discounted present value basis, the accounts receivable have a fair value of $2,600,000, and the long-term liabilities have a fair value of $8,000,000.
2. The current replacement cost of the parts inventory is $6,000,000.
3. The current replacement cost of the equipment is $19,500,000.
4. Squire occupies its service facilities under an operating lease with ten years remaining. The rent is below current market levels, giving the lease an estimated fair value of $1,250,000.
5. Squire has long-term service contracts with several large fleet owners. These contracts have been profitable; the present value of expected profits over the remaining term of the contracts is estimated at $2,000,000.
6. Squire has a skilled and experienced work force. You estimate that the cost to hire and train replacements would be $750,000.
7. Squire's trade name is well-known among fleet owners and is estimated to have a fair value of $200,000.

Required

a. Prepare the acquisition entry and a working paper to consolidate the balance sheets of Prince and Squire as of the date of acquisition.
b. If the acquisition was a merger, as in P2.5, Prince records Squire's assets and liabilities directly on its own books. Present Prince's entry to record the merger, and compare Prince's balance sheet immediately after the entry is booked with the consolidated balance sheet prepared in part *a*.

P3.12   Consolidation Policy for Equity Investments: U.S. GAAP and IFRS   Andrews Company, a   **LO 2, 5**
cement manufacturer, acquired all the voting common stock of Benson Company, a rug manufacturer, as part of a diversification program. As a result of a later decision to discontinue the diversification program and to concentrate on its primary line of business, Andrews divested all of its diversified businesses except for Benson. Andrews decided to retain an investment in Benson because it believed that Benson was well positioned for future growth and profitability. However, because of its current corporate strategy to commit capital resources only to its primary line of business, Andrews was unwilling to provide the capital needed to support the projected growth of Benson. Thus, Andrews caused Benson to issue additional shares of Benson's voting common stock in an initial public offering.

After Benson's initial public offering, Andrews' stockholding represented less than 50 percent of the total number of shares of Benson's voting common stock outstanding. But Andrews' shares were the largest block of Benson's voting common stock held by any single party, with the remainder widely held—no single party held more than 3 percent of the total number of shares of Benson's voting common stock outstanding. Benson had no other classes of equity securities or contingently issuable voting common stock.

Required

For each of the six cases below, indicate, with supporting reasons, what the consolidation conclusion would be under U.S. GAAP and under IFRS.

a. Andrews is able to elect a majority of Benson's board of directors solely as a result of exercising the voting rights of its large minority stockholding. Not all of Benson's stockholders exercise their right to vote, giving Andrews a majority of the votes cast. Following is information on votes cast in three separate cases (1), (2) and (3):

Case	Andrews' Percentage of Total Outstanding	Percentage of Total Outstanding That Voted	Andrews' Percentage of Votes Cast
(1)	49%	85%	58%
(2)	45%	85%	53%
(3)	40%	75%	53%

b. Instead of the facts in part *a*, Andrews is able to dominate the election of the board of directors through nominating its choices for board members, obtaining proxies from other stockholders, and convincing still other stockholders to cast their votes for its nominees. While Andrews' ability to dominate the composition of Benson's board of directors is largely due to its large minority stockholding, Andrews itself is not able to cast a majority of the votes as a result of ownership of voting rights. Following is information on votes cast in three separate cases (4), (5) and (6):

Case	Andrews' Percentage of Total Outstanding	Percentage of Total Outstanding That Voted	Andrews' Percentage of Votes Cast
(4)	35%	65%	20%
(5)	30%	60%	25%
(6)	25%	55%	20%

LO 4 P3.13 Working Backwards—Reconstruct Balance Sheet and Eliminating Entries Piedmont Corporation acquired all of the voting stock of Stearns Company. Below is information on acquisition costs, and the separate balance sheets of Piedmont and Stearns, as well as the consolidated balance sheet, *immediately after* the acquisition. All amounts are in thousands.

Cash paid to Stearns' former owners	$ 95,000
Fair value of stock issued to Stearns' former owners	120,000
Merger-related transactions costs, paid in cash	500
Stock registration fees on stock issued...	700
Fair value of earnout..	5,000

	Piedmont	Stearns	Consolidated
Current assets	$ 40,000	$ 15,000	$ 55,000
Plant assets, net.........................	360,000	140,000	470,000
Identifiable intangibles	—	—	100,000
Investment in Stearns.....................	220,000	—	—
Goodwill.................................	—	—	135,000
Total assets	$620,000	$155,000	$760,000
Liabilities................................	$220,000	$140,000	$360,000
Capital stock	300,000	40,000	300,000
Retained earnings	100,000	(25,000)	100,000
Total liabilities and equity.................	$620,000	$155,000	$760,000

Required

a. Prepare Piedmont's separate balance sheet just prior to the acquisition.
b. Reconstruct eliminating entries (E) and (R) to consolidate the balance sheet.
c. Prepare a schedule calculating the excess of acquisition cost over book value and its allocation to Stearns' identifiable net assets and goodwill.

P3.14 Consolidated Balance Sheet Working Paper, Identifiable Intangibles International Auto **LO 4** ✓
(IA) acquires all of the stock of Genuine Parts (GP) and reports the acquisition as a stock investment on
its own books. The acquisition involves the following payments. All amounts are in thousands.

Cash paid to GP shareholders.	$ 5,000
Cash paid to consultants and lawyers.	1,200
Fair value of new IA stock issued, 1,000 shares, $2 par	36,000
Stock registration fees, paid in cash	900
Fair value of earnings contingency.	250

The earnings contingency, if paid, will occur three years subsequent to the acquisition. The balance sheet
accounts of GP and IA, *just prior to the acquisition*, are as follows:

	International Auto	Genuine Parts	
	Book Value Dr (Cr)	Book Value Dr (Cr)	Fair Value Dr (Cr)
Current assets	$ 30,000	$ 1,000	$ 1,200
Fixed assets, net	420,000	27,000	20,000
Trademarks	89,000	3,400	6,000
Current liabilities.	(25,000)	(400)	(400)
Long-term liabilities	(350,000)	(26,000)	(25,000)
Common stock, par value	(8,000)	(500)	
Additional paid-in capital	(110,000)	(8,500)	
Retained earnings	(45,000)	2,000	
Accumulated other comprehensive income. . . .	(4,000)	1,400	
Treasury stock	3,000	600	
Total	$ 0	$ 0	

In addition to the assets reported on GP's balance sheet, the following previously unreported intangible
assets are identified. Note: Some of these intangibles may not be separately capitalized per *ASC Topic
805*.

	Fair value
Licensing agreements	$ 2,400
Skilled workforce	15,000
Order backlogs.	5,000
Future synergies between IA and GP supply chains	1,600

Required

a. Prepare a schedule calculating the excess of acquisition cost over GP's book value, and its allocation
   to GP's identifiable net assets and goodwill.
b. Prepare a consolidation working paper to consolidate IA and GP at the date of acquisition.
c. Prepare the consolidated balance sheet at the date of acquisition, in good form.

P3.15 Consolidated Balance Sheet Working Paper, Bargain Gain, Special Issues Packard Indus- **LO 4** ✓
tries acquires all of the stock of Steamobile Company for $20 million in cash, and reports the acquisition
as a stock acquisition on its own books. The balance sheet accounts of Packard and Steamobile, *immediately prior to the acquisition*, are as follows *(in thousands)*:

	Packard Book Value Dr (Cr)	Steamobile Book Value Dr (Cr)	Steamobile Fair Value Dr (Cr)
Current assets	$ 35,000	$ 5,000	$ 3,000
Fixed assets	500,000	150,000	140,000
Accumulated depreciation	(160,000)	(40,000)	—
Goodwill	—	35,000	—
Liabilities	(215,000)	(120,000)	(121,000)
Capital stock	(90,000)	(35,000)	
Retained earnings	(70,500)	5,800	
Accumulated other comprehensive income	500	(800)	
Total	$ 0	$ 0	

Steamobile has previously unreported identifiable intangibles with a fair value of $6 million that are separately capitalized per *ASC Topic 805*.

Required

a. Prepare a schedule calculating the excess of Steamobile's book value over acquisition cost, its allocation to Steamobile's identifiable net assets, and the amount of the bargain gain.
b. Prepare a consolidation working paper to consolidate Packard and Steamobile at the date of acquisition.
c. Prepare the consolidated balance sheet at the date of acquisition, in good form.

REVIEW SOLUTIONS

Review 1 Solution

Non-VIEs: Entities B and D would be consolidated. GM has majority ownership of the voting shares of these entities.

VIEs: GM consolidates entity F because it has the power to make decisions significantly affecting the entity's economic performance and may realize significant losses or benefits from its equity investment and loan guarantee. GM is not the primary beneficiary of entity E, due to shared power and interests. GM does not have decision-making power in entity G.

Review 2 Solution

(*in millions*)

Consolidation Working Paper	Accounts Taken From Books IBM Dr (Cr)	Accounts Taken From Books SoftCloud Dr (Cr)	Eliminations Dr	Eliminations Cr	Consolidated Balances Dr (Cr)
Cash and receivables	$ 800	$ 400			$ 1,200
Inventories	6,000	850		$ 50 (R)	6,800
Property, plant and equipment, net	25,000	2,900	(R) $ 600		28,500
Investment in SoftCloud	1,200	—		350 (E)	—
				850 (R)	
Favorable lease agreements	—	—	(R) 150		150
Goodwill	—	—	(R) 500		500
Accounts payable	(7,000)	(300)			(7,300)
Long-term debt	(22,000)	(3,500)		350 (R)	(25,850)
Common stock, par value	(100)	(10)	(E) 10		(100)
Additional paid-in capital	(2,500)	(200)	(E) 200		(2,500)
Retained earnings	(1,300)	(260)	(E) 260		(1,300)
Treasury stock	—	50		50 (E)	—
Accumulated other comprehensive income	(100)	70		70 (E)	(100)
Total	$ 0	$ 0	$1,720	$1,720	$ 0

4 Consolidated Financial Statements Subsequent to Acquisition

LEARNING OBJECTIVES

LO1 Explain the general process of periodic consolidation. (p. 119)

LO2 Describe the relation between equity method and consolidated balances. (p. 124)

LO3 Report subsequent year write-offs of acquisition date revaluations of subsidiary identifiable assets and liabilities. (p. 125)

LO4 Measure and report goodwill impairment losses. (p. 128)

LO5 Discuss IFRS for intangibles reporting and impairment testing. (p. 145)

LO6 Explain consolidation when the parent uses the cost method. (p. 148, appendix)

TIME WARNER INC.
www.timewarner.com

Time Warner Inc. is one of the largest media and entertainment conglomerates in the world. Its more than 1,000 subsidiaries include Turner Broadcasting System, Home Box Office Inc., and Warner Bros. Entertainment Inc., providing cable, internet, filmed entertainment, digital on-demand, music, and other services. Its organizational structure is the product of many acquisitions through the years, highlighted by combination with Turner Broadcasting System in 1996 and America Online in 2001.

Time Warner's December 31, 2013, balance sheet reports $30,563 million in goodwill, and identifiable intangible assets of $9,549 million. The goodwill and most of the identifiable intangibles were acquired in business combinations, and comprise almost 59 percent of Time Warner's total consolidated assets. Financial statement footnotes report 2013 amortization expense of $251 million and $97 million in impairment losses for the identifiable intangibles.

Time Warner acquired most of its subsidiaries in past years, sometimes many years ago. Each time they present financial statements, Time Warner's accountants must take the separate financial records of each subsidiary and consolidate them. How do their accountants perform this task? Does the passage of time since acquisition affect this process?

This chapter explains how a parent company, such as Time Warner, accounts for its investment in subsidiaries on its own books, the procedures needed to consolidate parent and subsidiary financial records, and methods used to measure appropriate amortization and impairment losses on acquired intangibles. *Source:* Time Warner Inc. annual report, 2013.

CHAPTER ORGANIZATION

Consolidation procedures in subsequent years	Revaluations of acquired assets: subsequent years	Illustration of consolidation in subsequent years	IFRS for acquired intangibles	Appendix: Consolidation using the cost method
• Equity method on parent's books • Consolidation eliminating entries • Basic consolidation example • Presentation of consolidated financial statements • Complete equity method as one-line consolidation	• Depreciation and amortization of previously-reported assets • Amortization and impairment testing of previously-unreported identifiable intangibles • Goodwill impairment • Illustration of amortization and impairment testing	• Consolidation after one year • Consolidation after two or more years	• Identifiable intangibles • Goodwill impairment testing	• Compare the cost and equity methods • Consolidation after one year • Consolidation after two or more years

INTRODUCTION

If a parent has a controlling interest in a legally separate subsidiary, it regularly presents consolidated financial statements that aggregate the financial records of the separate companies. Chapter 3 discussed procedures to consolidate financial statements at the *date of acquisition*. However, far more frequently accountants prepare consolidated statements for time periods *following* the date when the parent acquired the subsidiary. If consolidation is appropriate, the books of the parent and subsidiary must be consolidated at *every* financial reporting date.

Consolidating financial records of a parent and subsidiary at a date subsequent to acquisition raises many new challenges. How the parent reports its investment in the subsidiary on its own books over time affects consolidation procedures. On the acquisition date, consolidation working paper eliminations revalue the subsidiary's assets and liabilities to fair value. In subsequent years, revalued assets and liabilities change in reported value due to the passage of time, changing economic conditions, and transactions such as sales or other dispositions. The consolidated income statement includes results of the subsidiary's operations going forward from the acquisition date. Therefore, in subsequent years the accountant prepares a consolidated statement of income and comprehensive income and statement of cash flows, in addition to the consolidated balance sheet.

INTRODUCTION TO CONSOLIDATION PROCEDURES

We begin by describing and illustrating the general nature of the consolidation process at a date subsequent to the acquisition. The goal of this process, as discussed in Chapter 3, is to take the numbers reported on the books of the parent and the subsidiary, use a working paper to make changes necessary to remove intercompany relationships, and appropriately revalue the subsidiary's assets and liabilities.

LO1 Explain the general process of periodic consolidation.

In subsequent periods, the passage of time affects revaluations of subsidiary assets and liabilities. Suppose an acquisition occurs on January 1, 2014, when the subsidiary's equipment has a remaining life of ten years, a book value of $10,000,000, and a fair value of $15,000,000. On January 1, 2014, the consolidation process increases the plant and equipment account by $5,000,000. Now assume we are preparing consolidated financial statements at December 31, 2016, *three years later*. If the subsidiary still has the equipment, it is three years older. Using straight-line depreciation, the consolidation process adds a net value of only $3,500,000 to the plant and equipment account [= $5,000,000 − 3 × ($5,000,000/10)]. The consolidation process also affects consolidated expenses. The subsidiary reports depreciation expense of $1,000,000 (= $10,000,000/10) for 2016. Because consolidated depreciation expense, based on fair value at the date of acquisition, is $1,500,000 (= $15,000,000/10), the consolidation process adds $500,000 (= $5,000,000/10) to depreciation expense for each year, 2014 through 2023, if the subsidiary still holds the equipment.

As time passes, the investment account reported on the parent's books also changes. If the parent reports its investment using the **equity method**, the parent reports the subsidiary's adjusted net income on its own books by increasing the investment account. Subsidiary dividends received reduce the parent's investment account. The consolidation process removes these intercompany effects. Recall Chapter 1's discussion of the equity method, used for *external reporting* of significant influence stock investments. When the investor controls the investee, consolidated financial statements are prepared. To simplify the consolidation process, this text assumes the parent uses the **complete (full) equity method** to report the investment on its own books. Calculation of equity in net income of the investee using the equity method for external reporting differs from the complete equity method used *internally* by a parent company in two major ways:

- **Impairment losses on previously unreported tangible and intangible assets,** including goodwill, do not adjust equity in net income using the equity method for external reporting; equity in net income is reduced by these impairment losses using the complete equity method.

- **Unconfirmed profits on downstream sales** are deducted to the extent of the investor's *ownership interest* in the investee when computing equity in net income for external reporting; the complete equity method subtracts *all* unconfirmed downstream intercompany profits when computing equity in net income as reported on the parent's separate books.

If the parent does not use the complete equity method internally, additional eliminating entries are necessary to convert the parent's account balances to the complete equity method before proceeding with the consolidation. Chapters 4 through 6 discuss consolidation procedures based on the parent using the complete equity method on its own books. The appendix to this chapter discusses how the consolidation process changes when the parent uses the **cost method** to account for the investment on its own books.

Consolidation Eliminating Entries

At reporting dates after the acquisition date, we consolidate the subsidiary's assets and liabilities, and also its revenues, expenses, gains and losses. The consolidation process accomplishes the following goals:

- Eliminates equity method income reported on the parent's books and declared dividends on the subsidiary's books. These are intercompany items that are not appropriate when the parent and subsidiary are reported as one entity.

- Eliminates the stockholders' equity accounts reported on the subsidiary's books against the book value portion of the investment account reported on the parent's books.

- Adjusts the subsidiary's reported assets and liabilities for remaining acquisition date revaluations and eliminates the remainder of the investment balance.

- Adjusts reported expenses for current year revaluation write-offs.

We use a consolidation working paper to achieve these goals, with the following **eliminating entries**:

(C) Eliminate the current year's equity method entries, restoring the investment account to its balance at the beginning of the current year.

(E) Eliminate the subsidiary's beginning-of-year stockholders' equity account balances against the investment account.

(R) Eliminate the rest of the investment account, representing the beginning-of-year revaluation balance, and revalue the subsidiary's assets and liabilities as of the beginning of the year.

(O) Recognize current year write-offs of the subsidiary's asset and liability revaluations.

The acronym **CERO** may help you remember the four eliminating entries:

1. **Current**—eliminate the current year equity method entries.
2. **Equity**—eliminate the subsidiary's beginning-of-current-year equity balances.
3. **Revalue**—recognize the beginning-of-current-year fair value revaluations.
4. **Write-Off**—recognize current year revaluation write-offs.

Eliminating entries (E) and (R) parallel the entries introduced in Chapter 3, except that Chapter 3 uses *acquisition date* values to consolidate the financial statements at the date of acquisition. At any subsequent consolidation date, entries (E) and (R) eliminate the subsidiary's equity accounts and revalue its assets and liabilities as of the *beginning of the current year*. Then entry (O) adjusts the asset and liability revaluations to end-of-year values.

• •

Reporting Perspective

The parent company's use of the **complete equity method** facilitates the consolidation process by matching the parent's investment balance with the subsidiary's beginning-of-year equity and revaluations. Unless the investment account reflects the complete equity method, it will not be completely eliminated in eliminations C, E, and R. Further, we will see that use of the complete equity method results in the parent's net income and retained earnings equaling the consolidated amounts, maintaining consistency between the parent's books and the consolidated statements to the greatest extent possible. In practice, a parent company does not always use the complete equity method internally. If consolidated statements are prepared, the method used by the parent to account for its investments in subsidiaries does not affect the consolidated results. Details of the consolidation process differ, but the end result is the same. If the parent company uses a different method, such as the *cost method*, to report its investment internally, additional consolidation working paper entries, covered in the appendix to this chapter, are necessary to adjust the parent's accounts to the complete equity method before proceeding with the consolidation.

• •

Illustration of Consolidation Process

Suppose Time Warner pays $75,000,000 for Midwest Cable on January 1, 2015. Midwest Cable's book value is $10,000,000. The book values of Midwest Cable's net assets equal their fair values, except equipment has a fair value $15,000,000 higher than its book value, and Midwest Cable has previously unreported identifiable intangible assets valued at $2,000,000. Midwest's plant and equipment has a remaining life of 20 years, and the identifiable intangibles have a remaining life of four years. Straight-line depreciation and amortization are appropriate for both assets. Analysis of the acquisition follows:

Acquisition cost		$75,000,000
Book value of Midwest Cable		(10,000,000)
Cost in excess of Midwest Cable's book value		65,000,000
Differences between fair value and book value:		
Equipment.	$15,000,000	
Identifiable intangibles	2,000,000	(17,000,000)
Goodwill.		$48,000,000

Goodwill is subject to impairment testing, discussed later in this chapter. Assume goodwill is not impaired in 2015. Midwest reports net income of $5,000,000, other comprehensive income of $200,000, and declares and pays cash dividends of $1,000,000 to Time Warner in 2015. Time Warner uses the complete equity method to report its investment in Midwest Cable on its own books, and therefore reports equity in net income of Midwest Cable of $3,750,000, calculated as follows:

Midwest Cable's reported net income for 2015.	$5,000,000
Adjustments for revaluation write-offs:	
Equipment ($15,000,000/20)	(750,000)
Identifiable intangibles ($2,000,000/4)	(500,000)
Equity in net income of Midwest Cable	$3,750,000

Time Warner also reports Equity in Other Comprehensive Income of Midwest Cable of $200,000.

In addition to the initial acquisition entry, Time Warner makes the following entries on its own books during 2015, following the complete equity method:

Investment in Midwest Cable.	3,950,000	
Equity in net income of Midwest Cable.		3,750,000
Equity in other comprehensive income of Midwest Cable		200,000
To record equity in net income and other comprehensive income for 2015.		
Cash.	1,000,000	
Investment in Midwest Cable		1,000,000
To record dividends received in 2015.		

The investment account therefore has a December 31, 2015, balance of $77,950,000 (= $75,000,000 + $3,950,000 − $1,000,000).

On December 31, 2015, we prepare consolidated financial statements. The consolidation working paper in Exhibit 4.1 shows the preclosing accounts of Time Warner and Midwest Cable at December 31, 2015, in trial balance format. In journal entry form, the four eliminating entries needed to consolidate the 2015 financial statements of Time Warner and Midwest Cable are as follows:

(C)	Equity in net income of Midwest Cable	3,750,000	
	Equity in other comprehensive income of Midwest Cable.	200,000	
	Dividends.		1,000,000
	Investment in Midwest Cable		2,950,000
	To eliminate equity in net income and other comprehensive income on the parent's books, dividends on the subsidiary's books, and restore the investment account to its beginning-of-year value.		
(E)	Common stock, par	100,000	
	Additional paid-in capital	400,000	
	Retained earnings, January 1.	9,450,000	
	Accumulated other comprehensive income, January 1.	50,000	
	Investment in Midwest Cable		10,000,000
	To eliminate the subsidiary's beginning-of-year equity accounts against the investment account (see Exhibit 4.1 for balances).		
(R)	Plant and equipment, net.	15,000,000	
	Identifiable intangibles	2,000,000	
	Goodwill	48,000,000	
	Investment in Midwest Cable.		65,000,000
	To recognize the beginning-of-year revaluations and eliminate the remainder of the investment account balance.		
(O)	Operating expenses.	1,250,000	
	Plant and equipment, net		750,000
	Identifiable intangibles.		500,000
	To write off the equipment and identifiable intangibles revaluations for the current year, by recognizing additional depreciation and amortization expense.		

Exhibit 4.1 displays these eliminating entries, and the consolidated balance for each account.

EXHIBIT 4.1 Consolidation Working Paper for Time Warner and Midwest Cable
At December 31, 2015, Trial Balance Format

	Accounts Taken From Books Dr (Cr)		Eliminations		Consolidated Balances Dr (Cr)
	Time Warner	Midwest Cable	Dr	Cr	
Current assets	$ 19,000,000	$ 4,000,000			$ 23,000,000
Plant and equipment, net.	900,000,000	60,000,000	(R) $15,000,000	$ 750,000 (O)	974,250,000
Identifiable intangibles	—	—	(R) 2,000,000	500,000 (O)	1,500,000
Investment in Midwest Cable.	77,950,000	—		2,950,000 (C)	—
				10,000,000 (E)	
				65,000,000 (R)	
Goodwill	—	—	(R) 48,000,000		48,000,000
Current liabilities.	(10,000,000)	(10,000,000)			(20,000,000)
Long-term debt	(934,700,000)	(39,800,000)			(974,500,000)
Common stock, par	(500,000)	(100,000)	(E) 100,000		(500,000)
Additional paid-in capital	(19,500,000)	(400,000)	(E) 400,000		(19,500,000)
Retained earnings, January 1.	(19,200,000)	(9,450,000)	(E) 9,450,000		(19,200,000)
Accumulated other comprehensive income, January 1	(800,000)	(50,000)	(E) 50,000		(800,000)
Dividends	2,000,000	1,000,000		1,000,000 (C)	2,000,000
Sales revenue.	(600,000,000)	(150,000,000)			(750,000,000)
Equity in net income of Midwest Cable	(3,750,000)	—	(C) 3,750,000		—
Equity in other comprehensive income of Midwest Cable	(200,000)	—	(C) 200,000		—
Cost of goods sold.	400,000,000	115,000,000			515,000,000
Operating expenses	190,000,000	30,000,000	(O) 1,250,000		221,250,000
Other comprehensive income	(300,000)	(200,000)	—	—	(500,000)
Totals	$ 0	$ 0	$80,200,000	$80,200,000	$ 0

Consolidated Financial Statements

Using the working paper consolidated account balances in Exhibit 4.1, we prepare the following consolidated statement of comprehensive income, and the consolidated balance sheet.

TIME WARNER and MIDWEST CABLE
Consolidated Statement of Comprehensive Income
For Year Ended December 31, 2015

Sales revenue.	$750,000,000
Less: Cost of goods sold	515,000,000
Gross profit.	235,000,000
Less: Operating expenses	221,250,000
Net income	**13,750,000**
Plus: Other comprehensive income	500,000
Comprehensive income	$ 14,250,000

TIME WARNER and MIDWEST CABLE Consolidated Balance Sheet December 31, 2015			
Assets		**Liabilities and Stockholders' Equity**	
Current assets	$ 23,000,000	Current liabilities.	$ 20,000,000
Plant and equipment, net. . .	974,250,000	Long-term debt	974,500,000
Identifiable intangibles	1,500,000	Total liabilities.	994,500,000
Goodwill	48,000,000		
		Stockholders' equity	
		Common stock, par	500,000
		Additional paid-in capital	19,500,000
		Retained earnings	30,950,000
		Accumulated other comprehensive income	1,300,000
		Total stockholders' equity	52,250,000
Total assets	$1,046,750,000	Total liabilities and stockholders' equity . . .	$1,046,750,000

We calculate consolidated retained earnings and accumulated other comprehensive income at December 31, 2015, as follows, using the consolidated balances from the working paper and consolidated net income from the consolidated statement of comprehensive income:

Retained earnings, January 1.	$19,200,000
Plus: Consolidated net income	13,750,000
Less: Consolidated dividends	(2,000,000)
Retained earnings, December 31.	$30,950,000
Accumulated other comprehensive income, January 1.	$ 800,000
Plus: Other comprehensive income	500,000
Accumulated other comprehensive income, December 31.	$ 1,300,000

For convenience, in this illustration consolidated net income and comprehensive income are displayed on one statement of comprehensive income. Many companies use a two-statement format. The first page displays the components of net income, and a second page displays comprehensive income, starting with net income, and then adding and subtracting the various components of other comprehensive income to arrive at comprehensive income. The consolidation working paper trial balance format allows display of the financial statements in whatever format desired.

Complete Equity Method as One-Line Consolidation

LO2 Describe the relation between equity method and consolidated balances.

When Time Warner uses the complete equity method to report its investment in Midwest Cable, consolidated net income of $13,750,000 equals the net income Time Warner reports on its separate books ($13,750,000 = $600,000,000 + $3,750,000 − $400,000,000 − $190,000,000). Similarly, consolidated comprehensive income of $14,250,000 equals the comprehensive income Time Warner reports on its books ($14,250,000 = $13,750,000 + $200,000 + $300,000). Consolidated retained earnings at December 31, 2015 of $30,950,000 equals Time Warner's ending retained earnings reported on its own books ($30,950,000 = $19,200,000 + $13,750,000 − $2,000,000). Time Warner's separate accumulated other comprehensive income at December 31, 2015, is $1,300,000 ($800,000 + $200,000 + $300,000), the same as the consolidated balance. This is *not* a coincidence. Exhibit 4.2 shows that consolidated comprehensive income and the parent's comprehensive income have exactly the same components, packaged in different ways.

EXHIBIT 4.2 Equivalence of Parent's Income and Consolidated Income

Parent		Consolidated
Parent revenues Less: Parent expenses Plus: Equity in net income of subsidiary: Subsidiary revenues less subsidiary expenses, adjusted for revaluation write-offs		Parent revenues plus subsidiary revenues Less: Parent expenses plus subsidiary expenses, adjusted for revaluation write-offs
Parent net income	=	**Consolidated net income**
Plus: Parent's OCI Plus: Equity in subsidiary's OCI		Plus: Parent's OCI Plus: Subsidiary's OCI
Parent comprehensive income	=	**Consolidated comprehensive income**

The complete equity method is often called a "**one-line consolidation**" of the investee's financial results on the investor's books. The investment account is a one-line summary of the assets and liabilities of the investee, the equity in net income account is a one-line summary of the revenues and adjusted expenses of the investee, and the equity in other comprehensive income account is a one-line summary of the various components of the investee's other comprehensive income.

REPORTING REVALUATIONS OF SUBSIDIARY ASSETS AND LIABILITIES IN SUBSEQUENT YEARS

The acquisition date consolidation process included revaluation of the subsidiary's assets and liabilities at that date. Consolidation at a subsequent date requires recognition of write-offs of the reported revaluations over time. In the previous section's example, plant and equipment had a fair value $15,000,000 greater than book value at the acquisition date. When we prepare consolidated financial statements a year later, however, the equipment is a year older. At an estimated remaining life of 20 years and straight-line depreciation, the difference between fair and book value is now only $14,250,000 = [$15,000,000 − 1 × ($15,000,000/20)]. Consolidated operating expenses increase by $750,000 (= $15,000,000/20) to reflect the year's write-off.

> **LO3** Report subsequent year write-offs of acquisition date revaluations of subsidiary identifiable assets and liabilities.

The consolidation process includes adjustments to revalue assets and liabilities already on the subsidiary's books, such as plant and equipment or inventories. Previously unreported identifiable intangible assets, such as trademarks, brand names, or favorable lease agreements are also recognized. Because the price paid generally exceeds the fair value of the identifiable net assets acquired, goodwill usually appears on consolidated balance sheets. Whether tangible or intangible, we must measure the appropriate balances and changes in the value of these assets and liabilities over time, and report them in the consolidated financial statements. The reported changes for the current year appear in eliminating entry (O). This section describes the measurement and format of eliminating entry (O) for a variety of common revaluations.

Previously Reported Assets and Liabilities

Changes in revaluations of assets and liabilities already reported on the acquired company's books at the date of acquisition do not present new reporting challenges. As time passes, the revaluations are reported in the same way as the underlying assets or liabilities. Certain long-lived assets, such as land, inventories, and nonmarketable securities, remain at their reported values unless sold or impaired. Others, such as plant and equipment and finite-life intangibles, are systematically written off over their estimated lives. Next we discuss subsequent treatment of common revaluations of assets and liabilities reported on the subsidiary's books.

Inventories   Assume the fair value of a subsidiary's inventory is $1,000,000 and its book value is $800,000 when acquired on January 1, 2016. The subsidiary reports its inventory using the FIFO method, which assumes the beginning (oldest) inventory is sold first. Therefore, the subsidiary likely reports on its own books its January 1, 2016 inventory as completely sold during 2016 as follows:

Cost of goods sold..	800,000	
Inventory		800,000
To record sale of beginning inventory during 2016.		

On the 2016 consolidated income statement, cost of goods sold reflects the $1,000,000 fair value of the beginning inventory, and is $200,000 higher than the subsidiary's recorded value. The consolidation working paper includes an eliminating entry that revalues the cost of goods sold to $1,000,000, as follows:

(O)	Cost of goods sold	200,000	
	Inventory		200,000
	Eliminating entry to revalue cost of sales to fair value at the date of acquisition.		

This entry is part of eliminating entry (O) on the working paper, and does *not* appear on the subsidiary's books. Consolidation eliminating entries related to the inventory revaluation are not necessary in 2017 and beyond, since the subsidiary no longer carries the original inventory on its books. If the subsidiary uses LIFO, the beginning inventory is likely not reported as sold, and no eliminating entry (O) is appropriate.

Depreciable Assets   Assume the subsidiary reports equipment at a net book value of $50,000,000 on January 1, 2016, when its fair value is $70,000,000. The subsidiary appropriately depreciates this equipment on a straight-line basis, with a remaining life of 10 years, no residual value, and records depreciation expense of $5,000,000 (= $50,000,000/10) for the year 2016. On the consolidation working paper for 2016 and the next 9 years, eliminating entry (O) adjusts recorded depreciation expense to reflect the fair value of the equipment at the date of acquisition, as follows:

(O)	Depreciation expense.	2,000,000	
	Plant and equipment (or accumulated depreciation)		2,000,000
	Eliminating entry to revalue depreciation to reflect fair value at the date of acquisition; $2,000,000 = ($70,000,000 − $50,000,000)/10.		

This eliminating entry is required each year the subsidiary depreciates the equipment.

Long-Term Debt   The fair value of debt may differ from its book value at the date of acquisition. On January 1, 2016, assume the subsidiary reports $100,000,000 in 5 percent bonds payable, issued in a previous year at par, and due on December 31, 2025. Market interest rates are higher than 5 percent on January 1, 2016, and the fair value of the bonds is $90,000,000, a discount of $10,000,000.

The subsidiary appropriately reports $5,000,000 of interest expense (= $100,000,000 × 5%) on its own books during 2016. Assuming for convenience straight-line amortization of the discount over the bonds' remaining 10-year life, the 2016 consolidation working paper eliminating entry follows:

(O)	Interest expense	1,000,000	
	Bonds payable (or bond discount)		1,000,000
	Eliminating entry to amortize bond discount for 2016; $1,000,000 = $10,000,000/10.		

This eliminating entry is made each year the bonds remain outstanding.

Previously Unreported Identifiable Intangibles

The consolidated balance sheet reports a subsidiary's previously unreported identifiable intangible assets, if they meet the contractual or separability criteria of *FASB ASC Topic 805*. Examples include use rights, brand names, customer lists, and noncompetition agreements. *ASC Topic 350*, Intangibles—Goodwill and Other, provides the reporting requirements for these intangibles in periods after the acquisition date.

Intangibles may have **limited** or **indefinite** lives. Intangibles with limited lives are amortized over their useful lives. *Both* types of intangibles are subject to periodic impairment testing.

Intangible Assets with Limited Lives Limited life intangibles often include favorable lease agreements and customer lists. Standards similar to those generally applicable to depreciable assets are relevant here:

- The intangible is amortized over its estimated (limited) useful life.
- The amount to be amortized is the recorded amount of the asset less estimated residual value. Residual value is generally zero unless there is compelling market evidence to the contrary.
- The method of amortization reflects the pattern in which the economic benefits of the intangible are consumed. If a pattern of consumption cannot be readily determined, the straight-line method is used. Any subsequent change in the estimate of life or residual value follows the usual rules for a change in estimate.

In estimating the life of a recognized intangible asset, the accountant examines a variety of economic, legal, regulatory, contractual, competitive, and other factors, including:

- How the intangible asset will be used.
- The expected useful life of other assets to which the intangible may relate.
- Legal, regulatory, or contractual provisions that limit the useful life of the intangible asset, or that enable renewal of the life without substantial additional cost.
- Economic factors that may impact the useful life, such as competition, demand, and obsolescence.
- The costs necessary to maintain the useful life of the asset; very high maintenance costs suggest a short useful life.

If the estimated life changes, the remaining book value is amortized over the newly estimated remaining life.

Intangible Assets with Indefinite Lives If no factors appear to limit the intangible asset's life, then its life is deemed to be *indefinite*. To conclude that an intangible has an indefinite life does not mean it will last forever; it merely means that no life-limiting factors can be identified at this time. If circumstances change, the intangible should be reclassified as a limited life asset, subject to periodic amortization as explained above. Indefinite life intangibles can include brand names and franchises, and goodwill, discussed in a later section. Acquired in-process research and development costs are classified as indefinite-lived until the related projects are completed or abandoned.

Impairment Testing for Identifiable Intangibles Accounting for impairments of **limited life intangibles** is guided by *ASC Section 350-30-35*. A two-step process determines the impairment loss:

Step 1 Compare the **undiscounted cash flows** expected from the future use of the asset and its subsequent disposition with the asset's book value. If the sum of the future undiscounted cash flows is less than the asset's book value, impairment has occurred and we go on to the second step. If the book value is lower than the sum of the future undiscounted cash flows, no impairment has occurred.

Step 2 If Step 1 indicates impairment, the amount of impairment loss is the difference between the intangible asset's book value and the **present value of the cash flows** expected from the future use of the asset and its subsequent disposition.

For **indefinite life intangible assets**, a company has the *option* to do a qualitative assessment of whether it is *more likely than not* (more than 50 percent likely) that the intangible asset's fair value is less than its book value. This assessment requires consideration of appropriate indicators of value, and is similar to the qualitative assessment of goodwill, discussed in the next section. If qualitative assessment indicates impairment is likely, a quantitative test is performed. First the intangible asset's fair value is estimated. If fair value is less than book value, the loss is the difference between book and fair value. Note that the qualitative test is optional. If economic conditions indicate possible impairment, a company can skip the qualitative test and go straight to the quantitative analysis. Also note that the optional qualitative test does not apply to limited life intangibles.

BUSINESS APPLICATION   Time Warner's Identifiable Intangible Assets

Time Warner's 2013 consolidated balance sheet reports identifiable intangible assets totaling $9,549 million, of which $7,629 million have indefinite lives. Note 2 to the consolidated financial statements reports its December 31, 2013, limited-lived identifiable intangibles as follows:

(in millions)	Gross	Accumulated Amortization	Net
Intangible assets subject to amortization:			
Film library	$3,452	$(2,494)	$ 958
Brands, tradenames, and other intangible assets	2,156	(1,194)	962
Total	$5,608	$(3,688)	$1,920

Time Warner reported amortization expense of $251 million in 2013. It amortizes its film library using a "film forecast computation methodology," and other limited-lived intangibles are straight-line amortized over their useful lives. Time Warner also disclosed that it intends to reclassify indefinite-lived tradenames carried at approximately $586 million to limited-lived intangibles. These tradenames are connected with the Time, Inc. segment, an underperforming unit to be spun off as a separate company in 2014.

Time Warner recorded intangibles impairment losses of $97 million in 2013, mostly related to its Time, Inc. segment. In 2012 it reported $80 million in impairment losses related to its shutdown of Imagine, a Hindi general entertainment channel acquired for $126.5 million in 2009, which had performed poorly.

The expenses reported above are very large. Think about the role that judgment plays in determining the asset values, classification of whether they have limited or indefinite lives, and reported amortization and impairment losses. *Source:* Time Warner Inc. annual report, 2013.

Goodwill

LO4 Measure and report goodwill impairment losses.

FASB ASC Section 350-20-35 requires that goodwill—an indefinite life intangible—be regularly tested for **impairment**, using a unique process discussed below. Goodwill impairment losses are reported in the *operating section* of the income statement. If goodwill impairment losses are material, they appear as a separate line.

The Reporting Unit Concept   Goodwill is not a free-standing asset, but has meaning only in the context of a business unit. It represents a variety of intangible benefits connected with that business, beyond its tangible and identifiable intangible net assets. **Goodwill** is the residual value remaining after the acquisition cost in a business combination is assigned to the fair values of tangible and identifiable intangible assets acquired net of liabilities assumed. For purposes of impairment testing, the fair value of goodwill must be assessed in terms of the *reporting unit* to which the goodwill belongs.

A **reporting unit** for this purpose is usually an operating segment of the business, as defined by *ASC Topic 280,* Segment Reporting. *ASC para. 280-10-50-1* defines an operating segment as follows:

An **operating segment** is a component of an enterprise:

a. That engages in business activities from which it may earn revenues and incur expenses (including revenues and expenses relating to transactions with other components of the same enterprise),

b. Whose operating results are regularly reviewed by the enterprise's chief operating decision maker to make decisions about resources to be allocated to the segment and assess its performance, and

c. For which discrete financial information is available.

Assigning Goodwill to Reporting Units   Goodwill arising in a business combination is assigned to one or more reporting units, including **reporting units acquired** in the transaction and **existing reporting units** of the acquiring company.

Goodwill is assigned to *newly-acquired reporting units* the same way it is determined for the acquisition as a whole. The unit's goodwill is the difference between the fair value of the newly-acquired reporting unit and the fair values of identifiable assets and liabilities assigned to that unit.

When calculating the assignment of goodwill to *existing reporting units*, a "with and without" approach is used. The unit's fair value is estimated before (without) the business combination and again after (with) the business combination. The increase in fair value measures the goodwill assigned to that reporting unit, reflecting the expected benefits resulting from the combination.

The above procedures may not assign goodwill to individual reporting units in amounts that exactly equal the entire reported goodwill. If so, reasonable and consistent adjustments are made so that the exact amount of the total goodwill is assigned to the reporting units that benefit from the acquisition.

Assume that IBM acquires Softek Business Systems on January 1, 2016, at a cost of $840,000,000. Total goodwill from this acquisition is as follows:

Acquisition cost		$840,000,000
Fair value of identifiable net assets acquired:		
Previously reported assets.	$200,000,000	
Identifiable intangibles	800,000,000	
Liabilities.	(430,000,000)	570,000,000
Goodwill		$270,000,000

IBM acquires two new reporting units, Tech Services and Tech Software, and the combination is also expected to benefit the operations of one of IBM's existing reporting units, Global Services. All identifiable assets acquired and liabilities assumed are assigned to the two new units as follows:

	Tech Services	Tech Software	Total
Identifiable assets acquired	$700,000,000	$300,000,000	$1,000,000,000
Liabilities assumed.	(260,000,000)	(170,000,000)	(430,000,000)
Identifiable net assets assigned.	$440,000,000	$130,000,000	$ 570,000,000

The fair value of the Tech Services unit is estimated to be $630,000,000 and the fair value of the Tech Software unit is $160,000,000. Management estimates that the acquisition of Softek will increase the fair value of IBM's Global Services unit by $80,000,000. The preliminary assignment of goodwill to reporting units is:

	Tech Services	Tech Software	Global Services
Fair value of unit.	$630,000,000	$160,000,000	
Identifiable net assets assigned.	440,000,000	130,000,000	
Initial goodwill assignment	$190,000,000	$ 30,000,000	$ 80,000,000

Total assigned goodwill is $300,000,000 (= $190,000,000 + $30,000,000 + $80,000,000), which exceeds the $270,000,000 goodwill determined for the entire combination by $30,000,000, or ten percent of the total amount assigned [= ($300,000,000 − $270,000,000)/$300,000,000]. Although different adjustments may be defensible, one possibility is a ten percent reduction in the tentative allocation shown above. Implementing this adjustment results in the following assignment of goodwill, equaling the actual $270,000,000 goodwill for the combination:

	Tech Services	Tech Software	Global Services
Initial goodwill assignment.................	$190,000,000	$30,000,000	$80,000,000
10 percent reduction	(19,000,000)	(3,000,000)	(8,000,000)
Final goodwill assignment	$171,000,000	$27,000,000	$72,000,000

Goodwill Impairment   Goodwill resulting from a business combination should be tested for impairment *at least annually*, unless circumstances indicate the likelihood of impairment is remote. More frequent testing may be indicated based on new events or changing circumstances, such as:

- Significant downturn in the business climate
- Adverse legal or regulatory outcomes
- Unanticipated new competition
- Loss of key personnel
- Expectation that a reporting unit will be sold

Goodwill is tested for impairment at the reporting unit level. There are potentially *three steps* to the **goodwill impairment test**, as follows:

Step 0   A company has the *option* to qualitatively assess whether it is *more likely than not* (more than 50 percent likely) that a reporting unit's fair value is less than its book value. If not, the company is not required to test the reporting unit's goodwill for impairment. *ASC para. 350-20-35-3C* provides guidance on factors to consider in making this assessment, paraphrased below:

- **Macroeconomic conditions** such as general economic deterioration, limitations on accessing capital, fluctuations in foreign exchange rates, or other developments in equity and credit markets
- **Industry and market considerations** such as increased competition, a change in the market for the entity's products or services, or regulatory or political developments
- **Cost factors** such as increases in materials, labor, or other costs negatively affecting earnings and cash flows
- **Overall financial performance** such as negative or declining cash flows or declining performance relative to budgeted revenue or earnings
- **Changes in management**, key personnel, strategy, customers, or possible bankruptcy or litigation
- **Specific reporting unit issues**, such as a change in the composition of net assets, expectation of disposal, or recognition of goodwill impairment loss by a subsidiary that is part of the reporting unit.

Quantitative goodwill impairment testing is required only if the qualitative assessment reveals that it is more likely than not that the reporting unit's fair value is less than its book value. The quantitative test proceeds as follows:

Step 1   Estimate the **current fair value of the reporting unit** and compare it to its book value. If the fair value *exceeds* the book value, there is no impairment and the process stops. If the fair value is *less than* the book value, the reporting unit's goodwill *may be impaired*. We go to the second step to assess the amount of impairment of goodwill, if any.

Step 2   Estimate the **implied fair value of the reporting unit's goodwill** by repeating the process carried out at acquisition. Estimate the current fair values of identifiable net assets and subtract this total from the estimated fair value of the reporting unit to get the fair value of the goodwill. If the fair value of goodwill is less than its book value, the goodwill is impaired and a write-off is made. Once made, *write-offs are not reversed* in the future, even if the fair value of goodwill increases.

For any reporting unit at any time, the company has the "unconditional option" to skip Step 0 and go directly to Step 1 if desired. The company can subsequently resume using Step 0 at any time.

A reporting unit may have a zero or negative book value. Because fair value can never be negative, Step 1 assessment leads to no goodwill impairment. However, common sense suggests that a reporting unit with negative book value is *more* likely to have goodwill impairment. In *ASC para. 350-20-35-8A*, the FASB requires that when the reporting unit's book value is zero or negative, Step 2 must be performed when it is more likely than not that goodwill is impaired.

To illustrate goodwill impairment testing, return to the previous example. It is now one year later, December 31, 2016, and we test for possible goodwill impairment in 2016. Assume the company either decided to skip Step 0 or it concluded from its Step 0 qualitative analysis that it is more likely than not that the fair values of all three reporting units are less than book value. The following information is available at December 31, 2016:

Step 1	Tech Services	Tech Software	Global Services
Fair value of unit.	$700,000,000	$140,000,000	$1,000,000,000
Book value of unit.	(500,000,000)	(160,000,000)	(1,200,000,000)
Difference.	$200,000,000	$ (20,000,000)	$ (200,000,000)

Conclusion: Because the current fair values of Tech Software and Global Services are less than book value, goodwill assigned to these units may be impaired. Tech Services' goodwill is not impaired.

In Step 2, we compute the fair value of the goodwill at December 31, 2016, which we then compare to its current book value. Assume the December 31, 2016, fair values of the identifiable net assets of Tech Software and Global Services are $120,000,000 and $900,000,000, respectively. The Step 2 evaluation is as follows:

Step 2	Tech Software	Global Services
Fair value of unit.	$140,000,000	$1,000,000,000
Fair value of identifiable net assets of unit.	(120,000,000)	(900,000,000)
Fair value of goodwill	20,000,000	100,000,000
Goodwill book value.	27,000,000	72,000,000
Difference.	$ (7,000,000)	$ 28,000,000

Conclusion: Goodwill assigned to Tech Software is impaired by $7,000,000. Global Services' goodwill is not impaired.

We record an impairment loss of $7,000,000 for 2016 as part of eliminating entry (O) on the consolidation working paper, as follows:

(O)	Goodwill impairment loss	7,000,000	
	Goodwill.		7,000,000
	To record goodwill impairment loss for 2016.		

When goodwill is again tested for impairment in 2017, the book value of Tech Software's goodwill is $20,000,000 (= $27,000,000 − $7,000,000).

BUSINESS APPLICATION   **Time Warner's Reporting Units and Goodwill Impairment**

Time Warner reports $30,563 million in goodwill on its December 31, 2013, balance sheet, and assigns it to the following reporting units:

(in millions)	December 31, 2013
Turner.	$13,980
Home Box Office	7,431
Warner Bros.	5,990
Time Inc..	3,162
Total Time Warner	$30,563

In testing its goodwill for impairment in 2013, Time Warner elected not to perform the qualitative test. The quantitative goodwill impairment test did not result in recognition of any impairment losses. Time Warner discloses the following information concerning this test:

> The fair value of the Time Inc. reporting unit exceeded its carrying value by approximately 3%. No other reporting unit's fair value was within 10% of its carrying value . . . . For Time Inc., the significant assumptions utilized in the 2013 DCF analysis were a discount rate of 10.5% and a terminal revenue growth rate of 1.00%. Significant assumptions utilized for all other reporting units included discount rates that ranged from 9.5% to 10.0% and a terminal revenue growth rate of 3.25%. Significant assumptions utilized in the market based approach were market multiples of 7.5x for the Time Inc. reporting unit and market multiples ranging from 7.5x to 12.0x for the Company's other reporting units where a market-based approach was performed.

Because the fair value of each of its reporting units exceeded book value in Step 1 of the quantitative impairment test, Time Warner was not required to perform Step 2. Time Warner measures the fair value of its reporting units using discounted cash flows (DCF) and appropriate risk-adjusted discount rates and estimated revenue growth rates. Time Warner also uses a market-based approach for some units. This approach involves identifying public companies with characteristics similar to those of the unit and observing the relationship between their market value (stock price) and a measure of earnings performance, typically EBITDA. The same multiple is then applied to the unit's EBITDA to estimate its market value.

Time Warner's analysis highlights how difficult it is to estimate the numbers needed for impairment testing. Its footnote disclosure gives us some insight into this process.

> Determining fair value requires the exercise of significant judgment, including judgments about appropriate discount rates, perpetual growth rates, the amount and timing of expected future cash flows, as well as relevant comparable public company earnings multiples. The cash flows employed in the DCF analyses are based on the Company's most recent budgets and long range plans and, when applicable, various growth rates are assumed for years beyond the current long range plan period. Discount rate assumptions are based on an assessment of market rates as well as the risk inherent in the future cash flows included in the budgets and long range plans.

If you are Time Warner's auditor, how do you determine if its impairment losses are fairly presented? Evaluation requires a solid knowledge of Time Warner's activities and business environment. *Source: Time Warner Inc. annual report, 2013.*

Amortization and Impairment of Identifiable Intangibles and Goodwill: An Illustration

The following example illustrates how acquired identifiable intangibles and goodwill are reported in years subsequent to acquisition. Primus Telecommunications Group acquires all of the voting stock of Matrix Internet on January 1, 2017. The following intangibles, previously unrecorded by Matrix, are reportable on the consolidated financial statements:

Intangible asset *(in millions)*	Fair value	Useful life
Customer lists	$ 150	5 years
Brand names	240	4 years
Goodwill	3,200	Indefinite

The goodwill is appropriately allocated to two of Primus' reporting units, as follows *(in millions)*:

Broadband unit	$1,920
Wholesale carrier unit	1,280
Total goodwill	$3,200

Customer lists and brand names are straight-line amortized over their useful lives. It is now December 31, 2017, the end of the accounting year. We have the following information regarding these intangibles:

Intangible asset *(in millions)*	Total expected future cash inflows, undiscounted	Total expected future cash inflows, discounted
Customer lists	$100	$ 80
Brand names	200	125

(in millions)	Broadband	Wholesale Carrier
Fair value of unit	$17,600	$8,640
Book value of unit	15,040	8,960
Fair value of identifiable net assets	15,680	7,520

We must determine the 2017 amortization expense for the customer lists and brand names, and the appropriate impairment loss, if any, for all the intangibles.

Amortization expense on the customer lists and brand names is as follows *(in millions)*:

Customer lists	$150/5 = $30
Brand names	$240/4 = 60
Total amortization expense	$90

Because both customer lists and brand names have limited lives, we calculate impairment loss using the two-step process discussed on p. 127:

Identifiable intangible *(in millions)*	Book value	Step 1: Book value greater than undiscounted cash flow?	Step 2: Impairment loss = book value less discounted cash flow
Customer lists	$150 − $30 = $120	Yes ($120 > $100)	$120 − $80 = $40
Brand names	$240 − $60 = $180	No ($180 < $200)	—

Primus reports an impairment loss of $40,000,000 on the customer lists.

Suppose Step 0 of the goodwill impairment test indicates that book value more likely than not exceeds fair value for both reporting units. Goodwill impairment testing follows the process discussed on pp. 130–131:

Step 1 *(in millions)*	Broadband	Wholesale Carrier
Fair value of unit..	$17,600	$8,640
Book value of unit.....................................	(15,040)	(8,960)
Difference..	$ 2,560	$ (320)

Conclusion: Because the current fair value of Wholesale Carrier is less than its book value, goodwill assigned to this unit may be impaired. Broadband's goodwill is not impaired.

Step 2 *(in millions)*	Wholesale Carrier
Fair value of unit..	$8,640
Fair value of identifiable net assets of unit...............................	(7,520)
Current fair value of goodwill..	1,120
Book value of goodwill..	1,280
Difference...	$ 160

Conclusion: Goodwill assigned to Wholesale Carrier is impaired by $160 million.

Consolidation eliminating entry (O) is as follows:

(O)			
Amortization expense...		90,000,000	
Impairment loss on identifiable intangibles		40,000,000	
Goodwill impairment loss...		160,000,000	
Customer lists...			70,000,000
Brand names..			60,000,000
Goodwill..			160,000,000
To record amortization expense and impairment losses on previously unreported intangibles and goodwill for 2017.			

The $130,000,000 in amortization expense and impairment losses on customer lists and brand names can be combined with other operating items, such as general and administrative expenses, if appropriate. When the amount is material, the $160,000,000 goodwill impairment loss appears as a separate line in the operating section of the consolidated income statement.

• •

Reporting Perspective

The FASB added the qualitative assessment option (Step 0) to make impairment testing less onerous. Prior to 2012, all companies were required to compare the fair value of each indefinite life intangible and reporting unit to its book value. Companies complained that estimating the fair value of each intangible asset and reporting unit was costly and time consuming, and unnecessary when fair value was obviously higher than book value.

Critics claim that this option weakens the impairment test, by giving managers additional earnings management opportunities. The subjective nature of the qualitative assessment increases the ability to delay recognition of impairment losses. Management can also choose to perform the quantitative test in good years, but take the qualitative option in bad years, thus increasing the likelihood of impairment recognition when earnings are high and avoiding it when earnings are low.

continued

The new qualitative option may not result in time and cost savings. The subjective nature of this option can result in higher audit fees. Companies must develop a formal process for the qualitative assessment, and thoroughly document their reasons for not performing the quantitative test. When qualitative assessment reveals that fair value is only slightly above book value, the quantitative test may still be indicated.

Have companies taken advantage of Step 0? Which companies are more likely to opt out of impairment testing using Step 0? **Duff & Phelps**, a global valuation firm, conducted a study of 355 U.S. public companies for 2012 and 2013. They found that use of Step 0 increased from 33% in 2012 to 41% in 2013. As expected, companies with high market-to-book ratios were much more likely to opt out of impairment testing using Step 0, since fair value would likely be significantly higher than book value for these companies. *Source*: Duff & Phelps, *Goodwill Impairment Step 0 Study*, 2013.

Reporting Perspective

While FASB standards apply to public companies, private companies often prepare U.S. GAAP financial statements to satisfy creditors and other stakeholders. However, information needs of stakeholders in private companies are not the same as for public companies, and these stakeholders typically have alternate sources of information about a private company's performance. For private companies, the FASB recognized that the costs of implementing many of its standards likely exceed the benefits. In 2012, it established the **Private Company Council** (PCC), to develop U.S. GAAP alternatives for private companies.

One example is the goodwill impairment test. Although adding the optional qualitative step has the goal of making this test less onerous, the valuation process can still be very costly and complex. On the PCC's recommendation, in 2014 the FASB issued an Accounting Standards Update, effective in 2015, with these provisions:

- Goodwill is amortized on a straight-line basis over 10 years or less.

- Test goodwill for impairment at either the company or reporting unit level.

- Test goodwill for impairment only when a "triggering event" indicates that the fair value of the company or reporting unit is less than its book value.

- When testing the goodwill for impairment, the company has the option to perform a qualitative test. If impairment is more likely than not, the quantitative test only compares the company or reporting unit's fair value with its book value, rather than using a 2-step approach.

The private company goodwill impairment test is less costly because it does not require annual testing, allows testing at the overall company level, and never requires estimation of the fair value of the goodwill.

REVIEW 1 • Intangibles Impairment Testing

FineChannel Media Corporation reports several acquired intangible assets on its consolidated financial statements. At the end of the 2017 reporting year, each intangible is tested for possible impairment loss. The intangible assets and their current balances are as follows *(all amounts below in millions)*:

Intangible asset	Book value at December 31, 2017
Customer lists (limited life)	$ 250
Television rights (limited life)	100
Brand names (indefinite life)	400
Goodwill	1,750

Information related to impairment testing is as follows:

Total expected future undiscounted cash flows, customer lists	$ 240
Total expected future discounted cash flows, customer lists	225
Total expected future undiscounted cash flows, television rights	105
Total expected future discounted cash flows, television rights	65
Total expected future undiscounted cash flows, brand names	500
Total expected future discounted cash flows, brand names	380
Goodwill is assigned to the following reporting units:	
Cable	$1,000
Filmed Entertainment	200
Networks	550
Total	$1,750

FineChannel bypasses the qualitative assessment option for its indefinite life intangibles and goodwill impairment tests. Reporting unit information at December 31, 2017, is as follows:

	Cable	Filmed Entertainment	Networks
Fair value of unit	$ 2,000	$ 2,800	$ 6,200
Fair value of identifiable assets	20,000	15,000	30,000
Fair value of liabilities	19,500	13,350	24,050
Book value of unit	2,300	2,000	6,500

Required

Calculate the 2017 impairment losses on identifiable intangibles and goodwill, and prepare the eliminating entry (O) to record these losses.

Solutions are located after the chapter assignments.

COMPREHENSIVE ILLUSTRATION: CONSOLIDATION IN SUBSEQUENT YEARS

We now apply consolidation procedures to a more complex acquisition in years beyond the first year. Return to IBM's acquisition of DataFile, found in Chapters 2 and 3. IBM Corporation buys all of the voting stock of DataFile Inc. on July 1, 2015, the beginning of the fiscal year for both companies, for $25,000,000 cash. DataFile's book value on that date was $5,300,000. The analysis of the excess paid over book value from Chapter 3 appears below.

Acquisition cost		$25,000,000
Book value of DataFile		(5,300,000)
Cost in excess of DataFile's book value		19,700,000
Differences between fair value and book value:		
Current assets	$ (300,000)	
Plant and equipment, net	10,000,000	
Patents and copyrights	4,000,000	
Brand names	1,000,000	
Lease agreements	600,000	
Customer relationships	3,000,000	
Long-term debt	(2,000,000)	(16,300,000)
Goodwill		$ 3,400,000

Exhibit 4.3 contains information on DataFile's assets and liabilities. Estimated lives and write-off policies, identification of limited life and indefinite life intangible assets, and calculated impairment losses for specific intangibles and goodwill follow the requirements of *FASB ASC Topic 350*, as discussed in the previous section.

EXHIBIT 4.3 Revaluation Write-Off Information for DataFile Acquisition		
	Write-Off Policy	**Write-Off for Fiscal 2016**
Current assets	Revaluation pertains to inventory reported using FIFO	Full amount ($300,000), since beginning inventory is sold in 2016
Plant and equipment	25 years, straight-line	$10,000,000/25 = $400,000
Patents and copyrights	5 years, straight-line	$4,000,000/5 = $800,000
Brand names	Indefinite life	$100,000 impairment loss
Lease agreements	2 years, straight-line	$600,000/2 = $300,000
Customer relationships	3 years, straight-line	$3,000,000/3 = $1,000,000
Long-term debt	4 years, straight-line	$2,000,000/4 = $500,000
Goodwill.	Impairment testing	No impairment loss

Consolidation After One Year

It is now June 30, 2016, one year after the acquisition. DataFile reports net income of $3,000,000 and other comprehensive income of $40,000 for fiscal 2016 and declared and paid dividends of $400,000 to IBM during the year. IBM uses the complete equity method to report its investment in DataFile on its own books. Calculation of equity in the net income of DataFile for fiscal 2016 appears below.

DataFile's reported net income for fiscal 2016	$3,000,000
Adjustments for revaluation write-offs of:	
Current assets (cost of goods sold)	300,000
Plant and equipment (depreciation expense).	(400,000)
Patents and copyrights (amortization expense)	(800,000)
Brand names (impairment loss)	(100,000)
Lease agreements (amortization expense).	(300,000)
Customer relationships (amortization expense)	(1,000,000)
Long-term debt (interest expense)	500,000
Equity in net income of DataFile.	$1,200,000

After the initial acquisition entry, IBM makes the following entries on its own books during fiscal 2016:

Investment in DataFile	1,240,000	
Equity in net income of DataFile		1,200,000
Equity in other comprehensive income of DataFile.		40,000
To record equity in net income and other comprehensive income for fiscal 2016.		
Cash.	400,000	
Investment in DataFile.		400,000
To record dividends received in fiscal 2016.		

After these entries, the investment account has a June 30, 2016, balance of $25,840,000 (= $25,000,000 + $1,240,000 − $400,000). The reported balances from the books of IBM and DataFile at June 30, 2016, appear in the consolidation working paper in Exhibit 4.4. The eliminating entries, in journal entry form, are as follows:

(C)	Equity in net income of DataFile.	1,200,000	
	Equity in other comprehensive income of DataFile	40,000	
	Dividends.		400,000
	Investment in DataFile.		840,000

To eliminate equity in net income and other comprehensive income on the parent's books, dividends on the subsidiary's books, and restore the investment account to its beginning-of-year value.

(E)	Common stock, par	500,000	
	Additional paid-in capital	1,700,000	
	Retained earnings, July 1.	2,800,000	
	Accumulated other comprehensive income, July 1	300,000	
	Investment in DataFile.		5,300,000

To eliminate the subsidiary's beginning-of-year equity accounts against the investment account.

(R)	Plant and equipment, net.	10,000,000	
	Patents and copyrights	4,000,000	
	Brand names	1,000,000	
	Lease agreements	600,000	
	Customer relationships	3,000,000	
	Goodwill.	3,400,000	
	Current assets.		300,000
	Long-term debt.		2,000,000
	Investment in DataFile.		19,700,000

To recognize the beginning-of-year revaluations and eliminate the remainder of the investment account balance.

(O-1)	Current assets	300,000	
	Cost of goods sold		300,000

To adjust current year cost of goods sold to reflect inventory revaluation.

(O-2)	Operating expenses (depreciation)	400,000	
	Plant and equipment, net		400,000

To adjust current year depreciation expense to reflect plant and equipment revaluation.

(O-3)	Operating expenses (amortization).	2,100,000	
	Patents and copyrights		800,000
	Lease agreements.		300,000
	Customer relationships		1,000,000

To adjust current year amortization expense to reflect revaluations of limited life intangibles.

(O-4)	Long-term debt	500,000	
	Operating expenses (interest)		500,000

To adjust current year interest expense to reflect long-term debt revaluation.

(O-5)	Operating expenses (impairment loss).	100,000	
	Brand names.		100,000

To record brand names impairment for the current year.

EXHIBIT 4.4 Consolidation Working Paper for IBM and DataFile At June 30, 2016, Trial Balance Format

	Accounts Taken From Books Dr (Cr)		Eliminations		Consolidated Balances
	IBM	DataFile	Dr	Cr	Dr (Cr)
Current assets	$ 16,200,000	$ 3,000,000	(O-1)$ 300,000	$ 300,000 (R)	$ 19,200,000
Plant and equipment, net.	145,200,000	55,000,000	(R) 10,000,000	400,000 (O-2)	209,800,000
Patents and copyrights	2,500,000	800,000	(R) 4,000,000	800,000 (O-3)	6,500,000
Investment in DataFile	25,840,000	—		840,000 (C)	—
				5,300,000 (E)	
				19,700,000 (R)	
Brand names	—	—	(R) 1,000,000	100,000 (O-5)	900,000
Lease agreements	—	—	(R) 600,000	300,000 (O-3)	300,000
Customer relationships	—	—	(R) 3,000,000	1,000,000 (O-3)	2,000,000
Goodwill	—	—	(R) 3,400,000		3,400,000
Current liabilities.	(16,500,000)	(9,000,000)			(25,500,000)
Long-term debt	(89,900,000)	(41,860,000)	(O-4) 500,000	2,000,000 (R)	(133,260,000)
Common stock, par	(2,000,000)	(500,000)	(E) 500,000		(2,000,000)
Additional paid-in capital	(59,000,000)	(1,700,000)	(E) 1,700,000		(59,000,000)
Retained earnings, July 1	(16,000,000)	(2,800,000)	(E) 2,800,000		(16,000,000)
Accumulated other comprehensive income, July 1.	(1,000,000)	(300,000)	(E) 300,000		(1,000,000)
Dividends	1,000,000	400,000		400,000 (C)	1,000,000
Sales revenue.	(500,000,000)	(100,000,000)			(600,000,000)
Equity in net income of DataFile.	(1,200,000)	—	(C) 1,200,000		—
Equity in other comprehensive income of DataFile	(40,000)	—	(C) 40,000		—
Cost of goods sold.	420,000,000	65,000,000		300,000 (O-1)	484,700,000
Operating expenses	75,000,000	32,000,000	(O-2) 400,000	500,000 (O-4)	109,100,000
			(O-3) 2,100,000		
			(O-5) 100,000		
Other comprehensive income	(100,000)	(40,000)			(140,000)
Totals	$ 0	$ 0	$31,940,000	$31,940,000	$ 0

Using the working paper consolidated account balances in Exhibit 4.4, we prepare the following consolidated statement of comprehensive income for fiscal 2016, and the consolidated balance sheet at June 30, 2016.

IBM CORPORATION and DATAFILE, INC.
Consolidated Statement of Comprehensive Income
For Year Ended June 30, 2016

Sales revenue.	$600,000,000
Less: Cost of goods sold	484,700,000
Gross profit.	115,300,000
Less: Operating expenses	109,100,000
Net income	**6,200,000**
Plus: Other comprehensive income	140,000
Comprehensive income	$ 6,340,000

IBM CORPORATION and DATAFILE, INC.
Consolidated Balance Sheet
June 30, 2016

Assets		Liabilities and Stockholders' Equity	
Current assets	$ 19,200,000	Current liabilities.	$ 25,500,000
Plant and equipment, net. . . .	209,800,000	Long-term debt	133,260,000
Patents and copyrights	6,500,000	Total liabilities.	158,760,000
Brand names	900,000		
Lease agreements	300,000	Stockholders' equity	
Customer relationships	2,000,000	Common stock, par	2,000,000
Goodwill	3,400,000	Additional paid-in capital	59,000,000
		Retained earnings	21,200,000
		Accumulated other comprehensive income. . .	1,140,000
		Total stockholders' equity	83,340,000
Total assets	$242,100,000	Total liabilities and stockholders' equity	$242,100,000

We calculate consolidated retained earnings and accumulated other comprehensive income at June 30, 2016, as follows, using the consolidated balances from the working paper and consolidated net income from the consolidated statement of comprehensive income:

Retained earnings, July 1.	$16,000,000
Plus: Consolidated net income	6,200,000
Less: Consolidated dividends	(1,000,000)
Retained earnings, June 30	$21,200,000
Accumulated other comprehensive income, July 1.	$ 1,000,000
Plus: Other comprehensive income	140,000
Accumulated other comprehensive income, June 30	$ 1,140,000

Consolidation After Two Years

Now assume it is June 30, 2017, *two years* after the acquisition, and consolidated financial statements are again prepared. DataFile reports net income of $3,500,000 for fiscal 2017, an other comprehensive loss of $25,000, and declared and paid dividends of $200,000 to IBM during the year. There are no changes in depreciation and amortization policy for DataFile's plant and equipment and limited life intangibles. Year-end impairment testing in 2017 reveals no impairment loss for brand names, whereas goodwill is impaired by $700,000. Calculation of equity in the net income of DataFile for fiscal 2017 appears below.

DataFile's reported net income for fiscal 2017	$3,500,000
Adjustments for revaluation write-offs:	
Plant and equipment (depreciation expense).	(400,000)
Patents and copyrights (amortization expense)	(800,000)
Lease agreements (amortization expense).	(300,000)
Customer relationships (amortization expense)	(1,000,000)
Long-term debt (interest expense)	500,000
Goodwill (impairment loss)	(700,000)
Equity in net income of DataFile.	$ 800,000

IBM makes the following entries on its own books during fiscal 2017:

Investment in DataFile	775,000	
Equity in other comprehensive loss of DataFile	25,000	
Equity in net income of DataFile		800,000
To record equity in net income and other comprehensive income for fiscal 2017.		
Cash	200,000	
Investment in DataFile		200,000
To record dividends received in fiscal 2017.		

The investment account has a June 30, 2017, balance of $26,415,000 (= $25,840,000 + $775,000 − $200,000).

The reported balances from the books of IBM and DataFile at June 30, 2017 appear on the consolidation working paper in Exhibit 4.5. The reported retained earnings balance at July 1, 2016, for each company equals its reported July 1, 2015, balance plus 2016 net income less 2016 dividends, as reported on the books of each separate company. Similarly, the reported accumulated other income balance at July 1, 2016, for each company equals its reported July 1, 2015, balance plus 2016 other comprehensive income, as reported on each company's books. Eliminating entries, in journal entry form, are as follows:

(C)	Equity in net income of DataFile.	800,000	
	Equity in other comprehensive loss of DataFile		25,000
	Dividends.		200,000
	Investment in DataFile.		575,000
	To eliminate equity in net income and other comprehensive loss on the parent's books, dividends on the subsidiary's books, and restore the investment account to its beginning-of-year value.		
(E)	Common stock, par	500,000	
	Additional paid-in capital	1,700,000	
	Retained earnings, July 1.	5,400,000	
	Accumulated other comprehensive income, July 1	340,000	
	Investment in DataFile.		7,940,000
	To eliminate the subsidiary's beginning-of-year equity accounts against the investment account.		
(R)	Plant and equipment, net	9,600,000	
	Patents and copyrights	3,200,000	
	Brand names	900,000	
	Lease agreements	300,000	
	Customer relationships	2,000,000	
	Goodwill	3,400,000	
	Long-term debt		1,500,000
	Investment in DataFile.		17,900,000
	To recognize the beginning-of-year revaluations and eliminate the remainder of the investment account balance.		
(O-1)	Operating expenses (depreciation)	400,000	
	Plant and equipment, net		400,000
	To adjust current year depreciation expense to reflect plant and equipment revaluation.		
(O-2)	Operating expenses (amortization).	2,100,000	
	Patents and copyrights		800,000
	Lease agreements.		300,000
	Customer relationships		1,000,000
	To adjust current year amortization expense to reflect revaluations of limited life intangibles.		
(O-3)	Long-term debt	500,000	
	Operating expenses (interest).		500,000
	To adjust current year interest expense to reflect long-term debt revaluation.		
(O-4)	Operating expenses (impairment loss).	700,000	
	Goodwill.		700,000
	To record goodwill impairment for the current year.		

Eliminating entry (R) reports revaluations as of the beginning of the second year, revaluations that are now one year old. For example, the original plant and equipment revaluation is an increase of $10,000,000. Because the equipment is straight-line depreciated over 25 years, one year later the remaining revaluation is $9,600,000 [= $10,000,000 − 1 × ($10,000,000/25)]. Eliminating entry (O) reports the write-off for the current year.

If consolidation occurs after the end of the life of the revaluated asset or liability, related eliminating entries are no longer necessary. For example, the consolidated balance sheet reports an identifiable intangible, lease agreements, at the date of acquisition and at the end of fiscal 2017. Consolidated operating expenses for fiscal 2016 and 2017 reflect amortization expense on lease agreements. Because the lease agreements have a two-year life, consolidation working paper eliminations for fiscal 2018, the third year after acquisition, and any future years, do not recognize lease agreements in entry (R) or amortization of lease agreements in entry (O).

EXHIBIT 4.5 Consolidation Working Paper for IBM and DataFile At June 30, 2017, Trial Balance Format

	Accounts Taken From Books Dr (Cr)		Eliminations		Consolidated Balances
	IBM	DataFile	Dr	Cr	Dr (Cr)
Current assets	$ 17,000,000	$ 3,200,000			$ 20,200,000
Plant and equipment, net	160,000,000	62,000,000	(R) $ 9,600,000	$ 400,000 (O-1)	231,200,000
Patents and copyrights	2,400,000	600,000	(R) 3,200,000	800,000 (O-2)	5,400,000
Investment in DataFile	26,415,000	—		575,000 (C)	—
				7,940,000 (E)	
				17,900,000 (R)	
Brand names	—	—	(R) 900,000		900,000
Lease agreements	—	—	(R) 300,000	300,000 (O-2)	—
Customer relationships	—	—	(R) 2,000,000	1,000,000 (O-2)	1,000,000
Goodwill	—	—	(R) 3,400,000	700,000 (O-4)	2,700,000
Current liabilities	(18,000,000)	(10,000,000)			(28,000,000)
Long-term debt	(94,820,000)	(44,585,000)	(O-3) 500,000	1,500,000 (R)	(140,405,000)
Common stock, par	(2,000,000)	(500,000)	(E) 500,000		(2,000,000)
Additional paid-in capital	(59,000,000)	(1,700,000)	(E) 1,700,000		(59,000,000)
Retained earnings, July 1	(21,200,000)	(5,400,000)	(E) 5,400,000		(21,200,000)
Accumulated other comprehensive income, July 1	(1,140,000)	(340,000)	(E) 340,000		(1,140,000)
Dividends	1,200,000	200,000		200,000 (C)	1,200,000
Sales revenue	(550,000,000)	(110,000,000)			(660,000,000)
Equity in net income of DataFile	(800,000)	—	(C) 800,000		—
Equity in other comprehensive loss of DataFile	25,000	—		25,000 (C)	—
Cost of goods sold	450,000,000	68,000,000			518,000,000
Operating expenses	90,000,000	38,500,000	(O-1) 400,000	500,000 (O-3)	131,200,000
			(O-2) 2,100,000		
			(O-4) 700,000		
Other comprehensive (income) loss . .	(80,000)	25,000			(55,000)
Totals	$ 0	$ 0	$31,840,000	$31,840,000	$ 0

Using the working paper consolidated account balances in Exhibit 4.5, we prepare the following consolidated statement of comprehensive income for fiscal 2017, and the consolidated balance sheet at June 30, 2017.

IBM CORPORATION and DATAFILE, INC.
Consolidated Statement of Comprehensive Income
For Fiscal Year Ended June 30, 2017

Sales revenue..	$660,000,000
Less: Cost of goods sold	(518,000,000)
Gross profit..	142,000,000
Less: Operating expenses	(131,200,000)
Net income	**10,800,000**
Plus: Other comprehensive income.............................	55,000
Comprehensive income	$ 10,855,000

IBM CORPORATION and DATAFILE, INC.
Consolidated Balance Sheet
June 30, 2017

Assets		Liabilities and Stockholders' Equity	
Current assets	$ 20,200,000	Current liabilities........................	$ 28,000,000
Plant and equipment, net....	231,200,000	Long-term debt	140,405,000
Patents and copyrights	5,400,000	Total liabilities..........................	168,405,000
Brand names	900,000		
Customer relationships	1,000,000	Stockholders' equity	
Goodwill.................	2,700,000	Common stock, par	2,000,000
		Additional paid-in capital	59,000,000
		Retained earnings	30,800,000
		Accumulated other comprehensive income..	1,195,000
		Total stockholders' equity	92,995,000
Total assets	$261,400,000	Total liabilities and stockholders' equity	$261,400,000

We calculate consolidated retained earnings and accumulated other comprehensive income at June 30, 2017, as follows, using the consolidated balances from the working paper and consolidated net income from the consolidated statement of comprehensive income:

Retained earnings, July 1..	$21,200,000
Plus: Consolidated net income	10,800,000
Less: Consolidated dividends	(1,200,000)
Retained earnings, June 30	$30,800,000
Accumulated other comprehensive income, July 1...........	$ 1,140,000
Plus: Other comprehensive income.............................	55,000
Accumulated other comprehensive income, June 30	$ 1,195,000

REVIEW 2 • Consolidation in a Subsequent Year with Identifiable Intangibles

Time Warner acquired all of the stock of First Media for $1.2 billion in cash on January 1, 2015. First Media's book value was $350 million at the time, and the $850 million excess paid over book value is explained by the revaluations below. Information on reporting these items in subsequent years is also provided.

(in millions)	Book value	Fair value	Reporting policy
Inventories	$ 850	$ 800	LIFO; beginning inventory not reported as sold during 2015–2017.
Property, plant and equipment, net . . .	3,000	3,300	10 years, straight-line
Lease agreements	0	100	2 years, straight-line
Goodwill	0	500	Impairment calculated each year: 2015 and 2016: none; 2017: $100

During 2015 and 2016, First Media reported net income of $200,000,000 and $240,000,000, respectively, and paid no dividends. In 2017, First Media reported net income of $250,000,000 and paid dividends of $20,000,000. Time Warner uses the complete equity method to report its investment in First Media on its own books. The trial balances of Time Warner and First Media at December 31, 2017 (three years after the acquisition) appear in the consolidation working paper below.

Required

a. Calculate equity in net income of First Media, reported on Time Warner's 2017 income statement.
b. Complete the working paper and present the December 31, 2017, consolidated balance sheet and the consolidated statement of income for 2017, in good form.

Consolidation Working Paper

	Accounts Taken From Books Dr (Cr)		Eliminations		
(in millions)	Time Warner	First Media	Dr	Cr	Consolidated Balances Dr (Cr)
Cash and receivables.	$ 1,200	$ 450			
Inventories	7,200	1,000			
Property, plant and equipment, net	38,860	4,540			
Investment in First Media.	1,580	—			
Lease agreements	—	—			
Goodwill	—	—			
Accounts payable.	(7,800)	(670)			
Long-term debt	(35,000)	(4,300)			
Common stock, par	(120)	(10)			
Additional paid-in capital	(3,000)	(130)			
Retained earnings, Jan. 1.	(2,550)	(700)			
Treasury stock	—	50			
Dividends	100	20			
Sales revenue.	(10,000)	(2,000)			
Equity in net income of First Media	(120)	—			
Cost of goods sold.	8,500	1,600			
Operating expenses.	1,150	150			
Totals	$ 0	$ 0			$ 0

Solutions are located after the chapter assignments.

IFRS FOR ACQUIRED INTANGIBLES

LO5 Discuss IFRS for intangibles reporting and impairment testing.

While IFRS procedures to consolidate financial statements in subsequent years are similar to U.S. GAAP, there are differences in subsequent reporting of acquired intangibles. IFRS for acquired identifiable intangibles and goodwill is found in *IAS 38*, Intangible Assets, and *IAS 36*, Impairment of Assets.

Identifiable Intangibles

Chapter 3 noted that *IAS 38*'s criteria for reporting identifiable intangibles acquired in a business combination are similar to U.S. GAAP: to be reportable, the intangible must be either separable or contractual. Although these intangibles are generally carried at cost less appropriate accumulated amortization and impairment loss, IFRS also allows them to be reported at *fair value* in limited circumstances.

Intangibles Reported Using the Cost Model   As with U.S. GAAP, identifiable intangibles reported using the cost model may have **limited** or **indefinite lives**. Those with limited lives are amortized over the period during which the intangible is expected to produce cash flows for the company, using the same methods used for tangible depreciable assets such as plant and equipment. Even though residual value is usually zero, a third party may commit to buy the intangible at the end of its useful life, or the residual value can be based on an active market value. Estimates used to report periodic amortization should be reviewed regularly and revised as necessary. Any changes in these estimates affect future amortization, not past amortization. Intangibles deemed to have indefinite lives are not systematically amortized. The assumptions and estimations behind this judgment must be reassessed each reporting period. For example, a change in consumer tastes or economic conditions may change an indefinite-life trademark to one with a limited life.

Like U.S. GAAP, all identifiable intangibles reported at cost are subject to **impairment testing** under IFRS, regardless of whether they have limited or indefinite lives. The IFRS impairment testing procedure, covered in *IAS 36*, differs from U.S. GAAP procedures. Recall that for limited life intangibles, U.S. GAAP requires a two-step impairment test, where the intangible's book value is first compared with the sum of its future expected *undiscounted* cash flows. Only when the book value is greater do we go to the second step and measure the actual impairment loss as the difference between the book value and the future expected *discounted* cash flows. U.S. GAAP also allows an optional qualitative test for indefinite life tangibles. IFRS uses a **one-step test** for **all** intangible assets: book value is compared with the *greater* of the asset's **"value-in-use"** (generally the present value of future expected cash flows) or **net market value**, defined as fair value less selling costs. Using the Primus illustration of U.S. GAAP impairment testing of identifiable intangibles, covered earlier in this chapter, we repeat the relevant information for December 31, 2017, below:

Intangible asset (in millions)	Book value	Total expected future cash inflows, undiscounted	Total expected future cash inflows, discounted
Customer lists	$120	$100	$ 80
Brand names	180	200	125

Assuming there is no active market for the customer lists and brand names, value-in-use is the relevant measure, calculated as discounted future expected cash flows. Following IFRS, Primus reports the following impairment loss for 2017:

Customer lists	$120,000,000 − $80,000,000 = $40,000,000
Brand names	$180,000,000 − $125,000,000 = 55,000,000
Total impairment loss.	$95,000,000

Compare this loss with the $40,000,000 impairment loss reported in U.S. GAAP. Under U.S. GAAP, limited life intangibles must pass the first step, comparing book value with undiscounted cash flows, before any impairment loss is reported. Brand names do not pass the first step in our example. IFRS will likely report *greater* impairment losses for the same factual situations than U.S. GAAP.

Intangibles Reported Using the Revaluation Model   Unlike U.S. GAAP, IFRS allows identifiable intangibles to be "marked to market" in specific circumstances. The *IAS 38* definition of fair value is **market value**, which limits fair value reporting to intangibles that are traded in an active market. Unique intangibles, such as most patents, trademarks and customer relationships, are not likely to be actively traded. Most intangibles do not have active markets and are reported using the cost model.

Intangibles that have active markets may be reported at fair value. Examples include generic software, taxi licenses and production quotas. Companies report increases in value directly in "revaluation surplus," a component of other comprehensive income, unless they are reversals of previously reported impairment losses. Decreases in value similarly reduce the revaluation surplus, with reductions exceeding previous increases reported in net income.

For example, assume generic computer software with an active trading market is acquired in a business combination on January 1, 2016. Valued at $10,000,000 at the acquisition date, the software has a five-year estimated life, no residual value, and is reported using the revaluation model. Straight-line amortization is appropriate. On December 31, 2016, amortization expense of $2,000,000 is reported (= $10,000,000/5). If the software's fair value is now $12,000,000, it is revalued by $4,000,000 (= $12,000,000 − $8,000,000). The entries for 2016 are as follows:

Amortization expense.	2,000,000	
Computer software		2,000,000
To record amortization on the computer software for 2016.		
Computer software.	4,000,000	
Revaluation surplus (OCI)		4,000,000
To revalue the computer software to fair value as of December 31, 2016.		

Amortization expense in subsequent years is based on the revalued amount. If market value declines below carrying value, revaluation surplus is charged. Any value declines in excess of the surplus balance are charged to net income. For example, amortization expense for 2017 is $3,000,000 (= $12,000,000/4). If the fair value of the software on December 31, 2017, is $8,000,000, we make the following additional entry:

Revaluation surplus (OCI).	1,000,000	
Computer software		1,000,000
To revalue the computer software to fair value as of December 31, 2017;		
$1,000,000 = ($12,000,000 − 3,000,000) − $8,000,000.		

If instead fair value declined to $3,000,000, we charge $4,000,000 against the revaluation surplus in other comprehensive income and $2,000,000 against net income. Any remaining revaluation surplus is reclassified to retained earnings on sale or disposal of the software, and is never included in periodic net income.

Goodwill

IFRS goodwill impairment differs from U.S. GAAP goodwill impairment in two major ways:

● Goodwill is allocated to "cash generating units" (CGUs) rather than reporting units. A **CGU** is the smallest group of assets with independent cash inflows. Following U.S. GAAP, goodwill is assigned to "reporting units," generally operating segments that are regularly evaluated by top management. For a given firm, CGUs are likely to be smaller in size and greater in number than reporting units.

● Impairment loss is computed in one step, as the CGU's book value less its fair value. In contrast, following U.S. GAAP, if Step 0 is bypassed, or it is more likely than not that the reporting unit's book value exceeds its fair value, a two-step process is required. If the reporting unit's book value exceeds its fair value, a second computation determines the amount of goodwill impairment loss, as the difference between the fair value and the book value of the unit's goodwill.

Following IFRS, goodwill is tested for impairment at the CGU level at least annually. Goodwill is impaired if the CGU's book value exceeds its fair value, typically measured as the present value of the CGU's expected future cash flows. Because IFRS assumes that the lower overall fair value of the CGU resulted from a decline in the value of the CGU's goodwill, the amount of the goodwill impairment loss equals the *difference between the CGU's book value and fair value*. The CGU's other assets are written down only when its goodwill is completely written off.

BUSINESS APPLICATION Nokia's Goodwill Impairment: IFRS versus U.S. GAAP

The SEC requires foreign companies listed on U.S. exchanges to file financial and other information using Form 20-F. For years ending after November 15, 2007, companies using official IFRS are not required to include a reconciliation of IFRS information to U.S. GAAP. Thus, the reconciliation does not appear in Nokia Corporation's 2007 or 2008 filing; however, there is an explanation of differences in goodwill impairment in its 2006 filing, as follows:

Impairment of goodwill

Under IFRS, goodwill is allocated to "cash-generating units," which are the smallest group of identifiable assets that include the goodwill under review for impairment and generate cash inflows from continuing use that are largely independent of the cash inflows from other assets. Under IFRS, the Group recorded an impairment of goodwill of EUR 151 million related to Amber Networks in 2003 as the carrying amount of the cash-generating unit exceeded the recoverable amount of the unit.

Under U.S. GAAP, goodwill is allocated to "reporting units," which are operating segments or one level below an operating segment (as defined in FAS 131, Disclosures about Segments of an Enterprise and Related Information). The goodwill impairment test under FAS 142 compares the carrying value for each reporting unit to its fair value based on discounted cash flows.

The U.S. GAAP impairment of goodwill adjustment reflects the cumulative reversal of impairments recorded under IFRS that did not qualify as impairments under U.S. GAAP. Upon completion of the 2003 annual impairment test, the Group determined that the impairment recorded for Amber Networks should be reversed under U.S. GAAP as the fair value of the reporting unit in which Amber Networks resides exceeded the book value of the reporting unit. The annual impairment tests performed subsequent to 2003 continue to support the reversal of this impairment. The Group recorded no goodwill impairments during 2006 and 2005.

In 2003, Nokia reports IFRS goodwill impairment of €151,000,000 for its CGU, Amber Networks, but this CGU is part of a larger reporting unit under U.S. GAAP. Since the reporting unit's fair value exceeds its book value, no goodwill impairment is reported under U.S. GAAP. *Source:* Nokia Corporation Form 20-F, 2006.

The differences in goodwill impairment testing between IFRS and U.S. GAAP make it likely that goodwill impairment loss under IFRS is *higher* than under U.S. GAAP, especially with U.S. GAAP's addition of the optional Step 0 qualitative assessment. To illustrate, look again at the Primus illustration. Goodwill was initially allocated on January 1, 2017, to reportable segments, per U.S. GAAP, as follows *(in millions)*:

Broadband unit.	$1,920
Wholesale carrier unit.	1,280
Total goodwill.	$3,200

Assume Primus uses IFRS, and allocates goodwill to the following CGUs *(in millions)*:

Broadband internet	$ 320
Broadband data	1,600
Wholesale VoIP	960
Wholesale data services	320
Total goodwill	$3,200

On December 31, 2017, the following information is available:

(in millions)	Broadband internet	Broadband data	Wholesale VoIP	Wholesale data services
Fair value of unit	$8,000	$ 9,600	$4,800	$3,840
Book value of unit	4,800	10,240	5,440	3,520
Fair value of identifiable net assets	7,040	8,640	4,480	3,040

IFRS goodwill impairment loss for 2017 is calculated as follows:

(in millions)	Broadband internet	Broadband data	Wholesale VoIP	Wholesale data services
Fair value of CGU	$8,000	$ 9,600	$4,800	$3,840
Book value of CGU	4,800	10,240	5,440	3,520
Impairment	No	Yes	Yes	No
Impairment loss	—	$ 640	$ 640	—

Total IFRS goodwill impairment loss is $1,280 million (= $640 million + $640 million). Compare this number with the U.S. GAAP impairment loss of $160 million, calculated earlier in this chapter.

APPENDIX TO CHAPTER 4

Consolidation Eliminating Entries When the Parent Uses the Cost Method

LO6 Explain consolidation when the parent uses the cost method.

Because the parent's investment account is eliminated in consolidation, the method the parent uses to account for the investment on its own books does not affect consolidated balances. In Chapter 4 and subsequently in Chapters 5 and 6, we assume that the parent uses the complete equity method on its own books. However some parent companies use the *cost method*, because it simplifies the accounting on their own books. In this appendix, we explain the consolidation eliminating entries when the parent uses the **cost method** on its own books. We use IBM's acquisition of DataFile Inc., discussed in Chapter 4 pp. 136–143, to illustrate the eliminating entries.

Comparing the Cost and Complete Equity Methods

On July 1, 2015, the beginning of the fiscal year for both companies, IBM acquires all of the voting stock of Data-File Inc. for $25,000,000. DataFile's equity at the time is $5,300,000, consisting of $2,200,000 in capital stock, $2,800,000 in retained earnings, and $300,000 in accumulated other comprehensive income. An analysis of the resulting revaluations of DataFile's assets and liabilities is repeated here:

Acquisition cost		$25,000,000
Book value of DataFile		(5,300,000)
Cost in excess of DataFile's book value		19,700,000
Differences between fair value and book value:		
Current assets	$ (300,000)	
Plant and equipment, net	10,000,000	
Patents and copyrights	4,000,000	
Brand names	1,000,000	
Lease agreements	600,000	
Customer relationships	3,000,000	
Long-term debt	(2,000,000)	(16,300,000)
Goodwill		$ 3,400,000

Information on revaluation write-offs for fiscal 2016 is as follows:

	Write-Off Policy	Write-Off for Fiscal 2016
Current assets	Revaluation pertains to inventory reported using FIFO	Full amount ($300,000), since beginning inventory is sold in 2016
Plant and equipment	25 years, straight-line	$10,000,000/25 = $400,000
Patents and copyrights	5 years, straight-line	$4,000,000/5 = $800,000
Brand names	Indefinite life	$100,000 impairment loss
Lease agreements	2 years, straight-line	$600,000/2 = $300,000
Customer relationships	3 years, straight-line	$3,000,000/3 = $1,000,000
Long-term debt	4 years, straight-line	$2,000,000/4 = $500,000
Goodwill	Impairment testing	No impairment loss

During fiscal 2016, DataFile reports net income of $3,000,000, other comprehensive income of $40,000, and declares and pays dividends of $400,000. If IBM uses the complete equity method, it computes fiscal 2016 equity in net income as follows:

DataFile's reported net income for fiscal 2016	$3,000,000
Adjustments for revaluation write-offs of:	
Current assets (cost of goods sold)	300,000
Plant and equipment (depreciation expense)	(400,000)
Patents and copyrights (amortization expense)	(800,000)
Brand names (impairment loss)	(100,000)
Lease agreements (amortization expense)	(300,000)
Customer relationships (amortization expense)	(1,000,000)
Long-term debt (interest expense)	500,000
Equity in net income of DataFile.	$1,200,000

IBM records the equity in net income and other comprehensive income of DataFile as an increase in its investment account, and the dividends as a decrease in the investment account.

In contrast, if IBM uses the cost method, it records the dividends as income, and the *investment account remains at original cost*. The following summarizes IBM's entries under the cost and complete equity methods, for fiscal 2016:

Books of IBM

	Complete equity method		Cost method	
July 1, 2015				
Investment in DataFile	25,000,000		25,000,000	
Cash		25,000,000		25,000,000
Fiscal 2016				
Investment in DataFile	1,240,000		no entry	
Equity in net income of DataFile.		1,200,000		
Equity in other comprehensive income of DataFile		40,000		
Cash.	400,000		400,000	
Investment in DataFile		400,000		—
Dividend income.		—		400,000

When the parent uses the cost method, the eliminating entries are as follows:

(C)   Eliminate the parent's current year dividend income balance against the subsidiary's dividends account.

(A)   Adjust the parent's accounts to the beginning-of-year balances that would appear on its books if the parent used the complete equity method.

(E)   Eliminate the subsidiary's beginning-of-year stockholders' equity account balances against the investment account.

(R)   Eliminate the rest of the investment account, representing the beginning-of-year revaluations balance, and revalue the subsidiary's assets and liabilities as of the beginning of the year.

(O)   Recognize current year write-offs of the subsidiary's asset and liability revaluations.

Note that eliminating entries (E), (R), and (O) are identical to those used when the parent reports its investment using the complete equity method. Once we eliminate the intercompany dividend for the current year and adjust the parent's books to the complete equity method as of the beginning of the current year, the balances are at beginning-of-year amounts following the complete equity method, and consolidation can proceed as usual. In the next sections we illustrate these concepts using IBM's acquisition of DataFile.

Consolidation After One Year

The consolidated balances are the same whether IBM uses the complete equity method or the cost method to record its investment on its own books. However, if IBM uses the cost method, the consolidation eliminating entries illustrated on p. 138 must be adjusted, because IBM's accounts are slightly different: IBM does not report equity in net income and other comprehensive income of DataFile; it reports dividend income, and maintains its investment account at original cost, $25,000,000. Under the complete equity method, IBM's fiscal 2016 year-end investment balance is $25,840,000.

Consolidation eliminating entries for fiscal 2016, one year after the acquisition, are the same under the cost method as under the complete equity method, except for eliminating entry (C).

Consolidation eliminating entry (C)

		Complete equity method		Cost method	
(C)	Equity in net income of DataFile.	1,200,000		—	
	Equity in other comprehensive income of DataFile	40,000			
	Dividend income.		—	400,000	
	Dividends		400,000		400,000
	Investment in DataFile		840,000		—

Eliminating entries (E), (R), and (O) are identical to those illustrated in Chapter 4, p. 138. Note that when IBM uses the cost method, entry (C) eliminates the current year's dividend income recorded on IBM's books against DataFile's dividends account. Entries (E) and (R) are the same under both methods, because after elimination (C), the investment account is at its beginning-of-year balance, acquisition cost.

Consolidation After Two Years

In fiscal 2017, DataFile reports net income of $3,500,000, an other comprehensive loss of $25,000, and declares and pays dividends of $200,000. There are no changes in depreciation and amortization policy for DataFile's plant and equipment and limited life intangibles. Year-end impairment testing in fiscal 2017 reveals no impairment loss for brand names, whereas goodwill is impaired by $700,000. Following the complete equity method, IBM calculates fiscal 2017 equity in net income of DataFile as follows:

DataFile's reported net income for fiscal 2017	$3,500,000
Adjustments for revaluation write-offs:	
Plant and equipment (depreciation expense).	(400,000)
Patents and copyrights (amortization expense)	(800,000)
Lease agreements (amortization expense).	(300,000)
Customer relationships (amortization expense)	(1,000,000)
Long-term debt (interest expense)	500,000
Goodwill (impairment loss)	(700,000)
Equity in net income of DataFile.	$ 800,000

The following summarizes IBM's fiscal 2017 entries under the cost and complete equity methods:

Books of IBM

	Complete equity method		Cost method	
Investment in DataFile	775,000		no entry	
Equity in other comprehensive loss of DataFile.	25,000			
Equity in net income of DataFile.		800,000		
Cash.	200,000		200,000	
Investment in DataFile		200,000		—
Dividend income.		—		200,000

Under the complete equity method, IBM's investment account balance is $26,415,000. But the cost method maintains the investment balance at acquisition cost, $25,000,000. As done in the first year following acquisition, in eliminating entry (C) we eliminate IBM's dividend income account against DataFile's dividends account. To proceed with eliminating entries (E) and (R), though, we must also adjust the investment account to its beginning-of-year balance under the complete equity method. Using the complete equity method, the investment account increases by the excess of last year's equity in net income and other comprehensive income of DataFile over dividends received, or $1,200,000 + $40,000 − $400,000 = $840,000. IBM would have recorded $1,200,000 as net income and included it in its beginning retained earnings balance, and $40,000 as other comprehensive income and included it in its beginning accumulated other comprehensive income balance. In contrast, using the cost method IBM recorded $400,000 in dividend income and included it in its beginning retained earnings balance. Eliminating entry A below adds $840,000 to IBM's investment account, $800,000 to its beginning retained earnings account, and $40,000 to its beginning accumulated other comprehensive income account. This entry converts IBM's accounts to the same beginning-of-year balances resulting under the complete equity method.

To summarize, IBM must make the following eliminating entries when using the cost method:

Eliminating entries at June 30, 2017

(A) Investment in DataFile.	840,000	
Retained earnings, July 1		800,000
Accumulated other comprehensive income, July 1		40,000
To adjust the investment account, beginning retained earnings and accumulated other comprehensive income to their beginning-of-year amounts under the complete equity method.		
(C) Dividend income.	200,000	
Dividends.		200,000
To eliminate DataFile's current year dividends.		

Eliminating entries (A) and (C) convert IBM's accounts to the same beginning balances resulting when IBM uses the complete equity method, and we can proceed with remaining eliminations (E), (R), and (O).

The June 30, 2017, consolidation working paper showing IBM using the cost method appears below. Compare this working paper to Exhibit 4.5 on p. 142, which shows the working paper when IBM uses the complete equity method. Note that the consolidated balances are identical, and that elimination (A) adjusts IBM's beginning retained earnings and accumulated other comprehensive income to the complete equity method amounts shown in Exhibit 4.5. Elimination (C) does not change the investment account balance, and eliminations (E), (R), and (O) are identical to those required if IBM uses the complete equity method.

| | Accounts Taken From Books Dr (Cr) | | Eliminations | | Consolidated Balances |
	IBM	DataFile	Dr	Cr	Dr (Cr)
Current assets	$ 17,000,000	$ 3,200,000			$ 20,200,000
Plant and equipment, net	160,000,000	62,000,000	(R) $ 9,600,000	$ 400,000 (O-1)	231,200,000
Patents and copyrights	2,400,000	600,000	(R) 3,200,000	800,000 (O-2)	5,400,000
Investment in DataFile	25,000,000	—	(A) 840,000	7,940,000 (E)	—
				17,900,000 (R)	
Brand names	—	—	(R) 900,000		900,000
Lease agreements	—	—	(R) 300,000	300,000 (O-2)	—
Customer relationships	—	—	(R) 2,000,000	1,000,000 (O-2)	1,000,000
Goodwill	—	—	(R) 3,400,000	700,000 (O-4)	2,700,000
Current liabilities	(18,000,000)	(10,000,000)			(28,000,000)
Long-term debt	(94,820,000)	(44,585,000)	(O-3) 500,000	1,500,000 (R)	(140,405,000)
Common stock, par	(2,000,000)	(500,000)	(E) 500,000		(2,000,000)
Additional paid-in capital	(59,000,000)	(1,700,000)	(E) 1,700,000		(59,000,000)
Retained earnings, July 1	(20,400,000)	(5,400,000)	(E) 5,400,000	800,000 (A)	(21,200,000)
Accumulated other comprehensive income, July 1	(1,100,000)	(340,000)	(E) 340,000	40,000 (A)	(1,140,000)
Dividends	1,200,000	200,000		200,000 (C)	1,200,000
Sales revenue	(550,000,000)	(110,000,000)			(660,000,000)
Dividend income	(200,000)	—	(C) 200,000		—
Cost of goods sold	450,000,000	68,000,000			518,000,000
Operating expenses	90,000,000	38,500,000	(O-1) 400,000	500,000 (O-3)	131,200,000
			(O-2) 2,100,000		
			(O-4) 700,000		
Other comprehensive (income) loss	(80,000)	25,000			(55,000)
Totals	$ 0	$ 0	$32,080,000	$32,080,000	$ 0

In general, eliminating entry (A) converts the parent's cost method investment, retained earnings, and accumulated other comprehensive income to their complete equity method beginning-of-year balances. The amount of the adjustment to retained earnings is the cumulative excess of (1) equity in net income over (2) dividends received from the date of acquisition to the beginning of the current year, computed as follows:

Change in the subsidiary's retained earnings from the date of acquisition to the beginning of the current year (cumulative net income less dividends)

+/− cumulative write-offs of revaluations from the date of acquisition to the beginning of the current year

Amount of adjustment (A) to the parent's beginning retained earnings

To further illustrate eliminating entry (A), assume it is now June 30, 2018, three years since acquisition. Recall that DataFile's retained earnings balance at the date of acquisition was $2,800,000. As of June 30, 2017, DataFile's retained earnings is $8,700,000 (= $2,800,000 + $3,000,000 − $400,000 + $3,500,000 − $200,000). Calculation of the retained earnings adjustment amount in eliminating entry (A) is as follows:

Change in retained earnings, July 1, 2015 to June 30, 2017 ($8,700,000 − $2,800,000).	$5,900,000
Adjustments for revaluation write-offs for fiscal years 2016 and 2017:	
Plus FIFO inventory write-off to cost of goods sold.	300,000
Less plant and equipment depreciation ($400,000 × 2)	(800,000)
Less patents and copyrights amortization ($800,000 × 2).	(1,600,000)
Less brand names impairment loss($100,000 + $0)	(100,000)
Less lease agreement amortization ($300,000 × 2).	(600,000)
Less customer relationships amortization ($1,000,000 × 2)	(2,000,000)
Plus interest expense ($500,000 × 2).	1,000,000
Less goodwill impairment ($0 + $700,000)	(700,000)
Amount of retained earnings eliminating adjustment (A) for fiscal 2018	$1,400,000

DataFile's accumulated other comprehensive income balance at the date of acquisition was $300,000. As of June 30, 2017, this balance is $315,000 (= $300,000 + $40,000 − $25,000), an increase of $15,000. We now have the information needed to prepare eliminating entry (A).

Eliminating entry (A) at June 30, 2018

(A) Investment in DataFile.	1,415,000	
Retained earnings, July 1		1,400,000
Accumulated other comprehensive income, July 1		15,000
To adjust IBM's accounts to their beginning-of-year amounts under the complete equity method.		

In summary, if the parent uses the cost method to account for the investment in a subsidiary on its own books, the most straightforward approach is to adjust the parent's accounts to the complete equity method as of the beginning of the year, and eliminate the subsidiary's current year dividends against the parent's dividend income in elimination (C). The remaining eliminating entries are the same as if the parent used the complete equity method.

● ●

Reporting Perspective

The cost method may initially appear easier, as the parent only records dividends received from the subsidiary. As the discussion in this appendix shows, however, the need to calculate equity method income cannot be avoided. If the parent does not record equity method income on its own books, it must be incorporated, on a cumulative basis, into the consolidation eliminating entries, to arrive at the correct beginning balance for consolidated retained earnings.

● ●

REVIEW OF KEY CONCEPTS ●

Explain the general process of periodic consolidation. (p. 119) When a business combination is recorded as a stock acquisition, it is carried on the parent's books as an intercorporate investment. If consolidation is appropriate, the accounts of the parent and subsidiary must be consolidated **whenever financial statements are presented**. At any point in time subsequent to acquisition, a working paper is used to consolidate the assets, liabilities, equity, revenue and expense accounts of the parent and subsidiary. The consolidation process requires **four eliminating entries**, represented by the acronym **CERO**, as follows: (**C**) elimination of the parent's **C**urrent year equity method income and the subsidiary's intercompany dividends, restoring the investment account to its beginning-of-year balance; (**E**) elimination of the subsidiary's beginning-of-year stockholders' **E**quity accounts against the investment account; (**R**) recognition of the beginning-of-year **R**evaluation balances for the subsidiary's assets and liabilities and elimination of the remaining investment balance, and (**O**) writing **O**ff the revaluations for the current year.

LO 1

Describe the relation between equity method and consolidated balances. (p. 124) The method the parent uses to account for its investment in the subsidiary does not affect the consolidated statements, but does affect consolidation procedures. This text stresses the **complete equity method**, which reflects all consolidation adjustments and the parent's share of the subsidiary's comprehensive income and dividends, because use of this method simplifies

LO 2

the consolidation process. If the parent uses a different method, the consolidation process adjusts the parent's account balances to the complete equity method before proceeding.

LO 3 **Report subsequent year write-offs of acquisition date revaluations of subsidiary identifiable assets and liabilities. (p. 125)** Revaluations change in reported value as time passes. Revaluations of a subsidiary's previously reported net assets are accounted for in the same way as the underlying asset or liability. Previously unreported **identifiable intangibles** with **limited lives** are amortized over their useful lives, whereas those with **indefinite lives** are not amortized. Both types are periodically tested for impairment, following *FASB ASC Section 350-30-35*.

LO 4 **Measure and report goodwill impairment losses. (p. 128)** **Goodwill** is assigned to reporting units and is subject to **impairment testing** as described in *FASB ASC Section 350-20-35*. Goodwill impairment losses appear in the operating section of the consolidated income statement.

LO 5 **Discuss IFRS for intangibles reporting and impairment testing. (p. 145)** **IFRS** for intangibles reporting and impairment testing differs from U.S. GAAP. In limited circumstances, identifiable intangibles are reported at fair value and marked to market using a revaluation surplus account, reported in equity as a component of other comprehensive income. Impairment for identifiable intangibles is computed as the difference between reported carrying value and discounted future expected cash flows. Goodwill is allocated to cash generating units, and impairment is computed as the difference between the fair value of the unit and its book value.

LO 6 **Explain consolidation when the parent uses the cost method (p. 148, appendix)** If the parent uses the cost method to account for the investment in a subsidiary, the consolidation eliminating entries differ; the consolidated balances are not changed.

Assignments with the ✅ in the margin are available in Business Course.
See the Preface of the book for details.

MULTIPLE CHOICE QUESTIONS ·······································

Use the following information to answer questions 1–4 below:

On January 1, 2014, Portland Company acquired all of Salem Company's voting stock for $16,000,000 in cash. Some of Salem's assets and liabilities at the date of purchase had fair values that differed from reported values, as follows:

	Book value	Fair value
Buildings and equipment, net (20 years, straight-line).............	$ 11,000,000	$ 3,000,000
Identifiable intangibles (5 years, straight-line)	0	10,000,000

Salem's total stockholders' equity at January 1, 2014, was $4,000,000. It is now December 31, 2017 (four years later). Salem's retained earnings reflect the accumulation of net income less dividends; there have been no other changes in its retained earnings. Salem does not report any other comprehensive income. Cumulative goodwill impairment to the beginning of 2017 is $2,000,000. Goodwill impairment for 2017 is $500,000. Portland uses the complete equity method to account for its investment. The December 31, 2017, trial balance for Salem appears below.

	Salem Dr (Cr)
Current assets	$ 2,500,000
Plant assets, net...	28,000,000
Liabilities..	(10,000,000)
Capital stock	(2,000,000)
Retained earnings, January 1..................................	(16,000,000)
Sales revenue..	(14,000,000)
Cost of goods sold...	8,000,000
Operating expenses..	3,500,000
	$ 0

1. On the 2017 consolidation working paper, eliminating entry (R) reduces Investment in Salem by LO 1 ✓

    a. $3,100,000
    b. $5,200,000
    c. $6,400,000
    d. $8,000,000

2. On the 2017 consolidation working paper, eliminating entry (O) increases consolidated operating expenses LO 1 ✓
by

    a. $1,600,000
    b. $2,100,000
    c. $2,900,000
    d. $3,200,000

3. What is 2017 equity in net income of Salem, reported on Portland's books using the complete equity method? LO 2 ✓

    a. $ 400,000
    b. $ 900,000
    c. $1,200,000
    d. $2,500,000

4. On Portland's December 31, 2017, trial balance, what is the balance in its Investment in Salem account, us- LO 2 ✓
ing the complete equity method?

    a. $22,800,000
    b. $23,200,000
    c. $23,600,000
    d. $27,600,000

Use the following information to answer questions 5–8 below:

A company reports the following intangibles at December 31, 2016, *prior to* impairment testing:

	Book value
Customer lists	$1,500,000
Brand names	5,200,000
Goodwill	8,000,000

The customer lists have a limited life, and amortization expense has already been properly recorded. The brand names have indefinite lives. The goodwill is allocated to Divisions 1 and 2 for both U.S. GAAP and IFRS.

Assume the company bypasses the Step 0 qualitative assessment for both the brand names and the goodwill. On December 31, 2016, the following information is available:

	Division 1	Division 2
Book value of goodwill	$ 1,600,000	$ 6,400,000
Fair value of division	14,000,000	20,000,000
Book value of division	16,000,000	24,000,000
Fair value of identifiable net assets of division	13,000,000	12,000,000

Intangible asset	Total expected future cash inflows, undiscounted	Total expected future cash inflows, discounted
Customer lists	$1,600,000	$1,200,000
Brand names	4,000,000	3,400,000

⊘ LO 3   **5.** Impairment loss for 2016 for the customer lists and brand names, following U.S. GAAP, is

    a. $ 0
    b. $ 300,000
    c. $1,800,000
    d. $2,100,000

⊘ LO 4   **6.** Goodwill impairment loss for 2016, following U.S. GAAP, is

    a. $6,000,000
    b. $5,600,000
    c. $2,200,000
    d. $ 600,000

⊘ LO 5   **7.** Goodwill impairment loss for 2016, following IFRS, is

    a. $ 600,000
    b. $2,200,000
    c. $5,600,000
    d. $6,000,000

⊘ LO 5   **8.** Impairment loss for 2016 for the customer lists and brand names, following IFRS, is

    a. $ 0
    b. $ 300,000
    c. $1,800,000
    d. $2,100,000

⊘ LO 4   **9.** Which statement is *true* regarding the U.S. GAAP impairment test for limited life intangibles?

    a. If the intangible passes step 1, there is always an impairment loss in step 2.
    b. If the fair value of the intangible is less than its book value, there is always an impairment loss.
    c. U.S. GAAP impairment is likely to be greater than IFRS impairment.
    d. The impairment test for limited life intangibles is the same as the impairment test for indefinite life intangibles.

⊘ LO 6
(APPENDIX)   **10.** A parent uses the cost method to report its investment in a wholly-owned subsidiary, acquired on January 1, 2016. If it had used the complete equity method, the parent would have reported 2016 equity in net income of $500,000 and 2017 equity in net income of $550,000. The subsidiary's 2016 and 2017 dividends were $100,000 and $120,000, respectively. The subsidiary does not report any other comprehensive income. On the 2017 consolidation working paper, an adjusting entry is necessary to increase the parent's beginning retained earnings balance by

    a. $ 400,000
    b. $ 500,000
    c. $ 830,000
    d. $1,050,000

EXERCISES ●●●

LO 1, 3   E4.1   **Equity Method Accounting** George Corporation acquired all of the stock of Johnson Corporation on January 2, 2016. The book value of the net assets of Johnson on that date was $200 million and the fair values of Johnson's identifiable net assets equaled the book values, except for previously unreported developed technology valued at $25 million. The fair market value of the shares issued by George Corporation was $900 million. The developed technology is straight-line amortized over 5 years. For the year ended December 31, 2016, Johnson reported net income of $65 million and declared and paid dividends of $30,000,000.

Required

Prepare journal entries to record George's acquisition of Johnson and subsequent entries to the investment account for 2016, using the complete equity method. Assume goodwill impairment for 2016 is $10 million, and that the developed technology is not impaired.

E4.2 **Equity Method and Eliminating Entries, End of First Year**   On July 1, 2016, Prestige Commu-   LO 1, 3
nications acquired all of the voting stock of Southern Light Technologies for $300 million in cash. At the
date of acquisition, Southern Light's stockholders' equity accounts were as follows (*in millions*):

Capital stock	$ 26
Retained earnings	142
Accumulated other comprehensive income.	5
Treasury stock	(1)
Total	$ 172

At the date of acquisition, Southern Light's inventories and property, plant and equipment had a fair value
that was $2 million and $10 million lower than book value, respectively. It also had previously unreported
brand names, valued at $60 million, meeting the *ASC 805* criteria for separate capitalization. Southern
Light reports inventories using FIFO, its revalued plant and equipment had a 10-year remaining life,
straight-line, and the brand names are indefinite lived. Both companies have June 30 year-ends.

Southern Light reported $20 million in net income and $500,000 in other comprehensive income in
fiscal 2017, and declared and paid $2.5 million in cash dividends. Impairment testing at the end of fiscal
2017 reveals that Southern Light's brand names are impaired by $3 million and goodwill connected with
the acquisition is impaired by $5 million in 2017.

In your answers below, show all numbers in thousands.

Required

a.   Calculate equity in net income of Southern Light, appearing on Prestige Communication's books, for
fiscal 2017. Prestige uses the complete equity method to account for its investment.

b.   Prepare Prestige Communications' journal entries during 2017 to report its investment in Southern
Light, on its own books.

c.   Prepare the consolidation eliminating entries (C), (E), (R) and (O), required to consolidate Prestige
Communications' accounts with those of Southern Light Technologies at June 30, 2017.

E4.3 **Consolidation at End of First Year**   Peak Entertainment acquires its 100-percent-owned subsidiary   LO 1, 3 ✓
Saddlestone Inc. on January 1, 2016. In preparing to consolidate Peak and Saddlestone at December 31,
2016, you assemble the following information:

Value of stock given up to acquire Saddlestone: $10,000,000.
Direct merger costs: $250,000.
Saddlestone's stockholders' equity at acquisition: $7,200,000.
Fair value of earnings contingency agreement to be paid in cash: $300,000.
Fair value of previously unrecorded identifiable intangibles (5-year life): $2,000,000
Goodwill and identifiable intangibles are not impaired in 2016.
Saddlestone's net income in 2016: $3,000,000.
Saddlestone's dividends declared and paid in 2016: $1,000,000.

Required

a.   Prepare the 2016 journal entries made by Peak to record the acquisition and calculate and record
2016 equity in net income, using the complete equity method.

b.   Prepare the consolidation eliminating entries made at December 31, 2016.

E4.4 **Eliminating Entries After First and Second Years**   During 2017, Peerless Company's wholly-   LO 1, 3
owned subsidiary, Safeco Inc. reported net income of $1,600,000 and declared and paid dividends
of $600,000. Peerless acquired Safeco on January 2, 2017, at a cash cost of $8,000,000, which was
$1,000,000 in excess of the book value of net assets acquired. Safeco's equipment (five-year life) was
undervalued by $500,000. Its inventory, reported using FIFO, was undervalued by $200,000. The remaining $300,000 could not be allocated to identifiable assets and liabilities. Impairment testing indicates that
goodwill was impaired by $50,000 during 2017.

Required

a.   Prepare the journal entries recorded by Peerless in 2017 to record the acquisition and apply the complete equity method. Prepare the necessary eliminating entries to consolidate the financial statements
of Peerless and Safeco at December 31, 2017.

b.   Safeco reported net income of $2,000,000 and declared and paid dividends of $800,000 in 2018.
There was no further goodwill impairment. Prepare the journal entries recorded by Peerless in 2018

to apply the complete equity method. Prepare the necessary eliminating entries to consolidate the financial statements of Peerless and Safeco at December 31, 2018.

LO 1, 3   E4.5   Equity Method, Eliminating Entries, Several Years After Acquisition   Data for PlanetTwo Communications and its wholly-owned subsidiary, Stage 4 Networks, are given below. PlanetTwo acquired Stage 4 on January 1, 2009. PlanetTwo uses the complete equity method to report its investment in Stage 4, and its accounting year ends December 31.

(in thousands)	
Acquisition cost	$8,000
Stage 4's stockholders' equity, January 1, 2009	2,000
Stage 4's total reported net income, 2009–2016	7,000
Stage 4's total dividends paid, 2009–2016	1,000
Stage 4's reported net income, 2017	500
Dividends declared and paid by Stage 4, 2017	50
Allocation of excess of cost over book value to identifiable net assets, at acquisition date:	
Land	600
Buildings (20-year life, straight-line)	(800)
Identifiable intangibles (5-year life)	1,500
Long-term debt discount (10 years to maturity as of January 1, 2009)	100
Goodwill impairment loss, 2009–2016	200
Goodwill impairment loss, 2017	45

Required

a. Calculate the original goodwill reported for this acquisition.

b. Calculate the equity in net income for 2017, reported on PlanetTwo's books, using the complete equity method.

c. Calculate the balance in Investment in Stage 4 Networks at December 31, 2017, reported on PlanetTwo's books.

d. Prepare the eliminating entries necessary to consolidate the financial statements of PlanetTwo and Stage 4 for 2017.

LO 1, 3   E4.6   Consolidation after Several Years   On December 31, 2009, Adams Corporation acquired all of the stock of Baker Company. The fair value of Adams' shares used in the exchange was $7,500,000. At the time of acquisition, the book value of Baker's stockholders' equity was $5,000,000, and the fair value of Baker's building (25-year life) exceeded its book value by $1,000,000. From the date of acquisition to December 31, 2015, Baker had cumulative net income of $1,300,000 and declared and paid total dividends of $400,000. For 2016, Baker reported net income of $300,000 and declared and paid cash dividends of $100,000. Adams uses the complete equity method to account for its investment in Baker. There is no goodwill impairment loss for the period 2010 through 2015, but there is impairment loss of $100,000 in 2016.

Required

Prepare the working paper eliminating entries necessary to consolidate the financial statements of Adams and Baker at December 31, 2016.

LO 4   E4.7   Spin-Offs and Goodwill Impairment Losses   In 2014, **Time Warner, Inc.** spun off its wholly owned unit, **Time Inc.**, as an independent, publicly traded company. The spin-off was achieved by distributing new Time Inc. shares to the holders of Time Warner stock. The transaction was not taxable to Time Warner shareholders. Time Inc. is primarily engaged in magazine publishing and related operations. The business application in Chapter 4, describing Time Warner's accounting for goodwill, indicates that Time Inc. was one of the reporting units to which goodwill was allocated prior to 2014. Time Warner elected not to perform the qualitative test for goodwill impairment in 2013, but did not recognize any goodwill impairment losses in 2013. In answering the following questions, use the information provided here, as well as the information in the business application on p. 132.

TIME WARNER, INC.
[TWX]

Required

a. Why is goodwill assigned to reporting units? The business application indicates that $3,162 million in goodwill was assigned to the Time Inc. unit at December 31, 2013. What transactions and events determine the amount assigned to each reporting unit?

b. In general, how are goodwill impairment losses calculated? Why do you think Time Warner by-passed Step 0 in 2013? Why are no goodwill impairment losses reported in 2013?

c. How did Time Warner report Time Inc. in its consolidated financial statements in its 2013 financial statements? How do you think Time Warner reports its spin-off of Time Inc. in 2014?

d. How would Time Warner's goodwill impairment testing process change in 2014 as a result of the Time Inc. spin-off?

E4.8 Projecting Consolidation Eliminating Entries An acquisition takes place on January 1, 2015. At **LO 1, 3** December 31, 2015, you observe the following consolidation eliminating entries:

(R)	Identifiable intangibles	3,000,000	
	Land	2,000,000	
	Goodwill	15,000,000	
	Inventories		500,000
	Property and equipment, net		10,000,000
	Investment in Samson Company		9,500,000
(O)	Amortization expense	600,000	
	Impairment loss	200,000	
	Inventories	500,000	
	Property and equipment, net	1,000,000	
	Cost of goods sold		500,000
	Depreciation expense		1,000,000
	Identifiable intangibles		600,000
	Goodwill		200,000

Property and equipment and identifiable intangibles revaluations are written off on a straight-line basis, no residual value. Additional goodwill impairment losses of $400,000 are reported in 2018. Except for the inventories, none of the revalued assets are sold in future years.

Required

Prepare consolidation eliminating entries (R) and (O) on

a. December 31, 2017.

b. December 31, 2020.

c. December 31, 2025.

E4.9 Identifiable Intangibles and Goodwill, U.S. GAAP International Foods, a U.S. company, ac- **LO 3, 4** quired two companies in 2016. As a result, its consolidated financial statements include the following acquired intangibles:

Intangible asset	Date of acquisition	Fair value at date of acquisition	Useful life
Customer relationships	January 1, 2016	$ 4,000,000	4 years
Favorable leaseholds	June 30, 2016	8,000,000	5 years
Brand names	June 30, 2016	18,000,000	Indefinite
Goodwill	January 1, 2016	500,000,000	Indefinite

Goodwill was assigned to the following reporting units:

Asia	$100,000,000
South America	150,000,000
Europe	250,000,000
Total	$500,000,000

It is now December 31, 2017, the end of International Foods' accounting year. No impairment losses were reported on any intangibles in 2016. Assume that International Foods bypasses the qualitative option for impairment testing of goodwill and indefinite life intangibles.

Intangible asset	Sum of future expected undiscounted cash flows	Sum of future expected discounted cash flows
Customer relationships	$ 1,200,000	$ 900,000
Favorable leaseholds	6,000,000	4,400,000
Brand names	14,000,000	7,000,000

Reporting unit	Unit carrying value	Unit fair value	Fair value of identifiable net assets
Asia...............	$300,000,000	$400,000,000	$375,000,000
South America	200,000,000	350,000,000	280,000,000
Europe	600,000,000	500,000,000	385,000,000

Required

Compute 2017 amortization expense and impairment losses on the above intangibles, following U.S. GAAP.

⊘ LO 5   E4.10   Identifiable Intangibles and Goodwill, IFRS   Assume the same information as in E4.9, except that International Foods reports using IFRS and allocated its goodwill to the following cash generating units (CGUs):

E. Asia	$ 40,000,000
Indonesia	60,000,000
Brazil..	150,000,000
Mediterranean	150,000,000
Scandinavia	100,000,000
Total	$500,000,000

The following information is available at December 31, 2017:

CGU	Unit carrying value	Unit fair value	Fair value of identifiable net assets
E. Asia	$200,000,000	$150,000,000	$300,000,000
Indonesia	100,000,000	120,000,000	75,000,000
Brazil...............	130,000,000	140,000,000	100,000,000
Mediterranean	220,000,000	190,000,000	150,000,000
Scandinavia	300,000,000	230,000,000	200,000,000

Required

Compute 2017 amortization expense and impairment losses on the above intangibles, following IFRS.

LO 2, 3   E4.11   Consolidated Income Statement   When Parson Company acquired all of Soaper Company's stock on July 1, 2016, Soaper's inventory was undervalued by $160,000,000, plant assets with a 10-year life were overvalued by $200,000,000, and long-term debt which matures in five years was overvalued by $100,000,000. No goodwill arose in the combination. All of Soaper's depreciation and amortization charges are based on the straight-line method. The undervalued inventory was sold during the year ended June 30, 2017. The separate income statements of Parson and Soaper for the year ended June 30, 2017, follow *(amounts in millions)*.

	Parson	Soaper
Sales.	$5,000	$2,000
Equity in net income of Soaper	140	—
Total revenue	5,140	2,000
Cost of goods sold.	3,000	800
Depreciation expense.	500	140
Interest expense.	100	60
Other expenses	600	700
Total expenses	4,200	1,700
Net income.	$ 940	$ 300

Required

a. Prepare a consolidated income statement for Parson and Soaper for the year ended June 30, 2017.

b. Why is consolidated income the same as Parson's separately reported net income?

E4.12 Amortization and Impairment Testing of Identifiable Intangible Assets During the year ended July 27, 2013, **Cisco Systems, Inc.** acquired the following identifiable intangible assets through its purchase of two companies:

LO 3

CISCO SYSTEMS, INC.
[CSCO]

	Limited Lives				Indefinite Lives
	Technology		**Customer Relationships**		**IPR&D**
Acquired Company *(in thousands)*	**Useful life (in years)**	**Amount**	**Useful life (in years)**	**Amount**	**Amount**
NDS Group Limited	6.4	$807,000	7.4	$818,000	$94
Meraki, Inc..	8.0	259,000	6.0	30,000	—

Cisco acquired **NDS Group** at the beginning of fiscal 2013, and **Meraki, Inc.** at the end of the second quarter of fiscal 2013. Assume that Cisco separately tests identifiable intangibles acquired from each company for impairment, and collects the following information to conduct impairment tests at the end of fiscal 2013:

	Technology		Customer Relationships		IPR&D	
Acquired Company *(in thousands)*	**Sum of expected undiscounted cash flows**	**Sum of expected discounted cash flows**	**Sum of expected undiscounted cash flows**	**Sum of expected discounted cash flows**	**Sum of expected undiscounted cash flows**	**Sum of expected discounted cash flows**
NDS Group Limited . .	$700,000	$580,000	$680,000	$600,000	$100,000	$60,000
Meraki, Inc..	200,000	150,000	30,000	25,000	—	—

Round your answers below to the nearest thousand.

Required

a. Calculate amortization expense for the above identifiable intangibles for fiscal 2013. Intangibles are amortized on a straight-line basis starting in the month following acquisition.

b. Calculate impairment losses for fiscal 2013.

c. Determine the amounts reported on Cisco's fiscal 2013 balance sheet for technology, customer relationships, and in-process R&D.

LO 1, 3 **E4.13** **Equity Method Income and Working Paper Eliminations** Pace acquired Saber on January 1, 2016, attributing its $200 million excess of acquisition cost over book value to identifiable intangible assets valued at $40 million, with a 5-year life, and to goodwill. At that time Saber's stockholders' equity was $2,000 million. It is now December 31, 2017, and consolidation entries are prepared. The investment account balance on January 1, 2017 was $2,286 million. Saber reported net income of $150 million and declared and paid dividends of $30 million in 2017. Saber paid dividends of $25 million in 2016. Goodwill is not impaired in either year.

In your answers below, show amounts in millions.

Required

a. What was Saber's 2016 reported net income?
b. What was Saber's stockholders' equity on January 1, 2017?
c. Calculate Pace's equity in net income of Saber for 2017, using the complete equity method.
d. Prepare the eliminating entries needed to consolidate Pace and Saber at December 31, 2017.
e. Assume it is now December 31, 2021. Total goodwill impairment as of January 1, 2021 is $100 million, and there is no impairment for 2021. Saber still owns the identifiable intangibles. Prepare consolidation eliminating entries (R) and (O) for 2021.

LO 6 **E4.14** **Consolidation in First Year Using Cost Method** Assume the same information as in E4.2, ex-
(APPENDIX) cept Prestige Communications uses the cost method to account for its investment in Southern Light Technologies.

In your answers below, show all numbers in thousands.

Required

a. Prepare Prestige Communications' journal entries during 2017 to report its investment in Southern Light, on its own books.
b. Prepare the consolidation eliminating entries (C), (E), (R) and (O), required to consolidate Prestige Communications' accounts with those of Southern Light Technologies at June 30, 2017.

LO 6 **E4.15** **Consolidation After Several Years Using Cost Method** Assume the same information as in
(APPENDIX) E4.6, except Adams uses the cost method to account for its investment in Baker.

Required

Prepare the working paper eliminating entries necessary to consolidate the financial statements of Adams and Baker at December 31, 2016.

PROBLEMS ●●

LO 1, 3 **P4.1** **Condensed Consolidated Financial Statements One Year After Acquisition** Ponon Corpo-
ration acquired all of the stock of Santo Corporation on January 2, 2017, for $25,000,000 cash and debt. The book value of Santo's stockholders' equity was $10,000,000 and the resulting $15,000,000 excess of acquisition cost over book value was allocated as follows:

Account	Dr (Cr)	Amortization period
Inventory.	$2,000,000	(1)
Plant assets, net.	8,000,000	8 years
Patents (previously unrecorded).	1,500,000	4 years
Long-term debt	(1,000,000)	10 years
Goodwill.	4,500,000	(2)

(1) Santo uses the FIFO method of inventory valuation, and its beginning inventory was sold during 2017.
(2) Goodwill is impaired by $400,000 during 2017.

The following are the condensed financial statements of Ponon and Santo at December 31, 2017. Neither company declared dividends in 2017. Ponon uses the complete equity method to report its investment in Santo on its own books.

Condensed Balance Sheets

December 31, 2017	Ponon	Santo
Assets		
Cash and receivables............................	$ 4,500,000	$ 3,100,000
Inventory......................................	5,000,000	5,200,000
Plant assets, net...............................	8,000,000	12,000,000
Investment in Santo	26,365,000	—
Total assets	$43,865,000	$20,300,000
Liabilities and Stockholders' Equity		
Current liabilities..............................	$ 5,100,000	$ 2,000,000
Long-term debt	20,000,000	3,260,000
Capital stock	8,000,000	6,000,000
Retained earnings	10,225,000	8,840,000
Accumulated other comprehensive income...............	540,000	200,000
Total liabilities and stockholders' equity	$43,865,000	$20,300,000

Condensed Statements of Comprehensive Income

For Year Ended December 31, 2017	Ponon	Santo
Sales...	$30,000,000	$13,200,000
Equity in net income of Santo	1,325,000	—
Total revenues	31,325,000	13,200,000
Cost of goods sold..............................	18,000,000	4,000,000
Depreciation and amortization expense.................	2,000,000	3,200,000
Interest and other expenses.......................	5,400,000	1,000,000
Total expenses................................	25,400,000	8,200,000
Net Income....................................	5,925,000	5,000,000
Other comprehensive income	100,000	40,000
Comprehensive income..........................	$ 6,025,000	$ 5,040,000

Required

a. Prepare a schedule to compute the 2017 equity in net income of Santo.

b. Use a working paper to consolidate the trial balances of Ponon and Santo at December 31, 2017.

c. Prepare the December 31, 2017, consolidated balance sheet and 2017 consolidated statement of comprehensive income.

P4.2   Equity Method and Eliminating Entries Three Years After Acquisition   Puffin Industries ac-   LO 1, 2, 3 ✓
quired all of Sunset Coast Digital's stock on January 1, 2014, for $3,500,000, $2,100,000 in excess of
book value. At that time, Sunset Coast's inventory (LIFO) was overvalued by $500,000 and its plant
assets (10-year life) were overvalued by $1,000,000. The remaining excess of cost over book value is
attributed to undervalued identifiable intangible assets being amortized over 20 years. Sunset Coast depreciates plant assets and amortizes intangibles by the straight-line method. During the next three years
Sunset Coast reported total net income of $850,000 and paid out 50 percent in dividends. Puffin carries its
investment in Sunset Coast using the complete equity method. Sunset Coast's inventory increased each
year since it was acquired by Puffin, and Sunset Coast's reported net income for 2016 was $200,000.

Required

a. Compute Puffin's 2016 equity in net income of Sunset Coast.

b. Compute the balance in the Investment in Sunset Coast account at December 31, 2016, after all
equity method entries have been booked.

c. Prepare the working paper eliminating entries needed in consolidation at December 31, 2016.

d. If Puffin reports $600,000 net income from its own operations in 2016, what is consolidated net
income for 2016?

LO 1, 3   P4.3   Consolidation at End of First Year, Preacquisition Contingency   On January 2, 2016, Perkins Company acquired all of Sanders Corporation's stock for $4,000,000 cash, when the book value of Sanders' stockholders' equity was $2,200,000. Sanders reported $500,000 of net income and declared and paid dividends of $150,000 in 2016. Data related to the acquisition at January 2, 2016, appear below:

Out-of-pocket merger costs paid in cash by Perkins	$ 50,000
Excess of fair value of Sanders' inventory over book value.	80,000
Excess of fair value of Sanders' equipment over book value (10-year life, straight-line). . . .	200,000
Fair value of Sanders' previously unrecorded lawsuit liability	70,000
Fair value of Sanders' previously unrecorded in-process research and development	300,000
Acquisition-related restructuring costs paid in cash by Perkins	100,000

Sanders uses FIFO, and all of its beginning inventory was sold in 2016. The fair value of the previously unrecorded lawsuit liability increased to $85,000 by December 31, 2016, within the measurement period. Impairment tests show $100,000 in impairment for the in-process R&D and no impairment for the goodwill during 2016.

Required

a. Prepare a schedule to compute Perkins' equity in net income of Sanders Corporation for 2016 using the complete equity method, and prepare all entries related to the investment made by Perkins during 2016.
b. Compute the goodwill for this acquisition, after the measurement period adjustment.
c. Prepare the eliminating entries made in consolidation at December 31, 2016.

⊘ LO 1, 3   P4.4   Consolidated Balance Sheet Working Paper, Bargain Purchase (see related P3.4)   On January 1, 2016, Paxon Corporation acquired all of the outstanding common stock of Saxon Company for $1.8 billion cash. Paxon uses the complete equity method to report its investment. The trial balances of Paxon and Saxon at December 31, 2016, are shown below:

	Dr (Cr)	
(in millions)	**Paxon**	**Saxon**
Cash and receivables.	$ 3,100	$ 800
Inventory.	2,260	940
Long-term investments	—	—
Investment in Saxon.	2,158	—
Land	650	300
Buildings and equipment, net	3,600	1,150
Current liabilities.	(2,020)	(1,200)
Long-term debt	(5,000)	(450)
Common stock, par value	(500)	(100)
Additional paid-in capital	(1,200)	(350)
Retained earnings, January 1.	(2,410)	(845)
Dividends	500	100
Sales revenue.	(30,000)	(10,000)
Equity in net income of Saxon	(258)	—
Gain on sale of securities	—	(10)
Gain on acquisition.	(200)	—
Cost of goods sold.	26,000	8,000
Depreciation expense.	300	40
Interest expense.	250	25
Other operating expenses	2,770	1,600
Totals	$ 0	$ 0

Several of Saxon's assets and liabilities had fair values different from their book values at the acquisition date, as follows:

(in millions)	Fair value − Book value
Inventory (FIFO)	$100
Long-term investments (sold in 2016)	(50)
Land..	245
Buildings and equipment, net (20 years, straight-line).................	300
Long-term debt (overvalued), (5 years, straight-line)	(110)

Required

a. Prepare a schedule to compute equity in net income of Saxon for 2016, and the December 31, 2016 balance for Investment in Saxon, as reported on Paxon's books.

b. Use a working paper to consolidate the trial balances of Paxon and Saxon at December 31, 2016.

c. Prepare the consolidated balance sheet at December 31, 2016, and the consolidated income statement for 2016.

P4.5   **Goodwill Allocation and Impairment Testing**   Porter Corporation acquired Stewart Corporation on January 1, 2016, at a cost of $160 million. Stewart has three reporting units, Networks, Global Services, and Mobile Broadband. In addition, one of Porter's reporting units, U.S. Cellular, benefitted from the acquisition. Relevant data are as follows, at the date of acquisition (*in millions*):   **LO 4**

	Networks	Global Services	Mobile Broadband
Identifiable assets...........................	$50	$250	$125
Liabilities....................................	35	190	100
Fair value of unit............................	55	85	30

U.S. Cellular is expected to increase in value by $10 million because of the acquisition.

Assume qualitative assessment at December 31, 2016, indicates that it is more likely than not that book value exceeds fair value for all reporting units. On December 31, 2016, the following amounts were estimated for a quantitative analysis of goodwill impairment:

	Networks	Global Services	Mobile Broadband	U.S. Cellular
Fair value of unit....................	$50	$90	$25	$ 95
Fair value of identifiable net assets	20	65	23	87
Book value of unit..................	48	92	30	100

In your answers below, show all numbers in millions.

Required

a. Calculate the total goodwill for this acquisition, and its allocation to the four reporting units at January 1, 2016.

b. Calculate any goodwill impairment for 2016.

P4.6   **Intangible Assets and Goodwill: Amortization and Impairment**   In early 2015, Bowen Company acquired a new business unit in a merger. Allocation of the acquisition cost resulted in fair values assigned as follows: **LO 3, 4**

Intangible asset	Fair value	Estimated life
Customer lists	$ 500,000	5 years
Developed technology................................	800,000	10 years
Internet domain name	1,300,000	Indefinite
Goodwill[1]	6,200,000	Indefinite

[1] The goodwill is assigned entirely to the acquired business unit.

Impairment reviews at the end of 2015 and 2016 did not identify any impairment losses. After the business suffered a downturn during 2017, the year-end impairment review yielded the following information:

1. Customer lists are estimated to have undiscounted future cash flows of $250,000 and discounted future cash flows of $180,000.
2. Developed technology is estimated to have undiscounted future cash flows of $500,000 and discounted future cash flows of $420,000.
3. The internet domain name is estimated to have undiscounted future cash flows of $1,000,000 and discounted future cash flows of $750,000. Qualitative assessment indicates that it is more likely than not that the internet domain name is impaired.
4. Because of the economic downturn, Bowen bypassed qualitative assessment of the business unit (Step 0). The acquired business unit has a fair value of $17,000,000, a carrying amount of $18,500,000, and the fair value of its identifiable net assets is $14,200,000.

Required

Determine Bowen's amortization expense and impairment write-offs for 2017.

LO 1, 3 P4.7 Consolidation After Four Years   On January 1, 2014, Perth Company acquired all of Sharbot Company's voting stock for $16 million in cash. Some of Sharbot's identifiable assets at the date of acquisition had fair values that were different from reported values, as follows:

(in millions)	Fair value	Book value
Plant assets, net (20-year remaining life, straight-line)	$ 3	$11
Identifiable intangibles (5-year remaining life, straight-line)	10	0

Sharbot's total stockholders' equity at January 1, 2014, was $4 million. It is now December 31, 2017 (four years later). Cumulative impairment for the goodwill recognized on this acquisition, to the beginning of 2017, is $2 million. Goodwill impairment for 2017 is $0.5 million. Perth uses the complete equity method to account for its investment in Sharbot on its own books. December 31, 2017 trial balances for Perth and Sharbot appear below.

(in thousands)	Perth Company Dr (Cr)	Sharbot Company Dr (Cr)
Current assets	$ 5,000	$ 2,500
Plant assets, net	34,800	28,000
Intangibles	—	—
Investment in Sharbot	23,600	—
Liabilities	(22,000)	(10,000)
Capital stock	(15,000)	(2,000)
Retained earnings, Jan. 1	(25,000)	(16,000)
Sales revenue	(25,000)	(14,000)
Equity in net income of Sharbot	(400)	—
Cost of sales	20,000	8,000
Operating expenses	4,000	3,500
Total	$ 0	$ 0

In your answers below, show all amounts in thousands.

Required

a. Prepare the working paper to consolidate Perth and Sharbot's trial balances at December 31, 2017.
b. Prepare the consolidated income statement for 2017, and the consolidated balance sheet at December 31, 2017, in good form.

 LO 1, 3 P4.8 Consolidation Working Paper, Three Years After Acquisition (see related P3.2)   International Technology Inc. (ITI) acquired all of the voting stock of Global Outsourcing Corporation (GOC) on June 30, 2015, for $110 million in cash and stock, plus an earnings contingency payable at the end of the third year with a fair value of $2 million at the date of acquisition. Within the measurement period, the earnings contingency declined to a fair value of zero and the acquisition price was appropriately adjusted. Both companies have a June 30 year-end. At June 30, 2015, GOC's total stockholders' equity was $40 million, as follows *(in millions)*:

Common stock, par	$ 4
Additional paid-in capital	60
Retained earnings (deficit)	(25)
Accumulated other comprehensive income	3
Treasury stock	(2)
Total	$40

At the acquisition date, GOC's inventories were undervalued by $5 million, its property, plant and equipment was overvalued by $60 million, its reported patents and trademarks were undervalued by $10 million, and its long-term debt was undervalued by $3 million. GOC also had previously unreported identifiable intangibles: $5 million of advanced technology and $25 million of customer lists. GOC reports its inventory using the LIFO method, and purchases exceed sales every year. The acquisition date remaining lives of its assets and liabilities are as follows:

Property, plant and equipment, net	20 years
Patents and trademarks	5 years
Advanced technology	5 years
Customer lists	Indefinite
Long-term debt	3 years

The straight-line method is used for limited life assets. Impairment losses on the customer lists were $2 million in fiscal 2017 and $4 million in fiscal 2018. Goodwill impairment losses were $2 million in fiscal 2016, $3 million in fiscal 2017, and $2 million in fiscal 2018.

GOC reported net income of $15 million in fiscal 2016, and a net loss of $2 million in fiscal 2017. Neither company pays dividends. ITI uses the complete equity method to account for its investment in GOC on its own books. The trial balances of ITI and GOC at June 30, 2018, are as follows:

	Dr (Cr)	
(in millions)	ITI	GOC
Current assets	$ 232	$ 12
Property, plant and equipment, net	600	140
Identifiable intangible assets	1,100	30
Investment in GOC	127	—
Current liabilities	(175)	(10)
Long-term liabilities	(1,125)	(105)
Common stock, par	(22)	(4)
Additional paid-in capital	(580)	(60)
Retained earnings, July 1	(118)	12
Accumulated other comprehensive income, July 1	(16)	(4)
Treasury stock	8	2
Sales revenue	(2,000)	(900)
Equity in net income of GOC	(7)	—
Equity in OCI of GOC	(1)	—
Cost of goods sold	1,400	800
Operating expenses	580	88
Other comprehensive income	(3)	(1)
Totals	$ 0	$ 0

Required

a. Prepare a schedule that computes the June 30, 2018, investment in GOC balance and 2018 equity in net income on ITI's books.

b. Use a working paper to consolidate the trial balances of ITI and GOC at June 30, 2018.

c. Present the consolidated balance sheet at June 30, 2018, and the consolidated statement of comprehensive income for 2018.

LO 1, 3   P4.9   Working Paper Eliminating Entries, Partial Year Consolidation (see related P3.3)   On April 16, 2003, **Pfizer Inc.** traded $55,873 million fair value of stock for all of the stock of **Pharmacia**, in a stock acquisition. Pharmacia's stockholders' equity accounts at the date of acquisition totaled $7,236 million, and the $48,637 million excess of acquisition cost over book value was allocated as follows (*in millions*):

PFIZER INC.
[PFE]

Inventory.	$ 2,939
Long-term investments	40
Property, plant and equipment.	(317)
In-process research and development	5,052
Developed technology rights	37,066
Long-term debt premium.	(1,841)
Other assets	(15,606)
Goodwill.	21,304
Total	$48,637

Pfizer has a December 31 year-end, and Pharmacia's results of operations are included in the 2003 consolidated statements for the 8½ months following its acquisition. Reporting for the above revaluations during 2003 is as follows:

- Pharmacia's inventory was sold during 2003.
- Long-term investments remain on Pharmacia's books.
- Property, plant and equipment is depreciated over an average life of 20 years, straight-line.
- In-process research and development impairment for 2003 is $716 million.
- Finite-lived developed technology rights are valued at $31,596 million, and are amortized over an average life of 11 years, straight-line.
- Indefinite-lived developed technology rights are valued at $5,470 million, and no impairment loss is reported for 2003.
- Amortization of the long-term debt premium is $12 million.
- Other assets are written off over an average of 10 years, straight-line.
- Goodwill is not impaired during 2003.

Required (Round all numbers to the nearest million.)

a.   Assume Pharmacia reports net income of $5,000 million for the period April 16 to December 31, 2003, and pays no dividends. Calculate 2003 equity in net income of Pharmacia, recorded by Pfizer on its separate books using the complete equity method.

b.   Prepare the eliminating entries necessary to consolidate Pharmacia's 2003 financial results with Pfizer.

LO 4, 5   P4.10   Goodwill Impairment Testing, IFRS and U.S. GAAP   Following IFRS, **Nokia Corporation** allocates its goodwill to the cash-generating units that benefit from the business combinations generating the goodwill. In its 2013 Form 20-F, filed with the SEC, Nokia discloses the CGUs and the goodwill allocated to each (*in millions*):

NOKIA CORPORATION
[NOK]

CGU	Goodwill
HERE	€3,129
Radio Access Networks.	88
Global Services	91
Devices and Services.	1,417
Total goodwill.	€4,725

Nokia uses value-in-use to measure the fair values of HERE, Radio Access Networks, and Global Services, measured using discounted cash flows. Discount rates used in 2013 were as follows:

HERE	10.6%
Radio Access Networks.	10.8%
Global Services	10.3%

Nokia plans to sell the Devices and Services unit, and measures its fair value for goodwill impairment testing purposes at the agreed purchase price less estimated disposal costs.

Here is end-of-2013 information on Nokia's CGUs (*in millions*). Book values and the fair value of the Devices and Services unit are assumed.

	Fair value	Book value
HERE	€3,803	€3,800
Radio Access Networks......	3,096	2,800
Global Services	3,910	3,800
Devices and Services........	2,400	2,000

In your answers below, show all amounts in millions.

Required

a. Following IFRS, how is the "fair value" of a CGU defined? Does Nokia follow IFRS in measuring the fair value of its CGUs? Explain.

b. Why do you think the discount rates used for the three CGUs are different? Why is there no discount rate for the Devices and Services CGU?

c. Calculate Nokia's goodwill impairment loss for 2013.

d. What if the CGU book values were as follows (*in millions*):

HERE	€4,000
Radio Access Networks.......................................	3,000
Global Services	4,200
Devices and Services..	2,500

Calculate Nokia's goodwill impairment loss for 2013, per IFRS.

e. Now assume the same book values as in *d.*, and Nokia follows U.S. GAAP, reporting units are the same as CGUs, and Step 0 is bypassed. Assumed information on the fair values of identifiable net assets at the end of 2013 is (*in millions*):

HERE	€ 850
Radio Access Networks.......................................	2,600
Global Services	3,000
Devices and Services..	900

Calculate Nokia's goodwill impairment loss for 2013, per U.S. GAAP.

P4.11 **Complete Equity Method and Eliminating Entries, Four Years After Acquisition** On January 1, 2015, Peerless Network acquired all of the stock of Sound Telecom for $400 million in cash. At the date of acquisition, Sound Telecom's stockholders' equity was as follows (*in millions*): **LO 1, 3**

Capital stock	$10
Retained earnings	50
Accumulated other comprehensive income......................	2
Total..	$62

An evaluation of Sound Telecom's balance sheet at January 1, 2015, revealed that its plant assets (10-year remaining life) were overvalued by $40 million and it had previously unrecorded identifiable intangible assets (5-year remaining life) of $10 million. Goodwill from this acquisition was impaired by $5 million during 2015–2017, and by $1 million in 2018.

It is now December 31, 2018, four years after the acquisition. Sound Telecom reported total net income of $12 million during 2015–2017, and $5 million for 2018. It also reported total other comprehensive income of $1 million during 2015–2017, and $200,000 of other comprehensive loss in 2018. Sound Telecom declared and paid no dividends during this time period. Peerless Network reports its investment using the complete equity method. The following are the separate trial balances of Peerless and Sound Telecom at December 31, 2018.

(in thousands)	Peerless Network Dr (Cr)	Sound Telecom Dr (Cr)
Current assets	$ 175,000	$ 50,000
Plant assets, net	860,000	410,000
Identifiable intangibles	40,000	10,000
Investment in Sound Telecom	419,800	—
Liabilities	(898,500)	(390,200)
Capital stock	(50,000)	(10,000)
Retained earnings, Jan. 1	(490,000)	(62,000)
Accumulated other comprehensive income, Jan. 1	(25,000)	(3,000)
Sales revenue	(1,200,000)	(650,000)
Equity in net income	(6,000)	—
Equity in other comprehensive loss	200	—
Cost of sales	800,000	450,000
Operating expenses	375,000	195,000
Other comprehensive loss (income)	(500)	200
Total	$ 0	$ 0

In your answers below, show all numbers in thousands.

Required

a. Show how the following balances, appearing in the 2018 trial balances above, were calculated:
   (1) Equity in net income of Sound Telecom, appearing in Peerless Network's 2018 trial balance.
   (2) Sound Telecom's retained earnings and AOCI balances at January 1, 2018.
   (3) Investment in Sound Telecom at December 31, 2018, appearing in Peerless Network's trial balance.

b. Prepare the consolidation working paper to consolidate Peerless Network's trial balance accounts with those of Sound Telecom at December 31, 2018.

c. Present the consolidated balance sheet at December 31, 2018, and the consolidated statement of comprehensive income for 2018, in good form.

LO 4, 5 **P4.12** **Intangibles Under IFRS** **BT Group plc** is a global British telecommunications services company headquartered in London. Its financial statements are prepared using IFRS. For the year ended 31 March 2014, BT Group reports the following identifiable intangible assets:

BT GROUP [BT]

(in millions)	Customer Relationships and Brands	Telecoms Licences and Other	Internally Developed Software	Purchased Software
Cost	£394	£415	£3,156	£1,262
Accumulated amortization	(323)	(101)	(1,939)	(1,108)
Net	71	314	1,217	154

Required

a. Of the four types of identifiable intangibles reported, which are most likely to have been acquired in business combinations?

b. Would U.S. GAAP report the same balances as above for identifiable intangibles as IFRS? Explain.

c. Below are some assumed situations for BT Group's identifiable intangibles.
   (1) Assume that intangibles costing £40 million (10-year life), acquired 1 April 2015, are traded in an active market. BT Group amortizes them on a straight-line basis. On 31 March 2016, the market value of these items is £45 million. One year later, new developments reduce the market value to £30 million. Prepare all journal entries related to these intangibles, per IFRS, on 31 March 2016 and 2017. BT Group uses the revaluation approach for qualifying intangibles.

(2) Assume BT Group recognizes customer relationships valued at £2,500 million in a 1 April 2016 acquisition. These intangibles are straight-line amortized over 5 years, using the cost model. On 31 March 2017, the following information is gathered concerning these intangibles:

Sum of undiscounted expected future cash flows...............	£2,500 million
Present value of expected future cash flows (value-in-use).........	1,800 million
Net market value	1,500 million

Calculate the impairment loss recognized under IFRS and U.S. GAAP, assuming BT Group bypasses the qualitative assessment allowed under U.S. GAAP. What do you conclude about the relative impairment losses recognized under IFRS and U.S. GAAP?

P4.13 Consolidation After Acquisition, Revaluation Write-Off Issues (see related P3.9) In 2013, **AB InBev** acquired the remainder of the stock of **Grupo Modelo**, and began consolidating it as a wholly-owned subsidiary. Acquisition cost was $34,008 million. Grupo Modelo's equity balances at the date of acquisition were as follows (*in millions*):

LO 1, 3, 5
AB INBEV
[ABI]

Issued capital...	$ 200
Share premium..	1,300
Retained earnings	7,003
Accumulated other comprehensive income............................	700
Total	$9,203

Below is a summary of the date-of-acquisition revaluations of Grupo Modelo's identifiable net assets, and assumed subsequent measurement for each. Assume the acquisition took place at the beginning of 2013. All numbers are in millions.

(*in millions*)	Fair value – Book value	Subsequent measurement and other information as of 2016 year-end
Property, plant and equipment........	$ 99	10 year life, straight-line
Goodwill (on Grupo Modelo's books)...	(796)	No subsequent impairment losses reported by Grupo Modelo
Intangible assets	4,454	50% limited life, 5 years, straight-line; 50% indefinite life, impairment through 2015 = $500; no impairment in 2016
Investment in associates	(4)	Still held by Grupo Modelo
Current assets	4,333	FIFO inventories, sold in 2013
Trade and other payables	509	Accrued liabilities not reported on Grupo Modelo's books; expensed by Grupo Modelo in 2013 and 2014
Deferred tax liabilities..............	714	Differences between book and tax revaluation write-offs; $100 reversed through 2015, $20 reversed in 2016
Current liabilities..................	1,650	Accrued liabilities not reported on Grupo Modelo's books; expensed by Grupo Modelo in 2013

Goodwill of $19,592 million was recognized for this acquisition. The goodwill has not been impaired.

It is now December 31, 2016, four years after the acquisition, and you are preparing the working paper to consolidate Grupo Modelo with AB InBev. The following are the assumed trial balances of each company at that date. AB InBev's investment balance is reported using the complete equity method.

(in millions)	AB InBev Dr (Cr)	Grupo Modelo Dr (Cr)
Current assets	$15,000	8,000
Investment securities	300	10
Investment in associates	200	33
Investment in Grupo Modelo	41,237.8	—
Property, plant and equipment, net	18,000	15,000
Intangible assets	25,000	10,000
Goodwill	50,000	796
Current liabilities	(20,000)	(4,000)
Trade and other payables	(2,000)	(1,200)
Deferred tax liabilities	(9,800)	(2,200)
Employee benefit liability	(1,600)	(400)
Loans and borrowings	(52,568.1)	(5,731)
Issued capital	(1,700)	(200)
Share premium	(17,000)	(1,300)
Retained earnings, Jan. 1	(29,000)	(16,503)
Accumulated other comprehensive income, Jan. 1	(2,000)	(1,200)
Dividends	2,100	—
Revenue	(40,000)	(4,000)
Equity in net income of Grupo Modelo	(569.7)	—
Equity in OCI of Grupo Modelo	(100)	—
Equity in income of associates	(50)	(5)
Cost of sales	16,000	1,500
Operating expenses	10,000	2,000
Nonrecurring income	(5,000)	(1,000)
Finance expenses	2,000	200
Income tax expense	1,700	300
Other comprehensive income	(150)	(100)
Total	$ 0	$ 0

In your answers below, show all amounts in millions.

Required

a. Prepare a schedule to calculate AB InBev's equity in net income of Grupo Modelo, reported on its December 31, 2016, trial balance at $569.7 million.

b. Prepare a schedule to calculate AB InBev's investment in Grupo Modelo balance, reported on its December 31, 2016, trial balance at $41,237.8 million.

c. Prepare the December 31, 2016, consolidation working paper.

d. Prepare the 2016 consolidated statement of comprehensive income and the December 31, 2016, consolidated balance sheet, in good form.

LO 6 **P4.14** **Cost Method and Eliminating Entries Three Years After Acquisition**   Use the information
(APPENDIX) provided in P4.2, but assume that Puffin Industries uses the cost method to account for its investment in Sunset Coast Digital.

Required

Prepare the working paper eliminating entries needed in consolidation at December 31, 2016.

LO 6 **P4.15** **Cost Method and Eliminating Entries Four Years After Acquisition**   Use the information
(APPENDIX) provided in P4.11, but assume that Peerless Network uses the cost method to account for its investment in Sound Telecom.

Required

Prepare the working paper to consolidate the trial balances of Peerless Network and Sound Telecom at December 31, 2018.

REVIEW SOLUTIONS •••

Review 1 Solution

(*in millions*)

Impairment testing for identifiable intangibles:

Intangible asset	Undiscounted cash flows < Book value?	Impairment loss
Customer lists	$240 < $250? Yes	$250 − 225 = $25
Television rights	$105 < $100? No	NA
Brand names	NA	$400 − 380 = $20

Goodwill impairment testing:

	Cable	Filmed Entertainment	Networks
Fair value of unit.	$2,000	$2,800	$6,200
Book value of unit.	2,300	2,000	6,500
Fair value < Book value?.	Yes	No	Yes
Fair value of unit.	2,000		6,200
Fair value of identifiable net assets	500		5,950
Fair value of goodwill	1,500		250
Book value of goodwill.	1,000		550
Goodwill impairment	$ 0		$ 300

In summary, the consolidated income statement reports $45 million in identifiable intangibles impairment loss and $300 million in goodwill impairment loss. The eliminating entry to record the impairment is *(in millions)*:

(O)	Impairment loss: identifiable intangibles	45	
	Impairment loss: goodwill	300	
	Identifiable intangibles: customer lists		25
	Identifiable intangibles: brand names		20
	Goodwill.		300

• •

Review 2 Solution

a.

First Media reported net income for 2017	$250,000,000
Revaluation write-offs:	
Property, plant and equipment ($300,000,000/10).	(30,000,000)
Goodwill	(100,000,000)
Equity in net income of First Media	$120,000,000

b.

Consolidation Working Paper

(in millions)	Accounts Taken From Books Dr (Cr) Time Warner	First Media	Eliminations Dr	Cr	Consolidated Balances Dr (Cr)
Cash and receivables..........	$ 1,200	$ 450			$ 1,650
Inventories	7,200	1,000		$ 50 (R)	8,150
Property, plant and equipment, net	38,860	4,540	(R) $ 240	30 (O-1)	43,610
Investment in First Media.......	1,580	—		100 (C) 790 (E) 690 (R)	—
Lease agreements	—	—			—
Goodwill...................	—	—	(R) 500	100 (O-2)	400
Accounts payable............	(7,800)	(670)			(8,470)
Long-term debt	(35,000)	(4,300)			(39,300)
Common stock, par	(120)	(10)	(E) 10		(120)
Additional paid-in capital	(3,000)	(130)	(E) 130		(3,000)
Retained earnings, January 1....	(2,550)	(700)	(E) 700		(2,550)
Treasury stock	—	50		50 (E)	—
Dividends	100	20		20 (C)	100
Sales revenue...............	(10,000)	(2,000)			(12,000)
Equity in net income of First Media	(120)	—	(C) 120		—
Cost of goods sold...........	8,500	1,600			10,100
Operating expenses..........	1,150	150	(O-1) 30 (O-2) 100		1,430
Totals	$ 0	$ 0	$1,830	$1,830	$ 0

TIME WARNER and FIRST MEDIA
Consolidated Statement of Income
For Year Ended December 31, 2017 (in millions)

Sales revenue...	$12,000
Less: Cost of goods sold..	(10,100)
Gross profit...	1,900
Less: Operating expenses	(1,430)
Net income	**$ 470**

TIME WARNER and FIRST MEDIA
Consolidated Balance Sheet
December 31, 2017 *(in millions)*

Assets		Liabilities and Stockholders' Equity	
Current assets		Accounts payable	$ 8,470
Cash and receivables	$ 1,650	Long-term debt	39,300
Inventories	8,150	Total liabilities	47,770
Total current assets	9,800		
Noncurrent assets		Stockholders' equity	
Property, plant and equipment, net	43,610	Common stock, par	120
Goodwill	400	Additional paid-in capital	3,000
Total noncurrent assets	44,010	Retained earnings (1)	2,920
		Total stockholders' equity	6,040
Total assets	$53,810	Total liabilities and stockholders' equity	$53,810

(1) $2,550 + $470 − $100 = $2,920

5 Consolidated Financial Statements: Outside Interests

LAS VEGAS SANDS CORPORATION
www.lasvegassands.com

Las Vegas Sands Corporation (LVSC) owns and operates several entertainment destinations in Las Vegas, including The Venetian Las Vegas and The Palazzo. LVSC also owns several international properties, such as the Four Seasons Macao in Macau and the Marina Bay Sands in Singapore. LVSC incorporated in 2004 and lists its stock on the New York Stock Exchange.

LVSC presents financial statements that consolidate the parent company with more than eighty subsidiaries. One subsidiary, Sands China Ltd., owns and operates most of the Macau properties. In the equity section of LVSC's 2013 consolidated balance sheet, a "noncontrolling interest" of $1,835 million appears, comprising over 19 percent of LVSC's total equity. The 2013 consolidated income statement reports "net income attributable to noncontrolling interests" of $649 million. Footnotes to the annual report reveal that LVSC owns 70.2 percent of Sands China Ltd.; other investors own the remaining 29.8 percent.

Because companies are required to consolidate companies they control, this almost always means consolidation of any majority-owned company. While most subsidiaries are wholly-owned, a substantial number are not. The "noncontrolling interest" lines on LVSC's consolidated financial statements reflect the portion of the consolidated subsidiary, Sands China Ltd., that is not owned by LVSC. "Noncontrolling interest" on the balance sheet represents the equity of the noncontrolling shareholders. "Noncontrolling interest" on the income statement reports the noncontrolling shareholders' share of consolidated income.

In this chapter you will learn how to consolidate financial statements of a parent and its subsidiaries that are not wholly-owned. The existence of outside ownership in a subsidiary affects valuation of goodwill and consolidated shareholders' equity, and impacts the display of information on the consolidated financial statements. *Source:* Las Vegas Sands Corporation annual report, 2013.

CHAPTER ORGANIZATION

Noncontrolling interests at acquisition date	Noncontrolling interests in subsequent periods	Bargain purchases with noncontrolling interests	IFRS for noncontrolling interests	Consolidated statement of cash flows
• Estimate fair value of noncontrolling interests • Value goodwill • Eliminating entries • Consolidated balance sheet • Consolidating variable interest entities	• Calculate equity in net income and noncontrolling interest in net income • Eliminating entries • Consolidated statement of net income and comprehensive income	• Date of acquisition • Subsequent periods	• Alternative valuation of noncontrolling interests • Impact of alternative IFRS valuation on financial statements	• Major items affecting calculation of cash from operations • Preparing the consolidated cash flow statement

INTRODUCTION

When a parent has a controlling interest in a legally separate subsidiary, it regularly presents consolidated financial statements that aggregate the financial records of the separate companies. Previous chapters considered valuation and consolidation procedures when the parent acquires *all* of the voting interests in a subsidiary. This chapter discusses consolidation of less-than-wholly-owned subsidiaries.

Recall from Chapter 3 that "controlling interest" usually means ownership of a majority of the voting shares of another entity. However, regardless of ownership percentage, a controlling interest in another entity requires consolidation of that entity's assets, liabilities, revenues and expenses in its financial statements. The portion of the subsidiary's stock held by other investors is called the **noncontrolling interest**.

In the sections that follow, we see that even when the parent owns less than 100 percent of the subsidiary, it consolidates 100 percent of the subsidiary's assets, liabilities, revenues and expenses with its own accounts. On the consolidated balance sheet, the noncontrolling interest in the net assets of the subsidiary appears as a separate line in the equity section. Similarly, on the consolidated income statement the noncontrolling interest's share of the subsidiary's income appears as a separate line, representing that portion of consolidated income attributable to the noncontrolling interest.

Companies acquire a less-than-100-percent interest in a subsidiary for many reasons, for example:

* The subsidiary's previous owners want to retain an interest in the company.
* The acquirer does not want to invest the resources necessary to buy all of the acquiree's stock.
* The acquirer cannot convince all the stockholders to sell.
* A smaller investment suffices to achieve the acquirer's goals.

A noncontrolling interest also appears on the consolidated financial statements when a company determines it is the **primary beneficiary** of a **variable interest entity**. Recall from Chapter 3 that *FASB ASC Topic 810* requires the primary beneficiary of a variable interest entity to consolidate that entity, even if the primary beneficiary holds little or no equity interest in the entity. The consolidated balance sheet then reports a noncontrolling interest equal to its share of the difference between the variable interest entity's assets and liabilities. If the primary beneficiary has no equity interest, the noncontrolling interest equals the variable interest's total equity.

NONCONTROLLING INTERESTS AT ACQUISITION DATE

LO1 Consolidate a subsidiary with noncontrolling interests at the date of acquisition.

When the parent acquires a less-than-100-percent interest in a subsidiary, it reports its investment at acquisition cost. Acquisition cost includes the fair value of shares and debt issued, net of registration and issue costs, cash paid directly to the former shareholders of the acquired subsidiary, and any expected conditional payments. The consolidation working paper brings together the balance sheet accounts of the parent and the subsidiary, and reports the noncontrolling interest in the subsidiary's equity as a component of consolidated equity.

Valuation of Noncontrolling Interests and Goodwill at Acquisition

U.S. GAAP initially reports noncontrolling interests at **fair value**. Revaluations of acquired identifiable net assets are attributed to both the controlling and noncontrolling interests in proportion to ownership interests. Goodwill is separately attributed to each interest, typically in different proportions. An example illustrates the valuations.

Assume Admiral Casino & Resort pays $42,600,000 in cash for 80 percent of the stock of Gold Road Motor Inn, Inc., on January 1, 2015. The book values of Gold Road's net assets equal their fair values, except for previously unrecorded intangibles: customer lists, with a four-year life, straight-line amortization, valued at $5,000,000. Gold Road's book value of $10,000,000 consists of $2,500,000 of capital stock, $7,400,000 in retained earnings, and $100,000 in accumulated other comprehensive income. Admiral estimates the fair value of the 20 percent noncontrolling interest in Gold Road to be $8,400,000 at the acquisition date.

Total goodwill on this acquisition is $36,000,000, calculated as follows:

Acquisition cost	$42,600,000
Fair value of noncontrolling interest	8,400,000
Total fair value	51,000,000
Book value of Gold Road	(10,000,000)
Fair value in excess of Gold Road's book value	41,000,000
Difference between fair value and book value:	
Customer lists	(5,000,000)
Goodwill	$36,000,000

We allocate goodwill between the controlling and noncontrolling interest by first calculating goodwill attributed to the controlling interest, and then attributing the remainder to the noncontrolling interest.

Goodwill to controlling interest	
Acquisition cost	$42,600,000
Less controlling interest in the fair value of Gold Road's identifiable net assets:	
80% × ($10,000,000 + $5,000,000)	(12,000,000)
Controlling interest's share	$30,600,000
Goodwill to noncontrolling interest	
Total goodwill	$36,000,000
Less goodwill to controlling interest	(30,600,000)
Noncontrolling interest's share	$ 5,400,000

These goodwill allocations of 85 percent (= $30,600,000/$36,000,000) and 15 percent (= $5,400,000/$36,000,000) attribute goodwill to the controlling and noncontrolling interests when consolidating the financial statements in future years. Thus, the percentage ownership interests do not govern the goodwill allocation.

Measuring the Fair Value of Noncontrolling Interests

ASC para. 805-20-30-1 requires the acquiring company to value the noncontrolling interest in the subsidiary at its fair value at the acquisition date. The preceding example sets the estimated fair value of the noncontrolling interest at $8,400,000. How is this value determined? If there is an active market for the subsidiary's stock, the stock price at the acquisition date may be appropriate. If not, alternative valuation methods are used. *ASC paras. 805-20-30-7* and *8* provide some guidance, as follows:

> An acquirer sometimes will be able to measure the acquisition-date fair value of a noncontrolling interest on the basis of a quoted price in an active market for the equity shares not held by the acquirer. In other situations, however, a quoted price in an active market for the equity shares will not be available. In those situations, the acquirer would measure the fair value of the noncontrolling interest using another valuation technique.
>
> The fair values of the acquirer's interest in the acquiree and the noncontrolling interest on a per-share basis might differ. The main difference is likely to be the inclusion of a control premium in the per-share fair value of the acquirer's interest in the acquiree or, conversely, the inclusion of a discount for lack of control (also referred to as a noncontrolling interest discount) in the per-share fair value of the noncontrolling interest if market participants would take into account such a premium or discount when pricing the noncontrolling interest.

When public companies are involved, the current share price reflects transactions among noncontrolling shareholders. Such stockholders tend to be passive investors, earning a return from dividends and any future growth in the market price. Controlling owners, on the other hand, can direct business operations, set compensation and benefits, change capital structure, sell or merge the company, or even liquidate it. Because of all the powers a controlling owner has, a controlling ownership interest is worth more than a noncontrolling interest. The premium offered when a public company acquisition is proposed reflects, in part at least, the value the buyer assigns to acquiring control.

Because the stock of the company to be acquired is usually widely held by individual and institutional investors, the prospective buyer must offer a control premium large enough to induce sufficient numbers of existing noncontrolling holders to sell their stock. In the case of a nonpublic business, the seller may be the controlling owner, perhaps the sole owner. Such a seller is in a better position to capture the value of the control premium than the dispersed noncontrolling interests in most public companies.

Thus, the **current stock price** of a publicly-traded company reflects transactions among noncontrolling shareholders, and **is appropriate for valuing the noncontrolling interest**. Including a control premium in the acquirer's cost is reasonable, but deducting a discount for lack of control is not. If a valuation method such as capitalization of future returns is used to estimate the value of the company as a whole, it may be reasonable to deduct a discount for lack of control when valuing the noncontrolling interest.

Suppose an acquiree's current market price is $30 per share. The acquirer is willing to pay a 6.67 percent control premium, or $2 (= 6.67% × $30) per share to obtain the shares, and therefore pays $32 per share for 90 percent of the acquiree. The acquirer could logically value the noncontrolling interest at the acquiree's $30 per share market price. However, if the acquiree is not publicly traded, the acquirer may use one or more valuation techniques to estimate the value of the acquiree. If a business valuation method values the company at $32 per share, a discount of 6.25 percent [= 1 − (1/(1 + 0.0667))] may be applied to value the noncontrolling interest at $30 [= $32 × (1 − 0.0625)] per share.

In our initial illustration, Admiral pays $42,600,000 for 80 percent of Gold Road. The 20 percent noncontrolling interest's fair value is $8,400,000. If Gold Road has 1,000,000 outstanding shares, the noncontrolling interest is valued at $42 per share (= $8,400,000/200,000). The controlling interest's cost of $53.25 per share (= $42,600,000/800,000) reflects a control premium of about 27 percent [= ($53.25 − $42)/$42].

When an active market price is not available, acquirers use other valuation methods to estimate the fair value of both the controlling and noncontrolling interests in the acquiree. Business valuation methods include the following:

- Capitalization of expected future earnings or cash flows, where estimated future returns are discounted using an appropriate discount rate.
- Capitalization of excess earnings, where firm value is estimated as the fair value of tangible net assets plus capitalized earnings in excess of earnings attributable to the tangible assets.
- Direct comparison approach, using the terms of a similar acquisition, such as a multiple of book value, billings, or other appropriate measures.

ASC para. 805-20-50-1 requires disclosure of the following information for each business combination during the reporting period, in which the acquirer obtained less than 100 percent of the acquiree's equity interests:

- The fair value of the noncontrolling interest in the acquiree at the acquisition date.
- The valuation technique(s) and significant inputs used to measure the fair value of the noncontrolling interest.

Consolidation Eliminating Entries at Acquisition Date

Chapter 3 explained the eliminating entries required to consolidate a wholly-owned subsidiary at the date of acquisition:

> **(E)**   Eliminate the subsidiary's stockholders' equity accounts against the investment account.
>
> **(R)**   Eliminate the remainder of the investment account, representing the difference between acquisition price and the subsidiary's book value, and revalue the subsidiary's assets and liabilities from book value to fair value at the acquisition date.

When a noncontrolling interest is present, the eliminating entries accomplish the same goals as when the subsidiary is wholly-owned: eliminate the investment account and the subsidiary's equity accounts, and revalue the subsidiary's assets and liabilities to fair value at the date of acquisition. In addition, the eliminations create the noncontrolling interest in equity to be reported on the consolidated balance sheet. The date-of-acquisition noncontrolling interest in the subsidiary's net assets consists of its interest in the book value of the subsidiary, plus its interest in the revaluations that occur at the date of acquisition, including any goodwill. We modify eliminating entries (E) and (R) to allow for noncontrolling interests, as follows:

> **(E)**   Eliminate the subsidiary's stockholders' equity accounts, reducing the investment account and increasing the noncontrolling interest account according to each ownership interest's share of the subsidiary's equity.
>
> **(R)**   Revalue the subsidiary's assets and liabilities from book value to fair value at the acquisition date, reducing the investment account and increasing the noncontrolling interest account according to each ownership interest's share of the revaluations.

Eliminating entry (E) allocates the subsidiary's book value (equity) between the controlling interest—the investment account—and the noncontrolling interest, in proportion to their ownership interests. For example, if the parent owns 90 percent of the subsidiary, 10 percent of the subsidiary's equity is added to the noncontrolling interest. Eliminating entry (R) revalues the subsidiary's identifiable net assets, such as plant and equipment, previously unrecorded identifiable intangibles or liabilities, and acquired goodwill. The controlling and noncontrolling interests share revaluations in *identifiable net assets* in proportion to their ownership interests.

However, *goodwill* is allocated according to each interest's share in the goodwill. Goodwill is shared in proportion to ownership interests only when the acquisition price and the fair value of the noncontrolling interest are equal on a per share basis, which is unlikely. When there is a noncontrolling interest valuation discount, the goodwill allocation to the noncontrolling interest will be, on a percentage basis, *less* than its ownership interest. In our illustration, the noncontrolling interest in Gold Road is 20 percent, but it is allocated only 15 percent of the goodwill.

The acquisition date eliminating entries necessary to consolidate the balance sheets of Admiral and Gold Road appear below, in journal entry form.

(E)	Capital stock	2,500,000	
	Retained earnings	7,400,000	
	Accumulated other comprehensive income	100,000	
	Investment in Gold Road (80%)		8,000,000
	Noncontrolling interest in Gold Road (20%)		2,000,000
	To eliminate Gold Road's equity accounts against the book value		
	portion of the investment account and recognize the book value		
	of the noncontrolling interest.		
(R)	Customer lists	5,000,000	
	Goodwill	36,000,000	
	Investment in Gold Road		34,600,000
	Noncontrolling interest in Gold Road		6,400,000
	To revalue Gold Road's net assets to fair value and allocate the		
	revaluations to the controlling and noncontrolling interest.		
	$34,600,000 = (80% × $5,000,000) + $30,600,000.		
	$6,400,000 = (20% × $5,000,000) + $5,400,000.		

The consolidation working paper appears in Exhibit 5.1. Account balances other than the investment on Admiral's books and the equity accounts on Gold Road's books are assumed.

EXHIBIT 5.1   Consolidation Working Paper for Admiral and Gold Road, January 1, 2015

	Accounts Taken From Books Dr (Cr)		Eliminations		Consolidated Balances Dr (Cr)
	Admiral	**Gold Road**	**Dr**	**Cr**	
Current assets	$ 10,000,000	$ 4,000,000			$ 14,000,000
Equity investments	35,000,000	4,200,000			39,200,000
Plant and equipment, net	250,000,000	60,000,000			310,000,000
Investment in Gold Road	42,600,000	—		$ 8,000,000 (E)	—
				34,600,000 (R)	
Identifiable intangible assets	620,000,000	—	(R) $ 5,000,000		625,000,000
Goodwill	—	—	(R) 36,000,000		36,000,000
Current liabilities	(12,000,000)	(10,000,000)			(22,000,000)
Long-term debt	(920,600,000)	(48,200,000)			(968,800,000)
Capital stock	(5,000,000)	(2,500,000)	(E) 2,500,000		(5,000,000)
Retained earnings	(19,750,000)	(7,400,000)	(E) 7,400,000		(19,750,000)
Accumulated other comprehensive income	(250,000)	(100,000)	(E) 100,000		(250,000)
Noncontrolling interest	—	—		2,000,000 (E)	(8,400,000)
				6,400,000 (R)	
Totals	$ 0	$ 0	$51,000,000	$51,000,000	$ 0

Noncontrolling Interests in the Consolidated Balance Sheet

ASC Sections 810-10-45 and *55* provide authoritative guidance on presentation of noncontrolling interests in consolidated financial statements. On the **consolidated balance sheet**, the noncontrolling interest in the equity of a subsidiary appears as a **separate component of consolidated equity**. The equity section is divided between the controlling and noncontrolling interests. Controlling interests include separate lines for the parent's capital stock, retained earnings, accumulated other comprehensive income, and other equity accounts. *Noncontrolling interests appear on one line.* If there are multiple subsidiaries, noncontrolling interests may be presented in aggregate.

Admiral's consolidated balance sheet at January 1, 2015, the date of acquisition, appears below.

ADMIRAL CASINO & RESORT
Consolidated Balance Sheet
January 1, 2015

Assets		Liabilities and Stockholders' Equity	
Current assets	$ 14,000,000	Current liabilities.	$ 22,000,000
Equity investments	39,200,000	Long-term debt	968,800,000
Plant and equipment, net . . .	310,000,000	Total liabilities.	990,800,000
Identifiable intangibles	625,000,000		
Goodwill	36,000,000	Stockholders' equity	
		Admiral stockholders' equity:	
		Capital stock.	5,000,000
		Retained earnings.	19,750,000
		Accumulated other comprehensive income.	250,000
		Total Admiral stockholders' equity	25,000,000
		Noncontrolling interest	8,400,000
		Total stockholders' equity	33,400,000
Total assets	$1,024,200,000	Total liabilities and stockholders' equity	$1,024,200,000

Consolidating Variable Interest Entities

Recall that a company must consolidate an entity even if it has little or no equity ownership, when it is the entity's primary beneficiary. Companies that are primary beneficiaries of VIEs follow consolidation procedures outlined in *ASC paras. 810-10-30-1* and *2*. These procedures feature two valuation alternatives, depending on the prior relationship between the primary beneficiary (PB) and the VIE.

If the PB and the VIE are under *common control*, the assets and liabilities of the VIE are included on the consolidated balance sheet at **book value**. Entities under common control have common ownership and management. In that case, the VIE was not really "acquired" as it is already part of the corporate family, and there is no transaction to justify revaluation of the VIE's assets and liabilities. The book value of the VIE's net assets appears as noncontrolling interest. Consolidation eliminations delete the VIE's equity accounts and reclassify them as noncontrolling interests.

More typically, the primary beneficiary and the VIE do *not* have common ownership, although the PB has a financial relationship with the VIE. In the absence of common ownership, the assets and liabilities of the VIE, as well as the noncontrolling interest, are consolidated at **fair value** as of the date it is determined that the PB should consolidate the VIE. The consolidation working paper entries eliminate the VIE's equity accounts, revalue its identifiable assets and liabilities as appropriate, and establish the noncontrolling interest. Goodwill valuation follows *ASC Topic 805*, defined as the excess of acquisition cost and the fair value of noncontrolling interests over the fair value of identifiable net assets of the VIE. Consolidation of the VIE in subsequent years follows the requirements of *ASC Topic 810*, with no additional issues.

NONCONTROLLING INTERESTS IN SUBSEQUENT YEARS

LO2 Consolidate a subsidiary with noncontrolling interests in subsequent years.

Consolidating the accounts of the parent and subsidiary in periods after the acquisition requires that we consider the effect of the noncontrolling interest on consolidated income and comprehensive income, and changes in the equity value of the noncontrolling interest over time. The noncontrolling interest in net income is its share of subsidiary's reported net income, adjusted for the noncontrolling interest's share of revaluation write-offs. Noncontrolling interest on the balance sheet is its initial fair value, updated for its share of accumulated comprehensive income and dividends during the post-acquisition period.

Assume the parent uses the complete equity method in reporting the investment on its own books. Equity in net income is the controlling interest's share of the subsidiary's reported net income, adjusted for its share of revaluation write-offs. Equity in other comprehensive income is the controlling interest's share of the subsidiary's reported other comprehensive income. Equity in net income on the parent's books and noncontrolling interest in net income on the consolidated statement of income and comprehensive income involve parallel calculations, so we calculate both balances in one schedule. We continue with Admiral's 80 percent ownership of Gold Road.

Consolidation at End of the First Year

Suppose Gold Road reports net income of $5,000,000, other comprehensive income of $20,000, and declares and pays cash dividends of $600,000 in 2015, the first year following acquisition. Admiral uses the complete equity method to report its investment in Gold Road on its own books. Impairment testing reveals that the goodwill recognized in this acquisition is impaired by $500,000 during 2015.

Under the complete equity method, Admiral reports its share of Gold Road's 2015 net income and other comprehensive income on its own books. The schedule below simultaneously calculates the parent's equity in net income of the subsidiary reported on the parent's books, and the noncontrolling interest in the net income of the subsidiary reported on the consolidated income statement. The calculations are as follows:

	Total	Equity in net income	Noncontrolling interest in net income
Gold Road's reported net income for 2015	$5,000,000	$4,000,000	$1,000,000
Adjustment for revaluation write-offs:			
Customer lists ($5,000,000/4).	(1,250,000)	(1,000,000)	(250,000)
Goodwill (85:15 ratio)	(500,000)	(425,000)	(75,000)
Totals	$3,250,000	$2,575,000	$ 675,000

There is no specific authoritative guidance on how to allocate revaluation write-offs between the controlling and noncontrolling interests. This text assumes that write-offs of the subsidiary's asset and liability revaluations are shared *in the same proportions* used to assign the original revaluations. Because revaluations of identifiable net assets are attributed according to ownership interests, the write-off of customer lists is distributed in an 80:20 ratio. With 85 percent of the goodwill assigned to the controlling interest in our illustration, we allocate goodwill impairment losses in an 85:15 ratio.

Revaluation adjustments to the subsidiary's reported other comprehensive income are unlikely, so we split it in an 80:20 ratio, with $16,000 reported as equity in other comprehensive income on Admiral's books, and $4,000 reported as noncontrolling interest in other comprehensive income on the consolidated statement of comprehensive income.

In addition to the initial acquisition entry, Admiral makes the following entries on its own books during 2015:

Investment in Gold Road	2,591,000	
Equity in income of Gold Road		2,575,000
Equity in other comprehensive income of Gold Road.		16,000
To record equity in net income and other comprehensive income for 2015.		
Cash.	480,000	
Investment in Gold Road.		480,000
To record dividends declared and received in 2015		
($480,000 = 80% × $600,000).		

Given the $42,600,000 acquisition cost, the investment account has a December 31, 2015 balance of $44,711,000 (= $42,600,000 + $2,591,000 − $480,000).

The consolidation eliminating entries are similar to the **CERO** entries used to consolidate wholly-owned subsidiaries in subsequent years, covered in Chapter 4. However, we now add entry (N) to update the **N**oncontrolling interest for its share of the subsidiary's income and dividends for the current year. The eliminating entries are as follows:

(C) Eliminate the current year's equity method entries, restoring the investment account to its balance at the beginning of the current year.

(E) Eliminate the subsidiary's beginning-of-year stockholders' equity account balances, reducing the investment account and increasing the noncontrolling interest account according to each ownership interest's share of the subsidiary's beginning equity.

(R) Revalue the subsidiary's assets and liabilities as of the beginning of the year. Eliminate the remainder of the investment account, representing the controlling interest's beginning-of-year revaluation balance, and attribute the beginning-of-year net asset revaluations to the noncontrolling interest.

(O) Recognize current year write-offs of the subsidiary's asset and liability revaluations.

(N) Recognize the noncontrolling interest in net income and other comprehensive income. Update the noncontrolling interest in equity for its share of comprehensive income and dividends.

The consolidation working paper in Exhibit 5.2 shows the preclosing accounts of Admiral and Gold Road at December 31, 2015, in trial balance format. Here are the five eliminating entries needed to consolidate the 2015 financial statements of Admiral and Gold Road, in journal entry form:

(C)	Equity in net income of Gold Road	2,575,000	
	Equity in other comprehensive income of Gold Road	16,000	
	Dividends.		480,000
	Investment in Gold Road.		2,111,000
	To eliminate equity in net income and other comprehensive income on the parent's books, the parent's share of the subsidiary's dividends, and restore the investment account to its beginning-of-year value.		
(E)	Capital stock	2,500,000	
	Retained earnings, January 1.	7,400,000	
	Accumulated other comprehensive income, January 1.	100,000	
	Investment in Gold Road (80%)		8,000,000
	Noncontrolling interest in Gold Road (20%)		2,000,000
	To eliminate the subsidiary's beginning-of-year equity accounts against the beginning-of-year book value portion of the investment account and recognize the beginning-of-year book value of the noncontrolling interest.		
(R)	Customer lists	5,000,000	
	Goodwill.	36,000,000	
	Investment in Gold Road.		34,600,000
	Noncontrolling interest in Gold Road		6,400,000
	To revalue Gold Road's net assets to fair value and allocate the revaluations to the controlling and noncontrolling interest.		
	$34,600,000 = (80% × $5,000,000) + $30,600,000.		
	$6,400,000 = (20% × $5,000,000) + $5,400,000.		
(O)	Goodwill impairment loss.	500,000	
	Other operating expenses	1,250,000	
	Goodwill.		500,000
	Customer lists		1,250,000
	To write off the revaluations for the current year.		
(N)	Noncontrolling interest in net income	675,000	
	Noncontrolling interest in other comprehensive income	4,000	
	Dividends.		120,000
	Noncontrolling interest in Gold Road		559,000
	To recognize the noncontrolling interest in the subsidiary's comprehensive income and dividends for the current year.		

Exhibit 5.2 displays these eliminating entries and the consolidated account balances. Account balances unrelated to the discussion above are assumed.

EXHIBIT 5.2   Consolidation Working Paper for Admiral and Gold Road, December 31, 2015

	Accounts Taken From Books Dr (Cr)		Eliminations		Consolidated Balances Dr (Cr)
	Admiral	**Gold Road**	**Dr**	**Cr**	
Current assets	$ 10,880,000	$ 4,400,000			$ 15,280,000
Equity investments.	40,000,000	5,000,000			45,000,000
Plant and equipment, net.	260,000,000	55,000,000			315,000,000
Investment in Gold Road	44,711,000	—		$ 2,111,000 (C)	—
				8,000,000 (E)	
				34,600,000 (R)	
Identifiable intangible assets	600,000,000	—	(R) $ 5,000,000	1,250,000 (O)	603,750,000
Goodwill	—	—	(R) 36,000,000	500,000 (O)	35,500,000
Current liabilities.	(10,000,000)	(10,000,000)			(20,000,000)
Long-term debt	(909,970,000)	(39,980,000)			(949,950,000)
Capital stock	(5,000,000)	(2,500,000)	(E) 2,500,000		(5,000,000)
Retained earnings, January 1.	(19,750,000)	(7,400,000)	(E) 7,400,000		(19,750,000)
Accumulated other comprehensive income,					
January 1	(250,000)	(100,000)	(E) 100,000		(250,000)
Noncontrolling interest.	—	—		2,000,000 (E)	(8,959,000)
				6,400,000 (R)	
				559,000 (N)	
Dividends	2,000,000	600,000		480,000 (C)	2,000,000
				120,000 (N)	
Sales and other revenue.	(600,000,000)	(150,000,000)			(750,000,000)
Equity in net income of Gold Road	(2,575,000)	—	(C) 2,575,000		—
Equity in other comprehensive income of					
Gold Road.	(16,000)	—	(C) 16,000		—
Cost of goods sold.	400,000,000	115,000,000			515,000,000
Goodwill impairment loss.	—	—	(O) 500,000		500,000
Other operating expenses	190,000,000	30,000,000	(O) 1,250,000		221,250,000
Other comprehensive income	(30,000)	(20,000)			(50,000)
Noncontrolling interest in net income	—	—	(N) 675,000		675,000
Noncontrolling interest in other					
comprehensive income.	—	—	(N) 4,000		4,000
Totals	$ 0	$ 0	$56,020,000	$56,020,000	$ 0

Noncontrolling Interests in the Consolidated Statement of Income and Comprehensive Income

Following the requirements of *ASC Section 810-10-55*, the consolidated income statement reports consolidated net income in total and the portions attributable to the controlling and noncontrolling interest. In the statement of comprehensive income, total comprehensive income is similarly divided between controlling and noncontrolling interests. Either on the face of the income statement or in the notes, amounts of income from continuing operations, discontinued operations, and extraordinary items attributable to the controlling and noncontrolling interests are disclosed. However, earnings per share are shown *only for the controlling interest*. Using the consolidated account balances in Exhibit 5.2, the consolidated statement of income and comprehensive income for 2015 and the consolidated balance sheet as of December 31, 2015 follow.

ADMIRAL CASINO & RESORT
Consolidated Statement of Income and Comprehensive Income
For Year Ended December 31, 2015

Sales and other revenue.	$750,000,000
Less: Cost of goods sold	(515,000,000)
Gross profit.	235,000,000
Less: Goodwill impairment loss.	(500,000)
Other operating expenses	(221,250,000)
Consolidated net income.	**13,250,000**
Less: Noncontrolling interest in net income.	(675,000)
Net income attributable to Admiral	$ 12,575,000
Consolidated net income.	$ 13,250,000
Plus: Other comprehensive income	50,000
Consolidated comprehensive income	13,300,000
Less: Noncontrolling interest in comprehensive income (1).	(679,000)
Comprehensive income attributable to Admiral.	$ 12,621,000

(1) $675,000 + $4,000 = $679,000.

ADMIRAL CASINO & RESORT
Consolidated Balance Sheet
December 31, 2015

Assets			**Liabilities and Stockholders' Equity**		
Current assets	$	15,280,000	Current liabilities.	$	20,000,000
Equity investments.		45,000,000	Long-term debt		949,950,000
Plant and equipment, net. . .		315,000,000	Total liabilities.		969,950,000
Identifiable intangibles		603,750,000			
Goodwill		35,500,000	Stockholders' equity		
			Admiral stockholders' equity:		
			Capital stock.		5,000,000
			Retained earnings.		30,325,000
			Accumulated other		
			comprehensive income.		296,000
			Total Admiral stockholders' equity.		35,621,000
			Noncontrolling interest.		8,959,000
			Total stockholders' equity		44,580,000
Total assets		$1,014,530,000	Total liabilities and stockholders' equity		$1,014,530,000

Remember that the consolidated retained earnings and accumulated other comprehensive income balances displayed on the consolidated balance sheet are the amounts attributable to the *controlling interest*. The noncontrolling interest's share of each balance is included in the noncontrolling interest account, a separate equity account on the balance sheet. We calculate consolidated retained earnings and accumulated other comprehensive income at December 31, 2015, as follows, using the consolidated balances from the working paper and consolidated statement of income and comprehensive income:

Retained earnings, January 1.	$19,750,000
Plus: Net income attributable to Admiral	12,575,000
Less: Consolidated dividends	(2,000,000)
Retained earnings, December 31.	$30,325,000
Accumulated other comprehensive income, January 1.	$ 250,000
Plus: Other comprehensive income attributable to Admiral (2)	46,000
Accumulated other comprehensive income, December 31.	$ 296,000

(2) $50,000 − $4,000 = $46,000.

Consolidation at End of the Second Year

Now it is December 31, 2016, and we again consolidate the trial balances of Admiral and Gold Road. The December 31, 2016 preclosing trial balances appear on the consolidation working paper in Exhibit 5.3. Gold Road reports net income of $6,000,000, an other comprehensive loss of $10,000, and declares and pays cash dividends of $500,000 in 2016, the second year following acquisition. Goodwill is impaired by $200,000 during 2016.

Calculation of the parent's equity in net income of subsidiary, reported on the parent's books, and the noncontrolling interest in the net income of the subsidiary, reported on the consolidated income statement, proceeds as follows:

	Total	Equity in net income	Noncontrolling interest in net income
Gold Road's reported net income for 2016	$6,000,000	$4,800,000	$1,200,000
Adjustment for revaluation write-offs:			
Customer lists ($5,000,000/4)	(1,250,000)	(1,000,000)	(250,000)
Goodwill (85:15 ratio)	(200,000)	(170,000)	(30,000)
Totals	$4,550,000	$3,630,000	$ 920,000

Admiral makes the following entries on its own books during 2016:

Investment in Gold Road	3,622,000	
Equity in other comprehensive loss of Gold Road.	8,000	
Equity in net income of Gold Road		3,630,000
To record equity in net income and other comprehensive loss for 2016.		
Cash.	400,000	
Investment in Gold Road.		400,000
To record dividends declared and received in 2016		
($400,000 = 80% × $500,000).		

The investment account therefore has a December 31, 2016, balance of $47,933,000 (= $44,711,000 + $3,622,000 − $400,000).

On December 31, 2016, we prepare consolidated financial statements using these five eliminating entries to consolidate the 2016 financial statements of Admiral and Gold Road:

(C)	Equity in net income of Gold Road	3,630,000	
	Equity in other comprehensive loss of Gold Road		8,000
	Dividends.		400,000
	Investment in Gold Road.		3,222,000
	To eliminate equity in net income and other comprehensive loss on the		
	parent's books, the parent's share of the subsidiary's dividends, and		
	restore the investment account to its beginning-of-year value.		
(E)	Capital stock	2,500,000	
	Retained earnings, January 1.	11,800,000	
	Accumulated other comprehensive income, January 1.	120,000	
	Investment in Gold Road (80%)		11,536,000
	Noncontrolling interest in Gold Road (20%)		2,884,000
	To eliminate the subsidiary's beginning-of-year equity accounts against		
	the beginning-of-year book value portion of the investment account and		
	recognize the beginning-of-year book value of the noncontrolling interest.		
(R)	Customer lists	3,750,000	
	Goodwill	35,500,000	
	Investment in Gold Road.		33,175,000
	Noncontrolling interest in Gold Road		6,075,000
	To revalue Gold Road's net assets to fair value and allocate the		
	revaluations to the controlling and noncontrolling interest.		
	$33,175,000 = (80% × $3,750,000) + (85% × $35,500,000).		
	$6,075,000 = (20% × $3,750,000) + (15% × $35,500,000).		

continued

continued from prior page

(O)	Goodwill impairment loss.		200,000	
	Other operating expenses		1,250,000	
	Goodwill.			200,000
	Customer lists			1,250,000
	To write off the revaluations for the current year.			
(N)	Noncontrolling interest in net income		920,000	
	Noncontrolling interest in other comprehensive loss			2,000
	Dividends.			100,000
	Noncontrolling interest in Gold Road			818,000
	To recognize the noncontrolling interest in the subsidiary's comprehensive income and dividends for the current year.			

Exhibit 5.3 displays these eliminating entries, and each account's consolidated balance.

EXHIBIT 5.3   Consolidation Working Paper for Admiral and Gold Road at December 31, 2016

	Accounts Taken From Books Dr (Cr)		Eliminations		Consolidated Balances
	Admiral	**Gold Road**	**Dr**	**Cr**	**Dr (Cr)**
Current assets	$ 12,280,000	$ 8,900,000			$ 21,180,000
Equity investments	50,000,000	4,000,000			54,000,000
Plant and equipment, net	235,000,000	64,000,000			299,000,000
Investment in Gold Road	47,933,000	—		$ 3,222,000 (C)	—
				11,536,000 (E)	
				33,175,000 (R)	
Identifiable intangible assets	580,000,000	—	(R) $ 3,750,000	1,250,000 (O)	582,500,000
Goodwill	—	—	(R) 35,500,000	200,000 (O)	35,300,000
Current liabilities.	(13,000,000)	(12,000,000)			(25,000,000)
Long-term debt	(869,930,000)	(44,990,000)			(914,920,000)
Capital stock	(5,000,000)	(2,500,000)	(E) 2,500,000		(5,000,000)
Retained earnings, January 1	(30,325,000)	(11,800,000)	(E) 11,800,000		(30,325,000)
Accumulated other comprehensive income, January 1	(296,000)	(120,000)	(E) 120,000		(296,000)
Noncontrolling interest.	—	—		2,884,000 (E)	(9,777,000)
				6,075,000 (R)	
				818,000 (N)	
Dividends	2,000,000	500,000		400,000 (C)	2,000,000
				100,000 (N)	
Sales and other revenue.	(620,000,000)	(160,000,000)			(780,000,000)
Equity in net income of Gold Road	(3,630,000)	—	(C) 3,630,000		—
Equity in other comprehensive loss of Gold Road.	8,000	—		8,000 (C)	—
Cost of goods sold	410,000,000	120,000,000			530,000,000
Goodwill impairment loss.	—	—	(O) 200,000		200,000
Other operating expenses	205,000,000	34,000,000	(O) 1,250,000		240,250,000
Other comprehensive (income)/loss.	(40,000)	10,000			(30,000)
Noncontrolling interest in net income	—	—	(N) 920,000		920,000
Noncontrolling interest in other comprehensive loss	—	—		2,000 (N)	(2,000)
Totals	$ 0	$ 0	$59,670,000	$59,670,000	$ 0

Using the consolidated account balances in Exhibit 5.3, the consolidated statement of income and comprehensive income for 2016 and the consolidated balance sheet at December 31, 2016 appear next.

ADMIRAL CASINO & RESORT
Consolidated Statement of Income and Comprehensive Income
For Year Ended December 31, 2016

Sales and other revenue.	$780,000,000
Less: Cost of goods sold	(530,000,000)
Gross profit.	250,000,000
Less: Goodwill impairment loss.	(200,000)
Other operating expenses	(240,250,000)
Consolidated net income.	**9,550,000**
Less: Noncontrolling interest in net income.	(920,000)
Net income attributable to Admiral	$ 8,630,000
Consolidated net income.	$ 9,550,000
Plus: Other comprehensive income.	30,000
Consolidated comprehensive income	9,580,000
Less: Noncontrolling interest in comprehensive income (1).	(918,000)
Comprehensive income attributable to Admiral.	$ 8,662,000

(1) $920,000 − $2,000 = $918,000.

ADMIRAL CASINO & RESORT
Consolidated Balance Sheet
December 31, 2016

Assets		Liabilities and Stockholders' Equity	
Current assets	$ 21,180,000	Current liabilities.	$ 25,000,000
Equity investments.	54,000,000	Long-term debt	914,920,000
Plant and equipment, net.	299,000,000	Total liabilities.	939,920,000
Identifiable intangibles	582,500,000		
Goodwill	35,300,000	Stockholders' equity	
		Admiral stockholders' equity:	
		Capital stock.	5,000,000
		Retained earnings (2)	36,955,000
		Accumulated other	
		comprehensive income (3)	328,000
		Total Admiral stockholders' equity.	42,283,000
		Noncontrolling interest.	9,777,000
		Total stockholders' equity	52,060,000
Total assets	$991,980,000	Total liabilities and stockholders' equity	$991,980,000

(2) $30,325,000 + $8,630,000 − $2,000,000 = $36,955,000.
(3) $296,000 + $30,000 + $2,000 = $328,000.

Recall from Chapter 4 that consolidated comprehensive income may be reported in either a single statement or in two separate statements. For convenience, we illustrate examples in this text using the single statement format. In either case, net income and comprehensive income attributable to the controlling interest and noncontrolling interest are separately displayed. **Las Vegas Sands Corporation** uses the two-statement approach, displayed as follows in summary form.

LAS VEGAS SANDS CORP. AND SUBSIDIARIES
Consolidated Statements of Operations

	Year Ended December 31		
(in millions, except per share data)	**2013**	**2012**	**2011**
Revenues	$13,770	$11,131	$9,411
Operating expenses	(10,362)	(8,820)	(7,021)
Operating income	3,408	2,311	2,390
Other income (expense)	(264)	(248)	(295)
Income before income taxes	3,144	2,063	2,095
Income tax expense	(189)	(181)	(212)
Net income	2,955	1,882	1,883
Net income attributable to noncontrolling interests	(649)	(358)	(323)
Net income attributable to Las Vegas Sands Corp.	2,306	1,524	1,560
Preferred stock dividends and premiums	—	—	(290)
Net income attributable to common stockholders	$ 2,306	$ 1,524	$1,270
Earnings per share:			
Basic	$ 2.80	$ 1.89	$ 1.74
Diluted	$ 2.79	$ 1.85	$ 1.56

LAS VEGAS SANDS CORP. AND SUBSIDIARIES
Consolidated Statements of Comprehensive Income

	Year Ended December 31		
(in millions)	**2013**	**2012**	**2011**
Net income	$2,955	$1,882	$1,883
Currency translation adjustment	(90)	173	(33)
Total comprehensive income	2,865	2,055	1,850
Comprehensive income attributable to noncontrolling interests	(648)	(362)	(325)
Comprehensive income attributable to Las Vegas Sands Corp.	$2,217	$1,693	$1,525

The first statement displays components of net income. Note that earnings per share is calculated based on net income attributable to the controlling interest, adjusted for preferred stock interests. The second statement starts with total net income and adds in the other comprehensive income to arrive at comprehensive income, which is then split between noncontrolling and controlling interests.

Las Vegas Sands Corporation and subsidiaries report only one type of other comprehensive income, a currency translation adjustment. We cover this adjustment in Chapter 7 of this text. Large companies with diversified operations often report all four major categories of other comprehensive income: currency translation adjustments, unrealized gains and losses on AFS securities (covered in Chapter 1 of this text), gains and losses on hedge investments (covered in Chapters 8 and 9 of this text), and gains and losses related to defined benefit pension plans (covered in intermediate accounting texts). Subsidiaries generally do not report the size and variety of other comprehensive income items that the parent reports, and therefore the noncontrolling interests in other comprehensive income are often small.

Note that only the *controlling interest* in other comprehensive income is closed to accumulated other comprehensive income, reported in the equity section of the consolidated balance sheet. Las Vegas Sands reports $648 million in comprehensive income attributable to the noncontrolling interests. It also reports $649 million in net income attributable to the noncontrolling interests. How much of the $90 million currency translation loss is closed to accumulated other comprehensive income? Using the information provided, the noncontrolling interest's share of the translation loss is $1 million (= $649 million − $648 million). Therefore $89 million (= $90 million − $1 million) of the translation adjustment is closed to accumulated other comprehensive income.

BUSINESS APPLICATION   Noncontrolling Interests: Liability or Equity?

Current U.S. GAAP, effective in 2009, clearly requires noncontrolling interests to be reported in *consolidated equity*. Prior standards did not provide specific guidance on where these interests should be displayed on the balance sheet. In practice, most companies chose to report noncontrolling interests—at that time commonly labeled "minority interests"—in the unclassified "mezzanine section" between liabilities and equity.

However, not all noncontrolling interests are properly reported in equity. Consider the fiscal 2014 summary consolidated balance sheet of **Investors Real Estate Trust and Subsidiaries** (IRET).

(in thousands)

Total assets	$1,869,221
Total liabilities.	1,142,472
Redeemable noncontrolling interests—consolidated real estate entities	6,203
Investors Real Estate Trust shareholders' equity:	
Series A preferred shares	27,317
Series B preferred shares	111,357
Common shares	843,268
Accumulated distributions in excess of net income	(389,758)
Total Investors Real Estate Trust shareholders' equity	592,184
Noncontrolling interests	128,362
Total equity.	720,546
Total liabilities, redeemable noncontrolling interests and equity	$1,869,221

Note 19 to IRET's Form 10-K describes the nature of the company's redeemable noncontrolling interests:

> Redeemable noncontrolling interests on our Consolidated Balance Sheets represent the noncontrolling interest in a joint venture of the Company in which the Company's unaffiliated partner, at its election, could require the Company to buy its interest at a purchase price to be determined by an appraisal conducted in accordance with the terms of the agreement, or at a negotiated price. Redeemable noncontrolling interests are presented at the greater of their carrying amount or redemption value at the end of each reporting period.

ASC Topic 480 requires that redeemable noncontrolling interests be categorized outside of equity, if the company is required to buy them back at the discretion of the investor. This redemption feature creates an obligation, similar to debt. IRET also has a significant noncontrolling interest that is classified in equity, which presumably represents the outside equity interest in the Trust's subsidiaries. *Source:* Investors Real Estate Trust Form 10-K, fiscal 2014.

REVIEW 1 • Consolidation with Noncontrolling Interest at End of Third Year, U.S. GAAP

The trial balances of Admiral and Gold Road at December 31, 2017, *three* years after acquisition, appear in the consolidation working paper below.

	Accounts Taken From Books Dr (Cr)		Eliminations		Consolidated Balances
	Admiral	**Gold Road**	**Dr**	**Cr**	**Dr (Cr)**
Current assets	$ 14,000,000	$ 9,200,000			
Equity investments.	55,000,000	5,000,000			
Plant and equipment, net.	240,000,000	80,000,000			
Investment in Gold Road	54,297,000	—			
Identifiable intangible assets	550,000,000	—			
Goodwill	—	—			
Current liabilities.	(16,000,000)	(11,000,000)			
Long-term debt	(842,485,000)	(54,085,000)			
Capital stock	(5,000,000)	(2,500,000)			
Retained earnings, January 1.	(36,955,000)	(17,300,000)			
Accumulated other comprehensive income, January 1	(328,000)	(110,000)			
Noncontrolling interest.	—	—			
Dividends	2,500,000	800,000			
Sales and other revenue.	(700,000,000)	(200,000,000)			
Equity in net income of Gold Road	(7,000,000)	—			
Equity in other comprehensive income of Gold Road	(4,000)	—			
Cost of goods sold.	480,000,000	140,000,000			
Operating expenses	212,000,000	50,000,000			
Other comprehensive income	(25,000)	(5,000)			
Noncontrolling interest in net income . . .	—	—			
Noncontrolling interest in other comprehensive income.	—	—			
Totals	$ 0	$ 0			$ 0

There is no goodwill impairment during 2017.

Required

Prepare a consolidation working paper to consolidate the trial balances of Admiral and Gold Road, and present the 2017 financial statements in proper format.

Solutions are located after the chapter assignments.

NONCONTROLLING INTERESTS AND BARGAIN PURCHASES

LO3 Consolidate a subsidiary with noncontrolling interests when the acquisition is a bargain purchase.

In unusual cases an acquirer's acquisition cost is less than the fair value of the identifiable net assets acquired. Chapters 3 and 4 cover consolidation involving bargain purchases of wholly-owned subsidiaries. In the case of a partially owned subsidiary, the "bargain gain" or **gain on acquisition** is the difference between total firm value—acquisition cost plus the fair value of the noncontrolling interest—and the fair value of the acquiree's identifiable net assets, as follows:

> Fair value of identifiable net assets
> Less acquisition cost
> Less fair value of noncontrolling interest
>
> Gain on acquisition

ASC para. 805-30-25-2 requires that the bargain gain be *attributed entirely to the controlling interest.* In the year of acquisition, the parent reports the gain and closes it to retained earnings. In future years the gain remains as part of the parent's retained earnings, which are not eliminated in consolidation.

Bargain Purchase Consolidation at Date of Acquisition

Return to our earlier illustration, where Admiral Casino & Resort acquires an 80 percent interest in Gold Road Motor Inn, Inc. on January 1, 2015. Admiral pays $11,000,000 for its investment, and the fair value of the 20 percent noncontrolling interest in Gold Road is $2,500,000. All other information remains the same, including the fair values of all of Gold Road's identifiable net assets, which were carefully checked for accuracy.

The gain on acquisition is calculated below.

Book value	$10,000,000
Revaluation of identifiable net assets:	
Customer lists	5,000,000
Fair value of identifiable net assets	15,000,000
Less acquisition cost	(11,000,000)
Less fair value of noncontrolling interest	(2,500,000)
Gain on acquisition.	$ 1,500,000

Admiral makes the following entry on its own books to record the acquisition:

Investment in Gold Road	12,500,000	
Cash		11,000,000
Gain on acquisition of Gold Road		1,500,000
To record 80 percent acquisition of Gold Road.		

The date-of-acquisition eliminating entries are as follows:

(E)	Capital stock	2,500,000	
	Retained earnings	7,400,000	
	Accumulated other comprehensive income.	100,000	
	Investment in Gold Road (80%)		8,000,000
	Noncontrolling interest in Gold Road (20%)		2,000,000
	To eliminate Gold Road's equity accounts against the book value *portion of the investment account and recognize the book value* *of the noncontrolling interest.*		
(R)	Customer lists	5,000,000	
	Investment in Gold Road.		4,500,000
	Noncontrolling interest in Gold Road		500,000
	To revalue Gold Road's identifiable net assets to fair value, eliminate *the remaining investment balance and bring the noncontrolling interest* *to fair value. $4,500,000 = $12,500,000 − $8,000,000.* *$500,000 = $2,500,000 − $2,000,000.*		

In a bargain purchase, the investment account and noncontrolling interest do not reflect the total revaluation of the identifiable net assets because a bargain price was paid. We therefore set the amount credited to the investment in entry (R) equal to the amount necessary to eliminate its remaining balance. The amount credited to the noncontrolling interest in entry (R) is the amount needed to establish its fair value.

Bargain Purchase Consolidation at End of the First Year

Because the noncontrolling interest does not share in the gain, it also does not fully share in the revaluations of the acquired company's assets and liabilities. The most straightforward way to value the noncontrolling interest on the consolidated balance sheet in years subsequent to acquisition is to keep track of its value at the end of the previous year, and use elimination (R) to set the beginning-of-year value. At the end of the first year, the beginning-of-year value of the noncontrolling interest is of course its original estimated fair value. As before, Gold Road reports net income of $5,000,000, other comprehensive income of $20,000, and declares and pays cash dividends of $600,000 in 2015, the first year following acquisition.

Calculation of equity in net income and noncontrolling interest in net income for 2015 follows:

	Total	Equity in net income	Noncontrolling interest in net income
Gold Road's reported net income for 2015 . . .	$5,000,000	$4,000,000	$1,000,000
Adjustment for revaluation write-offs:			
Customer lists ($5,000,000/4).	(1,250,000)	(1,000,000)	(250,000)
Totals	$3,750,000	$3,000,000	$ 750,000

Because the gain on acquisition is attributed only to the parent, it is unlikely that the original revaluations of identifiable net assets are allocated between the controlling and noncontrolling interests in ownership proportions. However, for simplicity we assume that amortization of the customer lists is allocated according to ownership interests.

Admiral records equity in net income of $3,000,000, and its share of Gold Road's other comprehensive income and dividends for 2015. The investment account therefore has a December 31, 2015 balance of $15,036,000 (= $12,500,000 + $3,000,000 + $16,000 − $480,000).

The consolidation working paper in Exhibit 5.4 shows the preclosing accounts of Admiral and Gold Road at December 31, 2015, in trial balance format, for our bargain gain illustration. Following are the five eliminating entries needed to consolidate the 2015 financial statements of Admiral and Gold Road, in journal entry form:

(C)	Equity in net income of Gold Road	3,000,000	
	Equity in comprehensive income of Gold Road.	16,000	
	Dividends.		480,000
	Investment in Gold Road.		2,536,000
	To eliminate equity in net income and other comprehensive loss on the parent's books, the parent's share of the subsidiary's dividends, and restore the investment account to its beginning-of-year value.		
(E)	Capital stock	2,500,000	
	Retained earnings, January 1.	7,400,000	
	Accumulated other comprehensive income, January 1.	100,000	
	Investment in Gold Road (80%)		8,000,000
	Noncontrolling interest in Gold Road (20%)		2,000,000
	To eliminate the subsidiary's beginning-of-year equity accounts against the beginning-of-year book value portion of the investment account and recognize the beginning-of-year book value of the noncontrolling interest.		
(R)	Customer lists	5,000,000	
	Investment in Gold Road.		4,500,000
	Noncontrolling interest in Gold Road		500,000
	To revalue Gold Road's identifiable net assets to fair value, eliminate the remainder of the investment balance, and bring the noncontrolling interest to its beginning-of-year value of $2,500,000.		

continued

(O)	Operating expenses.	1,250,000	
	Customer lists		1,250,000
	To record the current year's amortization for customer lists.		

(N)	Noncontrolling interest in net income	750,000	
	Noncontrolling interest in other comprehensive income	4,000	
	Dividends.		120,000
	Noncontrolling interest in Gold Road		634,000
	To recognize the noncontrolling interest in the subsidiary's comprehensive income and dividends for the current year.		

Exhibit 5.4 displays these eliminating entries, and each account's consolidated balance.

EXHIBIT 5.4   Consolidation Working Paper for Admiral and Gold Road at December 31, 2015, Bargain Purchase

	Accounts Taken From Books Dr (Cr)		Eliminations		Consolidated Balances Dr (Cr)
	Admiral	**Gold Road**	**Dr**	**Cr**	
Current assets	$ 42,480,000	$ 4,400,000			$ 46,880,000
Equity investments.	40,000,000	5,000,000			45,000,000
Plant and equipment, net.	260,000,000	55,000,000			315,000,000
Investment in Gold Road	15,036,000	—		$ 2,536,000 (C)	—
				8,000,000 (E)	
				4,500,000 (R)	
Identifiable intangible assets	600,000,000	—	(R) $ 5,000,000	1,250,000 (O)	603,750,000
Current liabilities.	(10,000,000)	(10,000,000)			(20,000,000)
Long-term debt	(909,970,000)	(39,980,000)			(949,950,000)
Capital stock	(5,000,000)	(2,500,000)	(E) 2,500,000		(5,000,000)
Retained earnings, January 1.	(19,750,000)	(7,400,000)	(E) 7,400,000		(19,750,000)
Accumulated other comprehensive income, January 1	(250,000)	(100,000)	(E) 100,000		(250,000)
Noncontrolling interest.	—	—		2,000,000 (E)	(3,134,000)
				500,000 (R)	
				634,000 (N)	
Dividends	2,000,000	600,000		480,000 (C)	2,000,000
				120,000 (N)	
Sales and other revenue.	(600,000,000)	(150,000,000)			(750,000,000)
Equity in net income of Gold Road	(3,000,000)	—	(C) 3,000,000		—
Equity in other comprehensive income of Gold Road.	(16,000)	—	(C) 16,000		—
Cost of goods sold.	400,000,000	115,000,000			515,000,000
Operating expenses	190,000,000	30,000,000	(O) 1,250,000		221,250,000
Gain on acquisition.	(1,500,000)	—			(1,500,000)
Other comprehensive income	(30,000)	(20,000)			(50,000)
Noncontrolling interest in net income	—	—	(N) 750,000		750,000
Noncontrolling interest in other comprehensive income.	—	—	(N) 4,000		4,000
Totals	$ 0	$ 0	$20,020,000	$20,020,000	$ 0

Bargain Purchase Consolidation at End of the Second Year

December 31, 2016, preclosing trial balances of Admiral and Gold Road appear in the consolidation working paper in Exhibit 5.5. Gold Road reports net income of $6,000,000, an other comprehensive loss of $10,000, and declares and pays cash dividends of $500,000 in 2016.

Calculation of the parent's equity in net income of subsidiary, reported on the parent's books, and the noncontrolling interest in the net income of the subsidiary, reported on the consolidated income statement, is as follows:

	Total	Equity in net income	Noncontrolling interest in net income
Gold Road's reported net income for 2016	$6,000,000	$4,800,000	$1,200,000
Adjustment for revaluation write-offs:			
Customer lists ($5,000,000/4)	(1,250,000)	(1,000,000)	(250,000)
Totals	$4,750,000	$3,800,000	$ 950,000

After Admiral records equity in net income and other comprehensive loss of Gold Road and its share of Gold Road's dividends for 2016, the investment balance at December 31, 2016, is $18,428,000 (= $15,036,000 + $3,800,000 − $8,000 − $400,000). The five eliminating entries needed to consolidate the 2016 financial statements of Admiral and Gold Road, in journal entry form, follow:

(C)	Equity in net income of Gold Road	3,800,000	
	Equity in other comprehensive loss of Gold Road		8,000
	Dividends.		400,000
	Investment in Gold Road		3,392,000

To eliminate equity in net income and other comprehensive loss on the parent's books, the parent's share of the subsidiary's dividends, and restore the investment account to its beginning-of-year value.

(E)	Capital stock	2,500,000	
	Retained earnings, January 1.	11,800,000	
	Accumulated other comprehensive income, January 1	120,000	
	Investment in Gold Road (80%)		11,536,000
	Noncontrolling interest in Gold Road (20%)		2,884,000

To eliminate the subsidiary's beginning-of-year equity accounts against the beginning-of-year book value portion of the investment account and recognize the beginning-of-year book value of the noncontrolling interest.

(R)	Customer lists	3,750,000	
	Investment in Gold Road.		3,500,000
	Noncontrolling interest in Gold Road		250,000

To revalue Gold Road's net assets to fair value, eliminate the remaining investment balance, and bring the noncontrolling interest balance to its beginning-of-year value of $3,134,000.

(O)	Operating expenses	1,250,000	
	Customer lists		1,250,000

To record the current year's amortization for customer lists.

(N)	Noncontrolling interest in net income	950,000	
	Noncontrolling interest in other comprehensive loss		2,000
	Dividends.		100,000
	Noncontrolling interest in Gold Road		848,000

To recognize the noncontrolling interest in the subsidiary's comprehensive income and dividends for the current year.

EXHIBIT 5.5 Consolidation Working Paper for Admiral and Gold Road at December 31, 2016, Bargain Purchase

	Accounts Taken From Books Dr (Cr)		Eliminations		Consolidated Balances Dr (Cr)
	Admiral	Gold Road	Dr	Cr	
Current assets	$ 43,880,000	$ 8,900,000			$ 52,780,000
Equity investments.	50,000,000	4,000,000			54,000,000
Plant and equipment, net.	235,000,000	64,000,000			299,000,000
Investment in Gold Road	18,428,000	—		$ 3,392,000 (C)	—
				11,536,000 (E)	
				3,500,000 (R)	
Identifiable intangible assets	580,000,000	—	(R) $ 3,750,000	1,250,000 (O)	582,500,000
Current liabilities.	(13,000,000)	(12,000,000)			(25,000,000)
Long-term debt	(869,930,000)	(44,990,000)			(914,920,000)
Capital stock	(5,000,000)	(2,500,000)	(E) 2,500,000		(5,000,000)
Retained earnings, January 1.	(32,250,000)	(11,800,000)	(E) 11,800,000		(32,250,000)
Accumulated other comprehensive					
income, January 1	(296,000)	(120,000)	(E) 120,000		(296,000)
Noncontrolling interest.	—	—		2,884,000 (E)	(3,982,000)
				250,000 (R)	
				848,000 (N)	
Dividends	2,000,000	500,000		400,000 (C)	2,000,000
				100,000 (N)	
Sales and other revenue.	(620,000,000)	(160,000,000)			(780,000,000)
Equity in net income of Gold Road	(3,800,000)	—	(C) 3,800,000		—
Equity in other comprehensive loss					
of Gold Road	8,000	—		8,000 (C)	—
Cost of goods sold.	410,000,000	120,000,000			530,000,000
Operating expenses.	205,000,000	34,000,000	(O) 1,250,000		240,250,000
Other comprehensive (income)/loss.	(40,000)	10,000			(30,000)
Noncontrolling interest in net income	—	—	(N) 950,000		950,000
Noncontrolling interest in other					
comprehensive loss	—	—		2,000 (N)	(2,000)
Totals	$ 0	$ 0	$24,170,000	$24,170,000	$ 0

INTERNATIONAL FINANCIAL REPORTING STANDARDS FOR NONCONTROLLING INTERESTS

LO4 Explain IFRS for noncontrolling interests.

IFRS 3(R) presents IFRS for valuing and reporting noncontrolling interests in consolidated financial statements. Although IFRS agrees with U.S. GAAP that the noncontrolling interest should be reported at acquisition-date fair value, *IFRS 3(R)* actually allows the acquirer to choose between **two different valuation methods**:

1. Value the noncontrolling interest at **full fair value** at the acquisition date, as in U.S. GAAP.
2. Value the noncontrolling interest at its share of the **fair value of the subsidiary's identifiable net assets** at the acquisition date.

Using valuation method #2, the noncontrolling interest is not allocated any goodwill: only the controlling interest's share of goodwill is recognized. Therefore the IFRS alternative reports goodwill and noncontrolling interests at *lower amounts* on the consolidated balance sheet than under U.S. GAAP. When goodwill is impaired, IFRS noncontrolling interest in net income is *higher* than U.S. GAAP, since no goodwill impairment loss is charged against the noncontrolling interest.

Return to Admiral's acquisition of 80 percent of Gold Road's stock for $42,600,000. The alternative valuation method allowed by IFRS (#2) leads to this initial value of the noncontrolling interest:

Gold Road book value	$10,000,000
Revaluation of identifiable net assets:	
Customer lists	5,000,000
Fair value of identifiable net assets	15,000,000
Noncontrolling interest %.	× 20%
Noncontrolling interest	$ 3,000,000

Goodwill is attributed only to the parent, giving us the same goodwill amount attributed to the parent under U.S. GAAP:

Acquisition cost	$42,600,000
80% book value	(8,000,000)
80% revaluation: customer lists.	(4,000,000)
Goodwill	$30,600,000

To further illustrate the IFRS alternative valuation of noncontrolling interests, we consolidate the financial statements of Admiral and Gold Road at December 31, 2015, one year after acquisition. Assuming $425,000 goodwill impairment on the $30,600,000 in goodwill, as in the previous illustration, we calculate equity in net income and noncontrolling interest in net income as follows:

	Total	Equity in net income	Noncontrolling interest in net income
Gold Road's reported net income for 2015	$5,000,000	$4,000,000	$1,000,000
Adjustment for revaluation write-offs:			
Customer lists ($5,000,000/4).	(1,250,000)	(1,000,000)	(250,000)
Goodwill	(425,000)	(425,000)	—
Totals	$3,325,000	$2,575,000	$ 750,000

Here are the five eliminating entries needed to consolidate the 2015 financial statements of Admiral and Gold Road, in journal entry form:

(C)	Equity in net income of Gold Road	2,575,000	
	Equity in other comprehensive income of Gold Road	16,000	
	Dividends.		480,000
	Investment in Gold Road.		2,111,000
	To eliminate equity in net income and other comprehensive income on the parent's books, the parent's share of the subsidiary's dividends, and restore the investment account to its beginning-of-year value.		
(E)	Capital stock	2,500,000	
	Retained earnings, January 1	7,400,000	
	Accumulated other comprehensive income, January 1	100,000	
	Investment in Gold Road (80%)		8,000,000
	Noncontrolling interest in Gold Road (20%)		2,000,000
	To eliminate the subsidiary's beginning-of-year equity accounts against the beginning-of-year book value portion of the investment account and recognize the beginning-of-year book value of the noncontrolling interest.		
(R)	Customer lists	5,000,000	
	Goodwill	30,600,000	
	Investment in Gold Road.		34,600,000
	Noncontrolling interest in Gold Road		1,000,000
	To revalue Gold Road's net assets to fair value and allocate the revaluations to the controlling and noncontrolling interest. $34,600,000 = (80% × $5,000,000) + $30,600,000. $1,000,000 = (20% × $5,000,000).*		

continued

(O)	Goodwill impairment loss.	425,000	
	Other operating expenses	1,250,000	
	Goodwill.		425,000
	Customer lists		1,250,000
	To write off the revaluations for the current year.		
(N)	Noncontrolling interest in net income	750,000	
	Noncontrolling interest in other comprehensive income	4,000	
	Dividends.		120,000
	Noncontrolling interest in Gold Road		634,000
	To recognize the noncontrolling interest in the subsidiary's comprehensive income and dividends for the current year.		

Exhibit 5.6 displays these eliminating entries, and each account's consolidated balance.

EXHIBIT 5.6   Consolidation Working Paper for Admiral and Gold Road at December 31, 2015, IFRS Alternative

	Accounts Taken From Books Dr (Cr)		Eliminations		Consolidated Balances
	Admiral	**Gold Road**	**Dr**	**Cr**	**Dr (Cr)**
Current assets	$ 10,880,000	$ 4,400,000			$ 15,280,000
Equity investments.	40,000,000	5,000,000			45,000,000
Plant and equipment, net.	260,000,000	55,000,000			315,000,000
Investment in Gold Road	44,711,000	—		$ 2,111,000 (C)	—
				8,000,000 (E)	
				34,600,000 (R)	
Identifiable intangible assets	600,000,000	—	(R) $ 5,000,000	1,250,000 (O)	603,750,000
Goodwill	—	—	(R) 30,600,000	425,000 (O)	30,175,000
Current liabilities.	(10,000,000)	(10,000,000)			(20,000,000)
Long-term debt	(909,970,000)	(39,980,000)			(949,950,000)
Capital stock	(5,000,000)	(2,500,000)	(E) 2,500,000		(5,000,000)
Retained earnings, January 1.	(19,750,000)	(7,400,000)	(E) 7,400,000		(19,750,000)
Accumulated other comprehensive income, January 1	(250,000)	(100,000)	(E) 100,000		(250,000)
Noncontrolling interest.	—	—		2,000,000 (E)	(3,634,000)
				1,000,000 (R)	
				634,000 (N)	
Dividends	2,000,000	600,000		480,000 (C)	2,000,000
				120,000 (N)	
Sales and other revenue.	(600,000,000)	(150,000,000)			(750,000,000)
Equity in net income of Gold Road	(2,575,000)	—	(C) 2,575,000		—
Equity in other comprehensive income of Gold Road.	(16,000)	—	(C) 16,000		—
Cost of goods sold.	400,000,000	115,000,000			515,000,000
Goodwill impairment loss.	—	—	(O) 425,000		425,000
Other operating expenses	190,000,000	30,000,000	(O) 1,250,000		221,250,000
Other comprehensive income	(30,000)	(20,000)			(50,000)
Noncontrolling interest in net income	—	—	(N) 750,000		750,000
Noncontrolling interest in other comprehensive income.	—	—	(N) 4,000		4,000
Totals	$ 0	$ 0	$50,620,000	$50,620,000	$ 0

Compare the IFRS consolidated balances with the U.S. GAAP balances on the 2015 consolidated financial statements.

	IFRS	**U.S. GAAP**
Goodwill	$30,175,000	$35,500,000
Noncontrolling interest (balance sheet)	3,634,000	8,959,000
Noncontrolling interest in net income (income statement).	750,000	675,000

Goodwill is *lower* under IFRS because only the controlling interest's share is recognized. Noncontrolling interest in the equity section of the consolidated balance sheet is *lower* for the same reason. The difference in reported goodwill, $5,325,000 (= $35,500,000 − $30,175,000), is the noncontrolling interest's share of the ending goodwill balance under U.S. GAAP ($5,325,000 = 15% × $35,500,000). Noncontrolling interest in net income is *higher* under IFRS if there is any goodwill impairment during the year; the difference, $75,000 (= $750,000 − $675,000) is the noncontrolling interest's share of 2015 goodwill impairment under U.S. GAAP ($75,000 = 15% × $500,000). If there is no goodwill impairment, noncontrolling interest in net income based on the IFRS alternative equals U.S. GAAP.

Valuation of the noncontrolling interest using the IFRS alternative is more conservative. Rather than inferring the noncontrolling interest's share of goodwill from its acquisition-date fair value, the IFRS alternative reports only the parent's share of goodwill as revealed by its acquisition cost.

BUSINESS APPLICATION **IFRS and Nokia Corporation**

Nokia Corporation uses IFRS to present its financial statements. In 2007, Nokia and **Siemens AG** formed **Nokia Siemens Networks (NSN)** to combine the mobile and fixed-line telecommunications network equipment businesses of the two companies. Each corporation owned 50 percent of the new company, but Nokia consolidated NSN, because Nokia could appoint key officers and a majority of the Board of Directors. The €5,551 million reported cost of the acquisition was attributed to identifiable net assets of €3,995 million, and €1,556 million total goodwill. However, Nokia subtracted €753 "non-controlling interest in goodwill" to arrive at the €803 million goodwill reported on the consolidated balance sheet. Two major differences between IFRS and U.S. GAAP are illustrated.

- First, Nokia consolidated Nokia Siemens Networks. Under U.S. GAAP, the investment would probably not be consolidated since even though Nokia had effective control, it did not own the majority of the shares. The investment would instead have been reported as an equity investment.

- Second, Nokia reported only the controlling interest in goodwill. If Nokia followed current U.S. GAAP, total goodwill would have been reported and attributed to the controlling and noncontrolling interests. *Source:* Nokia Corporation, Form 20-F, December 31, 2007.

REVIEW 2 • Consolidation with Noncontrolling Interest at End of the Third Year, IFRS

Refer to the information in review problem #1, and now assume Admiral follows IFRS and uses the alternative method for valuing noncontrolling interests and goodwill. The consolidation working paper for 2017 is again presented below.

| | Accounts Taken From Books Dr (Cr) | | Eliminations | | Consolidated Balances |
	Admiral	Gold Road	Dr	Cr	Dr (Cr)
Current assets	$ 14,000,000	$ 9,200,000			
Equity investments	55,000,000	5,000,000			
Plant and equipment, net	240,000,000	80,000,000			
Investment in Gold Road	54,297,000	—			
Identifiable intangible assets	550,000,000	—			
Goodwill	—	—			
Current liabilities	(16,000,000)	(11,000,000)			
Long-term debt	(842,485,000)	(54,085,000)			
Capital stock	(5,000,000)	(2,500,000)			
Retained earnings, January 1	(36,955,000)	(17,300,000)			
Accumulated other comprehensive income, January 1	(328,000)	(110,000)			
Noncontrolling interest	—	—			
Dividends	2,500,000	800,000			
Sales and other revenue	(700,000,000)	(200,000,000)			
Equity in net income of Gold Road	(7,000,000)	—			
Equity in other comprehensive income of Gold Road	(4,000)	—			
Cost of goods sold	480,000,000	140,000,000			
Operating expenses	212,000,000	50,000,000			
Other comprehensive income	(25,000)	(5,000)			
Noncontrolling interest in net income . . .	—	—			
Noncontrolling interest in other comprehensive income	—	—			
Totals	$ 0	$ 0			$ 0

Assume that accumulated goodwill impairment to the beginning of 2017 is $595,000. There is no goodwill impairment during 2017.

Required

Prepare a consolidation working paper to consolidate the trial balances of Admiral and Gold Road, and present the 2017 financial statements in proper format.

Solutions are located after the chapter assignments.

CONSOLIDATED STATEMENT OF CASH FLOWS

Although not directly related to the topic of noncontrolling interests, we now discuss preparation of the **consolidated statement of cash flows**, one of a firm's required financial statements. This topic appears here because at this point in the text you have learned about the major issues affecting preparation of the consolidated statement of cash flows, such as revaluations and noncontrolling interests.

ASC Topic 230, Statement of Cash Flows, specifies the content and format of the statement, organized in sections showing the cash effect of *operating activities*, *investing activities*, and *financing activities*, and disclosure of material noncash transactions affecting investing or financing activities or both. Companies may use either the direct or indirect method to report cash flows from operating activities. The **direct method** converts each line on the income statement from accrual to cash basis: cash received from customers, cash paid for purchases, and so forth. When the direct method is used,

LO5 Prepare the consolidated statement of cash flows.

a reconciliation of net income to cash flow from operations is also required. The **indirect method** focuses on that reconciliation. It begins with net income, adds or subtracts those income statement items that did not affect operating cash, and adjusts for operating cash flows not reflected in net income by considering operating changes in current asset and current liability accounts. Because the indirect method is almost always found in practice, we use it to illustrate preparation of the statement of cash flows.

We do not duplicate the more complete discussions of the statement of cash flows found in intermediate accounting textbooks. Rather, we highlight particular items related to the consolidation process that affect the consolidated statement of cash flows.

Preparation of Consolidated Statement of Cash Flows

The consolidated statement of cash flows is most efficiently prepared from comparative consolidated balance sheets, consolidated statements of income and comprehensive income, and supplementary information. Attempts to prepare a consolidated statement of cash flows from the unconsolidated accounts of the parent and subsidiary are more difficult and require duplicative eliminating entries. The following items are frequently encountered in a consolidated statement of cash flows.

- When presenting cash provided by operations using the indirect method, start with **consolidated net income**, rather than consolidated income attributed to the parent, and adjust this balance for noncash and nonoperating items. If you start with consolidated income attributable to the parent, you must add (subtract) the noncontrolling interest in net income (loss), because it is a noncash deduction. Using consolidated net income avoids this adjustment. Similarly, other comprehensive income does not impact cash, as it consists primarily of unrealized gains and losses. Starting with consolidated net income, rather than comprehensive income, avoids adjustments for these noncash items.

- In determining cash provided by operations, we add back **goodwill impairment charges** arising in consolidation to consolidated net income. This deduction from net income does not use cash—it decreases a noncurrent asset, goodwill. Similarly, we add back amortization of previously unrecorded identifiable intangibles arising in consolidation to consolidated net income.

- **Dividends paid to noncontrolling shareholders**, as well as dividends paid to the parent's shareholders, are shown as cash used for financing activities.

- **Undistributed equity method income (loss)** from equity method investments is subtracted from (added to) net income in computing cash provided by operations. The accrual of equity method income increases long-term equity investments—noncurrent assets—and does not itself provide cash. Dividends received from such investments, however, represent a realization of the equity method income and do increase cash. Because these dividends are included in cash provided by operations, we subtract from net income the *undistributed* equity method income (not received in dividends) in arriving at cash provided by operations.

Consolidated Statement of Cash Flows: An Illustration

The following illustration is based on the data previously developed for Admiral Casino & Resort and its 80-percent-owned subsidiary, Gold Road Motor Inn, Inc., in Exhibits 5.2 and 5.3. Exhibit 5.7 shows comparative consolidated balance sheets for Admiral and Gold Road at December 31, 2016, and 2015, and a consolidated statement of income and comprehensive income for 2016. Exhibit 5.7 also provides supplementary information necessary to prepare the consolidated statement of cash flows for 2016, which appears in Exhibit 5.8.

EXHIBIT 5.7 Admiral and Gold Road Consolidated Financial Statements

ADMIRAL CASINO & RESORT
Comparative Consolidated Balance Sheets
December 31

	2016	2015
Assets		
Cash.	$ 3,400,000	$ 3,150,000
Receivables	8,800,000	9,300,000
Inventory.	8,980,000	2,830,000
Total current assets	21,180,000	15,280,000
Equity investments.	54,000,000	45,000,000
Plant and equipment, net.	299,000,000	315,000,000
Identifiable intangibles	582,500,000	603,750,000
Goodwill	35,300,000	35,500,000
Total noncurrent assets	970,800,000	999,250,000
Total assets	$991,980,000	$1,014,530,000
Liabilities and Stockholders' Equity		
Liabilities		
Current liabilities.	$ 25,000,000	$ 20,000,000
Long-term debt	914,920,000	949,950,000
Total liabilities.	939,920,000	969,950,000
Stockholders' equity		
Admiral stockholders' equity:		
Capital stock.	5,000,000	5,000,000
Retained earnings.	36,955,000	30,325,000
Accumulated other comprehensive income.	328,000	296,000
Total Admiral stockholders' equity.	42,283,000	35,621,000
Noncontrolling interest.	9,777,000	8,959,000
Total stockholders' equity	52,060,000	44,580,000
Total liabilities and stockholders' equity	$991,980,000	$1,014,530,000

ADMIRAL CASINO & RESORT
Consolidated Statement of Income and Comprehensive Income
For Year Ended December 31, 2016

Sales and other revenue.	$780,000,000
Less: Cost of goods sold	(530,000,000)
Gross profit.	250,000,000
Less: Goodwill impairment loss	(200,000)
Other operating expenses.	(240,250,000)
Consolidated net income.	**9,550,000**
Less: Noncontrolling interest in net income.	(920,000)
Net income attributable to Admiral	$ 8,630,000
Consolidated net income.	$ 9,550,000
Plus: Other comprehensive income.	30,000
Consolidated comprehensive income	9,580,000
Less: Noncontrolling interest in comprehensive income	(918,000)
Comprehensive income attributable to Admiral.	$ 8,662,000

Supplementary information

1. Other operating expenses include $30,000,000 depreciation expense on plant and equipment and $21,250,000 amortization expense on intangibles. Consolidated accumulated depreciation on plant and equipment for 2016 and 2015 is $175,000,000 and $160,000,000, respectively.
2. Sales and other income includes $3,000,000 gain on cash sales of plant and equipment.
3. Cash acquisitions of plant and equipment for 2016 were $40,000,000.
4. Sales and other revenue includes $10,000,000 income from equity method investments; $1,000,000 in cash dividends was received from those investments.
5. Cash dividends paid by Admiral during 2016 totaled $2,000,000. Cash dividends paid by Gold Road during 2016 totaled $500,000.

EXHIBIT 5.8   Admiral and Gold Road Consolidated Statement of Cash Flows

ADMIRAL CASINO & RESORT
Consolidated Statement of Cash Flows
For Year Ended December 31, 2016

Cash from operating activities		
Consolidated net income		$ 9,550,000
Add (subtract) items not affecting cash:		
Depreciation expense	$ 30,000,000	
Amortization expense	21,250,000	
Goodwill impairment loss	200,000	
Undistributed equity method income	(9,000,000)	42,450,000
Changes in current assets and liabilities:		
Decrease in receivables	500,000	
Increase in inventory	(6,150,000)	
Increase in current liabilities	5,000,000	(650,000)
Nonoperating item:		
Gain on sale of plant and equipment		(3,000,000)
Net cash flows from operating activities		48,350,000
Cash from investing activities		
Acquisition of plant and equipment	(40,000,000)	
Sale of plant and equipment (1)	29,000,000	(11,000,000)
Cash from financing activities		
Net decrease in long-term debt	(35,000,000)	
Dividends paid to controlling shareholders	(2,000,000)	
Dividends paid to noncontrolling shareholders	(100,000)	(37,100,000)
Net increase in cash		250,000
Cash balance, January 1		3,150,000
Cash balance, December 31		$ 3,400,000

(1) Cost of plant and equipment sold = $41,000,000 = ($315,000,000 + $160,000,000) + $40,000,000 − ($299,000,000 + $175,000,000). Accumulated depreciation on plant and equipment sold = $15,000,000 = $160,000,000 + $30,000,000 − $175,000,000. Thus, book value of plant and equipment sold = $41,000,000 − $15,000,000 = $26,000,000. Book value + gain on sale = cash received; $26,000,000 + $3,000,000 = $29,000,000.

REVIEW OF KEY CONCEPTS ●

LO 1 **Consolidate a subsidiary with noncontrolling interests at the date of acquisition. (p. 178)** Whenever an acquirer purchases less than 100 percent of an acquiree's stock, but controls the acquiree, the acquirer consolidates the accounts of the acquiree in its financial statements. That portion of the acquiree's equity not owned by the acquirer is the **noncontrolling interest**. *ASC Topic 805* outlines procedures for valuing noncontrolling interests, while *ASC Topic 810* provides the requirements for presenting these interests in the consolidated financial statements. Consolidated assets and liabilities include the subsidiary's balances, in full. The noncontrolling interest in the acquiree's accounts appears on a **noncontrolling interest line in the equity section of the consolidated balance sheet**—the portion of consolidated net assets attributable to noncontrolling interests. **Acquired goodwill** is the controlling interest's acquisition cost plus the fair value of the noncontrolling interest less the fair value of identifiable net assets acquired, and goodwill is attributed to the controlling and noncontrolling interests. The **fair value of the noncontrolling interest** may be the acquisition-date market price per share, if there is an active market for the stock. Alternative valuation methods such as discounted cash flow models and earnings multiples may be used. Generally the per-share acquisition price exceeds the per-share value of the noncontrolling interest due to a **control premium**. **Variable interest entities** (VIEs) commonly have noncontrolling interests. *ASC Topic 810* requires the VIE's primary beneficiary to consolidate the VIE's assets and liabilities at book value if the primary beneficiary and the VIE are under common control, and to report the noncontrolling interest at book value. More typically, if the two entities are not under common control, the VIE's assets, liabilities, and noncontrolling interest are initially reported at fair value.

Consolidate a subsidiary with noncontrolling interests in subsequent years. (p. 182) Consolidated rev- **LO 2** enues, expenses and other income-related accounts include the subsidiary's balances, in full. **A noncontrolling interest in net income line on the consolidated income statement**—the portion of consolidated net income attributed to noncontrolling interests—appears as a distribution of consolidated net income. It is calculated as the noncontrolling interest's share of the subsidiary's reported net income, adjusted for the noncontrolling interest's share of write-offs of revalued assets and liabilities. If the subsidiary reports other comprehensive income, a noncontrolling interest in comprehensive income line appears in the consolidated statement of comprehensive income. Consolidation eliminating entries are represented by the acronym **CERON**, as follows: **(C)** elimination of the parent's **C**urrent year equity method income and the subsidiary's intercompany dividends; **(E)** elimination of the subsidiary's beginning-of-year stockholders' **E**quity accounts, reducing the investment account and increasing the noncontrolling interest in equity account in proportion to ownership interests; **(R)** recognition of the beginning-of-year **R**evaluation balances for the subsidiary's assets and liabilities, with revaluations attributed to the controlling interest eliminating the remainder of the investment balance and revaluations attributed to the noncontrolling interest increasing the noncontrolling interest account; **(O)** writing **O**ff the revaluations for the current year; and **(N)** updating the **N**oncontrolling interest for its share of current year comprehensive income and dividends.

Consolidate a subsidiary with noncontrolling interests when the acquisition is a bargain purchase. **LO 3** **(p. 192) Gains on bargain purchases are attributed entirely to the controlling interest.** Because the subsidiary's net asset revaluations are not shared according to ownership interests, eliminating entry (R) removes the remaining investment balance and adjusts the noncontrolling interest to its value as of the end of the previous year.

Explain IFRS for noncontrolling interests. (p. 197) IFRS may differ from U.S. GAAP in the valuation of the **LO 4** noncontrolling interest and goodwill. Although IFRS allows valuation according to U.S. GAAP, companies may choose an alternative method that initially values the noncontrolling interest at its share of the fair value of the subsidiary's identifiable net assets, and reports only the controlling interest's share of goodwill.

Prepare the consolidated statement of cash flows. (p. 201) The **consolidated statement of cash flows** is most **LO 5** efficiently prepared from comparative consolidated balance sheets and the current consolidated income statement, plus supplementary information. The operating activities section starts with consolidated net income. Noncash items such as amortization expense on previously unrecorded intangibles and undistributed equity method income adjust consolidated income to arrive at cash from operating activities. The financing section reports cash dividends paid by the subsidiary to the noncontrolling interest as well as cash dividends paid by the parent.

Assignments with the ✓ in the margin are available in BusinessCourse. **See the Preface of the book for details.**

MULTIPLE CHOICE QUESTIONS ·····································

Use the following information to answer questions 1 – 7 below:

On January 1, 2015, Pomegranate Company acquired 90% of the voting stock of Starfruit Company for $91,700,000 in cash. The fair value of the noncontrolling interest in Starfruit at the date of acquisition was $6,300,000. Starfruit's book value was $13,000,000 at the date of acquisition. Starfruit's assets and liabilities were reported on its books at values approximating fair value, except its plant and equipment (10-year life, straight-line) was overvalued by $25,000,000. Starfruit Company had previously unreported intangible assets, with a market value of $40,000,000 and 5-year life, straight-line, which were capitalized following GAAP.

1. At the date of acquisition, consolidation eliminating entry (R) credits the noncontrolling interest in Starfruit **LO 1 ✓** Company in the amount of

   a. $1,500,000
   b. $5,000,000
   c. $6,300,000
   d. $8,500,000

Use the following additional information to answer questions 2 and 3 below:

Pomegranate uses the complete equity method to account for its investment in Starfruit on its own books. Goodwill recognized in this acquisition was impaired by a total of $2,000,000 in 2015 and 2016, and by $500,000 in 2017. It is now December 31, 2017, the accounting year-end. Here is Starfruit Company's trial balance at December 31, 2017:

	Dr (Cr)
Current assets	$ 28,200,000
Plant & equipment, net.	188,000,000
Intangibles	2,000,000
Liabilities.	(180,000,000)
Capital stock	(1,000,000)
Retained earnings, January 1.	(29,500,000)
Accumulated other comprehensive income, January 1.	(500,000)
Dividends	400,000
Sales revenue.	(24,000,000)
Cost of goods sold.	10,000,000
Operating expenses	6,500,000
Other comprehensive income	(100,000)
	$ 0

LO 2   **2.** On the 2017 consolidation working paper, eliminating entry (R) reduces the Investment in Starfruit by

    a. $ 3,600,000
    b. $64,800,000
    c. $68,200,000
    d. $81,000,000

LO 2   **3.** On the 2017 consolidated income statement, the noncontrolling interest in net income of Starfruit is

    a. $150,000
    b. $175,000
    c. $200,000
    d. $750,000

LO 4   **4.** If Pomegranate follows IFRS and uses the alternative method of valuing the noncontrolling interest, at the date of acquisition the noncontrolling interest in Starfruit appears in the equity section of the consolidated balance sheet in the amount of

    a. $7,800,000
    b. $6,300,000
    c. $2,800,000
    d. $1,300,000

LO 4   **5.** If Pomegranate follows IFRS and uses the alternative method of valuing the noncontrolling interest, the 2017 noncontrolling interest in comprehensive income of Starfruit is

    a. $185,000
    b. $300,000
    c. $210,000
    d. $200,000

Use the following information to answer questions 6 and 7 below:

Now assume Pomegranate paid only $20,000,000 to acquire 90% of Starfruit. The fair value of the noncontrolling interest at the date of acquisition was $2,000,000.

LO 3   **6.** At the date of acquisition, consolidation eliminating entry (R) credits the noncontrolling interest in Starfruit in the amount of

    a. $6,700,000
    b. $4,900,000
    c. $2,000,000
    d. $ 700,000

LO 3   **7.** On the 2017 consolidation working paper, eliminating entry (R) debits goodwill in the amount of

    a. $ 0
    b. $11,300,000
    c. $53,700,000
    d. $68,000,000

8. Which is the *best* way to measure the fair value per share of a subsidiary's noncontrolling interest?   **LO 1** ✓

   a.   The per share market value of the subsidiary's stock, in an active market, less a discount for lack of control
   b.   The price per share that the parent paid for the subsidiary's stock
   c.   The price per share that the parent paid for the subsidiary's stock, plus a premium for lack of control
   d.   The per share market value of the subsidiary's stock, in an active market

9. If the operating section of the consolidated statement of cash flows is displayed using the indirect method,   **LO 5** ✓
   which of the following is *not* an adjustment to consolidated net income?

   a.   Goodwill impairment loss
   b.   Noncontrolling interest in net income
   c.   Undistributed equity method income
   d.   Amortization expense on previously unreported identifiable intangibles

10. On the consolidated statement of cash flows, cash dividends paid to noncontrolling shareholders are   **LO 5** ✓

    a.   a cash outflow in the financing section.
    b.   an adjustment to income when the indirect method is used for the operating section.
    c.   a cash outflow in the investing section.
    d.   not reported.

EXERCISES ••

E5.1   **Date of Acquisition Consolidation Eliminating Entries**   Pennant Corporation acquired 80 per-   **LO 1** ✓
cent of Saylor Company's common stock for $12,000,000 in cash. At the date of acquisition, Saylor's
$3,000,000 of reported net assets were fairly stated, except land was undervalued by $200,000 and unrecorded in-process R&D was valued at $1,500,000. The estimated fair value of the noncontrolling interest is
$2,600,000 at the acquisition date.

   Required

   a.   Calculate total goodwill and its allocation to the controlling and noncontrolling interests.
   b.   Prepare the working paper eliminating entries needed to consolidate Pennant and Saylor at the date
        of acquisition.

E5.2   **Equity in Net Income and Noncontrolling Interest in Net Income**   Palm Resorts acquired its   **LO 2**
70 percent interest in Sun City on January 1, 2014, for $35,200,000. The fair value of the 30 percent non-
controlling interest at the date of acquisition was $9,800,000. Sun City's date-of-acquisition reported net
assets of $3,000,000 were carried at amounts approximating fair value, but it had unrecorded identifiable
intangibles, capitalizable per *ASC Topic 805*, valued at $5,000,000. These intangibles are determined to
have limited lives, amortized on a straight-line basis over five years. It is now December 31, 2017, and
Sun City reports net income of $8,000,000.

   Required

   Calculate equity in net income and the noncontrolling interest in net income for 2017, assuming goodwill
   from this acquisition is impaired by $2,000,000 in 2017.

E5.3   **Consolidation Eliminating Entries, Date of Acquisition and Two Years Later**   Plaza Hotels   **LO 1, 2**
acquired a 90 percent interest in Stardust Casinos on January 1, 2017 for $51,100,000. The fair value
of the 10 percent noncontrolling interest at the date of acquisition was $2,900,000. Stardust's date-of-
acquisition reported net assets were carried at amounts approximating fair value, except for these items:

   • Plant and equipment, 10-year life, straight-line, is overvalued by $6,000,000.
   • Previously unrecorded limited life identifiable intangibles, 4-year life, straight-line, were valued at
     $8,000,000.

   Stardust's equity accounts at the date of acquisition were as follows:

Capital stock	$ 300,000
Retained earnings	1,650,000
Accumulated other comprehensive income	50,000
Total	$2,000,000

Stardust reports net income of $4,000,000 and other comprehensive loss of $10,000 for 2018. Stardust reported net income of $2,800,000 and other comprehensive income of $25,000 in 2017. Stardust did not declare any dividends in either year. Goodwill from this acquisition is impaired by $200,000 during 2018, but was not impaired in 2017. Plaza Hotels follows U.S. GAAP.

Required

a.   Calculate the original goodwill for this acquisition and its allocation to controlling and noncontrolling interests. In what ratio is goodwill allocated between controlling and noncontrolling interests?

b.   Prepare the consolidation eliminating entries (E) and (R) at the date of acquisition.

c.   Prepare the consolidation eliminating entries (C), (E), (R), (O) and (N) at December 31, 2018.

LO 3   E5.4   Date of Acquisition Consolidation Eliminating Entries, Bargain Purchase   Peregrine Company acquired 80 percent of Sparrow Company's common stock for $22,000,000 in cash; fees paid to an outside firm to estimate the earning power of Sparrow and the fair values of its properties amounted to $3,000,000. Sparrow's equity consisted of $4,000,000 in capital stock, $20,000,000 in retained earnings, $1,500,000 in accumulated other comprehensive income, and $500,000 in treasury stock. Book values of Sparrow's identifiable assets and liabilities approximated their fair values except as noted below:

	Book value	Fair value
Land	$1,000,000	$ 200,000
Other plant assets, net.	6,000,000	8,000,000
Equity method investments	2,000,000	3,500,000
Long-term debt	4,000,000	4,700,000

Assume that the fair values above have been carefully evaluated for accuracy. The fair value of the noncontrolling interest is estimated to be $4,000,000 at the date of acquisition.

Required

a.   Calculate the gain on acquisition and prepare Peregrine's acquisition entry.

b.   Prepare the working paper eliminating entries needed to consolidate Peregrine and Sparrow at the date of acquisition.

✓ LO 2   E5.5   Consolidation Eliminating Entries at End of First Year (see related E4.3)   Peak Entertainment acquires 60 percent of its subsidiary Saddlestone Inc. on January 1, 2016. In preparing to consolidate Peak and Saddlestone at December 31, 2016, we assemble the following information:

• Value of stock given up to acquire Saddlestone: $10,000,000.
• Direct merger costs: $250,000.
• Saddlestone's stockholders' equity at acquisition: $7,200,000.
• Fair value of earnings contingency agreement to be paid in cash: $300,000.
• Fair value of previously unrecorded identifiable intangibles (5-year life): $2,000,000
• Goodwill and identifiable intangibles are not impaired in 2016.
• Fair value of the 40 percent noncontrolling interest at acquisition: $6,500,000.
• Saddlestone's net income in 2016: $3,000,000.
• Saddlestone's dividends declared and paid in 2016: $1,000,000.
• Peak uses the complete equity method to report the investment on its own books.

Required

a.   Calculate total goodwill and its allocation to the controlling and noncontrolling interests.

b.   Calculate equity in net income for 2016, as reported on Peak's books, and the noncontrolling interest in net income, as reported on the consolidated income statement for 2016.

c.   Prepare the consolidation eliminating entries made at December 31, 2016.

✓ LO 2   E5.6   Consolidation Eliminations Several Years After Acquisition   Paramount Corporation acquired its 75 percent investment in Sun Corporation in January 2012, for $2,910,000, and accounts for its investment internally using the complete equity method. At the acquisition date, total book value of Sun was $1,500,000, including $800,000 of retained earnings, and the estimated fair value of the 25 percent noncontrolling interest was $790,000. The fair values of Sun's assets and liabilities were equal to their carrying values, except for the following items:

	Fair value − Book value
Accounts receivable.	$ (100,000)
Inventory.	(125,000)
Equipment (10 years, straight-line).	(400,000)
Patents (5 years, straight-line)	200,000
Deferred tax liabilities (created as a result of the nontaxable acquisition) . . .	75,000

The receivables were collected and the inventory sold during the first three years following the acquisition. Deferred tax liabilities of $60,000 were reversed during 2012–2017. An impairment test made at the end of 2017 indicates a remaining value of $2,000,000 for the goodwill recognized as a result of the acquisition. Sun's stockholders' equity is $2,500,000, including $1,800,000 of retained earnings, at the end of 2017.

Required

a. Calculate the amount of goodwill initially recognized as a result of the acquisition, and its allocation to the controlling and noncontrolling interests.
b. Calculate the balance in the investment account, carried on Paramount's books, and the value of the noncontrolling interest, reported in the equity section of the consolidated balance sheet, as of the end of 2017.
c. Assume eliminating entry (C), to reverse Paramount's equity method entries for 2018, has been made. Prepare 2018 eliminating entries (E) and (R) to adjust Sun's assets to the correct values as of the beginning of 2018, eliminate the remainder of the investment, and recognize the beginning-of-2018 value of the noncontrolling interest.

E5.7 Consolidation Eliminating Entries Several Years After Acquisition On January 1, 2013, **LO 2**
Palomar Resorts acquired 65 percent of the stock of Sahara Hotel & Casino for $41.45 million in cash and stock. The date-of-acquisition fair value of the noncontrolling interest was $13.55 million. Sahara's book value on January 1, 2013, was $4 million, consisting of $2.5 million of capital stock and $1.5 million of retained earnings. An evaluation of Sahara's assets and liabilities revealed the following:

- Plant and equipment with a book value of $50 million had a fair value of $35 million. Remaining life 20 years, straight-line.
- Previously unrecorded favorable lease agreements had a fair value of $5 million. Remaining life 4 years, straight-line.
- Gaming licenses with a book value of $1 million had a fair value of $8 million. Remaining life 7 years, straight-line.
- Deferred tax liabilities related to the nontaxable acquisition were estimated at $3 million.

It is now December 31, 2017, 5 years since the acquisition. Sahara's January 1, 2017 retained earnings balance is $12 million. Goodwill impairment through the end of 2016 is $3.6 million, and goodwill impairment for 2017 is $1 million. Reversals of deferred tax liabilities through the end of 2016 are $2.2 million. During 2017, additional reversals total $300,000. Sahara reported net income of $2.55 million in 2017, and declared and paid $200,000 in dividends.

In your answers below, show amounts in thousands.

Required

a. Calculate goodwill at the date of acquisition, and its allocation to controlling and noncontrolling interests.
b. Calculate the December 31, 2017, balance for Palomar's investment in Sahara, assuming Palomar uses the complete equity method.
c. Prepare eliminating entries (C), (E), (R), (O) and (N) to consolidate the trial balances of Palomar and Sahara at December 31, 2017.

E5.8 Consolidation Working Paper, Date of Acquisition (see related E3.9) Below are the pre- **LO 1**
combination condensed balance sheets of Princecraft and Sylvan Companies just prior to Princecraft's acquisition of 90 percent of the voting shares of Sylvan for $43 million in cash. The book values of Sylvan Company's net assets approximate fair value. The noncontrolling interest in Sylvan has a fair value of $4,250,000.

	Princecraft Company	Sylvan Company
Cash.	$ 60,000,000	$ 2,000,000
Other current assets.	20,000,000	8,000,000
Property and equipment, net	70,000,000	15,000,000
Total assets	$150,000,000	$25,000,000
Total liabilities.	$ 30,000,000	$ 8,000,000
Common stock.	15,000,000	5,000,000
Additional paid-in capital	45,000,000	10,000,000
Retained earnings	60,000,000	2,000,000
Total liabilities and equity.	$150,000,000	$25,000,000

Required

a.   Calculate total goodwill and its allocation to the controlling and noncontrolling interests.
b.   Prepare the consolidation working paper at the date of acquisition.
c.   Prepare the consolidated balance sheet at the date of acquisition, in good form.

⊘ LO 1, 4   E5.9   Consolidation Eliminating Entries, Date of Acquisition: U.S. GAAP and IFRS   Plummer
Corporation acquired 90 percent of Softek Technologies' voting stock by issuing 2,000,000 shares of $2
par common stock with a fair value of $25,000,000. In addition, Plummer paid $500,000 in cash to the
consultants and accountants who advised in the acquisition. Softek's stockholders' equity at the date of
acquisition is as follows:

Common stock.	$ 200,000
Additional paid-in capital	8,000,000
Retained earnings	5,000,000
Accumulated other comprehensive income.	(800,000)
Treasury stock	(400,000)
Total	$12,000,000

Softek's assets and liabilities were carried at fair value except as noted below:

	Book value	Fair value
Plant assets, net.	$12,000,000	$9,000,000
Trademarks	—	1,500,000
Customer lists	—	1,000,000
Long-term debt	2,000,000	2,100,000

The fair value of the noncontrolling interest is estimated to be $2,500,000 at the date of acquisition.

Required

a.   Prepare the acquisition entry on Plummer's books and the working paper consolidation eliminating
entries at the date of acquisition, following U.S. GAAP.
b.   Prepare the working paper consolidation eliminating entries at the date of acquisition, following
IFRS and the alternative valuation method for noncontrolling interests.

LO 4   E5.10   Consolidation at Date of Acquisition, IFRS and U.S. GAAP   In 2013, **Deutsche Post DHL**
acquired 49 percent of the shares of **Compador Technologies GmbH**, Berlin, which develops sorting

DEUTSCHE POST
[DPW]

machines and software applications for mail services. The acquisition cost was €39 million, with an additional €1 million spent on transactions costs. Deutsche Post consolidates Compador because of potential voting rights. The fair value on Compador's noncontrolling interest at the date of acquisition is €38
million.

Following is information on Compador's identifiable net assets at the date of acquisition:

(in millions)	Dr (Cr)	
	Fair value	**Book value**
Noncurrent assets	€ 2.0	€2.2
Current assets	10.0	9.9
Current liabilities and provisions	(7.0)	(7.1)

In your answers below, show all amounts in millions.

Required

a.   Calculate total goodwill and the reported amount of noncontrolling interests at the date of acquisition, assuming Deutsche Post uses the IFRS alternative valuation method for noncontrolling interests.

b.   Prepare the consolidation eliminating entries at the date of acquisition.

c.   Calculate total goodwill and the reported amount of noncontrolling interests at the date of acquisition, assuming Deutsche Post uses the U.S. GAAP valuation method for noncontrolling interests.

d.   Prepare consolidation eliminating entries at the date of acquisition, assuming Deutsche Post uses the U.S. GAAP valuation method for noncontrolling interests.

E5.11   Consolidation Eliminating Entries, One Year After Acquisition, IFRS   Blue S.A., a French   **LO 4** telecommunications company, acquired a 45 percent interest in E-Minus for €65,000,000. Blue consolidates E-Minus because it has special voting rights that allow it to control E-Minus. The fair value of the noncontrolling interest at the date of acquisition was €70,000,000, and E-Minus' book value was €7,000,000. Its identifiable net assets were carried at amounts approximating fair value. One year later, E-Minus reports net income of €4,000,000, and declares and pays no dividends. Goodwill is not impaired.

Required

a.   Calculate total goodwill and the reported amount of noncontrolling interests at the date of acquisition, assuming Blue S.A. uses the IFRS alternative valuation method for noncontrolling interests.

b.   Prepare the consolidation eliminating entries necessary to consolidate the trial balances of Blue and E-Minus at the end of the first year, assuming Blue uses the complete equity method to report its investment in E-Minus on its own books.

E5.12   Consolidation at Acquisition Date, IFRS   Vivendi SA, headquartered in Paris, is a worldwide   **LO 1, 4** leader in digital entertainment. In 2009, **Maroc Telecom**, a subsidiary of Vivendi, acquired a 51 percent controlling interest in **Sotelma**, a Malian telecoms operator, for €278 million. The book value of Sotelma   **VIVENDI** at the date of acquisition was €35 million. The estimated fair value of Sotelma's noncontrolling interests   [VIVDY] was €208 million. Fair value adjustments to Sotelma's identifiable net assets were *(in millions)*:

MAROC TELECOM [MSPA]

License, depreciated over 8 years	€24
Customer bases, depreciated over 8 years	2
Deferred tax, net...	(3)
Total fair value adjustments	€23

Vivendi and its subsidiaries follow IFRS, and choose to value noncontrolling interests at fair value. Round all answers below to the nearest million.

Required

a.   Calculate total goodwill for this acquisition, and its allocation to the controlling and noncontrolling interests.

b.   Does the purchase price include a control premium? Explain.

c.   Prepare eliminating entries (E) and (R) required to consolidate Sotelma with Maroc Telecom at the date of acquisition.

d.   If Maroc Telecom had used the alternative method for valuing the noncontrolling interest, at what value would the noncontrolling interest be reported at the date of acquisition?

E5.13   Consolidated Balance Sheet, Date of Acquisition: U.S. GAAP and IFRS   Assume that   **LO 1, 4** **Microsoft Corporation** acquired 90 percent of the outstanding common stock of Powerline Technologies for $3,000,000 cash plus 200,000 shares of Microsoft's $10 par value common stock having a market value of $80 per share. Immediately prior to the acquisition, the trial balances of the two companies were as follows:

	Dr (Cr)	
	Microsoft	**Powerline**
Current assets	$10,000,000	$2,000,000
Plant and equipment, net.	35,000,000	7,000,000
Current liabilities.	(5,000,000)	(1,500,000)
Long-term liabilities	(20,000,000)	(3,000,000)
Common stock.	(3,000,000)	(100,000)
Additional paid-in capital	(5,600,000)	(1,450,000)
Retained earnings	(11,000,000)	(3,000,000)
Accumulated other comprehensive (income) loss.	(400,000)	50,000
	$ 0	$ 0

A review of the fair values of Powerline's assets indicates that current assets are overvalued by $500,000, plant and equipment is overvalued by $6,000,000, and previously unrecorded brand names have a fair value of $3,000,000. The fair value of the noncontrolling interest is $1,800,000.

Required

a. Calculate total goodwill and its allocation to the controlling and noncontrolling interests, following U.S. GAAP.
b. Prepare a working paper to consolidate the balance sheets of Microsoft and Powerline at the date of acquisition, following U.S. GAAP.
c. Assume Microsoft uses IFRS and the alternative valuation method for noncontrolling interests. Calculate total goodwill and repeat part b following IFRS.

✅ **LO 5**　**E5.14**　**Consolidated Cash Flow from Operations**　Consider the following data:

Consolidated net income	$20,000,000
Consolidated depreciation expense	3,000,000
Amortization of asset and liability revaluations:	
Previously unrecognized identifiable intangibles	1,400,000
Premium on long-term debt	(80,000)
(Net income − Dividends) reported by a 40-percent-owned equity investment	1,700,000
Decrease in noncash current operating assets	2,800,000
Decrease in current operating liabilities.	2,100,000

Required

Use the above data to prepare the operating cash flow section of a consolidated statement of cash flows, using the indirect method.

LO 5　**E5.15**　**Consolidated Cash Flow from Operations**　Consider the following data reported in the accounts of a parent company and its 80-percent-owned subsidiary:

(in thousands)	**Parent**	**Subsidiary**
Net income.	$1,000,000 (1)	$240,000
Depreciation expense.	175,000	38,000
Amortization expense.	50,000	—
Dividends paid in cash.	250,000	75,000
Income from equity method investments.	60,000	—
Cash dividends received from equity investments	35,000	—
Items appearing in eliminating entries:		
Revaluation write-offs:		
Depreciation expense	$ 3,000	
Amortization expense	15,000	
Goodwill impairment loss (2).	40,000	

(1) Parent's separate income only; does not include equity in net income of subsidiary.
(2) Goodwill impairment losses are shared with the noncontrolling interest in proportion to ownership interests.

Required

a. Calculate consolidated net income.

b. Prepare the cash flow from operating activities section of the consolidated statement of cash flows, starting with consolidated net income, using the indirect method. Assume no adjustment is required for changes in consolidated current asset and current liability accounts.

PROBLEMS ••

P5.1   **Consolidation Working Paper, Date of Acquisition**   On July 1, 2016, **The Hershey Company**   **LO 1** acquired 75 percent of the common stock of Bagota Organic Chocolates. The $1.2 billion purchase price was paid in cash and newly-issued debt securities. The acquisition entry is reflected below in the two companies' balance sheets just *after the acquisition*.

Balance Sheets at July 1, 2016		
(in millions)	**Hershey**	**Bagota**
Assets		
Current assets	$1,500	$ 325
Property, plant and equipment, net	1,600	600
Investment in Bagota	1,200	—
Patents and trademarks	1,300	75
Total assets	$5,600	$1,000
Liabilities and Stockholders' Equity		
Current liabilities	$1,600	$ 100
Long-term liabilities	1,900	400
Common stock, par value	300	10
Additional paid-in capital	1,950	200
Retained earnings	3,900	300
Treasury stock	(4,000)	—
Accumulated other comprehensive income (loss)	(50)	(10)
Total liabilities and stockholders' equity	$5,600	$1,000

Independent appraisals produced the following fair value estimates for certain of Bagota's previously recorded assets and liabilities. In addition, previously unreported customer-related intangibles have an estimated fair value of $30 million. Bagota's noncontrolling interest has an estimated fair value of $375 million.

(in millions)	**Fair value**	**Book value**
Property, plant and equipment, net	$400	$600
Patents and trademarks	120	75
Long-term liabilities	375	400

Required

a. Prepare a schedule to compute the total goodwill and its allocation to the controlling and noncontrolling interest.

b. Prepare a working paper to consolidate the balance sheets of Hershey and Bagota at July 1, 2016.

c. Prepare a formal consolidated balance sheet for Hershey and Bagota at July 1, 2016.

P5.2   **Consolidated Balance Sheet Working Paper, Date of Acquisition, Bargain Purchase (see**   **LO 3** **related P3.4)**   On January 1, 2016, Paxon Corporation acquired 80 percent of the outstanding common stock of the Saxon Company for $1 billion cash. The balance sheets of Paxon and Saxon, *immediately prior* to the combination, follow:

(in millions)		Paxon	Saxon
Assets			
Cash and receivables..		$2,860	$ 720
Inventory..		1,700	900
Long-term investments		—	300
Land...		650	175
Buildings and equipment	$3,400		
Less Accumulated depreciation..................	(1,000)	2,400	600 (net)
Total assets		$7,610	$2,695
Liabilities and Stockholders' Equity			
Current liabilities...		$1,500	$1,000
Long-term debt		2,000	400
Common stock, par value		500	100
Additional paid-in capital....................................		1,200	350
Retained earnings		2,410	845
Total liabilities and stockholders' equity		$7,610	$2,695

Several of Saxon's assets and liabilities had fair values that were different from their book values. Estimates of the fair values of these items follow:

(in millions)	Estimated fair value
Inventory..	$1,000
Long-term investments	250
Land...	420
Buildings and equipment, net	900
Long-term debt	290

The estimated fair value of the noncontrolling interest in Saxon is $200 million.

Required

a.   Calculate the gain on acquisition and prepare Paxon's entry to record the acquisition.
b.   Prepare a working paper to consolidate the balance sheets of Paxon and Saxon at January 1, 2016.
c.   Present the consolidated balance sheet, in good form, at the date of acquisition.

LO 1   P5.3   Consolidation Eliminating Entries, Date of Acquisition   Placer Company acquired a 75 percent interest in Summer Company for $8,000,000 in cash. The condensed balance sheets *immediately prior* to the acquisition are below:

	Placer	Summer	
(in thousands)	Book value	Book value	Fair value
Cash and receivables...........................	$10,000	$ 2,000	$1,800
Inventories	8,000	3,000	2,500
Plant assets, net...............................	12,000	5,000	4,000
Intangibles	2,000	1,000	0
Total assets	$32,000	$11,000	
Current liabilities..............................	$ 6,000	$ 2,500	$2,500
Noncurrent liabilities..........................	8,000	5,000	4,900
Common stock	5,000	500	
Retained earnings	13,000	3,000	
Total liabilities and stockholders' equity	$32,000	$11,000	

Additional information:

1. In addition to the above cash cost, out-of-pocket merger-related costs of $300,000 were paid in cash. ← *include-* ← *cash*
2. The merger agreement includes an earnings contingency agreement to be settled in cash; its fair value is $800,000.
3. It is determined that Summer has an unreported preacquisition contingency related to a pending lawsuit, consisting of a liability with an estimated present value of $400,000.
4. In-process research and development owned by Summer is worth $1,500,000.
5. The fair value of the 25 percent noncontrolling interest in Summer is $2,500,000.

Required

a. Prepare the acquisition entry made by Placer.
b. Prepare the working paper eliminating entries to consolidate the trial balances of Placer and Summer at the date of acquisition.

P5.4 **Consolidation Working Paper One Year After Acquisition, Bargain Purchase (see related P4.4)** On January 1, 2016, Paxon Corporation acquired 90 percent of the outstanding common stock of Saxon Company for $1,620 million cash. The fair value of the 10 percent noncontrolling interest in Saxon was estimated to be $180 million at the date of acquisition. Paxon uses the complete equity method to report its investment. The trial balances of Paxon and Saxon at December 31, 2016, appear below:

LO 3

	Dr (Cr)	
(in millions)	**Paxon**	**Saxon**
Cash and receivables....................................	$ 3,270	$ 800
Inventory..	2,260	940
Marketable securities..................................	—	—
Investment in Saxon...................................	1,962.2	—
Land...	650	300
Buildings and equipment, net	3,600	1,150
Current liabilities......................................	(2,020)	(1,200)
Long-term debt	(5,000)	(450)
Common stock, par value	(500)	(100)
Additional paid-in capital	(1,200)	(350)
Retained earnings, January 1.........................	(2,610)	(845)
Dividends...	500	100
Sales revenue..	(30,000)	(10,000)
Equity in net income of Saxon	(232.2)	—
Gain on sale of securities.............................	—	(10)
Cost of goods sold.....................................	26,000	8,000
Depreciation expense..................................	300	40
Interest expense.......................................	250	25
Other operating expenses	2,770	1,600
Totals	$ 0	$ 0

Several of Saxon's assets and liabilities had fair values different from their book values at the acquisition date, as follows:

(in millions)	Fair value − Book value
Inventory (FIFO)	$100
Long-term investments (sold in 2016)	(50)
Land..	245
Buildings and equipment, net (20 years, straight-line)......	300
Long-term debt (5 years, straight-line).....................	(110)

Required

a. Prepare a schedule computing the gain on acquisition.

b. Prepare a schedule calculating the equity in net income of Saxon for 2016, reported on Paxon's books, and the noncontrolling interest in net income for 2016, to be reported on the consolidated income statement for 2016.

c. Prepare a working paper to consolidate the trial balances of Paxon and Saxon at December 31, 2016.

LO 3 P5.5

Consolidation Working Paper Two Years After Acquisition, Bargain Purchase (see related P5.4) Refer to the information in P5.4. Now assume it is December 31, 2017, *two years* after the acquisition. The trial balances of Paxon and Saxon at December 31, 2017, appear below:

	Dr (Cr)	
(in millions)	**Paxon**	**Saxon**
Cash and receivables....................................	$ 3,000	$ 850
Inventory...	2,500	950
Investment in Saxon....................................	2,063.9	—
Land..	650	250
Buildings and equipment, net	5,905	1,440
Current liabilities.......................................	(2,500)	(1,000)
Long-term debt	(6,000)	(800)
Common stock, par value	(500)	(100)
Additional paid-in capital	(1,200)	(350)
Retained earnings, January 1.........................	(3,022.2)	(1,090)
Dividends	500	50
Sales revenue..	(35,000)	(12,000)
Equity in net income of Saxon	(146.7)	—
Cost of goods sold.....................................	30,000	9,500
Depreciation expense..................................	450	60
Interest expense..	300	40
Other operating expenses	3,000	2,200
Totals	$ 0	$ 0

Required

a. Prepare a schedule computing equity in net income of Saxon for 2017, reported on Paxon's books, and the noncontrolling interest in net income for 2017, to be reported on the consolidated income statement for 2017.

b. Prepare a working paper to consolidate the trial balances of Paxon and Saxon at December 31, 2017.

LO 2 P5.6

CAESAR'S ENTERTAINMENT CORPORATION [CZR]

Consolidation Working Paper, Second Year Following Acquisition On January 1, 2007, **Harrah's Entertainment, Inc.** acquired a 70 percent interest in the company that owned **Emerald Safari Resort** for $592 million in cash and stock. Harrah's is now part of **Caesar's Entertainment Corporation.** Assume the following information at the date of acquisition *(in millions)*:

Book value of Emerald Safari Resort	$580
Fair value of noncontrolling interest in Emerald Safari Resort............................	233
Fair value of previously unrecorded identifiable intangibles	100

The previously unrecorded identifiable intangibles have indefinite lives. In the years since this acquisition, intense competition and a declining economic outlook led to reduced projected performance for this property. Testing indicated impairment of the identifiable intangibles by a total of $40 million as of the end of 2014, and $10 million additional impairment occurred in 2015. The entire goodwill balance associated with this property has been written off prior to 2015. The December 31, 2015 trial balances of Harrah's and Emerald Safari Resort follow. Harrah's uses the complete equity method to report the investment on its own books.

(in millions)	Dr (Cr)	
	Harrah's Entertainment	Emerald Safari Resort
Current assets	$ 1,400	$ 200
Land, buildings, riverboats and equipment, net.	17,844.7	2,419
Intangible assets	2,500	800
Investment in Emerald Safari Resort	398.3	—
Current liabilities.	(1,500)	(300)
Long-term liabilities	(14,000)	(2,600)
Capital stock	(5,520)	(324)
Retained earnings, January 1.	(900)	(300)
Dividends	100	5
Casino revenues.	(6,600)	(2,200)
Food and beverage revenues.	(1,400)	(300)
Rooms revenues	(1,000)	(200)
Equity in net loss of Emerald Safari Resort	77	—
Direct casino, food and beverage, rooms expenses	7,200	1,800
General and administrative expenses	1,400	1,000
Totals	$ 0	$ 0

Required

a. Prepare a schedule to calculate the 2015 equity in net loss and the noncontrolling interest in the net loss of Emerald Safari Resort.

b. Prepare a consolidation worksheet to consolidate the December 31, 2015, trial balances of Harrah's Entertainment and Emerald Safari Resort.

P5.7 **Equity Method and Eliminating Entries Three Years After Acquisition (see related P4.2)** **LO 2**
Puffin Industries acquired 90 percent of Sunset Coast Digital's stock on January 1, 2014, for $3,150,000. At that time, Sunset Coast's stockholders' equity totaled $1,400,000, and the estimated fair value of the noncontrolling interest was $350,000. Sunset Coast's inventory (LIFO) was overvalued by $500,000 and its plant assets (10-year life) were overvalued by $1,000,000. The remaining excess of fair value over book value is attributed to undervalued identifiable intangible assets being amortized over 20 years. Sunset Coast depreciates plant assets and amortizes intangibles by the straight-line method. During the next three years Sunset Coast reported total net income of $850,000 and paid out 50 percent in dividends. Puffin carries its investment in Sunset Coast using the complete equity method. Sunset Coast's inventory increased each year since it was acquired by Puffin, and Sunset Coast's reported net income for 2016 was $200,000.

Required

a. Compute Puffin's 2016 equity in net income of Sunset Coast and the noncontrolling interest in net income of Sunset Coast for 2016.

b. Compute the balance in the investment in Sunset Coast account at December 31, 2016, after all equity method entries have been booked.

c. Compute the balance of noncontrolling interest, reported on the December 31, 2016, consolidated balance sheet.

d. Prepare the working paper eliminating entries needed to consolidate the trial balances of Puffin and Sunset Coast at December 31, 2016.

P5.8 **Consolidation Working Paper After Several Years** Consolidated Bottling Company acquired a **LO 2**
75 percent interest in Regional Bottling Partnership on January 1, 2008. Assume the following information related to this acquisition:

Acquisition price, paid by Consolidating Bottling Company, in cash	$72,000,000
Fair value of the 25 percent noncontrolling interest.	13,000,000
Book value of Regional Bottling Partnership at date of acquisition.	25,000,000

The excess of fair value over book value at the acquisition date is attributed to previously unreported franchise rights valued at $5,000,000, and to goodwill.

The franchise rights have indefinite lives, and total impairment losses for 2008 through 2016 are $1,000,000. There are no goodwill impairment losses for this period. Regional Bottling's business prospects declined during 2017, resulting in franchise rights impairment of $2,500,000 and goodwill impairment of $6,000,000. Consolidated Bottling uses the complete equity method to report its investment in Regional Bottling on its own books.

The trial balances of Consolidated Bottling and Regional Bottling at December 31, 2017, appear below:

	Dr (Cr)	
(in thousands)	**Consolidated Bottling**	**Regional Bottling**
Current assets	$ 160,000	$ 30,000
Property, plant and equipment, net	248,000	233,780
Franchise rights, net.	466,400	—
Investment in Regional Bottling	70,560	—
Current liabilities.	(120,000)	(20,000)
Long-term debt	(700,000)	(210,000)
Common stock.	(12,000)	(1,000)
Additional paid-in capital	(100,000)	(12,000)
Retained earnings, January 1.	(50,500)	(18,100)
Accumulated other comprehensive loss, January 1	13,000	100
Treasury stock	30,000	200
Dividends	2,000	—
Net sales.	(1,200,000)	(300,000)
Equity in net loss of Regional Bottling	5,025	—
Equity in other comprehensive loss of Regional Bottling.	15	—
Cost of sales.	760,000	175,000
Selling, delivery and administrative expenses	400,000	114,000
Impairment losses	500	—
Interest expense.	28,000	8,000
Other comprehensive (income) loss.	(1,000)	20
Totals	$ 0	$ 0

Required

a. Calculate goodwill for this acquisition, and its allocation to controlling and noncontrolling interests.

b. Prepare a schedule calculating the 2017 equity in net loss of Regional Bottling on Consolidated Bottling's books ($5,025,000) and the noncontrolling interest in the 2017 net loss to be reported on the consolidated income statement.

c. Prepare a schedule showing how the December 31, 2017 investment balance on Consolidated Bottling's books ($70,560,000) was calculated.

d. Prepare a consolidation working paper for December 31, 2017.

e. Present the consolidated financial statements, in good form, for 2017.

⊘ LO 5   P5.9   Consolidated Statement of Cash Flows   Sunny Valley Resort has owned 80 percent of Mountain Lodging, Inc. since Mountain Lodging's inception. The condensed consolidated balance sheets of Sunny Valley Resort at December 31, 2017 and 2016 and other relevant information follow:

SUNNY VALLEY RESORT AND SUBSIDIARY
Condensed Consolidated Balance Sheets
December 31

(in thousands)	2017	2016
Assets		
Cash..........	$ 600,000	$ 700,000
Other current assets........	1,400,000	1,000,000
Plant assets	4,000,000	4,200,000
Accumulated depreciation	(1,500,000)	(1,600,000)
Goodwill..........	300,000	330,000
Total assets	$4,800,000	$4,630,000
Liabilities and Stockholders' Equity		
Current liabilities........	$1,282,000	$1,550,000
Noncurrent liabilities........	1,800,000	1,700,000
Stockholders' equity—controlling interest........	1,430,000	1,100,000
Noncontrolling interest........	288,000	280,000
Total liabilities and stockholders' equity	$4,800,000	$4,630,000

Additional information for 2017 *(in thousands)*:

1. Consolidated net income to the controlling interest is $400,000.
2. Mountain Lodging reported net income of $120,000 on its own books, and paid $80,000 in dividends.
3. Consolidated depreciation expense was $350,000.
4. Plant assets with an original cost of $500,000 were retired from service and scrapped. Goodwill was impaired by $30,000.
5. Sunny Valley paid $70,000 in dividends.

Required

Prepare, in good form, a consolidated statement of cash flows for 2017.

P5.10 **Consolidated Statement of Cash Flows** Comparative consolidated balance sheets and the intervening income statement for Prime Casinos and its subsidiary Saratoga International Hotels are shown below:

LO 5

PRIME CASINOS and SARATOGA INTERNATIONAL HOTELS
Comparative Consolidated Balance Sheets
December 31

(in millions)	2017	2016
Assets		
Cash..........	$ 500	$ 200
Other current assets........	900	800
Property, plant and equipment........	3,100	2,500
Accumulated depreciation........	(1,000)	(800)
Goodwill..........	275	300
Total assets	$3,775	$3,000
Liabilities and Stockholders' Equity		
Current liabilities........	$ 900	$ 650
Long-term liabilities	950	800
Capital stock	700	500
Retained earnings	1,065	900
Noncontrolling interest........	160	150
Total liabilities and stockholders' equity	$3,775	$3,000

PRIME CASINOS and SARATOGA INTERNATIONAL HOTELS
Consolidated Statement of Income and Retained Earnings
For Year Ended December 31, 2017

Sales and other revenue.	$3,555
Cost of goods sold.	(1,700)
Operating expenses	(1,243)
Consolidated net income	612
Noncontrolling interest in net income	(12)
Controlling interest in net income	600
Retained earnings, January 1, 2017.	900
Dividends paid	(435)
Retained earnings, December 31, 2017.	$1,065

Additional information *(in millions)*:

1. Consolidated depreciation expense was $250.
2. During the year, plant assets of $675 were acquired for cash.
3. Operating expenses include $10 in losses on sale of plant assets for cash.

Required

Prepare, in good form, the consolidated statement of cash flows for the year ended December 31, 2017.

LO 4 **P5.11** **Consolidation Two Years After Acquisition, IFRS**   Rendezvous Resorts is a Swiss company with an 80 percent interest in Monaco Hotels, located in France. Rendezvous acquired its interest in Monaco on January 1, 2015, for €4 billion. Monaco's book value at the date of acquisition was €1 billion. Monaco's balance sheet reported its assets and liabilities at fair value, except for these items:

- Inventories (FIFO) were overvalued by €100 million.
- Property, plant and equipment (10-year life, straight-line) was undervalued by €400 million.
- Previously unreported identifiable intangibles (3-year life, straight-line) had a fair value of €300 million. These intangibles meet the IFRS criteria for capitalization.

It is now December 31, 2016. Rendezvous uses the complete equity method to account for its investment in Monaco on its own books and prepares consolidated financial statements using IFRS. Goodwill impairment losses were €100 million in 2015 and €200 million in 2016. The trial balances of Rendezvous and Monaco at December 31, 2016, are as follows:

	Dr (Cr)	
(in millions)	**Rendezvous Resorts**	**Monaco Hotels**
Current assets	€ 500	€ 900
Property, plant and equipment, net	3,000	2,000
Investment in Monaco	4,316	—
Identifiable intangibles	—	200
Liabilities.	(4,648)	(1,150)
Capital stock	(1,500)	(800)
Retained earnings, January 1.	(1,000)	(600)
Dividends	—	50
Sales revenue.	(5,000)	(3,500)
Equity in net income of Monaco.	(168)	—
Cost of sales.	4,200	2,500
Administrative and other operating expenses	300	400
Totals	€ 0	€ 0

Required

a. Calculate the total goodwill initially arising from this acquisition, using the IFRS alternative method of valuation.

b. Prepare a schedule calculating Rendezvous' equity in net income of Monaco and the noncontrolling interest in Monaco's net income for 2016.

c. Prepare a working paper consolidating the trial balances of Rendezvous and Monaco at December 31, 2016.

P5.12 Consolidation Several Years After Acquisition, IFRS Lily Bakeries, located in Belgium, specializes in biscuit and cake products. Lily owns 75 percent of Hearty Foods, a French company acquired on January 1, 2013, for cash and stock totaling €150 million. Hearty's book value at the date of acquisition was €70 million. Its assets and liabilities were fairly reported at the date of acquisition, except for these items: **LO 4**

(in thousands)	Book value	Fair value
Plant and equipment, net (10-year life, straight-line)............	€150,000	€100,000
Secret recipes (10-year life, straight-line).....................	—	40,000
Long-term debt (4-year life, straight-line).....................	30,000	28,000

It is now December 31, 2017. Impairment testing on the acquired goodwill reveals that total impairment during the years 2013–2016 was €2.5 million, and impairment in 2017 is €0.75 million. Lily uses the complete equity method to account for its investment internally. The December 31, 2017 trial balances of Lily and Hearty follow:

	Dr (Cr)	
(in thousands)	Lily Bakeries	Hearty Foods
Current assets	€ 35,000	€ 20,000
Plant and equipment, net.....................................	226,500	202,000
Investment in Hearty	176,750	—
Identifiable intangibles	100,000	10,000
Current liabilities	(30,000)	(25,000)
Long-term debt	(350,000)	(100,000)
Capital stock	(80,000)	(54,000)
Retained earnings, January 1.................................	(60,000)	(38,000)
Sales revenue..	(400,000)	(140,000)
Equity in net income of Hearty..............................	(11,250)	—
Cost of goods sold..	250,000	80,000
Operating expenses...	143,000	45,000
Totals	€ 0	€ 0

Lily follows IFRS and uses the IFRS alternative valuation for goodwill and noncontrolling interests.

Required

a. Calculate the total goodwill arising from this acquisition.

b. Prepare a schedule calculating Lily's equity in net income of Hearty and the noncontrolling interest in Hearty's net income for 2017.

c. Prepare a working paper consolidating the trial balances of Lily and Hearty at December 31, 2017.

P5.13 Consolidation Two Years After Acquisition Mirror Resorts, Inc., a U.S. company, acquires an 80 percent interest in Silver Nugget Company on January 1, 2016, for $80 million cash. The estimated fair value of the 20 percent noncontrolling interest in Silver Nugget is $18 million. Silver Nugget's book value at the date of acquisition is $10 million. Silver Nugget's recorded assets and liabilities are carried at fair value, but it has previously unrecorded intangibles valued at $20 million that are capitalizable under the requirements of *ASC Topic 805*. These intangibles have an estimated life of five years, straight-line. There are no identifiable intangible or goodwill impairments in either 2016 or 2017. Mirror Resorts uses the complete equity method to account for its investment in Silver Nugget. It is now December 31, 2017, and the trial balances of the two companies are as follows: **LO 2**

	Dr (Cr)	
(in thousands)	**Mirror Resorts**	**Silver Nugget**
Current assets	$ 35,000	$ 5,000
Plant and equipment, net...............................	216,600	140,000
Intangibles	350,000	51,050
Investment in Silver Nugget	86,440	—
Current liabilities......................................	(50,000)	(20,000)
Long-term debt	(600,000)	(150,000)
Common stock, par value	(500)	(100)
Additional paid-in capital	(6,000)	(5,500)
Retained earnings, January 1..........................	(25,000)	(17,700)
Accumulated other comprehensive (income) loss, January 1 .	(1,000)	200
Treasury stock	4,000	1,600
Dividends	2,000	1,500
Sales revenue..	(800,000)	(100,000)
Equity in net income of Silver Nugget	(1,600)	—
Equity in other comprehensive income of Silver Nugget	(40)	—
Cost of goods sold.....................................	650,000	80,000
Operating expenses....................................	140,000	14,000
Other comprehensive (income) loss....................	100	(50)
Totals	$ 0	$ 0

Required

a. Calculate equity in net income of Silver Nugget for 2017, as reported on Mirror Resorts' books, and the noncontrolling interest in net income of Silver Nugget, as reported on the consolidated income statement for 2017.

b. Prepare a working paper to consolidate the 2017 financial statements of Mirror Resorts and Silver Nugget.

LO 2   P5.14   Consolidation Working Paper One Year After Acquisition   On January 1, 2016, Pine Mountain Resorts acquires a 60 percent interest in Shawnee Peak Enterprises for $25.4 million in cash. The date-of-acquisition fair value of the noncontrolling interest in Shawnee is estimated at $11.6 million. Shawnee's book value at the date of acquisition is $2 million. Its reported assets and liabilities are carried at amounts approximating fair value, except property and equipment, with a remaining life of 10 years, straight-line, is overvalued by $5 million. Previously unrecorded licenses and certificates, with a remaining life of four years, straight-line, are valued at $8 million. Goodwill from this acquisition is impaired by $150,000 in 2016.

The December 31, 2016, trial balances of Pine Mountain and Shawnee are below. Pine Mountain uses the complete equity method to report the investment on its own books.

(in thousands)	**Pine Mountain Resorts** Dr (Cr)	**Shawnee Peak Enterprises** Dr (Cr)
Current assets	$ 5,000	$ 1,000
Property and equipment, net	70,000	12,000
AFS investments	2,000	800
Investment in Shawnee	25,538	—
Liabilities..	(82,577)	(9,895)
Capital stock	(100)	(9)
Retained earnings, January 1.........................	(13,700)	(1,985)
Accumulated other comprehensive income, January 1	(15)	(6)
Revenues	(28,000)	(4,000)
Equity in net income of Shawnee......................	(135)	—
Equity in other comprehensive income of Shawnee	(3)	—
Operating expenses...................................	22,000	2,100
Unrealized gains on AFS investments (OCI)...............	(8)	(5)
Total	$ 0	$ 0

For all answers, show amounts in thousands and use U.S. GAAP.

Required

a. Calculate the total goodwill for this acquisition and its allocation to the controlling and noncontrolling interest.

b. Calculate 2016 equity in net income of Shawnee, appearing on Pine Mountain's books, and 2016 noncontrolling interest in net income of Shawnee, appearing on the 2016 consolidated income statement.

c. Prepare a working paper to consolidate the trial balances of Pine Mountain and Shawnee at December 31, 2016.

d. Prepare a consolidated statement of income and comprehensive income for 2016, and a consolidated balance sheet at December 31, 2016, in good form.

P5.15 **Noncontrolling Interest in Comprehensive Income** In 2013, **Verizon Communications Inc.** owned 55 percent of **Verizon Wireless**, and the noncontrolling interest reported in Verizon's financial statements is **Vodafone Group Plc**'s 45 percent interest in Verizon Wireless. In 2014, Verizon bought Vodafone's 45 percent interest in Verizon Wireless, making it a wholly-owned subsidiary of Verizon. Below is selected financial statement information for Verizon, taken from its 2013 annual report. All amounts are in millions, except per share amounts.

LO 2

VERIZON
COMMUNICATIONS
INC.
[VZ]

VODAFONE
GROUP
[VOD]

Income Statement, Year Ended December 31, 2013:	
Operating Revenues	$120,550
Operating Expenses	
Cost of services and sales (exclusive of items shown below)	44,887
Selling, general and administrative expense	27,089
Depreciation and amortization expense	16,606
Total Operating Expenses	88,582
Operating Income	31,968
Equity in earnings of unconsolidated businesses	142
Other income and (expense), net	(166)
Interest expense	(2,667)
Income Before (Provision) Benefit for Income Taxes	29,277
(Provision) benefit for income taxes	(5,730)
Net Income	$ 23,547
Net income attributable to noncontrolling interest	$12,050
Net income attributable to Verizon	11,497
Net Income	$ 23,547
Basic Earnings Per Common Share	
Net income attributable to Verizon	$ 4.01
Weighted-average shares outstanding (in millions)	2,866
Diluted Earnings Per Common Share	
Net income attributable to Verizon	$ 4.00
Weighted-average shares outstanding (in millions)	2,874

Statement of Comprehensive Income, Year Ended December 31, 2013:	
Net income	$23,547
Other comprehensive income, net of taxes	
Foreign currency translation adjustments	60
Unrealized gain on cash flow hedges	25
Unrealized gain on marketable securities	16
Defined benefit pension and postretirement plans	22
Other comprehensive income attributable to Verizon	123
Other comprehensive loss attributable to noncontrolling interests	(15)
Total comprehensive income	$23,655
Comprehensive income attributable to noncontrolling interests	12,035
Comprehensive income attributable to Verizon	11,620
Total comprehensive income	$23,655

Excerpts from statement of changes in equity for 2013:

Noncontrolling Interest	
Balance at beginning of year	$52,376
Net income attributable to noncontrolling interest	12,050
Other comprehensive income (loss)	(15)
Total comprehensive income	12,035
Distributions and other	(7,831)
Balance at end of year	$56,580

Required

a. Assume the noncontrolling interest consists *entirely* of Vodafone's 45 percent interest in Verizon Wireless. What was Verizon Wireless' separate net income for 2013? What was Verizon Communications' separate net income for 2013?

b. The noncontrolling interest in other comprehensive income is a *loss* of $15. But other comprehensive income attributable to Verizon is a *gain* of $123. Explain this result.

c. Calculate the separate other comprehensive income or loss reported by Verizon Communications and Verizon Wireless.

d. Prepare consolidation eliminating entry (N) for 2013, assuming "distributions and other" are cash dividends declared.

REVIEW SOLUTIONS ••

Review 1 Solution

	Accounts Taken From Books Dr (Cr)		Eliminations		Consolidated Balances
	Admiral	**Gold Road**	**Dr**	**Cr**	**Dr (Cr)**
Current assets	$ 14,000,000	$ 9,200,000			$ 23,200,000
Equity investments.	55,000,000	5,000,000			60,000,000
Plant and equipment, net	240,000,000	80,000,000			320,000,000
Investment in Gold Road	54,297,000	—		$ 6,364,000 (C)	—
				15,928,000 (E)	
				32,005,000 (R)	
Identifiable intangible assets	550,000,000	—	(R) $ 2,500,000	1,250,000 (O)	551,250,000
Goodwill	—	—	(R) 35,300,000		35,300,000
Current liabilities.	(16,000,000)	(11,000,000)			(27,000,000)
Long-term debt	(842,485,000)	(54,085,000)			(896,570,000)
Capital stock	(5,000,000)	(2,500,000)	(E) 2,500,000		(5,000,000)
Retained earnings, January 1.	(36,955,000)	(17,300,000)	(E) 17,300,000		(36,955,000)
Accumulated other comprehensive income, January 1	(328,000)	(110,000)	(E) 110,000		(328,000)
Noncontrolling interest.	—	—		3,982,000 (E)	(11,368,000)
				5,795,000 (R)	
				1,591,000 (N)	
Dividends	2,500,000	800,000		640,000 (C)	2,500,000
				160,000 (N)	
Sales and other revenue.	(700,000,000)	(200,000,000)			(900,000,000)
Equity in net income of Gold Road	(7,000,000)	—	(C) 7,000,000		—
Equity in other comprehensive income of Gold Road	(4,000)	—	(C) 4,000		—
Cost of goods sold.	480,000,000	140,000,000			620,000,000
Operating expenses	212,000,000	50,000,000	(O) 1,250,000		263,250,000
Other comprehensive income	(25,000)	(5,000)			(30,000)
Noncontrolling interest in net income (1). .	—	—	(N) 1,750,000		1,750,000
Noncontrolling interest in other comprehensive income.	—	—	(N) 1,000		1,000
Totals	$ 0	$ 0	$67,715,000	$67,715,000	$ 0

(1) 20% × ($200,000,000 − $140,000,000 − $50,000,000 − $1,250,000) = $1,750,000.

ADMIRAL CASINO & RESORT
Consolidated Statement of Income and Comprehensive Income
For Year Ended December 31, 2017

Sales and other revenue.	$900,000,000
Less: Cost of goods sold	(620,000,000)
Gross profit.	280,000,000
Less: Operating expenses	(263,250,000)
Consolidated net income.	**16,750,000**
Less: Noncontrolling interest in net income.	(1,750,000)
Net income attributable to Admiral	$ 15,000,000
Consolidated net income	$ 16,750,000
Plus: Other comprehensive income	30,000
Consolidated comprehensive income	16,780,000
Less: Noncontrolling interest in comprehensive income (2).	(1,751,000)
Comprehensive income attributable to Admiral.	$ 15,029,000

(2) $1,750,000 + $1,000 = $1,751,000.

ADMIRAL CASINO & RESORT
Consolidated Balance Sheet
December 31, 2017

Assets		Liabilities and Stockholders' Equity	
Current assets	$ 23,200,000	Current liabilities.	$ 27,000,000
Equity investments	60,000,000	Long-term debt	896,570,000
Plant and equipment, net	320,000,000	Total liabilities.	923,570,000
Identifiable intangibles	551,250,000		
Goodwill	35,300,000	Stockholders' equity	
		Admiral stockholders' equity:	
		Capital stock.	5,000,000
		Retained earnings (3)	49,455,000
		Accumulated other	
		comprehensive income (4)	357,000
		Total Admiral stockholders' equity	54,812,000
		Noncontrolling interest.	11,368,000
		Total stockholders' equity	66,180,000
Total assets	$989,750,000	Total liabilities and stockholders' equity . . .	$989,750,000

(3) $36,955,000 + 15,000,000 − $2,500,000 = $49,455,000.
(4) $328,000 + $30,000 − $1,000 = $357,000.

Review 2 Solution

	Accounts Taken From Books Dr (Cr)		Eliminations		Consolidated Balances Dr (Cr)
	Admiral	Gold Road	Dr	Cr	
Current assets	$ 14,000,000	$ 9,200,000			$ 23,200,000
Equity investments	55,000,000	5,000,000			60,000,000
Plant and equipment, net	240,000,000	80,000,000			320,000,000
Investment in Gold Road	54,297,000	—		$ 6,364,000 (C)	—
				15,928,000 (E)	
				32,005,000 (R)	
Identifiable intangible assets	550,000,000	—	(R) $ 2,500,000	1,250,000 (O)	551,250,000
Goodwill	—	—	(R) 30,005,000		30,005,000
Current liabilities.	(16,000,000)	(11,000,000)			(27,000,000)
Long-term debt	(842,485,000)	(54,085,000)			(896,570,000)
Capital stock	(5,000,000)	(2,500,000)	(E) 2,500,000		(5,000,000)
Retained earnings, January 1	(36,955,000)	(17,300,000)	(E) 17,300,000		(36,955,000)
Accumulated other comprehensive income, January 1	(328,000)	(110,000)	(E) 110,000		(328,000)
Noncontrolling interest.	—	—		3,982,000 (E)	(6,073,000)
				500,000 (R)	
				1,591,000 (N)	
Dividends	2,500,000	800,000		640,000 (C)	2,500,000
				160,000 (N)	
Sales and other revenue.	(700,000,000)	(200,000,000)			(900,000,000)
Equity in net income of Gold Road	(7,000,000)	—	(C) 7,000,000		—
Equity in other comprehensive income of Gold Road	(4,000)	—	(C) 4,000		—
Cost of goods sold.	480,000,000	140,000,000			620,000,000
Operating expenses	212,000,000	50,000,000	(O) 1,250,000		263,250,000
Other comprehensive income	(25,000)	(5,000)			(30,000)
Noncontrolling interest in net income (1). . .	—	—	(N) 1,750,000		1,750,000
Noncontrolling interest in other comprehensive Income	—	—	(N) 1,000		1,000
Totals	$ 0	$ 0	$62,420,000	$62,420,000	$ 0

(1) 20% × ($200,000,000 − $140,000,000 − $50,000,000 − $1,250,000) = $1,750,000.

ADMIRAL CASINO & RESORT
Consolidated Statement of Income and Comprehensive Income
For Year Ended December 31, 2017

Sales and other revenue.	$900,000,000
Less: Cost of goods sold	(620,000,000)
Gross profit.	280,000,000
Less: Operating expenses	(263,250,000)
Consolidated net income.	**16,750,000**
Less: Noncontrolling interest in net income.	(1,750,000)
Net income attributable to Admiral	$ 15,000,000
Consolidated net income	$ 16,750,000
Plus: Other comprehensive income	30,000
Consolidated comprehensive income	16,780,000
Less: Noncontrolling interest in comprehensive income (2).	(1,751,000)
Comprehensive income attributable to Admiral.	$ 15,029,000

(2) $1,750,000 + $1,000 = $1,751,000.

ADMIRAL CASINO & RESORT
Consolidated Balance Sheet
December 31, 2017

Assets		**Liabilities and Stockholders' Equity**	
Current assets	$ 23,200,000	Current liabilities.	$ 27,000,000
Equity investments.	60,000,000	Long-term debt	896,570,000
Plant and equipment, net. . .	320,000,000	Total liabilities.	923,570,000
Identifiable intangibles	551,250,000		
Goodwill	30,005,000	Stockholders' equity	
		Admiral stockholders' equity:	
		Capital stock.	5,000,000
		Retained earnings (3)	49,455,000
		Accumulated other	
		comprehensive income (4)	357,000
		Total Admiral stockholders' equity	54,812,000
		Noncontrolling interest.	6,073,000
		Total stockholders' equity	60,885,000
Total assets	$984,455,000	Total liabilities and stockholders' equity . . .	$984,455,000

(3) $36,955,000 + 15,000,000 − $2,500,000 = $49,455,000.
(4) $328,000 + $30,000 − $1,000 = $357,000.

6 Consolidated Financial Statements: Intercompany Transactions

LEARNING OBJECTIVES

LO1 Prepare eliminating entries for intercompany service and financing transactions. (p. 230)

LO2 Describe elimination of unconfirmed profits and their effect on equity in net income and noncontrolling interest in net income. (p. 231)

LO3 Prepare eliminating entries for intercompany transfers of land. (p. 233)

LO4 Prepare eliminating entries for intercompany transfers of inventory. (p. 236)

LO5 Prepare eliminating entries for intercompany transfers of depreciable assets. (p. 240)

NIKE, INC.
www.nike.com

Nike, Inc. is a leading worldwide supplier of athletic clothing, footwear and equipment, headquartered in Portland, Oregon. Nike has over 150 subsidiaries, but as of 2014, its major subsidiaries are Converse, Inc., acquired in 2003, and Hurley International, acquired in 2002. Converse is known for the Chuck Taylor All Star basketball shoe. Hurley International produces and markets action sports clothing and accessories.

Note 1 to Nike's 2014 consolidated financial statements includes the following statement:

> The consolidated financial statements include the accounts of NIKE, Inc. and its subsidiaries (the "Company"). All significant intercompany transactions and balances have been eliminated.

Nike's consolidated financial statements present the results of transactions and events for Nike, Inc. and its subsidiaries as *one entity*. The financial statements do not report transactions *between* the parent company and its subsidiaries. Supply chain and financial transactions are likely to occur between Nike and its subsidiaries, especially since many of the subsidiaries distribute Nike products in other countries. To avoid creating additional complexities in the accounting system, the separate books of each company record these transactions the same way they record transactions with outside suppliers, customers, and other entities. When consolidating the financial statements of the parent and its subsidiaries, the accountant uses eliminating entries to remove the effects of these **intercompany transactions**.

In this chapter you will learn how to prepare consolidation eliminating entries that remove the effects of common intercompany relationships and transactions. *Source*: Nike, Inc. annual report, 2014.

CHAPTER ORGANIZATION

Intercompany service and financing transactions	Intercompany profits	Intercompany land sales	Intercompany merchandise sales	Intercompany sales of depreciable assets	Comprehensive illustration
• Intercompany revenues and expenses • Intercompany receivables and payables	• Unconfirmed profits • Effect on equity in net income and noncontrolling interest in net income	• Year of transfer • Subsequent years • Year of sale to outside party	• Unconfirmed profit in ending inventory • Unconfirmed profit in beginning inventory	• Year of transfer • Subsequent years • Year of sale to outside party	• Goodwill, equity in net income, noncontrolling interest in net income • Eliminations CIERON • Consolidation working paper and consolidated statements

INTRODUCTION

Affiliated companies often transact business with each other. Some companies acquire their suppliers or customers to create supply chain efficiencies. A parent and its subsidiaries may sell each other fixed assets, such as land or equipment, occasionally or in the normal course of business. The consolidated financial statements present the financial performance and status of the consolidated companies as a **single economic entity**. Consolidated statements do not reflect the effects of these intercompany transactions, just as transactions between divisions or segments of a company are not reported externally.

In the discussion below, we use the terminology introduced in Chapter 1 to distinguish between intercompany sales or transfers *from parent to subsidiary* and *from subsidiary to parent*, as follows:

- A **downstream** sale or transfer occurs when the parent sells to a subsidiary.
- An **upstream** sale or transfer indicates that a subsidiary is selling to the parent.

When goods or services are sold between affiliated companies, the consolidation process eliminates intercompany revenues and expenses. Neither arose out of transactions with outside parties, and both must be eliminated to avoid overstatement of consolidated revenues and expenses. Any related intercompany receivables and payables must also be eliminated.

Assets may be transferred among affiliates at a gain or loss to the selling company. If the buying company still holds these assets at the end of an accounting period, the asset balances include intercompany gains and losses. Since such gains and losses are not yet **confirmed** by transactions with outside parties, they must be eliminated and the asset balances adjusted in consolidation.

The consolidation eliminating entries discussed in this chapter add to the consolidation process discussed in Chapters 3, 4 and 5. We add step (I) to include all necessary **I**ntercompany eliminations. Because intercompany eliminations can affect the subsidiary's beginning retained earnings balance and the parent's beginning investment balance, step (I) appears *between steps (C) and (E)*, as follows:

(C) Eliminate the current year's equity method entries, restoring the investment account to its balance at the beginning of the current year.

(I) Eliminate the effects of upstream and downstream intercompany transactions.

(E) Eliminate the remainder of the subsidiary's beginning-of-year stockholders' equity account balances, reducing the investment account and increasing the noncontrolling interest according to each ownership interest's share of the subsidiary's remaining beginning equity.

(R) Revalue the subsidiary's assets and liabilities as of the beginning of the year. Eliminate the remainder of the investment account, representing the controlling interest's beginning-of-year revaluation balance, and attribute the appropriate beginning-of-year net asset revaluations to the noncontrolling interest.

(O) Recognize current year write-offs of the subsidiary's asset and liability revaluations.

(N) Recognize the noncontrolling interest in net income and other comprehensive income. Update the noncontrolling interest in equity for its share of comprehensive income and dividends.

The acronym **CIERON** may help you to remember the six elimination steps used in the consolidation process.

This chapter examines consolidation issues related to balances overstated or understated by intercompany transactions, and unconfirmed profits and losses arising out of intercompany services, financing, and transfers of land, inventory, and depreciable assets. Unconfirmed profits and losses also affect the calculation of the parent's equity in net income and, where appropriate, the noncontrolling interest in net income.

INTERCOMPANY SERVICE AND FINANCING TRANSACTIONS

LO1 Prepare eliminating entries for intercompany service and financing transactions.

In a strategic acquisition, a parent and subsidiary typically have complementary resources that lead to intercompany business transactions. **VF Corporation** acquired **The Timberland Company** in 2011. The merger augments VF's outdoor line and global market share, and Timberland's apparel offerings. VF and Timberland likely engage in significant supply chain transactions. **Brown Shoe Company**, known for its Famous Footwear retail outlets, has wholesale, retail, and development subsidiaries that support its supply chain. Transactions between these affiliates likely include borrowing and lending activities.

Intercompany service and financing transactions between a parent and a subsidiary result in offsetting account balances that must be eliminated in consolidation. Suppose Parrish Shoe Factory is a subsidiary of Jordan Athleticwear. During 2016, Jordan provides design services costing $650,000 to Parrish and bills Parrish $900,000 for these services. At year-end, Parrish still owes Jordan $100,000 for these services. In addition, Jordan loans $1,000,000 to Parrish. Interest on this loan, accrued and paid during 2016, is $50,000. The separate books of the two companies report the following accounts related to these transactions:

	Jordan	Parrish
Balance Sheet		
Accounts receivable	$ 100,000	—
Loan receivable	1,000,000	—
Accounts payable	—	$ 100,000
Loan payable	—	1,000,000
Income Statement		
Design revenue	900,000	—
Interest revenue	50,000	—
Design expense	650,000	900,000
Interest expense	—	50,000

The consolidated entity incurred design costs of $650,000 in developing its products. There are no other transactions with outside parties. Therefore only the $650,000 in design expenses should appear on the current consolidated financial statements. The step (I) eliminating entries needed to achieve this result are:

(I-1)	Accounts payable.	100,000	
	Accounts receivable		100,000
	To eliminate the intercompany receivable/payable.		
(I-2)	Loan payable	1,000,000	
	Loan receivable		1,000,000
	To eliminate the intercompany loan principal.		
(I-3)	Design revenue.	900,000	
	Design expense.		900,000
	To eliminate the intercompany service revenue/expense.		
(I-4)	Interest revenue	50,000	
	Interest expense		50,000
	To eliminate the intercompany interest revenue/expense.		

These eliminating entries are necessary to avoid overstating revenues, expenses, receivables and payables related to intercompany service and financing transactions. There is no effect on consolidated income.

INTERCOMPANY PROFITS

Elimination of intercompany profits on asset transfers within an affiliated group reflects the fundamental argument that, *since the parent and the subsidiary are under common control, transactions between them are not the result of arm's-length bargaining*. Therefore, any profits or losses recorded in such transactions are subject to **confirmation** via arm's-length transactions with external parties. *FASB ASC Section 810-10-45* clarifies that unconfirmed gains and losses on *all* intercompany transactions must be eliminated, whether they are upstream or downstream:

> As consolidated financial statements are based on the assumption that they represent the financial position and operating results of a single economic entity, such statements shall not include gain or loss on transactions among the entities in the consolidated group. *(para. 1)*

LO2 Describe elimination of unconfirmed profits and their effect on equity in net income and noncontrolling interest in net income.

Intercompany profits that require elimination relate only to transferred assets remaining **inside the affiliated group** at the end of the reporting period. These profits or losses are **not yet confirmed** by further sale to outside parties; confirmed profits require no elimination. Suppose Jordan acquired land sometime in the past at a cost of $1,000,000. During the current year, it sells the land to Parrish for $1,400,000. Prior to consolidation, a gain of $400,000 (= $1,400,000 − $1,000,000) appears on Jordan's books, and Parrish's books carry the land at $1,400,000. From a single-entity perspective, *no gain occurred*—the land was merely transferred internally, and should continue to be carried at its original cost of $1,000,000. The necessary eliminating entry made in consolidation for the year of sale is:

(I)	Gain on sale of land	400,000	
	Land.		400,000
	To eliminate the unconfirmed intercompany profit and reduce the land to		
	original acquisition cost.		

The land is reported in the consolidated balance sheet at $1,000,000, the original acquisition cost to the group, and the unconfirmed gain of $400,000 is eliminated. From a consolidated point of view, *the transaction is treated as if it never occurred*. However, since consolidation eliminating entries appear only on a working paper and are not booked, the $400,000 gain remains in Jordan's retained earnings, and the land remains at $1,400,000 on Parrish's books. Thus, the $400,000 intercompany gain must be eliminated in consolidation *each year* until it is *confirmed* through sale to an outside party.

Remember that only *unconfirmed* profits at year-end require elimination. In the above example, Parrish held the land at year-end. If Parrish sold the land to a third party for $1,600,000 during the current year, no elimination is required: Jordan reports a gain of $400,000 and Parrish reports a gain of $200,000. From a single-entity perspective, land costing $1,000,000 was sold for $1,600,000, a gain of $600,000. The consolidation process adds the parent and subsidiary gain balances to arrive at the correct gain on sale of land without any eliminating entries.

If the subsidiary has a noncontrolling interest, we must consider to what extent elimination of unconfirmed profits affects the noncontrolling interest. Elimination of intercompany profits arising in *downstream* sales affects *only the controlling interest's share of consolidated income*. Because the parent is the seller in the transaction, and records profit on a downstream sale, there is no effect on the subsidiary's net income and therefore no effect on any noncontrolling interest in net income. If the parent does not own 100 percent of the subsidiary, elimination of intercompany profits arising in *upstream* sales affects both the controlling and noncontrolling interests in consolidated income. The subsidiary is the seller in upstream sales, and records the intercompany profit, so elimination of that profit is shared between the controlling and noncontrolling interests. Because intercompany eliminations rarely affect other comprehensive income, we limit our discussion to their effects on net income.

Equity in Net Income and Noncontrolling Interest in Net Income

Recall from Chapter 4 that the complete equity method results in a **one-line consolidation**—if the parent uses the complete equity method, its separate net income equals consolidated net income attributed to the parent. Any adjustments made in consolidation that affect consolidated net income must also affect the parent's equity in net income. Therefore, unconfirmed intercompany gains and losses on upstream and downstream sales affect equity in net income. Specifically, the parent's share of any unconfirmed intercompany gains (losses) is deducted from (added to) its share of the subsidiary's reported net income in computing equity in net income.

The parent's unconfirmed intercompany profit on downstream sales seems to have nothing to do with the net income the parent accrues from its subsidiary. However, because these unconfirmed profits are eliminated in consolidation, they are also removed in determining equity in net income. If a consolidation eliminating entry affects consolidated net income, it must also affect equity in net income the same way. Otherwise the parent's separate net income, which includes equity in net income, will not equal the controlling interest's share of consolidated net income.

When the equity method is used for external reporting of unconsolidated investments, unconfirmed profits on downstream and upstream sales are deducted to the extent of the investor's ownership interests. In contrast, when the parent reports its controlling interest in a subsidiary *internally* using the complete equity method, the *entire* unconfirmed profit on **downstream transactions** is removed from equity in net income reported by the parent. If the subsidiary is not wholly owned, the *parent's share* of the unconfirmed profit on **upstream transactions** is removed from equity in net income. The noncontrolling interest in the subsidiary is affected only by *upstream* intercompany transactions because the subsidiary reports unconfirmed profits on upstream sales on its own books. With the noncontrolling interest sharing in the subsidiary's profits, removal of unconfirmed upstream profits affects the noncontrolling interest in net income.

To illustrate the above concepts, assume Jordan acquires 80 percent of Parrish on January 1, 2016. During 2016, Jordan sells merchandise costing $380,000 to Parrish for $400,000. Parrish still holds the merchandise in its inventory at year-end. The $20,000 profit on the intercompany transfer is *unconfirmed* until Parrish sells the merchandise to an outside customer. When computing Jordan's equity in the net income of Parrish, we make the adjustments for revaluation write-offs, and deduct an additional $20,000 to remove the downstream intercompany profit.

Suppose Parrish instead sells the merchandise to Jordan, recording a profit of $20,000, and Jordan still holds the merchandise in its inventory at year-end. Now the unconfirmed upstream profit is removed from both Jordan's equity in net income *and* the noncontrolling interest in net income reported on the consolidated income statement. We subtract Jordan's share of the unconfirmed profit, $16,000 (= 80% × $20,000), from equity in net income, and $4,000 from the noncontrolling interest in net income. The following chart summarizes the effects of intercompany transactions on equity in net income and the noncontrolling interest in net income.

Effects of Unconfirmed Intercompany Profits		
Transaction Type	**Equity in Net Income**	**Noncontrolling Interest in Net Income**
Downstream..............	Remove all unconfirmed profit	No effect
Upstream	Remove parent's share of unconfirmed profit	Remove noncontrolling interest's share of unconfirmed profit

INTERCOMPANY TRANSFERS OF LAND

LO3 Prepare eliminating entries for intercompany transfers of land.

Transfers of land between affiliated companies represent the most straightforward application of the concepts inherent in accounting for unconfirmed intercompany profits. Because land does not depreciate or affect accounts such as cost of sales, intercompany eliminations that remove the effects of land sales between parent and subsidiary are less complex than eliminations for intercompany merchandise and depreciable asset sales. Therefore these transfers are discussed first, to introduce the basic concepts of intercompany transactions and unconfirmed profits.

Eliminations in the Year of Transfer

In the year of transfer, the purchasing affiliate records the purchase of land at the price paid, and the selling affiliate recognizes a gain or loss on the intercompany sale. This gain or loss is included in the net income and ultimately in the retained earnings of the selling affiliate.

Since an unconfirmed intercompany gain or loss affects consolidated net income and is eliminated in consolidation, an equivalent elimination must be reflected in the parent's equity in net income. If the sale is downstream, all of the unconfirmed gain is deducted from equity in net income, thereby offsetting the gain reported on the parent's separate books. In the case of an upstream sale, the parent's share of the subsidiary's unconfirmed gain is deducted from equity in net income. This deduction offsets the parent's share of the gain reported on the subsidiary's separate books.

Assume that in 2016 Jordan sells land costing $2,000,000 to Parrish for $2,300,000. Parrish holds the land at year-end. The consolidation eliminating entry for this downstream transfer is:

Consolidation eliminating entry, year of transfer

(I)	Gain on sale of land	300,000	
	Land...		300,000
	To eliminate the unconfirmed intercompany profit and reduce the land to original acquisition cost.		

We make the same eliminating entry whether the transfer is upstream or downstream. However, the 20 percent noncontrolling interest in Parrish makes the upstream/downstream distinction important. Equity in net income, reported on Jordan's books, and noncontrolling interest in net income, reported on the consolidated income statement, are affected differently if Jordan sold the land to Parrish or Parrish sold the land to Jordan.

Effect of $300,000 Unconfirmed Intercompany Profit in Year of Transfer		
Transaction Type	**Equity in Net Income**	**20% Noncontrolling Interest in Net Income**
Downstream..............	Subtract $300,000	No effect
Upstream	Subtract $240,000	Subtract $60,000

Because consolidation eliminating entries are not posted to the books, the gain remains on the seller's books, as part of retained earnings, and the land remains overvalued on the purchaser's books. When we prepare the consolidated statements each year, working paper entries must be made to eliminate this transaction.

Eliminations in Subsequent Years

Eliminating entries for intercompany land transfers in subsequent years differ depending on whether the transfers are upstream or downstream.

Upstream Transfers   If the land was sold *upstream* in a prior period, we eliminate the unconfirmed gain from the *beginning retained earnings of the subsidiary*. Although we eliminated the gain on the prior period working paper, it remained intact on the subsidiary's books and was closed to its retained earnings in the year of sale. If Jordan still holds the land at the end of 2017, the consolidation eliminating entry is:

December 31, 2017, consolidation eliminating entry, upstream			
(I)	Retained earnings, beginning—Parrish	300,000	
	Land.		300,000
	To eliminate the unconfirmed upstream intercompany profit from a previous year and reduce the land to original acquisition cost.		

Eliminating the intercompany profit from Parrish's beginning retained earnings balance facilitates eliminating the investment account against Jordan's share of Parrish's stockholders' equity in (E), and automatically charges the noncontrolling interest for its proportional share of the unconfirmed profit.

To understand why Parrish's retained earnings are reduced in the above eliminating entry, suppose Jordan paid $80 million to acquire an 80 percent interest in Parrish on January 1, 2016. Parrish's book value was $100 million: capital stock of $75 million and retained earnings of $25 million. Because $80 million is 80 percent of $100 million, the acquisition is at book value and no revaluations are necessary. During 2016, Parrish reported net income of $5 million, including the gain of $300,000 on the intercompany sale of land, and paid no dividends. Jordan's December 31, 2016, investment balance is:

January 1, 2016, balance.	$80,000,000
Equity in net income, 2016:	
80% × ($5,000,000 − $300,000)	3,760,000
December 31, 2016, balance	$83,760,000

Thus, the investment account has been *reduced* by Jordan's share of the unconfirmed gain, $240,000 (= 80% × $300,000) via recognition of equity in net income, but Parrish's December 31, 2016, retained earnings balance, $30,000,000 (= $25,000,000 + $5,000,000), *includes* the $300,000 unconfirmed gain.

Step (E) of the consolidation process calls for eliminating the investment balance against the subsidiary's stockholders' equity *as of the beginning of the year*, and recognizing the noncontrolling interest's share of the subsidiary's beginning equity:

- Debit beginning balance of stockholders' equity—subsidiary
- Credit beginning balance of investment (parent's share of subsidiary's equity)
- Credit noncontrolling interest in subsidiary (noncontrolling interest's share of subsidiary's equity)

We computed the beginning investment balance for 2017 to be $83,760,000. The beginning noncontrolling interest balance for 2017 is:

January 1, 2016, balance	
$100,000,000 × 20%	$20,000,000
Noncontrolling interest in net income, 2016:	
20% × ($5,000,000 − $300,000)	940,000
December 31, 2016, noncontrolling interest	
balance	$20,940,000

Using the subsidiary's beginning-of-year book retained earnings balance, we do *not* have a balanced elimination for (E):

- Beginning balance of stockholders' equity—subsidiary = $105,000,000
  - = $100,000,000 + $5,000,000 in 2016 net income
- Beginning balance of investment = $83,760,000
- Beginning balance of noncontrolling interest = $20,940,000

Eliminating entry (I) above reduces Parrish's beginning retained earnings by $300,000, leaving a remaining balance of $104,700,000, which balances eliminating entry (E); $83,760,000 = 80% × $104,700,000.

Downstream Transfers   When *downstream* sales occur, in subsequent years we add the unconfirmed gain to the *investment account*. In this case, the total intercompany gain was originally charged against equity in net income and reduced the investment account. But there was no corresponding effect on the subsidiary's net income at the time of consolidation. As in the case of upstream sales, a discrepancy exists between the investment account and the subsidiary's stockholders' equity. We cannot adjust the subsidiary's retained earnings, because downstream transfers do not affect the subsidiary's net income and are not charged against the noncontrolling interest. For a balanced elimination in (E), the following eliminating entry (I) is made:

December 31, 2017, consolidation eliminating entry, downstream		
(I) Investment in Parrish	300,000	
Land.		300,000
To eliminate the unconfirmed downstream intercompany profit from a previous year and reduce the land to original acquisition cost.		

Continuing the above example, if Jordan sold the land to Parrish in 2016 at a profit of $300,000, the 2017 beginning investment balance is:

January 1, 2016, balance.	$80,000,000
Equity in net income, 2016:	
(80% × $5,000,000) − $300,000	3,700,000
December 31, 2016, balance.	$83,700,000

The beginning noncontrolling interest balance for 2017 is:

January 1, 2016, balance	
$100,000,000 × 20%	$20,000,000
Noncontrolling interest in net income, 2016:	
20% × $5,000,000.	1,000,000
December 31, 2016, balance.	$21,000,000

Using the parent's beginning-of-year book investment balance, we do not have a balanced elimination for (E):

- Beginning balance of stockholders' equity—subsidiary = $105,000,000
- Beginning balance of investment = $83,700,000
- Beginning balance of noncontrolling interest = $21,000,000

Eliminating entry (I) above increases Jordan's investment balance to $84,000,000, which balances eliminating entry (E); $84,000,000 = 80% × $105,000,000.

We continue to make elimination (I) in subsequent years' consolidations as long as the land remains in the consolidated entity, but intercompany land sales in previous years do not affect the parent company's current year equity in net income or the noncontrolling interest in current year consolidated net income.

Eliminations in Year of Sale to Outside Party

Sale of the land to an outside party in a subsequent year requires that the original intercompany gain be recognized in consolidated net income in that subsequent year. If the original intercompany gain was upstream, the working paper entry transfers the original intercompany gain out of the subsidiary's retained earnings and into current income. In the downstream case, the entry adds the gain back to the investment account from which it was previously deducted via equity in net income, and recognizes it as current income.

The parent's equity in net income in the year of external sale includes all of the now-confirmed downstream intercompany gain, or the parent's share of the now-confirmed upstream gain. If the intercompany sale was upstream, the noncontrolling interest in net income is increased by the noncontrolling interest's share of the now-confirmed intercompany gain.

Continuing our example, suppose the land was sold in 2018 for $3,000,000. Given that the original cost of the land to the consolidated entity was $2,000,000, a consolidated gain of $1,000,000 should be reported. The selling entity carries the land at $2,300,000, and reports a gain of $700,000. Recognizing the $300,000 intercompany gain in elimination (I) brings the total consolidated gain to its correct amount.

December 31, 2018, consolidation eliminating entry, upstream		
(I) Retained earnings, beginning – Parrish	300,000	
Gain on sale of land.		300,000
To include in current consolidated net income the previously recorded		
upstream gain now confirmed through external sale.		
December 31, 2018, consolidation eliminating entry, downstream		
(I) Investment in Parrish	300,000	
Gain on sale of land.		300,000
To include in current consolidated net income the previously recorded		
downstream gain now confirmed through external sale.		

These eliminations affect consolidated income, thereby affecting Jordan's equity in net income and the noncontrolling interest in net income. These effects are summarized as follows:

Effect of $300,000 Intercompany Profit Confirmed in Year of Sale to Outside Party		
Transaction Type	**Equity in Net Income**	**20% Noncontrolling Interest in Net Income**
Downstream.	Add $300,000	No effect
Upstream	Add $240,000	Add $60,000

Confirmation of the intercompany sale and removal of the land from the books mean that no further consolidation eliminating entries related to the land are needed.

INTERCOMPANY TRANSFERS OF INVENTORY

LO4 Prepare eliminating entries for intercompany transfers of inventory.

Transfers of inventory between affiliated corporations are quite common. Component parts are often manufactured by one affiliate and assembled by another. Or finished goods may be produced by one affiliate and marketed by another. In all such cases, preparation of consolidated statements requires elimination of intercompany revenues and expenses. If the intercompany transfer price differs from cost, and the goods remain in the affiliated entity at year-end, an unconfirmed gain or loss results.

To see the intuition behind required eliminations for intercompany inventory transfers, consider this example. During 2016, Jordan sells merchandise costing $1,000,000 to Parrish for $1,500,000. At the end of 2016, all of the merchandise remains in Parrish's inventory. This information is reported in the companies' separate books as follows:

	Jordan	Parrish
Balance sheet		
Inventory...	—	$1,500,000
Income statement		
Sales revenue...	$1,500,000	—
Cost of goods sold..	1,000,000	—

From a consolidated perspective, no transaction is reported unless it is with an outside party. Therefore the consolidated balance sheet must report Parrish's inventory at cost, $1,000,000, and no sales revenue or cost of goods sold appear on the consolidated income statement. The eliminating entries necessary to achieve this result are:

(I-1)	Sales..	1,500,000	
	Cost of goods sold		1,500,000
	To eliminate intercompany merchandise sales and purchases.		
(I-2)	Cost of goods sold.......................................	500,000	
	Inventory		500,000
	To eliminate unconfirmed profit from Parrish's ending inventory.		

Although the two eliminating entries above could be combined, separating them clarifies the two steps—elimination of gross intercompany sales and purchases, and elimination of unconfirmed profits in ending inventory.

Had Parrish sold all merchandise purchased from Jordan to outside customers by year-end, we only eliminate gross intercompany sales and purchases. If Parrish sold the inventory for $1,800,000 during 2016, the companies' separate books report the following:

	Jordan	Parrish
Balance sheet		
Inventory...	$ —	$ —
Income statement		
Sales revenue...	1,500,000	1,800,000
Cost of goods sold..	1,000,000	1,500,000

Because the consolidated financial statements report $1,800,000 in sales to outside customers, and cost of goods sold of $1,000,000, the following eliminating entry achieves this result:

(I)	Sales..	1,500,000	
	Cost of goods sold		1,500,000
	To eliminate intercompany merchandise sales and purchases.		

The principles involved in intercompany inventory profit eliminations parallel those encountered in eliminations arising from land transfers among affiliates. Nevertheless, the procedures may seem more complex because inventory is reflected in the income statement through cost of goods sold. There is no separate gain on sale of inventory on the income statement. Rather, the unconfirmed gain is part of the ending or beginning inventory balance, and is eliminated by adjusting cost of goods sold. Recall this familiar calculation:

$$\textbf{Cost of goods sold} = \textbf{Beginning inventory} + \textbf{Purchases} - \textbf{Ending inventory}$$

Eliminating intercompany profit in *ending* inventory *increases* cost of goods sold, whereas eliminating intercompany profit in *beginning* inventory *decreases* cost of goods sold. In addition, the total dollar amount of inventory transfers must be eliminated to avoid overstating consolidated sales revenue and cost of goods sold.

Unconfirmed Profit in Ending Inventory

The eliminating entry to remove unconfirmed profit in ending inventory is the same whether the parent or the subsidiary holds the inventory—in other words, whether the transaction was *upstream* or *downstream*. Unconfirmed profit is removed from the purchaser's ending inventory, increasing cost of goods sold. Suppose Jordan sold merchandise priced at $5,000,000 to Parrish during 2016, and at December 31, 2016, Parrish's ending inventory includes $840,000 purchased from Jordan. Jordan's markup is 20 percent of cost. The eliminating entries are:

December 31, 2016, consolidation eliminating entries		
(I-1) Sales...	5,000,000	
Cost of goods sold		5,000,000
To eliminate intercompany merchandise sale and purchases.		
(I-2) Cost of goods sold...	140,000	
Inventory		140,000
To eliminate unconfirmed intercompany profit in ending inventory; $140,000 =		
$840,000 − ($840,000/1.2).		

If Jordan's markup was 20 percent on *selling price*, the unconfirmed intercompany profit in elimination (I-2) is $168,000 (= 20% × $840,000). The entry to eliminate the unconfirmed profit in ending inventory is the same for upstream sales, in which Parrish sold the merchandise and it is now held in Jordan's year-end inventory.

Because the increase in cost of goods sold reduces consolidated income, adjustments must be made to Jordan's equity in net income and the 20 percent noncontrolling interest in net income:

Effect of $140,000 Unconfirmed Profit in Ending Inventory		
Transaction Type	**Equity in Net Income**	**20% Noncontrolling Interest in Net Income**
Downstream..............	Subtract $140,000	No effect
Upstream	Subtract $112,000	Subtract $28,000

Unconfirmed Profit in Beginning Inventory

Unconfirmed profits in the *ending* inventory of one period mean that next period's *beginning* inventory also reflects those profits. Working paper eliminations do not affect the companies' books, so at the next consolidation point cost of goods sold is *overstated by the previous year's unconfirmed profits*. A working paper elimination transfers these gains into current year income by reducing cost of goods sold. In effect, this procedure assumes that the profits are confirmed in the second year through the sale of the inventory to outside customers. Any such profits not actually confirmed during the current year are included in unconfirmed profits removed from the ending inventory. As in the earlier discussions concerning upstream and downstream sales of land, the offsetting debit is to beginning retained earnings of the subsidiary for upstream sales and to the parent's investment account for downstream sales. These adjustments are necessary for a balanced elimination for (E).

The need to transfer unconfirmed intercompany profits in beginning inventory into current year income also extends to the parent's equity in net income. Whereas unconfirmed intercompany profits in *ending* inventory were *deducted* from equity in net income, unconfirmed intercompany profits in *beginning* inventory, assumed confirmed in the current year, are *added* to equity in net income. As before, such adjustments are for the total amount of the profit in downstream sales, and for a proportional amount in upstream sales.

Continuing our illustration, if Parrish's beginning inventory for 2017 includes $840,000 purchased from Jordan—a *downstream* sale—the eliminating entry is:

December 31, 2017, consolidation eliminating entry, downstream		
(I) Investment in Parrish	140,000	
Cost of goods sold		140,000
To eliminate unconfirmed downstream intercompany profit in beginning inventory.		

If *Jordan's* beginning inventory for 2017 includes $840,000 purchased from *Parrish*—an *upstream* sale—the eliminating entry is:

December 31, 2017, consolidation eliminating entry, upstream		
(I) Retained earnings, beginning—Parrish	140,000	
Cost of goods sold		140,000
To eliminate unconfirmed upstream intercompany profit in beginning inventory.		

Because the decrease in cost of goods sold increases consolidated income, adjustments must be made to Jordan's equity in net income and the 20 percent noncontrolling interest in net income, as follows:

Effect of $140,000 Unconfirmed Profit in Beginning Inventory		
Transaction Type	**Equity in Net Income**	**20% Noncontrolling Interest in Net Income**
Downstream	Add $140,000	No effect
Upstream	Add $112,000	Add $28,000

Most companies employ a cost flow assumption such as LIFO (last-in, first-out) or FIFO (first-in, first-out). The intercompany profit elimination techniques discussed here are compatible with *any* cost-flow assumption. Our eliminations seem to imply a FIFO cost flow because any intercompany profit in beginning inventory is assumed confirmed and is added to current income.

Suppose, however, that LIFO was being used and, to simplify matters, that the ending LIFO inventory was unchanged from the beginning LIFO inventory. Therefore the beginning inventory was not sold during the year. Following our procedure, we *add* the beginning intercompany profit to current income, and *subtract* the ending intercompany profit. What is the effect on current income? Absolutely zero! The elimination of unconfirmed profit from beginning and ending inventories on the income statement has *no net effect* on current period income. Moreover, in making the elimination from ending inventory, we also remove the unconfirmed profit from the overstated inventory on the balance sheet. Under FIFO, of course, our procedure shows as confirmed the beginning intercompany profit and eliminates as unconfirmed any ending intercompany profit—precisely what is needed.

• •

Reporting Perspective

Recall from Chapter 1 that when used for external reporting, the equity method eliminates the investor's share of unconfirmed profits on intercompany merchandise sales. Intercompany revenues and cost of sales are *not* eliminated. Analysis of sales volume and gross margin can therefore be misleading, as the numbers used for analysis include the results of non-market transactions between affiliates. But when affiliates are consolidated, intercompany revenues and cost of sales reflect only transactions with outside customers. To illustrate, suppose an investor sells merchandise for $1 million to outside customers. Cost of sales is $800,000. The investor also sells merchandise costing $600,000 to its affiliate for $1 million. Suppose for simplicity that the affiliate makes no sales during the year. Using the equity method for an unconsolidated affiliate, the investor adjusts its equity in net income of the affiliate for the unconfirmed profit on merchandise sales, but does *not* adjust its sales or cost of sales numbers. Its gross margin on sales is 30 percent [= ($2,000,000 − $800,000 − $600,000)/$2,000,000]. If the investor controls and consolidates its affiliate, the intercompany sales and unconfirmed profits are eliminated. Gross margin on sales drops to 20 percent [= ($1,000,000 − $800,000)/$1,000,000]. Unlike the equity method, the consolidation process removes the effect of non-market sales from reported gross margin.

• •

BUSINESS APPLICATION   Crocs, Inc.

Crocs, Inc. designs and sells footwear, apparel, and related accessories. Its footwear comes in a variety of colors and is made from Croslite, a unique resin, producing casual shoes that are lightweight, soft and recyclable. Crocs' wholly-owned subsidiaries include **Jibbitz, LLC**, which makes charms that decorate Crocs shoes, and **Ocean Minded, LLC**, which designs, manufactures, markets and distributes beach and sport sandals. Because Jibbitz and Ocean Minded are subsidiaries, they maintain separate books that reflect all their transactions, including transactions with Crocs, Inc. These subsidiaries likely do business with Crocs on a regular basis, through merchandise and raw materials transfers and marketing services. For example, Crocs provides the foot beds necessary for production of Ocean Minded sandals, creating intercompany revenues, expenses, receivables and payables, and unconfirmed profits in the subsidiaries' beginning and ending inventories of foot beds. In preparing consolidated financial statements, the accountants at Crocs, Inc. must eliminate the effects of these intercompany transactions.

REVIEW 1   •   Intercompany Eliminations: Land and Merchandise Transfers

Protective Workshoes, Inc. owns 90 percent of the voting stock of Sandalite, Inc., acquired at book value several years ago. The fair value of the noncontrolling interest equaled 10 percent of Sandalite's book value. It is now December 31, 2017, and you are preparing the consolidated financial statements of Protective. The following information relates to its intercompany transactions with Sandalite.

1. Protective sold land costing $3,000,000 to Sandalite during 2015 for $3,500,000. Sandalite sold the land to an outside party for $3,300,000 in 2017.
2. Sandalite sells merchandise to Protective at a markup of 30 percent on cost. Protective sells merchandise to Sandalite at a markup of 20 percent on sales. Information on 2017 intercompany merchandise transactions is:

	Protective	Sandalite
Sales to affiliate	$14,000,000	$26,000,000
Beginning inventory balance purchased from affiliate	1,235,000	1,500,000
Ending inventory balance purchased from affiliate	1,378,000	1,125,000

Sandalite reported net income of $1,700,000 in 2017. Protective uses the complete equity method to report its investment in Sandalite on its separate books.

Required

a. Prepare eliminating entries (I) at December 31, 2017, in journal entry form.
b. Calculate Protective's equity in net income for 2017, and the consolidated noncontrolling interest in net income for 2017.

Solutions are located after the chapter assignments.

INTERCOMPANY TRANSFERS OF DEPRECIABLE ASSETS

LO5 Prepare eliminating entries for intercompany transfers of depreciable assets.

Though less common than intercompany inventory sales, transfers of depreciable assets between affiliates also require eliminating entries when preparing consolidated statements. The complication results from the way in which intercompany gains on depreciable assets are assumed confirmed. Recall that gains and profits arising on intercompany transfers of land and inventory *are confirmed when the items are sold to outsiders*. In contrast, *confirmation of intercompany gains on depreciable assets normally is linked to their depreciation*. As the book values of depreciable assets are written down, their services are assumed to be included in the goods and services sold externally by the purchasing affiliate. Because depreciation represents the expiration of assets' services, it also represents the "sale" of the assets' services to outsiders.

Reporting Perspective

For reasons of simplicity and materiality, we assume in this chapter that the gain or loss on intercompany transfers of noncurrent assets is confirmed through the write-off of the assets, whether it is in the form of depreciation, amortization, or impairment losses. This is, of course, not strictly true. If the purchasing affiliate is a manufacturing concern, and the asset is used in the manufacturing process, its write-off is included in the cost of the manufactured goods. For example, if a parent sells manufacturing equipment to its subsidiary, the subsidiary reports depreciation on that equipment as part of overhead, allocated to its work-in-process and finished goods inventories. The write-off affects income through cost of goods sold, and then only when the inventories are sold. Therefore the intercompany gain or loss is confirmed when the purchasing affiliate's inventory is *sold,* not when the write-off occurs. Similarly, for intercompany transfers of raw materials, profits are confirmed when merchandise containing the raw materials is sold, not when the materials are used. Our discussion above assumes that the cost of the use of the transferred asset affects income directly, and is not added to manufactured inventories that are sold at a later date. In practice, as long as the purchasing affiliate's manufactured inventory balances remain relatively stable, our simplifying assumption does not materially impact the result.

Objectives of the Eliminations

When one affiliate transfers a depreciable asset to another affiliate, the price charged to the purchasing affiliate typically differs from the asset's net book value (original acquisition cost less accumulated depreciation) to the selling affiliate. If the selling affiliate records a gain (loss) on the transfer, the resulting asset balance on the books of the purchaser is greater (less) than the net book value of the asset. The general objective in consolidation is to remove the effects of the intercompany transaction, treating it as if it had never occurred. From this general objective, we derive three specific objectives for our working paper eliminations:

- Eliminate the unconfirmed intercompany gain or loss.
- Eliminate the unconfirmed intercompany gain or loss from the amount of depreciation recorded by the purchasing affiliate—the difference between the annual depreciation expense recorded by the purchasing affiliate and the amount based on original acquisition cost.
- Restate the balances in the asset and accumulated depreciation accounts so that they are based on original acquisition cost.

Eliminations in Year of Transfer

Suppose that on January 2, 2016, Jordan sells equipment with a 10-year remaining life to Parrish for $4,500,000. The equipment originally cost Jordan $5,000,000 several years ago, and at the date of transfer total reported depreciation was $2,000,000. Jordan records a gain of $1,500,000 [= $4,500,000 − ($5,000,000 − $2,000,000)]. Assuming the equipment remains on Parrish's books at year-end and that Parrish uses straight-line depreciation, the separate companies report the following on their 2016 financial statements:

	Jordan	Parrish
Balance sheet, December 31, 2016		
Equipment	$ —	$4,500,000
Accumulated depreciation	—	450,000
2016 Income statement		
Depreciation expense.		450,000
Gain on sale of equipment	1,500,000	—

From a consolidated viewpoint, depreciation expense for 2016 based on original cost is $300,000 [= ($5,000,000 − $2,000,000)/10]. On December 31, 2016, the equipment is reported in consolidation at its original cost of $5,000,000, with accumulated depreciation of $2,300,000 [= $2,000,000 + $300,000]. The following eliminating entries accomplish these goals:

December 31, 2016, consolidation eliminating entries		
(I-1) Gain on sale of equipment	1,500,000	
Equipment		1,500,000
To eliminate unconfirmed gain on intercompany transfer of equipment.		
(I-2) Accumulated depreciation	150,000	
Depreciation expense		150,000
To eliminate the excess annual depreciation expense recorded by the purchasing affiliate; $150,000 = $1,500,000/10.		
(I-3) Equipment	2,000,000	
Accumulated depreciation.		2,000,000
To restate the asset and accumulated depreciation accounts to their original acquisition cost basis. The amount of adjustment equals the accumulated depreciation at the date of transfer.		

Taken together, the above entries restate the asset, accumulated depreciation, and depreciation expense accounts so that they reflect *original acquisition cost*. At the date of transfer, January 2, 2016, the unconfirmed gain is $1,500,000. As time passes, this gain is *confirmed* by *reducing depreciation expense* in the second entry above. Although the discussion above illustrates a downstream transfer of equipment, Parrish may also sell depreciable assets to Jordan. In the year of transfer, the eliminating entries are the same whether the transfer is downstream or upstream.

Because the eliminating entries affect consolidated income, they also affect Jordan's equity in net income and, if upstream, the 20 percent noncontrolling interest in net income. The intercompany gain on *downstream* transfers is *attributed to the parent*, affecting only the parent's equity in net income. On *upstream* transfers, the *gain belongs to the subsidiary*, affecting both the parent's equity in net income and the noncontrolling interest in consolidated income. Using the example above, equity in net income and noncontrolling interest in net income for 2016 are affected as follows:

Effect of $1,500,000 Unconfirmed Gain on Intercompany Transfers of Depreciable Assets (10-year life) Year of Transfer		
Transaction Type	**Equity in Net Income**	**20% Noncontrolling Interest in Net Income**
Downstream	Subtract $1,500,000	No effect
	Add $150,000	
Upstream	Subtract $1,200,000	Subtract $300,000
	Add $120,000	Add $30,000

Eliminations in Subsequent Years

At consolidation points subsequent to the year of sale, we make eliminations to achieve the three consolidation objectives previously discussed. Fortunately, only the entry made to eliminate the unconfirmed intercompany gain as of the beginning of the year differs from elimination entries made in the year of intercompany sale. The same entries made in the year of sale to eliminate the excess annual depreciation expense and accumulated depreciation and to restate the asset and accumulated depreciation accounts to their original cost basis are made at each subsequent consolidation point. Of course, the amount of excess depreciation expense eliminated each year is different when accelerated depreciation is used.

In the year of sale we first eliminated the entire gain and then recognized the amount confirmed by reducing depreciation expense. As with land and inventory transfers, in subsequent years the beginning-of-year unconfirmed gains on *upstream* sales are removed by *reducing the subsidiary's beginning retained earnings*. Beginning-of-year unconfirmed gains on *downstream* sales are eliminated by *increasing the investment account*.

Continuing our illustration, on December 31, 2017, suppose the purchasing affiliate still holds the equipment. If Jordan sold the equipment downstream to Parrish, eliminating entries (I) required in consolidation are:

December 31, 2017, consolidation eliminating entries, downstream

(I-1)	Investment in Parrish	1,350,000	
	Accumulated depreciation	150,000	
	Equipment		1,500,000
	To eliminate beginning-of-year unconfirmed gain on downstream intercompany transfer of equipment.		
(I-2)	Accumulated depreciation	150,000	
	Depreciation expense		150,000
	To eliminate the excess annual depreciation expense recorded by the purchasing affiliate.		
(I-3)	Equipment	2,000,000	
	Accumulated depreciation...............................		2,000,000
	To restate the asset and accumulated depreciation accounts to their original acquisition cost basis.		

If Parrish transferred the equipment to Jordan, the eliminating entries are:

December 31, 2017, consolidation eliminating entries, upstream

(I-1)	Retained earnings, beginning—Parrish	1,350,000	
	Accumulated depreciation	150,000	
	Equipment		1,500,000
	To eliminate beginning-of-year unconfirmed gain on upstream intercompany transfer of equipment.		
(I-2)	Accumulated depreciation.	150,000	
	Depreciation expense		150,000
	To eliminate the excess annual depreciation expense recorded by the purchasing affiliate.		
(I-3)	Equipment	2,000,000	
	Accumulated depreciation...............................		2,000,000
	To restate the asset and accumulated depreciation accounts to their original acquisition cost basis.		

Only the first upstream eliminating entry differs from the downstream eliminations. Whereas the upstream beginning-of-year unconfirmed gain reduces the subsidiary's beginning retained earnings, the downstream beginning-of-year unconfirmed gain increases the investment account.

Equity in net income and noncontrolling interest in net income for 2017 are affected by the reduction in depreciation expense as follows:

Effect of $1,500,000 Unconfirmed Gain on Intercompany Transfers of Depreciable Assets (10-year life) Subsequent Year		
Transaction Type	**Equity in Net Income**	**20% Noncontrolling Interest in Net Income**
Downstream...............	Add $150,000	No effect
Upstream	Add $120,000	Add $30,000

We repeat this consolidation procedure as long as the equipment remains within the consolidated entity. The unconfirmed gain eliminated from the investment account or the subsidiary's beginning retained earnings on a downstream or upstream transfer, respectively, equals the original gain less the confirmed portion of the gain as of the beginning of the year. For example, at December 31, 2018, the beginning-of-year unconfirmed gain is $1,200,000, or the original gain of $1,500,000 less the amounts confirmed through reduction in depreciation expense in 2016 and 2017, $150,000 + $150,000.

Eliminations in Year of Sale to Outside Party

Sale of the depreciable asset to an outside party in a subsequent year requires that the remaining uncon-firmed intercompany gain be recognized in consolidated net income in that subsequent year. If the original intercompany gain was *upstream*, the working paper entry transfers the beginning-of-year unconfirmed intercompany gain *out of the subsidiary's retained earnings* and into current income. In the *downstream* case, the unconfirmed gain is *added back to the investment account* from which it had been previously deducted via equity in net income, and is recognized in current income.

The parent's equity in net income in the year of external sale includes all of the now-confirmed downstream intercompany gain, or the parent's share of the now-confirmed upstream gain. If the inter-company sale was upstream, the noncontrolling interest in net income is increased by the noncontrolling interest's share of the now-confirmed intercompany gain.

Suppose Jordan originally sold the equipment to Parrish on January 2, 2016, and on January 2, 2018, two years later, Parrish sells the equipment to an outside party for $3,800,000. Parrish's books report a $200,000 gain on sale of equipment [= $3,800,000 − ($4,500,000 − 2 × ($4,500,000/10))]. *From the viewpoint of the consolidated entity*, the book value of the equipment on January 2, 2018, is $2,400,000 [= $3,000,000 − (2 × ($3,000,000/10)], and the 2018 gain on the sale is $1,400,000 (= $3,800,000 − $2,400,000). This eliminating entry corrects the $200,000 gain already reported on Parrish's books:

2018 consolidation eliminating entry, downstream		
(I) Investment in Parrish	1,200,000	
Gain on sale of equipment.		1,200,000
To recognize the remaining unconfirmed gain as confirmed.		

If Parrish originally sold the equipment to Jordan, this elimination corrects the $200,000 gain already reported on Jordan's books in 2018:

2018 consolidation eliminating entry, upstream		
(I) Retained earnings, beginning—Parrish	1,200,000	
Gain on sale of equipment.		1,200,000
To recognize the remaining unconfirmed gain as confirmed.		

This eliminating entry affects consolidated income, so the parent's equity in net income and noncontrol-ling interest in consolidated net income are adjusted as follows:

Effect of Remaining Unconfirmed $1,200,000 Gain on **Intercompany Transfers of Depreciable Assets** **Year of Sale to Outside Party**		
Transaction Type	**Equity in Net Income**	**20% Noncontrolling Interest in Net Income**
Downstream	Add $1,200,000	No effect
Upstream	Add $960,000	Add $240,000

Once the equipment is sold to an outside party, no eliminations are required in subsequent years.

REVIEW 2 • Intercompany Eliminations: Depreciable Asset Transfers

Refer to the information in review problem #1. Add the following additional information:

1. On January 2, 2014, Protective sold equipment with $10,000,000 original cost and accumulated deprecia-tion of $3,000,000 to Sandalite for $9,000,000. On that date the equipment had a remaining life of five years, straight-line. Sandalite still holds the equipment at December 31, 2017.

continued

2. On June 30, 2016, Sandalite sold a building costing $15,000,000, with accumulated depreciation of $2,000,000, to Protective for $10,500,000. On that date the building had a remaining life of 20 years, straight-line. Protective still holds the building at December 31, 2017.

Required

a. Prepare eliminating entries (I) at December 31, 2017, in journal entry form.
b. Calculate Protective's equity in net income for 2017, and the consolidated noncontrolling interest in net income for 2017.

Solutions are located after the chapter assignments.

INTERNATIONAL FINANCIAL REPORTING STANDARDS FOR INTERCOMPANY TRANSACTIONS

IFRS for consolidating the financial statements of a parent and its subsidiaries are found in *IFRS 10*, Consolidated Financial Statements. Like U.S. GAAP, financial statements consolidated under IFRS present the results as if the affiliated group is a single economic entity. Intergroup balances and transactions and unconfirmed profits in assets such as land, inventory and depreciable assets are eliminated in full. Therefore the procedures described in this chapter apply also to companies reporting using IFRS.

BUSINESS APPLICATION   Reconciling Intercompany Transactions

To perform intercompany eliminations, the records of the related parties must agree. If the parent reports a €500,000 receivable from its subsidiary, the subsidiary must report a €500,000 payable to the parent. Downstream merchandise sales recorded by the parent at €1,000,000 must initially be valued at €1,000,000 in the subsidiary's inventory account. However, in many cases errors, timing issues or differences in information systems cause parent and subsidiary records to disagree. Before eliminations can be made, intercompany transactions must be reconciled. A 2005 article in CFO Magazine provides a humorous comment on this process.

> "Mention intercompany transactions to finance managers, and most get a peculiar look on their faces—a look most readily compared to the soulless expression seen on prospective root-canal patients just before they disappear down the long hallway and into the dentist's lair. Admittedly, this may be something of an exaggeration (dentists don't have lairs). But reconciling intercompany transactions has never been a favorite pastime of finance department employees. While most accounting and financial consolidation packages include some capabilities for intercompany elimination or transaction monitoring, many programs track figures only at an aggregate level, requiring extensive analysis to resolve variances."

The article describes the situation at **Ferrero International Group**, headquartered in Luxembourg, and known for its Ferrero Rocher chocolates, Nutella chocolate hazelnut spread, and Tic Tac mints.

> In the past, workers at Ferrero's 50 subsidiaries manually input transaction data, with the balances keyed separately into the company's reporting system. This created a double loading of data (the preferred method for guaranteeing that mistakes make their way into a ledger).

Financial software and centralized systems facilitate reconciliation of intercompany transactions. In Ferrero's case, the consolidation department now has web access to detailed integrated information on intercompany transactions, allowing it to analyze the causes of discrepancies on a timely basis. (*Source*: Esther Shein, "Other Invoices, Other Rooms," *CFO Magazine*, July 1, 2005.)

COMPREHENSIVE ILLUSTRATION

We complete this chapter—and the mergers and acquisitions section of this text—with a comprehensive example illustrating many of the consolidation reporting concepts discussed in Chapters 3 through 6.

Adonis Corporation, a producer of sportswear, acquired 90 percent of the voting stock of Reelock Company, an athletic footwear manufacturer, on January 2, 2013, at an acquisition cost of $27,830,000. Reelock's book value was $2 million at the date of acquisition, and the estimated fair value of the noncontrolling interest was $2,170,000. Reelock's assets and liabilities were fairly reported except plant and equipment with a 10-year remaining life was undervalued by $7 million, long-term debt with a 4-year remaining term was overvalued by $400,000, and two previously unreported identifiable intangibles met the criteria for capitalization under *ASC Topic 805*: an order backlog with a 2-year life, valued at $1 million, and favorable leaseholds with a 5-year life, valued at $3 million. All revaluations are written off on a straight-line basis.

Goodwill arising from this acquisition is tested annually for impairment. Accumulated impairment for 2013–2015 was $1 million. Impairment for 2016 is $200,000.

Intercompany transactions between Adonis and Reelock are as follows:

- In 2014, Reelock sold land costing $5 million to Adonis for $5.5 million. In 2016, Adonis sold the land to a real estate investment firm for $6.5 million.

- Total 2016 retail merchandise sales by Reelock to Adonis (upstream) were $3 million. Adonis' January 1, 2016 inventory balance includes $400,000 in merchandise purchased from Reelock. Its December 31, 2016 inventory balance includes $450,000 purchased from Reelock. Reelock sells to Adonis at a 20 percent markup on sales. At year-end, Adonis owes Reelock $100,000 related to merchandise sales.

- Total 2016 retail merchandise sales by Adonis to Reelock (downstream) were $2 million. Reelock's January 1, 2016 inventory balance includes $300,000 in merchandise purchased from Adonis. Its December 31, 2016 inventory balance includes $240,000 purchased from Adonis. Adonis sells to Reelock at a 20 percent markup on cost. At year-end, Reelock owes Adonis $85,000 related to merchandise sales.

- On January 2, 2013 Adonis sold equipment costing $5 million with $3 million accumulated depreciation, and a 10-year remaining life, straight-line, to Reelock for $3.5 million. Reelock still holds the equipment.

- In 2016, Adonis charged Reelock $500,000 for marketing services costing $400,000. At year-end, Reelock owes Adonis $25,000 related to these services.

Exhibit 6.1 shows the consolidation working paper at December 31, 2016, with the separate account balances for Adonis and Reelock.

Total acquired goodwill and its allocation between the parent and noncontrolling interests is as follows:

Acquisition cost		$27,830,000
Fair value of noncontrolling interest		2,170,000
Total fair value		30,000,000
Book value of Reelock	$2,000,000	
Difference between fair value and book value:		
Plant and equipment	7,000,000	
Identifiable intangible: order backlog	1,000,000	
Identifiable intangible: favorable leaseholds	3,000,000	
Long-term debt	400,000	13,400,000
Total goodwill		$16,600,000
Goodwill to controlling interest		
Acquisition cost		$27,830,000
Less controlling interest in the fair value of Reelock's identifiable net assets:		
90% × $13,400,000		(12,060,000)
Controlling interest's share		$15,770,000
Goodwill to noncontrolling interest		
Total goodwill		$16,600,000
Less goodwill to controlling interest		(15,770,000)
Noncontrolling interest's share		$ 830,000

Adonis is therefore allocated 95 percent of the goodwill (= $15,770,000/$16,600,000).

We calculate 2016 equity in net income and noncontrolling interest in net income as follows:

	Total	Equity in net income	Noncontrolling interest in net income
Reelok's reported net income for 2016 (1)................	$2,000,000	$1,800,000	$200,000
Adjustments for revaluation write-offs:			
Plant and equipment ($7,000,000/10)	(700,000)	(630,000)	(70,000)
Favorable leaseholds ($3,000,000/5)	(600,000)	(540,000)	(60,000)
Long-term debt ($400,000/4)	(100,000)	(90,000)	(10,000)
Goodwill (95:5 ratio)	(200,000)	(190,000)	(10,000)
Adjustments for intercompany transactions:			
Upstream confirmed gain on land sale (2)	500,000	450,000	50,000
Upstream confirmed profit in beginning inventory (3)	80,000	72,000	8,000
Downstream confirmed profit in beginning inventory (4)	50,000	50,000	—
Upstream unconfirmed profit in ending inventory (5)........	(90,000)	(81,000)	(9,000)
Downstream unconfirmed profit in ending inventory (6)......	(40,000)	(40,000)	—
Downstream confirmed gain on sale of equipment (7).......	150,000	150,000	—
	$1,050,000	$ 951,000	$ 99,000

(1) Reelock's 2016 reported net income is $2,000,000 = $33,000,000 + $2,000,000 − $25,000,000 − $8,000,000; see Exhibit 6.1.
(2) $500,000 = $5,500,000 − $5,000,000.
(3) $80,000 = $400,000 × 20%.
(4) $50,000 = $300,000 − ($300,000/1.2).
(5) $90,000 = $450,000 × 20%.
(6) $40,000 = $240,000 − ($240,000/1.2).
(7) $150,000 = [$3,500,000 − ($5,000,000 − $3,000,000)]/10.

Based on the account balances reported in Exhibit 6.1, here are the eliminating entries needed to consolidate the 2016 financial statements of Adonis and Reelock, in journal entry form:

(C)	Equity in net income of Reelock..	951,000	
	Equity in other comprehensive income of Reelock	36,000	
	Investment in Reelock...		987,000
	To eliminate equity in net income and other comprehensive income on the parent's books and restore the investment account to its beginning-of-year value.		
(I-1)	Retained earnings, January 1..	500,000	
	Gain on sale of land...		500,000
	To recognize the confirmed gain on the upstream land sale.		
(I-2)	Sales revenue...	5,000,000	
	Cost of goods sold		5,000,000
	To eliminate intercompany sales and purchases ($5,000,000 = $3,000,000 + $2,000,000).		
(I-3)	Retained earnings, January 1..	80,000	
	Cost of goods sold		80,000
	To recognize the confirmed upstream profit in beginning inventory.		
(I-4)	Investment in Reelock	50,000	
	Cost of goods sold		50,000
	To recognize the confirmed downstream profit in beginning inventory.		
(I-5)	Cost of goods sold..	130,000	
	Current assets		130,000
	To eliminate the unconfirmed upstream and downstream profit in ending inventory ($130,000 = $90,000 + $40,000).		
(I-6)	Investment in Reelock	1,050,000	
	Accumulated depreciation..	450,000	
	Plant and equipment..		1,500,000
	To remove the unconfirmed beginning-of-year profit on downstream sale of equipment [$1,050,000 = $1,500,000 − (($1,500,000/10) × 3)].		

continued

continued from prior page

(I-7)	Accumulated depreciation	150,000	
	Operating expenses		150,000

To recognize the confirmed profit (excess depreciation) on downstream sale of equipment ($150,000 = $1,500,000/10).

(I-8)	Plant and equipment	3,000,000	
	Accumulated depreciation.		3,000,000

To restate the asset and accumulated depreciation accounts to their original acquisition cost basis.

(I-9)	Sales revenue.	500,000	
	Operating expenses		500,000

To eliminate the intercompany sale of marketing services.

(I-10)	Current liabilities.	210,000	
	Current assets		210,000

To eliminate intercompany receivables/payables ($210,000 = $100,000 + $85,000 + $25,000).

(E)	Capital stock	1,400,000	
	Retained earnings, January 1.	7,720,000	
	Accumulated other comprehensive income, January 1.	300,000	
	Investment in Reelock (90%).		8,478,000
	Noncontrolling interest in Reelock (10%)		942,000

To eliminate the subsidiary's beginning-of-year capital stock and accumulated other comprehensive income account and the remainder of its beginning retained earnings account against the beginning-of-year book value portion of the investment account, and recognize the beginning-of-year book value of the noncontrolling interest. [$7,720,000 = $8,300,000 − $500,000 (I-1) − $80,000 (I-3)].

(R)	Plant and equipment	7,000,000	
	Identifiable intangibles	1,200,000	
	Long-term debt	100,000	
	Goodwill	15,600,000	
	Accumulated depreciation.		2,100,000
	Investment in Reelock		20,400,000
	Noncontrolling interest in Reelock.		1,400,000

To revalue Reelock's net assets as of the beginning of the year and allocate the revaluations to the controlling and noncontrolling interest.
$20,400,000 = (90% × $6,200,000) + (95% × $15,600,000);
$1,400,000 = (10% × $6,200,000) + (5% × $15,600,000);
$6,200,000 = ($7,000,000 + $1,200,000 + $100,000 − $2,100,000).

(O)	Operating expenses	1,600,000	
	Accumulated depreciation.		700,000
	Identifiable intangibles.		600,000
	Long-term debt		100,000
	Goodwill.		200,000

To write off the revaluations for the current year.

(N)	Noncontrolling interest in net income	99,000	
	Noncontrolling interest in other comprehensive income	4,000	
	Noncontrolling interest in Reelock.		103,000

To recognize the noncontrolling interest in the subsidiary's comprehensive income.

Exhibit 6.1 displays these eliminating entries, and each account's consolidated balance. Using the consolidated account balances in Exhibit 6.1, we prepare the consolidated financial statements for 2016.

EXHIBIT 6.1 Consolidation Working Paper for Adonis and Reelock, December 31, 2016

	Accounts Taken From Books Dr (Cr)		Eliminations		Consolidated Balances
	Adonis	Reelock	Dr	Cr	Dr (Cr)
Current assets	$ 8,000,000	$ 2,040,000		$ 130,000 (I-5)	$ 9,700,000
				210,000 (I-10)	
Plant and equipment	100,000,000	30,000,000	(I-8) $ 3,000,000	1,500,000 (I-6)	138,500,000
			(R) 7,000,000		
Accumulated depreciation	(25,000,000)	(13,000,000)	(I-6) 450,000	3,000,000 (I-8)	(43,200,000)
			(I-7) 150,000	2,100,000 (R)	
				700,000 (O)	
Investment in Reelock	28,765,000	—	(I-4) 50,000	987,000 (C)	—
			(I-6) 1,050,000	8,478,000 (E)	
				20,400,000 (R)	
Identifiable intangible assets	—	—	(R) 1,200,000	600,000 (O)	600,000
Goodwill	—	—	(R) 15,600,000	200,000 (O)	15,400,000
Current liabilities.	(17,000,000)	(2,500,000)	(I-10) 210,000		(19,290,000)
Long-term debt	(66,278,000)	(4,500,000)	(R) 100,000	100,000 (O)	(70,778,000)
Capital stock	(2,000,000)	(1,400,000)	(E) 1,400,000		(2,000,000)
Retained earnings, January 1.	(24,000,000)	(8,300,000)	(I-1) 500,000		(24,000,000)
			(I-3) 80,000		
			(E) 7,720,000		
Accumulated other comprehensive income, January 1	(1,000,000)	(300,000)	(E) 300,000		(1,000,000)
Noncontrolling interest.	—	—		942,000 (E)	(2,445,000)
				1,400,000 (R)	
				103,000 (N)	
Dividends	500,000	—			500,000
Sales revenue.	(53,400,000)	(33,000,000)	(I-2) 5,000,000		(80,900,000)
			(I-9) 500,000		
Gains on asset sales	(1,500,000)	(2,000,000)		500,000 (I-1)	(4,000,000)
Equity in net income of Reelock.	(951,000)	—	(C) 951,000		—
Equity in other comprehensive income of Reelock.	(36,000)	—	(C) 36,000		—
Cost of goods sold.	38,000,000	25,000,000	(I-5) 130,000	5,000,000 (I-2)	58,000,000
				80,000 (I-3)	
				50,000 (I-4)	
Operating expenses.	16,000,000	8,000,000	(O) 1,600,000	150,000 (I-7)	24,950,000
				500,000 (I-9)	
Other comprehensive income	(100,000)	(40,000)			(140,000)
Noncontrolling interest in net income . . .	—	—	(N) 99,000		99,000
Noncontrolling interest in other comprehensive income.	—	—	(N) 4,000		4,000
Totals	$ 0	$ 0	$47,130,000	$47,130,000	$ 0

ADONIS CORPORATION AND SUBSIDIARY
Consolidated Statement of Income and Comprehensive Income
For Year Ended December 31, 2016

Sales revenue.	$80,900,000
Gains on asset sales	4,000,000
Cost of goods sold.	(58,000,000)
Operating expenses.	(24,950,000)
Consolidated net income.	**1,950,000**
Less: Noncontrolling interest in net income.	(99,000)
Net income attributable to Adonis	$ 1,851,000
Consolidated net income	$ 1,950,000
Plus: Other comprehensive income	140,000
Consolidated comprehensive income	2,090,000
Less: Noncontrolling interest in comprehensive income (1).	(103,000)
Comprehensive income attributable to Adonis	$ 1,987,000

(1) $99,000 + $4,000 = $103,000.

ADONIS CORPORATION AND SUBSIDIARY
Consolidated Balance Sheet
December 31, 2016

Assets		Liabilities and Stockholders' Equity	
Current assets	$ 9,700,000	Current liabilities.	$ 19,290,000
Plant and equipment, net of			
$43,200,000 accumulated			
depreciation	95,300,000	Long-term debt	70,778,000
Identifiable intangible assets	600,000	Total liabilities.	90,068,000
Goodwill	15,400,000	Stockholders' equity	
		Adonis stockholders' equity:	
		Capital stock.	2,000,000
		Retained earnings (2)	25,351,000
		Accumulated other comprehensive	
		income (3)	1,136,000
		Total Adonis stockholders' equity	28,487,000
		Noncontrolling interest.	2,445,000
		Total stockholders' equity	30,932,000
Total assets	$121,000,000	Total liabilities and stockholders' equity	$121,000,000

(2) $24,000,000 + $1,851,000 − $500,000 = $25,351,000.
(3) $1,000,000 + $140,000 − $4,000 = $1,136,000.

REVIEW OF KEY CONCEPTS •

LO 1   **Prepare eliminating entries for intercompany service and financing transactions. (p. 230)** Service and financing transactions between the parent and subsidiary require elimination of related receivables and payables, revenues and expenses. These eliminations are necessary to avoid duplicating balances, and involve no unconfirmed profits.

LO 2   **Describe elimination of unconfirmed profits and their effect on equity in net income and noncontrolling interest in net income. (p. 231)** Intercompany profit refers to the difference between the intercompany transfer price and the net book value to the selling affiliate. In consolidation, the entire amount of the unconfirmed intercompany profit is eliminated on the working paper. Elimination of unconfirmed intercompany profits on upstream sales—from subsidiary to parent—is proportionate between the controlling and noncontrolling interests, and the noncontrolling interest in net income is affected. Elimination of unconfirmed intercompany profit on **downstream sales**—from parent to subsidiary—is entirely against the parent's net income. Following the one-line consolidation concept, **equity in net income reflects the same eliminations of unconfirmed intercompany profits as those made in computing consolidated net income.** The parent's share of the subsidiary's reported net income is reduced by the total unconfirmed intercompany profits on downstream sales and by the parent's share of the unconfirmed intercompany profits on upstream sales.

Prepare eliminating entries for intercompany transfers of land. (p. 233) Eliminating entries for intercompany profits or losses on **transfers of land** remaining within the consolidated entity **restore the land balance to its original cost** and remove the unconfirmed gain or loss. When the intercompany gain or loss is confirmed through sale to a third party, an eliminating entry **reclassifies the gain or loss to consolidated net income.** **LO 3**

Prepare eliminating entries for intercompany transfers of inventory. (p. 236) Three eliminating entries for inventory sales between the parent and subsidiary are necessary to (1) remove duplication in sales and cost of sales, (2) confirm the intercompany markup on beginning inventory, and (3) remove the unconfirmed markup on ending inventory. **LO 4**

Prepare eliminating entries for intercompany transfers of depreciable assets. (p. 240) Intercompany profit on transfers of depreciable assets is **confirmed as the assets depreciate.** Eliminating entries restore the asset, accumulated depreciation and depreciation expense balances to amounts shown as if no intercompany transfer occurred. **LO 5**

Assignments with the ⊘ in the margin are available in BusinessCourse.
See the Preface of the book for details.

MULTIPLE CHOICE QUESTIONS ·······························

1. Suzlon, a subsidiary of Patni, provides services to Patni. During 2016, Suzlon charged $3,000,000 for services provided to Patni. Cost of the services provided was $2,100,000. How should the consolidated income statement report these services? **LO 1** ⊘

	Service revenue	Service expense
a.	$3,000,000	$0
b.	$3,000,000	$2,100,000
c.	$0	$2,100,000
d.	$0	$3,000,000

2. A parent makes an interest-bearing loan to its 90%-owned subsidiary in 2016, which is still outstanding in 2017. The eliminating entries (I) on the consolidation working paper for 2017, related to this loan, **LO 1** ⊘

   a. reduce investment in subsidiary by the amount of 2016's interest revenue.
   b. reduce the subsidiary's beginning retained earnings by the amount of 2016's interest revenue.
   c. reduce investment in subsidiary by the amount of interest owing at the end of 2017.
   d. have no effect on investment in subsidiary or the subsidiary's beginning retained earnings.

3. Petronet sells merchandise to its 80-percent-owned subsidiary Sonata at a markup of 20 percent on cost. During 2017, Petronet charges Sonata $4,000,000 for merchandise sales. Sonata's 2017 beginning inventory contains $540,000 in merchandise purchased from Petronet. Sonata's 2017 ending inventory contains $480,000 in merchandise purchased from Petronet. Petronet uses the complete equity method to record its investment in Sonata. How are Petronet's 2017 equity in net income of Sonata and 2017 consolidated income to the noncontrolling interest affected by intercompany merchandise transactions? **LO 2** ⊘

	Equity in net income	Noncontrolling interest in net income
a.	$10,000 increase	$0
b.	$ 8,000 increase	$2,000 increase
c.	$12,000 increase	$0
d.	$ 9,600 increase	$2,400 increase

4. Pentamedia owns 90 percent of Sesa. At the start of 2016, Sesa sold buildings carried at $4,000,000, net, to Pentamedia for $6,000,000. The buildings had a remaining life of 10 years and straight-line depreciation is used. Pentamedia uses the complete equity method to record its investment in Sesa. Pentamedia still owns the buildings. How are Pentamedia's 2017 equity in net income of Sesa and 2017 consolidated income to the noncontrolling interest affected by the intercompany sale of buildings? **LO 2** ⊘

	Equity in net income	Noncontrolling interest in net income
a.	$200,000 increase	$0
b.	$360,000 increase	$40,000 increase
c.	$400,000 increase	$0
d.	$180,000 increase	$20,000 increase

LO 3 5. A parent sells land costing $35,000 to a subsidiary in 2016 for $55,000. The subsidiary sells the land in 2018 to a third party for $85,000. On the consolidated income statement for 2018, the gain on sale of land should be reported at:

a. $20,000
b. $50,000
c. $30,000
d. $ 0

LO 3 6. A subsidiary sells land costing $1,000,000 to its parent in 2014 for $1,400,000. The parent owns 80 percent of the subsidiary's stock. In 2017, the parent sells the land to an outside party for $550,000. What eliminating entry (I) is required on the 2017 consolidation working paper?

a. Debit the subsidiary's beginning retained earnings and credit the loss on sale of land for $400,000.
b. Debit investment in subsidiary and credit the loss on sale of land for $400,000.
c. Debit the subsidiary's beginning retained earnings and credit the loss on sale of land for $450,000.
d. Debit investment in subsidiary and credit the loss on sale of land for $450,000.

LO 4 7. A subsidiary sells merchandise to its parent at a markup of 25% on cost. In 2017, the parent paid $500,000 for merchandise received from the subsidiary. By year-end 2017, the parent has sold $400,000 of the merchandise to outside customers for $450,000, but still holds the other $100,000 in its ending inventory. Which statement is **true** concerning how this information should be reported on the 2017 consolidated financial statements?

a. Consolidated sales should be $450,000.
b. The consolidated ending inventory balance should be $100,000.
c. Consolidated cost of goods sold should be $400,000.
d. Consolidated cost of goods sold should be $720,000.

LO 4 8. A parent sells $30,000,000 retail value of merchandise to its subsidiary during 2016. The subsidiary's beginning inventory for 2016 contains $1,000,000 in merchandise purchased from the parent, including a markup of $200,000. The subsidiary's ending inventory for 2016 contains $1,500,000 in merchandise purchased from the parent. The markup included in the ending inventory balance is $225,000. On the 2016 consolidation working paper, eliminations (I):

a. reduce ending inventory by $200,000.
b. reduce beginning retained earnings by $225,000.
c. reduce cost of goods sold by $225,000.
d. increase the parent's investment account by $200,000.

LO 5 9. At the beginning of 2015, a parent company sold a patent, carried on its books at $4,000,000, to its subsidiary for $3,000,000. The patent had a remaining life of five years and straight-line amortization is used. It is now the end of 2017, and the subsidiary still owns the patent. On the 2017 consolidation working paper, eliminations (I):

a. increase the patent by $800,000.
b. reduce the parent's investment account by $600,000.
c. increase the subsidiary's beginning retained earnings by $200,000.
d. reduce amortization expense by $400,000.

LO 5 10. At the beginning of 2013, a subsidiary sold equipment, carried on its books at $3,000,000, net, to its parent for $5,000,000. The equipment had a remaining life of 20 years and straight-line depreciation is used. It is now the end of 2016, and the parent still owns the equipment. On the 2016 consolidation working paper, eliminations (I):

a. reduce the parent's investment account by $1,700,000.
b. reduce the subsidiary's beginning retained earnings account by $1,600,000.
c. reduce depreciation expense by $100,000.
d. reduce net equipment by $2,000,000.

EXERCISES ••

E6.1 **Downstream Intercompany Land Transactions** Saucony Company, a wholly-owned subsid- **LO 3** iary of Puma Company, purchased a tract of land from Puma in 2016 for $4,000,000. Puma originally acquired the land for $1,500,000 and accounts for its investment in Saucony using the complete equity method.

Required

a. Assuming that Saucony still owns the land, give the working paper eliminations needed for the intercompany land sale when consolidated statements are prepared at the end of 2016 and 2017.

b. If Saucony sells the land to a third party for $6,500,000 in 2018, prepare the eliminations needed for the intercompany land sale when consolidated statements are prepared at the end of 2018.

E6.2 **Upstream Intercompany Land Transactions** Source Sandals is a subsidiary of Pony Industries. **LO 3** In 2016, Pony purchased land from Source for $8,000,000. Source had carried the land at $3,400,000 on its books, prior to the sale. Pony holds the land until 2020, when it sells it to an outside party for $3,000,000.

Required

a. Prepare the eliminating entry (I) for the intercompany land sale for each of the years 2016 and 2019.

b. Prepare the eliminating entry (I) for 2020, when the land is sold to an outside party. On the consolidated income statement, what amount appears as the gain or loss on the sale of the land?

E6.3 **Downstream Intercompany Merchandise Transactions** Sketchy Shoes is a subsidiary of Pa- **LO 4** ✓ cific Brands. Pacific routinely sells merchandise to Sketchy at a 25% markup on cost. Information on intercompany merchandise transactions is below *(in thousands)*:

Inventory balance on Sketchy's books, purchased from Pacific Brands, January 1, 2017......	$ 6,250
Inventory balance on Sketchy's books, purchased from Pacific Brands, December 31, 2017...	6,625
Total sales revenue recorded by Pacific Brands on merchandise sales to Sketchy in 2017.....	250,000

Required

a. Prepare the working paper eliminating entries related to these intercompany transactions at December 31, 2017.

b. Assume Sketchy sold merchandise acquired from Pacific Brands for $300,000 during 2017. What amounts appear on the separate books of Pacific Brands and Sketchy Shoes, relating to the intercompany merchandise transactions, for sales revenue and cost of goods sold? What are consolidated sales and cost of goods sold? Show how the eliminating entries in part *a* above adjust the balances reported on the separate books of the two entities to the correct consolidated balances.

E6.4 **Upstream Intercompany Merchandise Transactions** Jimmitz Inc. is a subsidiary of Krocker **LO 4** Gear. Jimmitz sells shoe accessories to Krocker at a 20% markup on cost. Information on these intercompany merchandise transactions is below *(in thousands)*:

Inventory balance on Krocker's books, purchased from Jimmitz, January 1, 2017	$ 10,800
Inventory balance on Krocker's books, purchased from Jimmitz, December 31, 2017	10,200
Total sales revenue recorded by Jimmitz on merchandise sales to Krocker in 2017	900,000

Required

a. Prepare the working paper eliminating entries related to these intercompany transactions at December 31, 2017.

b. Krocker sold shoes containing Jimmitz's shoe accessories during 2017. What amount did Krocker and Jimmitz record as cost of goods sold for the shoe accessories in 2017? What amount should appear in consolidated cost of goods sold for these shoe accessories? Show how the eliminating entries in part *a* adjust Krocker's cost of goods sold balance to the correct consolidated balance.

⊘ LO 5   E6.5   Downstream Intercompany Equipment Transactions On July 1, 2015, Pearl Industries sold administrative equipment with a book value of $600,000 to its subsidiary, Shiek Shoes, for $700,000. At the date of sale, the equipment had a remaining life of five years. It is being straight-line depreciated on Shiek's books. It is now December 31, 2017, the end of the accounting year, and you are preparing the working paper to consolidate the trial balances of Pearl and Shiek. Shiek still owns the equipment.

Required

a. Prepare the required eliminating entries for this intercompany equipment sale for the December 31, 2017, consolidation working paper.
b. It is now December 31, 2018. Prepare the required eliminating entries for this intercompany equipment transaction for the December 31, 2018, consolidation working paper.
c. Now assume that Shiek sells the equipment to an outside party for $500,000 on January 1, 2019. Prepare the required eliminating entries for the December 31, 2019, consolidation working paper.

LO 5   E6.6   Upstream Intercompany Building Transactions Shiek Shoes sold an administrative building to its parent, Pearl Industries, on January 1, 2015, for $8,000,000. At the time of sale, the building was carried on Shiek's books at original cost of $10,000,000, with $8,500,000 of accumulated depreciation. At the date of sale, the building had a remaining life of 20 years, and straight-line depreciation is appropriate. It is now December 31, 2017, the end of the accounting year, and you are preparing the working paper to consolidate the trial balances of Pearl and Shiek. Pearl still owns the building.

Required

a. Prepare the required eliminating entries for this intercompany building sale for the December 31, 2017, consolidation working paper.
b. What balances does Pearl report in its own trial balance for this building at December 31, 2017? Consider these balances: building, original cost; accumulated depreciation, building; depreciation expense, building. What balances should be reported on the consolidated trial balance? Show how the eliminating entries in part *a* adjust Pearl's book balances to the correct consolidated balances.

⊘ LO1   E6.7   Intercompany Financing Transactions Sessions Athletic Gear borrowed $5,000,000 from its parent, PF Consolidated Inc., at an interest rate of 5%. The loan was made on September 30, 2016, with interest due semiannually on March 31 and September 30 of each year, and principal due in 2020. PF's accounting year ends on December 31. You are doing the consolidation working paper at December 31, 2017. The loan is still outstanding, and Sessions has made interest payments as required.

Required

a. What balances appear in the December 31, 2017, trial balances of PF and Sessions with respect to this intercompany loan? What balances should appear on the consolidated financial statements?
b. Prepare the working paper eliminating entries needed for this intercompany loan at December 31, 2017.

LO 1   E6.8   Intercompany Service Transactions PF Consolidated Inc. provided consulting services to its subsidiary, Sessions Athletic Gear, during 2017. PF Consolidated charged $6,000,000 of travel, salary, overhead and supplies costs to its administrative expenses account, and charged Sessions $9,000,000 for the services. By December 31, 2017, the end of PF's accounting year, Sessions has paid all but $500,000 of the balance due to PF. Sessions categorizes the services as administrative.

Required

a. What balances appear in the December 31, 2017, trial balances of PF and Sessions with respect to these intercompany services? What balances should appear on the consolidated financial statements?
b. Prepare the working paper eliminating entries needed for these intercompany services at December 31, 2017.

LO 3, 4, 5   E6.9   Various Intercompany Transactions In consolidation of Perpetual Industries and Sand Hill Company at December 31, 2017, you assemble the following data related to unconfirmed intercompany profits:

	January 1, 2017	**December 31, 2017**
Land......................................	$2,500,000	$2,500,000
Merchandise inventory......................	1,400,000	3,200,000
Equipment	800,000	600,000

The equipment is carried on the purchasing affiliate's books at $7,200,000 with accumulated depreciation of $3,600,000 (straight-line, no salvage value) at December 31, 2017. Accumulated depreciation at the date of intercompany sale was $2,000,000; the original intercompany gain was $1,200,000.

Required

a. Assume that all of the above unconfirmed intercompany profits arose from *upstream* sales. Prepare the eliminating entries related to these intercompany transactions when consolidating the financial statements of Perpetual Industries and Sand Hill Company at December 31, 2017.

b. Repeat part *a* assuming that all of the above unconfirmed intercompany profits arose from *downstream* sales.

E6.10 Intercompany Transactions, Equity Method Income and Noncontrolling Interest   Putnam   **LO 2, 3, 4, 5**
Company owns 80 percent of Swaraj Company. The excess of acquisition cost over book value was attributed entirely to previously unrecorded identifiable intangibles. For 2017, Swaraj Company reported net income of $7,000,000 and declared and paid dividends of $2,000,000. Appropriate amortization of the previously unrecorded identifiable intangibles for 2017 is $1,750,000. The following information is available regarding intercompany transactions:

1. During 2017, Swaraj sold land to Putnam at a loss of $300,000. Putnam still holds the land at December 31, 2017.
2. Putnam's ending inventory at December 31, 2017, included merchandise acquired from Swaraj; the unconfirmed profit on this inventory was $600,000.
3. Putnam's ending inventory at December 31, 2016, included merchandise acquired from Swaraj; the unconfirmed profit was $350,000.
4. On January 3, 2014, Putnam sold equipment to Swaraj at a gain of $1,000,000; at the time of sale, the remaining life of this equipment was 10 years, straight-line. Swaraj still holds the equipment at December 31, 2017.

Required

a. Calculate Putnam Company's equity in net income for 2017 and the noncontrolling interest in net income for 2017.

b. Prepare the working paper eliminations made in consolidation at December 31, 2017, related to the intercompany transactions.

E6.11 Consolidated Income Statement, Intercompany Transactions   Condensed income state-   **LO 2, 4**
ments for Pon and its 80 percent-owned subsidiary, Star, appear below.

Condensed Income Statements	Pon	Star
Sales.	$9,000,000	$4,000,000
Equity in net income of Star.	508,000	—
Cost of goods sold.	(6,000,000)	(2,500,000)
Other expenses	(2,000,000)	(600,000)
Net income.	$1,508,000	$ 900,000

Intercompany sales are $1,000,000, unconfirmed intercompany profit in Pon's beginning inventory is $110,000 and unconfirmed intercompany profit in Star's ending inventory is $60,000. At the date of combination four years ago, previously unrecorded identifiable intangibles (8-year life, straight-line) of $800,000 were recognized. The total goodwill recognized at date of business combination is shared with the noncontrolling interest according to ownership interests. This year's goodwill impairment test indicates a $200,000 reduction in value.

Required

a. Prepare a schedule to compute Pon's equity in net income and the noncontrolling interest in net income.

b. Prepare a condensed consolidated income statement for Pon and Star.

LO 2, 4, 5   E6.12   Consolidated Net Income   The following information relates to **Brown Shoe Company** and its 51 percent-owned subsidiary, **B&H Footwear**, for fiscal 2016 *(in thousands)*.

Brown Shoe Company's net income from its own operations.	$50,000
B&H Footwear's net income from its own operations	20,000
Dividends paid by Shoes.com	8,000
Acquisition date overvaluation of inventory sold in fiscal 2016	900
Reduction in depreciation expense on equipment overvalued at acquisition date	300
Amortization of discount on long-term debt created at acquisition date	100
Impairment loss on in-process R&D capitalized at acquisition date	600
Confirmed downstream inventory profit in B&H Footwear's beginning inventory	700
Unconfirmed downstream inventory profit in B&H Footwear's ending inventory	400
Downstream loss on January 2 sale of patent to B&H Footwear; 5-year life.	500

Required

a.   Brown Shoe uses the complete equity method to account for its investment in B&H on its own books. Prepare a schedule calculating equity in net income of B&H, appearing on Brown Shoe's books, and noncontrolling interest in consolidated net income, appearing on the consolidated income statement for fiscal 2016.

b.   Prepare a schedule calculating consolidated net income and consolidated net income to the controlling interest for fiscal 2016.

LO 4   E6.13   Consolidation Working Paper Eliminations, Intercompany Merchandise Sales   Prance Athleticwear Company owns all of the voting stock of Stallion Shoes. Acquisition cost was $7 million in excess of Stallion's book value of $3 million, and the excess was attributed to indefinite lived identifiable intangibles of $2 million, and $5 million of goodwill. As of the beginning of the current year, the identifiable intangibles are impaired by $500,000, and goodwill is not impaired. There is no impairment of either intangible in the current year. Following is information on intercompany merchandise transactions between Prance and Stallion for the current year:

- Intercompany profit in Prance's beginning inventory, purchased from Stallion, is $300,000.
- Intercompany profit in Stallion's beginning inventory, purchased from Prance, is $400,000.
- Intercompany profit in Prance's ending inventory, purchased from Stallion, is $200,000.
- Intercompany profit in Stallion's ending inventory, purchased from Prance, is $250,000.
- Total sales from Stallion to Prance, at the price charged to Prance, were $7 million.
- Total sales from Prance to Stallion, at the price charged to Stallion, were $5 million.

Prance uses the complete equity method to account for its investment in Stallion on its own books. The separate trial balances for Prance and Stallion at the end of the current year are below.

(in thousands)	Prance Dr (Cr)	Stallion Dr (Cr)
Current assets	$ 2,500	$ 1,500
Plant and equipment, net.	350,000	250,000
Investment in Stallion.	12,050	—
Liabilities.	(353,300)	(245,500)
Capital stock	(2,000)	(1,000)
Retained earnings, beginning.	(6,000)	(4,000)
Sales revenue.	(275,000)	(150,000)
Equity in net income.	(1,250)	—
Cost of sales.	200,000	90,000
Operating expenses.	73,000	59,000
Total	$ 0	$ 0

Required

Prepare a working paper to consolidate the trial balances of Prance and Stallion. Label your eliminating entries (C), (I), (E), and (R).

**E6.14 Consolidation Working Paper Eliminations, Intercompany Merchandise Sales, Noncon- LO 4
trolling Interest** Paymore Shoes acquired 80 percent of the voting stock of Spire Footwear on February 1, 2014, for $21 million. The fair value of the noncontrolling interest at the acquisition date was $3 million. The excess of Spire's fair value over its $4 million book value was attributed to limited life identifiable intangible assets ($5 million, 5-year life) and goodwill. Paymore's fiscal year ends January 31. As of February 1, 2017, the goodwill and identifiable intangibles are not impaired. There is no impairment of either intangible in fiscal 2018. Spire transfers merchandise to Paymore on a regular basis, at a markup of 25% on cost. Following is information on intercompany merchandise transactions for fiscal 2018:

- Balance in Paymore's beginning inventory, purchased from Spire, $1,000,000.
- Balance in Paymore's ending inventory, purchased from Spire, $750,000.
- Total sales from Spire to Paymore, at the price charged to Paymore, $25 million.

Paymore uses the complete equity method to account for its investment in Spire on its own books. The separate trial balances for Paymore and Spire at January 31, 2018, are below.

(in thousands)	Paymore Dr (Cr)	Spire Dr (Cr)
Current assets	$ 10,000	$ 4,500
Plant and equipment, net	1,200,000	750,000
Intangibles	101,360	—
Investment in Spire	22,080	—
Liabilities	(945,000)	(745,000)
Capital stock	(28,000)	(3,000)
Retained earnings, beginning	(340,000)	(5,000)
Sales revenue	(1,200,000)	(300,000)
Equity in net income	(440)	—
Cost of sales	980,000	200,000
Operating expenses	200,000	98,500
Total	$ 0	$ 0

Required
a. Calculate the allocation of goodwill between controlling and noncontrolling interests.
b. Calculate the noncontrolling interest in net income for fiscal 2018.
c. Prepare a working paper to consolidate the January 31, 2018, trial balances of Paymore and Spire. Label your eliminating entries (C), (I), (E), (R), (O), and (N).

E6.15 Consolidation Working Paper Eliminations, Variety of Intercompany Transactions Pacif- LO 3, 4, 5
ic Athletic Corporation owns all of the voting stock of Solovair Apparel. Acquisition cost was $10 million in excess of Solovair's book value of $2 million, and the excess was attributed entirely to goodwill. As of the beginning of the current year, goodwill impairment is $4 million. Current year goodwill impairment is $200,000. Following is information on intercompany transactions between Pacific and Solovair for the current year:

- Pacific sold land to Solovair in a previous year at a gain of $300,000. Solovair sold the land to an outside party in the current year.

- Intercompany profit in Pacific's beginning inventory, purchased from Solovair, is $100,000.

- Intercompany profit in Pacific's ending inventory, purchased from Solovair, is $120,000.

- Total sales from Solovair to Pacific, at the price charged to Pacific, were $5 million.

- Solovair sold equipment with a book value of $2 million to Pacific three years ago for $4.5 million. The equipment had a remaining life of five years, straight-line. Pacific has held the equipment for three years as of the end of the current year.

The separate trial balances for Pacific and Solovair at the end of the current year follow:

	Pacific Dr (Cr)	Solovair Dr (Cr)
Current assets	$ 10,000,000	$ 4,000,000
Plant and equipment, net.	150,000,000	92,000,000
Investment in Solovair	15,305,000	—
Liabilities.	(145,860,000)	(85,375,000)
Capital stock	(1,000,000)	(500,000)
Retained earnings, beginning.	(20,000,000)	(8,400,000)
Accumulated other comprehensive income, beginning.	(200,000)	(100,000)
Sales revenue and gains	(200,000,000)	(50,000,000)
Equity in net income.	(2,180,000)	—
Cost of sales.	120,000,000	38,000,000
Operating expenses	74,000,000	10,400,000
Other comprehensive income	(40,000)	(25,000)
Equity in other comprehensive income	(25,000)	—
Total	$ 0	$ 0

Required

Prepare a working paper to consolidate the trial balances of Pacific and Solovair. Label your eliminating entries (C), (I), (E), (R), and (O).

PROBLEMS ••

LO 2, 4   P6.1

Consolidation Working Paper, Noncontrolling Interest, Intercompany Inventory Transactions   Peninsula Industries and Seaport Company, a 90-percent owned subsidiary, engage in extensive intercompany transactions involving raw materials, component parts, and completed products. Peninsula acquired its interest in Seaport several years ago, at a cost of $3,000,000. At that time, Seaport's book value was $2,000,000 and the fair value of the noncontrolling interest in Seaport was $275,000. The excess of acquisition cost over book value was attributed to previously unrecorded indefinite-lived intangibles, valued at $500,000, and to goodwill. As of January 1, 2016, the intangibles were impaired by $200,000 and the goodwill was impaired by $300,000. Impairment testing reveals no additional impairment of either asset in 2016. Intercompany sales for 2016 and the unconfirmed intercompany profits in the beginning and ending inventories of both companies are summarized below:

(in thousands)	Peninsula Industries	Seaport Company
Intercompany profit in inventory, January 1, 2016.	$ 100,000	$ 60,000
Intercompany sales to affiliate	2,200,000	3,700,000
Intercompany profit in inventory, December 31, 2016.	80,000	75,000

beg
end

Prior to consolidation at December 31, 2016, the separate condensed trial balances of the two companies are as follows:

(in thousands)	Dr (Cr)	
	Peninsula Industries	Seaport Company
Current assets	$ 1,950,000	$ 980,000
Investment in Seaport	4,192,000	—
Property, plant and equipment, net	5,810,000	5,130,000
Intangibles	4,315,000	—
Liabilities...	(4,900,000)	(2,100,000)
Capital stock	(3,000,000)	(1,200,000)
Retained earnings, January 1......................	(6,500,000)	(2,250,000)
Accumulated other comprehensive income, January 1..........	(200,000)	(50,000)
Dividends	1,000,000	400,000
Sales..	(15,000,000)	(6,000,000)
Equity in net income of Seaport...................	(813,000)	—
Cost of goods sold....................................	9,050,000	3,170,000
Operating expenses...................................	4,150,000	1,930,000
Other comprehensive income	(45,000)	(10,000)
Equity in other comprehensive income of Seaport	(9,000)	—
Totals	$ 0	$ 0

Required

a. Prepare a schedule to calculate total goodwill for this acquisition and its allocation to the controlling and noncontrolling interests.

b. Prepare a schedule to show how equity in net income of Seaport for 2016 was computed, and to compute noncontrolling interest in net income for 2016.

c. Prepare a working paper consolidating the trial balances of Peninsula and Seaport for 2016. Label your eliminating entries (C), (I), (E), (R), and (N).

P6.2   **Consolidation Working Paper, Noncontrolling Interest, Intercompany Merchandise Transactions**   Kellogg Company (Kellogg's) acquired 75 percent of the outstanding stock of Wholesome & Hearty Foods ("Wholesome") at the end of 2007, for cash and stock totaling $120 million. Wholesome's assets and liabilities were fairly reported at the date of acquisition, except for these items:

LO 2, 4

(in thousands)	Book value	Fair value
Plant & equipment, net (10-year life, straight-line)...............	$150,000	$135,000
Veggie burger recipe (10-year life, straight-line)	0	25,000
Long-term debt (4-year life, straight-line).....................	30,000	34,000

Wholesome's book value at the date of acquisition was $74 million, and the fair value of the 25% noncontrolling interest was $35 million. It is now December 31, 2016 (the end of the ninth year since acquisition). Impairment testing on the goodwill arising in this acquisition reveals that total impairment during 2008–2015 is $2 million, and impairment in 2016 is $1 million.

Wholesome sells merchandise and raw materials to Kellogg's at a markup of 30% on cost. Here is information on these intercompany sales *(in thousands)*:

Inventory, January 1, 2016, reported on Kellogg's books...........................	$10,400
Inventory, December 31, 2016, reported on Kellogg's books........................	13,000
Transfer price for 2016 sales from Wholesome to Kellogg's........................	60,000

Below are the separate trial balances of Kellogg's and Wholesome at December 31, 2016.

(in thousands)	Dr (Cr) Kellogg's	Wholesome
Current assets	$ 35,000	$ 20,000
Plant and equipment, net	262,650	192,000
Investment in Wholesome	128,850	—
Identifiable intangibles	100,000	10,000
Current liabilities	(30,000)	(25,000)
Long-term debt	(350,000)	(100,000)
Capital stock	(80,000)	(54,000)
Retained earnings, January 1	(57,750)	(38,000)
Sales revenue	(400,000)	(140,000)
Equity in net income of Wholesome	(1,750)	—
Cost of sales	250,000	65,000
Operating expenses	143,000	70,000
Totals	$ 0	$ 0

In your answers below, present all numbers in thousands.

Required

a. Calculate the initial goodwill arising from this acquisition, and its allocation to the controlling and noncontrolling interests.
b. Prepare a schedule computing Kellogg's equity in net income of Wholesome and noncontrolling interest in net income for 2016.
c. Prepare a working paper to consolidate the trial balances of Kellogg's and Wholesome at December 31, 2016. Label your eliminating entries (C), (I), (E), (R), (O), and (N).

LO 5   P6.3   Intercompany Transfers of Depreciable Assets   Placer Industries acquired 80 percent of SAS Shoes several years ago. Placer and SAS have made several intercompany transfers of depreciable assets over the years. Details are below.

- On June 30, 2012, Placer sold equipment with an original cost of $150,000 and accumulated depreciation of $40,000, to SAS for $200,000. The remaining life of the equipment was 8 years.
- On January 1, 2014, SAS sold a building with an original cost of $10,000,000 and accumulated depreciation of $1,000,000 to Placer for $6,000,000. The remaining life of the building was 20 years.
- On September 30, 2015, Placer sold equipment with an original cost of $700,000 and accumulated depreciation of $100,000 to SAS for $500,000. The remaining life of the equipment was 5 years.

It is now December 31, 2016, the end of Placer's accounting year. Placer uses the complete equity method to account for its investment in SAS on its own books. Straight-line depreciation is appropriate for the depreciable assets.

Required

a. Prepare the necessary consolidation working paper eliminating entries related to the above intercompany transactions at December 31, 2016.
b. Assume that the equipment that Placer sold to SAS on June 30, 2012, was sold to an outside party on January 1, 2017, for $125,000. Prepare the working paper eliminating entry needed at December 31, 2017, related to the sale of the equipment.

LO 2, 3, 4, 5   P6.4   Consolidated Financial Statements with Various Intercompany Transactions   Several years ago Puma Athletics acquired all of the outstanding stock of Serengeti Footwear. The acquisition cost was $40 million in excess of Serengeti's book value of $10 million, attributed to indefinite lived brand names with a fair value of $8 million, and goodwill. The brand names are unimpaired, but the goodwill was impaired by $2 million as of the beginning of the current year. There is no goodwill impairment in the current year. The following information relates to intercompany transactions:

- Puma's beginning inventory includes $500,000 of intercompany profit on goods purchased from Serengeti. Puma made no intercompany purchases during the current year and has no ending inventory of goods purchased from Serengeti. Serengeti's ending inventory includes $300,000 of intercompany profit on purchases of $4,000,000 from Puma.
- Serengeti's other expenses include a loss of $200,000 on an intercompany sale of land to Puma.

- Puma's other income reflects a $700,000 gain on the sale of machinery to Serengeti at the beginning of the year. At the date of sale, the machinery had a remaining life of five years; it is being straight-line depreciated.
- Several years ago, Puma recorded a gain of $250,000 on land sold to Serengeti for $600,000. Serengeti sold the land to an outside party during the year for $800,000. The gain is reflected in Serengeti's other income account.

The end-of-year trial balances of Puma and Serengeti are below. Puma uses the complete equity method to account for its investment in Serengeti on its own books.

(in thousands)	Puma Dr (Cr)	Serengeti Dr (Cr)
Cash and receivables.	$ 10,000	$ 4,000
Inventories	150,000	85,000
Land	200,000	120,000
Plant and equipment, net	600,000	380,000
Investment in Serengeti	64,540	—
Liabilities.	(750,250)	(561,800)
Capital stock	(2,000)	(1,500)
Retained earnings, beginning.	(267,000)	(24,500)
Dividends	1,000	—
Sales revenue.	(350,000)	(73,000)
Other income	(5,000)	(2,000)
Equity in net income.	(1,290)	—
Cost of sales.	275,000	47,000
Operating expenses	70,000	24,000
Other expenses	5,000	2,800
Total	$ 0	$ 0

Required

a. Prepare a schedule to calculate Puma's equity in net income of Serengeti, reported on its own books at $1,290,000.

b. Prepare a schedule to calculate Puma's investment in Serengeti, reported on its own books at $64,540,000.

c. Prepare a working paper to consolidate the trial balances of Puma and Serengeti at the end of the current year. Label your eliminating entries (C), (I), (E), and (R).

d. Present the consolidated income statement and balance sheet of Puma and its subsidiary, for the current year.

P6.5 **Equity in Net Income and Eliminating Entries—Intercompany Asset Transfers and Services** On January 2, 2015, Pohang Company acquired 80 percent of Suro Corporation's voting common stock for $1.25 billion. The fair value of the noncontrolling interest at the date of acquisition was $300 million. The $50 million excess of acquisition cost and noncontrolling interest over the book value of Suro was attributed entirely to goodwill. Suro reported net income of $150 million and $200 million in 2015 and 2016, respectively, paying out 40 percent of each period's earnings in dividends. Pohang reports its investment in Suro using the complete equity method. There is no goodwill impairment in 2015 or 2016. Information on intercompany transactions follows:

LO 1, 2, 3, 4, 5 ✅

1. On March 5, 2015, Suro sold a parcel of land to Pohang for $60 million; the land originally cost $45 million. Pohang continues to hold the land.

2. During 2016, Pohang and Suro recorded intercompany merchandise sales of $350 million, an amount equal to cost plus 25 percent. Suro's beginning inventory included $50 million of merchandise purchased from Pohang in prior years, while Pohang's ending inventory included $80 million of merchandise purchased from Suro.

3. On January 2, 2016, Suro sold a piece of machinery to Pohang for $60 million and recorded a gain of $25 million. Accumulated depreciation on the machinery amounted to $40 million at January 2. The machinery is being depreciated by the straight-line method over its remaining life of five years.

4. Pohang billed Suro $20 million for computer services during the year. The costs incurred by Pohang in supplying these services amounted to $15 million. On December 31, 2016, the unpaid portion of these intercompany services amounted to $3 million.

Required

a.   Prepare a schedule to compute Pohang's equity in net income of Suro and the noncontrolling interest in consolidated net income for 2016.

b.   Prepare the working paper eliminations to consolidate the accounts of Pohang and Suro at December 31, 2016.

LO 2, 4, 5   P6.6

Comprehensive Problem: Consolidation Working Paper and Financial Statements   Pierre Corporation acquired 75 percent of Selene Corporation's common stock for $20,100,000 on January 2, 2014. The estimated fair value of the noncontrolling interest was $5,900,000. Selene's book value at date of acquisition was $10,000,000, and its identifiable net assets were fairly stated except for previously unreported completed technology, valued at $4,000,000, with a remaining life of 5 years, straight-line. It is now December 31, 2017, and you are preparing consolidated financial statements for Pierre and Selene. Following is information on intercompany transactions:

1.   On January 2, 2015, Pierre sold equipment to Selene for $6 million and recorded a gain of $2 million. The equipment had a remaining life of 10 years at that time.

2.   Selene supplies Pierre with component parts for its products, at a markup of 20 percent on cost. During 2017, Selene made sales totaling $20 million to Pierre. Pierre had parts purchased for $1.8 million and $2.4 million in its 2017 beginning and ending inventory balances, respectively.

3.   Pierre sells materials to Selene for use in its manufacturing processes, at a markup of 20 percent on selling price. During 2017, Pierre made sales totaling $15 million to Selene. Selene had materials purchased for $3 million and $2.8 million in its 2017 beginning and ending inventory balances, respectively.

Goodwill arising from this acquisition was impaired by $3 million during the years 2014–2016, and no further goodwill impairment occurred in 2017. Pierre uses the complete equity method to report the investment in Selene on its own books. The separate December 31, 2017, trial balances of Pierre and Selene appear below, *before* Pierre's end-of-year adjustment to record its equity in Selene's net income and other comprehensive income for 2017.

	Dr (Cr)	
(in thousands)	**Pierre**	**Selene**
Cash	$ 1,000	$ 2,500
Receivables	5,600	10,000
Inventories	70,000	30,000
Investment in AFS securities	8,000	6,000
Plant and equipment, net	452,000	144,000
Investment in Selene	20,225	—
Current liabilities	(4,000)	(2,800)
Long-term debt	(489,825)	(163,700)
Capital stock	(5,000)	(2,000)
Retained earnings, January 1	(88,500)	(19,600)
Accumulated other comprehensive income, January 1	(1,500)	(400)
Dividends	40,000	3,000
Sales revenue	(150,000)	(50,000)
Cost of sales	100,000	35,000
Operating expenses	41,500	7,900
Unrealized losses on AFS securities (other comprehensive income)	500	100
Totals	$ 0	$ 0

Required

a.   Calculate the total goodwill arising from this acquisition and its percentage allocation to the controlling and noncontrolling interests.

b.   Prepare a schedule calculating Pierre's equity in the net income of Selene for 2017, and the noncontrolling interest in Selene's net income for 2017.

c.   Update Pierre's trial balance for its 2017 equity method entries and prepare a working paper consolidating the 2017 trial balances of Pierre and Selene.

d.   Present the consolidated financial statements of Pierre and Selene, in proper format.

P6.7 **Calculation of Investment and Consolidated Accounts Several Years After Acquisition** Pentland Shoe Company acquired 75 percent of Sketchers Inc.'s common stock on January 2, 2014 for $180 million. The fair value of the 25 percent noncontrolling interest was $50 million at the date of acquisition, and Sketchers' book value was $20 million. Sketchers' assets and liabilities were fairly stated, except for previously unreported customer-related intangible assets (5-year life, straight-line), capitalized under U.S. GAAP, and valued at $60 million. During the four years following the acquisition, Sketchers reported total net income of $140 million, declared and paid $12 million in dividends, and goodwill was impaired by $5 million. Pentland uses the complete equity method to account for its investment on its own books. The following intercompany transactions occurred: LO 2, 3, 4, 5

1. During 2014, Sketchers sold land carried on its books at $50 million to Pentland for $80 million. Pentland still holds the land.
2. Early in 2015, Pentland sold a patent recorded at $15 million to Sketchers for $25 million. Sketchers currently holds the patent and is amortizing it over a ten-year period.
3. Over the years since acquisition, total intercompany merchandise sales amounted to $400 million. Unconfirmed intercompany profits in the ending inventories of Pentland and Sketchers at December 31, 2017, are $20 million and $17 million, respectively.

Required

a. Prepare a schedule calculating consolidated retained earnings at December 31, 2017. Pentland's retained earnings from its own operations is $55 million. Hint: Consolidated retained earnings equals Pentland's separate retained earnings plus equity in net income for the years 2014–2017.
b. Calculate the balance in the investment account at December 31, 2017, reported on Pentland's books.
c. Calculate the balance in the noncontrolling interest, appearing in the equity section of the December 31, 2017, consolidated balance sheet.

P6.8 **Bonus Based on Adjusted Subsidiary Income** McDeer Equipment Company manufactures farm equipment. It has fifty co-owned dealership subsidiaries. McDeer owns 75 percent of each, and the local operator has a 25 percent equity interest. McDeer sells merchandise to the dealerships at a transfer price that reflects a 35 percent gross margin on sales, and finances dealership inventories at 80 percent of the purchase price. Financing bears 10 percent interest, and must be settled within 30 days of the dealer's sale of the merchandise. LO 1, 4

Western Nebraska Farm Supply, one of McDeer's dealer subsidiaries, acquires 80 percent of its merchandise from McDeer and 20 percent from other vendors, at markups similar to those charged by McDeer. For the year ended December 31, 2017, Western Nebraska Farm Supply presents the following income statement:

Sales revenue	$3,400,000
Cost of goods sold	2,500,000
Gross margin	900,000
Operating expenses	750,000
Income before taxes	$ 150,000

The dealership's balance sheet shows ending inventory of $680,000 and inventory financing due to McDeer of $720,000. Beginning-of-year balances were inventory of $300,000 and financing due of $380,000. Average financing indebtedness during the year was $600,000; interest expense is included in cost of goods sold.

Wendy Carr, the manager and 25 percent stockholder in Western Nebraska Farm Supply, receives a salary (included in operating expenses) and a bonus based on income. McDeer retains 40 percent for income taxes and corporate costs, and distributes 15 percent of the remainder to the local dealer as a bonus. Accordingly, Wendy expects a bonus of $13,500 (= $150,000 × 60% × 15%). However, McDeer bases the bonus on the dealership's income after adjustments to remove unconfirmed intercompany profits in the dealership inventory and interest paid to the parent company.

Required

Prepare a report computing Wendy Carr's bonus for 2017.

P6.9 **Consolidated Income Statement—Intercompany Transactions** Condensed income statements from their own operations for Portland Company and its 80 percent-owned subsidiary, Salem Company, follow. LO 2, 3, 4, 5

	Portland	Salem
Sales...	$40,000,000	$25,000,000
Other income	6,000,000	2,000,000
Total revenue	46,000,000	27,000,000
Cost of goods sold..	28,000,000	15,000,000
Operating expenses......................................	7,000,000	5,000,000
Other expenses	1,000,000	800,000
Total expenses	36,000,000	20,800,000
Net income (from own operations).....................	$10,000,000	$ 6,200,000

Additional information:

1. Salem's beginning inventory includes $650,000 of profit on goods purchased from Portland, and Portland's ending inventory includes $500,000 of profit on purchases of $4,000,000 from Salem.
2. Portland's other expenses include a $360,000 loss on a sale of depreciable assets to Salem at the beginning of the year. These assets have a 6-year remaining life at the date of intercompany sale and are depreciated by the straight-line method.
3. Salem's other income includes a $190,000 gain on sale of land to Portland.
4. Salem previously recorded a gain of $250,000 on a patent sold to Portland for $500,000. At that time the patent had a remaining life of 5 years. At the end of this year (three years later) Portland sold the patent externally for $420,000, reporting the gain in Portland's other income account.

Required

a. Prepare a schedule to compute Portland Company's equity in net income of Salem and the noncontrolling interest in consolidated income for the current year.
b. Prepare a consolidated income statement for Portland Company and Salem Company.

LO 1, 4, 5 **P6.10** **Comprehensive Intercompany Transactions** MC Enterprises began business some years ago as a franchiser of fast food restaurants known as The Mighty Chicken. Initially, all franchises were independently owned, but eventually the company began to buy individual franchises from owners who wanted to sell. MC Enterprises formed a wholly-owned subsidiary, Mighty Chicken Shops, to own and operate these repurchased franchises. Currently, there are 46 independently owned franchises, and 33 company-owned franchises held by the subsidiary. Following are condensed trial balances for MC Enterprises (the parent) and Mighty Chicken Shops (the subsidiary) at December 31, 2016:

	Dr (Cr)	
	MC Enterprises	**Mighty Chicken Shops**
Investment in Mighty Chicken Shops....................	$ 5,000,000	$ —
Other assets...	78,000,000	56,000,000
Liabilities..	(23,000,000)	(43,000,000)
Stockholders' equity, January 1........................	(46,000,000)	(7,000,000)
Sales revenue...	(140,000,000)	(89,000,000)
Franchise fee revenue	(15,000,000)	—
Interest revenue	(6,000,000)	—
Cost of goods sold..	98,000,000	57,000,000
Franchise fee expense	—	8,000,000
Interest expense...	3,000,000	4,000,000
Operating expenses (including depreciation)............	46,000,000	14,000,000
Totals	$ 0	$ 0

Mighty Chicken Shops' cost of goods sold consisted of beginning inventory of $10,000,000, purchases of $60,000,000, and ending inventory of $13,000,000. The subsidiary makes all of its purchases from the parent; the transfer price includes a 20 percent gross margin on sales for MC Enterprises. The gross margin percentage has been constant for several years. All of Mighty Chicken Shops' franchise fees and interest expense were paid to MC Enterprises and all of the subsidiary's debt is owed to the parent. MC Enterprises provides equipment at cost to all its franchisees, including those owned by Mighty Chicken Shops. The subsidiary currently has such equipment originally costing $20,000,000. On average, the equipment has a ten-year life and is currently half depreciated.

Required

Prepare appropriate consolidation eliminating entries (I) and (E) at December 31, 2016. There is no need to reverse equity in net income, as the parent did not record it. There are no revaluations since MC Enterprises formed Mighty Chicken Shops rather than acquiring it. Mighty Chicken Shops paid no dividends in 2016.

P6.11 **Consolidation of Equity Method Investments** The annual report of **Starbucks Corporation** for the year ended September 29, 2013, included information on seven investments in which Starbucks generally held a 50 percent ownership interest. Thus these investments were not consolidated, but were reported as unconsolidated equity method investments. Summary data for Starbucks and for its equity method investments is as follows:

LO 1, 4

STARBUCKS CORPORATION [SBUX]

Income Statement Data

(in millions)	Starbucks Corporation	Equity Method Investments
Revenues	$14,892.2	$3,018.7
Cost of sales and other operating expenses	(15,469.0)	(2,583.9)
Equity method income	251.4	—
Operating income.	(325.4)	434.8
Other income (expense), net	334.2	(76.8)
Net earnings	$ 8.8	$ 358.0

Balance Sheet Data

(in millions)	Starbucks Corporation	Equity Method Investments
Current assets	$ 5,471.4	$ 675.8
Noncurrent assets	6,045.3	783.3
Total assets	$11,516.7	$1,459.1
Current liabilities.	$ 5,377.3	$ 466.6
Noncurrent liabilities.	1,657.1	148.9
Total liabilities.	7,034.4	615.5
Shareholders' equity	4,482.3	843.6
Total liabilities and shareholders' equity	$11,516.7	$1,459.1

Equity method investments are carried as noncurrent assets on Starbucks' balance sheet at $450.9 million on September 29, 2013. The notes to the financial statements also disclose the following (edited to reflect fiscal year 2013 data only):

Also included (in the income from equity investees account) is our proportionate share of gross margin resulting from coffee and other product sales to, and royalty and license fee revenues generated from, equity investees. Revenues generated from these related parties, net of eliminations, were $205.1 million. Related costs of sales, net of eliminations, were $115.4 million. As of September 29, 2013, there were $48.3 million of accounts receivable on Starbucks' balance sheet from equity investees, primarily related to product sales and store license fees.

Required

a. Assume Starbucks determines that it controls the seven investments. Prepare a working paper to consolidate Starbucks' income statement and balance sheet with those of the seven companies. Assume that Starbucks owns 50 percent of each company, and that any excess of carrying value of equity investees over net book value is attributable to goodwill, which is shared equally between Starbucks and the noncontrolling interests. There is no goodwill impairment in 2013. The statement of cash flows reports that Starbucks received $195.2 million in dividends from the seven companies. Starbucks paid no dividends in 2013.

b. What percentage increase in total assets and in revenues would be reported by Starbucks had these seven companies been consolidated? Compute operating income and operating income as a percent of revenues for Starbucks and for the consolidated entity. Explain why they are different.

LO 4, 5 P6.12 Separate and Consolidated Balances, Intercompany Merchandise and Depreciable Asset Transactions   Peco Athletics and its subsidiary, Stetson Footwear, engage in intercompany transactions, as follows:

- Peco sells merchandise to Stetson at a markup of 35% on cost. In 2015, Peco sold merchandise to Stetson, charging a total of $16,875,000. Although Stetson did not have any merchandise purchased from Peco in its beginning inventory, it still holds $175,500 of this merchandise in its ending inventory. In 2016, Peco sold another $12,825,000 in merchandise to Stetson. Stetson held $148,500 of this merchandise in its ending inventory.
- At the beginning of 2015, Stetson sold machinery with an original cost of $900,000 and accumulated depreciation of $340,000 to Peco for $700,000. The machinery had a 7-year remaining life, and straight-line depreciation is appropriate. Peco still holds the machinery.

Required

a. For each of the items above, for each of the years 2015 and 2016, determine the accounts and balances reported in the end-of-year trial balances of the separate companies, the balances that should be reported in the consolidated accounts, and the eliminating entries necessary to convert the separate company balances to consolidated balances.

b. Now assume Peco sold the machinery to an outside party for $300,000 halfway through 2017. Determine the balances reported in the end-of-2017 trial balances of the separate companies, the correct consolidated balances, and the eliminating entries needed to convert the separate company balances to consolidated balances.

LO 2, 3, 4, 5 P6.13 Calculation of Investment Balance, Comprehensive Eliminating Entries, Variety of Intercompany Transactions   Poplar Outdoor Corporation owns 60 percent of the voting stock of Sugg Australia. Date-of-acquisition information is as follows:

- Acquisition cost: $39.5 million
- Fair value of the noncontrolling interest: $20.5 million
- Sugg's book value: $10 million
- Value of unreported acquired indefinite lived trademarks: $15 million.

As of the beginning of the current year, trademarks are impaired by $2 million, and goodwill impairment is $5 million. There is no current year impairment for the trademarks, but current year goodwill impairment is $1 million. Sugg reports net income of $1.5 million for the current year, and declares no dividends. Its total equity at the beginning of the year is $19 million.

Following is information on intercompany transactions between Poplar and Sugg:

- Sugg sold land to Poplar in the current year at a loss of $500,000. Poplar still owns the land.
- Intercompany profit in Poplar's beginning inventory, purchased from Sugg, is $200,000.
- Intercompany profit in Poplar's ending inventory, purchased from Sugg, is $290,000.
- Total sales from Sugg to Poplar, at the price charged to Poplar, were $6 million.
- Poplar sold administrative facilities with a book value of $8 million to Sugg two years ago, at the beginning of the year, for $7 million. The facilities had a remaining life of 10 years, straight-line. Sugg still uses the facilities.

Required

a. Prepare a schedule to compute equity in net income and noncontrolling interest in net income for the current year, assuming Poplar uses the complete equity method.

b. Compute the investment balance on Poplar's books at the end of the current year.

c. Prepare the current year eliminating entries (C), (I), (E), (R), (O), and (N), to consolidate the end-of-year trial balances of Poplar and Sugg.

P6.14 **Consolidation Working Paper Eliminations, Intercompany Merchandise Sales, Noncontrolling Interest, IFRS**   Pablo S.A. is a manufacturer of children's shoes, located in Spain. It owns 51 percent of the voting stock of Stabifoot, a specialty shoe manufacturer located in Belgium. Pablo acquired its interest in Stabifoot several years ago, and has consolidated Stabifoot in its financial statements since the date of acquisition. Per IFRS, Stabifoot's identifiable assets and liabilities were revalued to fair value at the date of acquisition. This process led to recognition of customer and distributor relationships valued at €40 million, and goodwill of €120 million. Pablo uses the IFRS alternative, and does not attribute goodwill to the noncontrolling interest. As of the beginning of the current year, the goodwill and identifiable intangibles are not impaired. Goodwill is impaired by €10 million in the current year. Pablo and Stabifoot engage in intercompany transfers of merchandise. Below is information on these transactions:

LO 2, 4

- Pablo sells merchandise to Stabifoot at a markup of 20% on price.
- Stabifoot sells merchandise to Pablo at a markup of 20% on cost.
- Balance in Pablo's beginning inventory, purchased from Stabifoot, €24 million.
- Balance in Pablo's ending inventory, purchased from Stabifoot, €26.4 million.
- Total sales from Stabifoot to Pablo, at the price charged to Pablo, €125 million.
- Balance in Stabifoot's beginning inventory, purchased from Pablo, €22.5 million.
- Balance in Stabifoot's ending inventory, purchased from Pablo, €25 million.
- Total sales from Pablo to Stabifoot, at the price charged to Stabifoot, €130 million.

Pablo uses the complete equity method to account for its investment in Stabifoot on its own books. The separate trial balances for the two companies for the current year are below.

(in thousands)	Pablo Dr (Cr)	Stabifoot Dr (Cr)
Current assets	€ 80,000	€ 60,000
Plant assets, net.	210,440	137,000
Intangibles	10,000	—
Investment in Stabifoot	178,236	—
Liabilities.	(286,300)	(89,000)
Capital stock	(2,000)	(1,000)
Retained earnings, beginning.	(187,000)	(99,000)
Sales revenue.	(800,000)	(500,000)
Equity in net loss	6,624	—
Cost of goods sold.	650,000	300,000
Operating expenses	140,000	192,000
Total	€ 0	€ 0

Required

a. Calculate Pablo's equity in net loss and the noncontrolling interest in net income for the current year.

b. Prepare a working paper to consolidate the trial balances of Pablo and Stabifoot. Label your eliminating entries (C), (I), (E), (R), (O), and (N).

P6.15 **Consolidation Working Paper Eliminations, Intercompany Transactions, Noncontrolling Interest, IFRS**   Adaris Group, headquartered in the UK, owns a 70 percent interest in Adaris Malaysia. The acquisition cost was £200 million. At the date of acquisition, 1 January 2012, Adaris Malaysia's book value was £60 million, and its identifiable net assets were carried at amounts approximating fair value. Goodwill recognized for this acquisition was impaired by £20 million during the period 2012–2014. Goodwill impairment for 2015, the current year, is £5 million. The following information relates to intercompany transactions:

LO 2, 3, 4, 5
⊘

- In 2013, Adaris sold land with a book value of £2 million to Adaris Malaysia for £3 million. Adaris Malaysia sold the land to an outside party in 2015 for £3.5 million.
- Adaris sells merchandise to Adaris Malaysia at a markup of 30% on cost. Adaris Malaysia's beginning inventory contains £11.7 million in merchandise acquired from Adaris. Its ending inventory contains £10.4 million in merchandise acquired from Adaris. Adaris sold merchandise priced at £260 million to Adaris Malaysia during 2015.

- On 30 June 2012, Adaris Malaysia sold equipment with a book value of £50 million to Adaris for £65 million. The equipment had a remaining life of five years, straight-line. Adaris still holds the equipment.

It is now 31 December 2015, the end of Adaris' accounting year. Adaris uses the complete equity method to account for its investment in Adaris Malaysia on its own books. Adaris also uses the IFRS alternative approach to valuing the noncontrolling interest in Adaris Malaysia. Below are the separate trial balances of Adaris Group and Adaris Malaysia at 31 December 2015.

(in thousands)	Adaris Group Dr (Cr)	Adaris Malaysia Dr (Cr)
Current assets	£ 35,000	£ 22,000
Plant assets, net	233,450	210,000
Investment in Adaris Malaysia	205,850	—
Liabilities	(300,000)	(120,000)
Capital stock	(40,000)	(30,000)
Retained earnings, beginning	(125,000)	(75,000)
Sales revenue and gains	(600,000)	(490,000)
Equity in net income	(3,300)	—
Cost of goods sold	430,000	210,000
Operating expenses	164,000	273,000
Total	£ 0	£ 0

Required

a. Calculate Adaris Group's equity in net income and the noncontrolling interest in net income for the current year.

b. Prepare a working paper to consolidate the trial balances of Adaris Group and Adaris Malaysia. Label your eliminating entries (C), (I), (E), (R), (O), and (N).

c. Present the consolidated income statement for 2015 and the consolidated balance sheet at 31 December 2015.

REVIEW SOLUTIONS ••

Review 1 Solution

a.

(I-1)	Investment in Sandalite	500,000	
	Gain on sale of land		500,000

To transfer unconfirmed downstream intercompany land sale gain to year of sale to outside party.

(I-2)	Sales	40,000,000	
	Cost of goods sold		40,000,000

To eliminate upstream and downstream merchandise sales; $40,000,000 = $14,000,000 + $26,000,000.

(I-3)	Retained earnings, beginning—Sandalite	285,000	
	Investment in Sandalite	300,000	
	Cost of goods sold		585,000

To remove intercompany profit from beginning inventory; $285,000 = $1,235,000 − $1,235,000/1.3; $300,000 = $1,500,000 × 20%.

(I-4)	Cost of goods sold	543,000	
	Inventory		543,000

To remove intercompany profit from ending inventory; $543,000 = $318,000 + $225,000; $318,000 = $1,378,000 − $1,378,000/1.3; $225,000 = $1,125,000 × 20%.

b. Protective acquired its 90% investment at book value, and the noncontrolling interest's fair value equaled book value at the date of acquisition. Therefore no revaluations appear, and no revaluation write-offs are necessary. The only items affecting equity in net income are intercompany transactions.

	Equity in net income	Noncontrolling interest in net income
Sandalite reported net income.	$1,530,000	$170,000
Confirmed gain on downstream sale of land	500,000	
Confirmed profit on downstream beginning inventory.	300,000	
Confirmed profit on upstream beginning inventory	256,500	28,500
Unconfirmed profit on downstream ending inventory	(225,000)	
Unconfirmed profit on upstream ending inventory	(286,200)	(31,800)
	$2,075,300	$166,700

Review 2 Solution

a. Add the following eliminations to those prepared for review problem #1:

Downstream equipment sale:

(I-1)	Investment in Sandalite	800,000	
	Accumulated depreciation	1,200,000	
	Equipment		2,000,000
	To eliminate beginning-of-year unconfirmed profit on intercompany transfer of equipment.		

(I-2)	Accumulated depreciation	400,000	
	Depreciation expense		400,000
	To eliminate the excess annual depreciation expense recorded by the purchasing affiliate; $400,000 = $2,000,000/5.		

(I-3)	Equipment	3,000,000	
	Accumulated depreciation.		3,000,000
	To restate the asset and accumulated depreciation accounts to their original acquisition cost basis.		

Upstream building sale:

(I-4)	Building	2,500,000	
	Retained earnings—Sandalite, January 1		2,437,500
	Accumulated depreciation.		62,500
	To eliminate beginning-of-year unconfirmed loss on intercompany transfer of building (½ year depreciation in 2016); $62,500 = ($2,500,000/20) × ½.		

(I-5)	Depreciation expense.	125,000	
	Accumulated depreciation.		125,000
	To adjust to cost the annual depreciation expense recorded by the purchasing affiliate; $125,000 = $2,500,000/20.		

(I-6)	Building	2,000,000	
	Accumulated depreciation.		2,000,000
	To restate the asset and accumulated depreciation accounts to their original acquisition cost basis.		

b.

	Equity in net income	Noncontrolling interest in net income
Sandalite reported net income.....................	$1,530,000	$170,000
Downstream confirmed gain on sale of land	500,000	—
Downstream confirmed profit on beginning inventory....	300,000	—
Upstream confirmed profit on beginning inventory	256,500	28,500
Downstream unconfirmed profit on ending inventory	(225,000)	—
Upstream unconfirmed profit on ending inventory	(286,200)	(31,800)
Downstream confirmed profit on equipment sale	400,000	—
Upstream confirmed loss on building sale.............	(112,500)	(12,500)
	$2,362,800	$154,200

7

Consolidating Foreign Currency Financial Statements

LEARNING OBJECTIVES

LO1 Apply translation and remeasurement procedures. (p. 277)

LO2 Describe how changing exchange rates affect financial analysis of international entities. (p. 295)

LO3 Explain procedures for consolidating international subsidiaries. (p. 297)

LO4 Apply IFRS translation requirements. (p. 302)

WAL-MART STORES, INC.
www.walmart.com

Wal-Mart Stores, Inc. has subsidiaries in many countries other than the U.S., including Argentina, Brazil, Canada, Chile, China, Costa Rica, El Salvador, Guatemala, Honduras, India, Japan, Mexico, South Africa and the United Kingdom. The accounts of these subsidiaries are included in Wal-Mart's consolidated financial statements. The accounts of an international subsidiary are usually measured in its local currency. For example, Wal-Mart's United Kingdom operations are reported in pounds sterling. How does Wal-Mart convert its subsidiaries' accounts into U.S. dollars for inclusion in its consolidated financial statements?

Are consolidation procedures for an international subsidiary different from the procedures for a U.S. subsidiary? How do changing exchange rates affect the consolidated financial statements? This chapter explains procedures for conversion and consolidation of the accounts of international subsidiaries, as well as the impact of changing exchange rates and translation methodologies on the financial statements.

CHAPTER ORGANIZATION

Converting foreign currency accounts	Translation and remeasurement procedures	Financial statement analysis	Consolidation of international subsidiaries	Currency conversion under IFRS
• The conversion process • The functional currency	• Translation procedures • Remeasurement procedures • Translation and remeasurement gains and losses • Highly inflationary economies • Illustration for an existing subsidiary • Statement of cash flows • Disclosures	• Profitability analysis • Short-term liquidity and long-term solvency	• Equity method entries • Consolidation at date of acquisition • Consolidation in subsequent years	• Translation and remeasurement • Hyperinflationary economies

INTRODUCTION

The global character of business presents challenges for corporate managers, professional accountants, and financial analysts. For a diversified corporation headquartered in the United States, two major problems faced by management are (1) controlling wide-ranging, geographically dispersed operations and (2) measuring the financial position and performance of its various divisions or subsidiaries. Several other difficulties are also common to multinational operations:

• Corporate headquarters located great distances from international operations.

• Books of account maintained in units of various currencies.

• Interest rates, inflation rates, and growth rates that vary widely across countries.

• Political conditions and economic institutions that differ among nations.

• Language and other cultural barriers to effective communication.

• Alternative accounting and reporting procedures.

When a U.S. company invests in a non-U.S. entity, the familiar concept of control determines the reporting for its investment. A multinational corporation with a controlling interest in an international subsidiary consolidates the subsidiary's financial results. The subsidiary usually prepares its financial statements in its local currency. Before consolidating its accounts with those of the U.S. parent, the subsidiary's financial information must be converted into U.S. dollars. Then the subsidiary's accounts are consolidated with those of the parent.

CONVERTING A SUBSIDIARY'S FOREIGN CURRENCY ACCOUNTS TO THE PARENT'S CURRENCY

This section discusses conversion of an international subsidiary's accounts to U.S. dollars, the currency in which its U.S. parent reports financial information. However, the concepts and procedures are equally applicable to a non-U.S. company desiring to change its reporting currency to U.S. dollars, an equity method investment in a non-U.S. company that is held by a U.S. investor, or non-U.S. branch operations of a U.S. company.

The financial statements of international subsidiaries owned by U.S. companies report the assets, liabilities, revenues, and expenses of these entities in their local currency. **Asda Stores Ltd.**, a British supermarket chain, has been a subsidiary of Wal-Mart since 1999. Asda reports its financial statements in pounds sterling. To consolidate Asda in Wal-Mart's financial statements, Wal-Mart must first convert Asda's financial statements to U.S. dollars, using **foreign exchange rates**.

A foreign exchange rate is the price of a unit of one country's currency expressed in units of another country's currency. Exchange rates are expressed in two ways: the amount of foreign currency that can be acquired per unit of domestic currency (the **indirect rate**), or the amount of domestic currency needed to acquire one unit of foreign currency (the **direct rate**). In the case of a U.S. company, the indirect rate is the foreign currency value per dollar, such as the number of yen per dollar, or the number of pounds sterling per dollar. An indirect rate of £0.64/dollar means that 0.64 pounds can purchase one dollar. The direct rate is the number of dollars needed to purchase one yen or pound. When the direct rate is $1.56/pound, $1.56 will buy one pound. Notice that the direct rate is the reciprocal of the indirect rate ($1.56 = $1/0.64). For an international subsidiary of a U.S. company, the direct rate is used to change the subsidiary's accounts into U.S. dollars.

Foreign currencies are traded on both **spot markets** and **forward markets** or **futures markets**. Transactions involving *immediate delivery* of the foreign currency are executed at **spot rates**. Transactions involving delivery of the foreign currency at some *later date* are executed at **forward rates**. Standardized contracts for future delivery trade at **futures rates**. When *more* U.S. dollars are required to buy one unit of foreign currency (the direct rate rises), the U.S. dollar is said to have **weakened** with respect to that currency. When *fewer* U.S. dollars are required (the direct rate falls), the U.S. dollar **strengthens**.

The Conversion Process

Generally accepted accounting principles for converting a subsidiary's financial information for consolidation with its parent are found in *ASC Topic 830*. First, we must identify the subsidiary's *reporting currency*, *local currency*, and *functional currency*. The **reporting currency** is the currency in which a parent reports its consolidated financial statements. Wal-Mart's reporting currency is the U.S. dollar. The **local currency** is the currency in which the subsidiary reports its accounts. Asda's local currency is the British pound. The subsidiary's **functional currency** is the currency in which the subsidiary conducts most of its transactions. In most cases, a subsidiary's functional currency is its local currency. Asda conducts business primarily with British customers and suppliers, and therefore its functional currency is its local currency, the British pound.

Sometimes a subsidiary does not record transactions in its functional currency. A subsidiary of a U.S. parent may be located in Hong Kong, but conducts most of its business with U.S. customers and suppliers. In that case its functional currency is the U.S. dollar, even though its accounts are measured in Hong Kong dollars. The Hong Kong subsidiary's functional currency is the same as the reporting currency, the U.S. dollar. Occasionally, a subsidiary of a U.S. parent may report its accounts in one currency and conduct business in another currency other than the U.S. dollar. Suppose a Swiss subsidiary of a U.S. parent records its accounts in Swiss francs and conducts business primarily in euros. Its local currency is the Swiss franc, its functional currency is the euro, and the reporting currency is the U.S. dollar.

The subsidiary's accounts expressed in its functional currency reflect the performance and financial health of the subsidiary, reported in its revenues, expenses, assets, liabilities, and equity, and the relationships between these accounts. Converting the subsidiary's accounts to U.S. dollars, the parent's currency, should not change the subsidiary's financial picture. The process of converting functional currency accounts to the reporting currency is known as **translation**. The FASB states the objectives of translation as follows:

a. Provide information that is generally compatible with the expected economic effects of a rate change on a reporting entity's cash flows and equity

b. Reflect in consolidated statements the financial results and relationships of the individual consolidated entities as measured in their functional currencies in conformity with U.S. generally accepted accounting principles. *(ASC para. 830-10-10-2)*

As we will see in subsequent sections, translation generally converts the subsidiary's functional currency accounts to U.S. dollars using the same or similar exchange rates, maintaining the functional currency relationships.

If the subsidiary's accounts are not expressed in its functional currency, before translation can occur the accounts must be converted into the subsidiary's functional currency. Because it conducts business primarily in a different currency, the local currency accounts do not adequately reflect the subsidiary's financial health and how it is affected by exchange rate changes. The process of converting local currency accounts to the functional currency is known as **remeasurement**. The FASB states the objective of remeasurement as follows:

> The remeasurement procedure is intended to produce the same result as if the entity's books of record had been maintained in the functional currency. *(ASC para. 830-10-45-17)*

The Swiss subsidiary of a U.S. parent conducts business in euros but maintains its accounts in Swiss francs. Remeasurement converts the subsidiary's accounts to their balances as if the Swiss subsidiary had actually recorded its transactions and adjustments in euros.

The process of converting an international subsidiary's accounts to dollars, the U.S. parent's reporting currency, occurs in one of three scenarios:

- **The subsidiary's functional currency is its local currency.** The subsidiary's accounts are *translated* to U.S. dollars. No remeasurement is needed.

- **The subsidiary's functional currency is the U.S. dollar.** The subsidiary's accounts are *remeasured* to U.S. dollars. No translation is needed.

- **The subsidiary's functional currency is another foreign currency.** The subsidiary's accounts are *remeasured* into the other currency. Then the accounts are *translated* into U.S. dollars.

A diagram of the conversion process follows:

Codification requirements follow from this basic objective: **preservation of the international entity's financial results and relationships expressed in its functional currency.** An international subsidiary that functions as a branch of a U.S. company, and regularly converts its cash flows to U.S. dollars, should report data equivalent to those reported had the U.S. parent entered into those foreign currency transactions directly. *Remeasurement*, which simulates the international entity's transactions as if they had all taken place in dollars, accomplishes this objective.

Alternatively, an international subsidiary of a U.S. company functioning primarily as a self-contained business unit, buying, selling, investing and financing in its own country and rarely converting these cash flows into U.S. dollars, should report data equivalent to those reported in the local currency. By multiplying all accounts by similar rates, *translation* largely accomplishes this goal by preserving local currency financial results and relationships.

Suppose Wal-Mart has a subsidiary, Euro-Mart, located in Germany. The subsidiary's accounts are maintained in euros, its local currency. If Euro-Mart's transactions are mostly *denominated* in euros—it does most of its business with customers and suppliers in euro countries, borrows and repays loans using euros, etc.—then Euro-Mart's functional currency is also the euro. When Wal-Mart consolidates Euro-Mart's accounts at the end of its reporting period, it *translates* Euro-Mart's local currency accounts into U.S. dollars. No remeasurement is required. If Euro-Mart's transactions are mostly denominated in U.S. dollars—it does most of its business with U.S. customers and suppliers and most transactions take place in U.S. dollars—then Euro-Mart's local currency accounts are *remeasured* into U.S. dollars. No translation is required. If Euro-Mart is located in Germany but most of its transactions are denominated in British pounds—it does most of its business with customers, suppliers, banks, etc. in the U.K.—then at the end of Wal-Mart's reporting period Euro-Mart's local currency accounts are first *remeasured* into British pounds, and then *translated* into U.S. dollars.

Before we discuss the mechanics of translation and remeasurement, we must determine the appropriate conversion process. This requires identifying the subsidiary's functional currency.

The Functional Currency

The Codification defines the functional currency as follows:

> An entity's **functional currency** is the currency of the primary economic environment in which the entity operates; normally, that is the currency of the environment in which an entity primarily generates and expends cash. *(ASC para. 830-10-45-2)*

The functional currency may be the international entity's **local currency, another foreign currency**, or the **U.S. dollar**. Exhibit 7.1 summarizes the economic indicators identified in *ASC Section 830-10-55* to be considered when determining an entity's functional currency. These indicators assess the extent to which the international entity is relatively self-contained or is an extension of the U.S. parent. In the end, determination of the functional currency is essentially a matter of *fact*.

EXHIBIT 7.1   Economic Indicators Influencing Determination of the Functional Currency

Economic Indicator	Functional Currency Probably is:	
	Local or Other Foreign Currency	**Parent's Currency ($)**
Cash flow	Cash flows are primarily in the foreign currency and do not have a direct impact on the parent's cash flows.	Cash flows have an impact on parent's cash flows on a current basis and are readily available for remittance to the parent company.
Sales price	Selling prices are determined primarily by local competition or governmental regulation, and not by short-term changes in exchange rates.	Selling prices are primarily determined by worldwide competition or international prices and respond to short-term changes in exchange rates.
Sales market	Active sales market for the entity's products is primarily local.	Sales market for the entity's products is primarily in the parent's country or sales contracts are denominated in the parent's currency.
Expenses	Costs of labor, materials, and so forth are primarily local costs.	Costs of labor, materials, and so forth are primarily costs for components obtained from the parent's country.
Financing	Financing is primarily denominated in the local currency and is serviced by foreign currency cash flows generated in the entity's country.	Financing is primarily from dollar-denominated obligations or parent company funds are needed to service debt obligations.
Intercompany	Volume of intercompany transactions and transactions is low, resulting in minimal relationship between the operations of the international entity and the parent.	Volume of intercompany transactions is high, resulting in substantial relationship between the operations of the international entity and the parent.

Source: *ASC para. 830-10-55-5*

Determination of the functional currency can generally be summarized as follows:

- An international entity whose operations are relatively self-contained and integrated within the country in which it is located normally uses the **local currency** of that country as its functional currency.

- An international entity whose operations are a direct and integral component or extension of a U.S. parent company's operations normally uses the **U.S. dollar** as its functional currency.

- An international entity located in one country but generating most of its cash flows in the currency of another country normally uses the **currency of the other country** as its functional currency.

TRANSLATION AND REMEASUREMENT PROCEDURES

This section summarizes the procedures used to remeasure a subsidiary's local currency accounts into its functional currency, and to translate the subsidiary's functional currency accounts to the U.S. parent's reporting currency, the U.S. dollar. Recall that when the subsidiary does business mostly in its local currency, its local currency is its functional currency and we only need to translate the subsidiary's accounts into U.S. dollars. When the subsidiary does business primarily in the U.S. parent's currency, its functional currency is the reporting currency and we only need to remeasure the subsidiary's accounts into U.S. dollars.

LO1 Apply translation and remeasurement procedures.

Conversion of the subsidiary's accounts to another currency requires the use of *current exchange rates* and *historical exchange rates*. The **current exchange rate** is the spot rate at the end of the current reporting period—the rate in existence on the balance sheet date. A **historical exchange rate** is a past spot rate, in existence when a particular transaction occurred. For recurring transactions, such as salaries and utilities, an **average exchange rate** may approximate historical rates.

Translation Procedures

When a subsidiary's functional currency is different from its parent's reporting currency, the subsidiary's functional currency accounts must be translated into the parent's reporting currency. However, the functional currency accounts best represent the financial health of the subsidiary.

> The **objective of translation** is to **maintain the financial statement results and relationships** as they exist in the functional currency statements.

To maintain the functional currency relationships between accounts, all of the subsidiary's **assets and liabilities** are translated to U.S. dollars using the exchange rate at the balance sheet date, the **current rate**. **Historical rates** are used to translate **contributed capital accounts** such as capital stock and additional paid-in capital. All **income statement accounts** are translated using the **exchange rate at the dates when these items are reported in income** as revenues, expenses, gains and losses.

Literal application of the requirement for translating income items requires identifying the exact date on which each income item is reported. It would be necessary to identify when each sale was made and when each expense was recognized during the year and use the exchange rate on that day to translate the revenue and expense balances to dollars. This level of detail is usually not cost effective, and therefore approximations are allowed. If a subsidiary's sales and expenses are recognized relatively evenly over the year, the **average exchange rate** for the year may be used to translate all income accounts. Average rates should be weighted according to the level of transactions. If a subsidiary's revenues and expenses are not recognized evenly, quarterly or monthly items may be translated at the average rate for the quarter or month, as appropriate.

Translating all asset and liability balances at the same (current) rate and income items at the same (average) rate generally achieves the objective of maintaining the relationships between accounts as measured in the subsidiary's functional currency. Income statement profitability ratios such as the gross profit percentage are similar whether based on functional currency balances or translated U.S. dollar balances. Liquidity ratios such as the current ratio are the same in the functional currency as in U.S. dollars. However, measures that combine balance sheet and income statement numbers, such as return on assets (income divided by average total assets) can be somewhat distorted by translation.

Remeasurement Procedures

Remeasuring the subsidiary's local currency accounts into its functional currency occurs when the subsidiary records its accounts in one currency but does most of its business in another currency. Therefore, the functional currency accounts reflect the financial health of the subsidiary.

> The **objective of remeasurement** is to show account balances **as if all transactions occurred in the functional currency**.

Balance sheet accounts measured at current money prices, also called **monetary assets and liabilities**, are remeasured using the exchange rate at the balance sheet date, the **current rate**. These are asset and liability balances that are fixed, in terms of currency units. Monetary assets and liabilities include cash, receivables, held-to-maturity investments, inventories carried at fair value and most liabilities. **Balance sheet accounts measured at historical prices**, such as plant and equipment, intangibles, inventories carried at cost, and capital accounts are remeasured at historical rates. Dividends are remeasured at the declaration rate. The remeasured retained earnings balance is an accumulation of remeasured income and dividend flows.

Generally assets carried at fair value are remeasured at the current rate, and assets carried at cost are remeasured at historical rates. However, remember that it is the **monetary assets** that are remeasured at the current rate, and they may not always be carried at fair value. A good example is held-to-maturity debt investments, carried at amortized cost. If the company intends to hold these investments to maturity, their value is derived from contractual interest and principal payments, making them monetary assets remeasured at the current rate.

Revenues and expenses are remeasured at **historical rates**, reflecting how these items would be recorded in the functional currency. For example, salary expenses are remeasured at the rates in effect when the salaries are accrued. Similar to translation, revenues and recurring out-of-pocket expenses such as salaries, utilities, and taxes may be remeasured using appropriate average rates if these accounts represent multiple inflows and outflows occurring fairly evenly. For example, if sales occur evenly throughout the year, a yearly average may be used. However, if most sales occur in December, the average rate for December should be used to remeasure most of the sales revenues. **Depreciation and amortization expenses, cost of goods sold**, and other write-offs of assets carried at cost are remeasured at the **rate in effect when the related asset was acquired**. For example, if Euro-Mart acquired a building for €5,000,000 in 2014, when the exchange rate was $1.25, and in 2016 reports €100,000 in depreciation expense on the building, the remeasured depreciation expense is $125,000, regardless of changes in the exchange rate over time.

Matching current rates to current prices and historical rates to historical prices achieves the remeasurement objective. Suppose Euro-Mart's functional currency is the U.S. dollar but its accounts are reported in euros. It acquires land when the exchange rate is $1.30, and records the land at €1,000,000. If its functional currency is the dollar, it probably used U.S. dollars to buy the land, and paid $1,300,000. Using the historical rate of $1.30 to remeasure the land account at any future date reports the account as if Euro-Mart had actually used U.S. dollars to acquire the land, which is likely what actually occurred.

Comparing Translation and Remeasurement

Exhibit 7.2 identifies the exchange rates used to translate or remeasure various major balance sheet and income statement accounts. To summarize the major differences between remeasurement and translation, we *remeasure* assets carried at cost using historical rates, but *translate* them using the current rate. Expenses related to assets carried at cost, such as cost of goods sold, depreciation and amortization expense, are *remeasured* using the rate when the asset was acquired. Expenses are *translated* at the rate when each income item appears in income, and therefore expenses related to using assets carried at cost are translated at the rate in effect when these items are included in expenses, *not* the rates when the assets were acquired.

Translation and Remeasurement Gains and Losses

From the above sections we know that an international subsidiary's local currency accounts are remeasured into its functional currency, if necessary, and then translated into the parent's reporting currency.

Current and historical exchange rates are used, as appropriate, to convert local currency accounts to the appropriate currency. **Gains and losses** result from both processes, due to changes over time in the rate used to convert an account.

EXHIBIT 7.2 Exchange Rates Used to Convert Financial Statement Items

	Remeasurement	Translation
Balance Sheet		
Cash and receivables...	C	C
Prepaid expenses...	H	C
Inventory at cost..	H	C
Inventory at market	C	C
Investments at cost	H	C
Investments at market	C	C
Property, plant and equipment.............................	H	C
Goodwill and other intangible assets.....................	H	C
Accounts payable...	C	C
Deferred income..	H	C
Long-term debt	C	C
Capital stock	H	H
Retained earnings	Note 1	Note 1
Dividends...	H	H
Income Statement		
Sales revenue...	Note 2	Note 4
Cost of goods sold...	H	Note 4
Out-of-pocket expenses	Note 2	Note 4
Amortization of prepaid expenses or deferred income	Note 3	Note 4
Depreciation, amortization, impairment losses	Note 3	Note 4

Notes:
C = Current rate; H = Historical rate
Note 1: Retained earnings is an accumulation of previous periods' translated or remeasured income less dividends.
Note 2: Remeasurement requires conversion of sales revenue and out-of-pocket expenses at the rates when incurred—the historical rates. However, these rates can generally be approximated by average rates.
Note 3: These accounts are remeasured at the same historical rates as the related assets or liabilities.
Note 4: Translation requires conversion of all revenues, expenses, gains and losses at the exchange rate when these items are recognized on the income statement. Theses rates can generally be approximated by average rates.

Suppose Wal-Mart establishes its German subsidiary, Euro-Mart, with the following initial balance sheet, measured in thousands of euros (€).

Cash............................	€ 10,000	Debt	€ 40,000
Other assets......................	90,000	Equity	60,000
Total assets	€100,000	Total liabilities and equity............	€100,000

If the direct exchange rate is $1.20/€, all initial account balances are multiplied by $1.20, and Euro-Mart's balance sheet in dollars *(in thousands)* is:

Cash............................	$ 12,000	Debt	$ 48,000
Other assets......................	108,000	Equity	72,000
Total assets	$120,000	Total liabilities and equity............	$120,000

As time passes and the exchange rate used to convert an account changes, a *gain or loss* occurs. In Euro-Mart's case, assume the U.S. dollar weakens against the euro, and the exchange rate rises to $1.30/€. If Euro-Mart's assets and liabilities continue to be converted to dollars using the current exchange rate, total assets, in dollars, are now $130,000 (= €100,000 × $1.30), an increase of $10,000 (= $130,000 − $120,000). Total assets increased in U.S. dollar equivalent, creating a *gain*. Total debt, in dollars, is now $52,000 (= €40,000 × $1.30), an increase of $4,000 (= $52,000 − $48,000). The debt increased in U.S. dollar amount, creating a *loss*.

The process of translation and remeasurement requires the use of both current and historical exchange rates. Those accounts converted using the *current rate* change in dollar equivalents, whereas those converted at *historical rates* remain fixed in dollar equivalents. Therefore a company's **exposure to translation and remeasurement gains and losses** comes from *those accounts converted at the current exchange rate*. In our example, total assets of €100,000 are multiplied by the current rate, which increases from $1.20 to $1.30, causing a $10,000 gain. If the assets were acquired when the exchange rate was $1.20, and they are converted to dollars using the historical rate, the balance in dollars stays at $120,000 (= €100,000 × $1.20), with no gain or loss. Therefore, the gain or loss is caused by a combination of the **exposed position**—those items converted using the current exchange rate—and **changes in the current exchange rate during the period.**

To calculate the gain or loss, the exposed position at the *beginning* balance sheet date is multiplied by the beginning-of-period current rate. The exposed position at the *ending* balance sheet date, which reflects increases and decreases during the period, is multiplied by the end-of-period current rate. Changes in the exposed position are converted at the rates in effect when the changes occur.

> **Translation and remeasurement gains and losses** arise because the *ending exposed position* is converted at the *current rate*, while the *beginning exposed position* is converted at the beginning-of-period rate and *all changes* during the current year are converted at *historical rates*.

Suppose Euro-Mart has a cash position of €1,000,000 on January 1, 2016, when the exchange rate is $1.25/€. Its cash position is unchanged at year-end, when the exchange rate is $1.35/€. If cash is converted using the current rate, Euro-Mart's gain on conversion of euros to dollars is:

	€	Rate	$
Beginning exposed position (cash)	€1,000,000	$1.25	$1,250,000
Change in exposed position	—		—
			1,250,000
Ending exposed position (cash)	€1,000,000	$1.35	−1,350,000
Gain			$ (100,000)

A **gain** arises because the exposed position is an *asset*, which *increased* in U.S. dollar terms. If the exposed position is a *liability*, a **loss** occurs.

Now assume Euro-Mart starts with a cash balance of €1,000,000, and receives €500,000 in cash on August 1, 2016, when the exchange rate is $1.32/€. Its ending cash balance is €1,500,000. Its gain on conversion of euros to dollars is:

	€	Rate	$
Beginning exposed position (cash)	€1,000,000	$1.25	$1,250,000
Change in exposed position	500,000	1.32	660,000
			1,910,000
Ending exposed position (cash)	€1,500,000	$1.35	−2,025,000
Gain			$ (115,000)

Euro-Mart's €1,000,000 is the equivalent of $1,250,000 at the beginning of the year, and $1,350,000 at the end of the year, a $100,000 gain. Similarly, €500,000 received during the year was originally worth $660,000. At the end of the year these euros are worth $675,000 (= €500,000 × $1.35), another $15,000 gain.

Companies usually have many more accounts than cash that are converted using the current rate. Remember that when the rate *increases*, a company *gains* from holding *assets* converted using the current rate, and *loses* from holding *liabilities* converted using the current rate. The opposite effects occur when the rate declines. Translation and remeasurement gains and losses derive from the overall exposed position.

Exposed position = Assets converted at the current rate − Liabilities converted at the current rate

Changes in the exposed position include *any transactions affecting the exposed position*. For example, if the exposed position is cash less all liabilities, the purchase of land for cash reduces the exposed position—cash decreases. But borrowing cash from the bank has no effect—the transaction increases cash and liabilities, with no change in *overall* exposed position.

Suppose Euro-Mart has the following account balances at January 1, 2016, converted using the current rate:

Cash...	€1,000,000
Accounts receivable...........................	3,000,000
Liabilities....................................	6,000,000

Euro-Mart's exposed position at January 1, 2016, is a €2,000,000 *net liability position* (= €1,000,000 + €3,000,000 − €6,000,000). During 2016, the following transactions affect Euro-Mart's exposed position:

1. Sales revenues of €5,000,000 occur when the rate is $1.27.
2. Inventory is purchased for €3,800,000 when the rate is $1.25.
3. Salaries of €1,600,000 are paid when the rate is $1.31.

Euro-Mart's exposed position at December 31, 2016, is a €2,400,000 net liability position (= − €2,000,000 + €5,000,000 sales revenues − €3,800,000 inventory purchases − €1,600,000 salaries paid). The loss on conversion of euros to dollars is calculated as:

	€	Rate	$
Beginning exposed position............................	€(2,000,000)	$1.25	$(2,500,000)
Change in exposed position:			
Sales revenues......................................	5,000,000	1.27	6,350,000
Inventory purchases.................................	(3,800,000)	1.25	(4,750,000)
Salaries paid.......................................	(1,600,000)	1.31	(2,096,000)
			(2,996,000)
Ending exposed position	€(2,400,000)	1.35	−(3,240,000)
Loss			$ 244,000

How do you know if the conversion process results in a gain or a loss? Although there are mechanical methods for answering this question, the best approach is an intuitive one: Compare the exposed position converted using historical rates with the exposed position converted using the current rate. If the current dollar amount of an exposed *liability* position is higher (lower), it is a loss (gain). If the current dollar amount of an exposed *asset* position is higher (lower), it is a gain (loss). In the above illustration, Euro-Mart's net liability position converted using historical rates is $2,996,000, while the same position converted using the current rate is $3,240,000. Therefore Euro-Mart's exposed net *liability* position is *higher*, creating a *loss*. The following table summarizes these relationships:

Exposed Position in Foreign Currency (FC)	Change in Value of U.S. Dollar	Adjustment
Asset......................................	Strengthens ($/FC falls)	Loss
Liability...................................	Strengthens ($/FC falls)	Gain
Asset......................................	Weakens ($/FC rises)	Gain
Liability...................................	Weakens ($/FC rises)	Loss

These gains and losses may have little economic significance. For example, suppose a British subsidiary of a U.S. company purchases merchandise from a U.K. supplier on credit and liquidates the payable with £10,000 generated from customers in the United Kingdom. Assuming that the direct exchange rate ($/£) *increases* by $.05, the dollar equivalent of the payable rises by $500, but the quantity of pounds sterling required to discharge it does not change. Has the U.S. firm incurred a loss when this happens? No economic loss has occurred.

A similar situation occurs when the subsidiary acquires plant assets in the U.K. using debt of £100,000. The debt is to be retired with pounds sterling generated in normal business operations. If the direct exchange rate ($/£) *falls* by, say, $.08, then $8,000 less is required to retire the debt. Has the U.S. firm realized a gain? As long as management intends to use pounds to retire the debt, there is no economic gain.

In cases such as these, there are neither actual nor intended conversions of dollars into foreign currency, and the changes in exchange rates are not relevant to performance. Such situations result in paper gains and losses with no immediate economic consequences. By contrast, when the U.S. firm uses dollars to liquidate foreign currency obligations, and purchases foreign currency to do so, the gain or loss measures the actual change in the number of dollars to be paid, a real economic effect. The difference in the actual economic impact of gains and losses resulting from converting a subsidiary's accounts to U.S. dollars is embodied in the translation and remeasurement reporting requirements for these gains and losses. We now discuss the specific calculation and reporting of translation and remeasurement gains and losses.

Translation When we translate a subsidiary's functional currency accounts to the U.S. parent's reporting currency, we convert all of the subsidiary's assets and liabilities to dollars using the current rate. Therefore the subsidiary's **exposure to translation gains and losses is its net assets, or equity**. Changes in equity, such as net income, dividends, and stock issuances, affect the subsidiary's exposed position. If a subsidiary has a positive net asset position—the most likely situation for solvent firms— and the direct rate increases, translation produces a gain due to the increased U.S. dollar equivalent of the subsidiary's net assets. Translation of an international subsidiary's accounts generally results in a gain when the U.S. dollar weakens with respect to the subsidiary's functional currency, and a loss when the U.S. dollar strengthens.

Recall that the subsidiary's financial health is best represented by its functional currency financial statements. Translation to the parent's reporting currency is necessary to consolidate the subsidiary's accounts with the parent, but has no economic implications for the subsidiary. Therefore the *translation gain or loss* is reported as a component of **other comprehensive income** and does not affect consolidated net income.

Remeasurement When we remeasure a subsidiary's local currency accounts to its functional currency, we convert the subsidiary's assets measured at current money prices, such as cash, receivables, held-to-maturity investments and investments and inventories carried at fair value, to dollars using the current rate. We also remeasure the subsidiary's liabilities using the current rate. Therefore, the subsidiary's **exposure to remeasurement gains and losses is its net assets carried at current money prices**. Revenues, out-of-pocket expenses, inventory and long-term asset purchases, dividends, and stock issuances affect the subsidiary's exposed position. Often a subsidiary has more liabilities than it has assets carried at current money prices, and it therefore has a negative exposed position. If the direct rate increases, remeasurement produces a loss due to the increased functional currency equivalent of the subsidiary's net exposed liability position. If the subsidiary's functional currency is the U.S. dollar, remeasurement of its accounts to dollars generally results in a loss when the U.S. dollar weakens with respect to the subsidiary's local currency, and a gain when the U.S. dollar strengthens.

Remeasurement converts the subsidiary's accounts to its functional currency, the currency in which it does most of its business. If a British subsidiary's functional currency is the U.S. dollar, for example, the subsidiary reports its liabilities in pounds but pays them in U.S. dollars. If the U.S. dollar strengthens against the pound, fewer U.S. dollars are needed to pay the liability, and the subsidiary has a real economic benefit. The *remeasurement gain or loss* has a real impact on the subsidiary's financial health, and is therefore **reported in income**, on the consolidated income statement.

BUSINESS APPLICATION Wal-Mart's International Subsidiaries

Footnotes to **Wal-Mart**'s 2014 annual report describe the method it uses to convert the accounts of its non-U.S. subsidiaries to U.S. dollars.

> The assets and liabilities of all international subsidiaries are translated from the respective local currency to the U.S. dollar using exchange rates at the balance sheet date. Related translation adjustments are recorded as a component of accumulated other comprehensive income (loss). The income statements of international subsidiaries are translated from the respective local currencies to the U.S. dollar using average exchange rates for the period covered by the income statements.

It is clear from this description that the functional currencies of all of Wal-Mart's international subsidiaries are their local currencies. How did the translation process affect Wal-Mart's 2014 other comprehensive income?

> For fiscal 2014, movements in currency exchange rates and the related impact on the translation of the balance sheets of the Company's subsidiaries in Japan, Canada, Brazil and Africa were the primary cause of a $2.8 billion net loss in the currency translation and other category of accumulated other comprehensive income (loss).

Remember that exposure to *translation* gains and losses comes from the net asset, or equity position of the subsidiaries, which is usually a positive exposure (net assets are typically greater than zero). Because Wal-Mart reported a *loss* on translation, we conclude that in fiscal 2014, the U.S. dollar *strengthened*, on average, against the currencies of Wal-Mart's subsidiaries. *Source:* Wal-Mart Stores, Inc. 2014 annual report.

BUSINESS APPLICATION Walt Disney's International Subsidiaries

The footnotes to Walt Disney Company and Subsidiaries' consolidated financial statements for 2013 describe its translation policy:

> The U.S. dollar is the functional currency for the majority of our international operations... For U.S. dollar functional currency locations, foreign currency assets and liabilities are remeasured into U.S. dollars at end-of period exchange rates, except for nonmonetary balance sheet accounts, which are remeasured at historical exchange rates. Revenue and expenses are remeasured at average exchange rates in effect during each period, except for those expenses related to the non-monetary balance sheet amounts, which are remeasured at historical exchange rates. Gains or losses from foreign currency remeasurement are included in income.

The accounts of Tokyo Disney Resort, Disneyland Paris, Hong Kong Disneyland Resort, and international locations of The Disney Stores are *translated*, but the accounts of most of Disney's subsidiaries are *remeasured*. It is interesting to note that although translation adjustments for subsidiaries whose functional currency is the local currency are separately disclosed in other comprehensive income, remeasurement gains and losses on the majority of Disney's subsidiaries whose functional currency is the U.S. dollar are combined with other items on its income statement, and are not separately disclosed. *Source:* Walt Disney Company and Subsidiaries, 2013 annual report.

Translation and Remeasurement Illustrated

To illustrate remeasurement and translation, we work through a simple example using the data in Exhibit 7.3. To clearly show the differing accounting results for each method, this example contains few transactions. Exhibit 7.4 shows the entries that Multiple Methods, Inc., a U.K. company, makes to record the events of 2016, and the resulting balance sheet and income statement or statement of comprehensive income. Remember that these entries are denominated in pounds sterling.

EXHIBIT 7.3   Data for Multiple Methods

MULTIPLE METHODS, INC.

Balance Sheet, January 1, 2016		June 30, 2016	December 31, 2016
Cash...........................	£ 50	1. Sell 1 unit for £120.	1. Record depreciation on furniture, £10.
Inventory (2 units @ £50)	100	2. Replace unit for £80.	
Furniture (5-year life).............	50	3. Pay other expenses of £30.	2. Close books and prepare financial statements.
	£200	4. Accrue other expenses of £20.	Assume FIFO for inventory.
Contributed capital...............	£200		

Exchange rates ($/£)

January 1, 2016	$2.00
Average for 2016	1.60
December 31, 2016	1.44

EXHIBIT 7.4   Entries and End-of-Year Financial Statements for Multiple Methods

MULTIPLE METHODS, INC.

Entries (in £)

June 30, 2016:

Cash..............................	120	
Sales...........................		120
Cost of goods sold..................	50	
Inventory........................		50
Inventory..........................	80	
Cash		80
Other expenses	30	
Cash		30
Other expenses	20	
Accounts payable.................		20

December 31, 2016:

Depreciation expense...............	10	
Furniture		10

Balance Sheet at December 31, 2016

Cash...............................	£ 60
Inventory (1 unit @ £50, 1 unit @ £80) ...	130
Furniture, net	40
Total assets	£230
Accounts payable....................	£ 20
Contributed capital..................	200
Retained earnings	10
Total liabilities and equity.............	£230

Income Statement for year ended December 31, 2016

Sales..............................	£120
Cost of goods sold..................	(50)
Other expenses	(50)
Depreciation expense................	(10)
Net income........................	£ 10

Remeasurement   Assume Multiple Methods' functional currency is the U.S. dollar, and it therefore **remeasures** its accounts to U.S. dollars. Calculation of Multiple Methods' remeasurement gain or loss requires the beginning and ending net assets carried at current money prices, and the transactions that affected these net assets during the year. In Multiple Methods' case, balances carried at current money prices are cash and accounts payable. Use the balance sheets for the beginning and end of the year to calculate beginning and ending exposure. To determine the changes in exposure during the year, consider the transactions that occurred and how they affected cash and accounts payable.

Calculation of Multiple Methods, Inc.'s remeasurement gain or loss for the year appears in Exhibit 7.5, panel A. In deciding whether the adjustment is a gain or loss, think clearly about the relationship between the ending exposed position remeasured at historical rates, $84.0, and the ending exposed position remeasured at the current rate, $57.6. Since the current equivalent is less than the historical amount, the company incurred a loss. Note that if the company's net assets carried at current money prices are a net *liability*, the same numbers produce a *gain*—a reduction in a net liability position.

EXHIBIT 7.5   Remeasurement and Translation Adjustments for Multiple Methods

MULTIPLE METHODS, INC.

Panel A. Calculation of Remeasurement Gain or Loss

	£	Rate	$
Exposed position, January 1 (Cash, £50)............................	£ 50	$2.00	$100.0
Changes in exposed position:			
Sales..	120	1.60	192.0
Inventory purchase.......................................	(80)	1.60	(128.0)
Other expenses...	(50)	1.60	(80.0)
			84.0
Exposed position, December 31 (Cash, £60 less accounts payable, £20)	£ 40	1.44	−57.6
Remeasurement loss (reported in income)...........................			$ 26.4

Panel B. Calculation of Translation Gain or Loss

	£	Rate	$
Exposed position, January 1 (Assets, £200 less liabilities, £0)	£200	$2.00	$400.0
Changes in exposed position:			
Net income......................................	10	1.60	16.0
			416.0
Exposed position, December 31 (Assets, £230 less liabilities, £20)	£210	1.44	−302.4
Translation loss (reported in OCI)...................................			$113.6

The year-end remeasured financial statements of Multiple Methods, Inc., appear in Exhibit 7.6, panel A. Note that the remeasurement loss calculated in Exhibit 7.5, panel A is shown on the remeasured income statement.

Translation   Assume Multiple Methods' functional currency is its local currency, the pound, and therefore **translation** of its accounts to U.S. dollars is appropriate. Calculation of Multiple Methods' translation adjustment requires the beginning and ending net assets position (assets less liabilities = equity), and the transactions that affected net assets during the year. Use the balance sheets for the beginning and end of the year to calculate beginning and ending net assets. To determine the changes in net asset position during the year, consider the events that affected equity. For Multiple Methods, the only change is net income. Other companies may have additional effects on equity during the year, such as dividends and capital stock transactions.

Calculation of Multiple Methods, Inc.'s translation adjustment for the year appears in Exhibit 7.5, panel B. In deciding whether the translation adjustment is a gain or loss, think clearly about the relationship between the ending exposed position translated at historical rates, $416.0, and the ending exposed position translated at the current rate, $302.4. Since the current dollar equivalent for net assets is less than its historical amount, the company reports a translation loss.

Translation of the year-end financial statements of Multiple Methods, Inc. appears in Exhibit 7.6, panel B. The translation adjustment calculated in Exhibit 7.5, panel B is part of 2016 other comprehensive income and reported in AOCI in the equity section of the translated balance sheet. This example has no beginning balance for AOCI, and no other items affecting this balance. In an actual company, there are likely to be other items affecting AOCI, such as unrealized gains and losses on AFS investments.

EXHIBIT 7.6 Financial Statements for Multiple Methods

MULTIPLE METHODS, INC.

Panel A. Remeasurement	£	Rate	$
Balance Sheet, December 31, 2016			
Cash	£ 60	$1.44	$ 86.4
Inventory, unit 2	50	2.00	100.0
Inventory, unit 3	80	1.60	128.0
Furniture, net	40	2.00	80.0
Total assets	£230		$394.4
Accounts payable	£ 20	1.44	$ 28.8
Contributed capital	200	2.00	400.0
Retained earnings	10	see I/S	(34.4)
Total liabilities and equity	£230		$394.4
Income Statement, Year Ended December 31, 2016			
Sales	£120	1.60	$192.0
Cost of goods sold	(50)	2.00	(100.0)
Other expenses	(50)	1.60	(80.0)
Depreciation expense	(10)	2.00	(20.0)
Remeasurement loss		see Exh. 7.5	(26.4)
Net income (loss)	£ 10		$ (34.4)

Panel B. Translation	£	Rate	$
Balance Sheet, December 31, 2016			
Cash	£ 60	$1.44	$ 86.4
Inventory, unit 2	50	1.44	72.0
Inventory, unit 3	80	1.44	115.2
Furniture, net	40	1.44	57.6
Total assets	£230		$331.2
Accounts payable	£ 20	1.44	$ 28.8
Contributed capital	200	2.00	400.0
Retained earnings	10	see I/S	16.0
Accumulated other comprehensive income		see Exh. 7.5	(113.6)
Total liabilities and equity	£230		$331.2
Statement of Comprehensive Income, Year Ended December 31, 2016			
Sales	£120	1.60	$192.0
Cost of goods sold	(50)	1.60	(80.0)
Other expenses	(50)	1.60	(80.0)
Depreciation expense	(10)	1.60	(16.0)
Net income	10		16.0
Translation loss (OCI)	—	see Exh. 7.5	(113.6)
Comprehensive income	£ 10		$ (97.6)

REVIEW 1 • Calculation of Remeasurement and Translation Gain or Loss

Seaco, Inc., is a Canadian subsidiary of Guardian Marine, a U.S. company. Seaco began operations on January 1, 2017, with assets consisting of a cash balance of C$411,200, obtained by issuing stock. Financial statements of Seaco as of December 31, 2017, are as follows, in Canadian dollars:

Balance Sheet, December 31, 2017		Income Statement For Year 2017	
Cash..........................	C$ 30,000	Sales.........................	C$404,000
Receivables	23,500	Beginning inventory	0
Inventories	42,500	Purchases....................	375,500
Equipment	369,500	Ending inventory..............	(42,500)
Accumulated depreciation	(27,500)	Cost of goods sold.............	333,000
Total assets	C$438,000		
		Gross margin	71,000
		Depreciation expense...........	(27,500)
Liabilities.....................	C$ 2,000	Other expenses	(18,700)
Capital stock	411,200		
Retained earnings	24,800	Net income....................	C$ 24,800
Total liabilities and equity.........	C$438,000		

Seaco acquired the equipment for cash when the exchange rate was $1.03. Merchandise purchases, sales and other expenses occurred evenly over the year. Exchange rates are as follows:

Date	Spot rate ($/C$)
January 1, 2017	$1.05
2017 average	0.98
December 31, 2017	0.93

Required

a. Assume Seaco's functional currency is the Canadian dollar. Calculate Seaco's 2017 translation gain or loss.
b. Assume Seaco's functional currency is the U.S. dollar. Calculate Seaco's 2017 remeasurement gain or loss.

Solutions are located after the chapter assignments.

• •

REVIEW 2 • Translation and Remeasurement of Foreign Currency Financial Statements

• •

Greco-Mart is a Greek subsidiary of United Stores, Inc., a U.S. company. Greco-Mart began operations on January 1, 2018. Its balance sheets for January 1 and December 31, 2018, are presented below, in euros:

Balance Sheets	January 1, 2018	December 31, 2018
Cash and receivables.............................	€ 10,000	€ 20,000
Inventories, at cost..............................	40,000	90,000
Noncurrent assets, net...........................	700,000	530,000
Total assets	€750,000	€640,000
Liabilities.....................................	€550,000	€420,000
Capital stock	200,000	200,000
Retained earnings	0	20,000
Total liabilities and equity........................	€750,000	€640,000

During 2018, the following events occurred:

1. Sales revenue was €2,000,000, earned evenly over the year.
2. Inventory purchases were €1,200,000, made evenly over the year.
3. Cost of goods sold was €1,150,000.
4. Out-of-pocket operating expenses were €650,000, incurred evenly over the year.
5. Depreciation expense on the equipment was €170,000.
6. Dividends of €10,000 were declared and paid when the exchange rate was $1.52/€.

Exchange rates are as follows:

Date	$/€
January 1, 2018	$1.40
2018 average	1.50
December 31, 2018	1.55

Required

a. Assume Greco-Mart's functional currency is the euro. Calculate the translation gain or loss for 2018, and prepare Greco-Mart's translated statement of comprehensive income for 2018 and balance sheet at December 31, 2018.

b. Assume Greco-Mart's functional currency is the U.S. dollar. Calculate the remeasurement gain or loss for 2018, and prepare Greco-Mart's remeasured income statement for 2018 and balance sheet at December 31, 2018.

Solutions are located after the chapter assignments.

Highly Inflationary Economies

International inflation rates significantly higher than U.S. inflation rates can cause the U.S. dollar value of the currency to fall dramatically, severely distorting translated financial results and relationships. Highly inflationary economies are frequently found in certain countries in South America, Africa and Asia.

When an international entity is located in a highly inflationary economy, and its functional currency is the local currency, translation causes the dollar value of assets, liabilities, revenues and expenses to significantly shrink over time, as the current and average exchange rates fall sharply. Thus local currency relationships are not preserved, as translation intends.

The Codification requires that an international entity located in a country with a **highly inflationary economy**, defined as **cumulative inflation of 100 percent or more over a three-year period**, use the U.S. dollar as its functional currency and **remeasure** its local currency accounts to the reporting currency. *(ASC para. 830-10-45-11)*

The Board stated that this decision was based on its belief that a local currency that "has largely lost its utility as a store of value cannot be a functional measuring unit." The FASB's pragmatic decision to require remeasurement to the reporting currency for international entities located in highly inflationary economies was also intended to preserve local currency results and relationships. When the local currency is more inflationary than the dollar, the dollar strengthens and the direct rate falls. Use of a highly inflationary local currency as the functional currency produces translated international asset balances that dwindle to nominal amounts. Of particular concern is the **disappearing plant phenomenon** in which land, factories and other plant assets seem to disappear in translation. Assuming the local currency account balances and the plant assets themselves remain unimpaired, the translated balances are meaningless.

Suppose the Brazilian real lost much of its value in U.S. dollars due to high inflation. A Brazilian subsidiary has plant assets of R$100,000,000 acquired when the exchange rate was $0.60/R$. With much lower inflation in the United States, the dollar strengthens and the direct exchange rate drops to $0.15/R$. Plant assets translated at the current rate shrink to $15,000,000 from $60,000,000, suggesting that only 25 percent of the assets remain when in fact 100 percent of the physical assets are still intact. In contrast, continued remeasurement at $0.60/R$, the historical rate, preserves the reported plant assets at $60,000,000.

> ### BUSINESS APPLICATION   Herbalife Ltd.'s Venezuelan Subsidiary
>
> **Herbalife Ltd.** is a U.S. global nutrition company whose products include weight management, fitness, and personal care products. Herbalife Venezuela is one of the subsidiaries included in Herbalife's consolidated financial statements. Since 2010, Venezuela has been classified as a highly inflationary economy. The following appears in Herbalife's 2013 annual report footnotes:
>
> > Pursuant to the highly inflationary basis of accounting under U.S. GAAP, Herbalife Venezuela changed its functional currency from the Bolivar to the U.S. dollar. Subsequent movements in the Bolivar to U.S. dollar exchange rate will impact the Company's consolidated earnings. Prior to January 1, 2010, when the Bolivar was the functional currency, movements in the Bolivar to U.S. dollar were recorded as a component of equity through other comprehensive income.
>
> Starting in 2010, Herbalife has remeasured its Venezuelan subsidiary's accounts to U.S. dollars. In 2013, a remeasurement loss of $15.1 million was included in selling, general and administrative expenses. Since remeasurement exposure to gains and losses comes from the effect of the devaluation of the Bolivar on Bolivar-denominated monetary assets and liabilities, it appears that Herbalife Venezuela's monetary assets exceeded its monetary liabilities in 2013. *Source*: Herbalife Ltd. 2013 consolidated financial statements.

Changing the Functional Currency

The Codification intends that determination of an entity's functional currency be a matter of *fact* and not a choice between accounting alternatives. Thus, the functional currency is changed only when significant new economic facts and circumstances clearly justify a different functional currency.

Because a change in an entity's functional currency is caused by changes in facts and circumstances, a change in conversion method is not a change in accounting principle. Thus, the change does not call for retrospective application to prior periods, as is otherwise required under *ASC Topic 250*. All changes are reported *prospectively*.

Change from Local Currency to U.S. Dollar   When the functional currency changes from the local currency to the U.S. dollar, translated assets and liabilities at the end of the prior period are the beginning remeasured book values. Last period's closing rate becomes the historical rate attached to items such as inventories, and property, plant and equipment. The cumulative translation adjustment balance as of the date of change remains in AOCI. This procedure applies if a subsidiary's functional currency is normally its local currency, but its economy becomes highly inflationary.

Change from U.S. Dollar to Local Currency   When the functional currency changes from the U.S. dollar to local currency, assets and liabilities are translated at the current rate. The **opening balance in the cumulative translation adjustment** equals the **difference between translated net assets and remeasured net assets**. This procedure applies if a subsidiary's economy becomes no longer highly inflationary, and translation is now appropriate.

Translation and Remeasurement of an Existing Entity

We now illustrate translation and remeasurement procedures when a U.S. parent acquires an international subsidiary at some point after it came into existence.

Domestic Corporation acquired all of the stock of International Company on January 1, 2016. International's comparative balance sheets for December 31 and January 1, 2016, and its income statement for 2016 follow. International Company has been in existence for several years, and reports in its local currency, the euro.

INTERNATIONAL COMPANY
Balance Sheet

	December 31, 2016	January 1, 2016
Assets		
Cash.	€ 600,000	€ 300,000
Receivables	600,000	700,000
Inventory.	800,000	1,000,000
Plant assets, net	2,300,000	2,000,000
Total assets	€4,300,000	€4,000,000
Liabilities and stockholders' equity		
Accounts payable	€ 840,000	€ 660,000
Long-term debt	1,260,000	1,340,000
Capital stock	800,000	800,000
Retained earnings	1,400,000	1,200,000
Total liabilities and stockholders' equity	€4,300,000	€4,000,000

INTERNATIONAL COMPANY
Income Statement
For Year Ended December 31, 2016

Sales.	€5,000,000
Cost of sales.	(2,250,000)
Depreciation.	(350,000)
Current operating expenses.	(1,700,000)
Net income.	€ 700,000

Relevant exchange rates are:

	$/€
January 1, 2016	$1.50
Average for 2016	1.55
December 31, 2016	1.60

International declared and paid €500,000 in dividends in 2016, when the exchange rate was $1.58. It purchased inventory of €2,050,000 evenly throughout 2016, and acquired plant assets of €650,000 when the exchange rate was $1.57. International reports inventory using FIFO, and purchased its December 31, 2016 inventory balance when the exchange rate was $1.58. Depreciation expense for 2016 consists of €300,000 related to plant assets acquired prior to January 1, 2016, and €50,000 related to plant assets acquired in 2016.

Exhibit 7.7 shows translation of International's 2016 account balances at December 31 and January 1, 2016, when its functional currency is the euro. Exhibit 7.8 displays remeasured financial information when International's functional currency is the U.S. dollar. Because Domestic acquired International on January 1, 2016, *the appropriate historical rate for any balances relating to transactions occurring prior to January 1, 2016, is the acquisition date exchange rate*, $1.50.

The International illustration highlights the differences between translation and remeasurement. Because the euro strengthened relative to the U.S. dollar during 2016,

- Translated total assets are higher, since the current rate is higher than historical rates.

- Translated cost of sales and depreciation expense are higher, since the average rate exceeds historical rates.

- Translation produces a *gain* on a net *asset* exposed position, reported as a component of OCI. But remeasurement produces a *loss* on a net *liability* position, reported in income.

EXHIBIT 7.7 International Company: Translation for the Year Ended December 31, 2016

Statement of Comprehensive Income

	€	Rate	$
Sales.	€5,000,000	$1.55	$7,750,000
Cost of sales.	(2,250,000)	1.55	(3,487,500)
Depreciation	(350,000)	1.55	(542,500)
Current operating expenses. . . .	(1,700,000)	1.55	(2,635,000)
Net income	700,000		1,085,000
Translation gain (OCI).	—	see below	225,000
Comprehensive income	€ 700,000		$1,310,000

Calculation of Translation Adjustment	€	Rate	$
Exposed position, January 1			
(€4,000,000 − €660,000 − €1,340,000).	€2,000,000	$1.50	$3,000,000
Changes in exposed position:			
Net income.	700,000	1.55	1,085,000
Dividends	(500,000)	1.58	(790,000)
			3,295,000
Exposed position, December 31			
(€4,300,000 − €840,000 − €1,260,000).	€2,200,000	1.60	−3,520,000
Translation gain			$ (225,000)

Balance Sheet

	December 31, 2016			January 1, 2016 (1)
	€	Rate	$	$
Assets				
Cash.	€ 600,000	$1.60	$ 960,000	$ 450,000
Receivables	600,000	1.60	960,000	1,050,000
Inventory.	800,000	1.60	1,280,000	1,500,000
Plant assets, net. . . .	2,300,000	1.60	3,680,000	3,000,000
Total assets	€4,300,000		$6,880,000	$6,000,000
Liabilities and stockholders' equity				
Accounts payable. . . .	€ 840,000	1.60	$1,344,000	$ 990,000
Long-term debt	1,260,000	1.60	2,016,000	2,010,000
Capital stock	800,000	1.50	1,200,000	1,200,000
Retained earnings . . .	1,400,000	see Note (2)	2,095,000	1,800,000
Accumulated other comprehensive income. . . .	—	see above	225,000	—
Total liabilities and stockholders' equity . . .	€4,300,000		$6,880,000	$6,000,000

(1) All January 1, 2016 accounts are translated at the exchange rate at acquisition date, $1.50.

(2) Retained earnings, January 1 . . . . . . €1,200,000 × $1.50 = $1,800,000
Plus net income. 1,085,000
Less dividends . . . . €500,000 × $1.58 = (790,000)
Retained earnings, December 31 . . . $2,095,000

Because the exchange rate rose to $1.60/€ from $1.50/€ during 2016, the dollar equivalents of euro balances increased. Remeasured net income is $21,000 higher due to (1) $74,000 (= $3,487,500 − $3,413,500) less in cost of sales and $14,000 (= $542,500 − $528,500) less in depreciation expense from applying lower historical rates for those items, offset by (2) a $67,000 remeasurement loss on the net liability exposed position.

EXHIBIT 7.8 International Company: Remeasurement for Year Ended December 31, 2016

Income Statement

	€	Rate	$
Sales..	€5,000,000	$1.55	$7,750,000
Cost of sales..	(2,250,000)	see below	(3,413,500)
Depreciation...	(350,000)	see below	(528,500)
Current operating expenses.............................	(1,700,000)	1.55	(2,635,000)
Remeasurement loss......................................		see below	(67,000)
Net income...	€ 700,000		$1,106,000

Calculation of Remeasurement Adjustment

	€	Rate	$
Exposed position, January 1			
(€300,000 + €700,000 − €660,000 − €1,340,000)......................	€(1,000,000)	$1.50	$(1,500,000)
Changes in exposed position:			
Sales...	5,000,000	1.55	7,750,000
Inventory purchases..................................	(2,050,000)	1.55	(3,177,500)
Plant assets purchases..............................	(650,000)	1.57	(1,020,500)
Current operating expenses.........................	(1,700,000)	1.55	(2,635,000)
Dividends...	(500,000)	1.58	(790,000)
			(1,373,000)
Exposed position, December 31			
(€600,000 + €600,000 − €840,000 − €1,260,000)......................	€ (900,000)	1.60	−(1,440,000)
Remeasurement loss.....................................			$ 67,000

Balance Sheet

	December 31, 2016			January 1, 2016 (1)
	€	Rate	$	$
Assets				
Cash...	€ 600,000	$1.60	$ 960,000	$ 450,000
Receivables..	600,000	1.60	960,000	1,050,000
Inventory..	800,000	1.58	1,264,000	1,500,000
Plant assets, net..	2,300,000	see below	3,492,000	3,000,000
Total assets..	€4,300,000		$6,676,000	$6,000,000
Liabilities and stockholders' equity				
Accounts payable.......................................	€ 840,000	1.60	$1,344,000	$ 990,000
Long-term debt..	1,260,000	1.60	2,016,000	2,010,000
Capital stock...	800,000	1.50	1,200,000	1,200,000
Retained earnings.......................................	1,400,000	See Note (2)	2,116,000	1,800,000
Total liabilities and stockholders' equity...........	€4,300,000		$6,676,000	$6,000,000

Remeasurement of Inventory and Plant Assets

	€	Rate	$
Inventory, January 1, 2016..............................	€1,000,000	$1.50	$1,500,000
Purchases...	2,050,000	1.55	3,177,500
Inventory, December 31, 2016..........................	(800,000)	1.58	(1,264,000)
Cost of sales...	€2,250,000		$3,413,500
Plant assets, net, January 1, 2016....................	€2,000,000	1.50	$3,000,000
Purchases...	650,000	1.57	1,020,500
Depreciation expense...................................	(350,000)	See Note (3)	(528,500)
Plant assets, net, December 31, 2016................	€2,300,000		$3,492,000

(1) All January 1, 2016 accounts are remeasured at the exchange rate at acquisition date, $1.50.

(2) Retained earnings, January 1 ...... €1,200,000 × $1.50 = $1,800,000
    Plus net income.................. 1,106,000
    Less dividends .... €500,000 × $1.58 = (790,000)
    Retained earnings, December 31 ... $2,116,000

(3) $528,500 = (€300,000 × $1.50) + (€50,000 × $1.57)

Converting the Statement of Cash Flows to the Reporting Currency

ASC para. 830-230-45-1 requires conversion of the statement of cash flows to the parent's currency to display "the reporting currency equivalent of foreign currency cash flows using the exchange rates in effect at the time of the cash flows." The objective is to **change foreign currency cash flows into dollars at the exchange rate(s) in effect when the cash flows occurred**, a result *not* affected by the company's choice of functional currency.

Although gains and losses accrue to all accounts that are translated or remeasured at the current rate, *only the portion of the gain or loss affecting cash is disclosed separately in the statement of cash flows.* Converting the foreign cash transactions to the reporting currency proceeds as follows:

- *Repetitive cash transactions*, such as payments for salaries and utilities, are converted at the *average rate*.

- *Large, discrete cash transactions*, such as dividend payments or proceeds from issuing securities, are converted at the *rate(s) in effect when they occurred*.

International Company's statement of cash flows for the year ended December 31, 2016, in euros and dollars, appears in Exhibit 7.9. Operating cash flows occur evenly throughout the year, and we assume retirement of long-term debt also occurs evenly. The $73,000 conversion gain accruing to cash appears in a separate schedule. *Cash flow from operations* is displayed using the direct method. We illustrate the indirect method reconciliation assuming International's functional currency is the euro.

Disclosures

ASC Section 830-30-50 requires companies to provide an analysis of changes in the cumulative translation adjustment during the year. These disclosures include the beginning and ending balance of cumulative translation adjustments, the translation adjustment for the current year and related income taxes, and any amounts transferred to income due to liquidation or sale of the subsidiary.

Wal-Mart's fiscal 2014 Consolidated Statement of Comprehensive Income illustrates the reporting for translation gains and losses related to its non-U.S. subsidiaries.

(in millions)	Fiscal Years Ended January 31,		
	2014	**2013**	**2012**
Consolidated net income.	**$16,695**	$17,756	$16,387
Less consolidated net income attributable to nonredeemable noncontrolling interest	**(606)**	(684)	(627)
Less consolidated net income attributable to redeemable noncontrolling interest	**(67)**	(73)	(61)
Consolidated net income attributable to Walmart	**16,022**	16,999	15,699
Other comprehensive income (loss), net of income taxes.			
Currency translation and other.	**(3,146)**	1,042	(2,758)
Derivative instruments	**207**	136	(67)
Minimum pension liability.	**153**	(166)	43
Other comprehensive income (loss), net of income taxes.	**(2,786)**	1,012	(2,782)
Less other comprehensive income (loss) attributable to nonredeemable noncontrolling interest. .	**311**	(138)	660
Less other comprehensive income (loss) attributable to redeemable noncontrolling interest.	**66**	(51)	66
Other comprehensive income (loss) attributable to Walmart	**(2,409)**	823	(2,056)
Comprehensive income, net of income taxes.	**13,909**	18,768	13,605
Less comprehensive income (loss) attributable to nonredeemable noncontrolling interest	**(295)**	(822)	33
Less comprehensive income (loss) attributable to redeemable noncontrolling interest	**(1)**	(124)	5
Comprehensive income attributable to Walmart	**$13,613**	$17,822	$13,643

Wal-Mart reports a currency translation *loss* of $3,146 million as a component of fiscal 2014 other comprehensive income (loss), and a *gain* of $1,042 million in fiscal 2013. On average, the U.S. dollar *strengthened* against the functional currencies of its non-U.S. subsidiaries in fiscal 2014, and *weakened* in fiscal 2013.

EXHIBIT 7.9 International Company: Converted Statement of Cash Flows

INTERNATIONAL COMPANY
Statement of Cash Flows
For Year Ended December 31, 2016

	€	Rate	$
Operating Activities			
Cash received from customers (1)	€5,100,000	$1.55	$ 7,905,000
Cash paid to suppliers (2).	(1,870,000)	1.55	(2,898,500)
Cash paid for operating expenses	(1,700,000)	1.55	(2,635,000)
Cash provided by operating activities	1,530,000		2,371,500
Investing Activities			
Acquisition of plant assets	(650,000)	1.57	(1,020,500)
Cash used by investing activities	(650,000)		(1,020,500)
Financing Activities			
Retirement of long-term debt.	(80,000)	1.55	(124,000)
Dividends paid	(500,000)	1.58	(790,000)
Cash used by financing activities	(580,000)		(914,000)
Change in cash.	300,000		437,000
Effect of exchange rate changes on cash (gain)		see below	73,000
Cash balance, January 1, 2016	300,000	1.50	450,000
Cash balance, December 31, 2016	€ 600,000	1.60	$ 960,000

Effect of Exchange Rate Changes on Cash

	€	Rate	$
Beginning cash balance	€ 300,000	$1.50	$ 450,000
Plus cash provided by operating activities.	1,530,000	1.55	2,371,500
Less cash used for investing activities.	(650,000)	1.57	(1,020,500)
Less retirement of long-term debt	(80,000)	1.55	(124,000)
Less dividends paid	(500,000)	1.58	(790,000)
			887,000
Ending cash balance	€ 600,000	1.60	−960,000
Effect of exchange rate changes on cash (gain)			$ (73,000)

Reconciliation of Net Income to Cash Provided by Operating Activities

	€	Rate	$
Net income.	€ 700,000	$1.55	$1,085,000
Depreciation expense.	350,000	1.55	542,500
Decrease in accounts receivable	100,000	1.55	155,000
Decrease in inventory.	200,000	1.55	310,000
Increase in accounts payable.	180,000	1.55	279,000
Cash provided by operating activities	€1,530,000		$2,371,500

(1) €5,100,000 = €5,000,000 + (€700,000 − €600,000)
(2) €1,870,000 = €2,250,000 − (€1,000,000 − €800,000) − (€840,000 − €660,000)

FINANCIAL ANALYSIS USING TRANSLATED AND REMEASURED INFORMATION

Translation and remeasurement of local currency accounts affect analysis and interpretation of an international subsidiary's financial picture in pervasive ways. This section discusses effects on ratio analysis and addresses the problem of interperiod comparisons. We focus on how a subsidiary's reported performance is affected by the way its accounts are converted to U.S. dollars.

LO2 Describe how changing exchange rates affect financial analysis of international entities.

Notice how translation and remeasurement impact components of financial statement data and influence ratios calculated with these data.

- Translated total assets are larger (smaller) than remeasured total assets when the exchange rate has been rising (falling) over time. This effect occurs because assets carried at historical cost are remeasured at historical rates, but are translated at the current rate.
- Disregarding the gain or loss from converting local currency accounts to U.S. dollars, translated income is larger (smaller) than remeasured income when the exchange rate has been falling (rising) over time. This effect occurs because depreciation, amortization and cost of sales are remeasured at historical rates, but are usually translated at the average rate.
- Remeasurement creates a gain or loss that affects net income, while the translation gain or loss appears in other comprehensive income and equity.

Measures of profitability, short-term liquidity and long-term solvency are all affected by the foreign currency conversion process. We first examine the DuPont Analysis, a common approach to assessing profitability.

Effects on Profitability: The "DuPont Analysis"

The basic **DuPont Analysis** disaggregates the *Return on Assets* ratio into *Return on Sales* and *Total Assets Turnover* ratios as follows.

$$\underset{\text{Return on Assets}}{\frac{\text{Income}}{\text{Average Total Assets}}} = \underset{\text{Return on Sales}}{\frac{\text{Income}}{\text{Sales}}} \times \underset{\text{Total Assets Turnover}}{\frac{\text{Sales}}{\text{Average Total Assets}}}$$

Return on assets measures the profitability of the firm's asset portfolio, **return on sales** measures the profitability of sales, and **total assets turnover** measures efficiency—the ability of the firm's asset portfolio to generate sales.

Although various measures of income are used by financial analysts, we prefer either after-tax operating income, approximated by: net income + [(1 − tax rate) × interest expense], or earnings before interest and taxes (EBIT). Use of income measures before interest expense rather than net income enables measurement of profitability before considering interest payments to suppliers of capital. In this way, the firm's operating and investing decisions are separated from its financing decisions. Using similar reasoning, remeasured *operating income* is calculated *before the remeasurement gain or loss*.

Relevant data from the International Company example for 2016 in Exhibits 7.7 through 7.9 are summarized below, followed by the profitability analysis calculations.

	€	$: Translation	$: Remeasurement
Sales.........................	€5,000,000	$7,750,000	$7,750,000
Operating income...............	700,000	1,085,000	1,173,000 (1)
Average total assets............	4,150,000 (2)	6,440,000 (3)	6,338,000 (4)

(1) $1,173,000 = $1,106,000 (net income) + $67,000 (translation loss) [see Exhibit 7.8]
(2) €4,150,000 = (€4,000,000 + €4,300,000)/2 [see balance sheets p. 290]
(3) $6,440,000 = ($6,000,000 + $6,880,000)/2 [see Exhibit 7.7]
(4) $6,338,000 = ($6,000,000 + $6,676,000)/2 [see Exhibit 7.8]

Currency	Profitability Analysis			
	Return on Assets	=	Return on Sales	× Total Assets Turnover
Euro	$\frac{700,000}{4,150,000}$	=	$\frac{700,000}{5,000,000}$	× $\frac{5,000,000}{4,150,000}$
	0.17	=	0.14	× 1.20
$ (translation)	$\frac{1,085,000}{6,440,000}$	=	$\frac{1,085,000}{7,750,000}$	× $\frac{7,750,000}{6,440,000}$
	0.17	=	0.14	× 1.20
$ (remeasurement)	$\frac{1,173,000}{6,338,000}$	=	$\frac{1,173,000}{7,750,000}$	× $\frac{7,750,000}{6,338,000}$
	0.19	=	0.15	× 1.22

When the international subsidiary's functional currency is the U.S. dollar, required remeasurement of local accounts into U.S. dollars presents a different picture of the subsidiary's profitability than that provided by the local currency accounts. However, when the subsidiary's functional currency is its local currency, the euro, translation of local currency accounts to U.S. dollars does not significantly change the profitability picture depicted by the local currency amounts.

In the International Company illustration, the U.S. dollar steadily weakens against the local currency, the euro. Historical rates are therefore lower than the average rate for the year, and the average rate is lower than the ending rate. Lower historical rates are used to remeasure some assets, cost of sales, and depreciation expense, causing remeasured operating income to be higher than translated operating income. Remeasured assets are lower than translated assets. Assuming the average rate approximates historical rates for revenues and out-of-pocket expenses, remeasured return on sales is higher than translated return on sales and remeasured assets turnover is higher than translated assets turnover.

Translated and remeasured ratios differ from local currency ratios if the local currency amounts in the numerator and denominator are multiplied by different rates. In remeasuring return on sales, operating income accounts are converted using average and historical rates, while sales is converted using the average rate. In remeasuring assets turnover, the numerator, sales, is multiplied by the average rate, but the denominator, assets, is multiplied by appropriate historical rates. For International Company, with the U.S. dollar steadily weakening against the euro, remeasured return on sales is greater than local currency return on sales, and remeasured assets turnover is greater than local currency assets turnover.

In contrast, translated ratios maintain local currency relationships. Translation of return on sales multiplies both the numerator and denominator local currency amounts by the average rate, so the ratio is unchanged by the translation process. In translating assets turnover, the numerator, sales, is multiplied by the average rate, and the denominator, assets, is an average of beginning and ending assets, converted using the beginning and ending rates respectively. Translated assets turnover differs from local currency assets turnover only to the extent that the average rate used to translate sales in the numerator differs from the average of the beginning and ending rates used to translate average total assets in the denominator.

Effects on Analysis of Short-Term Liquidity and Long-Term Solvency

Because translation and remeasurement generally lead to different U.S. dollar asset balances, income, and stockholders' equity accounts, other ratios employing those U.S. dollar amounts are also affected. For example, referring back to International Company's December 31, 2016, data in Exhibits 7.7 and 7.8, we make the following calculations:

Currency	Current Ratio	Total Liabilities/ Total Assets	Long-Term Debt/ Stockholders' Equity
Euro	$\frac{2,000,000}{840,000} = 2.38$	$\frac{2,100,000}{4,300,000} = 0.488$	$\frac{1,260,000}{2,200,000} = 0.573$
$ (translation)	$\frac{3,200,000}{1,344,000} = 2.38$	$\frac{3,360,000}{6,880,000} = 0.488$	$\frac{2,016,000}{3,520,000} = 0.573$
$ (remeasurement)	$\frac{3,184,000}{1,344,000} = 2.37$	$\frac{3,360,000}{6,676,000} = 0.503$	$\frac{2,016,000}{3,316,000} = 0.608$

In this example, remeasured ratios portray liquidity and solvency less favorably than the euro data suggest; the lower historical rates used to remeasure inventory and plant assets lower the ratio of current and total assets to current and total liabilities. Translated ratios preserve the local currency relationships exactly—*both numerator and denominator in local currency are multiplied by the same year-end current rate.*

The Codification justifies translation of local currency accounts to U.S. dollars when the subsidiary is relatively self-contained and independent by explaining that translation better preserves the financial results and relationships expressed in the subsidiary's local currency. Translation is required when the subsidiary's local currency is its functional currency. The above ratio analyses indicate that translation preserves these local currency relationships better than remeasurement.

Not all translated ratios, however, are identical to their functional currency counterparts. Significant changes in exchange rates and total assets cause ratios such as return on assets to diverge. Nevertheless, translated ratios avoid the potential large distortions that can occur when drastically different historical rates are used during remeasurement.

In contrast, remeasurement seeks to report the transactions of the subsidiary, recorded in its local currency, as if they were undertaken in the subsidiary's functional currency. If the subsidiary's functional currency is the parent's currency, the U.S. dollar, remeasuring local currency accounts into U.S. dollars at the exchange rates in effect when the transactions occurred produces ratio values equal to those resulting if the parent transacted directly with international suppliers and customers. The functional currency concept indicates that preserving local currency results and relationships are relatively unimportant when the subsidiary's functional currency is the U.S. dollar.

Reporting Perspective

The FASB approved the reporting standards for converting a subsidiary's accounts to the parent's currency in 1981, and these requirements are essentially the same today. Why have these standards stood the test of time? The FASB's conceptual framework provides a structure to guide board decisions on specific accounting issues. *SFAC 1* concludes that the principal objective of financial reporting is *usefulness to decision makers*, with particular emphasis on the role of financial information in assessing the amounts, timing, and uncertainty of future cash flows. In setting standards for converting an international subsidiary's financial information to the parent's reporting currency, the board focused on decision usefulness, not on an abstract theory that might be at odds with events' real economic impact. The *functional currency approach* seeks to match an entity's *economic exposure* to exchange rate movements with the *accounting exposure* that produces translation and remeasurement gains and losses. When a subsidiary's economic exposure is best measured by the viability of its operations, the exposed position of translation (net assets) applies. In contrast, when the subsidiary's economic exposure relates to specific monetary assets and liabilities, an exposed position focusing on those items leads to remeasurement gains and losses.

CONSOLIDATION OF INTERNATIONAL SUBSIDIARIES

This section explains the process for consolidating international subsidiaries. Although the procedures generally parallel those discussed in Chapters 3 through 5, additional issues related to changing exchange rates must be addressed. In the discussion following, we assume the subsidiary's financial information has already been remeasured to its functional currency, if necessary.

LO3 Explain procedures for consolidating international subsidiaries.

Equity Method Reporting

Under the complete equity method explained in Chapter 4, a parent company adjusts its investment account on its own books for its share of changes in the subsidiary's stockholders' equity. As part of that process, the parent records its share of the subsidiary's annual net income and other comprehensive income, if appropriate. The subsidiary's functional currency financial statements must therefore be translated into U.S. dollars before the U.S. parent books equity in net income and other comprehensive income.

The parent books its share of any dividend payment as a reduction of its investment account; dividends are translated at historical rates. The parent also adjusts its investment account for its share of the year's translation adjustment, which affects the subsidiary's OCI. The parent includes this amount as a component of its own OCI. These concepts are illustrated below.

The Consolidation Process

Translation of foreign currency financial statements occurs when the operations of international subsidiaries are to be included in the U.S. financial statements of the parent company. There are two major steps: (1) translate the subsidiary's functional currency accounts into U.S. dollars, and (2) consolidate the subsidiary using a consolidation working paper.

We illustrate the consolidation process for a subsidiary whose *functional currency is the local currency*, using the International Company illustration from earlier in the chapter. When the exchange rate is $1.50/€, Domestic Corporation pays $3,900,000, or equivalently €2,600,000, for all of the common stock of International Company on January 1, 2016. The balance sheet of International Company on January 1, 2016, is repeated below.

INTERNATIONAL COMPANY Balance Sheet at January 1, 2016	
Assets	
Cash	€ 300,000
Receivables	700,000
Inventory	1,000,000
Plant assets, net	2,000,000
Total assets	€4,000,000
Liabilities and stockholders' equity	
Accounts payable	€ 660,000
Long-term debt	1,340,000
Capital stock	800,000
Retained earnings	1,200,000
Total liabilities and stockholders' equity	€4,000,000

International Company's reported assets and liabilities approximate fair values. However, we discover previously unreported identifiable intangibles meeting the asset-recognition requirements of *ASC Topic 805*, with a fair value of €400,000. Analysis of the acquisition cost is:

	€	Rate	$
Acquisition cost	€2,600,000	$1.50	$3,900,000
Book value of International	(2,000,000)	1.50	3,000,000
Cost in excess of International's book value	600,000		900,000
Difference between fair value and book value:			
Identifiable intangibles	400,000	1.50	600,000
Goodwill	€ 200,000		$ 300,000

Consolidation at Date of Acquisition We translate International Company's assets, liabilities, and stockholders' equity using the spot rate at the acquisition date. Domestic Corporation's assumed balance sheet and International Company's translated balance sheet are shown in the consolidated working paper in Exhibit 7.10. In consolidation at the date of acquisition, we eliminate the translated stockholders' equity of International Company against the investment account in elimination (E), and revalue International's assets per the above schedule in elimination (R).

EXHIBIT 7.10   Consolidation Working Paper, Domestic Corporation and International Company, January 1, 2016

	Domestic Corporation Dr (Cr)	International Company Dr (Cr)	Eliminations Dr	Eliminations Cr	Consolidated Balance Sheet
Cash....................................	$ 800,000	$ 450,000			$ 1,250,000
Receivables	1,200,000	1,050,000			2,250,000
Inventory................................	4,000,000	1,500,000			5,500,000
Plant assets, net.........................	8,000,000	3,000,000			11,000,000
Investment in International Company.............	3,900,000	—		$3,000,000 (E)	—
				900,000 (R)	
Identifiable intangible assets	—	—	(R) $ 600,000		600,000
Goodwill.................................	—	—	(R) 300,000		300,000
Accounts payable..........................	(600,000)	(990,000)			(1,590,000)
Long-term debt	(1,400,000)	(2,010,000)			(3,410,000)
Capital stock	(8,000,000)	(1,200,000)	(E) 1,200,000		(8,000,000)
Retained earnings	(7,900,000)	(1,800,000)	(E) 1,800,000		(7,900,000)
Totals	$ 0	$ 0	$3,900,000	$3,900,000	$ 0

Consolidation Subsequent to Acquisition   At December 31, 2016, we again prepare consolidated statements. Domestic Corporation uses the complete equity method to account for its investment in International Company. The exchange rate is $1.60/€ at December 31, 2016. The average exchange rate for 2016 is $1.55/€. International Company declared and paid dividends when the exchange rate was $1.58/€.

The first step is to translate International's December 31, 2016, trial balance into U.S. dollars. Exhibit 7.11 shows the translation, using data from Exhibit 7.7.

EXHIBIT 7.11   Translation of International Company's Trial Balance, December 31, 2016

Trial Balances	€ Dr (Cr)	$/€	$ Dr (Cr)
Cash...	€ 600,000	$1.60	$ 960,000
Receivables	600,000	1.60	960,000
Inventory......................................	800,000	1.60	1,280,000
Plant assets, net...............................	2,300,000	1.60	3,680,000
Accounts payable..............................	(840,000)	1.60	(1,344,000)
Long-term debt	(1,260,000)	1.60	(2,016,000)
Capital stock	(800,000)	1.50	(1,200,000)
Retained earnings, January 1.....................	(1,200,000)	1.50	(1,800,000)
Dividends	500,000	1.58	790,000
Sales...	(5,000,000)	1.55	(7,750,000)
Cost of sales..................................	2,250,000	1.55	3,487,500
Depreciation expense...........................	350,000	1.55	542,500
Current operating expenses......................	1,700,000	1.55	2,635,000
Translation gain (OCI)...........................	—	See note 1	(225,000)
Totals	€ 0		$ 0

[1] See calculation in Exhibit 7.7.

The next step is to enter the account balances of the two companies in the consolidation working paper and make the required eliminating entries. Before continuing, however, examine how Domestic reports its investment in International on its own books.

Because Domestic uses the equity method to report the investment on its own books, the investment account is updated each year to reflect Domestic's share of International's net income, with necessary adjustments, and dividends. Assume that the previously unreported intangibles have an estimated life of four years, and that goodwill impairment is €20,000 during 2016. Domestic's equity in net income is calculated as follows:

International's reported net income ($1.55 × 700,000)	$1,085,000
Less revaluation write-offs:	
Amortization expense [$1.55 × (400,000/4)]	(155,000)
Goodwill impairment loss ($1.55 × 20,000)........................	(31,000)
Equity in net income for 2016	$ 899,000

The investment account is reduced by dividends of $790,000 (= $1.58 × 500,000). There is an additional change in International's stockholders' equity for 2016—the translation adjustment shown in OCI. The equity method reports Domestic's share of International's OCI as well as net income, and therefore increases the investment account by another $225,000. Domestic's entries appear below.

Investment in International Company.......................................	1,124,000	
Equity in net income of International Company		899,000
Equity in OCI of International Company		225,000
To record equity in net income and other comprehensive income for 2016.		
Cash...	790,000	
Investment in International Company		790,000
To record dividends received in 2016.		

Domestic's investment account now has a balance of $4,234,000 (= $3,900,000 + $1,124,000 − $790,000).

Working paper eliminations in journal entry format at December 31, 2016, are shown below, and the consolidation working paper is presented in Exhibit 7.12. Assets are translated at the current rate ($1.60), expenses are translated at the average rate ($1.55), and capital stock is translated at the acquisition date rate ($1.50).

(C)	Equity in net income of International Company.........................	899,000	
	Equity in OCI of International Company...............................	225,000	
	Dividends—International Company..............................		790,000
	Investment in International Company		334,000
(E)	Capital stock—International Company	1,200,000	
	Retained earnings, January 1—International Company..................	1,800,000	
	Investment in International Company		3,000,000
(R)	Intangible assets (1)...	640,000	
	Goodwill (2)...	320,000	
	Investment in International Company (3).........................		900,000
	Other comprehensive income		60,000
(O)	Amortization expense (4)	155,000	
	Goodwill impairment loss (5)	31,000	
	Other comprehensive income	6,000	
	Intangible assets (6)..		160,000
	Goodwill (7)		32,000

(1) $640,000 = €400,000 × $1.60
(2) $320,000 = €200,000 × $1.60
(3) $900,000 = Remaining Investment balance after eliminating entries (C) and (E).
(4) $155,000 = €100,000 × $1.55
(5) $31,000 = €20,000 × $1.55
(6) $160,000 = €100,000 × $1.60
(7) $32,000 = €20,000 × $1.60

EXHIBIT 7.12 Consolidation Working Paper, Domestic Corporation and International Company, December 31, 2016

	Domestic Corporation Dr (Cr)	International Company Dr (Cr)	Eliminations Dr	Eliminations Cr	Consolidated Balances Dr (Cr)
Cash.	$ 1,000,000	$ 960,000			$ 1,960,000
Receivables	3,208,000	960,000			4,168,000
Inventory.	5,000,000	1,280,000			6,280,000
Plant assets, net.	9,000,000	3,680,000			12,680,000
Investment in International Company.	4,234,000	—		$ 334,000 (C)	—
				3,000,000 (E)	
				900,000 (R)	
Identifiable intangible assets	—	—	(R) $ 640,000	160,000 (O)	480,000
Goodwill	—	—	(R) 320,000	32,000 (O)	288,000
Accounts payable.	(700,000)	(1,344,000)			(2,044,000)
Long-term debt	(2,100,000)	(2,016,000)			(4,116,000)
Capital stock	(8,000,000)	(1,200,000)	(E) 1,200,000		(8,000,000)
Retained earnings, January 1.	(7,900,000)	(1,800,000)	(E) 1,800,000		(7,900,000)
Dividends	—	790,000		790,000 (C)	—
Sales.	(25,000,000)	(7,750,000)			(32,750,000)
Equity in net income–International Company.	(899,000)	—	(C) 899,000		—
Equity in OCI—International Company	(225,000)	—	(C) 225,000		—
Cost of sales.	15,000,000	3,487,500			18,487,500
Depreciation expense.	—	542,500			542,500
Goodwill impairment loss.	—	—	(O) 31,000		31,000
Other operating expenses	7,382,000	2,635,000	(O) 155,000		10,172,000
Translation gain (OCI).	—	(225,000)	(O) 6,000	60,000 (R)	(279,000)
Totals	$ 0	$ 0	$5,276,000	$5,276,000	$ 0

The adjustments to OCI in eliminating entries (R) and (O) are caused by additional exposure to translation gains and losses through the consolidation process. The translation adjustment reflects exposure of the net asset position to changes in the exchange rate. When the net assets of International Company are *revalued and written off* in the eliminating entries, its *net asset position changes*, creating *additional translation gains or losses*. As can be seen from eliminating entries (R) and (O), the net translation gain caused by recognizing and writing off the revaluations is $54,000 (= $60,000 − 6,000), and, in the year following acquisition, can be independently calculated as follows:

	€	Rate	$
Revaluation (net assets), January 1, 2016	€600,000	$1.50	$900,000
Less revaluation write-offs:			
Amortization expense.	(100,000)	1.55	(155,000)
Goodwill impairment loss	(20,000)	1.55	(31,000)
			714,000
Revaluation (net assets), December 31, 2016	€480,000	1.60	−768,000
Translation gain attributed to revaluations.			$ (54,000)

The International illustration demonstrates that consolidation of international subsidiaries changes exposure to translation gains and losses. The resulting additional translation adjustments are reported in OCI.

REVIEW 3 • Consolidation of an International Subsidiary

Alti, a U.S. international discount supermarket chain, acquired all of the voting stock of Lodl, a German grocery chain, on January 2, 2017, for $14,000,000, when Lodl's book value was €3,000,000 and the spot rate was $1.40/ €. The excess of acquisition cost over book value was attributed to goodwill.

It is now December 31, 2017, and the spot rate is $1.30/€. The average rate for 2017 was $1.36/€. Lodl's December 31, 2017, trial balance, in euros, follows. There is no goodwill impairment in 2017. Lodl's functional currency is the euro.

	Dr (Cr)
Current assets	€ 1,500,000
Plant and equipment, net.	50,000,000
Liabilities.	(48,300,000)
Capital stock	(1,000,000)
Retained earnings, January 1.	(2,000,000)
Sales revenue.	(25,000,000)
Cost of goods sold.	12,000,000
Operating expenses	12,800,000
Total	€ 0

Required

a. Translate Lodl's December 31, 2017, trial balance into dollars.
b. Prepare Alti's journal entries for 2017, related to its investment in Lodl, using the complete equity method.
c. Prepare the eliminating entries necessary to consolidate Lodl with Alti at December 31, 2017.

Solutions are located after the chapter assignments.

IFRS FOR TRANSLATING AND CONSOLIDATING FOREIGN CURRENCY FINANCIAL STATEMENTS

LO4 Apply IFRS translation requirements.

IFRS for translating and consolidating the financial statements of international branches and subsidiaries is found in the following standards:

* *IAS 21*, The Effects of Changes in Foreign Exchange Rates
* *IAS 29*, Financial Reporting in Hyperinflationary Economies

Translation and Remeasurement

Similar to U.S. GAAP, *IAS 21* requires that an international subsidiary's accounts be remeasured to its functional currency before they are translated into the parent's currency, known as the **presentation currency**. IFRS remeasurement computes account balances as if all transactions had occurred in the functional currency.

If the subsidiary's functional currency is *not* hyperinflationary, translation of functional currency accounts into the presentation currency follows the translation procedures required in U.S. GAAP—assets and liabilities are translated at the end of year spot rate and capital accounts are translated at the rate when the shares were issued. Income accounts are translated at the rate on the date of each transaction; however if rates do not change significantly the average rate for the period may be used. Translation gains and losses caused by exchange differences are recognized in other comprehensive income.

Subsidiaries in Hyperinflationary Economies

A difference between IFRS and U.S. GAAP occurs when the subsidiary reports in the currency of a hyperinflationary economy. U.S. GAAP defines a "highly inflationary" economy in terms of the *inflation rate*, a cumulative inflation of about 100 percent or more over three years. In contrast, IFRS offers

BUSINESS APPLICATION   Foreign Currency Translation at Bayer Group

Bayer AG is a large global pharmaceutical company headquartered in Germany, with operations in the areas of health care, nutrition, and high-tech materials. Its consolidated financial statements are presented in euros and prepared using IFRS. In the footnotes to its 2013 financial statements, Bayer Group describes the translation process:

> The financial statements of the individual companies for inclusion in the consolidated financial statements are prepared in their respective functional currencies. . . . The majority of consolidated companies carry out their activities autonomously from a financial, economic and organizational point of view, and their functional currencies are therefore the respective local currencies. . . . In the consolidated financial statements, the assets and liabilities of companies outside the eurozone at the start and end of the year are translated into euros at closing rates. All changes occurring during the year and all income and expense items and cash flows are translated into euros at average monthly rates. Equity components are translated at the historical exchange rates prevailing at the respective dates of their first-time recognition in Group equity.
>
> The exchange differences arising between the resulting amounts and those obtained by translating at closing rates are recognized outside profit or loss as "Exchange differences on translation of operations outside the eurozone" (in other comprehensive income) or as "Exchange differences."

Note that Bayer uses "average monthly rates" to translate revenues and expenses, implying that there is sufficient variation in monthly volume to warrant using individual monthly rates instead of a simple yearly average.

Bayer has consolidated entities whose functional currency is not the euro located in countries all over the world, including the U.K, Switzerland, North America, and Asia/Pacific. To help in analysis, Bayer also discloses the variation in exchange rates against the euro, for major currencies:

Exchange Rates for Major Currencies		Closing rate		Average rate	
€/1/		2012	2013	2012	2013
ARS	Argentina	6.48	8.99	5.83	7.21
BRL	Brazil.	2.69	3.26	2.50	2.85
CAD	Canada.	1.31	1.47	1.28	1.37
CHF	Switzerland.	1.21	1.23	1.21	1.23
CNY	China	8.22	8.35	8.10	8.16
GBP	United Kingdom	0.82	0.83	0.81	0.85
JPY	Japan	113.61	144.72	102.38	129.20
MXN	Mexico	17.18	18.07	16.90	16.93
USD	United States	1.32	1.38	1.28	1.33

Bayer reports 2013 "exchange differences on translation of operations outside the euro zone" of €737 million, as a decrease in other comprehensive income. The 2013 ending balance in exchange differences is a €2,545 million reduction in accumulated other comprehensive income. In 2013 and cumulatively, the euro has generally *strengthened* against the functional currencies of Bayer's international subsidiaries. *Source:* Bayer Group Annual Report 2013.

characteristics indicating hyperinflation, which can be used to decide whether hyperinflation exists. *IAS 29* provides these characteristics:

• Local currency amounts held by the general population are immediately invested in non-monetary assets or in a more stable currency.

• Prices may be quoted in a different, more stable currency.

• Prices for credit sales and purchases reflect the expected loss in purchasing power during the credit period, even for short-term credit transactions.

- Prices, wage and interest rates are linked to a price index.
- The cumulative inflation rate over three years is near 100 percent.

If the subsidiary's functional currency *is* hyperinflationary, *IAS 29* requires that the subsidiary's accounts be *price-level adjusted* using a general price index such as a consumer or wholesale price index, before translation to the presentation currency. Suppose the price index was 100 on January 1, 2015, when a Venezuelan subsidiary purchased land for VEF100,000,000. On December 31, 2017, the price index is 350. The price-level-adjusted land balance is VEF100,000,000 × 350/100 = VEF350,000,000. Monetary accounts—generally cash, receivables and liabilities, whose value is fixed in currency units—are not adjusted, as they are already expressed in units of current purchasing power. Purchasing power gains and losses on monetary accounts are reported in income.

Once the subsidiary's accounts are converted to currency units of the same (current) purchasing power, they are translated to the presentation currency. When the presentation currency is the euro, and the December 31, 2017 exchange rate is €0.0004/VEF, the translated land balance is €140,000 (= VEF350,000,000 × €0.0004).

IFRS for subsidiaries with hyperinflationary functional currencies differs from U.S. GAAP. Instead of *adjusting* the subsidiary's functional currency accounts *to units of current purchasing power* and then *translating* to the presentation currency, U.S. GAAP requires the subsidiary's functional currency accounts to be *remeasured* to the parent's currency. In the example above, a Venezuelan subsidiary acquired land for VEF100,000,000 on January 1, 2015. Suppose that on January 1, 2015, the exchange rate was €0.0008/VEF. U.S. GAAP remeasures the land balance at €80,000 (= VEF100,000,000 × €0.0008). The difference between the IFRS translated land amount, €140,000, and the U.S. GAAP remeasured land amount, €80,000, is due to the relation between changes in the general purchasing power of the Venezuelan bolivar, and changes in the exchange rate between bolivars and U.S. dollars. To the extent that changes in the general purchasing power of the subsidiary's currency are *not* reflected in changes in the presentation currency exchange rate, IFRS balances differ from U.S. GAAP balances.

REVIEW OF KEY CONCEPTS

LO 1 **Apply translation and remeasurement procedures. (p. 277)** U.S. companies with subsidiaries in other countries must convert the accounts of those business units into U.S. dollars for inclusion in the consolidated financial statements. The subsidiary's local currency accounts are **remeasured** into its **functional currency**, and then **translated** into the parent's reporting currency, the U.S. dollar. Both procedures result in gains and losses from accounts converted using the **current rate**, which changes over time. Remeasurement presents the accounts as if the subsidiary's transactions were recorded in the functional currency. **Remeasurement gains and losses** have real economic effects, and are reported in income. Translation converts the functional currency accounts to the parent's reporting currency, the U.S. dollar, with the objective of maintaining the functional currency relationships between accounts. **Translation gains and losses** have little or no economic effect, and are reported in OCI. If a subsidiary's functional currency is **highly inflationary**, its accounts are remeasured into U.S. dollars to avoid distortions caused by extreme changes in exchange rates.

LO 2 **Describe how changing exchange rates affect financial analysis of international entities. (p. 295)** The subsidiary's financial picture is affected by the procedure used to convert its local currency accounts to dollars. **Profitability, liquidity, and solvency ratios** calculated using functional currency and translated information are generally the same, while ratios calculated using remeasured accounts will differ from the local currency ratios.

LO 3 **Explain procedures for consolidating international subsidiaries. (p. 297)** **Consolidation** of an international subsidiary's accounts with those of its parent requires (1) translation of the subsidiary's functional currency accounts into U.S. dollars, and (2) preparation of a consolidation working paper. Because the consolidation process typically requires **revaluation of a subsidiary's assets and liabilities** and subsequent write-offs, **additional translation gains and losses** occur.

LO 4 **Apply IFRS translation requirements. (p. 302)** **IFRS for remeasuring and translating the accounts of international subsidiaries** are similar to U.S. GAAP. A subsidiary's accounts are **remeasured into its functional currency**, and then **translated into the parent's presentation currency**. However, IFRS treatment in **hyperinflationary economies** uses **price-level adjustments** to remeasure the subsidiary's accounts to the functional currency before translation into the presentation currency.

Assignments with the ✓ in the margin are available in BusinessCourse.
See the Preface of the book for details.

MULTIPLE CHOICE QUESTIONS ··

1. A German subsidiary of a U.S. parent reports its accounts in euros. Its functional currency, however, is the   **LO 1** ✓
Swedish krona. You are responsible for changing the subsidiary's accounts into U.S. dollars in preparation
for consolidation. Which statement is *true* regarding this procedure?

   a. Remeasure the subsidiary's euro accounts into krona and then translate the krona accounts into U.S.
   dollars.
   b. Translate the subsidiary's euro accounts into krona and then remeasure the krona accounts into U.S.
   dollars.
   c. Remeasure the subsidiary's euro accounts into U.S. dollars.
   d. Translate the subsidiary's euro accounts into U.S. dollars.

2. At the end of 2017, an Italian subsidiary of a U.S. parent reports €1,000,000 in equipment purchased when   **LO 1** ✓
the exchange rate was $1.40, and €3,000,000 in equipment purchased when the exchange rate was $1.50.
The average exchange rate for 2017 is $1.35, and the beginning and ending rates for 2017 are $1.42 and
$1.31, respectively. If the Italian subsidiary's functional currency is the U.S. dollar, the equipment account,
in U.S. dollars, is

   a. $5,240,000
   b. $5,350,000
   c. $5,400,000
   d. $5,900,000

Use the following information to answer questions 3 and 4:

   A U.S. parent owns all of the stock of an Italian subsidiary. The subsidiary's January 1 and December
   31, 2017 trial balances are as follows, in euros:

	January 1, 2017 Dr (Cr)	December 31, 2017 Dr (Cr)
Cash, receivables.	€ 200,000	€ 180,000
Inventories, at FIFO cost	400,000	500,000
Plant & equipment, net.	1,600,000	1,300,000
Liabilities.	(1,400,000)	(1,080,000)
Capital stock	(200,000)	(200,000)
Retained earnings, beginning.	(600,000)	(600,000)
Dividends		100,000
Sales revenue.		(4,000,000)
Cost of goods sold.		2,300,000
Depreciation expense.		300,000
Out of pocket expenses.		1,200,000
	€ 0	€ 0

Sales, purchases, and recurring out of pocket expenses occurred evenly throughout the year. Exchange rates
($/€) are:

January 1, 2017	$1.45
Average for 2017	1.35
Rate when dividends declared.	1.32
December 31, 2017	1.30

3. Assume the subsidiary's functional currency is the euro. What is the translation gain or loss for 2017?   **LO 1** ✓

   a. $128,000 loss
   b. $134,000 loss
   c. $128,000 gain
   d. $134,000 gain

LO 1 4. Assume the subsidiary's functional currency is the U.S. dollar. What is the remeasurement gain or loss for 2017?

    a. $162,000 loss
    b. $ 30,000 loss
    c. $162,000 gain
    d. $ 30,000 gain

LO 2 5. A subsidiary's accounts are measured in euros. Assume the leverage ratio is ending total liabilities divided by ending total assets. The current ratio is ending current assets divided by ending current liabilities. The subsidiary's accounts must be converted to U.S. dollars for consolidation. If the U.S. dollar has been steadily *strengthening* against the euro, which statement is *true* concerning the subsidiary's financial ratios?

    a. Leverage in euros equals leverage remeasured from euros to dollars.
    b. Current ratio in euros equals current ratio translated from euros to dollars.
    c. Current ratio translated from euros to dollars is higher than current ratio remeasured from euros to dollars.
    d. Leverage remeasured from euros to dollars is higher than leverage translated from euros to dollars.

LO 2 6. Assume the U.S. dollar has been steadily *weakening* with respect to the euro. Your client, a U.S. company with a subsidiary in Germany, wants to know the **effect of the weakening dollar** on its consolidated financial statements. The subsidiary's functional currency is the euro. Which statement below is *false*?

    a. Sales revenue will increase.
    b. Translated net income will increase.
    c. Translated assets will be lower.
    d. Translated liabilities will be higher.

LO 3 7. A U.S. parent acquired its Singapore subsidiary at the beginning of 2017, for a price that is S$10,000,000 in excess of the subsidiary's book value. The excess paid was attributable to goodwill, which has not been impaired in the past, but is impaired by S$1,000,000 in 2017. The subsidiary's functional currency is the Singapore dollar. In 2017, the U.S. dollar has *strengthened* against the Singapore dollar. When doing eliminating entries (R) and (O) to consolidate the subsidiary with the parent at the end of 2017,

    a. there will be a credit to OCI in elimination (R) and a debit to OCI in elimination (O).
    b. there will be a debit to OCI in elimination (R) and a credit to OCI in elimination (O).
    c. there will be debits to OCI in both eliminations (R) and (O).
    d. there will be credits to OCI in both eliminations (R) and (O).

LO 3 8. A U.S. parent acquired all of the stock of its British subsidiary at the beginning of 2013, when the exchange rate was $1.50/£. The acquisition price exceeded the subsidiary's book value, and this excess was attributed to intangibles with a life of 5 years, valued at £400,000, and goodwill. The subsidiary's functional currency is the pound. In 2018, the subsidiary reports net income of £500,000 and pays no dividends. Goodwill impairment is £20,000. The beginning and ending exchange rates for 2018 are $1.60 and $1.70, respectively, and the average rate for 2018 is $1.65. The U.S. parent uses the equity method to account for its investment on its own books. The U.S. parent's 2018 equity in net income of subsidiary is

    a. $660,000.
    b. $720,000.
    c. $792,000.
    d. $825,000.

LO 4 9. A U.K. parent has a wholly owned subsidiary in Mexico, whose functional currency is the Mexican peso. The subsidiary reports plant and equipment of 10,000,000 pesos at the end of 2017. The Mexican economy is determined to be hyperinflationary at the beginning of 2017. The peso is worth £0.01 at the end of 2017. The plant and equipment was acquired when the exchange rate was £0.05. The general price-level index for Mexico rose from 100 to 400 during the time the subsidiary held the plant and equipment. The translated plant and equipment, following IFRS and U.S. GAAP, is

    a. £500,000 under IFRS and £500,000 under U.S. GAAP.
    b. £400,000 under IFRS and £500,000 under U.S. GAAP.
    c. £500,000 under IFRS and £100,000 under U.S. GAAP.
    d. £400,000 under IFRS and £100,000 under U.S. GAAP.

10. IFRS conversion of an international subsidiary's accounts to the parent's presentation currency is the same   **LO 4** ✓
as U.S. GAAP for *non*-hyperinflationary functional currencies,

     a.   with the exception that remeasurement gains and losses are reported in OCI.
     b.   with the exception that translation gains and losses are reported in income.
     c.   with the exception that translation is the only option; remeasurement is not allowed.
     d.   with no differences.

EXERCISES •••

E7.1   **Translation and Remeasurement of Inventory and Cost of Sales**   Shopwell is a U.K. grocery   **LO 1**
chain that is a subsidiary of Premium Products, a U.S. company. Premium's fiscal year ends January
31. On February 1, 2015, Shopwell's inventory balance consisted of £100,000 purchased when the exchange rate was $1.60/£, and £300,000 purchased when the exchange rate was $1.62/£. Shopwell made
purchases of £5,000,000 evenly throughout fiscal 2016, and its inventory on January 31, 2016, consisted
of £350,000 purchased when the exchange rate was $1.67/£. Shopwell's sales of inventory occurred
relatively evenly throughout fiscal 2016. The average exchange rate for fiscal 2016 was $1.64/£, and the
January 31, 2016, exchange rate was $1.70/£.

Required

     a.   Assume that Shopwell's functional currency is the pound. Calculate Shopwell's translated ending
inventory at January 31, 2016, and its translated cost of sales for fiscal 2016.
     b.   Now assume that Shopwell's functional currency is the U.S. dollar. Calculate Shopwell's remeasured ending inventory at January 31, 2016, and its remeasured cost of sales for fiscal 2016.

E7.2   **Translation and Remeasurement of Depreciable Assets**   Asda is a U.K. supermarket chain   **LO 1**
that is a subsidiary of **Wal-Mart Inc.**, a U.S. company. Wal-Mart's fiscal year ends January 31. On February 1, 2015, Asda reports facilities with original cost of £30 million and accumulated depreciation of
£15 million in its noncurrent assets, as follows:

- Buildings acquired at a cost of £25 million when the exchange rate was $1.50/£, with accumulated
depreciation of £12 million. The buildings are being depreciated on a straight-line basis over 25 years.
- Equipment acquired at a cost of £5 million when the exchange rate was $1.40/£, with accumulated
depreciation of £3 million. The equipment is being depreciated on a straight-line basis over 10 years.

Additional exchange rates:

February 1, 2015	$1.61
Average for fiscal 2016.	1.64
January 31, 2016	1.70

Asda still holds these facilities at January 31, 2016.

Required

     a.   Assume that Asda's functional currency is the pound. Calculate Asda's translated facilities, at cost,
and related accumulated depreciation, at January 31, 2016, and its translated depreciation expense
for fiscal 2016.
     b.   Now assume that Asda's functional currency is the U.S. dollar. Calculate Asda's remeasured facilities, at cost, and related accumulated depreciation, at January 31, 2016, and its remeasured depreciation expense for fiscal 2016.

E7.3   **Translation and Remeasurement of Account Balances**   U.S. Industries has a subsidiary in   **LO 1**
Switzerland. The subsidiary's financial statements are maintained in Swiss francs (CHF). Exchange rates
($/CHF) for selected dates are as follows:

January 1, 2015	$1.02	January 1, 2017	$1.05
January 1, 2016	1.04	December 31, 2017	1.09
		Average for 2017	1.06

The following items appear in the subsidiary's trial balance at December 31, 2017:

1. Cash in bank, CHF4,000,000.
2. Inventory on LIFO basis, CHF3,000,000. The inventory cost consists of CHF1,000,000 acquired in January 2015 and CHF2,000,000 acquired in January 2017.
3. Machinery and equipment, CHF11,000,000. A review of the records indicates that the company bought equipment costing CHF5,000,000 in January 2015 (20 percent of this was sold in January 2017) and additional equipment costing CHF7,000,000 in January 2016. Ignore accumulated depreciation.
4. Depreciation expense on machinery and equipment, CHF1,100,000 (depreciated over ten years, straight-line basis).

Required

Calculate the dollar amount for each of the above items, assuming the functional currency of the Swiss subsidiary is (*a*) the U.S. dollar and (*b*) the Swiss franc.

✅ LO 1   E7.4   Translation and Remeasurement Gain and Loss   Asda is a British supermarket chain owned by **Wal-Mart Stores, Inc.** Assume that the following data relate to Asda's activities for 2017 *(in millions)*.

Net monetary assets (liabilities), January 1, 2017	£ 700
Acquisition of plant assets for debt, February 15, 2017	1,000
Purchase of inventory made evenly during 2017	3,500
Collection of receivables outstanding at January 1, 2017	2,700
Sales made evenly during 2017	6,000
Cost of goods sold	3,300
Depreciation of assets acquired when the exchange rate was $1.80/£	400
Current operating expenses (excluding depreciation and amortization), incurred evenly during 2017	1,200
Refinancing or "rollover" of commercial paper	800

doesnot effect exposed position

Exchange rates ($/£) during 2017 are:

January 1, 2017	$1.65		Average for 2017		$1.72
February 15, 2017	1.70		December 31, 2017		1.76

Required

a. Assuming Asda's functional currency is the U.S. dollar, prepare a schedule to compute the remeasurement gain or loss for 2017.
b. Assuming Asda's functional currency is the pound, prepare a schedule to compute the translation gain or loss for 2017. Assume net assets on January 1, 2017, amounted to £1,200 million.

LO 1   E7.5   Translation and Remeasurement Gains and Losses   Massmart Holdings Ltd. is a South African subsidiary of **Wal-Mart Inc.**, selling high volume, low margin branded consumer goods to customers in twelve countries in Africa. Massmart's accounts are reported in South African rands (R). Assume that the following data relate to Massmart's activities for 2017 *(in millions)*.

Net monetary liabilities, beginning of year	R(15,000)
Net assets, beginning of year	5,400
Transactions during 2017:	
Sales	72,000
Inventory purchases	59,000
Depreciation and amortization	1,000
Cost of sales	61,000
Cash operating expenses	9,500
Dividends declared and paid	100
New long-term interest borrowings	300

Sales, inventory purchases, and cash operating expenses were reported evenly throughout the year. Exchange rates are as follows ($/R):

Beginning of 2017	$0.085
Average for 2017	0.090
End of 2017	0.095
Rate when assets related to depreciation and amortization were acquired	0.070
Rate when dividends declared....................................	0.094
Rate when long-term interest borrowings occurred	0.088

Required

a. Prepare a schedule to compute Massmart's 2017 remeasurement gain or loss, assuming Massmart's functional currency is the U.S. dollar.

b. Prepare a schedule to compute Massmart's 2017 translation gain or loss, assuming Massmart's functional currency is the South African rand.

E7.6   Effect of Translation and Remeasurement on Ratios   The following data relate to the Bainbridge Company's South African subsidiary, which maintains its records in the South African rand (R), its local currency.   **LO 2** ✓

		Translated amounts in $ when functional currency is	
	R	**$**	**R**
Sales...........................	R5,000,000	$ 750,000	$ 750,000
Operating income.....................	1,000,000	130,000	150,000
Average total assets....................	8,000,000	2,000,000	1,400,000

Required

a. Using the "DuPont Analysis," compute and disaggregate the subsidiary's return on assets into its return on sales and total asset turnover components under the three alternatives shown.

b. Explain whether the exchange rate ($/R) has been increasing or decreasing and how that change might affect the usefulness of these ratios. Assume that remeasured operating income does not include the remeasurement gain or loss.

E7.7   Remeasured and Translated Trial Balance   On January 2, 2016, Maddox Corporation, headquartered in the U.S., established a wholly-owned subsidiary in Mexico City. An initial investment of $1,000,000 was made on that date; the exchange rate was $0.10/peso. During 2016, the following cash transactions occurred at the Mexico City subsidiary. All amounts are in pesos (P).   **LO 1**

Facilities costs (January 2; 5-year life)	P1,000,000
Purchase of office equipment (April 1; 10-year life)	300,000
Sales..	12,000,000
Merchandise purchases..	9,000,000
Operating expenses	3,000,000

The exchange rate was $0.11/P in April when the office equipment and P2,000,000 of merchandise were purchased. Sales, other merchandise purchases, and operating expenses were assumed to have been made or incurred at an average exchange rate of $0.12/P. At year-end, the exchange rate was $0.15/P and the ending inventory (LIFO) amounted to P2,000,000. All depreciation and amortization is straight-line.

Required

a. Prepare the preclosing trial balance for the Mexico City subsidiary as of December 31, 2016, in U.S. dollars, the subsidiary's functional currency. Show all calculations.

b. Now assume the subsidiary's functional currency is the peso. Prepare the subsidiary's December 31, 2016, preclosing trial balance, in dollars.

E7.8   Change in Functional Currency   Oliver Corporation decided on January 1, 2017, that its Canadian subsidiary's functional currency is the Canadian dollar rather than the U.S. dollar. On that date, the net assets of its Canadian subsidiary amounted to C$20,000,000 and to $15,000,000 when remeasured; the exchange rate was $0.95/C$. During 2017, the Canadian subsidiary reported net income of C$2,500,000 and paid dividends of C$1,000,000. No other changes in owners' equity occurred.   **LO 1**

Required

Calculate the translation gain or loss for 2017, and the cumulative translation gain or loss at December 31, 2017. Relevant exchange rates were $0.98/C$ (average); $0.97/C$ (dividend declaration date); $0.99/C$ (December 31, 2017).

⊘ LO 1   E7.9   Translated and Remeasured Trial Balances   The Thode Company established a wholly-owned subsidiary in Saudi Arabia on January 1, 2016, when the exchange rate was $0.30/riyal (SAR). Of Thode's initial SAR200,000,000 investment, SAR100,000,000 was used to acquire plant assets (ten-year life) and SAR50,000,000 was used to acquire inventory. The remaining amount was initially held as cash by the subsidiary.

During 2016, the subsidiary reported net income of SAR20,000,000. Inventory purchases of SAR15,000,000 were made evenly during the year. It paid dividends of SAR10,000,000 on September 30, when the exchange rate was $0.255/SAR. No other transactions occurred between the subsidiary and the parent. The subsidiary's condensed income statement appears below:

Sales.	SAR85,000,000
Cost of goods sold (1)	(40,000,000)
Depreciation expense (2)	(10,000,000)
Other cash expenses	(15,000,000)
Net income.	SAR20,000,000

(1) Assume a FIFO inventory flow assumption.
(2) Relates solely to plant assets acquired on January 1, 2016.

The average rate during the year was $0.265/SAR. On the balance sheet date, it was $0.25/SAR.

Required

a.   Assuming the functional currency is the riyal, translate the subsidiary's preclosing trial balance at December 31, 2016, and prepare a schedule calculating the subsidiary's translation gain or loss for 2016.

b.   Assuming the functional currency is the U.S. dollar, remeasure the subsidiary's preclosing trial balance at December 31, 2016, and prepare a schedule calculating the subsidiary's remeasurement gain or loss for 2016.

LO 2   E7.10   Exchange Rate Changes and Return on Assets   Herbalife Ltd. has a subsidiary in Spain, **Herbalife International España, S.A.,** whose functional currency is the euro. Relevant translated data for the subsidiary appear below.

Date or Annual Period	Total Assets	Operating Income	Exchange Rate
January 1, 2017	$112,000,000	—	$1.40/€
2017 Average	—	$12,000,000	1.20/€
December 31, 2017	95,000,000	—	1.00/€
2018 Average	—	10,890,000	0.90/€
December 31, 2018	95,000,000	—	1.00/€

Required

a.   Calculate return on assets for 2017 and 2018 using both translated ($) and euro data.

b.   Explain whether translation has distorted the Spanish subsidiary's performance in 2018 compared with 2017. If so, explain how changes in the exchange rate contributed to the distortion.

LO 2   E7.11   Comparison of Financial Performance: Translation versus Remeasurement   Carrefour S.A. is a global retailer headquartered in France. Carrefour has a subsidiary in Hong Kong, **Carrefour Asia Ltd.,** which operates retail stores in Asia. Assume that Carrefour Asia Ltd. has a positive equity balance, and its monetary assets exceed its monetary liabilities. The euro has steadily strengthened against the Hong Kong dollar in the past few years.

CARREFOUR S.A.
[CRRFY]

Required

a.   Consider these two net income numbers for Carrefour Asia: net income remeasured from Hong Kong dollars into euros, and net income translated from Hong Kong dollars into euros. Which is larger? Explain your answer.

b.   Repeat the requirements of a. for Carrefour Asia's return on assets.

c. Repeat the requirements of *a*. for Carrefour Asia's current ratio and debt to assets ratio.

E7.12 Cash Flow Statement Conversion The Luh Company's 2017 cash flow statement appears below, in its functional currency, New Taiwan dollars (NT$). **LO 1**

THE LUH COMPANY Statement of Cash Flows For Year Ended December 31, 2017	
(in millions)	
Operating Activities	
Net income.	NT$100,000
Depreciation and amortization expense.	45,000
Gain on sale of long-term investments	(4,000)
Decrease in other current operating assets. . . .	24,000
Decrease in current operating liabilities. . . .	(32,000)
Cash provided by operating activities	133,000
Investing Activities	
Acquisition of plant assets.	(85,000)
Sale of long-term investments	50,000
Cash used in investing activities.	(35,000)
Financing Activities	
Retirement of long-term debt.	(98,000)
Issuance of common stock	170,000
Dividends paid	(65,000)
Cash provided by financing activities. . . .	7,000
Increase in cash	105,000
Cash balance, January 1, 2017	210,000
Cash balance, December 31, 2017	NT$315,000

Additional information:

1. Exchange rates: January 1, 2017: $0.042/NT$; December 31, 2017: $0.039/NT$; 2017 average: $0.04/NT$.
2. Changes in current operating assets and liabilities and dividend payments occurred at the average rate.
3. Common stock was issued and plant assets were acquired when the rate was $0.0423/NT$.
4. The long-term investments were sold and the long-term debt was retired when the rate was $0.0394/NT$.

Required

Convert the above statement of cash flows into dollars. Include a computation of the effect of exchange rate changes on cash.

E7.13 Consolidation of an International Subsidiary at Date of Acquisition Fairview Corporation, a U.S. company, has a wholly-owned subsidiary in Mexico. The subsidiary's functional currency is the Mexican peso, and translation to U.S. dollars is appropriate. The subsidiary was acquired for $18,000,000. The balance sheet of the subsidiary on the date of acquisition is as follows: **LO 3**

Mexican Subsidiary Balance Sheet at Date of Acquisition	
Assets	
Cash and receivables.	P 15,000,000
Inventories	35,000,000
Noncurrent assets, net.	75,000,000
Total assets	P125,000,000
Liabilities and stockholders' equity	
Liabilities.	P 25,000,000
Capital stock	80,000,000
Retained earnings	20,000,000
Total liabilities and stockholders' equity	P125,000,000

The fair values of the subsidiary's inventories are P50,000,000, and the fair values of the subsidiary's noncurrent assets are P70,000,000. All other amounts are reported at approximate fair value. The exchange rate at the date of acquisition is $0.10/peso.

Required

Present a schedule showing the calculation of goodwill for the acquisition, in U.S. dollars, and the entries necessary to consolidate the balance sheets of Fairview and its subsidiary at the date of acquisition.

LO 2, 3   E7.14   Translation and Remeasurement Gain or Loss Calculations and Consolidation   On September 10, 2017, the Globe Trading Company invested $3,000,000 to establish a small sales subsidiary in Lima, Peru. The subsidiary converted $3,000,000 into 10,000,000 new sols (S/) and opened a bank account in Lima. At December 31, 2017, the subsidiary reports the following trial balance:

Trial Balance	Dr (Cr)
Cash.	S/ 4,400,000
Equipment, purchased on September 10	2,700,000
Operating expenses.	2,900,000
Capital	(10,000,000)
Total	S/ 0

The subsidiary reports no depreciation on the equipment in 2017. The exchange rate was $0.33/S/ on December 31, 2017, and averaged $0.31/S/ during the period from September 10 to December 31, 2017. Other than the equipment purchase, all other payments occurred evenly over the period.

Required

a.   Assuming the functional currency of the sales subsidiary is the U.S. dollar, prepare a schedule to compute the remeasurement gain or loss in 2017.

b.   Assuming the functional currency of the subsidiary is the new sol, prepare a schedule to compute the translation gain or loss in 2017.

c.   For each functional currency alternative, give the entry or entries made by Globe at year-end, assuming Globe uses the complete equity method to report its investment in the sales subsidiary.

d.   Globe's trial balance at December 31, 2017, before year-end adjustments for its investment in the Lima subsidiary, is below. Prepare a working paper to consolidate the subsidiary, for each functional currency alternative.

	Dr (Cr)
Cash.	$ 500,000
Property, plant and equipment, net	22,000,000
Investment in subsidiary.	3,000,000
Liabilities.	(16,000,000)
Capital	(5,000,000)
Retained earnings, January 1.	(2,000,000)
Revenues	(15,000,000)
Expenses	12,500,000
Total	$ 0

LO 4   E7.15   Hyperinflationary Economies   Consider two companies with subsidiaries in Venezuela, a country that has been identified as hyperinflationary. U.S. Mart's reporting currency is the U.S. dollar, and it uses U.S. GAAP to consolidate its Venezuelan subsidiary. Euro Mart's presentation currency is the euro, and it uses IFRS to consolidate its Venezuelan subsidiary. For both companies, the functional currency of its subsidiary is the local currency.

Required

a.   Prior to identification of Venezuela as a hyperinflationary economy, both U.S. Mart and Euro Mart used the same procedures to convert nonmonetary accounts, such as plant assets, to the reporting or presentation currency. But because Venezuela has been identified as a hyperinflationary economy, these procedures now differ. Explain conversion procedures for plant assets following U.S. GAAP and IFRS, before and after Venezuela was identified as hyperinflationary.

b. Assume the Venezuelan subsidiary of each company has land reported at VEF10,000,000. U.S. Mart's subsidiary acquired its land when the exchange rate was $0.52/VEF. Euro Mart's subsidiary acquired its land when the exchange rate was €0.35/VEF. The price level index was 100 when both subsidiaries acquired their land. Currently the exchange rate is €0.10/VEF and the price level index is 400. Calculate how the land will be reported in the consolidated balance sheet of U.S. Mart and Euro Mart.

PROBLEMS ••

P7.1 **Translating and Remeasuring Selected Accounts** On January 1, 2016, Safetyway Group, a **LO 1** U.S. company, formed a Swiss subsidiary, TEurope AG. The subsidiary issued all of its currently out-standing common stock on that date. Selected accounts from its balance sheets on December 31, 2016 and 2017, all of which are shown in Swiss francs (CHF), are as follows:

	December 31	
(in millions)	**2017**	**2016**
Accounts receivable, net	CHF 40,000	CHF 35,000
Inventories, at cost.	80,000	75,000
Property, plant and equipment, net of accumulated depreciation of CHF31,000 at December 31, 2017 and CHF14,000 at December 31, 2016	163,000	150,000
Long-term debt	100,000	120,000
Common stock, 10,000 shares authorized, issued and outstanding 5,000 shares at December 31, 2017 and December 31, 2016	50,000	50,000

Additional information:
1. Exchange rates are as follows:

	$/CHF
January 1, 2016	$0.96
June, 2016	0.98
December 31, 2016	1.04
Average rate for 2016.	0.99
June, 2017	1.10
July 4, 2017	1.12
December 31, 2017	1.13
Average rate for 2017.	1.09

2. An analysis of inventories, for which the FIFO inventory method is used, is as follows:

	2017	**2016**
Inventory at beginning of year	CHF 75,000	—
Purchases (June 2017 and June 2016)	335,000	CHF375,000
Goods available for sale.	410,000	375,000
Inventory at end of year	(80,000)	(75,000)
Cost of goods sold.	CHF330,000	CHF300,000

3. On January 1, 2016, TEurope purchased land for CHF24,000 and plant and equipment for CHF140,000. On July 4, 2017, additional equipment was purchased for CHF30,000. Plant and equipment is depreciated on a straight-line basis over a ten-year period with no salvage value. A full year's depreciation is taken in the year of purchase.

Required

a. Prepare a schedule remeasuring the selected accounts above into U.S. dollars (the functional currency) at December 31, 2017, and December 31, 2016, respectively. Show supporting computations in good form.

b. Prepare a schedule translating the selected accounts above into U.S. dollars at December 31, 2017, and December 31, 2016, assuming the Swiss franc is the functional currency.

LO 1 P7.2

Existing Subsidiary—Remeasurement   Pennymarkets Corporation, a U.S. firm, acquired Super-Valu, on January 1, 2016. SuperValu is a Swedish company that has been in existence for several years, and whose functional currency is the U.S. dollar. Comparative account balances for January 1 and December 31, 2016, appear below, measured in krona (kr), the Swedish currency.

	Dr (Cr)	
Account Balances	**January 1**	**December 31**
Cash..	kr 175,000	kr 240,000
Accounts receivable, net	400,000	360,000
Plant and equipment, net....................	2,320,000	2,000,000
Accounts payable..........................	(535,000)	(200,000)
Notes payable	(800,000)	(600,000)
Capital stock	(400,000)	(400,000)
Retained earnings, January 1................	(1,160,000)	(1,160,000)
Sales.....................................	—	(1,200,000)
Depreciation expense.......................	—	320,000
Other expenses	—	640,000
Totals	kr 0	kr 0

Exchange rates in 2016 were:

Date	$/kr
January 1, 2016	$0.13
Average for 2016	0.14
December 31, 2016	0.16

Required

Remeasure SuperValu's 2016 ending trial balance into U.S. dollars. Include a schedule calculating the 2016 remeasurement gain or loss, appearing in 2016 income.

LO 1 P7.3

Existing Subsidiary—Translation   Refer to the information in problem P7.2, and assume Super-Valu's functional currency is the krona.

Required

Translate SuperValu's 2016 ending trial balance into U.S. dollars. Include a schedule calculating the 2016 translation gain or loss, appearing in other comprehensive income for 2016.

P7.4 **Statement of Cash Flows Conversion**   Costless Group has a subsidiary in France, ABC Stores.   **LO 1**
ABC Stores' beginning and ending trial balances, in its functional currency, the euro, are below.

(in thousands)	Dr (Cr) January 1	Dr (Cr) December 31
Cash...	€ 30,000	€ 40,000
Receivables	140,000	160,000
Inventories	200,000	400,000
Plant assets, net...	1,680,000	2,000,000
Accounts payable..	(150,000)	(200,000)
Loans payable	(600,000)	(1,000,000)
Capital stock	(500,000)	(500,000)
Retained earnings, January 1........................	(800,000)	(800,000)
Sales revenue..	—	(10,000,000)
Cost of goods sold......................................	—	6,000,000
Operating expenses.....................................	—	3,900,000
	€ 0	€ 0

Additional information (in thousands):
1. Plant assets costing €1,520,000 were acquired on July 6, when the exchange rate was $1.30/€.
2. Included in operating expenses is €1,200,000 in depreciation on plant assets.
3. Sales revenue, purchases, and out of pocket operating expenses were incurred evenly during the year.
4. Changes in receivables and accounts payable occurred evenly during the year. The accounts payable are amounts owed to merchandise suppliers.
5. ABC borrowed €400,000 when the exchange rate was $1.29/€.
6. Other exchange rates were: January 1, $1.28/€; December 31, $1.34/€; average for the year, $1.32/€.

Required

Prepare a statement of cash flows for ABC Stores, in euros, and then convert the statement into U.S. dollars. Use the direct format for the operating section of the statement. Include a computation of the effect of exchange rate changes on cash.

P7.5 **Translation and Ratio Analysis**   Suppose that on January 1, 2017, **La-Z-Boy Inc.** established a   **LO 1, 2**
subsidiary in Ireland, La-Z-Boy Ireland, to design, manufacture and distribute specialized furniture in the European market. Its condensed balance sheet at January 1, 2017, in euros, is below *(in thousands)*.

Assets		Liabilities and equity	
Cash.............................	€100,000	Liabilities.........................	€200,000
Plant assets, net................	300,000	Capital stock	200,000
Total assets	€400,000	Total liabilities and equity..........	€400,000

At December 31, 2017, La-Z-Boy Ireland reported the following condensed trial balance:

	Dr (Cr)
Cash...	€ 10,000
Merchandise inventory.................................	200,000
Plant assets, net...	250,000
Liabilities...	(220,000)
Capital stock	(200,000)
Sales..	(500,000)
Cost of sales...	320,000
Operating expenses.....................................	140,000
Total	€ 0

No dividends were declared or paid. Relevant exchange rates are as follows:

	$/€
January 1, 2017	$1.50
Average for 2017	1.30
December 31, 2017	1.10

Required

a. Prepare a translated 2017 statement of comprehensive income and balance sheet for La-Z-Boy Ireland as of December 31, 2017, assuming the subsidiary's functional currency is the euro. Include an analysis of the 2017 translation adjustment.

b. Assume that operating expenses include €50,000 of depreciation on the original plant assets, the merchandise inventory on hand at December 31 was acquired when the exchange rate was $1.15, and merchandise purchases and cash operating expenses were incurred evenly during 2017. Repeat the requirements of part *a*, assuming the subsidiary's functional currency is the U.S. dollar. Include a separate calculation of the remeasurement gain or loss for the year.

c. Compute the ratios of net income/sales and net income/total assets at December 31, 2017, using the euro financial statements and the translated and remeasured financial statements. Comment on the results.

d. Suppose the euro continues to weaken ($/€ continues to decline) in subsequent years. What will happen to the ratios computed in part *c*? Do the signals they provide indicate improving or deteriorating performance? Should La-Z-Boy's management use the ratios as justification for additional investments in La-Z-Boy Ireland?

✓ LO 1   P7.6   Translation and Remeasurement of Subsidiary Trial Balance   Costsave Corporation, a U.S. company, acquired Denner, a discount supermarket chain in Switzerland, on January 1, 2017. Denner is a subsidiary of Costsave, and its results are consolidated with those of Costsave in Costsave's financial statements. Denner's trial balances for January 1 and December 31, 2017, in Swiss francs (CHF) appear below.

	Dr (Cr)	
(in thousands)	January 1	December 31
Cash and receivables	CHF 25,000	CHF 30,000
Inventories	60,000	55,000
Plant and equipment, net	150,000	175,000
Accounts and notes payable	(125,000)	(120,000)
Common stock	(30,000)	(30,000)
Retained earnings, January 1	(80,000)	(80,000)
Dividends	—	20,000
Sales	—	(500,000)
Cost of sales	—	375,000
Operating expenses	—	75,000
Totals	CHF 0	CHF 0

Additional information:

1. Included in operating expenses is depreciation expense of CHF5,000.
2. Plant and equipment of CHF30,000 was purchased for cash during 2017, when the exchange rate was $1.04. Depreciation of CHF2,000 was taken on this purchase during 2017.
3. The ending inventory was purchased during the month of December.
4. Revenues, purchases, and operating expenses other than depreciation occurred evenly during the year.
5. Dividends were declared on December 31, 2017.
6. Exchange rates for 2017 were as follows ($/CHF):

January 1, 2017	$1.03
Average for 2017	1.06
Average for December 2017	1.08
December 31, 2017	1.09

It is now December 31, 2017, and Denner's accounts must be converted to U.S. dollars in preparation for consolidation.

Required

a. Denner's functional currency is the U.S. dollar. Prepare Denner's remeasured December 31, 2017 trial balance, and a schedule showing the computation of the remeasurement gain or loss for 2017.

b. Denner's functional currency is the Swiss franc. Prepare Denner's translated December 31, 2017 trial balance, and a schedule showing the computation of the translation gain or loss for 2017.

P7.7   Converting the Cash Flow Statement   Comparative balance sheets and the intervening statement of income for **Sears Canada Inc.** appear below. Sears Canada is a subsidiary of **Sears Holdings Corporation**, a U.S. corporation. All amounts are in Canadian dollars.

LO 1

SEARS CANADA INC.
[SCC]

SEARS HOLDINGS CORP.
[SHLD]

SEARS CANADA INC.
Comparative Balance Sheets

(in millions)	February 1, 2014	February 2, 2013
Assets		
Cash	C$ 514	C$ 400
Other current operating assets	903	974
Plant assets, net	975	1,393
Total assets	C$2,392	C$2,767
Liabilities and equity		
Accounts payable and accruals	C$ 798	C$ 906
Income taxes payable	52	1
Long-term debt	468	768
Total liabilities	1,318	1,675
Capital stock	15	15
Retained earnings	1,059	1,077
Accumulated other comprehensive income	—	—
Total stockholders' equity	1,074	1,092
Total liabilities and stockholders' equity	C$2,392	C$2,767

SEARS CANADA INC.
Statement of Income
For Year Ended February 1, 2014

(in millions)	
Sales and other income	C$4,671
Cost of goods sold	(2,548)
Operating expenses	(1,512)
Depreciation expense	(120)
Income tax expense	(44)
Net income	C$ 447

Sears Canada declared and paid dividends of $465 million during fiscal 2014. Exchange rates (U.S.$/C$) are as follows:

February 2, 2013	$0.99
Average, February 2, 2013 to February 1, 2014	0.95
February 1, 2014	0.88

Required

a. Prepare a statement of cash flows (indirect format) in Canadian dollars and U.S. dollars for the year ended February 1, 2014, and a computation of the effect of exchange rate changes on cash. Assume all investing and financing activities took place evenly throughout the year, other income includes gains of $100 million on dispositions of plant assets, and that Sears Canada's functional currency is the Canadian dollar.

b. Prepare a schedule computing the February 1, 2014 cumulative translation adjustment balance (the only component of AOCI), including computation of the translation adjustment for the year ended February 1, 2014. Assume that the beginning balance in AOCI was a gain of $60.

c. How would the converted cash flow statement differ if Sears Canada's functional currency was the U.S. dollar? Explain.

LO 1, 2   P7.8   Analysis of Translation Adjustment Disclosure   Grupo Comercial Chedraui is a food retailer headquartered in Mexico. While it has several subsidiaries, only one is located outside of Mexico. **Bodega Latina Co.** is a chain of self-service stores located in the U.S. Chedraui's consolidated accounts are reported in Mexican pesos (Mex$). Chedraui's statements of comprehensive income for 2011, 2012, and 2013 include the following line:

GRUPO COMERCIAL CHEDRAUI
[CHDRAUIB]

(*thousands of pesos*)	2013	2012	2011
Foreign currency translation gain (loss).........	Mex$3,373	Mex$(43,551)	Mex$71,811

The cumulative balance for the foreign currency translation gain component of accumulated other comprehensive income, at the beginning of 2011, was a gain of Mex$16,849 thousand.

Required

a. Is the Mexican peso or the U.S. dollar the functional currency of Chedraui's U.S. subsidiary? Explain your answer.

b. For each of the years 2011, 2012, and 2013, on average was the Mexican peso strengthening or weakening with respect to the U.S. dollar? How do you know?

c. Prior to 2011, on average was the Mexican peso strengthening or weakening with respect to the U.S. dollar? How do you know?

d. If Bodega Latina's functional currency had been the Mexican peso, would Chedraui's 2013 net income have been higher or lower? Clearly state your reasoning and any assumptions made.

LO 1   P7.9   Translated/Remeasured Trial Balances   On January 1, 2016, the U.K. subsidiary of U.S. International Corporation had the following condensed balance sheet, in pounds sterling (*in millions*):

Assets		Liabilities and equity	
Cash and receivables............	£2,000	Accounts payable..............	£2,100
Inventory (LIFO)	2,200	Long-term debt	1,200
Plant assets	1,600	Equity	2,100
Accumulated depreciation........	(400)		
Total assets	£5,400	Total liabilities and equity.........	£5,400

The exchange rate on January 1, 2016 was $2/£. Inventory and plant assets at January 1 were acquired when the exchange rate was $1.80/£. Plant assets costing £200 million were purchased when the exchange rate was $2.15/£. No depreciation was taken on these assets in 2016, and no transactions between the parent and the subsidiary occurred during 2016. At the end of 2016, the subsidiary reported the following trial balance:

(in millions)	Dr (Cr)
Cash and receivables..	£2,660
Inventory (LIFO)...	2,500
Plant assets..	1,800
Accumulated depreciation..	(560)
Accounts payable...	(2,200)
Long-term debt..	(1,100)
Equity, January 1...	(2,100)
Sales..	(4,000)
Cost of goods sold...	2,000
Depreciation expense..	160
Other operating expenses..	840
Total..	£ 0

The exchange rate when the new LIFO layer arose was $2.05/£ and the subsidiary purchased merchandise sold at an average exchange rate of $2.12/£. Sales and other operating expenses occurred evenly over the year. At year-end, the exchange rate was $2.20/£; the average for the year was $2.10/£.

Required

a. Prepare the remeasured December 31, 2016 trial balance of the U.K. subsidiary, assuming the dollar is the functional currency of the subsidiary. Assume the remeasured balance of equity on January 1, 2016 was $3,520 million. Prepare a schedule to calculate the remeasurement gain or loss for 2016.

b. Repeat part *a*, assuming the pound is the functional currency of the subsidiary. Assume the translated balance of equity on January 1, 2016, is $4,200 million. Prepare a schedule to calculate the translation gain or loss for 2016.

P7.10   **Translated and Remeasured Financial Statements**   StopnShop was organized in Hong Kong   **LO 1, 2** on January 1, 2017, with a capital stock issue that yielded HK$100 million. The exchange rate at that date was $0.10/HK$. Transactions for 2017 and the relevant exchange rates are shown below. The average exchange rate for 2017 was $0.12/HK$, and the ending exchange rate was $0.15/HK$.

- On January 5, equipment was purchased for HK$40 million in cash. The exchange rate was $0.11/ HK$. The equipment is straight-line depreciated over 10 years.
- Merchandise purchases of HK$250 million were made evenly throughout the year. StopnShop uses FIFO and its 2017 ending inventory cost HK$20 million and was acquired on December 20, when the exchange rate was $0.14/HK$. At year-end, StopnShop owed HK$25 million to suppliers.
- Merchandise sales of HK$260 million were made evenly throughout the year. At year-end, customers owed HK$10 million to StopnShop.
- Operating expenses of HK$25 million, paid in cash, were incurred evenly throughout the year.

Required

Prepare StopnShop's December 31, 2017 balance sheet and 2017 statement of comprehensive income, in U.S. dollars, assuming its functional currency is (a) the U.S. dollar, and (b) the Hong Kong dollar. Show the calculation of the 2017 remeasurement and translation gain or loss.

LO 3 **P7.11** **Consolidated Financial Statements with an International Subsidiary** On January 1, 2017, the Phillips Company acquired all of the outstanding shares of Standard, Ltd., a U.K. firm, for £8,000,000 in cash. At the end of 2017, the two companies presented the condensed financial statements below.

Balance Sheets
December 31, 2017

	Phillips	Standard
Assets		
Cash and receivables...........................	$ 2,100,000	£ 3,000,000
Inventory..	4,000,000	3,000,000
Property, plant and equipment, net	12,000,000	5,000,000
Investment in Standard	13,900,000	—
Total assets	$32,000,000	£11,000,000
Liabilities and Stockholders' Equity		
Current liabilities.................................	$ 8,000,000	£ 4,000,000
Long-term debt	4,000,000	1,000,000
Capital stock	10,000,000	2,000,000
Retained earnings	10,000,000	4,000,000
Total liabilities and stockholders' equity	$32,000,000	£11,000,000

Statements of Income and Retained Earnings
For Year Ended December 31, 2017

	Phillips	Standard
Sales...	$30,000,000	£10,000,000
Cost of goods sold................................	20,000,000	6,000,000
Depreciation.....................................	1,000,000	500,000
Other operating expenses	5,000,000	2,000,000
Total expenses...................................	26,000,000	8,500,000
Net income......................................	4,000,000	1,500,000
Dividends	(2,000,000)	(1,000,000)
Retained earnings, beginning........................	8,000,000	3,500,000
Retained earnings, ending	$10,000,000	£ 4,000,000

At date of acquisition, the exchange rate was $2/£. Standard's inventory and buildings were undervalued by £100,000 and £500,000, respectively. All of the undervalued inventory was sold during the year, and the buildings are depreciated over a 20-year life, straight-line. Other relevant information is as follows:

1. The exchange rate at the end of 2017 was $2.30/£. The average exchange rate for 2017 was $2.15/£.
2. Goodwill impairment during 2017 was £200,000.
3. Phillips reports its Investment in Standard using the complete equity method. However, neither equity in net income of Standard nor Phillips' share of the translation gain for 2017 have been booked. Intercompany dividends, declared when the exchange rate was $2.10/£, were credited to the investment account.

Required

Assuming the pound is Standard's functional currency, prepare a consolidated balance sheet and a consolidated statement of comprehensive income for Phillips and Standard. All supporting schedules and computations should be in good form.

LO 1, 4 **P7.12** **Hyperinflationary Economy, U.S. GAAP and IFRS** A subsidiary of a U.S. company began operations on January 1, 2017, in a country whose currency is identified as hyperinflationary. The subsidiary's local currency (LC) is its functional currency. The subsidiary's trial balances as of the beginning and end of 2017, in LC, are as follows (*in millions*):

	January 1, 2017 Dr (Cr)	December 31, 2017 Dr (Cr)
Cash.	LC10,000	LC125,000
Plant assets, net.	40,000	35,000
Liabilities.	—	(50,000)
Capital stock	(50,000)	(50,000)
Sales revenue.	—	(200,000)
Out of pocket operating expenses.	—	135,000
Depreciation expense.	—	5,000
	LC 0	LC 0

Sales and out of pocket operating expenses were incurred evenly throughout the year.

The general price-level index for the country in which the subsidiary operates is:

Date	Price-level index
January 1, 2017	100
2017 average	400
December 31, 2017	600

Exchange rates (U.S. $/LC) are:

Date	Exchange rate
January 1, 2017	$0.65
2017 average	0.15
December 31, 2017	0.10

Required

Present the subsidiary's balance sheet at December 31, 2017 and statement of comprehensive income for 2017, in U.S. dollars, following *(a)* U.S. GAAP, and *(b)* IFRS. Include schedules of any gain or loss on conversion.

P7.13   Remeasurement and Translation to Reporting Currency   Kreeger Group is a U.S. retailer with   **LO 1**
subsidiaries in several countries. One of its subsidiaries, Organic Unlimited, is headquartered in the U.K. but does most of its business in euro markets. The subsidiary was acquired on January 1, 2016. It is now December 31, 2016, and the subsidiary's beginning and ending trial balances, in pounds, are below.

	Dr (Cr)	
(in thousands)	January 1	December 31
Cash and receivables.	£ 10,000	£ 5,000
Inventories	75,000	85,000
Plant assets, net.	125,000	143,000
Accounts payable.	(20,000)	(18,000)
Loans payable	(70,000)	(80,000)
Capital stock	(50,000)	(50,000)
Retained earnings, January 1.	(70,000)	(70,000)
Sales revenue.	—	(600,000)
Cost of goods sold.	—	500,000
Operating expenses.	—	85,000
	£ 0	£ 0

Additional information:

1. Plant assets costing £30,000,000 were acquired on April 5, 2016.
2. Included in operating expenses is £12,000,000 in depreciation on plant assets. Of that amount, £2,000,000 is depreciation on the plant assets acquired in 2016.
3. Sales revenue, purchases, and out of pocket operating expenses were incurred evenly during the year.
4. Organic uses FIFO to report its inventory. The ending inventory was purchased on December 15, 2016.

Exchange rates were as follows:

	€/£	$/€
January 1, 2016	€1.12	$1.30
Average for 2016	1.18	1.25
April 5, 2016	1.14	1.28
December 15, 2016	1.19	1.23
December 31, 2016	1.20	1.22

Required

Convert Organic's December 31, 2016, trial balance to U.S. dollars in preparation for consolidation with its U.S. parent. Note that Organic's local currency is the pound, its functional currency is the euro, and its reporting currency is the U.S. dollar.

✔ LO 3   P7.14   Consolidating an International Subsidiary, Year of Acquisition   On February 1, 2016, Pathway Inc., a U.S. company, acquired all of the outstanding shares of Superbarn Supermarkets, an Australian chain, for A$100 million in cash. Superbarn's assets and liabilities were reported at amounts approximating fair value, but it had previously unrecorded intangible assets (5-year life, straight-line) valued at A$20 million. Superbarn's functional currency is the Australian dollar (A$). Pathway uses the complete equity method to record its investment in Superbarn on its own books. The January 31, 2017 trial balances of the two companies are below.

(*in thousands*)	Pathway Dr (Cr)	Superbarn Dr (Cr)
Cash and receivables	$ 15,000	A$ 5,000
Inventories	90,000	30,000
Plant and equipment, net	800,000	350,000
Investment in Superbarn	93,000	—
Liabilities	(874,000)	(345,000)
Capital stock	(25,000)	(10,000)
Retained earnings, February 1	(85,000)	(20,000)
Dividends	2,000	—
Sales revenue	(1,500,000)	(500,000)
Equity in net income of Superbarn	(3,600)	—
Equity in other comprehensive loss of Superbarn	2,600	—
Cost of goods sold	1,000,000	400,000
Operating expenses	485,000	90,000
	$ 0	A$ 0

Exchange rates:

February 1, 2016	$0.92/A$
Average for fiscal 2017	0.90/A$
January 31, 2017	0.85/A$

Goodwill arising from the acquisition of Superbarn was impaired by A$2 million in fiscal 2017.

Required

a. Prepare a working paper to consolidate the trial balances of Pathway and Superbarn for fiscal 2017.

b. Present the consolidated balance sheet and statement of comprehensive income for fiscal 2017, in good form.

P7.15 **Consolidating an International Subsidiary, Second Year Following Acquisition** Refer to **LO 3** the information in P7.14. It is now January 31, 2018, the end of the second year following Pathway's acquisition of Superbarn. The January 31, 2018, trial balances of the two companies are below.

(*in thousands*)	Pathway Dr (Cr)	Superbarn Dr (Cr)
Cash and receivables.	$ 18,000	A$ 6,000
Inventories	95,000	40,000
Plant and equipment, net.	920,000	400,000
Investment in Superbarn	91,050	—
Liabilities.	(990,500)	(399,000)
Capital stock	(30,000)	(10,000)
Retained earnings, February 1	(101,600)	(30,000)
Accumulated other comprehensive loss, February 1.	2,600	—
Dividends	1,500	—
Sales revenue.	(1,700,000)	(700,000)
Equity in net income of Superbarn.	(2,400)	—
Equity in other comprehensive loss of Superbarn	4,350	—
Cost of goods sold.	1,200,000	600,000
Operating expenses	492,000	93,000
	$ 0	A$ 0

Exchange rates:

February 1, 2017	$0.85/A$
Average for fiscal 2018.	0.80/A$
January 31, 2018	0.75/A$

There is no goodwill impairment in fiscal 2018.

Required

a. Prepare a working paper to consolidate the accounts of Pathway and Superbarn for fiscal 2018.

b. Present the consolidated balance sheet and statement of comprehensive income for fiscal 2018, in good form.

REVIEW SOLUTIONS ••

Review 1 Solution

a. Schedule of translation gain or loss

	C$	Rate	$
Beginning exposed position.	C$411,200	$1.05	$431,760
Change in exposed position:			
Net income	24,800	0.98	24,304
			456,064
Ending exposed position	C$436,000	0.93	−405,480
Translation loss (OCI)			$ 50,584

b. Schedule of remeasurement gain or loss

	C$	Rate	$
Beginning exposed position..................	C$411,200	$1.05	$431,760
Change in exposed position:			
Sales.....................................	404,000	0.98	395,920
Purchases.............................	(375,500)	0.98	(367,990)
Other expenses.........................	(18,700)	0.98	(18,326)
Equipment purchase....................	(369,500)	1.03	(380,585)
			60,779
Ending exposed position	C$ 51,500	0.93	−47,895
Remeasurement loss (earnings).............			$ 12,884

Review 2 Solution

a. Schedule of translation gain or loss

	€	Rate	$
Beginning exposed position..................	€200,000	$1.40	$280,000
Change in exposed position:			
Net income	30,000	1.50	45,000
Dividends	(10,000)	1.52	(15,200)
			309,800
Ending exposed position	€220,000	1.55	−341,000
Translation gain (OCI)......................			$ (31,200)

Statement of comprehensive income for 2018

	€	Rate	$
Sales revenue............................	€2,000,000	$1.50	$3,000,000
Cost of goods sold.......................	(1,150,000)	1.50	(1,725,000)
Out of pocket operating expenses...........	(650,000)	1.50	(975,000)
Depreciation expense......................	(170,000)	1.50	(255,000)
Net income..............................	30,000		45,000
Translation gain (OCI)......................	—	—	31,200
Comprehensive income...................	€ 30,000		$ 76,200

Balance sheet, December 31, 2018

	€	Rate	$
Cash and receivables....................	€ 20,000	$1.55	$ 31,000
Inventories	90,000	1.55	139,500
Noncurrent assets, net..................	530,000	1.55	821,500
Total assets	€640,000		$992,000
Liabilities..............................	€420,000	1.55	$651,000
Capital stock	200,000	1.40	280,000
Retained earnings	20,000	(1)	29,800
Accumulated other comprehensive income...	—	See schedule	31,200
Total liabilities and equity................	€640,000		$992,000

(1) $45,000 − $15,200 = $29,800.

b.   Schedule of remeasurement gain or loss

	€	Rate	$
Beginning exposed position..............	€ (540,000)	$1.40	$ (756,000)
Change in exposed position:			
Sales revenue........................	2,000,000	1.50	3,000,000
Purchases..........................	(1,200,000)	1.50	(1,800,000)
Out of pocket operating expenses........	(650,000)	1.50	(975,000)
Dividends	(10,000)	1.52	(15,200)
			(546,200)
Ending exposed position	€ (400,000)	1.55	−(620,000)
Remeasurement loss (earnings)...........			$ 73,800

Income statement for 2018

	€	Rate	$
Sales revenue.........................	€2,000,000	$1.50	$ 3,000,000
Cost of goods sold....................	(1,150,000)	See schedule	(1,716,500)
Out of pocket operating expenses..........	(650,000)	1.50	(975,000)
Depreciation expense...................	(170,000)	1.40	(238,000)
Remeasurement loss		See schedule	(73,800)
Net income (loss)	€ 30,000		$ (3,300)

Calculation of cost of goods sold

	€	Rate	$
Beginning inventory	€ 40,000	$1.40	$ 56,000
Purchases............................	1,200,000	1.50	1,800,000
Ending inventory.......................	(90,000)	1.55	(139,500)
Cost of goods sold.....................	€1,150,000		$1,716,500

Balance sheet, December 31, 2018

	€	Rate	$
Cash and receivables....................	€ 20,000	$1.55	$ 31,000
Inventories	90,000	1.55	139,500
Noncurrent assets, net.................	530,000	1.40	742,000
Total assets	€640,000		$912,500
Liabilities............................	€420,000	1.55	$651,000
Capital stock	200,000	1.40	280,000
Retained earnings	20,000	(2)	(18,500)
Total liabilities and equity..............	€640,000		$912,500

(2) − $3,300 − $15,200 = $(18,500).

Review 3 Solution

a. Trial balance, December 31, 2017

	€	Rate	$
Current assets	€ 1,500,000	$1.30	$ 1,950,000
Plant and equipment, net	50,000,000	1.30	65,000,000
Liabilities	(48,300,000)	1.30	(62,790,000)
Capital stock	(1,000,000)	1.40	(1,400,000)
Retained earnings, January 1	(2,000,000)	1.40	(2,800,000)
Sales revenue	(25,000,000)	1.36	(34,000,000)
Cost of goods sold	12,000,000	1.36	16,320,000
Operating expenses	12,800,000	1.36	17,408,000
Translation loss (OCL)	—	See schedule	312,000
Totals	€ 0		$ 0

Schedule of translation gain or loss

	€	Rate	$
Beginning exposed position	€3,000,000	$1.40	$ 4,200,000
Change in exposed position:			
Net income	200,000	1.36	272,000
			4,472,000
Ending exposed position	€3,200,000	1.30	−4,160,000
Translation loss (OCL)			$ 312,000

b.

Investment in Lodl	14,000,000	
Cash		14,000,000
To record the acquisition of Lodl's stock for $14,000,000.		
Equity in other comprehensive loss of Lodl	312,000	
Equity in net income of Lodl		272,000
Investment in Lodl		40,000
To record Lodl's 2017 net income and other comprehensive loss.		

The December 31, 2017, Investment balance is $13,960,000 (= $14,000,000 − $40,000).

c. Consolidation eliminating entries are:

(C)	Equity in net income of Lodl	272,000	
	Investment in Lodl	40,000	
	Equity in other comprehensive loss of Lodl		312,000
(E)	Capital stock	1,400,000	
	Retained earnings, January 1	2,800,000	
	Investment in Lodl		4,200,000
(R)	Goodwill (1)	9,100,000	
	Other comprehensive loss	700,000	
	Investment in Lodl (2)		9,800,000

(1) $9,100,000 = €7,000,000 × $1.30
(2) $9,800,000 = $13,960,000 + $40,000 − $4,200,000.

8 Foreign Currency Transactions and Hedging

LEARNING OBJECTIVES

LO1 Report import and export transactions and borrowing and lending denominated in foreign currency. (p. 330)

LO2 Report hedges of foreign-currency-denominated receivables and payables. (p. 341)

LO3 Report hedges of foreign-currency-denominated firm commitments. (p. 344)

LO4 Report hedges of foreign-currency-denominated forecasted transactions. (p. 349)

LO5 Report hedges of net investments in international operations. (p. 353)

LO6 Report speculative investments in foreign currency financial derivatives. (p. 354)

LO7 Describe IFRS for foreign currency transactions and hedging activities. (p. 356)

MCDONALD'S CORPORATION
www.mcdonalds.com

McDonald's Corporation is well-known for its Big Macs, Chicken McNuggets and Egg McMuffins. At the end of 2013, it had a presence in 119 countries, mainly through franchised restaurants. As a result, McDonald's transacts business in many different currencies. Revenues include sales by company-operated restaurants and rent and royalties paid by franchisees, with more than half coming from Europe, Asia/Pacific, the Middle East, and Africa.

McDonald's is a U.S. company, and it must report its activities in U.S. dollars. But a substantial amount of its revenues and expenses are denominated in other currencies, as described in this excerpt from its 2013 annual report:

> A significant part of the Company's operating income is generated outside the U.S., and about 40% of its total debt is denominated in foreign currencies. Accordingly, earnings are affected by changes in foreign currency exchange rates, particularly the Euro, British Pound, Australian Dollar and Canadian Dollar. Collectively, these currencies represent approximately 65% of the Company's operating income outside the U.S. If all four of these currencies moved by 10% in the same direction, the Company's annual diluted earnings per share would change by about 25 cents.

Foreign-currency-denominated transactions expose McDonald's to financial risk. McDonald's 2013 diluted earnings per share was $5.55, so a 25 cent effect due to changing currency values is significant. As exchange rates change, the U.S. dollar values of its foreign-currency-denominated revenues, expenses, receivables and payables also change. To reduce foreign currency risk and stabilize U.S. dollar values, McDonald's invests in various financial derivatives.

McDonald's represents one example of the global nature of business activities. The related reporting issues are relevant to virtually all U.S. companies. In this chapter, you learn about the nature of global transactions and related foreign currency risk, how companies manage this risk through investments in financial derivatives, and how companies report these activities in the financial statements. *Source:* McDonald's Corporation annual report 2013.

CHAPTER ORGANIZATION

Foreign currency transactions	Foreign currency risk and hedge investments	IFRS for foreign currency transactions and hedging
• Import and export transactions • Borrowing and lending transactions	• Types of risk and analysis of risk management investments • Reporting derivative investments under *FASB ASC Topic 815* • Hedges of receivables and payables • Hedges of firm commitments • Hedges of forecasted transactions • Hedges of net investments in international operations • Speculative investments • Footnote disclosures	• Criteria for hedge accounting • Differences between IFRS and U.S. GAAP • Footnote disclosures • FASB and IASB hedge accounting projects

FOREIGN CURRENCY TRANSACTIONS AND RISK

This chapter examines transactions between U.S. companies and international suppliers or customers, and ways to manage the resulting foreign exchange risk caused by changes in exchange rates. A U.S. company may be an exporter, selling its products to customers in other countries, or an importer, purchasing products from suppliers in other countries. When payments from international customers to the U.S. exporter are in dollars, we account for the export sale in the same way as domestic sales. Similarly, when the U.S. company pays international suppliers in dollars, the accounting for import purchases is identical to domestic purchases. But when the amount received from an international customer or paid to an international supplier is denominated in a foreign currency, there are new risks and accounting issues involved.

Chapter 7 explains that foreign currencies are traded on both **spot markets** and **forward markets** or **futures markets**. Transactions *involving immediate delivery* of the foreign currency are executed at **spot rates**. Transactions involving delivery of the foreign currency at some *later date* are executed at **forward rates**. Standardized contracts for future delivery trade at **futures rates**.

This chapter addresses issues involved when a U.S. company engages in transactions that are **denominated** (settled) in a foreign currency. When a U.S. exporter sells goods to a customer in Japan, and payment will be received in yen, how should the sale be recorded on the books of the exporter? If the customer is extended credit, and pays the exporter at a later date, how is the dollar equivalent of the sale affected if the foreign exchange rate changes between the time the sale is made and the payment is received in yen?

When a U.S. exporter sells to an international customer on credit, the U.S. company expects to receive the foreign currency at a future date. The U.S. company is exposed to *foreign exchange risk*, because the dollar equivalent of this future cash receipt likely will change due to changes in the foreign exchange rate. Similarly, a U.S. importer may purchase goods from an international supplier on credit. The U.S. importer is exposed to foreign exchange risk because the dollar equivalent of this future cash payment varies as the foreign exchange rate changes.

Changing exchange rates can be an advantage or a disadvantage. The dollar equivalent of foreign currency received from a customer or paid to a supplier may either increase or decrease. The U.S. importer or exporter can utilize financial instruments designed to *neutralize* the risks caused by changing exchange rates. Subsequent sections of this chapter discuss the accounting for import purchases and export sales, and the accounting for investments that neutralize, or **hedge**, foreign exchange risk.

Financial risk due to changing exchange rates can significantly impact the stability of a multinational company's financial results. Exhibit 8.1 shows how the value of the U.S. dollar changed in relation to other currencies in recent years. The numbers indicate how many U.S. dollars were needed to purchase one unit of foreign currency for immediate delivery (spot rates). When *more* U.S. dollars are required to buy one unit of foreign currency, the U.S. dollar is said to have **weakened** with respect to that currency. When *fewer* U.S. dollars are required, the U.S. dollar **strengthens**. Thus, in 2013, the dollar strengthened with respect to the Canadian dollar and Brazilian real, but weakened against the euro.

EXHIBIT 8.1   Foreign Exchange Rates (U.S. dollars per unit of foreign currency)

December 31	2007	2008	2009	2010	2011	2012	2013
$ price of a euro	$1.47	$1.41	$1.44	$1.42	$1.29	$1.32	$1.38
$ price of a Canadian dollar	1.02	0.82	0.95	1.00	0.98	1.00	0.93
$ price of a Brazilian real	0.57	0.43	0.57	0.59	0.54	0.49	0.42

FOREIGN CURRENCY TRANSACTIONS

LO1 Report import and export transactions and borrowing and lending denominated in foreign currency.

Import and export transactions and borrowing and lending in another currency have very similar characteristics. When importers and borrowers pay their obligations in foreign currency, they benefit when their currency strengthens against the other currency. When exporters and lenders receive payments in foreign currency, they benefit when their currency weakens against the other currency.

Import and Export Transactions

Import/export transactions—purchases from international suppliers and sales to international customers—present no particular accounting problem *if* all sales, purchases, payments, and receipts are denominated in dollars. In that case our international customers and suppliers do business in terms of the dollar, a currency foreign to *them*, and they accept the exchange rate risk. In any international transaction, at least one of the parties deals in a foreign currency. If a third currency is involved—for example if a U.S. company and a Japanese company specify that their transactions are settled in euros—then both parties deal in a foreign currency.

When a U.S. company makes a credit sale abroad and states the transaction price in foreign currency units, the dollar value of the account receivable may change before the foreign currency payment is received and converted into dollars. Similarly, when a U.S. company purchases goods from abroad on account at a price denominated in foreign currency units, the dollar amount owed may change before the U.S. company converts dollars into foreign currency and makes payment. These changes in the dollar value of receivables and payables generate *exchange gains and losses* to the U.S. firm that must be recognized at settlement and at intervening balance sheet dates.

Generally accepted accounting principles for import and export transactions denominated in a foreign currency are found in *ASC Topic 830,* Foreign Currency Matters. The initial sale or purchase transaction is recorded at its dollar equivalent, based on the foreign exchange spot rate in effect at the time of the transaction. Any *changes* in the dollar equivalent of the resulting receivable or payable are treated separately as **exchange gains or losses**, and do not affect the original dollar value of the sale or purchase. Exchange gains and losses are reported on the income statement. A summary of the accounting procedures for import or export transactions follows:

Reporting Import and Export Transactions Denominated in Foreign Currency

1. Restate the foreign currency invoice price into dollars using the appropriate foreign exchange spot rate and record the transaction in dollars.
2. Record an exchange gain or loss when the transaction is settled if exchange rate changes cause the number of dollars received or paid to differ from that originally recorded.
3. If the transaction is not settled at a balance sheet date, record an exchange gain or loss on the existing receivable or payable by adjusting it to the dollar equivalent implied by the spot rate at the balance sheet date.

Observe two objectives of these procedures. *First*, the accounting recognizes changes in the value of receivables and payables attributable to movements in the exchange rate. *Second*, fair value accounting applies, and the recognized value change is not deferred until eventual settlement if a balance sheet date occurs prior to settlement.

The following example illustrates the accounting for import and export transactions.

1. On October 16, 2016, **Gap Inc.**, a U.S. clothing company, purchased woolen sweaters at an invoice price of 17,000 New Zealand dollars (NZ$) from a New Zealand clothing manufacturer. The exchange rate was $0.82/ NZ$. Payment was to be made on December 16, 2016.

2016			
Oct. 16	Inventories	13,940	
	Accounts payable		13,940
	To record the purchase of sweaters from New Zealand;		
	$13,940 = $0.82 × NZ$17,000.		

2. On December 16, 2016, Gap purchased NZ$17,000 at an exchange rate of $.83/NZ$ and transmitted payment to the clothing manufacturer's bank in New Zealand.

2016			
Dec. 16	Exchange loss	170	
	Accounts payable		170
	To revalue the account payable to the current exchange rate;		
	$170 = ($0.83 − $0.82) × NZ$17,000.		
	Foreign currency	14,110	
	Cash		14,110
	To purchase sufficient foreign currency to pay the New		
	Zealand manufacturer; $14,110 = $0.83 × NZ$17,000.		
	Accounts payable.	14,110	
	Foreign currency		14,110
	To record payment of the liability to the New Zealand		
	manufacturer; $14,110 = $13,940 + $170.		

Consider the exchange loss recorded on December 16. Gap's liability to the New Zealand manufacturer was denominated in New Zealand dollars. Because the exchange rate *rose*, it took more U.S. dollars to purchase NZ$17,000, the dollar value of the liability *increased*, and Gap incurred a loss.

3. On December 20, 2016, Gap purchased wool scarves from a British mill for £40,000, when the exchange rate was $1.65/£. Payment is due on February 20, 2017.

2016			
Dec. 20	Inventories	66,000	
	Accounts payable		66,000
	To record the purchase of wool scarves from the U.K.;		
	$66,000 = $1.65 × £40,000.		

4. On December 22, 2016, Gap sold a quantity of deluxe wool coats to a Canadian concern for 9,800 Canadian dollars (C$). The exchange rate was $0.99/C$. Gap's terms are 90 days, net.

2016			
Dec. 22	Accounts receivable......................................	9,702	
	Sales		9,702
	To record the sale of coats to Canada;		
	$9,702 = $0.99 × C$9,800.		

5. On December 29, 2016, Gap purchased buttons costing 10,000 pesos (P) from a Mexican supplier. The exchange rate was $0.05/P; a check was mailed immediately.

2016			
Dec. 29	Inventories	500	
	Cash		500
	To record the cash purchase of buttons from Mexico;		
	$500 = $0.05 × P10,000.		

Because no time lapsed between the recording of the transaction and time of payment on December 29, there can be *no exchange gain or loss*.

6. Gap prepared financial statements at January 31, 2017, its fiscal year-end, and made the following adjusting entries. Exchange rates were $1.61/£ and $1.005/C$ at January 31, 2017.

2017			
Jan. 31	Accounts payable.......................................	1,600	
	Exchange gain....................................		1,600
	To revalue the liability to the British mill to the current		
	exchange rate; $1,600 = ($1.65 − $1.61) × £40,000.		
	The dollar value of this liability decreased to $64,400		
	(= $1.61 × £40,000).		
	Accounts receivable....................................	147	
	Exchange gain....................................		147
	To revalue the receivable from Canada to the current		
	exchange rate; $147 = ($1.005 − $0.99) × C$9,800. The		
	dollar value of this asset increased to $9,849 (= $1.005 ×		
	C$9,800).		

Contrast the two exchange gains accrued on January 31, 2017. Because the dollar *strengthened*, the direct exchange rate for pounds (£) *declined*, the dollar value of Gap's liability declined, and a gain resulted. The exchange rate for Canadian dollars *rose* by year-end (U.S. dollar *weakened*), also producing a gain. As the value of Canadian dollars rose, so did the U.S. dollar value of Gap's C$9,800 receivable from the Canadian firm.

7. Gap paid its obligation to the British mill on February 20, 2017. The exchange rate was $1.58/£.

2017			
Feb. 20	Accounts payable.......................................	1,200	
	Exchange gain....................................		1,200
	To revalue the account payable to the current exchange rate;		
	$1,200 = ($1.61 − $1.58) × £40,000.		
	Foreign currency	63,200	
	Cash		63,200
	To record the purchase of foreign currency to pay the British		
	mill; $63,200 = $1.58 × £40,000.		

Feb. 20	Accounts payable....................................	63,200	
	Foreign currency		63,200
	To record payment of the liability to the British mill;		
	$63,200 = $66,000 − $1,600 − $1,200.		

8. On March 20, 2017, payment was received from the Canadian customer on the sale of the coats. The exchange rate was $0.97/C$.

2017

Mar. 20	Exchange loss	343	
	Accounts receivable		343
	To revalue the receivable to the current exchange rate;		
	$343 = ($1.005 − $0.97) × C$9,800.		
	Foreign currency	9,506	
	Accounts receivable		9,506
	To record receipt of foreign currency from Canada in		
	payment of the receivable; $9,506 = $0.97 × C$9,800 =		
	$9,702 (original value) + $147 (exchange gain in fiscal 2017)		
	− $343 (exchange loss in fiscal 2018).		
	Cash..	9,506	
	Foreign currency		9,506
	To record exchange of the Canadian currency for U.S. dollars.		

To summarize, accounts receivable and accounts payable arising in international transactions are often denominated in a foreign currency and are recorded at the dollar equivalent of a fixed quantity of foreign currency. The specified foreign currency amount does not change. Because these receivables and payables are exposed to exchange rate risk, as the exchange rate changes their dollar equivalents also change. The display below summarizes the effects of changing exchange rates on the dollar equivalents of these exposed accounts and the resulting transaction gains and losses:

Effects of Changing Exchange Rates on Exposed Receivables and Payables Denominated in Foreign Currencies		
	Exchange Gains and Losses Due to Changes in Direct Exchange Rate	
Exposed Account	**Increase ($ Weakens)**	**Decrease ($ Strengthens)**
Accounts Receivable (AR)	AR increases; gain	AR decreases; loss
Accounts Payable (AP)...................	AP increases; loss	AP decreases; gain

The accounting for import and export transactions reflects the **two-transaction approach**. Under this approach, the dollar valuation of the inventories purchased from international suppliers or the revenue on sales made to international customers is unaffected by changes in the foreign exchange rate between the time the purchase or sale is made and the foreign currency is paid or collected. For example, Gap's purchase of sweaters on October 16, 2016, is valued at $13,940, even though Gap ends up paying $14,110 to settle the transaction. The exchange loss of $170 appears separately on the income statement. The FASB's position on this issue illustrates the traditional separation of operating transactions from financing transactions. When purchase of a building is financed by a mortgage, the cost of the building does not include interest on the mortgage. Similarly, the manner in which the import purchase is financed does not affect the cost of the inventory.

REVIEW 1 • Foreign-Currency-Denominated Import and Export Transactions

Fine Foods, Inc., a U.S. wholesaler, buys merchandise from suppliers in Germany, and pays the suppliers in euros. It also sells merchandise to customers in Italy, and receives payment in euros. Fine Foods' accounting year ends June 30. Exchange rates are as follows:

Date	Spot rate ($/€)
March 1, 2016	$1.35
April 1, 2016	1.40
June 30, 2016	1.42
July 15, 2016	1.43
August 15, 2016	1.45
August 31, 2016	1.48

Purchases of €1,000,000 are made on March 1, 2016. Fine Foods pays its German suppliers on August 15, 2016, and sells the merchandise to its U.S. customers on August 31, 2016. Sales of €100,000 are made on April 1, 2016. Fine Foods receives payment from its Italian customers on July 15, 2016.

Required
Calculate the following balances, appearing on Fine Foods' financial statements.
a. Accounts payable, on the June 30, 2016, balance sheet
b. Accounts receivable, on the June 30, 2016, balance sheet
c. Exchange gain or loss, on the fiscal 2016 income statement
d. Exchange gain or loss, on the fiscal 2017 income statement
e. Sales revenue, on the fiscal 2016 income statement
f. Cost of goods sold, on the fiscal 2017 income statement

Solutions are located after the chapter assignments.

Foreign Borrowing and Lending Transactions

Growth in the volume of international capital flows indicates that substantial investment funds move across national boundaries. U.S. companies engage in these and other investment transactions requiring foreign currency conversions:

- Investment in securities of international companies, banks, and governments.
- Borrowing from international lenders.
- Direct investment in international branches and subsidiaries.

Investments in securities of international entities often require the U.S. firm to convert dollars into foreign currency to acquire the security and then to convert the foreign currency into dollars when investment income is received and when the security matures or is sold. Similarly, borrowing internationally may mean that the U.S. firm borrows a quantity of foreign currency, converts it into dollars for use domestically, and later purchases sufficient foreign currency to repay the interest and principal. Direct investment in international branches and subsidiaries involves setting up a business operation, acquiring assets, and incurring debts in the country. Chapter 7 addresses the problems associated with converting these items for inclusion in U.S. company financial statements.

When an interest-bearing investment or note payable is denominated in another currency, what exchange rate should the U.S. firm use to convert the interest income or expense to U.S. dollars? Theoretically, the average exchange rate in effect while the interest is accruing should be used. Yet the receivable, payable, or collection or disbursement of cash when the accrued interest is recorded is translated at the current exchange rate. Taken together, these practices result in a discrepancy between the revenue or expense and the asset or liability when exchange rates fluctuate. We avoid this by converting interest income and expense at the *current spot rate when the interest is accrued*. After recording interest receivable and interest payable, exchange gains or losses can result from changes in the U.S. dollar value of the receivable or payable, due to changes in the exchange rate.

Consider a U.S. investment in an international bank certificate of deposit (CD). On August 15, 2016, Gap Inc. purchases a 90-day CD from a Swiss bank. The certificate has a face value of 1,000,000 Swiss francs (CHF), costs $1,250,000 (the spot rate is $1.25/CHF), and pays interest at an annual rate of 5 percent. The entry to record purchase of the CD is:

2016			
Aug. 15	Temporary investments	1,250,000	
	Cash		1,250,000
	To record purchase of a Swiss CD with face value of		
	CHF1,000,000; $1,250,000 = CHF1,000,000 × $1.25.		

On November 13, 2016, the certificate of deposit matures and Gap receives principal and interest of CHF1,012,500 [= CHF1,000,000 + 0.05(CHF1,000,000/4)] when the spot rate is $1.24/CHF. The following three entries record the exchange adjustment on the certificate, receipt of the foreign currency from the Swiss bank (including interest earned) and conversion of the Swiss francs into dollars.

2016			
Nov. 13	Exchange loss	10,000	
	Temporary investments.		10,000
	To recognize the exchange loss accrued on the certificate of		
	deposit; $10,000 = ($1.25 − $1.24) × CHF1,000,000.		
	Foreign currency ($1.24 × CHF1,012,500)	1,255,500	
	Temporary investments ($1,250,000 − $10,000)		1,240,000
	Interest income ($1.24 × CHF12,500).		15,500
	To record foreign currency received at maturity of the CD and		
	record the interest income converted at the current spot rate.		
	Cash.	1,255,500	
	Foreign currency		1,255,500
	To record the exchange of CHF1,012,500 for $1,255,500.		

Note that the interest accrued over ninety days, possibly at various exchange rates. However, because there was no previous accrual, we convert the interest income into dollars as of the date it is received by the U.S. company.

HEDGING FOREIGN EXCHANGE EXPOSURES

Importers and exporters, as well as borrowers and lenders in foreign currency, are exposed to *foreign exchange risk*. An importer or borrower faces the danger that the direct exchange rate will *rise* between the time the purchase or loan is made and the time the foreign currency obligation is paid, requiring the importer or borrower to use more dollars to purchase the foreign currency necessary to pay the obligation. An exporter or lender faces the risk that the direct exchange rate will *fall* between the time the exporter makes the sale or the lender lends the money, and the time the foreign currency is received, causing the exporter or lender to receive fewer dollars on conversion of the foreign currency received. There is also the chance in either case that rates will move in the U.S. company's favor.

Types of Foreign Exchange Risk

So far this chapter has concentrated on the risk associated with holding a receivable or payable denominated in a foreign currency. Here are several other situations that expose companies to foreign exchange risk.

- A company enters into a *firm agreement* to buy merchandise from an international supplier or sell merchandise to an international customer. Known as a **firm commitment**, in this situation the exposure to foreign exchange risk is in the future.
- A company buys regularly from international suppliers or sells to international customers and expects to do so in the future. Although such anticipated transactions are not in the form of firm

commitments, the foreign currency risk is just as real. These expected events are known as **forecasted transactions**.

- A company invests in an international subsidiary. When the subsidiary's accounts are translated or remeasured for consolidation with the parent, a gain or loss results. A **net investment in international operations** exposes the parent to foreign exchange risk.

- When a company believes it can predict the future movement of exchange rates, it may deliberately expose itself to exchange risk using **speculative investments**. For example, if a U.S. company believes the exchange rate for a particular currency will increase, it can invest in a CD denominated in the currency. If the exchange rate rises, it receives more U.S. dollars in principal and interest when the CD matures. If the rate falls, it receives fewer dollars.

Derivative Instruments Used in Hedging

Importers and exporters can **hedge**, or neutralize, foreign exchange risks by trading in the forward, futures or options markets. Hedging involves covering a foreign currency exposure by contracting in the forward market to purchase or sell foreign currency at a specified time in the future for a fixed price. In this way, managers neutralize the impact of changing exchange rates on the exposure by removing the uncertainty involved in not knowing how many U.S. dollars will be paid or received.

Forward and Futures Contracts   Contracting for future delivery of a foreign currency can involve either **forward contracts**—individual contracts negotiated with dealers—or **futures contracts**— standardized contracts traded on organized exchanges that generally require margin deposits. Both forwards and futures are examples of *derivatives*. In general, a **derivative** is a financial instrument that derives its value from some other financial item, such as a foreign currency rate, an interest rate, or a security price. For example, a forward contract that specifies the future purchase price of yen derives its value from the current market price of yen. The contract becomes more valuable as the market price of yen increases.

We concentrate here on forward contracts, the most basic derivative instruments commonly used to hedge foreign exchange risk. Other foreign-currency-denominated instruments, such as futures, option contracts, international loans and investments in international debt securities, can also function as hedges. Accounting for exchange gains or losses on such transactions parallels the forward contract case.

Refer to the **Gap Inc.** illustration discussed earlier in the chapter. On October 16, 2016, Gap agreed to pay a New Zealand manufacturer NZ$17,000 on December 16, 2016, for a purchase of sweaters. The October 16 exchange rate is $0.82/NZ$, but there is the risk that the exchange rate will increase or decrease by the time payment is to be made. Gap can remove this uncertainty by contracting with a foreign exchange broker on October 16, 2016, to buy NZ$17,000 in 60 days at a fixed price. This contract is called a **forward contract**, and prices for future delivery of currency are called **forward rates**.

If the forward rate for delivery of New Zealand dollars in 60 days is $0.81, Gap is no longer affected by the uncertainty of the future exchange rate. Gap now knows with certainty that it will pay $13,770 (= $0.81 × NZ$17,000) for the merchandise. In hindsight this arrangement was beneficial for Gap, because without the forward contract $14,110 would be paid on December 16, 2016.

Note carefully, however, that hedging with forwards neutralizes both the potential *losses* and the potential *gains* from changes in the exchange rate. If the spot rate *falls* to $0.78 on December 16, Gap is still required to fulfill the forward contract and pay $13,770 for the NZ$17,000 necessary to pay the obligation, even though without the forward contract only $13,260 (= $0.78 × NZ$17,000) would be paid for the needed currency on the spot market. By removing the uncertainty of decreases as well as increases in the exchange rate, the forward contract neutralizes both potential gains and potential losses.

Option Contracts   Foreign exchange **options** provide a hedge against the "downside risk" of foreign exchange losses, but without losing the chance to experience foreign exchange gains. The option holder has the right—but not the obligation—to buy or sell the contracted amount of foreign currency at a specified exchange rate called the **exercise price** or **strike price**. **Call options** give the holder the right to *buy* currency at a fixed price. **Put options** give the holder the right to *sell* currency at a fixed price. Option "holders" acquire options directly from option "writers," or indirectly from exchanges that facilitate options trading.

The option writer must follow through with selling or buying the currency if the option is exercised by the option holder. However, when it is not favorable to the option holder to exercise the option, the holder can let the option expire. Notice that the option writer incurs all of the risk of potential loss on the contract. For this reason, the option writer charges the holder a fee or **premium** as compensation for the risk undertaken.

To illustrate hedging with an option contract, look again at Gap Inc.'s purchase of sweaters on October 16, 2016, calling for payment of NZ$17,000 to be made on December 16, 2016. Gap can hedge the risk that the exchange rate will increase during this time interval by purchasing a 60-day call option giving Gap the right to buy NZ$ at a fixed price. Assume the option's strike price is $0.81, and the option costs Gap $400.

Call Option for NZ$17,000 with $0.81 Strike Price		
December 16, 2016, Spot Rate	Exercise?	Gap Pays
> $0.81	Yes	$13,770 = $0.81 × NZ$17,000
< 0.81	No	Spot rate

Thus Gap neutralizes the risk that the exchange rate will increase above $0.81. The cost of the currency needed to pay the NZ$17,000 debt will be $13,770 or less. If Gap used a forward contract with a forward rate of $0.81, the cost of the currency would be $13,770 exactly. By hedging with an option contract, the cost could be less if the spot rate goes below $0.81. Gap pays $400 to hedge the downside risk while retaining the opportunity for an upside gain.

Currency Swaps   In a **currency swap**, the parties to the agreement initially exchange currencies, or agree on a **notional** or **contractual** amount to be "exchanged," and then reverse the "exchange" at some future point in time. The parties agree on the exchange rates to be used at inception and completion of the swap. Payments in the foreign currency are also made at intermediate points during the swap, based on agreed-upon exchange rates. Although gross amounts are sometimes exchanged, usually only net cash flows actually change hands, based on exchange rate differentials, net of fees.

A typical currency swap occurs when a U.S. firm has international investments or recurring sales to international customers that generate periodic foreign currency cash inflows, and an international firm has U.S. investments or recurring sales to U.S. customers that generate periodic U.S. currency cash inflows. The U.S. firm wants to swap foreign currency for U.S. dollars on a periodic basis, and the international firm wants to swap U.S. dollars for foreign currency. The two firms agree to the terms of the swap. When the exchange and re-exchange of principal amounts at the beginning and end of the swap do not take place, the principal amount is referred to as *notional*. If they do occur, each firm has the option of immediately converting the unwanted foreign currency into its home currency. Because currency swaps are very similar to a series of forward contracts, the reporting requirements are the same as for forward contracts.

Decisions Involving Hedging   Even when hedges are effective, firms still must decide whether hedging is the best way to neutralize exchange rate risk. If the forward rate in a purchase contract is $1.40/€ and the spot rate is $1.50/€ when the firm liquidates its payable, the firm gained $0.10/€ by hedging while neutralizing the exchange rate risk. But if the spot rate is $1.35/€ at settlement, the firm lost $0.05/€ by hedging. A firm can avoid exchange rate risk by purchasing the foreign currency up front and either paying immediately or holding the currency until payment is due. In the latter case, the foreign currency could be temporarily placed in a foreign short-term interest-bearing investment until needed.

Suppose McDonald's Corporation has a €1,000,000 payable due in 60 days; the current spot rate is $1.40/€ and the 60-day forward rate is $1.41/€.

Case 1: Forward Contract. If McDonald's enters a 60-day forward purchase contract, $1,410,000 (= $1.41 × €1,000,000) is required when the contract matures to purchase €1,000,000 from the broker and liquidate the payable.

Case 2: Purchase € Now. By purchasing €1,000,000 now and holding the currency for 60 days (or paying now), McDonald's liquidates the payable for $1,400,000, a saving of $10,000 over the forward contract. However, interest is a relevant cost or benefit in this analysis. Although McDonald's can earn interest on the €1,000,000 by investing it in an international short-term interest-bearing instrument, by investing $1,400,000 in foreign currency now McDonald's gives up interest on possible alternative investments of the $1,400,000. If McDonald's must borrow to acquire the foreign currency, the interest expense on the loan must be taken into account.

Thus, the $10,000 savings on acquiring the €1,000,000 now represents only one part of the larger economic picture. McDonald's must consider all effects—additional interest revenue, interest expense, or interest lost—in evaluating the choice between a forward contract and purchasing the foreign currency now. A firm may also be able to neutralize exchange rate risk with a strategy that does not involve hedging. Be sure to consider all relevant costs when analyzing such situations.

BUSINESS APPLICATION   Natural Hedging

Investing in financial derivatives is not the only way a company can hedge against foreign exchange risk. Consider this excerpt from **McDonald's** 2013 annual report:

> . . . where practical, the Company's restaurants purchase goods and services in local currencies resulting in natural hedges.

Companies can avoid the effects of changing currency rates by doing business in the local currency and reducing the need to exchange currency. For example, McDonald's may receive euros from customers, and use these euros to pay suppliers. This type of activity is known as **natural hedging**. *Source:* McDonald's Corporation 2013 annual report.

Reporting Investments in Foreign Currency Derivatives

Generally accepted accounting principles for foreign currency forward, futures, swaps and option contracts, as well as other derivative financial instruments, are found in *ASC Topic 815,* Derivatives and Hedging.

Reporting Goals   The provisions in *ASC Topic 815* have the following general features, as applied to foreign exchange hedges:

- All investments in foreign currency forward or option contracts are shown on the balance sheet at their current *fair value*.
- If the contract is a qualifying hedge instrument, gains and losses due to changes in the fair value of the contract are recognized in the income statement *at the same time* the losses and gains on the exposure the contract is hedging are recognized. Thus, the neutralizing effect of the hedge is properly represented in the income statement by offsetting gains and losses.
- **Hedge accounting** changes the timing of gain and loss recognition so hedge and hedged item gains and losses appear on the same income statement, when normal accounting does not achieve this result.
- Hedges of firm commitments, such as contractual purchase or sale orders denominated in a foreign currency, are called **fair value hedges**. Hedges of forecasted transactions, such as anticipated purchases or sales denominated in a foreign currency, are called **cash flow hedges**.
- If the company does not completely hedge its foreign exchange risk, gains and losses due to its net (unhedged) exposure are shown in the income statement as foreign currency rates change.
- If a company invests in **speculative** derivatives, changes in their fair value are reported in the income statement as foreign currency rates change.

This and subsequent sections illustrate accounting for forward contracts in detail. The accounting for foreign exchange option contracts parallels the accounting for option contracts in the commodities and financial markets. Accounting for option contracts is analyzed in Chapter 9. Currency swaps are equivalent to a series of foreign currency forward contracts, and therefore are not separately discussed.

Calculating the Fair Value of a Foreign Currency Forward Contract   A **forward purchase contract** requires its holder to purchase foreign currency at a specified time in the future for a known price. An **importer** enters into a forward purchase contract so that, when an obligation to an international supplier comes due, the needed amount of foreign currency is available at a price agreed upon in advance. The fair market value of a forward purchase contract at any point in time derives from the

difference between the contracted forward rate and the current forward rate for delivery on the contracted date.

For example, suppose that on February 1 McDonald's enters into a forward contract to purchase C$100,000 for $0.97/C$ on April 1. Valuation of the forward contract follows:

Forward Purchase Contract—C$100,000 for Delivery April 1 at $0.97/C$		
Date	Forward rate for April 1 delivery	Value of forward contract asset (liability)
February 1	$0.97	$ 0 = [($0.97 − $0.97) × C$100,000]
March 1	0.99	2,000 = [($0.99 − $0.97) × C$100,000]
March 15	0.96	(1,000) = [($0.96 − $0.97) × C$100,000]

The value of the forward contract changes as the current forward rate for the contracted delivery date changes. Note that the forward purchase contract has a negative fair value when the forward rate for delivery of C$ on April 1 goes below $0.97 because the contract requires purchase of C$ at a higher cost than that now available on the market. To be completely accurate, since the forward contract involves cash flows that will occur in the future, the difference between the current forward rate and the contracted rate should be discounted to its present value. This chapter assumes that the effect of discounting is immaterial and ignores it.

The value changes that occur in forward contracts can be visualized with the help of familiar T-accounts. Think of a forward contract as having two sides: (1) *the current value of the currency involved*—a variable amount equal to the current forward rate multiplied by the currency amount, and (2) *the contract value of the currency*—the fixed obligation equal to the forward rate at inception (the contract rate) multiplied by the currency amount. In the case of forward currency purchases, the debit/asset side of the T-account is the current value of the currency to be received. The credit/liability side of the T-account is the fixed contract value that must be paid to the dealer for the currency. We can make the following observations about the forward contract T-account:

- At inception the two sides are equal—the current value of the currency equals its contract value and the contract itself has no net value.
- As time passes, the *current value side changes* but the contract value side does not.
- With a *forward purchase contract*, the *debit side* is the current value of the currency to be received; it changes with the current forward rate.
- The *credit side* is the fixed obligation to pay for the currency—the contract value—that *does not change*.
- When the forward rate increases, the value of the currency to be received rises above the contract value, and the contract has a net debit balance, which is an asset.
- When the forward rate decreases, the value of the currency to be received falls below the contract value, and the contract has a net credit balance, which is a liability.

The above value changes correspond with our intuition. An *increase* in the forward rate gives us the ability to buy the currency for less than its current value, an advantage (asset). A *decrease* in the forward rate means that we must buy the currency for more than its current value, a disadvantage (liability).

Recall that on February 1 McDonald's entered into a forward contract to purchase C$100,000 for $0.97/C$, with delivery to take place April 1. On March 1, the forward rate for delivery April 1 is $0.99. We depict these events in T-account format as follows:

Investment in Forward Purchase Contract		
	Current Value	Contract Value
February 1	$97,000 (= $0.97 × C$100,000)	$97,000 (= $0.97 × C$100,000)
Value change	2,000 [=($0.99 − $0.97) × C$100,000]	—
Balance March 1	$ 2,000	

Because the current dollar value of the currency to be received is higher than the contract obligation to be paid, the investment in forward contract is an asset.

A **forward sale contract** requires the holder to sell foreign currency at a specified time in the future for a known price. An **exporter** can hedge exposure to exchange rate changes by entering into a *forward sale contract* so that when international customers remit payments in foreign currency to the exporter, the foreign currency can be sold for a prearranged dollar amount. As with a forward purchase contract, the fair market value of a forward sale contract derives from the difference between the contracted forward rate and the current forward rate for delivery on the contracted date.

Suppose that on June 1 McDonald's enters into a forward contract to sell C\$100,000 for \$0.97/C\$ on August 1. On July 1, the forward rate for delivery of C\$ on August 1 is \$0.955, and the fair value of the forward contract is \$1,500 [= (\$0.97 − \$0.955) × C\$100,000]. The contract has value because it allows McDonald's to sell C\$ on August 1 for \$0.97, when the market price for delivery on August 1 is now \$0.955. In contrast, the forward sale contract has a negative fair value when the forward rate for delivery of C\$ rises above \$0.97.

As with the forward purchase contract, the above discussion on forward sales contracts can be visualized using a T-account. The forward sale contract has two sides: the current value is the obligation to deliver the foreign currency, and the contract value is the fixed amount to be received from the dealer in U.S. dollars. We can make the following observations:

- With a *forward sale contract*, the *credit side* is the *current value of the obligation to deliver the currency to the dealer*, which *changes with the current forward rate*. The debit side is the receivable from the dealer, which is the *fixed contract value*.

- When the forward rate increases, the current value of the obligation to deliver the currency rises above the contract value and the contract has a net credit balance, a liability.

- When the forward rate decreases, the current value of the obligation to deliver the currency falls below the contract value and the contract has a net debit balance, an asset.

The above value changes also correspond with our intuition. An increase in the forward rate means that we must sell the currency for less than its current value, a disadvantage (liability). A decrease in the forward rate gives us the ability to sell the currency for more than its current value, an advantage (asset).

Recall that on June 1 McDonald's entered into a forward contract to sell C\$100,000 for \$0.97/C\$, with delivery to take place August 1. On July 1, the forward rate for delivery on August 1 is \$0.955. We depict these events in T-account format as follows:

	Investment in Forward Sale Contract	
	Contract Value	**Current Value**
June 1................	\$97,000 (= \$0.97 × C\$100,000)	\$97,000 (= \$0.97 × C\$100,000)
Value change	—	(1,500) [= (\$0.955 − \$0.97) × C\$100,000]
Balance July 1	\$ 1,500	

Because the dollar contract value to be received is higher than the current value of the currency to be delivered, the investment in forward contract is an asset.

Reporting Gains and Losses on Forward Contracts   Because derivatives such as forward contracts are reported on the balance sheet at fair value, we must determine how the resulting unrealized gains and losses are reported. Reporting requirements depend on whether normal or hedge accounting is used. Normal accounting reports all changes in the value of the forward contract directly in earnings. If the forward contract qualifies for hedge accounting, under restrictive circumstances changes in the fair value of the contract may be deferred in other comprehensive income until the gain or loss can be matched with the loss or gain on the item being hedged, or gains and losses on the hedged transaction may be reported in income to match with losses and gains on the hedge investment, when normally they are not. Hedge accounting is illustrated in the next sections. Here we discuss how to determine whether a derivative qualifies for hedge accounting.

ASC Section 815-20-25 requires that qualified hedges be **documented as hedging a specific and recognized financial risk**, and also be **highly effective** in neutralizing the risk. The Codification does not specify a particular hedge effectiveness method, but the method must be "reasonable," be applied consistently, and must **assess the degree to which the hedge neutralizes risk**. Effectiveness is first evaluated when the hedge is initiated, and then periodically over time, to see if the investment still qualifies for hedge accounting. If the terms of the hedge and the hedged transaction are the same, it can be assumed that the hedge is effective. For example, a U.S. company may expect to pay €1 million to a supplier six months from now. If the company enters a forward contract that locks in the U.S. dollar price of €1 million, for delivery six months from now, the terms of the hedge and the hedged transaction exactly match.

In some cases, a hedge investment may be partially ineffective. If so, the ineffective change in its fair value is reported in income, using normal accounting. In this chapter, the terms of the forward contracts used to hedge foreign currency risk exactly match the terms of the transaction creating the risk. Therefore the hedge investments in this chapter are by definition highly effective. More discussion of the qualifications for hedge accounting appears in Chapter 9 of this text.

Using Forward Contracts to Hedge Import and Export Transactions U.S. importers and exporters whose payables and receivables are denominated in foreign currency face the risk that the U.S. dollar value of the payables and receivables will change as foreign currency rates change. Hedge investments lock in the U.S. dollar amounts paid or received.

> **LO2** Report hedges of foreign-currency-denominated receivables and payables.

Hedge accounting is not used when the hedged item is a foreign-currency-denominated receivable or payable. Receivables, payables and hedge investments are normally marked to market; therefore offsetting gains and losses automatically appear on the same income statement, using normal accounting.

Forward Purchase Contract: Hedge of Foreign-Currency-Denominated Payable Suppose that Gap Inc. purchases goods costing £1,000 from a British supplier on October 1, 2016, when the spot rate is $1.60/£. Payment in pounds is due on March 1, 2017. Because Gap's account payable is denominated in pounds, it exposes Gap to risk of exchange rate movements. To hedge this liability to the British supplier, a *forward purchase contract* calling for a foreign exchange broker to deliver £1,000 on March 1 is entered on October 1. If the forward rate for delivery on March 1 is $1.61/£, Gap "locks in" the dollar equivalent of the obligation to the British supplier at $1,610 (= $1.61 × £1,000) and is not affected by subsequent movements in the exchange rate.

An entry is required on October 1 to record the purchase of the goods. Gap makes *no entry* to record the forward purchase contract; it has a fair value of zero on October 1 because the contract price for delivery on March 1 equals the current forward rate for delivery on March 1. The entry on October 1 is:

2016			
Oct. 1	Inventories	1,600	
	Accounts payable		1,600
	To record the purchase of goods from the U.K.;		
	$1,600 = $1.60 × £1,000.		

On January 31, 2017, Gap's accounting year-end, entries are needed to record the change in fair value of both the account payable and the forward contract. If the spot rate on January 31, 2017, is $1.65 and the forward rate for delivery on March 1 is $1.66, Gap makes these entries:

2017			
Jan. 31	Exchange loss	50	
	Accounts payable		50
	To revalue the account payable to the current exchange rate;		
	$50 = ($1.65 − $1.60) × £1,000.		
	Investment in forward contract	50	
	Exchange gain.		50
	To record the change in fair value of the forward purchase		
	contract; $50 = ($1.66 − $1.61) × £1,000.		

Gap's income statement reflects the exchange *gain* on the forward purchase contract offsetting the exchange *loss* on the account payable exposure, because the forward purchase contract completely neutralizes the exchange risk caused by the import transaction. To the extent that forward rates and spot rates move together, the gains and losses will exactly offset. Otherwise, the hedge is partially ineffective and income is affected. On the balance sheet date, the forward purchase contract appears on the balance sheet as a *current asset* at its fair value of $50.

On March 1, the forward purchase contract is settled and the supplier is paid. The spot rate and, equivalently, the forward rate for delivery on March 1 are $1.68. First, Gap makes entries to "mark to market" both the account payable and the forward purchase contract:

2017			
Mar. 1	Exchange loss	30	
	Accounts payable		30
	To revalue the account payable to the current exchange rate;		
	$30 = ($1.68 − $1.65) × £1,000.		
	Investment in forward contract	20	
	Exchange gain......................................		20
	To record the gain in fair value on the forward purchase contract;		
	$20 = ($1.68 − $1.66) × £1,000.		

Thus for the period January 31 to March 1, forward rates and spot rates do not move exactly together, so the gain on the forward contract does not exactly offset the loss on the account payable. The net exchange loss of $10 for the period October 1 to March 1 can also be calculated as the difference between the spot and forward rates at the inception of the contract; $10 = ($1.61 − $1.60) × £1,000, since spot and forward rates must be equal on the delivery date.

At this point, we make entries to settle the forward contract and pay the British supplier:

2017			
Mar. 1	Foreign currency	1,680	
	Investment in forward contract		70
	Cash		1,610
	To record payment of $1,610 to the dealer, receipt of £1,000		
	valued at the current spot rate of $1.68, and fulfillment of the		
	forward purchase contract.		
	Accounts payable.......................................	1,680	
	Foreign currency		1,680
	To record payment to the British supplier; $1,680 =		
	$1,600 + $50 + $30.		

In retrospect, this hedge was beneficial to Gap. Rather than paying $1,680 on the spot market on March 1, Gap paid $1,610 under the forward contract. Even if Gap purchased the currency on the spot market on October 1 for $1,600, the forward contract cost only $10 more. Thus, Gap paid an additional $10 on a $1,600 obligation for the privilege of delaying payment for five months from October 1 to March 1, an annual interest rate of only 1.5 percent [= ($10/$1,600) × 12/5].

Forward Sale Contract: Hedge of Foreign-Currency-Denominated Receivable Suppose that Gap Inc. sold goods to a British customer on October 1, 2016, at a price of £2,000, when the spot rate was $1.60/£. Payment in pounds will be received on March 1, 2017. Because the account receivable is denominated in pounds, Gap is exposed to risk of exchange rate movements. To hedge this receivable from the British customer, a *forward sale contract* calling for delivery of £2,000 to a broker on March 1 is entered on October 1. If the forward rate for delivery on March 1 is $1.61/£, Gap "locks in" the dollar equivalent value of the receivable from the British customer at $3,220 (= $1.61 × £2,000), and is not affected by subsequent movements in the exchange rate.

Gap makes an entry on October 1 to record the sale of the goods, but no entry to record the forward sale contract, since it has a fair value of zero. The entry on October 1 is:

2016			
Oct. 1	Accounts receivable..	3,200	
	Sales revenue		3,200
	To record the sale of goods to the British customer;		
	$3,200 = $1.60 × £2,000.		

On January 31, 2017, Gap's accounting year-end, we record the change in fair value of both the account receivable and the forward contract. Assume the spot rate is $1.65 and the forward rate for delivery on March 1 is $1.66. Entries are as follows:

2017			
Jan. 31	Accounts receivable.....................................	100	
	Exchange gain.....................................		100
	To revalue the account receivable to the current exchange rate;		
	$100 = ($1.65 − $1.60) × £2,000.		
	Exchange loss	100	
	Investment in forward contract		100
	To record the loss in fair value on the forward sale contract;		
	$100 = ($1.66 − $1.61) × £2,000.		

Unlike the forward purchase contract discussed earlier in this section, the forward sale contract has a positive value when the current forward rate is *less than* the contracted rate. In the Gap example, the current forward rate is *greater than* the contracted rate. On the balance sheet date the forward sale contract appears on the balance sheet as a *current liability* at its fair value of $100.

On March 1, the British customer pays Gap and the forward sale contract is settled. Assume the spot rate and, equivalently, the forward rate for delivery on March 1 is $1.68. First, entries are made to mark to market both the account receivable and the forward sale contract:

2017			
Mar. 1	Accounts receivable.......................................	60	
	Exchange gain..		60
	To revalue the account receivable to the current exchange rate;		
	$60 = ($1.68 − $1.65) × £2,000.		
	Exchange loss	40	
	Investment in forward contract		40
	To record the loss in fair value on the forward sale contract;		
	$40 = ($1.68 − $1.66) × £2,000.		

At this point, the customer submits payment and Gap settles the forward contract with these entries:

2017			
Mar. 1	Foreign currency	3,360	
	Accounts receivable		3,360
	To record the payment by the British customer; $3,360 =		
	$3,200 + $100 + $60.		
	Cash..	3,220	
	Investment in forward contract	140	
	Foreign currency		3,360
	To record the delivery of the foreign currency to the dealer,		
	receipt of $3,220 as specified in the contract, and settlement of		
	the forward contract.		

In retrospect, the hedge was *not* beneficial to Gap. It could have sold the foreign currency in the spot market on March 1 for $3,360 rather than at the contracted price of $3,220. However, if spot prices had instead decreased over this period, the forward contract protects Gap from the resulting decline in the value of the receivable.

The following table summarizes the implications of changing exchange rates for the fair value of forward contracts.

Type of Contract	Fair Value of Forward Contracts Contract Rate (CR) vs Current Forward Rate (FR)	Net Income Statement Effect	Balance Sheet Disclosure
Forward purchase	FR > CR	Gain	Current Asset
Forward purchase	FR < CR	Loss	Current Liability
Forward sale.	FR > CR	Loss	Current Liability
Forward sale.	FR < CR	Gain	Current Asset

REVIEW 2 • Using Forward Contracts to Hedge Foreign-Currency-Denominated Import Transactions

Fine Foods, Inc., a U.S. wholesaler, buys merchandise from suppliers in Germany, and pays the suppliers in euros. Fine Foods' accounting year ends June 30. Exchange rates are as follows:

Date	Spot rate ($/€)	Forward rate for delivery August 15, 2016
March 1, 2016	$1.35	$1.37
June 30, 2016.	1.42	1.44
August 15, 2016.	1.45	1.45
August 31, 2016.	1.48	NA

On March 1, 2016, Fine Foods makes inventory purchases of €1,000,000, and enters into a forward purchase for delivery of €1,000,000 on August 15, 2016, to hedge its foreign currency risk. Fine Foods pays its suppliers on August 15, 2016, and sells the merchandise to its U.S. customers on August 31, 2016.

Required

Calculate the following balances, appearing on Fine Foods' financial statements.
a. Accounts payable, on the June 30, 2016 balance sheet
b. Investment in forward contract, on the June 30, 2016 balance sheet
c. Exchange gain or loss, on the fiscal 2016 income statement
d. Exchange gain or loss, on the fiscal 2017 income statement
e. Cost of goods sold, on the fiscal 2017 income statement

Solutions are located after the chapter assignments.

LO3 Report hedges of foreign-currency-denominated firm commitments.

Using Forward Contracts to Hedge Firm Foreign Currency Commitments   Many purchase or sale transactions are preceded by contractual agreements where both parties to the transaction commit to perform. For example, an exporter agrees to ship a specified quantity of goods on a preset future date, at a preset price. If the price is denominated in foreign currency, the exporter has the risk that the dollar equivalent value of the sale will decline between the time the commitment to ship is made and the time the payment is received. The exporter can hedge this risk by entering into a forward sale contract to lock in the dollar value of the sale, even before the shipment date.

An importer issues a purchase order obligating it to purchase goods from an international supplier at a contracted price denominated in foreign currency. The importer incurs a loss if the dollar equivalent of the purchase cost increases prior to payment. To hedge this risk, the importer can enter into a forward purchase contract to lock in the dollar cost of the purchase at the time the purchase order is issued.

Accounting for these situations is simplified when one separates the commitment period from the period when the recorded account payable or account receivable exposure exists. The *commitment period* begins when the purchase or sale agreement occurs and the forward contract begins. The *exposed asset or liability period* begins when the goods are received or delivered and the company records the purchase or sale. The time line below depicts the events for a *forward purchase contract*.

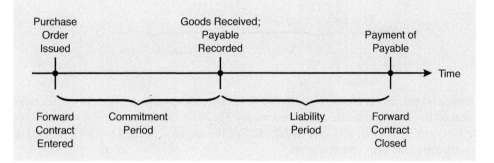

For hedges of firm commitments, normal accounting reports changes in hedge investment value on the income statement, but there is no offsetting change in value of the purchase or sale order. During the commitment period, we use *hedge accounting* to match hedge gains and losses with hedged item losses and gains.

ASC Section 815-20-35 specifies the accounting for forward contracts used as hedges of *firm foreign currency commitments*. The *ASC* glossary defines the commitments that qualify for hedge accounting.

A **firm commitment** is defined as an agreement with an unrelated party, binding on both parties and usually legally enforceable, with the following characteristics:

a. The agreement specifies all significant terms, including the quantity to be exchanged, the fixed price, and the timing of the transaction. The fixed price may be expressed as a specified amount of an entity's functional currency or of a foreign currency.

b. The agreement includes a disincentive for nonperformance that is sufficiently large to make performance probable.

The Codification requires that the gain or loss on a forward contract used to hedge a firm foreign currency commitment be recognized *currently in earnings*. The offsetting loss or gain on the firm purchase or sale commitment must also be recognized in earnings. But the commitment itself has not yet been recorded on the books because generally accepted accounting principles do not recognize purchase or sale orders as accounting events. Instead, a balance sheet account accumulates the losses or gains on the commitment, which is then *closed against the related sales revenue or inventory account* when the sale or purchase and related account receivable or payable are eventually booked. Because a firm commitment relates to a future transaction, valuation using forward rates is appropriate.

Forward Purchase Contract: Fair Value Hedge of a Foreign Currency Purchase Commitment   A firm foreign currency commitment exists when an importer issues a **purchase order** prior to actual receipt of the goods. Assume that on November 10, 2016, Gap Inc. issues a purchase order to Queens, Ltd., a U.K. exporter, to purchase apparel for £100,000. Delivery of the clothing to Gap is expected on February 20, 2017, and payment is due on March 10, 2017. This future payment of £100,000 is a firm foreign currency purchase commitment that Gap elects to hedge by purchasing £100,000 for delivery on

March 10, 2017, at a forward rate of $1.605/£. The commitment period runs from November 10, 2016, to February 20, 2017. The time line for this sequence of events is shown below:

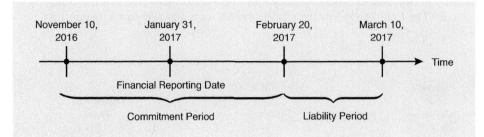

Gap makes no entries on November 10, 2016, because the purchase order is not recorded and the forward contract has no value at this time. On January 31, 2017, Gap's accounting year-end, the forward rate for delivery on March 10, 2017, is $1.625/£. Entries are now needed to mark to market both the forward contract and the firm commitment:

2017			
Jan. 31	Investment in forward contract	2,000	
	Exchange gain.		2,000
	To record the gain in fair value on the forward contract;		
	$2,000 = ($1.625 − $1.605) × £100,000.		
	Exchange loss	2,000	
	Firm commitment		2,000
	To record the loss on the firm commitment.		

The "firm commitment" account appears on the balance sheet as a current liability, representing the increased cost of the purchase commitment caused by the rising forward rate.

On February 20, the apparel is delivered to Gap. If the spot rate is $1.64/£ and the forward rate for delivery on March 10 is $1.645/£, Gap makes these entries:

2017			
Feb. 20	Investment in forward contract	2,000	
	Exchange gain.		2,000
	To record the gain in fair value on the forward contract;		
	$2,000 = ($1.645 − $1.625) × £100,000.		
	Exchange loss	2,000	
	Firm commitment		2,000
	To record the loss on the firm commitment.		
	Inventories	164,000	
	Accounts payable		164,000
	To record delivery of the apparel at the current spot rate of $1.64.		
	Firm commitment.	4,000	
	Inventories.		4,000
	To adjust the carrying value of apparel for the change in value		
	of the firm commitment during the commitment period.		

With the firm commitment gone, the forward contract hedges the recorded account payable. Now Gap accounts for the forward contract as a hedge of a foreign-currency-denominated liability, as discussed in the previous section on hedges of import and export transactions. If the spot rate on March 10 and, equivalently, the forward rate for delivery on March 10 is $1.635, Gap's entries to mark to market the account payable and the forward contract are:

2017
Mar. 10 | Accounts payable. 500
| Exchange gain . . . . | 500
| *To revalue the liability to Queens, Ltd. to the current exchange*
| *rate; $500 = ($1.64 − $1.635) × £100,000.*

Exchange loss 1,000
    Investment in forward contract 1,000
    To record the loss in fair value on the forward contract;
    $1,000 = ($1.645 − $1.635) × £100,000.

Gap records settlement of the forward contract and payment to Queens, Ltd. as follows:

2017
Mar. 10 | Foreign currency 163,500
| Investment in forward contract . . . . | 3,000
| Cash . . . . | 160,500
| *To record the payment of $160,500 to the broker, receipt*
| *of £100,000 valued at the current spot rate of $1.635, and*
| *settlement of the forward purchase contract; $3,000 = $2,000 +*
| *$2,000 − $1,000.*

Accounts payable 163,500
    Foreign currency 163,500
    To record the payment to the supplier.

To summarize, Gap uses the hedging process to fix the dollar amount of the liability to Queens, Ltd. at $160,500. Income is unaffected during the commitment period because the forward contract perfectly hedges the loss on the firm commitment. After the goods are delivered, a net loss of $500 on hedge activity arises because the change in the value of the forward contract, measured by the change in the forward rate, does not exactly match the change in the value of the account payable, measured by the change in the spot rate. The change in value of the purchase commitment during the hedging period reduces the inventory balance from $164,000 to $160,000, and is therefore recognized in earnings at a higher gross margin when the inventory is sold. If the commitment is for the purchase of a depreciable asset such as equipment, the change in value impacts earnings as the asset is depreciated.

Forward Sale Contract: Fair Value Hedge of a Foreign Currency Sale Commitment An exporter may contract to sell goods at a specified time in the future at a fixed price denominated in foreign currency. The exporter can hedge the risk that the dollar value of the sale will decline by entering a forward contract to sell the currency when received. If the contract begins prior to the time delivery of the goods is made, the forward contract hedges a firm commitment. The time line below depicts the events for a *forward sale contract*:

We illustrate the accounting with an example in which the sale transaction, collection, and settlement of the forward contract take place simultaneously. Therefore, the forward sale contract hedges only the foreign currency commitment; there is no asset to be hedged following the sale.

Suppose that Gap Inc. negotiated a cash sale of wool coats at a price of C$50,000 to Corsin, a Canadian retailer, on October 21, 2016. Payment is expected on March 19, 2017, at the same time the coats are delivered and the sale is recorded by Gap. The time line for this example appears below:

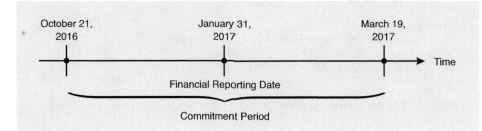

On October 21, 2016, the forward rate for delivery on March 19, 2017, is $0.98/C$. On January 31, 2017, the balance sheet date, the forward rate for delivery on March 19, 2017, is $0.975/C$, and on March 19, 2017, the spot rate is $0.96. No entries are required on October 21, 2016, because the forward contract has a fair value of zero and Gap does not record Corsin's order. Year-end adjusting entries are:

2017			
Jan. 31	Investment in forward contract	250	
	Exchange gain.		250
	To record the gain in fair value on the forward contract;		
	$250 = ($0.98 − $0.975) × C$50,000.		
	Exchange loss	250	
	Firm commitment		250
	To record the offsetting change in fair value of the firm		
	commitment.		

On March 19, 2017, Gap delivers the coats, receives payment from Corsin, and closes the forward contract.

2017			
Mar. 19	Investment in forward contract	750	
	Exchange gain.		750
	To record the gain in fair value on the forward contract;		
	$750 = ($0.975 − $0.96) × C$50,000.		
	Exchange loss	750	
	Firm commitment		750
	To record the offsetting loss in fair value on the firm commitment.		
	Foreign currency	48,000	
	Sales revenue		48,000
	To record the receipt of foreign currency and the sales revenue,		
	valued at the spot rate; $48,000 = $0.96 × C$50,000.		
	Firm commitment.	1,000	
	Sales revenue		1,000
	To adjust the sales revenue for the change in value of the firm		
	commitment.		
	Cash.	49,000	
	Investment in forward contract		1,000
	Foreign currency		48,000
	To record delivery of the foreign currency to the broker, and		
	settlement of the forward contract.		

REVIEW 3 • Using Forward Contracts to Hedge Foreign-Currency-Denominated Firm Commitments

Fine Foods, Inc., a U.S. wholesaler, buys merchandise from German suppliers, paying the suppliers in euros. Fine Foods' accounting year ends June 30. Here are the relevant exchange rates:

Date	Spot rate ($/€)	Forward rate for delivery August 15, 2016
March 1, 2016	$1.35	$1.37
June 30, 2016	1.42	1.44
August 15, 2016	1.45	1.45
August 31, 2016	1.48	NA

On March 1, 2016, Fine Foods sends a purchase order to a German supplier for €1,000,000 in merchandise, payable in euros, delivery to take place August 15, 2016. Also on March 1, Fine Foods enters into a forward contract for delivery of €1,000,000 on August 15. The forward qualifies as a hedge of a firm commitment. On August 15, Fine Foods closes the forward contract, takes delivery of the merchandise, and pays the supplier. The merchandise is sold to a U.S. customer on August 31.

Required

Calculate the following balances, appearing on Fine Foods' financial statements.
a. Firm commitment, on the June 30, 2016, balance sheet
b. Exchange gain or loss, on the fiscal 2016 income statement
c. Exchange gain or loss, on the fiscal 2017 income statement
d. Reported inventory amount, August 15, 2016
e. Cost of goods sold, on the fiscal 2017 income statement

Solutions are located after the chapter assignments.

Using Forward Contracts to Hedge Forecasted Transactions It is common practice for companies to invest in forward contracts to hedge planned purchase or sale transactions denominated in foreign currencies, even though there is no firm commitment involved. Normal accounting for hedges of forecasted transactions does not match hedge gains and losses against losses and gains on the forecasted transaction, because forecasted transactions are not recorded.

If the forward contract qualifies as a cash flow hedge of the forecasted transaction, *ASC Section 815-20-35* allows gains and losses due to changes in the fair value of such forward contracts to be reported in **other comprehensive income**, outside of earnings. These gains and losses are removed from accumulated other comprehensive income and recognized in earnings when the hedged forecasted transaction impacts earnings. This process matches the income effect of the hedge instrument against the income effect of the hedged item, using *hedge accounting*.

It is not possible to accurately recognize in the financial statements the changes in the fair value of the forecasted transaction as exchange rates change, as is the case with firm commitments, since the actual terms of the forecasted transaction are not yet known. Therefore, changes in the value of forward contracts used to hedge forecasted transactions are held in other comprehensive income to allow gains and losses on the hedge instrument to be matched against subsequent losses and gains on the hedged transaction.

Because hedge accounting in this case delays income statement recognition of gains and losses on the hedge instrument, hedges of forecasted transactions must meet stringent criteria. These criteria include:

- The forecasted transaction must be identified, probable, part of an established business activity, and expose the company to exchange risk.
- There is formal documentation of the hedging relationship and the entity's risk management strategy for undertaking the hedge.
- The hedging relationship is expected to be highly effective and is assessed on a regular basis.

LO4 Report hedges of foreign-currency-denominated forecasted transactions.

- The forecasted transaction involves an exchange with a third party external to the reporting entity, unless it is a forecasted intercompany foreign-currency-denominated transaction.

When these criteria are satisfied, the forward contract used to hedge the forecasted transaction qualifies as a *cash flow hedge*, and changes in its value are reported in other comprehensive income until the hedged transaction affects income. When these criteria are not satisfied, changes in the value of the forward contract are recognized currently in earnings.

Suppose Gap Inc. plans to purchase merchandise for €1,000,000 at the end of March, 2017, from a supplier in France. To hedge against a possible weakening of the dollar against the euro, Gap enters a forward purchase contract on December 2, 2016, for delivery of €1,000,000 on March 31, 2017, at a forward rate of $1.47/€. Because no cash changes hands initially, and the contract has no value at inception, no entry is made on December 2. On January 31, 2017, Gap's balance sheet date, the forward rate for delivery on March 31, 2017, is $1.472/€. The following entry marks to market the forward contract:

2017			
Jan. 31	Investment in forward contract	2,000	
	Other comprehensive income		2,000
	To record the gain in the fair value of the forward contract;		
	$2,000 = ($1.472 − $1.47) × €1,000,000.		

On March 31, 2017, Gap buys the foreign currency using the forward purchase contract and completes the forecasted transaction. If the spot rate is $1.482, these entries are made:

2017			
Mar. 31	Investment in forward contract	10,000	
	Other comprehensive income		10,000
	To record the gain in the fair value of the forward contract;		
	$10,000 = ($1.482 − $1.472) × €1,000,000.		
	Foreign currency	1,482,000	
	Investment in forward contract		12,000
	Cash		1,470,000
	To record the settlement of the forward contract.		
	Inventories	1,482,000	
	Foreign currency		1,482,000
	To record the merchandise purchase.		

The gain on the forward purchase contract remains in other comprehensive income until the forecasted transaction impacts earnings. In this case, the forecasted transaction affects earnings when the inventory is sold. Assume the inventory is sold on June 21, 2017, for $2,482,000. In addition to the usual entries to record sales revenue of $2,482,000 and cost of goods sold of $1,482,000, this entry recognizes the gain on the forward contract through a reduction in cost of goods sold, increasing the gross margin from $1,000,000 to $1,012,000:

2017			
June 21	Other comprehensive income	12,000	
	Cost of goods sold		12,000
	To reclassify as a component of current earnings the increase		
	in fair value of the forward contract used to hedge the now-		
	completed forecasted transaction.		

When the forward contract hedges a forecasted *sale* transaction, the gain or loss on the forward contract remains in other comprehensive income until the forecasted sale is made. At that point, it is reclassified out of accumulated other comprehensive income as an adjustment to sales revenue.

REVIEW 4 • Using Forward Contracts to Hedge Foreign-Currency-Denominated Forecasted Transactions

Fine Foods, Inc., a U.S. wholesaler, buys merchandise from German suppliers on a regular basis, and pays the suppliers in euros. Fine Foods' accounting year ends June 30. Exchange rates are as follows:

Date	Spot rate ($/€)	Forward rate for delivery August 15, 2016
March 1, 2016	$1.35	$1.37
June 30, 2016	1.42	1.44
August 15, 2016	1.45	1.45
August 31, 2016	1.48	NA

Fine Foods plans to buy merchandise from the supplier in mid-August, 2016. On March 1, it enters into a forward contract for delivery of €1,000,000 on August 15. The forward qualifies as a cash flow hedge of a forecasted transaction. On August 15, Fine Foods closes the forward contract, takes delivery of the merchandise, and pays the supplier. The merchandise is sold to a U.S. customer on August 31 for $2,000,000.

Required Prepare the journal entries to record the above events.

Solutions are located after the chapter assignments.

BUSINESS APPLICATION   McDonald's Cash Flow Hedges

McDonald's regularly receives payments from franchise operations in other countries which it can designate as forecasted transactions. These payments are denominated in the franchisees' local currencies. McDonald's uses cash flow hedges to reduce its exposure to changes in the value of these forecasted transactions. Footnotes to its 2013 financial statements describe the hedging relationships:

> To protect against the reduction in value of forecasted foreign currency cash flows (such as royalties denominated in foreign currencies), the Company uses foreign currency forwards and foreign currency options to hedge a portion of anticipated exposures.
>
> When the U.S. dollar strengthens against foreign currencies, the decline in value of future foreign denominated royalties is offset by gains in the fair value of the foreign currency forwards and/or foreign currency options. Conversely, when the U.S. dollar weakens, the increase in the value of future foreign denominated royalties is offset by losses in the fair value of the foreign currency forwards and/or foreign currency options.

In 2013, McDonald's reported in its statement of comprehensive income a $73.4 million other comprehensive loss on cash flow hedges, and a $35.9 million increase in other comprehensive income from reclassification of cash flow hedge losses to income. The vast majority of these adjustments relate to hedges of forecasted foreign currency transactions. When the transactions impact income, for example when McDonald's receives payments from franchisees in other countries, the losses are taken out of other comprehensive income, increasing nonoperating expenses. *Source:* McDonald's Corporation 2013 annual report.

Forward Contracts as Both Cash Flow and Fair Value Hedges   An importer or exporter may use the same forward contract to hedge a forecasted transaction through its cash settlement date. Such a forward contract starts as a cash flow hedge, and becomes a fair value hedge of a firm commitment or a recorded foreign-currency-denominated receivable or payable as time passes. The Codification requires that changes in the value of the forward contract be reported in other comprehensive income *throughout the hedging period*, even though the forward contract later becomes a fair value hedge. As changing exchange rates lead to gains and losses reported in earnings on the hedged item, a portion of other comprehensive income is reclassified to earnings as an offset.

Refer to the example just before Review 4, in which Gap hedges a €1,000,000 forecasted purchase from a supplier in France. Instead of paying for the merchandise on delivery on March 31, assume Gap expects to make payment on May 15, 2017. Assume also a May 15 delivery date for the forward contract, at a forward rate of $1.47. This forward contract hedges a forecasted transaction through March 31, and an exposed payable from March 31 to May 15.

If we assume the forward rate for May 15 delivery is $1.472/€, the adjusting entry to mark the forward contract to market on January 31, the company's balance sheet date, is the same as shown previously, with the $2,000 unrealized gain reported in other comprehensive income. On March 31, the company records delivery of the merchandise as before:

2017			
Mar. 31	Inventories	1,482,000	
	Accounts payable		1,482,000
	To record the purchase of the merchandise at the $1.482 spot rate.		

On May 15, when the spot rate is $1.485, the forward contract is settled and the supplier is paid, Gap makes these entries:

2017			
May 15	Investment in forward contract	13,000	
	Other comprehensive income		13,000
	To record the gain in fair value on the forward contract;		
	$13,000 = ($1.485 − $1.472) × €1,000,000.		
	Exchange loss	3,000	
	Accounts payable		3,000
	To revalue the payable to the current exchange rate;		
	$3,000 = ($1.485 − $1.482) × €1,000,000.		
	Foreign currency	1,485,000	
	Investment in forward contract		15,000
	Cash		1,470,000
	To record the settlement of the forward contract.		
	Accounts payable...	1,485,000	
	Foreign currency		1,485,000
	To record payment to the supplier.		

Because the forward contract became a hedge of the exposed payable on March 31, the Codification provides that an amount exactly offsetting the reported loss on the accounts payable be reclassified from other comprehensive income to earnings, as follows:

2017			
May 15	Other comprehensive income	3,000	
	Exchange gain..		3,000
	To reclassify a portion of the gain on the forward contract to		
	earnings, as an offset to the loss on the accounts payable.		

When Gap sells the merchandise on June 21, it reclassifies the remainder of the gain on the forward contract to earnings, as an adjustment to cost of goods sold:

2017			
June 21	Cost of goods sold..	1,470,000	
	Other comprehensive income	12,000	
	Inventory		1,482,000
	To recognize the cost of merchandise sold, and reclassify the		
	unrealized gain on the forward contract to earnings.		

• •

Reporting Perspective

ASC Topic 815 allows hedging gains and losses to be reported in many locations on the financial statements, including other comprehensive income, sales revenue, cost of sales, other operating expenses and various asset and liability accounts. As a result, it is difficult to develop a cohesive picture of a company's financial risks and the effectiveness of its hedge investments in neutralizing that risk. *ASC Topic 815* addresses this problem by requiring footnote disclosures that separate out and summarize the effects of hedging activities. These requirements are discussed later in the chapter.

• •

Hedge of Net Investment in an International Company   A U.S. company that invests in an international subsidiary is exposed to the risk that the value of its investment will change as exchange rates change. The company may hedge this foreign exchange risk with derivative investments or financial instruments denominated in the currency.

As studied in Chapter 7, exposure of a net investment in an international entity to exchange rate changes consists of the account balances that are converted to U.S. dollars using the current exchange rate. As the current exchange rate changes, the U.S. dollar value of these accounts changes, generating gains and losses. If an international subsidiary's functional currency is the local currency, the U.S. parent *translates* the accounts of the international subsidiary into U.S. dollars. All assets and liabilities are translated at the current rate. If the international subsidiary's functional currency is the U.S. dollar, the U.S. parent *remeasures* the accounts of the subsidiary into U.S. dollars. Monetary assets and liabilities are remeasured at the current rate.

The parent of an international subsidiary whose functional currency is the local currency is exposed to foreign exchange risk through the *net* assets—assets less liabilities—of the subsidiary. Since net assets are usually positive—total assets are greater than total liabilities—the parent's exposure is similar to that of an exporter, with a net "receivable" denominated in the foreign currency. Effective hedges of this currency risk include forward sale contracts, put options, and debt denominated in the same currency.

The parent of an international subsidiary whose functional currency is the U.S. dollar is exposed to foreign exchange risk through monetary assets less total liabilities. Since this exposure is usually negative—total liabilities are greater than monetary assets—the parent's exposure is similar to that of an importer, with a net "payable" denominated in the foreign currency. Effective hedges of this currency risk include forward purchase contracts, call options, and other investments, such as loans receivable, denominated in the same currency. These concepts are summarized below.

LO5 Report hedges of net investments in international operations.

	Foreign Currency Risk and Hedges	
Conversion Process	**Typical Exposure**	**Hedge Investments**
Translation	Assets − Liabilities > 0	Forward sale contracts Put options Foreign-currency-denominated debt
Remeasurement	Monetary assets − Liabilities < 0	Forward purchase contracts Call options Foreign-currency-denominated investments

ASC Topic 815 recognizes as hedges those forward contracts or other foreign currency investments or liabilities undertaken to neutralize the effect of exchange rate movements on a U.S. firm's investment in an international branch, an equity investee, or a subsidiary. If a hedge is so designated and is effective, it is viewed as an **economic hedge of a net investment in an international entity**.

Recall that a major goal of hedge accounting is to match gains and losses on the hedge investment with losses and gains on the hedged item in the same reporting period. When the international subsidiary's functional currency is its local currency, hedge accounting is needed to net the gain or loss on a hedge of the net investment in the subsidiary against the translation adjustment in OCI. When the international subsidiary's functional currency is the U.S. dollar, the gain or loss on a hedge of the net investment in the subsidiary offsets the remeasurement gain or loss in income using normal accounting. Hedge accounting is not needed to match hedge gains and losses against hedged investment losses and gains.

BUSINESS APPLICATION   McDonald's Net Investment Hedges

The functional currencies of **McDonald's** subsidiaries in Europe and Asia are generally their local currencies. Therefore McDonald's translates its subsidiaries' accounts into U.S. dollars, and the subsidiaries' net assets expose McDonald's to exchange risk. The footnotes to McDonald's 2013 annual report describe hedges of this exposure:

> The Company primarily uses foreign currency denominated debt (third party and intercompany) to hedge its investments in certain foreign subsidiaries and affiliates. As of December 31, 2013, $4.7 billion of the Company's third party foreign currency denominated debt, $4.2 billion of intercompany foreign currency denominated debt, and $827.4 million of derivatives were designated to hedge investments in certain foreign subsidiaries and affiliates.

Net investment hedges generated pre-tax losses of $401.2 million in 2013, reported in OCI on McDonald's statement of comprehensive income, as an offset to translation gains. We can conclude that the U.S. dollar *weakened*, on average, against the currencies of McDonald's subsidiaries, increasing the U.S. dollar value of the foreign currency denominated debt used to hedge investments in international subsidiaries, and resulting in losses on these hedges. *Source:* McDonald's Corporation 2013 annual report.

LO6 Report speculative investments in foreign currency financial derivatives.

Use of Forward Contracts for Speculation   Forward contracts entered for hedging purposes represent defensive measures to protect against adverse effects of exchange rate movements. In contrast, some firms sell or purchase foreign currency forwards for **speculative purposes**—to gain from anticipated changes in the exchange rate.

Because speculative forward contracts are by definition not hedge instruments, any gains and losses due to changes in their fair value are recognized currently in earnings. Having no offsetting loss or gain, speculative contracts increase earnings volatility.

Suppose a company expects the Canadian dollar (C$) to strengthen relative to the U.S. dollar, and decides to speculate by purchasing, on November 1, 2016, C$8,000,000 for delivery on March 29, 2017. The company will cover the contract by selling these Canadian dollars in the spot market when the forward contract matures on March 29, gaining if the rate increases, and losing if it falls. Assume that the company's accounting year ends on December 31. Relevant direct exchange rates ($/C$) are as follows:

Date	Spot rate	Forward rate for delivery March 29, 2017
November 1, 2016	$0.970	$0.940
December 31, 2016	0.965	0.935
March 29, 2017	0.932	0.932

The company records the events relating to this speculative forward contract, including sale of the Canadian dollars received from the forward contract, as follows:

2016			
Nov. 1	No entry at inception; the forward contract has no value.		
Dec. 31	Exchange loss	40,000	
	Investment in forward contract		40,000
	To record the loss in the fair value on the forward contract;		
	$40,000 = ($0.94 − $0.935) × C$8,000,000.		

The company's December 31, 2016, balance sheet reports the $40,000 balance in the investment as a *current liability*.

2017

Mar. 29	Exchange loss	24,000	
	Investment in forward contract		24,000
	To record the loss in fair value on the forward contract;		
	$24,000 = ($0.935 − $0.932) × C$8,000,000.		
	Foreign currency	7,456,000	
	Investment in forward contract	64,000	
	Cash		7,520,000
	To record settlement of the forward contract and receipt of		
	Canadian dollars valued at the spot rate of $0.932/C$.		
	Cash.	7,456,000	
	Foreign currency		7,456,000
	To record sale of Canadian dollars in the spot market at $0.932/C$.		

The total exchange loss recognized in the accounts, $64,000 (= $40,000 + $24,000), equals the net cash loss of $64,000 (= $7,520,000 − $7,456,000) from the speculative activity. The speculative contract results in a loss of $64,000 because the company must purchase C$8,000,000 under the contract for $0.94, and then sell that foreign currency on the spot market for $0.932. This company obviously did not possess sufficient insight on the future direction of exchange rates in this case.

Summary of Accounting for Foreign Currency Forward Contracts   The accounting for forward contracts requires reporting the contracts at fair market value in the financial statements. If the contract is a qualifying hedge, gains and losses on the contract and losses and gains on the hedged item are reported on the same period's income statement.

Hedges of accounts receivable or payable denominated in foreign currency do not require hedge accounting to achieve this result. The offsetting effects appear on the same income statement using normal accounting.

Hedge accounting is used for fair value hedges of firm foreign currency commitments and cash flow hedges of forecasted transactions. Fair value hedges of firm foreign currency commitments require concurrent recognition of commitment assets or liabilities. Gains and losses on forward contracts used as cash flow hedges of forecasted transactions accumulate in other comprehensive income until the forecasted transactions impact income. Gains and losses on speculative contracts are recognized currently in earnings as exchange rates change.

Derivatives Disclosure Requirements   The use of derivatives has grown dramatically over the years, and the instruments used can significantly affect financial performance. As we have seen in this chapter, the financial effects of foreign currency derivatives used for hedging and speculation are complex and not easily extracted from the financial statements. These effects are not separated out but are included in various accounts, such as sales revenue, cost of sales, administrative expenses and various asset and liability accounts. The related assets and liabilities are typically not separately listed on the balance sheet. As a result, financial statement readers rely on footnote disclosures to evaluate a company's performance with respect to derivatives activities and hedging.

Disclosures required by *ASC Topic 815* are designed to give financial statement readers a better view of the extent of a company's exposure to financial risk, its hedging activities, and the degree to which its financial risk is neutralized.

An entity with derivative instruments shall disclose information to enable users of the financial statements to understand:

    a.   How and why an entity uses derivative instruments

    b.   How derivative instruments and related hedged items are accounted for under *Topic 815*

    c.   How derivative instruments and related hedged items affect an entity's financial position, financial performance, and cash flows.

Source: *ASC para. 815-10-50-1*

Specific required disclosures include the following:

- Discussion of hedging activities organized by risk exposure, such as foreign currency risk, interest rate risk, and price risk
- Volume of derivative activity
- Location and fair value amounts of derivative instruments reported in the balance sheet
- Location and amount of gains and losses reported in the income statement

Chapter 9 provides further discussion of these disclosure requirements.

BUSINESS APPLICATION   Reporting Effects of Hedging Activities

McDonald's financial statements illustrate how the effects of hedging activities are scattered throughout the financial statements. The footnotes to its 2013 annual report disclose the fair values of its foreign currency derivative investments and where they are reported on its 2013 balance sheet:

(in millions)	
Derivatives designated as hedging instruments	
Prepaid expenses and other current assets.	$28.3
Accrued payroll and other liabilities	28.8
Derivatives not designated as hedging instruments	
Prepaid expenses and other current assets.	$ 9.3
Accrued payroll and other liabilities	23.8

Gains and losses on derivative investments are reported on McDonald's 2013 income statement in selling, general and administrative expenses, interest expense, and nonoperating (income) expense.

ASC Topic 815 requires footnote disclosure of the amount of gain or loss reported in income and in OCI for both the hedge instrument and the hedged item, by hedge type, to aid users in evaluating hedge performance. For 2013, McDonald's reports a pre-tax loss of $99.6 million in OCI from foreign currency cash flow hedges and $50.7 million in pre-tax losses reclassified from AOCI to income. OCI also includes a loss of $401.2 million on net investment hedges.

Although they meet *ASC Topic 815* requirements, McDonald's footnote disclosures for cash flow hedges are not particularly helpful in evaluating hedge performance. To what extent do hedge losses offset foreign currency gains on related hedged forecasted transactions? What gains on hedged net investments did the reported losses on net investment hedges offset? *Source:* McDonald's Corporation 2013 annual report.

The FASB issued a proposal in 2011, but waited until late 2014 to resume deliberations for a new hedge accounting standard to address criticisms of current hedge accounting standards. The IASB, on the other hand, finalized their new hedge accounting standard in 2014.

INTERNATIONAL FINANCIAL REPORTING STANDARDS FOR FOREIGN CURRENCY TRANSACTIONS AND HEDGING

LO7 Describe IFRS for foreign currency transactions and hedging activities.

IFRS for reporting foreign currency transactions and hedging appears in the following standards:

- *IAS 21*, The Effects of Changes in Foreign Exchange Rates
- *IFRS 7*, Financial Instruments: Disclosures
- *IFRS 9*, Financial Instruments

Hedge accounting requirements are the third and last phase of *IFRS 9*, published in 2014, which replaces *IAS 39*. The new standard is effective in 2018, but early adoption is allowed. This section discusses *IFRS 9* hedging requirements.

IFRS for import and export transactions, as well as borrowing and lending in foreign currency, is the same as U.S. GAAP. IFRS for derivatives and hedging has the same goals as U.S. GAAP, requiring all financial derivatives to be reported at fair value on the balance sheet. Changes in value are reported in income, unless the derivative is a cash flow hedge of a forecasted transaction. Changes in the value of cash flow hedges are reported in other comprehensive income, and released to income in the same time period in which the hedged item impacts income.

Qualifications for Hedge Accounting

IFRS 9's hedge accounting requirements focus on accurately reporting a company's risk management activities. There are two main qualifications for hedge accounting:

- Formal designation and documentation of the hedging relationship and the company's risk management objective and strategy.

- Demonstration of an economic relationship between the hedged transaction and the hedge investment, allowing the hedge investment to offset the hedged transaction's risk. This analysis can be quantitative or qualitative, and only occurs once, at the inception of the hedge; continuing evaluation of hedge effectiveness is not required.

Differences Between IFRS and U.S. GAAP

Both IFRS and U.S. GAAP categorize hedges as fair value, cash flow, and net investment hedges, and the accounting procedures for each category are generally the same. However, there are some differences, which have potentially significant implications for the financial statements.

Qualifications for Hedge Accounting   U.S. GAAP's standards for an investment to qualify for hedge accounting are considerably more restrictive than *IFRS 9* requirements. Major differences between *ASC Topic 815* and *IFRS 9* are:

- U.S. GAAP requires the hedge to be "highly effective," using quantitative evaluation of the degree to which changes in the value of the hedge offset changes in the value of the hedge transaction. IFRS's hedge criteria look to the company's risk management strategy and whether or not the investment fits with that strategy. An investment is therefore more likely to qualify for hedge accounting under IFRS than under U.S. GAAP.

- Under U.S. GAAP, hedge effectiveness must be assessed periodically throughout the hedging period, to see if the hedge still qualifies for hedge accounting. IFRS only requires assessment at inception.

- IFRS has a broader definition of investments and hedged items that are eligible for hedge accounting. For example, IFRS allows hedge accounting for hedges of groups of dissimilar transactions.

Hedge accounting standards have, in the past, been criticized as not reflecting actual risk management behavior, creating artificial income volatility by not allowing hedge accounting in situations where a company is effectively hedging its risk. *IFRS 9*'s more flexible provisions address this weakness, but U.S. GAAP has not yet changed in this area. The FASB began readdressing hedge accounting issues in late 2014, with the goal of developing standards that more accurately portray a company's hedging performance.

Basis Adjustments   The mechanics of accounting for fair value, cash flow, and net investment hedges are generally the same under U.S. GAAP and IFRS. However, when a company hedges a forecasted transaction that results in recognition of a nonfinancial item, U.S. GAAP and IFRS differ in the treatment of gains and losses on the hedge investment. A common example is a hedge of a forecasted purchase of a depreciable asset, payable in another currency. A company may use a forward contract to lock in the local currency value of the purchase, avoiding exchange rate risk.

Changes in the value of the cash flow hedge are reported in other comprehensive income under both U.S. GAAP and IFRS. The difference in reporting relates to the timing of reclassification of these gains and losses out of accumulated other comprehensive income. U.S. GAAP requires the hedge gains and losses to be reclassified to earnings as the hedged transaction affects earnings, when the asset is depreciated. *IFRS 9* requires reclassification of the entire net gain or loss as a **basis adjustment** to the asset. Although total reported income is the same, assets and equity are different, as illustrated next.

Fiat Group is headquartered in Turin, Italy, and reports its financial statements in euros. It plans to purchase equipment for $1,000,000 on June 30, 2017. On November 1, 2016, the Group enters a forward contract to purchase $1,000,000 for €700,000 on June 30, 2017, and designates the contract as a cash flow hedge of the equipment purchase. By December 31, 2016, the Group's year-end, the U.S. dollar has appreciated and the forward price for delivery of $1,000,000 is €750,000. The year-end adjusting entry, in euros, is:

2016			
Dec. 31	Investment in forward contract	50,000	
	Other comprehensive income		50,000
	To record the change in the fair value of the forward contract.		

On June 30, 2017, the U.S. dollar has appreciated further, and $1,000,000 can be purchased in the spot market for €820,000. The Group settles the forward contract and purchases the equipment.

2017			
June 30	Investment in forward contract	70,000	
	Other comprehensive income		70,000
	To record the gain in the fair value of the forward contract.		
	Equipment	820,000	
	Investment in forward contract		120,000
	Cash		700,000
	To settle the forward contract and acquire the equipment.		

Fiat Group then reclassifies the net gain on the forward as an adjustment to the equipment account.

2017			
June 30	Other comprehensive income	120,000	
	Equipment		120,000
	To reclassify the gain on the cash flow hedge as a basis adjustment.		

Because U.S. GAAP does not permit the basis adjustment, the equipment would be initially reported at €820,000. U.S. companies retain the gain or loss on cash flow hedges in accumulated other comprehensive income until the hedged item impacts income. In this case, the gain is reclassified to income over time as an adjustment to periodic depreciation expense on the equipment.

If the equipment has a two-year life, straight-line, entries to record depreciation for the six months ending December 31, 2017, under IFRS and U.S. GAAP, respectively, are:

2017			
Dec. 31			
IFRS	Depreciation expense.	175,000	
	Equipment.		175,000
	To record six months of depreciation on equipment;		
	€175,000 = €700,000/2 × ½.		

2017			
Dec. 31			
U.S. GAAP	Depreciation expense.	175,000	
	Other comprehensive income	30,000	
	Equipment.		205,000
	To record six months of depreciation on equipment;		
	€205,000 = €820,000/2 × ½ and €30,000 = €120,000/2 × ½.		

The table below summarizes financial statement disclosure for our example.

Fiat Group Selected Financial Statement Disclosures		
December 31, 2017	IFRS	U.S. GAAP
Depreciation expense................	€175,000	€175,000
Equipment, net.....................	525,000	615,000
AOCI............................	—	(90,000)

The income effect in the above example is the *same* whether the cash flow hedge gain remains in equity and adjusts depreciation, or is reclassified as an adjustment to the equipment. However, reported assets and equity are *lower* under IFRS.

Financial Instruments Disclosures

IFRS 7 and *IFRS 9* disclosure requirements seek to provide financial statement users with the information necessary to evaluate the risks resulting from the use of financial instruments, how these risks are managed, and how these instruments affect financial performance.

IFRS 9 requires more disclosures than currently required under *IFRS 7,* and focuses on providing financial statement users with information about a company's risk management activities. The disclosures are designed to provide information on three major hedging dimensions:

- The company's risk management strategy and how it is used to manage risk;
- How hedging activities affect the amount, timing and uncertainty of future cash flows; and
- The impact of hedging activities on financial performance, as portrayed in the financial statements.

Previous hedging standards allowed companies to scatter information on hedging activities throughout the financial statements. *IFRS 9* requires that disclosures be presented in a single note or in a separate section of the financial statements.

REVIEW OF KEY CONCEPTS ●●●●●●●●●●●●●●●●●●●●●●●●●●●●●●●●●

Report import and export transactions and borrowing and lending denominated in foreign currency. (p. 330) Import and export transactions and borrowing and lending abroad by domestic companies often generate **receivables and payables denominated in a foreign currency**. As the direct exchange rate—$/foreign currency—rises (falls), the number of dollars ultimately to be received or paid increases (decreases). Such changes in the dollar equivalents of receivables and payables generate **exchange gains and losses** reported in earnings by the domestic company as exchange rates change.
LO 1

Report hedges of foreign-currency-denominated receivables and payables. (p. 341) Changes in the value of **forward contracts** used to hedge foreign-currency-denominated receivables or payables are **reported in earnings as forward rates change**. To the extent that spot and forward rates move together, gains and losses on the forward contracts completely offset the losses and gains on the receivables and payables.
LO 2

Report hedges of foreign-currency-denominated firm commitments. (p. 344) Forward contracts can hedge firm commitments, such as purchase or sales orders denominated in foreign currency. Changes in the value of these forwards are reported in earnings, offsetting changes in the value of the firm commitments recognized for this purpose. The hedging gains or losses eventually **adjust the inventory balance or sales revenue**.
LO 3

LO 4 **Report hedges of foreign-currency-denominated forecasted transactions. (p. 349)** Changes in the value of forward contracts used to hedge forecasted purchases or sales denominated in foreign currency are initially recognized in **other comprehensive income**. When the hedged purchase or sale is reported in earnings, the hedging gain or loss is reclassified out of AOCI and **adjusts cost of sales or sales revenue**.

LO 5 **Report hedges of net investments in international operations. (p. 353)** Gains and losses on qualifying hedges of a company's net investment in an international subsidiary are matched with the related loss or gain on conversion of the subsidiary's accounts to the parent's currency. When the subsidiary's functional currency is the local currency, the translation gain or loss and the hedge loss or gain are both reported in other comprehensive income. When the subsidiary's functional currency is the parent's currency, the remeasurement gain or loss and the hedge loss or gain are both reported in income.

LO 6 **Report speculative investments in foreign currency financial derivatives. (p. 354)** Changes in the value of forward contracts not qualifying as hedges are **reported in earnings** as forward rates change.

LO 7 **Describe IFRS for foreign currency transactions and hedging activities. (p. 356)** **IFRS** for foreign currency denominated import and export transactions, borrowing and lending, financial instruments and hedging activities are similar to U.S. GAAP, although some differences in application include qualifications for hedge accounting, and **basis adjustments** for cash flow hedges.

Assignments with the ✓ in the margin are available in BusinessCourse.
See the Preface of the book for details.

MULTIPLE CHOICE QUESTIONS ••••••••••••••••••••••••••••••••

✓ **LO 1**   **1.** On May 20, 2016, when the spot rate is $1.28/€, a U.S. company buys merchandise from a supplier in Italy, at a cost of €100,000. The spot rate is $1.25/€ on June 30, the company's year-end. Payment of €100,000 is made on July 30, 2016, when the spot rate is $1.32/€. What is the effect on fiscal 2016 and fiscal 2017 income?

	Fiscal 2016	Fiscal 2017
a.	No effect	$4,000 exchange loss
b.	$3,000 exchange loss	$7,000 exchange gain
c.	No effect	$4,000 exchange gain
d.	$3,000 exchange gain	$7,000 exchange loss

✓ **LO 1**   **2.** On April 10, 2016, when the spot rate is $1.30/€, a U.S. company sells merchandise to a customer in Italy. The spot rate is $1.31/€ on June 30, the company's year-end. Payment of €100,000 is received on August 10, 2016, when the spot rate is $1.28/€. What is the effect on fiscal 2016 and 2017 income?

	Fiscal 2016	Fiscal 2017
a.	$1,000 exchange loss	$3,000 exchange gain
b.	No effect	$2,000 exchange loss
c.	No effect	$2,000 exchange gain
d.	$1,000 exchange gain	$3,000 exchange loss

Use the following forward and spot prices for Canadian dollars (C$) to answer questions 3–9 below. The prices are in U.S. dollars ($/C$).

	Spot rate	Forward rate for 4/15/17 delivery of Canadian dollars
November 15, 2016	$0.905	$0.895
December 31, 2016	0.965	0.950
March 1, 2017	0.920	0.915
April 15, 2017	0.940	0.940

3. On November 15, 2016, a U.S. company takes delivery of merchandise costing C$1,000,000 from a Canadian supplier and records an account payable. On the same date, the company enters a forward contract locking in the U.S. dollar purchase price of C$1,000,000, for delivery on April 15, 2017. The forward contract is closed and payment is made to the supplier on April 15, 2017. The company's accounting year ends on December 31. Assuming the company still holds the merchandise at December 31, 2016, at what amount is the merchandise reported? **LO 2** ✓

   a. $895,000
   b. $905,000
   c. $950,000
   d. $965,000

4. Use the information from question 3. What is the net exchange gain or loss for 2017? **LO 2** ✓

   a. $15,000 gain
   b. $25,000 loss
   c. $10,000 loss
   d. $25,000 gain

5. On November 15, 2016, a U.S. company issues a purchase order to a Canadian supplier for merchandise costing C$1,000,000. On the same date, the company enters a forward contract locking in the U.S. dollar purchase price of C$1,000,000, for delivery on April 15, 2017. The forward qualifies as a hedge of the firm commitment. Delivery of the merchandise takes place on March 1, 2017, and the forward contract is closed and payment is made to the supplier on April 15, 2017. How is the forward contract reported on the company's December 31, 2016, balance sheet? **LO 3** ✓

   a. $60,000 asset
   b. $60,000 liability
   c. $55,000 liability
   d. $55,000 asset

6. Use the information from question 5. After delivery, at what amount is the merchandise carried on the U.S. company's books? **LO 3** ✓

   a. $895,000
   b. $900,000
   c. $905,000
   d. $915,000

7. A U.S. company expects to buy merchandise from a Canadian supplier for approximately C$1,000,000, in the middle of April. On November 15, 2016, the company enters a forward contract locking in the U.S. dollar purchase price of C$1,000,000, for delivery on April 15, 2017. The forward qualifies as a hedge of the forecasted transaction. Delivery of the merchandise takes place on April 15, 2017, and the forward contract is closed and payment is made to the supplier. At what amount is the merchandise reported on delivery on April 15, 2017? **LO 4** ✓

   a. $895,000
   b. $905,000
   c. $940,000
   d. $950,000

8. Use the information from question 7. When the merchandise is sold, at what amount will the company report cost of goods sold? **LO 4** ✓

   a. $895,000
   b. $905,000
   c. $940,000
   d. $950,000

9. On March 1, 2017, a U.S. company enters a forward contract locking in the selling price of C$1,000,000, for delivery on April 15, 2017. The contract does not qualify for hedge accounting. What is the gain or loss on the forward contract that is reported on the company's 2017 income statement? **LO 6** ✓

   a. $ 5,000 loss
   b. $20,000 gain
   c. $25,000 loss
   d. $ 5,000 gain

⊘ LO 7 **10.** A UK company hedges its U.S. dollar purchase of equipment from a U.S. supplier using a forward contract exchanging pounds for U.S. dollars at a fixed rate. The forward qualifies as a hedge of a forecasted transaction. The company reports gains on the forward, and then closes the forward and buys the equipment. The company follows IFRS. Which statement is **true**?

    a. The IFRS company will report a lower equipment value on its balance sheet than if it followed U.S. GAAP.

    b. The IFRS company will report less total depreciation expense on the equipment than if it followed U.S. GAAP.

    c. The IFRS company will report a higher equipment value on its balance sheet than if it followed U.S. GAAP.

    d. The IFRS company will report more total depreciation expense on the equipment than if it followed U.S. GAAP.

EXERCISES ••

LO 1 **E8.1** **Recording Import Transactions** Pinnacle Foods imports a variety of items for resale to U.S. retailers. Following is a description of purchases and foreign-currency-denominated payments made in the last accounting period, plus the direct exchange rates for each date:

Country	Amount	Currency	Spot rate at purchase	Spot rate at payment
Australia	200,000	Australian dollar	$0.8800	$0.9100
Thailand	800,000	Baht	0.0350	0.0330
Hong Kong	5,000,000	Hong Kong dollar	0.1289	0.1178
Jordan	500,000	Dinar	1.4200	1.4500

Required

Prepare the journal entries made by Pinnacle, a U.S. company, to record the above purchase and payment transactions.

LO 1 **E8.2** **Recording Export Transactions** Daisy Brands, a U.S. company, sells items abroad. Daisy prices many of these transactions in the currency of the customer. Following are four such transactions made in the last accounting period, plus the direct exchange rates for each date:

Country	Amount	Currency	Spot rate at sale	Spot rate at collection
Argentina	250,000	Peso	$0.118	$0.121
Canada	400,000	Dollar	0.932	0.954
India	300,000	Rupee	0.016	0.013
South Africa	100,000	Rand	0.091	0.087

Required

Prepare the journal entries made by Daisy Brands to record the above sale and collection transactions.

⊘ LO 1 **E8.3** **Recording Import and Export Transactions** Homestyle Brands imports materials from other countries and exports finished products to customers throughout the world. Information regarding four such transactions occurring in the last accounting period, all denominated in units of foreign currency, is given below:

Country	Amount	Spot rate at transaction date	Spot rate at payment date
1. Import from Taiwan	100,000 Taiwan dollars	$0.033	$0.038
2. Import from Poland	600,000 zloty	0.300	0.285
3. Export to Brazil	400,000 reais	0.421	0.403
4. Export to Switzerland	950,000 Swiss francs	1.050	1.084

Required

Prepare the journal entries made by Homestyle Brands to record the above events on the transaction date and on the payment date.

E8.4 **Adjusting Entry at Balance Sheet Date** **Yum! Brands, Inc.** has the following receivables and **LO 1** payables denominated in foreign currencies, prior to closing on December 31. The spot rates at December 31 are also given.

Item	Current $ balance	FC balance	December 31 spot rate
1. Receivable	$ 75,000	1,000,000 Mexican pesos	$0.08
2. Receivable	220,000	225,000 Canadian dollars	0.95
3. Payable.	550,000	400,000 Jordan dinar	1.35
4. Payable.	50,000	200,000 Saudi Arabian riyal	0.26

Required

Prepare the adjusting entry recorded by Yum! Brands at December 31. Show all calculations.

E8.5 **Recording International Investment** To take advantage of high short-term interest rates, **Chipotle** **LO 1** **Mexican Grill, Inc.** purchased a 1,000,000 krona six-month certificate of deposit from a Swedish bank for $125,000 on October 1, 2016. The annual interest rate is 6 percent. Chipotle received the full principal and interest, in krona, on March 31, 2017, and immediately exchanged the krona for U.S. dollars at the current spot rate. Spot rates ($/krona) at December 31, 2016, and March 31, 2017, were $0.1445 and $0.1228, respectively. Chipotle is a calendar-year company, and accrues interest only at year-end.

Required

a. Prepare the journal entries recorded by Chipotle on October 1, 2016, December 31, 2016, and March 31, 2017.

b. What was the effective annual rate of return on this investment? Show calculations. Why is the effective annual rate different from 6 percent?

E8.6 **Hedging Exposed Liability Position** On March 15, 2017, Hunt Brands, a U.S. company, pur- **LO 2** chased merchandise from a South African company at a price of R1,000,000, payable in two months in rands. To hedge its exposed liability position, Hunt entered a forward contract for purchase of R1,000,000 on May 15, 2017. On May 15, Hunt closed the forward contract and used the rands to pay its supplier. The merchandise was sold to a U.S. customer for $110,000 in cash on June 5, 2017. Hunt's accounting year ends December 31.

Exchange rates ($/R) are as follows:

	Spot rate	Forward rate for delivery May 15, 2017
March 15, 2017	$0.0906	$0.0908
May 15, 2017	0.0909	—

Required

a. Prepare the journal entries Hunt Brands made on March 15, May 15, and June 5, 2017. Assume Hunt records cost of goods sold at the time of sale.

b. Calculate the cash gain or loss realized by Hunt Brands by hedging compared with not hedging.

E8.7 **Hedging Exposed Liability Position with Adjusting Entries** On December 1, 2017, Sizzler **LO 2** Foods, a U.S. company, purchased merchandise from a Hong Kong supplier at a price of HK$10,000,000, payable in three months in Hong Kong dollars. To hedge its exposed liability position, Sizzler entered a forward contract for purchase of HK$10,000,000 on March 1, 2018. On March 1, Sizzler closed the forward contract and used the Hong Kong dollars to pay its supplier. Sizzler's accounting year ends January 31.

Exchange rates ($/HK$) are as follows:

	Spot rate	Forward rate for delivery March 1, 2018
December 1, 2017	$0.1289	$0.1293
January 31, 2018	0.1299	0.1304
March 1, 2018	0.1303	—

Required

Prepare the journal entries Sizzler Foods made on December 1, 2017 and March 1, 2018 to record the above transactions, as well as its end-of-year adjusting entries on January 31, 2018.

LO 2 **E8.8** **Hedging Exposed Asset Position**   On September 3, 2017, Robin Franchises, a U.S. company, sold merchandise to a franchisee in the U.K., at a price of £8,000,000, payable in three months in pounds. To hedge its exposed asset position, on September 3, 2017, Robin entered a forward contract for delivery of £8,000,000 to the broker on December 3, 2017. On December 3, 2017, Robin received payment from the franchisee, and delivered the pounds to the broker to close the forward contract. Robin's accounting year ends December 31. Exchange rates ($/£) are as follows:

	Spot rate	Forward rate for delivery December 3, 2017
September 3, 2017	$1.6168	$1.6155
December 3, 2017	1.6150	—

Required

a. Prepare the journal entries Robin Franchises made on September 3, 2017 and December 3, 2017.
b. Calculate the cash gain or loss realized by Robin Franchises by hedging compared with not hedging.

LO 2, 3 **E8.9** **Hedged Purchase Commitment and Exposed Liability Position, with Adjusting Entries**   On November 20, 2017, International Foods, a U.S. company, agreed to purchase merchandise from a Hong Kong supplier at a price of HK$10,000,000. The merchandise will be delivered on January 10, 2018, and the amount owing is payable on April 10, 2018, in Hong Kong dollars. To hedge the expected future payment, International entered a forward contract for purchase of HK$10,000,000 on April 10, 2018. On January 10, 2018, the merchandise was delivered as promised. On April 10, International closed the forward contract and used the Hong Kong dollars to pay its supplier. International's accounting year ends December 31. Exchange rates ($/HK$) are as follows:

	Spot rate	Forward rate for delivery April 10, 2018
November 20, 2017	$0.1289	$0.1293
December 31, 2017	0.1299	0.1304
January 10, 2018	0.1301	0.1302
April 10, 2018	0.1303	—

Required

Prepare the journal entries International Foods made on January 10, 2018 and April 10, 2018 to record the above transactions, as well as its end-of-year adjusting entries on December 31, 2017.

LO 2, 3 **E8.10** **Hedged Sale Commitment and Exposed Asset Position**   On June 25, 2017, GlobalAgra Inc., a U.S. company, received a purchase order from a Swiss customer for delivery of merchandise on July 10, 2017, at a price of CHF10,000,000, payable in Swiss francs (CHF) on September 10, 2017. To hedge its exposure to exchange rate changes, on June 25, 2017, GlobalAgra entered a forward contract for delivery of CHF10,000,000 to the broker on September 10, 2017. The merchandise was delivered as scheduled. On

September 10, 2017, GlobalAgra received payment from the customer, and delivered the Swiss francs to the broker to close the forward contract. GlobalAgra's accounting year ends December 31. Exchange rates ($/£) are as follows:

	Spot rate	Forward rate for delivery September 10, 2017
June 25, 2017....................................	$1.0506	$1.0507
July 10, 2017	1.0510	1.0511
September 10, 2017............................	1.0512	—

Required

Prepare the journal entries GlobalAgra made on July 10, 2017, and September 10, 2017, to record the above transactions.

E8.11 **Hedged Sale Commitment and Exposed Asset Position, with Adjusting Entries** On December 10, 2017, Robin Franchises, a U.S. company, received a purchase order from a U.K. customer for delivery of merchandise on January 15, 2018. The price of the merchandise is £8,000,000, payable on March 15, 2018, in pounds. To hedge its exposure to exchange rate changes, on December 10, 2017, Robin entered a forward contract for delivery of £8,000,000 to the broker on March 15, 2018. The merchandise was delivered as scheduled. On March 15, 2018, Robin received payment from the customer, and delivered the pounds to the broker to close the forward contract. Robin's accounting year ends December 31. Exchange rates ($/£) are as follows:

LO 2, 3

	Spot rate	Forward rate for delivery March 15, 2018
December 10, 2017	$1.6168	$1.6166
December 31, 2017	1.6165	1.6163
January 15, 2018	1.6160	1.6158
March 15, 2018	1.6150	—

Required

Prepare the journal entries Robin Franchises made on January 15, 2018 and March 15, 2018 to record the above transactions, as well as its end-of-year adjusting entries on December 31, 2017.

E8.12 **Hedged Forecasted Purchase** Constellation Brands, a U.S. company, purchases merchandise from a German supplier on a regular basis. On April 1, 2016, Constellation purchased €14,000 for delivery on June 30, 2016, in anticipation of an expected purchase of merchandise for €14,000 at the end of June. The forward contract was a qualified hedge of a forecasted transaction. Constellation took delivery of the merchandise, settled the forward contract, and paid the German supplier €14,000 on June 30, 2016. The merchandise was subsequently sold in the U.S. on July 12, 2016, for $19,000 in cash. Relevant exchange rates ($/€) are as follows:

LO 4 ✓

	Spot rate	Forward rate for delivery June 30, 2016
April 1, 2016.....................................	$1.30	$1.28
June 30, 2016....................................	1.34	—

Required

Prepare the journal entries made by Constellation Brands on June 30 and July 12 concerning the above events. Assume Constellation Brands is a calendar-year company, and records cost of goods sold at the time of sale.

LO 4 **E8.13** **Hedged Forecasted Sale** Bectel, Inc. expects to sell merchandise for C$1,000,000 to a Canadian customer at the end of November, 2017. In anticipation of this forecasted transaction, on August 30, 2017, Bectel sold C$1,000,000 forward for delivery on November 30, 2017. Bectel made the sale as expected on November 30, and settled the forward contract. Relevant exchange rates ($/C$) are as follows:

	Spot rate	Forward rate for delivery November 30, 2017
August 30, 2017	$0.93	$0.97
November 30, 2017	0.98	—

Required

Prepare the journal entries made by Bectel on November 30 concerning the above events. Assume Bectel is a calendar-year company.

LO 5 **E8.14** **Hedge of Net Investment in International Operations** Below is an excerpt from the 2013 statement of comprehensive income of **Unilever Group** (in € millions):

UNILEVER GROUP [UN]

	2013	2012	2011
Other comprehensive income			
Items that may be reclassified subsequently into profit or loss:			
Currency translation gains/(losses) net of tax[a]	(999)	(316)	(703)

[a] Includes fair value gains (losses) on net investment hedges of €275 million [2012: €(160) million; 2011: €45 million].

Required

a. For each year 2013, 2012, and 2011, calculate the translation gain (loss) *before* the effects of hedging.
b. On average, did the euro strengthen or weaken against the currencies of Unilever's international subsidiaries during 2011–2013? Explain your answer.
c. The footnotes to Unilever's financial statements indicate that it mostly uses forward contracts to hedge its net investment in international operations. Does Unilever use forward *purchase* or forward *sale* contracts to hedge this risk? Explain.
d. How effective were Unilever's net investment hedges in each of the years 2013, 2012, and 2011?

LO 6 **E8.15** **Speculative Foreign Contracts** **Krispy Kreme Doughnuts, Inc.** has franchises operating outside the U.S. and invests in derivatives to hedge its foreign currency risk. Although it tries to hedge its various positions, on December 16, 2016, Krispy Kreme finds itself with the following unhedged forward contracts:

- Agreement to purchase 10,000,000 Hong Kong dollars (HK$) in 30 days at $0.13/HK$.
- Agreement to sell 10,000,000 Singapore dollars (S$) in 30 days at $0.84/S$.

Relevant exchange rates are:

30-day forward rates at December 16, 2016	$0.128/HK$	$0.834/S$
15-day forward rates at December 31, 2016	0.125/HK$	0.842/S$
Spot rates at January 15, 2017	0.131/HK$	0.836/S$

Required

a. What are the correct balances for the above contracts at December 16, 2016?
b. Prepare the journal entries made by Krispy Kreme on December 31, 2016, and January 15, 2017, assuming that the balances of the forward contracts are properly stated at December 16, 2016, and that the company closes its books on December 31.

PROBLEMS ••

P8.1 **Import/Export Transactions** Papa Pete's International is a U.S. food distributor that buys and sells   LO 1
merchandise in several non-U.S. currencies. Below is a summary of transactions occurring in 2017.

- Sales to Canadian customers, totaling C$1,000,000, occurred when the exchange rate was $0.93/C$.
  C$200,000 was for cash, but C$700,000 was paid by customers when the rate was $0.924/C$. The
  remainder is unpaid at year-end, when the rate is $0.922/C$.
- Sales to Italian customers, totaling €10,000,000, occurred when the exchange rate was $1.27/€. The
  company was paid €8,000,000 when the rate was $1.285. The remainder is unpaid at year-end, when
  the rate is $1.288.
- Purchases from Mexican suppliers, totaling Mex$3,000,000, occurred when the exchange rate was
  $0.075/Mex$. The company paid the suppliers Mex$2,700,000 when the rate was $0.0782/Mex$. The
  remainder is unpaid at year-end, when the rate is $0.0788/Mex$. Mex$2,800,000 of the merchandise
  was sold by Papa Pete's during 2017.
- Purchases from Hong Kong suppliers, totaling HK$4,000,000, occurred when the exchange rate was
  $0.129/HK$. The company paid the suppliers HK$3,400,000 when the rate was $0.123/HK$, and the
  remainder is unpaid at year-end, when the rate is $0.121/HK$. HK$3,600,000 of this merchandise was
  sold by Papa Pete's during 2017.

Required

Calculate the following amounts, appearing in Papa Pete's 2017 financial statements, related to the above
information. Show calculations clearly.

a. Accounts receivable and accounts payable, end of 2017
b. Sales revenue for 2017
c. Cost of goods sold for 2017
d. Inventory balance, end of 2017
e. Exchange gain or loss for 2017

P8.2 **Evaluation of Domestic and International Investments** The treasurer of Organic International   LO 1
Corporation is always on the lookout for short-term, high-yielding investments. Six-month low-risk domestic investments currently yield 3 percent per annum. Two international investments of comparable
risk are also being considered.

1. A six-month certificate of deposit issued by the Bank of England has a coupon rate of 3.5 percent per
    annum. The current exchange rate is $1.60 and is expected to be $1.595 at the end of six months ($/£).
2. A six-month certificate of deposit issued by the Bundesbank in Germany carries a coupon rate of 2.5
    percent per annum. The current exchange rate is $1.25 and is expected to be $1.254 at the end of 6
    months ($/€).

Required

Assuming that Organic has $1,000,000 to invest, and wants to maximize the number of dollars at the
end of six months, analyze the three alternative investments and make a recommendation. Support your
analysis with calculations.

P8.3 **Analysis of International Investments** Dale Food Company, a U.S. company, is considering put-   LO 1, 2
ting $10 million of its excess cash into a three-month investment. The following fixed return investments
have comparable risk. Dale is unwilling to be exposed to exchange rate risk, and therefore will enter a
forward contract to lock in, at the date of the initial investment, the U.S. dollar value of currency returned
to it at the end of three months.

- A three-month investment offered by a Singapore bank offers an annual interest rate of 4.5 percent.
  The spot rate is now $0.786, and the forward rate for delivery in three months is $0.803 ($/S$).
- A three-month investment offered by a Canadian investment bank offers an annual interest rate of 3.9
  percent. The spot rate is now $0.952, and the forward rate for delivery in three months is $0.981($/C$).

Required

Determine the annual rate of return on each investment.

P8.4 **Computation of Exchange Gain or Loss, Exposed Positions and Forward Contracts** In-   LO 1, 2
ternational Distributors, Inc., a U.S. company, is active in the import/export business. An analysis of
International's receivables, payables, and other assets (liabilities) prior to adjustment at December 31,
2017, disclosed the following:

Receivables	
U.S. customers.........	$ 100,000
Belgian customers (300,000 euros).........	385,000
Indian customers (1,200,000 rupees).........	19,500
Saudi Arabian customers (90,000 riyal).........	24,000
Total receivables.........	$ 528,500
Payables	
U.S. suppliers.........	$ (60,000)
Japanese suppliers (1,000,000 yen).........	(9,000)
Mexican suppliers (500,000 pesos).........	(38,120)
Total payables.........	$(107,120)
Other current assets (liabilities)	
Investment in forward purchase contract (for delivery of 500,000 pesos in 30 days at $0.0756).........	$ (525)
Investment in forward sale contract (for delivery of 300,000 euros in 60 days at $1.2785).........	480
Total other current assets (liabilities).........	$ (45)

Relevant exchange rates ($/FC) for the above currencies at December 31, 2017, are:

Currency	
Euro (spot rate).........	$1.27340
Euro (60-day forward rate).........	1.26840
Rupee (spot rate).........	0.01639
Riyal (spot rate).........	0.26660
Yen (spot rate).........	0.00925
Mexican peso (spot rate).........	0.07500
Mexican peso (30-day forward rate).........	0.07515

Required

a.   Prepare a schedule to compute the exchange gain or loss recognized by International Distributors in 2017. Record the needed adjusting entries.

b.   Comment on the hedge effectiveness of the two forward contracts.

LO 2   P8.5   Hedging, Leverage, Return on Assets   The Cheesecake Factory Inc.'s December 31, 2016 balance sheet shows total liabilities of $700 million and total assets of $1 billion; measured financial leverage is therefore 0.70. Included in current liabilities is $450 million (C$500 million) payable on April 1, 2017, to a Canadian supplier. Cheesecake Factory's management expects exchange rates to converge to $0.93/C$ on March 31, 2017 and April 1, 2017.

Required

Assuming that Cheesecake Factory's management always seeks to portray the most positive financial picture possible, assess the effects of the following actions. Disregard income taxes.

a.   On January 1, 2017, management enters into a 90-day forward contract to purchase C$500 million for $490 million. Compute the expected gain or loss from hedging compared with not hedging. Assuming total assets and liabilities are unchanged except as indicated by exchange rate movements, analyze how the hedge affects Cheesecake Factory's financial leverage when first quarter 2017 interim financial statements are issued.

b.   If Cheesecake Factory can borrow domestically at 4% per annum, evaluate the wisdom of using the forward contract described in part a above to neutralize the exchange rate risk.

c.   Cheesecake Factory's operating income for 2016 was $47.5 million; its annual return on average total assets (ROA) in 2016 was 5 percent. Cheesecake Factory projects the same relationship for 2017 at current exchange rates. Management considers purchasing C$500 million on January 1, 2017, for delivery in 90 days for $455 million to hedge the payable to the Canadian supplier. Cheesecake Factory projects total assets at $1.2 billion at March 31, 2017. Holding March 31, 2017 assets at $1.2

billion, analyze how hedging the payable, compared with not hedging, affects the first quarter ROA. Assume that foreign exchange gains and losses are part of operating income.

P8.6   **Recording a Hedged International Loan**   The Roderick Company, a U.S. company, borrowed £50 million from a London bank on December 16, 2017. The £50 million were immediately converted to dollars for use in the United States and were scheduled to be repaid with interest of £250,000 on January 15, 2018. To hedge the risk of an unfavorable change in the exchange rate, Roderick purchased £50.25 million for delivery on January 15, 2018. Roderick's accounting period ends on December 31. Exchange rates on various dates follow: **LO 1, 2**

	Spot rate	Forward rate for delivery January 15, 2018
December 16, 2017	$1.68	$1.71
December 31, 2017	1.66	1.69
January 15, 2018	1.63	—

Required

Prepare the journal entries made by Roderick on December 16, 2017, December 31, 2017, and January 15, 2018.

P8.7   **Import/Export Transactions and Hedged Commitment**   The following international transactions were entered into during 2017 by **Sysco Corporation**, the largest foodservice distributor in North America: **LO 1, 3** ✅

1. June 15, 2017: Entered into a firm commitment to purchase frozen pasta entrees from Italy which will be resold in the United States. The invoice price was €4,000,000, and delivery and payment were to be made in 60 days. Concurrently, €4,000,000 was purchased in the forward market for delivery in 60 days at the forward rate of $1.45. The goods were received, payment was made, and the forward contract was settled on August 14, 2017, when the spot rate was $1.43.
2. September 1, 2017: Canned products priced at 3,000,000 zloty were sold to a food distributor in Poland when the spot rate was $0.38. Payment was received on November 3, 2017, when the spot rate was $0.36, and the zloty were immediately converted to dollars.

Required

Prepare the 2017 journal entries made by Sysco Corporation relating to the above transactions. Sysco is a calendar year company.

P8.8   **Hedging a Foreign Currency Commitment—Effects on Income**   On October 1, 2017, Orchid Foods agreed to sell merchandise to a Swiss customer for 500,000 swiss francs (CHF). Delivery is to be made on November 30, 2017, and payment is to be received on January 31, 2018. Concurrently, Orchid Foods sold CHF500,000 forward for delivery on January 31, 2018, for a total contract price of $526,000. Orchid Foods closes its books annually on December 31. Current spot rates and forward rates ($/CHF) for delivery on January 31, 2018, are as follows: **LO 3**

	Spot rate	Forward rate
October 1, 2017	$1.004	$1.052
November 30, 2017	1.034	1.094
December 31, 2017	1.024	1.072
January 31, 2018	1.062	—

Required

a. Prepare all journal entries relative to the sale and the forward contract during 2017 and 2018.
b. Prepare a schedule showing the income statement effects of the above events in each of the two years.
c. Did Orchid Foods gain or lose from hedging the foreign currency commitment? Explain.

P8.9   **Hedging a Forecasted Purchase Transaction**   On September 1, 2016, Morton Industries, a U.S. company, decided to purchase merchandise from a supplier in Honduras for 10,000,000 lempira (L) at the end of January 2017. Morton plans to submit payment to the supplier on March 1, 2017, in lempira. Concurrently, Morton purchased L10,000,000 forward for delivery on March 1, 2017, for a total price of   **LO 4**

$482,000. This forward contract qualifies as a hedge of a forecasted transaction. On January 29, 2017, Morton took delivery of the merchandise. On March 1, 2017, the forward contract was settled and payment was made to the supplier. Morton is a calendar-year company. On April 8, 2017, the merchandise was sold to a U.S. customer for $600,000. Relevant exchange rates ($/L) are as follows:

	Spot rate	Forward rate for delivery March 1, 2017
September 1, 2016.	$0.0472	$0.0482
December 31, 2016	0.0481	0.0490
January 29, 2017	0.0563	0.0570
March 1, 2017	0.0596	—

Required

Prepare the journal entries to record the above events, including December 31, 2016 adjusting entries. Assume Morton records cost of goods sold at the time of sale.

✓ LO 4   P8.10   Hedging a Forecasted Sale Transaction   On December 10, 2017, Daisy Foods, a U.S. company, anticipates sales in the amount of A$25,000,000 to an Australian customer, payment in Australian dollars to be received at the end of May 2018. On December 10, 2017, Daisy Foods enters a forward contract for the sale of A$25,000,000 for a total price of $22,097,500 on May 31, 2018. The forward contract qualifies as a hedge of the forecasted sale. On March 1, 2018, Daisy delivered the merchandise to the Australian customer. On May 31, 2018, Daisy received A$25,000,000 from the customer, and delivered it to the broker to close the forward contract. Daisy Foods' accounting year ends January 31. Relevant exchange rates ($/A$) are as follows:

	Spot rate	Forward rate for delivery May 31, 2018
December 10, 2017	$0.8841	$0.8839
January 31, 2018	0.8832	0.8830
March 1, 2018	0.8798	0.8796
May 31, 2018	0.8750	—

Required

Prepare the journal entries to record the above events, including January 31, 2018 adjusting entries.

LO 4   P8.11   Hedge of Forecasted Transaction, Firm Commitment, and Foreign-Currency-Denominated Liability   Willson Leather Company, a calendar-year company, purchases merchandise from an Italian supplier on a regular basis. On November 1, 2016, Willson purchased €10,000,000 for delivery on March 1, 2017, in anticipation of an expected purchase of merchandise. The forward purchase qualifies as a cash flow hedge. On January 15, 2017, Willson issued a purchase order for €10,000,000 in merchandise, establishing a firm commitment. The merchandise was received on February 1, 2017. On March 1, 2017, Willson closed the forward and paid the supplier. On March 15, the merchandise was sold to a U.S. customer for $25,000,000. Exchange rates ($/€) are as follows:

	Spot rate	Forward rate for delivery March 1, 2017
November 1, 2016	$1.38	$1.41
December 31, 2016	1.39	1.42
January 15, 2017	1.40	1.43
February 1, 2017	1.43	1.45
March 1, 2017.	1.45	—

Required

Prepare the journal entries to record the above events. Assume Willson records cost of goods sold at the time of sale.

P8.12 **Interpretation of Financial Statement Disclosures**   Following are excerpts from the footnotes   **LO 1, 4**
to **IBM Corporation**'s 2013 financial statements:

**IBM
CORPORATION**
[IBM]

> The company's operations generate significant nonfunctional currency, third-party vendor payments
> and intercompany payments for royalties and goods and services among the company's non-U.S.
> subsidiaries and with the parent company. In anticipation of these foreign currency cash flows and
> in view of the volatility of the currency markets, the company selectively employs foreign exchange
> forward contracts to manage its currency risk.
>
> At December 31, 2013 and 2012, in connection with cash flow hedges of anticipated royalties
> and cost transactions, the company recorded net losses of $252 million and of $138 million (before
> taxes), respectively, in AOCI. Within these amounts $166 million and $79 million of losses, respec-
> tively, are expected to be reclassified to net income within the next 12 months, providing an offsetting
> economic impact against the underlying anticipated transactions.

Required

a.   Explain how IBM uses forward contracts to reduce currency risk related to anticipated royalties and
   cost transactions.
b.   If the hedges described above are **net forward sale contracts**, does IBM anticipate a net inflow or
   outflow of foreign currency related to its hedged royalty and cost transactions? Explain.
c.   Again assuming the hedges are net forward sale contracts, on average did the U.S. dollar strengthen
   or weaken with respect to the currencies hedged in 2013 and 2012? How do you know?
d.   For these cash flow hedges, where and when will the reclassification to income be recorded?

P8.13 **Accounting for Forward Contracts—Hedging and Speculation**   Futura Corporation, a   **LO 2, 3,** ✓
calendar-year corporation, is an active trader in foreign exchange, to hedge its international activities and   **4, 6**
for outright speculation. In particular, it is active in the forward market for krone (kr), the currency of
Denmark. On November 1, 2016, Futura entered into the following forward contracts. The contracts were
settled on January 29, 2017.

1.   Sold kr2,000,000 forward to hedge a forthcoming kr2,000,000 sale to a Danish firm; the sale price
   and January 29, 2017 delivery date have been negotiated and the customer will pay upon delivery.
2.   Purchased kr3,000,000 forward to hedge a forecasted purchase from a Danish supplier. Delivery and
   payment on the forecasted purchase takes place on January 29, 2017.
3.   Sold kr1,000,000 forward in anticipation of a fall in the spot rate.

Relevant exchange rates ($/kr) are as follows:

	November 1, 2016	December 31, 2016	January 29, 2017
Spot rate.	$0.162	$0.172	$0.192
Thirty-day forward rate. . .	0.145	0.165	0.185
Sixty-day forward rate . . .	0.125	0.145	0.190
Ninety-day forward rate . .	0.105	0.132	0.195

Required

a.   Prepare the journal entries made by Futura on December 31, 2016, and January 29, 2017, regarding
   the above transactions.
b.   Indicate how the above transactions would be disclosed on Futura's December 31, 2016, balance
   sheet and 2016 income statement.
c.   Comment on the specific use of the forward market by Futura.

P8.14 **Analyzing the Performance of an Import/Export Department**   William Johnston manages the   **LO 1, 2, 6**
import/export department of Bush Specialty Products. Because of the complexities of foreign currency
transactions and the continual changes in exchange rates, Bush's management is having difficulty determining exactly how Johnston's operation is performing. You have been called in as a consultant to give
advice on this performance-evaluation task.

   After you discuss the problem with Mr. Johnston, he produces the summary of his department's activities shown below. The letters FC identify foreign currency units, and exchange rates are defined as $/FC.

Import Transactions

Quantity—Part No.	Unit cost (FC)	Spot rate when purchased	Spot rate when paid	Unit selling price
2,000—K14.............	6.4	$0.83	$0.80	$ 7.75
17,000—KR08	10.0	0.49	0.58	6.00
5,000—L16.............	8.2	1.13	1.22	10.00
10,000—M29Q...........	25.2	0.37	0.32	9.20

Export Transactions

Quantity—Part No.	Unit selling price (FC)	Spot rate when sold	Spot rate when collected	Unit cost
14,000—A24.............	8.4	$0.27	$0.29	$ 1.98
6,000—DD2	12.5	2.00	1.92	24.00
20,000—A27.............	10.0	1.10	1.16	8.90
1,000—B23	14.6	0.63	0.58	8.50

Forward Contracts

Quantity of FC Purchased (Sold)	Spot rate at inception	Forward rate at inception	Spot rate at maturity	Purpose of contract
210,000................	$0.57	$0.62	$0.59	Hedge
(300,000)	0.88	0.90	0.87	Hedge
1,000,000................	0.28	0.25	0.22	Speculation
(1,000,000)	0.75	0.74	0.85	Speculation

Required

a. Prepare, in good form, schedules to calculate the profit contribution or loss realized by the import/export department.

b. Write a short memorandum to top management regarding your findings. Should Mr. Johnston be fired? Explain.

LO 5 **P8.15** **Hedge of Net Investment in an International Subsidiary** **PriceSmart, Inc.** is a U.S. company that operates international membership shopping warehouse clubs. Its subsidiaries are located in 13 countries, including Panama, Guatemala, Jamaica, and Nicaragua, and one U.S. territory, the U.S. Virgin Islands. Suppose PriceSmart hedges its net investment in its three Guatemalan subsidiaries. The quetzal is the Guatemalan currency.

PRICESMART, INC. [PSMT]

Required

a. If the functional currency of the Guatemalan subsidiaries is the U.S. dollar,
   1. What kinds of hedge investments are effective hedges of PriceSmart's foreign currency risk?
   2. If the value of the quetzal, in U.S. dollars, increases from $0.125 to $0.15, will PriceSmart report a gain or a loss on the hedges?
   3. Where in its financial statements will PriceSmart report gains and losses on hedges of its net investments?

b. If the functional currency of the Guatemalan subsidiaries is the quetzal,
   1. What kinds of hedge investments are effective hedges of PriceSmart's foreign currency risk?
   2. If the value of the quetzal, in U.S. dollars, increases from $0.125 to $0.15, will PriceSmart report a gain or a loss on the hedges?
   3. Where in its financial statements will PriceSmart report gains and losses on hedges of its net investments?

REVIEW SOLUTIONS ••

Review 1 Solution

a.   Accounts payable, June 30, 2016 = €1,000,000 × $1.42 = $1,420,000
b.   Accounts receivable, June 30, 2016 = €100,000 × $1.42 = $142,000
c.   Exchange gain or loss for fiscal 2016:
       Accounts payable: ($1.42 − $1.35) × €1,000,000 = $70,000 loss
       Accounts receivable: ($1.42 − $1.40) × €100,000 = $2,000 gain
d.   Exchange gain or loss for fiscal 2017:
       Accounts payable: ($1.45 − $1.42) × €1,000,000 = $30,000 loss
       Accounts receivable: ($1.43 − $1.42) × €100,000 = $1,000 gain
e.   Sales revenue, fiscal 2016 = €100,000 × $1.40 = $140,000
f.   Cost of goods sold, fiscal 2017 = €1,000,000 × $1.35 = $1,350,000

Review 2 Solution

a.   Accounts payable, June 30, 2016 = €1,000,000 × $1.42 = $1,420,000
b.   Investment in forward contract, June 30, 2016 = €1,000,000 × ($1.44 − $1.37)
       = $70,000 current asset
c.   Exchange gain or loss for fiscal 2016:
       Accounts payable: ($1.42 − $1.35) × €1,000,000 = $70,000 loss
       Forward contract: ($1.44 − $1.37) × €1,000,000 = $70,000 gain
       Net gain or loss is zero.
d.   Exchange gain or loss for fiscal 2017:
       Accounts payable: ($1.45 − $1.42) × €1,000,000 = $30,000 loss
       Forward contract: ($1.45 − $1.44) × €1,000,000 = $10,000 gain
       = Net loss of $20,000.
e.   Cost of goods sold, fiscal 2017 = €1,000,000 × $1.35 = $1,350,000

Note that cost of goods sold is valued at the spot rate at the time the inventory was purchased ($1.35), although it actually pays $1,370,000, through the forward contract, for the inventory.

Review 3 Solution

a.   Firm commitment, June 30, 2016 = €1,000,000 × ($1.44 − $1.37) = $70,000 current liability
b.   Exchange gain or loss for fiscal 2016:
       Firm commitment: ($1.44 − $1.37) × €1,000,000 = $70,000 loss
       Forward contract: ($1.44 − $1.37) × €1,000,000 = $70,000 gain
       Net gain or loss is zero.
c.   Exchange gain or loss for fiscal 2017:
       Firm commitment: ($1.45 − $1.44) × €1,000,000 = $10,000 loss
       Forward contract: ($1.45 − $1.44) × €1,000,000 = $10,000 gain
       Net gain or loss is zero.
d.   Reported inventory value, August 15 = currency paid adjusted for the firm commitment
       = [€1,000,000 × $1.45] − ($70,000 + $10,000) = $1,370,000
e.   Cost of goods sold, fiscal 2017 = $1,370,000

Review 4 Solution

2016

June 30

Investment in forward contract	70,000	
Other comprehensive income		70,000

To adjust the forward contract to the June 30 rate for delivery
on August 15; $70,000 = ($1.44 − $1.37) × €1,000,000.

2016

Aug. 15

Investment in forward contract	10,000	
Other comprehensive income		10,000

To adjust the forward contract to the August 15 spot rate;
$10,000 = ($1.45 − $1.44) × €1,000,000.

Foreign currency	1,450,000	
Investment in forward contract		80,000
Cash		1,370,000

To close the forward contract.

Inventory	1,450,000	
Foreign currency		1,450,000

To record the purchase of inventory.

2016

Aug. 31

Accounts receivable.......................................	2,000,000	
Sales revenue		2,000,000

To record the sale of inventory to the U.S. customer.

Cost of goods sold.......................................	1,370,000	
Other comprehensive income	80,000	
Inventory		1,450,000

To record cost of goods sold on the sale of inventory,
including adjustment for gains on forward contract used to
hedge the purchase.

Futures, Options and Interest Rate Swaps

LEARNING OBJECTIVES

LO1   Describe futures contracts and account for common futures transactions. (p. 380)

LO2   Explain options contracts and account for common options transactions. (p. 382)

LO3   Describe and account for interest rate swaps. (p. 392)

LO4   Discuss disclosure requirements for derivatives and hedging. (p. 397)

LO5   Discuss IFRS for derivatives and hedging. (p. 399)

THE KELLOGG COMPANY
www.kelloggs.com

Giant breakfast and snack foods manufacturer **The Kellogg Company** uses derivatives extensively to reduce the risks inherent in its everyday business. In the footnotes to its 2013 annual report, Kellogg's identifies these risks and describes its hedging strategy:

> The Company is exposed to certain market risks such as changes in interest rates, foreign currency exchange rates, and commodity prices, which exist as part of its ongoing business operations. Management uses derivative financial and commodity instruments, including futures, options, and swaps, where appropriate, to manage these risks. Instruments used as hedges must be effective at reducing the risk associated with the exposure being hedged and must be designated as a hedge at the inception of the contract.

In addition to hedges of foreign currency risk, Kellogg's uses commodity futures and options to lock in the costs of forecasted purchases of materials it uses in manufacturing its products:

> The Company is exposed to price fluctuations primarily as a result of anticipated purchases of raw and packaging materials, fuel, and energy. The Company has historically used the combination of long-term contracts with suppliers, and exchange-traded futures and option contracts to reduce price fluctuations in a desired percentage of forecasted raw material purchases over a duration of generally less than 18 months.

Kellogg's uses interest rate swaps to hedge its interest rate risk:

> The Company is exposed to interest rate volatility with regard to future issuances of fixed rate debt and existing and future issuances of variable rate debt. The Company periodically uses interest rate swaps, including forward-starting swaps, to reduce interest rate volatility and funding costs associated with certain debt issues, and to achieve a desired proportion of variable versus fixed rate debt, based on current and projected market conditions.

This chapter discusses various types of risk encountered by companies, the use of futures, options and swaps as hedging instruments to neutralize this risk, and the requirements for reporting hedging activities.

Source: The Kellogg Company 2013 annual report.

Derivatives and hedge accounting	Futures contracts	Option contracts	Interest rate swaps	Disclosure requirements	IFRS for derivatives and hedging
• Characteristics of derivatives • Accounting for derivatives and hedging transactions • Assessing hedge effectiveness	• Description and accounting events • T-account analysis • Illustrations of hedging transactions	• Definitions • Effects of price changes • Illustrations of hedging transactions	• Definitions and motivations • Accounting events • Illustrations of hedging transactions	• Required derivatives and hedging disclosures	• *IFRS 9* hedge accounting and disclosure requirements

DERIVATIVES AND HEDGE ACCOUNTING

Chapter 8 studied the use of forward contracts to hedge foreign exchange risk. This chapter discusses other types of risk and the derivative investments used to hedge this risk. *ASC para. 815-10-15-83* identifies four critical characteristics of derivatives:

1. Derivative values are tied to one or more **underlyings**—an interest rate, share price, foreign exchange rate, commodity price or other variable—that is subject to price changes. Kellogg's may purchase derivatives to lock in the future cost of oats used in its cereals. The derivatives' value is tied to the market price of oats.
2. A derivative specifies a face or **notional amount**. The notional amount is the number of bushels, pounds, shares, or other units specified in the contract. When Kellogg's uses a derivative contract to lock in the future price of one million bushels of oats, the notional amount is one million bushels.
3. Derivatives require **no initial net investment**, or a very small investment in relation to the total commitment. When Kellogg's agrees to buy one million bushels of oats in six months at a price of $3.50 per bushel, the total value of the contract is $3.5 million. However, Kellogg's typically pays little or nothing to enter the agreement.
4. Derivatives provide for a **net settlement** based on the interaction between the change in the underlying value and the notional amount. Suppose Kellogg's agrees to buy one million bushels of oats at $3.50 per bushel, and settles the contract by selling one million bushels when the per-bushel price is $3.75. Kellogg's receives a net cash payment of $250,000 [= ($3.75 − $3.50) × 1,000,000]; no delivery of oats takes place.

Futures, options and interest rate swaps possess these four characteristics. A **futures contract** "locks in" the purchase or sale of a specific amount of a commodity at a fixed price at a future delivery date. If Kellogg's enters a futures contract to *sell* 1,000,000 bushels of wheat at the fixed price of $8 per bushel, the contract gains value when the price of wheat falls below $8; a futures contract to *buy* wheat at a fixed price of $8 per bushel gains value when the price of wheat rises above $8.

Like a futures contract, an **option contract** locks in the future purchase or sale of a commodity at a fixed price. The option holder has the ability but not the obligation to buy or sell the commodity at the option price. If Kellogg's holds an option to buy wheat at $8 per bushel, and the price of wheat rises above $8, there is opportunity for gain and the option's value usually increases. Because options have no downside risk—Kellogg's can let the option expire if the price falls below $8—Kellogg's pays a premium to invest in the option.

A third common derivative is a "plain vanilla" **interest rate swap**, a contract in which Kellogg's may "swap" or exchange variable interest rate payments on its debt for fixed interest rate payments, or vice versa. When Kellogg's swaps variable payments for fixed payments, the swap gains value if interest rates rise because Kellogg's avoids payments at the higher variable rate.

With the foreign currency forward contracts discussed in Chapter 8, delivery is intended and occurs when settling the contract. A U.S. exporter settles a forward sale of euros by selling the euros acquired from customer sales and receiving dollars at the contract price. A U.S. importer settles a forward purchase of euros by using dollars to buy the euros necessary to pay its suppliers.

In contrast, futures, options and swap derivatives are typically settled with net cash payments, even when a delivery mechanism exists. A futures contract that locks in a purchase or sale is settled when the holder takes an opposite position. When Kellogg's enters a futures contract to sell wheat at $8 per bushel, and the price of wheat increases to $8.50, it can enter a contract to buy wheat at $8.50, paying $0.50 per bushel to settle the contract. When Kellogg's has an option to sell wheat at $8 per bushel, and the price of wheat increases to $8.50, it can let the option expire with no cash effect. When Kellogg's swaps variable payments at 4 percent for fixed payments at 4.5 percent, it makes a net cash payment of 0.5 percent of the debt principal at the interest payment date to settle the contract.

Accounting for Derivatives and Hedging Transactions

Generally accepted accounting principles for all derivatives and hedging activities are found in *ASC Topic 815*, Derivatives and Hedging. Chapter 8 discusses the general principles for reporting derivative investments and hedging activities, summarized below:

- All derivatives appear on the balance sheet at their current *fair value*. Unless the derivative is a qualifying hedge instrument, changes in value are reported in income as they occur.
- A derivative is a qualifying hedge instrument if it hedges a specific risk and is *effective* in hedging that risk.
- If the contract is a qualifying hedge instrument, gains and losses due to changes in the fair value of the contract are generally recognized in income *at the same time* the losses and gains on the exposure the contract is hedging are recognized. When the applicable accounting standards do not automatically match hedge gains and losses with hedged item losses and gains, *hedge accounting* changes the timing of gain and loss recognition to achieve matching.
- Derivatives qualifying as hedges of *exposed positions*, such as inventories and investments, and *firm commitments* to buy and sell these items, are *fair value hedges*. Changes in the value of fair value hedges and related hedged items are reported in income as they occur.
- Derivatives qualifying as hedges of *forecasted transactions*, such as planned purchases and sales of commodities, are *cash flow hedges*. Changes in the value of cash flow hedges are reported in other comprehensive income and reclassified to income when the hedged item is reported in income. Any portion of the derivative's gain or loss that is *not effective* in hedging the forecasted transaction is reported directly in income.

Hedge Accounting Qualifications

Hedge accounting allows deferral of gains and losses on derivative investments, and therefore can potentially be used to mislead financial statement readers, if used inappropriately.

Because **hedge accounting moves gains and losses between accounting periods**, such that the timing of realization and recognition differs, unwarranted use of hedge accounting creates opportunities for earnings management.

ASC Topic 815 therefore requires, for derivatives reported using hedge accounting, extensive documentation of the hedging relationship and hedge performance, both at inception and periodically throughout the investment period. At inception, formal documentation includes all of the following (*ASC Section 815-20-25*):

- The hedging relationship
- The entity's risk management objective and strategy for undertaking the hedge, including identification of the hedging instrument, the hedged item or transaction, the nature of the hedged risk, and the method used to assess the hedging instrument's effectiveness
- Determination of hedge effectiveness—the hedge must be **highly effective** in offsetting the hedged risk

A company using hedge accounting must evaluate whether the hedge still qualifies for hedge accounting whenever financial statements are prepared or at least every three months.

Assessing Hedge Effectiveness   A company must assess hedge effectiveness at inception and periodically throughout the investment period. *ASC Para 815-20-25-77* identifies the typical reasons a hedge is or becomes ineffective:

- **Differences in terms.** Kellogg's may hedge a forecasted purchase of oats, expected at the end of July, with a futures contract due in September.

- **Differences in basis.** Kellogg's may hedge its inventory of oats with a futures contract. The inventory's value changes with spot rates while the futures contract's value changes with futures rates. Spot and futures rates may not move in tandem.

A hedge's effectiveness depends on the extent to which changes in its value offset changes in the value of the exposed position, firm commitment, or forecasted transaction designated as the hedged item.

A common *measure of hedge effectiveness* divides the change in fair value of the hedging instrument by the change in fair value or cash flows of the hedged item, as follows:

$$\text{Hedge Effectiveness Measure} = \frac{\textbf{Change in fair value of hedge instrument}}{\textbf{Change in fair value of hedged item}}$$

Because one value change is a gain and the other is a loss, the *hedge effectiveness measure is negative.*

At inception, the analysis compares *expected* changes in value. Retrospective analysis looks at *actual* changes in value. *ASC Topic 815* does not specify a particular threshold of effectiveness. In practice, a range of -80% to -125% is often used to define effectiveness.

A company must define the value changes it uses to assess effectiveness. The value change can be the entire change in value of the hedge investment, or it can be only one part of that change. Consider this example. Kellogg's forecasts that it will buy 20 million bushels of corn in the spot market in two months. The spot price of corn is currently $3.60/bushel. To hedge the risk that the spot price will increase, Kellogg's invests in a futures contract that locks in the purchase price of corn at $3.598 per bushel in two months. At the end of two months, the spot price of corn is $3.61/bushel. If Kellogg's uses the *entire change* in the value of the hedge to assess effectiveness, it compares the change in value of the futures contract with the change in the cost of the forecasted purchase, both measured using futures rates. The calculation is as follows:

$$\frac{20 \text{ million} \times (\$3.61 - \$3.598)}{20 \text{ million} \times (\$3.598 - \$3.61)} = \frac{\$240,000}{\$(240,000)} = -100\%$$

The hedge is completely effective, and all value changes are reported using hedge accounting, i.e. all changes in the value of the futures contract are reported in other comprehensive income until the forecasted purchase affects income. On the other hand, Kellogg's could choose to specify the *spot price* component of the futures contract as the hedge. The calculation is:

$$\frac{20 \text{ million} \times (\$3.61 - \$3.60)}{20 \text{ million} \times (\$3.598 - \$3.61)} = \frac{\$200,000}{\$(240,000)} = -83\%$$

The hedge may still be assessed as effective, but if not, the ineffective part of the value change is reported in income. Consider another possibility: Kellogg's identifies the spot price change as the hedge, and also measures the value of the forecasted transaction using spot prices. The hedge is completely effective:

$$\frac{20 \text{ million} \times (\$3.61 - \$3.60)}{20 \text{ million} \times (\$3.60 - \$3.61)} = \frac{\$200,000}{\$(200,000)} = -100\%$$

But the futures contract actually increased in value by $240,000, not $200,000. Therefore the extra $40,000 gain is reported in income, not other comprehensive income.

As illustrated above, changes in the value of the hedge investment attributable to ineffectiveness are reported directly in income. This includes changes in value that are *excluded* from the assessment of effectiveness, as well as *ineffectiveness* within the defined measure of effectiveness. Choices concerning how hedges and hedged items are defined and measured, and which components of risk are hedged, are complex. In this chapter's illustrations we generally assume that all value changes are hedged, and that the hedges are highly effective.

FUTURES CONTRACTS

LO1 Describe futures contracts and account for common futures transactions.

Discussion in Chapter 8 focused on hedging with foreign currency *forward contracts*. *Futures contracts*—standardized contracts for future delivery—can also be used to lock in future foreign exchange rates, prices of commodities, interest rates and stock indexes. Most futures contracts are traded on organized exchanges. The largest futures exchanges, by number of contracts traded, include CME Group, Eurex Exchange, the National Stock Exchange of India, and NYSE Euronext.

Introduction to Futures Contracts

A **futures contract** is a legally-enforceable agreement between an investor and the clearinghouse of a futures exchange that:

- Obligates the investor to accept or make delivery of a standardized quantity of a commodity or financial instrument at a specified date, during a specified time period or to settle in cash.
- Can be canceled prior to the delivery date by entering into an identical but offsetting contract; e.g., cancel a purchased futures contract by selling an identical futures contract.

Commodity futures involve contracting for future delivery of commodities such as agricultural products, precious metals and oil at fixed prices. Their value changes with the market price of the commodity.

Interest rate futures lock in the future price of interest-bearing investments, typically low-risk securities such as *U.S. Treasury bills*, *Treasury bonds*, or *Eurodollars*. Companies intending to borrow money hedge against rising interest rates by investing in interest rate futures that lock in the selling price of the securities. If interest rates increase, the securities price falls. The company gains on the futures contract, offsetting its higher borrowing costs. Prices of interest rate futures are normally stated as a percentage of 100 or face value, and reflect the annual discount yield. Thus if the futures price is 96, the designated securities will be delivered at a yield of 4 percent ($= 100 - 96$).

Principal Differences Between *Forward Contracts* and *Futures Contracts*

- Futures are standardized exchange-traded contracts whereas forwards are tailored to specific needs and handled through dealers.
- Futures are normally closed out prior to maturity by entering an offsetting contract (without delivery) whereas forwards usually result in delivery.

Whether a given futures price change means an increase in value (gain) or decrease in value (loss), depends on whether futures are purchased (go **long** and *accept* future delivery) or sold (go **short** and *make* future delivery), as follows:

Changes in Fair Value of Futures Contracts			
Type of Contract	Change in Futures Price	Effect on Income	Balance Sheet Disclosure
Purchase (go long)	Increase	Gain	Current asset
Purchase (go long)	Decrease	Loss	Current liability
Sell (go short)	Increase	Loss	Current liability
Sell (go short)	Decrease	Gain	Current asset

Transacting in Futures Contracts

Actual sale and delivery of commodities or securities for which futures contracts exist occurs in cash or spot markets. As spot prices and futures prices usually move together, any gain or loss realized on the futures contract usually offsets the loss or gain caused by changes in spot prices of the related commodities or securities. Similar to the foreign currency forward contracts discussed in Chapter 8, at the inception of a futures contract the futures price differs from the spot price. The amount of the difference between the two prices is called *basis*.

Basis refers to the difference between an item's spot price and the corresponding futures price.

For example, when the cash (spot) price of a ton of soybean meal is $377 in June and the futures price for July delivery is $384, the July basis is "$7 under." Or when the spot price of crude oil is $90 per barrel (bbl.) and the September futures price is $88 per bbl., the September basis is "$2 over." Basis fluctuates over time as supply and demand conditions change in futures and spot markets. Because spot and futures prices may not move in perfect tandem, changes in basis mean that hedging may not perfectly offset the hedged risk.

Accounting Events in Futures Trading

An entity using futures contracts traded on an organized exchange encounters two types of accounting events prior to settlement of the contract:

1. An **initial margin deposit** is paid to the clearinghouse upon inception of the contract. The margin deposit ranges from less than 1 percent of face value on some interest rate futures contracts to over 10 percent on some commodity futures. Margin deposits are intended to guarantee performance, similar to a security deposit on an apartment.
2. At the end of each trading day, the clearinghouse values each outstanding contract at the closing price; i.e., **marks the contract to market.** The entity must either deposit additional funds with the broker—a realized loss—or receives cash or a credit to its account from the broker—a realized gain—for the change in the value of the contract.

The *initial margin deposit* is recorded as an asset—*Investment in Futures*. Subsequent changes in the amount deposited cannot fall below the *maintenance margin* required by the clearinghouse, which may be lower than the initial margin deposit. Thus if the initial margin deposit is 5 percent and the maintenance margin is 3 percent, the entity can incur losses without depositing additional collateral as long as the amount on deposit is at least 3 percent of the contract's value. The gain or loss arising when the contract is *marked to market* is added to or deducted from Investment in Futures. Two examples below illustrate the effects of price changes on long and short positions:

'Long' Example. Suppose Kellogg's purchases 100,000 bushels of oat futures (goes *long*) at $4.50 per bushel. When the oat futures close at $4.60 on the next day, Kellogg's realizes a *gain* of $10,000 [= ($4.60 − $4.50) × 100,000]—it would receive an additional $0.10 per bushel if it sold the futures for $4.60 to close out its long position.

'Short' Example. Suppose **General Mills, Inc.** sells (goes *short*) $1,000,000 face value interest rate futures (one-year Treasury bills) at 97. At the end of the next trading day, when the interest rate futures close at 97.5, General Mills realizes a *loss* of $5,000 [= (0.97 − 0.975) × $1,000,000]—it would pay $0.005 per dollar more if it purchased long futures contracts at 97.5 to close out its short position.

T-Account Analysis of Futures Contracts

T-accounts help us visualize the value changes that occur in futures contracts. Like forward contracts, a futures contract has two sides: (1) *the current value*—a variable amount equal to the current futures price multiplied by the notional amount—and (2) *the contract value*—the fixed obligation with the clearinghouse equal to the futures price at inception (contract price) multiplied by the notional amount. When long in futures, the debit side is the current value and the credit side is the contract value. When short in futures the sides are reversed. A futures contract account with a debit balance is an asset; a credit balance is a liability. We observe that:

- At inception the two sides are equal and the contract itself has no net value—the current value of the item to be delivered equals its contract value.
- As time passes the current value side changes but the contract value side remains constant.
- The *change* in the current value is posted to the current value side at reporting dates or when contracts are closed.
- A *long contract's* debit side—the current value of the item to be received—changes as the futures price changes. The credit side is the fixed contract value (obligation to the clearinghouse).
- A *short contract's* credit side—the current value of the item to be delivered—changes as the futures price changes. The debit side is the fixed contract value (amount due from the clearinghouse).
- Changes in the net balance represent the reported gains and losses.

In the "long" example just discussed, Kellogg's bought 100,000 bushels of oat futures at $4.50 per bushel. At the end of the next trading day the futures price closed at $4.60, producing a gain of $10,000 [= ($4.60 − $4.50) × 100,000]. These events are depicted as follows:

	Investment in Futures (Long)	
	Current Value	**Contract Value**
At inception	$450,000 (= $4.50 × 100,000)	$450,000 (= $4.50 × 100,000)
Value change	10,000 [= ($4.60 − $4.50) × 100,000]	—
Balance, next day.	$ 10,000	

In the "short" example just discussed, General Mills sold $1,000,000 face value of interest rate futures at 97. The futures price closed at 97.5 on the next trading day and produced a loss of $5,000 [= (0.975 − 0.97) × $1,000,000]. We post these events to our T-account as follows:

	Investment in Futures (Short)	
	Contract Value	**Current Value**
At inception	$970,000 (= 0.97 × $1,000,000)	$970,000 (= 0.97 × $1,000,000)
Value change	—	5,000 [= (0.975 − 0.97) × $1,000,000]
Balance, next day.		$ 5,000

To summarize, at inception the futures contract T-account has a zero balance. As the current futures price varies after inception, value changes that debit the account arise from gains whereas value changes that credit the account arise from losses.

Illustrations of Accounting for Futures Contracts

In the following examples, the futures contract is closed out prior to delivery. We ignore daily mark-to-market for convenience and recognize total realized gain or loss when each futures contract is closed. We also ignore brokerage commissions and other transaction costs.

Fair Value Hedge of an Exposed Asset **Del Monte Corporation** owns 100,000 bushels of corn carried in inventory at cost, $600,000, to be sold in the normal course of business in 90 days. Seeking to guarantee the current 90-day futures price of $700,000, Del Monte sells corn futures (goes *short*) for delivery in 90 days for $700,000 and designates the sale of corn futures as a *fair value hedge* of its corn inventory. The hedging derivative has the same terms as the hedged inventory and high effectiveness is assumed. We begin by recording a $60,000 margin deposit.

Investment in futures	60,000	
Cash		60,000
To record the initial margin deposit on the sale of $700,000 in commodity futures.		

By the end of the next accounting period, the futures price decreases to $650,000. At current prices, the fair value of the corn inventory also declines by $50,000. Del Monte closes out its short position by purchasing a corn futures contract at the then-current price of $650,000. This action locks in Del Monte's realized gain of $50,000 (= $700,000 − $650,000) and adds it to the deposit account at the brokerage. The next entries record the gain and closing of the futures contract.

Investment in futures	50,000	
Gain on hedging		50,000
To record in earnings the gain on the futures contract hedging existing inventory.		
Cash.	110,000	
Investment in futures.		110,000
To record receipt of cash from the broker, including the $60,000 initial margin, when the futures contract is closed out.		

Normally, Del Monte carries the corn inventory at cost. Because the futures contract is a qualified fair value hedge, Del Monte uses *hedge accounting* to match the loss on its corn inventory with the gain on the futures contract, with the following entry:

Loss on hedging.	50,000	
Inventory		50,000
To record in earnings the decrease in fair value of the hedged inventory.		

The $50,000 realized gain on this fair value hedge enters current earnings. Because the futures are hedging an existing asset, Del Monte reports the $50,000 loss from the decline in the corn inventory's market value in earnings and reduces inventory: the gain on the hedging instrument and the loss on the hedged inventory offset. When sold, Del Monte charges the reduced carrying value of the inventory to cost of goods sold and recognizes the gain as part of the gross profit on the sale.

In this example, Del Monte wished to lock in profit of $100,000 (= $700,000 − $600,000). If the corn is sold for $650,000, Del Monte achieves the anticipated profit. The $50,000 gain on the futures contract reduces the carrying value of the inventory to $550,000, and profit of $100,000 (= $650,000 − $550,000) results. Without hedging, profit on the sale of the inventory is only $50,000 (= $650,000 − $600,000).

Suppose the futures price does not exactly track the spot price because the basis changed. The futures price fell to $656,000 when the spot price fell to $650,000 and the $44,000 gain (= $700,000 − $656,000) on the short futures contract does not fully offset the $50,000 loss on the inventory. The hedge effectiveness measure (= change in fair value of the hedge instrument/change in fair value of the hedged item) is −0.88 [= $44,000/$(50,000)], high enough for hedge accounting to continue. But the net $6,000 loss (= $44,000 gain on futures − $50,000 loss on inventory) due to hedge ineffectiveness reduces earnings with no offset.

If basis changes cause the futures contract to no longer be effective, hedge accounting is discontinued. Gains and losses on the futures contract continue to be recorded in income, but no entries are made to record the offsetting changes in the value of the inventory.

Fair Value Hedge of a Firm Liability Commitment **Kraft Foods Group, Inc.** has a $1 million floating rate term loan payable every 91 days, with the interest rate set at the U.S. Treasury bill rate plus 0.75 percent, and designates the loan as a *firm commitment*. The current annual interest rate on Treasury bills is 2 percent, and Kraft therefore pays 2.75 percent (= 2 percent + 0.75 percent) on the loan.

When interest rates rise, the cost of the floating rate loan increases. To hedge against this possibility, when it takes the loan, Kraft sells (*goes short*) $1 million face value 91-day Treasury bill (interest rate) futures at 98 (= 100 − annual discount yield of 2 percent). Treasury bills sell at a discount from par that represents the interest to be earned at maturity, so there is no separate interest payment. When interest rates rise, the market value of the Treasury bills falls, and Kraft gains on its short position, offsetting the higher cost of its floating rate loan. When Kraft enters the futures contract, the clearinghouse requires a $1,500 margin deposit.

Investment in futures	1,500	
Cash		1,500
To record the initial margin deposit on the sale of $1 million face value 91-day		
Treasury bill futures.		

At the end of the 91-day period, the U.S. Treasury bill rate is 2.25 percent and the futures value is 97.75. Kraft realized a gain of $625 [= (0.98 − 0.9775)/4 × $1,000,000] on the short position. Kraft closes its short position and receives $2,125 (= $1,500 + $625).

Cash	2,125	
Investment in futures		1,500
Gain on hedging		625
To record the gain on the futures contract and close the position.		

The firm commitment to roll over the term loan has declined in value, because the market Treasury bill rate increased by 0.25 percent, from 2 percent to 2.25 percent. Kraft uses hedge accounting to record the loss on the firm commitment. Without hedge accounting, this entry would not be made.

Loss on hedging	625	
Firm commitment		625
To record the loss due to increase in borrowing cost of the loan.		

At this point Kraft rolls over the loan and closes the firm commitment liability to the new loan payable, creating a $625 premium on the new loan.

Short-term loan payable (old)	1,000,000	
Firm commitment	625	
Short-term loan payable (new)		1,000,000
Premium on short-term loan payable (new)		625
To roll over the floating rate loan and reclassify the firm commitment liability		
resulting from the hedge as a premium on the new loan payable.		

Kraft amortizes the $625 premium as a reduction in interest expense over the 91-day term of the new loan. The interest rate on the new loan is 3 percent (= 2.25 percent + 0.75 percent). The $625 gain on the futures exactly offsets the increased interest on the new loan, $625 [= (0.03 − 0.0275)/4 × $1,000,000]. Thus, Kraft maintains the old 2.75 percent rate for another 91-day period.

This hedge was effective because it locked in and extended the previous interest cost to the new financing period. Had interest rates fallen instead, the resulting increase in the futures price produces a loss on the short futures position. This loss offsets the reduced interest Kraft pays on the new loan. Kraft hedged against a rise in interest rates, but an effective hedge neutralizes both losses *and* gains.

Cash Flow Hedge of a Forecasted Purchase **Dean Foods** forecasts that it will need 100,000 pounds of Class III milk in 90 days to manufacture its products. To lock in the purchase price of the milk, it purchases 100,000 pounds of Class III milk (*goes long*) for delivery in 90 days at $16 per 100 pounds. The long futures position qualifies as a *cash flow hedge* of the forecasted purchase of milk, and is considered highly effective. Dean Foods is required to make a $500 margin deposit.

Investment in futures	500	
Cash		500
To record the initial margin deposit on the purchase of		
$16,000 (= $16 × 1000,000/100) in milk futures.		

At the end of the hedging period the futures price converges to the spot rate, which is $16.65/100 pounds, and Dean Foods realizes a gain of $650 on the hedge [= ($16.65 − $16.00) × 100,000/100].

Because the hedge qualifies for hedge accounting, this gain is reported in other comprehensive income until the hedged transaction affects income.

Investment in futures	650	
Other comprehensive income		650
To record the gain on the futures contract.		

Dean Foods closes the futures contract and buys Class III milk on the spot market.

Cash	1,150	
Investment in futures		1,150
To close the futures contract; $1,150 = $500 + $650.		
Inventory	16,650	
Cash		16,650
To record the purchase of 100,000 pounds of Class III milk at $16.65/100 pounds.		

This hedge effectively locked in the original milk price of $16 per 100 pounds. When products are sold containing the milk, the following entry records the cost of goods sold and reclassification of the hedging gain to income.

Cost of goods sold	16,000	
Other comprehensive income	650	
Inventory		16,650
To record the cost of milk in products sold.		

BUSINESS APPLICATION General Mills Hedge Accounting

Requirements for hedge accounting are rigorous and involve substantial cost. Companies must document their hedges and monitor effectiveness. The reporting standards and the financial terms of the hedges are often extremely complex. As a result, hedging activities often do not qualify for hedge accounting. An example is **General Mills, Inc.**'s hedges of commodity risk. Below is an excerpt from its fiscal 2014 10-K.

> We utilize derivatives to manage price risk for our principal ingredients and energy costs, including grains (oats, wheat, and corn), oils (principally soybean), dairy products, natural gas, and diesel fuel. Our primary objective when entering into these derivative contracts is to achieve certainty with regard to the future price of commodities purchased for use in our supply chain. We manage our exposures through a combination of purchase orders, long-term contracts with suppliers, exchange-traded futures and options, and over-the-counter options and swaps.
>
> We use derivatives to manage our exposure to changes in commodity prices. We do not perform the assessments required to achieve hedge accounting for commodity derivative positions. Accordingly, the changes in the values of these derivatives are recorded currently in cost of sales in our Consolidated Statements of Earnings.
>
> Although we do not meet the criteria for cash flow hedge accounting, we nonetheless believe that these instruments are effective in achieving our objective of providing certainty in the future price of commodities purchased for use in our supply chain.

Because General Mills does not use hedge accounting for its hedges of commodity price risk, changes in the fair values of its hedge investments may not appear in the same income statement as changes in the fair values of related hedged commodities, increasing income volatility. *Source:* General Mills, Inc. fiscal 2014 10-K.

REVIEW 1 • Accounting for Futures Contracts

Suppose on March 1, Kellogg's goes long in commodity futures and makes a $50,000 margin deposit. These contracts decline in value by $200,000 on March 31 when quarterly reports are prepared and increase in value by $300,000 on April 15 when the contracts are closed. Kellogg's then buys the commodity on the spot market for $10,180,000. On June 1, Kellogg's sells the commodity as part of its finished products.

Required

a. Suppose the commodity futures hedge a firm commitment to buy the commodity. Prepare the journal entries Kellogg's makes on March 1, March 31, April 15, and June 1.

b. Suppose the commodity futures hedge a forecasted purchase of the commodity. Repeat part *a*.

Solutions are located after the chapter assignments.

OPTION CONTRACTS

LO2 Explain options contracts and account for common options transactions.

Options can lock in a future price, but unlike futures contracts, **option contracts** are *one-sided* and require performance only when exercised. Options on individual securities and indexes, such as the S&P 500, ValueLine, and Gold/Silver indexes, are traded on organized exchanges. The CME Group (Chicago Mercantile Exchange Group), ICE (Intercontinental Exchange), and Eurex are among the largest options exchanges worldwide. Traders of most options execute agreements with the clearinghouses of those exchanges, not with each other as individuals.

An **option contract** *allows,* but *does not require,* its holder to buy (*call*) or sell (*put*) a commodity, security or other financial instrument at an *agreed-upon price* during an *agreed-upon time period* or on a *specific date*.

Definitions

The two basic types of options are *puts* and *calls*. A **put**, or *option to sell,* allows the *holder* to *sell* the optioned item to the *writer,* who is obligated to pay the agreed-upon price during the agreed-upon time period. In contrast, a **call**, or *option to buy*, allows the *holder* to *purchase* the optioned item from the *writer,* who is obligated to accept the agreed-upon price during the agreed-upon time period.

Suppose **Del Monte Corporation** pays $120 for a *call option* for 100 shares of **TreeHouse Foods, Inc.** stock, exercisable at the stock's current market price of $80 per share and expiring in 90 days. If the stock price stays at or below $80 during the 90 days, Del Monte does not exercise the right to buy, allows the call to expire and loses the $120. But if the stock rises above $80, say to $85, Del Monte can *exercise the call* by paying $8,000 for 100 shares of stock worth $8,500 or *sell the call.* The call is worth at least $500 [= ($85 − $80) × 100], because the stock's price is $5 *above* $80.

Suppose Del Monte invested in a *put option* with the above terms. Del Monte will exercise or sell the put only if the stock's price falls below $80. If the stock's price falls to $77, Del Monte can *exercise the put* by selling 100 shares of TreeHouse stock worth $7,700 for $8,000, or *sell the put.* The put is worth at least $300 [= ($80 − $77) × 100], because the stock's price is $3 *below* $80.

The *agreed-upon price* is referred to as the **strike price** or **exercise price**, and the *agreed-upon time period* is bounded by the *expiration date*. An **American option** can be exercised at any time during the agreed-upon time period, whereas a **European option** can be exercised only on the *expiration date*. Only American options are discussed in this text.

An option is **in the money** when it is profitable for the holder to exercise the option. Otherwise the option is **out of the money** or, when the optioned item's current market price equals the strike price, the option is **at the money**. A *put* is in the money when the strike price *exceeds* the current market price of the optioned item; a *call* is in the money when the strike price is *less than* the current market price of the optioned item.

For example, suppose the price of **J.M. Smucker Company** stock is $100 per share. A *call option* on Smucker stock with a strike price of $105 is *out of the money* because the holder could purchase the stock in the stock market for $100, less than the strike price of $105 to exercise the call and buy the stock from the option writer. But a *put option* at $105 is *in the money*, because the holder could sell the stock to the writer for $105, more than the $100 it would bring from sale in the stock market. These relations are summarized below.

Price Relation	In, Out or At the Money	
	Puts	Calls
Strike price > Price of optioned item................................	In	Out
Strike price < Price of optioned item................................	Out	In
Strike price = Price of optioned item................................	At	At

The option's price, or **premium,** includes the option's **intrinsic value**—the amount that the option is *in the money,* if any—and its **time value**—the excess of the premium over the option's intrinsic value. Because the probability that the option will be in the money increases as the expiration date grows more distant, the time value component of the premium is positively related to the time remaining to expiration.

Returning to the above options on Smucker stock with a $105 strike price, suppose the stock is currently priced at $100. On organized exchanges, we see that a *call option* on one share of Smucker stock expiring in 30 days, even though out of the money, is priced at $1.00. A *put option* with a $105 strike price, expiring in 45 days, is priced at $6.20. Because it has no intrinsic value, the call option's time value is its full price, $1.00. The put option is in the money, with an intrinsic value of $5 (= $105 − $100), and its time value is $1.20 (= $6.20 − $5.00). In general, the time value cannot be negative and reflects market participants' expectations about anticipated movements in the market price of the optioned item.

Effects of Price Changes of Optioned Items

The *holder* of a call bets that the price of the optioned item will rise, and the call *writer* bets against a price increase and takes the time value component of the premium to compensate for the risk. Although some option writers are net speculators, many take offsetting speculative positions to hedge their aggregate risk. Changes in the optioned item's price affect the option's intrinsic value only when the option is *at* or *in* the money. We summarize below how such changes affect the holder and writer when the option initially is in a neutral position—*at the money.*

Price of Optioned Item	Holder		Writer	
	Puts	Calls	Puts	Calls
Increases	—*	Gain	—*	Loss
Decreases...	Gain	—*	Loss	—*
* Holder's potential loss and writer's potential gain are limited to the initial premium.				

Accounting Events in Options Trading

Transacting in options contracts involves two types of accounting events prior to exercising the option or selling it.

1. Payment of the **initial premium** to the broker when purchasing the option. Not a margin deposit, this payment is for the option to buy (call) or sell (put) the optioned item.
2. The option is **marked to market** when exercised, sold and at financial statement dates. There is no daily cash settlement; until sold or exercised, gains and losses on options are *unrealized.*

The *premium paid* is recorded as an asset—*Investment in Options*. Mark-to-market gains and losses change the Investment in Options account.

Illustrations of Accounting for Options

Fair Value Hedge of an AFS Debt Security   On January 30, 2016, **H.J. Heinz Company** owns $3,000,000 face value 2.725 percent U.S. Treasury bonds due in 2026. Purchased at face value, Heinz classifies the bonds as *available for sale*. The bonds currently sell for 97 and yield about 3 percent. Concerned about rising interest rates and concurrent decreases in Treasury bond prices, Heinz purchases July 2016 *put options* on the bonds with a strike price of 100, designating them as an effective hedge of the bonds owned. Management designates the *intrinsic value component of the option as the hedging instrument*.

The premium is $3.04 per $100 of bonds, $91,200 [= $3.04 × ($3,000,000/$100)] for the 30,000 puts on $3,000,000 in bonds. Because the 100 strike price exceeds the bonds' current price of 97, the puts are *in the money* by $3.00. Thus the $3.04 option premium includes $3.00 of intrinsic value and $0.04 of time value. This entry records purchase of the Treasury bond puts.

2016			
Jan. 30	Investment in options...	91,200	
	Cash		91,200
	To record the purchase of put options to hedge Treasury bonds		
	owned; $91,200 = 30,000 × $3.04.		

When Heinz closes its books on April 30, 2016, the bonds are at 98 and the puts at $2.26 (= $2.00 of intrinsic value and $0.26 of time value). The options' $23,400 loss [= ($2.26 − $3.04) × 30,000] is reported in earnings. Concurrently, the bonds' fair value increased by $30,000 [= (0.98 − 0.97) × $3,000,000]. Because the bonds are designated as AFS, Heinz normally reports this increase in OCI. However, the put options qualify as a fair value hedge of the bonds. Because Heinz uses *hedge accounting* to match the options' loss with the bonds' gain, it reports the increase in the value of the bonds in earnings, not OCI. The $6,600 excess of the gain on the bonds over the loss on the options represents the increase in the time value of $6,600 [= ($0.26 − $0.04) × 30,000]. This net amount is recognized in earnings with no offset, and represents the change in option value that is not designated as a hedge.

2016			
April 30	Loss on hedging...	23,400	
	Investment in options		23,400
	To recognize the decline in the puts' value;		
	$23,400 = ($2.26 − $3.04) × 30,000.		
	Investment in bonds......................................	30,000	
	Gain on hedging		30,000
	To recognize the increase in fair value of the AFS bonds		
	attributable to the hedged risk. (Had the bonds not been hedged,		
	Heinz records the $30,000 gain in OCI.)		

Because management designated only the intrinsic value component of the option as the hedging instrument, the hedge was fully effective, with a hedge effectiveness measure of −1 [= ($30,000)/$30,000]. If the total option premium was designated as the hedging instrument, the hedge would no longer be highly effective: the hedge effectiveness measure would be −0.78 [= ($23,400)/$30,000], below the lower cutoff point of −0.8.

Now suppose that on July 1, 2016, Heinz Treasury bonds are at 95 and the firm closes the hedge by selling the put options for their current premium of $5.19. Because each put is in the money by $5.00, the proceeds include time value of $5,700 [= ($5.19 − $5.00) × 30,000]. We now record the gain on the options, the loss on the bonds, and sale of the puts.

2016			
July 1	Investment in options	87,900	
	Gain on hedging		87,900
	To record the increase in the options' fair value;		
	$87,900 = ($5.19 − $2.26) × 30,000.		
	Loss on hedging	90,000	
	Investment in bonds		90,000
	To record the decline in the fair value of the AFS bonds		
	attributable to the hedged risk; $90,000 [= (0.95 − 0.98) ×		
	$3,000,000]. (Had the bonds not been hedged, the loss enters		
	OCI).		
	Cash	155,700	
	Investment in options		155,700
	To record sale of the options; $155,700 = ($5.19 × 30,000).		

The overall *gain* of $60,000 on the 30,000 puts due to an increase in their intrinsic value from $3 to $5 offsets the decline in current value of the bonds by $60,000 [= (0.97 − 0.95) × $3,000,000]. After the puts are sold, the company netted a $64,500 cash gain (= $155,700 proceeds − $91,200 cost). Of this, $60,000 (= $90,000 increase in intrinsic value on July 1 − $30,000 premium paid on April 30) offsets the loss in carrying value of the bond investment to $2,850,000 (= 0.95 × $3,000,000) from $2,910,000 (= 0.97 × $3,000,000). The other $4,500—the increase in the time value from $1,200 to $5,700 when the options are sold—is recognized in earnings through its inclusion in the $64,500 net gain on the options. The change in the time value has no offset in income.

Fair Value Hedge of a Foreign Currency Firm Commitment Chapter 8 discusses forward contracts used to hedge foreign exchange risk. Here we illustrate hedging with foreign currency *options*. On September 1, 2017, when the spot rate is $0.85/A$ and the 120-day forward rate is $0.852/A$, **Beverage Distributors Company**, a U.S. company, issued a A$5,000,000 purchase order to an Australian company for 10,000 cases of Australian wine. To protect itself against a weakening U.S. dollar, Beverage Distributors pays $0.0105 each for December 2017 *call options* on A$5,000,000 with a strike price of $0.85—the entire premium is time value. Management designates the intrinsic value of the calls as a fair value hedge of a firm commitment, and records the purchase of the calls.

2017			
Sep. 1	Investment in options	52,500	
	Cash		52,500
	To record the purchase of call options to hedge a firm commitment		
	denominated in A$; $52,500 = $0.0105 × A$5,000,000.		

When the books are closed on September 30, the spot rate is $0.86/A$ and the 90-day forward rate is $0.862/A$, indicating a weakening U.S. dollar. Now $0.01 in the money, the calls sell for $0.017 and the time value component is $0.007. Beverage Distributors marks the calls to market and recognizes $32,500 [= ($0.0170 − $0.0105) × A$5,000,000] in earnings.

2017			
Sep. 30	Investment in options	32,500	
	Gain on hedging		32,500
	To revalue the call options to market.		

Concurrently, a firm commitment liability valued at the change in forward rate is established for the increase in the U.S. dollar cost of the wine purchase. The loss on the firm commitment due to the increase in the forward rate more than offsets the gain on the options.

2017			
Sep. 30	Loss on hedging..	50,000	
	Firm commitment		50,000
	To record the liability for the increased $ cost of settling the firm		
	commitment; $50,000 = ($0.862 − $0.852) × A$5,000,000.		

Suppose that on December 30, Beverage Distributors takes delivery of the wine, sells the options, and pays for the wine by buying Australian dollars in the spot market at $0.88/A$. The calls sell for their intrinsic value of $0.03. Beverage Distributors marks the calls to market, recognizing $65,000 [= ($0.03 − $0.017) × A$5,000,000] in earnings, and sells the options.

2017			
Dec. 30	Investment in options	65,000	
	Gain on hedging		65,000
	To revalue the call options to market.		
	Cash..	150,000	
	Investment in options		150,000
	To record the sale of the options; $150,000 = $0.03 × A$5,000,000.		

Beverage Distributors also adjusts the firm commitment for the additional loss due to the increase in the forward rate. At December 30, 120 days have passed and the spot rate equals the forward rate for delivery that day.

2017			
Dec. 30	Loss on hedging.......................................	90,000	
	Firm commitment		90,000
	To record the increased $ cost of settling the firm commitment;		
	$90,000 = ($0.88 − $0.862) × A$5,000,000.		

Beverage Distributors takes delivery of the wine, pays for it by buying Australian dollars at the $0.88 spot rate, and closes the firm commitment against the inventory balance.

2017			
Dec. 30	Inventory...	4,260,000	
	Firm commitment......................................	140,000	
	Cash		4,400,000
	To record delivery of the inventory, $4,400,000 payment to suppliers		
	(= $0.88 × A$5,000,000) and closing of the firm commitment.		

Because Beverage Distributors gained on its hedge of the purchase order, the inventory balance is $140,000 lower. This gain impacts earnings when the wine is sold.

Note that although the options increased in value by only $97,500, their intrinsic value, designated as the hedge, gained $150,000 [= ($0.03 − $0.00) × A$5,000,000]. The intrinsic value qualifies for hedge accounting through the firm commitment account. Because spot and forward rates do not change by exactly the same amount each period, there is a $10,000 difference (= $150,000 − $140,000) between the loss in the firm commitment value, valued according to changes in forward rates, and the gain in the options' intrinsic value, valued according to changes in spot rates. However, the options were still a highly effective hedge, as $150,000/$(140,000) = 107%.

Cash Flow Hedge with an Interest Rate Cap Companies can purchase an *interest rate cap* to protect against rising interest rates on their variable rate loans. Effectively a call option, an **interest rate cap** goes in the money when the variable rate rises above the cap's strike price—the rate specified in the cap agreement. Once in the money, the writer of the cap pays the holder the difference between the holder's variable rate interest and the cap rate. An interest rate cap is a *cash flow hedge:* it hedges against increased cash interest cost on the loans due to rising interest rates. The cap cannot hedge a firm commitment because future interest rates are unknown. Management normally designates the cap's intrinsic value as the hedging instrument.

Suppose that on January 2, 2016, **Seneca Foods Corporation** borrows $10 million from its bank for five years at prime plus 2 percent, a variable rate adjusted quarterly. Currently at 1.5 percent, Seneca Foods believes prime will rise during the life of its loan, and it buys a five-year, 4.5 percent interest rate cap from another bank for 0.5 percent per year to be paid in full immediately. This cap prevents the interest cost on the loan from going above 4.5 percent. The cap is out of the money and the entire premium is time value.

2016			
Jan. 2	Investment in interest rate cap..........................	250,000	
	Cash		250,000
	To record premium paid on a five-year 4.5% interest rate cap;		
	$250,000 = 0.005 × $10,000,000 × 5.		

Nine months later, prime increased to 3.5 percent, forcing Seneca Foods' variable rate to 5.5 percent during the last quarter of 2016, and the interest rate cap is now in the money. Suppose the cap's fair value decreased by $30,000 to $220,000: an increase in intrinsic value of $25,000 [= (0.055 − 0.045) × $10,000,000/4] and a $55,000 decrease in time value. The rise in intrinsic value hedges the higher interest cost on the loan whereas Seneca Foods reports the $55,000 decrease in time value in earnings as a loss on options. On December 31, 2016, Seneca Foods makes these end-of-period entries:

2016			
Dec. 31	Interest expense..........................	137,500	
	Cash		137,500
	To record interest paid to the bank for the last quarter of 2016;		
	$137,500 = 0.055 × $10,000,000/4.		
	Loss on options	55,000	
	Investment in interest rate cap		30,000
	Interest expense		25,000
	To record the loss in time value and the net decrease in the cap's		
	fair value, and reduce interest expense by the increase in the cap's		
	intrinsic value.		

Note that the net interest expense recorded above, $112,500 (= $137,500 − $25,000), allows Seneca Foods to report interest on the loan at 4.5 percent, the cap amount [= $112,500/($10,000,000/4)]. Later, the writer of the cap reimburses Seneca Foods for the excess interest it paid in the fourth quarter.

Cash.....................................		25,000	
Investment in interest rate cap			25,000
To record receipt of excess interest from the interest rate cap.			

REVIEW 2   •   Accounting for Option Contracts

On August 10, 2016, **TreeHouse Foods** invests in equity securities costing $3,000,000 and classifies them as AFS investments. On September 30, 2016, the value of the equity securities falls to $2,910,000, and TreeHouse pays $100,000 for March 2017 put options with a strike price of $3,000,000, as a fair value hedge of its equity investments. The intrinsic value of the options is designated as the hedging instrument. On December 31, 2016, TreeHouse's accounting year-end, the options have a fair value of $76,600 and the securities have a fair value of $2,940,000. TreeHouse sells the options on March 1, 2017, for $159,800, when the fair value of the securities is $2,850,000, and sells the securities for $2,900,000 on March 30, 2017.

Required

Prepare the journal entries made by TreeHouse on August 10, 2016, September 30, 2016, December 31, 2016, March 1, 2017, and March 30, 2017.

Solutions are located after the chapter assignments.

INTEREST RATE SWAPS

LO3 Describe and account for interest rate swaps.

Interest rate swaps are derivative financial instruments used primarily to lower financing costs, hedge interest rate risk, and for speculative purposes. They are a type of *financial swap,* in which two **counterparties** exchange cash flows over time. Interest rate swaps have fixed and variable cash flow components—one cash flow component changes in value and the other does not. When the variable cash flow component is an asset (liability), a gain (loss) results when that component increases in value.

In a **financial swap,** two end-users, or counterparties, negotiate a contract to exchange a series of cash flows at specified times and at specified prices. The counterparties may deal with each other directly or through an intermediary, such as a bank. The **principal amount** is the basis for calculating the swapped flows and often consists of assets or liabilities of the counterparties. Because the principal amount is normally not exchanged, it is called the **notional amount.**

An **interest rate swap** has the counterparties agree to exchange a fixed-rate interest obligation for a floating rate obligation, or the reverse, on existing or new debt typically denominated in the same currency. Only the net payment between the counterparties usually changes hands. In this way, swap users can effectively convert floating rate debt to fixed rate debt, and vice versa.

We discuss here the simplest "plain vanilla" interest rate swap, where a company swaps fixed interest payments on its debt for variable payments, or it swaps variable payments for fixed payments. The reasons for entering these swaps include:

- If a company wishes to avoid the risk of rising interest rates it may swap its floating rate interest obligations for fixed rate interest obligations.

- A bank with fixed rate investments, such as mortgages, may convert its floating rate interest payments to fixed payments to reduce its financial risk.

- A company that can borrow only at high fixed rates may swap its floating rate obligations to a counterparty able to borrow at low fixed rates.

- A company expects a decline in interest rates and swaps fixed for variable payments in anticipation of lower interest costs.

ASC Topic 815 treats *plain vanilla swaps that* **qualify as hedges** as follows:

- **Swap of fixed interest payments on fixed-rate debt for variable interest payments** (receive fixed/pay variable) is a **fair value hedge** because the fair value of the fixed-rate debt changes as market interest rates change. When market interest rates fall, the present value of all payments due on the debt increases, the fair value of the debt rises, and a loss occurs on the debt. This decline in interest rates also produces an increase in the present value of the fixed payments received in the swap, a gain that offsets the loss on the debt.

- **Swap of variable interest payments on variable-rate debt for fixed interest payments** (receive variable/pay fixed) is a **cash flow hedge** because, as interest rates change, the floating payments received in the swap hedge against unfavorable unknown future interest payments on the variable rate debt. When market interest rates rise, the present value of the fixed payments made in the swap falls, and a gain occurs on the swap. This gain will be offset by the larger floating interest payments on the floating rate debt when they occur in the future.

The floating rate is typically tied to a low-risk interest rate index. Common rate indexes include the **London Interbank Offered Rate (LIBOR)**—the average rate charged for loans between banks—or a Treasury bill rate. The positions of the counterparties and the movements of the swapped cash flows in a plain vanilla interest rate swap are described as follows and shown in Figure 9.1.

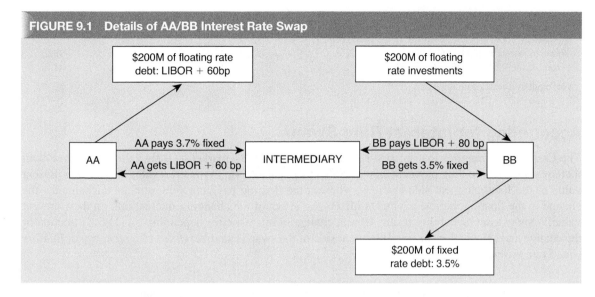

FIGURE 9.1   Details of AA/BB Interest Rate Swap

Assume that when the swap is entered, LIBOR stands at 2 percent or 200 *basis points*. A **basis point (bp)** is 1/100 of a percent in interest or 0.0001.

- AA has $200 million of existing debt with a floating rate equal to LIBOR + 60 bp (currently 2.6 percent). It wants to protect against increases in interest rates but cannot borrow directly at a fixed rate of less than 4 percent.

- BB also has $200 million of debt, but its debt carries a fixed coupon of 3.5 percent. Moreover, BB has $200 million of floating rate investments. It seeks to protect against decreases in interest rates which would cause its floating rate revenues to decline and its fixed rate expenses to become more onerous.

- Intermediary proposes this swap: it offers AA floating rate payments at LIBOR + 60 bp in exchange for fixed rate payments from AA at 3.7 percent; it offers BB fixed rate payments at 3.5 percent in exchange for floating payments from BB at LIBOR + 80 bp.

All payments are to be calculated on a notional amount of $200 million.

AA: Because AA pays LIBOR + 60 bp on its debt and receives LIBOR + 60 bp from intermediary, its net outflow is the 3.7 percent fixed payment to intermediary. AA becomes the *fixed rate payer* and the *floating rate receiver* in the swap. AA has an annual opportunity gain of $600,000 [= (0.04 − 0.037) × $200M] because the swap enables it to borrow fixed at 3.7 percent; 30 bp or 0.3 percent below its best direct fixed borrowing opportunity. By locking in this 3.7 percent rate, AA benefits directly if LIBOR goes above 3.1 percent (3.1 percent + 60 bp = 3.7 percent) but forgoes interest savings if LIBOR stays below 3.1 percent.

BB: The 3.5 percent fixed rate payment from intermediary offsets the 3.5 percent fixed rate payment BB makes on its debt. BB has *unlocked* its fixed rate and now pays LIBOR + 80 bp to intermediary. BB becomes the *floating rate payer* and the *fixed rate receiver* in the swap. Although BB directly benefits when LIBOR does not go above 2.7 percent (2.7 percent + 80 bp = 3.5 percent), it achieved its goal of stabilizing the relation between its floating rate revenues and its borrowing costs.

The swap produces a net spread of 40 basis points to intermediary. This spread's annual net cash inflow of $800,000 compensates intermediary for arranging the swap and for accepting the risk of default by either counterparty. The following display summarizes intermediary's cash inflows and outflows when LIBOR is 2 percent.

Fixed payment received from AA, 0.037 × $200M	$7.4M
Variable payment received from BB, 0.028 × $200M	5.6
Variable payment paid to AA, 0.026 × $200M.	(5.2)
Fixed payment paid to BB, 0.035 × $200M.	(7.0)
Net cash inflow to intermediary	$0.8M

Accounting for Interest Rate Swaps

The Codification requires that interest rate swaps be marked to market as their value changes. Recall that swaps have a floating payment side and a fixed payment side. As interest rates change, the present value of the fixed payment side changes, whereas the floating payment side remains unchanged—the change in the floating interest payments offsets the effect of the changing interest rate on their present value. A swap asset or liability results from a change in interest rates depending on (1) the direction of the change and (2) whether the fixed payment side of the swap is an *asset* (fixed rate *receiver*) or *liability* (fixed rate *payer*):

	Effect of Changing Interest Rates on Interest Rate Swap Value			
	Interest Rates Rise		**Interest Rates Fall**	
Fixed Payment Side	**Gain/ Loss**	**Change in Swap Asset/Liability**	**Gain/ Loss**	**Change in Swap Asset/Liability**
Fixed rate receiver	Loss	Asset down or liability up	Gain	Asset up or liability down
Fixed rate payer	Gain	Liability down or asset up	Loss	Liability up or asset down

To summarize, the *fixed rate receiver* hedging with a plain vanilla swap has a *fair value hedge* and reports a gain (loss) on the hedged fixed rate debt's fair value as interest rates rise (fall) that offsets the loss (gain) on the swap. The *fixed rate payer* hedging with a plain vanilla swap has a *cash flow hedge* and reports the gain (loss) on the swap when interest rates rise (fall).

Assessing Hedge Effectiveness

In principle, assessing the effectiveness of interest rate swaps that qualify as hedges involves dividing the change in the present value of the cash flows from the swap (the hedge) by the change in the present value of the cash flows from the hedged item. *ASC Topic 815* provides a **short-cut method** for interest rate swaps—when certain conditions are satisfied, full hedge effectiveness is assumed. Although the conditions for fair value and cash flow hedges differ somewhat (*paras. 815-20-25-102* through *111*), this short-cut method generally applies when the:

- notional amount of the swap matches the principal amount of the debt
- fair value of the swap is zero at inception
- expiration date of the swap matches the maturity date of the debt (*fair value hedges*)
- hedge applies only to all interest payments during the term of the swap and not to interest payments beyond the term of the swap (*cash flow hedges*)

BUSINESS APPLICATION **J.M. Smucker Company's Use of Interest Rate Swaps**

In recent years, interest rates declined to record low levels. Companies find they can reduce their interest payments by either borrowing at floating rates or using interest rate swaps to convert their fixed rate debt into lower variable rate debt. **The J.M. Smucker Company** uses an interest rate swap to change its payments on fixed rate debt into variable payments. This excerpt from its fiscal 2014 annual report provides specific details for this swap.

continued

During 2014, we entered into an interest rate swap on the 3.50 percent Senior Notes due October 15, 2021, which was designated as a fair value hedge and used to hedge against the changes in the fair value of the debt. We receive cash flows from the counterparty at a fixed rate and pay the counterparty variable rates based on LIBOR. The difference between the fixed-rate and variable-rate cash flows resulted in a reduction in interest expense for the year ended April 30, 2014. The interest rate swap was recognized at fair value in the Consolidated Balance Sheet at April 30, 2014, and changes in the fair value were recognized in interest expense. At April 30, 2014, the net gain position on the derivative instrument of $14.9 had no net impact to earnings, as the change in the fair value of the derivative was equal to the change in fair value of the underlying debt.

J.M. Smucker reported a *gain* on its receive fixed/pay variable interest rate swap in fiscal 2014, leading to the conclusion that interest rates *fell* during the time Smucker held the swap. *Source:* The J.M. Smucker Company 2014 annual report.

Accounting Events and Entries for Interest Rate Swaps

The accounting at **settlement** and **balance sheet dates** involves journalizing these events:

1. Interest expense on the hedged debt
2. Adjustment to interest expense—increase when making net payments to intermediary, decrease when receiving net payments from intermediary
3. Change in fair value of the swap hedge
4. Change in fair value of the hedged debt attributable to the hedged risk (fair value hedges)

We illustrate the entries using the swaps previously described.

BB Swap BB has fixed rate debt and swaps its fixed payments for variable payments. This receive fixed/pay variable swap is a *fair value hedge*. When market interest rates fall, the present value of the future payments on the debt increases, creating a loss on the fixed debt. This is offset by the gain from swapping its 3.5 percent fixed interest payments for lower variable interest payments. The gain and the loss are both reported in income.

BB's first entry records interest expense on the hedged debt.

Interest expense.	7,000,000	
Cash		7,000,000
To record periodic interest expense on BB's fixed rate debt;		
$7,000,000 = 0.035 × $200,000,000.		

BB then receives $1,400,000 [= (0.035 − 0.028) × $200M] net cash from intermediary to settle the swap.

Cash.	1,400,000	
Interest expense		1,400,000
To record cash received from intermediary to reduce interest expense under		
the terms of the swap.		

Suppose interest rates decline by 0.5 percent. Applying a lower discount rate to the future fixed debt payments results in a *higher* fair value for the fixed debt. Similarly, applying a lower discount rate to the future fixed payments received from intermediary increases their present value and results in a *higher* fair value for the swap. We assume the decline in interest rates results a $920,000 increase in the fair value of the debt and the swap.

Investment in swaps..	920,000	
Gain on hedging		920,000
To mark interest rate swap to market and record the gain produced by the		
decrease in interest rates.		

Loss on hedging..	920,000	
Long-term debt		920,000
To mark hedged fixed-rate debt to market and record the loss produced by the		
decrease in interest rates.		

AA Swap AA has variable rate debt and swaps its variable payments for fixed payments. This receive variable/pay fixed swap is a *cash flow hedge*. When market interest rates fall, the loss on swapping variable payments for fixed payments is reported in OCI. This loss is reclassified from AOCI to interest expense in the next period, to offset the lower variable interest expense.

AA's first entry records interest expense on the hedged debt at the 2.6 percent variable rate.

Interest expense...	5,200,000	
Cash		5,200,000
To record periodic interest expense on AA's floating rate debt;		
$5,200,000 = 0.026 × $200,000,000.		

AA then pays $2,200,000 [= (0.037 – 0.026) × $200M] net cash to intermediary to settle the swap.

Interest expense...	2,200,000	
Cash		2,200,000
To record cash paid to intermediary to settle additional interest under the terms		
of the swap.		

Suppose interest rates decline 0.5 percent. Applying a lower discount rate to the future fixed payments to intermediary increases their present value and results in a *lower* fair value for the swap. Assume the decline in the fair value of the swap is $900,000.

Other comprehensive income	900,000	
Investment in swaps		900,000
To mark interest rate swap to market and record the loss produced by the		
decrease in interest rates.		

Next year, AA makes a $4,200,000 (= 0.021 × $200M) interest payment on its variable rate debt, down from $5,200,000. We reclassify the $900,000 loss out of AOCI to offset the lower interest expense.

Interest expense...	5,100,000	
Other comprehensive income		900,000
Cash		4,200,000
To record cash paid to intermediary to settle additional interest under the terms		
of the swap.		

REVIEW 3 • Accounting for Interest Rate Swaps

On May 1, 2017, **H.J. Heinz Company** issues $100 million in 4 percent fixed rate debt, with interest payments due annually. On the same day, it enters into a 2-year $100 million notional amount receive fixed/pay variable interest rate swap, with settlement annually. The swap provides that the company receive payments at 4 percent and pay LIBOR + 60 bp. LIBOR is 2.2 percent at inception of the swap. On April 30, 2018, the market interest rate attributable to the debt increases, reducing the fair value of the debt by $450,000. The fair value of the swap also declines by $450,000 due to increasing interest rates. LIBOR increases to 2.3 percent for 2018.

Required

a. Prepare the journal entries to record the debt issuance on May 1, 2017 and all necessary entries at April 30, 2018. Heinz's accounting year ends April 30.

b. Suppose Heinz issues variable rate debt and entered into a receive variable/pay fixed interest rate swap. Explain how the entries at April 30, 2018, would differ from those you recorded in part *a*.

Solutions are located after the chapter assignments.

Reporting Perspective

The choice of whether to use hedge accounting for hedging activities involves a clear cost-benefit tradeoff:

- The substantial **cost** of documenting and monitoring complex financial relationships, and the risk that a company will misapply the standards and be required to restate its financial statements

- The **benefit** of smoother earnings, as the effects of the hedge and the hedged item appear in the same income statement

Broader application of the **fair value option** for financial instruments and other assets reduces the need for hedge accounting to achieve matching of gains and losses on hedges and hedged items. Using normal accounting for derivatives, realized and unrealized fair value changes appear on the income statement as they occur. When hedged items are reported using the fair value option, realized and unrealized gains and losses also appear on the income statement as they occur. Matching is achieved without using hedge accounting to change the timing of income recognition.

DISCLOSURE REQUIREMENTS

ASC Section 815-10-50 prescribes disclosures specifically for *derivatives and hedging activities*.

LO4 Discuss disclosure requirements for derivatives and hedging.

Derivatives and Hedging Disclosures

To set the overall context, entities must explain how and why they use derivatives, how they account for them, how derivatives and hedging activities affect financial position, performance and cash flows, and the risk exposure(s)—interest rate, credit, exchange rate, price, and the like. Some specific disclosure requirements are:

- For derivatives used for hedging, descriptions of risk management policies governing fair value, cash flow and foreign currency hedges, including the types of risks hedged, objectives of hedging activities and strategies for achieving those objectives.

- For derivatives not used for hedging, the objectives of such usage of derivatives.

- Net gain or loss recognized in earnings from (1) fair value and (2) cash flow hedges, including the amounts arising from hedge ineffectiveness and any derivative components excluded from hedge effectiveness assessment.

- Descriptions of transactions and events that will cause reclassification of gains and losses from other comprehensive income into earnings, and the estimated amount of such reclassifications over the next year.

- Maximum length of time covered by cash flow hedges of forecasted transactions.

- Amounts of gains and losses reclassified into earnings when cash flow hedges are discontinued.

- Net gain or loss on foreign currency hedges reported in accumulated other comprehensive income (AOCI).

- Analysis of the derivatives component of AOCI related to cash flow hedges, including beginning balance of accumulated gain or loss, current period net gain or loss, net amount reclassified into earnings, and ending balance of accumulated gain or loss.

These disclosures seek to inform the reader about a company's use of derivatives, the effectiveness of those used for hedging, and their impact on current earnings. They also seek to highlight derivatives' impact on OCI, and their likely effect on future earnings. How companies comply with these requirements affects their usefulness. For example, because quantitative information presented in tabular rather than narrative form can be more useful, and companies had not been providing enough of it, the Codification now requires tabular disclosures of the following kinds of quantitative information.

- Fair values of the different derivative types as assets and liabilities, hedges and non-hedges, and the balance sheet line items that include these values.
- Amounts of gains and losses and where reported—in income statement line items or OCI—presented separately for fair value and cash flow hedges and by type of derivative contract.

ASC para. 815-10-50-4E also requires tabular presentation of this information:

- Fair values of derivative contracts reported as assets and liabilities, separated by qualifying hedges and non-hedges, and by types of derivative contracts, and the balance sheet line items in which they are reported.
- Gains and losses on derivative contracts, separated by qualifying fair value and cash flow hedges and non-hedges, by types of derivative contracts, and by effective and ineffective portions on qualifying hedges.

As one might imagine, the resulting tables can be complex, possibly to the point where their complexity outweighs the well-meaning transparency goals motivating such presentations.

BUSINESS APPLICATION   J.M. Smucker Company Derivatives Disclosures

The **J.M. Smucker Company**'s tabular disclosure of derivatives clearly provides the information required by the Codification. The following table discloses the amounts and accounts where derivatives appear on Smucker's balance sheet, separated by hedges and non-hedges and by type of hedge.

(*in millions*)	April 30, 2014		
	Other Current Assets	Other Current Liabilities	Other Noncurrent Liabilities
Derivatives designated as hedging instruments:			
Commodity contracts	$23.4	$10.9	$ —
Interest rate contract	18.0	—	3.1
Total derivatives designated as hedging instruments	$41.4	$10.9	$3.1
Derivatives not designated as hedging instruments:			
Commodity contracts	$11.6	$ 5.8	$ —
Foreign currency exchange contracts	1.4	0.7	—
Total derivatives not designated as hedging instruments	$13.0	$ 6.5	$ —
Total derivative instruments	$54.4	$17.4	$3.1

Net gains and losses on cash flow hedges of commodity price risk, and where they are reported, appear next.

	2014
Gains recognized in other comprehensive income (effective portion)	$21.0
Losses reclassified from accumulated other comprehensive loss to cost of products sold (effective portion)	(20.3)
Change in accumulated other comprehensive income (loss)	41.3
Gains recognized in cost of products sold (ineffective portion)	1.4

continued

This table discloses net realized and unrealized gains on derivatives *not* designated as hedges. These gains are reported in cost of products sold.

	2014
Net gains on commodity contracts	$5.2
Net gains on foreign currency exchange contracts	3.3
Net gains recognized in cost of products sold (derivatives not designated as hedging instruments) . . .	$8.5

Although Smucker's follows the Codification requirements for its derivatives disclosures, readers may still have difficulty evaluating the effectiveness of its hedging strategy. *Source:* J.M. Smucker Company 2014 annual report.

DERIVATIVES AND HEDGING UNDER IFRS

LO5 Discuss IFRS for derivatives and hedging.

Because reporting requirements for derivatives and hedging activities are the same whether a company invests in foreign currency forward contracts or futures, options and swaps, Chapter 8's discussion of IFRS for derivatives and hedging applies to this chapter as well. IFRS for derivatives and hedging activities are found in *IFRS 7*, Financial Instruments: Disclosures, and in the hedge accounting sections of *IFRS 9*, Financial Instruments. Requirements for qualifying hedges and the mechanics of hedge accounting are similar to U.S. GAAP, except that IFRS allows use of the **basis adjustment** method for cash flow hedges of nonfinancial assets. Required disclosures are also similar.

IFRS 9 Hedge Accounting Requirements

As briefly summarized in Chapter 8, the IASB issued a new hedge accounting standard in 2014, effective in 2018 with early adoption allowed. This is the third and last phase of its financial instruments project. All three phases are included in *IFRS 9*. Chapter 8 provides an overview of *IFRS 9* hedging requirements. Here we elaborate on specific items pertaining to Chapter 9 topics.

Hedge Accounting Disclosures Because qualifications for hedge accounting are broader and more principles-based, they are also subject to increased judgment. Extensive disclosures of risk management and hedging activities, as well as hedging performance, are therefore required. The disclosures must be presented together, in a single note or section within the financial statements, to allow readers to more easily assess all aspects of hedging performance. Quantitative disclosures are categorized by hedged risk and contract type, and include detail on amounts reported in OCI and in income.

Accounting for Time Value and Basis Hedging instruments are usually not perfectly effective. Therefore income volatility can result, even when hedge accounting is used. Futures contracts hedging inventories change in value according to changes in futures rates, and the offsetting inventory value change is measured using changes in spot rates. The difference between futures and spot rates at the inception of the hedge is known as *basis*, and this difference impacts income even when the terms of the hedge match the hedged item exactly. Option value consists of *intrinsic value*, which is a perfect hedge of the related hedged item when terms match, and *time value*, which is related to price expectations and the passage of time. Usual practice excludes time value from hedge effectiveness assessment, and therefore changes in time value are reported directly in income. Companies have long criticized this requirement, as hedging with options often increases income volatility, misrepresenting the economics of hedging activities.

    IFRS 9 still allows basis and time value changes to be excluded from assessment of hedge effectiveness, but treats these differences as a "cost of hedging," to be deferred and later amortized to income. Regardless of whether the hedge is a fair value or cash flow hedge, the change in option time value or basis is reported in other comprehensive income and reclassified to income either over time or when the related transaction impacts income. This reduces income volatility, because the change in basis or time value is not necessarily linear, and recognition of changes as they occur, as required prior to *IFRS 9* hedging requirements, creates more volatility than systematic recognition over time.

Fair Value Hedges of Equity Investments Classified as FV-OCI Recall from Chapter 1 that *IFRS 9* allows certain equity investments to be classified as FV-OCI. These investments are reported at fair value on the balance sheet, and all value changes are included in other comprehensive income. These value changes are never reclassified to income. Similarly, *IFRS 9* allows changes in the value of fair value hedges of these equity investments to be reported in other comprehensive income. These hedge gains and losses are not reclassified to income.

The new IFRS hedge accounting requirements address many of the shortcomings of previous practice. Similarly, in 2014, the FASB is taking a new look at U.S. hedge accounting standards, with emphasis on correcting flaws in current *ASC Topic 815* provisions. The FASB does not, however, expect to develop hedge accounting standards that converge completely with IFRS.

REVIEW OF KEY CONCEPTS ●

LO 1 **Describe futures contracts and account for common futures transactions. (p. 380)** Similar to foreign currency forward contracts, **futures contracts** lock in the future purchase or sale price of a commodity or financial instrument. Companies use futures to avoid price risk on the expected future sale of inventories and forecasted purchases of commodities. Futures positions are normally settled by taking an opposite position; delivery rarely occurs. Changes in the value of futures used to hedge exposed positions or firm commitments are reported in income. Changes in the value of futures used to hedge forecasted transactions are reported in OCI and reclassified to income when the hedged transaction affects income.

LO 2 **Explain options contracts and account for common options transactions. (p. 386)** An **option contract** allows the holder to buy (call) or sell (put) the optioned commodity or financial instrument at a specified price (strike price) during a specified time period. The holder exercises or sells the option when it profits the holder by being in the money, and lets it expire when it is out of the money. Option value is composed of intrinsic value that measures the amount by which the option is in the money, and time value based on expectations of future prices. When hedging with options, option holders generally specify the intrinsic value as the hedge instrument; changes in time value are reported in income as they occur.

LO 3 **Describe and account for interest rate swaps. (p. 392)** Companies use **interest rate swaps** to change payments on variable rate debt into fixed payments, and vice versa. Receive fixed/pay variable interest rate swaps are fair value hedges; changes in the fair value of the swap and the hedged fixed rate debt are reported in income. Receive variable/pay fixed interest rate swaps are cash flow hedges; changes in the fair value of the swap are reported in OCI and reclassified as adjustments to future interest expense.

LO 4 **Discuss disclosure requirements for derivatives and hedging. (p. 397)** Companies are required to disclose the objectives of derivatives investments, where they are reported in the financial statements, and the expected impact on future income of reclassifications from AOCI. Information is categorized by hedge type and risk hedged.

LO 5 **Discuss IFRS for derivatives and hedging. (p. 399)** IFRS for derivatives and hedging is similar but not identical to U.S. GAAP. IFRS sometimes allows hedge accounting when U.S. GAAP does not, and vice versa. Unlike U.S. GAAP, in limited circumstances IFRS allows hedge gains and losses reported in AOCI to be reclassified as a **basis adjustment**. The hedge accounting requirements of *IFRS 9*, effective in 2018, make it easier for a hedge investment to qualify for hedge accounting, and depict hedging activities more accurately in the financial statements.

Assignments with the ✓ in the margin are available in BusinessCourse.
See the Preface of the book for details.

MULTIPLE CHOICE QUESTIONS ••••••••••••••••••••••••••••••••••

Use the following information to answer questions 1–3 below:

On December 1, 2017, Metallic Wonders Corporation has an inventory of metals carried at a cost of $1,000,000. The company plans to sell the inventory in about 60 days, and wishes to guarantee the current 60-day futures price of $1,400,000. On December 1, 2017, it takes a $1,400,000 short position in metal futures for delivery in 60 days. No margin deposit is required. The futures position is a qualified fair value hedge of the inventory, and the company elects to use hedge accounting. The company closes its futures position on January 31, 2018, and sells the metals on the spot market on February 5, 2018. The company's accounting year ends December 31.

Spot and futures prices for the inventory are:

	Spot price	Futures price on January 31, 2018
December 1, 2017	$1,340,000	$1,400,000
December 31, 2017	1,245,000	1,310,000
January 31, 2018	1,200,000	1,200,000
February 5, 2018	1,290,000	N/A

1. At what amount is the inventory reported on Metallic Wonders' December 31, 2017, balance sheet?　　**LO 1** ✓

   a. $ 905,000
   b. $ 910,000
   c. $1,000,000
   d. $1,250,000

2. At what amount is the investment in futures reported on Metallic Wonders' December 31, 2017, balance　　**LO 1** ✓
   sheet?

   a. $90,000 liability
   b. $95,000 asset
   c. $95,000 liability
   d. $90,000 asset

3. What is the gross margin on the February 5, 2018 sale of inventory?　　**LO 1** ✓

   a. $290,000
   b. $340,000
   c $430,000
   d. $490,000

4. GE stock has a current market value of $15. A call option in GE stock has a strike price of $11 and sells for　　**LO 2** ✓
   $6. Which statement is *false*?

   a. The time value of the option is $2.
   b. The call option could be hedging a company's investment in GE stock.
   c. The intrinsic value of the option is $4.
   d. If the market price of GE stock falls, the option will be less valuable.

Use the following information to answer questions 5–6 below.

Golden Corporation invests in a 4.9% interest rate cap to hedge $4,000,000 in variable rate debt, whose rate is set at LIBOR plus 20 bp. For the 6-month period ending December 31, 2016, LIBOR is 5%. For this same period, the cap's market value increases by $5,000.

5. How much does Golden receive in cash to settle the cap for the 6-month period ending December 31, 2016?　　**LO 2** ✓

   a. $ 6,000
   b. $ 12,000
   c. $ 94,000
   d. $100,000

✅ LO 2   **6.**   What is Golden's gain or loss on the cap (the change in time value) for the 6-month period ending December 31, 2016?

    a. $5,000 gain
    b. $6,000 loss
    c. $1,000 loss
    d. $5,000 loss

Use the following information to answer questions 7–10 below:

Sunny Corporation has $1,000,000 in fixed rate debt, with an annual interest rate of 4%, and interest payments due June 30 and December 31 of each year. On January 1, 2016, it entered a receive fixed/pay variable interest rate swap, where the variable rate is LIBOR. On January 1, 2016, LIBOR is 3.8%. On June 30, 2016, LIBOR declines to 3.5% and causes the variable rate to be reset at that time. The swap qualifies for hedge accounting.

✅ LO 3   **7.**   How much does Sunny pay or receive to settle the swap for the 6-month period ending June 30, 2016?

    a. $ 1,000 paid
    b. $20,000 received
    c. $19,000 paid
    d. $ 1,000 received

✅ LO 3   **8.**   Suppose the fixed rate debt changed in value by $80,000 as of June 30, 2016. How does Sunny record this change in value?

    a.   Gain reported in income
    b.   Loss reported in income
    c.   Loss reported in OCI
    d.   Not recorded

✅ LO 3   **9.**   Suppose the swap contract changed in value by $80,000 as of June 30, 2016. How does Sunny record this change in value?

    a.   Gain reported in income
    b.   Loss reported in income
    c.   Loss reported in OCI
    d.   Not recorded

✅ LO 3   **10.**   Suppose the same facts as above, except Sunny Corporation has variable rate debt, with interest payments at LIBOR, and enters a receive variable/pay fixed interest rate swap, with the annual fixed rate set at 4%. The swap changed in value by $80,000 as of June 30, 2016. How does Sunny record this change in value?

    a.   Gain reported in income
    b.   Loss reported in income
    c.   Loss reported in OCI
    d.   Not recorded

EXERCISES

LO 1   **E9.1**   **Fair Value Hedge: Short in Commodity Futures**   **American Italian Pasta Company** (AIPC) manufactures several varieties of pasta. On January 1, 2016, AIPC had excess commodity inventories carried at acquisition cost of $150,000. These commodities could be sold or manufactured into pasta later in the year. To hedge against possible declines in the value of its commodities inventory, on January 6 AIPC sold commodity futures, obligating the company to deliver the commodities in February for $160,000. The futures exchange requires a $10,000 margin deposit. On February 19, the futures price increased to $171,000 and the company closed out its futures contract. Spot prices continued to rise and AIPC sold its inventory for $173,500 in cash on March 2.

Required

    a.   Prepare the journal entries related to AIPC's futures contract and sale of commodities inventory. Assume a perpetual inventory system, that spot and futures prices move in tandem, and the futures position qualifies for hedge accounting.
    b.   By how much would AIPC's profit increase if the hedge was *not* undertaken?

E9.2 **Cash Flow Hedge: Long in Commodity Futures** The Hershey Company uses futures to lock **LO 1** ✓
in the cost of cocoa products it needs to produce its products. Hershey forecasts that it will need 500 tons
of cocoa in 90 days to manufacture its products. On February 10, 2016, it purchases 500 tons of cocoa
futures at $3,200/ton for delivery on May 10, 2016, and makes a $1,600 margin deposit. The long futures
position qualifies as a cash flow hedge of the forecasted purchase of cocoa, and is considered highly effective. On May 10, the spot price of cocoa is $3,250/ton, Hershey closes the contract and purchases 500
tons of cocoa on the spot market. Later in the year, products containing the cocoa are sold to retailers.

Required

Prepare the entries necessary to record the above events, including the cost of cocoa reported in cost of
goods sold when products containing the cocoa are sold. Hershey is a calendar-year company.

E9.3 **Hedge of Firm Commitment: Short in Commodity Futures** On May 1, 2017, Keister, Inc., **LO 1**
sells 100,000 units of commodity futures at $5/unit for delivery in 120 days and makes an initial margin
deposit of $10,000. Spot and futures prices move in tandem. Keister will buy the commodity from a sup-
plier in 90 days and, pursuant to a firm sale commitment, will sell it 30 days later at the prevailing spot
price. Keister designates the futures contracts to protect the proceeds to be received when the sale commitment is fulfilled and has a May 30 fiscal year-end.

Required

a. Prepare the journal entries made on May 1, on May 30 when the futures are selling at $4.80 per
unit, on July 29 when the futures are selling for $4.75 per unit and the commodity is purchased at a
total cost of $460,000, and on August 28 when the short position is closed out at $4.77 per unit. The
futures position qualifies for hedge accounting.
b. Assume the commodity is sold at the spot rate on August 28. Record the sale and cost of goods sold.

E9.4 **Economics of Hedging with Futures** Great Lakes Distributors buys 100,000 bushels of soybean **LO 1**
futures at $9.95 per bushel, to cover a commitment to deliver 100,000 bushels of soybeans to a customer
in 60 days at a price of $10.25 per bushel. No margin deposit is required. Spot and futures prices for
soybeans are equal and fluctuate between $9.50 and $10.40 per bushel. On the day of delivery to the customer, Great Lakes closes its futures position and buys soybeans in the spot market to fulfill its agreement
with the customer.

Required

a. Calculate the cost per bushel to Great Lakes if the spot price at the time of purchase is $9.50. Calcu-
late the cost per bushel if the spot price is $10.40.
b. Prepare the entries Great Lakes makes to record the above events if the spot price is $10.20 per
bushel on the day the futures contract is closed, Great Lakes buys the soybeans on the spot market,
and delivers them to the customer. The futures position qualifies as a fair value hedge of the firm
commitment to sell soybeans to the customer.
c. In this case, does hedge accounting lead to a different result than if hedge accounting were not used?
Explain.

E9.5 **Fair Value Hedge: Short in Interest Rate Futures** On June 1, 2017, Domino Foods borrows **LO 1**
$2 million in a floating rate term loan that rolls over every 91 days. The interest rate is set at the current
Treasury bill rate plus 0.95 percent, and is payable at the end of each 91-day period. To hedge the risk that
interest rates will increase, Domino sells $2 million face value 91-day Treasury bill futures at 98.5; the
price reflects the current Treasury bill rate of 1.5 percent. The futures position requires a $3,000 margin
deposit, and qualifies as an effective hedge of a firm commitment to roll over the floating rate loan. On
August 30, 2017, the end of the 91-day period, the Treasury bill rate is 1.25 percent and the interest rate
futures sell for 98.75. Domino rolls over the loan and closes its futures position. Domino is scheduled to
roll the loan over again on November 29, 2017, but does not hedge during this second period. Assume
that Domino is not required to pay additional cash to the broker to cover hedging losses before it closes
its position.

Required

Prepare the entries necessary to record the above events. Include entries to record interest expense at the
end of the first 91-day period and the second 91-day period.

LO 2   **E9.6**   **Cash Flow Hedge: Interest Rate Cap**   On July 1, 2016, **Molson Coors Brewing Company** borrowed $3 million for two years with interest paid semi-annually based on LIBOR adjusted semiannually. On that date, LIBOR is 2 percent per annum. To hedge against a possible rise in interest rates, on July 2 Molson Coors bought a two-year 2.05 percent interest rate cap for 0.075 percent per year, payable in full immediately. The intrinsic value of the cap is designated as the hedge instrument and the hedge is fully effective. LIBOR increased during the second half of 2016 and is reset to 2.15 percent for the first half of 2017. Molson Coors closes its books on December 31 and June 30. The cap's fair value is $3,500 on December 31, 2016, before the rate adjustment, and is $4,000 on June 30, 2017, when the time value component is $2,500.

Required

Prepare all journal entries related to the loan interest and the interest rate cap on July 2, 2016, December 31, 2016, and June 30, 2017.

⊘ LO 2   **E9.7**   **Fair Value Hedge: Put Options**   In 2016, Smithson Foods purchased $1,000,000 of 2.5 percent corporate bonds at par, and designated them as held-to-maturity investments. Throughout 2016, the market value of the bonds declined, but Smithson characterized the decline as temporary. On February 1, 2017, the bonds are selling at 98. To hedge against a further price decrease on the bonds, Smithson purchased for $3.10 per $100 of bonds, February 2018 put options on the bonds at a strike price of 101. The intrinsic value of the puts was designated as the hedge instrument. By June 30, 2017, Smithson's fiscal year-end, the bonds were selling at 99 and the puts for $2.30. On December 31, 2017, when the bonds were selling at 97, Smithson closed out its position by selling the puts for $4.20.

Required

Prepare Smithson Foods' journal entries during 2017 related to the puts and the hedged bonds.

LO 2   **E9.8**   **Cash Flow Hedge: Call Options**   On March 1, 2017, Prairie Farms forecasts that it will purchase 1,000,000 units of a commodity in six months. To hedge against rising prices, Prairie Farms invests in 1,000,000 September 2017 call options for the commodity. The call options have a strike price of $3.30 per unit, and cost $0.65 each. The current market price of the commodity is $3.25 per unit. The intrinsic value of the options is designated as the hedging instrument, and the option investment qualifies as a cash flow hedge of the forecasted purchase. On June 30, 2017, the market price of the commodity is $3.40 per unit, the options have a market price of $0.50 per unit, and Prairie Farms sells the options.

Required

Prepare the journal entry to record the sale of the options.

LO 2   **E9.9**   **Call Options Hedging Foreign Currency Debt**   Taking advantage of lower interest rates in the United Kingdom, Carlton Inc., a U.S. firm, borrowed £2,000,000 on July 1, 2016, to be repaid in one year. When the transaction occurred, the exchange rate was $1.50/£. To hedge against possible appreciation of the British pound, Carlton paid a premium of $0.014/£ for July 2017 call options on £2,000,000, with a strike price of $1.49/£. On December 31, 2016, when Carlton's books are closed, the exchange rate is $1.55/£, and the calls are selling for $0.069/£. On June 30, 2017, Carlton sells the calls for $0.12/£. The exchange rate at that time is $1.61/£.

Required

a.   Does hedge accounting apply in this situation? Explain.
b.   Prepare Carlton's journal entries made on July 1, 2016, December 31, 2016, and June 30, 2017, to recognize the calls' value changes and the exchange rate adjustments on the debt. Ignore interest on and repayment of the debt.

LO 2   **E9.10**   **Fair Value Hedge: Put Options**   On September 1, 2017, American Metals Distribution (AMD) has an inventory of 5,000 pounds of copper that it plans to sell on the spot market in three months. The inventory is carried at cost, and was purchased on the spot market at $3.25/lb. To hedge against a decline in market price, AMD invests in put options on 5,000 pounds of copper, expiring December 1, at a strike price of $3.20/lb, which is the current spot price. AMD pays $800 for the options, and designates the change in intrinsic value as the hedge. On November 1, 2017, the spot price is $3.18/lb, and AMD sells the options for $300. On December 16, 2017, AMD sells its inventory at the then-current spot price of $3.15/lb.

Required

Prepare AMD's journal entries to record the events of September 1, November 1, and December 16, 2017. AMD's accounting year ends December 31.

E9.11 **Interest Rate Swap: Profit and Default** On July 1, 2017, Queen Corp. and Prince, Inc. entered **LO 3** into an interest rate swap on a notional amount of $1 million. They accepted the following offer of Intermediary:

To Intermediary from Queen	LIBOR + 30 (floating)
To Intermediary from Prince...	3.4% (fixed)
To Queen from Intermediary	3.3% (fixed)
To Prince from Intermediary..	LIBOR + 20 (floating)

At inception of the swap, LIBOR = 3.3 percent. Due to an increase of 20 bp in the floating interest rate at the end of September, Queen Corp. defaulted and Intermediary honored its commitment to Prince, Inc. by continuing with the swap.

Required

a. What monthly profit, in dollars, was Intermediary making on the swap before default?

b. Is Intermediary losing money after the default? If so, how much?

E9.12 **Interest Rate Swap: Journal Entries** Refer to the data in E9.11. Assume that the floating rate is **LO 3** adjusted on October 1 and that default did *not* occur. Assume also that on September 30, 2017, the swap's fair value is a $75,000 liability to Queen, and the market value of Queen's fixed rate debt has declined in value by $75,000. Prince's swap has increased in value by $33,000.

Required

Prepare the journal entries made by Queen and Prince on September 30, 2017, when the first payments pursuant to the swap are made. Do not record the interest on the underlying debt.

E9.13 **Fair Value Hedge: Interest Rate Swap** On January 1, 2017, Greentree Foods borrowed $5 million **LO 3** of fixed rate debt at an annual rate of 3.5 percent, interest paid semiannually on June 30 and December 31 of each year, principal due on December 31, 2018. To hedge against falling interest rates, Greentree entered a receive fixed/pay variable interest rate swap at the Treasury bill rate plus 80 bp on a notional amount of $5 million, with the rate reset every six months. The Treasury bill rate was 3 percent on January 1, 2017. On June 30, 2017, the Treasury bill rate is 2.6 percent; the swap increased in value by $5,000 and the fair value of the fixed rate debt increased by the same amount. On December 31, 2017, the Treasury bill rate is 2.5 percent; the swap and fixed rate debt increased in value by another $1,000.

Required

Prepare the journal entries related to the debt and the swap for the year 2017.

E9.14 **Cash Flow Hedge: Interest Rate Swap** On January 1, 2017, Greentree Foods borrowed $5 mil- **LO 3** lion of variable rate debt at an annual rate equal to the Treasury bill rate plus 80 bp, interest paid semiannually on June 30 and December 31 of each year, principal due on December 31, 2018. The variable rate is reset every six months. To hedge against increasing interest rates, Greentree entered a receive variable/pay fixed interest rate swap, agreeing to pay a 3.5 percent fixed rate on a notional amount of $5 million. The Treasury bill rate was 3 percent on January 1, 2017. On June 30, 2017, the Treasury bill rate is 2.6 percent; the swap declined in value by $5,000. On December 31, 2017, the Treasury bill rate is 2.5 percent; the swap declined in value by another $1,000.

Required

Prepare the journal entries related to the debt and the swap for the year 2017.

E9.15 **Interest Rate Swap** On January 1, 2016, Marshall Corp. issues $10,000,000 in 4 percent fixed rate **LO 3** ✓ debt with interest payments due every six months. Concurrently, Marshall enters into an interest rate swap in which it receives 4 percent fixed and pays variable at *average* LIBOR + 60 bp on a notional amount of $10,000,000. On June 30, 2016, the market interest rate on comparable fixed rate debt is 3 percent and LIBOR declined to 2.2 percent. LIBOR averaged 2.7 percent during the six-month period. The estimated fair value of the swap to Marshall is $275,000 on June 30, 2016, and the fair value of the debt is $10,275,000.

Required

a. Prepare the journal entries made by Marshall on January 1 and June 30 in connection with the debt issuance, the periodic interest, and value changes in the swap and debt.

b. Suppose instead that Marshall issued variable rate debt and entered a swap in which it receives variable and pays fixed. If the market rate of interest on comparable fixed-rate debt declines on June 30, does Marshall record the fair value of the swap as an asset or a liability? Does Marshall recognize a gain or loss on the swap and what is its accounting treatment?

PROBLEMS ••

LO 1   P9.1   Commodity Futures: Fair Value Hedge   The Davis Company grows soybeans and processes them into soybean meal for eventual sale to food companies. Davis currently owns 10,000 tons of soybean meal, carried in inventory at a cost of $3,400,000. Soybean meal trades on the spot markets for $350 per ton; three-month futures are selling for $363 per ton. Davis expects to sell the 10,000 tons in 90 days. On August 1, 2017, Davis sells 10,000 tons of soybean meal futures to be delivered on October 30, 2017, at the $363 price. The price of Davis' futures contracts has advanced to $367 and the spot price is $354 on September 30, when the books are closed for interim reporting purposes. Davis closes out its short position on October 28, 2017, when the futures price is $361 per ton and the spot price is $348.

Required

a. Assuming that Davis deposits $75,000 margin with the broker on August 1, prepare the journal entries it makes on August 1, on September 30, and on October 28. Davis is required to maintain a minimum brokerage account balance of $75,000.

b. If Davis sells the soybean meal in the spot market on November 2, 2017, for $348.50 per ton, calculate its net cash gain or loss from the sale, taking into account the hedging transaction.

c. Suppose instead that Davis *purchased* the 10,000 tons of soybean futures on August 1, 2017, closing the long position on October 28, 2017. Calculate the net cash gain or loss on the long futures position and compare its accounting treatment with the gain or loss on the short futures position in part *a* above at October 28, 2017.

LO 1   P9.2   Interest Rate Futures: Cash Flow Hedge   As part of its cash management activities, Hilldale Brands regularly invests in 91-day Treasury bills. It purchased $1,000,000 face value of these bills on June 1 and, fearing lower interest rates when it rolls over these short-term investments, Hilldale purchases $1,000,000 face value Treasury bill futures at 96 to be delivered in 91 days and makes a $10,000 margin deposit. The futures qualify as a hedge of a forecasted transaction.

Required

a. Prepare the journal entries made on June 1, on the June 30 reporting date when the Treasury bill futures are selling at 97, and on August 30 when the old Treasury bills mature and the new ones are delivered. On August 30, Hilldale's futures contract is selling at 97.5.

b. Assume the new Treasury bills cost $993,750. Use calculations to show how the hedge enables Hilldale to report a 4 percent annualized return on the new Treasury bills even though they currently yield 2.5 percent annually.

LO 1   P9.3   Interest Rate Futures: Fair Value Hedge   Sanders Farms buys 10,450 bushels of corn each quarter to feed its chickens, at an average price of $5 per bushel. To finance these purchases, Sanders sells $1,000 face value Treasury bonds from its available-for-sale investment portfolio. The bonds are currently carried at 95, their current market value. Sanders sells Treasury bond futures at 95 on enough bonds to finance next quarter's corn purchases, and settles the contracts at 93 in three months. There is no margin deposit. The futures qualify as a fair value hedge of the bond investment.

Required

a. How many $1,000 face value Treasury bonds does Sanders sell each quarter to finance its corn purchases?

b. Prepare the journal entries to record the settlement of the futures contract, sale of Sanders' bonds, and purchase of the corn, assuming there is no intervening balance sheet date.

c. Now assume a balance sheet date occurs in 45 days, when the futures and the bonds are selling at 93.5. Prepare the required adjusting entries at the balance sheet date. How do the entries at settlement date change from your answer to part *b*?

⊘ LO 1   P9.4   Evaluating Hedging With Futures Contracts   A large farming company likes to firm up prices for its agricultural products. It anticipates harvesting and selling 1,000,000 bushels of a particular commodity in six months. News reports and changes in forecasts cause fluctuations in the spot price for the commodity. The current spot price is $5.00 per bushel. Futures contracts are available at $4.75 per bushel and six-month put option contracts with an exercise price of $5.00 per bushel are available for $0.35. A noninterest-bearing margin deposit of $200,000 is required if futures contracts covering the entire 1,000,000 bushels are sold. The company's current cost of borrowing is 4 percent per annum.

Required

a. Explain the advantages and disadvantages of hedging the harvest's value with futures contracts.
b. Calculate the spot price six months hence at which the company is indifferent between not hedging and hedging with futures contracts.
c. Assume the spot price stands at $5.25 per bushel when 1,000,000 bushels of the commodity are harvested (not sold) and that commodity inventories are carried at market. Explain, using calculations as needed, how the company's financial statements will differ without hedging compared to hedging with futures contracts.

P9.5   **Evaluating Hedging With Option Contracts**   Refer to the data in P9.4.   **LO 2**

Required

a. Explain the advantages and disadvantages of hedging the harvest's value with option contracts.
b. Calculate the spot price 6 months hence at which the company is indifferent between not hedging and hedging with option contracts.
c. Assume the spot price stands at $4.75 per bushel when 1,000,000 bushels of the commodity are harvested (not sold) and that commodity inventories are carried at market. Explain, using calculations as needed, how the company's financial statements will differ without hedging compared to hedging with option contracts.

P9.6   **Call Options: Cash Flow Hedge**   On July 1, 2017, **Kraft Foods Group, Inc.** forecasts that it will   **LO 2** purchase 500,000 pounds of Arabica coffee in three months. To hedge against rising prices, when the current spot price is $2.35/lb, Kraft invests in call options expiring October 1, 2017, for 500,000 pounds of coffee. The options have a strike price of $2.30/lb, and cost $225,000. The intrinsic value of the options is designated as the hedging instrument, and the option investment qualifies as a cash flow hedge of the forecasted purchase. On September 1, 2017, the spot price of the coffee is $2.45, and Kraft sells the options for $135,000. On October 1, 2017, Kraft buys 500,000 pounds of Arabica coffee in the spot market for $2.50/lb. It sells products containing the coffee the following month.

Required

a. Prepare the journal entries to record the events of July 1, September 1, and October 1, 2017.
b. When Kraft sells products containing the coffee, what amount does it include as the cost of the coffee, in cost of goods sold? Prepare the journal entry to record the cost of the coffee included in products sold.
c. Repeat the requirements of part *b*, assuming Kraft did not hedge the forecasted purchase of coffee.

P9.7   **Present Value Analysis of Interest Rate Cap and Journal Entries**   At July 1, 2016, Sunny   **LO 2** Orchards has $10,000,000 of debt due in four years with interest floating at prime. The rate is adjusted annually each July 1 and interest for the preceding year is payable on June 30. Sunny Orchards closes its books on June 30 and December 31 of each year. Prime currently stands at 4 percent annually and is expected to fluctuate between 2 percent and 8 percent over the next four years. On July 1, 2016, Sunny Orchards has the opportunity to invest in a 4-year interest rate cap with a strike price of 5 percent for $400,000 payable immediately.

Required

a. Suppose the prime rate is expected to be 6 percent on July 1, 2017, 8 percent on July 1, 2018, and stay at 8 percent for the remaining two years. Use a present value analysis to determine whether purchasing the cap is a good economic decision in this set of circumstances. *Hint:* Let the applicable prime rate(s) when the interest changes occur be the discount rate(s).
b. Suppose instead that the prime rate drops to 2 percent on July 1, 2017, and stays at 2 percent for the remaining three years. Use a present value analysis to determine whether the savings in interest cost (2 percent versus the original 4 percent) will offset the cost of the cap.
c. Assume the cap is purchased and prime rises to 6 percent on July 1, 2017. Prepare the journal entries made by Sunny Orchards to account for the periodic interest expense and the cap at December 31, 2017, and June 30, 2018. Assume that the fair value of the cap declines by $50,000 in each 6-month period.

LO 2   **P9.8**   **Fair Value Hedge: Put Options**   **Overhill Farms Inc.** has a large portfolio of marketable equity securities held as short-term investments. To protect against declines in the value of 10,000 shares of Tyson Foods Inc. common stock that Overhill holds, on November 1, 2016, Overhill Farms purchased 90-day put options for $35,000 on the 10,000 Tyson Foods shares it had purchased at $40. The exercise price is $40 and the shares are selling for $38 each. Overhill Farms designates the intrinsic value of the puts as the hedge instrument. Overhill Farms classifies the Tyson Foods shares as available-for-sale securities.

Required

a.   Prepare journal entries to record purchase of the puts and relevant events on November 1, 2016, and when the books are closed at December 31, 2016, the stock is selling for $35.50, and the options are selling for $50,000.

b.   Thirty days after the closing in part *a*, Overhill Farms decides to sell the 10,000 Tyson Foods shares for $32 each and to sell the put options for their intrinsic value of $80,000. Prepare the journal entries to record the sale, and calculate the net cash gain or loss realized on these sale transactions.

c.   How much of this net cash gain or loss is recognized in 2016 income? In 2017 income?

LO 2   **P9.9**   **Speculative Straddle: Journal Entries and Profit Calculation**   Fastbuck, Inc. trades put and call options on common stock. Acting on a tip, on January 31, 2017, Fastbuck wrote both calls and puts expiring on March 31—known as a **"straddle"**—on 5,000 shares of Exland Farm Services stock that was selling for $42 a share. March 2017 calls with a strike price of $45 were selling for $2; puts with the same terms were selling for $3.10. On February 28, when the price of Exland stock rose to $49 and the puts were selling at $0.80, Fastbuck sold the calls at $4.20. On March 31, Exland stock fell to $47 and the puts expired without being exercised.

Required

a.   Prepare journal entries to record writing the puts and calls and any other related accounting events including expiration of the puts. The books are closed monthly.

b.   Calculate Fastbuck's cash gain or loss on the straddle.

LO 1, 2   **P9.10**   **Futures and Options as Hedging Alternatives**   Companies seeking to hedge future purchases or revenue flows can often choose between futures contracts and option contracts. Sami Corp. projects purchasing 100 tons of a commodity in three months; its current spot price is $700/ton and the six-month futures price is $710/ton. Ninety-one day call options on the commodity at the money sell for $50.

Assume that Sami subsequently signs purchase orders for 100 tons to be delivered in three months at the then-current spot price, and hedges those firm commitments with six-month futures contracts requiring a $20,000 margin deposit. At the end of the three-month period, when the futures price is $690/ton, Sami closes its futures position and takes delivery of the 100 tons at the spot price of $682/ton.

Required

a.   What factors should Sami consider when deciding between hedging with futures versus options?

b.   Prepare summary journal entries to record all the events surrounding the firm commitment, the futures hedge and the eventual purchase of the 100 tons at the $682/ton spot price.

c.   Suppose that Sami does not sign purchase orders and instead uses option contracts to hedge its anticipated purchases, designating the options' intrinsic values as the hedge instrument. The option contracts remain out of the money and expire when Sami makes the spot market purchase at $682/ton. Prepare summary journal entries to record these events.

d.   Compute the cash gain or loss from hedging versus not hedging in parts *b* and *c*.

LO 2, 3   **P9.11**   **Evaluate Strategies to Hedge Against Rising Interest Rates**   Suppose **Apple, Inc.** has $100 million of two-year floating rate debt outstanding at LIBOR + 80 bp. In a swap, Apple can get LIBOR + 80 bp from intermediary in return for fixed payments to intermediary at 4 percent. Alternatively, Apple could purchase a 4 percent interest rate cap for the two years remaining until the debt matures. LIBOR is currently 3 percent.

Required

a.   Assume LIBOR remains at 3 percent for the next two years. Compute the maximum amount Apple would pay for the cap and be indifferent between the swap and the cap. Ignore discounting.

b.   Assume LIBOR does not remain at 3 percent for the next two years, and could go up or down. Explain the factors you would evaluate in deciding whether to make the swap or purchase the cap.

c.   Suppose Apple also could transact in $100 million notional amount of interest rate futures at 96; the discount yield on the futures closely tracks movements in LIBOR. If Apple decides on the futures, should they be bought or sold? What other factors would you consider?

P9.12 **Interest Rate Swap: Journal Entries and Valuation** Johnson & Johnson (J&J) has $10,000,000 **LO 3** of floating rate debt, with interest at LIBOR + 120 bp adjusted quarterly, and an equivalent amount of 2-year fixed-rate investments yielding 5 percent annually. J&J classifies the investments as held-to-maturity. To match fixed rate financing with its fixed-rate investments, J&J swaps 4 percent fixed payments to intermediary in exchange for LIBOR + 120 bp on the notional amount of $10,000,000 for 2 years. LIBOR is 2.8 percent.

Required

a. Prepare the entries made by J&J at the end of the first quarter to record interest expense.
b. After the swap is in effect one quarter, LIBOR rises to 3.3 percent and the variable payments rise to 4.5 percent. The swap and the hedged investments both change in value by $65,000. Prepare the entries made by J&J to record the value changes.
c. Prepare the entries made by J&J at the end of the second quarter to record interest expense.
d. Suppose the swap is not hedging fixed-rate investments, but instead hedges changing interest rates on debt. LIBOR rises to 3.3 percent at the end of the first quarter, and the swap changes in value by $65,000. Prepare the entry made by J&J to record this value change.

P9.13 **Critique Proposed Currency/Interest Rate Swap Arrangement** On June 25, 2016, Reno **LO 3** Company, a U.S. firm, will be taking out a £10,000,000 loan, due in three years and carrying an annual interest rate of LIBOR + 80 bp. In anticipation of the loan, a spot rate of $1.60/£ and LIBOR of 2 percent, Reno negotiates a currency swap and interest rate swap with Sterling Benteen, Ltd. (SB), a British firm. SB recently negotiated a fixed-rate dollar denominated loan. Proceeds from both loans will be converted into the home currency and used to finance projects in each company's home country. The two counterparties propose the following:

1. On June 25, 2016, Reno will receive £10,000,000 from SB in exchange for $16,000,000.
2. On June 24, 2019, Reno will receive $16,000,000 from SB in exchange for £10,000,000.
3. On June 24, 2017, 2018 and 2019, SB will pay Reno $480,000 (fixed at 3 percent annually) in exchange for sufficient £ to cover the annual interest on Reno's £10,000,000 floating rate loan.

Despite hours of staff work and pages of elegant analysis, you sense that there is something seriously wrong with this "deal."

Required

a. What is wrong with the above arrangements? Recast them into swaps sensible for Reno and SB.
b. After you recast the arrangements into sensible swaps, suppose throughout the year ended June 24, 2019, LIBOR is 3 percent and the spot rate is $1.50. For that year only, calculate the undiscounted number of dollars that Reno saved (lost) by entering these swaps as opposed to not entering them.

P9.14 **Interpreting Derivatives Disclosures** Refer to the information in the business application on **LO 4** pages 398–399, describing **J.M. Smucker Company**'s derivatives disclosures for fiscal 2014. In addition to the tabular disclosures, Smucker discloses the following information on its interest rate swaps (excerpts). Amounts are in millions.

J.M. SMUCKER COMPANY
[SJM]

During 2014, we entered into an interest rate swap which was designated as a fair value hedge and used to hedge against the changes in the fair value of the debt. The difference between the fixed-rate and variable-rate cash flows resulted in a reduction in interest expense for the year ended April 30, 2014. Changes in the fair value of the swap were recognized in interest expense. At April 30, 2014, the net gain position on the derivative instrument of $14.9 had no net impact to earnings, as the change in the fair value of the derivative was equal to the change in fair value of the underlying debt.

Included as a component of accumulated other comprehensive loss at April 30, 2014, were deferred losses of $4.8 related to the termination of prior interest rate swaps. We reclassified $0.6 of the loss... from other comprehensive income to interest expense during 2014.

Required

a. Identify the types of accounting Smucker uses for its commodity contracts, foreign currency exchange contracts, and interest rate contracts (i.e., fair value hedge accounting, cash flow hedge accounting, normal accounting).

b. Prepare the summary journal entry made in fiscal 2014 to record value changes for Smucker's commodity contracts designated as cash flow hedges.

c. Prepare the summary journal entry made in fiscal 2014 to record value changes for Smucker's derivatives that are not designated as qualified hedges.

d. Where are hedging gains and losses reported on Smucker's income statement? Where are gains and losses on derivatives not qualifying as hedges reported on Smucker's income statement? Comment on the appropriateness of Smucker's income statement display of derivatives gains and losses.

LO 3, 4   **P9.15**   **Interpreting Interest Rate Swap Disclosures**   The notes to **General Mills, Inc.**'s fiscal 2014 financial statements include the following information on its interest rate swaps:

GENERAL MILLS, INC.
[GIS]

(in millions)	May 25, 2014	May 26, 2013
Pay-floating swaps—notional amount......................	$250.0	$550.0
Average receive rate.....................................	0.9%	1.1%
Average pay rate.......................................	0.5%	0.4%

As of May 25, 2014, the pre-tax amount of cash-settled interest rate hedge gain or loss remaining in AOCI which will be reclassified to earnings over the remaining term of the related underlying debt follows:

(in millions)	Gain/(Loss)
5.2% notes due March 17, 2015	$ (0.4)
5.7% notes due February 15, 2017	(6.0)
5.65% notes due February 15, 2019	2.3
3.15% notes due December 15, 2021	(74.8)
3.65% notes due February 15, 2024	17.3
5.4% notes due June 15, 2040	(14.5)
4.15% notes due February 15, 2043	11.3
Net pre-tax hedge loss in AOCI..	$(64.8)

Required

a. Based on the data in the first table above, explain whether General Mills' swap position at the end of fiscal 2014 seems more or less beneficial than its position in fiscal 2013. Why do you think General Mills only has "pay-floating" swaps?

b. Look at the second table above. Are the notes payable listed there fixed or floating (variable) rate obligations? How do you know?

c. In the second table, the 3.15% notes are reported with a related $74.8 million loss, while the 3.65% notes are reported with a related $17.3 million gain. Explain the circumstances leading to a loss on one swap, and a gain on the other. Why does General Mills report a net pre-tax hedge *loss* of $64.8 million on these swaps?

d. What accounts are debited/credited when the swap gains and losses listed in the second table are reclassified to earnings?

REVIEW SOLUTIONS ••

Review 1 Solution

a. Fair value hedge

March 1	Investment in futures	50,000	
	Cash		50,000
	To record margin deposit on long futures position in fair value hedge.		

continued

March 31	Loss on hedging..	200,000	
	Cash		200,000
	To record decline in value of futures contracts and pay clearinghouse.		
	Firm commitment......................................	200,000	
	Gain on hedging		200,000
	To record the commitment asset resulting from the reduced cost to buy the commodity when it is eventually purchased.		
April 15	Cash...	350,000	
	Gain on hedging		300,000
	Investment in futures............................		50,000
	To record gain and concurrent settlement from clearinghouse.		
	Loss on hedging.......................................	300,000	
	Firm commitment		300,000
	To record the commitment liability resulting from increased cost to buy the commodity when it is eventually purchased.		
	Commodities inventory	10,180,000	
	Cash		10,180,000
	To record purchase of commodities on a cash market.		
	Firm commitment......................................	100,000	
	Commodities inventory		100,000
	To adjust inventory balance for commitment liability.		
June 1	Cost of goods sold....................................	10,080,000	
	Commodities inventory		10,080,000
	To record the sale of products containing the commodity.		

b. **Cash flow hedge**

March 1	Investment in futures	50,000	
	Cash		50,000
	To record margin deposit on long futures position in cash flow hedge.		
March 31	Other comprehensive income (loss on hedging)	200,000	
	Cash		200,000
	To record decline in value of futures contracts and pay clearinghouse.		
April 15	Cash...	350,000	
	Investment in futures............................		50,000
	Other comprehensive income		300,000
	To record gain and concurrent settlement from clearinghouse.		
	Commodities inventory	10,180,000	
	Cash		10,180,000
	To record purchase of commodities on a cash market.		
June 1	Cost of goods sold....................................	10,080,000	
	Other comprehensive income	100,000	
	Commodities inventory		10,180,000
	To record the sale of products containing the commodity.		

Review 2 Solution

2016			
Aug. 10	Investment in AFS securities	3,000,000	
	Cash		3,000,000
	To record purchase of AFS securities.		
Sept. 30	OCI	90,000	
	Investment in AFS securities		90,000
	To record decline in value to $2,910,000.		
	Investment in options	100,000	
	Cash		100,000
	To record purchase of options.		
Dec. 31	Loss on hedging	23,400	
	Investment in options		23,400
	To record decline in value to $76,600.		
	Investment in AFS securities	30,000	
	Gain on hedging		30,000
	To record increase in value to $2,940,000, using hedge accounting.		
2017			
Mar. 1	Investment in options	83,200	
	Gain on hedging		83,200
	To record increase in value to $159,800.		
	Loss on hedging	90,000	
	Investment in AFS securities		90,000
	To record decline in value to $2,850,000, using hedge accounting.		
	Cash	159,800	
	Investment in options		159,800
	To record sale of options.		
Mar. 30	Investment in AFS securities	50,000	
	OCI		50,000
	To record increase in value to $2,900,000.		
	Cash	2,900,000	
	Realized loss on sale of securities	40,000	
	OCI		40,000
	Investment in AFS securities		2,900,000
	To record sale of securities and release of unrealized loss from AOCI to income.		

Review 3 Solution

a. *(in thousands)*

2017			
May 1	Cash..	100,000	
	Long-term debt..................................		100,000
	To record debt issuance.		
2018			
April 30	Interest expense......................................	4,000	
	Cash		4,000
	To record periodic interest expense on fixed rate debt;		
	$4,000 = 0.04 × $100,000.		
	Cash...	1,200	
	Interest expense		1,200
	To record net cash payment from intermediary to settle the		
	swap; $1,200 = (0.040 − 0.028) × $100,000.		
	Long-term debt	450	
	Gain on hedging activity		450
	To record decline in fair value of the fixed rate debt.		
	Loss on hedging activity.............................	450	
	Investment in swap		450
	To record decline in fair value of the swap.		

b. If Heinz issues variable rate debt and enters a receive variable/pay fixed interest rate swap, the swap is a cash flow hedge. At the end of the year, if interest rates increase, the swap increases in value and the gain is credited to OCI. When Heinz makes next year's variable rate interest payment at the higher rate, the swap gain is reclassified from AOCI to offset the higher interest expense.

10 State and Local Governments: Introduction and General Fund Transactions

MECKLENBURG COUNTY, NORTH CAROLINA
www.charmeck.org

Mecklenburg County, North Carolina is the sixth largest urban region and the second largest financial center in the U.S. The county's largest city is Charlotte. Bank of America's headquarters are located in Mecklenburg County. Johnson & Wales University and the University of North Carolina both have campuses here. The county is also home to the NFL's Carolina Panthers and the NBA's Charlotte Bobcats.

Main funding sources for the county are property taxes and intergovernmental revenue received from state and federal grants. Major expenditures include the Charlotte-Mecklenburg Schools, Central Piedmont Community College, and the Mecklenburg Emergency Medical Services Agency.

Each year Mecklenburg County issues a Comprehensive Annual Financial Report (CAFR), detailing its financial status and activities. The county's 2013 CAFR reports a total net position deficit of over $92 million. The year's revenues exceeded expenses by $153 million, a decline from the $267 million surplus in 2012. Property tax revenues increased 0.2%, and sales tax revenues increased 3%, due to recapture of sales tax by the state. Interest revenue on investments fell 123%, a result of lower interest rates and less cash available for investment. While many expenses stayed flat, detention and court services increased 6% due to higher costs of jail management.

Who reads governmental financial statements? What kinds of information are provided? How do the financial statements differ from those of for-profit businesses? What accounting standards apply?

This chapter and the two that follow provide answers to these questions.

CHAPTER ORGANIZATION

Reporting for state and local governments	Fund structure	Accounting for the general fund	Illustration of general fund accounting
• External users of financial information • Sources of GAAP • GAAP hierarchy • Objectives of financial reporting • Reporting entity	• Governmental, proprietary and fiduciary activities • Fund types and financial statements • Basis of reporting	• Budgetary accounts • Property tax revenue • Purchase of goods and services • Supplies inventories • Interfund transactions • Capital assets and long-term debt • Closing entries • Encumbrances	• Record budget, transactions, and closing entries • Prepare financial statements

Chapters 10–12 explain reporting practices and requirements for *state and local governments*. A **government** can be a state, county, city, town, village, or school district, or a separate revenue-generating organization such as a toll road. When the term *municipality* is used to describe a government, **municipality** means a local government, such as a city, town or village. This chapter provides an overview of government reporting and discusses the accounting for day-to-day operating activities of state and local governments.

NATURE OF GOVERNMENT ACTIVITIES

Government at all levels is an increasingly important segment of the economy. As the scope and diversity of governmental services and programs expand, so too does the importance of governmental accounting and reporting. The internal and external structure of accounting and reporting for state and local governments reflects the operating environment, legal constraints, and goals of these governments. Because a government differs from a business on all these dimensions, the accounting and reporting policies are in many ways very different, although changes in external reporting requirements in the last decade moved the government reporting model closer to that of business reporting.

LO1 Describe the reporting environment for state and local governments.

Major factors differentiating a state or local government from a business include:

- Resources are from sources such as taxes, fees, and fines. The government has a legal right to collect taxes, which provide most governmental resources.
- There are no ownership interests in a government.
- A government must adhere to a legal budget. Expenditures cannot exceed amounts provided in the budget.
- Financial inflows are often legally required to be used in a particular way. For example, a bond issued for construction of a building must be used for that purpose. Citizens may be assessed a special tax to finance a street light project. A federal grant to operate a community center must be used for that purpose.
- The main objective of government is to provide services to citizens, usually on a nonprofit basis. The notion of "matching" governmental expenditures with revenues does not apply, since revenue often does not come from services provided. Profit is not a valid measure of performance for most governmental activities.
- Users of governmental financial statements are:
  - Credit market representatives, who determine bond ratings, provide bond insurance guaranteeing bond payments, and provide investment banking services

    ○ Elected and appointed officials of the government

    ○ Citizens, typically from budget advisory groups and "watchdog" organizations

    ○ Supervisory levels of government, such as a state controller monitoring county government financial performance

    ○ Public sector labor unions

• The **Governmental Accounting Standards Board** (GASB) sets accounting requirements for governmental external reporting. Many governments are legally required to follow GAAP and issue audited financial statements.

Activities of a government can be divided into three major categories: *governmental*, *proprietary*, and *fiduciary*. **Governmental activities** benefit the government or its citizens, and for the most part consist of primary services such as health and safety, economic assistance, education, culture and recreation, and legislative services. These activities typically do not generate significant inflows of resources, and are funded by income, sales, and property tax levies, and state and federal aid.

    Proprietary activities are similar to the activities of a business, in that goods and services are primarily financed by user fees, paid either by citizens or other departments within the government. User fees are usually set to approximate the cost of the goods or services provided. Examples are parking and recreational facilities, utilities, and motor pools.

    Fiduciary activities are those where the government holds resources in a custodial capacity for entities or individuals outside the governmental unit. For example, a local government collects sales taxes as an agent for the state, or a municipality funds and manages a pension plan for its employees.

• •

Reporting Perspective

Credit market representatives use municipal financial statements to evaluate the credit-worthiness of the governmental unit. The major forms of municipal debt obligations are bonds, notes, and leases. There are legal restrictions on the amount and types of debt a municipality can issue. Two basic types of bonds are *general obligation* and *revenue bonds*. **General obligation bonds** are secured by the full faith, credit, and general taxing powers of the municipality. Investors generally consider this form of debt to be the safest. **Revenue bonds** are secured by the pledge of specific revenues and, unlike general obligation bonds, usually contain bond covenants or restrictions. As an example, water revenue bonds may be issued to finance the construction of a water treatment plant. A portion of the connection fees and charges paid by users of the water system is pledged to pay the principal and interest on the bonds. Bond restrictions may require that the construction be completed, and that rates be sufficient to pay all costs, including bond debt service.

    Hybrid bond securities have characteristics of both general obligation and revenue debt, or possess other unique features. A common example is **guaranteed revenue bonds**, which are revenue bonds also backed by the full faith and credit of the municipality. If pledged revenues are insufficient to repay the debt, it is repaid with the municipality's general revenues. Municipalities may also issue **notes**, typically outstanding for periods of less than three years. Examples are tax, revenue, grant, and bond anticipation notes, and tax-exempt commercial paper. These notes are issued in *anticipation* of collecting expected taxes, revenue, grant revenue, or bond proceeds. **Bond anticipation notes** finance the start-up costs of a project for which the bonds cannot be issued immediately and are repaid from the subsequent bond issue proceeds.

    In general, the classification of debt is important because it determines which regulations and limitations apply. Both federal and state laws regulate the issuance and trading of municipal debt securities. Although nontaxable municipal bonds are exempt from most federal regulatory requirements of the 1933 and 1934 securities acts, they are not exempt from the antifraud provisions. State laws often limit the amounts and/or types of debt financing allowed by local governments. Some states only allow the issuance of revenue bonds, whereas others allow only general obligation bonds. Other states limit the amount of debt issued, and limits can vary depending on the type of debt.

• •

External Users of Governmental Financial Statements

External users of governmental financial statements include credit market representatives, elected officials, and citizens. Each group has different information needs.

Credit Market Representatives Organizations that provide financing to the government, in the form of bonds and loans, are interested in the government's ability to generate resources for required interest and principal payments. Important factors in this assessment include:

- Sources of revenues and expenditures by function and program
- Funding information on pensions and related liabilities
- Changes in all liabilities, including pending litigation and contingent liabilities
- Future financing plans
- Extent to which revenues from one program subsidize costs of another program
- Individual program or activity surpluses or deficits
- Material departures from GAAP
- Whether financial statements are audited on a timely basis
- Liquidity and flexibility of the governmental unit
- Evidence of management's performance
- Economic factors

Elected Officials and Citizens Citizens, legislators, unions and oversight officials focus on how much money a government has available to spend, how tax dollars are used, how much governmental services cost, sources of financing for various programs, and how current activities and plans affect future taxes and future ability to provide services. Financial information related to these concerns includes:

- Revenue sources and expenditures
- How much resources a government has available to spend
- Budget allocations for major programs and functions
- Comparison of actual results to the original budget
- Detailed capital improvement plans
- Costs of services in detail
- Percentage of total expenditures financed by taxes
- Impact of current performance on future tax rates and services

SOURCES OF GAAP FOR STATE AND LOCAL GOVERNMENTS

The **Governmental Accounting Standards Board** (GASB) issues authoritative standards on accounting and financial reporting by state and local governmental entities, including not-for-profit entities owned by or related to the government, such as state colleges and universities and public hospitals. Appointed and funded by the Financial Accounting Foundation, which also oversees the FASB, the GASB follows the same due process in establishing standards as the FASB. The GASB issues *Statements of Governmental Accounting Standards* (*SGAS*), *Statements of Governmental Accounting Concepts* (*SGAC*), *Interpretations*, and *Technical Bulletins*. Current accounting principles deemed authoritative by the GASB are organized into a publication entitled *Codification and Original Pronouncements*. The *Governmental Accounting Research System* (GARS Online) provides all standards and related literature in a searchable database. Similar to the FASB Codification, the *GASB Codification*, organized by topic, is available online.

The GASB does *not* establish GAAP for the *federal government*. Standards for federal government units are developed by the Office of Management and Budget (OMB), the Government Accountability Office (GAO), the Treasury Department, and the Federal Accounting Standards Advisory Board.

GAAP Hierarchy in Government Accounting

Although the GASB is *the* source of authoritative governmental accounting principles today, pronouncements of other standard-setting bodies and guidance of professional organizations remain relevant. Certain publications by the American Institute of Certified Public Accountants (AICPA) were embraced by the GASB in *SGAS 1*. The Government Finance Officers Association (GFOA) publishes a widely used source of nonauthoritative guidance: the GAAFR—*Governmental Accounting, Auditing and Financial Reporting*, also known as the "Blue Book." Moreover, the FASB has standards on issues not addressed by the GASB.

To advise governmental reporting entities of the authoritative ranking of accounting principles sources, *SGAS 55* establishes the following **GAAP hierarchy**.

Level 1   GASB *Statements* and *Interpretations*, including FASB and AICPA pronouncements adopted by the GASB.

Level 2   GASB *Technical Bulletins* and applicable AICPA *Industry Audit and Accounting Guides* and *Statements of Position* approved by the GASB.

Level 3   AICPA *Practice Bulletins* approved by the GASB and GASB Emerging Issues Task Force consensus positions.

Level 4   GASB *Implementation Guides* and practices commonly found in state and local government.

Level 5   Other accounting literature, such as GASB *Concepts Statements*, FASB pronouncements not specifically dealing with state and local governmental accounting, and accounting texts and articles.

A new GASB proposal, issued in 2014 and effective in 2015 if approved, changes the GAAP hierarchy to only two categories; Level 1: GASB *Statements*, and Level 2: GASB *Technical Bulletins, Implementation Guides*, and GASB-approved AICPA literature. The new standard would supersede *SGAS 55*.

OBJECTIVES OF FINANCIAL REPORTING

The GASB formalized the objectives of financial reporting by state and local governments in *SGAC 1*, Objectives of Financial Reporting. *SGAC 1* states that governmental financial reports should respond to the needs of the citizenry, their representatives (either elected or appointed members of oversight boards), and investors and creditors involved in the lending process. Paragraph 32 lists four specific **uses of financial reports** in making economic, social and political decisions, and in evaluating accountability:

> 1. Comparing actual financial results with the legally adopted budget.
> 2. Assessing financial condition and results of operations.
> 3. Determining compliance with finance-related laws, rules and regulations.
> 4. Evaluating efficiency and effectiveness. *(SGAC 1, para. 32)*

Note the stress on **accountability** in Items 1 and 3, in terms of fulfilling the budgetary plan and in complying with relevant laws, such as those specifying taxing and debt limits. Indeed, the GASB states that:

> Accountability is the cornerstone of all financial reporting in government . . . Accountability requires governments to answer to the citizenry—to justify the raising of public resources and the purposes for which they are to be used. *(SGAC 1, para. 56)*

Another key GASB concept is **interperiod equity**, a balanced budget notion stressing the need for users of governmental financial reports to "assess whether current-year revenues are sufficient to pay for the services provided that year and whether future taxpayers will be required to assume burdens for services previously provided." *(para. 60)*

Identifying the Reporting Entity

Financial information is to be presented for a **reporting entity**. For state or local governments, this entity could be a state, town, city, county, school district, water district, or fire protection district. Although a city or town may appear to be the reporting entity, additional legal entities often exist within a governmental unit or overlap it. For example, a school district may be a legally separate entity from the city or town in which it operates. A municipality may contain **special districts**—legally separate entities that provide a particular service such as sewers, sidewalks, street lighting, or fire protection to particular areas. Each entity likely has its own taxing authority, ability to issue debt, and other powers.

For state and local governments, the GASB concluded in *SGAS 14* that:

> The concept underlying the definition of the financial reporting entity is that elected officials are **accountable** to their constituents for their actions. *(para. 10)*

The financial statements should enable readers to assess the performance of elected officials, by including information on all activities for which these officials are accountable.

SGAS 14 defines the financial reporting entity as follows:

> The financial reporting entity consists of (a) the **primary government** and (b) its **component units**: organizations for which the primary government is **financially accountable**, and **other organizations** for which the nature and significance of their relationship with the primary government are such that exclusion would cause the reporting entity's financial statements to be misleading or incomplete. *(para. 12)*

The nucleus of a governmental financial reporting entity is the **primary government**, with a separate governing body elected by the citizenry. The primary government is a state government, municipality, township or county, or another entity such as a school district, if it satisfies all three conditions in paragraph 13 of *SGAS 14*.

1. It has a **separately elected** governing body.
2. It is **legally separate**.
3. It is **fiscally independent** of other state and local governments.

An organization is a **component unit** of a primary government when the primary government is financially accountable for it. According to *SGAS 14*, a primary government is financially accountable when it controls appointment of a voting majority of the organization's governing body and can **impose its will** on the organization's operations. Financial accountability also exists when the primary government can **derive financial benefits or financial obligations** from the organization.

Professional judgment is required to determine whether an organization is a component unit of a primary government. The decision is particularly difficult for financially independent *affiliated organizations* created to support the primary government's activities. *SGAS 39* provides additional guidance for these organizations. An **affiliated organization** is a component unit if it uses all or most of its resources to directly benefit the primary government or its component units, if the primary government has access to these resources, and the resources are significant to the primary government *(para. 5)*. A library foundation entirely benefitting and providing significant support to the library is a component unit of the library. A university alumni association that provides tuition and fee scholarships to students is a component unit of the university.

Presentation of Component Units   For financial reporting purposes, a component unit's information is either *blended* with that of the primary government, or *discretely presented* in the financial statements, depending on its relationship with the primary government. If the component unit's financial information is **blended** with the results of the primary government, it is not separately distinguishable. If a component unit's financial results are **discretely presented**, its results appear separately from the primary government, but are included in account totals.

Blended component units either have the same governing body as the primary government, or exist to provide services to the primary government *(SGAS 14, para. 53)*. Suppose a legally separate building authority issues tax-exempt bonds to finance a city's capital assets, and has a governing board appointed by the mayor, subject to city council approval. If the city funds the bond payments, the capital assets and the debt become the responsibility of the city, and the building authority is a blended component unit.

BUSINESS APPLICATION   **Reporting Entity for Mecklenburg County**

Mecklenburg County's CAFR reports the activities of its primary government, the county, and several component units. A county manager and elected Board of Commissioners govern the county. The county's three component units are all separate legal entities and discretely presented:

- The Public Library of Charlotte and Mecklenburg County is funded by general obligation bonds, for which the county is responsible. The county appoints six of the seven Library Board members.
- The Mecklenburg Emergency Medical Services Agency (Medic Agency) provides emergency medical services to county residents. Its Board consists of seven members; the county recommends one member, and health care agencies recommend the others. The county approves the Medic Agency's budget allocation.
- The Mecklenburg County Alcoholic Beverage Control Board (ABC Board) operates retail liquor stores in the county and investigates beverage control law violations. The county appoints its five-member Board. The ABC Board is obligated to distribute a portion of its resources to the county's general fund.

Discretely presented component units are relatively autonomous. Consider a public housing authority that provides subsidized housing. Its board is approved by the city council, but the city does not control the board's decisions. The board adopts its own budget, makes hiring decisions, sets rents, selects tenants, and issues bonds for which it is financially obligated. However, the city is obligated to provide significant funding as well. Because the city appoints the board and is a major source of funding, the housing authority is a discretely presented component unit.

SGAS 61 clarifies when an organization is a component unit and when it should be blended. Organizations are presented as component units when they are fiscally dependent on the primary government, and this relationship includes a financial benefit or burden. Component units are blended if they have the same governing body as the primary government, and have either a financial relationship with the primary government, or primary government management is operationally responsible for the component unit's activities.

FUND STRUCTURE

LO2 Identify the fund types and reporting methods for state and local governments.

A key aspect of accounting and reporting for state and local governments is the use of different reporting entities to account for resources subject to different restrictions. This structure often requires multiple journal entries to record a single transaction.

A typical governmental unit engages in most or all of the three types of activities discussed earlier in the chapter: *governmental*, *proprietary*, and *fiduciary*. Legislation and regulations often specify how resources are used. It may be stipulated that resources derived from local property taxes be spent in certain ways, resources derived from a bond issue in other ways, and resources received from federal programs in yet other ways. State and local government management is responsible for ensuring that resources are spent in the legally prescribed manner. This is the concept of **accountability** or **steward-ship**—the community entrusts management with resources, and management must carry out certain specified responsibilities with respect to their use.

Typical activities of a state or local government are:

Governmental activities:

- Collection of taxes, fees and fines
- Issuance of bonds and repayment of bond principal and interest
- Provision of primary services for which no user fees are collected, such as education, public safety, social and judicial services, administration
- Acquisition, construction, and disposition of long-lived assets, financed either by general resources, special assessments or long-term debt
- Special projects benefitting the public, funded by grants or other restricted resources

Proprietary activities:

- Provision of goods and services for which a cost-based fee is collected from the public, such as utilities, public transportation, parking facilities, recreational facilities, hospitals and colleges
- Provision of goods and services to other governmental units at cost by a central motor pool, central supplies activity, or similar activity

Fiduciary activities:

- Financial resources held in trust for others, such as public employee pensions
- Financial resources collected for and eventually disbursed to another governmental unit, such as state sales taxes collected by the county

Because of the need to adhere to legal requirements affecting the source and use of resources, and the large number and diversity of governmental activities, the financial reporting system of a single governmental entity is organized into several accounting entities, called *funds*.

> A **fund** is defined as a fiscal and accounting entity with a self-balancing set of accounts recording cash and other financial resources, together with all related liabilities and residual equities or balances, and changes therein, which are segregated for the purpose of carrying on specific activities or attaining certain objectives in accordance with special regulations, restrictions, or limitations. *(GASB, Codification, Section 1100.102)*

Instead of a single entity with one set of books, a typical government contains several entities, or funds, that have their own sets of books and issue financial statements. For external reporting purposes, however, the government presents financial statements on both a *fund basis*, and a *government-wide basis* that combines the activities of the various funds. Chapter 12 examines the external reporting requirements for state and local governments.

As **accounting segregations of financial resources**, funds become accountable for and exercise stewardship over resources. **Fund equity** measures the difference between a fund's assets and liabilities. Portions of fund equity are often designated for particular purposes. Total fund equity therefore consists of (1) an *unassigned portion*, indicating financial resources available for general spending, and (2) one or more *designated portions*, signifying amounts not available for expenditure or legally segregated for specific future uses.

An important focus of governmental financial reporting is demonstrating fiscal compliance. Operating statements report on whether financial resources received during a period cover expenditures, and whether spending complies with approved budgets. Division of resources into funds dedicated to spending for particular purposes is a control technique. Each fund keeps track of the flows of financial resources restricted to its specific activities. Financial reporting on fund activities reveals whether financial resources used complied with restrictions imposed by law or by third parties.

Fund Types

The financial affairs of a government are organized into groups of funds used for the various activities of a government. Individual funds belong to one of the following groups:

- **Governmental funds** account for most traditional governmental functions, and report on resources available to finance activities benefitting the government or its citizens.
- **Proprietary funds** account for a government's ongoing businesslike activities similar to those found in the private sector, where fees are charged for goods provided or services performed.
- **Fiduciary funds** account for resources held by the governmental unit in a trustee or agency capacity on behalf of individuals or other organizations outside the governmental unit, and which cannot be used to support the government or its programs.

A typical city government uses many or all of these fund types to account for its resources and activities, as described below.

Governmental Funds

General fund—Accounts for the basic services provided by city government, financed by general revenue, that are not required to be accounted for in another fund.

 a.   Resources come from property taxes, sales taxes, general state aid, fees, fines, and other general revenues.

 b.   Resources are used for city administration, police, fire protection, courts, streets, parks, sanitation, and other general services.

Special revenue funds—Account for specified activities of the city that benefit the public using revenue legally restricted to those activities.

 a.   Resources come from state or federal aid for specific purposes (for example, resources from federal programs used in public safety activities), taxes levied for certain purposes, grants, and public-purpose trusts. All resources are expendable.

 b.   Resources are used for the particular operations specified by the revenue source.

Capital projects funds—Account for the construction or acquisition of major capital assets used for governmental activities, including those financed by special assessments on property owners.

 a.   Resources come primarily from proceeds of bond issues. Other sources include state or federal aid, allocation of general fund revenues, or special tax assessments on property owners.

 b.   Resources are used for construction or acquisition of buildings, major equipment, and public improvements—commonly known as **infrastructure**—such as roads, bridges, and sewer systems.

Debt service funds—Account for the accumulation and payment of resources for principal and interest on the general long-term debt of the city.

 a.   Resources come from transfers from other funds, such as the general fund or the capital projects fund, from certain special assessment levies and from interest earned on investments.

 b.   Resources are used for payment of interest and principal; in some cases, resources are accumulated and invested to provide for future debt service payments.

Permanent funds—Account for activities and resources that are legally restricted—perhaps by trust agreement—to the expenditure of earnings for a specific purpose, with the principal remaining intact. *The specific purpose must benefit the government or its citizens*. Examples include a library fund that provides resources for the acquisition of public library materials, and a park fund that consists of resources held in trust for the maintenance of city parks.

 a.   Resources are derived from trusts or other legal agreements set up by individuals or private organizations. In contrast to special revenue funds, only the earnings may be used.

 b.   Resources are used for the particular activities specified by the trust agreement.

Proprietary Funds

Enterprise funds—Account for business-type activities, such as a city water department or a municipal golf course, that sell goods or services on a continuing basis to the public.

    a. Resources come from amounts charged to customers on a cost recovery basis, and from financing sources.

    b. Resources are used for the activity's operating expenses, capital expenditures and financing payments.

Internal service funds—Account for central services provided to other departments of the city on a cost-reimbursement basis; for example, a central supply unit that buys supplies in large quantities for distribution to various departments, or a central vehicle maintenance shop.

    a. Resources come from charges to and support from other city departments.

    b. Resources are used for operating expenses, capital expenditures and financing payments.

Fiduciary Funds

Pension trust funds—Account for resources held in trust for individuals enrolled in pension plans or other employee benefit plans.

    a. Resources come from employer and plan participant contributions, and investment income.

    b. Resources are used for pension benefits and administrative costs.

Investment trust funds—Account for the net assets of investors outside the governmental reporting entity, typically other governments, held in governmental investment pools.

    a. Resources come from investments and investment income.

    b. Resources are used for administrative costs, investment losses, and payments to investors.

Private-purpose trust funds—Account for the activities of all other trust agreements that benefit individuals, private organizations, or other governments, such as a fund holding resources from abandoned bank accounts and undeliverable amounts owed to individuals.

    a. Resources come from assets held in trust and from income on investment of assets.

    b. Resources are used for activities specified by the trust agreement, and for administrative costs and distributions.

Agency funds—Account for resources collected for and remitted to individuals, private organizations, or other governments, where the collecting government acts in a custodial capacity only. For example, a county may collect taxes for the school district.

    a. Resources come from collections on behalf of other entities, such as income taxes withheld from employees and certain special assessment levies.

    b. Resources are used for transmittal of amounts collected to other entities and for service of certain special assessment bond issues using collections from property owners.

    A comparison of the fund types with the activities of a state or local government reveals that these funds encompass all the activities of those governments. Although **a government always has one and only one general fund**, none, one, or several of each of the other fund types may exist. If a city has no construction projects underway, there are no capital projects funds. If three projects are currently under construction, the city may use three capital projects funds or combine all three projects in one capital projects fund.

REVIEW 1 • Identifying Funds

Required For each of the following transactions of a county government, identify which fund(s) is affected.

    a. Construction begins on a new double-span bridge across the river that bisects the county, and $200,000 is paid to contractors.

> *b.* The county collects sales taxes to be remitted to the state.
> *c.* The municipal swimming pool collects $40,000 in user fees.
> *d.* A new snowplow is purchased for road maintenance. The snowplow is expected to last 15 years.
> *e.* General tax revenues are collected from taxpayers. Some of these revenues are set aside for future payment of general obligation debt principal.
> *f.* Principal and interest on general obligation debt is paid.
> *g.* The municipal swimming pool purchases a new cover for its baby pool. The cover is expected to last 8 years.
> *h.* A state grant, legally restricted to the development of a new preschool program, is received in cash.
> *i.* An endowment is received in cash from a wealthy citizen. The principal of the endowment is not expendable, and income on the principal must be used to landscape one of the county parks.
>
> **Solutions are located after the chapter assignments.**

ACCOUNTING AND REPORTING BY FUNDS

We now consider the general accounting principles applicable to the fund entities discussed, and introduce the typical fund financial statements issued by the reporting government.

Accounting for Governmental Funds

Governmental funds—**general fund, special revenue funds, capital projects funds, debt service funds, and permanent funds**—use the *modified accrual basis* of accounting. The measurement focus is on accountability for the flow of financial resources. The GASB defines the flow of resources as **the flow of current financial resources**—cash, receivables, prepaid items, consumable goods such as supplies, and related current liabilities. Any transaction affecting current financial resources appears on the operating statement of a governmental fund. This statement is called the **Statement of Revenues, Expenditures, and Changes in Fund Balances**. Fund equity on the balance sheet of a governmental fund is called **fund balance**.

The **modified accrual basis of accounting** reflects the following reporting principles:

- **Revenues** are defined as *inflows of current financial resources*. Revenues are recognized when they are **measurable** and **available to finance expenditures of the current period**. Property taxes and intergovernmental grants are accrued as receivables and revenue before the cash is collected, if the uncollectible portion can be reasonably estimated, and amounts collected are expected to be available to liquidate current period obligations.

- Borrowings, and receipts of current financial resources from the sale of long-lived assets, are shown on the Statement of Revenues, Expenditures and Changes in Fund Balances, as **other financing sources**. Resources received from long-term borrowings are *not* shown as liabilities in the fund statements. Receipts from the sale of long-lived assets are reported in total without recognizing gain or loss.

- **Expenditures** are defined as *outflows of current financial resources*, and can be significantly different from full accrual expenses.

  ○ Payments of current financial resources for long-lived assets are treated as expenditures. Governmental funds do not capitalize long-lived assets or recognize depreciation.

  ○ Payments of current financial resources for long-term debt principal or interest are expenditures. Long-term debt does *not* appear as a liability and no liability is reduced when principal payments are made.

- Interest on long-term debt is accrued only in the period when it is expected to be paid.

- An excess of revenues over expenditures may reduce the taxes levied next year. Expenditures in excess of revenues burden taxpayers or reduce services in future years.

- **Interfund transactions** occur when governmental units engage in transactions between funds. These include, but are not limited to, **loans** and **transfers**. The general fund may loan money to the special revenue fund, with repayment expected within a few months. Or the general fund may transfer resources to an internal service fund to finance its expenditures. The balance sheet reports interfund loans as receivables and payables, typically labeled "due from" or "due to" a specific fund. Interfund transfers appear in the Statement of Revenues, Expenditures, and Changes in Fund Balances, as **other financing sources or uses**.

Fund statements for governmental funds are the **Statement of Revenues, Expenditures and Changes in Fund Balances**, the **Balance Sheet**, and the **Budgetary Comparison Schedule**, which compares budgeted and actual revenues, expenditures and other changes in fund balances for the general fund and any other fund that has a legally adopted budget.

Accounting for Proprietary Funds

For the proprietary funds—**enterprise and internal service funds**—the business concepts of revenue recognition and matching of expenses against revenues are appropriate, as these funds' operations are similar to those of private sector businesses. It is important to know the costs of services, because the fees charged to users—whether citizens or other departments within the government—are expected to cover those costs. Therefore, *full accrual accounting* is used.

Revenues are recognized when earned and measurable, and expenses are matched with revenues as product costs or recognized with the passage of time as period costs. Outlays for buildings and equipment are capitalized as assets and depreciated over their useful lives. Amounts borrowed through loans or bond issues are shown as liabilities and interest expense is accrued as owed.

Proprietary fund statements are the **Statement of Net Position**, the **Statement of Revenues, Expenses and Changes in Net Position**, and the **Statement of Cash Flows**. Revenues and expenses are classified as operating or nonoperating items. Fund net position on the balance sheet consists of three components: **net investment in capital assets**, **restricted**, and **unrestricted**.

Accounting for Fiduciary Funds

Fiduciary funds—**pension trust funds, investment trust funds, private-purpose trust funds, and agency funds**—account for governmental activities where resources are held in a trust or agency capacity for individuals or organizations outside the reporting government.

The *full accrual basis of accounting* is used to account for the activities of fiduciary funds. For example, *SGAS 45* requires full accrual of postemployment benefits. Agency funds accumulate resources held for disbursement to other entities. Assets are the resources accumulated in an agency capacity, and liabilities are the amounts owed to individuals or organizations. Agency fund assets equal liabilities. Standard financial statements for fiduciary funds are the **Statement of Fiduciary Net Position** and the **Statement of Changes in Fiduciary Net Position**. Agency funds do not report a net position and do not prepare a Statement of Changes in Fiduciary Net Position.

ACCOUNTING FOR THE GENERAL FUND

The general fund accounts for the government's routine operating activities. This section explains accounting procedures for the major activities of the general fund that are reported using the *modified accrual basis* of accounting.

The 2013 general fund balance sheet and statement of revenues, expenditures, and changes in fund balances for Mecklenburg County, appearing in Exhibits 10.1 and 10.2, illustrate the format of general fund financial statements. Because the general fund uses the modified accrual basis of reporting, its balance sheet has no long-term assets or liabilities. Assets include cash and investments, accounts receivable—mostly accrued state and federal aid—and taxes receivable. Liabilities include current payables and liabilities to be paid from restricted assets.

SGAS 65 classifies certain items previously reported as assets and liabilities as deferred outflows of resources and deferred inflows of resources. Deferred outflows of resources are roughly comparable to prepaid expenses in corporate accounting, while deferred inflows of resources are typically known as deferred revenues in businesses. Mecklenburg County's balance sheet shows $44,045,484 of deferred inflows of resources, which are taxes collected in advance of the fiscal year in which they are available to spend.

LO3 Prepare entries and financial statements for the general fund.

EXHIBIT 10.1 Mecklenburg County Balance Sheet—General Fund	

MECKLENBURG COUNTY, NORTH CAROLINA
General Fund Balance Sheet
June 30, 2013

Assets	
Cash and investments	$477,888,397
Interest receivable	972,931
Accounts receivable	62,763,320
Prepaid expenses	42,485
Accounts receivable—clinics	569,850
Less allowance for uncollectible claims	(558,451)
Taxes receivable	70,045,484
Less allowance for uncollectible taxes	(26,000,000)
Advances to other governmental agencies	735,973
Total assets	$586,459,989
Liabilities, deferred inflows of resources, and fund balances	
Liabilities	
Accounts payable and accrued liabilities	$ 72,160,124
Liabilities to be paid from restricted assets	2,015,079
Total liabilities	74,175,203
Deferred inflows of resources	44,045,484
Fund balances	
Restricted	
Stabilization by state statute	84,949,362
Health and human services	24,144
Committed	
Land use and environmental services	8,432,768
Detention and court support services	1,177,912
Administrative services	190,000
Capital reserves	19,000,000
Unassigned	354,465,116
Total fund balances	468,239,302
Total liabilities, deferred inflows of resources, and fund balances	$586,459,989

Fund balance is calculated as assets and deferred outflows of resources, less liabilities and deferred inflows of resources, and represents net resources available to spend. Mecklenburg County's general fund balance sheet illustrates that fund balance is divided among restricted, committed, and unassigned categories, separating the portion of fund balance set aside for specific purposes. *SGAS 54* requires five standard categories of fund balance, as follows:

- **Nonspendable** fund balance indicates amounts, such as inventories, that are not spendable.
- **Restricted** fund balance reports amounts that can only be spent consistent with stipulations of external resource providers.
- **Committed** fund balance reports amounts that can only be spent for purposes stipulated by formal action of the government's highest level of decision-making authority.
- **Assigned** fund balance indicates amounts intended to be used in specific ways. For funds other than the general fund, assigned fund balance is that portion of the fund balance available to that fund, and is not nonspendable, restricted or committed.
- **Unassigned** fund balance equals the portion of the *general fund's* fund balance that is not non-spendable, restricted, committed or assigned.

We discuss these fund balance categories in more detail in Chapters 11 and 12, and use these standard categories throughout Chapters 10–12.

The county's general fund operating statement displays revenues and expenditures, and other financing sources and uses. Most of Mecklenburg County's general fund revenues come from taxes. The largest

EXHIBIT 10.2 Mecklenburg County Operating Statement—General Fund		

MECKLENBURG COUNTY, NORTH CAROLINA
Statement of Revenues, Expenditures, and Changes in Fund Balances
General Fund
For Year Ended June 30, 2013

Revenues		
Taxes	$	822,443,026
Licenses and permits		20,886,622
Intergovernmental		150,599,921
Charges for services		61,994,383
Interest earned on investments		(4,743,835)
Administrative charges		2,544,040
Other		8,124,008
Total revenues		$1,061,848,165
Expenditures		
Current		
Customer satisfaction and management		13,587,103
Administrative services		72,332,559
Financial services		17,336,544
Land use and environmental services		42,141,451
Community services		61,255,426
Detention and court support services		133,529,202
Health and human services		252,497,144
Business partners		389,994,359
Total expenditures		982,673,788
Excess (deficiency) of revenues over (under) expenditures		79,174,377
Other financing sources (uses)		
Transfers in		754,400
Transfers out		(70,446,933)
Total other financing sources (uses)		(69,692,533)
Net change in fund balances		9,481,844
Fund balances—beginning of year		458,757,458
Fund balances—end of year	$	468,239,302

expenditure line is Business Partners, which include the Charlotte-Mecklenburg Schools, Central Piedmont Community College, and the Mecklenburg Emergency Medical Services Agency. The county also reports large general fund expenditures for Health and Human Services, and Detention and Court Support Services. All items reported on the general fund operating statement represent inflows and outflows of current financial resources and are closed to fund balance at year-end.

Budgetary Accounts

Accounting serves an important control function in state and local government, helping to ensure that resources are spent in compliance with legal requirements. Legal restrictions on spending are usually expressed in the form of a **budget** that prescribes both the total amount of spending allowed and the amounts in each expense category. A budget may be adopted by legislative/executive action or by popular vote, as in many school districts. Typically, any change in the total budget must be approved in the same way, whereas changes within the budget—transfers among budget components—usually require less formal approval. For example, a school board may approve budget transfers without voter approval.

At the beginning of the year, the general fund's budgeted revenues and budgeted expenditures are entered in **budgetary accounts** to aid in controlling revenues and expenditures. As actual revenues come in and resources are spent during the year, management compares these amounts with the budget to help ensure that, in each category of the budget, actual spending does not exceed the authorized amount. Recording budget data in the accounts is a key aspect of accounting for funds with legal budgets, and a major difference between governmental accounting and business accounting. In business, the budget is a managerial plan; in government, it is a legal constraint. The budget establishes legal spending limits that must not be exceeded.

Budget Entry A budget has two elements: budgeted revenues and budgeted expenditures. In state and local government, **Estimated Revenues** accounts for the former and **Appropriations** accounts for the latter. The budget entry debits Estimated Revenues because it represents the expected inflow of resources to the fund, roughly analogous to receivables. Similarly, the budget entry credits Appropriations because it represents the expected outflow of resources from the fund, roughly analogous to payables.

Some general fund inflows, such as proceeds from bond issues and sale of capital assets, and transfers in from other funds, are reported not as revenues, but as **other financing sources**. Similarly, some general fund outflows, such as transfers to other funds, are reported not as expenditures, but as **other financing uses**. The budget entry reports the budgeted amounts for these expected inflows and outflows as **Estimated Other Financing Sources and Uses**.

To illustrate, suppose that for 2017 Mecklenburg County budgets expenditures of $1,500,000,000 and other financing uses of $50,000,000. It budgets revenues of $1,520,000,000 and other financing sources of $30,000,000. Since budgeted outflows equal budgeted inflows, the budget is **balanced**. The budget entry is:

Estimated revenues	1,520,000,000	
Estimated other financing sources	30,000,000	
Appropriations		1,500,000,000
Estimated other financing uses		50,000,000
To record the 2017 (balanced) budget.		

The budget need not be balanced in a particular fiscal period. When a government plans to spend less than its anticipated revenue, the budget entry credits the unassigned fund balance.

Suppose Mecklenburg County expects revenues of $1,530,000,000, and all other budgeted amounts are as indicated above. Now the general fund plans to spend less than it receives and the budget entry increases its unassigned fund balance by $10,000,000.

Estimated revenues	1,530,000,000	
Estimated other financing sources	30,000,000	
Appropriations		1,500,000,000
Estimated other financing uses		50,000,000
Fund balance—unassigned		10,000,000
To record the 2017 (surplus) budget.		

Alternatively, suppose Mecklenburg County plans to spend more than its anticipated revenue, using resources accumulated in previous periods. If expected revenues are only $1,505,000,000, and all other budgeted amounts are as originally stated, the budget entry decreases its unassigned fund balance.

Estimated revenues	1,505,000,000	
Estimated other financing sources	30,000,000	
Fund balance—unassigned	15,000,000	
Appropriations		1,500,000,000
Estimated other financing uses		50,000,000
To record the 2017 (deficit) budget.		

After recording the budget, the unassigned fund balance account shows the **expected year-end balance**. In the last entry, showing total budgeted inflows of $1,535,000,000 and total budgeted outflows of $1,550,000,000, assume that the beginning fund balance was $105,000,000. After recording the budget, the fund balance is $90,000,000 (= $105,000,000 − $15,000,000). If the budgeted amounts are achieved, the actual year-end fund balance will also be $90,000,000.

Recording Property Tax Revenue

The modified accrual basis is used to account for property tax revenue. Because the government levies specific property tax amounts, the amount of revenue to be collected can be estimated with a reasonable degree of accuracy, and the probability of collection on a timely basis is very high. Thus, the government records property taxes as revenue when the taxes are levied, as long as the tax revenue is to be used in the same period that it is levied. Under the modified accrual basis, revenue is recognized in the period when the taxes are *available to be used*. "Available" means either collected during the period or expected to be collected soon enough after the period ends so that the revenues can be used to pay liabilities incurred during the period.

When taxes levied in 2016 are expected to be collected and used in 2016, they are reported as property tax revenue on the date levied. However, if taxes levied in 2016 are for use in 2017, the government reports the levied amount as **deferred inflows of resources** until 2017, when the money becomes available to spend. Mecklenburg County's June 30, 2013, general fund balance sheet in Exhibit 10.1 reports deferred inflows of resources of $44,045,484, representing taxes collected in fiscal 2013 for use in fiscal 2014.

The amount recorded as revenue is the gross amount of the tax levy, less an appropriate allowance for uncollectibles. Even though the gross amount of the levy is recorded as Taxes Receivable, the amount credited to revenues is the **net** amount the government expects to collect. This amount reflects the financial resources expected to be available for expenditure during the current period. Note the difference from business accounting that records gross revenue and accounts for bad debt expense separately. Because modified accrual accounting treats expenditures as outflows of current financial resources, bad debt "expense" is not an expenditure.

After a period of time, often by the end of the fiscal period, any uncollected taxes become delinquent. These taxes receivable should be reclassified to a Taxes Receivable—Delinquent account with a corresponding Allowance for Uncollectible Taxes—Delinquent. An adjusting entry sets the allowance equal to the amount expected to be uncollectible.

Suppose that Mecklenburg County levies a property tax of $950,000,000 that is expected to be 95 percent collectible. We first record the property tax levy:

Taxes receivable—current	950,000,000	
Allowance for uncollectible taxes—current.		47,500,000
Tax revenues		902,500,000
To record tax levy.		

Subsequent collection of $900,000,000 and declaration of uncollected amounts as delinquent are recorded as follows:

Cash	900,000,000	
Taxes receivable—current		900,000,000
To record collection of property taxes.		
Taxes receivable—delinquent	50,000,000	
Taxes receivable—current		50,000,000
To reclassify unpaid taxes as delinquent.		

The modified accrual basis provides that assessed but uncollected tax revenues be reported in the current year when they are measurable and expected to be collected early enough in the next year to be used to pay the current year's liabilities. The time limit for recognition of uncollected taxes as revenue is expected collection *60 days after the end of the year*. Suppose Mecklenburg County estimates at year-end that $15,000,000 of the $50,000,000 in uncollected taxes will be collected within 60 days. Tax revenues are therefore $915,000,000 (= $900,000,000 collected in cash and $15,000,000 expected to be collected within 60 days), and the allowance balance is $35,000,000. The following entry reclassifies the original allowance and adjusts the accounts accordingly:

Allowance for uncollectible taxes—current	47,500,000	
Tax revenues		12,500,000
Allowance for uncollectible taxes—delinquent		35,000,000
To recognize additional tax revenues, reclassify allowance for uncollectible taxes and reduce it to $35,000,000.		

In the next year, suppose Mecklenburg County collects $20,000,000 of the delinquent taxes and writes off the remainder. These entries record this activity:

Cash	20,000,000	
Taxes receivable—delinquent		20,000,000
To record collection of delinquent taxes.		
Allowance for uncollectible taxes—delinquent	35,000,000	
Taxes receivable—delinquent		30,000,000
Tax revenues		5,000,000
To write off uncollected delinquent taxes.		

The county records tax revenues of $5,000,000 related to last year's property taxes, because $5,000,000 more was collected than was estimated at the end of last year.

Following the modified accrual basis, if year-end uncollected taxes will be collected more than 60 days after the end of the fiscal year, they are not considered revenue of the current period, but are reported as Unavailable Revenues—Property Taxes, a deferred inflow of resources. Continuing the example above, suppose at year-end Mecklenburg County determines that of the $15,000,000 in collectible assessed taxes, $14,000,000 will be collected within 60 days and $1,000,000 will be collected more than 60 days later. It makes the following adjusting entry at year-end:

Allowance for uncollectible taxes—current	47,500,000	
Tax revenues		11,500,000
Unavailable revenues—property taxes (deferred inflows)		1,000,000
Allowance for uncollectible taxes—delinquent		35,000,000
To recognize additional tax revenues and unavailable revenues, reclassify the allowance for uncollectible taxes and reduce it to $35,000,000.		

In this case, tax revenues for the year are $914,000,000 (= $900,000,000 collected in cash + $14,000,000 expected to be collected early next year and available to pay this year's obligations). When the $1,000,000 is collected the following year, an adjusting entry reclassifies Unavailable Revenues—Property Taxes as revenues of the period in which they are collected.

After additional time passes, delinquent taxes become **tax liens**—legal claims against the taxed property—which may be satisfied by forcing sale of the property. The delinquent taxes are reclassified to a tax liens receivable account, with a corresponding allowance for uncollectibles. It is common practice to "fully reserve" tax liens by setting up an allowance equal to the amount of the receivable.

Purchase of Goods and Services

Acquisition of goods and services by a government typically involves three steps: (1) issuance of a purchase order or contract, (2) receipt of the goods or services, and (3) payment. In business accounting, only steps (2) and (3) are formally recorded in the accounting records. Unlike a business, a governmental unit has legal limits on its spending authority. Because of these legal restrictions, it is important to know not only the amount actually spent to date and the amount of unpaid bills, but also the amount of outstanding spending commitments. If no formal record is kept of purchase orders, the danger exists that the government will overcommit itself and exceed the legal spending authority. To aid in the control of expenditures, spending commitments, known as **encumbrances**, are recorded in the accounts.

Most counties receive significant funding from property taxes, based on the assessed valuation of property. Commonly, the property upon which taxes are based consists of real estate, such as vacant land, homes and business establishments. Mecklenburg County, however, also assesses property taxes on registered motor vehicles, boats, trailers, and income-producing personal property. In 2013, the total fair value of assessed property was $113,937 million and the total amount needed to be collected (the tax levy) was $902 million, resulting in a tax rate of $0.792 per $100 of assessed valuation [= ($902 million/$113,937 million) × $100]. For purposes of property tax assessment, the market value of real property in Mecklenburg County is updated (reassessed) every four years. In the reassessment year, the tax rate drops when the market value of assessed property increases. The tax rate then often increases during the years between reassessments, as the budget typically increases faster than the dollar value of assessed property. In Mecklenburg County, a reassessment occurred in 2011; however, due to economic changes impacting county residents, the county chose not to increase the tax rate from 2009–2011, and decreased it in 2012.

Recording Purchase Orders   Accounting for issuance of a purchase order requires the following:

- A debit to *Encumbrances* representing the charge against the fund's limited spending authority; encumbrances become expenditures when the goods or services ordered are delivered.

- A credit to *Fund Balance—Assigned* signifying restriction of a portion of the fund balance for the items ordered: these financial resources are set aside for a specific future use. The fund balance category used for encumbrances can be restricted, committed or assigned, depending on who authorized the expenditure. In this chapter, we assume outstanding encumbrances are appropriately reported in *Fund Balance—Assigned*.

Recording encumbrances does not create liabilities because the goods and services have not been delivered. Encumbrance entries are temporary, and are reversed when the goods or services are delivered.

Assume Mecklenburg County places an order for repair services on March 18, at an expected cost of $1,850,000. To formally record this commitment, an encumbrance entry is made on March 18, signifying that $1,850,000 of the repair services budget is no longer available for other purposes.

Encumbrances	1,850,000	
Fund balance—assigned		1,850,000
To record purchase order for repair services.		

Suppose that the repair services budget is $4,200,000 and that $800,000 was previously spent. Recording the $1,850,000 encumbrance tells county management that only $1,550,000 of the repair services budget remains available for use during the current period. This balance is often referred to as **available funds**.

Appropriations for repair services	$4,200,000
Expended to date	(800,000)
Unexpended balance	3,400,000
March 18 purchase order	(1,850,000)
Available funds	$1,550,000

Recording Receipt of Goods and Services   When the government receives goods or services and acknowledges liability for payment, it records *expenditures,* following the modified accrual approach. If an encumbrance was previously recorded, we reverse the amount originally encumbered, indicating that the purchase order is no longer outstanding, and then record the expenditure.

Recall that *expenditures* in modified accrual accounting signify *outflows of current financial resources*, unlike the recognition of *expenses* in business accounting, which measure consumption of resources in the process of earning revenue. To illustrate the difference, modified accrual accounting records an expenditure when financial resources are used to acquire office equipment; periodic depreciation expense is not recorded. Business accounting requires capitalization of resources used to acquire the office equipment, and recognizes consumption of that equipment over time through periodic depreciation expense.

Continuing our example, assume that by April 3 the repair services ordered on March 18 are received, accompanied by an invoice for $1,865,000. The two journal entries (1) reverse the previously recorded encumbrance, and (2) record the expenditure.

Fund balance—assigned	1,850,000	
Encumbrances		1,850,000
To reverse encumbrance entry.		
Expenditures	1,865,000	
Accounts payable		1,865,000
To record cost of repair services.		

The amount of the encumbrance and the amount of the expenditure need not be equal because the purchase order reflected an estimated cost of the goods or services. The reversing entry removes the *amount previously encumbered*, $1,850,000, and the expenditure entry records the *actual* cost of $1,865,000.

Supplies Inventories

The two acceptable methods of accounting for supplies inventories in the general fund and other governmental funds are the *consumption method*, which treats inventories as expenditures when *used*, and the *purchases method*, which treats them as expenditures when *purchased*.

The **consumption method** treats inventories as a financial resource, available to provide public service when "spent" or consumed, similar to cash. This method debits inventory when supplies are purchased, and debits expenditures when supplies are used, as in business accounting. Suppose that Mecklenburg County acquires supplies costing $21,000,000 during the year. The encumbrances recorded when the supplies were ordered are reversed upon delivery. Receipt of the supplies is recorded as follows:

Supplies inventory	21,000,000	
Accounts payable		21,000,000
To record purchase of supplies under the consumption method.		

If supplies costing $17,700,000 were consumed during the year, this entry summarizes the year's expenditures for the supplies consumed:

Expenditures	17,700,000	
Supplies inventory		17,700,000
To record supplies used under the consumption method.		

Recall that expenditures are closed at year-end, reducing unassigned fund balance. Because expenditures only include $17,700,000 in supplies used, an additional year-end adjusting entry signifies that $3,300,000 of fund balance is in the form of nonspendable inventories:

Fund balance—unassigned	3,300,000	
Fund balance—nonspendable		3,300,000
To adjust nonspendable fund balance for change in supplies inventory balance.		

In subsequent years, an adjusting entry records *changes* in the amount of supplies on hand at year-end. Suppose that in the following year, supplies are acquired for $24,000,000 and supplies costing $24,500,000 are consumed, reducing the supplies inventory to $2,800,000. Mecklenburg County records expenditures of $24,500,000 during the year, and at year-end the following adjusting entry reduces the nonspendable fund balance to $2,800,000.

Fund balance—nonspendable	500,000	
Fund balance—unassigned		500,000
To adjust nonspendable fund balance for change in supplies inventory balance.		

Under the **purchases method**, the cost of materials, supplies and other prepayments is charged to expenditures as the items are purchased. The method reflects the use of financial resources when these items are purchased, regardless of whether the materials or supplies are currently consumed. The purchases method itself recognizes no inventories of materials and supplies in the accounts. But when significant physical levels of inventory remain at year-end, this inventory must be reported on the balance sheet, increasing total fund balance by adding a nonspendable account.

To illustrate the *purchases method*, the supplies acquired at a cost of $21,000,000 in the previous example are recorded as expenditures when delivered:

Expenditures	21,000,000	
Accounts payable		21,000,000
To record purchase of supplies under the purchases method.		

The following year-end entry reports the supplies of $3,300,000 remaining in inventory:

Supplies inventory	3,300,000	
Fund balance—nonspendable		3,300,000
To record inventory of supplies at year-end under the purchases method.		

In subsequent years, changes in the amount of supplies on hand are recognized by making or reversing the above entry to record the changes. Using the same information as above for subsequent year supplies acquisition and consumption, Mecklenburg County records expenditures of $24,000,000 during the year for the supplies purchased, and at year-end the following adjusting entry reduces the inventory balance and the nonspendable fund balance to $2,800,000.

Fund balance—nonspendable	500,000	
Supplies inventory		500,000
To adjust inventory to current year-end balance of $2,800,000 under the *purchases method.*		

The **consumption method** follows regular business accounting—inventory is an asset when purchased and an expenditure when consumed. Since modified accrual accounting defines expenditures as *outflows of current financial resources*—cash, receivables and payables—under the consumption method inventories must be defined as current financial resources. Accordingly, purchase of inventories does not involve outflows of net current financial resources—instead, we exchange one current financial resource for another. Under the **purchases method**, current financial resources do **not** include inventories. Purchases of inventory are therefore a use of current financial resources and are recorded as expenditures.

Either the consumption or purchases method can currently be used in a governmental unit's external financial statements. However, the purchases method is typically used in general fund reporting because it is more consistent with modified accrual accounting.

Interfund Transactions

Transactions among funds—**interfund transactions**—are common in state and local government. These transactions are of two general types: loans and advances, and transfers.

Loans and Advances **Loans and advances** are temporary transfers from one fund to another, with authorization by statute or ordinance often required and repayment expected. These transfers are recorded as receivables or payables by the funds involved, with special account titles: *Due from Fund* and *Due to Fund*. Suppose a federal grant is awarded to a city to support a project to be accounted for in a special revenue fund. To cover project costs incurred prior to the actual receipt of the grant, the city might advance $800,000 from the general fund to the special revenue fund. This transaction is recorded in the *general fund* as follows:

Books of General Fund

Due from special revenue fund	800,000	
Cash		800,000
To record advance to special revenue fund.		

A parallel entry is required on the books of the *special revenue fund*:

Books of Special Revenue Fund

Cash	800,000	
Due to general fund		800,000
To record advance from general fund.		

Repayment of the advance triggers opposite entries by the general and special revenue funds.

Transfers   **Transfers** involve legally authorized payments of resources from the fund receiving the revenues (frequently the general fund) to the fund that will make the expenditures. Transfers may be recurring or capital contributions of a permanent equity nature. Transfers are reported in the statement of revenues, expenditures, and changes in fund balances as **other financing sources (uses)**. A proprietary fund reports an incoming permanent equity transfer in its statement of revenues, expenses and changes in net position as a capital contribution, shown as a separate item below nonoperating revenues and expenses. Examples of transfers include:

- Principal and interest payments on long-term debt originally issued by the general or capital projects funds are commonly made using general fund resources. Money is transferred from the general fund (*transfer out*) to the debt service fund (*transfer in*) that makes the debt-related expenditures.

- When a business activity such as the water department is partially subsidized by general fund resources, the general fund records a *transfer out*. The water department enterprise fund records receipt of the resources as a *transfer in*.

- A construction project is financed in part by a bond issue and in part by general fund resources transferred (*transfer out*) to the capital projects fund (*transfer in*).

- A city establishes an internal service fund and transfers general fund resources (*transfer out*) to provide the initial capital of the internal service fund (*capital contribution*).

- A construction project funded by a bond issue is completed and the related capital projects fund is closed. Cash remaining in the terminated capital projects fund is transferred (*transfer out*) to the debt service fund (*transfer in*).

Capital Assets and Long-Term Debt

Like all governmental funds, the general fund uses the modified accrual basis of accounting to report its transactions. A major difference between the modified accrual basis and business accounting is in the treatment of capital assets and long-term debt. Because the modified accrual basis emphasizes the *flow of current financial resources*, the balance sheet of the general fund reports unexpended financial assets and financial liabilities to be paid during the reporting period, but does *not* report capital assets or long-term debt. Capital assets cannot be expended, and long-term debt due beyond the current year does not require the use of current financial resources.

Accounting for Capital Assets   When acquiring a capital asset with general fund resources, the general fund reports the cost of the asset as an *expenditure*. Purchased and self-constructed assets are recorded at acquisition cost. If Mecklenburg County's general fund purchases highway equipment costing $4,000,000, this entry is made:

Capital outlay	4,000,000	
Accounts payable or cash.		4,000,000
To record the purchase of highway equipment.		

Capital outlay is reported as one of the *expenditures* in the statement of revenues, expenditures, and changes in fund balances.

Because the equipment is not recorded as an asset, the general fund does not report periodic depreciation on the equipment. When the equipment is sold by the general fund, the gross proceeds increase fund balance. If the equipment is sold at some future date for $1,500,000 in cash, this entry is made:

Cash.	1,500,000	
Proceeds from sale of capital assets		1,500,000
To record proceeds from sale of highway equipment.		

The fact that the capital assets have no book value in the general fund precludes recognizing a gain or loss on the sale. Instead, the gross proceeds are reported on the general fund's statement of revenues, expenditures, and changes in fund balances as part of *other financing sources*.

Accounting for Long-Term Debt   The general fund may incur long-term debt in the form of bonds of various types or long-term notes payable. As long as the government is liable for the general fund debt, inflows of current financial resources from debt issuances are recorded as *other financing sources* by the general fund. Outflows to pay principal and interest on the debt are recorded as expenditures. The following example uses long-term bonds to illustrate the accounting; similar procedures apply to other types of long-term debt.

Suppose Mecklenburg County's general fund issues $30,000,000 of long-term bonds to finance a service project. This event is recorded as follows:

Cash.	30,000,000	
Bond proceeds		30,000,000
To record proceeds of bond issue.		

The general fund reports bond proceeds on its statement of revenues, expenditures, and changes in fund balances as *other financing sources*.

Rather than transferring resources to a debt service fund, suppose the general fund pays principal and interest on the bonds directly. The general fund payments are $1,000,000 for principal and $400,000 for interest. The payments are recorded as follows:

Debt service: principal	1,000,000	
Debt service: interest	400,000	
Cash		1,400,000
To record payment of principal and interest on bonds.		

Outlays for both principal and interest appear as separate *expenditures* on the general fund's statement of revenues, expenditures, and changes in fund balances.

BUSINESS APPLICATION   Bond Refunding

In periods of falling interest rates, municipalities often find it cost effective to issue new debt at lower rates. An **advance refunding** issues new bonds in advance of the date that the original bonds can legally be paid off. Proceeds from the new bonds are placed with an escrow agent in an irrevocable trust to provide for all future debt requirements of the refunded debt, and the refunded debt is considered effectively retired (called "defeased").

Advance refundings can result in significant interest savings over the life of the refunded bonds. In 2013, Mecklenburg County issued $209,815,000 of general obligation refunding bonds at an interest rate of 1.75%, to refund debt paying substantially higher interest costs. The advance refunding resulted in a net savings of approximately $7.67 million to the county.

Closing Entries

Entries are prepared at the end of the reporting period to close all temporary accounts, *including the budgetary accounts*, to the fund balance. A single combined closing entry is possible, but use of two closing entries—one for revenues and other financing sources, and the other for expenditures and other financing uses—aids in understanding the process. These closing entries affect only the *unassigned* fund balance.

To illustrate the closing process, assume Mecklenburg County's budgeted revenues for 2017 are $1,505,000,000, estimated other financing sources are $30,000,000, budgeted expenditures are $1,500,000,000, and estimated other financing uses are $50,000,000. Actual revenues for the year are $1,507,000,000, actual expenditures amount to $1,488,300,000, outstanding encumbrances are $2,700,000 and actual other financing sources and uses are as budgeted. The following closing entries are made:

Revenues	1,507,000,000	
Other financing sources	30,000,000	
Estimated revenues		1,505,000,000
Estimated other financing sources		30,000,000
Fund balance—unassigned		2,000,000
To close revenues and estimated revenues to fund balance.		
Appropriations	1,500,000,000	
Estimated other financing uses	50,000,000	
Expenditures		1,488,300,000
Encumbrances		2,700,000
Other financing uses		50,000,000
Fund balance—unassigned		9,000,000
To close expenditures, encumbrances and appropriations to fund balance.		

These entries increase the unassigned fund balance by $11,000,000, because actual revenues exceeded the budget by $2,000,000, and actual expenditures and outstanding encumbrances were $9,000,000 less than planned. Recall the beginning-of-year budget entry:

Estimated revenues	1,505,000,000	
Estimated other financing sources	30,000,000	
Fund balance—unassigned	15,000,000	
Appropriations		1,500,000,000
Estimated other financing uses		50,000,000
To record the 2017 (deficit) budget.		

Whereas the fund balance was originally expected to decrease by $15,000,000, it actually decreased by only $4,000,000, as shown in this condensed budgetary comparison schedule:

	Budget	Actual	Variance— Favorable (Unfavorable)
Revenues and other financing sources	$1,535,000,000	$1,537,000,000	$ 2,000,000
Expenditures, encumbrances and other financing uses . . .	(1,550,000,000)	(1,541,000,000)	9,000,000
Change in fund balance—unassigned	$ (15,000,000)	$ (4,000,000)	$11,000,000

The $15,000,000 debit to the fund balance in the budget entry and the $11,000,000 total credits to the fund balance in the closing entries account for the actual $4,000,000 decrease during the year.

Outstanding Encumbrances at Year-End

Outstanding encumbrances at year-end are closed, even though the goods were not received as of year-end. Most jurisdictions honor outstanding purchase orders in the next period. Therefore, the amount reported as fund balance—assigned for outstanding encumbrances is *not closed* and remains as part of total assigned fund balance.

In our previous illustration, Mecklenburg County's general fund issued purchase orders amounting to $2,700,000 late in 2017 that are still outstanding at year-end. When the orders were issued, the encumbrance entry was:

Encumbrances	2,700,000	
Fund balance—assigned		2,700,000
To record purchase orders.		

As shown in the closing entries, outstanding encumbrances are closed to unassigned fund balance along with expenditures and other financing uses, while the related fund balance—assigned balance remains. The net effect reports $2,700,000 of the total fund balance as set aside for future payment of outstanding purchase orders. The accounting in the following year depends on how the government treats outstanding encumbrances in its budgetary accounts.

GAAP Budgetary Basis When the government uses the *GAAP budgetary basis*, outstanding encumbrances are *not* equivalent to expenditures of that year. A GAAP budgetary comparison schedule shows actual expenditures only, and appropriations are reduced by outstanding encumbrances. Next year, expenditures include the actual expenditure associated with last year's encumbrance, and appropriations include the outstanding encumbrance from last year, moving the appropriation and the expenditure to the year when the goods are received and the resources spent. The $2,700,000 encumbrances for purchase orders outstanding at the end of 2017 do not appear in the 2017 budgetary comparison schedule. At the beginning of 2018, the previously closed encumbrances are restored to the accounts, and the unassigned fund balance is increased, effectively reversing part of the 2017 closing entry:

Encumbrances	2,700,000	
Fund balance—unassigned		2,700,000
To restore encumbrances carried over from 2017.		

The expenditure signifying receipt in 2018 of the goods and services ordered in 2017 is recorded in the same manner as all other 2018 expenditures. Assume the actual expenditure related to the carryover encumbrance is $2,660,000. The $2,700,000 encumbrances are reversed, and the expenditure is recorded at the actual amount owed.

Fund balance—assigned	2,700,000	
Encumbrances		2,700,000
To reverse encumbrance entry.		
Expenditures	2,660,000	
Accounts payable		2,660,000
To record delivery of orders.		

In the GAAP budgetary comparison schedule, total 2018 expenditures include the actual $2,660,000 expenditure related to the carryover encumbrance, and total 2018 appropriations include the $2,700,000 carryover encumbrance.

Legal Budgetary Basis When the government uses the *legal budgetary basis*, outstanding encumbrances are equivalent to expenditures, since the obligation arises at the time of the purchase order. A budgetary comparison schedule at year-end compares actual expenditures *and* encumbrances to appropriations, including the portion for the outstanding encumbrance. The expenditure from the carryover encumbrance does not appear on the following year's budgetary comparison schedule.

The legal budgetary basis includes the $2,700,000 in encumbrances outstanding at the end of 2017 with expenditures in the 2017 budgetary comparison schedule. In the next year, the $2,660,000 expenditure related to the prior year outstanding encumbrance is recorded separately and closed against the portion of the prior year's fund balance assigned for encumbrances, not against the 2018 budget. When the goods and services ordered in 2017 are received in 2018 at a cost of $2,660,000, a separate expenditures account records completion of the transaction initiated in 2017:

Expenditures—prior year encumbrances...................................	2,660,000	
Accounts payable		2,660,000
To record invoices for goods and services ordered in 2017.		

At the end of 2018 an additional closing entry is required to close the prior year encumbrances:

Fund balance—assigned	2,700,000	
Expenditures—prior year encumbrances		2,660,000
Fund balance—unassigned..		40,000
To close encumbrances carried over from 2017 and related expenditures.		

The $40,000 credit to the unassigned fund balance effectively corrects the 2017 closing entry. Even though that entry charged $2,700,000 of 2017 encumbrances against the unassigned fund balance, the actual expenditure for these goods and services was $2,660,000.

Accounting for carryover encumbrances under these two alternative budgetary bases may be summarized as follows, using an encumbrance outstanding at the end of 2017. *Under both budgetary bases, outstanding encumbrances (the "encumbrances" account) are closed against the unassigned fund balance at year-end.*

1. The *GAAP budgetary basis* carries the encumbered amount into 2018:
   a. It is temporarily closed to the unassigned fund balance at the end of 2017, and reversed in 2018.
   b. It is not included in comparing budget to actual for 2017.
   c. The actual expenditure that occurs in 2018 is recorded as a regular 2018 expenditure.
   d. In comparing budget to actual for 2018, the 2018 budget includes the carryover encumbered appropriation from 2017.

2. The *legal budgetary basis* treats the encumbered amount in the budgetary comparison schedule as if it were an expenditure in 2017:
   a. It is closed to the unassigned fund balance in 2017.
   b. It is included in comparing budget to actual for 2017.
   c. The actual expenditure that occurs in 2018 is recorded separately from 2018 expenditures as "prior year," and is closed against the carried-over assigned fund balance; any difference is closed to the unassigned fund balance.
   d. It does not affect the 2018 comparison of budget to actual.

The general fund should report on the budgetary basis prescribed by the applicable laws and regulations in its jurisdiction to demonstrate legal compliance with those laws and regulations. However, GAAP-based financial statements **cannot** include encumbrances as expenditures. Therefore, if the legal budgetary basis is used, a **reconciliation to the GAAP basis** must be shown on the budgetary comparison schedule. See Chapter 12 for further explanation of this schedule.

COMPREHENSIVE ILLUSTRATION OF GENERAL FUND ACCOUNTING AND REPORTING

The following illustrates a county government's accounting for general fund activities, and presentation of year-end financial statements. Ranford County follows the *GAAP budgetary basis*, uses the *purchases method* for supplies inventory and does *not* recognize supplies inventory. Assume that the fiscal year for the Ranford County general fund is the calendar year. On January 1, 2016, the accounts of the general fund had the following balances:

RANFORD COUNTY
Trial Balance—General Fund
January 1, 2016

Accounts	Debit	Credit
Cash	$ 80,000,000	
Taxes receivable—delinquent	15,000,000	
Allowance for uncollectible taxes—delinquent		$ 12,000,000
Due from special revenue fund	10,000,000	
Accounts payable		8,000,000
Fund balance—unassigned		83,000,000
Fund balance—assigned		2,000,000
Totals	$105,000,000	$105,000,000

Assigned fund balance consists entirely of outstanding encumbrances. The 2016 general fund budget included revenues from the following sources:

Property taxes ($200,000,000 levied; 5% deemed uncollectible)	$190,000,000
State aid	30,000,000
Fees and licenses	8,000,000
Charges for services	12,000,000
Total estimated revenues	$240,000,000

Appropriations for 2016 included estimated expenditures for:

General services	$180,000,000
Maintenance	14,000,000
Supplies	18,000,000
Capital outlay	6,000,000
Total appropriations	$218,000,000

The general fund planned to transfer $28,000,000 to the debt service fund for payment of principal and interest on general obligation debt, and sell property for $7,000,000 during 2016.

Transactions During the Year

Ranford County records the events and transactions occurring during 2016 as follows:

1. The budget was recorded on January 2.

Estimated revenues	240,000,000	
Estimated other financing sources	7,000,000	
Appropriations		218,000,000
Estimated other financing uses		28,000,000
Fund balance—unassigned		1,000,000
To record 2016 budget.		

2. Taxes were levied.

Taxes receivable—current	200,000,000	
Allowance for uncollectible taxes—current		10,000,000
Tax revenues		190,000,000
To record property tax levy, estimated to be 95 percent collectible.		

3. The county received $30,000,000 in state aid.

Cash	30,000,000	
State aid revenues		30,000,000
To record aid received from state government.		

4. Delinquent taxes of $4,000,000 were received; the remainder of 2015 taxes were reclassified as tax liens and fully reserved.

Cash	4,000,000	
Taxes receivable—delinquent		4,000,000
To record collection of delinquent taxes.		
Tax liens receivable	11,000,000	
Taxes receivable—delinquent		11,000,000
To reclassify uncollected delinquent taxes as tax liens.		
Allowance for uncollectible taxes—delinquent	12,000,000	
Allowance for uncollectible tax liens		11,000,000
Tax revenues		1,000,000
To reclassify allowance for uncollectible taxes and fully reserve tax liens.		

5. The $28,000,000 authorized was transferred to the debt service fund.

Transfers out	28,000,000	
Cash		28,000,000
To record transfers to the debt service fund.		

6. Old equipment was sold for $7,300,000, and new equipment was purchased for $5,900,000.

Cash	7,300,000	
Proceeds from sale of capital assets		7,300,000
To record sale of old equipment.		
Capital outlay	5,900,000	
Cash		5,900,000
To record purchase of new equipment.		

7. Ranford County follows the GAAP budgetary basis for year-end encumbrances. Encumbrances outstanding at the end of 2015 were for general services, $2,000,000. The bill received in 2016 was $1,800,000, paid in cash.

Encumbrances	2,000,000	
Fund balance—unassigned		2,000,000
To restore encumbrances carried over from 2015.		
Fund balance—assigned	2,000,000	
Encumbrances		2,000,000
To reverse encumbrances.		
General services expenditures	1,800,000	
Cash		1,800,000
To record expenditures.		

8. Revenues of $21,300,000 were received as follows: $9,500,000 from fees and licenses, and $11,800,000 from charges for services.

Cash	21,300,000	
Fee and license revenues		9,500,000
Service revenues		11,800,000
To record revenues.		

9. Supplies of $18,000,000 were ordered.

Encumbrances...	18,000,000	
Fund balance—assigned......................................		18,000,000
To record supplies ordered.		

10. Cash expenditures were $40,300,000 for general services. Orders were issued for maintenance services, $14,000,000; for general services, $135,000,000.

General services expenditures......................................	40,300,000	
Cash		40,300,000
To record cash expenditures.		
Encumbrances...	149,000,000	
Fund balance—assigned......................................		149,000,000
To record encumbrances for goods and services ordered.		

11. Supplies ordered in transaction 9 were received and $18,000,000 in cash was paid to suppliers. Ranford County follows the *purchases method* of accounting for inventory expenditures.

Fund balance—assigned	18,000,000	
Encumbrances...		18,000,000
To reverse encumbrances.		
Supplies expenditures	18,000,000	
Cash		18,000,000
To record payment for supplies.		

12. Current taxes of $183,000,000 were collected.

Cash..	183,000,000	
Taxes receivable—current....................................		183,000,000
To record collection of current taxes.		

13. Invoices for goods and services ordered in transaction 10 and received were maintenance, $14,000,000, and general services, $136,000,000. Ranford paid a total of $152,000,000 on its 2016 accounts payable.

Fund balance—assigned	149,000,000	
Encumbrances...		149,000,000
To reverse encumbrances.		
Maintenance expenditures.......................................	14,000,000	
General services expenditures....................................	136,000,000	
Accounts payable		150,000,000
To record expenditures.		
Accounts payable...	152,000,000	
Cash		152,000,000
To record payment of accounts payable.		

14. Goods to be used in providing general services were ordered late in December for $1,300,000 but were not received in 2016.

Encumbrances...	1,300,000	
Fund balance—assigned......................................		1,300,000
To record encumbrances for goods ordered.		

15. Cash of $10,000,000 was received from the special revenue fund as repayment of a loan made in 2015.

Cash	10,000,000	
Due from special revenue fund		10,000,000
To record repayment of loan.		

16. Taxes uncollected at year-end were classified as delinquent. $2,000,000 of uncollected amounts are expected to be collected early in 2017.

Tax revenues	5,000,000	
Taxes receivable—delinquent	17,000,000	
Allowance for uncollectible taxes—current	10,000,000	
Taxes receivable—current		17,000,000
Allowance for uncollectible taxes—delinquent		15,000,000
To reclassify uncollected taxes as delinquent, adjust the related allowance account, and adjust tax revenues.		

The preclosing trial balance for Ranford County at December 31, 2016, appears as follows:

RANFORD COUNTY
Trial Balance—General Fund
December 31, 2016

Accounts	Debit	Credit
Cash	$ 89,600,000	
Taxes receivable—delinquent	17,000,000	
Tax liens receivable	11,000,000	
Encumbrances	1,300,000	
General services expenditures	178,100,000	
Maintenance expenditures	14,000,000	
Supplies expenditures	18,000,000	
Capital outlay	5,900,000	
Transfers out	28,000,000	
Estimated revenues	240,000,000	
Estimated other financing sources	7,000,000	
Allowance for uncollectible taxes—delinquent		$ 15,000,000
Allowance for uncollectible tax liens		11,000,000
Accounts payable		6,000,000
Tax revenues		186,000,000
State aid revenues		30,000,000
Fee and license revenues		9,500,000
Service revenues		11,800,000
Proceeds from sale of capital assets		7,300,000
Appropriations		218,000,000
Estimated other financing uses		28,000,000
Fund balance—unassigned		86,000,000
Fund balance—assigned		1,300,000
Totals	$609,900,000	$609,900,000

Closing Entries

Closing entries at December 31, 2016, are as follows:

Tax revenues	186,000,000	
State aid revenues	30,000,000	
Fee and license revenues	9,500,000	
Service revenues	11,800,000	
Proceeds from sale of capital assets	7,300,000	
Fund balance—unassigned	2,400,000	
Estimated revenues		240,000,000
Estimated other financing sources		7,000,000
To close revenues and other financing sources.		

Appropriations	218,000,000	
Estimated other financing uses	28,000,000	
General services expenditures		178,100,000
Maintenance expenditures		14,000,000
Supplies expenditures.		18,000,000
Capital outlay.		5,900,000
Encumbrances.		1,300,000
Transfers out		28,000,000
Fund balance—unassigned.		700,000
To close expenditures, other financing uses, and encumbrances.		

Financial Statements

The financial statements for the general fund of Ranford County can now be prepared. Ranford's **balance sheet** appears in Exhibit 10.3.

EXHIBIT 10.3   Ranford County Balance Sheet—General Fund

RANFORD COUNTY
Balance Sheet—General Fund
December 31, 2016
(in thousands)

Assets	
Cash.	$89,600
Taxes receivable—delinquent (net of $15,000 allowance for uncollectible taxes).	2,000
Tax liens receivable (net of $11,000 allowance for uncollectible tax liens)	—
Total assets	$91,600
Liabilities and fund balances	
Liabilities:	
Accounts payable.	$ 6,000
Total liabilities.	6,000
Fund balances:	
Assigned.	1,300
Unassigned	84,300
Total fund balances	85,600
Total liabilities and fund balances	$91,600

The general fund balance sheet is unclassified because modified accrual accounting excludes fixed assets and long-term debt. Thus, the assets of the general fund include only those able to be spent or otherwise consumed during the next fiscal period in carrying on the fund's activities. Similarly, the liabilities of the general fund are limited to claims to be paid during the next fiscal year. The total fund balance includes an assigned balance that signifies outstanding encumbrances at year-end.

Ranford's **statement of revenues, expenditures, and changes in fund balances** explains changes in the *total fund balance* and appears in Exhibit 10.4. Use of the *purchases method* for the supplies inventory includes supplies purchased during the year in expenditures. Reported fund balance does *not* include resources invested in supplies on hand at year-end because Ranford County does not recognize supplies inventory.

Revenues are classified by *source*. For the general fund, major sources of revenue include taxes, state aid, fees and licenses, and charges for services. *Expenditures* are often classified by character and function. Classification by *character* hinges on the time period (or periods) that the expenditures benefit. Common character classifications are *current expenditures*, *capital outlays*, and *debt service*. Classification by *function* identifies groups of related activities designed to accomplish a particular service or regulatory responsibility, such as general government, public safety, education, highways, sanitation, health, and recreation. Classification of expenditures by *object classes*—types of goods and services acquired—such as personnel compensation, supplies, and utilities is also common. Other financing sources and uses may include proceeds of long-term debt issues, proceeds from sales of capital assets, and transfers to or from the general fund.

EXHIBIT 10.4	Ranford County Statement of Revenues, Expenditures, and Changes in Fund Balances—General Fund

RANFORD COUNTY
Statement of Revenues, Expenditures, and Changes in Fund Balances
General Fund
For Year Ended December 31, 2016
(in thousands)

Revenues	
Property taxes	$186,000
State aid	30,000
Fees and licenses	9,500
Services	11,800
Total revenues	237,300
Expenditures	
General services	178,100
Maintenance	14,000
Supplies	18,000
Capital outlay	5,900
Total expenditures	216,000
Excess of revenues over expenditures	21,300
Other financing sources (uses)	
Proceeds from sale of capital assets	7,300
Transfers out	(28,000)
Total other financing sources (uses)	(20,700)
Excess of revenues and other financing sources over expenditures and other financing uses	600
Fund balances—January 1	85,000*
Fund balances—December 31	$ 85,600

* Unassigned fund balance	$83,000
Assigned fund balance	2,000
	$85,000

The operating statement reconciles the beginning and ending *total* fund balances of the general fund. This reconciliation may not be as straightforward as the reconciliation of beginning and ending retained earnings in a business, for the following reasons:

- If the *purchases method* is used to account for a government's inventories and inventories are significant, the change in the fund balance—nonspendable is included as part of the reconciliation, because this change in fund balance is not reported in the statement of revenues, expenditures, and changes in fund balances.

- If the *legal budgetary basis* is used to account for encumbrances, prior year expenditures are subtracted as part of the reconciliation, because they are not reported in the statement of revenues, expenditures, and changes in fund balances.

In addition to the statement of revenues, expenditures, and changes in fund balances, a parallel statement showing the comparison between budget and actual data is required. The format of this **budgetary comparison schedule** is similar to the format of the statement of revenues, expenditures, and changes in fund balances. For each item on the operating statement, the budgetary comparison schedule presents: (1) the original budgeted amount, (2) the final budgeted amount, after adjustment for legally authorized changes, and (3) the actual amount. An additional column reporting the variance between the final budget and actual amounts is encouraged but not required.

In the event the government uses a non-GAAP budgetary basis, "expenditures" likely include outstanding encumbrances. Because those "expenditure" amounts differ from the corresponding amounts in the statement of revenues, expenditures, and changes in fund balances, a reconciliation with GAAP is also required, as discussed in Chapter 12.

The budgetary comparison schedule for Ranford County, assuming the original budget was not changed during the year, appears in Exhibit 10.5. Because expenditures are legally limited by the budget, actual expenditures are less than or equal to budgeted expenditures.

EXHIBIT 10.5   Ranford County Budgetary Comparison Schedule—General Fund

RANFORD COUNTY
Budgetary Comparison Schedule—General Fund
For Year Ended December 31, 2016

(in thousands)	Budget	Actual	Variance—Favorable (Unfavorable)
Revenues			
Property taxes	$190,000	$186,000	$(4,000)
State aid	30,000	30,000	—
Fees and licenses	8,000	9,500	1,500
Services	12,000	11,800	(200)
Total revenues	240,000	237,300	(2,700)
Expenditures			
General services	180,000	178,100	1,900
Maintenance	14,000	14,000	—
Supplies	18,000	18,000	—
Capital outlay	6,000	5,900	100
Total expenditures	218,000	216,000	2,000
Excess of revenues over expenditures	22,000	21,300	(700)
Other financing sources (uses)			
Proceeds from sale of capital assets	7,000	7,300	300
Transfers out	(28,000)	(28,000)	—
Total other financing sources (uses)	(21,000)	(20,700)	300
Excess of revenues and other financing sources over expenditures and other financing uses	1,000	600	(400)
Fund balances—January 1	85,000	85,000	—
Fund balances—December 31	$ 86,000	$ 85,600	$ (400)

REVIEW 2 • General Fund Budget and Closing Entries, Financial Statements

Here is the December 31, 2016, pre-closing trial balance for the general fund of Eerie County, NY. The county uses the GAAP budgetary basis for encumbrances, of which $1,200 were outstanding at December 31, 2015.

	Debit	Credit
Cash.	$ 11,400	
Property taxes receivable.	64,000	
Allowance for uncollectible property taxes		$ 12,000
Due from other funds	3,000	
Accounts payable.		15,000
Due to other funds		4,000
Deferred inflows of resources		5,000
Fund balance—assigned		1,000
Fund balance—unassigned		50,000
Estimated revenues	700,000	
Estimated other financing sources.	30,000	
Appropriations		708,000
Estimated other financing uses		8,000
Revenues—property taxes.		300,000
Revenues—sales taxes		380,000
Expenditures	698,000	
Proceeds of general obligation debt		12,000
Proceeds from sale of capital assets		16,000
Transfers out	7,600	
Transfers in.		4,000
Encumbrances	1,000	
Totals	$1,515,000	$1,515,000

Assigned fund balance consists entirely of outstanding encumbrances.

Required
a. Prepare the budget entry made at January 1, 2016.
b. Compute the balance in fund balance—unassigned on December 31, 2015.
c. Prepare the required closing entries at December 31, 2016.
d. Prepare the statement of revenues, expenditures, and changes in fund balances for 2016.
e. Prepare the balance sheet at December 31, 2016.

Solutions are located after the chapter assignments.

REVIEW OF KEY CONCEPTS

LO 1 **Describe the reporting environment for state and local governments. (p. 415)** State and local governments differ in many ways from for-profit enterprises. Resources are derived from taxes, fees, fines and debt financing. A **legal budget** limits expenditures. The main purpose of the government is to provide services to the citizenry. External users of governmental financial statements include **credit market representatives, elected officials, public sector labor unions**, and **citizens**. Credit market representatives use the financial statements to judge the governmental unit's ability to generate resources to fund required interest and principal payments. Citizens and legislators are concerned with services provided, and how current activities and plans affect future taxes and ability to provide services. The **Governmental Accounting Standards Board (GASB)** sets accounting requirements for state and local governmental external reporting. The emphasis in external reporting is on **stewardship** and **interperiod equity**. Financial statements are prepared for the governmental **reporting entity**, which consists of the **primary government** (usually a state or local government) and its **component units**. Deciding which organizations comprise the reporting entity is primarily based on whether **financial accountability** exists.

LO 2 **Identify the fund types and reporting methods for state and local governments. (p. 420)** The government consists of several accounting entities known as **funds**, which correspond to the major activities of the government.

Although there is always one general fund, a particular government uses some or all of the other fund types, depending on its activities. The general, special revenue, capital projects, debt service, and permanent funds are known as **governmental funds**. These funds focus on sources, uses, and balances of **current financial resources** available to fund current expenditures, and use **modified accrual accounting**. Encumbrance and **budgetary accounts** aid in the control of resources. Required financial statements of governmental funds are the **statement of revenues, expenditures, and changes in fund balances**, the **balance sheet**, and the **budgetary comparison schedule**. Under the modified accrual basis of accounting, revenues represent **inflows of current financial resources**, excluding borrowings and transfers from other funds. Revenues are recognized when they are **measurable** and **available to finance expenditures in the current period**. Expenditures—outflows of current financial resources—are recognized when they are **measurable** and the **related liability is incurred**. The enterprise and internal service funds are known as **proprietary funds** because they are used to conduct business-type activities. Proprietary funds focus on determination of net income, financial position, and cash flows, and follow **full accrual accounting** as used in business. Required financial statements of proprietary funds are the **statement of revenues, expenses and changes in net position**, the **statement of net position**, and the **statement of cash flows**. **Fiduciary funds** account for resources held by the government in a custodial capacity for individuals or organizations outside the reporting government. These resources are not available to support government programs. Fiduciary funds are classified as **pension trust funds, investment trust funds, private-purpose trust funds**, and **agency funds**. All use accrual accounting. Agency funds record only assets and liabilities, and have no net position.

Prepare entries and financial statements for the general fund. (p. 425) The general fund's legal budget is recorded directly in the accounts using a **budget entry**. Property taxes are accrued when billed; **tax revenue** is reported net of estimated uncollectible amounts. Purchase orders are recorded as **encumbrances**, reducing available funds. **Interfund transactions** appear as temporary advances on the balance sheet or as transfers on the operating statement. Inventories of supplies can be accounted for by the **consumption method**, which recognizes expenditures when the supplies are used, or by the **purchases method**, which recognizes expenditures when the supplies are purchased. Alternative treatments also exist for **encumbrances outstanding at year-end**, depending on the budgetary basis used by the governmental unit. Under the **GAAP budgetary basis**, expenditures—including those related to carryover encumbrances—are charged against the budget for the year the *expenditures* are made. However, the budget is increased by the amount of the carryover encumbrance. Under the **legal budgetary basis**, expenditures are charged against the budget for the year the *encumbrances* are made. **Capital assets** acquired by the general fund and by other governmental funds are capital outlays, classified as *expenditures*. Depreciation is not recorded in governmental funds. Proceeds from the sale of capital assets are *other financing sources*. Proceeds from the issuance of **long-term debt** are *other financing sources*. Resources used to pay principal and interest on long-term debt are *expenditures*.

LO 3

Assignments with the ✔ in the margin are available in BusinessCourse.
See the Preface of the book for details.

MULTIPLE CHOICE QUESTIONS ••••••••••••••••••••••••••••••••••••

1. A county government annual report includes the activities of the primary government and its component units. Component units can be presented in the financial statements as blended or *discrete*. A discrete component unit is most likely to   **LO 1** ✔

    a. have the same governing body as the primary government.   *C*
    b. exist to provide services to the primary government.
    c. issue bonds for which the component unit is financially obligated.
    d. receive funding mostly from endowments from county citizens.

2. What is the highest authoritative source of generally accepted accounting principles for state and local governments?   **LO 1** ✔

    a. FASB   *C*
    b. AICPA
    c. GASB
    d. GFOA

3. The governmental funds statement of revenues, expenditures, and changes in fund balances will *never* report   **LO 2** ✔

    a. accrued pension costs.   *a*
    b. interest revenue.
    c. proceeds from issuing new bonds.
    d. property tax revenue.

✅ **LO 2**   **4.**   Which of the following funds is *not* a governmental fund?

    a.   Internal service fund

    b.   Debt service fund   *a*

    c.   Special revenue fund

    d.   Permanent fund

✅ **LO 3**   **5.**   Some of a county government's account balances at November 30, 2016 appear below. The government's fiscal year ends June 30, 2017.

Cash in bank	$ 100,000
Estimated revenues	20,000,000
Budgetary deficit	500,000
Revenues	8,000,000
Expenditures	7,600,000
Fund balance–assigned	75,000
Fund balance–unassigned	300,000

d

The assigned fund balance relates entirely to outstanding encumbrances. How much does the government have available to spend for the remainder of fiscal 2017?

    a. $ 300,000

    b. $ 325,000

    c. $12,325,000

    d. $12,825,000

Use the following information to answer questions 6 – 9 below. All numbers are in thousands.

Here is the preclosing December 31, 2017 trial balance for the general fund of Lancaster County:

	Debit	Credit
Cash	$ 371,000	
Taxes receivable	113,000	
Estimated revenues	1,290,000	
Estimated other financing sources	60,000	
General expenditures	1,015,000	
Capital outlay	25,000	
Debt service: principal payments	2,000	
Debt service: interest payments	8,000	
Transfers out	20,000	
Due from other funds	12,000	
Allowance for uncollectible taxes		$ 45,000
Accounts payable		50,000
Due to other funds		21,000
Property tax revenues		950,000
Speeding ticket revenues		400,000
Transfers in		8,000
Bond proceeds		50,000
Appropriations		1,085,000
Estimated other financing uses		22,000
Fund balance—unassigned		285,000
Totals	$2,916,000	$2,916,000

✅ **LO 3**   **6.**   What was the amount of fund balance—unassigned at the beginning of the year, *before* the budget entry?

    a. $ 20,000

    b. $ 42,000   *b*

    c. $ 80,000

    d. $102,000

✅ **LO 3**   **7.**   By how much do the *closing entries* at the end of 2017 increase fund balance—unassigned?

    a. $37,000

    b. $40,000   *d*

    c. $73,000

    d. $95,000

8. Total expenditures reported on Lancaster County's 2017 statement of revenues, expenditures and changes in fund balance are   **LO 3** ✓

   a. $1,015,000.
   b. $1,025,000.
   c. $1,048,000.
   d. $1,050,000.

   d

9. Total assets reported on Lancaster County's December 31, 2017 balance sheet are   **LO 3** ✓

   a. $439,000.
   b. $451,000.
   c. $472,000.
   d. $476,000.

   b

10. The Town of Pavilion's July 1, 2015 balance sheet reports the following property tax accounts: **LO 3** ✓

   b

Taxes receivable.	$70,000
Allowance for uncollectible taxes.	(49,000)
Taxes receivable, net	$21,000

   During fiscal 2016, $30,000 in cash is collected on fiscal 2015 taxes and the remainder are written off. The town levies fiscal 2016 property taxes in the amount of $1,000,000. It estimates that uncollectible property taxes for 2016 are $25,000. Cash collected for 2016 property taxes is $940,000. $15,000 of the remaining uncollected 2016 taxes are expected to be collected early in fiscal 2017. What are property tax revenues for fiscal 2016?

   a. $955,000
   b. $964,000
   c. $966,000
   d. $970,000

EXERCISES ••

E10.1 Identify Appropriate Fund   Following are some common activities or transactions of a state or local government.   **LO 2** ✓

   1. Public safety programs financed by state and federal grants.
   2. Proceeds of a state grant to be used to finance construction of a community center.
   3. Operations of a municipal swimming pool, financed by user fees.
   4. Accumulation of payroll deductions from local employees for health insurance premiums, to be remitted to various insurance companies.
   5. Activities of a central printing operation that provides services to various government agencies.
   6. Transactions of a state employee retirement plan.
   7. A town collects property taxes to be used for county services, and periodically remits these taxes to the county.
   8. Purchase of materials for the construction of a county courthouse.
   9. Payment of interest on general obligation bonds.
   10. Payment of salaries to municipal employees.
   11. Acquisition of books by a local public library, where the library is funded by a special property tax.
   12. Accumulation of money to be used to pay interest on general obligation bonds.
   13. Activities of a park trust, where income from non-spendable trust investments is restricted to the funding of maintenance costs for public parks.
   14. Accumulation of abandoned bank balances that have reverted to the town.

   Required

   Indicate the type of fund in which each activity or transaction should be recorded by a state or local government.

E10.2 Identify Appropriate Funds   Each of the following transactions relates to a city government: **LO 2**

   1. A sinking fund is set up to accumulate and invest resources for the retirement of a general bond issue maturing in ten years.

2. The city receives a $50,000 grant from the federal government to institute a meal delivery program for senior citizens.
3. New curbing is being installed on the south side of the city, with resources initially provided by the general fund. No debt is issued. Residents of the south side will pay for the cost of the curbing with an additional charge on their property tax bill during each of the next ten years.
4. Same as 3., except that initial financing is provided by issuing bonds for which the city is (a) liable or (b) not liable.
5. To remedy a flooding problem, the city plans a new drainage system in the northern part of the city, financed with a general bond issue.
6. The city establishes a retirement fund for its fire fighters, and sets aside 8 percent of the fire fighters' wages each year. The city administers the investment of funds and the payment of benefits.
7. Same as 6., except that the city pays a premium to an insurance company fully responsible for investment of funds and benefit payments.
8. The city set up a computer services division to handle payroll and other functions for all city agencies, for a fee.
9. Fifteen new police cars are purchased, as provided in the general budget.
10. Received state aid funds to be used for any of the city's general operations.
11. The city deducts federal income taxes from its employees' wages and periodically remits them to the federal government.
12. The city receives a $3,000,000 trust from a citizen. Income from trust investments must be used to maintain the public museum.
13. The city invests money received from other governments that pool their investments to increase return on excess funds invested.

Required

Identify the fund(s) affected by each of the above transactions.

LO 1 E10.3 Property Tax Rate and Revenues Steuben County anticipates appropriations of $10,500,000 and revenue from the state and other sources of $900,000. During the last fiscal year, the tax rate was $0.85 per $100 of assessed valuation, applied to property assessed at $1,000 million. Uncollectible property taxes are negligible. In the current year, the county's reassessment program increased the aggregate assessed value of property to $1,050 million.

Required

a. Compute the property tax revenue raised during the last fiscal year.
b. Compute the tax rate needed to balance the current budget.
c. Assume that the Steuben County charter requires a balanced budget and that increasing the tax rate is politically unacceptable. Compute the maximum amount of appropriations that can be funded by property taxes given the increase in assessed valuation.

LO 3 E10.4 Computing Available Funds As the newly-hired assistant controller for the **City of Columbia, Missouri**, you are working diligently to unravel the mysteries of governmental accounting. On your desk this morning is a memorandum from the controller asking you to advise her of the amount of available funds. After consulting your assistant and the city treasurer, you begin to analyze the following information.

(in thousands)	Dr (Cr)
Cash in bank	$ 40,000
Estimated revenue	4,000,000
Budgetary surplus	(200,000)
Revenue	(3,700,000)
Expenditures	2,500,000
Accounts payable	(300,000)
Fund balance—assigned	(225,000)
Fund balance—unassigned	(800,000)

Assigned fund balance consists of outstanding encumbrances.

Required

a. Calculate the funds available to be encumbered.
b. Suppose it is now August 31, close to the September 30 fiscal year-end. Operating costs occur evenly throughout the year. Do you expect to see an effort to cut next period's budget? Why?

E10.5 **Reconstruct Budget Entry, Compute Fund Balance** Suppose the following information relates **LO 3** to actual revenues and expenditures for the general fund of the **City of Farmington Hills, Michigan**:

	Actual	Over (Under) Budget
Revenues		
Property taxes	$28,896,909	$483,097
Licenses and permits	1,392,631	157,458
Fines	2,006,071	27,771
State-shared revenue	6,492,489	(150,332)
Fees and service charges	10,390,608	581,697
Miscellaneous	2,180,035	126,484
Expenditures		
Administration	19,786,590	(1,342,917)
Public safety	17,978,413	(926,681)
Public works	7,315,549	(278,188)

Required

a. What budget entry was made at the beginning of the year?
b. If the fund balance *before* the budget entry was $3,100,000, what is the fund balance after year-end closing entries?

E10.6 **Transactions, Closing Entries, and Budgetary Comparison Schedule** The January 1, 2016 **LO 3** balance sheet for the general fund of the Village of Owen, Texas is:

VILLAGE OF OWEN
General Fund Balance Sheet
January 1, 2016

(in thousands)

Cash	$30,000	Accounts payable	$13,000
Taxes receivable	20,000	Fund balance—unassigned	37,000
Total assets	$50,000	Total liabilities and fund balance	$50,000

Transactions for the village during 2016 were *(in thousands)*:

1. The village council approved a budget estimating revenues of $41,000 in property taxes and $10,000 in fees and service charges. The budget authorized expenditures of $51,000.
2. Collected receivables of $18,500 from last year and $26,500 of the 2016 tax levy.
3. Recorded encumbrances of $50,300. On December 31, 2016, purchase orders of $13,000 were outstanding.
4. Bills received exceeded the amounts encumbered by $200.
5. Mailed checks for $44,000 in payment of accounts payable.
6. Collected fees and service charges of $11,000.

Required

a. Prepare the journal entries to record the transactions during 2016.
b. Prepare closing entries at December 31, 2016.
c. Compute the unassigned fund balance at December 31, 2016.
d. Prepare a budgetary comparison schedule for 2016. Use the GAAP budgetary basis.

LO 3 **E10.7** **Property Tax Transactions** On July 10, the town of Salt Flats levied property taxes of $30,000,000. Based on past experience, town management estimated that the town will not collect 4 percent of the taxes. Taxes were due September 30, but $9,009,000 was received before that date from taxpayers taking advantage of the 1 percent discount for early payment. Salt Flats treats discounts given as a reduction of revenues. On January 1, the outstanding taxes due of $2,000,000 were declared delinquent; Salt Flats estimates that $200,000 of delinquent taxes will be collected early next year. By the end of the fiscal year, $300,000 of the delinquent taxes were collected and the rest were written off. No taxes receivable, either current or delinquent, existed at the beginning of the fiscal year. Actual expenditures of $25,000,000 equaled appropriations. All expenditures were cash transactions. The budget entry included $29,000,000 of estimated revenues. After the budget entry, the fund balance for the general fund was $5,200,000.

Required

a. Prepare the journal entries to record the property tax transactions and the expenditures.
b. State the balance sheet accounts and their respective balances relating to the property tax levy and collections as of the end of the fiscal year. Assume an $850,000 cash balance at the beginning of the fiscal year.

LO 3 **E10.8** **Inventory Accounting** General City's general fund reported a supplies inventory costing $500,000 at the beginning of the fiscal year. During the year, General City purchased materials and supplies on account for $13,000,000; $800,000 remains unpaid at year-end. Materials and supplies costing $450,000 are on hand at the end of the fiscal year.

Required

Prepare the summary journal entries made this year under the two allowable methods used by governmental funds to account for inventories.

LO 3 **E10.9** **Closing Entries** The Newberry County budget for the 2017 fiscal year included estimated revenues of $3,501,000 and appropriations of $3,449,000.

Required

Prepare the closing entries for 2017 under each of the following independent assumptions:

a. Actual revenues and expenditures equaled estimates.
b. Actual revenues were as expected, but appropriations exceeded actual expenditures by $22,000.
c. Actual revenues of $3,440,000 equaled actual expenditures.
d. The net effect of the closing entries on the fund balance was zero. Actual revenues were $3,495,000.

LO 3 **E10.10** **Carryover Encumbrances** The December 31, 2015, balance sheet for the general fund of Burnville showed an assigned fund balance of $1,900,000 for outstanding encumbrances. This figure represented $1,100,000 encumbered for office equipment and $800,000 for supplies. Early in 2016, the equipment and supplies were delivered and bills received for $1,170,000 and $795,000, respectively.

Required

Prepare the journal entries for 2016 relating to these events, using the

a. Legal budgetary basis.
b. GAAP budgetary basis.

LO 3 **E10.11** **Interfund Transactions** Suppose interfund transfers of the general fund of **Contra Costa County, California** for 2017 were as follows:

1. $2,000,000 advance to the Park Development special revenue fund, to permit initial expenditures under a project to be fully supported by a federal grant.
2. $1,500,000 to the Contra Costa County Fire Protection District (a special revenue fund) as the county's contribution to fire and emergency medical service activities for the year.
3. $500,000 from the Roads capital projects fund, unspent proceeds of a bond issue.
4. $3,000,000 to the County Hospital (enterprise fund), as the city's cost of services provided.
5. $2,900,000 to the Airport Fund (enterprise fund) to temporarily finance the maintenance of runways.
6. $2,000,000 from the Park Development special revenue fund, to repay the advance.

Required

For each of the above interfund transfers, state how the transaction is reported on the general fund's balance sheet and/or statement of revenues, expenditures, and changes in fund balances.

E10.12 Adjusting and Closing Entries, Balance Sheet The preclosing trial balance for the general fund **LO 3** of Graystone County is given below:

	Dr (Cr)
Cash..	$ 3,000,000
Taxes receivable—current	900,000
Allowance for uncollectible taxes—current	(400,000)
Supplies	180,000
Estimated revenues	12,000,000
Expenditures	9,700,000
Expenditures—prior year	330,000
Encumbrances	250,000
Due from other funds	210,000
Accounts payable...	(900,000)
Due to other funds	(150,000)
Deferred outflows of resources	(300,000)
Revenues	(13,700,000)
Appropriations	(10,000,000)
Fund balance—nonspendable......................................	(180,000)
Fund balance—assigned	(600,000)
Fund balance—unassigned	(340,000)
Total	$ 0

Additional information:

1. At year-end, all uncollected taxes are deemed delinquent and are fully reserved.
2. A physical count of inventory revealed $150,000 of supplies on hand.
3. Assigned fund balance consists of $250,000 in outstanding encumbrances at year-end, and $350,000 in prior year encumbrances.

Required

a. Prepare all year-end adjusting and closing entries for Graystone County's general fund.
b. Prepare a year-end balance sheet for Graystone County's general fund.

E10.13 General Fund Capital Asset and Long-Term Debt Transactions During the current year, the **LO 3** following transactions were recorded by the general fund of the City of Margate:

1. Acquired a new fire truck costing $3,420,000 in cash.
2. Sold for $75,000 old fire-fighting equipment acquired ten years ago for $750,000.
3. Paid interest and principal on long-term capital debt of $250,000 and $1,000,000, respectively.

Required

a. Prepare all journal entries made by the City of Margate's general fund for the above transactions.
b. State how each transaction is reported in the general fund financial statements.
c. Compute the effect of the foregoing on the general fund unassigned fund balance.

E10.14 Identifying the Reporting Entity These descriptions of organizations relate to a city government. **LO 1**

1. The public school district is a legally separate entity responsible for the administration of city schools and has a separate board elected by the public. The city council approves the school district's budget, levies taxes and issues debt on behalf of the school district. The city is legally liable for school district debt. The city also provides significant funding to the school district.
2. The housing authority is a legally separate entity that manages public housing in the city. The authority issues its own debt, payment on which is financed by housing rents. The city has no financial liability for the housing authority's debt. The city has input in choosing the authority's board, but does not appoint the board or control its decisions.
3. The waste disposal authority is a legally separate entity that operates the city landfill; its board is appointed and landfill rates are approved by the city council.
4. The sewer district provides sewage treatment services to several surrounding local governments, including the city. The city appoints a minority of the sewer district's board members. The district sets service rates and makes all decisions regarding its operations. Its operations are funded by property tax levies and user charges, and by debt for which it is legally liable.

5. The building authority is a separate legal entity whose board is appointed by the city. The authority issues bonds to finance construction of city capital assets. The city is legally liable for the bonds.

Required

For each organization described above, indicate whether it should be reported as a component unit of the city. If it is a component unit, should its financial information be blended with that of the city, or discretely presented? Justify your answers.

LO 3

STATE OF MICHIGAN

E10.15 Classifying General Fund Balance   The **State of Michigan** has the following outstanding amounts at the end of 2013, each of which affects fund balances in the general fund (*in millions*):

1. Inventory of $14 is held as of year-end.
2. The state intends to use $41,400 of its fund balance toward health and human services, and $96,547 toward transportation.
3. External legislation requires $117,000 to be set aside for public safety and corrections, $125,977 for education, and $134,000 for conservation of parks. In addition, the state's highest decision-making body decided to require that an additional $191,266 be held for public safety and corrections, $28,400 for conservation, and $714,000 for other purposes.
4. The state holds long-term notes receivable of $221,600, which cannot be immediately spent.
5. Remaining funds total $1,186,647 as of the end of the fiscal year.

Required

Prepare the State of Michigan's fund balances section of the general fund balance sheet.

PROBLEMS ••

⊘ LO 1   **P10.1   Determining the Reporting Entity**   The governmental reporting entity consists of a primary government and its component units. Various governmental structures are described below.

1. By a vote of 9-6, the Megalopolis City Council voted to establish a Convention Authority (CA). Megalopolis's mayor appoints the CA's governing board with the approval of city council. City council's direct financial commitment to the CA is limited to a $100,000 appropriation of seed money to be repaid from the CA's permanent financing as soon as possible. The CA's initial responsibility is to obtain the funding for a downtown convention center. Funding will likely come from a combination of federal development grant money, tax-exempt bonds issued and backed by the city, and corporate contributions.
2. Consider the same facts as in 1. except that the CA is authorized to issue its own bonds without city backing and may levy a small sales tax to support its activities. The CA's bond issues and sales taxes need not be approved by the city council but, as a matter of courtesy, council is advised of the CA's plans.
3. Many local communities in Gigantic County are served by volunteer fire departments. Each such fire department is a separate not-for-profit corporation governed by a board elected by and from its own membership. The county has a three-year contract with each fire department to pay for the department's fire-fighting services. Also, the county has historically paid for fire trucks and similar equipment used and owned by the fire departments.
4. The Winitville Board of Education is elected by the voters. This Board governs the Winitville School District and obtains an annual appropriation from the city to fund school district activities. The City of Winitville levies whatever taxes and issues whatever bonds it needs to fund its expenditures, including those attributable to the school district, and has no authority over the individual line items in the school district's budget.

STATE OF MICHIGAN

5. The **State of Michigan**, along with seven other states, participates in a joint venture to examine the water quality of the Great Lakes. Michigan is the largest contributor, and contributions to the **Great Lakes Protection Fund** (GLPF) are permanently restricted and are not available for disbursement. Each participating state is represented by two members on the GLPF's board of directors. The GLPF's financing and budgeting operations are controlled by the directors within requirements established by its own Articles of Incorporation.

STATE OF GEORGIA

6. The **Georgia Public Telecommunications Commission** is a legally separate entity within the **State of Georgia**. This commission is a public charitable organization created for the purpose of providing educational, instructional and public broadcasting services to the citizens of Georgia. The

budget of the commission must be approved by the state. The Board consists of three state officials designated by statute and six members appointed by the governor.

Required

For each of the above independent situations, identify the primary government and explain whether the other governmental enterprise is part of the primary government's financial reporting entity.

P10.2 **General Fund Entries and Financial Statements** The **City of Alexandria, VA** finances its op- LO 3 ✓
erations from revenues collected from property taxes, waste management fees, municipal court fines, and interest on investments. Alexandria maintains only a general fund. Suppose the following information is available for the year ended December 31, 2016:

1. Following is the general fund trial balance on January 1, 2016:

	Dr (Cr)
Investments	$ 5,000,000
Cash	2,500,000
Waste management supplies	515,000
Accounts receivable—waste management	550,000
Fund balance—nonspendable	(515,000)
Fund balance—unassigned	(8,050,000)
Total	$ 0

2. The budget for 2016, adopted by the town board, follows:

Property taxes	$3,200,000
Waste management costs	4,300,000
Court costs	950,000
Waste management revenues	3,700,000
Court fines	800,000
Salaries and operating expenditures	920,000
Investment income	400,000
Supplies expenditures	250,000
Miscellaneous expenditures	180,000

3. All property taxes were collected in cash. Waste management costs, all paid in cash, were $4,290,000. Court costs, all paid in cash, were $920,000.
4. Waste management revenues of $2,800,000 were billed during the year. All outstanding waste management bills on January 1, 2016, were collected during 2016. All 2016 billings were paid with the exception of $320,000, which were mailed to customers the last week of the year.
5. Court fines of $850,000 were collected in cash. Salaries and operating expenditures, all paid in cash, were $880,000. Investment income of $450,000 accumulates in the investments account until the investments mature. No investments matured in 2016.
6. Miscellaneous expenditures, all paid in cash, were $160,000.
7. Waste management supplies on hand at year-end were $265,000. The town uses the consumption method to report supplies.

Required

a. Prepare 2016 journal entries to record the above events and to close the books for the year.
b. Prepare a statement of revenues, expenditures, and changes in fund balances and the balance sheet for 2016.

P10.3 **General Fund Adjustments and Financial Statements** The books for the Town of Fountain LO 3
Inn are maintained by an inexperienced bookkeeper. All transactions were recorded in the town's general fund for the fiscal year ended June 30, 2017. The bookkeeper prepared the following trial balance:

TOWN OF FOUNTAIN INN
General Fund Trial Balance
June 30, 2017

	Debit	Credit
Cash.	$ 28,000,000	
Accounts receivable.	2,000,000	
Taxes receivable, current.	10,000,000	
Accounts payable.		$ 18,000,000
Appropriations		380,000,000
Expenditures	315,000,000	
Estimated revenues	460,000,000	
Revenues		440,000,000
Town property	19,000,000	
Bonds payable	40,000,000	
Fund balance		36,000,000
Totals	$874,000,000	$874,000,000

Additional information:

1. The accounts receivable balance was due from the town's golf course, representing an advance made by the general fund. Accounts for the municipal golf course operated by the town are maintained in a separate enterprise fund.
2. The total tax levy for the year was $300,000,000. The town's tax collection experience in recent years indicates an average loss of 5 percent of the net tax levy for uncollectible taxes. At year-end, all taxes receivable are considered delinquent and are fully reserved.
3. On June 30, 2017, the town retired at face value 4-percent general obligation serial bonds totaling $35,000,000. The bonds were issued on July 1, 2015, in the total amount of $150,000,000. Interest paid during the year was also recorded in the Bonds Payable account.
4. At the beginning of the year, the town council authorized a supply room with an inventory not to exceed $10,000,000. During the year, supplies totaling $14,000,000 were purchased and charged to Expenditures. The physical inventory taken at June 30, 2017, disclosed that supplies totaling $10,500,000 were used. The town uses the purchases method to report supplies, and supplies are reported in the balance sheet.
5. Expenditures for 2017 included $2,600,000 applicable to purchase orders issued in the prior year. Outstanding purchase orders at June 30, 2017, not recorded in the accounts, amounted to $4,500,000. The GAAP budgetary basis is used.
6. The amount of $9,000,000, due from the state for the town's share of state gasoline taxes, was not recorded in the accounts.
7. Equipment costing $8,000,000 was removed from service and sold for $1,000,000 during the year, and new equipment costing $20,000,000 was purchased. These transactions were recorded in the Town Property account.

Required

a. Prepare the adjusting and closing entries for the general fund of Fountain Inn.
b. Prepare a statement of revenues, expenditures and changes in fund balances and balance sheet for Fountain Inn's general fund.

P10.4 Reconstructing General Fund Journal Entries Suppose the general fund balance sheet for the **LO 3** City of Golden, Colorado, appears as follows:

CITY OF GOLDEN
General Fund
Balance Sheets at June 30

(in thousands)	2017	2016
Assets		
Cash.	$ 20,000	$ 22,000
Investments	40,000	48,000
Due from state government	60,000	—
Due from federal government.	—	98,000
Totals	$120,000	$168,000
Liabilities and fund balances		
Accounts payable.	$ 40,000	$ 32,000
Fund balance—assigned	—	18,000
Fund balance—unassigned	80,000	118,000
Totals	$120,000	$168,000

All numbers below are in thousands. Assigned fund balance consists of outstanding encumbrances. The following budget entry was made on July 1, 2016:

Estimated revenues	75,000	
Fund balance—unassigned	30,000	
Appropriations.		105,000
To record budget for fiscal 2017.		

Bills for the June 30, 2016, encumbrances were $2,000 less than the amount encumbered. Actual revenues were $15,000 less than budgeted. The legal budgetary basis is used for outstanding encumbrances. Investments were liquidated at book value.

Required

Reconstruct the journal entries, including closing entries, for the year ended June 30, 2017, for Golden's general fund.

P10.5 General Fund—Corrections, Adjustments, and Financial Statements During the fiscal year **LO 3** ending June 30, 2016, all transactions of Salleytown were recorded in the general fund due to the inexperience of the town's bookkeeper. The trial balance of Salleytown's general fund is as follows:

SALLEYTOWN
General Fund Trial Balance
June 30, 2016

(in thousands)	Debit	Credit
Cash.	$ 16,800	
Short-term investments	40,000	
Accounts receivable.	11,500	
Taxes receivable—current	30,000	
Accounts payable.		$ 50,000
Appropriations		520,000
Expenditures	382,000	
Estimated revenues	520,000	
Revenues		560,000
General property	85,400	
Bonds payable.	52,000	
Fund balance—unassigned		7,700
Totals	$1,137,700	$1,137,700

The following information is also available *(in thousands)*:

1. The accounts receivable of $11,500 includes $1,500 due from the town's water utility. Accounts for the municipal water utility operated by the town are maintained in a separate fund.
2. The balance in Taxes receivable—current is now considered delinquent, and the town estimates that $24,000 will be uncollectible.
3. On June 30, 2016, the town retired, at face value, 6-percent general obligation serial bonds totaling $40,000. The bonds were issued on July 1, 2011, at face value of $200,000. Interest and principal paid during the year ended June 30, 2016, were charged to bonds payable.
4. During the year, supplies totaling $128,000 were purchased and charged to expenditures. The town conducted a physical inventory of supplies on hand at June 30, 2016, and this physical count disclosed that supplies of $84,000 were used. The purchases method is used and ending inventory is recognized.
5. Expenditures for the year ended June 30, 2016, included $11,200 applicable to purchase orders issued in the prior year. Outstanding purchase orders at June 30, 2016, not recorded in the accounts, amounted to $5,000. The legal budgetary basis is used.
6. On June 28, 2016, the state revenue department informed the town that its share of a state-collected, locally shared tax would be $34,000.
7. During the year, equipment with a book value of $7,900 was removed from service and sold for $4,600. In addition, new equipment costing $90,000 was purchased. The transactions were recorded in general property.
8. During the year, 100 acres of land were donated to the town for use as an industrial park. The land had a value of $125,000. This donation was not recorded.

Required

a. Prepare the formal reclassification, adjusting, and closing journal entries for the general fund as of June 30, 2016.
b. Present, in good form, the general fund's statement of revenues, expenditures, and changes in fund balances for the fiscal year ended June 30, 2016.
c. Present, in good form, the general fund's balance sheet for the fiscal year ended June 30, 2016.

✔ LO 3   P10.6   Comprehensive General Fund Review   The Wayne City Council approved and adopted its general fund budget for 2016. The budget contained the following amounts:

Estimated revenues	$70,000,000
Appropriations	66,000,000
Authorized transfer to the Library debt service fund	3,000,000

During 2016, various transactions and events occurred which affected the general fund. The legal budgetary basis is used.

Required

For items 1–39, indicate whether the item should be **debited (D)**, **credited (C)**, or is **not affected (N)** in the general fund.

a. Items 1–5 involve recording the adopted budget
  1. Estimated revenues
  2. Fund balance—unassigned
  3. Appropriations
  4. Estimated other financing uses
  5. Expenditures
b. Items 6–10 involve recording the 2016 property tax levy. It was estimated that $500,000 would be uncollectible.
  6. Property taxes receivable—current
  7. Bad debt expense
  8. Allowance for uncollectibles—current
  9. Revenues
  10. Estimated revenues
c. Items 11–15 involve recording encumbrances at the time purchase orders are issued.
  11. Encumbrances
  12. Fund balance—assigned
  13. Expenditures
  14. Accounts payable
  15. Purchases

d. Items 16–20 involve recording expenditures that had been previously encumbered in the current year.
   16. Encumbrances
   17. Fund balance—assigned
   18. Expenditures
   19. Accounts payable
   20. Purchases

e. Items 21–25 involve recording the transfer made to the Library debt service fund. No previous entries were made regarding this transaction.
   21. Fund balance—assigned
   22. Due from Library debt service fund
   23. Cash
   24. Other financing uses
   25. Encumbrances

f. Items 26–36 involve recording the closing entries (other than encumbrances) for 2016.
   26. Estimated revenues
   27. Due to special revenue fund
   28. Appropriations
   29. Estimated other financing uses
   30. Expenditures
   31. Revenues
   32. Other financing uses
   33. Bonds payable
   34. Bad debt expense
   35. Depreciation expense
   36. Fund balance—assigned

g. Items 37–39 involve recording the closing entry related to $1,200,000 of outstanding encumbrances at the end of 2016.
   37. Encumbrances
   38. Fund balance—assigned
   39. Fund balance—unassigned

P10.7 **Comprehensive General Fund—Entries and Statements** Data relating to the general fund of **LO 3** the Quarryville School District are:

QUARRYVILLE SCHOOL DISTRICT
General Fund Balance Sheet
June 30, 2016

Assets		Liabilities and fund balances	
Cash.	$1,200,000	Accounts payable.	$ 30,000
Taxes receivable—current		Fund balances	
(net of $100,000 allowance for		Nonspendable	150,000
uncollectible taxes).	400,000	Assigned.	20,000
Inventory.	150,000	Unassigned	1,550,000
Total	$1,750,000	Total	$1,750,000

Additional information for fiscal 2017:

1. The fiscal 2017 budget included $3,200,000 in expected revenue, all from property taxes, estimated other financing uses of $200,000, and appropriations of $3,100,000. The tax levy was for $3,800,000.
2. Tax collections during fiscal 2017 were as follows:

Fiscal 2016 taxes.	$ 425,000
Fiscal 2017 taxes.	2,800,000

3. Taxes due at year-end are not considered delinquent but are 20-percent reserved. Unpaid 2016 taxes are written off as uncollectible.
4. Old school desks were sold for $10,000 in cash.
5. New desks were purchased for $500,000 in cash.
6. Vandalism to the schools resulted in $20,000 of unexpected repair and cleanup costs, paid in cash.

7. Salary expenditures by the general fund were $2,500,000 in cash.
8. Supplies on hand at year-end totaled $125,000, per annual physical inventory. Quarryville uses the consumption method.
9. Accounts payable of $25,000 were outstanding at the end of fiscal 2017, and $50,000 was encumbered for goods ordered but not yet received. The GAAP budgetary basis is used.
10. The 2016 encumbrance for $20,000 was canceled when the goods ordered were found to be defective.
11. Cash of $80,000 was paid to the enterprise fund, as the school district's support for its operating costs.

Required

a. Prepare all the fiscal 2017 journal entries and closing entries for the school district's general fund.
b. Prepare a fiscal 2017 statement of revenues, expenditures, and changes in fund balances and balance sheet for the general fund.

LO 2   P10.8   Employee Compensated Absences   Like most employees, governmental employees receive annual compensated sick leave, family leave, and vacation days. Often, employees are compensated for unused accumulated annual leave upon retirement or termination. Following is supplementary footnote information concerning governmental funds' compensated absences for the **State of South Carolina** for fiscal year 2013:

STATE OF SOUTH CAROLINA

Unpaid compensated absences as of July 1, 2012	$203,985,000
Unpaid compensated absences as of June 30, 2013	203,932,000

Required

Suppose that compensated absences are recorded in the general fund, and the general fund paid $65,000,000 to employees during fiscal 2013 for compensated absences.

a. Present the journal entry or entries necessary to record the above events in the general fund.
b. How would the above events be recorded if the general fund used full accrual accounting?
c. Comment on the value of the general fund balance sheet in evaluating South Carolina's future obligation for compensated absences.

LO 3   P10.9   General Fund Reporting   The following information is available concerning general fund activities of the City of Middletown for the year 2017. Middletown uses the GAAP budgetary basis to account for encumbrances.

1. The general fund budget for 2017 consisted of the following items:

Estimated property tax revenues	$8,500,000
Appropriations	8,800,000
Transfers to capital projects fund	200,000
Transfers to enterprise fund	50,000
Estimated bond proceeds	500,000

2. $78,000 in encumbrances were outstanding at the end of 2016.
3. Current property tax revenues of $8,500,000 were accrued at the beginning of the year, along with a current uncollectible portion of $100,000. The general fund reported equal balances of $25,000 in its delinquent property taxes receivable and uncollectible allowance accounts at the beginning of the year.
4. At the end of the year, current property tax receivables of $120,000 remained uncollected. The current uncollectible accounts balance was $40,000. Delinquent property taxes of $15,000 were collected during the year. The remaining delinquent balances were written off at the end of the year. The general fund's policy is to fully reserve any remaining current property taxes receivable and reclassify them as delinquent.
5. General obligation bonds with a face value of $500,000 were issued at par. Interest at 4% of principal and $20,000 of principal are due annually in 2018. These bonds will be used to finance a community project, which is reported in the general fund. Principal payments will be handled through the debt service fund, but interest payments will be paid through the general fund.
6. The general fund sold equipment with an original cost of $40,000 for $6,000, and purchased a building for $200,000 during 2017. Equipment with an original cost of $30,000 was retired during the year.
7. The transfers to the capital projects and enterprise funds were made as budgeted.

8. Actual expenditures (including the building purchase) for the year were $8,720,000, of which $80,000 related to encumbrances outstanding at the beginning of the year. Encumbrances outstanding at year-end were $130,000.

Required

Answer the following questions related to Middletown's general fund activities for 2017.

a. Present the beginning of 2017 budget and encumbrance entries. What is their net impact on fund balance—unassigned?
b. What is total property tax revenue for 2017? How much cash was collected from property taxes in 2017?
c. How much in bond interest payable should be shown on the general fund's year-end balance sheet?
d. Prepare the end of 2017 closing entries for the general fund.
e. Present a general fund budgetary comparison schedule for 2017.

P10.10 General Fund—Entries and Financial Statements The general fund trial balance for the City of **LO 3** Los Alvos at December 31, 2016, follows:

CITY OF LOS ALVOS
General Fund Trial Balance
December 31, 2016

(in thousands)	Debit	Credit
Cash.	$ 30,000	
Due from other funds	2,000	
Due from federal government.	10,000	
Property taxes receivable—delinquent	65,000	
Allowance for uncollectible taxes—delinquent		$ 40,000
Inventories	15,000	
Accounts payable.		30,000
Fund balance—nonspendable		15,000
Fund balance—assigned		6,000
Fund balance—unassigned		31,000
Totals	$122,000	$122,000

Assigned fund balance consists of outstanding encumbrances. The following information is available for the year 2017:

1. The general fund adopted the following budget for 2017:

Property tax revenues	$500,000
Licenses and fines	35,000
Federal grants	100,000
General government expenditures.	250,000
Human services expenditures	402,000
Transfers to other funds.	14,000

2. Property taxes totaling $500,000 were levied. Of this amount, $50,000 was estimated to be uncollectible. Collections during the year were $430,000 on currently levied taxes and $60,000 related to taxes declared delinquent in 2016. Delinquent taxes uncollected as of the end of 2017 were written off. All uncollected 2017 property taxes were classified as delinquent and $15,000 of these taxes are expected to be collected early in 2018.

3. The $10,000 federal grant accrued in 2016 was received in cash in early 2017. Of the $100,000 in federal grants expected and accrued in 2017, $85,000 was received in cash.

4. Cash received for licenses and fines totaled $34,000.

5. Cash payments for general government and human services activities were $234,000 and $400,000, respectively. At the end of the year, the accounts payable balance was $15,000 and inventories totaled $18,000. Accounts payable and inventories relate only to general government activities. Inventories costing $6,000, relating to encumbrances outstanding at the beginning of the year, were received during 2017. $4,000 in inventory purchase orders were outstanding at the end of the year.

6. Transfers of $14,000 were made to the city's debt service fund. The city's community center enterprise fund paid back a $2,000 cash advance provided by the general fund in 2016. The general fund provided $5,000 to the capital projects fund for temporary financing of a project; this amount is expected to be paid back in 2018.

7. The general fund received a $25,000 cash advance from the city nursing home (an enterprise fund) to cover its cash deficit. It is expected to be paid back next year.

The general fund uses the consumption method for inventory reporting, and the GAAP budgetary basis for year-end encumbrances.

Required

a. Prepare 2017 journal entries to record the above events in the general fund, and to close the books for the year.

b. Prepare the following financial statements for the City of Los Alvos general fund:
   (1) Statement of revenues, expenditures, and changes in fund balances for the year 2017
   (2) Balance sheet for the year ended December 31, 2017
   (3) Budgetary comparison schedule for the year 2017.

LO 3 P10.11 General Fund—Budget and Closing Entries, Financial Statements   Here is the December 31, 2017 pre-closing trial balance for the general fund of the **City of Akron, Ohio**. The city uses the GAAP budgetary basis for encumbrances, and $800 in encumbrances were outstanding at January 1, 2017.

(in thousands)	Debit	Credit
Cash.	$ 5,000	
Investments	14,000	
Property taxes receivable.	63,000	
Allowance for uncollectible property taxes		$ 27,000
Due from special revenue fund	9,000	
Accounts payable.		33,200
Due to internal service fund		7,600
Fund balance—assigned		500
Fund balance—unassigned		23,000
Estimated revenues	260,000	
Estimated other financing sources.	2,000	
Appropriations		257,000
Estimated other financing uses		4,800
Revenues—property taxes.		55,000
Revenues—income taxes.		180,000
Revenues—fines and licenses		18,000
Revenues—state grants.		6,000
Encumbrances	500	
Expenditures—general government.	130,400	
Capital outlay	11,000	
Transfers out	4,500	
Proceeds from sale of capital assets.		2,300
Debt service—interest	35,000	
Debt service—principal	80,000	
Totals	$614,400	$614,400

Assigned fund balance consists of outstanding encumbrances.

Required

a. Prepare the budget entry that was made at January 1, 2017.
b. Calculate the balance in fund balance—unassigned on December 31, 2016.
c. Prepare the required closing entries at year-end.
d. Prepare the general fund statement of revenues, expenditures, and changes in fund balances for 2017.
e. Prepare the general fund balance sheet at December 31, 2017.

P10.12 General Fund—Entries and Financial Statements   Below are the July 1, 2015, balances for the   **LO 3**
general fund of Montana County. The county's fiscal year ends June 30.

	Debit	Credit
Cash.	$120,000	
Taxes receivable—delinquent	22,500	
Allowance for uncollectible taxes—delinquent		$ 22,500
Due from special revenue fund	15,000	
Inventories	7,500	
Accounts payable.		7,500
Fund balance—assigned		3,000
Fund balance—nonspendable.		7,500
Fund balance—unassigned		124,500
Totals	$165,000	$165,000

Montana County uses the purchases method for inventories, and the GAAP budgetary basis for encumbrances outstanding at year-end. Assigned fund balance consists of outstanding encumbrances. The following events occurred in fiscal 2016:

1. Passed the 2016 budget, consisting of expected revenues from property taxes, fees and licenses of $370,500, expected state grants of $40,000, estimated expenditures of $370,000, and expected transfers out of $50,000. Accrued the state grants.
2. Levied property taxes of $300,000, of which 5 percent are estimated to be uncollectible. Collected $280,000 of these taxes.
3. Received $25,000 in state grants.
4. Collected $10,000 in fully reserved delinquent taxes; wrote off the remainder.
5. Transferred $50,000 to the special revenue fund.
6. Received $65,000 in cash for fees and licenses.
7. Received the inventories connected with purchase orders outstanding as of the end of fiscal 2015. The bill was $3,200.
8. Paid $8,000 to the capital projects fund, as a temporary loan.
9. Received $12,000 from the special revenue fund as partial repayment of a loan made in fiscal 2015.
10. Purchased inventories of $45,000 on account.
11. Made expenditures of $320,000 during the year. Purchase orders outstanding at year-end total $4,000.
12. Total accounts payable paid in fiscal 2015 amounted to $367,000. Included are amounts related to expenditures and inventory purchases.
13. Inventories on hand at year-end total $6,000.
14. Taxes uncollected at year-end are to be classified as delinquent and fully reserved.

Required

a. Prepare entries necessary at the beginning of the year to record the budget and make any other necessary adjustments or accruals.
b. Prepare entries necessary to record the events of the year and any year-end adjustments.
c. Prepare the necessary closing entries for June 30, 2016.
d. Present, in good form, the statement of revenues, expenditures and changes in fund balances for Montana County for fiscal 2016. Include a reconciliation of beginning and ending fund balances.
e. Present, in good form, the balance sheet for the general fund of Montana County for June 30, 2016.

P10.13 Capital Asset and Debt Transactions: Modified Accrual and Full Accrual Accounting   A   **LO 3**
major difference between modified accrual accounting used for the general fund and full accrual accounting
for businesses is the accounting for capital assets and long-term debt. Consider the following transactions:

1. At the beginning of 2014, the city purchased a new fire truck for $250,000. The fire truck has an estimated useful life of five years.
2. In 2014, the city issued $10 million of 30 year, 8% bonds at par.
3. In 2015, the city pays $400,000 of interest on the bonds issued in #2.
4. In 2015, the city repays $1,000,000 of bond principal for the bonds issued in #2.
5. At the end of 2017, the city sold the fire truck in #1 above for $40,000 cash.

Required

a.   Prepare the journal entries to record the above events in the general fund, using modified accrual accounting.

b.   How would the above events be recorded if the general fund used full accrual accounting? For capital assets, assume the straight-line depreciation method is used.

c.   How would the fire truck and bonds payable be presented in the 2015 balance sheet of the general fund using 1) modified accrual accounting and 2) full accrual accounting?

LO 1   **P10.14 Identify Appropriate Fund(s)**   The following activities occurred in the **City of Alexandria, Virginia**:

1.   General obligation bonds are issued, and the proceeds are to be used to finance construction of a new courthouse.
2.   General property taxes are accrued, and the property tax bills mailed to homeowners.
3.   Payment is made to a contractor for the construction of the new courthouse.
4.   A special property tax is levied on homeowners to pay for fire department services.
5.   Employees in the mayor's office are paid their bi-weekly salaries.
6.   A grant is received from the State of Virginia, to be used to purchase new equipment for the fire department.
7.   Fees are collected from residents who use the Chinquapin recreational facility.
8.   Two employees in the mayor's office pay a fee to borrow a city vehicle to drive to a governmental accounting conference.
9.   A long-time resident passes away, donating a large sum of money. Her will specifies that income from investment of this money is to be used toward children's services, while the principal is to remain intact.
10.   Fire department employees are paid their bi-weekly salaries.
11.   Excess resources remaining from construction of the new courthouse are transferred out, to be used to repay the bonds issued in #1 above.
12.   Principal and interest for a general obligation note are repaid.
13.   Monthly revenues for the city's water utility are accrued and the bills mailed to residents.
14.   The general fund loans money to the fire department fund.

Required

Identify the fund(s) affected by each of the above transactions.

LO 3   **P10.15 Budget and Closing Entries**   Budgetary comparison information for the budgeted line items in the general fund, taken from the 2013 CAFR for the **State of New York**, is as follows:

STATE OF NEW YORK

(*in millions*)	Budget	Actual	Variance with Budget
Revenues			
Taxes	$43,047	$43,282	$235
Miscellaneous	3,724	3,504	(220)
Federal grants	60	62	2
Total revenues	46,831	46,848	17
Expenditures			
Local assistance grants	39,776	39,760	16
State operations	8,094	7,856	238
General state charges	4,589	4,550	39
Total expenditures	52,459	52,166	293
Excess (deficiency) of revenues over expenditures	(5,628)	(5,318)	310
Other financing sources (uses)			
Transfers from other funds	12,231	11,934	(297)
Transfers to other funds	(6,916)	(6,793)	123
Net other financing sources (uses)	5,315	5,141	(174)
Excess (deficiency) of revenues and other financing sources over expenditures and other financing uses	$ (313)	$ (177)	$136

Required

For the general fund budgeted accounts shown above,

    a.   Prepare the 2013 budget entry for these items.
    b.   Prepare the closing entries.
    c.   What is the net effect on the general fund's fund balance—unassigned?
    d.   Evaluate New York State's performance for 2013.

REVIEW SOLUTIONS •••

Review 1 Solution

    a.   Capital projects fund
    b.   Agency fund
    c.   Enterprise fund
    d.   General fund, unless a designated capital projects fund makes such purchases
    e.   General fund for the revenues and transfer to the debt service fund; debt service fund for resources set aside for debt service
    f.   Debt service fund or general fund
    g.   Enterprise fund
    h.   Special revenue fund
    i.   Permanent fund

Review 2 Solution

a.

Estimated revenues	700,000	
Estimated other financing sources	30,000	
Appropriations		708,000
Estimated other financing uses		8,000
Fund balance—unassigned		14,000

b. In addition to the above budget entry, the following entry made in 2016 to reverse last year's closing of outstanding encumbrances is also included in the $50,000 trial balance amount:

Encumbrances	1,200	
Fund balance—unassigned		1,200

December 31, 2015, fund balance—unassigned = $50,000 − $14,000 − $1,200 = $34,800

c.

Revenues—property taxes	300,000	
Revenues—sales taxes	380,000	
Proceeds of general obligation debt	12,000	
Proceeds from sale of capital assets	16,000	
Transfers in	4,000	
Fund balance—unassigned	18,000	
Estimated revenues		700,000
Estimated other financing sources		30,000
Appropriations	708,000	
Estimated other financing uses	8,000	
Expenditures		698,000
Transfers out		7,600
Encumbrances		1,000
Fund balance—unassigned		9,400

continued

continued from prior page

d.

EERIE COUNTY GENERAL FUND
Statement of Revenues, Expenditures, and Changes in Fund Balances
For Year Ended December 31, 2016

Revenues:		
Property taxes		$300,000
Sales taxes		380,000
Total revenues		680,000
Expenditures		(698,000)
Excess of revenues over (under) expenditures		(18,000)
Other financing sources (uses):		
Proceeds from general obligation debt	$12,000	
Proceeds from sale of capital assets	16,000	
Transfers in	4,000	
Transfers out	(7,600)	
Total other financing sources (uses)		24,400
Excess of revenues and other financing sources over expenditures and other financing uses		6,400
Fund balances, January 1, 2016		36,000 (1)
Fund balances, December 31, 2016		$ 42,400 (2)

(1)	Fund balance—assigned	$ 1,200
	Fund balance—unassigned (from part *b*)	34,800
	Total fund balances, January 1, 2016	$ 36,000
(2)	Fund balance—assigned	$ 1,000
	Fund balance—unassigned	41,400
	Total fund balances, December 31, 2016	$ 42,400

e.

EERIE COUNTY GENERAL FUND
Balance Sheet
December 31, 2016

Assets	
Cash	$11,400
Property taxes receivable, net of $12,000 allowance	52,000
Due from other funds	3,000
Total assets	$66,400
Liabilities, deferred inflows of resources, and fund balances	
Liabilities	
Accounts payable	$15,000
Due to other funds	4,000
Total liabilities	19,000
Deferred inflows of resources	5,000
Fund balances	
Assigned	1,000
Unassigned	41,400
Total fund balances	42,400
Total liabilities, deferred inflows of resources, and fund balances	$66,400

State and Local Governments: Other Transactions

LEARNING OBJECTIVES

LO1 Describe accounting and reporting for special purpose activities. (p. 469)

LO2 Account for capital projects. (p. 472)

LO3 Account for debt service. (p. 478)

LO4 Account for proprietary activities. (p. 482)

LO5 Account for fiduciary activities. (p. 487)

LO6 Explain reporting for investments, compensated absences, landfills, leases, and debt refundings. (p. 490)

ALAMEDA COUNTY, CALIFORNIA
www.acgov.org

Alameda County, California is located on the east side of San Francisco Bay, and includes the cities of Oakland, Berkeley, Albany, Fremont, Livermore, Hayward and San Leandro. The University of California at Berkeley and California State University of the East Bay are located in the county, as well as the Oakland International Airport, Bay Area Rapid Transit System (BART), and the O.co Coliseum and Oracle Arena, home to Major League Baseball's Oakland Athletics, the NBA Golden State Warriors and the NFL Oakland Raiders.

Alameda County's 2013 CAFR reveals that the county manages the Alameda County Medical Center, provides flood control services, services general obligation and revenue bonds, has central transportation and information technology services for county business, and runs an investment fund that consolidates investments on behalf of school and community college districts, courts, and other special districts.

How does Alameda County account for these activities? Do they use full or modified accrual accounting? What do the financial statements for these activities look like? This chapter answers these questions and others concerning transactions of state and local governments in other funds besides the general fund.

CHAPTER ORGANIZATION

Special purpose activities	Capital projects	Debt service	Proprietary activities	Fiduciary activities	Investments, other liabilities, and debt refundings
• Special revenue funds • Permanent funds	• Basic transactions • Interactions with other funds • Financial statements	• Basic transactions • Interactions with other funds • Financial statements	• Enterprise funds • Internal service funds • Financial statements	• Trust funds • Agency funds • Financial statements	• Investments • Compensated absences • Landfills • Leases • Debt refundings

Whereas Chapter 10 explained the accounting for general fund operating activities, this chapter discusses accounting and reporting for governmental funds other than the general fund, i.e. special revenue, capital projects, debt service, and permanent funds. The chapter also discusses activities reported in proprietary funds and fiduciary funds. Funds other than the general fund report specific government activities, such as construction of roads and buildings, services provided to citizens for a fee, and external funding of specific projects.

The first sections of this chapter cover reporting for governmental funds other than the general fund. Recall from Chapter 10 that *SGAS 54* specifies five standardized categories of fund balance for governmental funds: *nonspendable*, *restricted*, *committed*, *assigned*, and *unassigned*. Unassigned fund balance is usually only reported by the general fund. The fund balance of other governmental funds is divided between the four other categories, as appropriate.

- The **nonspendable** category includes inventories, prepaid expenses, and resources legally or contractually required to remain intact, such as endowment principal.
- The **restricted** category contains amounts that can only be used for specific purposes, as specified by *external grant providers, contributors, creditors*, or by *laws and regulations of the other governments* providing the funds.
- **Committed** fund balance includes resources that can only be used for specific purposes, as authorized by the *highest level of the reporting government*. For a school district, for example, this authority might come from the district board of directors. Committed fund balance also includes resources intended to fulfill contractual obligations.
- **Assigned** fund balance contains residual resources not designated as nonspendable, restricted or committed. These amounts are *intended* for the specific purpose, expressed by the government or its delegate, such as a finance committee. But if the residual is negative, it appears as **unassigned** fund deficit.

To determine the balances in each category, first identify the nonspendable amounts. When restricted and unrestricted resources are available for expenditure, apply the government's spending priority policy, specifying the order in which resources are used, to calculate restricted fund balance. For the remainder of fund balance, apply the government's spending priority policy for use of committed or assigned resources.

ACCOUNTING FOR SPECIAL PURPOSE ACTIVITIES

State and local governments often obtain resources *restricted* by external resource providers or *committed* by the highest authority in the government, to be used for specified purposes other than capital projects and debt service. Examples include a state gasoline tax raised to fund repairs and improvements in the state transportation system, a property tax levy to finance refuse collection, and federal grants given to states to pay for particular social services programs. Alameda County has a Property Development Fund for the sale and development of surplus county land, a Flood Control Fund for resources received

LO1 Describe accounting and reporting for special purpose activities.

and used for provision of flood control services, and a Fish and Game Fund to account for fines received and used for fish and wildlife conservation.

Special Revenue Funds

A government may have restricted or committed resources that must be used for *activities that benefit the government and/or its citizens*, these resources are the *major ongoing revenue source* for these activities, and all the resources are *expendable*—available for expenditure. **Special revenue funds** account for the collection and expenditure of these resources. The accounting for special revenue funds parallels that of the general fund, except that the fund balance is restricted or committed, while the fund balance of the general fund can also be assigned and unassigned.

Suppose a county has a special revenue fund for flood control. The fund starts the year as follows:

Cash	$5,000,000	Fund balance—restricted	$2,000,000
		Fund balance—committed	3,000,000
Total assets	$5,000,000	Total fund balances	$5,000,000

Restricted fund balance is a state grant for flood control, and committed fund balance is amounts authorized by the highest level of county government for flood control.

During the year, expenditures for flood control are $4,000,000, and bills of $100,000 are unpaid at year-end. The county's policy is to spend restricted resources first. The flood control fund's year-end balance sheet appears below:

Cash	$1,100,000	Accounts payable	$ 100,000
		Fund balance—committed	1,000,000
Total assets	$1,100,000	Total liabilities and fund balance	$1,100,000

Permanent Funds

When resources are *nonexpendable*—expenditures are limited to investment income, and the principal remains intact—permanent funds account for the collection and expenditure of these resources. Permanent funds report income transactions separately from principal transactions. The principal part of the fund balance is *nonspendable*, and the income portion is *restricted* by the grantor or donor.

To illustrate the accounting for permanent funds, suppose that in fiscal 2016 a resident of Alameda County puts $1,000,000 in trust to support public library acquisitions. The trust specifies that income from trust investments be used to purchase books. A permanent fund is created to account for the activities of the trust, and the $1,000,000 is immediately invested. The Library Fund's entries follow:

Cash—principal	1,000,000	
Fund balance—nonspendable		1,000,000
To record receipt of library gift.		
Investments—principal	1,000,000	
Cash—principal		1,000,000
To record investment of library gift.		

During the year, investments earn $30,000 in cash interest, and the fund spends $25,000 for library acquisitions. Entries are:

Cash—income	30,000	
Investment income		30,000
To record earnings on investments.		
Expenditures	25,000	
Cash—income		25,000
To record library acquisitions.		

The closing entry for the Library Fund follows:

Investment income	30,000	
Expenditures		25,000
Fund balance—restricted		5,000
To close expenditures and income.		

In the permanent funds balance sheet, the fund balance distinguishes between nonspendable resources held in trust, and resources that are spendable but are restricted by the external resource provider for library acquisitions. Similarly, assets are reported as principal and income assets. The Library Fund's balance sheet appears in Exhibit 11.1.

EXHIBIT 11.1   Permanent Fund Balance Sheet

ALAMEDA COUNTY
Balance Sheet—Library Fund
June 30, 2016

Assets

Cash—income	$ 5,000
Investments—principal	1,000,000
Total assets	$1,005,000

Fund balances

Nonspendable	$1,000,000
Restricted	5,000
Total fund balances	$1,005,000

BUSINESS APPLICATION   Special Purpose Activities in State CAFRs

State and local governments report a wide array of funds for special purpose activities, reflecting their diverse environments and public concerns. The following is a sampling of the funds encountered in state Comprehensive Annual Financial Reports (CAFRs).

Special Revenue Funds

The **State of North Dakota** has a series of agriculture special revenue funds, such as a Milk Marketing Fund, Honey Promotion Fund, and a Beef Commission Fund. Such funds are used to promote the sale of North Dakota products. The **State of Mississippi**'s Rice and Soybean Promotion Fund collects fees charged for the sale of rice and soybeans. Revenue is used to promote the rice and soybean industries, through research, education and advertising. The **State of Alaska**'s Exxon Valdez Oil Spill Restoration Fund reports on how the $50 million restitution received by the state has been used for restoration projects related to the oil spill. Alaska also has a Fishermen's Fund that uses commercial fishing license fees to pay for emergency medical treatment of commercial fishermen.

Permanent Funds

The **State of Michigan**'s Children's Trust Fund uses investment earnings to support programs for the prevention of child abuse and neglect in the state. The Michigan Natural Resources Trust Fund uses interest income to acquire land and develop public recreational facilities. The **Texas** Permanent School Fund accounts for investments of the proceeds of land sales. All investment income is used to support Texas public schools. Texas also has a Permanent Health Fund for Higher Education that uses earnings on tobacco settlement monies for health care, tobacco education and enforcement. The **State of Alaska**'s Alaska Permanent Fund receives at least 25 percent of state mineral-related revenues. Resources are invested, and the income is distributed each year to qualified Alaskan citizens as their share of Alaska's natural resources. In 2013, the dividend was $900 per person.

ACCOUNTING FOR CAPITAL PROJECTS

LO2 Account for capital projects.

When a government acquires or constructs capital assets—land, buildings, equipment, or infrastructure such as sidewalks, sewers, roads, and bridges—reporting for these activities depends on the fund financing the asset.

The budget of a general or special revenue fund often includes appropriations for acquisitions of property and equipment, such as police cars and office equipment. Chapter 10 indicates that these funds, which use modified accrual accounting, report capital asset acquisitions as **capital outlays**, part of **expenditures.** For example, the entry to record the special revenue fund's purchase of equipment costing $50,000 in cash is:

Books of Special Revenue Fund

Capital outlay	50,000	
Cash		50,000
To record purchase of equipment.		

In contrast, acquisitions by a proprietary fund—enterprise or internal service fund—are recorded using full accrual accounting, the same as normal business accounting. A cash acquisition of $350,000 in new golf carts by a municipal golf course is recorded as follows:

Books of Enterprise Fund

Equipment	350,000	
Cash		350,000
To record purchase of golf carts.		

If the golf carts are straight-line depreciated over five years with no salvage value, the entry to record yearly depreciation is:

Depreciation expense.	70,000	
Accumulated depreciation.		70,000
To record annual depreciation on golf carts.		

Capital Projects

A government often engages in large capital projects involving construction of buildings or infrastructure. The projects can be financed by general obligation or revenue bonds issued to fund the construction, tax assessments on benefitted property owners, federal or state capital grants, or by transfers from other funds. Unless the project relates to an enterprise or internal service fund, a **capital projects fund** accounts for resources restricted, committed or assigned for capital outlay expenditures.

A separate capital projects fund may be established for each project or each type of asset. In some cases the fund is temporary, originating when the project begins, and ending when the capital asset is completed. However, governments commonly establish continuing capital projects funds for ongoing construction of particular types of assets such as roads or bridges.

Because the budget for a capital project typically requires formal approval, budgetary accounts are often used. If the project is to be financed by general obligation bonds, cost of initial work may be covered by a temporary advance from another fund or by short-term financing known as **bond anticipation notes**—short-term loans from a bank or other financial institution. Issuance of the long-term bonds produces the resources to repay these temporary loans. Any bond proceeds not used for the project are transferred to a debt service fund and used to pay principal and interest on the bonds. Even if the project is financed by multi-year property tax assessments, bonds typically provide up-front money to finance the project. The following chart lists major sources and uses of cash for capital projects funds.

Capital Projects Fund Cash Flows	
Sources of Cash	**Uses of Cash**
Bond anticipation notes (short-term)	Construction costs
Bond proceeds	Repayment of advances
Grants	Repayment of short-term financing
Advances or transfers from other funds	Investments
Investment proceeds	Transfers to other funds

Accounting for the Capital Projects Fund

Assume that in fiscal 2017 Alameda County decides to build a new addition to its main library, and accounts for the project in its Library Facilities capital projects fund. The expected $15,000,000 total cost of the project is to be funded by a $10,000,000 state grant and general obligation bonds of $5,000,000. The state grant and the bonds represent external restrictions on Library Facilities resources, and therefore the entire fund balance of this capital projects fund is *restricted*.

Budget Entry   Whether a budget entry is recorded depends on applicable local laws and regulations. If a budget entry is recorded, it appears as:

Books of Capital Projects Fund

Bonds authorized—unissued...	5,000,000	
Estimated revenues—state grant..	10,000,000	
Appropriations...		15,000,000
To record approval of library addition project.		

Bonds authorized—unissued and *estimated revenues—state grant* signify the resources budgeted for the project, similar to estimated revenues in the general fund.

Revenue Recognition   Capital projects funds typically recognize awarded grants as revenue, since collection is reasonably assured. The entry to record the grant revenue is:

Books of Capital Projects Fund

State grant receivable	10,000,000	
State grant revenue...		10,000,000
To record state grant awarded but not yet received.		

Temporary Financing   Initial resources for the project might be temporarily advanced from another fund to allow work to begin before issuing the bonds. We record a $500,000 advance from the general fund as follows:

Books of Capital Projects Fund

Cash...	500,000	
Due to general fund...		500,000
To record temporary advance from the general fund.		

Books of General Fund

Due from capital projects fund..	500,000	
Cash		500,000
To record temporary advance to the capital projects fund.		

Issuance of Bonds   When bonds finance a construction project, the proceeds must at least equal the amount budgeted. Therefore, the coupon rate on the bonds is typically at or above the interest rate demanded by investors, to ensure that the bond issue provides enough financing for the project. Legal provisions prescribe the use of any premium on a bond issue. The premium cannot be used on project construction costs, since the total cost of construction was previously authorized and cannot be increased unless approved by the same level of authority. The premium is typically applied toward paying the principal and interest on the bonds, and is therefore transferred to the debt service fund.

Assume bonds used to finance the library addition have a coupon rate of 5 percent and are issued at 102. The premium is to be transferred to the debt service fund for future payment of principal and interest.

Books of Capital Projects Fund

Cash..	5,100,000	
Bond proceeds		5,000,000
Due to debt service fund..		100,000
To record issuance of $5,000,000 face value bonds for $5,100,000.		

Bond proceeds appear as *other financing sources* on the capital project fund's statement of revenues, expenditures, and changes in fund balances. The following entries record transfer of the premium to the debt service fund.

Books of Capital Projects Fund

Due to debt service fund	100,000	
Cash		100,000
To record transfer of premium to the debt service fund.		

Books of Debt Service Fund

Cash..	100,000	
Transfers in		100,000
To record receipt of bond premium from capital projects fund.		

The capital projects fund could also record the premium as *other financing sources*, and its transmittal to the debt service fund as *transfers out*.

Partial Collection of Grant; Repayment of Advance
Alameda County receives half of the $10,000,000 state grant, and repays the advance from the general fund, as follows:

Books of Capital Projects Fund

Cash..	5,000,000	
State grant receivable		5,000,000
To record receipt of half of the state grant.		
Due to general fund	500,000	
Cash		500,000
To record repayment of advance from general fund.		

Books of General Fund

Cash..	500,000	
Due from capital projects fund		500,000
To record repayment of advance to capital projects fund.		

Investment of Excess Cash
Governments often temporarily invest bond proceeds and other resources not yet needed to fund construction. State laws typically restrict investments to U.S. Treasury or similar low-risk instruments. Laws also restrict the use of interest earned on such investments. Interest earned on temporary investments is typically used to offset future debt service payments.

Suppose that $2,000,000 is invested, and $60,000 of interest is earned and received for the year. State law requires such interest to be used for future debt service.

Books of Capital Projects Fund

Investments	2,000,000	
Cash		2,000,000
To record investment of excess cash.		
Cash	60,000	
Interest income		60,000
To record interest on investments.		
Transfers out	60,000	
Cash		60,000
To record transfer of interest to debt service fund.		

Books of Debt Service Fund

Cash	60,000	
Transfers in		60,000
To record transfer from capital projects fund.		

BUSINESS APPLICATION   Arbitrage Rebate

Governments often do not use bond proceeds immediately, and temporarily invest the cash until funds are used, such as when construction is complete. Municipal arbitrage occurs when a governmental entity invests its bond proceeds at an interest rate higher than the overall borrowing yield paid for the bond issue. This is possible because governments typically issue bonds at an interest rate that is much lower than that paid by businesses, due to their tax exempt status. As an example, if a school district issues bonds with an overall yield of 5.5% (by issuing tax exempt securities), and invests the proceeds in taxable securities that earn interest at a rate of 6.75%, the arbitrage profit percentage is 1.25%. Thus, governments could theoretically earn close to risk-free profits simply by issuing (and investing) large amounts of debt.

Lawmakers recognized the potential for perverse incentives, and IRS tax laws disallow earning arbitrage profits. Governments are required to calculate and return any arbitrage profits to the federal government, called **arbitrage rebate**. Because of the large amount of debt proceeds that are temporarily invested, capital projects funds are most often subject to arbitrage rebate. If governments do not voluntarily calculate (and return) arbitrage rebates, the bonds may lose their tax exempt status.

Awarding the Contract   After Alameda County receives bids for construction of the library addition, it awards a contract for $13,000,000 to the qualified low bidder. This constitutes an encumbrance, recorded as:

Books of Capital Projects Fund

Encumbrances	13,000,000	
Fund balance—restricted		13,000,000
To record award of contract for construction of library addition.		

Expenditure Recognition; Partial Payment   Construction contracts are usually paid as stages of construction are completed, and often provide for withholding a portion of each billing until the entire project is completed and passes inspection. Known as **retainage**, this provision helps protect against failure of the contractor to complete the project or against deficiencies that need to be remedied.

Assume receipt of $4,000,000 in invoices, representing partial completion of the encumbered construction contract, and that the contract provides for a 10 percent retainage. Entries for payment are:

Books of Capital Projects Fund

Fund balance—restricted..	4,000,000	
Encumbrances..		4,000,000
To reverse encumbrances for amount billed by contractor.		
Expenditures	4,000,000	
Contracts payable..................................		3,600,000
Contracts payable—retainage.....................		400,000
To record billing from contractor.		
Contracts payable	3,600,000	
Cash		3,600,000
To record payment to the contractor.		

Year-End Closing Entries   When the fiscal year ends on June 30, 2017, Alameda County makes the following closing entries:

Books of Capital Projects Fund

State grant revenue	10,000,000	
Bond proceeds...	5,000,000	
Interest income..	60,000	
Bonds authorized—unissued		5,000,000
Estimated revenues—state grant		10,000,000
Fund balance—restricted		60,000
To close actual against budgeted revenues and other financing sources.		
Appropriations	15,000,000	
Expenditures		4,000,000
Encumbrances....................................		9,000,000
Transfers out		60,000
Fund balance—restricted		1,940,000
To close actual expenditures, encumbrances and transfers against appropriations.		

Financial statements of the Library Facilities capital projects fund at June 30, 2017, appear in Exhibit 11.2. There are no other library facilities projects currently in process.

EXHIBIT 11.2   Financial Statements of Alameda County Capital Projects Fund

ALAMEDA COUNTY
Capital Projects Fund—Library Facilities
Statement of Revenues, Expenditures, and Changes in Fund Balances
For Year Ended June 30, 2017

Revenues	
State grant revenue	$10,000,000
Interest income..	60,000
Total revenues	10,060,000
Expenditures	
Contract expenditures	(4,000,000)
Excess of revenues over expenditures	6,060,000
Other financing sources (uses)	
Bond proceeds..	5,000,000
Transfers out...	(60,000)
Total other financing sources (uses)...	4,940,000
Excess of revenues and other financing sources over expenditures and other financing uses	11,000,000
Fund balance, June 30, 2016...	0
Fund balance, June 30, 2017...	$11,000,000

continued

ALAMEDA COUNTY
Capital Projects Fund—Library Facilities
Balance Sheet
June 30, 2017

Assets		Liabilities and fund balances	
Cash	$ 4,400,000	Contracts payable—retainage	$ 400,000
Investments	2,000,000	Fund balance—restricted.	11,000,000
State grant receivable	5,000,000		
Total assets	$11,400,000	Total liabilities and fund balances	$11,400,000

Completion of the Project   Because the budget for the entire project is usually established at the outset, at the beginning of fiscal 2018 we reestablish any carryover encumbrances and appropriations:

Books of Capital Projects Fund

Encumbrances	9,000,000	
Fund balance—restricted		9,000,000
To restore encumbrances closed at prior year-end.		
Fund balance—restricted.	11,000,000	
Appropriations.		11,000,000
To restore unspent appropriations for the year.		

Assume the contractor completes the library addition and it passes inspection. Alameda County makes all contracted payments and receives the remainder of the state grant. An additional $1,500,000 is paid for items not previously encumbered. Investments are liquidated without earning additional interest. The following entries record these events:

Books of Capital Projects Fund

Cash.	5,000,000	
State grant receivable		5,000,000
To record receipt of remainder of the state grant.		
Cash.	2,000,000	
Investments		2,000,000
To record liquidation of investments.		
Fund balance—restricted.	9,000,000	
Encumbrances.		9,000,000
To record reversal of encumbrances.		
Expenditures	10,500,000	
Contracts payable—retainage	400,000	
Cash		10,900,000
To record remaining expenditures and payments under contract, plus additional expenditures.		

The $500,000 cash balance remaining after completion of the project represents unspent bond proceeds. State law requires transfer of that balance to the debt service fund to pay principal and interest on the bonds:

Books of Capital Projects Fund

Transfers out	500,000	
Cash		500,000
To record transfer of unspent bond proceeds to debt service fund.		

Books of Debt Service Fund

Cash	500,000	
Transfers in		500,000
To record receipt of unspent bond proceeds from capital projects fund.		

The following entry closes the Library Facilities capital projects fund:

Appropriations	11,000,000	
Expenditures		10,500,000
Transfers out		500,000
To close expenditures and transfers out against appropriations.		

ACCOUNTING FOR GENERAL OBLIGATION DEBT

LO3 Account for debt service.

Treatment of long-term debt in the fund financial statements depends on the source of cash used for repayment, the fund making the payment, and the fund incurring the debt. Debt of *proprietary funds* is reported as a *liability of the fund itself*, and interest and principal payments follow business accounting procedures. Fiduciary funds typically do not issue long-term debt. Transactions involving general obligation debt—debt for which the government is liable and which is used to finance general operations or capital projects—are usually reported in two funds: the fund that receives the proceeds, and a *debt service fund* that services the debt. Debt proceeds increase the fund balance of the fund receiving the proceeds—usually the capital projects fund or the general fund. A **debt service fund** accounts for resources that are restricted, committed or assigned for payment of principal and interest on general obligation debt.

When *special assessment* construction activities are financed by debt for which only the affected property owners are liable, the periodic assessments are recorded as both assets and liabilities in an *agency fund*. The asset represents current amounts receivable from the property owners, and the liability represents current amounts due to the bondholders. Collection of assessments is recorded as a debit to cash and a credit to receivables. Payment to the bondholders is recorded as a debit to the liability and a credit to cash. A summary of the treatment of debt in the various funds statements appears below.

Long-term debt incurred by	Fund where liability is recorded	Source of resources to repay debt	Debt payment made from
General, special revenue, capital projects funds	Not recorded	General fund budget Special tax levies Bond premium Unspent bond proceeds	Debt service fund
Enterprise, internal service funds	Specific enterprise or internal service fund	Revenues from operations	Specific fund
Special assessment construction activities:			
Government liable for debt	Not recorded	Assessments on property owners	Debt service fund
Government not liable for debt	Not recorded	Assessments on property owners	Agency fund

General Obligation Debt

Funding for interest and principal payments on general obligation debt comes primarily from the general fund, or from special tax levies for debt payment. We saw earlier that some resources for general obligation debt payment are provided by bond premiums and unspent appropriations on capital projects. The chart below lists major sources and uses of cash in the debt service fund.

Debt Service Fund Cash Flows	
Sources of Cash	**Uses of Cash**
Budgeted transfers from general fund	Current payments of interest and principal on general obligation debt
Transfers from special revenue fund (special tax levies for debt service)	Investment for future principal and interest payments
Transfers from capital projects fund (bond premium, unspent bond proceeds, investment earnings)	
Special assessments	
Investment earnings	
Liquidation of investments	

Accounting for the Debt Service Fund

Governments often record a budget for estimated revenues and appropriations in the accounts of the debt service fund, even though the budget usually results from managerial design rather than from a legal approval process. The modified accrual basis of accounting precludes accounting and budgeting for accrued interest on long-term debt. Instead, appropriations include only interest due in the current year. A debt service fund may be used for either *serial bonds* or *term bonds*.

Serial bonds generally mature in equal annual installments over the life of the bond issue so that interest payments, and some principal payments, are made annually according to a predetermined schedule. Budgeted resource inflows are recorded as **estimated revenues** or **estimated financing sources.** Because these budgeted resource inflows normally equal the appropriations for interest and principal payments, the annual budget is typically balanced.

In contrast, **term bonds** mature at the end of the bond issue. Although only interest on term bonds is paid currently, sufficient resources must be available in the debt service fund to repay the principal of the bonds on their maturity date. When the debt service fund serves as a *sinking fund* for term bonds, the annual budget calls for the periodic inflows needed to fund current interest payments and future principal retirement. We use two estimated revenue accounts: **estimated transfers in** indicate the transfers needed from the appropriate funds, and **estimated earnings** reflect the estimated income from debt service fund investments.

When the debt service fund accumulates resources for future repayment of term bonds, annual appropriations differ from annual estimated revenues. During years in which resources are accumulated toward future principal payments, appropriations are less than estimated revenues. When an accumulation is expended in later years, appropriations exceed estimated revenues.

Illustration of Accounting for Term Bonds Suppose that in fiscal 2017 Alameda County establishes a debt service fund to make annual interest payments on the 5 percent, $5,000,000 general obligation bond issue to finance the library addition, and to accumulate resources for the future retirement of principal. The highest level of county government has authorized that all resources in the debt service fund be used for principal and interest payments. Therefore, the entire debt service fund balance is *committed*. Although the annual amount needed to fund principal retirement is frequently determined actuarially, we assume that an annual general fund transfer of $500,000 to the debt service fund suffices. Investment income for the year is estimated at $27,000. Assuming the only planned expenditure is the $250,000 interest payment on the bonds, the budget entry for the debt service fund follows:

Estimated transfers in.	500,000	
Estimated earnings.	27,000	
Appropriations.		250,000
Fund balance—committed		277,000
To record debt service fund budget.		

Assume that early in the year the debt service fund receives the $500,000 transfer from the general fund and immediately invests the cash received in interest-bearing securities.

Cash.	500,000	
Transfers in		500,000
To record transfer from general fund.		
Investments	500,000	
Cash		500,000
To record investments.		

Later in the year, the bond interest payment is made. To raise the needed cash, securities that cost $240,000 are sold for $250,000:

Cash.	250,000	
Investments.		240,000
Gains on investments		10,000
To record sale of securities.		
Debt service—interest	250,000	
Cash		250,000
To record payment of bond interest.		

At year-end, interest income accrued on the investments is $15,000, and $160,000 is transferred in from the capital projects fund:

Investments	15,000	
Interest income		15,000
To record earnings accrued on investments.		
Cash.	160,000	
Transfers in		160,000
To record cash transferred from capital projects fund.		

Because the modified accrual method precludes the debt service fund from accruing interest on long-term debt, there is no year-end adjusting entry for the bond interest accrued since the last payment date. Assuming that the fair values of investments equal their cost at year-end, closing entries for the debt service fund at June 30, 2017 are:

Transfers in.	660,000	
Gains on investments.	10,000	
Interest income.	15,000	
Estimated transfers in		500,000
Estimated earnings		27,000
Fund balance—committed		158,000
To close actual against budgeted revenues and other financing sources.		
Appropriations	250,000	
Debt service—interest.		250,000
To close actual expenditures against appropriations.		

The financial statements for the debt service fund appear in Exhibit 11.3.

Had *serial bonds* been issued instead of term bonds, the annual budget provides only for interest due and principal amount to be retired this fiscal year. Unless the bond indenture requires that the debt service fund also have a cash reserve to protect the bondholders, the budget is balanced.

EXHIBIT 11.3 Financial Statements of Alameda County's Debt Service Fund

ALAMEDA COUNTY
Debt Service Fund
Statement of Revenues, Expenditures, and Changes in Fund Balances
For Year Ended June 30, 2017

Revenues	
Gains on investments..	$ 10,000
Interest income...	15,000
Total revenues	25,000
Expenditures	
Debt service—interest	(250,000)
Excess of revenues over (under) expenditures	(225,000)
Other financing sources (uses)	
Transfers in...	660,000
Excess of revenues and other financing sources over (under) expenditures.....................	435,000
Fund balance, June 30, 2016...	0
Fund balance, June 30, 2017...	$435,000

ALAMEDA COUNTY
Debt Service Fund
Balance Sheet
June 30, 2017

Assets		Fund balance	
Cash............................	$160,000	Fund balance—committed.............	$435,000
Investments	275,000		
Total assets	$435,000	Total fund balance	$435,000

Interaction with Other Funds Below are the entries made by other funds to record the preceding events.

Books of General Fund

Transfers out	500,000	
Cash		500,000
To record transfer of appropriated contribution to debt service fund.		

Books of Capital Projects Fund

Due to debt service fund	100,000	
Cash		100,000
To transfer premium on bonds issued to debt service fund.		
Transfers out	60,000	
Cash		60,000
To record transfer of interest income on investments to debt service fund.		

Special Assessment Debt A government may finance some projects, such as water or sewer improvements, by assessing only those property owners that directly benefit. The project is financed by *special assessment debt*, and assessments on the property owners provide resources for debt service. When the government has no liability for the debt, an agency fund accounts for debt service transactions.

When the government is liable for special assessment debt in case of default by the property owners, the debt is reported like any other general obligation debt. A capital projects fund reports proceeds from debt issuance, and a debt service fund accounts for the assessments and debt payments.

BUSINESS APPLICATION   Tobacco Settlement Reporting

In the late 1990s, the major tobacco companies agreed to pay each of the states billions of dollars in compensation for tobacco-related health care costs. The annual payments vary with industry sales and profitability, and are made in perpetuity. Counties within each state receive a share of this settlement. The states and municipalities were expected to use these resources for medical care and health education. Because most governments could not wait for the yearly payments, they issued bonds to generate immediate resources, secured by revenues generated from the tobacco companies. This financial arrangement is another form of **securitization**, discussed in Chapter 3. Although many governments use their tobacco settlement money for health-related expenditures or for educating citizens about the dangers of smoking, others use these resources for unrelated purposes, such as closing budget deficits and building roads.

Tobacco settlement money is generally reported in special revenue, capital projects, and debt service funds. For example, **Alameda County, CA** uses a capital projects fund to report settlement money that finances construction of health care facilities. **Erie County, NY** reports activities funded with tobacco settlement money in both special revenue and capital projects funds. Both counties have separate debt service funds for the debt service connected with tobacco settlement bonds.

REVIEW 1 • Capital Projects and Debt Service Fund Transactions and Financial Statements

Following are selected transactions of the **City of Townsville**, during 2016 (its accounting year ends December 31):

1. A capital projects fund is established for the construction of a new garage for the highway department at an estimated cost of $5,000,000. The following sources provide funding: general obligation bond issue, $4,000,000, and state government grant, $1,000,000.
2. The general obligation bond issue yields a total of $4,100,000. The premium is transferred to the debt service fund for eventual payment of bond principal and interest.
3. The state government pays $900,000 on the grant.
4. A contract for $4,750,000 is awarded to the qualified low bidder.
5. Invoices of $2,300,000 are paid, less a 20% retainage.
6. The town makes $100,000 in interest and $40,000 in principal payments on the bonds, using a general fund transfer of $140,000.

Assume that capital project and debt service fund resources are *restricted*.

Required

For both the capital projects fund and the debt service fund,

a. Prepare journal entries to record the above events. Include the budget entry, entries made during the year, and closing entries.
b. Prepare the statement of revenues, expenditures, and changes in fund balances for 2016.
c. Prepare the balance sheet as of December 31, 2016.

Solutions are located after the chapter assignments.

ACCOUNTING FOR PROPRIETARY ACTIVITIES

LO4 Account for proprietary activities.

Proprietary funds report government activities that provide goods or services in return for a fee. Like business reporting, the emphasis in proprietary funds is on measuring income, financial position, and cash flows. There are two general types of proprietary funds—enterprise funds and internal service funds.

Enterprise funds account for provision of goods or services *to the general public*, including:

- Utilities—municipal water, gas, and electricity
- Sanitation—sewer systems and landfills
- Recreational facilities—golf courses, marinas, swimming pools, stadiums

- Lotteries
- Commercial facilities—airports, ports, and farmers' markets
- Transportation facilities—buses, rapid transit, parking and toll bridges
- Public hospitals and health clinics
- Public housing projects
- Public colleges

In addition to user charges, these activities are often subsidized by general governmental revenues. The principal source of revenue usually determines whether an enterprise fund or the general fund is used. If user charges provide most of the activity's revenue, the activity is accounted for in an enterprise fund; otherwise, the general fund is used.

Internal service funds account for provision of goods or services by *one department or agency of the government to another*, on a cost reimbursement basis. Centralized service functions are the most common examples, including such activities as:

- Maintenance and repair services
- Vehicle pool and transportation services
- Supply facilities
- Print shop
- Computing and information services

Centralizing such activities enables cost savings to be realized through more efficient use of equipment, volume purchasing, and other economies of scale. The internal service fund pays the cost of operating the central service facility and sets user charges to produce sufficient revenues to recover costs and to perpetuate the facility's activities.

Accounting for Enterprise and Internal Service Funds

Because enterprise and internal service funds use business accounting, revenues and expenses (*not* expenditures), including depreciation, are recognized using the full accrual basis. Enterprise and internal service funds account for their own capital assets and long-term debt, and often issue **revenue bonds** secured by the enterprise fund's operating revenues.

Statement of Net Position   The fund financial statements of enterprise and internal service funds follow those of business firms. The balance sheet, also called the **statement of net position**, has the same accounts and structure as a business balance sheet. Because proprietary funds have no capital stock and no stockholders, "equity" becomes "net position" that is displayed in three categories:

- Net investment in capital assets
- Restricted
- Unrestricted

The balance for "net investment in capital assets" is derived this way:

Cost of capital assets
Less accumulated depreciation—capital assets
Less outstanding principal of related debt
———————————————————————
Net investment in capital assets

The *related debt* includes only those debt proceeds invested in capital assets. Suppose a county parking division issued $10 million in bonds for a construction project, but only spent $2 million to date for construction. Net investment in capital assets includes only the $2 million invested in capital assets, net of $2 million in debt, or a net amount of zero.

Restricted net position is subject to external or governmental restrictions. Suppose a state government provides resources to a county recreation facility, for development of exercise programs. The county itself may impose legal spending restrictions on the fund's assets. For example, **Mecklenburg County, NC**'s Solid Waste enterprise fund reports net position restricted for landfill development and postclosure care.

Statement of Revenues, Expenses and Changes in Net Position Proprietary funds prepare the operating statement using full accrual accounting. The statement has the following categories:

- Operating revenues and expenses
- Nonoperating revenues and expenses
- Capital contributions and transfers

The **State of Minnesota** reports the activities of its state lottery in an enterprise fund. Its operating statement for fiscal 2013 appears in Exhibit 11.4.

EXHIBIT 11.4 Missouri State Lottery Enterprise Fund Operating Statement	
STATE OF MINNESOTA	
Statement of Revenues, Expenses, and Changes in Net Position	
State Lottery	
For the Year Ended June 30, 2013	
Operating revenues	
Scratch ticket sales	$363,835,268
Lotto ticket sales	196,562,316
Other income	92,321
Total operating revenues	560,489,905
Less: In-lieu-of-sales tax	36,425,843
Gross receipts	524,064,062
Direct costs:	
Scratch ticket prizes	248,336,306
Lotto ticket prizes	98,737,043
Online vendor expense	10,680,681
Ticket costs	8,076,972
Retailer commissions and incentives	33,483,145
Total direct costs	399,314,147
Gross profit	124,749,915
Operating expenses	
Advertising	6,876,833
Salaries and benefits	11,212,065
Promotion	1,562,398
Purchased services	1,643,988
Communication	560,299
Occupancy costs	1,455,021
Supplies and materials	1,150,457
Computer and Omnipoint maintenance	341,139
Depreciation	836,044
Other expense	590,080
Total operating expenses	26,228,324
Operating income	98,521,591
Nonoperating revenue (expense)	
Interest earned on investments	134,842
Unused compulsive gambling contribution	511,899
Payments to State:	
Compulsive gambling contribution from prize fund	(2,230,000)
Unclaimed prizes to State	(11,115,435)
Net proceeds to State	(85,822,897)
Total nonoperating expense	(98,521,591)
Change in net position	0
Net position at beginning of year	0
Net position at end of year	$ 0

Similar to many state lotteries, Minnesota's state lottery transfers a large portion of its excess of revenues over expenses—almost $86 million in 2013—to the state's general fund. The income helps support specific programs, such as environmental and other natural resources, as well as other general state operations. Other states, such as California and Missouri, use lottery resources to fund public education.

Statement of Cash Flows   Per *SGAS 9* and *SGAS 34*, the proprietary funds statement of cash flows reports the following categories:

- Cash flows from operating activities, presented using the direct method
- Cash flows from noncapital financing activities
- Cash flows from capital and related financing activities
- Cash flows from investing activities

The investing and financing cash flow classifications differ considerably from the classifications found on a statement of cash flows for a business. The items included in each category are summarized below.

Cash flows from operating activities
    Cash received from sales of goods and services
    Cash paid to suppliers, employees, etc. to provide goods and services
    Cash paid for other operating costs
Cash flows from noncapital financing activities
    Borrowings, repayment of borrowings and interest, and operating grants or transfers
       from other funds, for *other than* acquisition or improvement of capital assets
Cash flows from capital and related financing activities
    Borrowings, grants, special assessment levies, and other inflows, and repayment
       of debt and interest, related to acquisition of capital assets
    Payments to acquire capital assets
Cash flows from investing activities
    Purchase and sale of investments in equity and debt instruments
    Interest and dividends received in cash

Similar to requirements for businesses, a reconciliation of operating income to cash from operating activities is required. However, *SGAS 34* requires the direct method of reporting operating cash flows, whereas businesses can use either the indirect or direct method, and most businesses use the indirect approach.

Alameda County reports the activities of its motor pool in an internal service fund. Its statement of cash flows for fiscal 2013 appears in Exhibit 11.5.

BUSINESS APPLICATION   **Proprietary Activities in State CAFRs**

A sampling of enterprise and internal service funds reported in state CAFRs provides insight into the variety of business-type activities among the states.

Enterprise Funds

The **State of Hawaii** reports the following enterprise funds: the Department of Transportation-Airports Division, and the Department of Transportation-Harbors Division. The airports fund accounts for the operation of the state airports. The harbors fund supports water transportation, harbor operations, preservation of ocean shores and navigational safety. The **State of Texas** has a Texas Prepaid Tuition Plans enterprise fund which allows Texas families to lock in college costs at today's prices. **Alaska**'s Commercial Fishing Revolving Loan Fund supports the development and continued maintenance of commercial fishing gear and vessels. **California**'s State University Dormitory Building Maintenance and Equipment Fund accounts for student charges for housing, parking, and health services, and for revenue bond proceeds used to construct or acquire dormitories. The **State of Maine** has a State Ferry Service Fund that accounts for the operation of ferry services between the mainland and various islands.

continued

continued from prior page

Internal Service Funds

The **State of Georgia** has an internal service fund to account for management of state office buildings and maintenance of the Governor's Mansion and State Capitol grounds. **Michigan**'s Correctional Industries Revolving Fund reports on manufacturing and processing activities employing inmates of the state's correctional institutions.

EXHIBIT 11.5   Alameda County Internal Service Fund Statement of Cash Flows

COUNTY OF ALAMEDA, CALIFORNIA
Statement of Cash Flows
Motor Pool
For Year Ended June 30, 2013

(in thousands)

Cash flows from operating activities	
Internal activity—receipts from other funds	$ 8,806
Payments to suppliers	(5,973)
Payments to employees	(1,716)
Internal activity—payments to other funds	(1,202)
Net cash used in operating activities	(85)
Cash flows from noncapital financing activities	
Transfers in	160
Transfers out	(665)
Net cash used in noncapital financing activities	(505)
Cash flows from capital and related financing activities	
Acquisition of capital assets	(6,468)
Proceeds from sale of capital assets	278
Net cash used in capital and related financing activities	(6,190)
Cash flows from investing activities	
Interest received (paid) on pooled cash and investments	6
Net increase (decrease) in cash and cash equivalents	(6,774)
Cash and cash equivalents—beginning	6,774
Cash and cash equivalents—ending	$ 0
Reconciliation of operating income (loss) to net cash used in operating activities:	
Operating income (loss)	$(1,585)
Adjustments for non-cash activities:	
Depreciation	1,725
Changes in assets and liabilities:	
Other receivables	(330)
Accounts payable and accrued expenses	91
Compensated employee absences payable	3
Due to other funds	11
Total adjustments	1,500
Net cash used in operating activities	$ (85)

REVIEW 2 • Enterprise Fund Transactions and Financial Statements

A county water utility has the following post-closing trial balance at December 31, 2016 (its accounting year ends each December 31):

	Debit	Credit
Cash	$ 40,000	
Accounts receivable, net	75,000	
Supplies	3,500	
Capital assets.	120,000	
Accumulated depreciation		$ 62,000
Accounts payable.		10,000
Bonds payable		80,000
Net investment in capital assets		38,000
Unrestricted net position		48,500
Totals	$238,500	$238,500

Information for 2017:

1. The utility sent out water bills of $450,000 and collected $460,000.
2. Purchased supplies of $50,000; the ending inventory of supplies is $3,000.
3. Acquired capital assets of $25,000 for cash; depreciation expense was $4,000.
4. Incurred out-of-pocket operating expenses of $395,000; the ending accounts payable balance was $15,000.
5. Bond interest of $3,200 and principal of $5,000 were paid in cash.

Required

a. Prepare journal entries to record the events of 2017, including adjusting and closing entries.
b. Prepare the operating statement and statement of cash flows for 2017, in good form.
c. Prepare the statement of net position at December 31, 2017.

Solutions are located after the chapter assignments.

ACCOUNTING FOR FIDUCIARY ACTIVITIES

LO5 Account for fiduciary activities.

Fiduciary funds report financial activities where the government acts as a trustee or agent for others. Assets may *not* be used to support the government's programs. Fiduciary funds consist of two distinct elements: *trust funds* and *agency funds*. Both trust and agency funds involve resources collected, held, paid out, and/or managed by the government acting as a fiduciary for individuals and organizations outside the reporting government. However, the purpose and duration of fiduciary responsibility of the two fund types differ. Trust and agency funds use full accrual accounting, with some exceptions.

SGAS 34 specifies the following three types of **trust funds**:

- **Pension and other employee benefit trust funds** account for health insurance, pension, and other benefits to government employees.

- **Investment trust funds** account for investment pools where other governments invest excess cash on a short-term basis to earn additional income.

- **Private-purpose trust funds** account for all other trusts not benefitting the public in general. A common private-purpose trust fund reports unclaimed assets from abandoned bank accounts.

Agency funds report activities where the government acts in an *agency* capacity, collecting resources and remitting them to individuals or organizations outside the government. The two most common situations involving agency funds are employee deductions and tax collections. Deductions for federal and state taxes, health insurance, retirement contributions, union dues, and payroll savings are withheld from employees and periodically remitted to appropriate entities. Some states collect income taxes or sales taxes on behalf of a city or county. A county may collect property taxes on behalf of other legal entities—cities, towns, or special districts—within its jurisdiction.

Agency funds are also used to account for the *financing of special assessment activities* when the government itself has no liability for related debt. For example, a township issues bonds to finance the building of a road in a rural area. The property owners are liable for principal and interest payments on the bonds. The county collects assessments from the property owners and remits them to the bondholders, using an agency fund to report the collections and payments.

Accounting for Trust and Agency Funds

Accounting for the three types of trust funds is similar to the accounting for permanent funds, discussed earlier in this chapter. Full accrual accounting is used. The most common form of trust fund is the **pension trust fund**; its revenues include resources from the government, employees, and earnings on investments, and the majority of its expenses are in the form of retirement benefits.

Transactions in most agency funds fall into two categories: *collection* and *payment*. A **collection transaction** entry requires a debit to cash and a credit to an appropriate liability account; a **payment transaction** entry requires a debit to the liability and a credit to cash. Because these transactions use cash to create or settle liabilities, an agency fund has no revenues and expenses, and no net asset balance. Instead, it has offsetting assets and liabilities. Even fees charged by an agency fund as a collector of taxes for several jurisdictions are not revenue to the agency fund. Such fees are deducted from amounts due to the other jurisdictions and are recorded as liabilities due to the general fund of the government operating the agency fund.

Special Assessment Financing in an Agency Fund   Special assessment construction activities often require bonds to be issued to provide up-front cash needed for construction. The bonds are then serviced and retired over time as the special assessment money is collected periodically from the property owners.

Suppose a township decides to install new streetlights in a certain area. A ten-year 6 percent serial bond issue totaling $1,000,000 provides cash for construction. Residents in the affected area will be assessed $1,318,000 over ten years to retire the bonds and pay interest on the outstanding bonds, for which the government has no liability. The bonds are secured by commercial and residential buildings where the streetlights are located.

The serial bonds mature at the rate of $100,000 per year. Each year the assessments collected will be used to pay the $100,000 principal of the bonds maturing and the current year's interest on the outstanding bonds. Because the township has no liability for the bonds, an agency fund accounts for transactions related to the financing and the assessments. If the township has primary or residual liability for the bonds, a debt service fund accounts for the financing and assessment transactions.

The first year's assessments levied on the property owners are $160,000, which the township records in an agency fund. We assume uncollectible assessments are negligible; if estimated uncollectible amounts are significant, they are netted against the recorded asset and liability.

Assessments receivable—current	160,000	
Due to special assessment creditors		160,000
To record levy of special assessments.		

The year's assessments are collected, and used to pay the $100,000 of principal and $60,000 (= 0.06 × $1,000,000) of interest.

Cash	160,000	
Assessments receivable—current		160,000
To record collection of current assessments.		
Due to special assessment creditors	160,000	
Cash		160,000
To record payment of $100,000 of principal and $60,000 of interest.		

At the beginning of the next year, the second year's assessments are recorded. In this year, $154,000 is needed to retire $100,000 in bond principal and pay interest of $54,000 [= 0.06 × ($1,000,000 − $100,000)] on the $900,000 of bonds still outstanding.

	154,000	
Assessments receivable—current	154,000	
Due to special assessment creditors		154,000
To record the second year's assessments.		

The township makes similar sets of entries each year until all assessments are collected and all bond-holders are paid. The agency fund records only the *current* portion of assessments receivable each period. Recording future assessments would create a reported liability for the full amount of the debt, which contradicts the fact that the government is not liable for any of the debt.

Financial Statements for Fiduciary Funds *SGAS 34* as amended by *SGAS 63* requires that fiduciary fund activities be reported in a **statement of changes in fiduciary net position** and a **statement of fiduciary net position**. Because agency funds have no revenue and expenditure transactions, and no net position, agency fund activities are not reported in the statement of changes in fiduciary net position; only trust fund activities are reported in this statement. Trust fund net position is generally reported in total for each fund type.

If assets are held in an agency capacity pending distribution to *other funds within the government*, those assets are reported in the funds for which the assets are held, and not in a separate agency fund. Fiduciary funds only report on resources held for individuals or organizations *outside the reporting government*.

Alameda County reports each of the four fiduciary fund types—pension trust, investment trust, private purpose trust, and agency funds. Its investment trust fund accounts for investments made on behalf of external school and community college districts, courts, and other special districts. The private purpose trust fund reports management of assets belonging to conservatees of the county. Agency funds account for resources held in custody for others, including disputed property taxes receivable, payroll deductions, and federal and state funds to be distributed to local agencies. Summarized financial statements for Alameda County's fiduciary funds are in Exhibits 11.6 and 11.7.

EXHIBIT 11.6   Alameda County Statement of Changes in Fiduciary Net Position

COUNTY OF ALAMEDA, CALIFORNIA
Statement of Changes in Fiduciary Net Position
For Year Ended June 30, 2013

(in thousands)	Pension, OPEB, and Other Employee Benefit Trust Funds	Investment Trust Fund	Private Purpose Trust Fund
Additions:			
Employer and employee contributions................	$ 262,675	$ —	$ —
Contributions to pooled investments.................	—	6,981,733	—
Total contributions	262,675	6,981,733	—
Investment income:			
Interest and dividends	113,854	3,936	172
Net increase (decrease) in fair value of investments ...	614,690	(6,822)	(117)
Real estate and securities lending income...........	22,560	—	—
Total investment income	751,104	(2,886)	55
Less investment expenses.......................	39,238	—	—
Net investment income......................	711,866	(2,886)	55
Miscellaneous income	912	—	22,610
Total additions, net..........................	975,453	6,978,847	22,665
Deductions:			
Benefit payments...............................	361,252	—	—
Refunds of contributions	5,893	—	—
Administration expenses	14,098	—	—
Distribution of pooled investments.................	—	6,840,198	6,335
Other expenses	—	—	42,073
Total deductions.............................	381,243	6,840,198	48,408
Change in net position	594,210	138,649	(25,743)
Net position—beginning..........................	5,076,060	1,510,592	39,943
Net position—ending	$5,670,270	$1,649,241	$14,200

EXHIBIT 11.7   Alameda County Statement of Fiduciary Net Position

COUNTY OF ALAMEDA, CALIFORNIA
Statement of Fiduciary Net Position
June 30, 2013

(in thousands)	Pension, OPEB, and Other Employee Benefit Trust Funds	Investment Trust Fund	Private Purpose Trust Fund	Agency Funds
Assets:				
Cash and investments	$5,916,014	$1,696,536	$41,892	$185,185
Taxes receivable.	—	—	—	201,610
Interest and other receivables	63,202	1,345	1,815	110
Prepaid expenses.	—	3,959	—	9,785
Capital assets, net of depreciation.	5,563	—	14,011	—
Total assets	5,984,779	1,701,840	57,718	396,690
Liabilities:				
Accounts payable and accrued expenses	57,076	52,599	569	6,111
Securities lending obligation	257,433	—	—	—
Due to other governmental units	—	—	10,890	390,579
Notes and bonds payable	—	—	32,059	—
Total liabilities.	314,509	52,599	43,518	396,690
Net position:				
Restricted for pension	5,085,161	—	—	—
Restricted for postemployment medical benefits.	518,687	—	—	—
Restricted for other postemployment benefits.	64,356	—	—	—
Restricted for other purposes	2,066	1,649,241	14,200	—
Total net position	$5,670,270	$1,649,241	$14,200	$ —

ACCOUNTING FOR INVESTMENTS

LO6 Explain reporting for investments, compensated absences, landfills, leases, and debt refundings.

A government typically invests liquid assets on either a short-term or long-term basis. Amounts accumulated in the debt service fund for payment of term bond principal can be invested for several years. Bond proceeds for construction of capital assets can be temporarily invested by the capital projects fund. Permanent funds invest principal and use the income for specified activities benefitting the public. Trust funds, especially pension trust funds, typically invest in a variety of low-risk investments. The government can invest individually, or may combine resources with other governments in the form of an investment pool. State and local governments place legal restrictions on the types of investments made with governmental resources. Usually investments are restricted to low-risk securities such as obligations of the U.S. or state government, and highly rated commercial paper.

SGAS 31, Accounting and Financial Reporting for Certain Investments and for External Investment Pools, specifies that investments in debt or equity securities, mutual funds, external investment pools, options, warrants, and stock rights be reported at *fair value*. If a market price is not available, discounted cash flow or other estimation methods are used to determine fair value. *SGAS 31* applies to governmental, proprietary, and fiduciary funds. Investments appear on the fund's balance sheet or statement of net position.

Investment income appears as revenue in the fund's operating statement—the statement of revenues, expenditures, and changes in fund balances for governmental funds, the statement of revenues, expenses, and changes in net position for proprietary funds, or the statement of changes in net position for fiduciary funds. Investment income includes interest and dividend income, realized gains and losses on the sales of securities, as well as unrealized gains and losses on securities held at year-end. Governments often combine these amounts in the investment income line on the operating statement. The change in the fair value of investments may be listed as a separate component of investment income. However, unrealized gains and losses must not be reported separately from realized gains and losses. Alameda County's operating statement for fiduciary funds, Exhibit 11.6, reports that in fiscal 2013, the fair value of investments increased for the pension and other employee benefit trust funds, but decreased for the investment and private purpose trust funds.

Cases of poor investment management by governments have unfortunately been too common in the past. For example, in the early 1990s, **Orange County, California** ran a $20 billion investment pool which invested on behalf of 187 California municipalities. The county and its investment pool filed for bankruptcy court protection when the pool lost $1.7 billion on risky derivatives investments. In 2002, the Florida state pension system lost $335 million on its investment in **Enron** stock. From 2008 to 2011 **Jefferson County, Alabama** was on the brink of bankruptcy in part due to ill-conceived investments in interest rate swaps. Jefferson County finally declared bankruptcy in late 2011. *SGAS 31*'s fair value requirements allow more timely assessment of the financial condition of a government, since the financial effects of poor investment decisions are reported as values decline.

Derivatives Investments

Governments are subject to many of the same financial risks as businesses. A government that plans to purchase a commodity in the future takes the risk that commodity prices will increase. A government that issues variable rate debt takes the risk that interest rates will increase. Governments may hedge these risks using derivative instruments such as forwards, futures, options or swaps. We discuss the reporting for derivative instruments used by businesses in Chapter 9. *SGAS 53*, Accounting and Financial Reporting for Derivative Instruments, provides the reporting standards for derivatives used by governments. This section focuses on reporting investments in derivatives in the fund statements. Chapter 12 discusses reporting for investments in derivative instruments in the Comprehensive Annual Financial Report.

Derivatives differ from other investments because governments enter a derivatives agreement with little or no investment, and they can be settled early. A government may enter a futures contract fixing the price of wheat purchased in 120 days at $6 per bushel. The contract requires no initial investment, and the government may settle the contract at any time within the next 120 days by selling wheat at the current futures price. Suppose that after 30 days the government decides to settle the contract, when the 90-day futures price is $6.50 per bushel. The government receives a net payment of $0.50 per bushel by buying at $6.00 per bushel, per the futures contract, and selling at the market price of $6.50 per bushel.

SGAS 53 requires that derivatives be reported at *fair value* in a fund's *accrual-based* statement of net position. Unlike other investments, *this standard does not apply to governmental funds*, which use the modified accrual basis. *SGAS 53* divides derivatives into two types:

- A derivative used to generate income is reported using *SGAS 31* standards. Changes in fair value are reported on the fund's operating statement.

- Changes in the fair value of a derivative used as a *hedge investment* must be reported as *deferred inflows or outflows* on the fund's statement of net position.

In order to qualify as a hedge investment, the derivative's terms must match the terms of the hedged item and be effective in hedging the risk. A government issues 3-year variable rate bonds with a par value of $100 million. To hedge the risk that interest rates will rise, the government enters a 3-year receive variable/pay fixed interest rate swap with a notional value of $100 million, where a counterparty pays the government the variable interest it needs to pay its bondholders, and the government pays the counterparty a fixed rate. The swap hedges the government's interest rate risk by changing the variable rate to a fixed rate, and its terms match the terms of the government's debt.

Because governments commonly use interest rate swaps to hedge their interest rate risk on variable rate debt, we illustrate the hedge accounting requirements of *SGAS 53* using a receive variable/pay fixed interest rate swap. On July 1, 2015, Orleans County's enterprise fund issues 3-year $100,000,000 face value variable rate bonds, with interest paid annually on June 30, the end of the accounting year. The variable rate for fiscal 2016 is 5 percent. The county enters an interest rate swap, where the counterparty pays the county the variable interest it requires to pay its bondholders, and the county pays the counterparty 4 percent on a notional amount of $100,000,000. There is no initial investment and the swap has no value at inception. Orleans County's enterprise fund records the events of fiscal 2016 as follows:

2015			
July 1	Cash..	100,000,000	
	Bonds payable..		100,000,000
	To record issuance of variable rate bonds.		
2016			
June 30	Interest expense—bonds.......................................	5,000,000	
	Interest expense—counterparty		1,000,000
	Cash		4,000,000
	To record interest payments.		

Suppose the fair value of the swap rises from zero on July 1, 2015 to $2,800,000 on June 30, 2016. Because the swap qualifies as a hedge, the change in fair value is a *deferred inflow or outflow* on the proprietary fund's statement of net position:

2016			
June 30	Investment in swap	2,800,000	
	Deferred inflow—swap		2,800,000
	To report the change in swap fair value and report the swap		
	at fair value.		

The variable rate falls to 3 percent for fiscal 2017, and the fair value of the swap falls to $1,200,000. These entries report the events of fiscal 2017:

2017			
June 30	Interest expense—bonds.......................................	3,000,000	
	Interest expense—counterparty................................	1,000,000	
	Cash		4,000,000
	To record interest payments.		
	Deferred inflow—swap...	1,600,000	
	Investment in swap		1,600,000
	To report the change in swap fair value.		

The variable rate falls to 2.5 percent for fiscal 2018, and the swap expires and has no value on June 30, 2018:

2018			
June 30	Interest expense—bonds.......................................	2,500,000	
	Interest expense—counterparty................................	1,500,000	
	Cash		4,000,000
	To record interest payments.		
	Deferred inflow—swap...	1,200,000	
	Investment in swap		1,200,000
	To report the change in swap fair value.		

If the swap is settled early or no longer qualifies for hedge accounting, any deferred inflows or outflows are reclassified as investment income or loss in the operating statement.

Hedge accounting provides current year-end information by reporting derivative investments at fair value on the fund's statement of net position. However, the unrealized changes in fair value do not impact the fund's bottom line. Businesses report these value changes in other comprehensive income, and therefore avoid impacting income. Governments do not report other comprehensive income, but the deferred accounts on the statement of net position achieve the same result.

Because *SGAS 53* and other recent standards and proposals require the use of "deferred" accounts, the GASB issued *SGAS 63* to address proper display of these balances. Chapter 12 provides additional illustrations of the requirements of this standard.

ACCOUNTING FOR OTHER LIABILITIES AND DEBT REFUNDINGS

Like most organizations, governments engage in transactions and activities resulting in future payment obligations. Reporting for these activities differs significantly depending on whether the affected fund uses full or modified accrual accounting. We describe here the accounting and reporting for four common examples: compensated absences, landfill operations, leases, and debt refundings.

Compensated Absences

Governments offer various benefits to employees, such as vacation pay, paid holidays, and sick pay. When these costs are paid in the period earned, no particular reporting issues arise. In many cases, however, the benefits are paid in future periods. *SGAS 16* provides the reporting requirements for compensated absences.

Accounting and Reporting in Proprietary Funds   *SGAS 16* requires that proprietary funds recognize the liability for compensated absences as incurred, when employees perform the services on which the benefits are based. However, if the benefit depends on a future event, or on future services provided by the employee, no liability is recognized. Most sick leave is therefore not accrued, since payment of this benefit depends on the health of the employee, an unknown future event. Assume that for proprietary funds administrative employees, the year's estimated liability for compensated absences is $2,500,000. This entry accrues the expense and liability:

Administrative expense	2,500,000	
Liability—compensated absences		2,500,000
To record estimated compensated absences related to employee services performed this year.		

Subsequent benefit payments reduce the liability.

Accounting and Reporting in Governmental Funds   Because governmental funds use modified accrual accounting, only compensated absences expected to be paid with current financial resources are accrued in the current period. Although the entry is the same as for proprietary funds, the amount is likely much lower because the amount accrued is only that portion of the total benefits earned to be paid with current resources. Remaining benefits are reported as expenditures when actually paid.

Landfill Operations

Governments often operate landfill sites for the disposal of refuse. Although current operating activities pose no particular reporting issues, the U.S. Environmental Protection Agency established specific closure requirements for landfills that carry significant future costs. *SGAS 18* contains the reporting requirements for landfills.

    Landfill costs include current operating costs and estimated costs of closure and postclosure care. Costs of closure include equipment and facilities acquired at or near the date of closure, plus costs of capping the landfill. Postclosure care includes mandated monitoring and maintenance costs.

Accounting and Reporting in Proprietary Funds   When a proprietary fund accounts for the landfill, it allocates the estimated current cost of future closure and postclosure care to each period of landfill operation, based on usage. This approach is similar to the "units of production" depreciation method. Suppose the estimated current cost of closure and postclosure care is $20,000,000, $3,000,000 was reported in previous periods, and the landfill is 40 percent filled. Closure and postclosure costs recognized this period are $5,000,000 [= ($20,000,000 × 0.4) − $3,000,000], as follows:

Expense—landfill closure and postclosure care	5,000,000	
Liability—landfill closure and postclosure care		5,000,000
To record the current year's allocation of future closure and postclosure care costs.		

As actual closure and postclosure care costs are incurred, they are charged against the estimated liability. Proprietary funds also report expenditures for capital assets acquired for this purpose as reductions in the liability—which includes their estimated cost—and do not capitalize the assets.

Changes in estimates of future costs are handled prospectively as just described if the landfill is still in operation. Changes in estimates occurring after the landfill has closed are reported as current year costs, as they cannot be allocated over future periods.

Accounting and Reporting in Governmental Funds   When a governmental fund accounts for the landfill, it reports only costs requiring current financial resources in the current year. Since estimated closure and postclosure care costs are not incurred until the landfill closes, governmental funds do not report these costs while the landfill is in operation. The estimated future liability connected with the landfill does not appear in the governmental funds financial statements.

BUSINESS APPLICATION   **Compensated Absences and Landfill Liabilities**

Mecklenburg County, NC accounts for the operations of its landfill in a proprietary fund. The liabilities section of the fund's 2013 balance sheet reports $76,821 in current and $402,753 in long-term compensated absence liabilities related to landfill employees. Landfill development and postclosure care costs of $8,833,808 are listed as long-term liabilities. Current expenses include $40,088 in final closure and postclosure costs. There is no separate listing for compensated absences on the balance sheet or operating statement of Mecklenburg County's governmental funds. The county reports a liability for vacation pay/sick leave in the governmental funds balance sheet "only if the benefit has matured, for example, as a result of employee resignations and retirements." Mecklenburg County pays terminated employees one fourth of their unused sick leave. *Source:* Mecklenburg County June 30, 2013, CAFR.

Accounting for Leased Assets

Governments often enter into lease agreements for the use of long-term assets such as buildings and equipment. The proper accounting for leases depends on whether the lease is a *capital* or *operating lease* and whether the affected fund uses full or modified accrual accounting. State and local governments follow the provisions of *ASC Topic 840* concerning lease classification, which consider the lease agreement to be a capital lease when its terms transfer substantially all of the risks and benefits of ownership to the lessee. Proprietary funds use full accrual accounting for capital leases.

The following example illustrates general fund reporting for leases, using modified accrual accounting. Suppose that on January 1, 2017, Alameda County's general fund agrees to lease equipment for five years under these terms: $500,000 is due at the lease signing, and payments of $500,000 per year are due at the end of each of the next four years. The lease agreement reflects an implicit interest rate of 5 percent.

If the lease qualifies as a **capital lease**, the general fund records the lease as follows:

2017			
Jan. 1	Expenditures—capitalized leases	2,273,000	
	Other financing sources—capitalized leases		2,273,000
	To record the signing of the lease; $2,273,000 is the present value of the lease payments at 5 percent.		
	Expenditures—principal	500,000	
	Cash		500,000
	To record initial payment on the capital lease.		

The first entry records both expenditures and other financing sources at the present value of the lease payments. The rationale is that if the lease is a capital lease, it should be recorded as the purchase of a capital asset financed with debt. Thus, the government reports the amount borrowed as an other financing source, and the asset purchase as an expenditure. The payment at the end of 2017 is recorded as follows:

2017

Dec. 31	Expenditures—principal	411,350	
	Expenditures—interest	88,650	
	Cash		500,000

*To record the lease payment. The outstanding debt during 2017
is $1,773,000 (= $2,273,000 − $500,000) and the interest portion
of the payment is $88,650 (= 5% × $1,773,000).*

If the lease qualifies as an **operating lease**, the general fund treats the lease payments as rent. Each $500,000 lease payment is recorded as follows:

Expenditures—rent	500,000	
Cash		500,000

To record the operating lease payment.

Debt Refundings

Governments often issue new lower rate debt to replace higher rate debt, known as "refunding" or "defeasing" the old debt. The proceeds of the new bond issue are placed in escrow and invested until the money is needed to refund the old bonds. The bond contract usually specifies the investments and the schedule of payments to refund the old bonds. The scheduled principal and interest payments on the refunded debt continue to be paid from the escrow account until the call date. Reporting requirements for refunding of governmental fund debt are in *SGAS 7*, while proprietary fund refunding standards are in *SGAS 23* and *SGAS 65*.

When a government refunds general obligation debt, proceeds from the new debt issue usually go to the debt service fund, and are then transferred to the escrow account. For example, suppose a county issues $1,500,000 face value general obligation bonds, paying interest at a 3 percent rate, to refund bonds with a 5 percent interest rate. The bonds are issued at par. The debt service fund reports the issuance as follows:

Cash	1,500,000	
Other financing source—proceeds of refunding debt		1,500,000
To record issuance of new debt.		
Other financing use—payment to escrow agent	1,500,000	
Cash		1,500,000
To record payment to escrow agent		

Long-term governmental fund debt is not reported as a liability in the fund accounts. However, proprietary funds use full accrual accounting and report their long-term debts as liabilities. When proprietary fund debt is refunded, we must remove the liability for the old debt from the proprietary fund's accounts. There is usually a difference between the amount needed to retire the old bonds and the carrying value of the old bonds, due to a call premium and/or an unamortized premium or discount on the old debt. Suppose an enterprise fund has 7 percent bonds with a par value of $5,000,000 on its books at $4,900,000. The call premium is $200,000, so the enterprise fund pays the par value and the call premium to current bondholders, a total of $5,200,000. The enterprise fund issues new 3 percent bonds at a par value of $5,200,000 to finance the refunding. The summary entry to record the new debt issue and the refunding is:

Bonds payable, 5%	4,900,000	
Deferred outflow—refunding	300,000	
Bonds payable, 3%		5,200,000
To record refunding of debt.		

SGAS 65 requires that the difference between the reacquisition cost and the carrying value of the refunded debt be reported as a *deferred inflow or outflow* on the enterprise fund's balance sheet. This amount is amortized systematically as an adjustment to interest expense on the new bond issue. In this case, amortization of the deferred outflow increases interest expense on the new bonds.

BUSINESS APPLICATION   State of New York Debt Refundings

In fiscal 2014, the State of New York issued $6.6 billion in bonds, of which more than one third, $2.5 billion, was used to refund old debt. New York reports the activities of the State University of New York (SUNY) and the City University of New York (CUNY) in enterprise funds with a June 30 year-end. The 2013 balance sheet for SUNY and CUNY reports deferred outflows on refunding of $24 million and $69 million, respectively. This indicates that the amounts paid to refund debt exceeded the carrying value of the refunded debt. These outflows are debit balances that will be amortized as increases in interest expense on the new debt.

Although the governmental funds also report refunding activities, they do not result in deferred outflows or inflows because the original liability was never reported in those funds. New York's fiscal 2014 general debt service fund operating statement reports two items related to refunding, both in other financing sources (uses). Refunding debt issued of $770 million appears as an other financing source, and payments to escrow agents for refunding of $884 million appears as an other financing use. The net effect is a decrease in fund balances of $114 million. *Source*: State of New York 2014 CAFR.

REVIEW OF KEY CONCEPTS

LO 1 **Describe accounting and reporting for special purpose activities. (p. 469)** Resources collected and legally restricted for a particular purpose that benefits the public are reported in **special revenue** or **permanent funds**. A special revenue fund is used if the resources are **expendable**, and a permanent fund is used if the collected resources are **nonexpendable** but the income is expendable.

LO 2 **Account for capital projects. (p. 472)** **Construction activities** or major asset acquisitions are accounted for in the **capital projects fund**. Typical transactions include temporary financing, collection of debt proceeds, expenditures for construction, temporary investments, and transfers to other funds. Capital projects funds use modified accrual accounting.

LO 3 **Account for debt service. (p. 478)** The **debt service fund** accumulates resources and uses them for payment of principal and interest on **general obligation debt**. The debt service fund for **term bonds** typically also engages in investment activities. Debt service funds use modified accrual accounting.

LO 4 **Account for proprietary activities. (p. 482)** **Enterprise funds** account for the provision of goods or services to the public, in return for a fee. **Internal service funds** are used when the goods or services are provided to other departments or agencies within the government. Proprietary funds use full accrual accounting.

LO 5 **Account for fiduciary activities. (p. 487)** **Fiduciary funds** consist of **pension and other employee benefit trusts**, **investment trusts**, **private purpose trusts**, and **agency funds**, and report on activities related to individuals and entities outside the government.

LO 6 **Explain reporting for investments, compensated absences, landfills, leases, and debt refundings. (p. 490)** **Investments** by state or local governments are reported at **fair market value**, with income and realized and unrealized gains and losses reported in the fund's operating statement. Changes in the value of derivative investments used by proprietary or fiduciary funds to hedge financial risk appear as deferred gains and losses on the fund's statement of net position. Estimated liabilities for **compensated absences** and **future closure and postclosure costs of landfills** are recognized in proprietary funds statements. These liabilities are recognized in governmental funds only if they will be paid with current financial resources. **Leases** are classified as **capital** or **operating** leases following the requirements of *ASC Topic 840*. At inception, governmental funds report capital leases as expenditures and other financing sources, at the present value of the lease payments. Subsequent capital lease payments are reported as principal and interest expenditures. **Debt refunding** activities are reported in the other financing sources/uses section of the governmental funds operating statement. Proprietary funds report the difference between the cost of refunding and the carrying amount of the refunded debt as a deferred inflow or outflow on the balance sheet, which is amortized to interest expense in future years.

Assignments with the ✔ in the margin are available in BusinessCourse.
See the Preface of the book for details.

MULTIPLE CHOICE QUESTIONS ································

1. A county receives $10,000,000 from a private foundation. The foundation requires that the county maintain the principal of this endowment, and income from its investment must be used to maintain county parks. The county reports activities related to this endowment in a permanent fund. During the year, the county invests the $10,000,000, earns investment income of $300,000, and spends $280,000 on park maintenance. At year-end, how does the permanent fund report fund balance?   **LO 1 ✔**

   a.   Nonspendable $10,000,000 and restricted $20,000
   b.   Restricted $10,000,000 and committed $20,000
   c.   Restricted $10,000,000 and assigned $20,000
   d.   Nonspendable $10,000,000 and assigned $20,000

2. A county receives $10,000,000 from a private foundation. The foundation specifies that the $10,000,000 must be used for county park maintenance. The county reports activities related to this contribution in a special revenue fund. During the year, the county spends $1,000,000 on park maintenance. At year-end, how does the special revenue fund report fund balance?   **LO 1 ✔**

   a.   Nonspendable $10,000,000 and restricted $(1,000,000)
   b.   Restricted $10,000,000 and assigned $(1,000,000)
   c.   Restricted $9,000,000
   d.   Committed $9,000,000

3. A county capital projects fund receives resources of $8,000,000 from a bond issue and a state grant of $15,000,000, to build an administration building. Both funding sources are externally restricted to the capital project. During the year contracts are signed for $20,000,000. Contractors submit bills for $5,000,000 and the county pays $4,000,000. At year-end, how does the capital projects fund report fund balance?   **LO 2 ✔**

   a.   Restricted $4,000,000, committed $15,000,000
   b.   Restricted $3,000,000, committed $15,000,000
   c.   Restricted $18,000,000
   d.   Restricted $19,000,000

4. A capital projects fund buys equipment for $4,000,000. The equipment has a 4-year estimated life, straight-line, no residual value. The equipment is sold after 3 years for $200,000. Which statement is *true* regarding the effect on the capital project fund's operating statement in the year the equipment is sold?   **LO 2 ✔**

   a. $800,000 loss is reported in the nonoperating section.
   b. $200,000 proceeds are reported as other financing sources.
   c. $800,000 loss is reported as other financing uses.
   d. $200,000 proceeds are reported in the revenues section.

5. Which statement below is *false* concerning the reporting for bond issues in the fund statements of a government?   **LO 3 ✔**

   a.   Proceeds from bonds issued to finance capital projects are reported as other financing sources in the capital projects fund operating statement.
   b.   Payments of principal and interest on bonds issued by an enterprise fund are accounted for using a debt service fund.
   c.   Payments of principal on general obligation bonds are reported as expenditures in the debt service fund operating statement.
   d.   The principal of bonds issued to finance capital projects of an internal service fund is reported as a liability on the internal service fund's balance sheet.

6. The debt service fund makes a $10,000,000 payment on the principal of general obligation long-term debt. How is this reported on the financial statements of the debt service fund?   **LO 3 ✔**

   a.   Expenditure on the statement of revenues, expenditures and changes in fund balances
   b.   Expenditure on the statement of revenues, expenditures and changes in fund balances, and long-term debt on the balance sheet will be lower
   c.   Long-term debt on the balance sheet will be lower
   d.   Outflow of cash for financing on the statement of cash flows, and long-term debt on the balance sheet will be lower

LO 4   **7.** An enterprise fund buys equipment for $4,000,000. The equipment has a 4-year estimated life, straight-line, no residual value. The equipment is sold after 3 years for $200,000. Which statement is *true* regarding the reporting for the sale in the enterprise fund's operating statement?

    a. $800,000 loss is reported in the nonoperating section.
    b. $200,000 proceeds are reported as other financing sources.
    c. $800,000 loss is reported as other financing uses.
    d. $200,000 proceeds are reported in the revenues section.

LO 4   **8.** The net position section of the proprietary funds statement of net position is divided into which three categories?

    a. Unrestricted; temporarily restricted; permanently restricted
    b. Operating; nonoperating; restricted
    c. Reserved; assigned; unreserved
    d. Net investment in capital assets; restricted; unrestricted

LO 5   **9.** Agency funds do not appear in the statement of changes in fiduciary net position because

    a. agency funds are not fiduciary funds.
    b. they do not report on activities related to services to regular citizens.
    c. they are not major funds.
    d. agency funds have no net position.

LO 5   **10.** A sales tax is shared 50-50 between the county and the state. Businesses pay the county the full amount of the tax, and the county distributes half of the tax to the state. The county reports activities regarding the state's share of the sales tax in an agency fund. During 2016, the county collects $2,750,000 in sales taxes that belong to the state, and distributes $2,500,000 to the state. How are these activities reported by the county's agency fund?

    a. Revenues of $2,750,000 and expenditures of $2,500,000
    b. Net liability decrease of $250,000
    c. Liability increase of $2,750,000 and expenditures of $2,500,000
    d. Net liability increase of $250,000

LO 6   **11.** At the beginning of the fiscal year, a general fund leases property. The lease qualifies as a capital lease. At the time the lease is initiated, the present value of the future lease payments is $3,000,000. The lease agreement reflects an implicit interest rate of 4 percent. The first payment of $500,000 is made at the end of the fiscal year. On its operating statement for the year, the general fund reports

    a. other financing sources of $3,000,000 and a capital outlay expenditure of $500,000.
    b. a capital outlay expenditure of $500,000.
    c. a capital outlay expenditure of $3,000,000 and other financing sources of $3,000,000, an expenditure for interest of $120,000, and an expenditure for principal of $380,000.
    d. an expenditure for interest of $120,000.

LO 6   **12.** Landfill operations may be reported in a governmental fund or a proprietary fund. Assume an operating landfill is estimated to be 40 percent filled. Total expected future costs of closure and postclosure care are estimated at $5,000,000. Which statement below is *true*?

    a. If the landfill is reported in a governmental fund, the total liability for future closure and postclosure costs is reported at $2,000,000.
    b. If the landfill is reported in a governmental fund, the total liability for future closure and postclosure costs is reported at zero.
    c. If the landfill is reported in a proprietary fund, and previously reported closure and postclosure costs are $1,000,000, the total liability for future closure and postclosure costs is reported at $3,000,000.
    d. If the landfill is reported in a proprietary fund, the total liability for future closure and postclosure costs is reported at zero.

EXERCISES •

E11.1 Permanent Fund Transactions In March 2016, a resident of Randall City died, leaving her entire **LO 1** ✓
estate to the Randall City School District. The will specified that proceeds from the liquidation of her
estate are to be invested, and investment income used to provide scholarships for needy high school
students. Three students were to be selected each year by the school superintendent. At the date of the
donor's death, the fair market value of the estate was estimated to be $2,150,000. When liquidated in
December, the estate realized $2,200,000. Administrative costs of the estate in 2016 were $30,000. The
net proceeds were then transferred to the school district and were invested in appropriate securities. In
2017, income from investments was $130,000. Administrative costs (all related to income) were $3,000.
The first scholarships were awarded in 2017 for a total of $75,000. The investments are worth $2,250,000
at the end of 2017.

Required

Record the events described above in a permanent fund. Include closing entries.

E11.2 Capital Project Transactions On January 14, 2017, the city of Westport authorized a $1,000,000 **LO 2**
bond issue for the purchase of a building to be used as a community center. On May 3, the bonds were
issued at par, and on June 1, the building was purchased and paid for. On November 1, the general fund
paid the semiannual interest of $15,000 on the bonds.

Required

Record all necessary entries in the capital projects fund and the general fund for the above information.
State where each account is reported in the fund financial statements.

E11.3 Capital Project Transactions The **City of Fargo, North Dakota** authorized construction of a new **LO 2** ✓
levee to control flooding, on February 1, 2017. The $20,000,000 project will be financed by a bond issue
to be sold in March 2017. The city's fiscal year ends June 30. The following events occurred in fiscal
2017:

- February 10: The general fund advanced $500,000 to the capital projects fund to finance initial project
  planning.
- March 1: $350,000 was paid for initial planning.
- March 15: The bonds were issued at 101. The excess cash received was remitted to the debt service
  fund. The advance from the general fund was paid.
- March 20: The contract was awarded for $19,000,000.
- June 10: The contractors submitted bills for $3,000,000. The city applied its 10% retainage policy, and
  paid the net amount owed.

Assume all capital projects resources are restricted.

Required

a. Record all necessary entries in the capital projects fund for the above information, including closing
   entries.
b. Assuming this is the only project reported in the capital projects fund, prepare its statement of revenues, expenditures, and changes in fund balances and balance sheet for fiscal 2017.

E11.4 Capital Project Calculations The town of Kaley recently completed construction of a recreational **LO 2**
facility which was accounted for in a capital projects fund. Bonds were issued at the onset of the project
to finance construction. Legal constraints prevented use of the $800,000 premium on the bonds toward
construction costs. The premium has not yet been transferred to the debt service fund. Temporary investments of bond proceeds yielded a 3% return, or $2,424,000. Kaley awarded the construction contract for
the facility to the lowest bidder. The contract called for a 15% retainage. Kaley's books show $11,550,000
due the contractor pending final inspection. All other amounts due the contractor have been remitted. Assume interest on temporary investments remains in the capital projects fund.

Required

a. What was the face value of the bonds issued?
b. What was the amount of the contract awarded?
c. What was the original authorization for the project?
d. What is the total fund balance of the capital projects fund after closing entries?

LO 2   E11.5   Adequacy of Capital Project Authorization   The Board of Supervisors of Hanover Township authorized construction of a $10,000,000 community center. The township will contribute $1,000,000 from general fund revenues and bonds will be issued for the rest. Construction activities will last about eighteen months. The project is reviewed after six months when the construction manager indicates that the project is 41% complete and the township's $1,000,000 contribution was made. At that time, the following data from the capital projects fund are presented.

Cash—construction	$1,500,000
Short-term investments	5,000,000
Cash—debt service	150,000
Construction in progress	4,500,000
Bonds payable	9,000,000
Bond anticipation notes payable	1,000,000
Encumbrances (balance of construction contract)	6,500,000

Required

a.   At what amount were the bonds apparently issued?
b.   Calculate the apparent potential cost overrun.
c.   Identify the items above that are improperly reported in the capital projects fund.

LO 3, 6   E11.6   Debt Service Fund Transactions   The **City of Yuma, Arizona** accounts for debt service related to its $10,000,000 face value, 5% general obligation term bonds, issued July 1, 2016, in a debt service fund. The city's accounting year ends on June 30. Interest on the bonds is due each December 31 and June 30. The following events occur in fiscal 2017:

1.   The debt service fund budget called for $1,250,000 in transfers from the general fund, $20,000 in income on investments, and appropriations for the two semiannual interest payments.
2.   The general fund transferred $1,250,000 to the debt service fund on August 15. The debt service fund invested the cash.
3.   The debt service fund liquidated investments carried at $300,000 for $315,000 and made the December 31 interest payment.
4.   The debt service fund liquidated investments carried at $270,000 for $260,000 and made the June 30 interest payment.
5.   Dividend and interest income for the year, received in cash, was $45,000.
6.   At June 30, 2017, the debt service fund's investments had a fair value of $660,000.

Assume that all debt service fund resources are committed.

Required

a.   Prepare the journal entries to record the above events in the debt service fund. Include necessary closing entries.
b.   Prepare the debt service fund's statement of revenues, expenditures, and changes in fund balances and the year-end balance sheet for fiscal 2017.

LO 3   E11.7   Debt Service Fund Irregularities   A debt service fund's condensed trial balance at December 31, 2017 shows the following:

	Dr (Cr)
Cash	$1,000,000
Due from water utility (an enterprise fund)	200,000
Short-term investments	9,000,000
Estimated revenues	8,000,000
Expenditures	200,000
Interest payable	(200,000)
Water utility bonds payable	(8,000,000)
Appropriations	(200,000)
Fund balance—committed	(7,800,000)
Contributions from property owners	(2,200,000)
Total	$ 0

The water utility bonds were issued on July 1, 2017, and pay 5 percent interest annually on June 30. The contributions from property owners represent the proceeds from special assessment debt for which the government has no liability.

Required

Identify the apparent irregularities in the above debt service fund trial balance and suggest corrective action for them.

E11.8 **Internal Service Fund Financial Statements** At the beginning of fiscal year 2017, the City of **LO 4** ✓
Winston-Salem, North Carolina established a central supplies storehouse to provide various departments with supplies, tools, and operating equipment. The general fund contributed $15,000,000 (nonrefundable) to aid in the establishment of the supplies storehouse. It was agreed that the storehouse would charge other funds for the purchase price of supplies plus 20 percent. During the year, the storehouse purchased $13,000,000 of supplies, paid operating expenses of $1,500,000, and billed other funds for $14,400,000. All accounts are settled except $500,000 remaining to be collected from the general fund for supplies billed.

Required

a. Prepare the statement of revenues, expenses, and changes in net position for fiscal 2017, and the statement of net position at the end of fiscal 2017 for the central supplies storehouse.
b. State any effects of the transactions on the financial statements of the general fund of Winston-Salem. Assume the general fund bought supplies for $5,000,000, consumed $4,300,000 of supplies, uses the purchases method, and supplies balances are significant.

E11.9 **Enterprise Fund Profitability Analysis** Below are summary data for the first two years of operation **LO 4**
of an enterprise fund prepared under modified accrual accounting and business (full accrual) accounting.

(in thousands)	Modified Accrual Accounting		Business Accounting	
	Year 2	Year 1	Year 2	Year 1
Revenues	$1,100	$1,000	$1,300	$1,150
Expenditures/Expenses	4,000	3,500	1,000	900
Total assets	320	300	3,550	3,050
Fund balance/Net position	(3,400)	(500)	2,550	2,250

Required

a. For both the modified accrual and full accrual accounting data, perform a basic profitability analysis for Year 2 using the "DuPont Analysis" shown below.

$$\text{Return on assets} = \text{Return on revenues} \times \text{Total assets turnover}$$
$$\frac{\text{Income}}{\text{Average total assets}} = \frac{\text{Income}}{\text{Revenues}} \times \frac{\text{Revenues}}{\text{Average total assets}}$$

b. Which basis of accounting better reflects the profitability of the enterprise fund during Year 2? To what do you attribute the differences?

E11.10 **Special Assessment Project** After discussions with property owners residing on Bruce and Gar- **LO 3, 5**
rison Streets, the city council of **Hobson City, Alabama** authorized installation of street lights to better protect area citizens. Suppose total cost of the project is $3,300,000. Council will contribute $300,000 and ten-year term bonds will be issued to fund construction of the project. Hobson City can issue bonds paying 6 percent annually at par. The principal and interest will be repaid in ten equal annual assessments paid by the affected property owners. Because each annual assessment exceeds the interest due on the bonds, the excess is invested at 6 percent to retire the principal.

Required

a. Calculate the amount of the total annual assessment needed to pay the annual interest for ten years and retire the bonds.
b. Assume the government is liable for the bonds. Prepare the fund journal entries and identify the funds affected when the bonds are issued, the assessments are levied, the first assessment is collected, and the first interest payment is made.
c. Repeat b. assuming the government has *no* liability for the bonds.

LO 2   **E11.11**   **Capital Asset Transactions**   Suppose the **City of Naperville, Illinois** acquired the following capital assets in 2016:

1.   Land infrastructure improvements were paid by the general fund at a cost of $2,400,000.
2.   A used delivery van was purchased by the internal service fund at a cost of $10,000.
3.   A building was purchased for $20,000,000 by the capital projects fund to serve as a youth center. The purchase was financed by a 20-year bond issue.
4.   Machinery and equipment was purchased for $30,000 by the commuter parking enterprise fund. The purchase was financed by a bank loan.

Required

Prepare the entries needed to record the above transactions. For each entry, indicate the fund in which the entry is recorded, and how the asset, and liability if appropriate, are reported in the fund's balance sheet.

⊘ LO 6   **E11.12**   **Lease Transactions**   On July 1, 2016, suppose the **City of Olympia, Washington** leased a parking lot, agreeing to pay $400,000 at the start of the lease, and make five annual payments of $400,000 per year on June 30 of each subsequent year. The lease carries an interest rate of 4%. The county's fiscal year ends June 30, and the equipment is reported in the general fund.

Required

a.   Assume the lease qualifies as a capital lease. Prepare the entries to record the lease agreement and payments on July 1, 2016, June 30, 2017, and June 30, 2018.
b.   Assume the lease qualifies as an operating lease. Repeat the requirements in part *a*.
c.   Comment on the difference in total expenditures recognized under the two lease accounting methods.

LO 5   **E11.13**   **Agency Fund Transactions**   Suppose the **City of St. George, Utah**, decides to assist residents by installing sidewalks in their neighborhood. Construction will be financed by cash provided from a ten-year, 4 percent, serial bond issue for which the government has no liability. Bonds mature at a rate of $200,000 per year. Area residents are assessed over a ten-year period to cover bond principal and interest payments. Events are as follows:

1.   Serial bonds are issued, totaling $2,000,000.
2.   Assessments of $280,000 are levied on area residents to cover the first year's principal and interest payments.
3.   Assessments are collected and the first year's bond principal and interest are paid.

Required

Record the above events in an agency fund.

LO 4   **E11.14**   **Enterprise Fund Transactions**   **Frederick County, Maryland** maintains a sewer enterprise fund, which charges citizens for sewer fees, and opening (or "tapping") new sewer lines. Suppose the following activities occur:

1.   Residents are billed for $55,000 of sewer charges; a total of $52,000 is collected.
2.   Sewer supplies of $25,000 are purchased; $10,000 is paid in cash, and the balance is still outstanding.
3.   Capital improvements totaling $250,000 are made to existing sewer facilities. The improvements are financed by issuing a long-term note payable.
4.   Newly constructed homes are charged $5,500 for tap-in fees, to access sewer lines. Payment is received in cash.
5.   Semiannual interest of $25,000 and principal of $50,000 is paid on the note from #3.

Required

Record the above events in an enterprise fund.

LO 1   **E11.15**   **Special Revenue Fund Transactions**   The **City of Memphis, Tennessee** has a special revenue fund set up to account for funds received from the lease of park facilities within the Dr. Martin Luther King, Jr. Park. Funds are restricted for park operations. Suppose the following activities occur:

1.   The general fund provides funding of $36,000 to purchase picnic tables, half of which will be repaid in the future, and half is a permanent transfer. The tables are purchased from a local craftsman.
2.   Park fees of $15,000 are collected from residents, who pay in cash.
3.   Vandals spray paint graffiti on park benches, and a clean-up fee of $2,800 is paid.
4.   A $600 bill for lawn maintenance fees is received on account.
5.   Park employee wages of $1,500 are paid.

Required

Record the above events in a special revenue fund.

PROBLEMS ••

P11.1 **Special Revenue Fund** In 2016, Grand City established a special revenue fund to account for acqui- **LO 1**
sitions of wildlife by the city zoo.

During 2016, the following occurred:

1. Cash of $800,000 was transferred from the general fund and a federal grant of $800,000 was received.
2. Investments were purchased for $600,000 in cash.
3. Contracts for $1,200,000 for the acquisition of wildlife were signed. Animals, reptiles, and birds were delivered, and Grand City was billed for $1,200,000.
4. Investments yielded $30,000 in revenues. The investments were liquidated at cost.
5. Wildlife contract bills totaling $1,100,000 were paid.
6. Resources of $400,000 were reclassified for future transfer to the general fund.

The federal grant resources are restricted, while the general fund transfers and investment income are committed resources. City policy is to spend restricted resources first. The special revenue fund does not use budgetary accounts.

Required

a. Prepare all 2016 journal entries and closing entries for the special revenue fund.
b. Prepare the balance sheet for the special revenue fund as of December 31, 2016.

P11.2 **Reporting for Endowment** **Douglas County, Georgia** maintains a public education trust, which **LO 1**
reports restricted private contributions. Trust fund earnings are used to award grants and scholarships to assist students and support teacher excellence. Suppose that on January 1, 2015, the initial bequest was received from a wealthy citizen, consisting of the following:

Cash..	$ 25,000
Corporate bonds, $500,000 par value, 5 percent coupon paid annually, due on December 31 of each year, 6 percent yield to maturity, at current value	485,000

The cash was immediately invested in certificates of deposit yielding 3 percent, payable semiannually on July 1 and January 1 of each year. The county board also authorized a transfer of $30,000 to support the education fund during 2015. Education-related expenses in 2015 totaled $55,000, of which $50,000 was paid in cash. Assume that increases in the reported value of the investment represent spendable income.

Required

a. Identify the fund type used to report the Douglas County Education Trust Fund.
b. Assume income is received as expected. Prepare the fund's 2015 operating statement and December 31, 2015 balance sheet. Assume the fund accrues interest as earned and uses the effective interest method for the bond investment.

P11.3 **Capital Projects and Debt Service Activities** In fiscal 2016, the **County of Clackamas, Oregon** **LO 2, 3**
plans to issue $9,000,000 face value of 5 percent general obligation bonds to finance the expansion of the fire station plus equipment. Additional financing will be obtained from a federal grant. A capital projects fund will account for the activities relating to this project, and a debt service fund will account for resources used to make payments on the debt. The general fund will provide the resources to pay the annual interest payments. Suppose the following transactions occurred in each of the two years beginning October 1, 2015, and ending September 30, 2017.

Fiscal 2016

1. October 2: A budget was established for the fire station project as follows:

General obligation bonds...	$9,000,000
Federal grant	1,000,000

2. October 10: The general fund advanced $500,000 to cover planning activities.
3. October 15: $250,000 was spent for engineering and architectural work. The amount was not previously encumbered.
4. October 30: The general obligation bonds were issued at a total price of $9,090,000. The bonds mature on October 30, 2025, and interest is paid yearly. The bond premium is legally restricted to be used for bond payments, and is accordingly transferred to the debt service fund.

5. November 9: $800,000 of the federal grant proceeds was received.
6. December 1: Contracts were signed with several construction and fire equipment companies who will be responsible for various aspects of the project. All contracts provide for a 10 percent retainage. The contracts totaled $9,600,000.
7. May 15: The advance from the general fund was repaid.
8. September 30: Extensive work was done on the fire station during fiscal 2016, and the construction and equipment companies have submitted invoices in the amount of $8,200,000. $7,000,000 in cash has been paid as of year-end.

Fiscal 2017

1. October 2: $450,000 was transferred from the general fund to the debt service fund to cover its interest expenditure for the year.
2. October 30: Interest was paid on the bonds.
3. January 12: The remainder of the federal grant was received by the capital projects fund.
4. June 15: Additional invoices totaling $1,400,000 were received, representing the final billings of the contractors. $1,640,000 in cash was paid to contractors.
5. July 25: The fire station was accepted by the city. All contractors were paid in full, and the remaining balance was transferred to the debt service fund to finance future payments on the bonds.

Assume all resources of the capital project fund are restricted. Debt service fund resources are committed.

Required

a. Prepare the journal entries, including closing entries, for the capital projects and debt service funds for fiscal 2016 and 2017.
b. Prepare the balance sheet for the capital projects fund on September 30, 2016.
c. Prepare the balance sheet for the debt service fund on September 30, 2017.

LO 2, 3 P11.4 Capital Projects and Debt Service Activities The information below relates to the construction of a new recreation building in the city of Lander. Lander's fiscal year ends on June 30.

Fiscal 2016 transactions

1. A bond issue in the amount of $10,000,000 was authorized to provide funds for the construction. The bonds are to be repaid, in 20 annual installments, from a debt service fund, with the first installment due on June 30, 2016. Interest at 4 percent of face value is to be paid yearly on June 30.
2. An advance of $800,000 was received from the general fund to make a deposit on the land contract of $1,200,000. The deposit was made.
3. On July 1, 2015, bonds having a face value of $10,000,000 were sold for cash at 102, for an effective interest rate of 3.8 percent.
4. Contracts amounting to $7,800,000 were awarded to the lowest bidder for the construction of the recreation center.
5. The temporary advance from the general fund was repaid, and the balance on the land contract was paid.
6. The architect certified that work in the amount of $6,400,000 was completed, and submitted bills for that amount. $200,000 is to be held as retainage.
7. Bills paid by the treasurer relative to the completed work amounted to $6,200,000.
8. The bond premium was transferred to the debt service fund.

Fiscal 2017 transactions

9. Due to engineering modifications in the construction plans, the contract was revised to $8,800,000.
10. The recreation center was completed and billed at a further cost of $2,300,000. The building passed final inspection.
11. The treasurer paid all bills.
12. The cash balance remaining was transferred to the debt service fund.

Additional information:

1. Interest on the bond issue is paid directly from the general fund.
2. Budgeted and actual transfers from the general fund to the debt service fund are $450,000 in fiscal 2016 and $550,000 in fiscal 2017.
3. Cash accumulated in the debt service fund through transfers from the capital projects fund and the general fund was invested in certificates of deposit which yielded interest income of $5,000 in fiscal 2016 and $4,000 in fiscal 2017. Expected investment income on these investments was $5,000 in each year.
4. To meet the yearly bond principal payment, the debt service fund liquidated investments of $500,000 during each of the fiscal years 2016 and 2017. It paid installments on the bonds when due on June 30 of each year.

Assume recreation fund resources are restricted. Debt service fund resources are committed.

Required

a. Prepare the journal entries, including closing entries, for the recreation center capital projects fund for fiscal years 2016 and 2017.

b. Prepare the balance sheet for the recreation center fund on June 30, 2016.

c. Prepare the journal entries, including closing entries, for the debt service fund for fiscal years 2016 and 2017.

P11.5 **Evaluating Municipality Financial Condition**   Well-known examples of municipal financial prob-   **LO 2**
lems, such as **Jefferson County, Alabama** and **Harrisburg, Pennsylvania**, may have surprised capital market participants and other observers. Perhaps the modified accrual basis of accounting and the use of separate funds to report financial results complicate analysis of the relations between a government's sources and uses of financial resources and changes in its levels of fixed assets and debt. Governmental funds financial statements use modified accrual accounting. Modestly inappropriate uses of fungible financial resources in these funds can mask impending financial difficulties. Consider the five years of selected data for a hypothetical municipality shown below.

(in thousands)	2013	2014	2015	2016	2017
Estimated revenue—general fund	$3,400	$3,650	$3,800	$4,000	$4,100
Actual revenue—general fund	3,360	3,570	3,700	3,820	3,900
Short-term borrowings	200	250	310	370	500
Change in long-term debt—capital projects funds	440	600	620	550	580
Expenditures—capital projects funds	300	480	510	470	430
Fund balance (all governmental funds)	810	830	845	815	795

Required

a. Explain what is meant by "fungible financial resources."

b. Identify and explain any signals these data provide regarding the evolving financial condition of this municipality.

c. Discuss how the use of modified accrual accounting, rather than full accrual accounting, reduces the ability to evaluate the financial condition of a municipality.

P11.6 **Evaluating Status of Capital Project**   As a newly elected member of the Wannabe Area School   **LO 2**
Board, you are exhausted after listening to two hours of discussion on an obscure and inconsequential administrative issue. Now, at 11 PM, as part of the Business Manager's monthly report, a post-closing trial balance at the end of the first year of a two-year school construction project is circulated to update the Board. All financing authorized for the project has been recorded.

Because of your technical accounting background, you look sharply at the trial balance displayed below. While doing so, you recall that the Board just passed its largest budget ever, requiring a tax increase opposed by several citizens taxpayer groups.

WANNABE AREA SCHOOL DISTRICT
Middle School Extension Capital Projects Fund
Trial Balance at June 30, 2016

(in thousands)	Dr (Cr)
Cash in bank	$ 1,400
Supplies	750
Interest receivable	200
Temporary investments	9,700
Due from general fund	1,000
Accounts payable	(960)
Contracts payable	(1,340)
Fund balance—nonspendable	(750)
Fund balance—restricted	(12,600)
Fund balance—unassigned	2,600
Total	$ 0

Required

a. Another board member wants to move on to the next item of business. You object. Why?

b. Prepare an analysis designed to get the attention of your colleagues, citing specific items in the trial balance. Be sure to discuss the status of the project in relation to its budget.

LO 4 **P11.7** **Internal Service Fund** The **County of Lexington, South Carolina** operates a motor pool through an internal service fund to maintain all county-owned motor vehicles. Revenues come from fees charged for services provided. Suppose the post-closing trial balance for the motor pool at December 31, 2015, was as follows:

(in thousands)	Debit	Credit
Cash...	$18,000	
Receivable from general fund	3,000	
Materials and supplies......................................	8,000	
Capital assets, net of $7,600 accumulated depreciation.................	37,400	
Accounts payable...		$ 6,000
Net investment in capital assets		37,400
Unrestricted net position		23,000
Totals	$66,400	$66,400

The following information applies to the year ending December 31, 2016 *(in thousands)*:

1. Materials and supplies were purchased on account for $7,500.
2. The inventory of materials and supplies at December 31, 2016 was $6,500, which agreed with the physical count taken.
3. Salaries and wages paid to employees totaled $40,000, including fringe benefit costs.
4. A billing was received from an enterprise fund for utility charges totaling $3,000, and was paid.
5. Depreciation on the building, machinery and equipment was recorded in the amount of $3,800.
6. Machinery with an original cost of $1,200 and book value of $300 was sold for $100.
7. Transfers from the general fund, to support motor pool activities, were $200.
8. Billings to other departments for services rendered to them were:

General fund.	$36,000
Water and sewer fund	17,000
Special revenue fund..	9,000

9. Unpaid interfund receivable balances at December 31, 2016 were:

General fund.	$2,000
Special revenue fund..	500

10. Accounts payable at December 31, 2016 were $3,500.

Required

a. For the period January 1, 2016 through December 31, 2016, prepare journal entries to record all of the transactions in the motor pool fund accounts.

b. Prepare the closing entries for the motor pool fund at December 31, 2016.

c. Present, in good form, the December 31, 2016 balance sheet for the motor pool fund.

LO 4 **P11.8** **Critique Enterprise Fund Accounting** Two years ago, Mightyfine Township took over the swimming pool of a defunct private swim club and converted it into a community pool financed by user charges. Most user charges are in the form of low-cost family season passes sold to township residents; the fee charged to nonresidents is five times the fee charged to residents.

The township manager boasts about how he can provide such fine swimming facilities at a low cost to residents. He dismisses last year's dismal financial results—the first year the township ran the pool—as an aberration. During that year, a diving board and baby pool were added to the facilities. In his report to the Board of Supervisors, the manager presents the following schedule, taken from a subsidiary ledger in the township's general fund without adjustment.

MIGHTYFINE TOWNSHIP COMMUNITY SWIMMING POOL Operating Statement	
Season passes—residents.	$ 224,000
Season passes—nonresidents.	50,000
Daily admission fees.	13,000
Concessions, net	37,000
Total revenues	324,000
Salaries—pool manager and lifeguards.	228,000
Maintenance and repairs	67,000
Total expenditures	295,000
Excess of revenues over expenditures	$ 29,000
Notes:	
1. Fair value of original pool (20-year life)	$3,000,000
2. Cost of baby pool addition (25-year life)	500,000
3. Cost of diving board (10-year life)	150,000
4. Cost of rider to the township's liability insurance (paid by the township)	42,000

Required

a. Discuss the basis of accounting used in the above report.

b. What deficiencies in the report cause it to depart from GAAP?

c. Evaluate whether the township manager is justified in boasting. Support your evaluation with a numerical analysis.

d. A township resident who teaches accounting at Superfine University states that the pool is never crowded and that more revenue could be generated by reducing the cost of nonresident season passes from $200 per family to $120 per family. She estimates that the price elasticity of demand $[= -(\Delta q/q)/(\Delta p/p)]$ for a nonresident season pass is 2.5. Using the professor's numbers, calculate the additional revenue generated from lowering the cost of nonresident season passes.

P11.9 **Enterprise Fund Statement of Cash Flows** Below are the summarized financial statements of a **LO 4** state lottery for the year ended June 30, 2017.

STATE LOTTERY Statement of Revenues, Expenses and Changes in Net Position For Year Ended June 30, 2017	
(in thousands)	
Ticket sales.	$900,000
Prize expenses	(450,000)
Operating expenses	(180,000)
Operating income	270,000
Nonoperating items:	
Unrealized losses on investments	(2,000)
Loss on sale of capital assets	(5,000)
Transfers to state	(258,000)
Nonoperating expense	(265,000)
Change in net position	$ 5,000

STATE LOTTERY
Statement of Net Position
June 30, 2017 and 2016

(in thousands)	2017	2016
Cash and cash equivalents	$ 14,000	$ 21,000
Accounts receivable, net	39,000	25,000
Investments	42,000	38,000
Capital assets	51,000	60,000
Less accumulated depreciation	(13,000)	(12,000)
Totals	$133,000	$132,000
Current operating liabilities	$ 35,000	$ 40,000
Prize liabilities	86,000	85,000
Net position	12,000	7,000
Totals	$133,000	$132,000

Additional information (in thousands):

1. Accounts receivable are related to ticket sales.
2. Current liabilities relate to operating expenses.
3. Additional investments of $15,000 were made in 2017.
4. Depreciation expense on capital assets, included in operating expenses, was $3,000.
5. Capital assets of $14,000 were acquired in 2017.
6. Investments that matured in 2017 were liquidated at book value.

Required

Present the fiscal 2017 statement of cash flows. Include a reconciliation schedule.

⊘ LO 5   P11.10 Agency Fund   In compliance with a newly enacted state law, Dial County assumed the responsibility of collecting all property taxes for the county, as well as Eton City and Bart Township within the county, as of July 1, 2015. A composite property tax rate per $1,000 of assessed valuation was developed for the fiscal year ending June 30, 2016:

Dial County general fund	$ 60
Eton City general fund	30
Bart Township general fund	10
Composite tax rate	$100

When collected, the property taxes are distributed to the governmental units. Dial County established a tax agency fund to administer collection and distribution of taxes.

Additional information:

1. To reimburse Dial County for administrative costs of operating the agency fund, 2 percent of all tax collections are remitted to the Dial County general fund.
2. Tax bills sent out on July 1, 2015, for fiscal 2016, and estimated amounts to be collected are:

	Gross Levy	Estimated Amount to be Collected
Dial County	$36,000,000	$35,000,000
Eton City	18,000,000	17,400,000
Bart Township	6,000,000	5,600,000
Totals	$60,000,000	$58,000,000

3. As of September 30, 2015, the tax agency fund received $14,400,000 in tax payments. On October 1, the tax agency fund distributed the payments to the three governmental units.

Required

a. Prepare the journal entries made in the tax agency fund and in each of the three general funds to record the tax bills sent out July 1, 2015.

b. Calculate the amounts to be distributed to each of the three general funds on October 1, 2015.

c. Prepare the journal entries made in the tax agency fund to record the tax collection. Prepare the journal entries made to record the distribution made by the tax agency fund and by each of the three general funds to record receipt of payment on October 1, 2015.

P11.11 Reporting for Landfills Mecklenburg County, North Carolina's landfill is reported in a proprietary fund. On the county's 2013 CAFR, the liabilities section of the landfill's balance sheet reports landfill development and postclosure care costs in the amount of $8,833,808. Current expenses shown on the landfill's operating statement include $40,088 in development and postclosure costs.

LO 6

MECKLENBURG COUNTY, NORTH CAROLINA

Required

a. The financial statement footnotes state that the landfill is at 48 percent of capacity at the end of fiscal 2013. What is the current cost estimate of total closure and postclosure costs for the landfill? What total expense was reported in previous financial statements for closure and postclosure costs?

b. If the landfill had been reported in a governmental fund, what amounts would appear in the financial statements of governmental funds, related to the landfill?

c. The landfill is expected to close in 2030. Based on the analysis above, what average expense must be accrued each year from 2014 to 2030? Why do you think the expense reported in 2013 was so low?

P11.12 Budgeting for Various Funds The Laurens City Council passed a resolution requiring a yearly cash budget by fund for the city beginning with its fiscal year ending September 30, 2017. The city's financial director prepared a list of expected cash receipts and disbursements, shown below. The financial director is having trouble subdividing the receipts and disbursements by fund.

LO 1, 2, 3, 4, 5

Cash Receipts		Cash Disbursements	
Taxes:		Public services:	
General property	$ 685,000	General government	$ 671,000
School	421,000	Public safety	516,000
Franchise	223,000	School	458,000
	1,329,000	Sanitation	131,000
		Library	28,000
Licenses and permits:		Rental property	17,500
Business licenses	41,000	Parks	17,000
Automobile inspection permits	24,000		1,838,500
Building permits	18,000		
	83,000	Debt service:	
		General obligation bonds	618,000
Intergovernmental revenue:		Street construction bonds	327,000
Sales tax	1,012,000	School bonds	119,000
Federal grants	128,000	Sewage disposal plant bonds	37,200
State motor vehicle tax	83,500		1,101,200
State gasoline tax	52,000		
State alcoholic beverage licenses	16,000	Investments	358,000
	1,291,500	State portion of sales tax	860,200
Charges for services:		Capital expenditures:	
Sanitation fees	121,000	Sewer connection (assessed area)	114,100
Sewer connection fees	71,000	Civic center construction	73,000
Library revenues	13,000	Library construction	36,000
Park revenues	2,500		223,100
	207,500		
		Total disbursements	$4,381,000
Bond issues:			
Civic center	347,000		
General obligation	200,000		
Sewer	153,000		
Library	120,000		
	820,000		
Other:			
Proceeds from sale of investments	312,000		
Sewer assessments	50,000		
Rental revenue	48,000		
Interest revenue	15,000		
	425,000		
Total receipts	$4,156,000		

Additional information:

1. A bond issue was authorized for the construction of a civic center. Future civic center revenues are to account for 20 percent of the repayment of the debt. The remainder is to come from general property taxes.

2. A bond issue was authorized for additions to the library. The debt is to be paid from general property taxes.

3. General obligation bonds are paid from general property taxes collected by the general fund.

4. Ten percent of the total annual school taxes represents an individually voted tax for payment of bonds, the proceeds of which were used for school construction. School operations are accounted for in the general fund.

5. In 2014, a wealthy citizen donated rental property to the city. Net income from the property is to be used to assist in operating the library. The net cash increase attributable to the property is transferred to the library on September 30 of each year.

6. All sales taxes are collected by the city; the state receives 85 percent of these taxes. The state's portion is remitted at the end of each month.

7. Payment of the street construction bonds, for which the city has no liability, is to be made from assessments previously collected from the respective property owners. The proceeds from the assessments were invested and the principal of $312,000 is expected to earn $15,000 interest during the coming year.

8. In 2016, a special assessment in the amount of $203,000 was made on certain property owners for sewer construction. During fiscal 2017, $50,000 of this assessment is expected to be collected. The remainder of the sewer cost is to be paid from a $153,000 bond issue to be sold in fiscal 2017. Future special assessment collections will be used to pay principal and interest on the bonds, for which the city has residual liability.

9. All sewer and sanitation services are provided by a separate enterprise fund.

10. The federal grant is for fiscal 2017 school operations.

11. The proceeds remaining at the end of the year from the sale of civic center and library bonds are to be invested.

12. The state motor vehicle tax, state gasoline tax, and state alcoholic beverage license revenue represent the city's share of state revenues.

Required

Prepare a budget of cash receipts and disbursements by fund for the year ending September 30, 2017. Include all interfund cash transfers. Set up your solution in the following format:

Description	General Fund	Capital Projects Fund	Debt Service Fund	Permanent Fund	Agency Fund	Enterprise Fund
Cash receipts						
Cash disbursements						
Interfund transfers						
Net cash flow						

LO 1, 2, 4 **P11.13 Recording Various Fund Transactions** The following transactions take place within the town of Keough:

1. The general fund provides $100,000 to the Fire Department special revenue fund, and expects that half of the funds will be returned within six months.

2. The town issues $1,000,000 of general obligation bonds with an interest rate of 3 percent, due semi-annually. The funds are used to finance general operations.

3. The town issues $500,000 of 5 percent revenue bonds, which will be used to finance construction of a new addition for the fire station. A construction contract is signed totaling $480,000.

4. The Police Department, which is not financed by a specific revenue stream, is billed $25,000 for new equipment. The equipment is expected to last for five years.

5. The Keough town pool, which is financed through resident user fees, takes out a $50,000 note payable from a local bank and uses the money to purchase pool equipment. The note will be repaid over 5 years at 5 percent annual interest; the equipment is expected to last for 5 years.

6. The first semiannual interest installment is paid for the bonds issued in #2.

7. The Fire Department special revenue fund returns $25,000 to the general fund.

8. The town maintains a motor pool for town officials, who are charged to use vehicles for town business. The following departments are billed: Mayor's office $2,000; Fire Chief $500; Police Chief $500; Pool Manager $1,000.

9. The first installment of the note payable in #5 is paid, with $10,000 toward principal, and $2,500 of interest.

10. Any applicable depreciation is recorded for the assets purchased in #4 and #5 above. Assume the straight line depreciation method is used, and one year's depreciation is recorded, if appropriate.

Required

Record the above events in the proper fund. Designate the fund in which each transaction occurs.

P11.14 Enterprise Fund Transactions   Bedford Township, Michigan has a sewer facility, accounted for as an enterprise fund. Its statement of net position follows:

LO 4
BEDFORD
TOWNSHIP, MI

BEDFORD TOWNSHIP
Sewer Enterprise Fund
Statement of Net Position
June 30, 2013

Assets	
Current assets:	
Cash and cash equivalents.	$ 1,975,248
Receivables	1,375,068
Due from other funds	529,642
Prepaid expenses	10,331
Total current assets.	3,890,289
Long-term assets:	
Cash with fiscal agent.	6,597,649
Capital assets, less accumulated depreciation of $21,064,532.	20,858,231
Total long-term assets	27,455,880
Total assets	$31,346,169
Liabilities	
Current liabilities:	
Accounts payable and other payables	$ 136,286
Due to other funds	4,142
Current portion of bonds payable.	320,000
Total current liabilities.	460,428
Long-term liabilities:	
Bonds payable	5,635,000
Total liabilities.	6,095,428
Net position	
Net investment in capital assets	14,903,231
Restricted for sewer system replacement	8,331,071
Restricted for debt retirement	1,614,178
Unrestricted	402,261
Total net position	25,250,741
Total liabilities and net position	$31,346,169

During fiscal 2014, the following events occur:

1. The utility bills residents for sewer services totaling $3,166,045. All but $31,000 is subsequently collected in cash.

2. Penalties for late sewer payments total $52,978, collected in cash.

3. Contracted operations and maintenance fees of $2,354,227 are paid.

4. Depreciation expense on capital assets totals $748,504.

5. Office salaries of $99,166 are paid.

6. Old equipment with original cost of $600,000 and book value of $125,000 is sold at a loss of $30,000.
7. New sewer system replacement is purchased for $500,000, after issuing a five-year note payable for an equivalent amount.
8. Office supplies totaling $9,850 are purchased on account and used in operations.
9. Sewers for newly constructed homes are charged a total of $36,263 for "tap-in" fees. These fees have not been collected.
10. Cash paid for miscellaneous other nonoperating expenses totals $17,350. Prepaid expenses of $600 were written off to miscellaneous nonoperating expenses.
11. Cash is paid for the bond interest payment of $190,954, as well as for the current year bond principal payment owed.
12. Excess cash of $1,000,000 is invested in short-term investments; subsequently, interest revenue of $39,463 is accrued on investments.
13. The ending balance in accounts payable is $127,402. The ending balance in Due to Other Funds is $3,900. Other funds paid the sewer fund $25,000 for amounts owed on transactions from the previous year.
14. Out of the ending balance in bonds payable, $300,000 is considered current and due in fiscal 2015.

Required

a. Prepare the journal entries to record the above events in the enterprise fund, including closing entries.
b. Prepare the enterprise fund's statement of revenues, expenses, and changes in net position for fiscal 2014, and its statement of net position for June 30, 2014, in good form.

LO 6   P11.15 Debt Refundings and Swaps   On July 1, 2016, Lancaster County's Utilities enterprise fund issues $10,000,000 face value variable rate debt at par. The interest rate is set every six months, and is a 4 percent annual rate for the next six months. To hedge its interest rate risk, the county enters a receive variable/pay fixed interest rate swap, where every six months the county pays a counterparty a 4.5 percent annual fixed rate on a notional amount of $10,000,000, and the counterparty pays the county the amount necessary to pay the interest on the bonds. There is no initial investment and the swap has no value at inception. On December 31, 2016, the variable rate is reset to 3.5%. Since variable rates are expected to continue to fall, the fair value of the swap declines from zero to a liability of $20,000. On June 30, 2017, rates have continued to fall and the fair value of the swap has fallen by another $2,000 in the last six months. The county decides to refund the debt and close the swap. The call premium on the variable rate debt is $250,000. The county issues $10,250,000 of 5-year, 3.6 percent fixed rate debt to finance the refunding, and pays cash to close the swap. The county's accounting year ends June 30.

Required

a. Prepare the journal entries to record the above events on the books of the Utilities Fund.
b. Assume the difference between the reacquisition cost and the net carrying value of the variable rate debt is amortized on a straight-line basis over the life of the fixed rate debt. Prepare the journal entry to record the interest payment on December 31, 2017 on the books of the Utilities Fund.

REVIEW SOLUTIONS ••

Review 1 Solution

a. **Journal entries for capital projects fund:**

Bonds authorized—unissued	4,000,000	
Estimated revenues—state grant.	1,000,000	
Appropriations.		5,000,000
To record the budget entry.		
State grant receivable	1,000,000	
State grant revenue.		1,000,000
To accrue state grant.		
Cash.	4,100,000	
Bond proceeds		4,000,000
Due to debt service fund		100,000
To record bond issuance.		
Due to debt service fund	100,000	
Cash		100,000
To record remittance of bond premium to debt service fund.		
Cash.	900,000	
State grant receivable		900,000
To record partial receipt of state grant.		
Encumbrances.	4,750,000	
Fund balance—restricted		4,750,000
To record awarding of contract.		
Fund balance—restricted.	2,300,000	
Encumbrances.		2,300,000
To record reversal of encumbrances on bills received.		
Expenditures	2,300,000	
Contracts payable—retainage.		460,000
Cash		1,840,000
To record expenditures.		
Appropriations	5,000,000	
State grant revenue	1,000,000	
Bond proceeds.	4,000,000	
Expenditures		2,300,000
Encumbrances.		2,450,000
Bonds authorized—unissued		4,000,000
Estimated revenues—state grant		1,000,000
Fund balance—restricted		250,000
To close the books.		

Journal entries for debt service fund:

Estimated transfers in.	140,000	
Appropriations.		140,000
To record budget entry.		
Cash.	100,000	
Transfers in		100,000
To record transfer of bond premium from capital projects fund.		

continued

Cash...	140,000	
Transfers in		140,000
To record transfer from general fund.		
Debt service: interest	100,000	
Debt service: principal	40,000	
Cash		140,000
To record payment of principal and interest.		
Appropriations	140,000	
Transfers in...	240,000	
Debt service: interest.....................................		100,000
Debt service: principal....................................		40,000
Estimated transfers in		140,000
Fund balance—restricted		100,000
To close the books.		

b.

CITY OF TOWNSVILLE
Capital Projects Fund
Statement of Revenues, Expenditures, and Changes in Fund Balances
For Year Ended December 31, 2016

State grant revenue	$1,000,000
Expenditures	(2,300,000)
Excess of revenues over (under) expenditures	(1,300,000)
Other financing sources (uses):	
Bond proceeds...	4,000,000
Total other financing sources (uses).......................................	4,000,000
Excess of revenues and other financing sources over (under) expenditures and other financing uses.....................................	2,700,000
Fund balance—beginning	0
Fund balance—ending..	$2,700,000

Debt Service Fund
Statement of Revenues, Expenditures, and Changes in Fund Balances
For Year Ended December 31, 2016

Expenditures:	
Debt service: interest	$(100,000)
Debt service: principal	(40,000)
Total expenditures	(140,000)
Other financing sources (uses):	
Transfers in..	240,000
Excess of revenues and other financing sources over expenditures and other financing uses.....................................	100,000
Fund balance—beginning	0
Fund balance—ending..	$ 100,000

c.

CITY OF TOWNSVILLE
Capital Projects Fund—Balance Sheet
December 31, 2016

Cash	$3,060,000	Contracts payable—retainage	$ 460,000
State grant receivable	100,000	Fund balance—restricted	2,700,000
Total	$3,160,000	Total	$3,160,000

Debt Service Fund—Balance Sheet
December 31, 2016

Cash	$100,000	Fund balance—restricted	$100,000
Total	$100,000	Total	$100,000

Review 2 Solution

a.

Cash	460,000	
Accounts receivable		10,000
Water revenues		450,000
To record revenues and collection.		
Supplies expense	50,500	
Supplies		500
Cash		50,000
To record supplies purchased and used.		
Capital assets	25,000	
Cash		25,000
To record acquisition of capital assets.		
Depreciation expense	4,000	
Accumulated depreciation		4,000
To record depreciation on capital assets.		
Operating expenses	395,000	
Accounts payable		5,000
Cash		390,000
To record out-of-pocket operating expenses.		
Interest expense	3,200	
Bonds payable	5,000	
Cash		8,200
To record payment of bond principal and interest.		
Water revenues	450,000	
Unrestricted net position	2,700	
Supplies expense		50,500
Depreciation expense		4,000
Operating expenses		395,000
Interest expense		3,200
To close the books.		
Unrestricted net position	21,000	
Net investment in capital assets		21,000
To reclassify unrestricted net position to net investment in		
capital assets; $21,000 = $25,000 − $4,000.		

b.

WATER UTILITY
Statement of Revenues, Expenses, and Changes in Net Position
For Year Ended December 31, 2017

Water revenues		$450,000
Less operating expenses:		
Supplies	$ 50,500	
Depreciation	4,000	
Other operating expenses	395,000	(449,500)
Operating income		500
Nonoperating expense:		
Interest expense		(3,200)
Change in net position		(2,700)
Net position—beginning		86,500
Net position—ending		$ 83,800

WATER UTILITY
Statement of Cash Flows
For Year Ended December 31, 2017

Cash flows from operating activities	
Receipts from customers	$460,000
Payments to suppliers	(50,000)
Payments for operating expenses	(390,000)
Net cash from operating activities	20,000
Cash flows from noncapital financing activities	
Payments for interest	(3,200)
Payments for principal	(5,000)
Net cash used for noncapital financing activities	(8,200)
Cash flows from capital and related financing activities	
Acquisition of capital assets	(25,000)
Net decrease in cash	(13,200)
Cash—beginning	40,000
Cash—ending	$ 26,800

---

c.

WATER UTILITY
Statement of Net Position
December 31, 2017

Cash	$ 26,800	Accounts payable	$ 15,000
Accounts receivable	65,000	Bonds payable	75,000
Supplies	3,000	Net position:	
Capital assets	145,000	Net investment in capital assets	59,000
Accum. depreciation	(66,000)	Unrestricted	24,800
Total	$173,800	Total	$173,800

12 State and Local Governments: External Financial Reporting

LEARNING OBJECTIVES

LO1 Discuss the components of the Comprehensive Annual Financial Report. (p. 519)

LO2 Prepare government-wide financial statements. (p. 521)

LO3 Present the fund statements. (p. 525)

LO4 Describe the relation between government-wide and fund statements. (p. 539)

LO5 Explain the external reporting for infrastructure, investments, and defined benefit pension plans. (p. 543)

CITY OF ST. LOUIS, MISSOURI
www.stlouis.missouri.org

The **City of St. Louis**, Missouri, known for its Gateway Arch, is located at the confluence of the Mississippi and Missouri Rivers, and borders the State of Illinois. Home to Saint Louis University and Washington University, St. Louis also has a campus of the University of Missouri. Corporations headquartered in St. Louis include Energizer, Monsanto, Enterprise Rent-a-Car, and Hardee's. The city is famous for the Anheuser-Busch Breweries, now owned by AB InBev, and the St. Louis Cardinals.

The City of St. Louis issues an audited Comprehensive Annual Financial Report (CAFR), containing a full accrual-based balance sheet and operating statement, and separate financial statements for its various governmental, proprietary, and fiduciary activities. Each year the city receives the GFOA's Certificate of Achievement for Excellence in Financial Reporting, for publishing a CAFR that meets all professional and legal requirements. The CAFR is audited by KPMG LLP, following generally accepted auditing standards for governments, also known as the "Yellow Book."

The 2013 CAFR for the City of St. Louis reveals that it has over $3.4 billion in assets and over $2.1 billion in liabilities, government-wide. Total revenues were $1.002 billion, of which 53 percent came from taxes. But the cost of programs and services was $1.025 billion, resulting in a slight decrease in net position.

A government's CAFR presents financial statements for its governmental funds, proprietary funds, and fiduciary funds. Government-wide financial statements are also presented, on a full accrual basis. This chapter explains the GASB's requirements for the CAFR.

CHAPTER ORGANIZATION

External reporting model	Government-wide statements	Fund statements	Analysis and supplementary information	Accounting for infrastructure, investments and defined benefit pension plans
• MD&A • Government-wide statements • Fund statements • Notes and required supplementary information	• Statement of net position • Statement of activities	• Major funds • Governmental fund statements • Reconciliations to government-wide statements • Proprietary fund statements • Fiduciary fund statements	• Modified accrual versus full accrual information • Budgetary comparison schedules	• Asset capitalization requirements • Modified approach for depreciation • Income and hedge investments • SGAS 68 requirements for defined benefit pension plans

The external financial report of a state or local government is known as the **Comprehensive Annual Financial Report**, or **CAFR**, and is equivalent to a corporation's annual report to shareholders. *SGAS 34* prescribes the external reporting requirements for state and local governments, emphasizing readability and the use of full accrual accounting to report the full cost of governmental services. The GASB subsequently issued *SGAS 35*, requiring public colleges and universities to follow *SGAS 34*. Subsequent GASB statements clarify and extend the provisions of *SGAS 34*.

EXTERNAL REPORTING MODEL

Chapter 10 explains the three major users of governmental financial reports: investors and creditors, citizens, and legislative and oversight bodies. Traditionally, credit market representatives have the greatest interest in governmental financial reports, being concerned with the government's ability to meet obligations as they come due. Citizens, legislative and oversight bodies want to know how much money the government has available to spend, where tax dollars are going, costs of services, sources of funding for various programs, and the implications of the current level of services for future tax obligations.

LO1 Discuss the components of the Comprehensive Annual Financial Report.

Governments are expected to use resources for their intended purpose and to comply with legally enacted budgets. Fund financial statements report how current activities are financed, the amount of current financial resources available for future expenditures, how the period's budget compares with actual revenues and expenditures, and any significant changes in current financial position during the year.

The **measurement focus** in the governmental fund financial statements is on the **flow of current financial resources**, defined as cash, cash equivalents and receivables, net of payables and short-term debt. Revenues and other financing sources are inflows of current financial resources, and expenditures and other financing uses are outflows of current financial resources. Revenues earned but not yet available to finance expenditures in the current period are not recognized. Expenses accrued but not requiring current resources, such as depreciation, or interest to be paid in future years, are also not recognized.

This measurement focus underlies **modified accrual accounting**, and matches resources available to finance current period expenditures with outflows of current period resources. The difference between current assets and current liabilities, or fund balance, represents financial resources available for future expenditure. The **full accrual basis of accounting**, based on the **flow of economic resources**, is used for proprietary funds, where fee-for-service activities make it essential to know the *full cost* of services, not just those costs using current financial resources. Fiduciary funds also use the full accrual basis, with some exceptions.

In addition to the fund-based financial statements, *SGAS 34* requires a set of *full accrual* financial statements. The GASB believes full accrual **government-wide financial statements** provide more accurate and complete information about the full cost of services, results of operations, and financial position. Accrual basis reporting conveys more accurately the government's ability to maintain current service levels and the impact of current activities on future financial condition. Accrual-based statements report on the overall financial health of the primary government and its component units, and the government's ability to provide services now and in the future. The reporting requirements of *SGAS 34* parallel the changes in reporting for not-for-profit organizations that occurred in the mid-1990s, discussed in Chapter 13.

SGAS 34 requires, at a minimum, the following disclosures in the governmental unit's CAFR:

- Management's discussion and analysis (MD&A)
- Basic financial statements
  - ○ Government-wide financial statements
  - ○ Fund financial statements
  - ○ Notes to financial statements
- Required supplementary information (RSI) other than MD&A

Figure 12.1 shows the minimum requirements, per *SGAS 34, paragraph 7*.

FIGURE 12.1   Minimum External Reporting Requirements for State and Local Governments

Management's Discussion and Analysis

MD&A provides a readable overview and analysis of the government's financial performance for the year. Charts and graphs are encouraged. The discussion focuses on the short- and long-term financial performance of the primary government. MD&A introduces the basic financial statements, and is similar in content to that required by the SEC for public companies. Minimum requirements include:

- Overview of the information provided by the basic financial statements, including an explanation and comparison of the government-wide and fund statements.
- Condensed government-wide financial statements that compare the current year to the prior year, with analysis of the reasons for significant changes.
- Discussion of changes in the government's overall financial position and analysis of significant changes in the financial position of specific funds.
- Analysis of significant differences between original and final budget amounts and between budget and actual amounts for the general fund, and how those differences affect future services and liquidity.
- A description of capital expenditure commitments, changes in credit ratings, and the effect of debt limitations on the ability to finance future services or asset acquisitions.

GOVERNMENT-WIDE FINANCIAL STATEMENTS

The two required government-wide financial statements are the *statement of net position* and *statement of activities*. These statements report financial performance overall, and focus on *activities benefitting the government or its citizens*. Like a corporate balance sheet, the **statement of net position** reports the assets, liabilities, and net position of the government. The **statement of activities** reports revenues and expenses.

Both statements separately disclose resources and activities pertaining to *governmental activities* and *business-type activities*. **Governmental activities** are those primarily financed by taxes and intergovernmental transfers, and include the activities of governmental funds—general, special revenue, capital projects, debt service, and permanent funds—and internal service funds. **Business-type activities** are those financed at least partially by user fees and include only the activities of enterprise funds.

Although internal service funds use business accounting, they are included with governmental activities because their activities support other government departments. Fiduciary funds are **not** included in the government-wide statements, because the resources of fiduciary activities reported in agency and trust funds are not available to finance government programs and do not benefit citizens in general.

Unlike most of the fund financial statements discussed in Chapters 10 and 11, the government-wide financial statements use **full accrual accounting,** reflecting the GASB's *economic resources measurement focus*. Revenues, expenses, gains, losses, assets, and liabilities are reported using business accounting principles.

Land, buildings, equipment, infrastructure and similar items—termed **capital assets** by *SGAS 34*—are reported on the statement of net position at historical cost, net of accumulated depreciation. Depreciation expense on depreciable capital assets is reported in the statement of activities. **Infrastructure assets** are long-term stationary capital assets that can be maintained for a longer period than most capital assets. Examples include roads, bridges, and water and lighting systems. Governments may or may not depreciate infrastructure assets; see discussion later in the chapter.

All liabilities, including accrued interest and other obligations not requiring current financial resources, as well as pensions, bonds and other forms of long-term debt, are recognized in the statement of net position. Accrued interest expense and pension expense are reported in the statement of activities.

LO2 Prepare government-wide financial statements.

Government-Wide Financial Statements

Statements:
    Statement of net position (balance sheet)
    Statement of activities (operating statement)
Basis of reporting:
    Full accrual basis
Activities reported:
    Governmental activities
        Activities of governmental funds and internal service funds
    Business-type activities
        Activities of enterprise funds

Governmental funds report on a modified accrual basis, and do not report revenues, expenses, assets or liabilities unless they involve current flows of financial resources. These funds account for acquisition and disposition of capital assets and issuance and payment of long-term debt as changes in fund balance. Therefore, *major adjustments must be made to governmental fund financial information* so that governments can accurately report their activities in the full accrual government-wide financial statements.

Statement of Net Position

The **statement of net position**, which is equivalent to a balance sheet, reports the assets and liabilities of the primary government and its component units, both in total and separately by governmental and business-type activities. Presentation in order of liquidity, or in a classified format, is encouraged. Net position is presented in three categories:

- **Net investment in capital assets**: Capital assets net of depreciation, less debt incurred to acquire or improve the capital assets.
- **Restricted**: Unspent contributions, grants and loans subject to *external constraints* imposed by creditors, donors, or legislators.
- **Unrestricted**: Amounts not included in the other two categories. This category includes net position affected by internal restrictions imposed by management.

Internal transactions are common within and between the governmental, internal service, and enterprise funds, and lead to interfund receivables and payables or other "duplicate" balances. *SGAS 34* strives to minimize overstatement of assets and liabilities in the statement of net position, by requiring elimination of interfund receivables and payables in the governmental and business-type activities columns. However, the statement shows the net amounts owed *between the governmental and business-type activities* as offsetting internal balances. Because the government-wide statements do not include fiduciary funds, *amounts due from or to fiduciary funds* are reported as external balances.

Statement of Activities

The **statement of activities** reports all **changes in net position** during the year. Gross expenses are shown by function or program within the governmental or business-type categories. Specific revenues received for program services and/or grants and contracts are deducted from gross expenses. The net balance shows *how much each function or program uses or contributes to general revenues*, such as property taxes and other broad-based tax levies, unrestricted grants, and investment income. After adding general revenues, the "bottom line" reports the change in net position. Because program expenses are reported using full accrual accounting, they reflect full costs, not just amounts paid during the current period. Therefore the change in net position reflects the *degree to which the total costs of current services and activities are financed by total revenues for the period*.

Duplicate balances also may exist within the statement of activities. For example, when overhead expenses incurred by one function are allocated to other functions, the allocated overhead expenses should be reported only by the function to which they are allocated. To accurately report expenses and revenues by function, costs of goods and services provided between functions are reported as revenues by the selling function and expenses by the buying function.

Discussion of Government-Wide Statements

Exhibits 12.1 and 12.2 present the 2013 statement of net position and statement of activities, respectively, for the City of St. Louis, Missouri. Component units are combined into one column for brevity.

The primary government is the city. Blended component units include the Public Facilities Protection Corporation (PFPC), a self-insurance program; the St. Louis Municipal Finance Corporation (SLMFC), which acquires and finances city property; the St. Louis Parking Commission Finance Corporation (SLPCFC), which acquires and finances assets for the Parking Commission; and the Grand Center Municipal Parking Finance Corporation (MPFC), which manages parking services for Grand Center, the downtown arts and entertainment district. The activities of these blended units are reported in the primary government accounts.

Discretely presented component units are the St. Louis Development Corporation (SLDC), in charge of economic development in the city; the Metropolitan Police Department (SLPD), which funds police department activities; and the Solid Waste Management and Development Corporation (SWM-DC), which owns and leases a system of underground pipes providing pressurized steam to downtown municipal buildings.

Governmental activities reported in St. Louis' government-wide statements include general government operations, federal grants and other revenues legally restricted to specific purposes, capital projects, and debt service. Internal service activities also included in governmental activities are: the self insurance program, mail-handling services, and employee health insurance claims. St. Louis' business-type activities include its airport, water division, and parking division.

St. Louis' statement of activities in Exhibit 12.2 reports the 2013 cost of governmental programs and functions, net of related program revenues, at $580,826,000, funded by $535,678,000 in general tax revenues, from earnings, payroll, sales, property, and other taxes. The resulting shortfall is $45,148,000. Expenses of business-type activities were $233,325,000, but charges for services and other revenue

EXHIBIT 12.1   2013 Statement of Net Position, City of St. Louis, Missouri

CITY OF ST. LOUIS, MISSOURI
Statement of Net Position
June 30, 2013

(in thousands)	Primary Government			Component Units
	Governmental Activities	Business-Type Activities	Total	Total
Assets				
Cash and cash equivalents	$ 75,567	$ 94,277	$ 169,844	$ 14,378
Investments	7,961	44,256	52,217	500
Receivables, net.	157,004	25,581	182,585	17,547
Inventories	—	4,477	4,477	1,390
Restricted assets	66,465	214,282	280,747	2,850
Deferred charges	16,643	15,781	32,424	—
Internal balances	9,908	(9,908)	—	—
Other assets	50	2,268	2,318	1,411
Receivable from primary government	—	—	—	10,653
Receivable from component unit	1,844	—	1,844	—
Net pension asset.	42,327	—	42,327	—
Property held for development, net	—	—	—	17,003
Capital assets, net:				
Non-depreciable.	113,236	870,639	983,875	11,577
Depreciable	736,821	1,004,640	1,741,461	57,990
Total assets	1,227,826	2,266,293	3,494,119	135,299
Liabilities				
Accounts payable and accrued liabilities.	14,295	30,782	45,077	2,977
Accrued salaries and other benefits.	10,824	11,186	22,010	5,717
Accrued interest payable	94,473	20,428	114,901	—
Unearned revenue	2,603	4,388	6,991	1,475
Other liabilities	1,249	—	1,249	—
Payable to primary government	—	—	—	1,844
Payable to component units	10,653	—	10,653	—
Payable to other government agencies	4	55	59	—
Long-term liabilities:				
Due within one year	84,963	36,528	121,491	39,682
Due in more than one year	969,663	874,471	1,844,134	173,352
Total liabilities	1,188,727	977,838	2,166,565	225,047
Net position				
Net investments in capital assets.	502,818	1,033,922	1,536,740	59,699
Restricted:				
Debt service	—	112,642	112,642	—
Capital projects.	—	7,923	7,923	—
Passenger facility charges	—	29,134	29,134	—
Statutory restrictions	30,799	—	30,799	2,857
Unrestricted (deficit).	(494,518)	104,834	(389,684)	(152,304)
Total net position	$ 39,099	$1,288,455	$1,327,554	$ (89,748)

sources totaled $258,531,000 (= $236,165,000 + $751,000 + $21,615,000). The resulting surplus of $25,206,000 is primarily due to airport charges, grants and contributions in excess of expenses. After unrestricted investment earnings and transfers, the surplus for business-type activities is $22,372,000. The net effect is to decrease primary government net position by $22,776,000 (= $45,148,000 − $22,372,000).

The end-of-year total net position for the primary government, reported on the statement of activities as $1,327,554,000, is also reported on the statement of net position in Exhibit 12.1. Restricted and unrestricted net position of governmental activities is a deficit of $(463,719,000) (= $39,099,000 − $502,818,000). This means that for these activities, reported liabilities exceed reported assets.

EXHIBIT 12.2 2013 Statement of Activities, City of St. Louis, Missouri

CITY OF ST. LOUIS, MISSOURI
Statement of Activities
For Year Ended June 30, 2013

(in thousands)	Expenses	Program Revenues			Primary Government			Component Units
		Charges for Services	Operating Grants and Contributions	Capital Grants and Contributions	Governmental Activities	Business-Type Activities	Total	
Primary Government								
Governmental activities								
General government	$ 73,204	$ 33,375	$ 542	$ —	$ (39,287)	$ —	$ (39,287)	$ —
Convention and tourism	5,513	—	—	—	(5,513)	—	(5,513)	—
Parks and recreation	30,818	2,958	322	—	(27,538)	—	(27,538)	—
Judicial	52,232	21,542	1,856	—	(28,834)	—	(28,834)	—
Streets	68,402	26,012	87	630	(41,673)	—	(41,673)	—
Public safety	303,244	38,424	3,973	—	(260,847)	—	(260,847)	—
Health and welfare	61,162	1,041	34,336	—	(25,785)	—	(25,785)	—
Public service	62,301	2,906	1,926	14,252	(43,217)	—	(43,217)	—
Community development	77,530	5,332	21,740	—	(50,458)	—	(50,458)	—
Interest and fiscal charges	57,674	—	—	—	(57,674)	—	(57,674)	—
Total governmental activities	792,080	131,590	64,782	14,882	(580,826)	—	(580,826)	—
Business-type activities								
Airport	173,968	164,606	751	21,615	—	13,004	13,004	—
Water division	45,799	56,902	—	—	—	11,103	11,103	—
Parking division	13,558	14,657	—	—	—	1,099	1,099	—
Total business-type activities	233,325	236,165	751	21,615	—	25,206	25,206	—
Total primary government	$1,025,405	$367,755	$65,533	$36,497	$(580,826)	$ 25,206	$ (555,620)	—
Component units	$ 225,884	$ 15,009	$46,931	$ 2,464	$ —	$ —	$ —	$(161,480)

					Governmental Activities	Business-Type Activities	Total	Component Units
General revenues								
Taxes:								
Property taxes					$ 80,374	$ —	$ 80,374	$ —
Sales taxes					157,302	—	157,302	—
Earnings/payroll taxes					189,762	—	189,762	—
Other taxes					98,505	—	98,505	—
Unrestricted investment earnings					265	2,336	2,601	148
Support provided by the City					—	—	—	138,521
Extraordinary item—natural disaster					—	4,300	4,300	—
Transfers					9,470	(9,470)	—	—
Total general revenues and transfers					535,678	(2,834)	532,844	138,669
Change in net position					(45,148)	22,372	(22,776)	(22,811)
Net position—beginning of year					84,247	1,266,083	1,350,330	(66,937)
Net position—end of year					$ 39,099	$1,288,455	$1,327,554	$ (89,748)

REVIEW 1 • Prepare a Statement of Activities

We obtain the following information from the financial records of the Town of Scottsville for the year ended December 31, 2016 *(in thousands)*.

Expenses—water utility (enterprise fund)...	$ 700
Expenses—general government	3,500
Expenses—public safety	27,000
Expenses—education	45,600
General property taxes..	58,000
Grants and contributions—education	9,000
Interest on general long-term debt..	340
Charges for general government services	100
Charges for water services..	715
Charges for public safety services..	2,500
Charges for education services	1,100
State grants for public safety...	4,000
Gain on sale of general capital assets	50
Investment income—governmental activities	300
Beginning of year net position—governmental activities................................	90,000
Beginning of year net position—business-type activities	12,000

Required

Prepare, in good form, the government-wide statement of activities for the Town of Scottsville for the year 2016.

Solutions are located after the chapter assignments.

FUND FINANCIAL STATEMENTS

In addition to the government-wide statements, the CAFR includes financial statements for each of the government's fund types—governmental, proprietary, and fiduciary. Chapters 10 and 11 discuss in detail the preparation of these statements. This section summarizes the CAFR format requirements, including reconciliation of funds statement information to government-wide information. Recall from Chapters 10 and 11 that the fund statements differ in format and method of reporting, as follows:

LO3 Present the fund statements.

Fund Financial Statements

Governmental Funds: modified accrual basis
Balance sheet
Statement of revenues, expenditures, and changes in fund balances

Proprietary Funds: full accrual basis
Statement of net position
Statement of revenues, expenses, and changes in net position
Statement of cash flows

Fiduciary Funds: full accrual basis
Statement of fiduciary net position
Statement of changes in fiduciary net position

Major Funds

In the fund financial statements, *the general fund is always reported separately*. However, other individual **governmental** and **enterprise** funds are separately disclosed in columnar format only if they are *major funds*. The GASB specifies two tests for determining **major funds**:

1) The fund's total assets and deferred outflows, liabilities and deferred inflows, revenues *or* expenditures (expenses) are *at least ten percent* of the corresponding total for funds of that type—either governmental or enterprise, *and*

2) The same element that met the ten percent criterion is *at least five percent* of the corresponding total for all governmental and enterprise funds combined.

Note that funds must meet both thresholds to be considered a major fund. For example, suppose total assets of all governmental funds of a local government are $30,000,000, and total assets of all governmental and enterprise funds are $70,000,000. If a specific governmental fund's total assets are $3,500,000 or more, it is separately disclosed, since total assets of $3,500,000 or more meets both thresholds: 1) $3,000,000 (= 10% × $30,000,000) *and* 2) $3,500,000 (= 5% × $70,000,000). Alternatively, any governmental or enterprise fund may be reported as a major fund without meeting these criteria, if separate reporting of its activities is judged to be *relevant to financial statement readers*.

The financial results of **nonmajor** funds are combined in a separate column. Except for the general fund, fund information for governmental and enterprise funds is not disclosed by fund type unless there is only one fund within the fund type, *and* it is a major fund. *SGAS 34* requires that only *individual major funds* within a fund type be separately disclosed. Thus if a county has two of six special revenue funds meeting the major funds criteria, two columns appear on the fund financial statements to separately report the two major special revenue funds. The rest are combined in one column as nonmajor funds. If none of the county's capital projects funds meet the criteria for major funds, no separate information on capital projects funds is reported.

Separate reporting of major funds applies to governmental and enterprise funds, but *not* internal service funds or fiduciary funds. Internal service funds are reported *in total* on the proprietary funds financial statements. The fiduciary funds are separately reported *by fund type*—pension trusts, investment trusts, private-purpose trusts, and agency funds.

Governmental Funds Financial Statements

The governmental funds financial statements reflect modified accrual accounting, and report on the activities of the general, special revenue, capital projects, debt service, and permanent funds.

- The **balance sheet** shows current assets, current liabilities, deferred inflows and outflows of resources, and fund balances for the general fund, each major governmental fund, and the total balances of the nonmajor funds. A separate column reports the total assets, liabilities, deferred inflows and outflows and fund balances for all governmental funds. Per *SGAS 54*, fund balances are categorized as nonspendable, restricted, committed, assigned and unassigned.

- The **statement of revenues, expenditures, and changes in fund balances** shows operating results for each major governmental fund and totals for the nonmajor funds and for all governmental funds. Revenues are shown by source, and expenditures are categorized by program or function. Other financing sources and uses are separately listed.

The governmental funds financial statements for the City of St. Louis appear in Exhibits 12.3 and 12.4. The city has two major governmental funds other than the general fund—the capital projects fund and the grants special revenue fund. Most revenues come from taxes. Expenditures for public safety comprise about 37 percent of total governmental fund expenditures.

Because governmental funds use modified accrual accounting, they report capital asset acquisitions as *expenditures* (capital outlay), and long-term debt issuance as *other financing sources*. Expenditures exceeded revenues by $77,561,000, partially offset by $68,558,000 in net other financing sources, primarily from tax increment financing notes and transfers in from non-governmental funds. Governmental fund balances therefore declined by $9,003,000.

EXHIBIT 12.3 2013 Governmental Funds Balance Sheet, City of St. Louis, Missouri

CITY OF ST. LOUIS, MISSOURI
Balance Sheet
Governmental Funds
June 30, 2013

(in thousands)	General Fund	Capital Projects Fund	Grants Fund	Other Governmental Funds	Total Governmental Funds
Assets					
Cash and cash equivalents:					
Restricted................................	$ 5,024	$ 12,764	$ 2,816	$ 15,641	$ 36,245
Unrestricted............................	34,431	—	—	37,658	72,089
Investments:					
Restricted...............................	9,908	14,730	—	5,582	30,220
Unrestricted............................	2,346	1,530	324	3,644	7,844
Receivables, net of allowances:					
Taxes	86,059	3,019	—	43,038	132,116
Licenses and permits	2,517	—	—	205	2,722
Intergovernmental	3,421	1,925	9,282	875	15,503
Charges for services	3,697	32	—	1,545	5,274
Other..................................	334	13	—	32	379
Due from component units..................	1,844	—	—	—	1,844
Due from other funds	13,518	—	—	5,627	19,145
Total assets..............................	$163,099	$ 34,013	$12,422	$113,847	$323,381
Liabilities and fund balances					
Liabilities:					
Accounts payable and accrued liabilities	$ 3,456	$ 4,011	$ 5,162	$ 1,379	$ 14,008
Accrued salaries and other benefits	9,093	126	626	979	10,824
Due to component units....................	8,440	1,462	—	686	10,588
Due to other funds........................	4,481	1,991	6,696	1,423	14,591
Due to other government agencies	4	—	—	—	4
Advance to other funds	17,771	—	—	—	17,771
Deferred revenue	63,821	43	—	25,076	88,940
Unearned revenue	61	—	—	2,542	2,603
Other liabilities	1,314	—	—	—	1,314
Total liabilities	108,441	7,633	12,484	32,085	160,643
Fund balances:					
Nonspendable...........................	—	—	—	11	11
Restricted...............................	14,784	22,027	—	49,090	85,901
Committed..............................	8,054	28,939	—	28,188	65,181
Assigned	6,043	—	—	4,473	10,516
Unassigned	25,777	(24,586)	(62)	—	1,129
Total fund balances.......................	54,658	26,380	(62)	81,762	162,738
Total liabilities and fund balances	$163,099	$34,013	$12,422	$113,847	$323,381

Note: Columns are grouped as **Major Funds** (General Fund, Capital Projects Fund, Grants Fund) and **Nonmajor Funds** (Other Governmental Funds), with a **Total Governmental Funds** column.

EXHIBIT 12.4   2013 Governmental Funds Statement of Revenues, Expenditures, and Changes in Fund Balances, City of St. Louis, Missouri

CITY OF ST. LOUIS, MISSOURI
Statement of Revenues, Expenditures, and Changes in Fund Balances
Governmental Funds
For Year Ended June 30, 2013

(in thousands)	Major Funds			Nonmajor Funds	Total Governmental Funds
	General Fund	Capital Projects Fund	Grants Fund	Other Governmental Funds	
Revenues					
Taxes	$344,561	$18,992	$ —	$160,875	$524,428
Licenses and permits	18,358	—	—	6,001	24,359
Intergovernmental	21,203	14,771	66,355	4,960	107,289
Charges for services, net	35,760	300	—	16,287	52,347
Court fines and forfeitures	11,022	—	—	—	11,022
Investment income	192	30	—	43	265
Interfund services provided	5,531	—	—	—	5,531
Miscellaneous	4,799	414	—	8,301	13,514
Total revenues	441,426	34,507	66,355	196,467	738,755
Expenditures					
Current:					
General government	45,896	—	648	17,436	63,980
Convention and tourism	112	—	—	4	116
Parks and recreation	19,050	1,201	380	5,058	25,689
Judicial	47,137	—	1,897	2,815	51,849
Streets	32,714	3,648	72	944	37,378
Public Safety:					
Fire	70,582	—	—	1,013	71,595
Police	115,497	—	—	22,507	138,004
Police-pension	26,221	—	—	2,271	28,492
Other	47,609	—	5,448	7,121	60,178
Health and welfare	10,939	—	32,702	17,068	60,709
Public services	22,100	963	1	38,455	61,519
Community development	—	—	24,051	53,479	77,530
Capital outlay	16	36,534	—	364	36,914
Debt service:					
Principal	22,195	13,358	1,000	18,656	55,209
Interest and fiscal charges	12,633	6,606	156	27,759	47,154
Total expenditures	472,701	62,310	66,355	214,950	816,316
Deficiency of revenues over expenditures	(31,275)	(27,803)	—	(18,483)	(77,561)
Other financing sources (uses)					
Sale of capital assets	—	3	—	—	3
Issuance of leasehold revenue bonds	—	1,890	—	—	1,890
Issuance of tax increment financing notes	—	—	—	57,195	57,195
Transfers in	40,058	19,155	—	2,930	62,143
Transfers out	(9,995)	(1,042)	—	(41,636)	(52,673)
Total other financing sources (uses), net	30,063	20,006	—	18,489	68,558
Net change in fund balances	(1,212)	(7,797)	—	6	(9,003)
Fund balances:					
Beginning of year	55,870	34,177	(62)	81,756	171,741
End of year	$ 54,658	$26,380	$ (62)	$ 81,762	$162,738

Among the total governmental fund balances in Exhibit 12.3 of $162,738,000, the majority are restricted or committed, with only $1,129,000 unassigned. In the notes to its financial statements, the City of St. Louis explains how governmental fund balances are divided between the categories. **Restricted fund balance** contains amounts designated for a specific use by *constitution*, *external parties* such as creditors or grantors, or *legislation*. In St. Louis' total governmental funds restricted fund balance of $85,901,000, $34,141,000 is restricted to debt service, and $22,086,000 is restricted to redevelopment. **Committed fund balance** contains amounts formally designated by the City of St. Louis' *Board of Aldermen*, which comprise the city's highest level of decision-making authority. Out of total committed fund balances of $65,181,000, $12,131,000 is committed to health and welfare and $10,255,000 is committed to parks and recreation. **Assigned fund balance** contains amounts approved by the *Board of Estimate and Apportionment* for future use in specific projects. Amounts are designated for use in redevelopment and health and welfare projects, among others. Each government has its own policy for determining how to divide its fund balances between the categories required by *SGAS 54*.

Required Reconciliations Because the governmental funds statements reflect modified accrual accounting, they do not agree with the government-wide statements that follow full accrual accounting. *SGAS 34* requires (1) a *reconciliation of total governmental fund balances to the total net position of governmental activities*, and (2) a *reconciliation of the change in governmental fund balances to the change in total net position of governmental activities*.

Recall the major differences between modified accrual and full accrual accounting:

- Acquisitions of capital assets increase assets in the government-wide statements, but reduce fund balance—as expenditures—in the fund statements.

- Depreciation of general capital assets reduces net position in the government-wide statements, but is not reported in the fund statements.

- When capital assets of governmental funds are sold, the difference between the proceeds and the book value of the assets is reported as a change in net position—a gain or a loss—in the government-wide statements, but the total proceeds increase fund balance in the governmental fund statements.

- Issuance of long-term general obligation debt increases liabilities in the government-wide statements, but increases fund balance—as other financing sources—in the fund statements.

- Payments on long-term debt reduce liabilities in the government-wide statements, but reduce fund balance—as expenditures—in the fund statements.

- Governmental funds do not accrue any revenues or expenditures not involving flows of current financial resources, so accrued interest, compensated absences, pension and OPEB costs not currently using financial resources are not reported.

In addition to differences between modified and full accrual accounting, recall that *"governmental activities" on the government-wide statements include internal service funds, whereas "governmental funds" do not*. Therefore, reconciliation of governmental funds to governmental activities requires the addition of internal service funds information. Because internal service funds report on the full accrual basis, their data need not be adjusted.

Reconciliation of the Governmental Funds Balance Sheet to the Statement of Net Position This schedule appears with the governmental funds balance sheet. It reconciles the total fund balances on that statement with the balance reported for net position of governmental activities in the government-wide statement of net position. The general format of the reconciliation is:

Total fund balances, governmental funds	$XXX
+ Capital and other long-term assets used in governmental activities, net of accumulated depreciation . .	XXX
+ Receivables producing financial resources in future periods	XXX
− Long-term liabilities used to finance governmental activities	(XXX)
− Other payables not requiring current financial resources	(XXX)
+ Internal service fund net position included in the government-wide statement of net position but not included in the governmental funds balance sheet	XXX
Net position of governmental activities	$XXX

The 2013 reconciliation of governmental fund balances to net position of governmental activities for the City of St. Louis appears in Exhibit 12.5. Total fund balances—governmental funds, $162,738,000, is found on the governmental funds balance sheet in Exhibit 12.3. Total net position—governmental activities, $39,099,000, is on the government-wide statement of net position in Exhibit 12.1. The major reconciliation items are additions for net capital assets of $850,019,000 that were deducted from governmental fund balances but not from net position of governmental activities, and deductions for leasehold improvements and refunding revenue bonds of $473,403,000 that were added to governmental fund balances but not net position of governmental activities. The City adds $82,256,000 in tax receivables to be collected in future periods, recognized as assets on the full accrual basis but not reported using modified accrual accounting. Accrued compensated absences of $25,194,000 and interest payable of $94,473,000 are deducted because they are reported as liabilities on the statement of net position but not on the governmental funds balance sheet.

Reconciliation of the Governmental Funds Statement of Revenues, Expenditures, and Changes in Fund Balances to the Government-Wide Statement of Activities   This schedule appears with the governmental funds operating statement. It reconciles the total change in fund balances on that statement with the change in net position of governmental activities in the government-wide statement of net position. The general format of the reconciliation is:

Change in total fund balances, governmental funds	$XXX
+ Outlays for general capital assets	XXX
− Depreciation expense for general capital assets	(XXX)
+ Accrued revenues of governmental funds producing resources in future periods	XXX
− Long-term debt proceeds used to finance governmental activities	(XXX)
+ Repayments of long-term debt principal	XXX
− Accrued expenses of governmental funds using resources in future periods	(XXX)
+ Increase (− decrease) in internal service fund net position not included in the governmental funds operating statement but included in the government-wide statement of activities	XXX
Change in net position of governmental activities	$XXX

The 2013 reconciliation of the change in governmental fund balances to the change in net position of governmental activities for the City of St. Louis appears in Exhibit 12.6. The $(9,003,000) change in total fund balances—governmental funds, is found on the governmental funds statement of revenues, expenditures, and changes in fund balances in Exhibit 12.4. The $(45,148,000) change in net position—governmental activities, is on the government-wide statement of activities in Exhibit 12.2. The major reconciliation items are development and tax increment financing bonds and notes payable of $(57,195,000), depreciation expense of $(51,659,000), and annual principal payments on bonds and notes payable of $46,943,000.

EXHIBIT 12.5 **2013 Reconciliation, Governmental Funds Balance Sheet to Statement of Net Position, City of St. Louis, Missouri**

CITY OF ST. LOUIS, MISSOURI
Reconciliation of the Balance Sheet of Governmental Funds to the Statement of Net Position
June 30, 2013
(in thousands)

Total fund balances—governmental funds—balance sheet	$162,738

Amounts reported for governmental activities in the statement of net position are different because:

Capital assets and certain other assets used in governmental activities, which exceed capitalization threshold amounts (excluding internal service fund capital assets), are not financial resources and, therefore, are not reported in the fund financial statements.	850,019
The City reports a net pension asset on the statement of net position to the extent actual contributions to the City's retirement plans exceed the annual actuarial required contribution. This asset is not reported in the fund financial statements.	42,327
Various taxes related to fiscal year 2013 will be collected beyond the 60-day period used to record revenue in the fund financial statements. Revenue for this amount is recognized in the government-wide financial statements. . . .	6,684
Property taxes are assessed by the City on January 1st of each calendar year, but are not due until December 31st. Taxes assessed on January 1, 2013 and payable on December 31, 2013 are deferred within the fund financial statements. However, revenue for this amount is recognized in the government-wide financial statements.	82,256
Internal service funds are used by management to charge the costs of risk management and mailroom services to the individual funds, generally on a cost reimbursement basis. The assets and liabilities of internal service funds are included in governmental activities in the statement of net position.	1,427
Bond issuance costs are reported in the governmental funds financial statements as expenditures when debt is issued, whereas the amounts are deferred and amortized over the life of the debt on the government-wide financial statements.	16,643

Long-term liabilities applicable to the City's governmental activities are not due and payable in the current period and, accordingly, are not reported as liabilities within the fund financial statements. Interest on long-term debt is not accrued in governmental funds, but rather is recognized as an expenditure when due. All liabilities—both current and long-term—are reported on the government-wide statement of net position. Also, during the year, the City issued new debt and refunded some of its existing debt. Discounts, premiums, and deferred amounts on refunding are reported in the governmental fund financial statements when the debt was issued, whereas these amounts are deferred and amortized over the life of the debt on the government-wide financial statements. Balances as of June 30, 2013 are:

Accrued vacation and sick leave	(25,194)
Net pension obligation	(36,815)
Accrued interest payable	(94,473)
Joint venture financing agreement	(42,085)
Certificates of participation	(6,740)
Obligations with component unit	(53,015)
Capital leases-rolling stock	(13,698)
Leasehold improvement and refunding revenue bonds.	(473,403)
Development and TIF bonds and notes payable	(296,122)
General obligation bonds	(35,050)
Section 108 Loan Guarantee Assistance Programs	(39,530)
Fireman's Retirement EAN Note	(4,372)
Other long-term debt	(4,390)
Unamortized discounts	4,301
Unamortized premiums	(7,574)
Unamortized deferred amounts on refunding	5,165
Total net position—governmental activities—statement of net position	$ 39,099

EXHIBIT 12.6 2013 Reconciliation, Governmental Funds Operating Statement to Statement of Activities, City of St. Louis, Missouri

CITY OF ST LOUIS, MISSOURI
Reconciliation of the Statement of Revenues, Expenditures, and Changes in Fund Balances
of Governmental Funds to the Statement of Activities
For Year Ended June 30, 2013

(in thousands)

Net change in fund balances—governmental funds—statement of revenues, expenditures, and changes in fund balances	$ (9,003)

Amounts reported for governmental activities in the statement of activities are different because:

Governmental funds report capital outlays as expenditures. However, in the statement of activities, the cost of those assets, meeting the capitalization threshold, is allocated over their estimated useful lives and recorded as depreciation expense. Additionally, contributions of capital assets to the City are recorded as capital contributions on the statement of activities. This is the amount by which capital outlays and capital contributions, meeting the capitalization threshold, exceeded depreciation expense in the current year. Details of the reported amounts are as follows:

Capital outlay	$ 36,914
Capital contribution	261
Loss on disposal of capital assets	(305)
Depreciation expense.	(51,659)
	(14,789)

Revenues in the statement of activities that do not provide current financial resources are not reported as revenues in the fund financial statements. These amounts represent the extent to which revenues not providing current financial resources in the current fiscal year exceeded revenues not providing current financial resources in the prior fiscal year (which are recognized in the fund financial statements in the current year). Such amounts are attributable to the following factors:

Change in revenues received after the 60-day accrual period.	(2,924)
Property taxes due in the fiscal year following the fiscal year in which they were assessed.	1,376
	(1,548)

Internal service funds are used by management to charge the cost of risk management and mailroom services to the individual funds. The change in position of internal funds attributable to governmental activities is reported on the statement of activities.	(728)
The City reports a net pension obligation/asset on the statement of net position to the extent actual contributions to the City's retirement plans fall below/exceed the annual required contribution. This obligation/asset is not reported in the fund financial statements. Fluctuations in net pension obligations/assets are reported in the statement of activities..	(4,537)

Bond proceeds are reported as financing sources in governmental funds financial statements and thus contribute to the net change in fund balance. In the statement of net position, however, issuing debt increases long-term liabilities and does not affect the statement of activities. Similarly, repayments of principal is an expenditure in the governmental funds financial statements, but reduces the liability in the statement of position.

Debt issued during the current year:	
Development and tax increment financing bonds and notes payable.	(57,195)
Loan agreement with Forest Park Forever.	(1,890)
Repayments during the current year:	
Annual principal payments on bonds and notes payable	46,943
Annual principal payments on joint venture financing agreement.	4,080
Annual principal payments on capital lease	3,574
Annual principal payments on Certificates of Participation.	615
	(3,873)

Under the modified accrual basis of accounting used in the governmental funds financial statements, expenditures are not recognized for transactions that are not normally paid with expendable available financial resources. In the statement of activities, however, which is presented on the accrual basis of accounting, expenses and liabilities are reported regardless of when financial resources are available. In addition, interest on long-term debt is not recognized under the modified accrual basis of accounting until due, rather than as it accrues. This adjustment combines the net changes of the following:

Accrued vacation and sick leave	(147)
Accrued interest payable	(11,799)
Unamortized discounts.	(202)
Unamortized premiums	2,108
Deferred bond issuance costs, net of amortization	741
Unamortized deferred amounts on refunding.	(1,371)
	(10,670)

Change in net position—governmental activities—statement of activities	$(45,148)

Reporting Perspective

When reconciling the governmental funds financial statements, prepared on a modified accrual basis, to the government-wide statements, prepared using full accrual accounting, do you expect the fund balances to always be larger than the full accrual net position balances? A significant shortcoming of the modified accrual basis is that a government can improve its financial health by issuing long-term debt. This was a major motivation for requiring presentation of government activities on the full accrual basis. Long-term debt proceeds increase fund balances, but not net position. Borrowing to improve financial position is not a long-term solution to deficit spending. Governments that engage in this practice will likely report higher fund balances than net position. The City of St. Louis reconciliations are a case in point. In 2013, the fund balances of governmental funds declined by $9,003,000, while net position of governmental activities declined by $45,148,000, almost five times as much. The city covered much of its net deficit by issuing long-term debt. We should not, however, assume that all governments report the same pattern. For example, for the year ended June 30, 2013, the **City of St. George, Utah** reports a positive change in governmental fund balances of $9,276,296, and a *larger* positive change in net position of governmental activities of $25,046,956. In 2013, St. George's net capital outlays and debt principal repayments exceeded proceeds from debt issuance.

REVIEW 2 • Reconcile the Change in Fund Balances to Change in Net Position

We obtain the following information from Shasta County's financial records for 2017 *(in thousands)*:

1.	Net change in fund balances—governmental funds	$(2,200)
2.	Principal repayments—general obligation debt	5,600
3.	Accrued OPEB expense	100
4.	Cost of general capital assets acquired	14,000
5.	Proceeds from sale of general capital assets	300
6.	Loss on sale of general capital assets	10
7.	Accrued interest expense on general obligation debt	192
8.	Depreciation expense on general capital assets	3,800
9.	Proceeds from issuance of general obligation debt	9,300

Required

Prepare a reconciliation of change in fund balances—governmental funds, to change in net position—governmental activities. Shasta County has no internal service funds.

Solutions are located after the chapter assignments.

Proprietary Funds Financial Statements

Proprietary funds consist of enterprise and internal service funds. As with governmental funds, each major enterprise fund is shown separately and an aggregate total is reported for nonmajor enterprise funds. However, *only a single total for all internal service funds is shown*. The GASB believes that this reporting format allows readers to more easily reconcile the proprietary fund financial statements with the government-wide statements. Separate reporting of each fund type within the fund statements allows readers to relate the totals to those in the government-wide statements, since governmental activities on the government-wide statements include both governmental and internal service funds, and business-type activities report the results of enterprise funds. The following financial statements are required for proprietary funds:

- **Statement of net position**, with individual assets and liabilities classified according to liquidity, and net position reported in three categories as in the government-wide statements. Since proprietary funds use full accrual accounting, *no* reconciliation to the government-wide statements is needed. The total net position of all enterprise funds equals the total net position of business-type activities on the government-wide statement of net position.

- **Statement of revenues, expenses, and changes in net position**, with operating and nonoperating items separately categorized. Reporting a revenue or expense as operating or nonoperating depends on the government's policy, disclosed in the notes to the financial statements. Capital contributions received from other funds are reported separately, below nonoperating items. A reconciliation of the change in net position of proprietary funds to the change in net position shown on the government-wide statements is *not* needed, because both statements use full accrual accounting. The change in net position of enterprise funds on the statement of revenues, expenses, and changes in net position equals the change in net position of business-type activities on the government-wide statement of activities.

- **Statement of cash flows**, using the *direct* method to present cash from operating activities, and reconciliation of operating income to cash flow from operating activities, as in business reporting. Statement categories include cash flows from operating activities, cash flows from noncapital financing activities, cash flows from capital and related financing activities, and cash flows from investing activities. Chapter 11 discusses these categories in detail.

Because proprietary funds use full accrual accounting, any differences between the government-wide statements and proprietary funds statements should be due to differences in classification, not valuation.

The three required statements for the proprietary funds of the City of St. Louis, Missouri appear in Exhibits 12.7, 12.8, and 12.9. The city has three enterprise funds, all major funds—the Lambert-St. Louis International Airport, the Water Division, and the Parking Division. The proprietary funds operating statement in Exhibit 12.8 reports the 2013 change in enterprise fund net position as $22,372,000, which is the same as the change in net position of business-type activities reported in the government-wide statement of activities in Exhibit 12.2. Enterprise fund net position, reported in the proprietary funds balance sheet in Exhibit 12.7, is $1,288,455,000. The government-wide statement of net position in Exhibit 12.1 reports business-type net position at the same amount.

CITY OF ST. LOUIS, MISSOURI
Statement of Fund Net Position
Proprietary Funds
June 30, 2013

(in thousands)	Major Funds—Enterprise Funds				Internal Service Funds
	Lambert—St. Louis International Airport	Water Division	Parking Division	Total Enterprise Funds	
Assets					
Current assets					
Cash and cash equivalents........................	$ 17,867	$ 3,998	$ 7,545	$ 29,410	$ —
Restricted cash and cash equivalents	49,555	21,363	10,966	81,884	3,478
Investments					
Restricted investments...........................	33,051	—	—	33,051	—
Unrestricted investments	—	—	—	—	117
Receivables, net of allowances					
Intergovernmental...............................	121	—	—	121	1,000
Charges for services............................	7,376	9,929	129	17,434	10
Insurance recovery.............................	4,300	—	—	4,300	—
Passenger facility charges	3,638	—	—	3,638	—
Accrued interest	88	—	—	88	—
Prepaid assets	—	—	—	—	50
Due from other funds..............................	—	—	—	—	5,354
Advance from other funds	—	—	—	—	17,771
Inventories	2,245	2,232	—	4,477	—
Other current assets...............................	558	—	21	579	—
Total current assets	118,799	37,522	18,661	174,982	27,780
Noncurrent assets					
Cash and cash equivalents:					
Restricted cash and cash equivalents	36,031	2,604	—	38,635	—
Unrestricted cash and cash equivalents	—	12,393	—	12,393	—
Investments—unrestricted	44,256	—	—	44,256	—
Investments—restricted	108,312	—	4,874	113,186	—
Capital assets:					
Property, plant and equipment	1,603,311	284,668	83,559	1,971,538	112
Less accumulated depreciation	(796,977)	(141,162)	(28,759)	(966,898)	(74)
Net property, plant and equipment	806,334	143,506	54,800	1,004,640	38
Land and easements	755,023	1,238	22,903	779,164	—
Construction-in-progress	89,129	2,346	—	91,475	—
Capital assets, net.............................	1,650,486	147,090	77,703	1,875,279	38
Deferred charges and other assets, net	12,983	1,325	1,473	15,781	—
Other assets	1,689	—	—	1,689	—
Total noncurrent assets.........................	1,853,757	163,412	84,050	2,101,219	38
Total assets	1,972,556	200,934	102,711	2,276,201	27,818
Liabilities					
Current liabilities					
Accounts payable and accrued liabilities	9,490	1,246	537	11,273	287
Accrued salaries and other benefits.................	1,976	3,871	191	6,038	—
Accrued vacation and compensatory time benefits.....	3,252	1,743	153	5,148	—
Contracts and retainage payable	19,509	—	—	19,509	—
Accrued interest payable	20,205	103	120	20,428	—
Current portion of revenue bonds	30,465	3,765	2,298	36,528	—
Due to other funds	5,364	3,910	634	9,908	—
Due to other government agencies	—	—	55	55	—
Claims payable...................................	—	—	—	—	26,104
Deferred revenue	717	1,958	1,713	4,388	—
Total current liabilities.....................	90,978	16,596	5,701	113,275	26,391
Noncurrent liabilities					
Revenue bonds payable, net	782,581	3,820	63,601	850,002	—
Customer deposits...............................	—	1,854	—	1,854	—
Other liabilities	14,862	6,055	1,698	22,615	—
Total noncurrent liabilities......................	797,443	11,729	65,299	874,471	—
Total liabilities...................................	888,421	28,325	71,000	987,746	26,391
Net position					
Net investments in capital assets...................	881,435	139,505	12,982	1,033,922	39
Restricted:					
Debt service	95,625	4,598	12,419	112,642	—
Capital projects	7,923	—	—	7,923	—
Passenger facility charges	29,134	—	—	29,134	—
Unrestricted	70,018	28,506	6,310	104,834	1,388
Total net position	$1,084,135	$172,609	$ 31,711	$1,288,455	$ 1,427

EXHIBIT 12.8 2013 Proprietary Funds Statement of Revenues, Expenses, and Changes in Fund Net Position, City of St. Louis, Missouri

CITY OF ST. LOUIS, MISSOURI
Statement of Revenues, Expenses, and Changes in Fund Net Position
Proprietary Funds
For Year Ended June 30, 2013

(in thousands)	Major Funds—Enterprise Funds				Internal Service Funds
	Lambert—St. Louis International Airport	Water Division	Parking Division	Total Enterprise Funds	
Operating revenues					
Aviation revenues	$ 93,691	$ —	$ —	$ 93,691	$ —
Concessions	23,340	—	—	23,340	—
Water sales	—	52,586	—	52,586	—
Lease revenue	4,458	—	—	4,458	—
Parking, net	17,938	—	14,050	31,988	—
Charges for services	—	—	—	—	25,302
Intergovernmental revenue	—	—	—	—	891
Miscellaneous	—	2,872	595	3,467	—
Total operating revenues	139,427	55,458	14,645	209,530	26,193
Operating expenses					
Claims incurred	—	—	—	—	20,195
Premiums	—	—	—	—	1,550
Personal services	39,308	15,612	4,915	59,835	282
Material and supplies	6,335	9,405	175	15,915	4,894
Purchased power	—	2,953	—	2,953	—
Contractual services	34,391	5,975	1,063	41,429	—
Miscellaneous	97	3,553	1,167	4,817	—
Depreciation and amortization	48,890	5,051	2,758	56,699	6
Interfund services used	3,106	2,833	153	6,092	—
Total operating expenses	132,127	45,382	10,231	187,740	26,927
Operating income (loss)	7,300	10,076	4,414	21,790	(734)
Nonoperating revenues (expenses)					
Intergovernmental revenue	751	—	—	751	—
Investment income (expense)	2,137	(19)	218	2,336	—
Interest expense	(40,283)	(266)	(3,327)	(43,876)	—
Passenger facility charges	25,060	—	—	25,060	—
Amortization of bond issue costs	(1,558)	(72)	—	(1,630)	—
Loss on disposal of capital assets	—	(79)	—	(79)	(12)
Miscellaneous, net	119	1,444	12	1,575	—
Total nonoperating revenues (expenses), net	(13,774)	1,008	(3,097)	(15,863)	(12)
Income (loss) before transfers and capital contributions	(6,474)	11,084	1,317	5,927	(746)
Transfers in	—	—	908	908	—
Transfers out	(6,607)	(3,271)	(500)	(10,378)	—
Extraordinary item—natural disaster	4,300	—	—	4,300	—
Capital contributions	21,615	—	—	21,615	18
Change in net position	12,834	7,813	1,725	22,372	(728)
Total net position—beginning of year	1,071,301	164,796	29,986	1,266,083	2,155
Total net position—end of year	$1,084,135	$172,609	$31,711	$1,288,455	$ 1,427

CITY OF ST. LOUIS, MISSOURI
Statement of Cash Flows
Proprietary Funds
For Year Ended June 30, 2013

(in thousands)	Major Funds—Enterprise Funds				Internal Service Funds
	Lambert—St. Louis International Airport	Water Division	Parking Division	Total Enterprise Funds	
Cash flows from operating activities					
Receipts from customers and users.	$132,882	$54,633	$14,362	$201,877	$ —
Other operating cash receipts	—	—	160	160	—
Payments to suppliers of goods and services	(40,763)	(19,967)	(3,624)	(64,354)	(25,485)
Payments to employees	(39,374)	(15,706)	(4,924)	(60,004)	(280)
Payments for interfund services used	(2,708)	(3,272)	—	(5,980)	26,591
Net cash provided by operating activities.	50,037	15,688	5,974	71,699	826
Cash flows from noncapital financing activities					
Interest paid on share of bond pension liability	—	(206)	—	(206)	—
Transfers from the State of Missouri	—	—	12	12	—
Transfers from other funds	—	—	907	907	—
Transfers to other funds	(6,607)	(3,271)	(500)	(10,378)	—
Net cash provided by (used in) noncapital financing activities.	(6,607)	(3,477)	419	(9,665)	—
Cash flows from capital and related financing activities					
Cash collections from passenger facility charges	24,946	—	—	24,946	—
Receipts from federal financing assistance	27,687	—	—	27,687	—
Acquisition and construction of capital assets	(64,610)	(4,130)	(1,425)	(70,165)	—
Insurance recoveries	3,000	—	—	3,000	—
Proceeds from sale of surplus property	2,123	—	—	2,123	—
Cash paid for bond refunding	(41,819)	—	—	(41,819)	—
Proceeds from issuance of bond	34,839	—	—	34,839	—
Principal paid on revenue bond maturities	(30,655)	(3,895)	(2,236)	(36,786)	—
Cash paid for interest	(41,804)	(60)	(3,025)	(44,889)	—
Other capital and financing activities	—	1,411	—	1,411	—
Net cash used in capital and related financing activities	(86,293)	(6,674)	(6,686)	(99,653)	—
Cash flows from investing activities					
Purchase of investments	(285,232)	—	(9,517)	(294,749)	48
Proceeds from sales and maturities of investments.	355,149	—	9,517	364,666	—
Interest expense on cash and investments	—	(19)	—	(19)	—
Investment income	2,528	—	214	2,742	—
Net cash provided by (used in) investing activities.	72,445	(19)	214	72,640	48
Net increase (decrease) in cash and cash equivalents	29,582	5,518	(79)	35,021	874
Cash and cash equivalents:					
Beginning of year:					
Unrestricted.	37,737	27,778	11,503	77,018	2,604
Restricted	36,134	7,062	7,087	50,283	—
	73,871	34,840	18,590	127,301	2,604
End of year:					
Unrestricted.	49,555	33,756	10,966	94,277	3,478
Restricted	53,898	6,602	7,545	68,045	—
	$103,453	$40,358	$18,511	$162,322	$ 3,478
Reconciliation of operating income (loss) to net cash provided by operating activities:					
Operating income (loss)	$ 7,300	$10,076	$ 4,414	$ 21,790	$ (734)
Adjustments to reconcile operating income (loss) to net cash provided by operating activities:					
Depreciation and amortization	48,890	5,052	2,758	56,700	6
Changes in assets and liabilities:					
Receivables, net	(6,404)	115	(5)	(6,294)	(467)
Inventories	190	(92)	—	98	—
Prepaid assets	—	—	—	—	2
Other assets, net	193	—	20	213	—
Accounts payable, accrued liabilities, accrued salaries and other benefits.	(290)	551	153	414	253
Claims payable	—	—	—	—	901
Deferred revenue	236	(373)	(118)	(255)	—
Due to/from other funds	495	358	(1,243)	(390)	340
Advance to other funds	—	—	—	—	525
Customer deposits	—	76	—	76	—
Other long term liabilities.	(573)	(75)	(5)	(653)	—
Total adjustments	42,737	5,612	1,560	49,909	1,560
Net cash provided by operating activities	$ 50,037	$15,688	$ 5,974	$ 71,699	$ 826
Supplemental disclosure for noncash activities:					
Contributed capital	$ —	$ —	$ —	$ —	$ 18
Unrealized (loss) gain on investments	$ (340)	$ 79	$ 115	$ (146)	$ —

Fiduciary Funds Financial Statements

Fiduciary funds use full accrual accounting to report the resources and activities related to assets held in trust or in an agency capacity for entities or individuals outside the governmental unit. Separate columns appear for each of the four fiduciary fund types. No reconciliations to the government-wide statements exist, because those statements do not include fiduciary activities. Required financial statements are:

- **Statement of fiduciary net position.** The net position category generally shows only the balance of net position held in trust for others. Agency funds have no net position balance, because assets equal liabilities.

- **Statement of changes in fiduciary net position.** Only trust fund activities are reported, since agency funds do not report net position.

The City of St. Louis' pension trust funds and agency funds financial statements are shown in Exhibits 12.10 and 12.11. The pension trust funds report the city's activities as trustee of the three public employee retirement systems—the Firemen's Retirement System, the Police Retirement System, and the Employees' Retirement System. As expected, various investments comprise the majority of pension trust fund assets. Agency funds account for assets held on behalf of others, including taxes to be remitted to other governmental agencies, general insurance premiums, and bail bonds received from court defendants. Agency fund assets, consisting of cash, investments and accrued taxes receivable, equal agency fund liabilities, consisting of amounts due to or deposits held for others.

EXHIBIT 12.10   2013 Statement of Fiduciary Net Position, City of St. Louis, Missouri

CITY OF ST. LOUIS, MISSOURI
Statement of Fiduciary Net Position
Fiduciary Funds
June 30, 2013

(in thousands)	Pension Trust Funds	Agency Funds
Assets:		
Cash and cash equivalents—unrestricted	$ 24,407	$23,906
Cash and cash equivalents—restricted	—	1,729
Pension trust investments:		
Bonds	153,711	—
Domestic bond funds	77,777	—
Stocks	564,348	—
Mortgage-backed securities	14,301	—
Collective investment funds	438,379	—
Real estate equities and investment trust	140,620	—
Investment property	1,170	—
Hedge funds	86,357	—
Money market mutual funds and other short-term investments	65,999	—
Managed international equity funds	187,343	—
Total investments	1,730,005	—
Securities lending collateral	4,241	—
Receivables, net of allowances:		
Taxes	—	21,498
Contributions	13,093	—
Accrued interest	1,814	—
Other	1,822	1,295
Capital assets, net	1,199	—
Total assets	1,776,581	48,428
Liabilities:		
Accounts payable and accrued liabilities	2,056	1,565
Deposits held for others	329	17,569
Due to other governmental agencies	—	29,294
Securities lending collateral liability	4,241	—
Other liabilities	1,794	—
Total liabilities	8,420	48,428
Net position:		
Net position held in trust for pension benefits	$1,768,161	$ —

EXHIBIT 12.11   2013 Statement of Changes in Fiduciary Net Position, City of St. Louis, Missouri

CITY OF ST. LOUIS, MISSOURI
Statement of Changes in Fiduciary Net Position
Fiduciary Funds
For Year Ended June 30, 2013

(in thousands)	Pension Trust Funds
Additions	
Contributions:	
Members.	$ 6,743
Employer.	80,557
Investment income:	
Interest and dividends.	26,115
Net decline in fair value of investments	234,490
Investment income	260,605
Less investment expense.	(7,644)
Net investment income.	252,961
Total additions.	340,261
Deductions	
Benefits.	137,744
Refunds of contributions	5,116
Administrative expense.	3,254
Total deductions	146,114
Net increase	194,147
Net position held in trust for pension benefits:	
Beginning of year	1,574,014
End of year	$1,768,161

COMPARISON OF GOVERNMENT-WIDE AND FUNDS INFORMATION

How do the balances in the government-wide statements correspond with those reported in the funds statements? This section compares the governmental activities and business-type activities information reported on the government-wide financial statements with the information reported on the governmental funds and proprietary funds financial statements. Figure 12.2 summarizes the required fund financial statements and their relation to the government-wide financial statements.

LO4 Describe the relation between government-wide and fund statements

Governmental Activities

The government-wide statements report the assets and liabilities, revenues and expenses of governmental funds and internal service funds on a full accrual basis, as governmental activities. The funds statements report similar information, but governmental funds activities use modified accrual accounting, and internal service funds use full accrual accounting.

Compare some of the numbers reported for governmental activities on the statement of net position, Exhibit 12.1, with those reported for governmental funds and internal service funds in their respective fund balance sheets, Exhibits 12.3 and 12.7. Unrestricted cash and cash equivalents in the funds statements are $72,089,000 and $3,478,000 for governmental and internal service funds, respectively. The total, $75,567,000, matches the cash and cash equivalents reported in the government-wide statement of net position for governmental activities.

However, in the funds statements total assets are $323,381,000 for governmental funds and $27,818,000 for internal service funds, which are much lower than total assets of governmental activities in Exhibit 12.1 of $1,227,826,000. The difference of $876,627,000 is mainly explained by the net capital assets of $113,236,000 and $736,821,000 reported on the government-wide statement of net position. There are few internal service fund capital assets, so most relate to governmental funds, which do not report capital assets on the funds balance sheet.

FIGURE 12.2   Relation Between Fund and Government-Wide Financial Statements

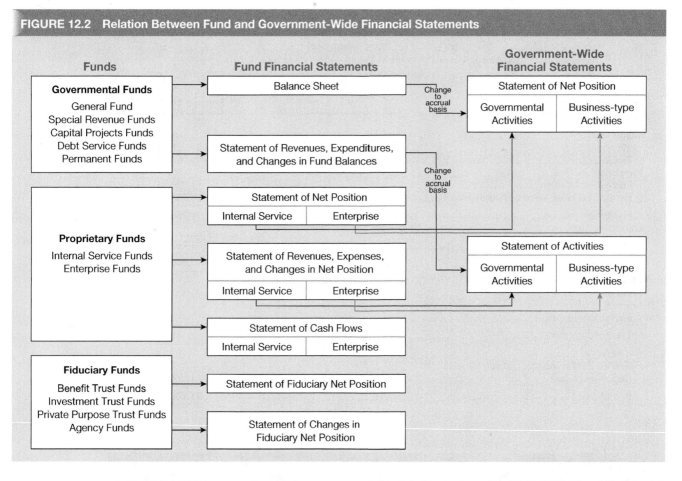

Total liabilities reported on the governmental funds balance sheet are $160,643,000, while internal service fund liabilities reported on the proprietary funds balance sheet are $26,391,000. These amounts are much lower than the $1,188,727,000 in total liabilities of governmental activities on the government-wide statement of net position, due to the fact that governmental funds do not report long-term liabilities.

On the government-wide statement of activities in Exhibit 12.2, the functional expense categories are similar to those listed on the statement of revenues, expenditures, and changes in fund balances for governmental funds in Exhibit 12.4. Functional expenses are typically greater than expenditures, since expenditures exclude such items as depreciation, accrued pension, and OPEB costs not requiring current financial resources. For example, general government *expenses* are $73,204,000 but general government *expenditures* are $63,980,000. Convention and tourism *expenses* are $5,513,000, but convention and tourism *expenditures* are only $116,000.

Business-Type Activities

The government-wide statements report the assets and liabilities, revenues and expenses of enterprise funds as business-type activities, and proprietary funds statements also report enterprise fund activities. Because both statements use full accrual accounting, the same information should appear in both sets of statements.

Compare some of the numbers reported for business-type activities on the statement of net position, Exhibit 12.1, with those reported for enterprise funds in the proprietary funds statement of net position, Exhibit 12.7. Total assets of business-type activities are $2,266,293,000, while total assets of enterprise funds are $2,276,201,000. Total liabilities of business-type activities are $977,838,000, and total liabilities of enterprise funds are $987,746,000. However, recall that the government-wide financial statements eliminate interfund receivables and payables, and the funds statements do not. We therefore expect the government-wide totals for assets and liabilities for business-type activities to be slightly lower than the enterprise funds totals reported on the funds statement of net position. The proprietary funds statement of net position reports $9,908,000 of enterprise fund liabilities due to other funds, an item not reported on the government-wide statement of net position. This amount explains the discrepancy between government-wide liabilities for business-type activities and enterprise fund liabilities (= $987,746,000 − $977,838,000).

The government-wide statement of activities reports total expenses of business-type activities as $233,325,000. On the proprietary funds statement of revenues, expenses, and changes in net position, total expenses of enterprise funds are also $233,325,000, after combining operating and nonoperating expenses (= $187,740,000 + $43,876,000 + $1,630,000 + $79,000).

NOTES AND REQUIRED SUPPLEMENTARY INFORMATION

Both the government-wide and fund financial statements use the same set of accompanying notes. The notes explain the information presented, including the measurement focus, asset capitalization policy, and details on capital assets, long-term debt, and endowment activities. Required supplementary information includes the MD&A, presented before the basic financial statements, as well as information that follows the financial statements and notes. Examples include a schedule of funding progress for retirement funds, and schedules comparing actual financial statement numbers with budgeted amounts.

Budgetary Comparison Schedules

Information presented after the basic financial statements includes **budgetary comparison schedules** for the general fund and each major fund with a legally adopted budget. These schedules report the original and final budgets, reflecting legislative and executive changes during the year, actual results, and a **reconciliation** of budget information to GAAP information.

The budgetary comparison schedule compares the legally budgeted revenues and expenditures for the government, based on applicable laws and regulations, with "actual" balances calculated on the same basis. If budgetary reporting methods differ from GAAP reporting requirements used to measure revenues and expenditures on the funds statements, another schedule reconciles the actual fund balances on the budgetary comparison schedule with the fund balances on the governmental funds balance sheet. Reconciling items include any or all of the following:

- **Entity differences.** Component unit results that appear in the fund financial statements but are not part of the legal budget.

- **Perspective differences.** The legal budget may include programs not reported in the governmental funds.

- **Basis differences.** Budget numbers may use the cash basis while the fund financial statements use the modified accrual basis of accounting.

- **Timing differences.** Year-end outstanding encumbrances are treated as expenditures for budget purposes, but not in GAAP-based fund financial statements.

The City of St. Louis has an annual budget for the general fund, debt service fund, capital projects fund, and several special revenue funds. The summarized 2013 budgetary comparison schedule for St. Louis' general fund appears in Exhibit 12.12. Overall, the final budgeted deficiency of revenues and other financing sources over expenditures and other financing uses was $(8,039,000), while the actual excess of revenues and other financing sources over expenditures and other financing uses was $5,622,000, for a positive variance of $13,661,000. Because the actual reported excess of $5,622,000 does not match the actual change in general fund balance of $(1,212,000) on the governmental funds operating statement in Exhibit 12.4, the footnotes provide the following reconciliation of the difference *(in thousands)*:

Budget basis	$ 5,622
Increase (decrease) due to:	
Revenue accruals	5,769
Expenditure accruals	(13,749)
Unbudgeted activities and funds	1,146
GAAP basis	$ (1,212)

For the City of St. Louis, the difference between the budget basis and GAAP basis of reporting is due to two factors:

- **Basis differences**—some revenues and expenditures are accrued prior to the cash receipt or payment under the GAAP modified accrual basis, while the budget uses the cash basis.

- **Perspective differences**—the budget does not include certain activities of the general, special revenue and capital projects funds, which are reported in the general fund financial statements.

EXHIBIT 12.12   Summarized 2013 Budgetary Comparison Schedule, General Fund, City of St. Louis, Missouri

CITY OF ST. LOUIS, MISSOURI
Schedule of Revenues, Expenditures, and Changes in Fund Balances—Budget and Actual
General Fund
For Year Ended June 30, 2013

(in thousands)	Original Budget	Final Revised Budget	Actual	Variance with Final Budget Favorable (Unfavorable)
Revenues				
Taxes	$347,675	$349,675	$354,046	$ 4,371
Licenses and permits	17,454	17,454	17,901	447
Intergovernmental	18,657	18,657	16,881	(1,776)
Charges for services	34,235	34,235	32,347	(1,888)
Court fines and forfeitures	7,622	7,622	10,896	3,274
Interest	1	1	28	27
Miscellaneous	3,966	3,966	3,570	(396)
Total revenues	429,610	431,610	435,669	4,059
Expenditures				
General government	46,497	47,069	46,769	300
Convention and tourism	147	147	114	33
Parks and recreation	19,312	19,312	19,107	205
Judicial	46,445	46,450	44,826	1,624
Streets	33,698	33,698	33,088	610
Public safety	142,745	142,410	143,370	(960)
Health and welfare	3,195	3,195	3,160	35
Public services	21,806	21,806	21,252	554
Debt service	25,911	27,699	27,969	(270)
Total expenditures	339,756	341,786	339,655	2,131
Excess of revenues over expenditures	89,854	89,824	96,014	6,190
Other financing sources (uses)				
Transfers in	35,186	35,186	35,708	522
Transfers to component units	(124,584)	(124,879)	(115,574)	9,305
Transfers out	(8,495)	(8,170)	(10,526)	(2,356)
Total other financing sources (uses)	(97,893)	(97,863)	(90,392)	7,471
Excess (deficiency) of revenues and other financing sources over expenditures and other financing uses	$ (8,039)	$ (8,039)	$ 5,622	$13,661

Another common reconciliation addresses outstanding year-end encumbrances, treated as expenditures in the legal budget at time of encumbrance, but not reported as expenditures until the goods or services are delivered in the following year. Chapter 10 introduced this reconciliation in its discussion of carryover encumbrances.

Suppose the budget basis excess of revenues and other financing sources over expenditures and other financing uses is $400,000, the beginning encumbrances balance was $12,000, and the ending encumbrances balance is $15,000. The reconciliation is as follows:

Revenues and other financing sources less expenditures and other financing uses—budget basis . . .	$400,000
Less beginning encumbrances.	(12,000)
Plus ending encumbrances	15,000
Revenues and other financing sources less expenditures and other financing uses—GAAP basis	$403,000

CAPITAL ASSETS, INFRASTRUCTURE, INVESTMENTS, AND DEFINED BENEFIT PENSION PLANS

Capital assets and investments typically comprise a significant part of a government's total assets. The modified accrual basis of reporting in the governmental funds leads to significant differences in how these items appear in the funds statements versus the government-wide statements.

LO5 Explain the external reporting for infrastructure, investments, and defined benefit pension plans.

Capital Assets and Infrastructure

SGAS 34 requires that the government-wide statements report **all capital assets** using full accrual accounting, including periodic recognition of depreciation expense. Gains and losses on sale or disposition of capital assets are reported in the statement of activities and equal the difference between proceeds and book value.

While proprietary funds always followed the above reporting requirements, governmental funds report purchases and sales of capital assets in the funds statements using modified accrual accounting. Purchases of capital assets are expenditures, and proceeds from sale of capital assets are other financing sources.

Depreciation on capital assets other than infrastructure follows usual business accounting methods, but the GASB also allows use of the **modified approach** for *infrastructure*—it need not be depreciated when preserved in good condition. The cost of *maintaining* the infrastructure—preserving its useful life—is instead reported as an expense. This modified approach for well-maintained infrastructure makes sense, because infrastructure is usually very long-lived. Bridges, roads, and water and sewer systems can last a hundred years or more. The traditional approach to allocating asset cost over an estimated useful life is therefore not as meaningful. Costs of increasing infrastructure capacity or efficiency are capitalized. Information on how the government accounts for infrastructure assets is reported in the required supplementary information.

Investments

Chapter 11 discussed reporting for investments in the fund statements. Following *SGAS 31*, all fund types, including governmental funds, report investments held for income at fair value on their balance sheet or statement of net position. Unrealized changes in investment value appear on the appropriate operating statement.

Some governments invest in derivative instruments, such as futures, options and swaps, both for income and to hedge their financial risk. *SGAS 53* requires that derivatives be reported at fair value in the government's proprietary and fiduciary accrual-based fund statements. *SGAS 53* also applies to the accrual-based government-wide financial statements. The government-wide statement of activities reports changes in fair value of derivatives held for income. Changes in fair value of derivatives used as qualified hedges are reported as *deferred inflows/outflows* on the government-wide statement of net position. If the derivative no longer qualifies as a hedge investment, all deferred amounts are reclassified to the statement of activities.

SGAS 53 does not apply to governmental funds. Therefore, the information reported in the government-wide statements for governmental funds' hedge investments will likely differ from the information reported in the governmental funds statements.

BUSINESS APPLICATION   City of New York Hedge Accounting

The **City of New York** uses derivative investments to hedge the financial risk from its variable rate interest payments. The liabilities section of the city's fiscal 2013 government-wide statement of net position reports primary government interest rate swaps of $100.884 million, which means the city reports unrealized losses totaling over $100 million on these swaps. Because the swaps qualify as hedge investments, the related unrealized loss is a component of deferred outflows of resources, reported on the asset side of the city's statement of net position, with no effect on the change in net position. All are receive variable/pay fixed swaps. Interest rates have fallen during the time the city has held these swaps, so they have lost value and are reported as liabilities. When interest rates fall, the city's net payment on the swaps increases, because the counterparties pay the city a lower variable rate, while the city continues to pay the counterparties the same fixed rate.

Recall from Chapter 11 that when a derivative no longer qualifies as a hedge investment, any value changes recorded in deferred inflows/outflows are reclassified to the statement of activities, affecting the change in net position. During fiscal 2013, the city partially refunded some of the variable rate bonds hedged with interest rate swaps. Therefore the swaps do not qualify as hedge investments. Footnotes to the city's fiscal 2013 financial statements indicate that the unrealized value changes associated with these swaps were reclassified from deferred inflows/outflows to investment revenue. *Source:* City of New York 2013 CAFR.

Defined Benefit Pension Plans

Governments commonly provide employees with defined benefit pension plans, which promise a specified monthly payment to retirees, based on their earnings history and length of employment. Standards for years prior to 2014 did not require accurate recognition of pension expenses and liabilities in the financial statements. Instead, the government-wide statements took a current funding orientation, and liabilities were only recognized for the difference between the annual required contribution and the employer's actual contributions. If employers were current on their annual contributions, no liability was reported. This is demonstrated by the 2013 Statement of Net Position for the City of St. Louis in Exhibit 12.1, which shows a net pension *asset* of $42,327,000 because the city's actual contributions exceeded required contributions.

Although actuarially determined liabilities were not recognized in the financial statements, *SGAS 25* required that pension plans report the actuarially determined information in required supplementary schedules. An example of this information is in Exhibit 12.13, for the City of St. Louis' Firemen's Retirement System, taken from the city's 2013 CAFR. It shows actuarially determined asset and liability amounts, as well as the pension plan's funding status, for the most recent actuarial valuation date.

EXHIBIT 12.13   Required Supplementary Information, Firemen's Retirement System City of St. Louis, Missouri

CITY OF ST. LOUIS, MISSOURI
Firemen's Retirement System of St. Louis
Schedule of Funding Progress
June 30, 2013

(amounts are in thousands)

Actuarial Valuation Date	Actuarial Value of System Assets (a)	Actuarial Accrued Liability (b)	Unfunded Actuarial Accrued Liability (UAAL) (b – a)	Funded Ratio (a/b)	Annual Covered Payroll (c)	UAAL as a Percentage of Covered Payroll [(b – a)/c]
10/1/12	$427,124	$453,529	$26,405	94.2%	$36,013	73.3%
10/1/11	404,101	430,755	26,654	93.8%	37,157	71.7%
10/1/10	407,028	439,352	32,324	92.6%	40,789	79.2%

SGAS 68, effective for years beginning after June 14, 2014, dramatically changed the pension amounts reported within the basic financial statements. Key changes include the following:

- The amount of the pension liability reported on the government-wide and proprietary fund statements significantly increases. The new amount to be reported is the **employer's total actuarial liability less the fiduciary fund net position**. Previously the amount reported in the government-wide and proprietary fund statements was the difference between the annual required contribution and actual contributions. Although the amounts will not be exactly the same, the City of St. Louis's reported actuarial accrued liability of $453,529,000 for its Firemen's Retirement System, shown in Exhibit 12.13, is similar to the amount reported under the new standard.

- Pension plan assets are valued at fair value, rather than the previous "smoothing" method, which reflected average asset market values over a long period of time, often up to five years.

- To increase comparability, all governments must use the same actuarial cost method. Previously governments chose among six different methods.

- More realistic discount rates are used to calculate the present value of the pension liability. Previously governments used the expected rate of return on investments to discount unfunded liabilities, and rates approaching 8 percent were common. An inflated rate understates the liability. The new standard allows use of the expected rate of return on investments to discount *funded* pension liabilities, but requires a lower municipal bond rate to discount *unfunded* liabilities, since resources to pay those liabilities would likely come from bond issues rather than investment earnings.

- Employers can no longer defer and amortize changes in benefits owed over very long periods of time, which in the past were often spread over 30 years. Most changes are now recognized in the period of change.

- Employers participating in multi-employer pension plans—those where a group of employers pool or share their pension obligations—now recognize their proportionate share of collective pension liabilities. Previously only the amount required to be paid into the plan was recognized, and employers were not required to recognize their share of the plan's actuarial liabilities.

These requirements pertain to the government-wide financial statements, and the fund statements that are prepared on a *full accrual basis*. The governmental fund financial statements use modified accrual accounting, and only report liabilities requiring current resources. *SGAS 68* requires governmental funds to only report a pension liability equal to the *expected future pension payment* to be funded by available financial resources.

SGAS 68 adds millions of dollars to governments' reported liabilities, making the actual costs of generous pension plans more transparent. State and local governments and Congress strongly opposed the new standard, because the increase in reported liabilities might result in downgrades in government credit ratings, making borrowing more expensive. Unrestricted net position is likely to shrink substantially, possibly increasing tax rates. Despite the opposition, the demand for more accurate information on pension obligations prevailed, and this standard is now effective.

Reporting Perspective

The increasing cost of government defined benefit pension plans has threatened to bankrupt some locales, such as the **City of Detroit**. Detroit's creditors recently attempted to recoup delinquent bond payments by trying to seize public assets such as the Detroit Institute of Arts museum pieces, which are owned by the city.

Compounding the problem of the large cost of government pension plans is that defined benefit pension plans often calculate employee retirement benefits based on the total compensation earned in workers' *final year of employment*. **Pension spiking** is when employees deliberately increase their final year of compensation by working massive hours of overtime, and cashing in accrued vacation and sick time accumulated over a number of years. Pension spiking artificially increases pension benefits to retirees, and can cost governments a significant amount of money. For example, the **State of California** recently reported losing approximately $800 million to pension spiking practices.

Some states have responded by more closely monitoring pension benefits, such as in the California State Teachers' Retirement System (CalSTRS). Audits of CalSTRS resulted in the return of approximately $1.5 million of illegal pension spiking. The Ohio Public Employees Retirement System investigates employee "outliers" who have an initial pension benefit that is out of proportion to the contributions they made while employed. The **State of Minnesota** has provisions that limit pension spiking, such as using a five-year window to calculate average salary, and preventing sick and vacation payments from inclusion as compensation.

Citizens groups are also more closely monitoring government employee pensions, which many view as overly generous and at times violating State laws. For example, the Goldwater Institute has threatened to sue the **City of Phoenix, Arizona** for allowing public safety personnel to use fringe benefits to spike their pensions, in violation of State laws.

REVIEW OF KEY CONCEPTS

LO 1   **Discuss the components of the Comprehensive Annual Financial Report. (p. 519)** The **external financial statements** of a state or local government are presented in the **Comprehensive Annual Financial Report**, or **CAFR**. *SGAS 34* requires **full accrual financial statements for the government as a whole**. These government-wide statements report on activities of the primary government and component units that provide services and programs to the public. Minimum financial disclosures are **management's discussion and analysis** (MD&A), the **basic financial statements**, and other **required supplementary information** (RSI). The MD&A introduces the financial statements and provides a readable overview and analysis of financial performance. The basic financial statements consist of government-wide statements, fund financial statements, and explanatory notes. RSI includes budgetary comparison schedules for governmental funds with legally-approved budgets, retirement plan funding status, and additional information on accounting for infrastructure assets.

LO 2   **Prepare government-wide financial statements. (p. 521)** The **government-wide statements** use full accrual accounting, report on the resources and activities benefitting the public, and report **governmental** activities and **business-type** activities separately. Governmental activities include governmental and internal service fund activities. Business-type activities consist of enterprise fund activities. Fiduciary fund activities are not included. The government-wide **statement of net position** shows assets, liabilities, and net position, including long-term assets and liabilities. The **statement of activities** shows the full costs of the government's various programs and activities. Specific revenues related to these programs, such as user fees and grants, are deducted to produce a net balance that indicates **how much each activity uses or contributes to revenues**. General revenues, such as property taxes, are added to obtain the change in net position for the year.

LO 3   **Present the fund statements. (p. 525)** **Fund financial statements** are presented for governmental, proprietary, and fiduciary funds. **Governmental fund financial statements** include a balance sheet and a statement of revenues, expenditures, and changes in fund balances, based on modified accrual accounting. **Proprietary fund financial statements** consist of a balance sheet, a statement of revenues, expenses, and changes in net position, and a statement of cash flows, using the direct method. **Fiduciary fund financial statements** include a statement of fiduciary net position and a statement of changes in fiduciary net position. Proprietary and fiduciary fund statements reflect full accrual accounting. Governmental and proprietary fund financial statements separately display only **major funds**, defined as the general fund, plus other individual governmental and enterprise funds that meet certain significance tests. Internal service funds are reported in total, and fiduciary funds are reported by fund type. Financial information on nonmajor funds is combined.

Describe the relation between government-wide and fund statements. (p. 539) The relation between government-wide and fund financial statements is disclosed to readers through **reconciliations** of (1) the total governmental fund balances to the total net position of governmental activities, and (2) the change in governmental fund balances to the change in net position of governmental activities. These reconciliations are needed to understand how the governmental funds use of modified accrual accounting differs from the government-wide statements use of full accrual accounting. The government-wide financial statements provide readers with information on the **long-term financial health** of the government, and the **full cost** of its programs and services. This information allows readers to better assess the future financial implications of current activities. **LO 4**

Explain the external reporting for infrastructure, investments, and defined benefit pension plans. (p. 543) Governmental funds' current acquisitions of infrastructure are reported in the government-wide statements using full accrual accounting. However, pre-1980 infrastructure need not be reported. Infrastructure depreciation can be measured using the **modified approach**, as the cost of **maintaining** infrastructure. Investments are reported at fair value. Unrealized gains and losses generally appear on the statement of activities. However, unrealized gains and losses on hedge investments are reported as deferred inflows and outflows on the statement of net position. *SGAS 68* requires governments to report the discounted present value of future pension payments of defined benefit pension plans in the government-wide and full accrual fund statements. **LO 5**

Assignments with the ⊘ in the margin are available in ᵐʸBusinessCourse.
See the Preface of the book for details.

MULTIPLE CHOICE QUESTIONS ∙∙∙∙∙∙∙∙∙∙∙∙∙∙∙∙∙∙∙∙∙∙∙∙∙∙∙∙∙∙∙∙

Use the following information to answer questions 1-4 below:

The following are some of the financial statements required in the **State of New York** CAFR:

1. Government-wide statement: statement of net position
2. Government-wide statement: statement of activities
3. Fund statement: balance sheet–governmental funds
4. Fund statement: statement of revenues, expenditures and changes in fund balances—governmental funds
5. Fund statement: statement of net position–proprietary funds
6. Fund statement: statement of revenues, expenses and changes in net position–proprietary funds

For each of the following balances related to the financial performance of the State of New York, indicate the number(s) of the statements on which the balance is reported.

1. Personal income tax revenue　　　　　　　　　　　　　　　　　　　　　　　　LO 1, 2 ⊘

    a. 6 only
    b. 2 only
    c. 4 only
    d. 2 and 4

2. Accrued postemployment benefit liability, governmental fund employees　　LO 1, 2 ⊘

    a. 1 and 3
    b. 1 only
    c. 3 only
    d. 5 only

3. Bonds payable, enterprise funds　　　　　　　　　　　　　　　　　　　　　LO 1, 2 ⊘

    a. 1 and 3
    b. 5 only
    c. 1 only
    d. 1 and 5

4. Depreciation expense on general fund assets　　　　　　　　　　　　　　　LO 1, 2 ⊘

    a. 2 and 4
    b. 2 only
    c. 2, 4 and 6
    d. 4 only

✅ LO 3   **5.** The following is information for a county (*in millions*):

Total governmental fund balances.	$138
Bonds payable—governmental funds	690
Accrued other postemployment benefit liabilities—governmental funds	130
Capital assets—governmental funds.	790
Accrued other liabilities—governmental funds.	128
Other long-term assets—governmental funds.	48

The net position of governmental activities is *(in millions)*

   a. $ 28
   b. $ 248
   c. $1,568
   d. $ 172

✅ LO 3   **6.** The following information is available concerning the financial activities of the **State of New York** for fiscal 2013 (*in millions*):

STATE OF NEW YORK

Net change in fund balances–governmental funds	$ 136
Depreciation expense on general capital assets, net of gains on asset disposal	384
Proceeds from disposal of capital assets of governmental funds.	373
Revenues of governmental funds that do not provide current financial resources	564
Repayments of principal on general long-term debt	6,291
Proceeds from issuance of general long-term debt.	5,412
Expenses of governmental funds, other than depreciation, not requiring current financial resources	2,767
Capital outlays—governmental funds	1,883

The fiscal 2013 change in net position—governmental activities is *(in millions)*

   a. $(62)
   b. $(904)
   c. $(2,128)
   d. $ 2,294

✅ LO 4   **7.** A county uses the legal budgetary basis to report encumbrances. Information for its latest fiscal year is as follows:

Encumbrances outstanding at the beginning of the year	$ 50,000
Encumbrances outstanding at the end of the year	75,000
Excess of revenues and other financing sources over expenditures and other financing uses, legal budgetary basis.	860,000

What is the excess of revenues and other financing sources over expenditures and other financing uses, using the GAAP budgetary basis?

   a. $810,000
   b. $835,000
   c. $885,000
   d. $935,000

✅ LO 4   **8.** A county's 2016 operating statement for governmental funds reports transportation expenditures of $19,000,000. The government-wide statement of activities reports transportation expenses of $55,000,000. Which one of the following items would *not* explain why the government-wide statement reports a higher number than the governmental funds statement?

   a. The $19,000,000 does not include depreciation on transportation-related equipment.
   b. The $55,000,000 includes accrued pension costs earned this year by transportation-related employees.
   c. The $19,000,000 does not include expenses not paid in cash this year.
   d. The $55,000,000 includes temporary loans made by the transportation-related funds.

9. A governmental fund reports derivative investments that qualify for hedge accounting. How are unrealized **LO 5** ✓
   gains and losses on these investments reported in the government-wide financial statements?

   a. They are not reported.
   b. They appear on the governmental funds balance sheet as part of fund balance—nonspendable.
   c. Unrealized gains appear on the statement of net position as deferred inflows and unrealized losses appear as deferred outflows.
   d. Unrealized gains appear on the statement of net position as deferred outflows and unrealized losses appear as deferred inflows.

10. A county's general fund bought equipment for $50,000. The equipment was estimated to have a 10-year life, **LO 5** ✓
    straight-line, no salvage value. Four years later, it sold the equipment for $18,000. In the year of the sale, the
    government-wide statement of activities will report

    a. Loss on sale of capital assets of $12,000
    b. Proceeds from sale of capital assets of $18,000
    c. Loss on sale of capital assets of $32,000
    d. Proceeds from sale of capital assets of $32,000

EXCERISES ·

E12.1 **Fund and Government-Wide Reporting** Consider the following transactions of Dillingham **LO 2, 3**
County:

1. General obligation bonds of $10,000,000 are issued at par to finance the cost of a new fire station.
   The fire station is built for $9,925,000, and remaining cash of $75,000 is transferred for future payment of the debt principal.
2. An old police vehicle with a book value of $5,000 is sold for $2,000. A new vehicle is purchased
   using general revenues of $50,000. Police activities are reported as part of general operations.
3. A municipal golf course issues $750,000 in bonds to finance its activities. The bonds are expected to
   be paid using golf course revenues.
4. A central publishing shop, which services municipal agencies on a fee-for-service basis, purchases
   equipment for $15,000.
5. Equipment is purchased by a fund dedicated to enhanced 911 service, at a cost of $300,000. This
   service is funded by a property tax levy for that purpose.
6. Downloadable electronic books costing $15,000 are purchased by a local public library. The acquisition is financed by a trust fund set up by a wealthy citizen, using income from investments. The
   principal of the trust must remain intact. Public library activities are reported in the general fund.
7. Same as 6., but there is no restriction on spending the principal of the trust.

Required
For each of the above transactions, prepare journal entries necessary to record the transactions in both the
fund financial statements and the government-wide financial statements for Dillingham County. For the
government-wide entries, indicate whether the item is reported in governmental or business-type activities. For the fund entries, indicate which fund is affected.

E12.2 **Fund and Government-Wide Reporting** Consider these transactions of the City of Somerville: **LO 2, 3**

1. An investment pool that accumulates and invests money contributed by other governments invests
   $200,000 in securities.
2. Interest totaling $90,000 is paid on bonds used to finance sewer construction, where the bonds are
   the liability of the affected property owners, and the interest payment is financed by a special assessment on the property owners.
3. Property tax bills of $4,200,000 are sent out, to be used to finance primary government services. All
   bills are considered collectible.
4. Payment of $75,000 is made for the costs of public park programs, where the resources are provided
   by income from a grant provided by a private philanthropic institution. The principal of the grant
   must remain intact.
5. $70,000 in benefits are paid by an unemployment compensation benefit plan, funded by employers
   and required to cover its costs. Benefits are paid to all eligible citizens.
6. Interest of $65,000, due next year, is accrued on bonds used to finance a city parking garage that
   charges parking fees to the public.

7. Interest of $50,000, due next year, is accrued on bonds that finance general government activities.

Required

For each of the above transactions, prepare entries necessary to record the transactions in both the fund financial statements and the government-wide financial statements of the City of Somerville. For the government-wide entries, indicate whether the item is reported in governmental or business-type activities. For the fund entries, indicate which fund is affected.

⊘ LO 2, 3   E12.3   Fund and Government-Wide Financial Statements   Below is information on the financial performance of the City of Leland:

1. Depreciation expense on municipal parking garage assets
2. Gains on the sale of general fund county snowplowing equipment
3. Payroll deductions to be paid to tax authorities
4. Depreciation expense on general fund assets
5. Payments for general obligation debt principal

Required

Indicate on which of the city's financial statement(s) we would report each item of information. Choose from the following list of financial statements:

a. Government-wide statement of net position
b. Government-wide statement of activities
c. Statement of revenues, expenditures and changes in fund balances–governmental funds
d. Statement of revenues, expenses and changes in net position–proprietary funds
e. Statement of net position—fiduciary funds

LO 2, 3   E12.4   Transaction Reporting in Fund and Government-Wide Statements   Each transaction relates to the activities of Lancaster County.

1. General obligation bonds, due in 20 years, are issued for $10,000,000 in cash. The bonds are used to finance the building of a new community center. The total cost of the community center is $12,000,000.
2. Principal of $500,000 and interest of $25,000 are paid on general obligation debt. This debt was not used to finance capital assets.
3. Snow removal equipment is purchased by the general fund at a cost of $150,000.
4. Equipment with original cost of $300,000 is sold for $40,000. The equipment had a 5-year life when purchased, and was sold after 4 years. The county uses straight-line depreciation when appropriate. The equipment was used in general government operations.
5. The county collects $225,000 in property taxes to be remitted to the town.
6. Investments are made using $550,000 withheld from paychecks of county workers to finance their pension plan.
7. The investments in transaction 6 increase in value by $11,000 during the year, although the investments are not liquidated.
8. Cash of $200,000 is received from a citizen, to be held in trust and used for scholarships for local citizens to attend local universities. All amounts received are spendable.

Required

Indicate how each transaction is reported in Lancaster County's (a) fund statements, and (b) government-wide statements. Identify (i) the statement affected, (ii) the account where the item appears, and (iii) its classification if necessary. For example, assets purchased by the general fund appear as capital assets (governmental activities) on the statement of net position, and as general fund expenditures on the governmental funds statement of revenues, expenditures, and changes in fund balances. For the fund statements, assume whenever necessary that the relevant fund qualifies as a major fund.

LO 2, 3   E12.5   Transaction Reporting in Fund and Government-Wide Statements   Consider the following transactions of Daley County:

1. General property taxes of $4,500,000 are levied and collected.
2. Grants of $850,000 are received from the state to finance public safety programs.
3. Investment income of $55,000 is earned on investments of a debt service fund.
4. Investment income of $85,000 is earned on investments made using money received from a generous citizen. The money is held in trust to finance acquisitions of the public art gallery, outlays are limited to earnings and the original contribution cannot be spent.

5. User fees of $45,000 are received from operations of the community pool.
6. Depreciation on public safety equipment is $35,000 for the year.
7. Investment income of $25,000 is earned on government investments of excess cash. The income is not restricted.
8. The motor pool submits $32,000 in charges for vehicle use to other units in the government.
9. Current year accrued interest on general long-term debt is $30,000, and is not due for several years.

Required

Indicate how each transaction is reported in Daley County's (a) fund statements, and (b) government-wide statements. Identify (i) the statement affected, (ii) the account where the item appears, and (iii) its classification if necessary. For example, assets purchased by the general fund appear as capital assets (governmental activities) on the statement of net position, and as general fund expenditures on the governmental funds statement of revenues, expenditures, and changes in fund balances. For the fund statements, assume whenever necessary that the relevant fund qualifies as a major fund.

E12.6   Choice of Fund Type   Following are descriptions of actual funds found in state CAFRs.   **LO 1**

1. The Financial Institutions Deposits Fund is used to account for security deposits held by the **State of**   **STATE OF**
Michigan's Treasurer on behalf of banks which operate trust departments. Deposits are in the form   **MICHIGAN**
of securities or other acceptable assets.
2. Michigan's Second Injury Fund insures carriers and self-insured employers against certain workers' compensation losses. The fund is supervised by the administrator who is appointed by the fund's Board of Trustees. Revenue consists of assessments on insurance carriers and self-insured employers.
3. The **State of Iowa**'s Rebuild Iowa Infrastructure Fund accounts for resources directed by the Gen-   **STATE OF IOWA**
eral Assembly for public infrastructure related expenditures.
4. Iowa's Scholarship and Tuition Grant Reserve Fund receives surplus monies for scholarships and grants at the end of each fiscal year to cover over-expenditures in the scholarship and grant accounts.
5. The Alcoholic Beverage Control Board operates facilities in the **State of Alabama** for the distribu-   **STATE OF**
tion and sale of alcoholic beverages to the public.   **ALABAMA**
6. Alabama's Air Transportation Fund provides air transportation for state personnel and maintenance facilities for state aircraft, on a cost-reimbursement basis.

Required

For each item, identify the type of fund, and the method of accounting.

E12.7   Reporting Capital Assets in the Government-Wide and Fund Statements   Landon County   **LO 3, 4, 5**
reports all capital asset activities used in general government operations in its general fund. The following changes related to capital assets occurred during 2016:

	Beginning	Increases	Decreases	Ending
Capital assets, original cost	$3,200,000	$450,000	$(382,000)	$3,268,000
Accumulated depreciation	(1,300,000)	(225,000)	250,000	(1,275,000)
Capital assets, net	$1,900,000	$225,000	$(132,000)	$1,993,000

Capital assets were acquired for cash, and $150,000 in cash was received from the sale of capital assets during 2016.

Required

How will the above information be reported in the government-wide and governmental funds financial statements?

LO 3   **E12.8**   **Major Funds**   Olean County uses the following capital projects funds for acquisition or construction of capital facilities:

Capital Projects Fund	Assets	Liabilities	Revenues	Expenditures
Buildings, equipment and improvements. . . .	$40,000	$25,000	$190,000	$180,000
Highways, roads, bridges and equipment . . .	55,000	40,000	220,000	150,000
Olean County Medical Center	30,000	32,000	260,000	240,000

Total balances for governmental, enterprise, internal service, and fiduciary funds are:

Governmental funds.	$500,000	$460,000	$2,000,000	$1,890,000
Enterprise funds.	200,000	120,000	3,500,000	2,710,000
Internal service funds.	45,000	42,000	320,000	300,000
Fiduciary funds.	410,000	390,000	1,200,000	1,050,000

Required

Which of the capital projects funds, if any, are reported as major funds in Olean County's CAFR?

LO 3   **E12.9**   **Reconciliation of Governmental Funds Balance Sheet to Government-Wide Statement of Net Position**   Below is the June 30, 2017, governmental funds balance sheet for Collins County *(in thousands)*:

Assets	
Cash.	$200,000
Property taxes receivable, net	128,000
State grant receivable	100,000
Investments	150,000
Total	$578,000
Liabilities and fund balances	
Accounts payable.	$175,000
Fund balance—restricted.	20,000
Fund balance—assigned for capital projects.	200,000
Fund balance—assigned for debt service	80,000
Fund balance—unassigned	103,000
Total	$578,000

Additional information (in thousands):

1.   The county owns capital assets with original cost of $430,000 and accumulated depreciation of $150,000.
2.   Total accrued compensated absences and OPEB costs are $65,000.
3.   Total bonds payable outstanding is $250,000.
4.   Accrued interest payable on bonds is $3,000.
5.   Internal service fund net position is $5,000.

Required

Prepare a reconciliation of governmental funds fund balances to governmental activities net position as of June 30, 2017.

LO 3   **E12.10**   **Reconciliation of Governmental Funds Statement of Revenues, Expenditures, and Changes in Fund Balances to Government-Wide Statement of Activities**   The following is the June 30, 2017, governmental funds statement of revenues, expenditures, and changes in fund balances for Collins County *(in thousands)*:

Revenues

Property taxes	$ 650,000
Fines and licenses	100,000
Investment revenue	4,000
Grants	230,000
Total	984,000

Expenditures

General government	320,000
Health and safety	330,000
Education	260,000
Capital outlay	70,000
Debt service: interest	10,000
Debt service: principal	90,000
Total	1,080,000
Excess of revenues over (under) expenditures	(96,000)

Other financing sources (uses)

Bond proceeds	125,000
Proceeds from sale of capital assets	15,000
Total	140,000
Excess of revenues and other financing sources over expenditures and other financing uses	$ 44,000

Additional information (in thousands):

1. Depreciation for 2017 on governmental funds' capital assets is $40,000.
2. Pension and OPEB costs incurred during 2017 total $95,000.
3. Accrued interest expense for 2017 is $3,000.
4. Change in internal service fund net position for 2017 is $800.
5. The book value of capital assets sold was $20,000.

Required

Prepare a reconciliation of governmental funds change in fund balances to governmental activities change in net position for the year ended June 30, 2017.

E12.11 Reconciliation of Budgetary Basis to GAAP Basis Erie County, New York uses the legal budgetary basis to report the change in fund balances in its general fund budgetary comparison schedule. It reports the following information for the year ended December 31, 2013 *(in thousands)*:

LO 4

ERIE COUNTY, NEW YORK

Excess of revenues and other financing sources over expenditures and other financing uses—budgetary basis	$1,293
Encumbrances, January 1, 2013	3,523
Encumbrances, December 31, 2013	2,458

Required

Present a reconciliation of the budgetary basis to the GAAP basis of operating results.

E12.12 Reporting Compensated Absences in Government-Wide and Fund Statements Dare County, NC reports the following information about its compensated absence liabilities for fiscal 2013:

LO 4

DARE COUNTY, NORTH CAROLINA

(in thousands)	Governmental Activities	Business-Type Activities
July 1, 2012, balance	$2,516	$251
Additions	1,031	106
Reductions	(1,046)	(109)
June 30, 2013, balance	$2,501	$248

Assume that liability reductions were cash payments to employees, and that internal service fund compensated absences included in governmental activities are as follows:

(in thousands)	Internal Service Fund
July 1, 2012, balance	$60
Additions	82
Reductions	(87)
June 30, 2013, balance	$55

Required

How is the above information reported in the government-wide and fund financial statements?

LO 4

E12.13 Reconciliation of Budgetary Basis to GAAP Basis Following is the condensed fiscal 2013 statement of budget and actual revenues, expenditures, and changes in fund balances for the **City of Los Angeles'** general fund.

CITY OF LOS ANGELES, CA

(in thousands)	Budget	Actual	Variance
Revenues	$4,303,112	$4,380,762	$ 77,650
Expenditures	4,305,534	4,108,628	196,906
Other financing sources (uses)	2,422	(130,551)	(132,973)
Excess of revenues and other financing sources over expenditures and other financing uses	$ —	$ 141,583	$141,583

The 2013 governmental funds statement of revenues, expenditures and changes in fund balances reports a change in fund balances of $152,873,000 for the general fund. The following information is available concerning budgetary basis and modified accrual basis reporting differences for the general fund (*in thousands*).

Encumbrances reported as budgetary expenditures	$270,843
Prior year encumbrances expended in current year	235,917
Expenditures reported in the general fund operating statement but not in the budget	3,245
Interfund repayments, net of borrowings, reported as "transfers" in the budget, but as "due from/to other funds" in the governmental funds financial statements	8,678
Amount by which revenues less expenditures, measured for budget purposes as amounts received/paid, exceed revenues less expenditures, measured using the GAAP basis	29,069

Required

Prepare a reconciliation of the budgetary basis to GAAP basis for the excess of revenues and other financing sources over expenditures and other financing uses for the general fund.

LO 3

E12.14 Major Funds Information for fiscal 2017 for Cuyahoga County's enterprise and governmental funds is as follows:

(in thousands)	Assets	Deferred Outflows	Liabilities	Deferred Inflows	Revenues	Expenses
Water Fund	$ 605	$ 35	$ 400	$ 20	$ 1,380	$ 1,380
Sewer Fund	245	—	195	5	310	300
Airport Fund	1,100	50	930	25	950	970
Harbor Fund	480	—	475	2	625	622
All enterprise and governmental funds	9,500	200	9,450	150	13,000	12,500

Required

Identify the enterprise funds that meet the thresholds to be reported as major funds in the enterprise fund financial statements. Show your work clearly.

E12.15 Investments Information on Tillman County's investments for the year 2017 is as follows: **LO 5**

Dividend and interest income, governmental funds.	$4,000,000
Dividend and interest income, enterprise funds.	500,000
Realized gains on sale of investments, governmental funds	650,000
Unrealized losses on investments, governmental funds	(6,000)
Unrealized losses on investments, enterprise funds	(45,000)
Accumulated unrealized gains on derivative hedge investments, governmental funds	10,000
Accumulated unrealized losses on derivative hedge investments, governmental funds.	(2,000)
Accumulated unrealized gains on derivative hedge investments, enterprise funds	25,000
Accumulated unrealized losses on derivative hedge investments, enterprise funds.	(100,000)

Required

a. For each item above, determine if it is reported in Tillman County's fund financial statements. For each item that is reported, identify the financial statement in which it is reported, and how the item is categorized.

b. Show how Tillman County reports the above information in its government-wide statement of net position and statement of activities.

PROBLEMS •

P12.1 Reconcile Fund Statements to Statement of Net Position The following information is taken **LO 3** ⊘
from the financial records of Jackson City at December 31, 2017:

Total fund balances—governmental funds	$ 51,000,000
Total net position—enterprise funds	12,000,000
Total net position—internal service funds	3,000,000
Total net position—fiduciary funds	6,000,000
Total capital assets, net of depreciation—governmental funds.	135,500,000
Total capital assets, net of depreciation—enterprise funds.	71,000,000
Total capital assets, net of depreciation—internal service funds.	9,000,000
Total long-term debt—governmental funds.	75,000,000
Total long-term debt—enterprise funds.	35,000,000
Total long-term debt—internal service funds.	8,400,000

Required

Prepare a reconciliation of total fund balances—governmental funds, as reported on the governmental funds balance sheet to net position—governmental activities, as reported on the government-wide statement of net position.

⊘ LO 3 **P12.2** **Reconcile Fund Statements to Statement of Activities** The following information is taken from the financial records of Bretton City for the year 2017:

Change in total fund balances—governmental funds	$ 90,000
Change in net position—enterprise funds	50,000
Change in net position—internal service funds	4,000
Change in net position—fiduciary funds	25,000
Total capital assets, net of depreciation—governmental funds	1,065,000
Total capital assets, net of depreciation—enterprise funds	500,000
Total capital assets, net of depreciation—internal service funds	175,000
Capital outlays—governmental funds	85,000
Capital outlays—enterprise funds	30,000
Capital outlays—internal service funds	26,000
Depreciation expense on general capital assets	45,000
Book value of general capital assets sold	110,000
Proceeds on sale of general capital assets	35,000
Revenues of governmental funds not providing current financial resources	21,000
Revenues of enterprise funds not providing current financial resources	6,000
Revenues of internal service funds not providing current financial resources	3,000
Expenses of governmental funds not requiring current financial resources, other than depreciation	15,000
General long-term debt balance	260,000
Proceeds from issuance of general long-term debt	73,000
Repayments of general long-term debt	116,000

Required

Prepare a reconciliation of the change in total fund balances—governmental funds, as reported on the governmental funds operating statement, to the change in net position—governmental activities, as reported on the government-wide statement of activities.

LO 2 **P12.3** **Government-Wide Statement of Activities** Consider the following information for the City of Daysville for the year ended December 31, 2017.

Expenses—parking garage (enterprise fund)	$ 1,100,000
Expenses—general government	26,000,000
Expenses—public safety	19,000,000
Expenses—health and sanitation	9,000,000
General property taxes	32,000,000
Unrestricted grants and contributions	5,000,000
Interest on general long-term debt	550,000
Charges for general government services	14,000,000
Charges for parking services	1,500,000
Charges for public safety services	900,000
Charges for health services	4,500,000
State grants for public safety	5,000,000
Gain on sale of general capital assets	50,000
Investment income—governmental activities	75,000
Beginning of year net position—governmental activities	18,000,000
Beginning of year net position—business-type activities	550,000

Required

Prepare, in good form, the government-wide statement of activities of Daysville for the year 2017.

P12.4 Government-Wide Statement of Net Position The City of Gardenvale records financial activities in a general fund and a community center (enterprise) fund. Consider the following information for the city for the year ended December 31, 2016:   **LO 2**

General property taxes levied	$15,000,000
General property taxes collected..	14,900,000
Community center user fees, collected in cash....................................	1,200,000
Investment income earned—general fund, received in cash......................	230,000
Capital assets purchased with cash—general fund.............................	540,000
Capital assets purchased using loans—general fund	410,000
Capital assets purchased with cash—community center	25,000
Fair value of investments—general fund, December 31, 2016	14,090,000
General long-term debt principal payments, in cash (1)	300,000
General long-term debt interest payments, in cash...........................	50,000
Total expenses of governmental programs (2)................................	15,500,000
Total expenses of community center programs (3)	1,205,000
Governmental program expenses paid in cash	14,920,000
Community center program expenses paid in cash	1,178,000
State grant received in cash, restricted for use in community center programs........	20,000
Sales taxes collected in cash, to be remitted to state.........................	1,700,000
Sales taxes remitted to state	1,692,000

(1) Payments reduce debt used to finance capital assets.
(2) Includes $500,000 of depreciation expense on capital assets.
(3) Includes $30,000 of depreciation expense on capital assets.

The December 31, 2015, statement of net position for the City of Gardenvale is as follows:

	Governmental Activities	Business-type Activities	Total
Assets			
Cash....................................	$ 1,500,000	$ 40,000	$ 1,540,000
Taxes receivable.........................	1,000,000	—	1,000,000
Investments	14,000,000	—	14,000,000
Capital assets, net	85,000,000	560,000	85,560,000
Total assets	101,500,000	600,000	102,100,000
Liabilities			
Accounts payable........................	1,000,000	25,000	1,025,000
Long-term debt	40,000,000	200,000	40,200,000
Total liabilities..........................	41,000,000	225,000	41,225,000
Net position			
Net investment in capital assets	50,000,000	380,000	50,380,000
Restricted for community center projects	—	6,000	6,000
Unrestricted	10,500,000	(11,000)	10,489,000
Total net position	$ 60,500,000	$375,000	$ 60,875,000

Required

Prepare, in good form, the 2016 government-wide statement of net position for the City of Gardenvale.

P12.5 Budgetary Comparison Schedule Reconciliation Dare County, North Carolina's Water Fund is an enterprise fund. The county presents a budgetary comparison schedule for the Water Fund, using the modified accrual basis to report actual revenues in excess of expenditures and other financing uses of $1,002,026. The following information is available for fiscal 2013:   **LO 4**

DARE COUNTY, NORTH CAROLINA

1. Water Fund asset depreciation: $2,096,094.
2. Compensated absences payable decreased by $2,579.
3. Inventory decreased by $30,005.
4. Water Fund asset amortization: $53,402.
5. Debt principal payment: $1,275,000.
6. Capital outlay: $4,991,655.

7.   Accrued interest payable decreased by $5,135.
8.   OPEB payable increased by $339,835.

Required

Prepare a schedule reconciling the $1,002,026 revenues in excess of expenditures and other financing uses, prepared on a modified accrual basis, to the change in net position, as reported on the Water Fund's operating statement.

LO 2   P12.6   **Government-Wide Statement of Net Position**   Central City reports the following balances at September 30, 2017, its fiscal year-end, using full accrual accounting:

(in thousands)	Governmental Activities	Business-Type Activities
Assets		
Cash and cash equivalents..........................	$150,000	$ 40,000
Property taxes receivable, net	130,000	—
Due from business-type activities	12,000	—
Supplies	35,000	2,000
Capital assets:		
Depreciable, net	300,000	120,000
Nondepreciable.................................	62,000	19,000
Liabilities		
Accounts payable.................................	34,000	21,000
Accrued current liabilities	8,000	4,000
Due to governmental activities	—	12,000
Bonds payable	200,000	56,000

Additional information (in thousands):

1.   All bonds were used to acquire capital assets.
2.   Governmental activities consist of the general fund, a special revenue fund for grants, a capital projects fund, and a debt service fund. At September 30, 2017, the special revenue fund has $35,000 in net position restricted to grant-related activities, the capital projects fund has $220,000 in net position restricted to capital projects, and the debt service fund has $140,000 in net position restricted to debt service, all calculated on a full accrual basis.
3.   Business-type activities consist of the parking garage and community center. $1,000 in parking garage net position is restricted to specific facility improvements.

Required

Prepare a government-wide statement of net position for Central City as of September 30, 2017, in good form.

LO 2   P12.7   **Statement of Activities**   **Dare County, North Carolina** reports the following information for the fiscal year ended June 30, 2013 *(in thousands)*:

DARE COUNTY, NORTH CAROLINA

Property tax revenues	$53,350
Sales tax revenues..	16,281
Hotel occupancy, alcoholic beverage, and other general tax revenues	13,553
Unrestricted investment loss—general	13
Unrestricted investment loss—business-type activities	42
Special item: hedge termination loss—general government	3,160
Transfers from water department to general government	457
General government expenses	12,368
Public safety expenses..	26,306
Economic development, human services, cultural and recreational expenses.................	25,093
Environmental protection expenses..	8,596
Education and transportation expenses	21,155
Interest on general long-term debt..	3,041
Water department expenses	11,326
Charges for services—general government..	1,803

continued

Charges for services—public safety	3,658
Charges for services—economic development, human services, cultural and recreational	3,489
Charges for services—environmental protection.	1,850
Charges for services—water department	11,388
Grants and contributions—general government	394
Grants and contributions—public safety	170
Grants and contributions—economic development, human services, cultural and recreational . . .	6,630
Grants and contributions—environmental protection	101
Grants and contributions—education and transportation	355

Dare County has one enterprise fund, its water department.

Required

Prepare, in good form, the government-wide statement of activities for Dare County for the fiscal year ending June 30, 2013.

P12.8   Major Funds   Lenox County provides the following information on its governmental and enterprise funds: **LO 3** ✓

Fund	Assets	Liabilities	Revenues	Expenditures/ Expenses
General fund.	$ 80,000	$ 72,000	$680,000	$783,000
Grants special revenue fund	55,000	43,500	200,000	97,000
Parks and recreation special revenue fund .	2,000	1,300	40,000	42,000
Licensed gaming special revenue fund	8,000	7,000	65,000	62,000
Roads capital projects fund	14,000	12,000	200,000	203,000
Bridges capital projects fund	35,000	30,000	120,000	115,000
Buildings capital projects fund.	40,000	30,000	100,000	98,000
Water enterprise fund.	210,000	200,000	890,000	780,000
Airport enterprise fund	650,000	620,000	950,000	953,000

Required

In the *governmental funds* financial statements, which of these funds are reported separately as major funds? Show calculations.

P12.9   Long-Term Liabilities in the Government-Wide and Fund Statements   The City of Fre-   **LO 4** ✓
mont's fiscal year ends June 30. The city issued the following general obligation bonds:

1. On July 1, 2014, the city issued 5 percent, $100,000 face value, 10-year bonds for $92,640, to yield 6 percent. Interest is payable on June 30 of each year.
2. On January 1, 2016, the city issued 5 percent, $100,000 face value, 10-year bonds for $108,115, to yield 4 percent. Interest is payable on December 31 of each year.

Required

a. Determine the amounts reported in the government-wide statement of activities and statement of net position for fiscal year 2017, related to the bonds.
b. Determine the amounts reported in the governmental funds statement of revenues, expenditures, and changes in fund balances and balance sheet for fiscal year 2017, related to the bonds.

P12.10 Fund and Government-Wide Financial Statements   Below are various types of information on   **LO 2, 3**
the financial performance of the Town of Granville:
1. General property taxes collected.
2. Depreciation expense on general long-term assets.
3. Amount of general long-term debt outstanding.
4. Costs of providing public service programs.
5. Amounts on hand for future payment of general obligation debt.
6. Payroll deductions collected for health insurance, to be remitted to a private insurance carrier.
7. Amounts collected as user fees that fully fund community center day-care programs for the public.
8. Cost of general long-term assets purchased this year.

9. Investments held by a pension trust fund.
10. Gain on sale of public park land.

Required

Indicate which of Granville's financial statement(s) would report each item of information, according to *SGAS 34*. Choose from the following list of financial statements:

a. Government-wide statement of net position
b. Government-wide statement of activities
c. Governmental funds balance sheet
d. Governmental funds statement of revenues, expenditures, and changes in fund balances
e. Proprietary funds statement of net position
f. Proprietary funds statement of revenues, expenses, and changes in net position
g. Proprietary funds statement of cash flows
h. Fiduciary funds statement of fiduciary net position
i. Fiduciary funds statement of changes in fiduciary net position

LO 4

CITY OF ST. LOUIS, MISSOURI

P12.11 Analysis of the City of St. Louis CAFR   Refer to the 2013 financial statements of the **City of St. Louis**, appearing in Exhibits 12.1 through 12.12.

Required

a. The statement of net position (Exhibit 12.1) and the statement of activities (Exhibit 12.2) divide financial information into governmental and business-type activities. The activities of which fund(s) are included in each category?

b. Compare the statement of net position (Exhibit 12.1) with the balance sheet for governmental funds (Exhibit 12.3). Explain the major differences in assets and liabilities reported.

c. Compare the statement of activities (Exhibit 12.2) and the statement of revenues, expenditures, and changes in fund balances for governmental funds (Exhibit 12.4).
    1. Explain differences in the categorization of revenues on each statement.
    2. The statement of revenues, expenditures, and changes in fund balances lists two expenditures that do not appear as expenses of governmental activities on the statement of activities. Identify the two items, and explain why they are not reported on the statement of activities.
    3. The statement of revenues, expenditures, and changes in fund balances reports several items as "other financing sources (uses)." Where is each of the items reported on the government-wide financial statements?
    4. The statement of activities lists streets expenses at $68,402,000, while the statement of revenues, expenditures, and changes in fund balances lists streets expenditures at $37,378,000. Why are these two numbers different?

d. Where are the amounts reported in the proprietary fund statement of revenues, expenses, and changes in fund net position (Exhibit 12.8) shown in the statement of activities?

e. Where are the amounts reported in the statement of fiduciary net position (Exhibit 12.10) shown in the government-wide financial statements?

LO 3   **P12.12 Capital Leases in Government-Wide and Fund Statements**   Oceanside County's fiscal year ends June 30. The county leased equipment during fiscal 2017, as follows:

1. The general fund signed a 4-year lease on July 1, 2016, with payments of $15,000 to be made each June 30.
2. The water department enterprise fund signed a 5-year lease on July 1, 2016, with payments of $10,000 to be made each June 30.

Both leases qualify as capital leases, at an interest rate of 4 percent. When appropriate, the equipment is straight-line depreciated with no residual value.

Required

a. How is each lease reported in the fund statements for fiscal 2017?
b. How is each lease reported in the government-wide statements for fiscal 2017?

LO 3, 4, 5

CITY OF KANSAS CITY, MISSOURI

P12.13 Fund Balances, Net Position, Long-Term Debt and Investments   The **City of Kansas City, Missouri** reports the following selected information on its April 30, 2013 CAFR, all balances as of the end of the 2013 fiscal year (*in thousands*):

Net position of internal service funds.	$ 5,303
Accrued interest payable on long-term debt	58,242
Capitalized general obligation bond issue costs	11,102
Accrued other post employment benefits liability	50,428
Revenues not to be received in cash within 60 days	56,019
Governmental capital assets less accumulated depreciation	4,144,737
Accumulated decline in fair value of hedging derivatives	26,889
Total accrued compensated absences	29,188
Unamortized premium on bond issues	37,918
Deferred discount on bond issues	9,430
Deferred charges on refunding.	36,858
Accumulated pension obligations	43,600
Long-term bonds and notes payable.	1,577,168

Required

a. All but one of the items listed above appear on Kansas City's reconciliation of April 30, 2013 fund balances of governmental funds to net position of governmental activities. For each item, explain why it appears (or does not appear) in the reconciliation and whether it is added or subtracted.

b. Kansas City's April 30, 2013 fund balances of governmental funds is $386,930,000. Prepare a reconciliation to net position of governmental activities.

c. Look at St. Louis, Missouri's reconciliation of governmental fund balances to net position of governmental activities, appearing in Exhibit 12.5 in the chapter. In St. Louis' reconciliation, governmental fund balances are significantly higher than net position of governmental activities. However, your reconciliation in b. shows that for Kansas City, the opposite is true. What causes the difference?

P12.14 Reconciliation of Government-Wide and Fund Financial Statements Dallas County, Texas **LO 3, 4**
reports the following selected information on its September 30, 2013 CAFR (*in thousands*):

DALLAS COUNTY, TEXAS

Net change in fund balances—governmental funds	$25,291
Salary expenditures of governmental funds.	4,367
Capital expenditures of governmental funds	55,629
Depreciation expense on capital assets of governmental funds	18,210
Depreciated cost of capital assets sold by governmental funds	704
Unrealized gains on fiduciary fund investments.	276
General revenues of governmental funds not providing current resources	15,610
Compensated absences earned in excess of payments made, governmental funds	221
Other postemployment benefits of governmental funds	55,122
Other expenses of governmental funds not requiring current resources.	20,403
Accrued interest revenue of fiduciary funds.	132
General obligation debt principal repayment.	20,075
Face value of general obligation debt issued.	35,825
Premium on general obligation debt issued.	4,423
Face value of advance refunding bonds issued by governmental funds.	10,515
Premium on advance refunding bonds issued by governmental funds.	1,669
Payment to advance refunded bond escrow agent.	11,440
Amortization of general obligation bond issuance costs	873
Amortization of general obligation bond premium.	1,982
Increase in net position, internal service funds	878

Required

Prepare Dallas County's fiscal 2013 reconciliation of net change in fund balances—governmental funds to change in net position—governmental activities.

P12.15 Fund and Government-Wide Financial Statements The June 30, 2013 CAFR for the **City of** **LO 2, 3**
Los Angeles reports the following account balances.

CITY OF LOS ANGELES, CA

1. Net investment in capital assets
2. Taxes receivable
3. Accrued compensated absences payable
4. Deferred outflows of resources, derivative instruments
5. Property tax revenues
6. Net expense, governmental activities

7. Fund balance, assigned
8. Nonoperating revenues
9. Depreciation and amortization
10. Capital assets, trust funds
11. Investment income, trust funds
12. Issuance of long-term debt (for the year)
13. Accumulated depreciation
14. Unrealized losses on investments
15. Cash and pooled investments, agency funds

Required

Each of the above items appears as an account title in the City of Los Angeles' financial statements. Below is a list of the financial statements in the city's CAFR. For each item, indicate the letter or letters of the financial statements displaying the account title. The item can be on one statement or more than one statement.

a. Government-wide statement of net position
b. Government-wide statement of activities
c. Governmental funds balance sheet
d. Governmental funds statement of revenues, expenditures, and changes in fund balances
e. Proprietary funds statement of net position
f. Proprietary funds statement of revenues, expenses, and changes in net position
g. Fiduciary funds statement of net position
h. Fiduciary funds statement of changes in net position

REVIEW SOLUTIONS

Review 1 Solution

TOWN OF SCOTTSVILLE
Statement of Activities
For Year Ended December 31, 2016

		Program Revenues		Net (Expense) Revenue and Changes in Net Position		
(in thousands) Functions/Programs	Expenses	Charges for Services	Grants & Contributions	Governmental Activities	Business-Type Activities	Total
Governmental activities:						
General government	$ 3,500	$ 100	$ —	$ (3,400)	$ —	$ (3,400)
Public safety	27,000	2,500	4,000	(20,500)	—	(20,500)
Education	45,600	1,100	9,000	(35,500)	—	(35,500)
Interest on long-term debt	340	—	—	(340)	—	(340)
Total governmental activities	76,440	3,700	13,000	(59,740)	—	(59,740)
Business-type activities:						
Water utility	700	715	—	—	15	15
Total primary government	$77,140	$4,415	$13,000	$(59,740)	$ 15	$ (59,725)

General revenues		
Property taxes	58,000	—	58,000
Investment income	300	—	300
Gain on sale of assets	50	—	50
Total	58,350	—	58,350
Excess (deficiency) of revenues over expenses	(1,390)	15	(1,375)
Net position—beginning	90,000	12,000	102,000
Net position—ending	$88,610	$12,015	$100,625

Review 2 Solution

Net change in fund balances—governmental funds	$(2,200)
Plus cost of general capital assets acquired	14,000
Less depreciation expense on general capital assets	(3,800)
Less proceeds on sale of general capital assets	(300)
Less loss on sale of general capital assets	(10)
Plus principal repayments—general obligation debt	5,600
Less proceeds from issuance of general obligation debt	(9,300)
Less accrued OPEB expense	(100)
Less accrued interest expense	(192)
Change in net position—governmental activities	$ 3,698

LEARNING OBJECTIVES

LO1 Prepare financial statements of private not-for-profit (NFP) organizations in proper format. (p. 568)

LO2 Report all types of contributions received. (p. 572)

LO3 Report investments in financial securities. (p. 580)

LO4 Describe major reporting issues for specific NFPs. (p. 586)

LO5 Evaluate financial information provided by NFPs. (p. 589)

BETA ALPHA PSI
www.bap.org

Beta Alpha Psi is an honors organization, recognizing and promoting academic excellence and achievement in accounting, finance and information systems. Beta Alpha Psi's activities include regional and annual meetings, and case and chapter competitions supporting professionalism, service, and public responsibility. Founded in 1919, there are more than 300 Beta Alpha Psi chapters on college and university campuses in the U.S., New Zealand and Australia, with over 300,000 members initiated since its inception.

Although not-for-profit organizations are not subject to the reporting requirements of the stock exchanges, their donors and other funding sources generally expect financial disclosure in the form of audited financial statements, following GAAP. Each year Beta Alpha Psi provides an audited annual report, consisting of a statement of activities, a statement of financial position, and a statement of cash flows.

The goals and activities of private NFP organizations differ in many ways from those of for-profit entities. How do the reporting requirements for private NFP organizations compare with the standards you learned in your principles and intermediate accounting courses? How do the financial statements differ? This chapter discusses the accounting and reporting by private not-for-profit organizations.

CHAPTER ORGANIZATION

Financial reporting display model	Accounting for contributions received	Accounting for investments	Comprehensive illustration	Reporting for specific NFPs	Evaluate financial information
• Statement of financial position • Statement of activities • Statement of cash flows	• Unconditional and unrestricted cash contributions • Contributions of goods and services • Temporarily restricted contributions • Conditional contributions • Permanently restricted contributions • Contributions of long-lived assets • Annuity and life income contributions • Contributions received on behalf of others	• Gains and losses • Investment income • Endowments	• Record transactions • Prepare financial statements	• Voluntary health and welfare organizations • Colleges and universities • Health care organizations	• Strengths and weaknesses of reporting requirements • FASB NFP reporting project

CHARACTERISTICS OF PRIVATE NOT-FOR-PROFIT (NFP) ORGANIZATIONS

Private (nongovernmental) NFP organizations share the following characteristics:

- Significant amounts of the organization's resources come from providers who expect no payment or economic benefits proportionate to the resources provided.
- The organization's primary mission is to contribute to society, *not* to generate a profit.
- There are no ownership interests that can be sold, transferred, or redeemed, or that convey entitlement to a share of resources in the event the organization is liquidated. The NFP is usually owned by its members or a legal foundation, and is run by a board of directors or trustees.

Private NFP organizations generally fall into these categories:

Voluntary health and welfare organizations (VHWOs). These organizations generate the majority of their support from voluntary contributions and grants, and offer their services to the general public. Services include social welfare, health, or community activities. Examples include the **American Heart Association,** the **Salvation Army,** the **YMCA,** and **Habitat for Humanity.**

Colleges and universities. This category includes private not-for-profit colleges and universities. Support comes mainly from student tuition and fees, alumni contributions, grants and private endowments, and state and federal funding.

Hospitals and other health care organizations. These organizations include private not-for-profit hospitals, nursing homes, health maintenance organizations, medical groups, ambulatory care facilities, and clinics. Major support comes from patient charges, including third party payments, contributions, endowments and grants.

Other private NFP organizations. These include private NFP elementary and secondary schools, social and political groups, churches, museums, and civic, fraternal, and professional organizations. The **American Automobile Association, Beta Alpha Psi,** and the **American Institute of Certified Public Accountants** are examples.

This chapter covers the reporting requirements for *private* NFP organizations. Private NFPs may receive a significant amount of public funding, but they are run by a nongovernmental group. The FASB issues reporting standards for these organizations. *Public* NFPs must follow the accounting requirements of the GASB, covered in Chapters 10, 11 and 12.

When deciding whether the FASB requirements for NFP reporting apply to a particular organization, one must consider two important issues: Is the organization under the jurisdiction of a private group, or is it a governmental entity? If private, is it a not-for-profit or a for-profit organization? The latter question cannot be answered merely by identifying the nature of the services rendered and the funding sources. For-profit forms of voluntary health and welfare organizations, elementary and secondary schools, and health care organizations also exist.

NFP REPORTING ENVIRONMENT

FASB reporting standards apply to private NFPs; public NFPs follow GASB standards. Differing reporting requirements have been troubling in the past, since it does not seem reasonable that similar public and private NFPs should report different types of information. Why should the reporting requirements for **The Ohio State University** differ from the requirements for the **University of Dayton**? In recent years the GASB has worked to bring the reporting requirements for public NFPs and state and local governments closer to the requirements for private NFP entities. *SGAS 34* outlines the external reporting requirements for state and local governments, studied in Chapter 12 of this text. *SGAS 35* applies the same requirements to public colleges and universities. These requirements are similar to the external reporting requirements for private NFPs studied in this chapter.

Most major FASB reporting requirements for private NFP organizations emerged in the 1990s. These standards are now part of *FASB ASC Topic 958*, Not-For-Profit Entities. FASB *Statement of Financial Accounting Concepts No. 4*, Objectives of Financial Reporting by Nonbusiness Organizations, and sections of *FASB Statement of Financial Accounting Concepts No. 6*, Elements of Financial Statements provide the reporting framework.

External Financial Reporting Requirements: General Concepts

Years ago, much like the governmental funds statements studied in Chapters 10–12, NFPs provided their stakeholders with segregated financial information by funds—pools of resources segregated by purpose—that focused on stewardship over these resources. The financial data allowed readers to track resources received and expended for particular functions and activities.

The financial climate and information demands on NFPs changed over the last few decades. NFPs now look to external financial markets to finance escalating costs, and solicit contributions from corporations and foundations, as well as individuals. As the number of NFPs grows, there is greater competition for limited resources, and donors demand accurate and complete information to support their own resource allocation decisions. This demand for financial accountability encouraged the FASB to develop accounting and reporting requirements that provide external readers with useful and readable financial statements for the NFP organization as a complete entity. As a result, external financial statements report on the organization as a whole, on a full accrual basis, and provide more understandable and user-friendly information on the entire organization's performance and financial condition.

Goals of Financial Reporting by NFPs Unlike for-profit businesses, NFPs are not expected to generate a net profit from their activities. However, they are expected to use contributions for their intended purposes, choose activities that effectively further the organization's goals, and operate efficiently. Users of an NFP's financial statements should be able to find evidence on these dimensions of performance. Contributors, lenders, organization members, charity watchdog groups, managers, and the general public are potential users.

Contributors and watchdog groups are interested in what part of each dollar contributed is spent on administration and fund-raising, and how much the organization spends on its prime mission. Charity watchdog groups monitor spending, and evaluate organizations on various dimensions of financial performance.

Lenders are concerned with the organization's ability to meet obligations as they come due. An NFP's bond ratings are affected by management, governance, debt structure and history, as well as its revenue and expense base and financial condition. To assess credit-worthiness, lenders need information on the amount of the organization's assets available to meet debt payments and planned and unplanned expenditures. Lenders also assess the stability and expected future level of revenue sources.

External users want to know whether the organization's activities are above-board and within its mission, whether the organization is fiscally responsible, and whether it can continue to provide services and pay its bills in the future. These concepts form the basis for current GAAP for NFPs.

BUSINESS APPLICATION   Charity Watchdog Groups

The standards developed by two watchdog groups—the Council of Better Business Bureaus and the American Institute of Philanthropy—provide insight into the financial information demanded by external readers. The **Council of Better Business Bureaus**—www.give.org—rates charities according to 20 standards, divided into standards of governance and oversight, measuring effectiveness, finances, and solicitations and informational materials. The "finances" section lists seven standards:

- Spend at least 65% of total expenses on program activities.
- Spend no more than 35% of "related contributions" on fund-raising. Related contributions are those received as a result of fund-raising efforts.
- Avoid accumulating resources that could be used for current program activities. Unrestricted net assets available for use should not be more than three times the size of the past year's expenses or three times the size of the current year's budget, whichever is higher.
- Make available to all, on request, complete annual financial statements prepared in accordance with generally accepted accounting principles.
- Include in the financial statements a breakdown of expenses that shows the portions of these expenses allocated to program, fund-raising and administrative activities.
- Accurately report expenses, including joint cost allocations, in the financial statements.
- Have a board-approved annual budget for the current fiscal year that outlines projected expenses for major program activities, including fund-raising and administration.

The **American Institute of Philanthropy** (AIP)—www.charitywatch.org—publishes a Charity Rating Guide, which rates charitable organizations using the following statistics:

- Percent of total expenses spent on charitable programs: In AIP's view, 60% or greater is reasonable for most charities.
- Cost to raise $100 in related contributions: $35 or less is considered reasonable in most cases.
- Years of available assets, measuring how long a charity could continue to operate at current levels without additional fund-raising: Organizations having available assets of over three years of operating expenses receive a negative rating.

Overall Reporting Concepts   *FASB Concepts Statement No. 4* presents the basic principles and objectives of NFP reporting. The three broad objectives are:

- Financial information should be useful to contributors, lenders, suppliers, organization members, oversight bodies, and managers in making resource allocation decisions—either how much to give to the organization, or how much to allocate to alternative activities within the organization.
- Financial information should be useful in evaluating the services provided by the organization and in determining its ability to continue to provide these services.
- Financial information should be useful in assessing the performance of management.

FASB *Concepts Statement No. 6* partitions the **net assets** ("equity") section of an NFP's balance sheet into **three classes**:

- **Permanently restricted net assets.** Contributions or other net inflows where donor-imposed restrictions limit use indefinitely.

- **Temporarily restricted net assets.** Contributions or other net inflows subject to donor-imposed restrictions that expire either through the passage of time or by actions of the organization.
- **Unrestricted net assets.** All other net assets.

These principles and objectives were implemented in the contributions and financial statement requirements of *ASC Topic 958*. The financial statements must include information on the organization's assets, liabilities, and net assets, transactions affecting net assets, how the organization obtains and uses cash, and its service efforts.

FINANCIAL REPORTING DISPLAY MODEL

LO1 Prepare financial statements of private not-for-profit (NFP) organizations in proper format.

The FASB Codification calls for a common structure in financial reporting that provides financial results for the entity as a whole. Accordingly, an NFP organization's required financial statements are a **statement of financial position**, a **statement of activities**, and a **statement of cash flows**.

Statement of Financial Position

The statement of financial position presents the assets, liabilities, and net assets of the organization. Important features are:

- Assets and liabilities are classified in order of liquidity.
- **Basic concepts of business accounting** are followed in **valuing assets and liabilities**, except for investments in debt and equity securities, where *ASC Subtopic 958-320* requires that fair values be used for *all* investments in debt and equity securities with determinable fair values.
- **Cash or other assets donor-restricted** in a way that **limits their use** over the long-term, such as for construction of long-term assets or as permanent endowments, should be **reported separately** from unrestricted cash and other assets that are available for current use.
- Net assets must be presented in the **three net asset categories** discussed above.

Beta Alpha Psi's 2014 statement of financial position in Exhibit 13.1 reports unrestricted and temporarily restricted net assets, but has no endowments. Most assets and all liabilities are current; the organization does not own property, plant or equipment or engage in any long-term borrowing.

Statement of Activities

The statement of activities shows **changes in each of the net asset categories** during the year. Important features are:

Contributions and Other Inflows

- **Inflows**—from contributions, sales, and so forth—**are revenues, reported as increases in the appropriate net asset category.** For example, unrestricted donations increase unrestricted net assets; contributions restricted by the donor for use in a particular time period or for a particular purpose increase temporarily restricted net assets; contributions where the donor stipulates that the principal is to be kept intact and only the income earned on the contribution is to be used, increase permanently restricted net assets.
- As **donor-imposed temporary restrictions** are met, either because the stipulated time passed or the contributions were used for the intended purpose, temporarily restricted net assets decrease and unrestricted net assets increase. These items appear separately on the statement of activities as **net assets released from restrictions** with equal amounts shown as reductions in temporarily restricted net assets and increases in unrestricted net assets. By definition, there can be no release of permanently restricted net assets, unless donor-imposed restrictions change.

Expenses

- **Expenses are reported as reductions in the unrestricted net assets category only.** Use of restricted resources is reported first as **net assets released from restrictions**—moved from the

EXHIBIT 13.1   Beta Alpha Psi 2014 Statements of Financial Position

BETA ALPHA PSI
Statements of Financial Position

For Years Ended	April 30, 2014	April 30, 2013
Current assets		
Cash and cash equivalents	$1,923,292	$1,638,399
Investments	145,000	186,000
Accounts receivable	93,177	63,210
Prepaid expenses and other assets	61,369	19,866
Total current assets	2,222,838	1,907,475
Investments	94,000	145,000
Web site development, net of accumulated amortization of $170,595 and $168,851	189,715	231,963
Total assets	$2,506,553	$2,284,438
Liabilities		
Accounts payable	$ 161,964	$ 93,286
Unearned revenue	41,510	43,910
Total liabilities	203,474	137,196
Net assets		
Unrestricted	2,218,049	2,053,736
Temporarily restricted	85,030	93,506
Total net assets	2,303,079	2,147,242
Total liabilities and net assets	$2,506,553	$2,284,438

temporarily restricted category to the unrestricted category—with the related expense then shown as a reduction in unrestricted net assets. *No expenses appear in the other net asset categories.*

- **Expenses are classified functionally**, separating out expenses of each major program or service, and **showing support costs**—administrative, membership development, and fund-raising—**separately**.

- **Administrative costs** are those not specifically related to a particular program, fund-raising activity, or membership development activity, but are required for the organization's continued operations. Administrative costs include accounting, financing, and business management costs.

- **Membership development costs** include costs of soliciting prospective members, collection of dues, and membership relations.

- **Fund-raising costs** are costs incurred to persuade potential donors to make contributions, such as the costs of fund-raising campaigns, including the cost of preparing and distributing printed material. It is important to provide readers with an accurate breakdown of fund-raising costs, since donors have an avid interest in the proportion of their contributions spent on programs versus fund-raising.

- Organizations often use an activity for both mission-related and fund-raising purposes. Those organizations incurring such *joint costs* must disclose the fact that costs have been allocated between functional categories, and the amounts allocated to each classification.

- For **voluntary health and welfare organizations**, a **natural** or object **classification of expenses**— for example, salaries, rent, depreciation—**is required** in addition to the functional classification. These organizations must show expenses separately by functional *and* natural classification in matrix format. Other organizations are encouraged but not required to show a natural classification of expenses. Exhibit 13.7, presented later in the chapter, illustrates this disclosure.

Investments in Securities

- The FASB Codification requires that **investments in debt and equity securities** be valued at **fair market value**. Changes in investment values are shown in the statement of activities. Unless they are donor-restricted, value changes are reported as changes in unrestricted net assets. Similarly, investment income is unrestricted unless the donor specifically says otherwise.

Format

• The general format of the statement of activities shows **changes in each of the three classifications of net assets**, with the change in net assets as the "bottom line." However, **NFPs are encouraged to include additional classifications** within their operating statement, which provide better disclosure of the organization's performance. For example, changes in net assets may be classified as operating and nonoperating, recurring and nonrecurring, or realized and unrealized.

Beta Alpha Psi's 2014 statement of activities in Exhibit 13.2 reports changes in unrestricted and temporarily restricted net assets. Most unrestricted revenues come from membership fees and charges

---

EXHIBIT 13.2   Beta Alpha Psi 2014 Statements of Activities

BETA ALPHA PSI
Statement of Activities

For Years Ended	April 30, 2014	April 30, 2013
Changes in unrestricted net assets		
Revenue and support:		
Membership fees	$ 724,180	$ 645,040
Associates program contributions	195,000	184,000
Chapter maintenance fees	85,500	83,400
Annual student convention	305,648	253,663
Charter and petition fees	7,000	9,000
Regional meetings	166,690	145,620
Interest income	3,437	5,131
Contributed services	60,400	64,480
Net assets released from restrictions	215,002	204,192
Miscellaneous	3,260	5,501
Total unrestricted revenue and support	1,766,117	1,600,027
Expenses		
Annual student convention	477,118	345,425
Community service day	32,771	50,000
Board of directors meetings	38,089	28,245
Chapter installations and visitations	712	6,839
Banners and gavels	3,225	4,274
Regional meetings	259,735	278,957
Superior Chapter Award Program	40,700	37,125
Best practice awards	29,625	29,750
Diversity awards	13,250	11,500
Faculty advisor awards	25,000	25,000
Gold Challenge awards	30,000	22,500
Project Run With It awards	12,000	12,000
BIPOY awards	6,000	6,000
Ethics awards	19,000	15,000
Miscellaneous	5,859	5,039
Total program expenses	993,084	877,654
General and administrative	608,720	559,561
Total expenses	1,601,804	1,437,215
Change in unrestricted net assets	164,313	162,812
Change in temporarily restricted net assets		
Contributions	206,526	216,675
Net assets released from restrictions	(215,002)	(204,192)
Change in temporarily restricted net assets	(8,476)	12,483
Change in net assets	155,837	175,295
Net assets, beginning of year	2,147,242	1,971,947
Net assets, end of year	$2,303,079	$2,147,242

for the annual student convention and regional meetings. Expenses are categorized functionally, with amounts spent for chapter awards, the annual student convention and regional meetings clearly displayed. The statement of activities reports 2014 temporarily restricted contributions of $206,526 and net assets released from restrictions of $215,002. Footnotes indicate that temporarily restricted net assets received and released from restrictions relate to contributions received to finance chapter awards. Temporarily restricted net assets were released from restrictions in 2014 and 2013 when spent on the following donor-restricted chapter awards:

	2014	2013
Best practice awards	$ 29,625	$ 29,750
Faculty advisor awards	25,000	25,000
Community service day	22,771	40,000
Superior chapter awards program	40,700	37,125
Diversity awards	13,250	11,500
Project Run With It awards and program expenses	28,656	17,317
Gold Challenge awards	30,000	22,500
Ethics awards	19,000	15,000
BIPOY awards	6,000	6,000
Totals	$215,002	$204,192

These awards are financed by various accounting firms, including Deloitte, McGladrey, KPMG, Ernst & Young and Moss Adams LLP.

Unspent temporarily restricted net assets at year-end appear on the statement of financial position in Exhibit 13.1. For 2014 and 2013 these amounts are $85,030 and $93,506, respectively, in the following awards categories:

	2014	2013
Best practice awards	$ 9,375	$11,850
Faculty advisor awards	13,800	38,800
Superior chapter awards program	2,150	2,150
Inclusive leadership awards	—	8,750
Project Run With It	33,975	25,956
Community service day	25,730	—
BIPOY awards	—	6,000
Totals	$85,030	$93,506

Statement of Cash Flows

The statement of cash flows follows the usual business format for reporting cash flows from operations, investing, and financing, except for the following special features for NFPs:

- Contributions and income that are **donor restricted for long-term purposes**, such as plant assets and endowment, are reported as **financing cash flows**.

- Proceeds from the **sale of donated financial assets**, such as securities, are reported as **operating cash flows**, if they are sold immediately after they are received and the donor did not restrict their use to long-term purposes.

- The **reconciliation** of income to operating cash flows appears as a reconciliation of the **change in total net assets**—the "bottom line" of the statement of activities—to **cash from operations**.

Either the direct or indirect method of reporting cash from operating activities is allowed. The comprehensive illustration later in the chapter uses the direct method, and the required reconciliation of the change in assets to cash from operations illustrates the indirect method.

Beta Alpha Psi's statement of cash flows in Exhibit 13.3 reports operating and investing activities. Like most businesses, it presents operating cash flow via the indirect method that reconciles the change in net assets to cash from operations.

EXHIBIT 13.3 Beta Alpha Psi 2014 Statements of Cash Flows

BETA ALPHA PSI
Statements of Cash Flows

For Years Ended	April 30, 2014	April 30, 2013
Operating activities		
Change in net assets	$ 155,837	$ 175,295
Adjustments to reconcile change in net assets to net cash provided by (used in) operating activities:		
Amortization	64,950	1,744
Changes in operating assets and liabilities:		
Accounts receivable	(29,967)	(12,130)
Prepaid expenses and other assets	(41,503)	3,678
Accounts payable	68,678	(206,189)
Unearned revenue.	(2,400)	6,540
Net cash provided by (used in) operating activities	215,595	(31,062)
Investing activities		
Capital expenditures	(22,702)	(131,949)
Proceeds from maturation of investments.	186,000	237,000
Purchase of investments	(94,000)	(145,000)
Net cash provided by (used in) investing activities	69,298	(39,949)
Net increase (decrease) in cash and cash equivalents	284,893	(71,011)
Cash and cash equivalents, beginning of year	1,638,399	1,709,410
Cash and cash equivalents, end of year	$1,923,292	$1,638,399

ACCOUNTING FOR CONTRIBUTIONS RECEIVED

LO2 Report all types of contributions received.

NFPs measure contributions at *fair value* and recognize them as increases in **unrestricted, temporarily restricted**, or **permanently restricted net assets**, as described above. Contributions received may be in cash, other assets, forgiveness of liabilities, and qualified volunteer services. According to the ASC glossary, a contribution is "an **unconditional transfer** of cash or other assets to an entity or a settlement or cancellation of its liabilities in a voluntary *nonreciprocal transfer* by another entity acting other than as an owner." **Unconditional** implies that there are no circumstances under which the contribution would be returned. A **nonreciprocal transfer** signifies that the donor receives nothing of significant value in return. Therefore if a donor receives goods or services, other than a minor thank-you item, the "contribution" is *payment for goods or services*, and normal business accounting is appropriate.

Unconditional and Unrestricted Cash Contributions

Unconditional and unrestricted cash contributions have no donor-imposed conditions or restrictions. An example is the cash deposited in Salvation Army kettles at the holiday season. Conditions or restrictions of contributions are *donor-imposed* conditions or restrictions *only*. If the Board of the NFP organization decides to set aside unrestricted contributions for a designated purpose, such as funding a particular program or accumulating a sinking fund for repayment of debt, the contributions are still unrestricted.

Unconditional contributions of cash not subject to donors' restrictions are recorded as increases in *unrestricted net assets* on the statement of activities. Suppose Beta Alpha Psi receives a contribution of $1,000, for general use, from a recent accounting graduate. The journal entry to record this unconditional contribution of cash is:

Cash.	1,000	
Contribution revenue—unrestricted		1,000
To record unconditional cash contribution of $1,000.		

Unconditional and Unrestricted Contributions of Goods and Services

Unconditional contributions of goods not subject to donors' restrictions are reported as increases in unrestricted net assets, at fair market value on the date contributed. An NFP organization is required to make good faith estimates of the value of goods received. This may require independent appraisal information.

Organizations such as the **Salvation Army** and **Goodwill Industries** receive a significant amount of contributions in the form of used clothing, furniture and appliances. These items are sold either in thrift stores or to brokers. The Salvation Army and Goodwill Industries must value these contributions at fair value when received. Of course, this does not require estimation of the value of all contributions when received. Most contributions are received and liquidated in the same accounting period, and fair value is the amount received on liquidation. Only those contributions received in one period and sold in another period require appraisal.

Revenue from contributed goods not subject to donors' restrictions increases unrestricted net assets on the statement of activities. Suppose a company donates office supplies with a fair value of $5,000 to Beta Alpha Psi, with no restrictions as to use. The entry to record this unconditional contribution of goods is:

Office supplies	5,000	
Contribution revenue—unrestricted		5,000
To record an unconditional contribution of office supplies.		

Unconditional contributions of services increase unrestricted net assets when the services:

- Create or enhance nonfinancial assets or
- Require specialized skills, are provided by individuals possessing those skills, and are typically purchased if not provided by donation. Services requiring specialized skills are provided by accountants, architects, carpenters, doctors, electricians, lawyers, nurses, plumbers, teachers, and other professionals.

Contributed services that do not meet the above criteria are not recognized. Specialized services that do not create or enhance nonfinancial assets, and would otherwise be purchased, are valued at the *fair value of the services rendered*. Services that create or enhance nonfinancial assets, such as services donated by a contractor to build an addition to the organization's community center, are valued at the *fair value of the asset created*.

Unless the service creates or enhances a nonfinancial asset, the entry to record unconditional contributions of services typically involves both an increase *and* a decrease in unrestricted net assets, as it simultaneously recognizes revenue and expense. Suppose Beta Alpha Psi receives organizational support from the AICPA for its annual conference, in the form of professional consulting services, valued at $3,000. The entry to record this unconditional contribution of services is:

Annual convention expenses	3,000	
Revenues from contributed services—unrestricted		3,000
To record the donation of consulting services.		

Annual convention expenses reduce unrestricted net assets, while revenues from contributed services increase unrestricted net assets on the statement of activities.

Beta Alpha Psi records services that create or enhance nonfinancial assets, such as donated services of a contractor in building a new conference facility, valued at $800,000, in this way:

Building	800,000	
Revenue from contributed services—unrestricted		800,000
To record services donated to construct a new conference facility.		

BUSINESS APPLICATION   **Contributions of Services**

Most NFPs rely on volunteers for everyday operations and delivery of services. Here are two examples of the reporting for these contributions:

Habitat for Humanity International's 2013 consolidated financial statements reveal the following:

> A substantial number of volunteers have made significant contributions of their time to Habitat's program and supporting services. The value of this contributed time is not reflected in the consolidated financial statements since it does not require a specialized skill. However, certain other contributed services that require specialized skills, where provided by individuals possessing those skills and otherwise needing to be purchased if not provided by donation, are recognized as revenue and expense.

Beta Alpha Psi's 2014 financial statements recognize the efforts of students and faculty, but do not report these contributions:

> The Organization recognizes contribution revenue for certain contributed services received at the fair value of those services. Those services include facilities and organizational support...furnished by the American Institute of Certified Public Accountants. In addition, a significant amount of time, for which no value has been assigned because it does not meet the criteria for recognition, was volunteered by professionals, professors and students to the activities of the Organization.

Donor-Imposed Temporary Restrictions

Donors may impose two types of **temporary restrictions** on their contributions: *time restrictions* and *use restrictions*. The most common **time-restricted contributions** are unconditional **promises**, discussed below. Future payments in multi-year pledges are automatically time-restricted. With a **use-restricted contribution**, the donor specifies that the contribution be used for a particular purpose. This restriction may be explicitly stated by the donor or inferred because of the way the contribution was solicited. For example, a donor makes a donation to a private university, stipulating that the donation be used to finance scholarships for accounting students. Alternatively, the accounting department solicits contributions in a scholarship fund drive. Although the donor may not specifically state the restriction, donations to the fund drive are implicitly restricted to scholarship use.

Both time and use restrictions are **temporary restrictions** since the restrictions disappear either with the passage of time or by using the contributions for the intended purpose. Temporarily restricted contributions initially increase temporarily restricted net assets. When the restriction is met, net assets are released from temporarily restricted to unrestricted net assets. Suppose Beta Alpha Psi receives $20,000 donor-designated to fund best practice awards to the chapters, and then makes the awards. Entries are:

Cash.	20,000	
Contribution revenue—temporarily restricted		20,000
To record the cash contribution.		
Net assets released from restrictions—temporarily restricted.	20,000	
Net assets released from restrictions—unrestricted		20,000
To record the release of net assets.		
Best practice awards (expense).	20,000	
Cash		20,000
To record distribution of cash awards.		

Contribution revenue increases temporarily restricted net assets on the statement of activities. The "net assets released" accounts reduce temporarily restricted net assets and increase unrestricted net assets, respectively. If the expenditure of restricted funds is an expense, it reduces unrestricted net assets. The expenditure is capitalized as an asset if the contribution was donor-restricted to a building fund and the expenditure was a payment to a contractor.

As a practical matter, when donations restricted to a particular use are used for this purpose in the same accounting period, organizations need not first classify the donations as temporarily restricted and then release them from restrictions when the expenditures are made. Although the reporting is technically not as accurate, such donations may be included with unrestricted net assets in the period received.

Unconditional Promises An **unconditional promise** to give in the future, having **verifiable documentation**, is reported in the period the promise is given, as an increase in unrestricted, temporarily restricted, or permanently restricted net assets. The promise appears as a receivable, valued at *realizable value*, *net of estimated uncollectible amounts*. Contributions expected to be collected over more than one year are measured at present value.

Most promises to contribute over more than one year are recorded as *time-restricted contributions*. Because the organization does not receive the payments immediately, their use is automatically restricted to the period(s) in which payment is received. Thus if the promise has the documentation allowing it to be recorded in the period the promise is made, the contribution revenue is temporarily restricted.

As an example of an unconditional promise that qualifies for recognition in the year the promise is made, suppose a donor agrees in writing to contribute $5,000 per year to Beta Alpha Psi for the next five years. Using a discount rate of 10 percent, when the agreement is signed Beta Alpha Psi makes the following entry:

Contributions receivable	18,954	
Contribution revenue—temporarily restricted		18,954
To record the present value of the written agreement. At a 10% discount rate,		
$18,954 is the present value of an annuity of $5,000 per year for five years. The		
promise is assumed to be 100% collectible.		

Each year, Beta Alpha Psi recognizes interest on the receivable and the $5,000 cash donation. The interest is included in *contribution revenue*, not interest income, and accumulates in temporarily restricted net assets until the donation becomes available for use (*ASC para. 958-310-45-2*). Entries for the first year are:

Contributions receivable	1,895	
Contribution revenue—temporarily restricted		1,895
To record interest earned on outstanding contributions receivable;		
$1,895 = 10% × $18,954.		
Cash	5,000	
Contributions receivable		5,000
To record the donor's cash contribution for the year.		
Net assets released from restrictions—temporarily restricted	5,000	
Net assets released from restrictions—unrestricted		5,000
To record satisfaction of the time restriction.		

NFP organizations must keep careful records of promises and payments, and make judgments as to their collectibility and whether the promise is backed by verifiable documentation. Clearly a donor's written agreement to contribute $5,000 per year for the next five years is recognized as revenue in the year the agreement is signed. Just as clearly, a phone pledge during a telethon, where the potential donor asks to "think it over" before making the donation, is not immediately recognized. However, other situations may not be as clear.

Sufficient verifiable documentation supporting recognition of contribution revenue includes written agreements, pledge cards, or follow-up written confirmations of oral agreements. It is important to distinguish an intention from a promise. Even though an individual indicates that the organization is a beneficiary in his or her will, the will may be legally modified before death. Thus this intention to give is not recognized as revenue by the organization. However, if the individual dies without modifying the will, the organization recognizes the contribution as revenue after probate, prior to receiving the bequest.

Donor-Imposed Conditions

A donor-imposed **condition** refers to an uncertain future event that could void the contribution. Conditional and documented *promises* to give are recognized as receivables and contribution revenue *in the period the condition is met*. When a donor makes the contribution *before* the condition is met, the organization recognizes a liability. Suppose a donor promises in writing to contribute $1,000,000 to Beta Alpha Psi if contributions by others total $1,000,000. When that condition is met, Beta Alpha Psi records the $1,000,000 promise as revenue. If the donor pays $1,000,000 to the organization *before* the condition is met, entries are:

Cash	1,000,000	
Refundable contributions		1,000,000
To record the receipt of a conditional contribution as a liability because the		
required condition has not been met.		
Refundable contributions	1,000,000	
Contribution revenue—unrestricted		1,000,000
To record contribution revenue when the condition is met, assuming the		
contribution has no donor-imposed restrictions.		

Donations made *after* the condition is met are immediately recognized as contribution revenue.

Donor-Imposed Permanent Restrictions

Donors of permanently restricted contributions generally stipulate that the principal of the donation be maintained, and any income earned on investment of the principal may be unrestricted, or restricted to a particular purpose or time period. The amount donated is a **permanent endowment** and increases permanently restricted net assets. Income on the endowment is either unrestricted or temporarily restricted, depending on the donor's wishes.

Suppose a large CPA firm gives $1,000,000 to Beta Alpha Psi in 2015. The $1,000,000 principal is to be left intact, and income earned on the principal must be used to fund annual faculty advisor awards. Beta Alpha Psi invests the $1,000,000 in securities that generate income of $50,000 in 2016. This $50,000 is paid out in faculty advisor awards in 2017. The entries are:

2015		
Restricted cash	1,000,000	
Contribution revenue—permanently restricted		1,000,000
To record receipt of the permanent endowment.		
Investment in securities	1,000,000	
Restricted cash		1,000,000
To record investment in securities.		
2016		
Cash	50,000	
Investment income—temporarily restricted		50,000
To record the investment income.		
2017		
Net assets released from restrictions—temporarily restricted	50,000	
Net assets released from restrictions—unrestricted		50,000
To record release of funds from temporary restrictions.		
Faculty advisor awards (expense)	50,000	
Cash		50,000
To record use of the funds for the donor-specified purpose.		

The faculty advisor award expense reduces unrestricted net assets on the statement of activities.

BUSINESS APPLICATION   Net Assets of The American National Red Cross

The American National Red Cross provides support in national and international emergency situations. Programs include armed forces emergency services, biomedical services, community, domestic disaster, and international relief and development services. Biomedical services include collection and distribution of blood and blood products, and related testing and research facilities. The Red Cross' June 30, 2013, balance sheet reports the following net assets for 2012 and 2013:

(in thousands)	2013	2012
Unrestricted net assets	$398,444	$133,687
Temporarily restricted net assets.	861,605	757,513
Permanently restricted net assets	730,008	704,023

Included in temporarily restricted net assets are contributions to support recovery from specific natural disasters. In the fiscal year ended June 30, 2013, these natural disasters included wildfires, floods and tornadoes in the United States, and a massive typhoon in the Philippines. In addition, the Red Cross continues to provide assistance for previous years' disasters, such as the 2010 Haiti earthquake and 2012's Hurricane Sandy which severely damaged the U.S. Atlantic coast. When an NFP organization collects contributions that are donor-specified to support a particular program or activity, the unspent balance of contributions is reported in temporarily restricted net assets. The footnotes to its 2013 financial statements report that about $260 million of the Red Cross' temporarily restricted net assets at June 30, 2013, are designated for international relief and development services.

Contributions of Long-Lived Assets

Donations of long-lived assets, valued at fair market value at the date of donation, may increase unrestricted net assets or temporarily restricted net assets. When the *asset's use is donor-restricted*, either by use or time, the donation increases *temporarily restricted net assets*. If the *organization intends to liquidate the assets*, the donation is most likely an increase in *unrestricted net assets*.

When the donor does not stipulate how long or in what capacity the organization must use the donated asset, reporting procedures depend on whether the organization has a consistent policy with respect to donations of long-lived assets. Organizations that have a policy of treating such contributions as *time restricted* meet that restriction over time as the asset depreciates. *ASC para. 958-605-45-6* also requires organizations to follow the same policy with respect to cash contributions donor-restricted to the acquisition of long-lived assets. In the absence of a policy, donations of long-lived assets without donor restrictions increase unrestricted net assets.

Suppose a former Beta Alpha Psi chapter president, now a successful partner in a large CPA firm, donates a building with a fair market value of $1,500,000 to Beta Alpha Psi, with no restrictions on use. Beta Alpha Psi has a policy of recognizing such contributions as time restricted. Straight-line depreciation is based on the building's estimated 15-year life, with no salvage value. Entries are:

Building	1,500,000	
Contribution revenue—temporarily restricted		1,500,000
To record receipt of the building.		
Net assets released from restrictions—temporarily restricted.	100,000	
Net assets released from restrictions—unrestricted		100,000
To record release of restrictions as the building depreciates.		
Depreciation expense.	100,000	
Accumulated depreciation—building		100,000
To record depreciation expense on the building.		

Organizations that initially record the contribution as unrestricted do not need the entry to release net assets in connection with depreciation recognition.

Organizations also receive donations of nondepreciable assets, such as land or artworks. Contributions of land are recorded at fair value as increases in permanently restricted, temporarily restricted, or unrestricted net assets, depending on donor stipulations and organization policy. Organizations are *not* required to report revenue for donations of works of art or items of historical value that meet these criteria:

- They are held for public exhibition, education, or research in furtherance of public service rather than financial gain
- They are protected, not used as collateral for loans, cared for, and preserved
- They are subject to an organizational policy that requires the proceeds from sales of collection items to be used to acquire other items for collections. (ASC glossary definition of "collection," and *ASC para. 958-605-25-19*)

Contributions not reported as revenue are also not capitalized as assets.

Annuity and Life Income Contributions

NFPs often use *annuity or life income agreements* to raise funds. A donor makes a contribution of money or other resources that is recorded at fair market value. In exchange, the organization agrees to make periodic payments, either to the donor or to other specified individuals, over several time periods. When the periodic payment is a fixed amount, we have an *annuity agreement*; when the payment is defined as the amount of income earned on the contributed assets, we have a *life income agreement*.

In an **annuity agreement**, the present value of the annuity payments is recorded as a liability. The difference between the amount contributed and the present value of the annuity payments is the value of the agreement to the organization, and increases net assets. If this amount becomes part of a permanent endowment when the agreement terminates, the increase is to permanently restricted net assets. If it is available for restricted purposes, or available for unrestricted use when the agreement terminates, it initially increases temporarily restricted net assets.

In a **life income agreement**, future payments to beneficiaries equal future income, and the present value of the liability is zero. Thus the entire contribution initially increases either temporarily or permanently restricted net assets, depending on the donor's intent.

Annuity Agreement Illustration   Suppose that a retired accounting professional with a remaining life expectancy of nine years donates $500,000 to Beta Alpha Psi under an annuity agreement. She is to receive $70,000 annually for life, with the first payment occurring in one year. Using a 6 percent discount rate, the present value of the liability equals $70,000 × present value of an ordinary annuity of nine years at 6% = $70,000 × 6.8017 = $476,119. Once the agreement terminates, Beta Alpha Psi has unrestricted access to the value of the annuity in excess of the present value of the related obligation. The initial entry is:

Cash..	500,000	
Annuity payable...		476,119
Contribution revenue—temporarily restricted		23,881
To record the contribution and corresponding annuity agreement.		

Suppose further that the $500,000 was invested and earned 8 percent. Entries for the first year are:

Investments	500,000	
Cash		500,000
To record investment of the $500,000.		
Cash..	40,000	
Investment income		40,000
To record income for the year from investments; $40,000 = $500,000 × 8%.		

Interest expense for the year of $28,567 (= $476,119 × 6%) is recognized on the annuity payable. Since expenses can only be reported in unrestricted net assets, an entry releases the restricted net assets before the expense can be recognized.

Net assets released from restrictions—temporarily restricted...............	28,567	
Net assets released from restrictions—unrestricted..................		28,567
To record release of net assets.		
Interest expense...	28,567	
Annuity payable..	41,433	
Cash..		70,000
To record interest expense on the annuity obligation and reduction in the annuity liability.		

Life Income Agreement Illustration Assume the $500,000 contribution described above is made under a *life income agreement*. Beta Alpha Psi has no initial liability, because the donor will receive whatever income is generated each year. The entries for a life income agreement are:

Cash..	500,000	
Contribution revenue—temporarily restricted..................		500,000
To record contribution under a life income agreement.		
Investments...	500,000	
Cash..		500,000
To record investment of the $500,000.		
Cash..	40,000	
Life income payable..................................		40,000
To record the 8% income for the year from investments, and related obligation to donor.		
Life income payable...	40,000	
Cash..		40,000
To record payment of current income to donor per agreement.		

Contributions Received on Behalf of Others

An NFP organization may collect contributions for distribution to other NFP organizations. For example, the **United Way** encourages donors to designate their contributions for specific unaffiliated organizations. A church collects contributions from members to support an unaffiliated missionary organization.

Accounting for such transactions hinges on whether the recipient organization is a **donee** or end user that benefits from the contribution or merely an **intermediary** that accepts the contribution on behalf of another organization. If a recipient organization is a donee, the contribution is recorded as **contribution revenue**. But when the recipient organization serves as an agent that collects assets for distribution to specified unaffiliated organizations, the amount received is recorded as a **liability**, not a contribution. The specified beneficiaries record the contribution as revenue.

Suppose you make a contribution to the United Way, and specify that your donation is to support the **American Cancer Society**. The United Way records your donation as a liability, and, when informed, the American Cancer Society records a receivable and contribution revenue. When the cash is transferred to the American Cancer Society, the liability on the United Way's books and the receivable on the American Cancer Society's books are extinguished. However, if you give United Way the *right* to redirect your money to other beneficiaries, or if you do not specify a particular beneficiary, United Way becomes a donee and treats your donation as contribution revenue. When the money is eventually distributed, United Way records it as *contributions made* (expense) and the organization receiving the contribution records the revenue.

If you make a contribution to an organization, and specify that the money is to be used by an **affiliated organization**, the recipient organization treats your contribution as temporarily restricted revenue. Perhaps you make a cash contribution to a private foundation that controls two organizations. One organization provides scholarships to college students interested in accounting careers. The other organization supports programs to encourage high school students to pursue accounting careers. If you specify that your contribution is to be used to support college scholarships, the foundation records your contribution as temporarily restricted revenue.

REVIEW 1 ● Accounting for Contributions

Suppose **Make-A-Wish Foundation** has the following contribution-related transactions during 2017:

1. On January 2, a donor promises, in writing, to contribute $1,000 each year for the next five years, starting on December 31, 2017. The appropriate discount rate is 5%. On December 31, the Foundation receives the first payment.
2. A donor contributed $50,000 in cash in 2016, to fund wishes related to baseball. During 2017, three baseball-related wishes are granted, costing $35,000.
3. A donor contributes equipment with a fair value of $100,000 and useful life of 5 years. Make-A-Wish's policy is to report donations of long-lived assets as temporarily restricted. One year of depreciation is recorded in 2017.
4. Donations of services are as follows: Legal services performed by a lawyer, valued at $40,000; development of architectural plans for a new administrative facility by an architect, $25,000; fund-raising activities by families of wish recipients, $10,000.

Required

Prepare entries to record the above events occurring in 2017. Specify how each category of net assets is affected.

Solutions are located after the chapter assignments.

ACCOUNTING FOR INVESTMENTS

LO3 Report investments in financial securities.

NFP organizations frequently invest endowment and other restricted resources on a long-term basis, and invest unrestricted resources on a temporary basis. *Purchased investments* are recorded at *cost* and *donated investments* at *fair value when received*. *ASC Subtopic 958-320* specifies the post-acquisition accounting for investments held by NFP organizations.

All investments in *equity securities with determinable fair values* and *all debt securities* are reported at **fair (market) value**. Unrealized gains and losses are reported in the statement of activities. Note that no distinction is made between securities held for trading, available-for-sale, and held-to-maturity, as specified for investments held by business entities. Realized and unrealized gains and losses on purchased investments are categorized as changes in unrestricted, temporarily restricted, or permanently restricted net assets, depending on the existence of donor restrictions or applicable laws. If no donor-specified restrictions exist, all value changes are changes in unrestricted net assets, even if the NFP Board's policy is to restrict such value changes to a particular use.

When the donation is a **specific investment**, such as 5,000 shares of AT&T common stock, and the donor specifies that the shares be held as a permanent endowment, any change in their value is a change in permanent net assets. Because the shares themselves are the permanent endowment, their value is permanently restricted, regardless of how that value changes. Changes in the value of the securities do not impact unrestricted net assets.

If the donation is $40,000 in **cash**, donor-restricted as a permanent endowment, and the organization invests the cash in equity securities, gains and losses on the securities increase or reduce unrestricted or temporarily restricted net assets, depending on the donor's wishes, leaving the value of the permanent endowment unchanged at $40,000.

Reporting Perspective

NFP reporting differs from for-profit accounting because the goals of reporting and the types of transactions are different—NFPs typically generate most revenues from donor contributions, and donor restrictions must be accurately represented. However, NFP reporting is actually quite similar to normal business accounting in terms of asset acquisitions and write-offs, revenue and expense recognition, and the like. However, NFP reporting for **financial investments** and **hedging** is fundamentally different from normal business accounting.

continued

NFP organizations are required to report *all* financial investments in debt and equity securities at fair market value, with the changes in value reported in the statement of activities in the appropriate category of net assets. The net asset category affected depends on whether or not there are *donor restrictions* on the unrealized gains and losses. In contrast, normal business accounting for investments currently uses a three-portfolio approach: such investments are assigned to the trading, available-for-sale or held-to-maturity portfolios based on *management's intent*. Value changes for trading securities are reported in income, while value changes for AFS securities are reported in other comprehensive income. In contrast, held-to-maturity debt investments are carried at amortized cost, since changes in value are irrelevant when management intends to hold these securities for the principal and interest payments.

Normal business accounting allows hedge accounting for derivatives used to hedge financial risks, allowing the gains and losses on hedge investments to match against the losses and gains on the hedged items. For example, unrealized gains and losses on derivatives used to hedge a forecasted purchase of inventory are deferred in other comprehensive income and reclassified to income when the inventory is sold. In contrast, *hedge accounting is not available to NFP organizations*. Changes in the value of derivative investments are reported on the statement of activities as they occur, regardless of whether they are hedge investments or not. This undoubtedly leads to artificial volatility in the NFP's bottom line, as gains on hedges may be reported in a different period than losses on hedged items. In recent years the GASB has recognized the need for hedge accounting for state and local governments, by allowing gains and losses on certain hedge investments to be reported on the balance sheet as deferred inflows/outflows, rather than impacting changes in net position. However, to date the FASB has not addressed the issue of hedge accounting for NFPs.

BUSINESS APPLICATION   **Hedging Activities of The American National Red Cross**

The American National Red Cross holds derivatives, in the form of swaps and options, to hedge its exposure to interest rate, currency, commodity and equity risk. For example, it uses equity collars to hedge the risk that its equity portfolio will lose value. All contracts are valued at fair value, with unrealized gains and losses reported as changes in unrestricted, temporarily restricted, or permanently restricted net assets, as appropriate.

In 2013, the Red Cross includes net losses of $140,000 on its commodity and equity derivatives in investment income. In its schedule showing in which category of net assets investment income is reported, it does not separate out investment income for derivatives. However, out of total net unrealized investment gains of about $96 million, about half were reported in unrestricted net assets and only 4 percent were reported in permanently restricted net assets. *Source:* The American National Red Cross 2013 consolidated financial statements.

REVIEW 2   •   Reporting for Investments

On January 1, 2016, the Gatehouse Foundation has the following equity investments, reported at fair value:

1. Securities valued at $100,000. The securities are investments of excess cash. At year-end, the securities have a fair value of $65,000. Dividend income for 2016 is $4,000.
2. Securities valued at $48,000. The securities were purchased several years ago with $55,000 in cash permanently restricted by the donor. Income must be used to fund the Foundation's publications and brochures. At year-end, the securities have a fair value of $42,000. Dividend income for 2016 is $2,500.
3. Securities valued at $75,000. The securities were contributed in 2015; fair value at the time of donation was $70,000. The donor specified that the securities were to be held by the Foundation. There is no restriction on income. At year-end, the securities have a fair value of $78,000. Dividend income for 2016 is $6,000.

Required

Prepare a schedule showing how the dividend income and unrealized gains and losses on these securities are reported on the Foundation's statement of activities. Indicate the effect on each category of net assets.

Solutions are located after the chapter assignments.

COMPREHENSIVE ILLUSTRATION OF NFP ACCOUNTING: NORTHEASTERN HEART SOCIETY

This section illustrates many of the accounting and reporting requirements for NFP organizations. It records typical transactions for the year and prepares the financial statements in good form.

The Northeastern Heart Society supports research, education, and public awareness programs on the prevention of heart disease. The Society's resources are generated from contributions, bequests, and grants. A trial balance at December 31, 2016, appears below.

	Dr (Cr)
Cash	$11,700,000
Pledges receivable, net of $1,600,000 allowance for uncollectibles	6,400,000
Investments	72,000,000
Land	2,000,000
Equipment, net of accumulated depreciation	2,400,000
Accounts payable.	(3,300,000)
Net assets—unrestricted	(19,200,000)
Net assets—permanently restricted.	(72,000,000)
Total	$ 0

The following events occur during 2017:

1. Contributions pledged by the public during 2017 amounted to $130,000,000, of which $115,000,000 was collected during the year. In addition, $6,700,000 of the $8,000,000 in gross pledges outstanding at January 1 were collected; the balance was written off. The Society records pledges at gross and provides an allowance for uncollectibles equal to 20 percent of pledges outstanding at year-end. Pledges are recorded at full value because collection usually occurs within one year. Revenue of $4,600,000 was earned from programs which the Society conducted for employees of various corporations.

Cash	115,000,000	
Pledges receivable	15,000,000	
Contributions—unrestricted		130,000,000
To record contributions and cash collections for 2017.		
Cash	6,700,000	
Pledges receivable		6,700,000
To record collection of receivables outstanding on January 1, 2017.		
Allowance for uncollectible pledges.	1,300,000	
Pledges receivable		1,300,000
To write off the remaining January 1, 2017 pledges receivable balance.		
Bad debt expense (general administration)	2,700,000	
Allowance for uncollectible pledges		2,700,000
To adjust the allowance for uncollectible pledges account to its correct ending balance of $3,000,000 (= 20% × $15,000,000); prior to adjustment the allowance stood at $300,000 (= $1,600,000 beginning balance − $1,300,000 write-offs).		
Cash	4,600,000	
Educational program revenue—unrestricted.		4,600,000
To record revenue from educational programs.		

2. Cash disbursements amounted to $115,500,000 in 2017, as follows:

Research	$ 40,000,000
Public awareness programs.	35,000,000
Corporate programs.	3,500,000
General administration	19,500,000
Fund-raising	17,500,000
Total	$115,500,000

Accounts payable increased from $3,300,000 to $4,800,000; all unpaid invoices at beginning and end of year relate to general administration costs.

Expenses—research	40,000,000	
Expenses—public awareness programs	35,000,000	
Expenses—corporate programs	3,500,000	
Expenses—general administration	21,000,000	
Expenses—fund-raising	17,500,000	
Cash		115,500,000
Accounts payable		1,500,000
To record expenses for 2017.		

3. Early in 2017 the Society received a federal grant of $20,000,000 to expand its public awareness programs into smaller communities where it had not been active. The grant period expires on March 31, 2018. During the last half of 2017, $14,300,000 was spent on the project under the terms of the grant; the balance of $5,700,000 is designated by the grantor for expenditure in 2018 and remains temporarily restricted.

Cash	20,000,000	
Federal grant support—temporarily restricted		20,000,000
To record receipt of the federal grant.		
Net assets released from restrictions—temporarily restricted	14,300,000	
Net assets released from restrictions—unrestricted		14,300,000
To record release of assets from temporary restrictions.		
Expenses—public awareness programs	14,300,000	
Cash		14,300,000
To record expenditures for designated programs.		

4. The Society's permanent endowment contains donor-restricted money to be used for research scholarships. Several years ago, the Society received a $50,000,000 bequest to establish this fund. The donor stipulated that the principal be maintained intact, with income used for research scholarships. Subsequent bequests and contributions increased the principal of the fund to $72,000,000 at the beginning of 2017. During 2017, contributions of $350,000 and a bequest of $1,000,000 added to principal. Investment income of $8,000,000 was earned. At year-end, all but $500,000 of the 2017 principal addition was invested in certificates of deposit. Endowment cash held at year-end is separately categorized.

Restricted cash	1,350,000	
Contributions—permanently restricted		1,350,000
To record support designated for endowment.		
Investments	850,000	
Restricted cash		850,000
To record purchase of investments; $850,000 = $1,350,000 − $500,000.		
Cash	8,000,000	
Investment income—temporarily restricted		8,000,000
To record income from investments.		

5. In 2017, $7,500,000 was spent for research scholarships, pursuant to the fund restrictions.

Net assets released from restrictions—temporarily restricted	7,500,000	
Net assets released from restrictions—unrestricted		7,500,000
To record release of assets from temporary restrictions.		
Expenses—research scholarships	7,500,000	
Cash		7,500,000
To record disbursement of scholarship funds.		

6. During 2017, construction began on an office building estimated to cost the Society $40,000,000. The Society borrowed $30,000,000 from the bank on a short-term building loan. During 2017, construction costs were $24,000,000, and $2,800,000 in interest was paid on the loan. Investment of excess cash balances in time deposits yielded $770,000 in interest revenue; the Society's board of directors authorized the use of this money for unanticipated construction costs. Office equipment depreciation of $300,000 was charged to general administration.

Cash.	30,000,000	
Loan payable.		30,000,000
To record financing for the building.		
Construction in progress	24,000,000	
Cash		24,000,000
To record construction activity during 2017.		
Interest expense—general administration	2,800,000	
Cash		2,800,000
To record interest expense on the loan (assumed not capitalized).		
Cash.	770,000	
Investment income—unrestricted		770,000
To record interest revenue on investments of excess cash.		
Expenses—general administration.	300,000	
Accumulated depreciation.		300,000
To record depreciation on the office equipment.		

The statement of activities for Northeastern Heart Society for the year ended December 31, 2017, the statement of financial position at December 31, 2017, and the statement of cash flows for the year ended December 31, 2017, appear in Exhibits 13.4, 13.5, and 13.6. An analysis of expenses, by natural and functional classification, appears in Exhibit 13.7.

EXHIBIT 13.4   Northeastern Heart Society Statement of Activities

NORTHEASTERN HEART SOCIETY
Statement of Activities
For Year Ended December 31, 2017

Change in unrestricted net assets:	
Revenues and support:	
Contributions	$130,000,000
Educational programs.	4,600,000
Investment income	770,000
Net assets released from program restrictions	21,800,000
Total unrestricted revenues and support	157,170,000
Expenses:	
Research programs	47,500,000
Public awareness programs	49,300,000
Corporate programs	3,500,000
General administration	26,800,000
Fund-raising	17,500,000
Total expenses	144,600,000
Increase in unrestricted net assets	12,570,000
Change in temporarily restricted net assets:	
Grants.	20,000,000
Investment income	8,000,000
Net assets released from program restrictions	(21,800,000)
Increase in temporarily restricted net assets	6,200,000
Change in permanently restricted net assets:	
Contributions	1,350,000
Increase in net assets.	20,120,000
Net assets, January 1, 2017.	91,200,000
Net assets, December 31, 2017.	$111,320,000

EXHIBIT 13.5 Northeastern Heart Society Statement of Financial Position

NORTHEASTERN HEART SOCIETY
Statements of Financial Position
December 31, 2017 and 2016

Assets	2017	2016
Cash	$ 32,670,000	$11,700,000
Pledges receivable, net	12,000,000	6,400,000
Restricted cash	500,000	—
Investments	72,850,000	72,000,000
Land	2,000,000	2,000,000
Equipment, net	2,100,000	2,400,000
Construction in progress	24,000,000	—
Total assets	$146,120,000	$94,500,000
Liabilities and net assets		
Liabilities		
Accounts payable	$ 4,800,000	$ 3,300,000
Loan payable	30,000,000	—
Total liabilities	34,800,000	3,300,000
Net assets		
Unrestricted	31,770,000	19,200,000
Temporarily restricted	6,200,000	—
Permanently restricted	73,350,000	72,000,000
Total net assets	111,320,000	91,200,000
Total liabilities and net assets	$146,120,000	$94,500,000

EXHIBIT 13.6 Northeastern Heart Society Statement of Cash Flows

NORTHEASTERN HEART SOCIETY
Statement of Cash Flows
For Year Ended December 31, 2017

Cash flows from operating activities	
Contributions	$121,700,000
Investment income	8,000,000
Program revenue	4,600,000
Grant support	20,000,000
Interest revenue	770,000
Interest expense	(2,800,000)
Program expenditures	(137,300,000)
Net cash from operating activities	14,970,000
Cash flows from investing activities	
Investments	(850,000)
Construction	(24,000,000)
Net cash used for investing activities	(24,850,000)
Cash flows from financing activities	
Loan proceeds	30,000,000
Endowments	1,350,000
Net cash from financing activities	31,350,000
Increase in cash	21,470,000
Cash balance, January 1, 2017	11,700,000
Cash balance, December 31, 2017	$ 33,170,000

Reconciliation of Change in Net Assets
To Net Cash from Operating Activities

Increase in net assets	$ 20,120,000
Adjustments:	
Depreciation expense	300,000
Endowment contributions	(1,350,000)
Increase in pledges receivable, net	(5,600,000)
Increase in accounts payable	1,500,000
Net cash from operating activities	$ 14,970,000

EXHIBIT 13.7   Northeastern Heart Society Statement of Functional Expenses

NORTHEASTERN HEART SOCIETY
Statement of Functional Expenses
For Year Ended December 31, 2017

| | Program Services | | | Supporting Services | | |
	Research	Public Programs	Corporate Programs	General Administration	Fund-Raising	Total Expenses
Salaries...............................	$ 8,700,000	$20,500,000	$2,800,000	$14,000,000	$ 2,700,000	$ 48,700,000
Fees.................................	—	—	—	—	7,000,000	7,000,000
Supplies............................	4,500,000	2,300,000	—	1,000,000	1,000,000	8,800,000
Utilities.............................	2,000,000	8,000,000	—	1,500,000	3,000,000	14,500,000
Occupancy.........................	1,500,000	1,500,000	500,000	2,000,000	500,000	6,000,000
Maintenance.......................	3,500,000	2,000,000	—	1,500,000	—	7,000,000
Printing.............................	2,000,000	9,000,000	—	—	3,000,000	14,000,000
Travel...............................	4,000,000	4,000,000	200,000	—	300,000	8,500,000
Conferences.......................	3,500,000	2,000,000	—	1,000,000	—	6,500,000
Research grants...................	10,300,000	—	—	—	—	10,300,000
Scholarships.......................	7,500,000	—	—	—	—	7,500,000
Interest.............................	—	—	—	2,800,000	—	2,800,000
Bad debts..........................	—	—	—	2,700,000	—	2,700,000
Depreciation.......................	—	—	—	300,000	—	300,000
Totals..............................	$47,500,000	$49,300,000	$3,500,000	$26,800,000	$17,500,000	$144,600,000

REPORTING ISSUES FOR SPECIFIC NOT-FOR-PROFIT ORGANIZATIONS

LO4 Describe major reporting issues for specific NFPs.

This section discusses reporting issues specific to each of the three specific types of NFP organizations. Detailed guidelines may be found in such publications as the AICPA Audit and Accounting Guide—*Not-for-Profit Entities*, which is updated regularly, and in *ASC Topic 954*, Health Care Entities.

Voluntary Health and Welfare Organizations

VHWOs, such as **Habitat for Humanity International**, generate most of their resources from **public support**—contributions, bequests, and grants—and revenues from providing goods and services. Donors to VHWOs take a strong interest in the distinction between program service expenses, and administrative and fund-raising expenses. The discussion earlier in the chapter on the functional classification of expenses and treatment of joint educational and fund-raising costs is particularly applicable to VHWOs.

Accounting for revenues and expenses related to providing goods and services should be carefully separated from activities related to contributions. VHWOs follow revenue recognition principles from regular business accounting in accounting for the sale of goods or services. For example, the **YWCA** provides childcare services to the public, and **Goodwill Industries** does contract work for local businesses. Revenue on such services and contracts is recognized when earned, and expenses are recognized when resources are consumed, using business accounting principles. All such activities are changes in unrestricted net assets.

Colleges and Universities

Private colleges and universities derive much of their resources from student tuition and fees, contributions, contracts, endowment income and grants. Tuition revenue is typically shown gross, with adjustments such as scholarships and waivers shown as either revenue deductions or as expenses. If the tuition adjustments are in return for services provided, such as tuition waivers for graduate teaching assistantships, the adjustments are shown as expenses. If the tuition adjustments do not involve any services, as with scholarships, the adjustments are revenue deductions. Functional classifications of expenses include the following: **education costs**, such as faculty salaries, supplies, and classroom facility costs, **support costs**, such as student services and maintenance, and **self-supporting services**, such as dormitories, food service, and health service.

Colleges and universities must be especially diligent in tracking donations restricted to particular uses. They usually have a **permanent endowment** consisting of funds that are donor-restricted indefinitely, with the income either unrestricted or donor-restricted for particular purposes. For example, a business school endowment may restrict endowment income to expenditures for upgrading the accounting curriculum. Donors often establish an **annuity fund**, where the university must pay a specified amount each year to the donor, with any excess remaining when the agreement terminates going to the university. A **life income fund** pays the donor the income on fund investments for life, with the remainder going to the university upon the donor's death.

Health Care Organizations

The business environment for health care organizations has changed substantially over the years, causing changes in the information required to make decisions. These organizations face significant pressure from escalating operating costs and competition. Most hospital bills are paid by third parties such as Medicare, Medicaid, and insurance carriers. Third-party payers reimburse providers using flat rates for many services based on the patient's diagnosis, not the actual treatment cost incurred. These third-party payers require detailed analyses of costs incurred to develop reasonable reimbursement rates by diagnosis. Cost information is also used to rank health care providers. These rankings help determine whether a particular health care facility qualifies for reimbursement, and can strongly influence its ability to attract patients.

Operating revenues consist of **patient service revenue**, generated from patient charges, and **revenue from research grants and auxiliary services** such as the cafeteria and gift shop. Amounts realizable from third-party payers are typically less than gross revenues. On the statement of activities, gross patient service revenue appears first, with provisions for contractual and other adjustments deducted from gross revenue to determine net patient service revenue.

Charity care must be distinguished from *bad debt expense*. **Charity care** represents services performed with no expectation that payment will be received, and is separately reported at *cost*; no revenue or profit is recognized on charity care. Services provided to patients, with the expectation that payment will be received, are recorded as patient service revenue. Uncollectible portions of this patient service revenue are typically shown separately as **bad debt expense** and not netted against revenue.

Medical malpractice claims and similar liabilities are reported at the gross amount expected to be paid. Amounts expected to be reimbursed through insurance are reported as receivables and are not netted against the liability.

Health care expenses fall into the following major classifications: nursing services, other professional services, general services, administrative services, uncollectible accounts, and depreciation. The AICPA Audit and Accounting Guide—*Health Care Entities,* updated annually, provides detailed guidance.

• •

Reporting Perspective

NFPs merge with or acquire other NFPs with about the same frequency as for-profit businesses. NFPs combine to improve the quality and efficiency of services, expand the types of services offered, gain access to better funding opportunities, or enter new geographic areas.

Prior to 2010, combinations of NFP organizations were exempted from the guidance in *ASC Topic 805,* Business Combinations, and instead followed the old requirements of *APB Opinion 16* (1970). An Accounting Standards Update, effective in 2010, recognizes the unique features of NFPs, and provides specific guidance for NFP mergers and acquisitions in *ASC Topic 958,* Not-for-Profit Entities. This guidance differs from business accounting for mergers and acquisitions as follows:

• If an NFP organization obtains control of another entity, the combination is an **acquisition**, and the valuation requirements of *ASC Topic 805* apply. The acquiring NFP reports the acquired NFP's assets and liabilities at fair value, including previously unreported intangibles. However, the accounting

continued

treatment of the excess of acquisition cost over the fair value of identifiable net assets acquired depends on the nature of the acquired NFP. If the acquiree operates like a business, charging fees to cover costs, the acquirer recognizes this difference as *goodwill*. If the acquiree is primarily supported by contributions, the acquirer reports the excess as a *separate charge* in its statement of activities. Although a business records a bargain purchase gain on its income statement when the fair value of identifiable net assets acquired exceeds the acquisition cost, an acquiring NFP records an *inherent contribution received*, as a credit in its statement of activities.

Valuation of the acquired organization's assets and liabilities at fair value is appropriate if the acquirer takes control. Because goodwill is not as relevant to donors' assessment of organizations funded primarily by contributions, acquisition cost in excess of the fair value of identifiable net assets acquired is immediately expensed. For organizations that do recognize goodwill, the FASB is currently evaluating whether current standards for goodwill impairment testing are appropriate to NFPs. Due to cost concerns, the FASB may decide to allow NFPs to follow standards similar to those now allowed for private companies.

- If two or more NFP organizations give up control to create a new entity with a new governing board, the combination is a **merger**. The new entity accounts for the merger using the *carryover method*— the assets and liabilities of the merging organizations are combined at the amounts reported on their separate financial statements at the merger date, and are not recorded at fair value. No "goodwill" or "bargain purchase" issues arise.

NFP organizations often combine to improve services to the public or to otherwise further their mission. An NFP acquirer frequently pays nothing for the acquired NFP's net assets. Because of the unique nature of NFP combinations, the FASB decided to allow the new entity to carry over the merged entities at book value.

BUSINESS APPLICATION   **Consolidation Policy of The American National Red Cross**

The American National Red Cross presents *consolidated* financial statements. In its summary of significant accounting policies, its consolidated entities are described as follows:

> The accompanying consolidated financial statements present the consolidated financial position and changes in net assets, functional expenses and cash flows of the Organization. The Organization has national and international programs that are conducted by its headquarters, biomedical services, and chartered local chapters. Also included in the consolidated financial statements are the net assets and operations of Boardman Indemnity Ltd., a 100% owned captive insurance subsidiary, and ARC Receivables Company, LLC, a wholly owned bankruptcy-remote special purpose entity.

Note 11 explains the consolidated special purpose entity's function.

> The Organization has an asset securitization program. The program is structured to sell the eligible biomedical hospital account receivables, without legal recourse, to a third party investor, through a wholly owned bankruptcy-remote special purpose entity . . . The Organization continues servicing the sold receivables. Proceeds received under the securitization program are treated as secured borrowings.

The Red Cross determines which entities to consolidate in its financial statements using the same standards as a normal business. Its consolidated entities are wholly-owned, indicating control. *Source*: The American National Red Cross 2013 consolidated financial statements.

EVALUATION OF EXTERNAL REPORTING FOR NFP ORGANIZATIONS

The FASB requirements for NFPs are supported by some and criticized by others. This section discusses both sides of the major issues, in terms of the impact of the requirements on the external reader's ability to evaluate the financial performance of NFPs.

LO5 Evaluate financial information provided by NFPs.

Strengths of External Reporting Requirements

The strengths of the external reporting model for NFPs include standardization, completeness and comparability between types of NFP organizations.

- The requirements provide a **standardized presentation** of financial performance and condition by all NFP organizations. Prior to these standards, each type of NFP organization had its own presentation methodology. In addition, disclosures were often omitted, such as the statement of cash flows and a functional classification of expenses.

- The external reporting model does not preclude an NFP from **tailoring its financial statements** to meet readers' needs. For example, although the "bottom line" on the statement of activities is the change in net assets, the NFP may include a measure of operating performance that it feels best reflects its activities.

- The presentation requirements focus on the **entity as a whole**. Creditors, donors, members, and other interested readers prefer to evaluate the performance of the entire organization.

- Restricted contributions and changes in the value of investments appear on the financial statements on a more **timely basis**, providing full information to financial statement users.

Criticisms of External Reporting Requirements

Criticism of the FASB requirements generally follows one major theme—that the required reporting of changes in net assets can cause readers of the financial statements to *overestimate resources available for organization activities*.

- Investments in debt and equity securities are reported at fair value rather than at cost. Unrealized gains can be misinterpreted as funds available for the organization's activities.

- Contributions are reported as revenue in the period they are promised, not when received. Critics contend that financial statements are misleading to the extent that promised contributions not yet available are shown as increases in net assets, especially when multi-year pledges are involved.

- Recognition of contributions in the period received has special complications for those organizations receiving large amounts of contributions in the form of goods, such as used clothing. The Codification requires that these organizations estimate the market value of contributions when received, which may be subject to a high degree of error.

- Restricted contributions are recognized as increases in net assets in the period received. Critics say that these contributions are not revenues until the period the restrictions are met and they become available for use. Showing them as increases in net assets can be misleading, even though they are segregated under temporarily restricted net assets.

- Donations of long-lived assets are recognized as increases in net assets in the period received. The full fair value of the asset is shown as revenue in the period received, but the asset will benefit many periods in the future. Even though the organization may treat such donations as temporarily restricted, critics feel that this causes a mismatching of revenues with expenses, and overstates the resources available to fund program services.

- Net assets are classified according to donor restrictions, not internal organization restrictions. Critics feel that classification by management intention provides a more meaningful presentation of resources available for future use. In practice, income on restricted funds is often used for the same purpose as the original restricted funds, but unless the income is donor-restricted, it appears as an increase in unrestricted assets.

- Assets are not classified according to intended use. Critics feel that assets to be used as a part of operations should be clearly separated from those assets which are held as part of a restricted endowment.

- Organizations find it difficult to distinguish between restrictions and conditions. Restricted contributions are shown as increases in net assets, while conditional contributions are shown as increases in liabilities. A contribution to a building fund may be considered restricted, in the sense that the donor intends that it be used to finance building construction. On the other hand, the contribution is conditional in the sense that if total contributions are too low, plans to build may be scrapped and the money returned.

Many of the criticisms of FASB reporting requirements for NFPs are mitigated by additional disclosures. Although it is true that GAAP requires that the statement of activities present the change in each of the categories of net assets and the change in total net assets, organizations are encouraged to show other measures of performance. If an organization feels that its "bottom line" change in net assets is not an accurate reflection of the change in resources available for future activities, it can show a subtotal in the statement of activities, or provide a more detailed presentation of changes in unrestricted net assets. *ASC 958* suggests these possible classifications: operating and nonoperating, expendable and nonexpendable, earned and unearned, recurring and nonrecurring.

Current Developments in NFP Reporting

The FASB is currently considering a change in NFP financial statement presentation, focusing on net asset classifications and footnote disclosures. No proposal or update has been issued as of late 2014, but some of the FASB's conclusions are described below.

- Change the net asset classifications to only two: **net assets with donor-imposed restrictions**, and **net assets without donor-imposed restrictions**. This classification structure focuses on how and when the NFP's resources can be used, rather than on whether restrictions are temporary or permanent.

- On the statement of activities, report results on two aspects of performance: a **mission** dimension and an **availability** dimension. The mission, or operating, section reports resources available and used to carry out the NFP's main activities, the mission of the organization. For example, for the Red Cross it would be disaster relief, biomedical services, etc. The availability section includes nonoperating activities, such as financing and investing income and gains and losses, as well as resources unavailable for current operations, either because of donor restrictions or internal limitations imposed by the governing board.

- All NFPs must report expenses **by function and by nature**, either in the statement of activities or in the footnotes, and explain how costs are allocated between program and support classifications.

- On the statement of cash flows, the **direct method is required** for cash flows from operating activities, but the **reconciliation** of the change in net assets to cash from operating activities **is no longer required**.

- Several types of cash inflows and outflows are **classified differently on the statement of cash flows**, to better align with the operating/nonoperating format of the statement of activities. For example, dividends and interest received on investments move from operating to investing activities, and interest paid on debt moves from operating to financing activities. Cash received and paid for sales and purchases of operating assets moves from investing to operating activities. Cash gifts that are donor-restricted for acquisition of operating assets move from financing to operating activities.

The purpose of the FASB's NFP project is to provide better information to interested readers of an NFP's financial statements, by improving the net asset classification structure and information provided about the NFP's liquidity, financial performance and cash flows.

A summarized excerpt of its 2013 statement of activities illustrates how **The American National Red Cross** presents changes in unrestricted net assets:

(in thousands)	**Unrestricted**
Operating revenues and gains	$3,355,375
Operating expenses:	
Program services	3,054,869
Supporting services	325,714
Total operating expenses.	3,380,583
Change in net assets from operations	(25,208)
Nonoperating gains	42,670
Pension-related changes other than net periodic benefit cost	247,295
Change in net assets	$ 264,757

The Red Cross reports a $264,757,000 increase in unrestricted net assets for 2013. However, its operating performance is a deficit of $25,208,000. Many NFPs separate their statement of activities into operating and nonoperating sections to enhance disclosure to financial statement readers.

REVIEW OF KEY CONCEPTS

Prepare financial statements of private not-for-profit (NFP) organizations in proper format. (p. 568) Three financial statements are required: a **statement of financial position**, a **statement of activities**, and a **statement of cash flows**. The **statement of financial position** reports the organization's net assets classified as **unrestricted**, **temporarily restricted**, or **permanently restricted**. The **statement of activities** reports **changes in each of the three net asset categories. Expenses** are reductions in **unrestricted net assets** only, whereas **revenues** can appear in each category. The **statement of cash flows** reconciles the change in total net assets to cash flow from operating activities. Cash flows from investing and financing activities complete the analysis of the change in cash and cash equivalents during the period.   **LO 1**

Report all types of contributions received. (p. 572) Contributions increase unrestricted net assets unless donor-restricted. **Temporary restrictions** take the form of **time** or **use restrictions**. When donor restrictions on contributions expire, **net assets are released** by reducing temporarily restricted net assets and increasing unrestricted net assets. If the donor stipulates that the principal of the donation be maintained, it is added to permanently restricted net assets. **Promises to contribute** are recognized when they are **supported by verifiable documentation. Contributions of services** are recognized when they meet conditions prescribed in the Codification. When an organization acts as an **agent** in collecting contributions intended for other unaffiliated organizations, the contributions increase **liabilities** and not contribution revenue.   **LO 2**

Report investments in financial securities. (p. 580) **Investments** held by NFP organizations are reported at **fair market value**. Value changes and investment income are reported in the statement of activities as changes in unrestricted net assets unless subject to donor restrictions.   **LO 3**

Describe major reporting issues for specific NFPs. (p. 586) All NFP organizations follow the same FASB requirements for financial statement presentation. Donors to **VHWOs** take particular interest in the distinction between program service and administrative and fund-raising expenses. Revenues and expenses related to providing goods and services are reported separately. **Colleges and universities** report gross tuition revenue, with scholarships as revenue adjustments. Expenses include tuition waivers as compensation for student work assignments. **Health care organizations** typically show patient service revenue gross, with contractual adjustments as revenue deductions. Estimated uncollectibles appear as bad debt expense, and charity care is reported at cost.   **LO 4**

Evaluate financial information provided by NFPs. (p. 589) The NFP reporting model **standardizes** reporting for the **entity as a whole**, while allowing flexibility in categorizing revenues and expenses. Critics claim that the   **LO 5**

requirements **overstate reported revenue**. They believe that unrealized increases in investment value, documented promises, donated services, restricted contributions and contributions of long-lived assets should not be considered revenue because such items are not available to fund current programs. The FASB is currently considering major changes in financial statement format and disclosure to improve readers' ability to evaluate an NFP organization's performance and resource availability.

Assignments with the ✅ in the margin are available in BusinessCourse.
See the Preface of the book for details.

MULTIPLE CHOICE QUESTIONS ·································

Use the following information to answer questions 1–5 below.

Geneva Preschool provides free instruction for children from low-income families. Its January 1, 2016, trial balance is as follows:

	Debit	Credit
Cash..	$ 100,000	
Equipment & furnishings, net........................	1,500,000	
Building, net...	3,500,000	
Accounts payable.......................................		$ 200,000
Net assets—unrestricted..............................		3,400,000
Net assets—temporarily restricted..................		1,500,000
	$5,100,000	$5,100,000

Activities for 2016:

a. Unrestricted cash contributions were $4,500,000.

b. On January 1, 2016, a donor made a documented promise of $500,000, to be paid at the end of 2018 (3 years later). Using a 5 percent discount rate, the present value of this promise is $431,918.

c. Each year, Geneva collects donor-restricted contributions to purchase technology for educational programs. During 2016, $200,000 was received and $500,000 was spent. Geneva expenses technology purchases.

d. Out-of-pocket operating expenses for the year were $4,200,000. The year-end accounts payable balance, all related to operating expenses, was $150,000.

e. A licensed CPA did all of Geneva's required financial statements and IRS forms for free. Fair value of these services is $25,000. Parents of students donated their time to lead preschool classes in safety and nutrition. The fair value of their time is $5,000.

f. Depreciation for the year on equipment and furnishings was $250,000. Depreciation on the building was $600,000.

✅ LO 1   **1.** How do Geneva's 2016 financial statements report the out-of-pocket operating expenses described in item *d.* above?

	Statement of Activities	Statement of Cash Flows
a.	$4,250,000 reduction in unrestricted net assets	$4,250,000 cash for operating activities
b.	$4,200,000 reduction in unrestricted net assets	$4,250,000 cash for operating activities
c.	$4,200,000 reduction in temporarily restricted net assets	$4,200,000 cash for operating activities
d.	$4,250,000 reduction in temporarily restricted net assets	$4,200,000 cash for operating activities

✅ LO 1   **2.** On Geneva's 2016 statement of cash flows, a reconciliation of the change in net assets to cash from operating activities requires *adding* which of the following adjustments to change in net assets?

a. $50,000 change in accounts payable

b. $25,000 contribution of services

c. $850,000 depreciation expense

d. $431,918 promises to contribute

3. Geneva's 2016 statement of activities reports item *e.* as follows: **LO 2** ✓

   a. $25,000 increase in unrestricted net assets (contributions) and $25,000 decrease in unrestricted net assets (expenses)
   b. $30,000 increase in unrestricted net assets (contributions) and $30,000 decrease in unrestricted net assets (expenses)
   c. $25,000 increase in temporarily restricted net assets (contributions)
   d. Not reported

4. Geneva's 2016 statement of activities reports item *b.* as follows: **LO 2** ✓

   a. $431,918 increase in temporarily restricted net assets
   b. $431,918 increase in temporarily restricted net assets and $21,596 increase in unrestricted net assets
   c. $453,514 increase in temporarily restricted net assets
   d. This promise is not reported until the contribution is received.

5. Item *c.* affects Geneva's net assets in 2016 as follows: **LO 2** ✓

   a. $500,000 net decrease in unrestricted net assets, $300,000 net decrease in temporarily restricted net assets
   b. $500,000 net decrease in unrestricted net assets, $500,000 net decrease in unrestricted net assets
   c. No change in unrestricted net assets, $200,000 net increase in temporarily restricted net assets
   d. No change in unrestricted net assets, $300,000 net decrease in temporarily restricted net assets

6. At the beginning of 2017, a private not-for-profit museum receives a donation of equity securities valued at   **LO 3** ✓
   $10,000,000. The donor specifies that the securities be held as a permanent endowment, and income from the securities is restricted to the purchase of Native American artifacts. The securities have a fair value of $9,500,000 at the end of 2017. The museum reports the $500,000 decline in the value of the securities as

   a. a reduction in permanently restricted net assets.
   b. a reduction in temporarily restricted net assets.
   c. a reduction in unrestricted net assets.
   d. not reported.

7. At the beginning of 2017, a private not-for-profit museum receives a donation of $10,000,000. The donor   **LO 3** ✓
   specifies that the donation be held as a permanent endowment, and income from its investment can be used for any purpose. The museum invests the $10,000,000 in equity securities. The securities have a fair value of $9,500,000 at the end of 2017. The museum reports the $500,000 decline in the value of the securities as

   a. a reduction in permanently restricted net assets.
   b. a reduction in temporarily restricted net assets.
   c. a reduction in unrestricted net assets.
   d. not reported.

8. On its statement of activities, a private NFP hospital reports charity care   **LO 4** ✓

   a. at cost.
   b. at the fair value of services rendered.
   c. at fair value net of cost to provide services.
   d. in the footnotes to its financial statements, not on the statement of activities itself.

9. Critics of the FASB's reporting requirements for NFPs have a common concern, that current GAAP for not-   **LO 5** ✓
   for-profit organizations

   a. does not accurately recognize pledges of contributions.
   b. misreports the actual value of investments.
   c. does not recognize all donations of services.
   d. overstates resources available for spending.

10. Which of the following is *most likely* your major concern when auditing an NFP?   **LO 5** ✓

    a. The NFP is overstating pledges receivable.
    b. The NFP is understating fund-raising expenses.
    c. The NFP is overstating investment income.
    d. The NFP is understating cash contributions.

EXERCISES ••

LO 2   **E13.1**   **Reporting Donations**   The **Orange County Rescue Mission, Inc.,** receives the following donations:

1. A donor contributes cash, with no restrictions or conditions.
2. An accountant provides services in maintaining organization records.
3. Volunteers provide services in staffing the local soup kitchen.
4. A donor signs an agreement promising to contribute cash next year.
5. A donor contributes land. The Mission has no accounting policy regarding donations of long-lived assets.
6. A donor contributes cash, specifying that it be used to support a program to teach life skills to battered women.

Required

For each of the above donations, identify the effect on net assets. Use one of the following alternatives for each donation:

    UR   affects unrestricted net assets
    TR   affects temporarily restricted net assets
    PR   affects permanently restricted net assets
    N   does not affect net assets

⊘ LO 2   **E13.2**   **Reporting Donations**   Dunning College, a private college in northern Idaho, receives the following donations:

1. A parent of a current accounting student contributes $5,000,000, with the stipulation that the donation be used to fund a new building for the business school. The college does not know whether it can accumulate enough additional resources to go ahead with the project.
2. An accounting alumnus contributes $500,000 to the accounting department. The alumnus stipulates that the principal of the contribution remain intact, and any investment income be used to fund a speaker series on current accounting issues. The college invests the $500,000 in securities, and earns income of $15,000. The $15,000 is used to pay transportation costs and speaker fees.
3. A retired recruiter from a local CPA firm notifies the college that her will states that $1,000,000 of her estate be paid to the accounting department of the college, with no restrictions on use.
4. An alumnus promises to contribute $50,000 if the college can raise $50,000 from other sources. The college raises the $50,000 and the alumnus contributes the additional $50,000.
5. A student donates a van valued at $20,000, specifying that the van be used to transport disabled students from their dorms to class.
6. The car in item 5. depreciates by $2,000.
7. Cash contributions to the college total $12,000,000. The college's Board sets aside $600,000 for repairs to the administration building.

Required

For each of the above items, prepare the appropriate journal entry or entries. If the item affects net assets, specify which category of net assets is affected.

LO 2   **E13.3**   **Donated Building**   On January 1, 2016, the **YWCA** receives a donated building with a fair market value of $50 million. The donor specifies that the building is to be used to house international families until they obtain permanent housing. The YWCA estimates that the building has a remaining useful life of 20 years, uses straight-line depreciation, and is a calendar year organization.

YWCA

Required

Prepare the journal entries necessary in 2016 and 2017 to account for this donation and subsequent depreciation. If the entry affects net assets, indicate which category of net assets is affected.

⊘ LO 3   **E13.4**   **Accounting for Investments**   In 2016, Western Community Hospital, a private facility, receives donated securities with a fair market value of $400,000. The donor specifies that the securities be held as a permanent endowment, and investment income earned on these securities can be used for any purpose. The securities have a fair market value of $405,000 at the end of 2016, and $396,000 at the end of 2017. Dividend income earned on the securities is $15,000 in each of the two years.

Required

a. Prepare the journal entries to record the above events in 2016 and 2017. Indicate the balance in each account and its placement in the financial statements.
b. Assume the same facts as above, except the donation was $400,000 in cash, and the hospital invested the $400,000 in securities. How do the entries in *a.* change?

E13.5 Reporting Pledged and Restricted Contributions Consider the following contributions to private not-for-profit organizations: **LO 2** ✓

1. Pledge cards signed by church members pledge $3,000,000 to a facilities improvement campaign. Church officials expect that 90 percent of the pledges will be collected, and collection is expected within one year.
2. A university phone-a-thon produces $75,000 of "intentions to give;" respondents have 30 days to think it over.
3. A prominent alumnus pledges $5,000,000 to support the MS in accounting program in a local university, conditional on the program becoming separately accredited by the AACSB.
4. Contributors sign pledge cards for $150,000 to support ongoing programs at a local teaching hospital. The $150,000 is expected to be received at the end of two years. The appropriate discount rate is 5%.
5. A college receives cash gifts of $250,000 restricted by the donors to a new graduate program in mathematical finance. College officials believe $1,000,000 is needed before the new program can begin.

Required

State whether each of the above items is recognized as a contribution. If recognized, give the amount of contributions revenue and whether it is unrestricted or temporarily restricted. If it is not recognized, explain why.

E13.6 Recognition of Donations Hopeville Retreat is a private not-for-profit organization that counsels   **LO 2**
former drug addicts in readjusting to productive community life. Donations provide the major support for Hopeville Retreat. During 2016, the following gifts were received:

1. Cash from the semiannual fund-raising campaign, $4,000,000.
2. Cash donations from rehabilitated clients, $100,000.
3. Clothing donated by a department store. Cost to the store was $5,000; market value was $7,000.
4. A flat-screen television, valued at $800, donated by a friend of the Retreat.
5. Medication, donated by a pharmaceutical company. Cost of the medication was $3,000; market value was $5,000.
6. Accounting services for necessary paperwork and record-keeping performed by a CPA, valued at $7,000.
7. Door-to-door fund solicitation time donated by high school students, as part of their school community service requirement. Their time is estimated to be worth $2,800 when valued using minimum wage rates.
8. Free radio announcements of the fund-raising campaign given by a local radio station. The normal charge for advertisements of comparable length is $1,000.

Required

For each item, indicate at what amount the donation is recorded on the books of Hopeville Retreat, and where it would appear in its statement of activities.

E13.7 Effect of Transactions on Net Assets Suppose the Institute of Management Accountants   **LO 1, 2**
(IMA) incurs the following transactions:

1. A gift of cash is received with no stipulations as to use.
2. The IMA borrows money to finance construction of a new office building.
3. Money is collected from participants for the future annual conference.
4. The Board of Directors sets aside money for distribution to universities as awards for best management accounting doctoral dissertations.
5. An automobile is donated; the donor specifies that the automobile is to be used in transporting staff on official organization business.
6. Depreciation is computed on the automobile in 5.
7. Cash is set aside to repay the loan in 2.
8. Gently used accounting textbooks are collected for future distribution to inner city high schools.

Required

For each item, indicate the category of net assets affected, if any.

E13.8 Promises of Future Gifts On July 1, 2015, Rajeev Gupta, a wealthy alumnus of Clearwater Uni-   **LO 2**
versity, promises in writing to contribute $10,000 at the beginning of each of the next five fiscal years to finance the yearly continuing education requirements for accounting faculty. The university's fiscal year runs from July 1 to June 30. Accounting faculty spend the $10,000 each year, starting in fiscal 2017, on continuing education programs.

Required

Prepare journal entries to report this donation throughout its 5-year life. A 4 percent discount rate is appropriate. If the entry affects net assets, indicate the net asset category affected.

LO 3   **E13.9**   **Temporary Investments**   The National Leukemia Society maintains a portfolio of temporary equity investments, representing investment of excess cash. At December 31, 2016, the Society holds the following securities:

Security	Cost	Fair Value
300 shares of Alpha Corporation	$ 20,000	$ 21,000
1,000 shares of Beta, Inc	300,000	298,000
200 shares of Sigma Company	42,000	49,000

Quarterly dividends paid in 2017 on each investment were as follows:

Alpha Corporation	$1.50/share
Beta, Inc.	0.40/share
Sigma Company.	1.60/share

At December 31, 2017, fair values of the above securities are as follows. No securities were bought or sold during 2017.

	Fair Value
300 shares of Alpha Corporation	$ 19,700
1,000 shares of Beta, Inc	304,000
200 shares of Sigma Company	46,800

Required

Prepare a schedule showing the investment income recognized on the Society's 2017 statement of activities, including any unrealized gains or losses. Indicate in what category of net assets the investment income is reported.

LO 1, 2, 4   **E13.10**   **College Transactions**   San Rafael College's transactions include the following:

1. An alumna donates cash for the purchase of accounting research software.
2. An alumna donates cash, stipulating that income generated by investment of the cash be paid to the donor during her lifetime. At the donor's death, the gift and all future income belong to the college.
3. An alumna donates cash, stipulating that income generated by investment of the cash be used for accounting student scholarships. The principal is to remain intact.
4. A student center is constructed.
5. Salaries to faculty are paid.
6. Tuition scholarships are made to students.
7. Tuition waivers are granted to students who work as teaching assistants.
8. Student activity fees for independent student organizations are collected with tuition payments.
9. Depreciation on college facilities is recognized.

Required

For each item, identify the accounts affected and for all changes in net assets, their placement on the college's statement of activities.

LO 1, 2, 4   **E13.11**   **College Journal Entries**   Following are transactions of Canton College:

1. The college's general fund-raising campaign generates written pledges of $800,000. Past history shows pledges to be 90 percent collectible. Cash collection is expected within one year.
2. A previously recorded unrestricted pledge is received, $7,000.
3. A staff member borrows $1,000 from the college and signs a note for repayment within one year.
4. Previously collected student activity fees of $6,000 are transferred to independent student organizations.
5. Salaries of $500,000 are paid to employees. An accrual had not been recorded.
6. A loan of $100,000 is taken to buy audiovisual equipment.
7. An $800 scholarship is awarded from funds donor-restricted to scholarships.

Required

For each of the above transactions, record the journal entry and, if appropriate, indicate where each item appears on the college's statement of activities.

E13.12 Annuity/Life Income Transactions   On January 1, 2016, Pauline Doyle gave Rocky Mountain   **LO 2**
College $600,000 in cash with the provision that the cash be invested in income-producing securities. Actuarial estimates set Doyle's life expectancy at 20 years from the date of the gift. The annual discount rate is 3 percent. Rocky Mountain College invested the $600,000 in securities earning 4 percent in cash dividends in 2016.

Required

Record all 2016 events relating to Pauline Doyle's gift, under each of the following *independent* arrangements.

a.   The college is to pay Pauline Doyle $20,000 every December 31 of her remaining life. Upon Doyle's death, remaining resources become available to the college with no restrictions as to use.
b.   The college is to pay Pauline Doyle all earnings of the principal for life. Upon Doyle's death, remaining resources become available to the college with no restrictions as to use.

E13.13 Critique of Statement of Activities Format   Your accounting firm audits the financial statements   **LO 1**
of the Sioux Falls Society for the Preservation of Prairie Dogs, a private not-for-profit organization. Your job is to review the format of the Society's operating statement for the year. Here is the statement:

SIOUX FALLS SOCIETY FOR THE PRESERVATION OF PRAIRIE DOGS
Statement of Activities
For Fiscal Year Ended June 30, 2017

	Unrestricted net assets	Temporarily restricted net assets	Permanently restricted net assets
Revenues, gains and other support:			
Contributions	$215,000	$180,000	$350,000
Fees	150,000	—	—
Investment income	1,500	25,000	—
Gains on investments	2,000	1,000	5,000
Net assets released from restrictions	150,000	(45,000)	(85,000)
Total revenues, gains, and other support	518,500	161,000	270,000
Expenses:			
Salaries	130,000	25,000	—
Supplies	75,000	10,000	—
Rent	290,000	—	—
Total expenses	495,000	35,000	—
Net profit	23,500	126,000	270,000
Beginning net assets	102,000	140,000	460,000
Ending net assets	$125,500	$266,000	$730,000

Required

There are five different reporting errors in this statement. Identify each error. Assume the numbers are correct.

E13.14 In-Kind Contributions   In its fiscal 2013 consolidated financial statements, **Make-A-Wish Founda-**   **LO 2**
tion of America reports the following in-kind contributions of assets and services, included in its statement of activities:

MAKE-A-WISH
FOUNDATION

Wish related	$ 6,973,235
Professional services	410,276
Advertising and media	5,932,281
Investments	65,703
Total	$13,381,495

Related program or supporting services expenses were recorded totaling $13,315,792 in 2013.

Required

a. How did Make-A-Wish decide which contributed services to report in its statement of activities? How were they valued? How were the investments valued?

b. Prepare the journal entry Make-A-Wish made to report its 2013 in-kind contributions. For accounts reported on the statement of activities, indicate which category of net assets is affected.

LO 1 **E13.15 Statement of Cash Flows** Current year cash receipts and payments for the Walker Aquarium, a private NFP organization, appear below (*in thousands*).

1. Unrestricted cash contributions: $6,000.
2. Collections of documented promises: $65.
3. Permanently restricted cash endowments received: $45.
4. Grant received from a private trust, restricted to special programs: $500. $425 is spent on these programs.
5. Cash paid to acquire equipment: $200.
6. Cash paid for investments in securities: $150. Securities with a book value of $30 were sold for $35.
7. Donor-restricted cash accumulated in prior years, spent for programs: $150; spent for equipment, $125.
8. Program, fund-raising, and administrative expenses: $5,700; accounts payable increased $40 during the year, and equipment depreciation included in expenses was $50.
9. Investment income, received in cash: $20.

Required

Prepare a statement of cash flows for Walker Aquarium, in good form. The beginning cash balance was $120.

PROBLEMS ••

LO 1, 2, 3 **P13.1** **Journal Entries and Financial Statements** The Southside Counseling Center was established on January 10, 2016, to provide a variety of counseling services to community residents, including marital and family counseling and treatment for alcoholism and drug abuse. The center's initial resources were provided by a private foundation in the form of a $2,500,000 capital grant. Of this sum, the foundation designated $1,000,000 for building and equipment and $750,000 for the establishment of a special program for counseling parolees. The following transactions occurred during 2016:

1. Contributions of $1,200,000 were received through the local United Way campaign, and an additional $200,000 was received in direct contributions. Of the direct contributions, $20,000 was for the parolees' program and $50,000 was for the building fund; the remaining $130,000, of which $60,000 was in the form of documented pledges expected to be collected within one year, was unrestricted. The pledges are estimated to be 85% collectible. Any bad debt expense is allocated to administrative expense.
2. Out-of-pocket operating expenses for the year were $1,400,000. Of the total, $950,000 are program expenses, $350,000 are administrative expenses, and the remainder are fund-raising expenses. $100,000 of the expenses were unpaid at year-end.
3. The special parolees' program had not yet begun as of December 31, 2016. All resources dedicated to this program were invested in short-term securities. Investment income for the year, which was reinvested, was $30,000. There are no unrealized gains or losses on the securities.
4. The center obtained a $2,400,000 mortgage to purchase a building, and obtained a $300,000 3-year note to purchase equipment. The center also used the designated capital grant to finance these purchases; the total cost of the building and equipment was $3,700,000.
5. Interest of $140,000 was accrued and paid on the mortgage and note, all allocated to administrative expense.
6. Depreciation on the building and equipment is $190,000, all allocated to program expenses.

Required

a. Prepare journal entries to record the transactions for 2016.

b. Prepare Southside's statement of activities for 2016 and its statement of financial position at December 31, 2016.

P13.2 Recognition of Contributions The following events relate to **Habitat for Humanity International**'s activities. If appropriate, assume a discount rate of 6 percent per annum.   **LO 2** ✔

1. In a telephone solicitation, a potential donor says he will contribute $500 in 30 days.
2. In a telephone solicitation, a potential donor requests that a pledge card be mailed, suggesting that a $250 contribution may be forthcoming.
3. A potential donor makes a documented promise to contribute $100,000 when Habitat for Humanity has raised $100,000 in matching funds; $40,000 in matching funds has been raised to date.
4. Same as 3. except that the potential donor promises to contribute up to $100,000 by giving $1 for each $1 of matching funds raised.
5. A group of college students helps build a house for Habitat for Humanity in inner city Los Angeles; Habitat for Humanity estimates the value of the group's services at $10,000.
6. A potential donor signs an agreement to contribute $15,000 now and $15,000 at the beginning of each of the next four years, to help pay for general operating expenses.
7. A donor contributes $200,000, stating that half is to be used to restore and build houses in upstate New York this year, and half is to be used for the same purpose next year.
8. At the beginning of the year, a donor contributes a building worth $4,000,000 and requires that it be used to house Habitat for Humanity's administrative offices over the building's 20-year remaining estimated useful life.
9. A registered plumber volunteers her services to install plumbing in several Habitat for Humanity houses. The plumber's services are valued at $5,000.
10. A donor contributes $1,000,000 face value of 4 percent bonds as an endowment to Habitat for Humanity. Income generated from the bonds is to be used to buy appliances for new houses. Donated between interest payment dates, the bonds' $1,060,000 value includes accrued interest of $25,000.

Required

In each case, identify (a) whether the item should be recorded as a contribution and (b) if recorded, the dollar amount of the item to be reported as a change in unrestricted, temporarily restricted, or permanently restricted net assets.

P13.3 Journal Entries and Financial Statements The Learning Circle is a private organization that provides after-school and summer tutoring and educational activities to children from low-income families. The organization is funded by member dues and contributions. Following is Learning Circle's trial balance at July 1, 2015:   **LO 1, 2**

	Debit	Credit
Cash.	$ 60,000	
Dues receivable	5,000	
Supplies	25,000	
Land	200,000	
Building, net	500,000	
Equipment, net.	260,000	
Accounts payable.		$ 35,000
Unrestricted net assets		820,000
Temporarily restricted net assets.		195,000
Totals	$1,050,000	$1,050,000

Cash receipts and payments for fiscal 2016 are:

Receipts:	
Collection of dues.	$102,000
Contributions	210,000
Grants.	270,000
Disbursements:	
Tutoring programs	245,000
After-school programs	310,000
Fund-raising	36,000

Additional information:

1. Depreciation for the year is $25,000 for the building and $35,000 for the equipment; depreciation is allocated equally between tutoring and after-school programs.
2. The grants were restricted to a new tutoring program for inner city teens. Of the amount received in fiscal 2016, $150,000 was spent for the specified program (included in expenditures above).
3. Supplies of $16,000 were on hand at the end of fiscal 2016. All supplies relate to the tutoring programs.
4. Dues of $8,000 were uncollected as of June 30, 2016.
5. The July 1, 2015, balance in temporarily restricted net assets consists of grants restricted to after-school programs. These grants were spent for the specified programs in fiscal 2016 (included in expenditures above).
6. The July 1, 2015, accounts payable balance was paid during fiscal 2016, and consisted of bills related to tutoring programs. Accounts payable at year-end total $60,000, of which $45,000 are bills related to tutoring program activities, and the remainder relates to after-school program activities.

Required

a. Record the transactions and adjustments for the fiscal year ended June 30, 2016.
b. Prepare The Learning Circle's statement of activities for fiscal year 2016, and its statement of financial position as of June 30, 2016.

LO 1, 2, 3   P13.4   Presentation of Corrected Financial Statements   The Chicago History Museum is a privately funded institution that promotes the history of Chicago and Illinois. It receives support from memberships, fees, grants and investment income. Suppose that the Museum's *unadjusted trial balance* at June 30, 2016, is as follows:

	Debit	Credit
Cash	$ 2,800,000	
Assets restricted to investment in plant assets	40,000,000	
Pledges receivable, net	53,000,000	
Supplies	4,500,000	
Land, buildings, and equipment, net	65,000,000	
Investments	12,500,000	
Accounts payable.		$ 2,200,000
Notes payable		80,000,000
Net assets—unrestricted, July 1, 2015		17,600,000
Net assets—temporarily restricted, July 1, 2015.		35,000,000
Contributions—unrestricted.		60,000,000
Contributions—temporarily restricted		44,700,000
Investment income—unrestricted		300,000
Expenses—exhibitions and programs	39,000,000	
Expenses—membership and development	1,000,000	
Expenses—administrative	8,000,000	
Expenses—building operations	14,000,000	
Totals	$239,800,000	$239,800,000

Additional information:

1. At the end of fiscal 2016, documented pledges were received in the amount of $5,000,000 per year for the next 10 years. These pledges have not been recorded. The appropriate discount rate is 4%, and no amounts are estimated to be uncollectible.
2. In fiscal 2015, the Museum received and properly recorded as restricted contributions a documented pledge in the amount of $10,000,000 per year for five years, to cover operating expenses. In fiscal 2016, the Museum recorded receipt of the first $10,000,000 installment as an unrestricted contribution. The appropriate discount rate is 4%.
3. The Museum recorded a $2,500,000 conditional contribution received in 2016 as an unrestricted contribution. The condition has not been met as of the fiscal year-end.
4. The Museum used $27,500,000 in donations restricted to the building fund for construction activities. This was recorded as an increase in land, buildings and equipment. The Museum also spent $4,000,000 in donations restricted to specific program activities, recorded as an increase in expenses for exhibitions and programs. Both expenditures reduced cash.

5. The following donated services were not recorded. Estimated fair values are in parentheses.
   - Tax and other financial services performed by CPAs ($500,000)
   - Maintenance services provided by neighborhood volunteers ($800,000)
   - Contractor services for construction of the building ($10,000,000)
6. The investments held at year-end have a fair value of $15,000,000. Investment gains are donor-restricted to specific program activities.

Required

a. Record the entries necessary to correct The Chicago History Museum's June 30, 2016 trial balance.
b. Prepare, in good form, The Chicago History Museum's fiscal 2016 statement of activities and its June 30, 2016, statement of financial position.

P13.5 Hospital Transactions The following information was taken from the books of Garden Court Hospital for the year ended December 31, 2018:   **LO 1, 2, 3, 4**

1. The hospital received $70,000,000 in cash from patients it cared for during the year. Another $35,000,000 is due from patients, and $20,000,000 is due from various insurance companies, all at standard charge rates. Revenues from other nursing services amounted to $3,000,000 and revenues from other professional services were $4,000,000. Only $2,500,000 of those revenues were collected in cash during the year. Other revenue, mostly from cafeteria sales, amounted to $1,500,000, received in cash. Except for cafeteria sales, all revenues flowed through accounts receivable.
2. Garden Court has certain agreements with various insurance companies under which standard rates were adjusted downward by $1,900,000. Garden Court is also involved in a community assistance program; the hospital provided $1,600,000 of charity and other free services costing $2,000,000 and billed at $3,800,000. These items were included as part of revenues in 1. Cost of the charity care is included in 4. An allowance for uncollectible accounts was established based on one percent of all revenue flowing through accounts receivable in 2018. Receivables written off in 2018 were $900,000.
3. Supplies costing $6,000,000 were ordered and received in 2018; however, only half have been paid for as of the end of 2018. A pharmaceutical company donated medicinal supplies with a fair value of $1,600,000. In addition, an appliance company donated a large refrigeration unit; its fair market value was $8,000,000.
4. Garden Court's principal expense categories are salaries and wages, supplies, and other operating expenses. An allocation of these expenses among the principal service categories shows the following:

	Wages and Salaries	Supplies	Other Expenses
Nursing services.	$2,500,000	$1,800,000	$2,000,000
General health care services	2,100,000	1,600,000	1,500,000
Professional services	1,200,000	1,200,000	1,700,000
Auxiliary services	2,600,000	800,000	1,000,000
Totals	$8,400,000	$5,400,000	$6,200,000

Of these expenses, $200,000 of wages and $900,000 of other operating expenses remain unpaid at year-end.

5. Early in 2018, Garden Court received a gift to be used for conducting research on a deadly and intractable disease. Of the $5,000,000 received, $2,800,000 was expended on the research. Another $2,000,000 was invested in bonds and earned interest of $100,000. The donor specified that investment income is restricted for the designated research purposes.
6. A friend of the hospital donated securities worth $25,000,000. The securities are to be held and 75 percent of the income is restricted for research on brain diseases; the balance is available for current operating expenses. During 2018, $1,900,000 in dividends were received and $1,500,000 was expended on the designated research.
7. The hospital is replacing its scanning equipment. Volunteers conducted a fund-raising campaign to finance the new equipment and raised $18,000,000 in cash. In order to cover the $50,000,000 cost of the equipment, a $32,000,000 loan was obtained. The hospital purchased the new equipment in late November. Sale of the old equipment (book value, $2,000,000) yielded $1,650,000 in proceeds.

Required

Prepare journal entries to record the transactions of Garden Court Hospital for 2018.

LO 1, 2, 3, 4 **P13.6** **Hospital Statement of Activities** The following information pertains to the activities of Montclair Hospital for the year ended December 31, 2018.

1.

Gross patient service revenue	$80,000,000
Charity allowances	15,000,000
Contractual discounts to third party payers	5,000,000

The hospital calculates a provision for uncollectibles at 5 percent of net patient service revenue.

2. Fair market value of noncash donations:

Volunteer workers in public-relations campaign	$200,000
Medical supplies donated by a pharmaceutical firm	800,000

3. Operating expenses, of which $3,000,000 are unpaid at year-end:

Professional patient care	$33,000,000
General services	9,500,000
Nursing services	10,000,000
Administrative services	3,500,000

4. The hospital conducts various educational programs for which it received fees of $500,000 during 2018.
5. The cafeteria and gift shop reported profit of $120,000 on sales of $1,320,000; operating costs are recorded as administrative expenses and are included in 3.
6. A retired doctor provided $1,000,000 to be used in validating the accuracy of a new cholesterol testing procedure. The funds were spent this year. In addition, $2,800,000 was spent for health education programs, using donor-restricted funds donated last year. Both expenditures were recorded as general services expenses.
7. In July, a donor established a trust in the amount of $6,000,000. Income from the trust is to be paid to the hospital until the donor's death. At that time, the principal is to be given to a local university. A local bank is appointed as trustee. Income received by the trust, and due to be distributed in 2018, amounted to $100,000. As of December 31, the bank had remitted only $60,000 to the hospital.
8. A donor's will provided for a bequest to the hospital of common stock of a public company. When the donor died on March 15, the stock was worth $1,500,000; at year-end it was worth $1,270,000.
9. A new X-ray machine was purchased for $4,000,000, using unrestricted cash.

Required

Prepare Montclair Hospital's 2018 statement of activities. Ignore beginning and ending net asset balances.

LO 1, 2 **P13.7** **Transactions and Financial Statements** Irvine Services is a private organization that provides community services for the prevention of substance abuse. The following events occur in 2016:

1. Cash contributions of $450,000 are received. Of this amount, $200,000 is donor-designated for educational program activities. The rest is unrestricted.
2. Contributions of $290,000 are promised to the organization during the year. Irvine has signed agreements from the donors that payment will be received in early 2017. It is estimated that 90 percent of these promises are collectible. Due to the short collection period, it is not necessary to report these promises at present value.
3. A donor contributes securities valued at $150,000, with the stipulation that the securities be held intact. The income is unrestricted. The value of the securities at year-end is $146,000. Dividends received on the securities during 2016 is $10,000.
4. Cash expenses for the year are:

General services	$ 30,000
Program services	480,000
Fund-raising	90,000

Included in the program services expenses above are $200,000 from contributions made last year which were donor-designated for educational program activities, and $160,000 from contributions made this year (see 1. above) which were donor-designated for educational program activities.

5. Volunteers contributed services as follows:
   - A local CPA provided accounting and payroll services valued at $6,000.
   - A contractor donated his services to finish the upper floor in the organization's office building. The fair value of these services is $50,000.

Required

Prepare Irvine Services' statement of activities for 2016. Beginning balances of unrestricted, temporarily restricted, and permanently restricted net assets were $230,000, $450,000, and $290,000, respectively.

P13.8 Accounting for Investments   The American Hereditary Disease Association, a private organization supporting research and education related to hereditary diseases, holds the following long-term investments at December 31, 2015:   **LO 3**

December 31, 2015	Market Value
Investment in mortgage bonds	$ 900,000
Investment in debt securities	1,500,000
Investment in equity securities	6,200,000

All debt investments were purchased at par value.

Notes:
1. The mortgage bonds were donated several years ago; the donor stipulated that the securities be held as a permanent endowment, and income on the securities be used for research projects relating to sickle cell disease. The market value of these securities was $870,000 when donated.
2. The debt securities are a recent investment of permanently restricted cash contributions of $1,500,000. There are no donor restrictions on investment income, gains or losses.
3. The equity securities are investments of permanently restricted cash contributions of $6,500,000. The donor specified that income and gains be restricted to community education programs on Crabbe's Disease.
4. Income on investments during 2016 was:

Interest on bonds	$ 45,000
Interest on debt securities	60,000
Dividends on equity securities	325,000

5. Market values at December 31, 2016 are:

Investment in bonds	$ 892,000
Investment in debt securities	1,700,000
Investment in equity securities	7,200,000

Required

Show how the events of 2016 are reported in the American Hereditary Disease Association's statement of activities. Identify the effect on each category of net assets.

P13.9 Statement of Activities   Suppose the information below was taken from the records of the **Milwaukee Art Museum, Inc.** All information pertains to activities for the year 2016.   **LO 1, 2, 3**

Restricted contributions	$ 9,200,000
Unrestricted contributions	56,000,000
Investment income	4,000,000
Expenses—administrative	3,900,000
Expenses—membership development	6,000,000
Expenses—fund-raising	1,500,000
Expenses—educational programs	40,000,000
Expenses—research	15,000,000

Additional information:

1. The Museum holds investments in debt and equity securities. The investment income listed above represents cash receipts of interest and dividends on these investments. $2,500,000 of this amount is donor-restricted to educational programs. The rest is unrestricted. In addition, $500,000 of interest and dividends has accrued as of year-end. All accrued investment income is unrestricted.

2. The investments in debt and equity securities held by the Museum increased in value by $900,000 during 2016. Of this amount, $400,000 relates to shares of stock donated several years ago, where the donor specified that the shares be held as a permanent endowment. $200,000 relates to perma-nently restricted cash that was invested in securities, with gains and income restricted to research activities, and $300,000 was unrestricted. The value of all these securities at the beginning of 2016 was significantly above their cost or donated value.

3. Included in educational programs expenses is $3,500,000 funded by contributions in past years that were restricted to educational programs. The Museum has just completed a capital campaign to raise money for a new wing to house the works of Wisconsin native Georgia O'Keeffe. During 2016, $4,000,000 was spent to begin construction on the new wing. All funds used were donor-restricted to the capital campaign.

4. All cash received from contributions was recorded as restricted or unrestricted contributions. Restricted contributions include $600,000 in permanently restricted contributions; the rest are temporarily re-stricted. In addition, documented unrestricted pledges of $2,200,000 were received in 2016, estimated to be 100 percent collectible. Of the cash contributions received in 2016, $1,200,000 recorded as unre-stricted contributions relate to pledges made in 2015 and are included in contributions revenue.

5. The beginning balances of net assets are as follows: Unrestricted, $22,000,000; temporarily restrict-ed, $24,000,000; permanently restricted, $6,000,000.

Required

Prepare Milwaukee Art Museum's 2016 statement of activities.

LO 1, 2   **P13.10 Complete Financial Statements**   The information below was taken from the records of Greenvale Community Day Care Center, a private not-for-profit organization, for the year 2016. The Center pro-vides free day care to low-income families.

1. Trial balance as of January 1, 2016:

Cash.	$ 100,000
Contributions receivable	152,000
Equipment and furnishings, net	2,500,000
Building, net	3,500,000
Accounts payable.	(220,000)
Salaries and wages payable.	(42,000)
Net assets—unrestricted	(5,010,000)
Net assets—temporarily restricted.	(980,000)
Total	$ 0

2. Unrestricted pledges of $4,250,000 were made during 2016, of which $4,200,000 was collected. In addition, the pledges outstanding on January 1, 2016, were collected in cash.

3. The Center won a state grant of $1,000,000 to support a new preschool program. To date, $600,000 of the grant has been received, and $300,000 has been spent on the program. Of the $300,000 spent, $100,000 was for salaries and wages and $200,000 was for equipment.

4. Donor-restricted resources are accumulated to purchase computers and software for child devel-opment programs. During the year, $350,000 was received for child development programs, and $400,000 was spent; $350,000 on computers and $50,000 for software. The Center capitalizes the computers and expenses the software.

5. Cash paid for salaries and wages during the year totaled $3,300,000. The balance of accrued salaries and wages as of year-end is $72,000. Salaries and wages are attributed as 20 percent administrative and 80 percent program services.

6. Expenses for utilities, food, and supplies totaled $750,000 for the year, all for program services. The year-end balance for accounts payable, all related to utilities, food, and supplies, is $170,000.

7. Depreciation for the year on equipment and furnishings, including the computers in 4. above, was $240,000. Depreciation on the building was $550,000. All depreciation is 25 percent administrative and 75 percent program services.

8. $250,000 in state grant money was temporarily invested in short-term debt securities near the end of the year. No interest revenue was earned on these investments in 2016, and their fair value at year-end equaled cost.

Required

Prepare, in good form, a statement of activities, statement of financial position, and statement of cash flows, using the direct method, for Greenvale Community Day Care Center for the year 2016. In the statement of cash flows, include a reconciliation of change in net assets to net cash provided by operating activities.

P13.11 Statement of Activities for a University Buena Vista University is a small private liberal arts university in Iowa. Suppose the following transactions and events occurred in 2016.   **LO 1, 2, 3, 4**

1. $180,000,000 in tuition was charged to students.
2. $24,000,000 in scholarships were awarded. In addition, tuition waivers for teaching assistantships totaled $12,000,000.
3. Securities were donated to the university. At the time of donation, the securities had a fair value of $15,000,000. The donor specified that the university must retain the securities, but any income is unrestricted. The securities increased in value to $18,000,000 by year-end.
4. Salaries and overhead for the year was as follows:

Instruction	$120,000,000
Research programs	24,000,000
Student services	6,000,000
Administration	12,000,000

5. Grants received from outside agencies totaled $2,000,000, and are unrestricted.
6. Cash gifts were received as follows: restricted to programs: $6,000,000, and restricted to the capital fund: $3,600,000.
7. The university spent $650,000 for building construction, financed by the capital fund. Program spending financed by restricted gifts totaled $5,200,000.
8. Investment income totaled $420,000. Of that amount, $280,000 is donor-restricted to programs, and $60,000 is restricted by the Board of Trustees to research programs.

Required

Prepare, in good form, the 2016 statement of activities for Buena Vista University. Assume beginning balances of net assets are $3,800,000 unrestricted, $4,000,000 temporarily restricted, and $22,000,000 permanently restricted.

P13.12 Prepare Complete Financial Statements The Make-A-Wish Foundation is a privately funded VHWO that grants wishes to children with life-threatening illnesses. Since 1980, it has reached over 300,000 children worldwide through a network of thousands of volunteers. Suppose the Foundation's trial balance as of January 1, 2017, follows: **LO 1, 2, 3, 4**

MAKE-A-WISH FOUNDATION
Trial Balance
January 1, 2017

(in thousands)	Dr (Cr)
Cash	$ 40,000
Contributions receivable	20,000
Property and equipment, net	12,000
Investments	120,000
Accounts payable	(8,000)
Notes payable	(1,000)
Unrestricted net assets	(135,000)
Temporarily restricted net assets	(30,000)
Permanently restricted net assets	(18,000)
Total	$ 0

Transactions and events for 2017 are as follows *(dollars in thousands)*:

1. Cash contributions of $157,500 were received. They consist of:
   (a) $150,000 received from the public as general contributions, either through the mail or at special fund-raising events.

(b) $6,000 in grants, of which $5,000 is designated for purchase of property and equipment, $50 is a permanent endowment, and $950 is unrestricted.

(c) $1,500 in permanent endowments received from the public.

2. The contributions receivable outstanding on January 2, 2017, represent the present value of promises to contribute, discounted at 5 percent. On December 31, 2017, $15,000 was received related to these promises. These promises are undesignated.

3. Additional promises to contribute $8,000 were made on January 2, 2017, to be received over the next five years. The present value of these contributions at January 2, 2017, discounted at 5 percent is $6,000. These promises were properly recorded as contributions receivable. At the end of 2017, $2,000 was received in cash on these promises. These contributions are undesignated.

4. The investments on hand at January 1, 2017 are:

(a) A donor contributed securities several years ago; fair value at January 1, 2017, is $15,000. The securities are permanently restricted. The fair value of the securities at December 31, 2017, is $12,000.

(b) $2,000 fair value of securities represent investment of permanently restricted cash contributions of $2,000 at the end of 2016. The fair value of these securities at December 31, 2017, is $1,500.

(c) The remainder of $103,000 fair value of securities are investments of excess cash and have a fair value of $98,000 at December 31, 2017.

(d) No securities were sold in 2017.

5. Undesignated endowments of $4,000 were donated during 2017, and the cash was invested in securities. There are no unrealized gains or losses on these investments in 2017.

6. Property and equipment of $12,000 was purchased in 2017. The $5,000 grant in 1. above was used to buy some of the property.

7. Investment income, received in cash, totaled $7,000. Of this amount, $2,000 is income restricted to specific wish fulfillment.

8. Expenses for 2017 were:

Wish granting	$150,000
Chapter support	10,000
Fund-raising	30,000
Management and general	16,000
Total	$206,000

$20,000 of this total represents spending for donor-specified activities. Also included is $1,500 depreciation on Foundation property. Accounts payable increased by $800 during 2017.

9. Volunteers supplied the following services to the Foundation:

(a) $6,000 fair value of management and general services, meeting the criteria for recognition.

(b) Public service announcements with a fair value of $32,000, that don't meet the criteria for recognition.

Required

a. Present Make-A-Wish Foundation's 2017 statement of activities and December 31, 2017, statement of financial position, in good form.

b. Present Make-A-Wish Foundation's 2017 statement of cash flows, in good form. Use the direct approach for the operating section, and provide a reconciliation of change in net assets to cash from operating activities.

LO 2 **P13.13 Promised Contributions**   In its fiscal 2013 consolidated financial statements, **The American Red Cross** reports the following information concerning contributions receivable (*in thousands*):

THE AMERICAN RED CROSS

	2013	2012
Amounts receivable within one year	$82,390	$71,778
Amounts receivable in 1 to 5 years, net of present value discount	12,205	16,030
Total contributions receivable before allowance for uncollectible amounts	94,595	87,808
Less allowance for uncollectible amounts	(2,087)	(1,767)
Contributions receivable, net	$92,508	$86,041

Amounts presented above have been discounted to present value using various discount rates ranging between 0.13% and 5.53%. Promises to be received in one year are not discounted to present value. The allowance for uncollectible amounts relates to the promises to be received in one year.

Suppose the Red Cross recorded new promises receivable within one year in the amount of $80 million, with $1.2 million estimated to be uncollectible. The present value of new promises receivable in 1 to 5 years totaled $10 million. During fiscal 2013, promises receivable in 1 to 5 years increased in value by $1 million due to the passage of time.

Required

a. Explain how the Red Cross determined the discount rates it used to report the present value of its contributions receivable in 1 to 5 years. Why does it use a discount rate of only 0.13% to record some promises, but 5.53% for others?
b. What amount of promises did the Red Cross write off as uncollectible in 2013?
c. How much cash did the Red Cross collect on promises receivable within one year?
d. How much cash did the Red Cross collect on promises receivable in 1 to 5 years?
e. Prepare the journal entries to record the above information. For items appearing on the statement of activities, indicate the category of net assets affected.

P13.14 Prepare Complete Financial Statements The information below was taken from the records **LO 1, 2, 3** of the International Society of Accounting Professionals, a private NFP organization, for the year 2017. The Society promotes the accounting profession through public events and member benefits. All dollar amounts below are in thousands.

The Society's trial balance at January 1, 2017, is as follows:

Cash.	$ 225
Investments	850
Contributions receivable	200
Buildings and equipment, net	4,000
Accounts payable.	(300)
Unrestricted net assets	(2,300)
Temporarily restricted net assets.	(1,700)
Permanently restricted net assets	(975)
	$ 0

Activities for 2017 are listed below. The Society reports expenses in three categories on its statement of activities: programs, administrative, and fund-raising.

1. Unrestricted cash contributions were $5,200.
2. Documented promises to contribute were received at the beginning of 2017. Their present value is $350, using a 4 percent discount rate. No cash was received during 2017 on these promises.
3. The contributions receivable of $200 outstanding at the beginning of 2017 are promises that were discounted at a 3 percent rate. At the end of 2017, $75 in cash is received on these promises. There are no donor restrictions on these contributions.
4. Permanently restricted cash endowments of $250 were received in 2017. The cash was immediately invested in securities. There are no donor restrictions on income or gains and losses.
5. The Society received a state grant of $500, restricted to the development of a special exhibit on accounting practice. The Society spent $400 in cash on the exhibit, all designated as program expenses.
6. Donor-restricted resources are accumulated for specific events. During the year, $200 of donor-restricted cash, received in previous years, was spent. Half was for program expenses and the other half was for equipment.
7. Out-of-pocket operating expenses for the year were $5,000. The year-end accounts payable balance, all related to operating expenses, was $280. Operating expenses are mostly joint costs, and are allocated 60 percent to programs, 30 percent to administrative, and 10 percent to fund-raising.
8. Depreciation for the year on buildings and equipment was $800. All depreciation is allocated as follows: 60 percent to programs, 35 percent to administrative, and 5 percent to fund-raising.
9. The following donated services were provided in 2017:
    a. Contractors donated services to build an addition to the building, fair value $160.
    b. CPAs donated services to handle payroll, taxes, and legal documents, fair value $75. These services are considered administrative.
10. Investment income for the year is $25, all received in cash. There are no donor restrictions on investment income.

11. The securities with a balance of $850 at the beginning of the year are a permanent endowment of securities; a donor gave these securities to the Society with the stipulation that they were not to be sold. The fair value of these securities at year-end is $835. The securities in 4. have a fair value of $270 at year-end.

Required

Prepare, in good form, the following financial statements for the International Society of Accounting Professionals.

a. Statement of activities for 2017.

b. Statement of financial position for 2017.

c. Statement of cash flows for 2017. Use the direct method for the operating activities section, and provide a reconciliation of change in net assets to cash from operating activities.

LO 1, 2, 3 **P13.15 NFP Financial Statements**   The mission of New York City's **American Museum of Natural History** is to "discover, interpret, and disseminate, through scientific research and education, knowledge about human cultures, the natural world, and the universe." Suppose its trial balance on June 30, 2016, is as follows (*in thousands*):

	Debit	Credit
Cash.	$ 40,000	
Contributions receivable	23,000	
Investments	540,000	
Plant and equipment, net.	470,000	
Accounts payable.		$ 23,000
Loans payable		310,000
Net assets—unrestricted		330,000
Net assets—temporarily restricted.		250,000
Net assets—permanently restricted.		160,000
	$1,073,000	$1,073,000

Activities for fiscal 2017 are listed below. Expenses are divided between **three categories** on the Museum's statement of activities: programs, administrative, and fund-raising. The Museum divides its statement of activities into operating and nonoperating items. All numbers are in thousands.

1. Cash received from contributions and grants was as follows: $113,000 unrestricted, and $98,000 donor-restricted to specific program-related research and exhibitions.

2. Documented promises with a present value of $8,000 were received. The increase in the present value of all promises during fiscal 2017 was $3,000. Cash received related to promises was $12,000.

3. Investments at the beginning of the fiscal year consist of $140,000 investments of excess cash, $100,000 donated securities that are permanently restricted, and $300,000 of permanently restricted cash that was invested in securities. All income, gains and losses are unrestricted. The following activities relate to these investments:

    a. $50,000 of investments of excess cash were sold during the year for $55,000.

    b. The donated securities increased in value to $115,000.

    c. The securities acquired with permanently restricted cash increased in value to $306,000.

4. $94,000 in cash received in the past from temporarily restricted contributions was spent during fiscal 2017 for program-related research and exhibitions.

5. Out-of-pocket operating expenses for the year, not including the expenditures in 4., were $150,000. The year-end accounts payable balance, all related to operating expenses, was $21,000. Operating expenses are allocated 60% to program services, 30% to administrative services, and 10% to fund-raising activities.

6. Donated legal and financial services had a fair value of $3,000, and were properly recognized as contributions per *ASC 958*. These services are classified as administrative. Contractors donated services with a fair value of $5,000 to build an addition to museum facilities.

7. Depreciation for the year on plant and equipment was $35,000. Depreciation is allocated 40% to programs and 60% to administrative. Plant and equipment with a book value of $22,000 was sold for $18,000.

8. Interest expense on the loans was $15,000, paid in cash. Principal payments of $8,000 were made. Interest is classified as administrative expense.

Required

a. Prepare the journal entries to record the events of fiscal 2017.
b. Prepare, in good form, the following financial statements for the American Museum of Natural History:
   (1) Statement of activities for fiscal 2017
   (2) Statement of financial position at June 30, 2017

REVIEW SOLUTIONS ··

Review 1 Solution

1.
Contributions receivable	4,330	
Contribution revenue—temporarily restricted		4,330
To record a documented pledge, discounted at 5%; $4,330 =		
$1,000 × 4.33, the present value of a 5-period ordinary annuity		
of $1 discounted at 5% per period.		
Contributions receivable	217	
Contribution revenue—temporarily restricted		217
To record increase in value of pledge; $217 = 5% × $4,330.		
Cash	1,000	
Contributions receivable		1,000
To record receipt of pledge payment.		
Net assets released from time restriction—temporarily restricted	1,000	
Net assets released from time restriction—unrestricted		1,000
To record release of time restriction for pledge payment.		

2.
Net assets released from use restriction—temporarily restricted	35,000	
Net assets released from use restriction—unrestricted		35,000
To record release of use restriction.		
Wish-granting expenses (reduces unrestricted net assets)	35,000	
Cash		35,000
To record cash expenditures for wishes.		

3.
Equipment	100,000	
Contributions revenue—temporarily restricted		100,000
To record contribution of equipment.		
Net assets released from time restriction—temporarily restricted	20,000	
Net assets released from time restriction—unrestricted		20,000
To record release of restriction for donated equipment depreciation.		
Depreciation expense (reduces unrestricted net assets)	20,000	
Accumulated depreciation		20,000
To record depreciation on donated equipment.		

4.
Administrative expenses (reduces unrestricted net assets)	40,000	
Property (asset)	25,000	
Contributed services (increases unrestricted net assets)		65,000
To record contributed services. Volunteer services for fund-raising		
do not meet recognition criteria.		

Review 2 Solution

GATEHOUSE FOUNDATION
Statement of Activities
For Year Ended December 31, 2016

		Unrestricted	Temporarily Restricted	Permanently Restricted
1.	Unrealized loss.	$(35,000)	—	—
	Dividend income.	4,000	—	—
2.	Unrealized loss.	(6,000)	—	—
	Dividend income.	—	$2,500	—
3.	Unrealized gain.	—	—	$3,000
	Dividend income.	6,000	—	—

Note: In part 2, the Foundation invested the donor's permanently restricted cash donation. The original donation amount is permanently restricted and the Foundation accepts the risk of value changes, affecting its unrestricted net assets.

14 Partnership Accounting and Reporting

LEARNING OBJECTIVES

LO1 Distinguish between the characteristics of a partnership and a corporation. (p. 613)

LO2 Record the formation of a partnership. (p. 619)

LO3 Allocate partnership income to partners. (p. 620)

LO4 Record the admission of a partner. (p. 624)

LO5 Record the retirement of a partner. (p. 630)

LO6 Determine appropriate cash distributions in partnership liquidations. (p. 633)

SUBURBAN PROPANE PARTNERS, L.P.
www.suburbanpropane.com

Suburban Propane Partners is a publicly traded limited partnership; its limited partnership interests trade like shares on the New York Stock Exchange under the symbol SPH. The company is engaged in the nationwide marketing and distribution of propane, fuel oils and refined fuel. It is the third largest retail marketer of propane in the U.S., serving more than 1.2 million active residential, commercial, industrial, and agricultural customers from approximately 750 locations in 41 states. As a publicly traded company, Suburban Propane Partners files financial reports with the SEC. Owners of its shares (units) receive cash distributions and are taxed on their share of Suburban's profits. Unlike corporate income, partnership income is not separately taxed.

Although most publicly-traded companies are organized as corporations, some are structured as partnerships. Most of these are limited partnerships, with a general partner (which itself may be a corporation) and a large number of limited partners. Suburban Propane has over 60 million units outstanding.

In this chapter you will learn how accounting for partnerships differs from corporations. The primary differences are in the accounting for equity interests. *Source:* Suburban Propane Partners, L.P. annual report, 2013.

CHAPTER ORGANIZATION

Distinguish between the characteristics of a partnership and a corporation	Record the formation of a partnership	Allocate partnership income to partners	Record the admission of a partner and the retirement of a partner	Determine appropriate cash distributions in partnership liquidations
• Characteristics of a partnership • Relations of partners to others • Partners' property rights • Limited partnerships • Partnership reporting issues	• Bonus approach • Goodwill approach	• Measuring partnership net income • Salaries and bonus to partners • Interest on capital accounts • Percentage allocation	• Admission by purchase of existing interest and by investment of new capital • Bonus and goodwill methods for admission • Retirement using personal assets and partnership assets • Bonus and goodwill methods for retirement	• Priorities for payments and rights of creditors • Simple liquidations • Installment liquidations • Calculation of safe payments • Preparing a cash distribution plan

INTRODUCTION

Despite the popularity of the corporate form of business organization, most businesses in the United States are sole proprietorships or partnerships. These business forms are easier and less costly to establish than forming a corporation. In addition, while a corporation is a separate taxable entity, the income from a sole proprietorship or a partnership is taxed directly to the owners. Relatively few partnerships are public entities like Suburban Propane; most are small, non-public entities. Financial information is still important to creditors and to the partners themselves. This chapter examines the partnership form of business organization and the applicable accounting procedures.

CHARACTERISTICS OF A PARTNERSHIP

The organizational and operational rules for partnerships derive from two sources: *law*—the **Uniform Partnership Act (UPA)**, and *contract*—the **partnership agreement**. The UPA has governed partnerships since 1914. It establishes law for partnership creation, rights and obligations between the partners, and between the partners and parties with whom the partnership does business. It also establishes rules for partnership dissolution. Substantial revisions in the 1990s updated and clarified the UPA's provisions, and, in particular, **established the partnership as an entity**, separate from its partners. The partnership holds assets, and the partners have an interest in the partnership. This concept makes it easier for the partnership to transfer property, and for partners to withdraw without requiring dissolution of the partnership. Partnerships are subject to the laws of the particular state in which they are organized. All states except Louisiana have adopted either the original UPA or the revised UPA.

LO1 Distinguish between the characteristics of a partnership and a corporation.

The Uniform Partnership Act defines a **partnership** as "an association of two or more persons to carry on as co-owners a business for profit."

Some implications of this definition are:

- The **actions** of individuals as they jointly conduct a business activity and share profits and losses **legally create a partnership** even if no formal agreement among the individuals exists.

- A partnership is considered to be an **entity distinct from the individual partners**.

- **Co-ownership of property**, even if that property is income-producing, **does not necessarily create a partnership**. For example, three individuals who jointly own a rental property do not constitute a partnership. The rental property is deemed a passive investment, not an ongoing business activity. However, the greater the activity by the owners, the more likely the entity becomes a partnership.

The term *persons* in this definition is not limited to individuals. Corporations or other legal entities may be partners. For example, Suburban Propane's general partner is Suburban Energy Services Group LLC.

Relations of Partners to Others

Each partner is considered an agent of the partnership. For most transactions, any one partner can act for the entire partnership and can legally enter into contracts that also bind the other partners. Known as **mutual agency**, this characteristic is of great convenience to partners in transacting business. Because one partner may act for the entire partnership, outsiders know that any partner they deal with legally represents the entire partnership. Mutual agency also imposes a risk on individual partners, as they are bound by the actions of fellow partners.

Although any one partner may enter into transactions on behalf of the partnership, all partners are liable for the partnership's obligations. Partners are **liable jointly and severally**; the partnership group is liable for the partnership obligations and each partner has personal liability which could extend to the entire partnership obligation. Creditors of the partnership can seek to collect the full amount of the partnership debt from a single partner. Because partners' obligations are not limited to their investments in the partnership—personal assets are also at risk—partners assume **unlimited liability**. To reduce personal liability, many partnerships are now organized under limited liability company (LLC) or limited liability partnership (LLP) laws, not under the partnership laws.

Relations Among Partners

The UPA provides that the rights and duties of the partners in relation to the partnership shall be determined, subject to any agreement between them, by the following rules:

- **Each partner shall be repaid all contributions**, whether capital or advances (loans) to the partnership, and **share equally in the profits and surplus** remaining after all liabilities, including those to partners, are satisfied. Each partner must contribute toward the losses sustained by the partnership according to each partner's share in the profits.

- **The partnership must compensate (indemnify) every partner** for payments made and personal liabilities reasonably incurred by a partner in the ordinary and proper conduct of its business, or for the preservation of its business or property.

- A partner who makes any payment or advance beyond the amount of capital which the partner agreed to contribute, **shall be paid interest** from the date of payment or advance.

- A partner shall **receive interest** on the capital contributed only from the date when repayment should be made.

- All partners have **equal rights** in the management and conduct of the partnership business.

- **No partner is entitled to compensation** for conducting partnership business, except that a surviving partner is entitled to reasonable compensation for services in winding up the partnership affairs.

- **No person can become a member** of a partnership **without the consent** of all the partners.

- Any difference arising as to ordinary matters connected with the partnership business may be decided by a **majority of the partners**; but no act in contravention of any agreement between the partners may be done rightfully without the consent of all the partners.

The partnership agreement may modify the above statutory rules. For example, the partners could agree to divide profits and losses in unequal shares. When no specific agreement exists, however, the provision of the UPA regarding equal sharing applies.

Partners' Property Rights

The UPA defines two specific property rights which a partner possesses:

1. The partner possesses a **partnership interest**—a right to a share of the capital and profits. This right to a share of profits and to receipt of distributions is transferable by the partner to another party. Such a transfer does not confer partner status on the recipient, give the recipient any managerial rights in the partnership, or entitle the recipient to financial or business information from the partnership.
2. The partner has a **right to participate in managing the partnership**. However, a partner is not a co-owner of partnership property, and has no transferable interest in such property.

Contractual Provisions: The Partnership Agreement

The **partnership agreement**, sometimes referred to as the **articles of partnership**, is a contract among the partners. On certain matters, such as the allocation of income among partners, the contractual agreement takes precedence over the provisions of the UPA. On other matters, such as the rights of outside parties, the agreement cannot be at variance with the law. In general, the partnership agreement deals with the following matters:

- Characteristics of the partnership, such as its name, nature of its business activity, location, duration, and fiscal year.
- Methods of allocating partnership income to the partners.
- Procedures for admitting new partners and for settling a partner's interest upon withdrawal or death, including life insurance to be carried on partners and buy-sell agreements.

Limited Partnerships

The discussion thus far focuses on **general partnerships** in which all partners can participate in the management of the firm and all are liable for the partnership's obligations. Another type of partnership, the **limited partnership**, has both general partners (at least one) and limited partners. The general partner(s) manage the firm and have all the rights and obligations previously discussed. The limited partners invest capital and have the right to a specified share of income or loss but have no right to participate in management. Their liability for the partnership's obligations is limited to their investment in the partnership.

Limited partnerships are often used when large amounts of investment capital are needed and tax treatment as a partnership is desired. A general partner initiates the project, such as real estate development or natural resource exploration, and finances it by selling limited partnership interests to investors. The general partner acquires the needed capital without relinquishing management control, and investors acquire a right to share in income without bearing any personal responsibility for partnership liabilities. Limited partnerships can have a variety of governance and ownership structures. Three popular limited partnerships are known as LLCs, LLPs, and MLPs.

A **limited liability company (LLC)** combines many of the organizational and tax treatments of a general partnership with the limited liability protection of a corporation. Like a corporation, an LLC has articles of organization, and in many states, a governing board. LLC owners also have limited liability for partnership obligations. Like a partnership, an LLC's income is passed through to its partners, avoiding double taxation of income and dividends and offering tax benefits for partnership losses. LLCs can be managed by their owners or by professional managers. There is no limit on the number of owners, which can include corporations.

The **limited liability partnership (LLP)** retains the tax benefits and many of the organizational features of a LLC. However, corporations cannot be owners, and, of greater importance, at least one of the managing partners must be liable for the partnership's obligations. Other partners and investors can enjoy limited liability as long as they are not active managers. Organizations offering professional services, such as law firms, group medical practices, and CPA firms, are almost always organized as LLPs. If a CPA firm is organized as an LLP, an individual partner involved in a negligent audit is personally liable, but a partner not involved in the engagement in any way is not personally liable.

The **master limited partnership (MLP)** retains the tax benefits of limited liability partnerships, but their shares trade on markets, like common stock, increasing the partnership's ability to raise funds, and making it easier for investors to buy and sell ownership interests. The MLP has a general partner that manages the business in return for some form of incentive pay. The limited partners own shares (units) in the MLP, and receive cash distributions. To avoid federal taxation of partnership income, 90 percent or more of an MLP's income must come from natural resources, commodities, or real estate related transactions. Suburban Propane is organized as an MLP.

In recent years, most general partnerships converted their legal status to LLC, LLP, or MLP. However, the major characteristics of partnership operations and accounting procedures for these forms of partnerships follow those of the general partnership.

Reporting Perspective

Many partnerships are small local businesses with few partners. In such cases, mutual agency and joint and several liability may be manageable characteristics; each partner is likely to be aware of the actions of the other partners. But some partnerships, such as international CPA firms, are large national or international enterprises with hundreds or thousands of partners. Mutual agency and joint and several liability may cause major problems in these firms. For example, suppose a partner in the Los Angeles office of a CPA firm presides over an audit failure that leads to a large liability judgment against the firm. Under general partnership law, every partner in the firm, whether in New York or Grand Rapids, Michigan, has potential personal liability for the judgment, even though he or she had absolutely no involvement with the failed audit.

Historically, professionals such as CPAs, attorneys and physicians were not allowed to limit personal liability by organizing their affairs as corporations. Creation of the LLC and LLP forms of organization largely remedies the problem of joint and several liability for professionals. Under these newer organizational arrangements, partners involved in a particular engagement are personally liable for damages arising out of that engagement but their liability does not extend to their partners who are not involved in the engagement.

BUSINESS APPLICATION   Tax Benefits of Master Limited Partnerships

Remember that partners are taxed on partnership *income*, not distributions. For tax purposes, the excess of distributions over taxable income reduces the investor's cost basis, with no tax effect until the investment is sold. MLPs are in the natural resources, commodities, or real estate sectors, and take particular advantage of the various tax credits and deductions the IRS makes available to stimulate the economy. Since their cash distributions are based on distributable cash flow, these distributions are often considerably higher than reported income. The excess cash distribution reduces the basis of the investment, and is taxed at the investor's personal tax rate only when the investment is sold. This makes investment in an MLP more valuable to the investor, who receives current cash distributions but defers much of the related tax effect.

Comparison of Corporate and Partnership Forms of Organization

Each form of partnership organization possesses advantages and disadvantages. A general partnership ceases to exist legally when a new partner enters or an existing partner retires or dies, but the partnership agreement can provide for continued business operations seemingly unaffected by changes in partnership personnel. All partners must consent to transfers of ownership interests. In a limited partnership, the entity ceases to exist when a general partner is no longer present. Interests of the limited partners are freely transferable whereas changes in the general partner's interest are subject to consent of all other partners. The tax law treats all qualified partnerships as **conduits**. Transactions with tax effects pass through to the partners; no income tax is levied on the partnership itself. This feature may or may not be a benefit, depending on the tax status of the partners.

A corporation is formed under a charter granted by a governmental entity. Shareholders have no personal liability for the corporation's debts, and have no right to participate in management, although they do elect the corporation's governing board of directors. The life of a corporation is generally unlimited and shares are freely transferable. Most corporations are taxable entities, as are those partnerships that possess corporate characteristics. Because income taxes are levied on the corporation and on certain distributions to shareholders, "double taxation" can result.

Partnership Reporting Issues

Partnership financial information is used by the partners, its creditors, and tax authorities (Internal Revenue Service). Being a business entity, a partnership uses regular business GAAP. Partnerships and corporations use the same standards for revenue and expense recognition and asset and liability valuation. There are, however, a few important areas where partnership accounting differs from corporate accounting.

Like a corporation, a partnership is a separate accounting entity distinct from the individual partners. However, the partners are often actively involved in the firm; they are not absentee owners. This fact influences the concept of net income for a partnership as well as the treatment of owners' equity. Corporate owners' equity is reflected in several accounts—common stock, additional paid-in capital, and retained earnings—but a corporation does not maintain separate equity accounts for each stockholder. Partnership equity, on the other hand, is recorded in **capital accounts** that reflect the partners' shares of invested capital and undistributed earnings. A separate capital account is maintained for each partner. These accounting considerations also apply to sole proprietorships, with only a single capital account for the sole proprietor.

Income Allocations Versus Payments to Partners   When discussing the distribution of partnership income to the individual partners, one must distinguish between:

1. **Allocations to partners**, which are *credits* to the partners' capital accounts for their respective shares of partnership income (or debits for their shares of partnership loss).
2. **Payments to partners**, which are *debits* to their capital accounts reflecting the transfer of resources from the partnership to the partners. These payments are often called **drawings**.

Measuring Partnership Income   Although partnerships employ the same revenue and expense recognition criteria as corporations, net income has a special meaning in a partnership. In corporate accounting, net income signifies the *return to the corporation*; the return to the owners/shareholders comes in dividends and capital gains. In partnership accounting, however, net income signifies the *return to the owners/partners*. In addition to being investors, partners may also render personal services in the day-to-day conduct of business and may loan money to the partnership. It can be difficult to separate these roles. Stockholders of a corporation may also be employees of, or lenders to, that corporation, but these roles are more distinct; salaries and interest paid to them are subtracted from revenue in computing corporate net income.

Accounting and tax requirements necessitate a careful distinction between the corporate entity and the individual, along with a distinction among the individual's possible roles as stockholder, employee, and lender. These distinctions are not particularly useful in a partnership because a partnership does not have the formal legal status of a corporation and is not a taxable entity.

When partners have multiple involvement in the financial affairs of the partnership—as investors, employees, and lenders—it can be difficult to distinguish among: (1) compensation for services performed, (2) interest on loans, and (3) return on capital invested. Certain income allocations may be called *salaries*, other allocations *interest*, and still others *shares of profit*. The lack of arm's-length transactions in valuing these allocations causes the various role distinctions to be disregarded—all income allocations to partners are considered to be divisions of partnership net income. In other words, net income of a partnership is determined *before* any allocations are made to partners; allocations such as *salaries and interest to partners are not treated as expenses*. Similarly, net income of a sole proprietorship is the return to the proprietor; *no compensation to the proprietor is subtracted*.

Another area of difference between corporation and partnership net income is the treatment of income taxes. As noted earlier, a corporation is a taxable entity, but a partnership is a conduit through which income flows to the individual partners. The individual partners include their share of partnership income—their allocations—and any special tax-treatment items on their personal income tax returns. *The income statement of the partnership does not report income tax expense*.

Partnership Income Allocations Once the partnership's net income is determined, it must be allocated among the individual partners. Because all allocations to partners are viewed as divisions of partnership net income, partnership agreements frequently consider the various roles—investor, employee, lender—that partners hold. The partnership agreement should specify the income allocation rules. These rules may be simple or complex, sometimes calling for salary, interest, and bonus allocations. If the partnership agreement is silent, the law requires income to be divided equally among all partners.

Capital Changes Another important issue in accounting for partnerships involves changes in the capital structure. Such changes include initial formation of partnerships, investments and withdrawals by the partners, subsequent entry and exit of individual partners, and eventual liquidation of partnerships. Partnerships frequently report these events in a schedule of changes in capital accounts, similar to the corporate statement of changes in stockholders' equity.

Summary of Reporting for Partnership Operations Corporate accounting standards for revenue and expense recognition and asset and liability valuation generally apply to partnerships. As a result, accounting matters specific to partnerships focus on events affecting the capital accounts that represent the owners' equity accounts. These accounts combine invested capital and undistributed income and are impacted by:

1. **Investment of capital.** An individual partner's capital account is affected not only by the partner's own investment, but also by the investments of new partners and retirements of existing partners.
2. **Allocation of net income.** As stated, partnership net income—the return to the partners—is determined before subtracting any compensation to the partners. Then the partnership's net income is allocated to the partners in accordance with the partnership agreement, or in equal shares if the partners have not agreed otherwise. The income shares are credited to the partners' capital accounts. When a loss occurs, the partners' loss shares are debited to their capital accounts.
3. **Withdrawal of capital.** Amounts withdrawn by partners from invested capital or undistributed income allocations are debited to each partner's capital account. When withdrawals are made in anticipation of income allocations, they are debited to separate **drawing accounts** for each partner that are closed at year-end to the capital accounts. For example, if partner Burns draws $500 per month to help with living expenses, the following entry is made monthly:

Drawing—Burns...	500	
Cash		500
To record monthly drawing.		

At year-end, the balance in the drawing account is closed, as follows:

Capital—Burns...	6,000	
Drawing—Burns		6,000
To close drawing account to capital; $6,000 = $500 × 12.		

Use of drawing accounts is optional; withdrawals may be directly debited to the capital accounts.

• •

Reporting Perspective

In Chapter 3 of this text, we learned that when a company follows GAAP, its financial statements must include, or consolidate, the accounts of all entities it controls. The company may have a financial relationship with a limited partnership, and therefore must determine whether the partnership should be included in its consolidated financial statements. Typically a general partner of a limited partnership consolidates the partnership, since the general partner has the authority to make decisions within the partnership. However, if the limited partners can block the general partner's decisions through **kick-out** or **participating rights**, the general partner may not control the partnership. Each situation requires careful analysis to identify the controlling entity, and clear documentation of the process used to determine whether or not to consolidate.

• •

FORMATION OF THE PARTNERSHIP

Accounting for the formation of a partnership requires setting values for assets contributed by the partners and establishing the initial capital account balances. Assets contributed to a partnership in exchange for a capital interest are recorded at fair market value. Issues arise when one or more partners contribute identifiable assets with a relative fair value that differs from their stated interest in the partnership. For example, two partners may contribute cash of $500,000 and $800,000, respectively, for equal interests in the partnership.

LO2 Record the formation of a partnership.

Bonus and Goodwill Approaches

Establishing the opening balance in each partner's capital account can be complicated even though fair market values of the contributed assets are known. The simplest approach sets each partner's capital account equal to the fair market value of net assets invested. Suppose Prince and Quinn form a partnership. Prince invests $30,000 cash, and Quinn invests land and a building having a combined fair market value of $75,000, subject to a $35,000 mortgage that the partnership assumes. Thus Quinn invested net assets with fair market value of $40,000 (= $75,000 − $35,000). When each partner's capital account is set equal to net assets invested at fair market value, we have:

Cash.	30,000	
Land and building.	75,000	
Mortgage payable		35,000
Capital—Prince		30,000
Capital—Quinn		40,000
To record formation of partnership.		

Alternatively, the partners could specify a capital percentage for each partner that provides each partner with an agreed-upon percentage interest in initial total partnership capital. This approach could generate several different entries to record the partnership's formation, depending on the agreement between Prince and Quinn. One approach assigns the total capital based on the agreed-upon capital percentages of the respective partners. Suppose that Prince and Quinn decide that each will have a 50 percent interest in the partnership's initial capital. Perhaps the reason the partners agreed on equal capital balances while making unequal tangible investments is that one partner, Prince in this case, brings certain talents, contacts, or other intangible benefits to the partnership.

Because Prince invested $30,000 and Quinn invested $40,000, they must decide how to apply their capital percentages to determine their opening capital balances. Two approaches are possible:

1. **Bonus approach**: divide the total capital of $70,000 according to the capital percentages, in this case equally, and credit each partner with $35,000. This situation implies a capital transfer, or *bonus*, of $5,000 from Quinn to Prince. Under the **bonus approach to partnership formation,** the entry is:

Cash.	30,000	
Land and building.	75,000	
Mortgage payable		35,000
Capital—Prince		35,000
Capital—Quinn		35,000
To record formation of partnership under the bonus approach.		

2. **Goodwill approach**: assume that Prince contributes enough intangible assets in the form of talents and contacts to bring the investments, and the capital balances, into the desired relation. We record this intangible asset, called **goodwill**, in an amount sufficient to achieve the desired relation among the capital accounts. Quinn's contribution of $40,000 of tangible net assets establishes the amount that Prince's investment must meet. In the current example, we need to record $10,000 (= $40,000 − $30,000) of goodwill to make Prince's investment equal to Quinn's. Under the **goodwill approach to partnership formation**, the entry is:

Cash.	30,000	
Land and building.	75,000	
Goodwill	10,000	
Mortgage payable		35,000
Capital—Prince		40,000
Capital—Quinn		40,000
To record formation of partnership.		

When forming a partnership, the partners must specify which accounting approach is to be used. Choice of method depends on the extent to which the partners agree to recognize the goodwill certain partners may bring to the partnership, and whether one or more partners are willing to be credited for an amount that is less than the fair value of the assets they contribute.

When an existing business entity, currently operated as a proprietorship, becomes that partner's investment in the partnership, revaluation of proprietorship assets may be necessary to reflect the fair market value of assets being transferred to the partnership, and intangible assets may be recognized. After settling these matters, the partners record their investments in an entry signifying formation of the partnership.

REVIEW 1 • Formation of a Partnership

Abel, Baker and Cahn form an insurance agency, as equal partners. Abel invests $100,000 cash; Baker invests $30,000 cash and has extensive experience in the insurance industry. Cahn invests a building worth $200,000, subject to a mortgage of $125,000, and office equipment having a fair value of $17,000.

Required

a. Record the formation of the partnership under the bonus method.
b. Record the formation under the goodwill method.

Solutions are located after the chapter assignments.

ALLOCATION OF PARTNERSHIP INCOME TO PARTNERS

LO3 Allocate partnership income to partners.

As previously discussed, partnership net income does not reflect expenses for partners' salaries or interest. Because such provisions are considered in allocating partnership net income among the individual partners, a multifactor allocation procedure may be used. Although partners may agree to use any factors, three common ones are:

1. A **salary factor**, representing compensation for the personal services a partner provides to the operations of the partnership.
2. An **interest factor**, a return on the capital each partner has invested.
3. A **percentage factor**, the agreed income-sharing ratio to allocate income or loss remaining after providing for any salaries and interest.

Salaries to Partners

Allocations of net income in the form of salary allowances are typically established by the partnership agreement. This agreement usually specifies (1) each partner's amount or (2) a formula, such as a bonus formula, based on the time, effort, or experience that each partner contributes to the business. For example, the DEF partnership might agree that D's annual salary is $200,000, E's is $50,000, F receives no salary, and any remaining income or loss is to be divided equally among the partners. Suppose partnership net income for the year is $370,000. The allocation first provides for the $250,000 in salaries and then divides the remaining $120,000 in the income-sharing ratio, yielding the following allocation of partnership net income:

	D	E	F	Total
Salaries	$200,000	$50,000	$ 0	$250,000
Balance	40,000	40,000	40,000	120,000
Net allocation	$240,000	$90,000	$40,000	$370,000

The partnership agreement should specify whether salary and other allocations are to be **fully implemented**, even if they exceed partnership net income. *We assume full implementation unless otherwise stated.* In the DEF example, assume that net income is $160,000 and that salaries are to be fully implemented. Because the $250,000 salary allocation exceeds net income; the $90,000 "loss" is then allocated by the income-sharing ratio, as follows:

	D	E	F	Total
Salaries	$200,000	$ 50,000	$ 0	$250,000
Balance	(30,000)	(30,000)	(30,000)	(90,000)
Net allocation	$170,000	$ 20,000	$(30,000)	$160,000

When partners' salaries or other income allocation devices are not fully implemented, the partnership agreement must specify the order for applying the various devices. The partners could agree to first implement salaries, followed by interest on capital balances, and so forth. Moreover, the partners must agree on a procedure for partial implementation of any income-sharing device. In the above example, income of $160,000 is not enough to implement even the salaries, let alone any other income allocation device. Two of the many possible approaches are (1) allocate D's salary first or (2) allocate using D's $200,000 salary and E's $50,000 salary in the proportion that the salary of each bears to total salaries of $250,000. Using the proportional basis in (2), the $160,000 of income is allocated as follows:

	D	E	F	Total
Net allocation	$128,000*	$ 32,000**	$ 0	$160,000

* $128,000 = ($200,000/$250,000) × $160,000
** $ 32,000 = ($50,000/$250,000) × $160,000

Bonus to Partners

Allocation of net income to partners for services rendered may reflect a bonus based on profit, perhaps in addition to a fixed salary. In discussing various bonus relationships, we use the following symbols:

   X = Net income before bonus
   B = Amount of bonus
   Y = Net income after bonus (= $X - B$)
   R = Percentage rate of bonus

When we define the bonus as a percentage of net income before the bonus, we have:

   $B = RX$

When the bonus is defined as a percentage of the net income that remains *after* the bonus, we have a somewhat more complex formula:

   $B = RY$
   $B = R(X - B)$
   $B = RX/(1 + R)$

For example, assume net income before the bonus is $300,000 and the bonus rate is 25 percent of net income after the bonus, an amount currently unknown. Using the above formula, we calculate the bonus as follows:

   $B = RX/(1 + R)$
   $B = (0.25 \times \$300,000)/1.25$

B = \$75,000/1.25
B = \$60,000

We can verify that the \$60,000 bonus is 25 percent of Y, the \$240,000 of net income after the bonus (Y = \$300,000 − \$60,000).

Many other bonus possibilities exist, including different percentages based on different levels of income. Or the bonus could be determined after implementing one income-sharing device, such as salaries, but before implementing another, such as interest on capital accounts.

Interest on Partners' Capital Accounts

Allocations of net income may also reflect interest allowances on partners' capital accounts. A specified interest rate is usually applied to *weighted average capital balances*. Suppose a partner's capital account has a balance of \$60,000 on January 1, additional capital of \$200,000 is invested on March 1, and \$20,000 is withdrawn on September 1. The *weighted average capital balance* for the year is:

Period	Capital Balance	Fraction of Year	Weighted Average
January 1–February 28.	\$ 60,000	2/12	\$ 10,000
March 1–August 31	260,000	6/12	130,000
September 1–December 31	240,000	4/12	80,000
Total			\$220,000

If the specified interest rate is 8 percent, \$17,600 (= 0.08 × \$220,000) of the partnership net income is allocated to this partner for interest on the average capital balance.

As with salary allocations to partners, any interest-based allocation of net income may be fully implemented, even if it exceeds total net income. Any remaining income or loss created by previous allocations is divided according to the percentages in the income-sharing ratio.

Percentage Allocation by Income-Sharing Ratio

A percentage allocation formula, or **income-sharing ratio**, always exists for a partnership. Although the entire net income of the partnership can be allocated by this percentage formula, some income may be allocated by salaries, by interest, or both. In the latter case, the amount of partnership net income remaining after full implementation of salaries and interest, whether positive or negative, is allocated by the income-sharing ratio.

The partnership agreement sets forth the income-sharing ratio. Although a single set of percentages is typically applied to all forms of income, the partners may agree to divide different types of income, or expense, in different ways. When the partnership agreement fails to specify an income-sharing ratio, the Uniform Partnership Act provides that all partners share equally.

Comprehensive Illustration of Partnership Net Income Allocation

Thomas, Underwood, and Vickers are partners in a printing firm. Their partnership agreement contains the following income allocation provisions:

- Thomas devotes two days per week to partnership business and receives an annual salary of \$150,000. Underwood and Vickers work full time and receive annual salaries of \$350,000 and \$300,000, respectively.

- Vickers, who is responsible for sales, receives a bonus equal to 10% of any net income, before allocations, in excess of \$1,000,000.

- The partners receive 10% interest on their weighted average capital balances, before considering allocations of salaries and bonus.

- After implementing these three allocations, allocate any remaining income or loss 50% to Thomas, 30% to Underwood, and 20% to Vickers.

Suppose that partnership net income for 2016 was $1,500,000. The partners' capital balances at the beginning of the year were: Thomas, $690,000; Underwood, $400,000; and Vickers, $400,000. Underwood invested another $100,000 on March 31, 2016. At the end of each quarter, the partners withdrew a total of $60,000, divided according to the income-sharing percentages—Thomas withdrew $30,000, Underwood $18,000, and Vickers $12,000. Thomas withdrew an additional $180,000 on October 31, 2016. Exhibit 14.1 shows the allocation of 2016 income.

EXHIBIT 14.1 Illustration of Income Allocation

	Thomas	Underwood	Vickers	Total
Salaries.	$150,000	$350,000	$300,000	$ 800,000
Bonus*	—	—	50,000	50,000
Interest**	61,500	44,800	38,200	144,500
				994,500
Balance***	252,750	151,650	101,100	505,500
Totals	$464,250	$546,450	$489,300	$1,500,000

*Bonus is 10 percent of $500,000 (=$1,500,000 − $1,000,000)

**Weighted average capital is calculated as follows. 10% of the weighted average capital is the amount of interest.

	Thomas	Underwood	Vickers
January 1–March 31	$690,000 × 3/12 = $172,500	$400,000 × 3/12 = $100,000	$400,000 × 3/12 = $100,000
April 1–June 30	660,000 × 3/12 = 165,000	482,000 × 3/12 = 120,500	388,000 × 3/12 = 97,000
July 1–September 30	630,000 × 3/12 = 157,500	464,000 × 3/12 = 116,000	376,000 × 3/12 = 94,000
October 1–October 31	600,000 × 1/12 = 50,000	446,000 × 1/12 = 37,167	364,000 × 1/12 = 30,333
November 1–December 31	420,000 × 2/12 = 70,000	446,000 × 2/12 = 74,333	364,000 × 2/12 = 60,667
Weighted average	$615,000	$448,000	$382,000

***The balance of $505,500 is allocated 50% to Thomas, 30% to Underwood, and 20% to Vickers.

Schedule of Changes in Capital Accounts

Partnerships frequently summarize the events affecting the partners' capital accounts during an accounting period in a **schedule of changes in capital accounts**. Exhibit 14.2 illustrates this schedule using the information for the year ended December 31, 2016, for Thomas, Underwood, and Vickers.

EXHIBIT 14.2 Schedule of Changes in Capital Accounts

Event	Capital Accounts			
	Thomas	Underwood	Vickers	Total
Beginning balance, January 1	$690,000	$400,000	$400,000	$1,490,000
Investment, March 31	—	100,000	—	100,000
Drawings, March 31	(30,000)	(18,000)	(12,000)	(60,000)
Drawings, June 30	(30,000)	(18,000)	(12,000)	(60,000)
Drawings, September 30	(30,000)	(18,000)	(12,000)	(60,000)
Withdrawal, October 31	(180,000)	—	—	(180,000)
Income allocation, December 31*	464,250	546,450	489,300	1,500,000
Drawings, December 31	(30,000)	(18,000)	(12,000)	(60,000)
Ending balance, December 31	$854,250	$974,450	$841,300	$2,670,000

*From Exhibit 14.1.

When the schedule of changes in capital accounts is included with the formal financial statements prepared by a partnership, items such as Drawings appear in total on a single line.

REVIEW 2 • Income Allocation

The Abel, Baker & Cahn Insurance Agency completed its first year of operations, earning a net income of $177,000. Assume the bonus method was used to record the formation of the partnership (see Review Problem 1). Abel is Baker's father-in-law; Abel is not active in the business, but agreed to invest to help get the agency under way. Baker is the manager of the agency and the primary salesperson. Cahn also sells insurance, but he is less experienced than Baker. The partnership agreement provides that Abel receives 15 percent interest on his beginning-of-year capital balance. Baker receives an annual salary of $80,000 and a 10 percent bonus on partnership income above $100,000. Cahn receives 8 percent interest on beginning-of-year capital and a $40,000 salary. Remaining profits are divided equally. All salary, bonus, and interest provisions are to be fully implemented.

Required
a. Determine the allocation of the partnership's net income.
b. Assume that salaries and the bonus were distributed in cash to the appropriate partners. Calculate the capital balances at year end.

Solutions are located after the chapter assignments.

ADMISSION OF A NEW PARTNER

LO4 Record the admission of a partner.

A new partner may be admitted to a partnership with the consent of the continuing partners. The new partner may gain admission through purchase of an existing partnership interest, or by investing new capital.

In the illustrations that follow, assume the partnership of Arthur Associates has this balance sheet at June 30, 2017:

ARTHUR ASSOCIATES
Balance Sheet
June 30, 2017

Various assets	$140,000	Liabilities.	$ 50,000
		Capital	
		Arthur $31,000	
		Bradley 26,000	
		Crowe 33,000	90,000
Total assets	$140,000	Total liabilities and capital	$140,000

Assume further that the partners' income-sharing ratio is as follows: Arthur, 50%; Bradley, 20%; and Crowe 30%.

Admission by Purchase of an Existing Partnership Interest

A new partner may enter an existing partnership by purchasing the interest of one or more existing partners. Such a transaction occurs between the old and new partners as individuals and usually has no direct effect on the partnership accounts. This parallels the case in which one individual sells shares of stock in a corporation to another individual. Only the two individuals are involved in the transaction; the corporation makes no entry other than to update its stockholder records. In a similar manner, when one individual buys an existing partnership interest, the only partnership entry usually needed transfers the capital account from the old partner to the new.

Transfer of Capital Interests   The usual method of accounting for a purchase of an existing partnership interest is to transfer the capital balance of the selling partner to a new capital account established for the entering partner. The amount of the entry is the existing capital balance of the selling partner, which may be different from the selling price.

Purchase from One Partner   Suppose that on July 1, 2017, Findley purchases Crowe's entire partnership interest for $45,000. The partnership records the transfer of Crowe's capital balance to Findley as follows:

Capital—Crowe	33,000	
Capital—Findley		33,000
To record transfer of partnership interest from Crowe to Findley.		

The $45,000 purchase price has no bearing on the partnership entry. Crowe realized a gain of $12,000 on the sale of the partnership interest, assuming Crowe's basis is $33,000. The cost (and tax basis) of Findley's partnership interest is $45,000, despite the fact that the partnership books show the capital account as $33,000. Findley's cost of $45,000 has no effect on any capital-based distributions the partnership makes. However, the $45,000 cost affects the amount of taxable gain or loss recognized by Findley when that partnership interest is sold.

Purchase from Several Partners   A new partner may purchase a portion of the interest of several partners. Suppose that Grogan buys a 25 percent interest in Arthur Associates by purchasing 25 percent of each partner's interest for $28,000. We could simply record the transfer of 25 percent of each partner's capital interests to Grogan.

Capital—Arthur	7,750	
Capital—Bradley	6,500	
Capital—Crowe	8,250	
Capital—Grogan		22,500
To record transfer of 25% interest to Grogan.		

The debits to the capital accounts of the three existing partners represent 25 percent of their respective capital balances. As before, the $28,000 purchase price has no bearing on the entry. The three existing partners recognize gains or losses as individuals on the sale of part of their partnership interests.

A new income-sharing ratio must be established for the four partners. We typically assume that the contract for the new partnership specifies that (1) the new partner's percentage of income is the same as the capital balance percentage and (2) the old partners maintain their income-sharing relationship. After Grogan joins the firm, therefore, the partners share income as follows: Arthur, 37.5%; Bradley, 15%; Crowe, 22.5%; and Grogan, 25%. These percentages are based on the fact that the old partners now own 75% of the partnership: Arthur has 50% of 75%, or 37.5%; Bradley has 20% of 75%; and Crowe has 30% of 75%.

Recognition of Implied Goodwill   Admission of a new partner by purchase of an existing partnership interest is usually recorded by transferring capital accounts as described above. Another approach involves recognizing implied goodwill. Under this approach, we use the purchase price to infer the value of the entire partnership. To illustrate, again consider the case where Grogan buys 25 percent of each partner's interest for $28,000.

If Grogan is willing to pay $28,000 for a 25 percent interest in the partnership, the entire partnership must be worth $112,000 (= $28,000/0.25). But the partnership books show only $90,000, the total capital of Arthur, Bradley, and Crowe. This implies that $22,000 (= $112,000 implied total value – $90,000 recorded capital) of unrecorded assets exist. We call these unrecorded assets *goodwill*, unless we have evidence that other identifiable assets are undervalued. We first record the goodwill, apportioning a share to each existing partner according to the established income-sharing ratio of 50% for Arthur, 20% for Bradley, and 30% for Crowe. The entry to record the **implied goodwill** is as follows:

Goodwill	22,000	
Capital—Arthur		11,000
Capital—Bradley		4,400
Capital—Crowe		6,600
To record implied goodwill.		

We now make the entry transferring 25 percent of each partner's capital to Grogan:

Capital—Arthur (25% × 42,000)	10,500
Capital—Bradley (25% × 30,400)	7,600
Capital—Crowe (25% × 39,600)	9,900
Capital—Grogan	28,000
To record transfer of 25% interest to Grogan.	

Under the implied goodwill approach, the credit to the new partner's capital account equals the amount paid to acquire the interest. Unless the agreement covering the purchase of partners' interests specifically provides for recognizing implied goodwill on the partnership books, the transfer of capital interests method should be used.

Admission by Investment of New Capital

A new partner may enter an existing partnership by investing directly in the partnership: the new partner contributes an agreed-upon amount of assets—cash, property, or services to the partnership. In return, the new partner receives an agreed-upon share of capital at date of entry and a specified share of subsequent income and loss. This agreed-upon capital percentage is used to establish the new partner's initial capital balance. Thereafter, the income percentage guides the division of subsequent profits and losses among the partners. In many cases, the capital percentage and income percentage are equal. When they are not equal, their use is guided by the following rule:

Capital percentage (capital-sharing ratio) is used to establish the value of the firm and the total amount of goodwill.

Income percentage (income-sharing ratio) is used to allocate goodwill or bonus to partners and to allocate income.

The partnership records the investment of assets by the new partner, the capital account of the new partner, and any adjustments needed to reconcile the two. When the investment by the new partner equals the new partner's capital percentage times the new capital (old capital plus assets invested) no accounting problem exists. For example, suppose that on July 1, 2017, Edwards invests $10,000 in Arthur Associates in exchange for a 10 percent interest in capital and income (hereafter referred to as a 10 percent interest). We have the following:

1. Investment by Edwards = $10,000.
2. Edwards' share of new capital = 10% × ($90,000 old capital + $10,000 invested by Edwards) = 10% × $100,000 = $10,000.

Since Items 1 and 2 are equal, we make the following entry:

Assets...	10,000	
Capital—Edwards		10,000
To record investment by Edwards.		

When the new partner does not invest an amount equal to the capital share, the amount of the investment may be more or less than the share of new capital. Consider the following cases:

Case A
Edwards invests $9,000 for the 10% interest:

1. Investment by Edwards = $9,000.
2. Edwards' share of new capital = 10% × ($90,000 + $9,000) = $9,900.

Case B
Delano invests $12,000 for a 10% interest:

1. Investment by Delano = $12,000.
2. Delano's share of new capital = 10% × ($90,000 + $12,000) = $10,200.

In Cases A and B above, the investment differs from the computed share of capital. When this situation occurs, the disparity must be reconciled in one of two ways before the entry recording the investment can be made.

1. Consider the share of capital amount (item 2 in Cases A and B) to be the correct amount credited to the new partner's capital account. The difference between this amount and the amount invested is treated as an adjustment of the existing partners' capital accounts. This is known as the **bonus method of admission**.

2. Consider the invested amount (item 1 in Cases A and B) to be the correct amount credited to the new partner's capital account. Bring the investment and the share of capital (item 2) amounts into agreement by inferring the existence of intangible assets and adding these either to the capital of the new partner or to the capital of the existing partners. This is known as the **goodwill method of admission**.

The partnership agreement should specify the methods to be used when admitting a new partner to the partnership. The following sections discuss and illustrate both methods.

Bonus Method of Admission   The bonus method of admission avoids revaluing assets and recognizing goodwill when a new partner enters.

Under the **bonus method of admission**, the total capital of the new partnership after admission of the new partner equals the capital before admission plus the investment of the new partner. The new partner's capital account is credited with the agreed-upon share of the total capital.

Suppose that the new partner's investment is less than the computed share of capital, as in Case A above, where Edwards invests $9,000 but receives a $9,900 share in capital. In such a situation, the existing partners have some reason for admitting Edwards at this less-than-fair-share price. Perhaps Edwards brings some important talents or resources to the firm, and to obtain these the existing partners subsidize Edwards' admission by giving a $9,900 share for only $9,000. The $900 difference is charged against the existing partners' capital accounts in their income-sharing percentages. Here is the entry to record Edwards' admission for a 10 percent interest with an investment of $9,000:

Cash.	9,000	
Capital—Arthur.	450	
Capital—Bradley	180	
Capital—Crowe	270	
Capital—Edwards		9,900
To record Edwards' admission under the bonus method.		

The Edwards admission, in which the new partner's investment is less than the computed capital balance, results in a **bonus to the new partner**.

Suppose the new partner's investment is more than the computed share of capital, as in Case B above, where Delano invests $12,000 for a $10,200 share in total capital. Here the existing partners are able to command a premium when admitting a new partner. Perhaps the assets of the partnership are worth more than their book value. Perhaps the partnership has above-average earning potential. Or perhaps the existing partners wish to be compensated for the risk and effort they incurred in establishing the firm. In any event, to gain admittance Delano must contribute not only a fair share of assets, $10,200, but another $1,800 that is credited to the capital accounts of the existing partners in their income-sharing percentages. The entry to record Delano's admission for an investment of $12,000 in exchange for a 10% interest, is as follows:

Cash.	12,000	
Capital—Arthur		900
Capital—Bradley		360
Capital—Crowe.		540
Capital—Delano.		10,200
To record Delano's admission under the bonus method.		

The Delano admission, in which the new partner's investment is more than the computed capital balance, results in a **bonus to the existing partners**.

Goodwill Method of Admission   The goodwill method of admission specifically provides for asset revaluation and goodwill recognition supported by the amount of the new partner's investment.

> The **goodwill method of admission** attributes the difference between the amount invested by the new partner and the share of capital initially calculated to the presence of unrecorded intangible assets or other undervalued assets. This method reconciles the difference by recording these unrecorded or undervalued assets.

Any goodwill recorded in admitting a new partner is evaluated periodically for impairment.

Goodwill to the New Partner   Suppose the new partner's investment of tangible assets is less than the initially computed share of capital, as in Case A above, where Edwards invests $9,000 cash for a $9,900 share in net assets. To explain this imbalance, we infer that Edwards brings something more to the firm than $9,000 cash—perhaps some special skills or talents—such that the existing partners will admit Edwards as a 10 percent partner for $9,000. Calculation of the goodwill proceeds as follows:

1. Calculate the total value of the new firm implied by the capital of the existing partners. In the current example, existing capital amounts to $90,000. Because the existing partners will have a 90 percent interest in the new partnership, the total value of the new partnership must be $100,000 (= $90,000/0.9).
2. Calculate the new partner's share of this total value. In the current example, Edwards' share is $10,000 (10 percent of $100,000).
3. The goodwill invested by the new partner is the difference between the share of the firm's calculated value and the amount of tangible assets invested. In this example, Edwards invested $1,000 of goodwill (= $10,000 share of firm's value − $9,000 cash invested).

The entry to record Edwards' admission follows:

Cash.	9,000	
Goodwill.	1,000	
Capital—Edwards		10,000
To record Edwards' admission under the goodwill method with goodwill to new partner.		

Goodwill to the Existing Partners   Suppose that the new partner's investment of tangible assets is more than the initially computed share of capital, as in Case B above, where Delano invests $12,000 cash for a $10,200 share in net assets. Perhaps this imbalance results from the net assets of the existing partnership being understated. Some of the firm's tangible assets may have market values in excess of their book values. Or the firm may have unrecorded goodwill in the form of established customers, product recognition, and skillful management. The fact that a new partner will pay more than book value for a partnership interest supports the notion that undervalued or unrecorded assets exist. We bring the new partner's investment into balance with the share of net assets, acknowledging these unrecorded asset amounts, calculated as follows:

1. Calculate the total value of the new firm implied by the new partner's investment. In the current example, the fact that Delano invests $12,000 for a 10 percent interest implies a total value of the new partnership of $120,000 (= $12,000/0.10).
2. Calculate the amount by which assets are understated. In this example, net assets are recorded at $90,000. Delano's investment of $12,000 brings the total to $102,000. Because we calculated the value of the new firm to be $120,000, assets are understated by $18,000 (= $120,000 − $102,000).
3. Revalue reported assets and record previously unreported identifiable intangible assets as appropriate to correct the $18,000 understatement of assets. If objective evidence supporting these revaluations is not available, the full amount of the understatement is allocated to goodwill.

The following entry is used to record Delano's admission, assuming the $18,000 understatement of assets is attributed entirely to goodwill:

Cash..	12,000	
Goodwill..	18,000	
Capital—Arthur...		9,000
Capital—Bradley..		3,600
Capital—Crowe...		5,400
Capital—Delano...		12,000
To record Delano's admission under the goodwill method with goodwill to existing partners.		

Effects of Bonus and Goodwill Methods on Partners' Capital

In general, the bonus and goodwill methods do not yield the same capital balances for the individual partners or the same total capital for the partnership.

Total Partnership Capital after Admission of New Partner	
Bonus Method	**Goodwill Method**
Total capital before admission + Amount invested by new partner	Total capital before admission + Amount invested by new partner + identifiable asset revaluations and goodwill recorded

Compare the bonus and goodwill results obtained in the illustrations for Arthur Associates. The total capital before admission was $90,000. New partner Edwards invested $9,000. Under the goodwill method, $1,000 of goodwill was attributed to Edwards. The capital balances after admission follow:

	Bonus Method	Goodwill Method
Arthur..	$30,550	$ 31,000
Bradley	25,820	26,000
Crowe..	32,730	33,000
Edwards..	9,900	10,000
Totals...	$99,000	$100,000

In the other illustration, new partner Delano invested $12,000. Under the goodwill method, $18,000 of goodwill was attributed to the existing partners. The capital balances after admission follow:

	Bonus Method	Goodwill Method
Arthur..	$31,900	$ 40,000
Bradley	26,360	29,600
Crowe..	33,540	38,400
Delano	10,200	12,000
Totals...	$102,000	$120,000

Evaluation of Bonus and Goodwill Methods

In comparing the bonus and goodwill methods, we find the rationales for the discrepancy between investment and share of net assets to be similar, but the accounting conclusions are quite different. An investment *smaller* than the computed share of net assets—Case A in the preceding illustrations—is explained in terms of the intangible benefits the new partner brings to the firm. The goodwill method recognizes these intangibles as an asset. The bonus method transfers capital from the existing partners to the new partner, to obtain these intangible benefits for the firm.

An investment *larger* than the computed share of net assets—Case B in the preceding illustrations—is explained in terms of understated or unrecorded asset values presently existing in the partnership. The goodwill method records these increases in asset values and the bonus method transfers capital from the new partner to the existing partners, to obtain an interest in these assets.

In sum, both the bonus and goodwill methods deal with the presence of unrecorded assets signaled by the amount invested by an incoming partner. The bonus method is conservative in that it avoids recording intangible assets whose presence and value are difficult to verify and which may have no realizable value upon liquidation. However, the goodwill approach has a better theoretical foundation. Because admission of a new partner creates a new economic entity, a new basis of asset accountability is appropriate. The transaction that occurs—investment by an outsider, the new partner—provides the basis for revaluing partnership assets.

RETIREMENT OF A PARTNER

LO5 Record the retirement of a partner.

A partner may leave a continuing partnership due to retirement, death, or other reasons. The Uniform Partnership Act uses the term **dissociation** to characterize this form of ownership change. There is a settling up with the dissociated partner or his/her estate, based on the fair value of the partnership at the date of dissociation. Accounting for the change in ownership depends on whether the dissociated partner is paid by the continuing partners, using their personal assets, or by the partnership, with partnership assets.

Purchase with Personal Assets

Suppose the remaining partners, as individuals, purchase the interest of the retiring partner with their personal assets. This transaction, between the retiring partner and the remaining partners, occurs outside the partnership; the partnership need only transfer the capital balances. To illustrate, the partners in KLM Associates have capital balances and income-sharing percentages as follows:

Partner	Capital Balance	Income Share
Keenan	$ 75,000	45%
Ludlow	60,000	30%
Morris	30,000	25%
Totals	$165,000	100%

If Keenan and Ludlow buy Morris' interest for $60,000, Morris' $30,000 capital balance must be transferred to Keenan and Ludlow. If the purchasers retain their relative income-sharing ratio (45:30, or 3:2), $18,000 is credited to Keenan and $12,000 to Ludlow, as follows:

Capital—Morris	30,000	
Capital—Keenan		18,000
Capital—Ludlow		12,000
To record Morris' retirement and purchase of her interest by Keenan and Ludlow.		

This treatment is similar to procedures discussed earlier for admitting a new partner by purchase of an existing interest. In that case, however, the purchase transaction with an outside party could lead to recognition of implied goodwill on the partnership books. No outside party is involved in this retirement case; all participants are partners. Without an arm's-length transaction, the existence of credible market value to support goodwill recognition is unlikely.

Purchase with Partnership Assets

Now suppose the retiring partner receives assets directly from the partnership in settlement of that individual's capital interest.

Determination of Payment to Retiring Partner Settlement with a retiring partner should reflect the fair value of the partner's interest, but one cannot expect this value to equal the balance in the retiring partner's capital account. The partnership agreement should prescribe an equitable approach for setting the payment to the retiring partner. When forming the partnership, the partners should agree upon a method of valuing a partner's interest in the event of dissociation. They could use a formula, such as "five times the partner's average share of income over the preceding three years, plus the balance in the capital account." Or they could base the value on an outside appraisal of the partnership's net assets. When the partnership agreement does not address these issues, the parties must agree on valuation procedures at the time of retirement.

Accounting for Retirement The retiring partner's capital account must be removed from the partnership books, and any differences between the payment and the capital balance accounted for. We first assume that the retiring partner is paid with partnership cash. When the payment includes other partnership assets, those assets are adjusted to fair market value before recording their distribution to the retiring partner. Any difference between fair market value and book value is entered in the partners' capital accounts according to their income-sharing percentages.

Accounting for a partner's retirement via distribution of partnership assets is similar to accounting for admission of a new partner via direct investment in the partnership. Where payment to the retiring partner equals that partner's capital balance, the entry is as follows:

Capital—Retiring Partner	XXX	
Cash (or other assets)		XXX
To record retirement of partner.		

When the payment does not equal the capital balance, we account for the difference by either the bonus or goodwill method.

Bonus Method Suppose the partners agree to pay Morris $55,000. Under the bonus method, the $25,000 difference between the $55,000 payment and the $30,000 balance in Morris' capital account is transferred from Keenan and Ludlow to Morris. This entry records the bonus.

Capital—Keenan	15,000	
Capital—Ludlow	10,000	
Capital—Morris		25,000
To record retirement bonus to Morris.		

The bonus is charged against Keenan and Ludlow in their respective income shares (45:30, or 3:2). The next entry records the payment to Morris and removes Morris' capital account.

Capital—Morris	55,000	
Cash		55,000
To record retirement payment to Morris.		

When Morris receives *less* than the $30,000 capital balance, the difference is transferred from Morris to Keenan and Ludlow. For example, if Morris is paid $22,000, we record the retirement as follows:

Capital—Morris	30,000	
Capital—Keenan		4,800
Capital—Ludlow		3,200
Cash		22,000
To record Morris' retirement under the bonus method.		

Now the bonus of $8,000 (= $30,000 − $22,000) is credited to the remaining partners in their 3:2 income-sharing ratio, with $4,800 credited to Keenan and $3,200 to Ludlow.

Goodwill Method   The goodwill method calls for asset revaluations when a positive or negative difference exists between the settlement amount and the retiring partner's capital balance. A positive difference means that existing assets are written up, identifiable intangible assets or goodwill are recorded, or both. Alternatively, a negative difference means that existing assets are written down.

Two interpretations of the goodwill method exist: the *partial goodwill approach* and the *total goodwill approach*. Either can be applied to upward or downward asset revaluations. Use of the retirement payment to justify asset revaluations is less supportable in the retirement case than in the admission case because the retirement transaction is with one of the partners and is not arm's-length. Moreover, if the retirement payment includes an inducement to buy out an unproductive or dissident partner, it may not be evidence of undervalued assets or goodwill at all.

The **partial goodwill approach** limits revaluations of assets triggered by a partner's retirement to the difference between the settlement price and the retiring partner's capital account. When the payment exceeds the capital balance, we first revalue any identifiable undervalued assets and attribute any remaining difference to goodwill. When the payment is less than the capital balance, we first write down overvalued assets to the extent of the difference. Asset revaluations under the partial goodwill approach are charged or credited only to the retiring partner's capital account. In contrast, the **total goodwill approach** calls for a revaluation of the entire partnership, with the change in value to be charged or credited to the capital accounts of all partners according to their income-sharing ratio.

Illustration of Goodwill Approaches   Returning to the example of Morris' retirement from KLM Associates, assume that Morris receives $55,000, that Morris' capital account balance is $30,000, and that the partners determine that identifiable assets are appropriately valued. The *partial goodwill approach* calls for recognizing $25,000 of goodwill—the difference between the settlement price and the capital balance. The *total goodwill approach* follows the logic that if $25,000 of goodwill is attributable to Morris' 25 percent interest, then total goodwill of the firm is $100,000 (= $25,000/0.25) This entire amount should be recognized and allocated to the partners according to their income-sharing percentages. The *total goodwill approach* yields total partnership capital, before Morris' retirement, of $265,000, the original $165,000 capital plus $100,000 of goodwill.

Exhibit 14.3 illustrates application of these two variations of the goodwill method under three independent assumptions regarding Morris' retirement from KLM Associates.

EXHIBIT 14.3 Comparison of Partial and Total Goodwill Approaches: KLM Associates				
Assumption	**Partial Goodwill Approach**		**Total Goodwill Approach**	
Excess payment is attributed to goodwill				
Morris' retirement payment is $55,000	Goodwill 25,000		Goodwill 100,000	
	Capital—Morris. . . .	25,000	Capital—Keenan. . .	45,000
			Capital—Ludlow . . .	30,000
			Capital—Morris. . . .	25,000
	Capital—Morris 55,000		Capital—Morris 55,000	
	Cash	55,000	Cash	55,000
Excess payment is attributed to undervalued land $15,000 and to goodwill				
Morris' retirement payment is $55,000	Land 15,000		Land 15,000	
	Goodwill 10,000		Goodwill 85,000	
	Capital—Morris. . . .	25,000	Capital—Keenan. . .	45,000
			Capital—Ludlow . . .	30,000
			Capital – Morris. . . .	25,000
	Capital—Morris 55,000		Capital—Morris 55,000	
	Cash	55,000	Cash	55,000
Difference is attributed to overvalued land				
Morris' retirement payment is $22,000	Capital—Morris 8,000		Capital—Keenan 14,400	
	Land	8,000	Capital—Ludlow. 9,600	
			Capital—Morris 8,000	
			Land	32,000
	Capital—Morris 22,000		Capital—Morris 22,000	
	Cash	22,000	Cash	22,000

Accountants should evaluate the propriety of revaluing assets and recognizing goodwill upon retirement on a case-by-case basis. The lack of an arm's-length transaction and the presence of motives for "excess" payments that do not signify the presence of asset revaluations and goodwill must be kept in mind. Accountants should insist that other evidence supporting the amounts of revaluations and goodwill recognized be provided to substantiate amounts recorded.

REVIEW 3 • Retirement of a Partner and Admission of a New Partner

The Abel, Baker and Cahn Agency is established and has a successful first year. Abel wishes to resign from the partnership. It is agreed that he will receive his original $100,000 investment, plus 20 percent of the partnership's net income to date, $177,000. (See Review Problem 2 for information on the partners' income-sharing and capital balances.)

Required

a. Record Abel's resignation using the bonus approach.
b. Record Abel's resignation using the partial goodwill approach.
c. Record Abel's resignation using the total goodwill approach.

Subsequent to Abel's resignation, which was recorded by the total goodwill approach, the remaining partners admit Dexter as a 20 percent partner in exchange for a cash investment of $28,000. Dexter brings skills in insurance fields different from those of Baker and Cahn.

d. Record Dexter's admission using the bonus approach.
e. Record Dexter's admission using the goodwill approach.

Solutions are located after the chapter assignments.

PARTNERSHIP LIQUIDATIONS

Previous discussion in this chapter assumes the partnership continues after a change in ownership. In this section the partnership is dissolved and its net assets are liquidated. Reasons for this type of termination include:

LO6 Determine appropriate cash distributions in partnership liquidations.

- Bankruptcy of the partnership.
- Partners agreed that the partnership would exist for a limited time or until a certain purpose was accomplished. For example, a partnership is created to buy a tract of land and to develop and sell subdivision lots; when all lots are sold and paid for, the partnership is dissolved.
- Desire to terminate an unsuccessful partnership.
- Partners wish to pursue other activities.
- Conversion to a sole proprietorship by the remaining partner.
- Reorganization as a corporation.

Accounting for partnership liquidations emphasizes the proper sequence of distributions to the partners when the liquidation extends over a period of time. The proper sequence preserves equity among the partners, particularly when the proceeds do not cover all partners' investments.

Priorities for Payments

The sequence of liquidating distributions must consider: (1) outside creditors'claims against partnership assets, and (2) partners'claims on partnership assets resulting from loans of personal assets to the partnership, investments in the partnership, and the right to share in undistributed income of the partnership.

Liquidation distributions go first to outside creditors and then to partners. When considering partners' claims, the sequence of liquidation distributions can be more complicated. The law identifies three subcategories of partners' claims: partners' loans, partners' invested capital, and partners' undistributed income. However, there is little difference between partners' invested capital and the undistributed income, closed annually to the capital accounts. Partners' drawings typically do not specify whether they are withdrawals of capital or income. There is also little practical difference between partners' loans or partners' invested capital, even though loans to the partnership are to be paid off before invested capital.

Partnership law requires partners to contribute sufficient capital to cover a **capital deficiency**—a debit balance in the capital account. If a partner with a capital deficiency made loans from personal assets to the partnership, then the **right of offset** applies the loan payable balance to the deficiency. Thus if the partner has insufficient invested capital, the loan payable to the partner, instead of being paid off first, becomes another component of invested capital and increases the capital balance. Similarly, a loan receivable from a partner decreases the capital balance.

Suppose Partner A has a capital deficiency—an amount due to the partnership—of $8,000 and also made a loan to the partnership of $10,000. The *right of offset* enables Partner A to receive $2,000 of the liquidation proceeds. Similarly, if the partnership has a loan receivable from a partner, the right of offset calls for the loan to increase the capital deficiency.

Although more complexity may exist in particular cases, we use the **following two-step priority sequence for distribution of cash in a partnership liquidation**:

1. Outside creditors
2. Partners' combined loans and capital

In partnership liquidations, therefore, the first concern is to meet obligations to outside creditors. After providing for payment of outside creditors, we focus on the proper sequence for distributing, to the partners, any remaining cash arising during the liquidation process.

Rights of Creditors

Both partnership creditors and individual partners' creditors have legal rights to available resources during a partnership liquidation. *Creditors of the partnership* must first seek payment of their claims from partnership assets. If the partnership is technically insolvent, the partnership creditors may seek payment from any partner; therefore, the partnership is technically solvent so long as any individual partner is solvent. Thus a partner can be individually liable for any and all claims against the partnership.

Creditors of an individual partner must first seek payment of their claims from the individual. If the individual is insolvent, creditors have a claim against all of that partner's assets, including the partnership interest. Such claims are not limited to the individual's insolvency. The creditor that obtains a judgment against the individual may petition the court for a *charging order*. A **charging order** specifies that any partnership payments to which the individual partner becomes entitled shall be made to the creditor. These payments include distributions of profits and withdrawals of capital. The debtor remains as a partner and the creditor does not assume any of the rights of partnership. A charging order amounts to a lien on the partner's interest until the judgment is repaid.

When a creditor's claim is so large that there is no prospect that the partnership distributions will repay it within a reasonable time, the court may order **foreclosure**, sale of the partnership interest for the benefit of the creditor. As previously discussed, a partnership interest is transferable property. The purchaser of that interest does not automatically become a partner, but does acquire the rights to distributions held by the previous partner.

When the partnership and all partners are insolvent, the relative rights of partnership creditors and individual creditors to the assets of the various parties become important. Partnership creditors and individual creditors have equal standing with respect to the assets of an insolvent partner. Partnership creditors retain their priority over individual creditors with respect to *partnership assets*, but all unsecured parties have equal claim to an individual's assets.

Simple Versus Installment Liquidations

Liquidation of a partnership may be carried out in several ways.

- All assets may be sold in a single transaction, at a going-business price.
- The assets may be sold in a single transaction at distress prices, perhaps at a bankruptcy auction.
- Some assets might be sold individually over a period of time, as buyers for specific items are found, while other assets, such as receivables and prepayments, are collected or otherwise consumed.
- The partners may seek distribution of cash as it becomes available, before all assets are liquidated.

The timing of cash distributions to partners influences the accounting procedures. In a **simple liquidation** or **lump-sum liquidation**, all assets are sold before any cash distributions to partners. When cash distributions to partners occur before the sale of assets is complete, an **installment liquidation** exists. Some assets are sold and some cash is distributed, then additional assets are sold and more cash is distributed, and so on, producing a series of payments to the partners.

Simple Liquidations

Determining the proper distribution of cash to partners of a liquidating partnership can be straightforward or complex. Even in the *simple liquidation* situation, any partners that have initial capital deficiencies or develop them during the liquidation complicate settlement.

Successful Liquidating Partnerships   One views a liquidating partnership as *successful* when all partners receive a return of capital. This means that the sale of partnership assets produces either a net gain, or a net loss small enough that no capital deficiencies result. In this case, proper distribution of cash to outside creditors and to partners is easily accomplished.

Suppose that the JKL partnership has the following balance sheet immediately prior to liquidation.

JKL PARTNERSHIP Balance Sheet			
Cash	$12,000	Liabilities	$17,000
Other assets	48,000	Capital—J	21,000
		Capital—K	6,000
		Capital—L	16,000
Total assets	$60,000	Total liabilities and capital	$60,000

The three partners share income in a 2:1:1 ratio. If the other assets are sold for $64,000 and the resulting $16,000 gain is allocated to the partners, the accounts show the following:

Cash	$76,000	Liabilities	$17,000
		Capital—J [$21,000 + (0.5 × $16,000)]	29,000
		Capital—K [$6,000 + (0.25 × $16,000)]	10,000
		Capital—L [$16,000 + (0.25 × $16,000)]	20,000
Total assets	$76,000	Total liabilities and capital	$76,000

With sufficient cash to pay off the outside creditors, and no capital deficiencies, the $76,000 can be distributed in amounts equal to the liability and capital balances: $17,000 to the outside creditors, $29,000 to J, $10,000 to K, and $20,000 to L.

Unsuccessful Liquidating Partnerships   An unsuccessful liquidating partnership occurs when losses from the sale of assets result in one or more capital deficiencies. Suppose a partner has a capital deficiency, after offsetting any loans payable to that partner against the debit balance in the capital account. The partner may invest resources sufficient to remedy the deficiency such that enough assets are then available to pay the creditors and the other partners. If the deficient partner cannot invest enough to eliminate the deficiency, the deficiency is allocated to the other partners before assets are distributed.

Suppose that the pre-liquidation balance sheet of the XYZ partnership is:

XYZ PARTNERSHIP
Balance Sheet

Cash............................	$ 10,000	Liabilities............................	$ 20,000
Loan receivable—Z	8,000	Loan payable—X	6,000
Other assets......................	100,000	Loan payable—Y	4,000
		Capital—X	41,000
		Capital—Y	10,000
		Capital—Z	37,000
Total assets	$118,000	Total liabilities and capital	$118,000

The partners share income and loss in a 5:3:2 ratio, respectively. If the other assets are sold for $30,000, we allocate the $70,000 (= $100,000 − $30,000) loss on the sale as follows:

	Capital Accounts Before Loss	Loss Allocation		Capital Accounts After Loss
Partner X...............	$41,000	(0.5 × $70,000) =	$(35,000)	$ 6,000
Partner Y	10,000	(0.3 × $70,000) =	(21,000)	(11,000)
Partner Z...............	37,000	(0.2 × $70,000) =	(14,000)	23,000
Totals	$88,000		$ 70,000	$18,000

Thus Y has a capital deficiency of $11,000, before considering the loan payable to Y of $4,000.

Since the partnership owes $4,000 to Y, $7,000 is Y's net deficiency. If Y invests $7,000, and we offset Y's loan against the capital account, the accounts appear as follows. The cash balance of $47,000 equals the original $10,000 plus the $30,000 sale proceeds and Y's $7,000 investment.

Cash............................	$47,000	Liabilities...........................	$20,000
Loan receivable—Z	8,000	Loan payable—X	6,000
		Capital—X	6,000
		Capital—Y	0
		Capital—Z	23,000
Total assets	$55,000	Total liabilities and capital	$55,000

After offsetting the loan receivable from Z against Z's capital account, the cash is distributed as follows:

Outside creditors	$20,000
Partner X...	12,000
Partner Y	0
Partner Z ($23,000 − $8,000)..	15,000
Total cash distributed..	$47,000

Now suppose that Y is personally insolvent. Because Y cannot invest any resources to remedy the deficiency, after the $4,000 owed to Y is offset against Y's capital account the accounts show the following:

Cash............................	$40,000	Liabilities...........................	$20,000
Loan receivable—Z	8,000	Loan payable—X	6,000
		Capital—X	6,000
		Capital—Y	(7,000)
		Capital—Z	23,000
Total assets	$48,000	Total liabilities and capital	$48,000

Because Y is unable to invest further, X and Z must absorb Y's deficiency. We allocate Y's $7,000 deficiency to X and Z in the 5:2 income-sharing ratio, charging X with $5,000 and Z with $2,000, producing these new account balances:

Cash	$40,000	Liabilities	$20,000
Loan receivable—Z	8,000	Loan payable—X	6,000
		Capital—X	1,000
		Capital—Y	0
		Capital—Z	21,000
Total assets	$48,000	Total liabilities and capital	$48,000

After offsetting the $8,000 loan receivable against Z's capital account and adding the $6,000 loan payable to X's capital account, the $40,000 cash is distributed as follows:

Outside creditors	$20,000
Partner X	7,000
Partner Y	0
Partner Z ($21,000 − $8,000)	13,000
Total cash distributed	$40,000

In summary, **simple partnership liquidations** use the following sequence of accounting procedures:

1. Determine the gain or loss on the sale of assets.
2. Allocate the gain or loss to the partners' capital accounts according to the income-sharing ratio.
3. Subtract loans receivable from capital accounts.
4. Add loans payable to capital accounts.
5. Record any investments by partners in response to capital deficiencies.
6. Allocate any remaining deficiencies to partners with positive capital account balances. If this step produces new capital deficiencies, repeat Steps 5 and 6.
7. Distribute the cash.

Installment Liquidations

The preceding sections focused on simple liquidations characterized by sale of all assets before distributing any cash to the partners. All gains and losses were realized and allocated to the partners' capital accounts. Suppose, however, that the partners request cash distributions before all assets are sold. Because the net gain or loss on future asset sales is unknown, how to distribute cash to the partners as it becomes available is not immediately evident. Outside creditors have the first claim and they must be paid before distributing any cash to the partners. Once the creditors are paid, we need a method for determining an equitable distribution of available cash to the partners. The two general approaches—determination of *safe payments* and preparation of a *cash distribution plan*—yield the same results.

Safe Payment Approach The **safe payment approach** determines how the cash available in a single installment is to be distributed. The calculation, repeated prior to distribution of each installment, relies on two simple and highly conservative assumptions:

1. All *remaining assets will be a total loss*: no more cash will be realized.
2. *Deficient partners will not invest any additional resources*: other partners will be charged with those deficiencies.

To illustrate the safe payment approach, assume that the ABC partnership decided to terminate business and liquidate its assets. Assets will be sold or otherwise converted into cash over a period of time, and the partners intend to distribute cash as it becomes available. The partners share income and loss in a 4:4:2 ratio and the pre-liquidation balance sheet is:

ABC PARTNERSHIP
Balance Sheet

Cash..........................	$ 3,000	Liabilities.........................	$ 30,000
Receivables	30,000	Loan payable—A	20,000
Inventory........................	47,000	Capital—A	86,000
Land...........................	25,000	Capital—B	140,000
Building, net.....................	72,000	Capital—C	41,000
Equipment, net..................	140,000		
Total assets	$317,000	Total liabilities and capital	$317,000

Suppose that half of the receivables are collected and that the entire inventory is sold for $35,000. After distributing the realized loss of $12,000 (= $47,000 − $35,000) on the inventory to the capital accounts ($4,800 to A, $4,800 to B, and $2,400 to C), the accounts show the following:

Cash ($3,000 + $15,000 + $35,000)	$ 53,000	Liabilities.........................	$ 30,000
Receivables	15,000	Loan payable—A	20,000
Land	25,000	Capital—A	81,200
Building, net.....................	72,000	Capital—B	135,200
Equipment, net..................	140,000	Capital—C	38,600
Total assets	$305,000	Total liabilities and capital	$305,000

If the partners distribute the $53,000, the outside creditors get the first $30,000. How is the remaining $23,000 to be distributed?

First, we combine the partners' loans with the partners' capital accounts. In this example, the $20,000 loan payable to A is combined with A's capital balance of $81,200. *Second,* we assume that all remaining noncash assets will result in a total loss, which is allocated by the income-sharing ratio. When additional expenses are anticipated as part of the liquidation process, these should also be included in the loss allocation. Book values of these remaining assets—receivables, land, building, and equipment—total $252,000. If these produce a total loss, the partners' capital accounts are affected as follows:

	Capital Accounts Before Loss	Loss Allocation		Capital Accounts After Loss
Partner A (includes $20,000 loan) ...	$101,200	(0.4 × $252,000) =	$(100,800)	$ 400
Partner B	135,200	(0.4 × $252,000) =	(100,800)	34,400
Partner C	38,600	(0.2 × $252,000) =	(50,400)	(11,800)
Totals	$275,000		$(252,000)	$23,000

Third, we assume that Partner C cannot invest additional capital and allocate C's $11,800 deficiency equally to A and B since they have equal (4:4) income shares, leading to the following:

	Capital Accounts Before Deficiency Allocation	Deficiency Allocation		Capital Accounts After Deficiency Allocation
Partner A	$ 400	(0.5 × 11,800) =	$(5,900)	$ (5,500)
Partner B	34,400	(0.5 × 11,800) =	(5,900)	28,500
Partner C	(11,800)		—	0
Totals	$23,000		$(11,800)	$23,000

Fourth, we assume that A cannot invest additional capital, and allocate A's entire $5,500 deficiency to B, resulting in the following capital balances:

Partner A	$ 0
Partner B	23,000
Partner C	0
Total	$23,000

The $23,000 is therefore distributed entirely to Partner B. This is called a **safe payment** because it is based on the *worst possible circumstances*; namely, that no more cash will be generated by the sale of assets and that deficient partners are unable to invest additional capital. Following distribution of $30,000 to the creditors and $23,000 to Partner B, the accounts show the following:

Receivables	$ 15,000	Loan payable—A	$ 20,000
Land	25,000	Capital—A	81,200
Building, net	72,000	Capital—B ($135,200 − $23,000)	112,200
Equipment, net	140,000	Capital—C	38,600
Total assets	$252,000	Total liabilities and capital	$252,000

When more cash becomes available at the next stage in the liquidation, another safe payment is computed. Suppose that $6,000 of receivables is collected, the remaining receivables are uncollectible, and the equipment is sold for $90,000. After recording these transactions, including the $96,000 cash receipt, allocation of the $9,000 (= $15,000 − $6,000) loss from uncollectible receivables and the $50,000 (= $140,000 − $90,000) loss on sale of equipment to the partners in the 4:4:2 ratio, we have the following:

Cash	$ 96,000	Loan payable—A	$ 20,000
Land	25,000	Capital—A	57,600
Building, net	72,000	Capital—B	88,600
		Capital—C	26,800
Total assets	$193,000	Total liabilities and capital	$193,000

As before, assume no recovery of the remaining assets having total book value of $97,000 (= $25,000 + $72,000) and allocate this potential loss to the partners as shown below:

	Capital Accounts Before Loss	Loss Allocation		Capital Accounts After Loss
Partner A (includes $20,000 loan)	$ 77,600	(0.4 × $97,000) =	$(38,800)	$38,800
Partner B	88,600	(0.4 × $97,000) =	(38,800)	49,800
Partner C	26,800	(0.2 × $97,000) =	(19,400)	7,400
Totals	$193,000		$(97,000)	$96,000

Because this loss creates no capital deficiencies, the $96,000 is distributed: $38,800 to A, $49,800 to B, and $7,400 to C. After this cash distribution, an updated balance sheet is prepared, the next batch of assets is sold, and so forth, until the liquidation is complete. The safe payment approach to cash distribution in installments is a fairly easy procedure. Its principal disadvantages are that (1) new calculations must be made for each installment distribution and (2) no information on future installment distributions is provided. The cash distribution plan, discussed next, remedies these disadvantages.

Cash Distribution Plan As an alternative to calculating safe payment at each cash installment, we can focus on the ability of the partners to absorb future losses at the beginning of the liquidation process.

The resulting **cash distribution plan** provides a sequence of cash distributions satisfying safe payment criteria. Once prepared, we use the plan to determine how to distribute available cash.

The balances of the partners' capital accounts continue to be critical for determining cash distributions according to this plan. Throughout partnership accounting, we noted that partners' shares of capital and profits are not necessarily the same. Conceptually, the cash distribution plan integrates the partners' income shares and capital balances to develop standard measures of ability to absorb future losses.

This concept can be understood with a simple example. Suppose Black and Jones share profits and losses equally, but Black's capital account has a balance of $45,000, while Jones' capital account has a balance of $30,000. Despite the fact that they are equal partners for income-sharing purposes, Black has more capital, due to Black's having either invested more or withdrawn less than Jones. Fairness suggests that when the partnership is liquidated, Black should receive $15,000 before Jones receives anything so as to equalize their capital positions. Once Black's capital is reduced to $30,000, they should share any remaining cash in accordance with their equal income-sharing ratio. Thus the following cash distribution plan applies in this simple situation:

Jones' and Black's Cash Distribution Plan

1. All liabilities are paid.
2. Black receives the next $15,000.
3. Any further distributions are divided equally between Black and Jones.

When several partners with different income-sharing percentages liquidate their partnership in installments, derivation of the cash distribution plan requires the more formal approach explained in the following display. The logic is the same as in the simple example above: cash distributions should follow a sequence designed to bring the capital accounts of the partners into proper alignment with respect to each other. This means that the partner having the *largest capital balance relative to his or her income percentage* will be the first to receive cash. In the preceding example, Black, with more capital and a 50 percent income percentage, received the first distribution. After equalizing all the imbalances in relative capital strength, subsequent distributions are made to all partners in proportion to their income percentages.

The **cash distribution plan** is prepared before liquidation begins and incorporates the following steps:

1. **Standardize** the capital relationship among the partners by dividing each capital balance by that partner's income-sharing percentage. The results provide a **measure of each partner's ability to absorb losses** that may occur during liquidation. The larger a partner's standardized capital balance, the greater is that partner's ability to absorb losses before his or her capital balance is eliminated.

2. **Equalize** the standardized capital balances in steps. Begin with the largest balance, and determine the adjustment (subtraction) needed to equalize it with the next largest. Continue this process until all standardized capital amounts are equal. These equalization adjustments signify the **incremental amounts of loss** which can be absorbed by partners with larger standardized capital balances over what can be absorbed by partners with smaller standardized balances.

3. **Convert** the equalization adjustments back into the respective partners' capital accounts by multiplying each adjustment, in the order made, by that partner's income-sharing percentage. This gives the amounts and priorities of cash distributions to the partners.

4. **Organize** the results of Step 3 into a formal cash distribution plan. Remember to provide first for payment of all outside creditors.

Cash Distribution Plan Illustration To illustrate preparation of a more complex cash distribution plan, refer to the ABC Partnership discussed in the previous section. Prior to the liquidation process, the right-hand side of the balance sheet appeared as follows:

ABC PARTNERSHIP Liabilities and Capital	
Liabilities..	$ 30,000
Loan payable—A..	20,000
Capital—A..	86,000
Capital—B..	140,000
Capital—C..	41,000
Total..	$317,000

The partners share income in a 4:4:2 ratio. As before, A's capital of $86,000 and loan of $20,000 are combined prior to proceeding, so that Partner A has total capital of $106,000.

First, standardize the capital accounts to find each partner's *loss-absorption ability* by dividing each partner's actual capital by the income-sharing percentage:

	Actual Capital	Income Percentage	Standardized Capital
Partner A	$106,000	0.4	$265,000
Partner B	140,000	0.4	350,000
Partner C	41,000	0.2	205,000

This calculation tells us that when we standardize for the different income shares, Partner B has the greatest amount of relative capital, and Partner C has the least. Partner B can absorb the greatest amount of loss, and Partner C the least amount. It is reasonable to expect that B will receive money first, then A, then finally C.

Second, equalize the standardized capital balances, starting with the largest:

	Partner A	Partner B	Partner C
Standardized capital..	$265,000	$350,000	$205,000
a. Equalize B with A..	—	(85,000)	—
	$265,000	$265,000	$205,000
b. Equalize A and B with C.................................	(60,000)	(60,000)	—
Totals...	$205,000	$205,000	$205,000

This process is repeated until the standardized capital balances of all partners are equalized. *Each adjustment represents incremental loss-absorption ability.* Thus B can absorb a partnership loss on liquidation of $85,000 more than A, and $145,000 (= $85,000 + $60,000) more than C. When the equalization process is complete, all partners have the same loss-absorption ability remaining.

Third, convert these adjustments back into actual capital balances as follows:

	Partner A	Partner B	Partner C
a.....................	—	$85,000 × 0.4 = $34,000	—
b.....................	$60,000 × 0.4 = $24,000	$60,000 × 0.4 = $24,000	—

This calculation indicates that after paying the $30,000 of liabilities, Partner B receives $34,000, and then Partners A and B each receive $24,000. These distributions equalize the standardized capital balances of each partner, and convert their actual capital balances to their 4:4:2 income-sharing ratio. Any further distributions of cash should be made according to this income-sharing ratio.

Exhibit 14.4 shows a worksheet combining the second and third steps. The left side of the worksheet shows the equalization of standardized capital to determine the partners' incremental loss-absorption abilities. The right side shows the conversion back to the partners' actual capital account balances. The amounts on the left side are multiplied by the respective income percentages to get the figures on the right side. The adjustments equalizing the standardized capital represent the predetermined sequence of cash distributions that bring the partners' capital accounts into line with the income-sharing ratio.

EXHIBIT 14.4   Worksheet for Cash Distribution Plan

	Equalization of Standardized Capital				Actual Capital Accounts and Cash Distributions		
	Partner A	Partner B	Partner C		Partner A (40%)	Partner B (40%)	Partner C (20%)
Standardized capital.............	$265,000	$350,000	$205,000	Actual capital	$106,000	$140,000	$41,000
a. Equalize B with A..............	—	(85,000)	—	Cash paid	—	(34,000)	—
	$265,000	$265,000	$205,000		$106,000	$106,000	$41,000
b. Equalize A and B with C.........	(60,000)	(60,000)	—	Cash Paid	(24,000)	(24,000)	—
	$205,000	$205,000	$205,000		$ 82,000	$ 82,000	$41,000

Fourth, organize the results into a formal cash distribution plan, such as that shown below, that indicates how to distribute any amount of cash that becomes available. Remember that distributions are *cumulative:* each distribution starts where the previous one ended.

ABC Partnership's Cash Distribution Plan

Distribution	Amount	Payment Made to
1.....................	First $30,000	Creditors
2.....................	Next $34,000	Partner B
3.....................	Next $48,000	Partners A and B in equal amounts up to $24,000 each
4.....................	Any further amount	Partners A, B and C in 4:4:2 ratio

Equivalence of Cash Distribution Plan and Safe Payments   To illustrate the equivalence of the cash distribution plan and safe payments, recall that we calculated the proper safe payment distribution of the first two installments in the liquidation of the ABC partnership—$53,000 ($30,000 to the creditors and $23,000 to B) and $96,000 ($38,800 to A, $49,800 to B and $7,400 to C). We now use the cash distribution plan to verify the safe payment amounts.

First, consider the $53,000. The cash distribution plan calls for paying the first $30,000 to creditors and the next $34,000 to Partner B. Available cash of $53,000 permits us to complete the first distribution— to pay the creditors $30,000—and to partially complete the second distribution—to pay Partner B $23,000 of the required $34,000, as follows:

Creditors...	$30,000
Partner B	23,000
Total...	$53,000

Second, we have $96,000 to distribute. We must complete the second distribution called for by the plan—to pay Partner B an additional $11,000 (for a total of $34,000)—before moving to the third distribution. According to the cash distribution plan, we perform the following steps:

1. Pay $11,000 to Partner B to complete the second distribution, leaving $85,000 (= $96,000 − $11,000) available to pay out.
2. Divide the next $48,000 equally between A and B, completing the third distribution indicated by the plan, and leaving cash of $37,000 (= $85,000 − $48,000) to be paid.
3. Divide the $37,000 among A, B, and C in the 4:4:2 income-sharing ratio, as specified by the fourth and final distribution in the plan.

Proper payment of the entire $96,000 is summarized here:

| | | **Payment Made To** | | |
Distribution	Amount	Partner A	Partner B	Partner C
1................	$11,000	$ 0	$11,000	$ 0
2................	48,000	24,000	24,000	0
3................	37,000	14,800	14,800	7,400
Totals	$96,000	$38,800	$49,800	$7,400

Observe that this result is identical to that achieved by the safe payment approach.

Deviations from the Plan and Distributions in Kind Not all available cash needs be paid to the partners immediately. Cash may be retained for anticipated liquidation expenses or other purposes. Both the safe payment approach and the cash distribution plan—which is actually a *schedule of safe payments*—specifically direct the distribution of *cash* in a partnership liquidation.

Occasionally, though, temporary deviations from the safe payments determined by either approach occur. For example, suppose a specific asset is distributed to a partner in lieu of cash, and the value of the asset exceeds the amount to which that partner is entitled. Subsequent payments must be adjusted in favor of other partners until the excess is absorbed. We illustrate how distribution of a noncash asset in liquidation can temporarily disrupt scheduled safe payments by using the following hypothetical cash distribution plan.

Distribution	Amount	Payment Made to
1............................	First $10,000	Creditors
2............................	Next $16,000	Partner D
3............................	Next $30,000	Partners D and E in 6:3 ratio
4............................	Any further amount	Partners D, E and F in 6:3:1 ratio

Suppose that when considering the third distribution, E receives a truck worth $14,200 in lieu of the $10,000 cash, effectively receiving an advance on the fourth distribution. Appropriate payments to D and F in a 6:1 ratio must be made before making the fourth distribution in the 6:3:1 ratio. The excess payment of $4,200 to E ($= \$14,200 - \$10,000 = 3 \times \$1,400$) is remedied in the fourth distribution by paying $8,400 to D ($= 6 \times \$1,400$) and $1,400 to F ($= 1 \times \$1,400$) before E receives any further payment. In other words, of the next $14,000 considered in the fourth distribution, E's share of $4,200 ($= 0.3 \times \$14,000$) was *prepaid* as part of the truck value. D and F are paid the remaining $9,800 ($= \$14,000 - \$4,200$) in their 6:1 ratio. When more than $9,800 in cash is available in the fourth distribution, the excess is paid in the 6:3:1 ratio.

If we are working with individually calculated safe payments, distributing the truck to E could serve to prepay some of the next safe payment to which E is otherwise entitled. If so, calculation of that next safe payment is modified to incorporate the effect just illustrated on the cash distribution plan.

When dealing with partnership liquidations occurring over an extended period of time, the accountant must ensure an equitable distribution of partnership assets. Consideration must be given to actual and prospective losses on sales of assets and to the potential inability of partners to remedy capital deficiencies. These factors are considered, either directly or indirectly, in the two procedures discussed for installment liquidations—the safe payment approach and the cash distribution plan.

REVIEW 4 • Termination of the Partnership

After 15 years of operation, the Abel, Baker and Cahn Agency is sold to new owners, as the existing partners either wish to retire or to pursue other business interests. The partnership has $65,000 of liabilities and capital accounts as follows: Baker (40% interest) $325,000; Cahn (40% interest), $180,000; Dexter (20% interest), $65,000. The agency's assets are sold for $800,000, which will be paid in four equal installments of $200,000.

Required
Determine the distribution of each $200,000 installment.

Solutions are located after the chapter assignments.

REVIEW OF KEY CONCEPTS •••••••••••••••••••••••••••••••••

LO 1   **Distinguish between the characteristics of a partnership and a corporation. (p. 613)** Partnerships differ from corporations with respect to the rights and liabilities of their owners, and in certain aspects of accounting, particularly the measurement of net income. **Partnership law** specifies the general conditions under which partnerships operate. Many specific details are subject to the contractual terms established by the partners in the **partnership agreement**.

LO 2   **Record the formation of a partnership. (p. 619)** In the **formation of a partnership**, assets are recorded at **fair market value**. Initial capital balances may be based on amounts actually invested or on a pre-established capital ratio. In the latter case, either the **bonus** or **goodwill** approach is applied to reconcile any difference between the amount invested and the calculated share of capital.

LO 3   **Allocate partnership income to partners. (p. 620)** Because **net income of a partnership** represents **return to the partners**, it excludes deductions for salaries or interest to partners. Salaries, bonuses, interest on capital accounts, and percentage formulas all may be used to **allocate** net income to partners. **Full implementation** of such allocations is common.

LO 4   **Record the admission of a partner. (p. 624)** **Admission of a new partner** may occur by **purchase of an existing interest** or **direct investment in the partnership**. In the case of a purchase, transfer of capital accounts is the usual accounting method. In the case of investment, either the bonus or goodwill approach is used to account for any difference between the new partner's investment and the share of capital acquired. The **bonus** and **goodwill approaches** reflect different conceptual views of the nature of admission of a new partner. The **bonus method** recognizes **transfers of capital among partners**. The **goodwill method** calls for **asset revaluations**, often in the form of intangibles.

LO 5   **Record the retirement of a partner. (p. 630)** The interest of a **retiring partner** may be purchased with the **personal assets** of one or more of the remaining partners or with **partnership assets**. In the latter case, the **bonus** and **goodwill** approaches are used to account for any difference between the payment to the retiring partner and the amount of the retiring partner's capital account. When the **partial goodwill** approach is used in retirement, asset revaluations are recognized only in connection with the **retiring partner's interest**. Use of the **total goodwill** approach infers asset revaluations pertaining to **all partners**, based on capitalizing the excess of the payment to the retiring partner over the retiree's capital balance.

LO 6   **Determine the appropriate cash distributions in partnership liquidations. (p. 633)** If the partnership is to be **liquidated**, the **rights of creditors** are based on the applicable law. Loans payable to partners and loans receivable from partners are combined with those partners' capital balances under the **right of offset**. When a partner has a **capital deficiency**, that partner is obligated to invest additional assets in the partnership to remedy the deficiency; if this is impossible, the deficiency is allocated to the other partners in their income-sharing ratio. A **simple** or **lump-sum liquidation** occurs when all assets are sold before any cash is distributed to the partners. In an **installment liquidation**, cash is paid to the partners before the sale of assets is complete. Either the **safe payment approach** or the **cash distribution plan** provide for equitable division of each cash distribution among the partners. Both methods address the partners' relative abilities to absorb a total loss on all remaining assets and produce the same sequence of cash payments.

Assignments with the ⊘ in the margin are available in ᵐʸBusinessCourse.
See the Preface of the book for details.

MULTIPLE CHOICE QUESTIONS •••••••••••••••••••••••••••••••

⊘ **LO 1**   **1.** In a partnership, *mutual agency* means that

   a.   one partner is designated as agent, to act for all partners.
   b.   any partner may act on behalf of the partnership.
   c.   partners have unlimited liability for partnership debts.
   d.   partners are co-owners of partnership property.

⊘ **LO 1**   **2.** In which form of partnership organization do partnership shares trade on public exchanges?

   a.   General partnership
   b.   LLC
   c.   MLP
   d.   none

⊘ **LO 1**   **3.** In computing the net income of a partnership, expenses include operating expenses and

   a.   partners' loan interest and partners' salaries.
   b.   partners' loan interest but not partners' salaries.
   c.   partners' salaries but not partners' loan interest.
   d.   no items related to partners.

Use the following information to answer questions 4 and 5 below.

Two individuals form a partnership. Amos invests $75,000 and Bemus invests $25,000, but each is to have an equal interest in partnership capital.

4. Under the bonus method, capital credited to Amos would be   LO 2 ✓

   a. $75,000.
   b. $50,000.
   c. $37,500.
   d. $25,000.

5. Under the goodwill method, capital credited to Bemus would be   LO 2 ✓

   a. $25,000.
   b. $37,500.
   c. $50,000.
   d. $75,000.

6. The Muldoon Partnership consists of three partners, Adam, Dawn, and Lorrie. The partnership agreement   LO 3 ✓
   provides for annual salaries of $40,000 to Dawn and $60,000 to Lorrie. Residual profits are shared in a 3:3:4
   ratio. Salaries are to be fully implemented, even if partnership net income is less than total salaries. Partnership net income for the year is $140,000. Adam's share of net income is

   a. $14,000.
   b. $12,000.
   c. $42,000.
   d. $ 4,000.

Use the following information to answer questions 7–12 below.

The balance sheet of the Troy Partnership at September 30, 2016, shows:

Various assets	$500,000	Various liabilities.	$100,000
		Capital, Thomas	160,000
		Capital, Renee	120,000
		Capital, Oscar.	80,000
		Capital, Yvonne	40,000
TOTAL	$500,000	TOTAL	$500,000

The partners share income equally. Consider each question independently.

7. Zeke invests $150,000 and is admitted as an equal partner. The bonus method is used. Capital accounts of   LO 4 ✓
   the partners after Zeke's admission are

   a. Thomas $160,000, Renee $120,000, Oscar $80,000, Yvonne $40,000, Zeke $150,000.
   b. Thomas $172,500, Renee $132,500, Oscar $92,500, Yvonne $52,500, Zeke $100,000.
   c. Thomas $170,000, Renee $130,000, Oscar $90,000, Yvonne $50,000, Zeke $110,000.
   d. Thomas $210,000, Renee $170,000, Oscar $130,000, Yvonne $90,000, Zeke $150,000.

8. Zeke invests $150,000 and is admitted as an equal partner. The goodwill method is used. Capital accounts of   LO 4 ✓
   the partners after Zeke's admission are

   a. Thomas $160,000, Renee $120,000, Oscar $80,000, Yvonne $40,000, Zeke $150,000.
   b. Thomas $172,500, Renee $132,500, Oscar $92,500, Yvonne $52,500, Zeke $100,000.
   c. Thomas $170,000, Renee $130,000, Oscar $90,000, Yvonne $50,000, Zeke $110,000.
   d. Thomas $210,000, Renee $170,000, Oscar $130,000, Yvonne $90,000, Zeke $150,000.

9. Renee decides to retire as a partner. The remaining partners agree to pay Renee $300,000 from partnership   LO 5 ✓
   funds, and to use the bonus method. The capital accounts of the remaining partners after Renee's retirement are

   a. Thomas $160,000, Oscar $80,000, Yvonne $40,000.
   b. Thomas $60,000, Oscar $(20,000), Yvonne $(60,000).
   c. Thomas $100,000, Oscar $20,000, Yvonne $(20,000).
   d. Thomas $90,000, Oscar $10,000, Yvonne $0.

☑ **LO 5**   **10.**   Renee decides to retire as a partner. The remaining partners agree to pay Renee $300,000 from partnership funds, and to use the partial goodwill method. The capital accounts of the remaining partners after Renee's retirement are

    a.   Thomas $160,000, Oscar $80,000, Yvonne $40,000.
    b.   Thomas $400,000, Oscar $320,000, Yvonne $280,000.
    c.   Thomas $260,000, Oscar $180,000, Yvonne $140,000.
    d.   Thomas $220,000, Oscar $140,000, Yvonne $100,000.

☑ **LO 6**   **11.**   The Troy Partnership decides to terminate operations and liquidate. To begin the process, assets with a book value of $292,000 are sold for $184,000. Under a safe payment approach, how much will be distributed to the partners?

    a.   Thomas $62,000, Renee $22,000, Oscar $0, Yvonne $0
    b.   Thomas $92,000, Renee $92,000, Oscar $0, Yvonne $0
    c.   Thomas $87,000, Renee $47,000, Oscar $25,000, Yvonne $25,000
    d.   Thomas $46,000, Renee $46,000, Oscar $46,000, Yvonne $46,000

☑ **LO 6**   **12.**   Under a cash distribution plan, how would the first $150,000 be distributed?

    a. $100,000 to creditors, $50,000 equally among the four partners
    b. $100,000 to creditors, $50,000 equally among Thomas, Renee, and Oscar
    c. $100,000 to creditors, $50,000 equally to Thomas and Oscar
    d. $100,000 to creditors, $45,000 to Thomas, $5,000 to Renee

EXERCISES ••

LO 2   **E14.1**   **Partnership Formation**   On June 7, 2016, Cheng and Morales, two recent graduates of Upper State University, formed a computer consulting firm. Cheng contributed an extensive, up-to-date computer installation, valued at $100,000. This equipment had been financed by a bank loan; the partnership assumed the current balance of $25,000. Cheng also invested $5,000 cash. Morales had recently inherited a small office building, valued at $150,000 and encumbered by a mortgage debt of $35,000. Morales transferred both the building and the debt to the partnership. Cheng's extensive computer skills coupled with Morales' sales and customer service skills suggest a profitable future for the firm. They agreed to share profits in the ratio of 40 percent for Cheng and 60 percent for Morales, in part because of Morales' larger investment.

Required

Compute the balance in each partner's capital account on June 7, 2016, and record the partnership formation entry if the:

    a.   Partners do not specify any capital relationship.
    b.   Partners agree that each is to have a 50 percent interest in partnership capital, and they specify the bonus approach to recording the formation.
    c.   Partners agree that each is to have a 50 percent interest in partnership capital, and they specify the goodwill approach to recording the formation.

☑ **LO 2**   **E14.2**   **Partnership Formation**   Max, Nat and Roberta formed a partnership to operate a dry-cleaning business. They agreed to share initial capital and subsequent income in a 3:2:1 ratio. Each partner's contributions to the new venture are listed next.

    Max: $20,000 cash, dry-cleaning equipment worth $150,000 and the ability to keep the equipment in good operating condition.

    Nat: $40,000 cash and extensive experience in the dry-cleaning business.

    Roberta: $15,000 cash and a 2-year $60,000 note, payable to the firm, with 6 percent interest on the unpaid balance.

Required

    a.   Record the formation using the goodwill approach.
    b.   Record the formation using the bonus approach.

LO 3   **E14.3**   **Partnership Income Allocation**   Whitman and Greene are partners in a real estate venture. At January 1, 2017, their respective capital balances were $165,000 and $190,000. Their partnership agreement provides that Whitman is to receive a guaranteed salary of $85,000, and that remaining profits after the salary are to be shared equally. Partnership operations for the year 2017 resulted in a net income of $60,000. Whitman's salary is paid in cash during the year, but there are no other withdrawals or capital changes. Assume full implementation.

Required

a. Compute the balance of each partner's capital account at December 31, 2017.
b. Compute the balance of each partner's capital account at December 31, 2017, assuming partnership net income was $105,000.

E14.4 Partnership Income Allocation—Various Options   The January 1, 2017, balance sheet of the   **LO 3** ✓
partnership of Linda Kingston and Jeannette Allen is shown below.

Assets		Liabilities and Capital	
Cash.............	$ 20,000	Liabilities..............	$ 60,000
Other assets...........	180,000	Capital—Kingston	56,000
		Capital—Allen............	84,000
Total assets	$200,000	Total liabilities and capital	$200,000

The partnership reported revenues of $80,000 and expenses of $55,000 for 2017. Neither partner withdrew funds from the partnership during the year. Kingston invested $8,000 in the firm on June 28, 2017.

Required

Compute the December 31, 2017, capital balance for each partner under each of the following assumptions:

a. The partnership agreement does not specify how income is to be divided.
b. The partnership agreement specifies that Kingston receives 65 percent of income and Allen 35 percent.
c. The partnership agreement specifies that income is divided equally after paying each partner 10 percent interest on her weighted average capital balance.
d. The partnership agreement specifies that Kingston and Allen receive salaries of $12,000 and $8,000, respectively, and that each partner receives 5 percent interest on her capital balance at the beginning of the year. Salary and interest allocations are to be fully implemented. Any remaining income is to be divided equally.

E14.5 Multiple Income Allocation Provisions   Partners Johnson, Kane and Lehman agreed to the follow-   **LO 3**
ing provisions for sharing profit or loss from their partnership:

1. Johnson, Kane and Lehman receive salaries of $55,000, $45,000, and $62,000, respectively.
2. Interest on average capital investment is credited at the rate of 8 percent per annum.
3. Residual profit or loss is shared in the ratio 5:2:3.
4. All provisions are to be fully implemented.

The average capital investments for the year are:

Johnson	$200,000
Kane............	280,000
Lehman...........	100,000

Required

a. Prepare a schedule to allocate partnership income of $252,000.
b. Repeat part a for income of $150,000.
c. Suppose Johnson, as managing partner, is entitled to a bonus of 20 percent of profit after the bonus but before other allocation provisions. Prepare a schedule to allocate partnership income of $252,000.

E14.6 New Partner Admission: Purchase of Existing Interest   The capital balances for the partnership   **LO 4**
of Ajeet, Rahul, and Suresh are as follows:

Capital—Ajeet	$360,000
Capital—Rahul........	300,000
Capital—Suresh	450,000

The partnership profit-sharing ratio is 3:2:5. A new partner, Harish, enters the partnership by purchasing existing interests in the partnership.

Required

Prepare the journal entry to record Harish's admission to the partnership, and compute the new capital balances, in each of the following cases.

a. Harish pays Ajeet $400,000 for his entire interest in the partnership. There is no revaluation of partnership assets.

b. Harish pays the three partners a total of $350,000 for 20 percent of each of the partners' interests. There is no revaluation of partnership assets.

c. Repeat part *b*, assuming revaluation of partnership assets by recording goodwill.

LO 4 E14.7 Partner Admission: Investment of New Capital   The capital balances for the partnership of Liang, Tan, and Wu are as follows:

Capital—Liang	$ 50,000
Capital—Tan.	250,000
Capital—Wu	140,000

The partnership profit-sharing ratio is 1:6:3. A new partner, Gao, enters the partnership by investing cash directly in the partnership.

Required

Prepare the journal entry to record Gao's admission to the partnership, and compute the new capital balances, in each of the following cases.

a. Gao invests $60,000 for a 12 percent interest in the partnership.

b. Gao invests $50,000 for a 12 percent interest in the partnership. The bonus method is used.

c. Gao invests $72,000 for a 12 percent interest in the partnership. The goodwill method is used, and any revaluation is attributed to goodwill.

⊘ LO 4 E14.8 Admission of New Partner   Following is the condensed balance sheet of Martinez, O'Neill and Clemens, partners who share profits or losses in the ratio of 2:3:5.

Cash.	$ 48,000		Liabilities.	$200,000
Other assets	752,000		Capital—Martinez.	108,000
			Capital—O'Neill	176,000
			Capital—Clemens	316,000
Total assets	$800,000		Total liabilities and capital	$800,000

Required

a. Assume that the partnership's assets and liabilities are fairly valued as shown. The partners wish to admit Jeter as a partner with a 40 percent interest in capital, profits, and losses. They require Jeter to invest an amount such that bonus or goodwill adjustments are not needed. How much should Jeter invest for the 40 percent share?

b. Assume instead that the existing partners, all of whom contemplate retirement relatively soon, decide to sell Jeter 40 percent of their respective partnership interests for a total payment of $320,000. This payment will be made proportionately to Martinez, O'Neill, and Clemens. The partners agree that implied goodwill is to be recorded prior to the transaction with Jeter. What are the capital balances of the four partners after the transaction with Jeter?

LO 5 E14.9 Partner Retirement: Various Cases   The capital balances for the partnership of Diaz, Isidro, and Nelson are as follows:

Capital—Diaz	$1,500,000
Capital—Isidro	900,000
Capital—Nelson	600,000

The partners share income in a 2:4:4 ratio. Nelson decides to retire. Diaz and Isidro continue the partnership, sharing income in a 2:4 (1:2) ratio.

Required

Prepare the journal entry or entries to record the retirement of Nelson in each of the following scenarios:

a. Diaz and Isidro use their personal assets to buy Nelson's interest for $800,000.
b. The partners agree to pay Nelson $750,000 of partnership cash. The bonus method is used.
c. Same as *b.*, but the partial goodwill approach is used.
d. Same as *b.*, but the total goodwill approach is used.
e. The partners agree to pay Nelson $450,000 of partnership cash. The difference is attributed to over-valued plant and equipment, and the total goodwill approach is used.

E14.10 Post-Retirement Capital Balances   On April 30, 2017, the partnership of ABC Associates had the   **LO 5**
following balance sheet:

Total assets, at cost.	$500,000
Loan payable to Atkins.	$195,000
Capital—Atkins.	60,000
Capital—Bodkins	110,000
Capital—Calkins.	135,000
Total liabilities and capital	$500,000

The partners share income in a 2:3:5 ratio. Atkins is retiring as of April 30, 2017. The partnership's assets have been appraised at $650,000, and the partnership records the appraised value. The partnership agrees to pay $150,000 for Atkins' capital interest. Atkins' loan will remain, and will continue to be paid, with interest, over the next several years. No goodwill is to be recorded in connection with Atkins' retirement.

Required

Calculate the capital balances of Bodkins and Calkins immediately after recording the retirement of Atkins, using the bonus method.

E14.11 Retirement: Bonus and Goodwill Calculations   Ellery Stevens, senior partner in a rapidly grow-   **LO 5**
ing local CPA firm, has decided to retire. His share in the firm's profits and losses is 30 percent and his capital account has a balance of $190,000. Total capital of the firm is $600,000. Under the partnership agreement, Stevens will receive $250,000 upon retirement.

Required

a. Calculate the bonus to Stevens and the total capital of the firm after Stevens' retirement.
b. What balance sheet accounts will change after Stevens' retirement, and by what amounts, if the partial goodwill approach is used?
c. If the total goodwill method is used, calculate the amount of goodwill recognized and the total capital of the firm after Stevens' retirement.

E14.12 Lump-Sum Liquidation   Three university students, Cho, Kenney, and Martinez, operated a success-   **LO 6**
ful business, renting furniture and appliances to students residing in dormitories and off-campus apartments. The three are now graduating and wish to sell the business before beginning their respective careers. They shared profits in a 7:5:4 ratio. The partnership's current balance sheet is as follows:

Cash.	$ 6,000	Accounts payable.	$ 60,000
Receivables	25,000	Loan payable—Kenney	10,000
Loan receivable—Cho	15,000	Capital—Cho	27,000
Rental equipment, net	140,000	Capital—Kenney.	28,000
		Capital—Martinez.	61,000
Total assets	$186,000	Total liabilities and capital	$186,000

Another student group, organized as a corporation, wants to buy the business. Their offer of $105,000 for the equipment and $12,000 for the receivables is accepted. After receipt of the $117,000, the liabilities are paid and the partnership is liquidated.

Required

How much does each partner receive?

LO 6 **E14.13 Rights of Creditors** The following are data for the AB Partnership and for A and B as individuals. Assume that A and B are equal partners.

AB Partnership	Case 1	Case 2
Cash	$48,000	$31,000
Liabilities	42,000	51,000
Capital—A	3,000	(8,000)
Capital—B	3,000	(12,000)
Partner A		
Cash	10,000	30,000
Liabilities	17,000	17,000
Partner B		
Cash	50,000	15,000
Liabilities	9,000	16,000

Required

For each case, indicate how the assets of the partnership and the assets of each partner are applied if creditor claims are satisfied as fully as possible.

LO 6 **E14.14 Safe Payment Calculation** Partners Rane, Snow, and Hale share profits and losses in the ratio of 5:3:2, respectively. The partners vote to dissolve the partnership when its assets, liabilities, and capital are as follows:

Cash	$ 10,000	Liabilities	$100,000	
Other assets	500,000	Capital—Rane	120,000	
		Capital—Snow	180,000	
		Capital—Hale	110,000	
Total assets	$510,000	Total liabilities and capital	$510,000	

The partnership will be liquidated over an extended period of time. As cash becomes available, it will be distributed to the partners. The first sale of noncash assets having a book value of $200,000 realizes $135,000.

Required

Use the safe payment approach to determine the amount of cash to be distributed to each partner after this sale.

LO 6 **E14.15 Cash Distribution Plan** At the time they decided to liquidate their partnership, Whitehead, Ellis and Riley had capital balances of $65,000, $45,000 and $80,000, respectively. Liabilities were $50,000 and the balance sheet showed a note receivable from Ellis in the amount of $30,000. The partners share income in a 5:3:2 ratio.

Required

Prepare a schedule showing how cash is to be distributed as it becomes available during the liquidation process.

PROBLEMS ●

LO 2 **P14.1 Partnership Formation: Working Backward** Brian and two other friends from his MS in Accounting program at Quality State University decide to form a CPA firm specializing in forensic accounting. The three had worked for different Big Four firms for several years and accumulated a wealth of experience as well as a variety of other assets the new firm could use. After agreeing on a 2:3:1 capital and income ratio, the three listed what they intend to contribute to the new firm:

Brian: Cash ($50,000), office and computer equipment ($30,000), knowledge of potential client base.
Jennifer: Cash ($40,000), specialized forensic skills
Eric: Note payable to the firm ($60,000), extensive computer audit experience

Pro-forma capital balances under three formation scenarios follow.

	Scenario #1	Scenario #2	Scenario #3
Capital—Brian	$152,000	$100,000	$125,000
Capital—Jennifer	148,000	25,000	50,000
Capital—Eric	60,000	55,000	85,000

Required

a. In each scenario, identify the flow of bonuses or the amount and beneficiaries of goodwill recorded.

b. Discuss the relative advisability of the three scenarios, paying particular attention to their effects on the new firm's future profitability and leverage (or credit-worthiness).

P14.2 **Partnership Formation**   Augustus Berrini, the sole proprietor of the Berrini Company, is planning to   **LO 2** expand the company and establish a partnership with Fiedler and Wade. The partners plan to share profits and losses as follows: Berrini, 50 percent; Fiedler, 25 percent; Wade, 25 percent. They also agree that the beginning capital balances of the partnership will reflect this same relationship.

Berrini asked Fiedler to join the partnership because his many business contacts are expected to be valuable during the expansion. Fiedler is also contributing $28,000. Wade is contributing $11,000 and a block of marketable securities which the partnership expects to liquidate as needed during the expansion. The securities, which cost Wade $42,000, are currently worth $57,500.

Berrini's investment in the partnership is the Berrini Company. The balance sheet for the Berrini Company appears below. He plans to pay off the notes with his personal assets. The other partners have agreed that the partnership will assume the accounts payable and the mortgage. The three partners agree that the inventory is worth $85,000; the equipment is worth half its original cost; the building and land are worth $65,000 and $25,000, respectively; and the allowance established for uncollectible accounts is correct.

BERRINI COMPANY
Balance Sheet
Date of Partnership Formation

Assets		Liabilities and owner's equity	
Cash.........................	$ 7,000	Accounts payable..................	$ 53,000
Accounts receivable (net).........	48,000	Notes payable	7,000
Inventory.....................	72,000	Mortgage payable	55,000
Equipment (net of $12,000		Total liabilities....................	115,000
accumulated depreciation)......	18,000	Owner's equity	
Building (net of $20,000		Capital, Berrini	85,000
accumulated depreciation)......	40,000		
Land........................	15,000		
Total assets	$200,000	Total liabilities and owner's equity....	$200,000

Required

Prepare the balance sheet of the partnership on the date of formation under each of the following independent assumptions:

a. The partners agree to follow the bonus approach to record the formation.

b. The partners agree to follow the goodwill approach to record the formation.

P14.3 **Partners' Disputes over Income Allocation**   Nathan, Daniel and Kaitlyn generally get along well   **LO 3** as business associates in their consulting firm. Recently, however, the income-sharing provisions of their partnership agreement have become contentious. These provisions require partnership net income to be shared as follows:

	Salary	Interest on Capital	% of Remainder
Nathan	$90,000	4%	20%
Daniel	75,000	4%	30%
Kaitlyn..................	0	20%	50%

Note: Salary and interest provisions are to be implemented in that order only to the extent of the available income.

Kaitlyn was originally to have been a silent partner, an investor without active participation in the business. Daniel, on the other hand, was to have had a large voice in business decisions as well as a modest capital investment. As it turns out, Daniel has been shunted to the side whereas Kaitlyn appears to be running the business much of the time. Nathan spends a lot of time on practice development and generates few chargeable hours.

In the last three years, partnership income and partners' average capital balances were:

Partnership Net Income			Average Capital Balances		
2016	**2015**	**2014**	**Nathan**	**Daniel**	**Kaitlyn**
$140,000	$205,400	$250,000	$40,000	$70,000	$180,000

Required

a. Explain why the income-sharing provisions have become contentious.

b. Would a provision allowing Kaitlyn a 25 percent bonus of net income before any allocations satisfy her? What would Daniel's reaction be?

c. Suppose the partners adopt the provision in part *b* for 2017 except that the bonus is based on 25 percent of net income before allocations but after the bonus. Net income for 2017 amounts to $220,000 and average capital balances are unchanged. Compare the 2017 income allocations with and without the bonus. Comment on the income redistribution you observe.

LO 3   P14.4   Income Allocation; Schedule of Changes in Capital Accounts   The December 31, 2016, balance sheet for the Greystone Partnership appears below:

GREYSTONE PARTNERSHIP
Balance Sheet
December 31, 2016

Assets		Liabilities and Capital	
Cash..........................	$ 35,000	Accounts payable................	$186,000
Accounts receivable.............	200,000	Long-term liabilities	250,000
Equipment	240,000	Capital—Burstein................	154,000
Buildings.....................	300,000	Capital—Reeves.................	250,000
Land.........................	125,000	Capital—Sills	60,000
Total assets	$900,000	Total liabilities and capital	$900,000

Additional information:

1. The partners agreed that each will earn 5 percent interest on his or her beginning-of-year capital balance.
2. Salaries are as follows: Burstein, $60,000; Reeves, $75,000; and Sills, $40,000.
3. Sills is to receive a bonus of 15 percent of income before salaries, bonus, and interest to partners.
4. Any income remaining after salaries, bonus, and interest to partners is to be allocated equally.
5. During 2016, Burstein withdrew $10,000 from the firm. All other allocations to Burstein for salary, interest, and profit were retained in the business.
6. Reeves withdrew all but $25,000 of 2016 allocations.
7. In 2016 Sills withdrew $35,000 and all salary, bonus, interest, and profit allocations.
8. Total capital balances at the beginning of the year were $400,000.
9. Income for 2016 after deducting interest to partners but before deductions for salaries and bonus was $280,000.

Required

a. Calculate the capital balances at January 1, 2016.

b. Prepare a schedule of changes in capital accounts for the partners in the Greystone Partnership for 2016.

P14.5 **Tax Consequences of Investments in MLPs**   At the beginning of 2015, an investor purchases 5,000   **LO 1**
exchange-traded units of **Transocean Partners**, a deepwater drilling company organized as a Master Limited Partnership, at a cost of $125,000. Per-unit allocations of taxable income and cash distributions for
2015, 2016, and 2017 take place at the end of each year, and are as follows:

	2015	2016	2017
Taxable income	$0.40	$0.36	$0.50
Cash distributions	1.20	1.50	1.60

The investor's personal marginal tax rate is 35 percent, and the relevant capital gains rate is 15 percent.
The investor sells the investment for $140,000 at the end of 2017.

Required

a.   Prepare a schedule of the yearly after-tax return, in dollars, for this investment, for each of the years
2015, 2016, and 2017.
b.   Calculate the amount of taxes the investor owes related to the sale of the investment at the end of
2017.
c.   Calculate the present value of the investor's savings from delaying the tax on excess cash distributions until the sale of the investment, using a 10 percent discount rate.

P14.6 **Financial Statement Effects of Partnership Expansion**   Graham and Hyde currently share profits   **LO 4**
and losses in a 3:1 ratio and are considering admitting Ingalls as a new partner with a 20 percent interest in
capital and profits and losses. The different approaches to accounting for partnership expansion affect the
financial statements of the new partnership. Condensed balance sheets for the Graham/Hyde partnership and
the Graham/Hyde/Ingalls partnership under alternative admission approaches appear below.

	G/H	G/H/I #1	G/H/I #2	G/H/I #3	G/H/I #4
Cash and receivables	$ 37,000	$ 37,000	$ 77,000	$ 77,000	$ 49,000
Other assets	142,000	142,000	142,000	222,000	150,000
Total assets	$179,000	$179,000	$219,000	$299,000	$199,000
Accounts payable	$ 48,000	$ 48,000	$ 48,000	$ 48,000	$ 48,000
Long-term debt	51,000	51,000	51,000	51,000	51,000
Capital—Graham	50,000	40,000	62,000	110,000	50,000
Capital—Hyde	30,000	24,000	34,000	50,000	30,000
Capital—Ingalls	—	16,000	24,000	40,000	20,000
Total liabilities and capital	$179,000	$179,000	$219,000	$299,000	$199,000

Required

a.   As a user of financial statements in credit-granting or investment decisions, which of the above balance sheets look strongest? Discuss any red flags that whet your appetite for additional information.
b.   Explain whether Ingalls will likely prefer a particular alternative. Which one?
c.   Reconstruct the journal entries recording the four alternatives.

P14.7 **Investment Club: Admission and Income Allocation**   The Lucky Investment Club is a partner-   **LO 3, 4, 6**
ship of about 20 individuals who jointly invest in securities as a hobby. All are equal partners. There are
occasional admissions of new partners who join the Club and occasional departures from the Club as individuals relocate or lose interest in Club activity. Thus the exact number of partners fluctuates somewhat
over time. The Club maintains its books on a cost basis to facilitate its income tax reporting. Since it has
no public reporting requirements, it chooses not to follow GAAP for marketable securities. However,
upon admission, a new partner must invest an amount equal to a proportionate share of the fair market
value of the Club's assets after the admission. Neither goodwill nor bonus is recorded upon admission of
a new partner.

On January 1, 2017, the books of the Lucky Investment Club showed cash of $3,200 and a portfolio
of securities with a cost of $78,300 and a fair market value of $122,800. The Club has no liabilities, and
has 18 partners.

On January 2, 2017, Grant and Lee are admitted to the Club, each investing cash equal to a 1/18 share of the Club's assets at fair market value, prior to their investment of new cash. During 2017, the Club earned interest and dividends of $4,200. Each of the 20 partners invested $500 in new funds. Two securities were sold; each had been bought in 2015:

Security	Cost	Fair Market Value January 1, 2017	Selling Price
A.	$ 3,000	$ 6,600	$ 8,600
B.	11,000	9,200	8,200
Totals	$14,000	$15,800	$16,800

$40,000 was invested in new securities during 2017. The fair market value of the portfolio at December 31, 2017, was $166,000.

Required

a.   How much must Grant and Lee each invest on January 2, 2017?

b.   Allocate the Club's 2017 income among Grant, Lee, and the other 18 partners as a group.

c.   In January 2018, a major stock market rally increases the portfolio value to $228,000. Club members vote to sell the entire portfolio and disband the Club. How much will Grant, Lee, and the other 18 partners as a group each receive?

LO 4   P14.8   Admission of New Partner   Blackman and Coulter are highly successful criminal attorneys, practicing law in a partnership. Each earns approximately $600,000 annually, sharing profits equally. Since the firm has minimal capital needs, they withdraw most of their earnings. Their capital balances currently stand at $30,000 for Blackman and $40,000 for Coulter.

Xavier is a young staff attorney who has been with the firm for eight years. Xavier's research skills and case strategy plans have contributed significantly to the firm's success, but Xavier lacks the courtroom skills to be successful as a criminal trial attorney. Xavier currently receives an annual salary of $150,000.

Blackman and Coulter both anticipate retiring in ten years, at which point the firm will disband. To induce Xavier to remain with the firm over the next ten years, Blackman and Coulter propose to admit Xavier as an equal partner. Blackman and Coulter will admit Xavier in exchange for a payment equal to Xavier's increased earnings, discounted at 20 percent.

Required

Assuming continuation of current earnings levels, how much must Xavier pay to be admitted to the partnership?

⊘ LO 5   P14.9   Retirement of Two Partners   Thirty years ago, five mechanics formed a partnership and established an automobile repair shop. Two of the partners, Decker and Groth, are now retiring. The other three partners, Farmer, Wang, and Lux, are continuing the partnership. The original agreement called for an equal division of income. The remaining partners plan to continue this arrangement. The following balance sheet is prepared for the partnership as of the retirement date:

Cash	$130,000	Accounts payable	$175,000
Accounts receivable	160,000	Loan payable	80,000
Inventory of parts	80,000	Capital—Decker	100,000
Equipment, net	180,000	Capital—Groth	80,000
Building, net	60,000	Capital—Farmer	140,000
Land	50,000	Capital—Wang	20,000
		Capital—Lux	65,000
Total assets	$660,000	Total liabilities and capital	$660,000

All partners agreed that Decker should receive $130,000 for his interest in the business and Groth should receive $110,000. Farmer proposed the bonus method for recording the retirements. Wang objects to this method and suggests the partial goodwill approach.

Required

a. Prepare the journal entry to record the retirements under the bonus method.
b. Prepare the journal entry to record the retirements under the partial goodwill approach.
c. Why does Wang object to the bonus method of accounting?
d. Regardless of the accounting method employed, what immediate problem for the business can you identify at the time of retirement? Propose a solution to this problem.

P14.10 Financial Statement Effects of Retirement/Admission   Moore, Mills, Sinclair & Co. (MMS)   **LO 4, 5** is a rapidly-growing regional CPA firm. It actively recruits new staff accountants at major colleges and universities and aggressively pursues exceptional partners and near-partners at other CPA firms. Concurrently, MMS's founders have been retiring. Moore left last year and Mills and Sinclair are contemplating retiring soon. Prior to retirement of Mills and Sinclair, who each have a 20 percent share in profits and losses, the firm's condensed balance sheet appears as follows:

MOORE, MILLS, SINCLAIR & CO.
Balance Sheet
December 31, 2016

Cash and cash equivalents	$ 178,000
Accounts receivable—clients	430,000
Notes receivable—Sinclair	100,000
Prepayments	60,000
Fixed assets, net	500,000
Goodwill, net	800,000
Total assets	$2,068,000
Trade payables	$ 47,000
Accrued liabilities	209,000
Notes payable—1st National Bank	600,000
Notes payable—Moore	200,000
Capital—Mills	270,000
Capital—Sinclair	195,000
Capital—Other Partners	547,000
Total liabilities and capital	$2,068,000

After some discussion, the firm agrees to pay Mills $350,000 upon retirement, intending to borrow the cash to do so from 1st National Bank. Shortly thereafter, Luh, a highly competent and entrepreneurial information systems specialist, is offered a 10 percent interest in capital and profits for a $50,000 cash investment.

Required

a. Discuss the ways in which the methods of accounting for the retirement could weaken the above balance sheet, and illustrate with calculations.
b. Suppose Mills' retirement is accounted for by the total goodwill method. After Mills' retirement is recorded by the total goodwill approach, prepare pro-forma balance sheets for MMS that reflect Luh's admission under the two alternative admission methods.
c. Briefly describe the principal differences between the two balance sheets in part *b*. Which seems to portray the healthier firm? Why?

P14.11 Partnership Liquidation—Safe Payments   Several years ago, Ann Dennis, Jill Edwards, Lee   **LO 6** ✓ Lacy, and Sarah Ingram formed a partnership to operate the Deli Sisters Cafe. Rerouting of bus lines caused declines in patronage to the extent that the partners have agreed to dissolve the partnership and liquidate the assets. The November 2, 2017, balance sheet of the Deli Sisters Cafe and other data appear below. The partnership agreement did not specify how profits and losses were to be shared.

DELI SISTERS CAFE
Balance Sheet
November 2, 2017

Cash..........................	$ 30,000	Liabilities.......................	$ 50,100
Supplies	15,000	Loan—Ingram...................	20,000
Equipment	150,000	Capital—Dennis	52,000
Fixtures.......................	40,000	Capital—Edwards...............	45,000
		Capital—Lacy...................	19,900
		Capital—Ingram	48,000
Total assets	$235,000	Total liabilities and capital	$235,000

Additional information:

1. During November, sold half of the fixtures for $5,000. Sold equipment with a book value of $30,000 for $22,000.
2. During December, paid all outside creditors. A neighboring restaurant bought Deli Sisters Cafe's supplies at 80 percent of cost. Sold the remaining fixtures for $8,000.
3. During January, sold equipment with a book value of $40,000 for $28,000.

Required

Following the safe payment approach, specify how cash is to be distributed at the end of November, December, and January.

LO 6 **P14.12 Partnership Liquidation—Safe Payments** Partners Dodge, Edsel, Ford and Harley share income in a ratio of 8:5:4:3, respectively. On January 1, 2017, they decide to terminate operations and begin a process of liquidation. The partnership's trial balance on that date shows the following:

	Debit	Credit
Cash...	$ 32,000	
Accounts receivable..	87,000	
Loan receivable—Edsel	25,000	
Inventory...	55,000	
Land..	30,000	
Equipment	112,000	
Truck	37,000	
Bank loan payable		$ 75,000
Accounts payable..		48,000
Loan payable—Dodge		80,000
Capital—Dodge		71,000
Capital—Edsel		42,000
Capital—Ford..		53,000
Capital—Harley		9,000
Totals	$378,000	$378,000

To maximize proceeds, assets were sold over a three-month period. At the end of each month, available cash, less an amount retained to cover estimated future expenses, was distributed to the partners. The liquidation proceeded as follows:

January 2017:
1. Returned inventory costing $10,000 to the supplier, who granted a credit of $8,500 against the open accounts payable.
2. Collected $45,000 of the accounts receivable; collection of the remainder is uncertain.
3. Sold the remaining inventory to a competitor for $30,000.
4. Sold the equipment for $80,000.
5. Paid liquidation expenses of $5,500.
6. Paid the bank loan and the remaining accounts payable in full.
7. Retained $20,000 of cash for potential future obligations and liquidation expenses.

February 2017:
1. Collected $15,000 of the accounts receivable, and the remainder is determined to be uncollectible.
2. Transferred the truck to Dodge in exchange for a $30,000 reduction in the partnership's loan obligation to Dodge.

3. Paid liquidation expenses of $3,000.
4. Retained $10,000 of cash for potential future obligations and liquidation expenses.

March 2017:
1. Sold the land for $125,000.
2. Paid liquidation expenses of $8,000.
3. Distributed all remaining cash.

Required

Prepare a schedule to compute the safe installment payments to the partners at the end of January, February, and March 2017.

P14.13 Close Books and Prepare Cash Distribution Plan Arnold, Bell and Crane agree to liquidate **LO 3, 6** their partnership as soon as possible. The partnership agreement calls for salaries of $50,000 and $70,000 for Arnold and Bell, respectively; any remaining profit or loss is divided in a 2:5:3 ratio. The preclosing trial balance for the partnership at July 31, 2017, the end of the firm's fiscal year, is:

Account	Debit	Credit
Cash.	$ 95,000	
Other assets	350,000	
Liabilities.		$114,000
Loan payable—Crane.		36,000
Capital—Arnold		85,000
Capital—Bell.		70,000
Capital—Crane.		40,000
Sales.		732,000
Operating expenses	520,000	
Drawings—Arnold	60,000	
Drawings—Bell.	27,000	
Drawings—Crane	25,000	
Totals	$1,077,000	$1,077,000

Required

a. Prepare a schedule showing the balances in the capital accounts prior to liquidation.
b. Prepare a cash distribution plan for the liquidation.
c. Compute the amount that must be realized from the other assets to liquidate the liabilities and drive all capital accounts to zero.

P14.14 Analysis of Liquidation Scenario Partners Green and Blue have operated a coin laundry business **LO 6** in a strip shopping center for several years. Their income-sharing ratio is 3:2. The business was generating decent operating cash flow but in the last 18 months, cash flow declined precipitously. On alternate days each partner empties the coins from the laundromat's machines and deposits them in the bank.

Green is experiencing personal financial problems relating to a messy divorce and investments that went "in the tank." She is urging Blue to sell out and liquidate their partnership. The following trial balance is prepared by the partners' accountant.

	Dr (Cr)
Cash.	$ 2,300
Supplies and prepayments	900
Equipment	42,000
Accumulated depreciation	(17,000)
Accounts payable.	(1,350)
Loan payable—Blue.	(11,000)
Sales.	(25,000)
Operating expenses	13,000
Depreciation expense.	6,000
Capital—Green.	(5,000)
Capital—Blue.	(4,850)
Totals	$ 0

In addition, the partnership has a noncancellable lease (remaining term: 2 years) on the building where the laundromat is located, classified as an operating lease under *ASC Topic 840*. The monthly payments of $500 are based on an implicit annual interest rate of 9 percent and are consistently made on time. The lessor requires a $10,000 payment to release the lessees.

Required

a. Identify the weakness in the partnership's internal control which could produce the pattern of declining cash flow.

b. If the partners decide to liquidate, explain whether they should pay the $10,000 or the present value of the remaining lease payments.

c. Determine the ending capital balances and prepare a cash distribution plan for the liquidation.

d. How much must be realized on the sale of the supplies and prepayments and equipment before Green receives any of the liquidation proceeds? Do you think it is likely that Green will receive any proceeds? Explain.

LO 4, 6   **P14.15 Evaluation of Partnership Opportunities**   Reitmyer, Simon, and Trybus are partners in a real estate partnership. The partnership's balance sheet shows:

Cash..........................	$ 20,000	Mortgages payable...............	$300,000
Rental properties, net.............	700,000	Capital, Reitmyer (40%)...........	200,000
		Capital, Simon (40%).............	150,000
		Capital, Trybus (20%).............	70,000
Total assets	$720,000	Total liabilities and capital	$720,000

The partners are contemplating terminating their business, as they no longer wish to spend the time involved in managing the properties. Further, several properties are in need of renovation. They believe that the properties could be sold on a piecemeal basis for a total of $1,200,000. After paying off the mortgage debt, the remaining cash would be distributed to the partners.

Don and Mary Usher have approached the partnership with a proposal. Don is experienced at property maintenance and renovation, and Mary is experienced in property management. They are interested in getting into the real estate rental business. Both are currently employed, but they have little capital to invest. They offer $50,000 to be admitted as a 40 percent partner; the three existing partners would continue as partners, but would be relieved of all operating responsibilities. Each year for the next ten years, each old partner would receive a "salary" of $40,000 out of partnership earnings, though they would not be expected to render any services.

Because they would retain a collective 60 percent ownership, they could block any actions by Don and Mary that they deemed inadvisable. Their interests would be further protected by a security interest in the rental properties, though it would be subordinated to any present and future mortgage debt. At the end of the ten years, their remaining partnership interests would be transferred to the Ushers for $1,000 each. The Ushers could accelerate the process at any time by prepaying the future payments, at a 10 percent discount rate. The existing partners could terminate the agreement at any time and buy out the Ushers for a price of $50,000 times the number of years the agreement had been in effect. However, if the existing partners did not receive their specified salaries for two years, they could terminate the agreement without any payment due the Ushers.

Required

For each of the following five scenarios, determine the amount to be received, in present value terms, by each partner. Use a 10 percent discount rate.

a. Ushers' offer is not accepted. The properties are sold and the partnership is liquidated.

b. Ushers' offer is accepted and the agreement is completely fulfilled over the ten-year time span.

c. Ushers' offer is accepted. Despite their efforts, the Ushers are not able to turn the properties into money-makers, and have defaulted on the payments due the old partners for years 3 and 4. At the end of year 4, the old partners invoke their termination rights. The mortgage debt has grown to $400,000, as money was borrowed to finance renovations. It is estimated that the sales value of the various properties has fallen to $950,000.

d. Ushers' offer is accepted, and the Ushers have been quite successful in making the properties profitable. All payments to the old partners have been made as scheduled. However, tensions between the Ushers and the prior partners have escalated, due to different approaches to property management. By the end of year 5, the old partners are ready to invoke their termination rights, pay the Ushers the required buyout, and liquidate the partnership. The properties have an expected resale value of

$2,000,000, and mortgage debt stands at $650,000. However, before the old partners act, the Ushers borrow money and exercise their prepayment rights.

e.   Same as part *d* above, except that the Ushers do not exercise their prepayment rights.

REVIEW SOLUTIONS •••

Review 1 Solution

Net assets invested amount to $222,000 ($130,000 cash, $200,000 building, $17,000 office equipment, less $125,000 mortgage payable).

a.   Under the bonus method, $74,000 of capital (= $222,000/3) is credited to each partner. The entry to record the formation is:

Cash...	130,000	
Building	200,000	
Office equipment	17,000	
Mortgage payable......................................		125,000
Capital, Abel		74,000
Capital, Baker		74,000
Capital, Cahn...		74,000
To record formation of partnership under the bonus method.		

b.   Under the goodwill method, Abel's investment of $100,000 for a 1/3 interest would establish the value of the partnership at $300,000, resulting in goodwill of $78,000 (= $300,000 − $222,000). The entry to record the formation is:

Cash...	130,000	
Building	200,000	
Office equipment	17,000	
Goodwill...	78,000	
Mortgage payable......................................		125,000
Capital, Abel		100,000
Capital, Baker		100,000
Capital, Cahn...		100,000
To record formation of partnership under the goodwill method		

Review 2 Solution

a.   Baker's bonus, 10 percent of net income over $100,000, is $7,700 (= 10 percent × $77,000). Abel receives interest of $11,100 (= 15 percent × $74,000) and Cahn receives interest of $5,920 (=8 percent × $74,000). After the salaries, bonus, and interest are allocated, $32,280 remains to be shared equally.

Partner	Salary	Bonus	Interest	Balance	Total
Abel	—	—	$11,100	$10,760	$ 21,860
Baker	$ 80,000	$7,700	—	10,760	98,460
Cahn.............	40,000	—	5,920	10,760	56,680
Totals	$120,000	$7,700	$17,020	$32,280	$177,000

b.   Capital balances at year-end:

Partner	Beginning Capital	Income Allocation	Distributions	Ending Capital
Abel	$ 74,000	$ 21,860	—	$ 95,860
Baker	74,000	98,460	$ 87,700	84,760
Cahn.............	74,000	56,680	40,000	90,680
Totals	$222,000	$177,000	$127,700	$271,300

Review 3 Solution

Abel receives $135,400 (= $100,000 original investment plus $35,400 (= 20 percent × $177,000)). Abel's capital balance is $95,860. Thus Abel receives $39,540 (= $135,400 − $95,860) in excess of capital balance.

a. Under the bonus approach, Baker and Cahn each transfer $19,770 (= $39,540/2) of capital to Abel. The entries are:

Capital, Baker.	19,770	
Capital, Cahn	19,770	
Capital, Abel		39,540
To record transfer of capital to Abel under the bonus method.		
Capital, Abel	135,400	
Cash		135,400
To record payment to Abel.		

b. Under the partial goodwill approach, the $39,540 excess payment to Abel is recorded as goodwill.

Goodwill	39,540	
Capital, Abel		39,540
To record partial goodwill based on payment to Abel.		
Capital, Abel.	135,400	
Cash		135,400
To record payment to Abel.		

c. Under the total goodwill approach, the $39,540 excess payment for Abel's 1/3 interest is multiplied by 3 to get total goodwill of $118,620.

Goodwill	118,620	
Capital, Abel		39,540
Capital, Baker		39,540
Capital, Cahn.		39,540
To record total goodwill based on payment to Abel.		
Capital, Abel.	135,400	
Cash		135,400
To record payment to Abel.		

Following Abel's withdrawal, recorded by the total goodwill approach, the partnership's capital is $254,520 (Baker $124,300 (= $84,760 + $39,540) and Cahn $130,220 (= $90,680 + $39,540)). Dexter is admitted as a 20 percent partner for an investment of $28,000. Total net assets of the partnership after Dexter's admission is $282,520 (= $254,520 + $28,000).

d. Under the bonus approach, Dexter's share of capital is $56,504 (= 20 percent × $282,520), which exceeds Dexter's investment by $28,504 (= $56,504 − $28,000). This amount, shared equally, is a bonus from Baker and Cahn to Dexter. The entry is:

Cash.	28,000	
Capital, Baker.	14,252	
Capital, Cahn	14,252	
Capital, Dexter.		56,504
To record admission of Dexter under the bonus method.		

e. Under the goodwill approach, the value of the partnership based on the capital of Baker and Cahn is $318,150 (= $254,520/0.8). Thus Dexter's 20 percent share is $63,630 (= 20 percent × $318,150) and Dexter is presumed to have invested goodwill of $35,630 (= $63,630 − $28,000). The entry is:

Cash...	28,000	
Goodwill...	35,630	
Capital, Dexter..		63,630
To record admission of Dexter under the goodwill method.		

Review 4 Solution

Partners' capital is $570,000 (= $325,000 + $180,000 + $65,000) and partnership assets are $635,000 (= $570,000 capital + $65,000 liabilities). The sale of partnership assets for $800,000 yields a gain on $165,000 (= $800,000 − $635,000). Preparation of a cash distribution plan, as shown below, indicates the following sequence of distributions:

First $65,000 to creditors
Next $145,000 to Baker
Next $100,000 to Baker and Cahn in equal amounts
All remaining funds to Baker, Cahn, and Dexter in 4:4:2 ratio

Cash Distribution Plan:

	Baker	Cahn	Dexter
Capital balances after gain......................	$391,000	$246,000	$ 98,000
Standardized capital (divide by partner's percentage)...	$977,500	$615,000	$490,000
Equalize Baker with Cahn	(362,500)		
Balance..	$615,000	$615,000	$490,000
Equalize Baker and Cahn with Dexter	(125,000)	(125,000)	
Balance..	$490,000	$490,000	$490,000

Convert back into profit sharing ratios:

1. Baker receives first $145,000 (= $362,500 × 0.40)
2. Baker and Cahn then receive $50,000 each (= $125,000 × 0.40)
3. All partners share remaining cash in 4:4:2 ratio

The allocation of each distribution is as follows:

	Assets	Liabilities	Baker (40%)	Cahn (40%)	Dexter (20%)
Balances.......................	$635,000	$65,000	$325,000	$180,000	$65,000
Gain on sale	165,000	—	66,000	66,000	33,000
Balances after gain.............	800,000	65,000	391,000	246,000	98,000
First installment	(200,000)	(65,000)	(135,000)	—	—
Balances.......................	600,000	0	256,000	246,000	98,000
Partial second installment, to bring into 4:4:2 alignment	(110,000)	—	(60,000)	(50,000)	—
Balances.......................	490,000	0	196,000	196,000	98,000
Remainder of second installment.....	(90,000)	—	(36,000)	(36,000)	(18,000)
Balances.......................	400,000	0	160,000	160,000	80,000
Third installment.................	(200,000)	—	(80,000)	(80,000)	(40,000)
Balances.......................	200,000	0	80,000	80,000	40,000
Fourth installment...............	(200,000)	—	(80,000)	(80,000)	(40,000)
Balances.......................	$ 0	$ 0	$ 0	$ 0	$ 0

15 Bankruptcy and Reorganization

LEARNING OBJECTIVES

LO1 Explain the basic legal aspects of bankruptcy. (p. 664)

LO2 Prepare a statement of affairs for a Chapter 7 bankruptcy. (p. 665)

LO3 Prepare a statement of realization and liquidation. (p. 670)

LO4 Account for a company undergoing Chapter 11 reorganization. (p. 674)

LO5 Describe accounting for other forms of reorganization. (p. 683)

QUIZNOS

www.quiznos.com

Quiznos (legal name QIP Holder LLC) is a sandwich chain, based in Denver, Colorado, known for their toasted subs. Their outlets are concentrated in shopping malls and highway rest stops. Quiznos was founded in 1981 with one restaurant, and by 2007 had grown to over 5,000 locations in the U.S., Canada, and many other countries. Quiznos' ownership has varied over the years, starting as a sole proprietorship, then a privately held corporation, going public in 1994, and going private again in 2001. In 2006, a private equity firm acquired a 49% interest through a leveraged buyout, saddling Quiznos with $950 million in additional debt.

Starting in 2007, sales began slowing down and many Quiznos stores closed. Competition from other fast-food restaurants such as Chipotle, Panera and Subway cut market share. In 2012, two creditors gained control of the company through a debt restructuring and attempted to reverse the downward trend in sales. However, they were not successful and Quiznos filed for Chapter 11 bankruptcy protection in 2014. The reorganization plan calls for eliminating two thirds of Quiznos' debt, or $400 million, by replacing existing debt with a combination of new debt and equity. Current equity shares will be canceled. Quiznos continues to operate as it implements the plan, which includes other changes to improve operations, such as reducing food costs and making restaurant improvements.

When a company is unable to pay its creditors in a timely manner, they may file for Chapter 11 bankruptcy protection, where creditors agree to debt reductions and restructuring, and the company makes changes to cut costs and streamline operations. The company then emerges from bankruptcy protection. However, if the creditors do not agree on the planned restructuring, and changes in operations are not successful, the company may liquidate under Chapter 7 of the Bankruptcy Code. In that case, the company ceases to exist, and proceeds from the sale of its assets are distributed to its creditors.

There are many reporting issues relating to bankruptcy and reorganization. In Chapter 7 liquidation, it is important to keep track of asset sales and distribute the proceeds according to the legal rights of creditors and owners. In Chapter 11 reorganization, the company continues to operate, and income items related to reorganization must be clearly separated from normal operations. Once reorganization is complete, the company generally emerges with a "fresh start" balance sheet, displaying revalued assets and a new capital structure. There are other alternatives to bankruptcy and reorganization, such as quasi-reorganization, which streamlines asset values and resets retained earnings to zero, and troubled debt restructurings, where the company negotiates privately with specific creditors to change the terms of outstanding debt. This chapter covers the major reporting requirements for bankruptcy, reorganization, quasi-reorganization and troubled debt restructurings.

CHAPTER ORGANIZATION

Legal aspects of bankruptcy	Accounting for Chapter 7 bankruptcy (liquidation)	Accounting for Chapter 11 bankruptcy (reorganization)	Accounting for other forms of restructuring
• Chapters 7, 11 and 13 of Bankruptcy Code • Legal process of Chapter 7 liquidation • Legal process of Chapter 11 reorganization	• Categories of liabilities • Categories and valuation of assets • Statement of affairs • Statement of realization and liquidation	• Reporting during reorganization • Determining reorganization value • Fresh start reporting	• Quasi-reorganization • Troubled debt restructuring

Many firms encounter serious financial difficulties that threaten their continued existence. Well-known examples include Chrysler, General Motors, American Airlines, Enron, and Lehman Brothers. Among the actions possible in the face of serious financial problems are liquidation, reorganization, and debt restructuring. *Liquidation* and *reorganization* usually proceed under the provisions of the bankruptcy laws, while debt restructuring typically involves a private agreement between a debtor and a creditor. This chapter examines the accounting and reporting implications of these actions.

Estates and trusts are entities created to manage assets on behalf of others. One common example is the estate of a deceased individual: an executor manages the estate's assets until they are distributed to the decedent's beneficiaries. Similarly, trusts can manage assets on behalf of someone unable to manage their own assets, such as a child or an infirm person. The estate concept also applies to the management of the assets of a financially ailing firm in bankruptcy until the assets can be properly distributed to creditors, bondholders, and stockholders.

In the case of a bankrupt firm, a **trustee** or **receiver** responsible primarily to the creditors of the firm must repay as much of their claims as possible, consistent with the security agreements contained in debt contracts and with the provisions of bankruptcy law. The trustee or receiver has secondary responsibility to the stockholders and seeks to preserve as much of their ownership equity as possible.

Adherence to laws affecting firms in bankruptcy proceedings influences the accounting for these entities. These laws safeguard the interests of creditors while the trustee or receiver manages the firm's assets. The accountant's mission of reporting on the management of the assets to the concerned parties involves accounting and special reporting that show how the trustee's responsibilities have been met. To carry out this reporting responsibility, the accountant must consider the legal framework that constrains the operation of bankrupt firms.

The **trustee/receiver** is responsible for payment of claims:

- First to creditors
- Second to stockholders

LEGAL ASPECTS OF BANKRUPTCY

LO1 Explain the basic legal aspects of bankruptcy.

A firm in financial difficulty can pursue several possible courses of action: initiate formal actions under federal bankruptcy law, or less formal actions outside the judicial system. The least formal action has the firm agree with one or more creditors to **restructure** debt—to modify the terms or to settle the debt at less than full payment. When several creditors agree to debt restructuring, the process often leads to a **composition** or **creditors' composition agreement**. In a somewhat more formal procedure, an **assignment for the benefit of creditors** has the firm voluntarily transfer its assets to a trustee, who liquidates the assets and offers partial payment to the creditors on a *pro rata* basis. Creditors accept the offer and discharge the remaining debt, or they reject the offer and initiate proceedings to force the firm into involuntary bankruptcy.

Federal law provides the legal process and remedies for **bankruptcy**, the condition that individuals and business firms face when unable to meet their debts. The bankruptcy process seeks to provide relief and protection to debtors, and to satisfy creditors, either by *liquidating and distributing the debtor's assets* to its creditors, or by *restructuring the organization to continue operations* in a way that offers better prospects for generating sufficient cash flows to satisfy obligations to creditors.

Federal bankruptcy law consists primarily of the *Bankruptcy Act of 1898,* its subsequent revisions, and case law. Major revisions included the *Chandler Act of 1938,* and the *Bankruptcy Reform Act of 1978* that remains the basis for much of current bankruptcy law. Most bankruptcy legislation between 1978 and 2005 dealt with administrative matters and the authority of bankruptcy judges. Major new legislation appeared in the *Bankruptcy Abuse Prevention and Consumer Protection Act of 2005*, that was generally viewed as making bankruptcy more difficult for individual and corporate debtors.

Three different situations are referred to as Chapter 7, 11, and 13 proceedings. It is common to refer to specific provisions by their chapter number.

Chapter 7, applicable to both individuals and firms, provides for **liquidation** of the debtor's assets to pay the creditors. A trustee takes control of the firm's assets, sells them and distributes the proceeds to creditors on a *pro rata* basis. A completed liquidation process results in most remaining debts being **discharged**—cancelled with the creditor having no further claim. Debts not discharged include certain taxes, alimony and child support, and certain student loans. This non-discharge applies mostly to individuals and these claims remain valid against the individual's future income. Chapter 7 proceedings are **voluntary** when initiated by the debtor, **involuntary** when initiated by one or more creditors.

Chapter 11 is most commonly used by business firms, although it also applies to individuals. Chapter 11 provides for **reorganization**, whereby the firm continues in business without liquidating its assets. The firm develops an equitable plan that modifies the rights and interests of its creditors and stockholders and often restructures its business operations. If a plan of reorganization allows the firm to remain in possession of its assets, the firm is called a **debtor-in-possession** and management usually continues to operate the business. To be implemented, the reorganization plan must be approved by creditors representing two-thirds of the dollar claims and a creditors' committee supervises administration of the plan. Creditors may agree to settle for partial payment, to lengthen the payment period, to modify terms, or to accept equity in place of debt. Creditors often prefer reorganization to liquidation because the prospects of collecting what the firm owes tend to improve when the company continues to operate instead of selling its assets.

Chapter 13 of the Bankruptcy Code applies the reorganization concept to an *individual debtor* with a regular income. Rather than liquidating the debtor's assets, a **repayment plan** is worked out with creditors. The 2005 bankruptcy legislation cited earlier made significant changes to individual bankruptcy that reduces the frequency with which a person can file for bankruptcy protection. This text does not examine Chapter 13 proceedings.

Bankruptcy filings are a common occurrence. According to U.S Bankruptcy Court statistics, in 2013 about 1.1 million bankruptcy petitions were filed, a 12% decline from 2012. In 2005, before the change in the bankruptcy laws, over 2,000,000 petitions were filed. In 2013, 33,212 petitions were filed by business entities and 1,038,720 by nonbusiness entities, primarily individuals. Of the various types, about 730,000 filings fell under Chapter 7 of the Bankruptcy Code, 9,000 filings under Chapter 11, and 330,000 filings under Chapter 13.

Legal Process of Chapter 7 Liquidation

The legal process of a Chapter 7 bankruptcy begins with filing a petition in the federal bankruptcy court. This petition states that the debtor cannot meet obligations and requests that the provisions of the bankruptcy law be applied. When the debtor files the petition, it is a **voluntary petition**; when filed by creditors, it is an **involuntary petition**. The law requires that a specified number of creditors having a significant amount of claims against the firm must agree to file an involuntary petition.

When accepted by the bankruptcy judge, a properly filed petition subjects the debtor to an orderly process. Individual creditors cannot enforce liens or judgments, or repossess assets of the debtor. Rather, the claims of all creditors are processed and satisfied, to the extent possible, by applying the provisions of the law. The desire to be subject to this orderly process rather than face the lawsuits, repossessions, and liens of individual creditors explains why some debtors file voluntary petitions.

Chapter 7 mandates appointment of a **trustee** to take possession of the debtor's assets, convert them to cash over a period of time, and distribute cash to creditors according to their legal rights and priorities. Usually, the cash is insufficient to pay all debts fully. The trustee distributes all assets before **discharging** and releasing the debtor from all remaining debts. At that point the debtor company ceases to exist.

Legal Process of Chapter 11 Reorganization

The Chapter 11 reorganization process also begins when the debtor firm files a petition with the bankruptcy court. This filing begins the **reorganization proceeding** designed to preserve the company as a going concern while maximizing the recovery by creditors and stockholders.

Critical to the reorganization process is the **plan of reorganization**, a proposal to restructure the debt and equity interests of the company and fashion the entity that will emerge as the continuing operating firm. In a Chapter 11 filing the debtor usually remains in possession, although the court appoints a trustee when there is cause to do so. After the debtor proposes a reorganization plan, affected parties may respond and offer alternative plans. Ultimately, the bankruptcy court confirms the plan that it finds to be *feasible,* in the *best interests of the creditors*, and *fair and equitable* to any creditors unwilling to accept it. Once confirmed, the plan of reorganization binds all parties, including those that originally objected to it. Remaining corporate debts are not legally discharged as in a Chapter 7 liquidation.

FINANCIAL REPORTING FOR CHAPTER 7 LIQUIDATION

The financial reports for a Chapter 7 bankruptcy liquidation fall into two categories:

1. The **statement of affairs**, a balance sheet, shows the debtor firm's assets at their likely recoverable value, and the liabilities according to the legal status of the claims.

2. The **statement of realization and liquidation**, an operating statement, shows how the trustee has managed the bankrupt firm's assets on behalf of the creditors.

Statement of Affairs

The **statement of affairs** is a statement of financial condition for a company entering a Chapter 7 bankruptcy. Because such a company is no longer a going concern, **estimated realizable values** replace historical costs and going-concern fair values as the amounts reported for the debtor firm's assets. Thus the statement shows the amounts likely to be realized to satisfy creditors' claims.

LO2 Prepare a statement of affairs for a Chapter 7 bankruptcy.

Reporting the Debtor's Liabilities   The statement of affairs presents a firm's liabilities in order of legal priority for repayment. Liabilities are organized into four categories:

1. **Fully secured liabilities.** The creditor has a lien on specific assets with estimated realizable values *equal to or greater than* the amount of the liability. For example, a bank holds a $700,000 mortgage secured by a bankrupt firm's building. The building has an estimated realizable value of $1,000,000. Because the $1,000,000 proceeds expected from the sale of the building exceed the

mortgage amount, the mortgage is **fully secured**, and the bank is a **fully secured creditor**. The bank receives $700,000 of the proceeds from the sale of the building before other creditors' claims are addressed.

2. **Partially secured liabilities.** The creditor has a lien on specific assets with estimable realizable values *less than* the amount of the liability. For example, a finance company holds a $200,000 note secured by equipment of a bankrupt firm with an estimated realizable value of only $90,000. The note is only **partially secured**, and the finance company is a **partially secured creditor**. The finance company receives the full proceeds from the sale of the equipment; other creditors have no claim on these proceeds. The remaining $110,000 owed to the finance company is unsecured debt.

3. **Unsecured liabilities with priority.** These are obligations where the creditor has no lien on any specific assets of the bankrupt firm, but Section 507 of the Bankruptcy Code identifies the claims as having priority by *law* over other unsecured creditors. These claims are considered **unsecured liabilities with priority**. Common priority claims against bankrupt businesses include the following, in order of payment priority.

   • Administrative expenses of the trustee, including accounting and legal costs, as well as compensation to the trustee for work performed.

   • Unpaid compensation to employees, from services rendered within 180 days of filing for bankruptcy.

   • Amounts due to employee benefit plans, from services rendered within 180 days of filing for bankruptcy.

   • Amounts paid to the bankrupt firm by its customers, for goods or services that were not delivered.

   • Income, property, employment, excise, or sales taxes owed to the government.

   The Code sets forth limits on priority claims for compensation, pensions, and amounts owing to customers. These limits are inflation-adjusted, and vary from year to year.

4. **Unsecured liabilities.** These are claims with no liens and no priority status, and are considered **unsecured**. This category includes the unsecured portion of partially secured liabilities, for example the $110,000 owed to the finance company above, that is not secured by the equipment.

Reporting the Debtor's Assets   The statement of affairs also presents the realizable value of the bankrupt firm's assets, in order indicating how the proceeds from their sale are used to pay claims. Assets are organized into three categories:

1. **Assets pledged to fully secured creditors.** Assets may be pledged as security for a particular liability. If the estimated realizable value of the assets *equals or exceeds* the amount of the liability, the liquidation of these assets can yield resources used to pay unsecured liabilities. The building with an estimated realizable value of $1,000,000 that secures a $700,000 mortgage liability illustrates an asset pledged to a fully secured creditor. After paying the $700,000 mortgage, $300,000 remains for unsecured creditors.

2. **Assets pledged to partially secured creditors.** Assets may be pledged as security for particular liabilities, where the realizable value of the asset is *less than* the amount of the liability. Liquidation of the asset yields resources used for partial payment of the liability; nothing remains for the unsecured creditors. The remaining liability is unsecured. The equipment with a realizable value of $90,000 that secures a $200,000 loan payable illustrates an asset pledged to a partially secured creditor. The remaining $110,000 of the note is unsecured.

3. **Free assets.** Assets may not be pledged as security for any particular liability, and proceeds from their sale are thus available to meet the claims of unsecured creditors. Called *free assets*, this category also includes the value of assets pledged to fully secured creditors, in excess of the related liabilities. The building with a realizable value of $1,000,000, that is pledged as security for a $700,000 mortgage, has two components: a $700,000 asset pledged to fully secured creditors, and a $300,000 free asset, available to unsecured creditors.

Format of the Statement of Affairs   The statement of affairs presents assets and liabilities organized into the categories just discussed. Secured claims and corresponding assets are offset so that the statement of affairs shows both the *total amount of free assets* and the *total amount of unsecured liabilities*. We net these two amounts to show the **estimated deficiency to unsecured creditors**—the amount by which the unsecured liabilities exceed the assets available to pay them. An example statement of affairs appears in Exhibit 15.1.

The **liability section** is developed first, and displays creditors' claims and unsecured liabilities. Unsecured liabilities include the excess of partially secured debt ($155,000) over the realizable value of pledged assets ($80,000), plus unsecured debts ($315,000). Fully secured debts are displayed, but not included in the computation of unsecured liabilities, as they are paid using the proceeds from pledged assets. Unsecured liabilities with priority are also displayed, but not included in the computation of unsecured liabilities. Unsecured liabilities with priority are paid before other unsecured liabilities, and are offset against free assets in the asset section of the statement of affairs.

EXHIBIT 15.1   **Format of the Statement of Affairs**

X CORPORATION
Statement of Affairs *(In thousands)*
Date

Book Value		Estimated Realizable Value	Free Assets
$320	Assets pledged to fully secured creditors: (list)	$340	
	Less: Liabilities to fully secured creditors	(275)	$ 65
60	Assets pledged to partially secured creditors: (list)	$ 80	
400	Free assets: (list).		137
	Total free assets.		202
	Less: Unsecured liabilities with priority		(24)
	Net free assets		178
	Estimated deficiency to unsecured creditors.		212
$780	Total unsecured liabilities.		$390

Book Value		Creditors' Claims	Unsecured Liabilities
$275	Fully secured creditors: (list).	$275	
155	Partially secured creditors: (list)	$155	
	Less: Value of pledged assets	(80)	$ 75
24	Unsecured creditors with priority: (list).	$ 24	
315	Unsecured creditors: (list)		315
11	Stockholders' equity		—
$780	Total unsecured liabilities.		$390

The **asset section** displays the realizable value of assets pledged to fully and partially secured creditors, as well as unpledged assets. **Total free assets** consist of the value of unpledged assets ($137,000) plus the value of assets pledged to fully secured creditors, in excess of related liabilities ($65,000). **Unsecured liabilities with priority** ($24,000) are subtracted from total free assets to yield **net free assets** ($178,000). Net free assets are available to pay unsecured liabilities without priority ($390,000), which was calculated in the liabilities section of the statement. In this illustration, $178,000 is expected to be available to pay unsecured debts totaling $390,000, resulting in an **estimated deficiency to unsecured creditors** of $212,000 (= $390,000 − $178,000). In this example, unsecured creditors can expect to be paid about $0.46 (= $178,000/$390,000) per dollar of debt. This calculation is known as the **expected recovery percentage** for unsecured creditors. Note that priority claims, though unsecured, are netted out of the $178,000 available to unsecured creditors, since they are paid in full before other unsecured debts can be paid. They are also not included in the $390,000 of total unsecured liabilities.

The format of the statement of affairs highlights the key aspects of bankruptcy reporting. Because estimated realizable values are more relevant than historical costs for a company that is no longer a going concern, we present information directly related to the debtor's ability to repay the various classes of creditors. Reported book values are also often shown, since they tie the statement of affairs to the conventional historical cost balance sheet, and indicate the expected gains and losses upon liquidation.

Illustration of Statement of Affairs   Bristol Corporation enters Chapter 7 bankruptcy proceedings on October 31, 2017. Bristol's unclassified balance sheet on that date shows the following information:

BRISTOL CORPORATION
Balance Sheet
October 31, 2017

Assets		Liabilities and stockholders' equity	
Cash.................................	$ 4,000	Accounts payable....................	$134,000
Marketable securities.................	7,000	Loan payable	100,000
Accounts receivable..................	27,000	Equipment note payable	30,000
Inventory............................	63,000	Accrued wages.......................	41,000
Land	15,000	Taxes payable	12,000
Building	135,000	Mortgage payable	94,000
Equipment	163,000	Stockholders' equity	14,000
Goodwill............................	11,000		
Total assets	$425,000	Total liabilities and stockholders' equity ..	$425,000

A firm may enter bankruptcy even though it has positive stockholders' equity if the firm cannot meet its debt obligations. Reported total assets may be greater than liabilities, but all assets are not available to pay obligations. In addition, reported asset values, based on the going concern assumption, may overstate amounts expected to be realized on liquidation.

Suppose Bristol's assets have the following realizable values:

Cash..	$ 4,000
Marketable securities..	9,000
Accounts receivable...	20,000
Inventory...	44,000
Land and building...	190,000
Equipment	63,900
Goodwill...	—
Total..	$330,900

Bristol's assets cannot cover its $411,000 (= $425,000 − $14,000) in liabilities. The receivables and inventory are pledged as security for the $100,000 loan and the land and building secures the $94,000 mortgage. A machine with an estimated realizable value of $22,000 and a book value of $20,000 secures the $30,000 equipment note payable. The priority liability balances are within legal limits.

The statement of affairs for Bristol appears in Exhibit 15.2 and shows net free assets of $97,900, unsecured liabilities of $178,000, and an estimated deficiency to unsecured creditors of $80,100. The **expected recovery percentage** for Bristol's unsecured creditors is 55 percent, calculated below.

$$\text{Expected recovery percentage} = \text{Net free assets/Unsecured liabilities}$$

$$= \$97,900/\$178,000$$

$$= 55 \text{ percent}$$

EXHIBIT 15.2   Statement of Affairs for Bristol Corporation

BRISTOL CORPORATION
Statement of Affairs
October 31, 2017

Book Value		Estimated Realizable Value	Free Assets
$150,000	Assets pledged to fully secured creditors:		
	Land and building.	$190,000	
	Less: Mortgage payable.	94,000	$ 96,000
	Assets pledged to partially secured creditors:		
27,000	Accounts receivable.	20,000	
63,000	Inventory.	44,000	
20,000	Equipment	22,000	
	Total assets pledged to partially secured creditors	$ 86,000	
	Free assets:		
4,000	Cash.	$ 4,000	
7,000	Marketable securities	9,000	
143,000	Equipment	41,900	
11,000	Goodwill	0	54,900
	Total free assets.		150,900
	Less: Unsecured liabilities with priority		53,000
	Net free assets		97,900
	Estimated deficiency to unsecured creditors.		80,100
$425,000	Total unsecured liabilities.		$178,000

Book Value		Creditors' Claims	Unsecured Liabilities
	Fully secured creditors:		
$ 94,000	Mortgage payable	$ 94,000	
	Partially secured creditors:		
100,000	Loan payable	100,000	
	Less: Value of accounts receivable and inventory	64,000	$ 36,000
30,000	Equipment note payable	30,000	
	Less: Value of machine	22,000	8,000
	Unsecured creditors with priority:		
41,000	Accrued wages.	41,000	
12,000	Taxes payable	12,000	
	Total unsecured creditors with priority.	$ 53,000	
	Unsecured creditors:		
134,000	Accounts payable.		134,000
14,000	Stockholders' equity		0
$425,000	Total unsecured liabilities.		$178,000

Bristol's unsecured creditors can expect to receive 55 cents per dollar owed to them by the bankrupt firm. Fully secured creditors will receive the full amount owed them, as will the unsecured creditors with priority. The partially secured creditors receive less than 100 percent of what they are owed, but more than the percentage received by unsecured creditors. We can calculate the total recovery expected by the two partially secured creditors in this example, as follows:

Loan payable of $100,000:	
Secured portion (full recovery) value of pledged assets..	$64,000
Unsecured portion (partial recovery) $36,000 × 55%	19,800
Total recovery...	$83,800

Equipment note payable of $30,000:	
Secured portion (full recovery) value of pledged asset................................	$22,000
Unsecured portion (partial recovery) $8,000 × 55%	4,400
Total recovery...	$26,400

Thus the loan creditor recovers 83.8 percent (= $83,800/$100,000), and the equipment note creditor recovers 88 percent (= $26,400/$30,000).

REVIEW 1   ●   Chapter 7 Liquidation

Baines Corporation is undergoing liquidation under Chapter 7 of the bankruptcy code. Baines reports total liabilities of $820,000 and its assets have a liquidation value of $650,000. Of those assets, $300,000 are pledged as security on debt obligations of $220,000, and another $120,000 are pledged as security on $180,000 of liabilities. Unsecured liabilities with priority amount to $30,000.

Required

Calculate net free assets and the expected recovery percentage for unsecured creditors.

Solutions are located after the chapter assignments.

Statement of Realization and Liquidation

LO3 Prepare a statement of realization and liquidation.

The **statement of realization and liquidation** provides a complete record of the **receiver's transactions** during a period of time. Whereas the statement of affairs set forth the creditor claims and the expected realizable values of assets as the firm entered bankruptcy, the realization and liquidation statement reports on assets sold and liabilities paid during the liquidation process.

One task of the receiver is to **realize the assets**—to convert the noncash assets into cash to pay creditors. The process of realization takes several forms. Certain operating activities of the firm continue for a time and provide cash or other assets. Some assets are realized in normal business operations, such as collection of customer receivables. Other assets are realized through sale. Because the receiver acts in the best interest of the creditors, he or she selects the means of realization that provides the greatest return to the creditors. As a result, the realization process can extend over a considerable period of time, while gains and losses on asset sales occur, expenses are incurred, and revenues are earned.

Format of the Statement of Realization and Liquidation   Various formats are found in practice; Exhibit 15.3 shows one possibility. The statement focuses only on the realization of noncash assets and the liquidation of liabilities.

The assets realized and liabilities liquidated are reported at actual amounts received or paid. Assets to be realized are reported at book value. The differences between book value and cash received or paid appear in the gain/loss sections of the statement.

EXHIBIT 15.3   Format of the Statement of Realization and Liquidation

X CORPORATION
(Name of Receiver or Trustee)
Statement of Realization and Liquidation
(Time Period Covered)

Assets to be realized:	Assets realized:
(List and amounts)	(List and amounts of proceeds)
Assets acquired:	Assets not realized:
(List and amounts)	(List and amounts)
Liabilities liquidated:	Liabilities to be liquidated:
(List and amounts of payments)	(List and amounts)
Liabilities not liquidated:	Liabilities incurred:
(List and amounts)	(List and amounts)
Gain on realization or liquidation:	Loss on realization or liquidation:
COMBINED TOTAL	COMBINED TOTAL

A *balance sheet* and a *statement of estate deficit* should accompany the realization and liquidation statement. The **balance sheet of the trustee** has the following format:

Trustee
Balance Sheet

Cash.................................	$ X	Liabilities not liquidated	$XX
Assets not realized (book value).............	XX	Estate deficit.............................	X
Total assets	$XX	Total liabilities and equity.................	$XX

A **statement of estate deficit** shows the periodic revenues, expenses, gains, and losses that produce a net change in the estate deficit. The initial balance of the estate deficit is the stockholders' equity of the firm, and subsequent transactions by the receiver increase or decrease this amount. Note the concept of *estate* used here; *the receiver acts as fiduciary to manage the assets of the bankrupt firm on behalf of its creditors.* The statement of estate deficit is analogous to a statement of changes in owners' equity of a going concern. One format of this statement appears next:

Statement of Estate Deficit

Revenues	$X	
Gains	X	$XX
Expenses	X	
Losses	X	XX
Net Change in estate deficit.................................		X
Estate deficit—beginning of period		X
Estate deficit—end of period		$XX

• •

Reporting Perspective

When reporting changes in the estate deficit, a firm in receivership or bankruptcy must consider whether to recognize depreciation. When the firm continues its operating activities, recognition of depreciation is appropriate to measure the results of operations. If few or no operating activities are being conducted—often the case when assets are being sold and liabilities settled—no depreciation charges should be recorded.

• •

Illustration of Statement of Realization and Liquidation   Joanne Willis is appointed receiver of the Weeks Corporation, a company in bankruptcy. Her responsibilities are to administer the bankrupt firm, to realize the assets, and to liquidate the liabilities. At the time of her appointment, the company's balance sheet appears as follows; none of the liabilities are secured.

WEEKS CORPORATION Balance Sheet March 31, 2016			
Cash............................	$ 1,000	Accounts payable....................	$27,000
Accounts receivable.................	6,000	Accrued wages......................	5,000
Inventories	11,000	Notes payable	40,000
Equipment, net.....................	35,000	Stockholders' equity	(19,000)
Total assets	$53,000	Total liabilities and equity.............	$53,000

Willis takes control of the company's assets and has a statement of affairs prepared to show the estimated realizable values of the company's assets, and the estimated recovery by each class of creditors. She then establishes accounting records for herself as trustee. Her initial entry records the assets and liabilities that she is administering at their book values:

Cash...	1,000	
Accounts receivable..	6,000	
Inventories	11,000	
Equipment	35,000	
Estate deficit...	19,000	
Accounts payable		27,000
Accrued wages		5,000
Notes payable		40,000
To record assets and liabilities of Weeks Corporation, administered by Receiver Joanne Willis.		

Suppose that during the next three months, the following six transactions occur:

1. Collected $3,300 in settlement of $5,000 of accounts receivable; the remaining $1,000 is expected to be collectible.
2. Sold for $6,400 inventory items having a book value of $8,000.
3. Sold for $12,000 a machine with a book value of $7,000.
4. Paid the accrued wages.
5. Accrued administrative expenses of $4,000.
6. Made an initial payment of 20 cents per dollar of indebtedness to the unsecured creditors.

Receiver Willis records these transactions as follows:

1.			
	Cash..	3,300	
	Loss on realization	1,700	
	Accounts receivable		5,000
	To record collection of receivables.		

2.			
	Cash..	6,400	
	Loss on realization	1,600	
	Inventory		8,000
	To record sale of inventory.		

3.			
	Cash..	12,000	
	Equipment..		7,000
	Gain on realization.......................................		5,000
	To record sale of machine.		

continued

4.

Accrued wages.	5,000	
Cash		5,000
To record payment of wages.		

5.

Administrative expenses	4,000	
Accrued expenses.		4,000
To accrue expenses of trustee.		

6.

Accounts payable.	5,400	
Notes payable	8,000	
Cash		13,400
To record partial payment of 20 percent of amount due to unsecured		
creditors; $13,400 = 0.2 × ($27,000 + $40,000).		

The statement of realization and liquidation, along with the receiver's balance sheet and the statement of estate deficit at June 30, 2016, appear in Exhibit 15.4.

EXHIBIT 15.4   Receiver's Financial Statements

WEEKS CORPORATION
Joanne Willis, Receiver
Statement of Realization and Liquidation
For Three Months Ended June 30, 2016

Assets to be realized:			**Assets realized:**			
Accounts receivable	$ 6,000		Accounts receivable	$ 3,300		
Inventory.	11,000		Inventory.	6,400		
Equipment.	35,000	$ 52,000	Equipment.	12,000	$ 21,700	
Assets acquired:			**Assets not realized:**			
None			Accounts receivable	1,000		
			Inventory.	3,000		
			Equipment.	28,000	32,000	
Liabilities liquidated:			**Liabilities to be liquidated:**			
Accounts payable	5,400		Accounts payable	27,000		
Accrued wages.	5,000		Accrued wages.	5,000		
Notes payable.	8,000	18,400	Notes payable.	40,000	72,000	
Liabilities not liquidated:			**Liabilities incurred:**			
Accounts payable	21,600		Accrued expenses		4,000	
Notes payable.	32,000					
Accrued expenses	4,000	57,600				
Gain on realization		5,000	Loss on realization		3,300	
Combined total.		$133,000	Combined total.		$133,000	

WEEKS CORPORATION
Joanne Willis, Receiver
Balance Sheet
June 30, 2016

Cash.	$ 4,300	Accounts payable.	$21,600
Accounts receivable.	1,000	Notes payable	32,000
Inventory.	3,000	Accrued expenses	4,000
Equipment	28,000	Estate deficit.	(21,300)
Total assets	$36,300	Total liabilities and equity.	$36,300

continued

continued from prior page

EXHIBIT 15.4 Receiver's Financial Statements

WEEKS CORPORATION
Joanne Willis, Receiver
Statement of Estate Deficit
June 30, 2016

Gain on realization		$ 5,000
Loss on realization	$ 3,300	
Administrative expenses	4,000	7,300
Net change in estate deficit		(2,300)
Estate deficit, March 31, 2013		(19,000)
Estate deficit, June 30, 2013		$(21,300)

FINANCIAL REPORTING FOR CHAPTER 11 REORGANIZATION

LO4 Account for a company undergoing Chapter 11 reorganization.

Because the bankruptcy process of Chapter 7 results in the *liquidation* of the firm, financial reporting focused on the realizable value of assets and the priority of settling liability claims. The bankruptcy process of Chapter 11, on the other hand, results in the *reorganization* of the firm and its continued operation in restructured form. Financial reporting emphasizes the various aspects of restructuring, including disposition and revaluation of assets, settlement and modification of liabilities, and changes in equity interests. Reporting requirements are found in *FASB ASC Topic 852*, Reorganizations.

Reporting During the Reorganization Process

Unlike a Chapter 7 proceeding, which envisions liquidation, the going concern assumption continues to be valid in a Chapter 11 reorganization. Thus, changes in the existing historical cost valuation of assets and liabilities are not normally needed. The two major areas affected concern the *presentation of liability information* and the *distinction between operating transactions and transactions associated with the reorganization process*.

Reporting Liabilities During a Reorganization During reorganization, the balance sheet should separately classify the amount of liabilities *subject to compromise*. A liability is **subject to compromise** if it is a *prepetition* liability and is *not* fully secured. A **prepetition liability** arose *prior to filing* for Chapter 11 protection, or arose after filing but resulted from pre-bankruptcy events and is allowed by the court as a prepetition claim. An example of the latter is a liability incurred *after filing* for prematurely terminating a lease that existed prior to filing.

The balance sheet of the firm in reorganization reports the total amount of liabilities subject to compromise under a separate caption, with disclosure of the major categories of these claims in the notes to the financial statements. Because payments on these liabilities cease upon initiating reorganization, pending development of a settlement plan, a current/noncurrent classification is not used. No payment of these liabilities is likely while the firm is in reorganization. On the other hand, the firm pays liabilities *not* subject to compromise on a timely basis, and reports them in the usual current and noncurrent categories.

Reporting liabilities subject to compromise separately from those not subject to compromise does not affect *valuation*. All liabilities are reported at the amounts expected to be *allowed* by the court, generally the existing book value, even though many of these liabilities are eventually *settled for lesser amounts*.

BUSINESS APPLICATION   The Crystal Cathedral

Bankruptcy is not limited to business enterprises; not-for-profits enter bankruptcy as well. The **Crystal Cathedral**, which took its name from the 10,000-plus panes of glass on its façade, was a Protestant Christian church in Orange County, California, known for its "Hour of Power" broadcasts. It filed for bankruptcy in 2010, with over $50 million in debts. Its major asset was its campus and its distinctive building. Numerous bidders emerged for the property, including Chapman University and retailer Hobby Lobby. In 2012, the property was sold to the Roman Catholic Diocese of Orange County for $57.5 million. Over the next several years the Diocese renovated the property and renamed the main building as Christ Cathedral.

Recognition of Reorganization Items   The firm undergoing reorganization must next identify revenues, expenses, gains, and losses resulting from reorganization, and separate these items from the results of ongoing operations. The following elements are among those likely to appear as **reorganization items** on the income statement:

- Legal, accounting, and other costs directly resulting from the reorganization process.
- Gains and losses from asset dispositions, except that gains and losses from *disposals of a business segment* are reported according to the provisions of *ASC Subtopic 205-20*.
- Gains and losses resulting from adjusting existing book values of liabilities to the *amounts likely to be allowed* by the court.
- Adjustments resulting from recording liabilities brought about by the reorganization process, such as cancellation of a purchase contract.
- Interest income. Because debt payments are typically halted during the reorganization process, pending the development and approval of the reorganization plan, a temporary accumulation and investment of cash is likely; the interest earned is deemed to be a reorganization item.

Settlements of prepetition liabilities do not normally occur *during* the reorganization process, and hence are not likely to appear in the category of reorganization items. Such settlements are governed by the reorganization plan, and are recorded as the firm *emerges from reorganization*, discussed later.

   Although interest expense is included as an operating item rather than a reorganization item, the full contractual amount of interest is not likely to be recorded. Interest expense is recorded during reorganization only to the extent that it is *actually paid, or accrued when likely to be allowed as a claim*. Differences between contractual amounts of interest and recorded amounts should be disclosed in the notes to the financial statements.

   The **statement of cash flows** also separately identifies reorganization items. A separate section for reorganization items, such as professional fees and interest revenue, appears in the operating activities section. We suggest reporting operating cash flows by the *direct method* to facilitate the separation of cash flows relating to the reorganization. The investing activities section reports proceeds from asset sales resulting from the reorganization process. Finally, the financing activities section distinguishes between payment of prepetition and postpetition liabilities.

Major differences in financial statements during reorganization:

- Liabilities subject to compromise are shown as a separate line on the balance sheet.
- Current/noncurrent classification of liabilities is not employed for liabilities subject to compromise.
- Liabilities are recorded at amounts expected to be allowed by the court.
- Reorganization items are shown separately from the results of ongoing operations on the income statement.
- Reorganization items are also shown separately on the statement of cash flows.

Illustration of Financial Reporting During Reorganization Manson Corporation filed a petition for relief under Chapter 11 of the bankruptcy laws in April 2016. The company continued to operate while developing a plan of reorganization, and is considered a **debtor-in-possession**. The company considers all its prepetition liabilities to be subject to compromise, except for a mortgage secured by the company's headquarters building.

During the remaining months of 2016, Manson sold excess equipment and vehicles for $75,000, resulting in a $30,000 loss. Termination of a warehouse lease resulted in a $25,000 cancellation penalty. Other reorganization items included $42,000 paid for professional fees and $6,000 received in interest revenue. No prepetition liabilities were paid after the filing date, except for $13,000 in wages and customer warranty claims approved by the bankruptcy court. Manson's financial statements at December 31, 2016, appear as follows.

MANSON CORPORATION
(Debtor-in-Possession)
Balance Sheet
December 31, 2016

Current assets		Current liabilities (postpetition).....		$ 360,000
Cash.........................	$ 150,000	Long-term liabilities (prepetition,		
Accounts receivable..............	320,000	fully secured):		
Inventories	550,000	Mortgage payable.............		800,000
Prepaid expenses...............	70,000	Liabilities subject to compromise...		2,500,000
	1,090,000	Stockholders' equity		
Property, plant and equipment, net ..	2,390,000	Preferred stock...............	$400,000	
Intangible assets	120,000	Common stock................	100,000	
		Retained earnings	(560,000)	(60,000)
Total assets	$3,600,000	Total liabilities and equity.........		$3,600,000

The following liabilities are **subject to compromise**:

15% notes payable, partially secured by inventories and receivables	$1,000,000
Bank loan payable, unsecured..	300,000
Taxes payable (priority claims)...	150,000
Accounts payable and other liabilities	1,050,000
Total	$2,500,000

The income statement for the year is as follows:

MANSON CORPORATION
(Debtor-in-Possession)
Income Statement
For Year Ended December 31, 2016

Revenues		$3,100,000
Expenses		(2,980,000)
Income before reorganization items and taxes		120,000
Reorganization items:		
Professional fees	$(42,000)	
Loss on sale of equipment and vehicles	(30,000)	
Lease termination penalty......................................	(25,000)	
Interest revenue	6,000	(91,000)
Income before taxes...		29,000
Income tax expense...		(10,000)
Net income..		$ 19,000

The following condensed statement of cash flows illustrates presentation of the reorganization items. Because the filing of the Chapter 11 petition temporarily halts payments on prepetition debt, the company's cash balance increased substantially. Balances not related to reorganization activities are assumed.

MANSON CORPORATION (Debtor-in-Possession) Statement of Cash Flows For Year Ended December 31, 2016		
Cash flows from operating activities		$ 64,000
Operating cash flows from reorganization items:		
Interest received	$ 6,000	
Professional fees paid	(42,000)	(36,000)
		28,000
Cash flows from investing activities:		
Capital expenditures.	(10,000)	
Proceeds from sale of equipment and vehicles due to reorganization	75,000	65,000
Cash flows from financing activities:		
Net short-term borrowing (postpetition).	50,000	
Payments of prepetition debt authorized by court.	(13,000)	37,000
Net increase in cash.		$130,000

The reporting just illustrated applies while the company is in the reorganization process. As seen in the next section, different reporting considerations apply when the company *emerges from reorganization* as a restructured entity.

Reporting After Reorganization

The key element in the firm's **emergence from reorganization** as a new, restructured entity is the **confirmation of the plan of reorganization** by the Bankruptcy Court. Once confirmed, the plan binds all parties, even those creditors unwilling to agree to it. The confirmed plan typically provides for the *compromise* of prepetition liabilities and for reduction or elimination of prior equity interests. If certain conditions are met, the emerging firm is considered a *new entity for accounting purposes*.

Reorganization Value   In the new entity, assets must equal liabilities plus equity interests; any retained earnings deficit is eliminated. An important element affecting what the creditors and equity holders will receive under the reorganization plan is the value of the assets in the reorganized firm. **Reorganization value** is defined as the amount a willing buyer would pay for the *assets* of the firm immediately *after* the restructuring; essentially, reorganization value approximates the *fair value of the assets*.

The emerging firm classifies its assets into two groups for purposes of estimating the reorganization value. Some assets are needed to carry on the operations of the new entity; other assets (called **excess assets**) are scheduled for disposition. Fair value of the *excess assets* is measured by the *expected proceeds from disposition. Assets to be employed in the new entity*, taken as a whole, are considered to have a fair value equal to the *discounted cash flows* expected from the operation of the new entity. Thus:

$$\text{Reorganization value} = \begin{array}{l} \text{Expected proceeds from sale of } \textit{excess assets} \\ + \text{ Present value of future cash flows from the new} \\ \quad \text{entity's } \textit{operating assets} \end{array}$$

The reorganization value establishes the total amount that the plan provides for liabilities and equity interests. Thus reorganization value can also be expressed in terms of the components of the right-hand side of the balance sheet.

Reorganization value =	Postpetition liabilities (in full)
	+ Fully secured prepetition liabilities
	+ Compromised amount of other prepetition liabilities
	+ Valuation of new equity interests

New Basis of Accounting: Fresh Start Reporting   When certain conditions are met, the entity emerging from reorganization is deemed to be sufficiently distinct from the old entity to conclude that a **new basis of accounting** is appropriate for the entity's assets and liabilities. Financial reporting after adopting this new basis of accounting is referred to as **fresh start reporting**, initiated when these conditions are satisfied:

- Reorganization value of the entity's assets is *less than* the total amount of all postpetition liabilities plus all allowed prepetition claims, and

- The pre-confirmation holders of existing voting shares will receive *less than 50 percent* of the voting shares in the new entity.

The first condition requires that the asset value to be recorded—*reorganization value*—be less than prepetition liabilities allowed plus postpetition liabilities. This means that the compromised amount of prepetition liabilities is less than amounts allowed by the courts. The resulting write-downs of debt demonstrate that an economic revaluation in fact occurred. The second condition requires that there be a *change of control* of the entity, which also supports the conclusion that assets and liabilities should be revalued.

Fresh start reporting requires the new values of reported assets to equal reorganization value. Identifiable assets are valued at fair market value, following the business combinations standards found in *ASC Topic 805*, and discussed in Chapter 2 of this text. Previously unreported intangibles are reported if they meet the contractual or separability criteria. Expected benefits from operating loss carryforwards are also included as identifiable assets. If reorganization value *exceeds* the total of the fair values of identifiable assets, the difference is reported as **goodwill**. Because the reorganization value of assets is less than allowed liabilities, recognition of a bargain gain is unlikely.

Fresh start reporting also typically involves reducing or eliminating existing liability and equity amounts. The new entity reports each liability at its *fair value*. Deferred taxes are reported pursuant to *ASC Topic 740*.

Entries to reflect fresh start reporting are made *on the books of the predecessor entity* to close out the reorganization process and to establish the new basis of accountability for the assets, liabilities, and equities of the new entity. These entries accomplish three objectives:

1. **Record the discharge of debt**: Eliminate the existing *liabilities subject to compromise* and record the *payments, new debt securities, and new equity securities* received by these creditors. Typically, the payments and new securities are *less than* the previously recorded amounts, leading to a **gain on debt discharge**.

2. **Record the new interests of the former equity holders**: Delete the old equity and establish the new equity interests, which are typically *much less than* the old interests. The difference produces a temporary increase in additional paid-in capital.

3. **Record the asset value adjustments and eliminate the existing deficit**: Increase or decrease assets to their fair market values determined in the allocation of reorganization value, and record goodwill as appropriate. Canceling the deficit, net of the gain on discharge of debt recorded earlier, typically produces a charge against additional paid-in capital.

These entries reflect the provisions of the confirmed plan of reorganization that restructure the interests of the creditors and equity holders, and establish the new basis of accounting for the emerging entity. When it proves impossible to formulate an acceptable plan of reorganization, the company does not emerge from reorganization as a restructured firm and heads toward Chapter 7 liquidation.

BUSINESS APPLICATION   General Motors Fresh Start Reporting and Goodwill

When **General Motors** emerged from reorganization in 2009, it applied fresh start reporting to its assets and liabilities. While GM had reported no goodwill prior to the reorganization, $30.5 billion in goodwill appeared on its balance sheet following reorganization. GM explains this as follows:

> When applying fresh start reporting, certain accounts, primarily employee benefit and income tax related, were recorded at amounts determined under specific U.S. GAAP rather than fair value and the difference between the U.S. GAAP and fair value amounts gave rise to goodwill, which is a residual. If all identifiable assets and liabilities had been recorded at fair value upon application of fresh start reporting, no goodwill would have resulted.

GM reported some of its liabilities at amounts that were higher than fair value. Therefore identifiable net assets were less than reorganization value, and goodwill was reported. As a reader of GM's financial statements, how much credence would you have attached to GM's reported goodwill balance of $30.5 billion? When an organization has just emerged from reorganization, it seems unlikely that its "goodwill" has much value. This view is supported by GM's subsequent reporting for this goodwill—impairment testing reduced the goodwill balance to $0.1 billion as of December 31, 2013. *Source:* General Motors 2013 annual report.

Reporting Perspective

Fresh start reporting after Chapter 11 reorganization requires estimation of reorganization value, which equals the expected proceeds from selling excess assets plus the value of operating assets. Methods used to measure the value of operating assets parallel those used for asset valuation in business acquisitions and impairment testing of tangible and intangible assets. Since these are operating assets, used within the business, discounted cash flows rather than market values are appropriate. The cash flow projections are based on the expected results of implementing the reorganization plan, and are significantly affected by judgments regarding the amount and timing of cash flows, the discount period, and the discount rate used.

Illustration of Fresh Start Reporting After Reorganization   Continuing with the earlier example of the Manson Corporation, suppose Manson adopts a plan of reorganization on January 1, 2017, that provides for the following:

1. The company's main building will be sold; future operations will be conducted in rented facilities. Proceeds from sale of the building (book value, $1,100,000) of $1,000,000 will fully pay the $800,000 mortgage.

2. After reflecting the above planned transaction, Manson estimates its reorganization value at $2,580,000, consisting of the following:

Cash in excess of normal operating requirements.	$ 250,000
Net realizable value of excess assets available for disposition	30,000
Present value of discounted operating cash flows of the emerging entity	2,300,000
Total reorganization value	$2,580,000

3. Its reorganized capital structure has these components:

Postpetition liabilities	$ 360,000
Note payable to IRS	100,000
Senior secured debt (12%, 10 years)	700,000
Subordinated debt (14%, 7 years)	950,000
Common stock	220,000
Total	$2,330,000

Observe that the total capital of $2,330,000 equals the reorganization value of $2,580,000 less the excess cash of $250,000, assumed paid to creditors immediately.

4. Settlement of the $2,500,000 of liabilities subject to compromise as follows:

a. Exchange the 15 percent notes payable of $1,000,000 for (1) $150,000 immediate cash payment, (2) $500,000 of senior secured debt, (3) $250,000 of subordinated debt, and (4) 20 percent of the new common stock issue.

b. Exchange the $300,000 bank loan for (1) $50,000 immediate cash payment, (2) $100,000 of senior secured debt, (3) $100,000 of subordinated debt, and (4) 10 percent of the new common stock issue.

c. Settle the taxes payable of $150,000 by (1) $50,000 immediate cash payment and (2) two additional annual payments of $50,000, with interest at 15 percent.

d. Exchange the $1,050,000 accounts payable and other liabilities for (1) $100,000 of senior secured debt, (2) $600,000 of subordinated debt, and (3) 50 percent of the new common stock issue.

5. Prior equity interests are adjusted as follows:

a. The existing preferred stock is canceled; the preferred stockholders receive 15 percent of the new common stock issue.

b. The existing common stock is canceled; the common stockholders receive 5 percent of the new common stock issue.

The emerging entity satisfies the *two conditions for fresh start reporting*:

- Reorganization value of $2,580,000 is less than the total amount of all postpetition liabilities ($360,000) plus all allowed prepetition claims ($2,500,000), and

- Pre-confirmation holders of the existing voting shares received less than 50 percent of the voting shares in the new entity (20 percent in this case).

Entries to Record the Restructuring Entries to reflect the above transactions follow. First, under provision 1 of the plan, record the sale of the building and repay the mortgage.

Cash	1,000,000	
Loss on sale of building	100,000	
Property, plant and equipment, net		1,100,000
To record sale of building		
Mortgage payable	800,000	
Cash		800,000
To record full settlement of the fully-secured liability.		

Next, pursuant to plan provision 4, record settlement of the prepetition liabilities subject to compromise.

Liabilities subject to compromise	2,500,000	
Cash		250,000
Senior secured debt		700,000
Subordinated debt		950,000
Note payable to IRS		100,000
Common stock (new)		176,000
Gain on discharge of debt		324,000
To record settlement of prepetition liabilities according to terms of the plan of reorganization.		

The $176,000 credit to common stock represents the 80 percent share of the new equity of $220,000, specified in provision 3, granted to various creditors under terms of the reorganization plan. Because the total cash, new debt securities, and equity granted to the prepetition creditors fell short of the total claims by $324,000, this amount appears as a gain on discharge of debt.

Restructuring the interests of the prior stockholders—plan provision 5—involves eliminating their existing interests, recording their new interests, and temporarily crediting additional paid-in capital with the difference.

Preferred stock.	400,000	
Common stock (old).	100,000	
Common stock (new).		44,000
Additional paid-In capital.		456,000
To record the elimination of existing equity interests and creation of new equity		
interests ($44,000 = 0.2 × new common stock equity of $220,000).		

The final step is the revaluation of assets of the emerging entity called for by provision 2 of the plan. After recording the building sale, total assets are $2,700,000:

Total assets at December 31, 2016 (from the balance sheet	
immediately prior to emerging from reorganization).	$3,600,000
Less: Book value of building sold	(1,100,000)
Plus: Cash from sale, net of mortgage repayment.	200,000
Total assets after building sale.	$2,700,000

Given the $2,580,000 reorganization value, assets must be written down by $120,000. Assume that estimates of the assets' fair values result in the following adjustments to pre-reorganization book values:

Accounts receivable are reduced from a book value of	
$320,000 to an estimated collectible value of $260,000.	$ (60,000)
Inventory is reduced from $550,000 to $450,000	(100,000)
Property, plant and equipment is increased from $1,290,000 to $1,380,000.	90,000
Intangibles are written off.	(120,000)
	(190,000)
Goodwill	70,000
Net adjustment to book values	$(120,000)

The following **reorganization entry** reflects these adjustments, the elimination of the deficit net of gains and losses recorded above, and the reduction in the paid-in capital created by the restructuring of equity interests.

Property, plant and equipment.	90,000	
Goodwill	70,000	
Gain on discharge of debt	324,000	
Additional paid-in capital	456,000	
Accounts receivable		60,000
Inventories.		100,000
Intangible assets		120,000
Loss on sale of building.		100,000
Deficit on December 31, 2016 balance sheet		560,000
To adjust asset values to reorganization value and eliminate deficit.		

After posting these entries, Manson's balance sheet appears as follows:

MANSON CORPORATION
Balance Sheet
January 1, 2017

Assets		Liabilities and equity	
Cash	$ 100,000	Postpetition	$ 360,000
Accounts receivable	260,000	Current portion of long-term debt ...	255,700
Inventories	450,000	Current liabilities	615,700
Prepaid expenses	70,000		
		Long-term liabilities	
Current assets	880,000	Senior secured debt	700,000
Property, plant and equipment, net	1,380,000	Subordinated debt	950,000
Goodwill	70,000	Note payable	100,000
			1,750,000
		Less current portion	(255,700)
			1,494,300
		Stockholders' equity	
		Common stock	220,000
		Retained earnings	0
Total assets	$2,330,000	Total liabilities and equity	$2,330,000

BUSINESS APPLICATION   Trump Entertainment Resorts

Emerging from Chapter 11 does not guarantee future success. Nor is there any law against multiple filings. Donald Trump and various organizations with which he has been connected are a good illustration. Trump Entertainment Resorts and its predecessors have filed for bankruptcy *four times*. In 1988, Trump financed the purchase of the Taj Mahal Casino in Atlantic City, New Jersey, using junk bonds. By 1991, unable to pay the high interest on the bonds, he filed for bankruptcy. In 2004, his company Trump Hotels & Casino Resorts filed for bankruptcy, and as a result bondholders traded some of their debt for equity and Donald Trump reduced his equity ownership. The name of the company changed to Trump Entertainment Resorts, which filed for bankruptcy in 2009, owing $1.2 billion. As part of the debt restructuring, Donald Trump's ownership interest was again reduced. In late 2014, Trump Entertainment Resorts again filed for bankruptcy. Although four Chapter 11 reorganization filings may at first glance appear to be a way to avoid paying amounts owed to creditors, the creditors themselves undoubtedly view this more positively. The alternative would be to liquidate, and a working casino is likely to generate more cash flow than selling it.

REVIEW 2   •   Chapter 11 Reorganization

Instead of filing under Chapter 7, Baines Corp. (see Review Problem 1) decides to reorganize under Chapter 11 of the bankruptcy code. Postpetition liabilities of $275,000 were incurred during the reorganization process. Adding the company's prepetition liabilities gives total liabilities of $1,095,000 (= $820,000 + $275,000). As Baines prepares to emerge from reorganization, it has $90,000 in cash, and the present value of future operating cash flows is $800,000. The prepetition liabilities will be discharged as follows:

- Fully-secured creditors ($220,000) will receive $40,000 in cash and $180,000 in 10 percent senior secured debt.
- Partially secured creditors ($180,000) will receive $20,000 in cash, $100,000 in 10 percent senior secured debt, $40,000 in subordinated debt, and 10 percent of the equity in the reorganized company.
- Unsecured creditors with priority ($30,000) will be paid in cash.
- Unsecured creditors ($390,000) will receive $250,000 in subordinated debt and 70 percent of the equity of the reorganized company.
- Prior stockholders will receive 20 percent of the equity of the reorganized company.

Required

Determine how much gain will be recorded on the settlement of debt.

Solutions are located after the chapter assignments.

OTHER FORMS OF RESTRUCTURING

To this point, the chapter examined formal actions under the bankruptcy laws to deal with firms in financial difficulty: liquidation under Chapter 7 and reorganization under Chapter 11 of the Bankruptcy Code. We now briefly consider accounting for two other forms of restructuring.

LO5 Describe accounting for other forms of reorganization.

Quasi-Reorganization

A *quasi-reorganization* normally does not involve a restructuring of debt. The usual situation is that the company has accumulated a deficit in retained earnings, and believes that its asset values are overstated and that future amortization of these overstated amounts will continue to produce losses. The **quasi-reorganization** uses fresh start accounting to accomplish the following:

- Write assets down to fair values further increasing the deficit.
- Restructure the common stock equity to create enough additional paid-in capital to absorb the deficit in retained earnings, reducing the per-share par value, reducing the number of shares, or both.
- Eliminate the deficit against the additional paid-in capital so that retained earnings has a zero balance.

Because a quasi-reorganization changes the interests of equity holders, formal stockholder approval is needed. Creditor approval is not needed, however, as debts are left unchanged. Further, there is no immediate effect on cash flows. The motivation for the quasi-reorganization is to enhance the prospects of profitable operations in the future and thereby create the ability to pay dividends, not possible with negative retained earnings. Past circumstances that produced the deficit imply that recorded asset values will not be recovered by future operations, and should be written down. To accomplish this, stockholders voluntarily restructure their own holdings.

The major impact on **post-quasi-reorganization financial reporting** is the establishment of a "new" retained earnings account, with an initial balance of zero, dated to show that the accumulation of retained earnings begins from the effective date of the restructuring. Dating the retained earnings account continues until enough time has passed so that the quasi-reorganization is no longer deemed significant in understanding the company's financial statements.

Troubled Debt Restructuring

As an alternative to the overall debt restructuring provided by bankruptcy law, a specific obligation may be restructured by negotiation between debtor and creditor. Such a restructuring is called a **troubled debt restructuring** when, in view of a debtor's financial difficulties, a creditor grants a concession to the debtor that it otherwise would not grant. The creditor seeks to make the best of a poor situation, hoping that the concession raises the probability or amount expected to be collected. The concession typically includes one or more of the following:

- Accepting noncash assets from the debtor, such as receivables or real estate, in full or partial settlement of the debt.
- Accepting an equity interest in the debtor in full or partial settlement of the debt.
- Modifying the terms of the obligation, by reducing the interest rate, extending the maturity date, reducing the principal amount, forgiving accrued interest, or some combination of the foregoing.

A troubled debt restructuring involves an **economic loss** to the creditor—the fair values of assets or equity interests accepted are *less than* the creditor's investment in the debt obligation being settled. However, modifying the terms of a debt obligation in response to changing market conditions, reduced risk, or competition from other lenders is *not* considered a troubled debt restructuring, even though the lender suffers an economic loss. For a troubled debt restructuring to occur, the modification must be one not granted under normal circumstances and be motivated by realization that collectibility is threatened in the absence of some concessions. Accounting principles for troubled debt restructurings are specified in *ASC Subtopics 470-60* and *310-40*. Two conditions must exist for a transaction to be considered a troubled debt restructuring. The debtor must be experiencing financial difficulties, and the restructuring must constitute a concession by the creditor.

Accounting by Debtors   When assets are transferred in settlement of debt, the resulting gain to the debtor is likely to have two components. One component, the difference between the *fair value of the asset surrendered* and the asset's *carrying value*, is reported as a **gain or loss on asset disposition**. The second component, the difference between the *fair value of the asset surrendered* and the *carrying value of the debt settled*—face value plus accrued interest plus or minus unamortized premium, discount, or issue costs—is reported as a **gain on restructuring**. This latter gain is typically treated as an ordinary item.

When the debtor exchanges an equity interest for partial forgiveness of a debt, the debtor records the new equity at its fair value. The difference between the fair value of the equity granted and the carrying value of the debt settled also constitutes a *gain on restructuring*.

A modification of terms produces no adjustment to the carrying value of the debt unless the *total undiscounted future cash payments* specified by the new terms are *less than* the present carrying value. In this case, the debtor reduces the carrying value to the new total of the undiscounted future cash payments, and a gain on restructuring is recorded. When no reduction of carrying value is required, the change in terms is reflected *prospectively,* by modifying annual interest expense. The effective interest approach is used to calculate interest expense, so the carrying value of the debt declines over time until it equals the principal amount owed at maturity.

REVIEW OF KEY CONCEPTS ••

LO 1   **Explain the basic legal aspects of bankruptcy. (p. 664)** The **bankruptcy laws** provide two approaches for firms unable to meet their obligations. **Chapter 7** provides for **liquidation**—termination of operations and disposition of the firm's assets to pay creditors. **Chapter 11** provides for **reorganization**—continuation of operations while a plan is developed to restructure both creditor claims and equity interests so that the emerging entity has a prospect of profitable operations.

LO 2   **Prepare a statement of affairs for a Chapter 7 bankruptcy. (p. 665)** The trustee of **firms in liquidation** prepares a **statement of affairs** to show the financial condition of the company. Assets are valued at **estimated realizable value** and are classified according to any security interests held by creditors. Liabilities are classified according to their **legal preference**. The statement shows the **estimated deficiency to unsecured creditors**, the difference between the liabilities and the estimated realizable value of the assets.

LO 3   **Prepare a statement of realization and liquidation. (p. 670)** The **statement of realization and liquidation** details the activities of the **receiver or trustee** in administering the estate of the bankrupt firm during the liquidation process.

LO 4   **Account for a company undergoing Chapter 11 reorganization. (p. 674)** **Firms in reorganization** continue their accounting on a **going-concern basis**. Liabilities are classified to distinguish prepetition from postpetition claims, and to focus on those liabilities **subject to compromise**. During the reorganization phase, payments on prepetition liabilities are generally suspended while a **plan of reorganization** is developed. This plan restructures the interests of creditors and stockholders to enable the firm to continue to operate. When the company **emerges from reorganization** after approval of the plan, a **new accounting entity** results when **reorganization value** is less than total liabilities and prior stockholders have less than 50 percent of the voting shares in the new entity. **Fresh start reporting** follows from meeting these conditions and establishes a new basis of accountability for the firm's assets, liabilities, and equity interests.

LO 5   **Describe accounting for other forms of reorganization. (p. 683)** Restructurings may also occur in less formal ways, without resort to the bankruptcy laws. A **quasi-reorganization** revises asset values and restructures the equity interests to eliminate a deficit in retained earnings and enhance the prospects of future profitability. A **troubled debt restructuring** involves an agreement between a debtor and a creditor to settle a liability or modify its terms in light of the debtor's financial difficulties.

Assignments with the ✅ in the margin are available in myBusinessCourse.
See the Preface of the book for details.

MULTIPLE CHOICE QUESTIONS ···

1. Under the provisions of Chapter 7 of the bankruptcy laws   LO 1 ✅

   a.   all of a company's debts are forgiven.
   b.   the company attempts to continue operations by restructuring its finances.
   c.   the company ceases operations, disposes of assets, and settles its liabilities.
   d.   the company is taken over by the creditors.

2. Under the provisions of Chapter 11 of the bankruptcy laws   LO 1 ✅

   a.   all of a company's debts are forgiven.
   b.   the company attempts to continue operations by restructuring its finances.
   c.   the company ceases operations, disposes of assets, and settles its liabilities.
   d.   the company is taken over by the creditors.

Use the following information to answer questions 3 and 4 below.

Inho Corporation has fully secured liabilities of $300,000 and unsecured liabilities of $1,500,000, of which $250,000 have legal priority. Inho's assets are expected to realize $1,000,000; of these, $420,000 is pledged to the fully-secured creditors.

3. Inho's net free assets amount to   LO 2 ✅

   a. $1,000,000.
   b. $ 700,000.
   c. $ 580,000.
   d. $ 450,000.

4. The estimated deficiency to Inho's unsecured creditors is   LO 2 ✅

   a. $800,000.
   b. $700,000.
   c. $500,000.
   d. $450,000.

Use the following information to answer questions 5 and 6 below.

Borden Corporation is undergoing a Chapter 7 liquidation. Currently, it has cash of $130,000, inventory of $650,000, and equipment of $775,000. It owes an unsecured bank loan payable of $500,000 and unsecured accounts payable of $1,600,000. During the current month, the Receiver sells Borden's entire inventory to a liquidator for $290,000. The entire cash balance is then distributed to unsecured creditors.

5. Borden's statement of realization and liquidation shows   LO 3 ✅

   a.   gain on liquidation of $1,680,000.
   b.   assets not realized of $360,000 for inventory and $775,000 for equipment.
   c.   assets to be realized of $1,555,000 (cash, inventory, and equipment).
   d.   loss on realization of $360,000.

6. The receiver's payment to the bank is   LO 3 ✅

   a. $500,000.
   b. $420,000.
   c. $100,000.
   d. $290,000.

Use the following information to answer questions 7 and 8 below.

Mannheim Corporation is ready to emerge from Chapter 11 bankruptcy under a reorganization plan accepted by all parties. Mannheim's balance sheet shows:

Various assets	$2,000,000	Prepetition liabilities, fully secured...............	$ 400,000
		Prepetition liabilities subject to compromise.......	1,360,000
		Postpetition liabilities	820,000
		Stockholders' equity	(580,000)
TOTAL	$2,000,000	TOTAL	$2,000,000

LO 4 **7.** There are no excess assets. The present value of future cash flows from the reorganized company's operating assets is $2,370,000. Mannheim's reorganization value is

a. $2,370,000.
b. $2,000,000.
c. $2,580,000.
d. $1,760,000.

LO 4 **8.** New equity interests in the reorganized company are $160,000. The compromised amount of Mannheim's prepetition liabilities is

a. $1,360,000.
b. $1,390,000.
c. $2,210,000.
d. $ 990,000.

LO 5 **9.** Jones Inc. has common stock of $3,000,000, additional paid-in capital of $200,000, and a retained earnings deficit of $1,440,000. As part of a quasi-reorganization, Jones writes down its assets by $800,000. To eliminate its deficit, Jones must reduce its common stock account by

a. $1,240,000.
b. $1,440,000.
c. $2,040,000.
d. $2,240,000.

LO 5 **10.** Kiefer Company has negotiated with its major creditor to undertake a troubled debt restructuring. Under the agreement, Kiefer transfers a parcel of real estate in full settlement of a debt of $1,800,000. The real estate has a carrying value on Kiefer's books of $920,000 and a fair value of $1,460,00. As a result of this transaction, Kiefer reports

a. $340,000 gain on debt restructuring.
b. $880,000 gain on asset disposition.
c. $880,000 gain on debt restructuring.
d. $540,000 gain on debt restructuring.

EXERCISES ••

LO 2 **E15.1** **Statement of Affairs** The following information is available for Dennison Company, which is entering bankruptcy proceedings.

Net realizable values of Dennison's assets:

Cash	$ 5,000
Accounts receivable	15,000
Inventory	65,000
Equipment	100,000

Dennison has the following claims against it:

Accounts payable to suppliers	$60,000
Priority liabilities	22,000
Note payable, secured by equipment with a realizable value of $60,000	50,000
Loan payable, secured by equipment with a realizable value of $20,000	80,000

Required
Prepare a statement of affairs for Dennison Company, in good form.

E15.2 **Deficiency to Unsecured Creditors** Consider the following information for Evans, Inc. when the   **LO 2**
company entered bankruptcy proceedings:

Account	Balance per Books Dr (Cr)
Cash.	$ 31,700
Accounts receivable.	646,800
Inventory.	320,000
Prepaid expenses.	10,600
Buildings, net	750,000
Equipment, net.	123,500
Goodwill	88,000
Wages payable.	(77,300)
Taxes payable	(30,900)
Accounts payable.	(967,300)
Notes payable	(205,400)
Common stock.	(1,200,000)
Retained earnings—deficit.	510,300
Total	$ 0

Inventory with a book value of $240,000 and realizable value of $175,000 is security for notes payable of
$145,000. The equipment secures the remaining notes payable. Expected realizable values of the assets are:

Accounts receivable.	$300,000
Inventory.	200,000
Buildings.	250,000
Equipment	40,000

The prepaid expenses and goodwill have a realizable value of zero. The entire wages payable balance is
a priority liability.

Required

Compute the estimated deficiency to unsecured creditors.

E15.3 **Statement of Affairs** Dellwood Corporation is experiencing difficulty in paying its bills and is con-   **LO 2** ✓
sidering filing for bankruptcy. Current data as of September 30, 2017, show the following:

Assets	Estimated Realizable Value
Cash.	$ 20,000
Accounts receivable.	325,000
Inventory—materials.	100,000
Inventory—finished goods	400,000
Land	200,000
Building	1,100,000
Trucks.	45,000
Equipment	200,000

Liabilities	Book Value	Secured by
Accounts payable.	$800,000	
Bank loan	275,000	80% of receivables
Wages payable.	140,000	
Taxes payable	75,000	
Truck loan.	70,000	Trucks with $30,000 estimated realizable value
Mortgage payable	600,000	Land and building
Loan payable	450,000	Finished goods
Note payable	750,000	

All of the wages payable have priority.

Required

Prepare a statement of affairs.

LO 2   E15.4   Bankruptcy Calculations   Faced with an inability to meet its current debt payments, The Selbert Company entered bankruptcy on April 30, 2017. The appointed trustee will liquidate the company and pay the creditors in accordance with the provisions of the bankruptcy laws. Selbert's balance sheet on April 30, 2017, shows the following:

THE SELBERT COMPANY
Balance Sheet
April 30, 2017

Assets		Liabilities and equity	
Cash.	$ 3,200	Accounts payable.	$131,900
Accounts receivable.	71,000	Loan payable to bank.	60,000
Notes receivable.	50,000	Notes payable to suppliers.	83,900
Inventories	108,600	Accrued wages.	94,700
Prepaid expenses.	17,200	Accrued taxes	70,000
Land and buildings, net	172,000	Mortgage payable	195,000
Equipment, net.	113,500	Common stock.	100,000
Goodwill, net	28,000	Retained earnings	(172,000)
Total assets	$563,500	Total liabilities and equity.	$563,500

Additional information:

1. The trustee estimates that 60 percent of the accounts receivable will be collected, and she has agreed to settle the notes receivable for $42,500. The notes receivable serve as collateral for the loan payable to the bank.
2. The inventories will likely be sold to a competitor, at 40 percent of book value.
3. Other than a $2,000 insurance refund, no recovery of prepaid items is expected.
4. Appraised at $300,000, the land and buildings are pledged as security on the mortgage.
5. The equipment is expected to be sold for $40,000.
6. The notes payable to the suppliers are unsecured.
7. Accrued wages do not exceed statutory limits per employee.

Required

Compute the following:

a. Estimated gains and losses on asset dispositions.
b. Amount of priority claims.
c. Estimated payments to fully and partially secured creditors.
d. Expected recovery percentage to unsecured creditors.

LO 3   E15.5   Statement of Realization and Liquidation   Dong Company declares bankruptcy and the appointed trustee begins liquidation. Here is Dong's balance sheet as it enters liquidation.

Assets	
Cash.	$ 20,000
Receivables	85,000
Inventories	150,000
Buildings and equipment	200,000
Total assets.	$455,000

Liabilities and equity	
Accounts payable.	$175,000
Wages and taxes payable	45,000
Loans payable	260,000
Equity	(25,000)
Total liabilities and equity	$455,000

None of the liabilities are secured. The following transactions occur over the next six months:

1. Customers paid in full $35,000 of receivables; collection attempts indicate that 60 percent of the remaining receivables are collectible.
2. Inventory with a book value of $80,000 was sold for $45,000.
3. Equipment with a book value of $70,000 was sold for $50,000.
4. Legal, accounting, and trustee fees total $28,000.
5. The trustee pays all priority claims.

Required

Prepare a statement of realization and liquidation for the six month period, and a balance sheet and statement of estate deficit as of the end of the six month period.

E15.6 Journal Entries for Bankruptcy Trustee The balance sheet of the Binder Company immediately prior to entering bankruptcy proceedings and a balance sheet prepared during liquidation follows: **LO 3** ✅

BINDER COMPANY
Balance Sheet
June 30, 2016

Cash.........................	$ 2,000	Accounts payable.................	$ 40,000
Accounts receivable..............	10,000	Accrued wages*.................	7,000
Inventories	30,000	Taxes payable	8,000
Equipment, net..................	53,000	Notes payable**.................	70,000
Land.........................	15,000	Stockholders' equity	(15,000)
Total assets	$110,000	Total liabilities and equity...........	$110,000

* Amounts due do not exceed statutory limits per employee.
** Of the notes payable, $25,000 are secured with inventory having a book value of $25,000. The remaining notes payable and the accounts payable are unsecured.

BINDER COMPANY, Alfred Wade, Trustee,
Balance Sheet
December 31, 2016

Cash.........................	$ 9,250	Accounts payable.................	$30,000
Equipment, net..................	53,000	Notes payable	41,250
		Estate deficit....................	(9,000)
Total assets	$62,250	Total liabilities and equity...........	$62,250

The inventory was sold at 60 percent of its book value. Eighty percent of the accounts receivable were collected; the rest were written off.

Required

Reconstruct the journal entries made by Alfred Wade, Trustee for Binder Company, from June 30 to December 31, 2016.

E15.7 Statement of Realization and Liquidation At January 1, 2017, the records of Sharon Thomson, **LO 3** trustee in bankruptcy for Davis Corporation, showed the following:

	Dr (Cr)
Cash......................................	$ 17,700
Assets not realized:	
Land......................................	40,000
Building....................................	217,000
Equipment..................................	68,000
Patents....................................	21,600
Liabilities not liquidated:	
Accounts payable............................	(400,000)
Loans payable	(120,000)
Estate deficit................................	155,700

During January, Thomson sold equipment having a book value of $30,000 for $12,500, and sold the patents for $40,000. Thomson was paid $2,500 as a trustee's fee, and $62,400 was distributed proportionately to the creditors.

Required

Prepare a statement of realization and liquidation for January and a balance sheet and statement of estate deficit as of January 31, 2017.

LO 3   E15.8   Reconstruct Realization and Liquidation Transactions   A trustee's statement of realization and liquidation is presented below:

Assets to be realized:			**Assets realized:**			
Accounts receivable.........	$ 15,000		Accounts receivable.........	$ 9,000		
Inventory..................	41,000		Inventory..................	18,000		
Equipment	88,000	$144,000	Equipment	23,000	$ 50,000	
Assets acquired:			**Assets not realized:**			
None			Accounts receivable.........	6,000		
			Inventory..................	20,000		
			Equipment	72,000	98,000	
Liabilities liquidated:			**Liabilities to be liquidated:**			
Notes payable		45,000	Accounts payable...........	90,000		
			Notes payable	160,000	250,000	
Liabilities not liquidated:			**Liabilities incurred:**			
Accounts payable...........	90,000		None			
Notes payable	110,000	200,000				
Gain on realization		7,000	Loss on realization		3,000	
Gain on liquidation		5,000				
Combined total.............		$401,000	Combined total.............		$401,000	

Required

Reconstruct, in journal form, the trustee's transactions for the period.

✔ LO 4   E15.9   Liabilities During Reorganization   Francona Corporation is undergoing reorganization under the provisions of Chapter 11 of the bankruptcy code. Francona is currently continuing in operation as a debtor-in-possession while a plan of reorganization is developed. The following occurred during the reorganization period:

1.   Liabilities existing at the time of filing the petition for reorganization are $2,000,000, all unsecured. The full amount of these liabilities is expected to be allowed by the court, although the eventual settlement is projected to be about 70 percent of face value. $800,000 of these liabilities were previously reported as current, and the remainder were long-term liabilities.
2.   Liabilities of $500,000 were incurred since filing the petition. These are all current liabilities.
3.   Legal costs connected with the reorganization process amounted to $150,000.
4.   Sold two company cars, generating $40,000 in cash and a $2,000 loss.
5.   Cancelled a contract to purchase a new machine and forfeited the company's $50,000 deposit.

Required

Describe how each of the above would be presented on Francona's financial statements during reorganization. Give the specific statement and caption for each item.

LO 4   E15.10   Calculation of Reorganization Value   Weihong Corporation is about to emerge from a Chapter 11 reorganization. Assets of the emerging entity have a total book value of $3,000,000. Of these, assets with a book value of $600,000 are not needed to operate the emerging entity and will be sold for an expected price of $460,000. The remaining assets will be used in operations. Operations are expected to generate an annual net cash flow of $350,000. This amount is projected for the next five years; a discount rate of 10 percent is deemed appropriate.

Required

Calculate Weihong Corporation's reorganization value. For convenience, assume the operating cash flows take place at the end of each year.

E15.11 Fresh Start Reporting   Rudolph Corporation is about to emerge from a Chapter 11 reorganization.   **LO 4**
The following data are available:

Reorganization value of assets	$6,000,000
Prepetition liabilities—allowed claims	5,000,000
Prepetition liabilities—expected settlement (value of cash, debt securities, and equity securities to be given in settlement)	4,600,000
Postpetition liabilities	1,200,000

Pre-confirmation equity structure:
   Preferred stock (nonvoting), 50,000 shares
   Common stock (voting), 450,000 shares

New equity structure:
   All existing stock canceled
   New voting common stock issued as follows:
      35 percent to prepetition creditors
      35 percent to previous preferred stockholders
      30 percent to previous common stockholders

Required

Is Rudolph Corporation entitled to adopt fresh start reporting for the emerging entity? Explain.

E15.12 Reorganization Entries and Balance Sheet   Here is the balance sheet of AB Electronics, on July   **LO 4**
1, 2017, the date it filed for Chapter 11 reorganization.

Assets	
Cash	$ 10,000
Receivables, net	115,000
Inventories	200,000
Buildings and equipment	200,000
Intangible assets	600,000
Total assets	$1,125,000

Liabilities and equity	
Accounts payable	$ 300,000
Notes payable (8%), due in 2 years	100,000
Loan payable (7%), due in 18 months	500,000
Capital stock	250,000
Retained deficit	(25,000)
Total liabilities and equity	$1,125,000

Provisions of the reorganization plan are as follows:

1. Write down reported assets to reflect actual value to the company, with balances as follows: Receivables, $100,000; buildings and equipment, $150,000; inventories are fairly valued but intangibles should be written off.
2. Exchange the 8% notes for $50,000 of senior secured debt, and 20% of the new common stock.
3. Exchange the 7% loan for $100,000 of senior secured debt, $100,000 of subordinated debt, and 40% of the new common stock.
4. Exchange the accounts payable for $75,000 of senior secured debt and 10% of the new common stock.
5. The old capital stock is canceled and replaced with a new common stock issue valued at $135,000. The retained deficit is eliminated.

Required

Prepare the journal entries to record the restructuring, and present AB Electronics' balance sheet immediately after the restructuring.

LO 5 **E15.13 Quasi-Reorganization** Zoyhofski Corporation has incurred losses for several years, and currently has a $620,000 deficit in retained earnings. It has 40,000 shares of $10 par value common stock issued and outstanding, and has additional paid-in capital of $500,000. Due to a permanent decline in its economic prospects, Zoyhofski believes its assets are overvalued. As part of a quasi-reorganization, a $250,000 writedown is proposed to reflect the changed conditions. The present $10 par common stock is to be exchanged for a new issue bearing a $1 par value; each stockholder will receive one new share for every eight old shares.

Required
a. Prepare journal entries to record the quasi-reorganization.
b. Prepare the stockholders' equity section of Zoyhofski's balance sheet after the quasi-reorganization.

LO 5 **E15.14 Troubled Debt Restructuring** Bakert Company's $1,000,000 note payable to a private investor just matured. Interest was not paid on the note for the past three years and accrued interest now totals $300,000. Bakert is in serious financial difficulty and is unable to pay off the note. In an attempt to help the company survive, the company and the investor agree to the following:

1. Bakert transfers a parcel of vacant land to the investor in settlement of $400,000 of the total obligation. The land has a book value of $150,000, and $400,000 is a reasonable estimate of its fair value.
2. Bakert issues $300,000 par value of 10 percent cumulative preferred stock in settlement of $300,000 of the obligation.
3. The remaining $600,000 of the total obligation is replaced by a five-year note in the principal amount of $300,000, with interest at 12 percent.

Required
Prepare journal entries to record these arrangements for Bakert Company.

LO 5 **E15.15 Troubled Debt Restructuring** Wolfconn Company is having financial difficulties. It has a note payable with a principal amount of $5,000,000, due in three years, plus accrued interest of $750,000 that has not been paid. The note carries an interest rate of 6 percent. Wolfconn and the holder of the note negotiate a restructuring of the note, with the following terms:

- Principal amount is $3,000,000, payable in five years.
- Interest on the note is payable at the end of each of the five years, at a rate of 10 percent per annum.

Required
a. Prepare the entry to record the restructuring of the debt.
b. Suppose the new note had a principal amount of $4,000,000, payable in five years, with interest at 10 percent payable at the end of each of the five years. How would this restructuring be recorded?

PROBLEMS ●

LO 2 **P15.1 Statement of Affairs** The following items of information appear on the statement of affairs of Shaw Corporation:

1. Estimated deficiency to unsecured creditors, $72,000.
2. Unsecured liabilities with priority, $37,000.
3. Assets pledged to fully secured creditors ($200,000) exceed the related liabilities by $40,000.
4. Liabilities to partially secured creditors, $83,000.
5. Assets not pledged to any creditors, $185,000.
6. Total assets, book value $523,000, estimated realizable value $435,000.

Required
Determine the following amounts:

a. Assets pledged to partially secured creditors.
b. Total unsecured liabilities (excluding those with priority).
c. Total liabilities.
d. Total stockholders' equity.

LO 2 **P15.2 Calculation of Expected Distributions** Gorgan Corporation is entering bankruptcy proceedings. Here is its balance sheet, with estimated realizable values provided for the assets.

	Book Value	Estimated Realizable Value
Assets		
Cash....	$ 4,000	$ 4,000
Accounts receivable....	80,000	65,000
Inventories.....	130,000	90,000
Buildings and equipment....	500,000	220,000
Total assets.....	$714,000	
Liabilities		
Wages and taxes payable.....	$ 35,000	
Unearned revenue—customer deposits....	20,000	
Accounts payable....	100,000	
Note payable, secured by all inventories....	50,000	
Mortgage payable, secured by all buildings and equipment....	350,000	
Total liabilities....	555,000	
Equity		
Capital stock.....	10,000	
Retained earnings.....	149,000	
Total equity....	159,000	
Total liabilities and equity....	$714,000	

All priority liabilities are within the legal limits for collection.

Required

a. How much, in dollars, is expected to be available to creditors upon liquidation of the corporation?
b. Calculate the expected recovery percentage for unsecured creditors.
c. How much, in dollars, can each of the classes of creditors expect to receive? Note that the total equals your answer to *a*, except for possible rounding errors.
d. Calculate the expected recovery percentage for partially secured creditors.

P15.3 **Statement of Affairs**   The Janes Corporation has filed a petition for protection under Chapter 7 of the   **LO 2**
bankruptcy laws. Its financial data as of March 10, 2017, the filing date, are as follows.

Assets	
Cash.....	$ 12,000
Accounts receivable, net.....	82,000
Inventory of raw materials.....	112,000
Inventory of finished goods.....	158,000
Prepaid advertising and insurance.....	14,000
Marketable securities, fair market value at December 31, 2016.....	27,000
Land.....	50,000
Building, net.....	675,000
Machinery and equipment, net.....	238,000
Goodwill.....	50,000
Total assets.....	$1,418,000
Liabilities and equity	
Accounts payable.....	$ 370,000
Bank loan payable.....	113,000
Accrued federal taxes payable.....	150,000
Accrued salaries and wages payable.....	60,000
Notes payable.....	250,000
Mortgage payable.....	422,000
Common stock.....	120,000
Retained earnings (deficit).....	(67,000)
Total liabilities and equity.....	$1,418,000

Additional data:

1. The cash balance includes $2,000 of NSF customer checks; collection of these is unlikely.

2. Accounts receivable include $36,000 in numerous small balances under $500. These customers would probably take advantage of Janes' bankruptcy filing and never pay, knowing that the amount owed is too small to justify collection procedures.

3. Accounts receivable also include $8,000 of credit balances owed to customers for deposits for future services.

4. The inventory of raw materials could be sold for $65,000, or could be converted into finished goods at an additional cost of $46,500. These finished goods have a normal selling price of $210,000 (but see next item).

5. The inventory of finished goods has a normal selling price of $240,000, but when sold in bankruptcy to a liquidator, these goods are likely to yield only 55 percent of the normal selling price.

6. The prepaid advertising ($6,000) has no refund clause in its contract. The prepaid insurance ($8,000) has a cancellation value at the filing date of $1,700, but by the time bankruptcy proceedings are completed and the policy could safely be terminated, it is likely to have expired.

7. Since December 31, 2016, the marketable securities declined in value by $6,000.

8. The land and building have an estimated selling price of $700,000; the machinery and equipment have an estimated selling price of $85,000.

9. The goodwill balance results from an acquisition eight years ago, and has no liquidation value.

10. The notes payable are secured by the accounts receivable and by the current inventory of finished goods. The mortgage payable is secured by the land and building. All other liabilities are unsecured.

11. All priority liabilities are within statutory limits.

12. Janes is defendant in a lawsuit, not reported on its balance sheet. A loss of $50,000 is probable, of which half will be covered by insurance.

13. Janes has noncancelable operating leases for several vehicles used in its business; $100,000 of lease payments remain. However, the leases can be terminated early by paying half the remaining balance. *Hint:* Early termination may not always be the best option. Remember to evaluate the lease payment with and without the option.

14. Expected legal, accounting, and administrative costs of the bankruptcy are $120,000.

Required

a. Prepare a statement of affairs.

b. Compute the estimated settlement per dollar of unsecured liabilities.

LO 2   P15.4   Statement of Affairs   Bridges Furniture Store is finding it increasingly difficult to meet its obligations despite satisfactory sales volume and profitability. Bridges cannot meet its working capital requirements for inventory and payments on current liabilities. Finally, after pledging all of its installment receivables, Bristol failed to meet the bills due on October 10, 2017. Management feels that if the company could obtain an extension of time in which to pay its obligations it could meet its liabilities in full. The corporation arranged for a meeting of creditors to determine whether the company should be granted an extension or be forced into bankruptcy.

The pre-closing trial balance for the current calendar year of the company on September 30, 2017, follows:

	Debit	Credit
Cash.	$ 6,360	
Installment receivables, pledged	645,000	
Allowance for doubtful installment receivables		$ 40,320
Accounts receivable.	62,490	
Allowance for doubtful accounts		3,150
Inventories, January 1, 2017	453,450	
Prepaid insurance	4,470	
Autos and trucks	67,140	
Accumulated depreciation, autos and trucks		44,880
Furniture and equipment	37,500	
Accumulated depreciation, furniture and equipment.		6,420
Buildings.	269,280	
Accumulated depreciation, buildings.		22,590
Land	30,720	
Organization costs	2,640	
Trade accounts payable.		396,300
Furniture and equipment loan payable.		17,400
Installment loan on auto and trucks.		30,000
Bank loan, secured by installment receivables		483,750
Taxes payable (prior years)		42,660
Accrued salaries and wages		14,040
Accrued interest.		32,970
Notes payable, stockholder		300,000
Mortgage payable, 6%.		147,000
Capital stock		300,000
Retained earnings	195,870	
Sales.		2,126,700
Purchases.	1,582,890	
Other expenses and income, net	650,370	
Totals	$4,008,180	$4,008,180

Further investigation produced the following additional data:

1. Depreciation, allowances for doubtful accounts, prepaid and accrued items are all adjusted as of September 30, 2017.
2. All installment receivables are pledged with the bank on September 30, 2017, the bank had deducted its interest to date and loaned the company loan 75 percent of the face amount of the receivables. Bridges estimates that a forced liquidation will result in a loss of $120,000 of the receivables' face amount.
3. Accounts receivable are not pledged, and Bridges estimates collectibility of $49,500 on a liquidation basis.
4. Since January 1, 2017, the company made a gross profit of 33 1/3 percent but the inventory on hand will likely provide only $300,000 in a forced liquidation.
5. Cancellation of the insurance will provide $2,970.
6. All autos and trucks are pledged as security for an installment loan, and their total market value is $24,000.
7. The store was remodeled in 2016, and the furniture and equipment are financed by a loan; the furniture and equipment is pledged as security for the loan. Because of its specialized nature, Bridges estimates that a forced sale would realize no more than $15,000.
8. The land and buildings are subject to a 6 percent mortgage, on which interest on the outstanding mortgage balance has been paid to July 30, 2017. It is estimated the property could be sold for $225,000.
9. The accrued salaries and wages do not exceed statutory limits.
10. The notes payable to stockholders are not subordinated to general creditors. The notes carried a 6 percent rate of interest, but no interest has been paid since December 31, 2015.
11. Bridges estimates the cost of liquidation proceedings to be $15,000.

Required

a. Prepare a statement of affairs for Bridges Furniture Store as of September 30, 2017.
b. Compute the percentages of recovery by the unsecured creditors and the partially-secured creditors if Bridges Furniture Store is forced into bankruptcy.

LO 3   P15.5   Statement of Realization and Liquidation   Barnwell Corporation had a history of profitable operations until recently encountering serious difficulty paying its bills. Attempts to acquire bank financing have been unsuccessful, due to the advanced age and ill health of the firm's sole owner and manager, Amos Barnwell, as have attempts to sell the company. Faced with the prospect of the firm's bankruptcy, Barnwell's creditors met and proposed the following terms to Mr. Barnwell:

1. Operations will be continued until the present raw materials and work-in-process inventories are used or completed and sold.
2. The creditors will advance $9,000 to finance the necessary operating costs. Repayment is due when operations cease.
3. A trustee will be appointed by the creditors to manage the remaining operations and subsequent liquidation.

Amos Barnwell agreed to these terms and on August 1, 2016, Frank Carrington was appointed trustee. The company's balance sheet on that date showed the following:

BARNWELL CORPORATION
Balance Sheet
August 1, 2016

Cash.	$ 397		Accounts payable.	$ 37,933
Accounts receivable.	6,093		Common stock, $10 par.	30,000
Raw materials inventory.	24,000		Additional paid-in capital	60,000
Work-in-process inventory.	51,600		Retained earnings	12,783
Finished goods.	8,550			
Equipment, net.	50,076			
Total assets	$140,716		Total liabilities and equity.	$140,716

During the first six months of Carrington's term as trustee, the following occurred:

1. The creditors advanced the company $9,000.
2. Purchased additional raw materials on account for $9,450.
3. Incurred expenses on account of $22,500. Paid expenses of $31,732, of which $24,937 was for labor. All expenses are charged to work in process.
4. Expended cash in the amount of $1,125 for new equipment.
5. Of the accounts receivable outstanding on August 1, $570 is deemed uncollectible. The balance was collected.
6. Recorded depreciation of $1,500 and charged it to work in process.
7. Collected sales on account of $108,450 during the 6-month period.
8. No equipment was sold.

On January 31, 2017, account balances are as follows: accounts receivable (new), $5,073; accounts payable (new), $133; raw materials, $3,000; and finished goods, $45,000.

Required
a. Prepare a schedule showing transactions affecting the cash account of Barnwell Corporation. *Hint:* While not required, computation of the transactions affecting the remaining asset accounts and the accounts payable account will facilitate the preparation of the statement of realization and liquidation in part *b*., below.
b. Prepare a statement of realization and liquidation for Barnwell Corporation for the six-month period ending January 31, 2017.

✓ LO 3   P15.6   Statement of Realization and Liquidation   Comfort Mattress Corporation, a retailer, decided to liquidate in the face of an extreme cash shortage. By agreement with creditors, a receiver was appointed to manage the liquidation. Upon appointment, the receiver found the company's financial condition to be as follows:

COMFORT MATTRESS CORPORATION
Balance Sheet
March 17, 2016

Cash........................	$ 15,000	Accounts payable..................	$485,000
Accounts receivable.............	120,000	Loan payable (secured by inventory)..	225,000
Inventory of merchandise.........	500,000	Note payable (secured by fixtures)....	60,000
Store fixtures, net...............	150,000	Stockholders' equity	15,000
Total assets	$785,000	Total liabilities and equity...........	$785,000

From March 17 through June 30, the following occurred:

1. Collected accounts receivable of $80,000; the remaining accounts are deemed to be uncollectible.
2. Held a "going out of business sale." Sold inventory costing $310,000 for $298,000. Paid expenses of conducting the sale, amounting to $75,000.
3. Sold the remaining inventory to a liquidator for $60,000.
4. The receiver terminated the store's lease; the lease provides for a termination penalty of $25,000, which was accrued.
5. Sold the store fixtures at auction for a net of $40,000.
6. Accrued the receiver's fee of $50,000.
7. Paid the secured creditors to the extent of the realized value of their security.

Required

a. Prepare a statement of realization and liquidation as of June 30, 2016.
b. Compute the remaining cash and determine how it is disbursed, assuming no further expenses.

P15.7 Statement of Realization and Liquidation Below is the balance sheet of Cognitotech Corporation, **LO 3** at the time it declared bankruptcy and began liquidation.

Cash......	$ 1,000
Receivables, net....	45,000
Supplies	15,000
Prepaid expenses.....	4,000
Equipment, net.....	150,000
Intangibles	200,000
Total assets.....	$415,000
Accounts payable.....	$150,000
Wages and taxes payable	35,000
Deferred revenue: customer deposits	20,000
Loans payable	225,000
Capital stock	5,000
Retained deficit	(20,000)
Total liabilities and equity....	$415,000

All priority claims are within legal limits. The following information relates to activities during the first six months of liquidation, overseen by the trustee.

1. $30,000 of the receivables reported in the beginning balance sheet were collected; it is estimated that 10% of the remaining receivables are uncollectible.
2. Supplies with a book value of $6,000 were sold for $4,000. It is estimated that the remaining supplies can be sold for 50 percent of book value.
3. Prepaid expenses consist of deposits with suppliers; $3,000 was received and the rest were written off.
4. The priority claims were paid in cash.
5. Equipment with a book value of $60,000 was sold for $35,000. It is estimated that the remaining equipment will be sold for 40 percent of book value.
6. The intangibles were written off as worthless.

Required

a. Prepare a statement of realization and liquidation for the six-month period.
b. The remaining liabilities are unsecured. Estimate the recovery percentage for these liabilities.

LO 4 **P15.8 Accounting and Reporting During Reorganization** On April 1, 2018, the Axell Corporation petitioned for reorganization under Chapter 11 of the bankruptcy laws. The company's **liabilities** at that date consisted of the following:

Accounts payable to trade creditors	$1,000,000
Loan payable to bank (unsecured)	200,000
Note payable on equipment (uncertain as to whether the value of the equipment equals the amount of the note)	175,000
Mortgage payable on building (fully secured)	1,000,000
Accrued interest on mortgage (payments are in arrears)	150,000
Total	$2,525,000

The company's assets were as follows:

Cash	$ 70,000
Accounts receivable, net	500,000
Equipment, net	400,000
Land and building, net	1,500,000
Investment (equity method)	195,000
Total	$2,665,000

During the next eight months, the company continued to operate while developing the reorganization plan. It made no payments on its prepetition liabilities during this period. The following transactions occurred between April 1 and December 31:

1. Sales amounted to $1,500,000, with net cash collections of $1,100,000.
2. Operating expenses (including selling, general, and administrative expenses) were $1,200,000. Of this amount, $800,000 was paid in cash, $50,000 represented depreciation of equipment, and $75,000 represented depreciation of building.
3. Interest of $30,500 accrued on the company's liabilities: $4,000 on the loan, $1,500 on the note, and $25,000 on the mortgage. None of this amount was paid. Axell expects that half of each amount will be allowed as a claim.
4. Accrued income taxes of $40,000 for the period April 1 through December 31, and made estimated tax payments of $35,000.
5. Earned interest on cash balances of $1,000.
6. Accrued $120,000 in legal and accounting fees connected with the reorganization.
7. The accounts payable existing at April 1 include a $100,000 invoice from a subcontractor that is subject to dispute. It is expected that one-half of this amount is likely to be allowed as a claim.
8. Sold the investment in May for $250,000 cash. No further adjustments to the investment account were recorded after April 1. This sale did not constitute a disposal of a business segment.
9. Settled an employment contract with the company's executive vice president and agreed on $150,000 of deferred compensation. The $150,000 is likely to be allowed as a claim.

Required

Prepare Axell's December 31, 2018, balance sheet and its income statement and statement of cash flows for the period ended December 31, 2018. Use the direct method for the operating section of the statement of cash flows.

LO 4 **P15.9 Classification of Liabilities in Reorganization** The Spring Hill Corporation entered Chapter 11 reorganization on March 19, 2017. At December 31, 2017, the accountant prepared the following list of liabilities, and seeks your assistance in determining the amount to classify as liabilities subject to compromise in the December 31, 2017, balance sheet:

1. The balance of accounts payable to suppliers is $742,000 on December 31, and was $588,000 on March 19. The company's attorney instructed that no payments are to be made on the March 19 balances.
2. In April, the company terminated leases on several executives' automobiles, incurring a cancellation penalty of $26,000 that remains unpaid.

3. Accrued legal fees of $90,000. An $8,000 balance existed on March 19; the remainder was incurred since that date, in connection with the reorganization proceedings.
4. Notes payable for trucks amount to $57,000. An additional $7,000 in accrued interest accumulated, as no payments were made on the note since March 19. The market value of the trucks is estimated to be $50,000 to $70,000.
5. An unsecured line of credit loan from First National Bank has a balance of $150,000, plus $15,000 interest accrued since March 19.
6. Negotiated a new line of credit loan with Second National Bank after Spring Hill filed for reorganization. The current balance of this loan, including accrued interest, is $70,000.
7. The mortgage payable on the company's land and building stands at $350,000, plus $20,000 interest accrued since March 19. The land and building have an estimated market value of $500,000.
8. Canceled maintenance contracts, at an agreed cancellation charge of $10,000 that is not yet paid.

Required

Prepare the liabilities section of the December 31, 2017, balance sheet, in good form. Remember to separately classify liabilities subject to compromise.

P15.10 Reorganization Value   Lopez Corporation is emerging from Chapter 11 reorganization proceedings. The company's balance sheet shows total assets of $10,000,000. Liabilities subject to compromise amount to $8,000,000, and fully secured liabilities are $2,000,000. Liabilities incurred since filing the reorganization petition amount to $1,000,000. The plan of reorganization identifies assets not needed in the new operation that have a $1,500,000 book value. These assets will be sold in the near future for an expected $500,000. The remaining assets will be used in the new operations of the emerging company; the estimated present value of their future cash flows is $7,900,000. The plan also provides for the new equity interests in the emerging company to be valued at $950,000; 70 percent of this equity will be held by unsecured prepetition creditors, with the remainder held by the former stockholders of Lopez.   **LO 4**

Required

a. Determine the reorganization value.
b. Determine the amount of gain on the restructuring of the company's debt.
c. Prepare a summary balance sheet after implementing the reorganization plan.

P15.11 Emerging from Reorganization   Salem-Winston Corporation is emerging from reorganization proceedings under Chapter 11 of the bankruptcy laws. The company's balance sheet shows total assets of $4,000,000, liabilities subject to compromise of $3,800,000, and postpetition liabilities of $900,000. For purposes of determining reorganization value, Salem-Winston has the following: **LO 4** ✓

Excess cash (accumulated because no payments were made on prepetition debt during the reorganization period)	$ 500,000
Net realizable value of excess assets available for disposition (book value is $120,000)	100,000
Present value of future operating cash flows of the emerging entity	2,800,000
Total	$3,400,000

The new capital structure of Salem-Winston will be as follows:

Postpetition liabilities	$ 900,000
Senior secured debt (10%, 15-year maturity)	1,600,000
Subordinated debt (13%, 8-year maturity)	350,000
Common stock	50,000
Total	$2,900,000

The creditors represented in the amount of liabilities subject to compromise receive an immediate cash payment of $500,000 (the excess cash), all of the new debt securities, and 60 percent of the new common stock. The existing equity holders receive 40 percent of the new common stock.

Required

a. Does Salem-Winston qualify for fresh start reporting? Explain.
b. Prepare journal entries to record Salem-Winston's emergence from reorganization.
c. Present Salem-Winston's post-reorganization balance sheet.

⊘ LO 5   **P15.12 Quasi-Reorganization**   The Hassani Corporation has the following balance sheet:

Current assets	$ 700,000	Current liabilities.	$ 600,000
Noncurrent assets	3,600,000	Long-term liabilities	2,950,000
		Common stock ($10 par)	1,700,000
		Retained earnings	(950,000)
Total assets	$4,300,000	Total liabilities and equity	$4,300,000

Company profitability has been marginal, in part due to book values of noncurrent assets that do not adequately reflect the reduced earning power of the assets. To give its balance sheet a better basis for future profitability, the company decides to undertake a quasi-reorganization. Hassani writes down noncurrent assets to their fair value of $3,000,000 and replaces the current common stock with 100,000 shares of a new issue having a $1 par value.

Required
a. Prepare journal entries to record the quasi-reorganization.
b. Prepare a balance sheet following the quasi-reorganization.

LO 5   **P15.13 Troubled Debt Restructuring**   Herbert Company holds a variety of investment assets (land and securities) in addition to its operating assets. The company is experiencing cash flow problems because of marginally-profitable operations and a substantial operating debt burden. The investments produce very little cash flow, although the market values appreciated substantially. The current balance sheet follows:

Operating assets	$2,000,000	Accounts payable.	$1,500,000
Land	700,000	Notes payable	300,000
Securities	1,200,000	Loan payable	500,000
		Officer loan.	600,000
		Accrued liabilities	300,000
		Stockholders' equity	700,000
Total assets	$3,900,000	Total liabilities and equity	$3,900,000

Reluctantly, management decided to use some of its investment assets to reduce its operating debt burden, and negotiated the following agreements with creditors:

1. Settled the $300,000 note payable, currently secured by operating assets, by the transfer of securities with a fair market value of $290,000 (book value = $140,000). The creditor agreed to the $10,000 discount to get immediate settlement of the note, which does not mature for another two years.
2. Settled the unsecured $500,000 bank loan, maturing in seven years, by the transfer of securities having a fair market value of $450,000 and a book value of $300,000. The bank agreed to the settlement because it can currently lend funds at a higher interest rate.
3. Settled the officer's loan of $600,000, plus $60,000 accrued interest, by the transfer of a parcel of land worth $600,000 (book value = $125,000).
4. Suppliers representing $1,200,000 of accounts payable agreed to accept a two-year, 8 percent note in the amount of $1,200,000.

Required
Record the journal entries for the above transactions, and prepare Herbert Company's balance sheet following the restructuring. Assume a 30 percent tax rate when accruing income taxes on reported gains.

LO 5   **P15.14 Troubled Debt Restructuring**   Thornson Company owes principal and interest on a loan from Pacific Financial Bank, but due to financial difficulties it has not been able to make timely payments. Pacific Financial agrees to the following restructuring of the terms of the loan:

• Principal amount is $750,000, payable at the end of two years.
• Interest is payable at the end of each of the two years, at a rate of 8 percent per annum.

Required

a. Assume that the carrying value of the loan plus accrued interest, on the books of Thornson Company, is $777,500. Prepare the entry, if any, to record the restructuring of the debt.

b. What is the effective interest rate on the new loan? *Hint:* The effective rate is the discount rate where the present value of the future payments equals the carrying value of the debt. Round your answer to the nearest whole percent.

c. Record the first year's interest payment on the new loan, using the effective interest method.

d. Record the second year's interest payment, and the principal payment.

P15.15 Quasi-Reorganization   Here is the balance sheet of Gordon Company, which has experienced sig-   **LO 5**
nificant losses over the last few years.

Current assets	$ 40,000
Buildings, net	500,000
Equipment, net	400,000
Total assets	$940,000
Current liabilities	$100,000
Long-term liabilities	240,000
Common stock, $5 par	500,000
Additional paid-in capital	140,000
Retained deficit	(40,000)
Total liabilities and equity	$940,000

Gordon's shareholders agree to a quasi-reorganization to eliminate the retained deficit and write down the company's buildings and equipment to amounts that better approximate their value in generating future returns.

Required

a. Assume the buildings are written down to $300,000 and the equipment is written down to $350,000. The reorganization plan reduces the par value of the common stock to eliminate the retained deficit. At what par value per share will the retained deficit be eliminated?

b. Now assume the reorganization plan calls for the shareholders to accept one share of $2 par common stock for every two shares of $5 par stock held. What is the maximum amount the company can write down its buildings and equipment and still eliminate the retained earnings deficit?

c. Assume the reorganization plan calls for reducing the buildings and equipment by 25%, and the par value of the stock is cut in half. Present the post-reorganization balance sheet.

REVIEW SOLUTIONS •••

Review 1 Solution

Assets pledged to fully-secured creditors	$300,000
Less: Liabilities to fully-secured creditors	220,000
Available as free assets	80,000
Unpledged assets (= $650,000 − $300,000 − $120,000)	230,000
Less: Unsecured liabilities with priority	(30,000)
Net free assets	$280,000
Liabilities to partially-secured creditors	$180,000
Less: Assets pledged to partially-secured creditors	120,000
Unsecured portion	60,000
Unsecured liabilities (= $820,000 − $220,000 − $180,000 − $30,000)	390,000
Total unsecured liabilities	$450,000

Net free assets of $280,000 are available to pay unsecured claims of $450,000. The expected recovery percentage is $280,000/$450,000 = 62.22 percent.

Review 2 Solution

The company has $890,000 in assets ($90,000 cash plus $800,000 present value of future cash flows). With new liabilities of $845,000 (= $275,000 postpetition liabilities + $280,000 10 percent senior secured debt + $290,000 subordinated debt), the value of the new equity is $45,000.

The entry to record settlement of the prepetition debt follows:

Liabilities to fully-secured creditors	220,000	
Liabilities to partially-secured creditors	180,000	
Unsecured liabilities with priority	30,000	
Unsecured liabilities	390,000	
Cash		90,000
10% senior secured debt		280,000
Subordinated debt		290,000
Equity (= 80% × $45,000 assigned to creditors)		36,000
Gain on debt discharge.		124,000

Thus, a gain of $124,000 is recognized on debt discharge.

16 The SEC and Financial Reporting

UNITED STATES SECURITIES AND EXCHANGE COMMISSION
www.sec.gov

Advanced accounting students are familiar with standard-setting organizations such as the Financial Accounting Standards Board (FASB) and the International Accounting Standards Board (IASB). They also know that the federal government plays a standard-setting role, primarily through the Securities and Exchange Commission (SEC). Because it has the statutory authority (1) to set accounting principles and (2) to regulate the securities markets, the SEC deserves detailed consideration in an advanced financial accounting course.

Complying with SEC regulations in professional practice requires highly specialized expertise, and many professional accountants dedicate themselves to becoming experts in this field. It represents another important way for the professional to contribute to sound financial reporting and efficient securities markets.

One reason that investors rely on published financial reports relates to the SEC's **full disclosure** mission of providing the capital markets with all material financial information about public companies. Companies listed on U.S. stock exchanges, whether they are U.S. or international entities, are subject to extensive requirements regarding reporting standards, financial reports, other financial and nonfinancial disclosures, auditing policies, and corporate governance. Most of these requirements affect the responsibilities of professional accountants. This chapter describes these requirements, as well as current accounting, auditing, and governance issues involving the SEC.

CHAPTER ORGANIZATION

Introduction to the SEC	SEC organization and structure	Registration of new securities	Periodic reporting requirements	Corporate accountability and governance	SEC and accounting standards
• Establishing the SEC • Relevant securities legislation • Definition of "security"	• Divisions and offices • Accounting and auditing pronouncements	• 1933 Act requirements • Registration statement and forms • Underwriting scenarios	• EDGAR system • Annual report (10-K) • Regulation S-X • Quarterly report (10-Q) • Special reports (8-K)	• Audit committees • Antifraud provisions and insider trading • Proxy statements • Dodd-Frank Act	• SEC/FASB relationships • The SEC and IFRS

Legislation charges the SEC with monitoring securities markets and keeping investors informed of developments affecting publicly-traded companies, primarily through requirements emphasizing full disclosure.

SEC action to significantly *increase regulation* has typically been triggered by events with harmful impacts on investors and the economy. The accounting scandals of the late 20th century and early 21st century led Congress to enact the **Sarbanes-Oxley Act of 2002**, giving the government authority over accounting and auditing standards, as well as broad monitoring powers over audit firms, through the **Public Company Accounting Oversight Board** (PCAOB). The 2008 credit crisis gave rise to the **Dodd-Frank Wall Street Reform and Consumer Protection Act** of 2010, which increases regulation over financial services markets. In both cases, the perceived weaknesses of self-regulation led to government intervention. In the case of accounting standards, the government, while retaining final authority, still relies on the FASB to develop standards. In addition, the PCAOB adopted many of the standards of the AICPA, which developed auditing standards prior to the creation of the PCAOB.

Most of the SEC's *financial reporting enforcement actions* involve *misreporting revenues*. High-profile instances of reporting **fictitious revenues** include **HealthSouth Corporation**, charged in 2003 with booking nonexistent sales revenues to meet market expectations, and **Ahold N.V.**, charged in 2004 with inflating revenues by overstating expected vendor payments for promotional allowances. **Satyam Computer Services**, known as India's Enron, fraudulently inflated revenues for many years before its chairman was charged by Indian law enforcement in 2009. PricewaterhouseCoopers audit affiliates were fined $6 million in an SEC enforcement action, for not following basic audit practices, and agreed not to accept new U.S.-based clients for six months. **Premature revenue recognition** cases include **i2 Technologies** and **Computer Associates International**, both charged in 2004 with recognizing revenue from software contracts up front, even though the agreements required significant future support services to customers, and **Raytheon Company**, charged in 2006 with booking revenue from the sale of unfinished aircraft. Companies sometimes **misrepresent revenues**, leading investors to incorrectly infer that the revenues are from stable and growing sources. **Tenent Healthcare Corporation** was charged in 2007 with failure to disclose that significant revenue came from a loophole in the Medicare reimbursement system. **Dell, Inc.** reported revenue derived from large payments from Intel, made to ensure that Dell continued to use Intel as their CPU supplier, but reported the payments as customer product sales, viewed more favorably by investors. The SEC charged Dell in 2010 with failure to provide investors with material information, and as a result Dell paid a $100 million fine; two of its executives paid lesser fines.

Companies can also **understate expenses** to inflate reported income. Earlier in this century, **WorldCom, Inc.** was charged with capitalizing $3.8 billion in costs that should have been expensed. **America Online Inc.** was found to have violated GAAP by capitalizing costs of acquiring new subscribers. Other schemes involve asset and liability misstatements and the use of reserves to smooth income. Companies often use a combination of methods to achieve their reporting goals. The SEC's case against **General Electric**'s reporting methods was settled in 2009 for $50 million. GE used improper **hedge accounting** to report losses on interest rate swaps in OCI instead of earnings, and at the same time used multiple schemes to prematurely report revenues on locomotives and spare parts sales.

ESTABLISHMENT OF THE SEC AND KEY SECURITIES LEGISLATION

LO1 Discuss why the SEC was established and the principal legislation it enforces.

Long before the accounting scandals of the early 21st century and 2008's near melt-down in the credit and financial markets, the 1929 stock market crash started a financial panic unparalleled in American history. Stock market averages lost about **50 percent** of their value during the autumn of 1929. The averages hit bottom in 1932, having lost about **80 percent** of their pre-crash levels. By contrast, the 2008 crisis saw market averages drop about **40 percent** from pre-crisis levels.

Establishment of the SEC

Following the 1929 crash, considerable discussion ensued as to the role the federal government might play in regulating the issuance and trading of securities. Several years of debate led to passage of the Securities Act of 1933 and the Securities Exchange Act of 1934. The latter Act established the Securities and Exchange Commission. Securities legislation was conceived during the worst financial and social crisis in our history and became part of a much broader program of social reform that promised to give a New Deal to the average American at a time when the economy was prostrate. Twenty-five percent of the labor force was unemployed in 1933. Four thousand banks failed that year, and 252,400 nonfarm properties were foreclosed. The gross national product in 1933 declined to 53 percent of its 1929 level.

Securities Legislation and the SEC

The SEC's mission is to administer federal legislation that promotes efficient capital allocation by ensuring that securities markets function fairly and honestly. Embedded in the SEC's mission are (1) protection of investors by requiring full disclosure of material information by issuers of securities, and (2) prevention of fraudulent activities in securities trading and markets. The SEC is charged with administering, either directly or indirectly, these federal securities laws, discussed in detail below:

- Securities Act of 1933
- Securities Exchange Act of 1934
- Public Utility Holding Company Act of 1935
- Trust Indenture Act of 1939
- Investment Company Act of 1940
- Investment Advisers Act of 1940
- Securities Investor Protection Act of 1970
- Foreign Corrupt Practices Act of 1977
- Insider Trading Sanctions Act of 1984
- Private Securities Litigation Reform Act of 1995
- Sarbanes-Oxley Act of 2002
- Emergency Economic Stabilization Act of 2008
- Dodd-Frank Wall Street Reform and Consumer Protection Act of 2010

The **Securities Act of 1933** deals primarily with the issuance of new securities. It regulates the public offering of securities and prohibits (subject to certain exemptions) the offering and sale of securities unless they are registered with the government as well as fraudulent or deceptive practices in the offering or sale of securities. The **Securities Exchange Act of 1934** established the **Securities and Exchange Commission,** granting it jurisdiction over the securities markets. The 1934 Act governs trading in securities once they are issued and outstanding. This Act authorizes the government, through the SEC, to establish accounting, reporting, and disclosure requirements for publicly-owned corporations, and prohibits deceptive and manipulative practices in the purchase or sale of securities.

Although the 1933 and 1934 Acts are the primary focus of our discussion, several other laws related to the securities markets contribute to the work of the SEC. To prevent abuse of the holding company device in controlling and manipulating public utility operating companies, the **Public Utility Holding Company Act of 1935** was enacted. This Act requires public utility holding companies to register with the SEC, provides for SEC-influenced reorganization of such holding companies when dictated by the public interest, and calls for equitable distribution of voting power among security holders in a public utility system. The **Trust Indenture Act of 1939** deals with the issuance of bonds. It requires a formal trust agreement, or *indenture,* specifying the rights of the bondholders, and provides for the appointment, by the issuing company, of an independent trustee to represent the bondholders.

The **Investment Company Act of 1940** regulates investment companies, such as *open-end mutual funds* and *closed-end investment companies.* When such companies register with the SEC, they fulfill certain disclosure requirements involving their investment policies and management fees, and solicit shareholder participation in company policy. **The Investment Advisers Act of 1940** requires those who provide paid advice to the public concerning securities to register with the SEC. Activities of such advisers are also regulated; for example, they may not receive a share of the gains in their clients' portfolios.

The **Securities Investor Protection Act of 1970** created the Securities Investor Protection Corp. (SIPC), which insures customer accounts held by brokers. The SIPC must file annual reports and financial statements with the SEC, and all of its activities are subject to SEC inspection. The **Foreign Corrupt Practices Act of 1977** (FCPA), enacted to stop U.S. companies from making illegal payments to foreign entities, requires companies to maintain accurate accounting records and to maintain a system of effective internal accounting controls. Provisions of the FCPA that are administered by the SEC apply to all companies that register with or report to the commission. Another key law, the **Insider Trading Sanctions Act of 1984,** drastically increased penalties assessed for violating insider trading rules. Under this legislation the SEC can seek fines of up to the greater of $1 million or three times the profits gained or losses avoided by those insiders who inappropriately use material nonpublic information.

The **Private Securities Litigation Reform Act of 1995** limits the liability of public accountants to their "fair share" in certain securities suits. It also creates new safe harbors—protection against lawsuits—that apply to certain forward-looking financial information reported by registrants to the SEC and illegal acts reported by auditors to the SEC.

Congress enacted the **Sarbanes-Oxley Act of 2002 (SOX)** in the wake of numerous financial reporting scandals and corporate governance failures in the early years of the 21st century. SOX requires new reports on internal controls, top management certifications of financial statements filed with the SEC, and created the *Public Company Accounting Oversight Board,* to monitor auditing firms and set auditing standards.

The **Emergency Economic Stabilization Act of 2008** allowed the government to "bail out" banks holding subprime mortgages, and eventually other organizations, notably **General Motors.** One provision reminds the SEC of its ability to suspend or modify accounting standards, in this case the FASB's mark-to-market fair value accounting rules provided in *FASB ASC Topic 820.* Some observers believe that the financial crisis was worsened by requiring banks to book large losses on securities normally traded in markets that simply froze up and became inactive. Later the FASB issued additional guidance relaxing some of the strict mark-to-market interpretations that had been controversial. Also related to the 2008 financial crisis, the **Dodd-Frank Act of 2010** substantially expanded the SEC's role in monitoring financial services markets.

Definition of a Security

The Securities Act of 1933 established a broad definition of the meaning of a **security,** as follows:

Any note, stock, treasury stock, bond, debenture, evidence of indebtedness, certificate of interest or participation in any profit-sharing agreement, collateral trust certificate, preorganization certificate or subscription, transferable share, investment contract, voting trust certificate, certificate of deposit for a security, fractional undivided interest in oil, gas, or other mineral rights, or, in general, any interest or instrument commonly known as a "security," or any certificate of interest or participation in, temporary or interim certificate for, receipt of, guarantee of, or warrant or right to subscribe to or to purchase, any of the foregoing. *(Sec. 2.1)*

The law provided several categories of securities that are exempt from the SEC's registration and reporting rules, although other provisions, such as the antifraud rules, generally apply to these securities. The following are among the **exempt securities:**

- Securities issued or guaranteed by federal, state, or local governments.

- Securities issued or guaranteed by a bank or savings and loan association. These securities, however, are subject to the provisions of the 1934 Act.

- Commercial paper, that is, short-term notes (original maturity not exceeding nine months) issued for working capital purposes.

- Securities issued by not-for-profit organizations. These also are subject to the provisions of the 1934 Act.

Subsequent legislation and litigation clarified the securities status of financial instruments. In *SEC v. W. J. Howey Co.* (1946), the court concluded that the basic question to be addressed in deciding whether a financial instrument is a *security* is whether "the person invests his money in a common enterprise and is led to expect profits solely from the efforts of the promoter or a third party." Thus interests in real estate condominiums, interests in oil drilling programs, variable annuities (where the return depends on the performance of a portfolio of securities), and commodity option contracts have all been held to be securities. But bank certificates of deposit, savings and loan "shares," life insurance policies, and notes representing ordinary bank loans are not securities. Because the definition of a security is so broad, many financial transactions fall under the jurisdiction of the securities laws.

ORGANIZATION AND STRUCTURE OF THE SEC

LO2 Examine the SEC's organization and structure.

The SEC administers and enforces the federal securities laws, and consists of five commissioners, collectively known as the *commission*. The president of the U.S. nominates commissioners subject to Senate confirmation, with one commissioner appointed each year for a staggered five-year term. No more than three of the five commissioners can be from the President's political party. As an independent, nonpartisan agency, the SEC is not part of the legislative or executive branches of government. It is funded by a combination of user charges and congressional appropriations. The commission has a large support staff of accountants, attorneys, economists, IT specialists, and many others.

The SEC is organized into five divisions. The division most frequently encountered by accountants is the **Division of Corporation Finance.** This division primarily administers the disclosure requirements of the securities laws and also participates in matters concerning proxy statements and tender offers. It processes and reviews registration statements and filings of quarterly and annual financial reports. The Division does not review every filing, but focuses on weaknesses in disclosures that might mislead investors. These reviews sometimes result in **restatements** of filed financial reports, which often have devastating effects on a company's share value. These restatements generally result from the misapplication of accounting standards. Common errors include timing of revenue recognition, lease accounting, hedge accounting, equity-based compensation, deferred taxes, and classification of investments. See also the discussion of misleading accounting practices at the beginning of this chapter.

The **Division of Enforcement** is charged with enforcing the securities laws. It investigates possible violations by market participants, such as corporate officers, brokers, financial analysts, and accountants. The division makes recommendations to the Justice Department concerning administrative proceedings, injunctions, and criminal prosecution.

The **Division of Trading and Markets** oversees the operations of the secondary securities markets, where already-outstanding securities are traded, and monitors trading activities and stock market operations. The **Division of Investment Management** regulates investment companies, such as mutual funds and exchange-traded funds, registered investment advisers, and certain insurance products. The **Division of Economic and Risk Analysis** supports all SEC activities through identification of new market practices, issues and concerns, and using economic modeling and data analytics to evaluate the costs and benefits of SEC initiatives.

Several staff offices serve as technical advisors to the commission. The staff office best known to accountants is that of **Chief Accountant of the SEC.** The Chief Accountant is the SEC's expert on accounting principles, auditing standards, and financial disclosures, supervises preparation of SEC accounting and auditing pronouncements, and reviews Division of Enforcement investigations of questionable accounting and auditing practices. The Chief Accountant serves as the link between the SEC and the accounting profession, has oversight powers over the FASB and the PCAOB, and expresses the SEC's views in speeches, papers, and appearances before standard-setting groups. The Divisions of Corporation Finance, Enforcement, and Investment Management also have their own Chief Accountant's office supporting the division.

BUSINESS APPLICATION   SEC Enforcement Initiatives

In 2013, the SEC's Division of Enforcement created the **Financial Reporting and Auditing Task Force**, charged with developing techniques to identify potential cases involving accounting fraud. Methodologies include review of restatements, analysis of performance trends, and modeling tools, including the **Accounting Quality Model**, which identifies filings most likely to contain misleading information. This task force works with the Division's **Center for Risk and Quantitative Analytics** (CRQA) to find cases of potential misreporting.

These initiatives are part of a general upswing in SEC enforcement activity, focusing on expanding the SEC's reach throughout the financial community. SEC "omnipresence" is expected to be achieved through

- Using the resources of other organizations, as well as whistleblowers;
- Focusing on the gatekeepers—boards of directors, audit committees, and auditors;
- Encouraging respect for the law by enforcement of even small cases; and
- Leveraging the expertise of the Financial Reporting and Auditing Task Force to deal with complex and time consuming cases.

SEC Pronouncements on Accounting and Auditing

Recall that the goal of the SEC is to promote efficient allocation of capital by helping to maintain honest and fair securities markets. One important means for accomplishing this goal is by disclosures that communicate relevant information about securities to market participants. This in turn should lead to improved methods of security analysis and increased public confidence in the securities markets. Although the SEC generally delegates its authority to set accounting principles—recognition, measurement and accounting disclosure issues—to the FASB, it occasionally imposes additional requirements on its registrants, asks the FASB to deal with specific accounting issues, and frequently comments on accounting and auditing matters. The SEC communicates its views on accounting and auditing-related matters in formal published pronouncements and through less formal methods, as follows.

- *Financial Reporting Releases (FRR or FR)* are formal pronouncements of the commission and are somewhat analogous to FASB *Codification*. By law, the SEC has the power to establish accounting and reporting standards for companies with securities under its jurisdiction. The *FRR*s therefore are viewed as the highest-ranking authoritative source of accounting principles for publicly-held companies.
- *Staff Accounting Bulletins (SAB)* are similar but not identical to FASB *Technical Bulletins*. *SAB*s are issued by the SEC staff, including the Chief Accountant, without due process, and without a vote by the commission, and represent the staff's current position on various accounting issues in SEC filings.
- *Accounting and Auditing Enforcement Releases (AAER)* report disciplinary or other enforcement actions against accountants and others whose conduct affects public companies' financial reporting. Unlike the *SAB*s, all *AAER*s require an affirmative vote by the SEC commissioners.
- **Private rulings** to companies concerning particular transactions. Referred to as *no-action* and *interpretive letters,* these rulings indicate that the SEC will not object if a transaction is handled in the proposed manner.
- **Informal statements** by commissioners or top staff, such as the Chief Accountant. These statements, often in the form of speeches or written releases, convey informally the views of key individuals on certain matters. This format is frequently used to express views on matters being considered by the FASB or by the accounting profession.

REVIEW 1 • Mission and Organization of the SEC

Required

a. Explain why the SEC exists and its fundamental mission.

b. Describe three pieces of legislation that the SEC is responsible for, other than the 1933 and 1934 Acts.

c. Describe in your own words the meaning of "security," and comment on whether that meaning is broad enough to encompass virtually all instruments likely to be traded in financial markets.

d. How does the SEC fulfill its statutory responsibility to set accounting and reporting standards?

Solutions are located after the chapter assignments.

REGISTRATION OF NEW SECURITIES

LO3 Describe principal SEC requirements for registering new securities.

The key feature of the **Securities Act of 1933** is the set of requirements for registration of new security issues, a direct response to the deceptive and manipulative environment frequently encountered by investors in the 1920s and early 1930s. Because the SEC acts as a conduit for information provided by issuers of securities to other market participants, the **full disclosure requirement** for new security issues of public companies provides adequate and accurate disclosure of material facts concerning the company and the securities it proposes to sell. Thus, investors may make a realistic appraisal of the merits of the securities and exercise informed judgment in determining whether or not to purchase them.

The 1933 Act provides, with few exemptions, that no security may be offered or sold to the public unless it is registered with the SEC. Most corporate equity and publicly-held debt securities are registered. Achieving registration does not mean that the SEC passes judgment on the merits of the security; rather, it means only that certain disclosure requirements have been satisfied. Thus the SEC performs *compliance reviews,* not *merit reviews.* The 1933 Act also sets forth the registration procedure and establishes liabilities for misstatements or omissions.

A prospective issuer becomes an SEC **registrant** and must file a **registration statement**—the set of documents needed to register securities—with the SEC. The registration statement consists of two parts: (1) a *prospectus* that must be furnished to each purchaser of the security, and (2) other information and exhibits that must be publicly available but need not be supplied to each investor. The **prospectus** describes the issuing company, its business operations and risks, its financial statements, historical financial information, the securities to be sold, and the expected uses of the proceeds. Typically, a **registration team** consisting of the issuer's chief financial officer and legal counsel, and the underwriter (investment banker) and underwriter's counsel, prepares the registration statement. The registrant's independent public accountant reviews and audits information in the registration statement.

Although a registration statement could become effective as early as 20 days after being filed, companies generally delay the effective date pending notification that the SEC will declare the registration statement "effective." The SEC's Division of Corporation Finance takes about 30 days to review the statement to see if it meets disclosure requirements. Reviews may be complete or partial, and the issuing company may receive a **letter of comment** stating any suggestions or criticisms. Responses to SEC comments and amendments to the registration statement frequently create additional 20-day waiting periods and delay the effective date. Even a cursory SEC review, however, does not waive the registrant's obligation to provide complete and accurate disclosures. Once the registration statement becomes effective, the issuer may sell the securities to the public.

Reporting Perspective

To help promote their securities before the registration process becomes effective, companies distribute *preliminary prospectuses,* with those words stamped in red on the cover, to a small group of potential investors. Because changes are often made to these red-stamped preliminary prospectuses after SEC review, they became known as **red herrings**. This term dates back at least to 19th century Britain where fugitives pulled strong smelling herrings that turned red after being smoked across the path to divert pursuing dogs to a false trail.

Form S-1, the basic form for the registration of new issues, consists of lists of required disclosures. Other commonly used forms are short **Form S-3** used by issuers meeting specified criteria and **Form S-4** for securities issued in exchanges, such as debt exchanges, and in business combinations. Companies may be able to file the simpler Form S-3 if they already filed an annual Form 10-K. The logic is that since information about such companies is already available to the market, less additional information is needed from them than from the company going public for the first time.

Financial data presented in a registration statement include a balance sheet dated within 90 days of filing, statements of comprehensive income and statements of cash flows for the past three years, and summaries of operations for the past five years. Such data must be accompanied by an auditor's report covering at least through the end of the last fiscal year. The period from the last audited statement to the date of the most recent interim period ending before the registration statement, known as the **stub period,** is generally covered by an accountant's review. Accountants also commonly write **comfort letters** to the underwriter providing negative assurance on nonfinancial statement information contained in the registration statement.

There are two major exemptions to the above detailed registration requirements. One is for "small" offerings: various rules limit the maximum dollar size and number of investors allowed under this provision. The second exemption is for **private placements,** securities issued to a single investor or small group of investors who have access to the kind of information otherwise disclosed during registration. Institutional investors such as insurance companies and pension funds frequently absorb private placements.

The flow of the securities in a typical issuance is

$$\text{Issuer} \rightarrow \text{Underwriter} \rightarrow \text{Dealer} \rightarrow \text{Public}$$

The underwriter advises the company about the terms and structure of the issue, and markets the securities to the public under one of three types of arrangements.

- A **firm commitment** underwriting means that the underwriter buys the entire issue at a fixed price, and it is responsible for selling the issue to dealers, who will in turn sell it to the public. The underwriter bears the risk that the issue will not find market acceptance at the asking price.

- A **best efforts** underwriting means that the underwriter sells as many shares as possible, receiving a commission based on sales. The issuing company bears the risk of nonacceptance in the market.

- An **all-or-none** underwriting means that if the underwriter is unable to sell all, or a predetermined portion, of the issue, then the issue may be cancelled and the subscribed but unsold shares are rescinded. This arrangement relieves the issuing company of the risk that not enough capital will be raised to sustain the project or projects for which the securities are being sold.

After a new security issue is registered and sold, it normally is traded in a secondary market. Depending upon the size and nature of the issue, it may be traded *over-the-counter* by dealers or listed and traded on one of the organized securities exchanges. The issuing company has a continuing obligation to the SEC, and to the public, to provide full and complete disclosure of relevant information, and must satisfy the SEC's periodic reporting requirements.

PERIODIC REPORTING REQUIREMENTS

The **Securities Exchange Act of 1934** subjects issuers of currently traded securities to the same "full disclosure" philosophy that the 1933 Act applies to newly offered securities. Thus issuers of currently traded securities also are SEC registrants that file periodic reports with the SEC so that important information about issuers' affairs becomes public. The periodic reporting requirements of the SEC cover all companies that have securities listed on a national securities exchange, along with all companies that have more than 500 stockholders and more than $10,000,000 in assets.

LO4 Explain the periodic reporting requirements for SEC registrants.

EDGAR

Most documents filed with the SEC are available to the public through its online **Electronic Data Gathering, Analysis, and Retrieval System (EDGAR).** EDGAR allows users to search for filing information according to company name, country, most recent filings, filing type, and other attributes. Most documents are available in multiple formats. Many documents must be filed in Interactive Data format using the **eXtensible Business Reporting Language (XBRL)**. XBRL codes the data in financial statements, allowing users to download selected data directly to spreadsheets, for use in their specific analyses.

The principal reports currently made by issuers to the SEC are the annual report (Form 10-K), quarterly reports (Form 10-Q), and special reports (Form 8-K) filed within a short period after specified events occur. Contents of these reports are largely governed by two sets of regulations: *Regulation S-X* addresses accounting and financial statement requirements for both annual and quarterly reports, and *Regulation S-K* covers all other disclosures.

The Annual Report: Form 10-K

The annual report to the SEC, or **Form 10-K,** is an extensive document presenting financial statements and a variety of disclosures and descriptive information. Exhibit 16.1 outlines the structure of the Form 10-K annual report. Note that financial statements comprise only one of the categories of information; financial disclosures and a variety of nonfinancial information account for the remainder.

In the interest of standardizing reporting and disclosure, a company's annual financial report to its stockholders must conform to SEC financial statement requirements set forth in Regulation S-X. Moreover, the SEC specifies that other SEC-required disclosures be included in the annual report to stockholders. Such information can be *incorporated into the 10-K report by reference* to the annual report to shareholders.

EXHIBIT 16.1 Structure and Contents of Form 10-K

Item	Description
Part I	
1	Description of the business
1A	Risk factors
1B	Unresolved staff comments
2	Description of properties
3	Legal proceedings involving the company
4	Mine safety disclosures
4A	Executive officers
Part II	
5	Market price of common stock, dividends, and related stockholder matters
6	Selected financial data
7	Management's discussion and analysis of financial condition and results of operations
7A	Quantitative and qualitative disclosures about market risk
8	Financial statements and supplementary financial information
9	Changes in and disagreements with accountants on accounting and financial disclosure
9A	Controls and procedures
Part III	
10	Directors and executive officers
11	Executive compensation and transactions with executives
12	Security ownership by certain beneficial owners and by management
13	Certain relationships and related-party transactions
14	Principal accountant fees and services
Part IV	
15	Exhibits
Signatures	
Certification	

Filing deadlines for Forms 10-K and 10-Q depend on the market capitalization (public float) of the filer. The table below summarizes the requirements.

Size of filer (public float)	Deadline for 10-K filing	Deadline for 10-Q filing
Large accelerated filer: $700 million or more	60 days after year-end	40 days after end of quarter
Accelerated filer: between $75 million and $700 million . . .	75 days after year-end	40 days after end of quarter
Non-accelerated filer: less than $75 million	90 days after year-end	45 days after end of quarter

The 10-K is signed by the company, its principal executive officer, its principal financial officer, its principal accounting officer (usually the controller), and a majority of the board of directors, signifying the broad responsibility of officers and directors for proper reporting and disclosure. To further emphasize this responsibility, Section 302 of the Sarbanes-Oxley Act requires that CEOs and CFOs certify the accuracy and completeness of their companies' financial reports with personal sworn statements. SOX Section 404 requires similar certifications on the adequacy of internal controls in general and "internal control over financial reporting" in particular.

As stated, **Regulations S-X** and **S-K** set forth the accounting, reporting, and disclosure requirements for preparing the 10-K. Regulation S-X governs Item 8 in Exhibit 16.1—financial statements and supplementary financial information—whereas Regulation S-K governs the other items. The following brief discussion of the content of many of the 10-K items indicates the broad range of information required by the SEC, extending far beyond that commonly found in the annual financial report to stockholders.

Item 1A: Risk Factors   Item 1A requires disclosure of risk factors specific to the registrant's securities. These risk factors include but are not limited to: short operating history, lack of recent profitable periods, weak financial position, risky business-specific conditions and concerns over marketability of the registrant's securities.

BUSINESS APPLICATION   Target Corporation's 2014 10-K, Item 1A

In 2013, **Target Corporation** opened 124 stores in Canada, their first non-U.S. expansion; initial results have not met expectations. In late 2013, Target was the victim of a large and well-publicized security breach involving customers' credit and debit card information, likely causing the major decline in retail sales Target experienced during the fourth quarter of 2013. In Item 1A, Target's fiscal 2014 10-K identifies these events, among others, as risk factors. Here are some of the risk factors Target included.

- If we are unable to positively differentiate ourselves from other retailers, our results of operations could be adversely affected.

- If we are unable to successfully develop and maintain a relevant and reliable multichannel experience for our guests, our sales, results of operations and reputation could be adversely affected.

- Our earnings are highly susceptible to the state of macroeconomic conditions and consumer confidence in the United States.

- Interruptions in our supply chain or increased commodity prices and supply chain costs could adversely affect our gross margins, expenses and results of operations.

- The data breach we experienced in 2013 has resulted in government inquiries and private litigation, and if our efforts to protect the security of information about our guests and team members are unsuccessful, future issues may result in additional costly government enforcement actions and private litigation and our sales and reputation could suffer.

- If we do not positively differentiate the Target experience and appeal to our new Canadian guests, our financial results could be adversely affected.

Item 1B: Unresolved Staff Comments   Item IB describes any material questions the SEC has raised on reports filed in the past, which remain unresolved over an extended period of time.

Item 2: Description of Properties   Item 2 contains descriptions of the location and general character of the company's principal plants; oil, gas, or other mineral deposits; and other physical properties. Users of the report need these physical descriptions to appreciate what lies behind the dollar amounts of plant assets reported in the corporate balance sheet. Property descriptions may be brief or very detailed.

Item 3: Legal Proceedings   Item 3 describes significant legal proceedings involving the company. Because this disclosure is usually more detailed than that presented in the annual report to stockholders, interested readers become better informed about the company's potential legal exposure and may be able to sense the adverse effects of significant liabilities lying beneath the surface.

Item 5: Stock Prices and Dividends   Data in Item 5 include the number of shareholders, and information on dividends, stock repurchases, and shareholder return over the past few years. Companies are encouraged to make a statement that dividends will or will not be paid in the near future.

Item 6: Selected Financial Data   Item 6 presents summaries of financial data to highlight trends in the company's financial condition and operating results, and to provide a basis for evaluating the company's performance and financial position in the current year. These summaries include, for each of the past five years, at least the following:

- Net sales or operating revenues
- Income or loss from continuing operations
- Income or loss per share
- Total assets
- Long-term obligations and redeemable preferred stock
- Cash dividends declared per common share

Companies may disclose additional items that they believe are informative with respect to trends in their financial condition and operating results. Companies often use this item to display "non-GAAP" performance measures, which exclude certain nonoperating and/or noncontinuing items, presumably to provide investors with additional information useful in predicting future performance.

Item 7: Management's Discussion and Analysis   The MD&A's principal objective is to allow the reader to examine the company through the eyes of management. It represents management's opportunity, indeed obligation, to provide analytical commentary on the current state of the company's business operations and likely significant future developments. The key areas to be discussed are *liquidity, capital resources,* and *trends or uncertainties.*

   Liquidity refers to the company's ability to generate adequate amounts of cash to meet its needs. Registrants identify any known commitments or events that will significantly affect liquidity, or any major uncertainties that, if realized, will have a material effect on liquidity. When major liquidity problems exist, management should discuss actions it is taking or plans to remedy the problems.

   Capital resources involve both sources of long-term funding and expenditures on long-term assets. Registrants discuss major commitments or plans for capital expenditures, such as plant expansions, pollution control equipment, or energy-saving investments. Discussion also includes trends or anticipated changes in the sources of long-term capital—debt, equity, and off-balance-sheet forms of financing.

   With respect to **trends or uncertainties**, registrants disclose any unusual or infrequent events or transactions that materially affected income, factors that may significantly affect revenues—whether favorably or unfavorably—and events expected to change the relationship between costs and revenues. Registrants explain significant year-to-year changes in line items on the financial statements.

   Certain items are required to be presented in the MD&A, if appropriate. Many of these items have been added as a response to misleading reporting practices. For example, required disclosure of off-balance-sheet arrangements followed from implementation of the Sarbanes-Oxley Act, and disclosure of investment impairment testing originated in the aftermath of the credit crisis. Required disclosures include:

- **Segment information**: Discuss performance by business segments, as appropriate to understanding the business as a whole, and when a segment contributes disproportionately to overall performance.
- **Prospective information**: Disclose known trends, demands, commitments, events or uncertainties that are likely to materially impact liquidity.
- **Off-balance-sheet arrangements**: Disclose, in a separately captioned section of the MD&A, obligations and contractual arrangements not reported on the balance sheet. Relevant items include unconsolidated variable interest entities, and agreements with customers, suppliers, financial institutions, derivatives counterparties, and lessors.
- **Contractual obligations**: Provide a tabular presentation of contractual obligations, disclosing payments due for each type of contract over the next few years. Examples include long-term debt, lease obligations, and purchase obligations.

- **Critical accounting policies and estimates**: Identify the accounting policies that significantly influence reported performance and require the most subjective judgments, to inform readers concerning the impact of these judgments on financial statements.

- **Income taxes**: Discuss the effect of new tax laws and uncertain tax positions on company performance, including the likelihood of realizing deferred tax assets, and the amount and timing of deferred tax settlements.

- **Investments**: Explain how the company determines whether a decline in value is impairment (other-than-temporary).

- **Pensions**: Discuss the nature of the company's pension plans, deferred gains and losses, the validity of assumptions used, and the amounts and timing of future funding requirements.

Item 7A: Quantitative and Qualitative Disclosures about Market Risk   This item seeks to help financial statement users assess the reasons that companies use derivative financial instruments, and the likely exposure to market risk created by companies' positions in derivatives and other financial instruments. **Market risk** is the risk of loss from adverse movements in interest rates, exchange rates, commodity prices, and the like.

BUSINESS APPLICATION   **Microsoft Corporation's 2014 10-K, Item 7A**

Microsoft Corporation's 10-K for fiscal 2014 includes the following discussion of market risk (Item 7A):

> We are exposed to economic risk from foreign currency exchange rates, interest rates, credit risk, equity prices, and commodity prices. A portion of these risks is hedged, but they may impact our consolidated financial statements.
>
> We use a value-at-risk ("VaR") model to estimate and quantify our market risks. VaR is the expected loss, for a given confidence level, in the fair value of our portfolio due to adverse market movements over a defined time horizon. The distribution of the potential changes in total market value of all holdings is computed based on the historical volatilities and correlations among foreign currency exchange rates, interest rates, equity prices, and commodity prices, assuming normal market conditions.
>
> The VaR is calculated as the total loss that will not be exceeded at the 97.5 percentile confidence level or, alternatively stated, the losses could exceed the VaR in 25 out of 1,000 cases. Total one-day VaR for the combined risk categories was $333 million at June 30, 2014 and $350 million at June 30, 2013.

Microsoft provides a one-day VaR for each of its risk categories, as follows:

			Year ended June 30, 2014		
Risk Categories (in millions)	**June 30, 2014**	**June 30, 2013**	**Average**	**High**	**Low**
Foreign currency	$179	$199	$215	$287	$117
Interest rate	73	85	82	91	73
Equity.	176	181	208	246	173
Commodity.	17	19	18	21	16

Why is the sum of the one-day VaR amounts for the four risk categories greater than the $333 million total one-day VaR at June 30, 2014? Portfolio diversification reduces the combined risk.

Registrants group their market risk sensitive instruments into those entered into (1) "for trading purposes" and (2) "for purposes other than trading" and have the flexibility to choose at least one of three alternative approaches to estimating and communicating market risk.

- **Tabular presentation** of estimated fair values and expected cash flows of derivatives and other financial instruments by expected maturity date.

- **Sensitivity analysis** indicates, for a selected time period, potential losses in future cash flows, earnings, or fair values from hypothetical changes of at least 10% in relevant interest and currency exchange rates, commodity prices, etc.

- **Value at risk (VAR)** indicates the potential loss, as in a sensitivity analysis, that has a selected likelihood of occurrence. For example, VAR could estimate the maximum loss expected to occur over the next ten days with probability ≤ 0.05.

Item 9: Changes in and Disagreements with Accountants   One area of concern is the extent to which firms replace their outside auditors because of disagreements over accounting or financial disclosure matters. A change of accountants is a special event that calls for filing a special report in accordance with the rules for Form 8-K (discussed later in this chapter). The report must indicate whether the registrant and the former auditors disagreed on an issue concerning auditing procedures, accounting principles, or financial statement disclosures. When such an 8-K was filed within the past 24 months, Item 9 of the annual 10-K must disclose, for the transactions or events under dispute, the difference between the company's reporting method and that proposed by the former auditors.

Registrants replacing auditors must also disclose (1) former auditors' concerns that remain unresolved, (2) the substance of consultations with new auditors before their appointment and (3) whether the former auditors resigned or were discharged.

Item 9A: Controls and Procedures   Here we find the report of the registrant's CEO and CFO about the effectiveness of the registrant's internal controls and procedures, and management's evaluation of the effectiveness of internal controls over financial reporting, required by SOX Section 404.

Item 10: Directors and Executive Officers   Item 10 identifies the registrant's directors, executive officers, and certain other key employees, along with their business experience. It also requires disclosure of any family relationships among directors and executive officers and any involvement of directors or executive officers in certain legal proceedings.

Item 11: Executive Compensation and Transactions   Item 11 describes various aspects of officer and director compensation. Executive compensation is disclosed in total and for each top executive, including salary, bonus, and equity awards. Registrants present narrative descriptions of deferred compensation plans, pension and profit-sharing plans, stock option plans, and the like, and any proposed changes in officer and director compensation.

Item 12: Security Ownership   Item 12 discloses the security holdings of major stockholders and management of the company.

Item 13: Certain Relationships and Related Transactions   Registrants describe significant transactions, including indebtedness, with related parties, such as executives and directors of the registrant, owners of more than 5% of the registrant's voting stock, and immediate family members of these individuals. In addition, certain business relationships and ownership interests involving directors or director nominees are to be disclosed.

Item 14: Principal Accountant Fees and Services   This item relates to concerns over independence of a registrant's public accountant. It requires disclosure of aggregate fees billed by the principal accountant in each of the last two fiscal years for audit fees, audit-related fees, tax fees, and all other fees. The registrant must also describe its audit committee's procedures for approving such fees and the percentages of fees other than audit fees that the audit committee approved.

Certifications   As stated earlier, to emphasize the responsibility of top management for the veracity of their companies' financial reports, first the SEC and then SOX Sections 302 and 404 require personal sworn statements by the registrant's CEO and CFO in three areas: (1) accuracy and completeness of financial statements, (2) effectiveness of internal controls and procedures related to financial reporting, and (3) deficiencies in and changes to internal controls, including corrective actions. In Section 302(a)(3), SOX requires the CEO and CFO to certify that the annual and quarterly reports "fairly present" the company's results of operations and financial condition, regardless of conformance with GAAP.

Regulation S-X

Regulation S-X governs the form and content of financial reporting to the SEC and related matters and is a collection of rules derived from original SEC pronouncements. Together with FASB pronouncements, Regulation S-X prescribes the body of accounting and reporting principles to be followed in SEC filings.

Regulation S-X is organized into the several articles outlined in Exhibit 16.2. Article 2 concerns the qualifications and actions of accountants. Disciplinary actions sanctioning the improper or unprofessional work of accountants who practice before the SEC are generally brought under *Rule 102(e)* of the Commission's Rules of Practice, often referred to as *Rule 2(e)*. Articles 3 and 4 present the broad accounting and reporting rules applicable to most companies. Article 10 deals with interim reports and Article 12 prescribes disclosure of detailed information in schedules included in the 10-K report. Many of the other articles address accounting and reporting issues appropriate to particular industry types.

EXHIBIT 16.2   Contents of Regulation S-X

Article	Contents
1	Application of Regulation S-X
2	Qualifications and reports of accountants
3	General instructions as to financial statements
3A	Consolidated and combined financial statements
4	Rules of general application
5	Commercial and industrial companies
6	Registered investment companies
6A	Employee stock purchase, savings, and similar plans
7	Insurance companies other than life insurance
8	Financial statements of smaller reporting companies
9	Bank holding companies
10	Interim financial statements
11	*Pro forma* financial statements
12	Form and content of schedules

BUSINESS APPLICATION   Auditor Conduct and the Credit Crisis

In the aftermath of the credit crisis of 2008, the SEC's Division of Enforcement brought action under Rule 102(e), charging some auditors of bankrupt companies with "improper professional conduct." Under Rule 102(e), improper professional conduct can occur in any of these circumstances:

- **Intentional or knowing** conduct, including reckless conduct;

- A single instance of **highly unreasonable conduct** resulting in violation of professional standards, in which the accountant **should know** that heightened scrutiny is warranted;

- Repeated instances of unreasonable conduct, each resulting in a **violation of applicable professional standards**, indicating a **lack of competence** to practice before the Commission.

The SEC charged the management of failed banks and other financial institutions with fraud, for misreporting loan losses, and charged the auditors with misconduct, for relying on management's information about the quality of the loans. A notable case involves **TierOne Bank**, which incurred millions of dollars in loan losses and eventually filed for bankruptcy. The SEC brought charges against three bank executives, and also two KPMG auditors, who in 2013 were charged with improper professional conduct under Rule 102(e). The SEC accused the auditors of "rubber stamping" the bank's loan loss estimates and ignoring "the red flags surrounding the bank's troubled real estate loans." *Source:* SEC press release, January 9, 2013

SEC accounting rules generally parallel generally accepted accounting principles (GAAP) issued by the FASB. Section 101 in the SEC's *Codification of Financial Reporting Policies* endorses the work of the FASB. The SEC automatically accepts pronouncements of the FASB unless the SEC issues its own pronouncement on the particular subject. Historically, most accounting standard-setting has been done directly by the private sector with SEC oversight, even though the SEC has the statutory authority to set accounting principles. The SEC accepts and encourages this procedure, except in a few cases where the SEC acted first to spur the private standard-setting body into action on some pressing matter.

Section 108 of SOX authorizes the SEC to recognize as generally accepted any accounting principles established by a standard-setting body that meets the Act's requirements. The FASB meets these requirements. Presently the FASB is the SEC's "official" accounting standard-setter, but SOX leaves the door open for the SEC to recognize the work of other standard-setters such as the IASB, that meet SOX's requirements. Required attributes include independence, adequate funding, and the ability to identify and consider important issues on a timely basis.

General Accounting and Reporting Rules   Article 3 of Regulation S-X prescribes the financial statements to be prepared and the time periods covered. Registrants generally provide:

- Audited consolidated balance sheets as of the end of the two most recent fiscal years
- Audited consolidated statements of income and comprehensive income and cash flows for the three most recent fiscal years
- Analysis of changes in the stockholders' equity accounts shown in the balance sheet for the three most recent fiscal years as a separate financial statement or a footnote schedule

Article 4 of Regulation S-X deals with selected accounting and reporting matters applicable to companies in general, independent of their industry. For example, *foreign private issuers* can file financial statements using official IFRS without any reconciliations to U. S. GAAP. The SEC also accepts foreign security issuers' financial statements prepared according to a comprehensive set of accounting principles other than U.S. GAAP or IFRS, but requires Form 20-F reconciliations of net income and stockholders' equity to U.S. GAAP. Examples of how Article 4 treats specific items appear in the following paragraphs.

Notes to the financial statements must provide summarized balance sheet and income statement information for certain significant unconsolidated subsidiaries and equity method investees. SEC rules for presenting *income tax expense* go beyond GAAP's tax allocation requirements and require separate disclosure of temporary differences whose effect exceeds 5% of the total tax expense. And the SEC requires a reconciliation of the amount reported as income tax expense and the amount computed by multiplying income before tax by the statutory federal tax rate. This often-difficult-to-understand reconciliation aids in determining the difference between the *statutory tax rate* and the registrant's *effective tax rate*.

Registrants disclose significant transactions with *related parties,* such as management, principal owners and affiliated companies. These rules encompass the provisions set forth in *ASC Topic 850,* Related Party Disclosures, and *Statement on Auditing Standards No. 6,* Related Party Transactions. When separate financial statements are prepared for the registrant or certain investees and subsidiaries, those statements must disclose amounts eliminated and not eliminated in the related consolidated statements. Similarly, the effect of intercompany profits/losses not eliminated in the separate statements shall be disclosed. Material related party items, such as receivables, payables, revenue, expense, gain or loss, or cash flows, must be identified on the face of the respective financial statement, not merely in the notes.

Schedules of Information   Article 12 of Regulation S-X requires schedules that provide considerable detail on several items. Their purpose is to enhance understanding of the financial statements through disclosure of details behind, and analysis of changes in, certain account balances. In general, schedules are required for the following items:

- Condensed financial information of the registrant (for certain bank holding companies).
- Valuation accounts; e.g., allowance for bad debts and valuation allowance for deferred tax assets.
- Real estate and accumulated depreciation.
- Mortgage loans on real estate.
- Supplemental insurance information.

The Quarterly Report: Form 10-Q

Firms required to file an annual report with the SEC must also file quarterly reports prescribed in Form 10-Q. Such quarterly reporting is intended to provide investors and others with an *update of the most recently filed 10-K report*. Quarterly reports are therefore not stand-alone documents and are not designed to forecast the next 10-K. Rather, they foster timely disclosure of important developments affecting the registrant such that the annual report should contain few major surprises. Registrants file the 10-Q report within 45 days after the end of each of the first three quarters of the company's fiscal year; no fourth quarter report is required. Quarterly report filing dates are 40 days after the end of the quarter for large accelerated and accelerated filers.

ASC Topic 270, Interim Reporting, *ASC Topic 250*, Accounting Changes and Error Corrections, and *ASC Subtopic 740-270*, Income Taxes—Interim Reporting, are the primary sources of accounting principles for interim reports. The SEC requires that quarterly data be presented in the annual reports of all registrants. Although these data need not be audited, the independent accountant checks for consistency between these data and those previously subjected to the auditor's review procedures. Quarterly reports are typically much shorter than the annual report. Form 10-Q contains:

- Balance sheets at the end of the quarter and the end of the prior fiscal year
- Quarterly and year-to-date statements of income and comprehensive income for the current quarter and the same quarter of the prior year
- Cumulative year-to-date statements of cash flow for the current and prior fiscal years

The statements may have fewer captions than the annual statements. Smaller accounts may be combined under one caption, as long as the general format of the statements is maintained; e.g., do not combine current items with noncurrent items.

Selected other disclosures also appear in the 10-Q, such as the **MD&A.** Others include legal proceedings, changes in the company's securities, defaults on senior securities, and matters reported on Form 8-K during the quarter. The extensive financial disclosures found in the annual report are not required on a quarterly basis.

Special Reports: Form 8-K

The SEC requires that registrants file a special report or *current report* known as **Form 8-K** within four days of the occurrence of events significant to investors, such as those in Exhibit 16.3.

Whether or not to file a Form 8-K is often a matter of judgment, especially for events reported under Item 8.01. **Target Corporation**'s massive data breach occurred in late 2013, when over a two-week period thieves stole information on 40 million debit and credit cards from Target customers. Target eventually issued an 8-K concerning this event, but not until late February 2014. The 8-K identified the data breach as one of many risk factors. In part, Target reported the following:

> The data breach we experienced in 2013 has resulted in government inquiries and private litigation, and if our efforts to protect the security of personal information about our guests and team members are unsuccessful, future issues may result in additional costly government enforcement actions and private litigation and our sales and reputation could suffer.
>
> A significant disruption in our computer systems and our inability to adequately maintain and update those systems could adversely affect our operations and our ability to maintain guest confidence.
>
> We experienced a significant data security breach in the fourth quarter of fiscal 2013 and are not yet able to determine the full extent of its impact and the impact of government investigations and private litigation on our results of operations, which could be material. *Source:* Target Corporation 8-K, February 26, 2014.

Financial statements normally do not accompany Form 8-K. But when the 8-K reports a major acquisition, the 8-K filing includes the acquired company's financial statements.

EXHIBIT 16.3   Events Reported on Form 8-K

Item 1.01	Entry into a material definitive agreement
Item 1.02	Termination of a material definitive agreement
Item 1.03	Bankruptcy or receivership
Item 2.01	Completion of acquisition or disposition of assets
Item 2.02	Results of operations and financial condition
Item 2.03	Creation of a direct financial obligation or an obligation under an off-balance-sheet arrangement of a registrant
Item 2.04	Triggering events that accelerate or increase a direct financial obligation or an obligation under an off-balance-sheet arrangement
Item 2.05	Costs associated with exit or disposal activities
Item 2.06	Material impairments
Item 3.01	Notice of delisting or failure to satisfy a continued listing rule or standard; transfer of listing
Item 3.02	Unregistered sales of equity securities
Item 3.03	Material modification to rights of security holders
Item 4.01	Changes in registrant's certifying accountant
Item 4.02	Non-reliance on previously issued financial statements or a related audit report or completed interim review
Item 5.01	Changes in control of registrant
Item 5.02	Departure of directors or certain officers; election of directors; appointment of certain officers; compensatory arrangements of certain officers
Item 5.03	Amendments to articles of incorporation or bylaws; change in fiscal year
Item 5.04	Temporary suspension of trading under registrant's employee benefit plans
Item 5.05	Amendments to the registrant's code of ethics, or waiver of a provision of the code of ethics
Item 5.06	Change in shell company status
Item 6.01	Asset-backed security informational and computational material
Item 6.02	Change of servicer or trustee
Item 6.03	Change in credit enhancement or other external support
Item 6.04	Failure to make a required distribution
Item 6.05	Securities act updating disclosure
Item 7.01	Regulation FD disclosure
Item 8.01	Other events

REVIEW 2 • Registration and Periodic Reporting Requirements

Required

a. Summarize the process for registering new security issues with the SEC, including the forms used, the accountant's role, and the mechanics of typical underwriting.

b. Although Form 10-K is probably the best-known SEC filing, it contains much non-accounting information that is governed by Regulation S-K. Indicate which items governed by Regulation S-K relate to accounting and reporting.

c. Regulation S-X governs the financial statement information in the 10-K. Explain why Articles 3 and 4 are particularly important.

d. Explain the purpose of Form 8-K and comment briefly on the importance of Items 2.03, 2.04 and 4.01.

Solutions are located after the chapter assignments.

CORPORATE ACCOUNTABILITY AND GOVERNANCE

LO5 Describe the SEC's role in corporate accountability and governance.

In addition to concerns over corporate *accounting,* capital market participants show considerable interest in the broader notion of corporate *accountability.* Complying with SEC requirements for periodic financial reporting helps the corporation fulfill its obligation to be accountable for its actions. How a corporation conducts its affairs and relates to its security holders, employees, and the public are major aspects of corporate accountability. The SEC plays an important role, both directly and indirectly, in setting guidelines for corporate accountability and governance.

One of its indirect influences appeared in the *Foreign Corrupt Practices Act (FCPA)* of 1978 that prohibits certain activities in the conduct of international transactions. This Act also requires management to maintain accurate books and records that will reveal any illegal transactions, and to maintain an adequate system of internal control to reduce the occurrence of such transactions. Despite this apparently clear requirement, note that SOX revisits much of the same territory.

The blockbuster Sarbanes-Oxley (SOX) legislation was enacted in 2002 in response to a series of corporate accounting scandals. One major provision of SOX established the **Public Company Accounting Oversight Board (PCAOB)** to regulate and monitor auditing firms, subject to SEC oversight. In an early decision, the PCAOB received authority to assume the AICPA's role in setting auditing standards for audits of public companies.

Another major SOX provision addresses auditor independence and conflict-of-interest concerns by severely limiting the types of non-audit services that CPA firms can provide to audit clients. Section 201 of SOX prohibits services such as bookkeeping, design and installation of financial information systems, internal audit outsourcing, and any other services that the PCAOB decides to prohibit. Finally, the growing importance of properly functioning committees of a company's board of directors leads us to summarize below some of the principal provisions of SOX relating to key board committees, especially the audit committee, and to director independence.

Audit Committees

The **board of directors** plays an important role in the governance of the corporation. Three key board committees are (1) the *audit committee,* (2) the *nominating committee* and (3) the *compensation committee*. Although SOX deals only with audit committees, as discussed below, the NYSE requires that all three committees be separate and composed of independent directors that cannot be current or prior employees of the firm or have other insider relationships. NASDAQ rules actually increase the influence of a company's independent directors.

The Dodd-Frank Act (2010) reaffirms these independence requirements. It also extends them to compensation committees' use of outside consultants.

The **audit committee** makes sure that management fulfills its responsibilities for accounting, reporting, controlling the operations, and safeguarding the assets of the corporation. It monitors the financial accounting and reporting system as well as the external and internal audit functions. Mandatory audit committee responsibilities include hiring the independent auditor and approving fees for audit and non-audit services. The auditor reports to the audit committee.

One significant implication of the independent director requirement for the three board committees mentioned above is that the company's Chief Executive Officer (CEO) can no longer serve on, and perhaps dominate, these committees. The independence and effectiveness of many corporate boards should increase as a result. Section 301 of SOX defines independence, makes the audit committee "directly responsible" for arrangements with and oversight of the company's external audit firm, and requires its active involvement in the company's financial reporting and internal control systems.

Although it is responsible to either the audit committee or management, the **internal audit department** needs direct access to the audit committee for special problems, and the audit committee can use the internal audit department for special investigations. The audit committee also interacts with top management on financial accounting, reporting, and control issues.

Antifraud Provisions and Insider Trading

A broad set of rules known as the **antifraud provisions**, found in both the 1933 and 1934 Acts, promotes fair capital markets that allocate resources efficiently. These rules seek a "level playing field" for all capital market participants by prohibiting fraud, deceit, and manipulative practices in the issuance or trading of securities. For example,

- A corporation cannot issue false or misleading statements about the company or its stock. Underwriters of a stock issue cannot artificially stimulate demand or hold back stock in order to profit from a price rise.
- Prohibited corporate mismanagement includes issuing corporate stock for less than adequate compensation.
- Registrants cannot easily make mergers or acquisitions against minority shareholders' interests.

Insider trading is a special type of fraud that refers to the purchase or sale of a company's stock by individuals who have access to information not yet available either to those with whom they are dealing or to the market in general. An *insider* may be a company officer, director, major stockholder, or anyone else who utilizes confidential nonpublic information for the purpose of trading in securities. The exact definitions of *insider* and *inside information,* however, are still unsettled and are the subjects of many legal proceedings.

A major objective of the securities laws is to promote full disclosure of material information to all participants in the market. Trading by insiders having access to special knowledge compromises this objective. Although one cannot completely prevent use of inside knowledge, certain rules help to constrain it. One 1934 Act rule requires officers, directors, and stockholders who directly or indirectly own more than 10% of a class of equity securities—*beneficial owners*—to report their holdings and transactions in these securities to the SEC. As a public record, this report discloses completed insider transactions. A second rule permits the company, or a stockholder acting on the company's behalf, to sue to recover "*shortswing profit*" earned by an insider from "in-and-out trading"—either purchase-sale or sale-purchase—within a six-month period.

Proxy Statements

Proxy statements are communications to shareholders of matters for shareholder action, such as election of directors, appointment of the independent auditor, a change in the corporate charter or bylaws, issuance of new securities, or approval of a business combination. The proxy statement discusses these matters and advises the shareholder of the voting procedure. When security issuances and business combinations are considered, accountants become involved to provide the proxy statement with the most recent annual report containing financial statements presented in accordance with Regulation S-X.

Because voting on policy matters frequently occurs at the stockholders' annual meeting that many stockholders cannot attend, management often solicits their voting right, or **proxy.** The proxy statement seeks to provide shareholders with the information they need to decide how to assign their proxies. SEC regulation of proxy statements follows from its emphasis on full disclosure and the belief that the capital markets work better when registrants' managers are accountable to the stockholders.

The proxy statement also provides a mechanism for action on *stockholder proposals not supported by management*. Notice of such a proposal must be given to the company at least 90 days prior to the mailing of the proxy statement. Stockholders' proposals must be personally presented at the annual meeting by a stockholder unless management previously agreed to put the proposal on the ballot. In addition, the proxy statement often contains detailed information on nonvoting matters, such as board committees, litigation, management compensation plans (including the amount of compensation paid to top management), and related-party transactions.

BUSINESS APPLICATION   **Shareholder Proposals**

In recent years, increasing numbers of investors have presented shareholder proposals related to governance, social, and environmental issues. 2014 proxy season data reveal that the successful proposals—those achieving majority shareholder support—focused on corporate governance issues. Below is a selection of issues that succeeded in 2014, based on data from 432 shareholder proposals.

- Majority voting in director elections
- Board declassification
- Elimination of supermajority vote requirements
- Shareholders' ability to call special meetings
- Independent chair
- Proxy access
- Shareholder approval of shareholder rights plan
- No accelerated vesting of equity awards upon a change of control

Source: Institutional Shareholder Services

The Dodd-Frank Act

One consequence of the 2008–2009 financial crisis, driven by improper identification and pricing of risks in many mortgage-backed securities, was the collapse of some banks and the bailout of others. In 2010, Congress passed the **Dodd-Frank Wall Street Reform and Consumer Protection Act**, which provides for stronger regulation of the financial services industry. Although this Act focuses on governance of financial services, its provisions, particularly the compensation-related regulations, also affect accountants.

The purpose of the Dodd-Frank Act is stated as follows (paraphrased):

- To promote the financial stability of the United States by improving accountability and transparency in the financial system,
- To end "too big to fail,"
- To protect the American taxpayer by ending bailouts, and
- To protect consumers from abusive financial services practices.

Provisions of the Dodd-Frank Act include establishment of new and powerful regulatory organizations, covering various aspects of financial markets, with a special focus on oversight of financial entities whose potential failure would be particularly harmful to the economy ("too big to fail"). Responsibilities and powers of existing financial market regulatory organizations, including the SEC and the Federal Reserve, are also affected. Provisions of the Dodd-Frank Act include the following:

- Creation of the **Financial Stability Oversight Council**, to provide comprehensive monitoring of the U.S. financial system and identify and neutralize financial risks to the economy.
- Creation of a **Bureau of Consumer Financial Protection** within the Federal Reserve, to help consumers get the clear, accurate information they need to shop for financial products, and protect them from abusive and deceptive practices.
- Creation of an **Office of Credit Rating Agencies** within the SEC, providing new regulations promoting transparency and accountability for credit rating agency practices.
- Registration of large **hedge funds** and various **investment advisors and brokers**, making them subject to federal regulation and SEC enforcement.
- Limits on trading and service activities for banking entities (**Volcker Rule**), to prevent the kinds of speculative investments that contributed to the 2008–2009 bank failures.
- Regulation of **derivatives markets** and participants.
- **Whistle blowers** with information about security violations can provide information to the government and receive a financial reward.
- **Governance regulations** affecting all public companies, including shareholder approval of **executive compensation** ("say on pay"), clawback provisions, which provide for repayment of executive compensation as a result of accounting restatements, and disclosure of company policies for incentive-based compensation.

THE SEC AND ACCOUNTING STANDARDS

We previously mentioned that although the Securities Exchange Act of 1934 gave the SEC the statutory authority to set accounting standards for companies under its jurisdiction, the SEC historically left the bulk of this task to the FASB.

    The SEC actively oversees the standard-setting process and continually reviews registrants' filings. In most cases the SEC accepts the FASB's standards. However, in other cases the SEC either influences the FASB to take a particular action, or imposes its own standards. A few recent cases involving the interaction between the FASB and the SEC are described below.

    Stock options are currently required to be expensed at fair value when granted, using an appropriate valuation method. Prior to this standard, however, most companies did not expense stock options.

LO6 Explain the SEC's role in accounting standards development and global standards convergence.

When the FASB first proposed the new standard in the mid-1990s, companies that used options as a significant form of compensation lobbied vigorously against it, as it would greatly lower their reported income. Even Congress took the position that this new standard would hurt the economy. Surprisingly, the SEC sided with Congress and the business community on this issue, and influenced the FASB to issue a weaker standard in 1995, making expensing optional. This dual reporting continued for several years before the FASB took the upper hand and in 2004 issued a revised standard making expensing mandatory. That standard appears in *ASC Topic 718*.

The SEC put pressure on the FASB after the Enron accounting scandal, pushing it to get its project on **consolidating special purpose entities** on the "fast track." That guidance emerged quickly in 2003 and now appears in *ASC Topic 810*. As discussed in Chapter 3 of this text, this standard continues to be modified with the goal of consolidating any entity a company controls.

In 2009 the SEC completed a Congressionally-mandated study of the FASB's standards on **mark-to-market accounting**, found in *ASC Topic 820*, and its application to valuation of financial instruments. This study was motivated by concern over the effects of fair value accounting on financial institutions, market responses to investment write-offs, and the usefulness of the information to investors. The study's main conclusion was that fair value accounting standards provide useful information and should not be suspended. However, in the midst of the crisis, markets for financial instruments became very limited. The SEC persuaded the FASB to develop new guidelines allowing valuation of these investments using normal market prices, allowing banks to avoid catastrophic write-downs.

A major ongoing SEC initiative relates to potential **convergence of U.S. GAAP and IFRS**. In 2008, the SEC proposed a "roadmap" that would require all U.S. public companies to file under IFRS in 2014, following a phase-in beginning with certain 2010 filings. However, the initial fervor over rapid adoption of or convergence with IFRS has significantly abated, with major differences still remaining. Accounting for business acquisitions is one example of almost complete convergence. Consolidation of special purpose entities and classification of and impairment testing for financial instruments are areas where U.S. GAAP and IFRS diverge, with no indication of convergence in the near future.

Clearly, the SEC's statutory authority requires it to remain an active participant in the accounting standard-setting process. Even though the SEC is a key player in the financial reporting process, it consistently looks to the FASB to develop standards. Like the FASB, though, the SEC faces its own challenges related to the bureaucratic nature of its operations and its dependence on Congress for sufficient financial resources to adequately carry out its multidimensional mission of investor protection.

REVIEW 3 ● Corporate Accountability and Governance, SEC Intervention in Standard-Setting

Required

a. Briefly explain the nature of fraudulent financial reporting and the ethical dilemma it poses.

b. Explain why strong audit committees are so important to good corporate governance.

c. Twenty-four years after Congress passed the Foreign Corrupt Practices Act (1978) requiring companies to maintain accurate books and records and an adequate system of internal control, Congress passed the Sarbanes-Oxley Act (2002), which contains similar provisions. Comment on whether this tells us anything about the state of corporate accountability in the U.S.

Solutions are located after the chapter assignments.

REVIEW OF KEY CONCEPTS ●●●●●●●●●●●●●●●●●●●●●●●●●●●●●●

LO 1 **Discuss why the SEC was established and the principal legislation it enforces. (p. 706)** The 1929 stock market crash and ensuing economic depression led Congress to legislate governmental oversight for the financial markets and the companies with securities traded on those markets. Congress enacted the **Securities Act of 1933** to regulate the issuance of new securities. The subsequent **Securities Exchange Act of 1934** regulates the trading of already-issued securities and establishes the **Securities and Exchange Commission (SEC)**. The SEC is responsible for the administration and enforcement of the federal securities laws including the 1933 and 1934 Acts.

Examine the SEC's organization and structure. (p. 708) The SEC is an independent non-partisan agency **LO 2** funded by a combination of user charges and congressional appropriations. It is organized into five divisions with the **Division of Corporation Finance** being most relevant to accountants. Of its several supporting staff offices, the **Office of the Chief Accountant** has the most effect on the financial reporting process. The SEC has statutory authority to establish accounting and reporting principles for publicly held companies. Although it relies heavily on the private sector for standard-setting—currently the FASB—the SEC does issue its own pronouncements—*Financial Reporting Releases (FRR), Accounting and Auditing Enforcement Releases (AAER)* and *Staff Accounting Bulletins (SAB)*.

Describe principal SEC requirements for registering new securities. (p. 710) The 1933 Act provides, with few **LO 3** exemptions, that **no security may be offered or sold to the public unless it is registered with the SEC.** A prospective issuer becomes an SEC **registrant** and must file a **registration statement**—the set of documents needed to register securities—that includes a **prospectus** and other information. The SEC does not pass judgment on the merits of the security and can be said to perform **compliance reviews, not merit reviews.** Typically, a **registration team**, consisting of the issuer's chief financial officer, legal counsel and independent public accountant, and the underwriter (investment banker) and underwriter's counsel, prepares the registration statement.

Explain the periodic reporting requirements for SEC registrants. (p. 711) Companies under SEC jurisdiction **LO 4** file annual reports **(Form 10-K)**, quarterly reports **(Form 10-Q)**, and special reports **(Form 8-K)** when certain events occur. The contents of these reports are largely governed by **Regulation S-X**, which covers accounting and financial statement requirements, and **Regulation S-K**, which covers all other disclosures.

Describe the SEC's role in corporate accountability and governance. (p. 720) Besides its role in accounting **LO 5** and reporting, the SEC also plays an important role in **corporate governance.** It provides **proxy statement** requirements, encourages **audit committees**, and regulates **insider trading.** The landmark **Sarbanes-Oxley Act of 2002** made several reforms in the financial reporting process and strengthened the SEC's authority. These include the **Public Company Accounting Oversight Board** that reviews audit firms and sets auditing standards, top management sworn certifications of financial reports filed with the SEC, limits on non-audit services that external auditors can provide to audit clients, and reports on the effectiveness of registrants' internal controls over financial reporting.

Explain the SEC's role in accounting standards development and global standards convergence. (p. 723) The **LO 6** SEC has a history of involvement in accounting standard-setting. It continues to oversee the movement toward **adoption of or convergence with IFRS** although timetables have been fluid. The SEC monitors the work of the FASB, contributes to it on a continuing basis, and occasionally overrules it.

Assignments with the ✓ in the margin are available in ᵐʸBusinessCourse.
See the Preface of the book for details.

MULTIPLE CHOICE QUESTIONS ••••••••••••••••••••••••••

1. The SEC was established in 1934 to help regulate the United States securities market. Which of the follow- **LO 1 ✓** ing statements is *true* concerning the SEC?

   a. The SEC prohibits the sale of speculative securities.
   b. Registration with the SEC guarantees the accuracy of the registrant's prospectus.
   c. The SEC's initial influence and authority has diminished in recent years as stock exchanges have become more organized and better able to police themselves.
   d. The SEC regulates only securities offered for public sale.

2. Which of the following acts gives the SEC the ultimate power to suspend trading in a security, delist a secu- **LO 1 ✓** rity, and prevent brokers and dealers from working in the securities market?

   a. Securities Investors Protection Act of 1934
   b. Securities Act of 1934
   c. Securities Exchange Act of 1934
   d. Investment Company Act of 1940

3. Assuming that all other criteria regarding the issuing organization and its "security" are met, which one of **LO 1 ✓** the following is not a "security" under the jurisdiction of the SEC?

   a. A trust certificate
   b. A municipal bond
   c. An oil drilling venture participation unit
   d. A limited partnership share

✅ LO 2 **4.** Which of the SEC's organizational units—divisions and principal offices—reviews the registration statements, annual reports, and proxy statements filed with the commission?

    a. Office of the Chief Accountant
    b. Division of Corporation Finance
    c. Division of Enforcement
    d. Division of the Comptroller

✅ LO 2 **5.** *Financial Reporting Releases (FRRs)* and *Staff Accounting Bulletins (SABs)* are two pronouncements issues by the SEC. How do *FRRs* and *SABs* differ?

    a. *FRRs* are part of the 1934 Securities Exchange Act while *SABs* are not.
    b. *SABs* represent the official rules of the SEC while *FRRs* do not.
    c. *SABs* represent amendments to Regulation S-X, *FRRs* do not.
    d. *FRRs* represent requirements applicable to the form and content of financial statements filed with the SEC, *SABs* represent accounting interpretations followed by the SEC.

✅ LO 3 **6.** Which of the following statements related to registration of new securities is *false*?

    a. Registration of new securities is governed by the Securities Act of 1933.
    b. Form S-1, the basic form for new security registration, is an elaborate checklist of rules to be followed and questions to be answered.
    c. A "private placement" may be exempt from detailed registration requirements.
    d. The independent public accountant reviews and audits information included in the registration statement.

✅ LO 4 **7.** Which of the following statements related to the SEC's periodic reporting requirements is *false*?

    a. Form 10-K, the annual report, is governed only by *Regulation S-X*, not *Regulation S-K*.
    b. Financial statements in Form 10-Q, the quarterly report, follow typical interim reporting principles contained in *ASC Topic 270*.
    c. Required Form 10-Q financial statements include balance sheets, statements of income and comprehensive income and cash flow statements.
    d. Form 10-Q financial statements may include fewer line items than those in Form 10-K.

✅ LO 4 **8.** A significant event affecting a company registered under the Securities and Exchange Act of 1934 should be reported on which of the following?

    a. Form 10-K
    b. Form S-1
    c. Form 8-K
    d. Form 11-K

✅ LO 5 **9.** An audit committee of the board of directors consisting of outside directors should be objective in arbitrating disputes between a company's top management and the external auditor because audit committee members

    a. have no direct responsibility for the results of a company's operations.
    b. have only limited contacts with the external auditor.
    c. rely on senior management's opinions to resolve disputes with the external auditor.
    d. are required by the Securities Exchange Act of 1934 to oversee the progress of the annual external audit.

✅ LO 6 **10.** The role of the SEC regarding financial accounting for public companies is that the SEC does which of the following?

    a. Promulgates generally accepted accounting principles
    b. Regularly adopts requirements that conflict with FASB pronouncements
    c. Makes regulations and rules pertaining to filings with the SEC but not to annual or quarterly reports to shareholders
    d. Makes regulations and rules pertaining more to disclosure outside the financial statements than to the setting of accounting principles

EXERCISES •

E16.1 **Multiple Choice—Securities Laws and SEC Functions** These questions involve the federal **LO 1, 2** securities laws and the organization, structure, and authority of the SEC.

Required

a. Which of the following are *not* requirements imposed by the Securities Exchange Act of 1934 and its amendments?
   1. Proxy solicitation requirements.
   2. Prospectus requirements.
   3. Insider trading requirements.
   4. Accounting, recordkeeping, and internal control requirements.

b. Which of the following laws requires companies to maintain accurate accounting records and a system of effective internal accounting controls?
   1. Securities Exchange Act of 1934
   2. Securities Investor Protection Act of 1970
   3. Foreign Corrupt Practices Act of 1977
   4. Dodd-Frank Act of 2010

c. Which of the following is *not* a purpose of the Securities Exchange Act of 1934?
   1. To establish federal regulation over securities exchanges and markets.
   2. To prevent unfair practices on securities exchanges and markets.
   3. To discourage and prevent the use of credit in financing excessive speculation in securities.
   4. To approve the securities of corporations that are to be traded publicly.

d. Which of the following categories is *not* registered by the SEC?
   1. Securities brokers who deal in over-the-counter markets.
   2. Securities brokers who deal only in interstate markets.
   3. Public accounting firms.
   4. Securities exchanges.

E16.2 **Multiple Choice—SEC Reporting Requirements** These questions involve SEC reporting **LO 4** requirements.

Required

a. Nonfinancial statement disclosures are specified in which of the following?
   1. Regulation S-K
   2. *Financial Reporting Releases*
   3. *Staff Accounting Bulletins*
   4. Regulation S-X

b. Which of these items is *not* required by the SEC in either the Securities Act of 1933 or the Securities Exchange Act of 1934?
   1. Identification of directors and executive officers with the principal occupation and employer of each.
   2. Identification of the principal markets in which the firm's securities are traded.
   3. Range of market prices and dividends for each quarter of the two most recent fiscal years.
   4. Comfort letter to the underwriter and legal counsel from the company's independent accountant.

c. SEC regulations provide for a procedure known as *incorporation by reference*. Which of the following best illustrates the concept of *incorporation by reference*?
   1. A partnership is incorporated by reference to the U.S. Tax Code.
   2. The incorporation of a proprietorship or partnership.
   3. Inclusion of information on officers' remuneration in Form 10-K by reference to the same information in the shareholders' proxy statement.
   4. Footnote reference to market data per share since incorporation.

d. The SEC requires Form 8-K to be filed with the commission within four days after the end of the month in which a significant event transpired. However, financial statements accompany Form 8-K only under certain conditions. Which event requires financial statements to accompany Form 8-K?
   1. A material default on a senior security.
   2. A write-down, write-off, or abandonment of assets.
   3. A major business acquisition.
   4. A change in the registrant's certifying accountants.

⊘ LO 4 **E16.3** **Multiple Choice—SEC Reporting Requirements** These questions involve SEC reporting requirements.

Required

a. What is the name of the SEC's online database of company filings?
   1. XBRL
   2. DRVA
   3. VaR
   4. EDGAR

b. What is a "non-accelerated filer"?
   1. A company with fewer than five employees.
   2. A company having a public float of less than $75 million.
   3. A not-for-profit organization.
   4. A financial services organization.

c. Which one of the following items need *not* be filed with Form 10-Q?
   1. Matters reported on Form 8-K during the quarter.
   2. A description of legal proceedings.
   3. Income statements for the most recent quarter and for the equivalent quarter from the preceding year, and year-to-date data for both years.
   4. An audit report from an independent accountant.

LO 4 **E16.4** **Multiple Choice—SEC Reporting Requirements** These questions involve SEC reporting requirements.

Required

a. Which of the following describes Regulation S-X?
   1. Specifies the information that can be incorporated by reference from the annual report into the registration statement filed with the SEC.
   2. Specifies the regulations and reporting requirements of proxy solicitations.
   3. Provides the basis for generally accepted accounting principles.
   4. Specifies the general form and content of financial statements filed with the SEC.

b. Which section of Form 10-K is used for management's discussion and analysis of financial condition and results of operations?
   1. Item 7
   2. Item 8
   3. Item 1A
   4. Item 4A

c. Within four days after any event of material importance to the stockholders occurs, a company must file a Form 8-K with the SEC to disclose the event. Which of these is an example of the type of event to be disclosed?
   1. Salary increases to the officers.
   2. A change in projected earnings per share from $12 to $12.11 per share.
   3. The purchase of bank certificates of deposit.
   4. Acquisition of a large subsidiary.

d. Which of these events does not require a company to file a Form 8-K?
   1. Acquisition or disposition of a significant amount of assets.
   2. Change in certifying public accountants.
   3. Election of new vice-president of finance to replace the retiring incumbent.
   4. Default in the payment of principal, interest, or sinking fund installment.

⊘ LO 5 **E16.5** **Multiple Choice—Corporate Governance** These questions relate to corporate governance.

Required

a. Formation and meaningful utilization of an audit committee of the board of directors is required of publicly traded companies that are subject to the rules of which of the following?
   1. Securities and Exchange Commission.
   2. Financial Accounting Standards Board.
   3. New York Stock Exchange.
   4. National Association of Securities Dealers.

b. The SEC's antifraud rules prohibit trading on the basis of inside information of a business corporation's stock by which of these?
1. Officers.
2. Officers and directors.
3. Officers, directors, and beneficial holders of 10% of the corporation's stock.
4. Anyone who bases his or her trading activities on inside information.

c. Shareholders may ask or allow others to enter their vote at a shareholders meeting that they are unable to attend. The document furnished to shareholders to provide background information for their vote is a
1. registration statement.
2. proxy statement.
3. 10-K report.
4. prospectus.

E16.6   Multiple Choice—SEC and Accounting Standards   These questions examine the role of the **LO 5, 6**
SEC in establishing accounting and reporting standards.

Required

a. Two important topics concerning the SEC are the role it plays in developing accounting principles and the impact the SEC has on the accounting profession and business in general. Which statement concerning the SEC's authority relative to accounting practice is *false?*
1. The SEC has the statutory authority to regulate and to prescribe the form and content of financial statements and other reports it receives.
2. Regulation S-X of the SEC is the principal source relating to the form and content of financial statements to be included in registration statements and financial reports filed with the SEC.
3. The SEC has little, if any, authority over disclosures in corporate annual reports mailed to shareholders with proxy solicitations. Here, the type of information disclosed and the format to be used are left to the discretion of management.
4. If the SEC disagrees with some presentation in the registrant's financial statements but the principles used by the registrant have substantial authoritative support, the SEC may accept footnotes to the statements in lieu of correcting the statements to the SEC view, provided the SEC has not previously expressed its opinion on the matter in published material.

b. After the Enron accounting scandal, the SEC encouraged the FASB to quickly develop a new standard on what topic?
1. Consolidation of special purpose entities
2. Convergence with IFRS
3. Mark-to-market accounting for financial instruments
4. Valuation of equity-based compensation

E16.7   Multiple Choice—Registration of Securities   These questions involve registration of new secu-   **LO 3**
rity issues with the SEC.

Required

a. In the registration and sale of new securities issues, the SEC
1. provides a rating of the investment quality of the security.
2. may not allow the registration to go effective if it judges the security's investment risk to be too great.
3. allows all registrations to go effective if the issuing company's external accountant is satisfied that disclosures and representations are not misleading.
4. makes no guarantees regarding the registration statement's material accuracy.

b. In cases of false or misleading disclosure in a registration statement that the SEC has allowed to become effective in conjunction with the public sale of securities, investors have the potential for legal recourse (for example, damage suits) against all of the following *except*
1. the Securities and Exchange Commission.
2. the issuing entity.
3. the underwriter (managing broker) of the sale.
4. the issuing entity's external accountant.

c. Which of the following is *not* required for the registration statements filed under the Securities Act of 1933?
1. Nature and history of the issuer's business
2. Description of the securities being registered
3. Estimate of the net proceeds and the expected uses of the proceeds
4. Financial forecasts for the next two fiscal years

    d. The 1933 Securities Act provides for a 20-day waiting period between the filing and effective dates of the registration. During this waiting period the registrant is prohibited from engaging in which of these activities?
1. Preparing any amendments to the registration statement.
2. Accepting offers from potential investors to purchase securities being registered.
3. Placing an advertisement indicating who will accept orders for the securities being registered.
4. Issuing a prospectus in preliminary form.

LO 4

FORD MOTOR COMPANY
[F]

E16.8 **Risk Factors** Download the 2013 10-K of **Ford Motor Company** and find Item 1A, describing Ford's risk factors.

Required

List five of Ford's significant risk factors.

LO 4, 5

E16.9 **Possible Effect of SOX on the SEC's Designation of Standard-Setting Bodies**

Required

Write a short essay speculating on how SOX changes the SEC's traditional delegation of its statutory authority to set accounting standards to private-sector standard-setting bodies in the U.S. Consider the implications of the PCAOB and Section 108's recognition of the SEC's authority and ability to designate standard-setting bodies.

LO 5

MICROSOFT CORPORATION
[MSFT]

E16.10 **Reporting Insider Trades** On November 3, 2014, William H. Gates III filed a Form 4 with the SEC in which he reported some insider transactions in **Microsoft Corporation** stock.

Required

Access that Form 4 and answer these questions.
a. Give the title of Form 4.
b. How many shares did Mr. Gates sell and for what reason?
c. How many shares are owned by Mr. Gates after these transactions?

LO 4

MICROSOFT CORPORATION
[MSFT]

E16.11 **Use of Form 8-K** **Microsoft Corporation** filed a Form 8-K with the SEC on July 17, 2014, that described an event of potential significance to investors.

Required

Access that Form 8-K and answer these questions.

a. Briefly describe the event reported on that Form 8-K.
b. From the list of Microsoft's 2014 SEC filings of Form 8-K, what are the two most common events reported?

LO 4

THE COCA-COLA COMPANY
[KO]

E16.12 **Form 10-K Item 6** Download the 2013 10-K of **The Coca-Cola Company**. Item 6, "Selected Financial Data," contains a table that includes net operating revenues for the years 2009–2013, and other information. There was a decline in net operating revenues between 2012 and 2013, and a significant increase over the period 2009 to 2011.

Required

Explain the reasons given for the changes in net operating revenues over this period.

LO 4, 5

E16.13 **Effects of Sarbanes-Oxley Act on Financial Reporting Requirements** The Sarbanes-Oxley Act was enacted to enhance the proper functioning of the securities markets.

Required

Briefly describe three aspects of the Sarbanes-Oxley Act that are designed to improve the financial reporting process.

LO 4

TARGET CORPORATION
[TGT]

E16.14 **Form 10-K Items 6 and 7** Download the 10-K of **Target Corporation** for the fiscal year ended February 1, 2014, and find items 6 and 7, selected financial data and management's discussion and analysis. Note that Target labels its fiscal year ended February 2014 as "2013."

Required

a. In item 6, 2013 sales revenues are *lower* than 2012 sales revenues, yet in item 7 Target says sales *increased* in 2013. Explain these two apparently conflicting pieces of information.
b. What was Target's GAAP diluted earnings per share for 2013? What was Target's "adjusted" diluted earnings per share? Explain why the two numbers are different, and the reason Target gives for providing the non-GAAP earnings per share information.

E16.15 **Item 9A Controls and Procedures**   Download the fiscal 2014 10-K of **Oracle Corporation** and find Item 9A.   **LO 4**

**ORACLE
CORPORATION**
[ORCL]

Required

   a. Summarize the information provided by Oracle in Item 9A.

   b. Evaluate the information provided. Do you find this information to be useful?

PROBLEMS ••

P16.1 **Origins and Objectives of Securities Legislation**   During the late 1920s, about 55% of all personal savings in the United States were used to purchase securities. Public confidence in the business community was extremely high as stock values doubled and tripled in short periods of time. People believed the road to wealth was through the stock market, and everyone who was able participated. Thus, the public was severely affected when the Dow Jones Industrial Average fell 89 percent between 1929 and 1933. The public outcry arising from this decline in stock prices motivated Congress to enact major federal laws regulating the securities industry.   **LO 1**

Required

   a. Research the 1929 stock market crash, and describe the investment practices of the 1920s that contributed to the erosion of the stock market.

   b. Explain the basic objectives of each of the following:

      1. Securities Act of 1933.

      2. Securities Exchange Act of 1934.

   c. Subsequent legislation resulted from abuses in the securities industry. Explain the major provisions of each of the following:

      1. Foreign Corrupt Practices Act of 1977.

      2. Insider Trading Sanctions Act of 1984.

P16.2 **Annual Reports to Stockholders and Form 10-K**   Public companies usually provide financial information in two formats: the 10-K, and the annual report to stockholders.   **LO 4**

Required

   a. What is Form 10-K, and who requires that it be completed?

   b. What information not normally included in the company's annual report could be ascertained from the 10-K?

   c. Indicate three items of financial information often included in annual reports that are not required for the 10-K.

P16.3 **Quarterly Reports to the SEC**   The SEC sets forth specific guidelines as to what information must be included on Form 10-Q, the quarterly report to stockholders.   **LO 4**

Required

   a. Corporations are required by the SEC to file a Form 10-Q.

      1. What is Form 10-Q, and how often is it filed with the SEC?

      2. Explain why the SEC requires corporations to file Form 10-Q.

   b. Discuss the disclosure requirements pertaining to Form 10-Q with specific regard to the following:

      1. Condensed balance sheet.

      2. Statement of income and comprehensive income.

      3. Statements of cash flows.

      4. Management's discussion and analysis of the interim period(s).

      5. Footnote disclosures.

P16.4 **Special Reports to the SEC**   To accomplish its regulatory objectives, the SEC requires that public companies register their securities and periodically prepare and file Forms 8-K, 10-K, and 10-Q.   **LO 4**

Required

   a. With regard to Form 8-K, discuss

      1. the purpose of the report.

      2. the timing of the report.

      3. the role of financial statements in the filing of the report.

    b. Identify five circumstances under which the SEC requires the filing of Form 8-K.

    c. Discuss how the filing of Form 8-K fosters the purpose of the SEC.

    d. Explain whether the SEC passes judgment on securities based on information contained in periodic reports.

LO 5   **P16.5**   **Audit Committees**   Although audit committees are now very much a part of the corporate governance landscape, their evolution spans many decades. Today's audit committees reflect SEC recommendations, stock exchange listing requirements and the mandates of Section 301 of SOX.

Required

    a. Explain the role the audit committee generally assumes with respect to the annual audit conducted by the company's external auditors.

    b. Identify duties other than those associated with the annual audit that might be assigned to the audit committee by the board of directors.

    c. Discuss the relationship that should exist between the audit committee and a company's internal audit staff.

    d. Explain why board members appointed to serve on the audit committee should be outside (independent of management) board members.

LO 5   **P16.6**   **Proxy Statements**   The SEC was given the authority to regulate proxy solicitation by the Securities and Exchange Act of 1934. SEC regulations require that a proxy statement be distributed by a registrant's management to each shareholder shortly before the annual shareholders meeting.

Required

    a. Explain the purpose of proxy statements.

    b. Identify four types of events or actions for which proxy statements normally are solicited.

    c. Identify the conditions that must be met in order to have a dissident shareholder proposal included in a proxy statement.

LO 3   **P16.7**   **Registration of New Securities**   In business for about twenty years, Trapper Inc.'s finance committee has been discussing alternative ways of financing a major proposed facilities expansion. Both short-term and long-term notes were ruled out because of high interest rates. Chief financial officer Bob Smith said, "It boils down to either bonds, preferred stock, or additional common stock." Maria Garza, a consultant helping in the financing decision, stated, "Regardless of your choice, you will have to file a Registration Statement with the SEC." Dave Brown, Trapper's chief accountant for the past five years, stated, "I've coordinated the filing of all the periodic reports required by the SEC—10-Ks, 10-Qs, and 8-Ks—and see no reason why I can't also prepare a Registration Statement."

Required

    a. List the circumstances in which a firm files a Registration Statement with the SEC.

    b. Explain the registration process's objectives given in the Securities Act of 1933.

    c. Identify and explain the SEC regulations and publications Dave Brown would use for guidance in preparing the Registration Statement.

LO 6   **P16.8**   **Role of the SEC in Standard Setting**   Many organizations and individuals influenced the development of accounting theory and practice over a long period of time. Today the most important source of accounting rules is the private-sector independent FASB, based in Norwalk, CT.

Required

    a. What official role does the SEC have in the development of financial accounting theory and practice?

    b. Explain the relationship between the FASB and SEC with respect to the development and establishment of financial accounting theory and practices.

LO 5   **P16.9**   **Role of the PCAOB**   The Sarbanes-Oxley Act of 2002 created a new entity, the PCAOB, to govern audit firms. Use information from the PCAOB web site and the chapter to answer the questions below.

Required

    a. When does an audit firm come under the jurisdiction of the PCAOB?

    b. What are the main activities of the PCAOB?

    c. What is the relationship between the PCAOB and the AICPA?

P16.10 Corporate Governance Guidelines Go to the website for **AIG (American International Group)**, the much-maligned insurance giant that got into a lot of trouble over credit default swaps, examine AIG's Corporate Governance Guidelines, and answer these questions.

LO 5

AMERICAN
INTERNATIONAL
GROUP, INC
[AIG]

Required

a. How does the document distinguish between the roles of management and the board of directors in running AIG's business operations?

b. What percentage of the board is to be filled by "independent" directors, as defined in the New York Stock Exchange's listing standards?

c. What do the Guidelines say about former CEOs of AIG serving on the board?

d. List three particular requirements of AIG's audit committee discussed in Section IX of the Guidelines.

P16.11 PCAOB Inspections Go to the PCAOB website and download its 2013 inspection report for **PricewaterhouseCoopers LLC**, dated June 19, 2014. Answer the questions below.

LO 5

Required

a. What are the major sections of the report? Briefly describe the contents of each section.

b. Not all engagement deficiencies are described in the report. How did the PCAOB decide which deficiencies to include in its report?

c. Review the description of deficiencies by issuer, found in Part 1A. In general, what are the major audit procedure deficiencies identified?

d. Identify the major types of transactions and balance sheet items that resulted in deficiencies.

e. Does the existence of audit deficiencies imply the financial statements of these issuers are misstated? Explain.

P16.12 Registration Statement **Facebook, Inc.** filed an amended Form S-1 on May 16, 2012.

LO 3

FACEBOOK, INC.
[FB]

Required

a. Describe the amount and average offering price of the issued shares covered by this Form S-1.

b. Calculate the registration fee as a percent of maximum offering price.

c. What does Facebook plan to do with the money raised through this IPO?

d. Identify the public accounting firm involved and describe the permission they are providing.

REVIEW SOLUTIONS ••

Review 1 Solution

a. The SEC's fundamental mission is investor protection, principally by requiring registrants to publicly disclose all material facts and circumstances and prevent or correct deceptive and fraudulent practices in securities trading. Because no such investor protections, at least at the federal level, existed before the 1929 stock market crash, Congress realized in the early 1930s such protections needed to be enacted.

b. The text cites ten such pieces of legislation. Although any three could be chosen for discussion, we offer:

1. The **Investment Company Act of 1940** requires investment companies, including mutual funds (but not hedge funds) to register with the SEC and disclose their investment policies and management fees, and to solicit shareholder participation in company policy.

2. The **Private Securities Litigation Reform Act of 1995** limits the liability of public accountants to their "fair share" in certain securities suits and protects registrants from lawsuits related to certain forward-looking financial information and illegal acts reported by auditors to the SEC.

3. The **Sarbanes-Oxley Act of 2002** requires reports on internal controls, top management certifications of financial statements filed with the SEC, and created the *Public Company Accounting Oversight Board (PCAOB)* to monitor auditing firms and set auditing standards.

c. The statutory definition is very broad, referring to ANY note, stock, bond and the like and, in general, any interest or instrument commonly known as a "security," including ANY certificate to subscribe to or to purchase, any of the foregoing. Any financial instrument that promises a return or protection from loss, other than insurance policies, and involves a third party, is likely to be a "security."

d. Although the SEC relies on the FASB to set accounting standards, it occasionally issues its own pronouncements, such as *FRRs* and *SABs*, and influences the standard-setting process through its participation in that process.

Review 2 Solution

a. A prospective issuer registers with the SEC registrant and files a registration statement that consists of two parts: (1) information generally included in a prospectus, which must be furnished to each purchaser of the security, and (2) other information and exhibits, which must be publicly available but need not be supplied to each investor.

   The independent CPA is part of the registration team that also includes the issuer's chief financial officer, legal counsel, the underwriter (investment banker) and the underwriter's counsel. Form S-1 is the basic registration form although Forms S-3 and S-4 are used in certain circumstances. The underwriter advises the issuer and markets the securities to the investing public under one of three alternative arrangements.

b. Certainly items 6 (selected financial data) and 7 (MD&A) relate to accounting and reporting. Also items 7A (disclosures about market risk of derivatives), 9 (changes and disagreements with accountants) and 9A (reports on internal controls and specifically internal controls over financial reporting), deal with various aspects of accounting and reporting.

c. Article 3 prescribes the audited financial statements to be prepared and the time periods covered, generally consolidated balance sheets as of the end of the two most recent fiscal years, consolidated statements of income, comprehensive income, and cash flows for the three most recent fiscal years, and analysis of changes in the stockholders' equity accounts shown in the balance sheet for the three most recent fiscal years as a separate financial statement or a footnote schedule

   Article 4 deals with selected accounting and reporting matters applicable to companies in general, independent of their industry. It provides for the usual form, order, and terminology, and addresses issues related to filings by foreign private security issuers.

d. In addition to annual (10-K) and quarterly (10-Q) reporting, registrants must file an 8-K within four days of any event deemed significant enough to be of interest to investors, including proposed business combinations and large transactions in securities. Items 2.03 and 2.04 call for timely reporting of creation or expansion of "direct" (on balance sheet) financial obligations or liabilities and "off-balance sheet" financial obligations that effectively create liabilities for registrants. Item 4.01 alerts investors to a change in the registrant's independent public accountant and the circumstances surrounding it, perhaps raising concerns about the credibility of financial reporting before or after the change.

Review 3 Solution

a. Fraudulent financial reporting is intentional or reckless conduct that results in materially misleading financial statements.

   But at what point do discretionary transactions entered at year-end to produce a particular reporting result that seems to overemphasize the positive in the underlying economics, become fraudulent? Intent must usually be proven in fraud cases. The ethical dilemma arises when the boss asks for a "credit" when there should be a "debit" or specifies the timing and amount of transactions or event recognition that have significant financial statement effects, or whenever the accountant senses even a hint of impropriety.

b. The audit committee makes sure that management fulfills its responsibilities for accounting, reporting, and controlling the operations and safeguarding the assets of the corporation. It monitors the financial accounting and reporting system as well as the external and internal audit functions, hires the independent auditor, and the auditor reports to it. The internal audit department needs direct access to the audit committee for special problems, and the audit committee can use the internal audit department for special investigations.

   A weak audit committee will overlook or deliberately ignore problems, fail to confront top management on financial accounting, reporting, and control issues, and not take advantage of an effective internal audit function. Strong audit committees composed of truly independent, financially savvy directors should contribute to good corporate governance primarily by fostering credible external financial reporting that creates trust with investors and creditors.

c. Sadly, the passage of time appears to have eroded the spirit if not the letter of the Foreign Corrupt Practices Act—it seemed less relevant to the financial reporting environment of the first few years of the 21st century. As seen, though, the Act relates to more than foreign corrupt practices. Those responsible for corporate accountability, including the independent public accountants, may need periodic reminders of their obligations to the public. The fact that certain provisions of SOX were deemed necessary despite the apparent redundancy with the FCPA is unfortunate.

Index